A Companion to Budd

Blackwell Companions to Philosophy

This outstanding student reference series offers a comprehensive and authoritative survey of philosophy as a whole. Written by today's leading philosophers, each volume provides lucid and engaging coverage of the key figures, terms, topics, and problems of the field. Taken together, the volumes provide the ideal basis for course use, representing an unparalleled work of reference for students and specialists alike.

Already published in the series:

1. The Blackwell Companion to Philosophy, Second Edition
Edited by Nicholas Bunnin and Eric Tsui-James
2. A Companion to Ethics
Edited by Peter Singer
3. A Companion to Aesthetics, Second Edition
Edited by Stephen Davies, Kathleen Marie Higgins, Robert Hopkins, Robert Stecker, and David E. Cooper
4. A Companion to Epistemology, Second Edition
Edited by Jonathan Dancy, Ernest Sosa, and Matthias Steup
5. A Companion to Contemporary Political Philosophy (two-volume set), Second Edition
Edited by Robert E. Goodin and Philip Pettit
6. A Companion to Philosophy of Mind
Edited by Samuel Guttenplan
7. A Companion to Metaphysics, Second Edition
Edited by Jaegwon Kim, Ernest Sosa, and Gary S. Rosenkrantz
8. A Companion to Philosophy of Law and Legal Theory, Second Edition
Edited by Dennis Patterson
9. A Companion to Philosophy of Religion, Second Edition
Edited by Charles Taliaferro, Paul Draper, and Philip L. Quinn
10. A Companion to the Philosophy of Language
Edited by Bob Hale and Crispin Wright
11. A Companion to World Philosophies
Edited by Eliot Deutsch and Ron Bontekoe
12. A Companion to Continental Philosophy
Edited by Simon Critchley and William Schroeder
13. A Companion to Feminist Philosophy
Edited by Alison M. Jaggar and Iris Marion Young
14. A Companion to Cognitive Science
Edited by William Bechtel and George Graham
15. A Companion to Bioethics, Second Edition
Edited by Helga Kuhse and Peter Singer
16. A Companion to the Philosophers
Edited by Robert L. Arrington
17. A Companion to Business Ethics
Edited by Robert E. Frederick
18. A Companion to the Philosophy of Science
Edited by W. H. Newton-Smith
19. A Companion to Environmental Philosophy
Edited by Dale Jamieson
20. A Companion to Analytic Philosophy
Edited by A. P. Martinich and David Sosa
21. A Companion to Genethics
Edited by Justine Burley and John Harris
22. A Companion to Philosophical Logic
Edited by Dale Jacquette
23. A Companion to Early Modern Philosophy
Edited by Steven Nadler
24. A Companion to Philosophy in the Middle Ages
Edited by Jorge J. E. Gracia and Timothy B. Noone
25. A Companion to African-American Philosophy
Edited by Tommy L. Lott and John P. Pittman
26. A Companion to Applied Ethics
Edited by R. G. Frey and Christopher Heath Wellman
27. A Companion to the Philosophy of Education
Edited by Randall Curren
28. A Companion to African Philosophy
Edited by Kwasi Wiredu
29. A Companion to Heidegger
Edited by Hubert L. Dreyfus and Mark A. Wrathall
30. A Companion to Rationalism
Edited by Alan Nelson
31. A Companion to Pragmatism
Edited by John R. Shook and Joseph Margolis
32. A Companion to Ancient Philosophy
Edited by Mary Louise Gill and Pierre Pellegrin
33. A Companion to Nietzsche
Edited by Keith Ansell Pearson
34. A Companion to Socrates
Edited by Sara Ahbel-Rappe and Rachana Kamtekar
35. A Companion to Phenomenology and Existentialism
Edited by Hubert L. Dreyfus and Mark A. Wrathall
36. A Companion to Kant
Edited by Graham Bird
37. A Companion to Plato
Edited by Hugh H. Benson
38. A Companion to Descartes
Edited by Janet Broughton and John Carriero
39. A Companion to the Philosophy of Biology
Edited by Sahotra Sarkar and Anya Plutynski
40. A Companion to Hume
Edited by Elizabeth S. Radcliffe
41. A Companion to the Philosophy of History and Historiography
Edited by Aviezer Tucker
42. A Companion to Aristotle
Edited by Georgios Anagnostopoulos
43. A Companion to the Philosophy of Technology
Edited by Jan-Kyrre Berg Olsen, Stig Andur Pedersen, and Vincent F. Hendricks
44. A Companion to Latin American Philosophy
Edited by Susana Nuccetelli, Ofelia Schutte, and Otávio Bueno
45. A Companion to the Philosophy of Literature
Edited by Garry L. Hagberg and Walter Jost
46. A Companion to the Philosophy of Action
Edited by Timothy O'Connor and Constantine Sandis
47. A Companion to Relativism
Edited by Steven D. Hales
48. A Companion to Hegel
Edited by Stephen Houlgate and Michael Baur
49. A Companion to Schopenhauer
Edited by Bart Vandenabeele
50. A Companion to Buddhist Philosophy
Edited by Steven M. Emmanuel
51. A Companion to Foucault
Edited by Christopher Falzon, Timothy O'Leary, and Jana Sawicki
52. A Companion to the Philosophy of Time
Edited by Heather Dyke and Adrian Bardon
53. A Companion to Donald Davidson
Edited by Ernest Lepore and Kirk Ludwig
54. A Companion to Rawls
Edited by Jon Mandle and David Reidy
55. A Companion to W.V.O Quine
Edited by Gilbert Harman and Ernest Lepore
56. A Companion to Derrida
Edited by Zeynep Direk and Leonard Lawlor
57. A Companion to David Lewis
Edited by Barry Loewer and Jonathan Schaffer
58. A Companion to Kierkegaard
Edited by Jon Stewart
59. A Companion to Locke
Edited by Matthew Stuart
60. A Companion to Ayn Rand
Edited by Allan Gotthelf and Gregory Salmieri

A Companion to Buddhist Philosophy

Edited by

Steven M. Emmanuel

WILEY Blackwell

This paperback edition first published 2016

Edition history: John Wiley & Sons, Inc. (hardback, 2013)

Registered Office
John Wiley & Sons Ltd, The Atrium, Southern Gate, Chichester, West Sussex, PO19 8SQ, UK

Editorial Offices
350 Main Street, Malden, MA 02148-5020, USA
9600 Garsington Road, Oxford, OX4 2DQ, UK
The Atrium, Southern Gate, Chichester, West Sussex, PO19 8SQ, UK

For details of our global editorial offices, for customer services, and for information about how to apply for permission to reuse the copyright material in this book please see our website at www.wiley.com/wiley-blackwell.

Library of Congress Cataloging-in-Publication Data

A companion to Buddhist philosophy / edited by Steven M. Emmanuel.
pages cm – (Blackwell companions to philosophy ; 139)
Includes bibliographical references and index.
ISBN 978-0-470-65877-2 (hardback) ISBN 978-1-119-14466-3 (paperback)
1. Buddhist philosophy. I. Emmanuel, Steven M., editor of compilation.
B162.C66 2013
181′.043–dc23

2012036590

A catalogue record for this book is available from the British Library.

Cover image: Statue of Buddha, Sukhothai, Thailand. Photo © Paul Davis.

Set in 10/12.5 pt Photina by SPi Global, Pondicherry, India
Printed and bound in Singapore by C.O.S. Printers Pte Ltd

2 2016

Are not the mountains, waves, and skies, a part
Of me and of my soul, as I of them?
– Lord Byron

Contents

Notes on Contributors xi

Acknowledgments xviii

List of Abbreviations xix

Introduction 1
Steven M. Emmanuel

Part I Conceptual Foundations 11

1 The Philosophical Context of Gotama's Thought 13
Stephen J. Laumakis

2 *Dukkha,* Non-Self, and the Teaching on the Four "Noble Truths" 26
Peter Harvey

3 The Conditioned Co-arising of Mental and Bodily Processes within Life and Between Lives 46
Peter Harvey

Part II Major Schools of Buddhist Thought 69

4 Theravāda 71
Andrew Skilton

5 Indian Mahāyāna Buddhism 86
James Blumenthal

6 Tibetan Mahāyāna and Vajrayāna 99
Douglas Duckworth

7 East Asian Buddhism 110
Ronald S. Green

Part III Themes in Buddhist Philosophy 127

A. Metaphysics 129

8 Metaphysical Issues in Indian Buddhist Thought 129
Jan Westerhoff

9 Emptiness in Mahāyāna Buddhism: Interpretations and Comparisons 151
David Burton

10 Practical Applications of the *Perfection of Wisdom Sūtra* and Madhyamaka in the Kālacakra Tantric Tradition 164
Vesna A. Wallace

11 The Huayan Metaphysics of Totality 180
Alan Fox

12 Forms of Emptiness in Zen 190
Bret W. Davis

13 Between the Horns of Idealism and Realism: The Middle Way of Madhyamaka 214
Graham Priest

B. Epistemology 223

14 A Survey of Early Buddhist Epistemology 223
John J. Holder

15 Reason and Experience in Buddhist Epistemology 241
Christian Coseru

16 The Three Truths in Tiantai Buddhism 256
Brook Ziporyn

17 "Spiritual Exercise" and Buddhist Epistemologists in India and Tibet 270
Matthew T. Kapstein

18 Yogic Perception, Meditation, and Enlightenment: The Epistemological Issues in a Key Debate 290
Tom J. F. Tillemans

C. Language and Logic 307

19 Language and Logic in Indian Buddhist Thought 307
Brendan S. Gillon

20 Buddhist Philosophy of Logic 320
Koji Tanaka

21 Candrakīrti on the Limits of Language and Logic 331
Karen C. Lang

22 On the Value of Speaking and Not Speaking: Philosophy of Language in Zen Buddhism 349
Steven Heine

23 The Voice of Another: Speech, Responsiveness, and Buddhist Philosophy 366
Richard F. Nance

D. Philosophy of Mind 377

24 Mind in Theravāda Buddhism 377
Maria Heim

25 Philosophy of Mind in Buddhism 395
Richard P. Hayes

26 Cognition, Phenomenal Character, and Intentionality in Tibetan Buddhism 405
Jonathan Stoltz

27 The Non-Self Theory and Problems in Philosophy of Mind 419
Joerg Tuske

E. Ethics and Moral Philosophy 429

28 Ethical Thought in Indian Buddhism 429
Christopher W. Gowans

29 Character, Disposition, and the Qualities of the *Arahats* as a Means of Communicating Buddhist Philosophy in the *Suttas* 452
Sarah Shaw

30 Compassion and the Ethics of Violence 466
Stephen Jenkins

31 Buddhist Ethics and Western Moral Philosophy 476
William Edelglass

F. Social and Political Philosophy 491

32 The Enlightened Sovereign: Buddhism and Kingship in India and Tibet 491
Georgios T. Halkias

33 Political Interpretations of the *Lotus Sūtra* 512
James Mark Shields

34 Socially Engaged Buddhism: Emerging Patterns of Theory and Practice 524
Christopher S. Queen

35 Comparative Reflections on Buddhist Political Thought: Aśoka, Shambhala and the General Will 536
David Cummiskey

Part IV Buddhist Meditation 553

36 Buddhist Meditation: Theory and Practice 555
Charles Goodman

37 Seeing Mind, Being Body: Contemplative Practice and Buddhist Epistemology 572
Anne Carolyn Klein

38 From the Five Aggregates to Phenomenal Consciousness: Towards a Cross-Cultural Cognitive Science 585
Jake H. Davis and Evan Thompson

Part V Contemporary Issues and Applications 599

39 Buddhism and Environmental Ethics 601
Simon P. James

40 Buddhism and Biomedical Issues 613
Damien Keown

41 War and Peace in Buddhist Philosophy 631
Sallie B. King

42 Buddhist Perspectives on Human Rights 651
Karma Lekshe Tsomo

43 Buddhist Perspectives on Gender Issues 663
Rita M. Gross

44 Diversity Matters: Buddhist Reflections on the Meaning of Difference 675
Peter D. Hershock

Further Reading 693

Index 696

Notes on Contributors

James Blumenthal is Associate Professor in the Philosophy Department at Oregon State University and founding faculty member at Maitripa College, Portland. He is the author of numerous articles and books on Buddhism, including *The Ornament of the Middle Way: A Study of the Madhyamaka Thought of Śāntarakṣita* (Snow Lion, 2004), editor of *Incompatible Visions: South Asian Religions in History and Culture* (University of Wisconsin Press, 2006), and co-author (with Geshe Lhundup Sopa) of *Steps on the Path to Enlightenment: A Commentary on Tsongkhapa's Lamrim Chenmo*, Vol. 4: *Samatha* (Wisdom, 2012). In 2004 he had the honor of translating Nāgārjuna's "Sixty Stanzas of Reasoning" for His Holiness the Dalai Lama on the occasion of his public lectures on the text in Pasadena, California.

David Burton is Senior Lecturer in the Department of Theology and Religious Studies at Canterbury Christ Church University in the UK. Along with a number of articles, he has published two books: *Buddhism, Knowledge and Liberation: A Philosophical Study* (Ashgate, 2004) and *Emptiness Appraised: A Critical Study of Nāgārjuna's Philosophy* (RoutledgeCurzon, 1999).

Christian Coseru is Associate Professor in the Department of Philosophy at the College of Charleston, South Carolina. He is the author of several articles on Buddhist philosophy and a book, *Perceiving Reality: Consciousness, Intentionality, and Cognition in Buddhist Philosophy* (Oxford University Press, 2012).

David Cummiskey is Professor of Philosophy at Bates College, Lewiston, Maine. He is the author of *Kantian Consequentialism* (Oxford University Press, 1996), and his recent articles include "Competing Conceptions of the Self in Kantian and Buddhist Moral Theories," in *Cultivating Personhood: Kant and Asian Philosophy* (Walter de Gruyter, 2010), "The Law of Peoples," in *The Morality and Global Justice Reader* (Westview Press, 2011), and "Dignity, Contractualism, and Consequentialism," in *Utilitas*, 20/4 (2008).

Bret W. Davis is Associate Professor of Philosophy at Loyola University Maryland. Among his books are *Heidegger and the Will: On the Way to Gelassenheit* (Northwestern University Press, 2007); co-edited with Brian Schroeder and Jason M. Wirth, *Japanese and Continental Philosophy: Conversations with the Kyoto School* (Indiana University Press,

2011); and co-edited with Fujita Masakatsu, *Sekai no naka no Nihon no tetsugaku* (Japanese Philosophy in the World) (Showado, 2005). He has also published numerous articles in English and in Japanese on continental and comparative philosophy, on the Kyoto School, and on Zen.

Jake H. Davis is a doctoral student in philosophy and cognitive science at the Graduate Center of the City University of New York, visiting faculty at the Barre Center for Buddhist Studies, Massachusetts, and a visiting scholar in psychiatry at Brown University. He trained in Buddhist theory and meditative practice under the meditation master Sayadaw U Pandita of Burma and served for a decade as an interpreter between Burmese and English for meditation retreats in Burma and abroad.

Douglas Duckworth is Assistant Professor in the Department of Philosophy and Humanities at East Tennessee State University. He is the author of *Mipam on Buddha-Nature: The Ground of the Nyingma Tradition* (SUNY Press, 2008) and *Jamgön Mipam: His Life and Teachings* (Shambhala, 2011). He also translated Bötrül's *Distinguishing the Views and Philosophies: Illuminating Emptiness in a Twentieth-Century Tibetan Buddhist Classic* (SUNY Press, 2011).

William Edelglass is Professor of Philosophy and Environmental Studies at Marlboro College, Vermont. Previously he taught at the Institute of Buddhist Dialectics in Dharamsala, India. He has published widely in Indian and Tibetan Buddhist philosophy, environmental philosophy, and contemporary continental philosophy. He is co-editor of the journal *Environmental Philosophy* and of *Facing Nature: Levinas and Environmental Philosophy* (Duquesne University Press, 2012), *Buddhist Philosophy: Essential Readings* (Oxford University Press, 2009), and *The Oxford Handbook of World Philosophy* (2010).

Alan Fox is Professor of Asian and Comparative Philosophy and Religion in the Philosophy Department at the University of Delaware. He has published on Chinese Buddhism and philosophical Daoism. His publications include "Self-Reflection in the *Sanlun* Tradition: *Madhyamika* as the Deconstructive Conscience of Buddhism," in the *Journal of Chinese Philosophy* (March 1992), "Process Ecology and 'Ideal Dao,'" in the *Journal of Chinese Philosophy* (March 2005), and "Dushun's *Huayan Fajie Guan Men* (*Meditative Approaches to the Huayana Dharmadātu*)," in *Buddhist Philosophy: Essential Readings* (Oxford University Press, 2009).

Brendan S. Gillon is Professor of Linguistics at McGill University. He has research interests in the history of logic and metaphysics in India, Sanskrit linguistics, and natural language semantics, and has published extensively in all of these areas. He is editor of *Logic in Earliest Classical India* (Motilal Banarsidass, 2010) and co-editor of *Semantics: A Reader* (Oxford University Press, 2004). In collaboration with Richard Hayes, he has translated the first 38 verses and their prose commentary of Dharmakīrti's Svarthanumana chapter of the *Pramanavarttika*.

Charles Goodman is Associate Professor in the Philosophy Department and the Department of Asian and Asian-American Studies at Binghamton University. He is the author of several published articles on Buddhist philosophy and of the book *Consequences of Compassion: An Interpretation and Defense of Buddhist Ethics* (Oxford University Press, 2009).

Christopher W. Gowans is Professor of Philosophy at Fordham University. He is the editor of *Moral Disagreements* (Routledge, 2000) and *Moral Dilemmas* (Oxford University Press, 1989) and the author of *Philosophy of the Buddha* (Routledge, 2003).

Ronald S. Green is Assistant Professor in the Department of Philosophy and Religious Studies at Coastal Carolina University, South Carolina. He is an editor of a book series on religions and social engagement which includes *Buddhist Roles in Peacemaking: How Buddhism can Contribute to Sustainable Peace* (Blue Pine Books, 2009). His research focuses on East Asian developments of Yogācāra and tantric Buddhist philosophy.

Rita M. Gross, before her retirement, was for twenty-five years Professor of Comparative Studies in Religion at the University of Wisconsin–Eau Claire. She is a well-known Dharma teacher and the author of many books and articles. Her best-known books are *Buddhism after Patriarchy* (SUNY Press, 1993), *Feminism and Religion: An Introduction* (Beacon Press, 1996), and *A Garland of Feminist Reflections: Forty Years of Religious Exploration* (University of California Press, 2009). She was co-editor of *Buddhist–Christian Studies* for ten years and has been active in inter-religious discussion.

Georgios T. Halkias is Research Fellow and Coordinator of Religions of Central Asia at the Centre of Religious Studies at the Ruhr University in Bochum and a Fellow at the Oxford Centre of Buddhist Studies. Among his publications are *Luminous Bliss: A Religious History of Pure Land Literature in Tibet* (University of Hawaiʻi Press) and a number of articles on Tibetan and Central Asian Buddhism and history and interdisciplinary studies in religion.

Peter Harvey is Emeritus Professor of Buddhist Studies at the University of Sunderland in the UK. His research focuses on early Buddhist thought and practices and Buddhist ethics. He is the editor of *Buddhist Studies Review* and the author of *An Introduction to Buddhism: Teachings, History and Practices* (Cambridge University Press, 1990, 2nd edn 2012), *The Selfless Mind: Personality, Consciousness and Nirvana in Early Buddhism* (Curzon Press, 1995), and *An Introduction to Buddhist Ethics: Foundations, Values and Practices* (Cambridge University Press, 2000). He is currently working on *Spiritual Nobility in Early Buddhism: Noble Path, Noble Persons, and the Four True Realities that They See.*

Richard P. Hayes is Associate Professor of Philosophy at the University of New Mexico. He earned his doctorate in Sanskrit and Indian studies at the University of Toronto. He has taught in the departments of Philosophy and Religious Studies at the University of Toronto and McGill University and as Numata guest professor of Buddhism at Leiden University.

Maria Heim is Associate Professor of Buddhist Studies at Amherst College, Massachusetts. She holds a BA from Reed College and a PhD in Sanskrit and Indian studies from Harvard University. She works on South Asian Buddhism, particularly on Theravāda, and is currently focusing on the thought of Buddhaghosa. She is interested in moral psychology and is completing a book on Theravāda understandings of agency and intention in the different canonical and commentarial genres of the Pāli literature.

Steven Heine is Professor of Religious Studies and History as well as Associate Director of the School of International and Public Affairs and Director of Asian Studies at Florida International University. His research specialty is the origins and development of Zen Buddhism, especially the life and teachings of Dōgen, founder of the Sōtō sect. He has published two dozen books, including The *Zen Poetry of Dōgen* (Tuttle, 1997) and, with Oxford University Press, *Opening a Mountain* (2002), *Did Dōgen Go to China?* (2006), *Zen Masters* (2010), and *Dōgen: Textual and Historical Studies* (2012).

Peter D. Hershock is Director of the Asian Studies Development Program at the East–West Center in Honolulu, Hawai'i. His research has focused mainly on using Buddhist conceptual resources to address contemporary issues. Among his books are *Liberating Intimacy: Enlightenment and Social Virtuosity in Ch'an Buddhism* (SUNY Press, 1996), *Reinventing the Wheel: A Buddhist Response to the Information Age* (SUNY Press, 1999), *Chan Buddhism* (University of Hawai'i Press, 2005), *Buddhism in the Public Sphere: Reorienting Global Interdependence* (Routledge, 2006), and *Valuing Diversity: Buddhist Reflection on Realizing a More Equitable Global Future* (SUNY Press, 2012).

John J. Holder is Associate Professor of Philosophy at St. Norbert College, Wisconsin. He is the author of *Early Buddhist Discourses* (Hackett, 2006), a volume containing English translations of Pāli discourses that are essential for the study of early Buddhist philosophy. He has also published articles on early Buddhist epistemology, ethics, and social theory. His research focus is on comparative philosophy, specifically comparing early Buddhism and classical American pragmatism with the aim of developing a naturalistic theory of aesthetics and religious meaning.

Simon P. James is Senior Lecturer in Philosophy at Durham University in the UK. He is the author of *Zen Buddhism and Environmental Ethics* (Ashgate, 2004), *The Presence of Nature: A Study in Phenomenology and Environmental Philosophy* (Palgrave, 2009), and (with David E. Cooper) *Buddhism, Virtue and Environment* (Ashgate, 2005).

Stephen Jenkins is Professor of Religious Studies at Humboldt State University. His research is focused on Buddhist concepts of compassion, their philosophical grounding, and their ethical implications. His current work explores these themes in justifications of warfare, penal codes, compassionate killing, tantric *sādhanas* for killing, and the Aśokan edicts.

Matthew T. Kapstein is currently Director of Tibetan Studies at the École Pratique des Hautes Études in Paris and Numata Visiting Professor of Buddhist Studies in the Divinity School of the University of Chicago. His publications include *The Tibetan Assimilation of Buddhism: Conversion, Contestation, and Memory* (Oxford University Press, 2000), *Reason's Traces: Identity and Interpretation in Indian and Tibetan Buddhist Thought* (Wisdom, 2001), *The Tibetans* (Blackwell, 2006), and, in the Clay Sanskrit Series, *The Rise of Wisdom Moon* (New York University Press, 2009).

Damien Keown is Emeritus Professor of Buddhist Ethics at Goldsmiths College, University of London. His main research interests are theoretical and applied aspects of Buddhist ethics, with particular reference to contemporary issues. He is the author of many books and articles, among them *The Nature of Buddhist Ethics* (Palgrave, 2001), *Buddhism and Bioethics* (Palgrave, 2001), *Buddhism: A Very Short Introduction*

(Oxford University Press, 2000), *Buddhist Ethics: A Very Short Introduction* (Oxford University Press, 2006), and the *Oxford Dictionary of Buddhism* (2003). In 1994 he founded the *Journal of Buddhist Ethics* with Charles S. Prebish, with whom he also co-founded the Routledge Critical Studies in Buddhism Series, and co-edited the *Routledge Encyclopedia of Buddhism*.

Sallie B. King is Professor of Philosophy and Religion at James Madison University, Virginia. She is the author of *Buddha Nature* (SUNY Press, 1991), *Journey in Search of the Way: The Spiritual Autobiography of Satomi Myodo* (SUNY Press, 1993), *Being Benevolence: The Social Ethics of Engaged Buddhism* (University of Hawai'i Press, 2005), and *Socially Engaged Buddhism* (University of Hawai'i Press, 2009). She is co-editor (with Christopher S. Queen) of *Engaged Buddhism: Buddhist Liberation Movements in Asia* (SUNY Press, 1996) and (with Paul O. Ingram) of *The Sound of Liberating Truth: Buddhist–Christian Dialogues in Honor of Frederick J. Streng* (Curzon Press, 1999).

Anne Carolyn Klein is Professor of Religious Studies at Rice University and a founding director and resident teacher of the Dawn Mountain Center, Houston. Her work centers on the Tibetan Buddhist tradition and its Indian roots, with a special interest in the interplay between intellectual understanding and contemplative practice. She is the author or translator of six books, notably *Heart Essence of the Vast Expanse: A Story of Transmission* (Snow Lion, 2010) and the recently republished *Meeting the Great Bliss Queen* (Snow Lion, 2008).

Karen C. Lang is Professor of Indian Religions in the Department of Religious Studies and two-time Director of the Center for South Asian Studies at the University of Virginia. Her publications include *Four Illusions: Candrakīrti's Advice for Travelers on the Bodhisattva Path* (Oxford University Press, 2003) and *Āryadeva's Catuḥśataka: On the Bodhisattva's Cultivation of Merit and Knowledge* (Akademisk Forlag, 1986), as well as numerous articles on Buddhist philosophy and literature. She has been a member of the team that produced the first English translation of Tsongkhapa's *The Great Treatise on the Stages of the Path to Enlightenment*. Her primary research and translation interests focus on the work of the seventh-century Indian Buddhist philosopher Candrakīrti.

Stephen J. Laumakis is Professor of Philosophy and Director of the Aquinas Scholars Honors Program at the University of St. Thomas in St. Paul, Minnesota. Among his publications are articles in *East–West Connections: Review of Asian Studies*, the *Modern Schoolman*, *American Catholic Philosophical Quarterly*, and a book, *An Introduction to Buddhist Philosophy* (Cambridge University Press, 2008).

Richard F. Nance is Assistant Professor of South Asian Buddhism in the Department of Religious Studies at Indiana University. He has published work in the *Journal of Indian Philosophy*, *Religion Compass*, and the *Journal of the International Association of Buddhist Studies*, and is the author of *Speaking for Buddhas: Scriptural Commentary in Indian Buddhism* (Columbia University Press, 2012).

Graham Priest is Boyce Gibson Professor of Philosophy at the University of Melbourne, Distinguished Professor at the Graduate Center, City University of New York, and Arché Professorial Fellow at the University of St. Andrews. His books include

In Contradiction (Nijhoff, 1987), *Beyond the Limits of Thought* (Clarendon Press, 2002), *Towards Non-Being* (Clarendon Press, 2005), *Doubt Truth to be a Liar* (Clarendon Press, 2006), and *Introduction to Non-Classical Logic* (Cambridge University Press, 2008).

Christopher S. Queen is Lecturer on Buddhism and World Religions at Harvard University. Among his publications are *Engaged Buddhism: Buddhist Liberation Movements in Asia* (with Sallie King; SUNY Press, 1996); *American Buddhism: Methods and Findings in Recent Scholarship* (with Duncan Williams; Curzon Press, 1999); *Engaged Buddhism in the West* (Wisdom 2000); and *Action Dharma: New Studies in Engaged Buddhism* (with Charles Prebish and Damien Keown; RoutledgeCurzon, 2003).

Sarah Shaw has membership of the Faculty of Oriental Studies and Wolfson College, Oxford University, and is an honorary fellow of the Oxford Centre for Buddhist Studies. She is the author of a number of books on Buddhist meditation and narrative, including *Buddhist Meditation: An Anthology of Texts from the Pali Canon* (Routledge, 2006) and *Introduction to Buddhist Meditation* (Routledge, 2008). She is also co-editor (with Linda Covill and Ulrike Roesler) of *Lives Lived, Lives Imagined: Biographies of Awakening* (Wisdom, 2010).

James Mark Shields is Assistant Professor of Comparative Humanities and Asian Thought at Bucknell University, Lewisburg, Pennsylvania, and Research Associate at the Reischauer Institute for Japanese Studies, Harvard University. He is the author of *Critical Buddhism: Engaging with Modern Japanese Buddhist Thought* (Ashgate, 2011) and co-editor (with Victor Sōgen Hori and Richard P. Hayes) of *Teaching Buddhism in the West: From the Wheel to the Web* (Routledge, 2003). He is currently working on a book manuscript entitled *Warp and Woof: Modernism and Progressivism in Japanese Buddhism, 1886–1936.*

Andrew Skilton is a Senior Research Fellow in the Department of Theology and Religious Studies at King's College London and Spalding Fellow at Clare Hall, Cambridge. His research focuses on textual sources from Indian and South-East Asian Buddhism in Sanskrit and Pāli.

Jonathan Stoltz is Associate Professor of Philosophy at the University of St. Thomas in St. Paul, Minnesota. He has authored papers on Buddhist epistemology in numerous journals, including *Philosophical Quarterly*, *Philosophy East and West*, and the *Journal of the International Association of Buddhist Studies*. He is currently writing a book on philosophy of mind in twelfth-century Tibetan Buddhism.

Koji Tanaka is Senior Lecturer in the Department of Philosophy at the University of Auckland, New Zealand. A specialist in logic and Buddhist philosophy, he contributed "A Dharmakirtian Critique of Nagarjunians" to *Pointing at the Moon* (Oxford University Press, 2009) and is a co-author of *Moonshadows: Conventional Truth in Buddhist Philosophy* (Oxford University Press, 2011).

Evan Thompson is Professor of Philosophy at the University of Toronto. He is the author of *Mind in Life: Biology, Phenomenology, and the Sciences of Mind* (Harvard University Press, 2007), co-author of *The Embodied Mind: Cognitive Science and Human*

Experience (MIT Press, 1991), and co-editor of *Self, No Self? Perspectives from Analytical, Phenomenological, and Indian Traditions* (Oxford University Press, 2010).

Tom J. F. Tillemans is Emeritus Professor of Buddhist Studies at the University of Lausanne, Switzerland. He is the author of many books and articles on Buddhism and currently serves as editor in chief of the "84000" (see http://84000.co), a long-term project to translate Buddhist canonical literature.

Joerg Tuske is Associate Professor in the Philosophy Department at Salisbury University in Maryland. His main interest lies in Sanskrit philosophy, especially in the debate about the *ātman*. His publications include "Teaching by Example: An Interpretation of the Role of *Upamana* in Early Nyaya Philosophy," in *Asian Philosophy* (2008), and "Dignaga and the Raven Paradox," in the *Journal of Indian Philosophy* (1998).

Karma Lekshe Tsomo is Associate Professor in the Department of Theology and Religious Studies at the University of San Diego, where she teaches courses on Buddhism, world religions, comparative religious ethics, and death and afterlife. She studied Buddhism in Dharamsala, India, for 15 years and received a doctorate in comparative philosophy from the University of Hawai'i at Manoa, with research on death and identity in China and Tibet. Her publications include *Sisters in Solitude: Two Traditions of Buddhist Monastic Ethics for Women* (SUNY Press, 1996), *Into the Jaws of Yama, Lord of Death: Buddhism, Bioethics, and Death* (SUNY Press, 2006), and a number of edited volumes on women in Buddhism.

Vesna A. Wallace is Professor of Buddhist Studies in the Department of Religious Studies at the University of California, Santa Barbara. Her areas of research are Indian Buddhism and Mongolian Buddhism. She has published three books related to the Kālacakratantra and a series of articles on the Kālacakra tantric tradition and Mongolian Buddhism.

Jan Westerhoff is Lecturer in Philosophy at the University of Durham and Research Associate in the School of Oriental and African Studies, University of London. He is the author of numerous articles and books on Buddhism, including *The Dispeller of Disputes: Nāgārjuna's Vigrahavyāvartanī* (Oxford University Press, 2010) and *Nāgārjuna's Madhyamaka: A Philosophical Investigation* (Oxford University Press, 2009).

Brook Ziporyn is Professor of Chinese Philosophy, Religion, and Comparative Thought at the Divinity School of the University of Chicago and Visiting Professor at the National University of Singapore. His published books include *Evil and/or/as the Good: Omnicentrism, Intersubjectivity, and Value Paradox in Tiantai Buddhist Thought* (Harvard University Press, 2000), *The Penumbra Unbound: The Neo-Taoist Philosophy of Guo Xiang* (SUNY Press, 2003), *Being and Ambiguity: Philosophical Experiments with Tiantai Buddhism* (Open Court, 2004) and *Zhuangzi: The Essential Writings with Selections from Traditional Commentaries* (Hackett, 2009).

Acknowledgments

A volume such as this is only possible because of the efforts of many talented people. I would therefore like to express my sincere gratitude to the contributors, with whom it has been both an honor and a great pleasure to collaborate on this project. I would also like to thank Caroline Richmond for her careful editorial work in preparing the final manuscript for publication, and Sue Leigh for her patient diligence in seeing the volume through the final stages of production.

List of Abbreviations

Bibliographical

AKB Vasubandhu, *Abhidharmakośa-bhāṣyam.* Trans. L. M. Pruden from Louis de La Valleé Poussin's French translation of *Abhidharmakośabhāṣyam.* 4 vols. Berkeley, CA: Asian Humanities Press, 1991.

AN *Aṅguttara Nikāya: The Book of the Gradual Sayings.* Trans. F. L. Woodward and E. M. Hare. 5 vols. London: PTS, 1932–6; *The Numerical Discourses of the Buddha.* Trans. Bhikkhu Bodhi. Boston: Wisdom, 2012.

BW Bhikkhu Bodhi, *The Buddha's Words: An Anthology of Discourses from the Pali Canon.* Boston: Wisdom, 2005.

CŚ *Āryadeva's Catuḥśataka: On the Bodhisattva's Cultivation of Merit and Knowledge.* Trans. Karen Lang. Copenhagen: Akademisk Forlag, 1986.

Dhp. *Dhammapada: The Word of the Doctrine.* Trans. K. R. Norman. London: PTS, 1997; *The Dhammapada.* Trans. V. Roebuck. London: Penguin, 2010.

Dhs. *Dhammasangani: A Buddhist Manual of Psychological Ethics.* Trans. C. A. F. Rhys Davids. Third edn. London and Boston: PTS, 1974.

Dhs-a *Aṭṭhasālinī*: Commentary on the *Dhammasangaṇī. The Expositor*. Trans. Pe Maung Tin. 2 vols. London: PTS, 1920–1.

DN *Dīgha Nikāya: Dialogues of the Buddha.* Trans. T. W. Rhys Davids and C. A. F. Rhys Davids. 3 vols. London: PTS, 1899–1921; *Long Discourses of the Buddha.* Trans. M. Walshe. Second rev. edn. Boston: Wisdom, 1996.

DN-a *Dīgha Nikāya Aṭṭhakathā (Sumaṅgalavilāsinī).* Commentary on DN.

It. *The Itivuttaka.* Trans. P. Masefield. London: PTS, 2000.

J *The Jātaka, or, Stories of the Buddha's Former Births.* Ed. E. B. Cowell. 7 vols. Cambridge: Cambridge University Press, 1895–1907; London PTS, 1972 [*Jātakas* cited by number].

MĀ *Introduction to the Middle Way: Candrakīrti's Madhyamakāvatāra.* Trans. Padmakara Translation Group. Boston and London: Shambhala, 2004.

Miln. *Milindapañha: Milinda's Questions.* Trans. I. B. Horner. 2 vols. London: PTS, 1963–4.

MMK *The Fundamental Wisdom of the Middle Way.* Trans. and Commentary Jay L. Garfield. Oxford: Oxford University Press, 1995.

MN *Majjhima Nikāya: The Collection of the Middle Length Sayings.* Trans. I. B. Horner. 3 vols. London: PTS, 1954–9; *The Middle Length Discourses of the Buddha.* Trans. Bhikkhu Ñāṇamoli and Bhikkhu Bodhi. Boston: Wisdom, 1995.

MN-a *Majjhima Nikāya Aṭṭhakathā (Papañcasūdanī).* Commentary on MN.

Patis. *Paṭisambhidā-magga: The Path of Discrimination.* Trans. Bhikkhu Ñāṇamoli. London: PTS, 1982.

PP *Mūlamadhyamakakārikās de Nāgārjuna avec la Prasannapadā Commentaire de Candrakīrti.* Trans. Louis de La Vallée Poussin. Osnabrück: Biblio Verlag, 1970 [reprint].

SB Rupert Gethin, *Sayings of the Buddha: A Selection of Suttas from the Pali Nikāyas.* Oxford and New York: Oxford University Press, 2008.

SN *Saṃyutta Nikāya: The Book of the Kindred Sayings.* Trans. C. A. F. Rhys Davids and F. L. Woodward. London: PTS, 1917–30; *The Connected Discourses of the Buddha.* Trans. Bhikkhu Bodhi. Boston: Wisdom, 2005.

Sn *Sutta-nipāta: The Group of Discourses.* Trans. K. R. Norman. Second edn. London: PTS, 2001.

T *Taishō shinshū daizōkyō: The Taishō Tripiṭaka.* Ed. Takakusu Juniro et al. Tokyo: Taishō issaikyō kankō-kai, 1914–32. [Taishō is a definitive version of the Chinese Buddhist canon standardized in Japan during the Taishō period.] Online edn: Chinese Buddhist Electronic Text Association (CBETA), www.cbeta.org/.

Thag. *Thera-gāthā: Elders' Verses.* Trans. K. R. Norman. Vol. 1. London: PTS, 1969.

TS *The Tattva-saṃgraha of Śāntarakṣita with the Commentary (Pañjikā) of Kamalaśīla.* Trans. Ganganatha Jha. Vols. 1–2. Delhi: Motilal Banarsidass, 1986.

Ud. *The Udāna.* Trans. P. Masefield. London: PTS, 1994.

Vibh. *Vibhaṅga: The Book of Analysis.* Trans. U. Thittila. London: PTS, 1969.

Vibh-a Commentary on *Vibhaṅga: Dispeller of Delusion.* Trans. Bhikkhu Ñāṇamoli. 2 vols. London: PTS, 1996.

Vin. *Vinaya Piṭaka: The Book of the Discipline.* Trans. I. B. Horner. 6 vols. London: PTS, 1938–66.

Vism. Buddhaghosa, *Visuddhimagga: The Path of Purification.* Trans. Bhikkhu Ñāṇamoli. Onalaska, WA: BPS Pariyatti, 1999.

General

Ch. Chinese
Gk Greek
Jp. Japanese
K. Korean
P. Pāli
PTS Pali Text Society
Skt Sanskrit
Tb. Tibetan

Introduction

STEVEN M. EMMANUEL

The task of producing a comprehensive, single-volume treatment of Buddhist philosophy presents certain editorial challenges, not the least of which is the problem of how to do justice to the sheer breadth and diversity of a tradition that spans some two and a half millennia. The following introductory remarks are intended to shed some light on the considerations that shaped the structure and content of this volume.

The Buddha and Buddhist Philosophy

Buddhism is a living tradition that traces its origins to the life and teachings of Siddhattha Gotama (Skt Siddhārtha Gautama), the historical Buddha. Not much is known with any certainty about the life of the founder. Even his dates, conventionally given as 566–486 BCE, are a subject of ongoing scholarly debate.[1]

The earliest accounts of the Buddha's life are fragmentary, and though more complete biographical narratives begin to appear around the first century CE, these later versions of the story are highly embellished and in some cases offer conflicting accounts of events. While these texts are of enormous importance to Buddhist tradition, they present challenges for the historian who is interested in separating myth from fact. That said, the picture we have of the historical Buddha is a composite based on what scholars have been able to infer from a combination of early Buddhist sources, archeological evidence, and general historical information about the culture and traditions of Indian society of the period.[2]

Another salient fact for us is that the Buddha did not commit any of his teachings to writing. According to tradition, 500 *arahats* (awakened disciples) assembled at Rājagaha several months after the Buddha's death to recite the teachings as they had been heard. These were divided into two collections: the first containing rules for

A Companion to Buddhist Philosophy, First Edition. Edited by Steven M. Emmanuel.

monastic conduct (*vinaya-piṭaka*); the second containing discourses delivered by the Buddha and his close disciples (*sutta-piṭaka*). Over time a third collection of "higher teachings" developed (*abhidhamma-piṭaka*). These contained detailed lists and expositions of concepts found in the discourses and were aimed at giving a more precise philosophical formulation of the Buddha's teachings.

As Buddhism gradually spread across the Indian subcontinent, versions of these teachings were orally preserved in various schools. Only much later were they written down in collections of scriptural texts.

The history of the formation of the Buddhist scriptural canon remains largely obscure to modern scholarship. The "Pāli canon" of the Theravāda school was one of the earliest to be written down. According to Theravāda tradition, this occurred in Sri Lanka in the latter half of the first century BCE. Other early schools produced canons in various Middle Indian dialects (Gethin 1998, 41–2). Important elements of these canons have been preserved in Sanskrit and in Chinese translation. However, the Pāli canon is the only one to have survived intact in its original Indian language. These texts, commonly referred to as the *Tipiṭaka*, form the scriptural basis of the southern tradition of Buddhism.

As Buddhist thought spread to China (beginning in the first century CE) and then to Tibet (beginning in the seventh century CE) it continued to be translated and interpreted through other cultural lenses and, to greater and lesser degrees, shaped by its encounters with other systems of thought. These encounters produced many new expressions of Buddhism, which differed from one another on philosophical points as well as matters of practice. Textual sources for the eastern and northern traditions of Buddhism are contained in Chinese and Tibetan canons respectively. While both of these collections contain translations of materials that have counterparts in the Pāli canon, they also contain a unique body of literature known as the Mahāyāna scriptures, which reflect important shifts in thinking that had begun already within the early Indian Buddhist community.

As the name Mahāyāna ("greater vehicle") implies, these scriptures purport to describe a superior path, according to which the ultimate aim of spiritual practice is not the fulfillment of one's own nirvanic aspirations, which Mahāyānists associated with the enlightenment realized by the *arahat*, but the complete and perfect awakening attained by the Buddha himself. This path is illustrated in Mahāyāna writings by the bodhisattva, who vows to work for the liberation of all beings. Some of these writings, known as the *Prajñāpāramitā Sūtras* ("Perfection of Wisdom Sūtras"), point to a more profound wisdom that can be attained through deep contemplation on the "emptiness" of all things.

In addition to the Mahāyāna scriptures, the Tibetan canon includes a distinctive body of tantric writings of Indian origin.[3] These esoteric teachings set out practical methods for realizing the supreme goal described in the Mahāyāna scriptures – for example, yogic practices, rituals, meditations using sacred mantras, and visualizations. As such, Tantric Buddhism is commonly understood to represent a third path of practice referred to as Vajrayāna.

Western scholarship has traditionally regarded the earliest portions of the Pāli canon as the most authoritative and reliable source for understanding early Buddhism.[4] The justification for this relies greatly on the Theravādin account of its provenance, which traces the canon back to a recension of the scriptures brought to Sri Lanka around 250 BCE, thereby securing its claim to being a faithful representation of the word of the Buddha. However, the supposed primacy of the Theravāda canon has been the object of much critical scrutiny in recent years. Scholars have challenged what they regard as unwarranted assumptions about the monolithic character of Theravāda tradition, as well as the presumed reliability of the canon as a source for understanding what Buddhists in earlier times actually believed and practiced (see Blackburn 2001 and Schopen 1997). There is considerable doubt surrounding the supposition that the Pāli texts, as we now have them, are a verbatim transcription of an oral version dating to the middle of the third century BCE. The content of surviving fragments from other early canons, though quite similar to the Pāli texts, is sufficiently different to suggest an ongoing process of composition and redaction. Many scholars would concur with the general assessment of Luis O. Gómez:

> Transmitted and edited through the oral tradition, the words of the Buddha and his immediate disciples had suffered many transformations before they came to be compiled, to say nothing of their state when they were eventually written down. We have no way of determining which, if any, of the words contained in the Buddhist scriptures are the words of the founder. . . . Evidently, the Pali canon, like other Buddhist scriptures, is the creation, or at least the compilation and composition, of another age and a different linguistic milieu. As they are preserved today, the Buddhist scriptures must be a collective creation, the fruit of the effort of several generations of memorizers, redactors, and compilers.
>
> (Gómez 2002, 55)

Along the same lines, Steven Collins has persuasively argued that the Pāli canon, understood as a "closed list of scriptures with a special and specific authority as the avowed historical record of the Buddha's teaching," did not pre-exist the Theravāda school, but was rather a product of it (Collins 1990, 72). Indeed, the creation of that canon continued at least through the fifth century CE, and "like most other religious Canons was produced in the context of dispute, here sectarian monastic rivalries" (ibid., 76–7). We might also note in this connection that a large portion of the Mahāyāna scriptures were already in circulation by the fifth century CE. All this points to a far more complicated (less linear) picture of the development of Buddhism than one might infer from the traditional Theravāda account.

Given the complex history of these texts, we should be wary of attempts to recover a more authentic or original form of Buddhism from canonical sources. This attitude has greatly influenced the presentation of Buddhism in contemporary scholarship, where it is now customary to stress the plurality of Buddhist thought and practice. In response to concerns about the perceived over-reliance on canonical writings, and in particular the narrowing effect of this textual-critical approach on research and teaching, scholars have increasingly begun to look to other sources, including "oral and vernacular traditions, epigraphy, ritual, patterns of social and institutional evolution, gender, lay and folk traditions, art, archeology and architecture" (Cabezón 1995, 262–3), which they believe offer a more accurate account of the actual practice of Buddhism.

Still, the gravitational pull of the canonical texts remains strong, especially in presentations of Buddhist philosophy. Every general survey pays close attention to the discourses of the *sutta-piṭaka* (the so-called Pāli Nikāyas) or to their counterparts in the Chinese canon (where they are called "Āgamas"). It is generally accepted that these texts are an important source for understanding how Buddhist thinkers in the early centuries of the Common Era framed their own philosophical inquiries. As Rupert Gethin observes:

> The failure to appreciate this results in a distorted view of ancient Buddhism, and its subsequent development and history both within and outside India. From their frequent references to and quotations from the Nikāyas/Āgamas, it is apparent that all subsequent Indian Buddhist thinkers and writers of whatever school or persuasion, including the Mahāyāna – and most certainly those thinkers such as Nāgārjuna, Asaṅga, and Vasubandhu, who became the great Indian fathers of east Asian and Tibetan Buddhism – were completely familiar with this material and treated it as the authoritative word of the Buddha.
>
> (Gethin 1998, 44)

Gethin goes on to note that, while interpretive disagreements inevitably arose, the authority of the texts was never in question.

To recognize the teachings presented in the Nikāya/Āgama material as in some sense "foundational" to the history of Buddhist philosophy does not, of course, commit us to parochial assumptions concerning the primacy of one textual tradition relative to others, or to claims about how accurately those texts reflect the actual words of the historical teacher. Still less does it commit us to the view that Buddhist philosophy is reducible to the views presented in those texts.

Introductions to Buddhist philosophy vary a good deal in the scope and depth of the coverage they offer. Some are limited to an exposition of the discourses contained in the early canonical writings, which are commonly presented as the "basic" or "essential" teachings of the Buddha (e.g., Gowans 2003), while others begin with the basic teachings, then proceed to show how these ideas were developed in later schools (e.g., Siderits 2007).

There are differences too in the way the authors approach the question of attribution. In his well-known study entitled *What the Buddha Taught* (1959), Walpola Rahula aims to give "a faithful and accurate account of the actual words used by the Buddha as they are to be found in the original Pali texts of the *Tipiṭaka*" (xi). However, the approach taken by Christopher W. Gowans in *Philosophy of the Buddha* (2003, 14) is more circumspect:

> The distance from the Buddha's mouth to the texts we now possess is considerable . . . and there is much room for modification and misunderstanding. To a limited extent, modern scholarship may inform us when texts are more or less likely to accurately represent what the Buddha really thought. But there is little prospect that we will ever know in detail how closely extant texts correspond to his actual teaching.

The question of attribution continues to be a contentious one in the secondary literature. According to Richard Gombrich, the core teachings of Buddhism exhibit a coherence that compels us to see them as the work of a single mind. "One remarkable brain," he claims, "must have been responsible for the basic ideology. The owner of that brain happens to be known, appropriately, as the Buddha, the 'Awakened'" (Gombrich 2009, 17).[5] This view parallels that of Étienne Lamotte, who, half a century earlier, remarked that "Buddhism could not be explained unless we accept that it has its origin in the strong personality of its founder" (Lamotte 1988, 639). Both statements are reactions to what the authors see as a facile dismissal of the textual evidence. Gombrich explains:

> It should go without saying that we are not bound to take what a Pali text – or any other text in the world – says at face value. But our initial working hypothesis has to be that the text is telling the truth, and in each case where we do not believe it, or doubt it, we must produce our reasons for doing so. There will be innumerable such cases and all kinds of reasons. But if we just dismiss what the text tells us *a priori*, there is no subject. If there is no subject, no one should be employed to teach it – and good riddance.
>
> (Gombrich 2009, 96)[6]

Surely the canonical texts must be accorded some evidential weight regarding claims about the origin of their content, even if the history of their formation makes it impossible to distinguish precisely between what the founder actually taught and what the texts report. To suppose that the redactors and compilers of the textual tradition merely invented most or all of those ideas and put them in the mouth of a charismatic teacher is as uncharitable as it is implausible. In any event, the texts are what we have, and they have been received by the tradition as embodying the wisdom of the historical Buddha.

More important, perhaps, than the question of attribution is the originating concern from which the teachings arose. The Buddha portrayed in the canonical texts was preoccupied with one central problem: how to overcome *dukkha*, the suffering or deep unsatisfactoriness that pervades human experience. This problem is the central focus of the *Dhammacakkappavattana Sutta* ("Setting in Motion of the Wheel of Dhamma"), which establishes the soteriological aim at the heart of all Buddhist thought and practice. Presented as the Buddha's first public teaching following his awakening at Bodh Gaya, this *sutta* lays out a conceptual framework for understanding the true causes of suffering and the path of practice that leads to the cessation of suffering. Although this teaching is said to express the profound insight into the nature of reality attained by Gotama Buddha upon his awakening – and indeed can be fully grasped only by those who have themselves attained awakening – it is elaborated in various discourses by means of key concepts such as impermanence, non-self, and conditioned co-arising. These concepts, and the contemplative path that leads to the direct awareness of the realities described by them, would become the focus of rigorous philosophical examination and debate.

It is useful to bear in mind here that the Buddha of the canonical texts embraced a thoroughly pragmatic attitude regarding the value of teachings. He warned against the inherent danger of becoming attached to any teaching for its own sake. The value of the Dhamma must be understood in the context of its practical purpose: to facilitate liberation, the realization of *nibbāna* (Skt *nirvāṇa*). In this respect, the Buddha likened his Dhamma to a raft: the usefulness of the teaching lies in helping us to reach the other shore. But once there, we must let it go (MN.I.134–5).[7]

In the same spirit of pragmatism, the Buddha urged others not to believe anything merely on the basis of established tradition, the presumed authority of scripture, or reason alone, but to accept only what can be confirmed by experience (see the *Kālāma Sutta*, AN.I.188–93). He did not invite mere intellectual assent, but encouraged instead a deeper moral, spiritual, and intellectual engagement with the existential problem of suffering. This process, if earnestly undertaken, inevitably opens the door to new questions and new ways of conceptualizing both the path of Buddhist practice and its goal. Indeed, it is the history of this engagement that produced the immensely rich and diverse tradition of thought we call Buddhist philosophy.

As we noted at the outset, Buddhism is a living tradition. To take this idea seriously is to recognize that, while it has its origins in the seminal teachings attributed to the historical Buddha, those teachings have always been the subject of interpretation and analysis. Even the codified version of the teachings preserved in the textual canon is to some extent the product of a history of interpretation that had been underway for centuries before being written down. That we cannot come any closer to the mind of the historical Buddha than through this tradition of interpretation and critical engagement should be of little concern to those who wish to study Buddhist philosophy.

Buddhist Philosophy in Focus

The central insight attained by the Buddha can be stated briefly as follows: all phenomena are conditioned, transitory, and devoid of any essence or "self" that remains unchanged over time. All phenomena arise within a complex network of mutually conditioning causes and effects. As the Buddha succinctly put the point: "When this exists, that comes to be; with the arising of this, that arises. When this does not exist, that does not come to be; with the cessation of this, that ceases'" (MN.III.64; Ñāṇamoli and Bodhi 1995, 927). According to this view, nothing in the world of our experience can be said to exist as an independent, unconditioned reality.

Applying this insight to human nature, we observe that a person is merely a collection of psycho-physical elements or "aggregates" (*khandhas*) – body, feelings, perceptions, volitions, consciousness – that give rise to a causal pattern we identify as a particular individual. It does not follow from the relative stability of this pattern, however, that there must be an underlying essence. When we look more closely, we see that both the mental and the physical phenomena that make up a person are constantly changing. Physical change is, of course, apparent in the natural process of aging. But careful observation of the mind, where we might hope to encounter the unifying core of personal identity, reveals nothing more than a perpetual succession of thoughts, ideas, and emotions.

This analysis is similar in some respects to the position advanced by David Hume, who reasoned that the thing we call a "self" is

> nothing but a bundle or collection of different perceptions, which succeed each other with an inconceivable rapidity, and are in a perpetual flux and movement. Our eyes cannot turn in their sockets without varying our perceptions. Our thought is still more variable than our sight; and all our other senses and faculties contribute to this change; nor is there any

> single power of the soul, which remains unalterably the same, perhaps for one moment. The mind is a kind of theatre, where several perceptions successively make their appearance; pass, re-pass, glide away, and mingle in an infinite variety of postures and situations. There is properly no simplicity in it at one time, nor identity in different; whatever natural propension we may have to imagine that simplicity and identity.
>
> (Hume 1978, 252–3)[8]

While Hume was concerned primarily to make a theoretical point, the Buddha's analysis has a therapeutic and soteriological purpose. The doctrine of non-self (*anattā*) is key to understanding the causes of *dukkha* and its cessation.

A principal cause of the suffering or unsatisfactoriness denoted by *dukkha* is "thirst" (*taṇhā*), the endless craving or desire that shapes our self-centered pursuit of happiness in the world. "Thirst" accounts for a wide range of physical, emotional, and psychological ills. According to the Buddha, these ills are the inevitable result of the desire to cling to things that are, by their very nature, impermanent and changing.

We experience *dukkha* most immediately in the form of aging, sickness, and death. But everything in the world of human experience – including our thoughts and feelings, the people and things we cherish, the myriad situations and events that occur in the course of our lives – is conditioned in this way: it arises interdependently, undergoes a process of change, and passes away. By clinging to these things we only renew the conditions of our own suffering, thereby perpetuating the samsaric cycle of birth, death, and rebirth. To escape suffering, one must abandon the "identity view" (MN.I.434).

The path that leads to the cessation of *dukkha* is a threefold practice involving the cultivation of wisdom, moral training, and concentration (meditation). This practice prepares the way for direct insight into the causes of suffering:

> Whatever exists therein of feeling, perception, formations, and consciousness, he sees those states as impermanent, as suffering, as a disease, . . . as not self. He turns his mind away from those states and directs it towards the deathless element thus: "This is the peaceful, this is the sublime, this is the stilling of all formations, the relinquishing of all attachments, the destruction of craving, dispassion, cessation, Nibbāna."
>
> (MN.I.437; Ñāṇamoli and Bodhi 1995, 541)

Though this insight clearly reflects a deeper metaphysical understanding of the mental and physical processes that condition sentient experience, the Buddha does not explicitly draw any ontological conclusions regarding the ultimate nature of those phenomena. In fact, as he is portrayed in the discourses, the Buddha is notably reluctant to engage in purely theoretical inquiries, as he seems to regard these as a diversion from useful discussion and analysis, and possibly even a hindrance to the pursuit of liberation.[9]

That the Buddha does not venture into questions of an ontological nature indicates how closely his interest in metaphysical and epistemological issues is tied to soteriological ends. In this regard, his approach to philosophy is similar to that of the ancient Hellenistic philosophers, for whom there was no point to philosophical discourse if it did not "expel the suffering of the soul."[10] The similarities between Buddhist and Hellenistic thought have been well noted by contemporary writers.[11]

Nevertheless, as we noted earlier, critical engagement with the ideas presented in the discourses produced a vigorous tradition of philosophical inquiry, which, though motivated by the same soteriological goal, was broader in its scope and analytical methods.[12] This began with the Abhidhamma movement and was developed further by way of critical reactions to the Abhidhamma in diverging schools of Buddhist thought. In this vast and varied body of writings we find rigorous conceptual analyses of reality, truth, and knowledge; detailed investigations of the nature of mind and consciousness; reflections on ethics and moral psychology; and ideas about the statecraft and the conditions for flourishing in society.

Aim and Structure of the Volume

An exhaustive account of our subject would fill perhaps several volumes of a comparable size. However, in keeping with the general aim of the Companion series we have endeavored to present a broad survey of the most important ideas, problems, and debates in the history of Buddhist philosophy.

The volume is arranged in five parts. Part I features three introductory chapters on the conceptual foundations of Buddhist philosophy, beginning with a discussion of the intellectual context of Gotama's thought. This sets up presentations of the Buddha's foundational teachings on *dukkha* and the path that leads to liberation, as well as the closely related doctrine of conditioned co-arising. We depart here from the customary practice of beginning with an account of the Buddha's life, partly because our focus is philosophical and partly because biographies are readily available in electronic and printed sources.[13]

Part II presents a general survey of the three living traditions of Buddhist thought: Theravāda, Mahāyāna, and Vajrayāna. Focusing mainly on bringing out key philosophical differences, these discussions provide a useful overview of the major figures and texts associated with the various schools.

The chapters comprising Part III are organized by section under topical headings familiar to students of Western philosophy. It should be noted, however, that Buddhist philosophy is not as neatly delineated as this taxonomy would suggest. For example, Buddhist thinkers do not in practice distinguish between epistemology and logic, since they treat inference as one of two sources of knowledge (the other being perception). We have introduced a soft division between these sections for the purpose of isolating more specific questions about both the role that meaning plays in inference and how Buddhist logicians might have conceived of a philosophy of logic. Other chapters in the "Language and Logic" section explore Buddhist reflections on the limits of language.

Our purpose in presenting the material this way is not to divest Buddhist thought of its native idioms, but rather to help readers understand the characteristic ways in which Buddhist thinkers have addressed issues of perennial concern to Western philosophers. There is a conscious attempt throughout the volume to create a mainstream bridge between the Buddhist and Western traditions. To this end, many chapters in the volume are written from a comparative perspective. It is hoped that this approach will not only encourage a better understanding and appreciation of Buddhist philosophy but also suggest natural ways to incorporate it in the Western syllabus.

Part IV contains a set of chapters on the theory and practice of Buddhist meditation. Although other chapters in the volume include some discussion of the role of contemplative practice in various traditions of Buddhism, the focus here is on explaining the meditation process and its special value as a mode of inquiry. The concluding chapter offers a cross-cultural look at the relevance of Buddhist meditation to contemporary neuroscience and theories of consciousness.

Finally, in Part V we turn to an examination of contemporary developments in Buddhist philosophy. These chapters extend the discussion of Buddhist social, political, and ethical thought as it applies to environmental and biomedical issues, war and peace, human rights, gender, and diversity.

Notes

1 For a summary of this debate, see Prebish (2008).
2 For a helpful discussion of this issue, see Gethin (1998, 7–27).
3 Esoteric teachings are also represented in the Chinese Zhenyan tradition.
4 Among contemporary scholars, this view is perhaps best represented in the work of Richard Gombrich (1988, 1996, and esp. 2009, ch. 7).
5 Peter Harvey agrees: "There is an overall harmony to the Canon, suggesting 'authorship' of its system of thought by one mind" (Harvey 2012, 3).
6 This is similar to the "Principle of Testimony" articulated by Richard Swinburne: "The special considerations that lead us to doubt a subject's reports of his experiences are evidence that generally or in matters of a particular kind he misremembers or exaggerates or lies. But, in the absence of such positive evidence, we have good grounds to believe what others tell us about their experiences" (Swinburne 2004, 322).
7 It was understood, of course, that in order to test the teachings one would need to proceed on the basis of some provisional trust or confidence (*saddhā*) in their salvific efficacy.
8 Compare Derek Parfit's updated version of Hume's argument in Parfit (1984).
9 This issue is explored in Ruegg (1995, 149–53).
10 Epicurus, as quoted in Porphyry, *To Marcella* 31. Translated in Long and Sedley (1987, 155).
11 See, for example, Gowans (2003, 42–6), as well as his essay "Medical Analogies in Buddhist and Hellenistic Thought: Tranquillity and Anger," in Ganeri and Carlisle (2010, 11–34).
12 This included questions of an ontological nature. See Ronkin (2005) for a detailed discussion of the development of Buddhist metaphysics in the Abhidhamma.
13 Two concise biographies of the Buddha's life are Carrithers (1983) and Strong (2001). For a presentation of the Buddha's life based on Pāli canonical texts, the reader may consult Ñāṇamoli (1992).

References

Blackburn, Anne M. (2001). *Buddhist Learning and Textual Practice in Eighteenth-Century Lankan Monastic Culture*. Princeton, NJ: Princeton University Press.

Cabezón, José Ignacio (1995). Buddhist Studies as a Discipline and the Role of Theory. In *Journal of the International Association of Buddhist Studies* 18, 231–68.

Carrithers, Michael (1983). *The Buddha: A Very Short Introduction*. Oxford: Oxford University Press.
Collins, Steven (1990). On the Very Idea of the Pali Canon. In *Journal of the Pali Text Society* 15, 89–126.
Ganeri, Jonardon, and Carlisle, Clare (eds) (2010). *Philosophy as Therapeia*. Royal Institute of Philosophy, Supplement no. 66. Cambridge: Cambridge University Press.
Gethin, Rupert (1998). *The Foundations of Buddhism*. Oxford: Oxford University Press.
Gombrich, Richard (1988). *Theravāda Buddhism: A Social History from Ancient Benares to Modern Colombo*. London: Routledge & Kegan Paul.
Gombrich, Richard (1996). *How Buddhism Began: The Conditioned Genesis of the Early Teachings*. London: Athlone Press.
Gombrich, Richard (2009). *What the Buddha Thought*. London: Equinox.
Gómez, Luis O. (2002). Buddhism in India. In *The Religious Traditions of Asia: Religion, History and Culture*. Ed. J. M. Kitagawa. London and New York: RoutledgeCurzon, 41–96.
Gowans, Christopher W. (2003). *Philosophy of the Buddha*. London: Routledge.
Harvey, Peter (2012). *Introduction to Buddhism: Teachings, History and Practices*. Second edn. Cambridge: Cambridge University Press.
Hume, David (1978). *A Treatise of Human Nature*. Second edn. Oxford: Clarendon Press.
Lamotte, Étienne (1988). *History of Indian Buddhism*. Trans. Sara Webb-Boin. Louvain: Institut Orientaliste.
Long, A. A., and Sedley, D.N. (1987). *The Hellenistic Philosophers*. Vol. 1. Cambridge: Cambridge University Press.
Ñāṇamoli, Bhikkhu (1992). *The Life of the Buddha*. Kandy, Sri Lanka: Buddhist Publication Society.
Ñāṇamoli, Bhikkhu, and Bodhi, Bhikkhu (trans.) (1995). *The Middle Length Discourses of the Buddha*. Boston: Wisdom.
Parfit, Derek (1984). *Reasons and Persons*. Oxford: Clarendon Press.
Prebish, Charles (2008). Cooking the Buddhist Books: The Implications of the New Dating of the Buddha for the History of Early Indian Buddhism. In *Journal of Buddhist Ethics* 15, 1–21.
Rahula, Walpola (1974). *What the Buddha Taught*. Rev. edn. New York: Grove Press.
Ronkin, Noa (2005). *Early Buddhist Metaphysics: The Making of a Philosophical Tradition*. London and New York: RoutledgeCurzon.
Ruegg, D. Seyfort (1995). Some Reflections on the Place of Philosophy in the Study of Buddhism. In *Journal of the International Association of Buddhist Studies* 18, 145–81.
Schopen, Gregory (1997). *Bones, Stones, and Buddhist Monks: Collected Papers on the Archaeology, Epigraphy, and Texts of Monastic Buddhism in India*. Honolulu: University of Hawai'i Press.
Siderits, Mark (2007). *Buddhism as Philosophy: An Introduction*. Indianapolis: Hackett.
Strong, John S. (2001). *The Buddha: A Short Biography*. Oxford: Oneworld.
Swinburne, Richard (2004). *The Existence of God*. Second edn. Oxford: Oxford University Press.

Part I

Conceptual Foundations

1

The Philosophical Context of Gotama's Thought

STEPHEN J. LAUMAKIS

Some Fundamental Problems

Although it is de rigueur to begin any account of Buddhism with the "received" biography of its founder, Siddhattha Gotama, or, as he is more commonly known, the Buddha or the Awakened One, there are at least a half dozen fundamental problems with this practice. First, like Jesus and Socrates, the Buddha never wrote anything – about either himself or his teachings. Second, his supposed teachings were compiled anywhere from a hundred to a few hundred years after his death. Third, the canonical teachings that ultimately informed the "received" view of his life contain numerous conflicting and, in fact, contradictory accounts of his life. Fourth, there is no scholarly doubt that the supposed teachings of the Buddha underwent various changes, editions, and developments as they passed from an oral tradition to a written record. Fifth, there are ongoing scholarly debates over exactly what – if anything at all – can be said with any degree of certainty with respect to what the man who became the Buddha actually thought or taught given the previous issue. And, sixth, the "received" view of his life fails to consider the historical and intellectual contexts in and from which his supposed teachings emerged.

If the foregoing problems were not enough to make one stop and think about what we really know about the Buddha and his teachings, there is the additional question about whether what the Buddha thought and taught is philosophy, religion, both, or neither.

Nevertheless, despite these problems, recent scholarship has begun to shed some light on the social, cultural, historical, and intellectual contexts in and from which the Buddha and Buddhism arose. In order to take advantage of this work and sidestep the thorny issues associated with the supposed biography of the Buddha and the debate over whether Buddhism is a philosophy, a religion, both, or neither, this essay will

A Companion to Buddhist Philosophy, First Edition. Edited by Steven M. Emmanuel.

instead provide an account of his intellectual biography by analyzing the philosophical context in and from which his thought and teachings emerged.

Indian "Views" of Reality

As I have argued elsewhere (Laumakis 2008), perhaps one of the easiest ways of understanding the basic elements of classical Indian thought – and Siddhattha Gotama's reaction to it – is to think of them as a collection of intellectual insights in a series of transitions in what we might call the "Indian Way" of seeing and understanding reality (Koller 2006). Conceived of in this way, it is helpful to think of the ancient Indians as offering us at least three distinct conceptual frameworks or "views" of reality.

The first "view," what we might call the understanding of the Dasyus, or the pre-Aryan or "pre-Vedic view" of things, seems to have countenanced belief in many gods, nature worship, fertility rituals, concerns about purification, and some basic ideas about both an afterlife and the possibilities of reincarnation. According to some scholars, the last two points, in particular, appear to be anchored in simple observations about the cycle of birth–life–death in nature, the phases of the moon, the seasons of the year, and obvious family resemblances. Recent archeological evidence also supports the claim that the Dasyus appear to have been vegetarians who engaged in ascetic practices and yogic meditation.

The second Indian "view," the understanding of the Aryans and the Vedas, builds upon this early view of things and seems to have formalized it with ritual sacrifices and celebrations, the production of sacred texts (supposedly not composed by humans) – concerned with the "wisdom" of poet-seers and hearers to whom it was revealed, and liturgical formulae and chants about what had been seen and heard. This second view also contains the "philosophical" (or merely human) reflections and speculations of the Upanishads.

The third and final "view," what we might call the post-Vedic understanding of reality, is actually a more sustained, careful, and detailed working out of the individual elements of the pre-Vedic and Vedic views of things. This rather complex understanding of reality includes a clarification and specification of the roles of the gods (or a denial of their existence) and their relation to the ultimate, single source of all things (i.e., Brahman), a delineation of the details of the *varṇa*/color and caste systems, an account of the stages of life (i.e., studying under a teacher or being a student; returning home to marry and raise a family as a householder; relinquishing daily affairs to one's son by retiring and beginning meditative practices; and, finally, leaving home to live and die in the forest as an ascetic) and the various aims of life (i.e., *dharma*/virtue or moral righteousness, *artha*/wealth and success, *kāma*/pleasure and fulfilling material desires, and *mokṣa*/liberation or achieving salvation). It also contains more serious reflection on the cyclical nature of birth–life–death (samsara) and the notions of rebirth and the prospects of release or liberation from this cosmic cycle.

At a more fine-grained level of consideration, this third "view" includes what scholars have identified as the nine *darśanas* ("schools" or "viewpoints") of classical Indian thought – i.e., Sāṃkhya, Yoga, Mīmāṃsā, Vedānta, Nyāya, Vaiśeṣika, Jain, Cārvāka, and Buddhist views (See Mohanty 2000, 153–8). Finally, it involves an elucidation of the notions and relations of the "self" and society and social regulation through the ideas of norms, duties, obligations, virtues, karma, and Dharma.

Indian Philosophy and/or Indian Religion?

What begins to emerge from this series of "views" is, I think, a rather rich and complex understanding of reality that includes features that are both "philosophical" and "religious"/"theological"[1] in the typical Western senses of these terms. In fact, before delving into the philosophical details of these views, I think it is possible to get a preliminary sense of the intellectual context and cultural milieu that supported the social and philosophical development of Siddhattha Gotama and his emergence as the historical Buddha.

For example, the Dasyu beliefs in many gods, nature worship, and fertility and purification rituals are clearly (by common Western standards) "religious" kinds of beliefs. These same "religious"/"theological" beliefs are also part of the "Vedic view" of the Aryans who formalized them with ritual texts and the Brahmanical priesthood. But it is also important to recall that this same "Vedic view" includes the purely "philosophical" reflections and arguments of the Upanishads. In fact, when conceived of as a whole, it is useful to think of the Vedas as a complex, simultaneously religious and philosophical reconciliation, merging the pre-Vedic and Aryan views of reality.

The Vedas themselves contain virtually every element and theme of the "pre-Vedic view" of the Dasyus as well as the wisdom of their own seers and hearers: hymns for deities, rules for fire sacrifices, music, poetry, magic rituals, and ideas about *ṛta* (order), karma (Skt *karma*: action and its consequences), samsara, and the afterlife.

The Upanishads, on the other hand, continue to develop these themes in a more strictly "philosophical" or purely rational way. In fact, it is this philosophical working out of the same themes and their logical implications as the "post-Vedic view" of reality that provides the immediate historical, cultural, and intellectual context within which the life and teachings of Siddhattha Gotama were formed.

As a result, I think it is safe to say that the "post-Vedic view" that was formed both during and after the life of Siddhattha is what we in the West would call "Indian philosophy" strictly and properly speaking. It is to a finer-grained analysis of this context that we now turn our attention.

Siddhattha Gotama's Cultural and Intellectual Context

Like many great thinkers, Gotama was born into a rich, complex, and dynamic social and historical setting. On the one hand, he inherited an Indian culture rich in philosophical and religious beliefs and practices. Not only were his contemporaries interested in securing the material goods necessary both for basic subsistence and for making one's way through the various stages of life noted above, but they were also profoundly interested in trying to understand the meaning and purpose of life and the fundamental nature of reality in order to realize – in the appropriate kinds of ways – the various aims of life.

In fact, Sue Hamilton (Hamilton 2001, 1) has pointed out that in India it was traditionally believed that the activity of philosophizing was directly associated with one's personal destiny. She also notes that what we in the West tend to distinguish as "religion" and "philosophy" was actually combined in India in people's attempts to understand both the meaning and structure of life and the fundamental nature of reality. In other words, in India, especially at the time when Gotama was alive, the two activities of doing philosophy and practicing religion were actually two interrelated or interdependent aspects of the same inner or spiritual quest.

In addition to his personal and cultural wealth, Gotama was born into a society in the midst of great social and political changes. Putting aside for the moment concerns about the actual dates of his birth and death, there is little doubt that he lived at a time when the certainties of traditional ways of thinking and living – in other words, when a historically nomadic and pastoral tribal society morphs into a predominantly agrarian one – were being challenged by the new and unsettling problems arising out of the breakdown of tribal federations and the development of powerful monarchies and emerging urban centers. In other words, Gotama lived in the midst of a transition from an agrarian, village-based economy to a city-based form of life with all of its attendant problems and possibilities (Gombrich 1988).

Yet, as was the case with the many great thinkers who lived before and after him, Gotama's life may be seen as the fortuitous coming together of the right man with the right abilities at the right time in the right circumstances bringing about a truly amazing solution to a very complex set of challenges. It is precisely this image of an appropriately qualified person and a portentous opportunity fortuitously and "karmically" coming together – what Peter Hershock (Hershock 1996, 110) refers to as "virtuosity" – that I want to employ as a heuristic to help explain the cultural and philosophical context for the emergence of Buddhism.

Basic Elements of the Pre-Vedic View – The Remote Origins of Gotama's Thought

As we have seen, the Dasyu or "pre-Vedic view" of reality (c. 2500 BCE), which is supported not by primary texts but rather by archeological evidence and the writings of their successors, is rooted in nature worship and beliefs in multiple gods. Other features of this *darśana* include purification and fertility rituals, vegetarianism, asceticism, yoga, and some rudimentary ideas about an afterlife and the possibility of rebirth. Although it is not possible to be certain about how these basic beliefs were formed, it is not difficult to imagine an ancient agricultural people and their ordinary problems and concerns.

To begin, it is obvious that the basic facts of every human life include practical concerns about food, clothing, and shelter. There are also environmental concerns about one's life and safety in the face of nature and its power, as well as concerns about the dangers posed by wild animals and other human beings. Once these basic biological needs and environmental concerns are met and addressed, it is easy to see how and why ancient peoples would have turned their attention to deeper "metaphysical" questions about the ultimate end and purpose of living and dying, since these are the basic facts of life.

The Meaning, Purpose, and End of Life

It goes without saying that little reflection is required for one to realize that many things in the world are beyond human control, and it is often difficult, if not impossible, to know or predict future events and circumstances, such as the weather and seasons and natural disasters. However, it is also quite clear that many of these very same forces and events in nature seem to follow general patterns, even predictable cyclical patterns. The sun rises and sets, the moon waxes and wanes, the tides rise and fall, and the seasons come and go in relative order and stability. It should not be difficult to imagine ancient Indians being concerned with questions about the source or sources of this apparent order and pattern. Furthermore, it is easy to imagine them asking if the order itself is real or merely apparent. Finally, one could imagine them asking themselves, if things are not in their control, then might or must there be something that does control or explain the order and pattern.

The best available evidence seems to indicate that the ancient Dasyu way of understanding and dealing with the ordinary questions and problems of life was to recognize some superhuman or divine sources of power behind or within natural forces and events. They also seem to have realized that nature itself exercised a kind of control over human affairs. The Dasyus recognized the immutable and inexorable truth that humans are born, live, and die, but they also appear to have held the view – based on their burial practices – that death was not the end of life. It is, however, unknown whether they distinguished clearly between rebirth in a different world in some other location or simply rebirth in this world at some future time. Whether they had considered some kind of causal (i.e., karmic) explanation of either possible rebirth scenario is unclear as well.

Seeds and Fruit: Actions and their Consequences

Consider, for a moment, the same data of experience that we have been highlighting, especially in an agricultural community setting. The sun rises and sets, the moon waxes and wanes, the tides rise and fall, and the seasons come and go in relative order and stability. Humans, plants, and animals are born, grow, mature, and die. Humans interact with one another and the world around themselves, and events and outcomes seem to follow regular patterns. The same kinds of seeds produce the same kinds of trees, which in turn produce the same kinds of fruit and the same seeds all over again. The same kinds of animals produce the same kinds of offspring and the results of similar kinds of human actions tend, always or almost always, to be the same, and, for that matter, even predictably so. In general, when I do action A to object B at time T, the result is always, or nearly always, the same. How can one make sense of this?

One ancient Indian account, whose origin and roots are unknown, is to claim that the similarities in outcomes that we experience in our interactions with nature and other human beings are best explained by appealing to the agricultural idea of seeds and their fruits. Actions, whether human or natural, like seeds, produce fruits or outcomes or effects, based on the kinds of seeds they are. Orange seeds produce orange trees that produce oranges that once again produce orange seeds. Dogs produce dogs that produce more dogs. Humans produce humans that produce more humans. So, by extension, human actions produce outcomes or results that are causally determined by the kind of actions they are. "Good" actions produce "good" effects and "bad" actions produce "bad" effects. In general, effects follow from their causes in the same way that fruit follows from seeds. In other words, according to the ancient Indians, the world and events happening around us seem to follow law-like, regular patterns.

Whether this regularity is real, or apparent and merely perceived, whether it is a necessary relation or merely a statistical probability or correlation, whether it is a real feature of the world or the result of a psychological habit built up over time in human observers, the fact remains that the ancient Indians used the idea of karma to make sense out of and explain what was happening around them. Like the idea of rebirth, the idea of karma provides a plausible and rational explanation for things and events that are happening around us. Moreover, these ideas seem to have been among the most basic insights of the "Indian way" of understanding reality. In fact, they provided the foundation for Gotama's philosophical reflections.

Basic Elements of the Vedic View: The Source of Gotama's Philosophical Concerns

What I am calling the "Vedic view" of reality (c. 1500–500 BCE) is an understanding of life and reality that emerged from a complex cultural and intellectual process of absorption, assimilation, rejection, and revision of Dasyu beliefs and practices. Although there is much historical ignorance and uncertainty about both the geographical origins of the Aryans as a people and culture and their subsequent arrival and impact on the Indus Valley civilization of the Dasyus, there is no doubt that during the second millennium BCE the Aryans, who spoke and wrote a form of proto-Sanskrit, replaced the Dasyus as the dominant people of the Indus Valley.

The basic elements of the Aryan account of the purpose and meaning of life and the fundamental nature of reality are recorded in the Vedas, the Brahmanas, the Aranyakas, and later the Upanishads. These elements, which were "heard" and "remembered" by seer-poets and sages, include an initial polytheism (later replaced by the monism/monotheism of the Upanishads) and formalized ritual fire sacrifices performed by priests or Brahmans. Other features of this *darśana* are a gradual acceptance of vegetarianism, non-violence, asceticism, yoga, karma, and belief in rebirth and the cyclical nature of reality and existence.

Just as there are serious scholarly doubts and uncertainties about the formation of the "pre-Vedic view," there are similar problems and questions about exactly how the basic features of the "Vedic view" were formed. Nevertheless, the elements of what I am calling the "Vedic view" have the notable advantage of being recorded in written texts.

The texts themselves seem to indicate that the religious and philosophical beliefs and practices of the Aryans underwent two distinct but related types of development. On the one hand, they appear to have absorbed and eventually replaced Dasyu beliefs and practices. On the other hand, they seem to have undergone an internal development and deepening penetration of vision and understanding of their own insights. In other words, what I want to suggest is that the "Vedic view" sublated the pre-Vedic Dasyu "view" while simultaneously, over a period of some five hundred to a thousand years, deepening its own insight and understanding of reality and the meaning, purpose, and end of life. Nonetheless, it is important to keep in mind that what I call the "Vedic view" is in reality something far more complex and complicated than the single name I employ to denominate it. In fact, this "view" includes a relative spectrum of historically distinct beliefs about important philosophical concepts and ideas.

Despite this oversimplification, I think this way of presenting the "Vedic view" has the advantage of capturing most, if not all, of the important religious and philosophical ideas that came to form the immediate historical, intellectual, and cultural context from which and against which the teachings of Siddhattha Gotama arose.

Basic Elements of the Post-Vedic View: The Immediate Context of Gotama's Thought

The post-Vedic "view" (after 500 BCE) was a more careful, rigorous, and systematic rational working out of the details of the pre-Vedic and Vedic accounts of things. It was also the source of the nine classical "schools" of Indian philosophy. In fact, it is helpful to think of this third conceptual framework as being constituted by the individual views of its nine schools in the same way that white light is the product of the seven colors of the visible spectrum. Each individual color or school has its own unique features and history, and when appropriately harmonized they – in good Buddhist understanding – interdependently give rise to the "post-Vedic view" of things.

As we have already noted, this rather complex "view" included a clarification and specification of the roles of the various deities of the pre-Vedic and Vedic views (or their non-existence) and their relations to the ultimate, single source of all things (i.e., Brahman of the Upanishads), a delineation of the details of the *varṇa*/color and social caste systems, and the enumeration of the stages of life and the various possible aims of individual lives. It also contained more serious and sustained philosophical reflection and, in fact, vigorous disagreement – in which Gotama participated – over the possible outcomes of the cyclical nature of birth–life–death as well as the notions of rebirth and the prospects of release or liberation from this cosmic cycle. Finally, it involved more sustained philosophical debate about the notions and relations of the "self" and society (i.e., metaphysical and epistemological thinking) and social regulation (i.e., ethical thinking) through the increasingly complex ideas of norms, duties, obligations, virtues, karma, and Dharma.

It bears repeating that the living social reality and history of all of this was clearly far more complex and complicated than my simple distinguishing of Indian thought into three "views" would indicate. In fact, the division of Indian thought into the nine classical *darśanas* is itself a simplification of a richer and more complex spectrum of historically and philosophically distinct views. Moreover, when we turn our attention to these various "schools" we encounter a number of ideologically distinct and mutually exclusive accounts of the meaning and purpose of life and the fundamental nature of reality. In short, what is commonly designated as the teachings of Siddhattha Gotama is actually just one of these nine competing points of view.

Nevertheless, it is important to keep in mind that the *darśanas* themselves represent, in rather broad strokes, a full spectrum of both logical and real possible positions with respect to the fundamental ideas contained in the pre-Vedic, Vedic, and post-Vedic "views." In the light of the initial sketches of the three "views" already presented, we may now consider these other systems in more detail as constituting the immediate philosophical context of Gotama's thought.

Nine *Darśanas*

It may be helpful to begin our consideration of the nine classical "schools" of Indian thought by noting that the Buddhist tradition[2] itself refers to no fewer than 62 kinds of "wrong views" on matters as diverse as the past, the self, the world, pleasure, the mind, good and bad, chance, the future, life after death, nirvana, and even the teaching on interdependent arising.

From what has already been said about the history of the three "views," it should not be surprising that the roots of Indian philosophical orthodoxy are traced to the Vedas and the Upanishads. In fact, the traditional and perhaps the easiest way of capturing the distinctions among the classical schools of Indian philosophy is to categorize them as "orthodox" and "unorthodox" or "heterodox," based on whether they accept or reject the basic "truth" of the Vedas and the Upanishads.[3]

These are, after all, the first written texts that convey the basic elements of what one might call "the Indian view of the world." Not only were these texts and their words regarded by the religious leaders of ancient India, the Brahmans, as the primary sources of truth about the ultimate meaning and purpose of life and the fundamental nature of reality, but they also were compiled by those with the power, both materially and spiritually, to confirm their truth and insure their acceptance and continuing influence. It should not be surprising, therefore, to see the religious and philosophical landscape of India, especially at the time of the Buddha, defined by one's relationship to the "Vedic view" of reality.

Six "Orthodox" *Darśanas*

According to the Indian tradition, six *darśanas* are recognized as "orthodox." These are the Sāṃkhya, Yoga, Mīmāṃsā, Vedānta, Nyāya, and Vaiśeṣika systems.

According to the Sāṃkhya view, whose name means reason or discriminating knowledge, reality, which is ultimately dualistic (i.e., consists of two irreducible modes of being or existence) in nature, can be classified into 25 categories of matter (*prakṛti*) and spirit (*puruṣa*) – the two most basic principles of being. This view also maintained that reality consists of three elements – water, fire, and air – as well as three qualities (*guṇas*) that helped to explain the material constitution of things – lightness or mental activity (*sattva*), energy or activity (*rajas*), and inertia or dullness (*tama*).

This view, which is sometimes described as an atheistic naturalism (Mohanty 2000, 4–5), admitted an eternal self, numerically distinct for each individual. As Mohanty claims, "In its mature form, it developed a theory of evolution of the empirical world out of the original, undifferentiated nature" (ibid., 5). In fact, the three qualities or *guṇas* of material being, which were originally in a state of equilibrium, were disturbed by contact with spirit or *puruṣa*. The subsequent evolution of the physical world is a progressive and uneven scattering or intermingling of the three *guṇas* and spirit. In order to avoid the logical and metaphysical problem of something coming from nothing, the causal mechanism of this activity is explained by arguing that effects pre-exist in their causes. At the same time, each unique, individual spirit experiences attachment to its materially composite body as a result of failing to distinguish its true "spirit-self" from the composite that is itself a product of nature and its causes. According to this view, release from this condition or *mokṣa*, which is a return to the state of an unmixed spirit, is achieved by realizing or coming to know that the "spirit-self" is really metaphysically different from matter and nature.

Over time, this speculative metaphysical view of the world came to be paired with the more practical or ethically focused system of Yoga. According to the Yoga view of things, ontological dualism is metaphysically correct, but it also recognizes that, in addition to matter and individual spirits, there is a divine/supreme being, a God/Self that exists. Following the Sāṃkhya idea that there is a real metaphysical difference between spirit and matter, the Yoga view insists that the composite being leads the true spirit-self to mistake itself for the composite. The solution to this misidentification, and ultimately to release or *mokṣa*, is the development of discriminating insight or knowledge that is achieved through the disciplined meditation of yoga. It is the practice of yoga meditation that enables the true self to overcome its ignorance and liberate itself from its bondage and attachment to the material and physical.

The third (and fourth) classical Indian school is called Mīmāṃsā, which means exegesis. Without getting too detailed, it should be noted that this system is traditionally divided into an early (Purva Mīmāṃsā) and later (Uttarā Mīmāṃsā or Vedānta) version. In general, holders of this view, at least in its earliest version, disagree with the Sāṃkhya and Yoga belief that knowledge alone is sufficient for release from bondage. According to the early version of this *darśana*, ritual practice is what is essential for *mokṣa*. At the same time, however, those who maintain this early view appear to be ambivalent about the existence of God or a supreme being. On the one hand, they reject typical arguments for God's existence but, on the other hand, they also recognize an ontological category of potency or power that seems to include supernatural agency. Nevertheless, the most important element of the Mīmāṃsā vision of reality (taken as a whole) is its rather elaborate system for understanding and interpreting the Vedas.

As part of their science of interpretation, Mīmāṃsā thinkers believe that words themselves are the ultimate source of knowledge and that they serve as a direct means of truth. They also argue that true cognition originates from multiple sources, among them perception, logical inferences, verbal utterances, simple comparison, and postulation. As Koller points out, the chief concern of Mīmāṃsā philosophers, at least in its early version, is to work out a theory of knowledge that accommodates scriptural testimony as a valid means of knowledge and, on that basis, to provide a science of scriptural interpretation that captures and explains the meaning and truth of the Vedas, especially the ritualistic Brahmanas (see Koller 2006, 247).

The later Mīmāṃsā or Vedānta philosophers focused their attention on the more philosophical and non-ritualistic Upanishads. While initially accepting the authority of the early Vedas, the Uttarā Mīmāṃsā emphasized knowledge, instead of ritual, as the means to liberation. However, at least some Vedānta thinkers insisted that ritual-type devotion was a means of relating to and knowing Brahman. Not surprisingly, following the Upanishads, they argued that Brahman is the ultimate reality, that the "true self" is metaphysically identical to Brahman, and that knowledge of this truth was essential for *mokṣa*.

Taken together, the two versions of the Mīmāṃsā exegetical system represent the ritual and gnostic branches of the Brahmanical tradition, whose roots can be traced back to the fifth century BCE. These complementary halves of the Vedic and post-Vedic view ultimately came to be known as the action/*karma* and knowledge/*jñāna* interpretations of the Vedas.

The fifth and sixth classical systems of Indian thought are the Nyāya and Vaiśeṣika views. The Nyāya *darśana* is fundamentally concerned with questions and problems in logic. Its roots may be traced back to the belief that faulty reasoning and/or logical mistakes are the causes of suffering and attachment, and that one can arrive at the truth and ultimately liberation by correcting fallacious reasoning. In order to root out mistakes in reasoning, Nyāya thinkers analyzed reality into various logic-based categories, all of which could be proven to exist. In fact, the philosophers of this school worked out an entire epistemological theory of logic, rational argumentation, and proof, as well as an account of valid knowledge. Their ideas in logic and epistemology were subsequently adopted by their "sister system," the Vaiśeṣika, from whom the Nyāya borrowed their metaphysical views of reality and the self. This sharing of ideas led in time to a nominal joining of the views as the Nyāya-Vaiśeṣika.

The Vaiśeṣika contribution to the union was an account of the particularities of all real things. Their pluralistic realism, which involved an atomistic theory of the material world, was rooted in six ontological categories: substance, quality, action, universality, particularity, and inherence. They employed these categories to demonstrate the incompatibility of spirit and matter. They also claimed that "God" made the physical world out of pre-existent elemental substances. More importantly, they argued that through logical analysis one could arrive at a sound knowledge of all things, including the mind and the true eternal self, and that such knowledge was the only source of liberation from attachment and enslavement to matter.

These six *darśanas* or viewpoints of the Vedas and the Upanishads are collectively referred to as the *āstika* – "so-sayers" (Renard 1999, 90) – systems because they are in general agreement, despite their particular differences, with respect to their acceptance of the authority and truth of what I call the "Vedic view" of the purpose and meaning of life, as well as the fundamental nature of reality. Their acceptance of the Vedas and the Upanishads also justifies their designation as the "orthodox" schools. The remaining three classical systems of Indian thought, the Jain, the Cārvāka, and the Buddhist *darśanas*, are collectively referred to as the *nāstika* – "deniers or rejecters" (ibid.) – systems because each, in their own unique way, rejects the authority and truth of the Vedic scriptures and tradition.

Three "Heterodox" *Darśanas*

According to the Jain view of things, there is a sharp distinction between spirit and matter or souls and bodies. The first kind of beings, spiritual beings (*jiva*), are alive, and the second kind of beings, material beings or non-spiritual beings, (*ajiva*) are not alive. Bondage to the cycle of birth, life, death, and rebirth for spiritual beings is caused by their karmic actions.

The specifics of this account of rebirth involve the idea that karmic actions by spiritual beings causally produce material particles that are attracted to the soul's spiritual energy and thereby bind themselves to the spiritual self. The continuing union of the soul and matter that results from karmic action is itself caused by both ignorance and attachment that result from the passions, wants, and desires of spiritual beings. There is, however, a way out of the soul's bondage, through the practice of moral living, meditation, and great ascetic austerities. In fact, the ultimate cause of release is the acquisition of knowledge or insight into the soul's samsaric situation by way of a kind of awakening or extraordinary insight into the true, pure, and unsullied nature of the soul or self.

This profound insight also includes the recognition that the only way to experience liberation is to destroy, by ascetic mortification – preferably in a monastic setting – the accumulated "material" karmic consequences of prior actions and avoid all future karmic action. In addition to these ethical and metaphysical claims, Jain thinkers reject the sacrificial rituals of the Vedas as well as the monism of the Upanishads.

From the epistemic point of view, the Jains claimed that reality has an infinity of aspects, and that all truth claims can be confirmed by perception, logical inference, or verbal testimony. As a result of their ontological pluralism, they also claimed that all truths are relative to a specific frame of reference. In other words, every claim or proposition is true from a certain point of view and false from some other point of view.

Given this account of the basic features of their view of reality, it should not be surprising that the Jains deny the existence of a single "God" or divine being but simultaneously affirm the existence of multiple gods or divine beings. In fact, Jain thinkers insist that each individual soul or spirit has the capacity, through severe ascetic practice, to develop infinite consciousness or omniscience, infinite power or omnipotence, and absolute happiness or eternal bliss. All that is necessary for this ultimate achievement is sufficiently severe ascetic practices that eliminate impure and harmful thoughts, words, and deeds.

The second "heterodox" classical Indian view is the Cārvāka *darśana*. According to this materialist "school," only material things exist, and, as a result, there are no immaterial beings and hence no spiritual selves. Since matter is the only reality, there is no afterlife (precisely because there is no existence beyond the physical, material world) and, consequently, no karma, no karmic bondage, and no possibility of *mokṣa* or nirvana. Like all materialists, Cārvāka thinkers maintained that the only reliable source of knowledge is sense experience, and that the goal of life is the pursuit of pleasure and the avoidance of pain.

While individual materialists disagreed about the number and kind of basic material elements from which all material things are composed, they appear to be unanimous in their denial of *mokṣa* or nirvana and affirmation of causal determinism and fatalism. One such thinker, Gosala, claimed that human beings have no freedom to act precisely because all outcomes are causally predetermined by fate, or the laws of material interactions. According to this view, despite the internal introspective experience of choice, the actual outcome of events is necessitated by the prior physical conditions that give rise to it.

Such a view is, as Gotama saw, obviously at odds with the hedonistic claim which suggests that the purpose of life is to pursue pleasure and avoid pain, because the notions of pursuit and avoidance seem to presuppose, or at least assume, choice or some form of non-determinism. Perhaps it was this inconsistency and other uncertainties about the metaphysics of the self and karma and *mokṣa* that led some materialists to defend a complete skepticism with regard to any true knowledge about the meaning and purpose of life as well as the fundamental nature of reality.

The Buddha, as we know, had a different view of each of these matters. Yet it was within the context of these competing views[4] and their ongoing debates and disagreements that Siddhattha Gotama worked out his own unique philosophical views and eventually became the Awakened One.

Notes

1 For an interesting and persuasive analysis of this distinction, see Fitzgerald (2000). For more on the ongoing debate about the status of religious studies and for other views of the matter, see *Religious Studies Review* 27/2 (2001) and 27/4 (2001).

2 *Brahmajala Sutta*: *The Supreme Net* (DN.I.1–46; Walshe 1995). The Buddha not only compares these wrong views to a fishnet but also refers to them as a net of views that catches and holds those who hold them.

3 It should be noted that, even though it is misleading to suggest that both sets of texts share the exact same "view" of reality, I have combined them as part of the "Vedic view" in order to simplify a rather complex situation.

4 It is important to keep in mind that the "orthodox"/"heterodox" distinction is just one of many different ways of conceptualizing the relationships among the various philosophical *darśanas* of ancient India. Obviously, there are other possible ways of distinguishing the numerous schools – for example, according to their metaphysical beliefs (about the whole of reality, or about its parts – i.e., the nature of the human person, the soul or spirit or self, nirvana, etc.), their epistemological beliefs (about the nature, origin, and limits of knowledge), or their ethical beliefs (about the goals of human living, the elements of the good human life, the standards of morality, karma, etc.).

References

Fitzgerald, T. (2000). *The Ideology of Religious Studies*. New York: Oxford University Press.

Gombrich, R. (1988). *Theravada Buddhism: A Social History from Ancient Benares to Modern Colombo*. London: Routledge & Kegan Paul.

Hamilton, S. (2001). *Indian Philosophy: A Very Short Introduction*. Oxford: Oxford University Press.

Hershock, P. D. (1996). *Liberating Intimacy: Enlightenment and Social Virtuosity in Ch'an Buddhism*. Albany: State University of New York Press.

Koller, J. M. (2006). *The Indian Way: An Introduction to the Philosophies and Religions of India*. Second edn. Upper Saddle River, NJ: Pearson/Prentice-Hall.
Laumakis, S. J. (2008). *An Introduction to Buddhist Philosophy*. Cambridge: Cambridge University Press.
Mohanty, J. N. (2000) *Classical Indian Philosophy*. Lanham, MD: Rowman & Littlefield.
Renard, J. (1999). *101 Questions and Answers on Buddhism*. New York: Gramercy Books.
Walshe, M. (trans.) (1995). *The Long Discourses of the Buddha: A Translation of the Digha Nikaya*. Boston: Wisdom.

2

Dukkha, Non-Self, and the Teaching on the Four "Noble Truths"[1]

PETER HARVEY

After reflection on the limitations faced by any sentient being as subject to "aging, sickness and death" (MN.I.163), the person who became known as "the Buddha" or "Awakened One" sought that which was in various ways beyond these. After his awakening/enlightenment experience, in which he is seen to have experienced that which is the unborn, unaging, unailing, deathless (Skt *nirvāṇa*; P. *nibbāna*),[2] he went on to teach others how to experience this. The problem of suffering had prompted his own quest for awakening, and its solution naturally became the focus of his teachings. He sometimes summarized these by saying simply, "Both in the past and now, I set forth just this: *dukkha* and the cessation of *dukkha*" (e.g., MN.I.140). The Pāli word *dukkha* (Skt *duḥkha*) encapsulates many subtleties of meaning, but its application spans pain, suffering, disappointment, frustration, things going badly, hassle, unease, anxiety, stress, dis-ease, unsatisfactoriness, non-reliability of people and things, limitation, imperfection. It sums up the problematic aspects of life: its mental and physical pains, obvious or subtle, and also the painful, stressful, unsatisfactory aspects of life that engender these.

The Pāli term for the Buddha's teachings is *Dhamma* (Skt *Dharma*), though this term also refers to the *basis* of his teachings – the nature of reality as known by him, the path of practice which he taught, and its culmination in *nirvāṇa*. *Dhamma* is a difficult word to translate, but may be understood as the "Basic Pattern" of things. The term is also used in the plural (and in Roman script without an initial capital letter) for the basic patterns or processes of reality found within this overall Basic Pattern.

In what is portrayed as his first sermon (Vin.I.10–12),[3] the *Dhamma-cakka-ppavatana Sutta* (DCPS),[4] the Buddha highlighted four key aspects or dimensions of existence to which one needs to become attuned so as to become deeply spiritually transformed and end *dukkha*: (i) the features of life which exemplify *dukkha*; (ii) the key cause for why we experience such pains; (iii) the reality of an end to *dukkha* by ending what causes it; and (iv) a path of practice leading to this. He referred to each of these four as an

A Companion to Buddhist Philosophy, First Edition. Edited by Steven M. Emmanuel.

"*ariya-sacca*" (Skt *ārya-satya*), which has generally come to be translated as "Noble Truth." While the Mahāyāna Buddhist tradition later came to see the *ariya-saccas* as preliminary to higher teachings, as found in the early *sutta* (Skt *sūtra*) collections known as the Pāli Nikāyas of the Theravāda school or the āgamas (Chinese translations of similar early texts), they are subjects of an advanced teaching intended for those who have been spiritually prepared to have them pointed out. When teaching lay persons, the Buddha frequently began with a "step-by-step discourse":

> that is, i) talk on giving (*dāna*), talk on moral virtue (*sīla*: Skt *śīla*), talk on the heaven worlds [positive rebirths as the fruit of generosity and moral restraint]; ii) he made known the danger, the inferior nature of and tendency to defilement in sense-pleasures, and the advantage of renouncing them [by moral discipline, meditative calming, and perhaps ordination]. When the Blessed One knew that the householder Upāli's mind was ready, open, without hindrances [desire for sense-pleasures, ill-will, dullness and lethargy, restlessness and worry, and vacillation], inspired and confident, then he expounded to him the elevated *Dhamma*-teaching of the Buddhas: *dukkha*, its origin, its cessation, the path.
>
> (MN.I.379–80)[5]

If the mind is not calm and receptive, talk of *dukkha* may be too disturbing, leading to states such as depression, denial, and self-distracting tactics. The Buddha's own discovery of the *ariya-saccas* was from the fourth *jhāna* (Skt *dhyāna*), a state of profound meditative calm (MN.I.249), after he had first used this state as a basis for remembering many of his past lives and for seeing how beings were reborn according the ethical quality of their actions (*karma*). These first two insights can be seen to have prepared the way for the third, as an overview of wandering for countless lives in the various realms of rebirth according to karma would naturally lead to an enhanced awareness both of the forces leading to repeated rebirths and of their attendant *dukkha*. While rebirths in the (long-lasting but not eternal) hell-realms, or as a frustrated ghost or as some kind of animal/bird/fish/insect, are more obviously unpleasant, the relatively pleasant human realm and various heavenly rebirths are also seen to end in death and have their various pains.

Pāli and Sanskrit make a fair use of compound expressions – perhaps not as much as in German, but more than in English. In such compounds, words other than the last one have no indication of whether they are singular or plural, or how exactly they relate to the last word, as the component words relate in different ways according to compound type. Nevertheless, context is usually a good guide to "unpacking" compounds, just as in English we know how to make sense of compound words such as doorway, red-eyed, lamplight, etc. The translation of the compound expression "*ariya-sacca*" as "Noble Truth" (e.g., Anderson 1999), while well established in English-language literature on Buddhism, is the "least likely" of the possible meanings (Norman 1997, 16). To unpack and translate "*ariya-sacca*," one needs to look first at the meanings of each word and then how they are most plausibly related. The term *sacca* (Skt *satya*) is regularly used in the sense of "truth," but, just as its adjectival use can mean either "true" or "real," so its noun meaning can be either "truth" *or* "reality" – a genuinely real existent. The Sanskrit word *satya* is related to the word *sat*, "existence/being," and both can have religious connotations. In the pre-Buddhist *Upaniṣads*, *Sat* (Being) is equated with *Ātman*/Self and *Brahman*, seen respectively as the unchanging essence of a person and the world, and in the twentieth century Mahātma Gandhi called his method of non-violent social change *Satyāgraha*, "holding onto Truth."

In "*ariya-sacca*," *sacca* is a noun, and there are three reasons why its meaning here cannot be "truth." Firstly, it is said that the second *ariya-sacca* (the origination of *dukkha*) is to be abandoned (SN.V.422): surely, one would not want to abandon a "truth," but one might well want to abandon a problematic "reality." Secondly, it is said that the Buddha understood " 'This is the *dukkha ariya-sacca*,' " not "The *ariya-sacca* 'This is *dukkha*' " (SN.V.422), which would be the case if *sacca* here meant a *truth* whose content was expressed in the words in quote marks. Thirdly, in some *suttas* (e.g. SN.V.425), the first *ariya-sacca* is explained by identifying it with a kind of existent (the bundles of grasping-fuel – see below), not by asserting a form of words that could be seen as a "truth." In normal English usage, the only things that can be "truths" are propositions – i.e., something that is expressed in words (spoken, written, thought). It seems odd to describe an item in the world, whether physical or mental, as itself a "truth." "Truth" (and falsity) potentially comes into it only when we try to give a correct description of what there is. Something *said* about *dukkha*, even just "this is *dukkha*," can be a "truth," but *dukkha* itself can only be a true, genuine *reality*.[6] Hence "true reality" is here best for "*sacca*," which still keeps a clear connection to "truth" as the other meaning of *sacca*.

What of the term *ariya*? As a noun, this means "noble one." In Brahmanism (which evolved into Hinduism), the term referred to members of the top three of the four social classes, denoting purity of descent and social superiority. In Buddhism it is used in a spiritual sense: the Buddha is "the Noble one" (SN.V.435), and other "Noble ones" are those who are partially or fully awakened and those well established on the path to these states:

- Stream-enterers: the first of those with direct experiential insight into all four *ariya-saccas*, so that they have uprooted certain spiritual fetters (Self-identity view (see below), clinging to practices and vows, and vacillation), cannot be reborn at less than a human level, and will become fully enlightened within seven lives at most (AN.I.235).
- Once-returners: those whose insight has weakened the fetters of desire for sense-pleasures and ill-will, whose future rebirths can only include one in the sense-desire realms of humans and the lower heavens.
- Non-returners: those who have ended the latter two fetters, and can only be reborn in the higher heavens, where they in time become fully enlightened.
- *Arahats* (Skt *arhat*): those who are fully enlightened, having ended the final fetters of attachment to any heavenly realms or experiences, restlessness, conceit and ignorance. They have experienced *nirvāṇa* in life, brought *dukkha* to an end, and cannot be reborn in any form. Their state "in" *nirvāṇa* beyond death is beyond description.
- In each of the above cases, there are also those whose insight places them as definitely set to attain the relevant state.

To make clear the spiritual sense of the term *ariya*, and that being a "Noble one" is something one attains rather than something to which one is born,[7] the translation "the Spiritually Ennobled" seems most apposite: a person who has been uplifted and purified by deep insight into reality. As an adjective, *ariya* means "noble," hence the

Buddhist path, the practice of which makes ordinary people into Noble ones, is itself clearly said to be "noble."

While a "truth" might be "noble" or, for those who have insight into it, "ennobling," the case is different when *sacca* means a "true reality." Insofar as one of the *ariya-saccas*, the origin of *dukkha*, is to be abandoned, this is hardly "noble" or "ennobling." In this context, *ariya* must mean "the spiritually ennobled," and the compound "*ariya-sacca*" must mean "true reality *for* the spiritually ennobled."[8] The *ariya-saccas* are the most significant categories of existence, and only the spiritually ennobled recognize their full import. Correct identification of them, and deep insight into their nature, is what makes a person spiritually ennobled. Of course, teachings *about* these true realities are still seen as truths, but such teachings are not themselves the "*ariya-saccas*."

The Four True Realities for the Spiritually Ennobled (more briefly, Realities for the Noble Ones), and statements which point to these realities, such as "This is *dukkha*," form the structural framework for all higher teachings of early Buddhism. They are: (i) *dukkha*, "the painful," encompassing the various forms of "pain," gross or subtle, physical or mental, to which we are all subject, along with painful things that engender these; (ii) the origination (*samudaya*, i.e., cause) of *dukkha*, namely craving (*taṇhā*; Skt *tṛṣṇā*); (iii) the cessation (*nirodha*) of *dukkha* by the cessation of craving (this cessation being equivalent to *nirvāṇa*); and (iv) the Noble Eight-Factored Path (*magga*; Skt *mārga*) that leads to this cessation. The DCPS says that the first of the four is "to be fully understood"; the second is "to be abandoned"; the third is "to be personally experienced"; the fourth is "to be developed/cultivated" (*bhāvitabba*). To "believe in" the *ariya-saccas* may play a part, but not the most important part. At the end of the DCPS, one of the Buddha's hearers, Kondañña, becomes a Stream-enterer, yet he responds not with *belief in* the *ariya-saccas* but with a kind of transformed vision: the "stainless *Dhamma*-eye" arises, and he has insight into the nature of these four crucial realities and their relationship: that, as *dukkha* has an identifiable cause, it can be ended.

The same fourfold structure of ideas (x, origination of x, its cessation, path to its cessation) is also applied to a range of other phenomena, such as the experienced world (*loka*; SN.I.62). This structure may also have been influenced by, or itself influenced, the practice of early Indian doctors: (i) diagnose an illness, (ii) identify its cause, (iii) determine whether it is curable, and (iv) outline a course of treatment to cure it. The first True Reality is the metaphorical "illness" of *dukkha* (Vibh-a.88), and the Buddha is seen as fulfilling the role of a spiritual physician. Having "cured" himself of *dukkha*, he worked to help others to do likewise.

Dukkha as the First True Reality for the Spiritually Ennobled: The Painful

Let us now examine what is said on this first True Reality, for without understanding the central concept of *dukkha* one is hindered from understanding the others. In the DCPS, the Buddha said:

> Now *this*, monks, for the spiritually ennobled, is the painful (*dukkha*) true reality (*ariya-sacca*): [i] birth [i.e., being born] is painful, aging is painful, illness is painful, death is

> painful; [ii] sorrow, lamentation, (physical) pain, unhappiness and distress are painful; [iii] union with what is disliked is painful; separation from what is liked is painful; not to get what one wants is painful; [iv] in brief, the five bundles of grasping-fuel are painful.
>
> (SN.V.421)

The *Atthasālinī*, a Theravādin commentary, says that the word *dukkha* is used in a variety of senses, such as: painful feeling (*dukkha-vedanā-*); basis of pain (*dukkha-vatthu-*), as in "birth is *dukkha*"; painful object (*dukkhāramaṇa-*), as in "material form is *dukkha*" (SN.III.69); condition for *dukkha* (*dukkha-paccaya-*), as in "*dukkha* is the accumulation of evil (*dukkho pāpassa uccayo*)" (Dhp.117); place (*-ṭṭhānā*) of *dukkha*, as in "how *dukkha* are the hells (*dukkhā nirayyā*)" (MN.III.169).

The word *dukkha* has been translated in many ways, with "suffering" as the most common, so that the above passage is generally translated, "Now this, monks, is the noble truth of suffering: birth is suffering . . . ," but "suffering" is an appropriate translation only in a general, inexact sense. The English word "suffering" is a noun (as in "his suffering is intense"), a present participle (as in "he is suffering from malaria"), or an adjective (as in "the suffering refugees"). If one translates "birth is suffering," it does not make sense to take "suffering" as a noun, as it is not the case that birth, etc., are themselves *forms of* suffering – they can only be occasions for the arising of the experience of suffering, things which often entail it. Nor can "suffering" be here meant as a present participle – it is not something that birth *is doing*; and as an adjective "suffering" applies only to people. However, in the passage on the first True Reality, *dukkha* in "birth is *dukkha* . . ." *is* an adjective – as shown by the fact that the grammatical gender changes according to the word it qualifies – but is not applied to a person or to people. The best translation here is by the English adjective "painful," which can apply to a range of things.

In fact, the basic everyday meaning of "*dukkha*" as a noun is "pain" as opposed to "pleasure" (*sukha*). These, with neither-*dukkha*-nor-*sukha*, are the three kinds of feeling (*vedanā*), with *dukkha* explained as covering both physical pain – *dukkha* in the narrowest sense (DN.II.306) – and unhappiness (*domanassa*), mental pain (SN.V.209–10). Similarly, in English, "pain" refers not just to physical pain but also to mental distress, both of these being covered by the second part of the phrase the "pleasures and pains of life." One also talks of difficult situations or persons as "a pain" – clearly in the sense of a mental pain, not a physical one. In the DCPS, something to which the adjective *dukkha* is applied is "painful" in the sense of being in some way troublesome or problematic, either obviously (e.g., physical pain, not getting what one wants) or only on investigation (e.g., being born). It applies to all those things which are unpleasant, stressful, unsatisfactory, imperfect, and which we would like to be otherwise. Those things that have these qualities can then be described as "the painful," which seems to be the meaning of the "*dukkha*" that is then explained above as "birth is painful . . ." Here "the painful" means both mental or physical pains and the aspects of life that engender these.

The first features described as "painful" in the above DCPS quote, (i), are basic biological aspects of being alive, each of which can be traumatic (BW.20–36). The *dukkha* of these is compounded by the rebirth perspective of Buddhism, for this involves repeated re-birth, re-aging, re-sickness, and re-death. The second set of features refer to physical or mental pains that arise from the vicissitudes of life. The third set of features point to the fact that we can never wholly succeed in keeping away things, people, and situations that we dislike, in holding on to those we do like, and in getting what we want. The changing, unstable nature of life is such that we are led to experience dissatisfaction, loss, and disappointment: in a word, frustration. The fourth feature will be discussed below.

Is Buddhism "pessimistic" in emphasizing the unpleasant aspects of life? Buddhism teaches that transcending the stress of life requires a fully realistic assessment of its pervasive presence. One must accept that one is "ill" if a cure is to be possible: ignoring the problem only makes it worse. It is certainly acknowledged that what is "painful" is not exclusively so (SN.III.68–70). The pleasant aspects of life are not denied, but it is emphasized that ignoring painful aspects leads to attachment, while calmly acknowledging the painful aspects have a purifying, liberating effect. Thus the Buddha says in respect of each of the five aspects of body and mind:

> The pleasure and gladness that arise in dependence on it: this is its attraction. That it is impermanent, painful (*dukkha*), and subject to change: this is its danger. The removal and abandonment of desire and attachment for it: this is its transcending.
>
> (AN.I.258–9; BW.192)

Happiness is real enough, and the calm and joy engendered by the Buddhist path help effectively to increase it, but Buddhism emphasizes that all forms of happiness (bar that of *nirvāṇa*) are fleeting. Sooner or later, they slip through one's fingers and can leave an aftertaste of loss and longing. In this way, even happiness is to be seen as *dukkha*. This can be more clearly seen when one considers another classification of forms of *dukkha*: the painfulness of (physical and mental) pain (*dukkha-dukkhatā*), the painfulness of conditioned phenomena (*saṇkhāra-dukkhatā*), and the painfulness of change (*viparanāma-dukkhatā*; SN.IV.259, SN.V.57, DN.III.216). The Theravādin commentator Buddhaghosa explains the first as "bodily and mental painful feeling," the third as "(bodily and mental) pleasant feeling, because they are a cause for the arising of *dukkha* when they change," and the second as "equanimous feeling and the remaining conditioned phenomena of three planes (of existence) because they are oppressed by rise and fall" (Vism.499). Hence, at SN.II.53, Sāriputta says: "Friend, there are these three feelings. What three? Pleasant feeling, painful feeling (*dukkhā vedanā*), neither-painful-nor-pleasant feeling. These three feelings are impermanent; whatever is impermanent is *dukkha*," and the Buddha says, "This is another method of explaining in brief that same point: 'Whatever is felt is (included) within *dukkha*.' " When a happy feeling passes, it often leads to mental pain due to change, and, even while it is occurring, the wise recognize it as subtly painful in the sense of being a limited, conditioned, imperfect state, one which is not truly satisfactory. This most subtle sense of *dukkha* is sometimes experienced in feelings of a vague unease at the fragility, transitoriness, and unsatisfactoriness of life.

Nevertheless, if *dukkha* is perceived in the right way, it is said to lead to "faith" or "trustful confidence" (*saddhā*; Skt *śraddhā*) in the Buddha's teachings (SN.II.30). From faith, other states successively arise which are part of the path to the end of *dukkha*: gladness, joy, happiness, meditative concentration, and deepening states of insight and detachment. This suggests that some initial understanding of *dukkha* supports a spiritual practice that leads to greater insight into it and ultimately liberation from it.

To what extent is "this is *dukkha*" a *description*, and to what extent is it a *judgment?* Many words have aspects of both. For example, "liar" is a description which also contains an implicit judgment. When something is said to be "*dukkha*" as it is a physical or mental pain, the descriptive aspect of its meaning is predominant, though there is an implied "this is unfortunate." When something is said to be "*dukkha*" due to being conditioned, limited, and imperfect, the judgmental aspect is to the fore, for that which is *dukkha* is here clearly being unfavorably compared to what is unconditioned and unlimited, namely *nirvāṇa*. The clear message is: if something is *dukkha*, do not be attached to it. At this level, *dukkha* is whatever is not *nirvāṇa*, and *nirvāṇa* is that which is not *dukkha*. This does not lead to a useless circular definition of the two terms, for *dukkha* is that which is conditioned, arising from other changing factors in the flow of time, and *nirvāṇa* is that which is unconditioned.

The Five Bundles of Grasping-Fuel: The Factors of Personality

When the DCPS summarizes its outline of *dukkha* by saying, (iv) "in brief, the five bundles of grasping-fuel are painful," it is referring to what is *dukkha* in the subtlest sense. The five "bundles of grasping-fuel" (*upādāna-kkhandha*; Skt *upādāna-skandha*) are the five factors which make up a "person." Buddhism holds, then, that none of the phenomena which comprise personal existence is free from some kind of painfulness. Each factor is a "group," "aggregate," or "bundle" (-(*k*)*khandha*) of related states, and each is an object of "grasping" (*upādāna*) so as to be identified as "me", "I," "myself." They are also just referred to as the *khandhas*.

The translation of *upādāna-kkhandha* as "groups of grasping" is often found, but it can be misleading. Grasping, *upādāna*, is a specific mental state which would best be classified as an aspect of the fourth *khandha* (the constructing activities: see below); so there are not five groups that are each *types* of grasping. Thus "groups (as objects of) grasping" is better. Nevertheless, there are hidden nuances in the word *upādāna*. Its derivation indicates that its root meaning is "taking up." While it often has the abstract meaning of "grasping," it also has a concrete meaning as "fuel": the "taking up" of which sustains a process such as fire. Richard Gombrich comments that the *suttas* are rich in fire-related metaphors due to the importance of fire in Brahmanism, and then argues that the term *upādāna-kkhandha* is also part of this fire imagery (Gombrich 1996, 66–8). The *upādāna-kkhandhas*, then, can each be seen as a "bundle of fuel" (ibid., 67) which "burn" with the "fires" of *dukkha* and its causes (SN.II.19–20). They are each sustaining objects of, or fuel *for*, grasping (cf. Thanissaro 1999, ch. 2). The translation "bundles of grasping-fuel" captures these nuances.

That the spiritually ennobled see even the factors making up a person as *dukkha* shows that their understanding of reality is rather different from that of ordinary people (who are also unlikely to see being born as *dukkha*). Hence it is said that, while the world sees the flow of agreeable sense-objects as pleasurable, and the ending of this as *dukkha*, the spiritually ennobled see the transcending of the *khandhas* and sense-objects as what is truly pleasurable (Sn.759–62 and SN.IV.127): *nirvāṇa* as the blissful state beyond all conditioned phenomena of the round of rebirths.

To aid understanding of *dukkha*, Buddhism gives details of each of the five factors in its analysis of personality (Hamilton 1996). All but the first of these "bundles" are mental in nature, for they lack any physical "form":

1 *rūpa*, "(material) form": This refers to the material aspect of existence, whether in the outer world or in the body of a living being. It is said to be comprised of four basic elements or forces – solidity (literally, "earth"), cohesion ("water"), heat ("fire"), and motion ("wind") – and forms of subtle, sensitive matter derived from these (e.g., the visual sensitivity of the eye). From the interaction of these, the body of flesh, blood, bones, etc., is composed.
2 *vedanā*, or "feeling": This is the hedonic tone or "taste" of any experience – pleasant, painful (*dukkha*), or neutral. It includes both sensations arising from the body and mental feelings of happiness, unhappiness, or indifference.
3 *saññā* (Skt *saṃjñā*), which processes sensory and mental objects, so as to classify and label them, for example, as "yellow," "a man," or "fear." It is "perception," "cognition," mental labeling, recognition, and interpretation – including misinterpretation – of objects. Without it, a person might be conscious but would be unable to know *what* he was conscious of.
4 the *saṅkhāras* (Skt *saṃskāra*), or "constructing activities" (also rendered "volitional formations," "mental formations," and "karmic activities"): These comprise a number of processes which initiate action or direct, mould, and give shape to character. The most characteristic one is *cetanā*, "will" or "volition," which is identified with karma (AN.III.415), literally, "action," that which brings later karmic results. There are processes which are ingredients of all mind-states, such as sensory stimulation and attention, ones which intensify such states, such as energy, joy, or desire-to-do, ones which are ethically "skillful" or "wholesome" (*kusala*; Skt *kuśala*), such as mindfulness and a sense of moral integrity, and "unskillful" ones, such as greed, hatred, and delusion.
5 *viññāṇa* (Skt *vijñāna*), "(discriminative) consciousness": This includes both the basic awareness of a sensory or mental object and the discrimination of its aspects or parts, which are actually recognized by *saññā*. One might thus also see it as perceptual "discernment." There are six types according to whether it is conditioned by eye, ear, nose, tongue, body, or mind-organ. It is also known as *citta*, the central focus of personality which can be seen as "mind," "heart," or "thought." This is essentially a "mind set" or "mentality," some aspects of which alter from moment to moment, but others recur and are equivalent to a person's character. Its form at any moment is set up by the other mental *khandhas*, but in turn it goes on to determine their pattern of arising, in a process of constant interaction.

Much Buddhist practice is concerned with the purification, development, and harmonious integration of the five "bundles" that make up a "person," through the cultivation of virtue and meditation. In time, however, the fivefold analysis is used to enable a meditator gradually to transcend the naïve perception – with respect to "himself" or "another" – of a unitary "person" or "self." In place of this, there is set up the contemplation of a person as a cluster of changing physical and mental processes, or *dhammas* (Skt *dharma*), thus undermining grasping and attachment, which are key causes of suffering.

Phenomena as Impermanent and Non-Self[9]

Though the DCPS emphasizes *dukkha*, this is in fact only one of three related characteristics or "marks" of the five *khandhas*. These "three marks" (*ti-lakkhaṇa*; Skt *tri-lakṣaṇa*) of all conditioned phenomena are that they are impermanent (*anicca*; Skt *anitya*), painful (*dukkha*; Skt *duḥkha*), and non-Self (*anattā*; Skt *anātman*).[10] Buddhism emphasizes that change and impermanence are fundamental features of *everything*, bar *nirvāṇa*. Mountains wear down, material goods wear out or are lost or stolen, and all beings, even gods, age and die (MN.II.65–82; BW.207–13). The gross form of the body changes relatively slowly, but the matter which composes it is replaced as one eats, excretes, and sheds skin cells. As regards the mind, character patterns may be relatively persistent, but feelings, moods, ideas, etc., can be observed to change constantly. The ephemeral and deceptive nature of the *khandhas* is expressed in a passage which says that they are "void, hollow": "Material form is like a lump of foam, and feeling is like a bubble; perception is like a mirage, and the constructing activities are like a banana tree [lacking a core, like an onion]; consciousness is like a (magician's) illusion" (SN. III.142; BW.343–5).

It is because things are impermanent that they are also *dukkha*. Because they are impermanent and in some sense painful, moreover, they are to be seen as *anattā*, non-Self. When something is said to be *anattā*, the kind of "self" it is seen not to be is clearly one that would be permanent and free from all pain, however subtle – so as to be happy, self-secure, independent. While Pāli and Sanskrit do not have capital letters, in English it is useful to signal such a concept with a capital: Self.

The term *anattā* is a noun, in the form of the word for Self, *attā* (Skt *ātman*), prefaced by the negative prefix *an*, meaning that what is *anattā* has nothing to do with "self" in a certain sense: it is neither a Self, nor what pertains or belongs to such a thing (*attaniya*, SN.III.33–4; SN.IV.54), as "mine," or what contains Self or is contained in it (MN.I.300; SN.III.127–32). It is "empty (*suñña*; Skt *śūnya*) of Self or what pertains to Self" (SN.IV.54; BW.347). While *anattā* is often rendered simply as "not-Self," this translation captures only part of its meaning, as it misses out the aspect of not being anything that pertains to a Self, which "non-Self" includes.

This important teaching was introduced by the Buddha in his "second sermon," the *Anatta-lakkhaṇa Sutta* (Vin.I.13–14; SN.III.66–8; BW.341–2). Here he explained, with respect to each of the five *khandhas*, that, if it were truly Self, it would not "tend to sickness," and it would be totally controllable at will, which it is not. Moreover, as each *khandha* is impermanent, *dukkha*, and of a nature to change, it is inappropriate to consider it as "This is mine, this am I, this is my Self" – and doing so will lead to *dukkha*, due to the gap between how things are and how one is struggling to portray them.

The spiritual quest was seen by the Buddha's contemporaries largely as the search for identifying and liberating a person's true Self. Such an entity was postulated as a person's permanent inner nature, the source of true happiness, and the autonomous "inner controller" (Skt *antaryamin*) of a person's actions and inner elements and faculties. It would also need to be in full control of itself. In Brahmanism, this Self was seen as a universal Self (*Ātman*) identical with *Brahman*, the ground and essence of the world, while in Jainism, for example, it was seen as the individual "Life principle" (*Jīva*). The Buddha argued that anything subject to change, anything not autonomous and totally controllable by its own wishes, anything involved with the disharmony of mental pain, could not be such a perfect true Self or what pertained to it. Moreover, to take anything as being such is to lay the basis for much suffering; for what one fondly takes as one's permanent, essential Self, or its secure possession, actually changes in undesired ways. While the *Upaniṣads* recognized many things as being not-Self, they felt that a real, true Self could be found. They held that when it was found, and known to be identical to *Brahman*, the basis of everything, this would bring liberation. In the Buddhist *suttas*, though, literally *everything* is seen as non-Self, even *nirvāṇa*. When this is known, then liberation – *nirvāṇa* – is attained by total non-attachment. Thus both the *Upaniṣads* and the Buddhist *suttas* see many things as not-Self, but the *suttas* apply it, indeed non-Self, to *everything*.

The teaching on phenomena as non-Self is intended to undermine not only the Brahmanical or Jain concepts of Self but also much more commonly held conceptions and deep-rooted feelings of I-ness. To feel that, however much one changes in life from childhood onwards, some essential part remains constant and unchanged as the "real me," is to have a belief in a permanent Self. To act as if only *other* people die, and to ignore the inevitability of one's own death, is to act as if one had a permanent Self. To relate changing mental phenomena to a substantial self which "owns" them: "*I* am worried . . . happy . . . angry," is to have such a Self-concept. To build an identity based on one's bodily appearance or abilities, or on one's sensitivities, ideas and beliefs, actions or intelligence, etc., is to take them as part of an "I."

The non-Self teaching can easily be misunderstood and misdescribed, so it is important to see what it is saying. The Buddha accepted many conventional usages of the word "self" (also "*attā*"), as in "yourself" and "myself." These he saw as simply a convenient way of referring to a particular collection of mental and physical states. But, within such a conventional, empirical self, he taught that no permanent, substantial, independent, metaphysical Self could be found. This is well explained by an early nun, Vajirā:[11] just as the word "chariot" is used to denote a collection of items in functional relationship, but not a special part of a chariot, so the conventional term "a being" is properly used to refer to the five *khandhas* relating together. None of the *khandhas* is a "being" or "Self"; these are simply conventional labels used to denote the collection of functioning *khandhas*.

The non-Self teaching does not deny that there is continuity of character in life, and to some extent from life to life. But persistent character traits are due merely to the repeated occurrence of certain *cittas*, or "mind-sets." The *citta* as a whole is sometimes talked of as an (empirical) "self" (e.g., Dhp.160; cf. 35), but while such character traits may be long-lasting, they can and do change, and are thus impermanent, and so "non-Self," insubstantial. A "person" is a collection of rapidly changing and interacting mental and physical processes, with character patterns reoccurring over time. Only partial control can be exercised over these processes; so they often change in undesired ways, leading to suffering. Impermanent, they cannot be a permanent Self. Being "painful," they cannot be a true, autonomous "I," which would contain nothing that was out of harmony with itself.

While *nirvāṇa* is beyond impermanence and *dukkha*, it is still non-Self. This is made clear in a recurring passage (e.g., at AN.I.286–7), which says that all *saṇkhāras*, here meaning conditioned phenomena, are impermanent and *dukkha*, but that "all *dhammas*" are non-Self. "*Dhamma*" (Skt *dharma*) is a word with many meanings in Buddhism, but here it refers to any basic component of reality. Most are conditioned, but *nirvāṇa* is the unconditioned *dhamma*; both conditioned and unconditioned *dhammas* are non-Self. While *nirvāṇa* is beyond change and suffering, it has nothing in it which could support the feeling of I-ness; for this can arise only with respect to the *khandhas*, and it is not even a truly valid feeling here (DN.II.66–8; Harvey 1995, 31–3).

That said, it should be noted that, while "all *dhammas* are *anattā*" – "everything is non-Self" – clearly implies that there is no Self, the word *anattā* does not *itself* mean "no-Self" – i.e., does not itself mean "there is no Self." It simply means that what it applies to is not a Self or what pertains to it. Moreover, the non-Self teaching is not in *itself* a denial of the existence of a permanent self; it is primarily a practical teaching aimed at the overcoming of grasping. Indeed, when asked directly if "self" (in an unspecified sense) exists or not, the Buddha was silent, as he did not want either to affirm a permanent Self or to confuse his questioner by not accepting self in any sense (SN.IV.400–1). A philosophical denial of "Self" is just a view, a theory, which may be agreed with or not. It does not necessarily get one actually to examine all the things with which one actually *does* identify, consciously or unconsciously, as Self or essentially "mine." This examination, in a calm, meditative context, is what the "non-Self" teaching aims at. It is not so much a conceptual idea as something to be *done*, applied to actual experience, so that the meditator actually *sees* that "*all dhammas* are non-Self." A mere philosophical denial does not encourage this, and may actually mean that a person sees no need for it.

While the *suttas* have no place for a metaphysical Self, seeing things as *non-Self* is clearly regarded as playing a vital soteriological role. The concept of "Self" and the associated deep-rooted feeling of "I am" are utilized for a spiritual end. The non-Self teaching can in fact be seen as a brilliant device which uses a deep-seated human aspiration, ultimately *illusory*, to overcome the negative products of such an illusion. Identification, whether conscious or unconscious, with something as "what I truly and permanently am," or as inherently "mine," is a source of grasping or attachment; such attachment leads to frustration and a sense of loss when what one identifies with changes and becomes other than what one desires. The deep-rooted idea of "Self," though, is not to be attacked, but used as a measuring-rod against which all phenomena should be compared, so as to see them as falling short of the perfections implied in the idea of Self. This is to be done through a rigorous experiential examination of the phenomena that we *do* identify with as "Self," "I," or "mine": as each of these is examined, but is seen actually to be non-Self, falling short of the ideal, the intended result is that one should let go of any attachment to such a thing. In doing this, a person finally comes to see *everything* as non-Self, thereby destroying all attachment and attaining *nirvāṇa*. In this process, it is not necessary to give any philosophical "denial" of Self; the idea simply withers away, as it is seen that no actual instance of such a thing can be found anywhere (MN.I.138; SB.161–5).

Overall, it can be said that: (i) in the changing, empirical self, no permanent Self can be found; (ii) yet one of the constructing activities is the "I am conceit" (*asmi-māna*) – the gut feeling or attitude that one is or has a real Self, a substantial I, expressed in self-preoccupation, self-importance, and ego-feelings; (iii) as a person develops spiritually, their empirical self becomes stronger as they become more centered, calm, aware, and open; (iv) in this process, awareness of all the factors of personality as non-Self undermines grasping, and so makes a person calmer and stronger; (v) at the pinnacle of spiritual development, the liberated person is free of all the causes of *dukkha*, and thus lacks any "I am" conceit, yet has a *mahattā*, "great (empirical) self" (It.28–9; Harvey 1995, 55–8): they are strong, spiritually developed people.

Sensitivity to the above variation in self-language should help one avoid incoherence in presenting ideas relating to the non-Self doctrine. Students sometimes say odd things such as: "Buddhism teaches that there is no self. . . . The self is the five *khandhas* . . . but these are to be seen as not-self." Again, while Pāli and Sanskrit lack capital letters, the use of them helps signal the difference, clearly implicit in the *suttas*, between an accepted empirical self and a metaphysical Self which is never accepted.[12]

Buddhism sees no need to postulate a permanent Self, and it accounts for the functioning of personality, in life and from life to life, in terms of a stream of changing, conditioned processes. As explained in chapter 23, THE CONDITIONED CO-ARISING OF MENTAL AND BODILY PROCESSES, rebirth does not require a permanent Self or substantial "I," but *belief* in such a thing is one of the things that causes rebirth.

The Second True Reality for the Spiritually Ennobled: The Origin of the Painful

In the DCPS, the Buddha talks of the second True Reality thus:

> Now *this*, monks, for the spiritually ennobled, is the originating-of-the-painful (*dukkha-samudaya*) true reality. It is this craving (*taṇhā*; Skt *tṛṣṇā*) which leads to renewed being, accompanied by delight and attachment, seeking delight now here, now there; that is, craving for sense-pleasures, craving for being, craving for non-existence.

So the key origin or cause of *dukkha* is "*taṇhā*." This literally means "thirst" and clearly refers to demanding, clinging desires which are ever on the lookout for gratification, "now here, now there," in the changing, unreliable world, demanding that things be like this . . . and not like that. . . . It contains an element of psychological compulsion, a driven restlessness ever on the lookout for new objects on which to focus: *I want*, *I want* more, *I want* different. This propels people into situations which open them to pain, disquiet, and upset. We like things to be permanent, lasting, reliable, happy, controllable, and belonging to us. Because of such longings, we tend to look on the world as if it were like this, in spite of the fact that we are repeatedly reminded it is not. We are good at ignoring realities: spiritual ignorance. Thus arise what are called the "inversions" (*vipallāsa*; Skt *viparyāsa*) of mind, of perception or view: looking on what is impermanent as if it were permanent; looking on what is *dukkha* as if it were happiness, or happiness-inducing; looking on what is not a permanent I/Self or its possession as if it were one (AN.II.52). Such a distorted outlook means that we continue to grasp at things which, by their nature, cannot *actually* satisfy our longings. Thus we continue to experience frustration.

Taṇhā, then, is not just any "desire," but a driven desire rooted in delusion. Desire, though, can be also be wise, wholesome, and for good things (Webster 2005b). *Chanda*, or desire-to-act, can be either unwholesome, like *taṇhā*, or wholesome, and it is a key ingredient of one of the four *iddhi-pādas*, or "bases of success," which aid spiritual development (Gethin 2001, 81–103).

The stronger a person *craves*, though, the greater the frustration when the demand for lasting and wholly satisfying fulfilment is perpetually disappointed by a changing and unsatisfactory world. Also, the *more things* a person craves, the more opportunities for frustration, *dukkha*. Craving also brings pain as it leads to quarrels, strife, and conflict between individuals and groups (DN.II.59–61) and motivates people to perform various actions with karmic results shaping further rebirths, with their attendant *dukkha*.

The DCPS identifies three types of craving: craving for sensual pleasures (*kāma-taṇhā*), craving for being (*bhava-taṇhā*), and craving for non-existence (*vibhava-taṇhā*). The second type refers to the drive for ego-enhancement based on a certain identity and for some mode of eternal life after death as *me*. The third is the drive to get rid of unpleasant situations, things, and people. In a strong form, it may lead to the impulse for suicide, in the hope of annihilation. Such a craving, ironically, helps cause a further rebirth, whose problems will be as bad as, or worse than, the present ones. In order to overcome *dukkha*, the Buddhist path aims not only to limit the expression of craving but ultimately to use calm and wisdom to uproot it completely from the psyche.

Besides craving, another important cause of *dukkha* is "views" (*diṭṭhi*; Skt *dṛṣṭi*). The Buddha focused much critical attention on views concerning "Self," which he saw as leading to attachment and thus suffering. Such views can take many forms, but he felt that many of them locate a substantial Self somewhere in the five *khandhas*, regarding any one of them as being Self, owned by Self, within Self, or having Self within it, leading to 20 such views in all (SN.III.1–5; SB.216–20). Each of these is known as a "view on the existing group" (*sakkāya-diṭṭhi*; Skt *satkāya-dṛṣṭi*), sometimes also translated as "personality view." However, as the meaning is a view which sees a Self-essence as somehow related to the "existing group" – the five *upādāna-kkhandhas* (MN.I.299) – perhaps the best gloss is "Self-identity view." The non-acceptance of any of these views in the *suttas* means, for example, that, with regard to material form, the body, it is not truly appropriate to say "I am body," "the body is mine," "body is part of my Self," "I am in the body." Indeed, it is said that the body does not "belong" to anyone: it simply arises due to past karma (SN.II.64–5). Its associated mental states do not "own" it.

Even when specific views regarding "Self" have been transcended, a subtle kind of "conceit" (*māna*) still remains as a vague and non-specific feeling of I-ness with respect to the *khandhas* (SN.III.127–32; BW.402–6). "Conceit" is the basic attitude of "I am":

deep-rooted self-centeredness, self-importance, or egoism, which is concerned about how "I" measure up to "others" as "superior," "inferior," or "equal" – another key cause of *dukkha*.

A further summary of the causes of *dukkha* is "attachment (*rāga*: sensual and other forms of lust), hatred (P. *dosa*; Skt *dveṣa*) and delusion (*moha*)," with attachment and hatred equivalent to craving for and craving to be rid of something, and delusion equivalent to spiritual ignorance (P. *avijjā*; Skt *avidyā*). This ignorance is an ingrained misperception of reality that fails to see and understand the True Realities for the Spiritually Ennobled (MN.I.54), and which sustains a series of conditions, including craving and grasping, that lead to *dukkha*: the conditioned co-arising sequence.

The Third and Fourth True Realities for the Spiritually Ennobled: The Cessation of the Painful, and the Path to This

The third True Reality is described in the DCPS as follows:

> Now *this*, monks, for the spiritually ennobled, is the ceasing-of-the-painful true reality. It is the remainderless fading away and cessation of that same craving, the giving up and relinquishing of it, freedom from it, non-reliance on it.

That is: the ending of thirst for the "next thing," so as to give full attention to what is here, now; abandoning attachments to past, present, or future; freedom that comes from contentment; not relying on craving so that the mind does not fixate on anything, adhering to it, roosting there. When craving and other related causes thus come to an end, *dukkha* ceases. This is equivalent to *nirvāṇa* (P. *nibbāna*), also known as the "unconditioned" or "unconstructed" (*asaṇkhata*; Skt *asaṃskṛta*; SN.IV.360–73), the ultimate goal of Buddhism (Collins 1982). As an initial spur to striving for *nirvāṇa*, craving for it may play a role (AN.II.145; Webster 2005b, 134–5), but this helps in the overcoming of other cravings, is generally replaced by a wholesome aspiration, and is completely eradicated in the full experience of *nirvāṇa*: *nirvāṇa* is attained only when there is total non-attachment and letting go.

Nirvāṇa literally means "extinction" or "quenching," being the word used for the "extinction" of a fire. The "fires" of which *nirvāṇa* is the extinction are described in the "Fire sermon" (SN.IV.19–20; BW.346; SB.222–4). This teaches that everything internal and external to a person is "burning" with the "fires" of attachment, hatred, and delusion and of birth, aging, and death. Here the "fires" refer both to the causes of *dukkha* and to *dukkha* itself. *Nirvāṇa* during life is frequently defined as the destruction of the three "fires" or defilements (e.g., SN.IV.251; BW.364). When one who has destroyed these dies, he or she cannot be reborn and so is totally beyond the remaining "fires" of birth, aging, and death, having attained final *nirvāṇa*. When the Buddha was asked if an enlightened person, after death, "is," "is not," both or neither of these, he set the questions aside as irrelevant to the spiritual quest, and as all infected with the idea of Self. There has been much speculation on what the Buddha's silence on this matter might imply (Harvey 1995, 208–10, 239–45; 2013, 78–80).

The fourth True Reality is described thus:

> Now *this*, monks, for the spiritually ennobled, is the true reality which is the way leading to the cessation of the painful. It is this noble eight-factored path, that is to say, [1] right view, [2] right resolve, [3] right speech, [4] right action, [5] right livelihood, [6] right effort, [7] right mindfulness, [8] right mental unification.

The DCPS also describes this path as a "middle way" (*majjhimā paṭipadā*; Skt *madhyama pratipad*) that avoids two extremes: the pursuit of sensual pleasures and self-mortification. The path involves wisdom (factors 1 and 2), moral virtue (3–5), and meditative training (6–8) (MN.I.301). It works on both a cognitive and an affective level, with both inward and external aspects. It is also practiced initially at an ordinary level, with benefits in this and future lives, and then at a "transcendent" (*lokuttara*; Skt *laukottara*) level, which leads to the noble states, culminating in arahatship (MN.III.71–8; Gethin 2001, 190–226; Harvey 2013, 81–7).

The Cessation of *Dukkha*

Both during life and beyond death, *nirvāṇa* pertains to the *arahat*, who has overcome the "disease" of *dukkha* and attained complete mental health (AN.II.143). But in what sense has an *arahat* attained the "cessation" of *dukkha*? To address this question, it is useful to remind ourselves of the key aspects of *dukkha*:

i birth – i.e., being born – which inevitably leads to:
ii aging, illness, death: features of life that entail physical and mental pain;
iii sorrow, lamentation, (physical) pain, unhappiness, and distress: mental and physical pains;
iv union with what is disliked, separation from what is liked, not to get what one wants: various frustrations;
v the five bundles of grasping-fuel: the conditioned, impermanent, and non-Self factors of personality.

These can then be grouped thus:

a physical pain and features of life entailing this;
b mental pains and frustration;
c impermanent, conditioned factors of personality, mental and physical.

Now an *arahat* or buddha will be free of (a) once their present, final rebirth ends, but until then they are still embodied beings who periodically experience physical pain: "the five (sense-) faculties still remain, through which . . . he undergoes the pleasant and the unpleasant, he experiences pleasure and *dukkha*" (It.38).

However, they are in the main free of (b). It is said that the Buddha remained mindful and clearly comprehending in the face of intense pain from a foot injury, and so did not become distressed (SN.I.27). The balanced detachment of the *arahat*'s mind is such that he and the almost enlightened Non-returner are free of aversion (*paṭigha*) to physical pain, and so add no mental pain in response to it: "he does not sorrow, grieve or lament, he does not weep . . . and become distraught." One who adds mental pain in response to physical pain is said to be like a person shot with one arrow then being shot with a second arrow (SN.IV.208–9). Indeed, any Noble person, from a Stream-enterer upwards, is not "afflicted in mind" when "afflicted in body." This is because they are free of Self-identity view – they do not relate to any of the *khandhas* as Self or as related to Self – so undesired change in any of the *khandhas* (whether bodily or mental ones) does not lead to experiencing "sorrow, lamentation, pain, unhappiness and distress" (SN.III.2–4). An ordinary person (not yet a Noble person) lusts after pleasant feelings and grieves over unpleasant ones; in that a pleasant feeling "invades his mind and remains," this is because his "body (*kāya*)" is not developed; in that the painful feeling "invades his mind and remains," this is because his mind (*citta*) is not developed (MN.I.239–40). Here the commentary explains that "development of the body" refers to insight (*vipassanā*) into pleasant feeling as impermanent, subtly painful (unsatisfactory), and non-Self, while "development of the mind" refers to the development of calm (*samatha*) by deep meditative concentration. This illustrates how the Buddhist path works on both cognitive and affective roots of suffering, insofar as both delusion and craving, and their mutual supporting, need to be undone. The *arahat* remains ever calm and does not identify with pain or pleasure as "mine," but sees them simply as non-Self passing phenomena, as well as withdrawing from physical pain in meditative concentration. As is said in the second century CE *Avadāna-śataka* (II.384; Dayal 1970 [1932], 15), "the sky and the palm of his hand were the same to his mind." Even faced with the threat of death, the *arahat* is unruffled. In this situation, the *arahat* Adhimutta disconcerted a potential assailant by fearlessly asking why he should be perturbed at the prospect of the end of the constituents of "his" personality: he had no thought of an "I" being here, but just saw a stream of changing phenomena (Thag.715–16). Indeed, anyone who shows any hint of fear, conceit, anger, or any other negative states cannot be an *arahat* (MN.I.317; cf. Miln.207–8, 186–8; Vism.634–5).

The *arahat* Sāriputta says that "There is nothing in the world through the change and alteration of which sorrow, lamentation, pain, unhappiness and distress might arise in me," even if such change was the death of his teacher, the Buddha – though he would acknowledge the loss of a source of welfare for the world (SN.II.274). Accordingly, it is said that, when the Buddha died, those disciples who were not *arahats* grieved, while the *arahats* "endured mindfully and clearly aware, saying, 'All conditioned things are impermanent – what is the use of this?' " (DN.II.158). Sāriputta also taught that, for one who is discontented (*anabhirati*), wherever he goes and whatever posture he is in, he does not experience happiness (*sukha*) and pleasure – unlike one who is contented (AN.V.121).

That said, enlightened ones are not seen as indifferent to their physical needs. In his final illness, the Buddha could be insistent about these. At one time he becomes extremely thirsty, and asks Ānanda three times for some water to drink after the latter delays bringing some as the available water is muddy – though Ānanda then finds it unmuddy, the implication being that this is by the Buddha's power (DN.II.128–9).

Perhaps more surprising is that the Buddha is occasionally described in a way implying he experienced mental pain – not in response to physical pain, but in response to an actual or potential situation. In his final year, he was once asked by Ānanda about the rebirth destiny of 12 local people. Having given answers in each case, the Buddha then says, "Ānanda, it is not remarkable that one who has attained a human state should die, but that you should come to the *Tathāgata* to ask the destiny of each of these who have died, that is a *vihesā* to him" (hence he tells Ānanda a way to work out the answer to such questions for himself; DN.II.93). The Pali Text Society *Pali–English Dictionary* defines *vihesā* as "vexation, annoyance, injury, worry" and says it is related to the word *vihiṃsā*, "hurting, injuring, cruelty, injury." In this context, though, it probably means something like a tiring, troublesome thing – that the Buddha had not experienced *annoyance* is shown by the fact that he had actually answered the 12 questions just put to him; but, for an old man, many such questions would indeed be tiring. Indeed the commentary (DN-a.II.544) here explains that what is meant is that answering such questions would be "a weariness for the body (*kāya-kilamatha*)."

Elsewhere, the Buddha says that, just as a doctor whose medicine had failed to cure the blindness of a man would experience "weariness (*kilamatha-*) and distress (*vighāta*)," so would it be a "weariness (*kilamatho*) and trouble (*vihesā*)" for him (MN.I.510) if he taught his disciples how to attain the "health" of *nirvāṇa*, but none of them did so. Indeed, soon after his enlightenment, when he was considering teaching others what he had discovered, he initially hesitated to do so, as he thought that people were so wrapped up in their worldly concerns that they would not understand the profound, subtle, and hard to understand realities he had experienced, such that teaching people would be a "weariness and trouble" for him (MN.I.168; Webster 2005a). In such a case, physical tiredness would no doubt be involved, but were *everyone* genuinely unable to understand the Buddha (something the Buddha then saw was not the case), then his teaching them would be a pointless exercise, like hitting one's head against a brick wall. Such an action would clearly be not the act of a wise person, or, indeed, the act of one with compassion for all beings, including himself. This does imply, though, that an enlightened person can experience not only physical pain but at least some mental pains: the pain involved in doing a pointless task or one that taxed their resources of physical and mental energy, especially if these were low as a result of age and/or illness.

The *arahat* is free of any "distress (*vighāta*)" from other sources: "the distresses and fevers that arise from sense-desire [or ill-will, cruelty, visible forms, or the existing group (*sakkāya*: the *khandhas* (MN.I.299)], and he does not feel that feeling" (DN. III.240). Yet the *Milindapañha* slightly overstates the case when it says that the *arahat* feels bodily painful feelings but not mental painful feelings (Miln.445). Here, though, its later explanation shows that it has in mind only mental pain in response to physical pain:

> An *Arahat*'s mind is developed, sire, well developed, it is tamed, well tamed, it is docile and obedient. On his being assailed by a painful feeling he grasps it firmly thinking that it is not permanent; he fastens his mind to the post of concentration, and when his mind is fastened to the post of concentration it does not quiver or shake, but is steadfast and composed, although his body, owing to the diffusion of the perturbation of the feeling, bends, contorts itself and rolls about.
>
> (Miln.254)

Arahats can, then, like non-enlightened experienced meditators, periodically experience deep meditative states, the *jhānas*, which are free of physical pain and can be very joyful or peaceful. These states are still conditioned and impermanent, though, and so come under type (c) *dukkha*. Moreover, intense physical pain may prevent a person being able to attain *jhāna* or to remain in *jhāna* (cf. SN.I.120–4).

The Buddha, when he had suffered a bout of intense pain that he had endured while mindful and clearly aware, without becoming distressed (*avihaññamāno*; DN.II.99), goes on to say that, he, in his eightieth year, is now:

> old, worn out . . . Just as an old cart is made to go by being held together with straps, so the *Tathāgata*'s body is kept going by being strapped up. It is only when the *Tathāgata*, from not attending to any perceptual signs (*nimitta*), from the cessation of certain feelings, having attained the signless (*animitta*) mental concentration, dwells there, that the *Tathāgata*'s body (*kāya*) knows comfort (*phāsukato*).
>
> (DN.II.100)

The signless state is one where the mind of a Noble person attends to *nirvāṇa* as itself "signless" (Harvey 1986; 1995, 193–7), and it may be this state to which the Buddha alludes when he says that he is able, without moving his body, to "stay experiencing nothing but happiness (*sukha-*) for up to seven days and nights" (MN.I.94). The later Theravāda tradition certainly sees the attainment of the "fruit" states which know *nirvāṇa* as attained by Noble ones "for the purpose of abiding in happiness here and now" (Vism.700).

As for type (c) *dukkha*, this ends when the conditioned *khandhas* end at death. The *khandhas* are impermanent and, "whatever is impermanent, that is painful (*dukkha*)" (SN.II.53), so, when an *arahat* dies, it should be seen that the *khandhas* have simply ended, and that these were impermanent and *dukkha* (SN.III.112). In addition, when an *arahat* first experiences *nirvāṇa* during life, or later returns to this experience, there is also access to a state beyond type (c) *dukkha*. For the developed Theravāda tradition, this is explained as a direct *seeing and knowing* of *nirvāṇa* as a signless, timeless, and unconditioned realm, though the consciousness of the *arahat* that knows this is still conditioned. There are various suggestions in the Pāli *suttas*, though, that the *arahat*'s full experience of *nirvāṇa* in life is one where consciousness, free of attachment to any object, is able to become entirely objectless and unconditioned, and to itself *be nirvāṇa*, the timeless unborn, the deathless (Harvey 2013, 79–80; 1995, 180–226).

So, we have seen how, in the early Buddhist texts, *dukkha* in its various senses is brought to an end for an enlightened person. Their ending of craving, and the ignorance by which it is conditioned, mean that the ups and downs of life do not upset their calm equanimity, as they are no longer tied to these variable states by grasping and aversion. They also have access to blissful meditative states. Yet they still experience physical pain and can become physically tired and mentally weary at draining repeated questions or the prospect of a fruitless task. Such final limitations and their painfulness end, though, with the end of rebirth – that no longer has craving to cause it – as well as being periodically experienced in life.

This then raises the question of whether saying that something is *dukkha* means that it is: (i) *by its very nature* "painful" or (ii) "painful" *when reacted to with grasping or aversion*. Both seem to be implied in the *suttas* of the Pāli Nikāyas: grasping at anything leads to psychological pain (as what one grasps at does not remain as one wants it to), and aversion makes pain worse, but also conditioned things are to be seen, in themselves, as *dukkha* in the sense of being impermanent and conditioned, hence limited and imperfect. They may also, in a straightforward sense, be forms of physical or mental pain.

The path of early Buddhism and the Theravāda school aims initially at lessening the mental pain that the vicissitudes and stresses of life can produce, then at ending the great majority of mental pain, but ultimately at ending the round of rebirths, conditioned existence, and both its physical pains and its more subtly painful nature. The Mahāyāna tradition, though, does not see things of the world as painful *by their very nature*, for when truly understood with wisdom they are seen as non-different from *nirvāṇa*. Hence the idea developed in the Mahāyāna that a buddha, and those advanced on the bodhisattva path leading to buddhahood, could remain in, or in contact with, the world in what is known as "non-abiding" (*apratiṣṭhita*) *nirvāṇa*, clinging neither to the world of rebirths nor to *nirvāṇa* as something supposedly separate from this (Nagao 1991; Williams 2009, 60, 185–6).

Notes

1 Note that two-thirds of this chapter overlaps with part of chapter 3 in the author's *Introduction to Buddhism: Teachings, History and Practices*. Second edn. Cambridge: Cambridge University Press, 2013. This material is included here with permission.
2 On the whole, Pali versions of terms are given first in this chapter, except in the case of *nirvāṇa*, as this is well known in English.
3 Whether or not this was historically so.
4 SN.V.420–4 (BW.75–8; SB.243–6; Harvey 2007); Skt *Dharma-cakra-pravartana Sūtra*.
5 Translations are the author's own, in some cases as modifications of published translations.
6 In a few contexts, such as "in truth, in reality," "truth" and "reality" can be synonyms, but in general they are not, and it aids clarity to translate *sacca* as "reality" in contexts where this is the force of its meaning.
7 Unless one had already become, e.g., a Stream-enterer in a past life.
8 Harvey (2007, 2009a); and Karl Brunnholzl (2010, 680–1) argues for "realities of the noble ones" from Sanskrit and Tibetan sources.
9 See Collins (1982); Harvey (1995, 17–108; 2009b, 265–74); Siderits (2003).
10 E.g., SN.III.44–5 (BW.342–3); SN.IV.46–7 (SB.224–5); SN.IV.133–5 (BW.346–7).
11 SN.I.135; cf. Miln.25–8.
12 Though the Mahāyāna contains some flirting with "Self" language in relation to the Buddha-nature (Williams 2009, 103–28).

References

Anderson, C. (1999). *Pain and its Ending: The Four Noble Truths in the Theravāda Buddhist Canon*. London: Curzon Press.

Brunnholzl, Karl (2010). *Gone Beyond: The Prajñāpāramitā Sūtras, the Ornament of Clear Realization and its Commentaries in the Tibetan Kagyu Tradition*. Ithaca, NY: Snow Lion.

Collins, S. (1982). *Selfless Persons: Imagery and Thought in Theravāda Buddhism*. Cambridge: Cambridge University Press.

Dayal, H. (1970 [1932]). *The Bodhisattva Doctrine in Buddhist Sanskrit Literature*. London: Routledge & Kegan Paul; repr. Delhi: Motilal Banarsidass.

Gethin, R. M. L. (2001). *The Buddhist Path to Awakening*. Oxford: Oneworld.

Gombrich, R. F. (1996). *How Buddhism Began: The Conditioned Genesis of the Early Teachings*. London, and Atlantic Highlands, NJ: Athlone Press.

Hamilton, S. (1996) *Identity and Experience: The Constitution of the Human Being According to Early Buddhism*. London: Luzac Oriental.

Harvey, P. (1986). Signless Samādhis in Pāli Buddhism. In *Journal of the International Association of Buddhist Studies* 9, 25–52.

Harvey, P. (1995). *The Selfless Mind: Personality, Consciousness and Nirvana in Early Buddhism*. London: Curzon Press.

Harvey, P. (2007). *Dhammacakkappavattana Sutta: The Discourse on the Setting in Motion of the Wheel (of Vision) of the Basic Pattern: The Four Realities for the Spiritually Ennobled Ones*. Trans., with notes, at: www.accesstoinsight.org/tipitaka/sn/sn56/sn56.011.harv.html.

Harvey, P. (2009a). The Four Ariya-saccas as "True Realities for the Spiritually Ennobled" – the Painful, its Origin, its Cessation, and the Way Going to This – Rather than "Noble Truths" Concerning These. In *Buddhist Studies Review* 26, 197–227. DOI: 10.1558/bsrv.v26i2.197.

Harvey, P. (2009b). The Approach to Knowledge and Truth in the Theravāda Record of the Discourses of the Buddha; Theravāda Philosophy of Mind and the Person; Theravāda Texts on Ethics. In *Buddhist Philosophy: Essential Readings*. Ed. W. Edelglass and J. L. Garfield. Oxford: Oxford University Press, 175–85, 265–74, 375–87.

Harvey, P. (2013). *An Introduction to Buddhism: Teachings, History and Practices*. Second edn. Cambridge: Cambridge University Press.

Nagao, G. (1991). *Mādhyamika and Yogācāra: A Study of Mahāyāna Philosophies: Collected Papers of G. M. N. Nagao*. Albany: State University of New York Press.

Norman, K. R. (1997). *A Philological Approach to Buddhism*. London: School of Oriental and African Studies.

Siderits, M. N. (2003). *Personal Identity and Buddhist Philosophy: Empty Persons*. Aldershot, and Burlington, VT: Ashgate.

Thanissaro Bhikkhu (1999). *The Mind Like Fire Unbound*. Barre, MA: Dhamma Dana, and at: www.accesstoinsight.org/lib/modern/thanissaro/likefire/index.html.

Webster, D. (2005a). The Weary Buddha or Why the Buddha Nearly Couldn't Be Bothered. In *Buddhist Studies Review* 22, 15–25.

Webster, D. (2005b). *The Philosophy of Desire in the Buddhist Pali Canon*. London and New York: RoutledgeCurzon.

Williams, P. (2009). *Mahāyāna Buddhism: The Doctrinal Foundations*. Second edn. London and New York: Routledge & Kegan Paul.

3

The Conditioned Co-arising of Mental and Bodily Processes within Life and Between Lives[1]

PETER HARVEY

The Centrality of Conditioned Co-arising

A common inscription on Buddhist monuments goes:

> Of those states that proceed from a cause (*hetu*),
> The *Tathāgata* has told the cause.
> And that which is their stopping (*nirodha*):
> The great renunciant has such a teaching
>
> (Vin.I.40)

A doctrine strongly related to the Four True Realities for the Spiritually Ennobled (usually called "Noble Truths"), particularly the second (the origin of *dukkha*), is that of *paṭicca-samuppāda* (P.; Skt *pratītya-samutpāda*). This has been variously translated as: Dependent Origination, Conditioned Arising, Conditioned Co-arising.[2]

The understanding of conditioned co-arising is so central to Buddhist practice and development that the Buddha's chief disciple, Sāriputta, said, "Whoever sees Conditioned Co-arising sees *Dhamma*, whoever sees *Dhamma* sees Conditioned Co-arising" (MN.I.191). Moreover, after his enlightenment, the Buddha is said to have reflected on what he had discovered, initially feeling that it was too subtle for others to understand:

> This *Dhamma* won by me is profound (*gambhīra*), difficult to see, difficult to understand, peaceful, sublime, beyond the scope of mere reasoning (*atakkāvacara*), subtle, to be experienced by the wise. But this generation is delighting in clinging (to the familiar) . . . so that this were a matter difficult to see, that is to say specific conditionality (*idappaccatyatā*), Conditioned Co-arising. This too were a matter difficult to see, that is to say the stilling (*samatha*) of all constructing activities, the renunciation of all attachment, the destruction of craving, dispassion, stopping (*nirodha*), *Nirvāṇa*.
>
> (MN.I.167)

A Companion to Buddhist Philosophy, First Edition. Edited by Steven M. Emmanuel.

This specifies conditioned co-arising and *nirvāṇa* (P. *nibbāna*) as two aspects of the subtle and profound Dhamma, "beyond the scope of mere reasoning" that was the focus of the Buddha's experience of awakening. This implies that conditioned co-arising and *nirvāṇa* are in some way closely related. *Nirvāṇa* is the stopping, or transcending, of conditioned co-arising.

The Buddha also taught that rebirth continues until direct insight into conditioned co-arising is attained (DN.II.55).

The Principle of Conditionality

In its abstract form, the doctrine states:

> That being, this comes to be;
> from the arising (*uppāda*) of that, this arises;
> that being absent, this is not;
> from the cessation (*nirodha*) of that, this ceases.
> (SN.II.28, 70, 78, 95, 96)

In its simplest sense, this is the principle of conditionality, applied to all processes, events, and "things," physical or mental, in the universe: they arise and exist due to the presence of certain conditions and cease once their conditions are removed; nothing (except *nirvāṇa*) is independent. The doctrine thus complements the teaching that no permanent, independent self can be found. The above abstract principle is always introduced as a prelude to an enumeration of the 12 conditioned and conditioning links (*nidānas*), culminating in the arising of *dukkha*, hence as an abstraction of an overall pattern from a series of instances of it. The principle can also, then, be seen at work in other examples of conditionality.

The standard version of conditioned co-arising, as a series of 12 *nidānas* is seen for example at Vin.I.1:

> Then the Blessed One, during the first watch of the night paid attention to Conditioned Co-arising in forward (*anuloma*, i.e., arising/*uppāda*) and reverse (*paṭiloma*, i.e., cessation/*nirodha*) mode:
>
> from [1] (spiritual) ignorance (*avijjā*) as condition (*paccaya*) are the constructing activities/volitional activities/karmic formations/fabrications (*saṅkhāras*);
>
> from [2] the constructing activities as condition is consciousness (*viññāṇa*);
>
> from [3] consciousness as condition is name-and-form/mind-and-body/the sentient body (*nāma-rūpa*);
>
> from [4] name-and-form as condition are the six sense-spheres (*āyatanas*);
>
> from [5] the six sense-spheres as condition is stimulation/contact/impingement (*phassa*);
>
> from [6] stimulation as condition is feeling (*vedanā*);
>
> from [7] feeling as condition is craving (*taṇhā*);

> from [8] craving as condition is grasping/clinging (*upādāna*);
>
> from [9] grasping as condition is becoming (*bhava*);
>
> from [10] becoming as condition is birth (*jāti*);
>
> from [11] birth as condition is [12] old age and dying, grief, lamentation, physical pain, unhappiness and distress come into being. Such is the arising (*samudaya*) of this whole painful bundle (*dukkha-kkhandha*).
>
> But from the fading away without remainder of (spiritual) ignorance is the cessation/stopping (*nirodha*) of the constructing activities;
>
> from the cessation/stopping of the constructing activities is the cessation/stopping of consciousness;
>
> [etc., until we come to:]
>
> from the cessation/stopping of birth, old age and dying, grief, lamentation, physical pain, unhappiness and distress cease. Such is the cessation of this whole painful bundle.

This sequence may be explained from link (1) through to (12) or the explanation may start at (12), then specify (11) as its crucial condition, and so on, back to (1). After the formula is given in either versions of this forward/arising (*anuloma*) mode, it follows in reverse/cessation (*paṭiloma*) mode. In this form, it describes how the cessation of *dukkha* comes about due to the complete cessation of spiritual ignorance and the consequent cessation of each following *nidāna*.

The Meaning and Nature of Conditioned Co-arising

In the term *paṭicca-samuppāda*, *samuppāda* comes from *sam*, "together," and *uppāda*, "arising." As explained by the fifth-century Theravādin commentator Buddhaghosa, this means that something can only arise when its conditions are gathered together (Vism.521). Something arises together with its conditions. *Paṭicca* means "conditioned," "having fallen back on," "grounded on," being derived from *paṭi-i*, from which comes the verb *pacceti*, "it falls back on." From the same root comes the word *paccaya*, "condition" or "foundation." Synonyms for *paccaya* are *nidāna*, "ground," *hetu*, "cause," *samudaya*, "origin," *āhāra*, "nutriment," and *upanisa*, "support." Thus a *paccaya* is a supporting ground which helps to set off and feed that which it conditions. *Paṭicca-samuppāda* thus means something like conditioned co-arising, grounded co-arising, arising together with conditions.

What of the term *nirodha*, "stopping" or "cessation," in the conditioned co-arising formula? Does this refer to the stopping of a *particular* instance of "birth," for example, or to the stopping of the *whole* process of births in a person? It is clear that the latter is meant. DN.II.57 talks of "if there were absolutely no birth at all . . . with the cessation of birth, could aging-and-death appear?" As one Theravādin commentary (MN-a. II.308) puts it, "stopping" is equivalent to "non-arising (*an-uppāda*)": it is the stopping of the process of the rise and fall of instances of, say, feeling. Conditioned phenomena are both constantly arising and passing away, but are also subject to final "stopping" or "cessation." The emphasis is on how *types* of things arise, so that they can be changed or stopped.

Conditioned Co-arising, the Four True Realities for the Spiritually Ennobled, and Spiritual Practice

Before looking individually at the 12 links, some general remarks are in order. The teaching explains how *dukkha*, the first True Reality for the Spiritually Ennobled, comes about, this originating set of conditions being the second True Reality for the Spiritually Ennobled; and the formula in reverse/cessation mode describes the cessation of *dukkha*, namely *nirvāṇa*, the third True Reality (AN.I.177). It is also said that the Noble Eightfactored Path, the fourth True Reality, is the way going to the cessation of each of the 12 links, and thus of *dukkha* (SN.II.43).

Note that the twelfth link is summarized as "this whole painful bundle (*dukkha-kkhandha*)," which reminds us that the teaching on the first True Reality for the Spiritually Ennobled ends by saying, "in short, these five bundles (*khandha*) of grasping-fuel (*upādāna*) are painful."

In some texts, each of the 12 links are given the same treatment as *dukkha* in the Four True Realities for the Spiritually Ennobled, for example:

> From the arising of (spiritual) ignorance is the arising of the constructing activities; from the stopping of (spiritual) ignorance is the stopping of the constructing activities. This Noble Eightfold Path is itself the course leading to the stopping of the constructing activities . . .
>
> (SN.II.43)

The Four True Realities for the Spiritually Ennobled relating to *dukkha* can be seen as an application of the principle of conditioned co-arising focused particularly on *dukkha*. Its structure – phenomenon, its key condition, cessation of the phenomenon from the cessation of its key condition, the systematic path of positive conditions leading to this – is permeated with the principle of conditionality, which runs through the whole of Buddhist thought and practice.

There is even a version of conditioned co-arising (SN.II.30) which continues beyond link 12 to say that, based on *dukkha*, faith (*saddhā*; Skt *śraddhā*) arises, and then on through various successive states which are part of the path to the end of *dukkha*. The doctrine thus unites the four True Realities and makes possible a methodological science of moral and spiritual life. By becoming aware of how one is conditioned, one can come to alter the flow of conditions by governing, suspending, or, for skilful ones, intensifying them so as to reduce *dukkha*, and ultimately stop it entirely by transcending the conditions: reconditioning, then de-conditioning.

Nirvāṇa is the stopping of the entire sequence of conditions mapped out in the conditioned co-arising teaching. With the arising of the Dhamma-seeing Dhamma-eye at stream-entry, which knows "whatever is of the nature to arise (*samudaya-dhamma*), all that is of the nature to stop (*nirodha-dhamma*)," there is insight into both the way in which the *nidānas* arise in the conditioned co-arising sequence, and that these conditionally arisen *dhammas* are of such a nature that they can be stopped/transcended in the "stopping/cessation" that is *nirvāṇa*. The Dhamma-eye thus sees the four True Realities for the Spiritually Ennobled in seeing: conditioned *dukkha* states, how they arise, how they stop when their conditions stop, and the Noble Eightfold Path (itself the "best of all conditioned states," AN.II.34) as the way to this. The Stream-enterer knows all the conditions and how they can be stopped, and so "stands squarely before the door of the deathless" (SN.II.43): he or she can "see" the *nirvāṇa* that will later be fully experienced at arahatship.

While the path that leads to the experiencing of *nirvāṇa* is conditioned, *nirvāṇa* itself is unconditioned/unconstructed (*asaṅkhata*), just as a mountain is not dependent on the path that leads to it (Miln.269). As the "unborn, unbecome, unmade, unconstructed" (Ud.80–1), it is "not co-arisen (*asamuppanaṃ*)" (It.37–8). *Nirvāṇa* is not something that is conditionally arisen, but is the stopping of all such processes.

Conditioned Co-arising, Non-Self, and the *Khandhas*

Besides explaining the origin of *dukkha*, the formula also explains karma, rebirth, and the functioning of personality, all without the need to invoke a permanent self. No substantial self can be found which underlies the *nidānas*, owning and operating them: they simply occur according to conditions. Thus it is inappropriate to ask, for example, "who craves?," but appropriate to ask what craving is conditioned by, the answer being "feeling" (SN.II.14). Just as Buddhism looks at "how?" rather than "why?" questions, it also looks at "how?" rather than "who?" questions. Nevertheless, in the context of moral discourse, it treats any particular conditioned stream of mental and physical processes as a "person" who is held (except for extenuating circumstances) responsible for "his" or "her" actions. Hence, you are responsible for your actions even though no essential "You" can be found who is their agent.

While the five *khandha* doctrine is an analysis of the components of personality in static form, the 12 *nidāna* formula is a synthesis, which shows how such components arise (SN.II.28) and interact dynamically to form the living process of personality, in one life and from life to life. Each of the five *khandhas* also occurs in the *nidāna* formula. Consciousness, constructing activities, and feeling occur in both lists. Material form (*rūpa*) is the same as the "body" (part of link 4), and perception (*saññā*) is part of "mind" (*nāma*); in the form of misinterpretation, it is also tantamount to spiritual ignorance.

The 12 Links (*nidānas*)

The 12 *nidānas* are individually explained at SN.II.2–4, and considerable detail is also given in a section of the *Mahā-nidāna Sutta* (DN.II.55–63).[3]

*(Spiritual) Ignorance (*avijjā; *Skt* avidyā*)*

Ignorance complements and supports craving in the causation of *dukkha*. It shows the effects that mis-seeing has, according to Buddhism, and the importance of seeing things "as they really are."

The *nidāna* of spiritual ignorance is defined as unknowing (*aññāṇa*) with regard to the Four True Realities for the Spiritually Ennobled (SN.II.4). As the principle of conditioned co-arising underlies these truths, the first link can be seen, ironically, to be ignorance of this very principle. Conditioned co-arising, then, is a process which can operate only in ignorance of itself. Once a person fully understands it, it can be stopped. The "ignorance" referred to is not lack of information but a more deep-seated misperception of reality, which can be destroyed only by direct meditative insight. It is given as the first link due to its fundamental influence on the process of life, but is itself conditioned by sensual desire, ill will, dullness and lethargy, restlessness and worry, and vacillation: the five hindrances to meditative calm. These are in turn conditioned by bad conduct of body, speech, or mind (AN.V.113), hence such karmically harmful constructing activities feed back to help sustain spiritual ignorance.

Buddhism, then, sees the basic root of the pain and stress of life as spiritual ignorance, rather than sin, which is a willful turning away from a creator God. Indeed, it can be regarded as having a doctrine of something like "original sinlessness." While the mind is seen as containing many unskillful tendencies with deep roots, "below" these roots it is radiant: "Monks, this mind (*citta*) is brightly shining (*pabhassara*; Skt *prabhāsvara*), but it is defiled by adventitious defilements" (AN.I.10). That is, the deepest layer of the mind is bright and pure (though not yet immune from being obscured by defilements). This represents, in effect, the potentiality for attaining *nirvāṇa* – but defilements arise through inept interaction of the mind with the world. The idea of defilements as "arriving" or "adventitious" is related to their non-Self nature: they are not an intrinsic part of person, so can be transcended. Even a newborn child is not seen as having a wholly pure mind, however, for it is said to have unskillful latent tendencies (*anusaya*; Skt *anuśaya*) which are carried over from a previous life (MN.I.433). In the calm of deep meditation, the depth-radiance of the mind is experienced at a conscious level as the process of meditation suspends the defiling five hindrances, just as a smelter purifies gold ore so as to attain pure gold (SN.V.92). More than a temporary undefiled state of mind is necessary for awakening, however. For this, there must be destruction of the four "taints" or "cankers" (*āsava*; Skt *āśrava*): the most deeply rooted spiritual faults, which are likened to festering sores, leeching off energy from the mind, or intoxicating influxes on the mind. These are the taints that flow in relation to sense-desire, becoming, views, and spiritual ignorance, which are seen as conditioning, and being conditioned by, spiritual ignorance (MN.I.54–5).

One can see ignorance, indeed ignore-ance, as a misperception which beclouds the basic radiance of mind. One can perhaps see craving as leading to the willful ignoring of things that one has, in part of one's mind, or at some past time, realized. People are good at forgetting. This is one reason why Buddhism emphasizes mindfulness, which includes an element of careful "bearing in mind."

Constructing Activities (the saṅkhāras; *Skt* saṃskāras*)*

The second *nidāna*, "constructing activities" (Harvey 1995, 122–4), are actions of body, speech, or mind (SN.II.4) expressed in both karmically fruitful (generally translated as "meritorious") and karmically harmful actions of body, speech, and mind (DN. III.217).[4] Ignorance can be seen to condition active impulses in that all actions are performed from the perspective of a particular way of perceiving and construing the world, an outlook and set of beliefs, which provides a motivating framework: a person acts in response to the "world" as it appears to him or her. Prior to enlightenment, all actions will be in some way affected by misperceptions, or at least by correct beliefs which are not based on direct perception, so as to be in some way narrow or incomplete. Actions can bring positive fruits if they are based on *some* degree of insight into reality, such as the principles of karma or impermanence. In a person who has destroyed spiritual ignorance, though, actions no longer have the power to "construct" any karmic results.

The main "constructing activity" is will (*cetanā*) (SN.II.39–40), that which initiates actions. As it is conditioned, but not rigidly determined, by past events, it has a relative freedom. For example, the arising of anger need not lead on to angry behavior if a person becomes watchfully aware of it, so as to lessen its power. This is because the act of mindfulness brings about a change in the current conditions operating in the mind (Harvey 2007).

SN.II.65–6 talks of the constructing activities in terms of willing (*ceteti*), planning, and having an underlying or latent tendency (*anusaya*) towards something:

> What one wills (*ceteti*), what one plans (*pakappeti*), and what one has a tendency towards (*anuseti*): This is an object (*ārammaṇa*) for the maintenance of consciousness. There being an object, there is a support (*patiṭṭhā*) for consciousness. When that consciousness is supported and grows, there is the production of renewed becoming (*puna-bbhava*) in the future. [The following *Sutta* says instead, "there is a descent of name-and-form" here.] When there is the production of renewed becoming in the future, there is future birth, aging and death, sorrow, lamentation, pain, unhappiness and distress. Such is the origination of this whole painful bundle.

The same is said to happen if one only plans and has a tendency, or just has a tendency. Having an underlying tendency thus appears to be seen as the most deep-seated and stubborn constructing activity – one that possibly underlies the operation of all the rest, as an unconscious latent disposition. Elsewhere, the seven *anusayas* are listed as those of sense-desire, aversion, views, uncertainty, conceit, attachment to becoming, and ignorance. The above passage goes on to say that, without even a latent tendency, consciousness has no object or support, and so does not "grow" so as to produce future rebirth and hence more *dukkha*.

*Consciousness (*viññāṇa; *Skt* vijñāna*)*

This *nidāna* is the same as the fifth *khandha*. The most important but not the only context in which constructing activities condition consciousness is in the generation of consciousness in a future life; for it is said that the "evolving" or "conducive" (*saṃvattanika*) consciousness is the crucial link between rebirths (MN.II.262). At death, the momentum set up by constructing activities (including craving) is not cut off, but impels the evolving flux of consciousness to spill over beyond one life and help spark off another.

Constructing activities condition consciousness in that they generate tendencies whose momentum tends to make a person become aware of, or think of, certain objects (Harvey 1995, 124–30). For example, if one has decided (a mental action) to look for a certain article to buy, such as a house, one's mind will automatically notice related things, such as advertisements and "for sale" notices, that were previously not even mentally registered, as suggested by the above passage (SN.II.65–6). What one is conscious of, and thus the form of one's consciousness, depends on one's volitions and tendencies. The SN.II.65–6 passage shows that the constructing activities condition consciousness by giving it a certain direction, so that it turns towards a certain object, or kinds of objects, on which to "settle." This provides it with a supporting and maintaining object, so that it is consciousness *of* that. The object is an "opportunity" (another meaning of *ārammaṇa*, translated above as "object") for consciousness to continue to arise, a focus of preoccupation, in which there has been volitional energy invested, where consciousness turns for its sustenance and continuation. A similar point seems to be made at MN.I.115, which says: "whatever one ponders and reflects on much [e.g., sense-pleasures], towards that is the inclination of the heart."

As consciousness is also conditioned by its objects (and the sense organs), the version of conditioned co-arising in the *Mahā-nidāna Sutta* (DN.II.63) gives "name-and-form" (*nāma-rūpa*) – i.e. perceived meaningful forms, mental and physical phenomena as objects – as the first link in the chain, followed by consciousness then *nāma-rūpa* again, here as mind-and-body, and on through the remaining links as in the standard version. The DN.II.63 passage, then, has consciousness conditioned by the mental and physical phenomena onto which the constructing activities direct it as supporting objects. The conditioning of consciousness by its objects is also seen in a common passage:

> Visual-consciousness, your reverences, arises conditioned by eye and visual forms; the meeting of the three is stimulation (*phassa*); from stimulation as condition is feeling (*vedanā*) . . . [then parallel statements for the other sense channels].
>
> (SN.II.73)[5]

A person, then, consists of a dynamic interplay between consciousness and the body of other mental and physical states that are either the objects of consciousness or its facilitating complements. In the vortical interplay between consciousness and *nāma-rūpa* (Harvey 1995, 116–21), the whole complex of the 12 links of conditioned co-arising and the realm of language is spun out:

> just this, namely *nāma-rūpa*, is the cause, ground, origin and condition of consciousness. Thus far, then, can we trace birth and decay, death and passing away and being reborn, thus far extends the way of designation (*adhivacana-*), of language (*nirutti-*), of concepts (*paññatti-*), thus far is the sphere of understanding (*paññāvacara*), thus far the round (of rebirth) goes as far as can be discerned here, namely *nāma-rūpa* together with consciousness.
>
> (DN.II.63–4)

Consciousness hangs around *nāma-rūpa*, the other four *khandhas*, as its "home" (SN. III.9–10). True renunciation, non-attachment to this conditioned "home," opens up the possibility of radical "homelessness": the realm of the unconditioned, *nirvāṇa*.

When there is no craving or grasping, consciousness can be like a sunbeam that lands nowhere, being "unsupported (*appatiṭṭhita*)" (SN.II.101–5). This simile suggests that consciousness that has "stopped," being no longer meshed in the network of conditions, does not stop existing, any more than a radiant sunbeam does when it is not obstructed by anything.

*Name-and-Form/Mind-and-Body/Sentient Body (*nāma-rūpa*)*

This is literally "name and form." This term already had a currency in the (non-Buddhist) Brahmanical *Upaniṣads*. At *Bṛhadāraṅyaka Upaniṣad* 1.4.7, it means the name and visible appearance of a person, though these are seen to veil the immortal breath within (Br.Up.1.6.3). In *Chāndogya Upaniṣad* 6.1.4–6, "name" is what differentiates different things made from the same kind of substance – e.g., clay or iron. In a famous passage at *Muṇḍaka Upaniṣad* 3.2.8, *nāma-rūpa* means something like individuality:

> As the rivers flow on and enter into the ocean
> giving up their names and appearances,
> So the knower, freed from name and appearance,
> reaches the heavenly Person, beyond the very highest.
> (Olivelle 1996, 276)

Bṛhadāraṇyaka 3.2.12 sees a person's "name" as going with him or her (if unliberated, presumably) after death, as a key ingredient of their particular identity. "Name" is the expression of intention and thought through speech (*Chāndogya Upaniṣad* 7.1–5), while speech grasps names as sight grasps visible appearances and hearing grasps sounds (*Kauṣītaki Upaniṣad* 3.4).

In Buddhism, "name/mind" consists of feeling, perception, will, stimulation, and attention, and "form"/body consists of the physical elements (SN.II.3): together these are equivalent to the four *khandhas* other than consciousness (Vibh.136). The name/mind factors specified can be seen as essential aspects of what makes a person sentient, recognizing and responding to objects – thus the commentator Buddhaghosa, punning, says "it is '*nāma*' because of bending (*namanato*) towards objects" (Vism.558). Thus one might translate *nāma-rūpa* as "sentient body," or "sentience and body," in Buddhist contexts: the body and accompanying mental states which provide sentience. The sense of individual existence, as in the *Upaniṣads*, can also be seen to be meant.

The "sentient body" develops in the womb once the flux of consciousness "descends" into the womb, and continues to do so provided that consciousness does not depart (DN. II.62–3). Indeed the Sarvāstivāda tradition saw name-and-form as embryonic life prior to the development of the senses (AKB.III.21–4). The embryo starts to develop when there has been intercourse at the right time of the month, and there is an available being who is ready to be reborn (MN.I.265–6). Outside the womb, the sentient body continues unless consciousness is cut off (DN.II.63), for consciousness, vitality (*āyu*), and heat make a body alive and sensitive (MN.I.295–6). Together, consciousness and the sentient body encompass all five *khandhas* of personality, and the interaction between them is seen to be the crux of the process of life and suffering:

> Indeed, consciousness turns back round onto name-and-form, it does not go beyond. Only in this way can one be born, or grow old, or die, or fall away from one's past existence, or be reborn: that is to say, insofar as consciousness is conditioned by name-and-form, name-and-form is conditioned by consciousness, the six sense-bases are conditioned by name-and-form. . . .
>
> (DN.II.32)

Here one sees interactive vortex of consciousness and the sentient body, as in the *Mahā-nidāna Sutta*.

The Six Sense-Bases (āyatanas) *and Stimulation (*phassa; *Skt* sparśa*)*

The next *nidāna* is the six sense-bases or sense-media (*āyatanas*), which are the five physical sense organs and the mind organ (*mano*; Skt *manas*), the latter being seen as that which is sensitive to mental objects (*dhammas*) – i.e., objects of memory, thought, imagination, and the input of the five senses. The six sense-bases are conditioned by the sentient body, as they can only exist in a living sentient organism.

In turn the sense-bases condition stimulation, which is the "meeting" of a sense, its object, and the related kind of consciousness (MN.I.111). DN.II.62 omits the sense-bases and goes directly from the sentient body to stimulation, which shows that any analysis in terms of a sequence of conditions can be varied in its detail: the "standard" 12 links are just one way of doing this.

"Contact" is a fairly literal translation for *phassa*, but suggests that a purely physical meeting of sense and object is meant, overlooking the involvement of consciousness. "Impingement" or "impression" are possibilities but "stimulation" signals more the aspect of an initial mental registration. DN.II.62 explains that *phassa* involves both a "resistance" (*paṭigha-*) and "designation" (*adhivacana-*) form. That is, *phassa* entails *both* a physical "contact" in the "meeting" of sense and object and a mental "designative contact" in the involvement of consciousness.

Buddhism emphasizes that, whatever the external physical world is like, the "world" (*loka*) of our actual lived experience is one built up from the input of the five senses, interpreted by the mind organ (SN.IV.95). As this interpretation is, for most people, influenced by spiritual ignorance, our "lived world" is skewed and not in harmony with reality. Such a world is fraught with *dukkha*, but it is conditioned and can be transcended: "I declare that this fathom-long carcass, which is percipient and endowed with mind-organ, contains the world, and the origin of the world, and the cessation of the world [*Nirvāṇa*], and the way leading to the cessation of the world" (SN.I.62). This can be seen as about the Four True Realities for the Spiritually Ennobled, with "the world" replacing "*dukkha*."

*Feeling (*vedanā*) and Craving (*taṇhā; *Skt* tṛṣṇā*)*

"Feeling" is the same as the second *khandha*, and refers simply to the pleasant, unpleasant, or neither-pleasant-nor-unpleasant feeling-tone that is an aspect of any experience. This arises in direct response to stimulation in one of the six sense-channels. It in turn conditions the arising of craving, which is highlighted in the teaching on the True Realities for the Spiritually Ennobled as the key condition for *dukkha.*

Depending on what feelings arise, there is craving (*taṇhā*; Skt *tṛṣṇā*) to enjoy, prolong, or get rid of them. While one cannot help what feelings arise initially from sensing something, the extent of craving (and type of accompanying feeling) in response to them is modifiable. People take feeling very seriously, thirsting for the pleasant, trying to push away the unpleasant, and having an attitude of indifference or confusion towards the neutral. Indeed, at MN.III.285 it is said:

> When one is touched by pleasant feeling, if one delights in it, welcomes it, and remains holding on to it, then the underlying tendency (*anusaya*) to attachment (*rāga*) lies within one. When one is touched by painful feeling, if one sorrows, grieves and laments, weeps while beating one's breast and becoming distraught, then the underlying tendency to aversion (*paṭigha-*) lies within one. When one is touched by neither-painful-nor-pleasant feeling, if one does not understand it as it really is: the origination, the disappearance, the gratification, the danger, and the transcending in regard to that feeling, then the underlying tendency to ignorance (*avijjā*) lies within one.[6]

The *suttas* see this as an important aspect of how attachment, hatred, and delusion, the roots of *dukkha*, are sustained. More complex responses also occur. In reaction to some kinds of unpleasant experience, people become unsettled and confused, and so seek solace by going in search of some pleasant feeling to become attached to . . . like a baby sucking a dummy. In response to neutral feeling, a person may respond with boredom and wanting something to happen, or may like it, and fall into a somewhat dull state. People are often hooked or hijacked by feelings into one or other kind of response. But such responses, while deeply ingrained, are not the only, or most skillful, ones that can occur.

The *suttas* give various descriptions of the way in which mental states arise and operate in the six sense-channels, in response to objects of the six senses. MN.I.111–12 says:

> Visual-consciousness, your reverences, arises conditioned by eye and visual forms; the meeting of the three is stimulation (*phassa*); from stimulation as condition is feeling (*vedanā*); what one feels (*vedeti*) one perceives/interprets/labels (*sañjānāti*); what one perceives one thinks about (*vitakketi*); what one thinks about one elaborates (*papañceti*); what one elaborates is the origin of the interpretations and reckonings (*-saññā-saṅkhā*) [that come] from elaboration which assail a man in regard to visual forms discernible by the eye, past, future or present.
>
> [This is then repeated in a parallel way for the other five sense-channels.]

In this description of the perceptual process, after feeling, the terms change from nouns to verbs – "from stimulation as condition is feeling; what one feels one perceives" – i.e., active responses to experience start to occur. The response may be some form of craving, but MN.I.111–12 talks particularly of the activity of "elaboration" (*papañca*) which generates assailing "interpretations and reckonings (*-saññā-saṅkhā*)." This is reminiscent of spiritual ignorance, which is a form of misperception. The arising of feeling is a crucial phase in experience, for the next phase may involve either craving or ignorance, or both of these – key causes of *dukkha*. Hence the importance placed on understanding that all forms of feeling are to be seen as in a sense *dukkha* (unsatisfactory or in some sense painful), so as to engender a more skillful, less habitual response to them, which is not attachment, aversion, or ignore-ance. Regarding all feeling as *dukkha*/painful is not about generating actual aversion to feeling. Aversion is dislike directed at something. Buddhism encourages, rather, an attitude of letting go, disenchantment, turning away (P. *nibbidā*).

Unskillful response to feelings also feeds the attitude of "I am": "the uninstructed ordinary person, touched by feeling born of stimulation by spiritual ignorance, thinks 'I am' " (SN.III.46). The *Mahā-nidāna Sutta* (DN.II.66–9) examines the views that "my Self" is feeling, something without feeling, or something that possesses feeling, and sees all as problematic (Harvey 1995, 31–3; 2009, 270–1).

*Grasping (*upādāna*)*

This term is also found in the expression *upādāna-kkhandha*, bundle/aggregate of grasping-fuel. Craving conditions grasping or clinging: having reached for something, one seeks to hold onto it, to wallow in a certain craving-based state. The four forms of grasping are those directed at sensual pleasures (*kāma*), views (*diṭṭhi*; Skt *dṛṣṭi*), conduct/precepts and vows (*sīla-bbatūpadāna*), and Self doctrines (*atta-vāda*) (SN.II.3).

Grasping at sensual pleasures is simply an intensification of sensual craving: the mind wanting to hold on to the object of desire such that the whole mind-set is colored by sense-desire and it loses its center of balance. Grasping at views is seen by the Theravādin Abhidhamma text, the *Dhammasaṅgaṇī* (sections 1214–17), as relating to views other than those on Self (probably to make sense of the latter being separately listed as a focus of grasping). Grasping at a Self doctrine are those views which are forms of grasping at one or other aspect of the body–mind complex as "Self" or "pertaining to Self," as in "Self-identity view (*sakkāya-diṭṭhi*)."

"Views" are beliefs, theories, opinions, or worldviews, especially when they become fixed or dogmatic, so that one identifies fully with a way of looking at something, a way of explaining it (Fuller, 2005). One's attachment is then such that one is wounded if that theory is criticized, and one is willing to be underhand or not fully honest in defense of the theory. One is also limited in one's vision by the theory or belief: it is like a pair of blinkers which enable one to see only certain things, narrowing one's whole outlook on life, like a blind man who mistakes the part of an elephant that he has felt for the whole of what an "elephant" is (Ud.67–9); it may contain some truth, but one needs always to be open to a deepening of that truth or to a balancing by a complementary one. The Buddha was clearly very wary of mere theories or "views," holding that they led to quarrels (AN.I.66) and conceit (Sn.842–3). Such views are seen as hidden forms of self-assertion, which lead to conflict with those of other opinions, be this in the form of verbal wrangling or ideological wars and bloody revolutions. In this context, it is worth noting that the atrocities carried out by Hitler, Stalin, and the Khmer Rouge were initiated by people who were convinced of a theory which demanded and "justified" their actions. Indeed, Buddhism holds that wrong view feeds bad behavior

(AN.I.30–2; BW.213–14) and that the worst way of doing a bad act is if it is accompanied by a view that perversely sees it as "right" (Harvey 2000, 55–6).

To be sure, there are what might be called "Buddhist views," such as belief in the goodness of giving and in karma and rebirth: that what one does *matters*. Such beliefs are termed "ordinary" (*lokiya*) "right view," and, though they lead in the right direction, they are still associated with clinging (MN.III.72), as they can be clung to if not tested by wisdom (MN.I.133). One should not even cling to the view that all views displease one, but get rid of whatever view one has and not take up any other (MN.I.497–8). Views, as all else in the conditioned world, are seen to be arisen according to conditions, to be impermanent, and to bring *dukkha* if clung to (AN.V.187–8). Wisdom (*paññā*; Skt *prajñā*), analytically directed intuitive insight, though, is said to be "transcendent" (*lokuttara*) "right view" (MN.III.72), and is such that, when it knows, for example, that "all *dhammas* are non-Self," this is "well seen, as it really is" (AN.V.188), in a way that goes beyond all speculative reasoning or acceptance of ideas from others. The true aim, then, is not to have a view or belief, even if it happens to be true, but to have direct knowledge "not dependent on another" (SN.III.135) – in other words, to replace a viewpoint with a direct seeing.

Sīla-bbatūpadāna, literally "grasping at conduct/precepts (*sīla*) and vows," is sometimes translated as grasping at "rite-and-ritual," but this is a translation probably influenced by Protestant dislike of rituals. From a Buddhist perspective, one cannot assess a ritual, or someone's use of it, unless one assesses the extent to which it encourages wholesome/skillful, or unwholesome/unskillful, states of mind. Bhikkhu Bodhi's translation of the *Saṃyutta Nikāya* ("The Connected Discourses of the Buddha") talks of grasping at "rules and observances."

As regards grasping at vows: this would clearly relate to certain customs of the Buddha's day, where ascetics vowed to carry out various penances – e.g., the vow to behave like a dog or an ox (MN.I.378). More generally, "grasping at conduct and vows" could be seen as any form of thinking: if only I do something *this* way, then everything will be all right. It is over-expectation as regards what guidelines or ethical precepts can provide and can lead to over-rigidity and harping guilt when a precept is infringed. It is making a rule something important only in its own right, rather than also as a help towards something else. This grasping might show itself in regard to politics, religious ritual, personal habits and preferences, and even moral precepts and meditational guidelines.

Looking at the four forms of grasping, one can see that they are focused on pleasant experiences, ideas, or actions. Any of these can be objects of clinging, attachment, and rigidity.

The Theravādin commentarial tradition sometimes picks out views, craving, and the "I am conceit (*asmi-māna*)" as representing the causes of *dukkha* and sees the contemplation: "this is not mine, this is not I am, this is not my Self" as counteracting, respectively, craving ("this is mine"), conceit ("I am"), and views ("this is my Self").

Besides the above ways in which craving leads to grasping, the *Mahā-nidāna Sutta* (DN.II.58–62) has a long aside on craving, spelling out a sequence of conditions set off by it that relate to possessiveness and quarrelling; this again highlights its destructive effect. AN.III.399–401 highlights the way that craving acts as a "sempstress," stitching together various things so as to attach one to new situations and rebirths.

*Becoming or Being (*bhava*)*

Bhava is the noun from the verb meaning "is," *bhavati* (or, in shortened form, *hoti*), often used to say that something "is" something else – e.g., "the Brahmin is a minister" – rather than being from the verb *atthi*, to exist, from which comes the word *atthitā*, "existence." Many people translate *bhava* as "becoming," to emphasize the dynamic nature of existence according to Buddhism. "Being" would be a possible translation except for the fact that in English it can have metaphysical associations. Moreover "*a* being" is used to translate *satta* (Skt *sattva*), which is from the same root as *atthi*.

The *suttas* are brief in their description of *bhava*. The term is also part of the word *puna-bbhava*, "re-becoming," a common term for rebirth. Several passages see it as relating to the three spheres of Buddhist cosmology: those of the sense-desire realm of human and lesser rebirths, and the meditation-related realms of (elemental) form and the formless. A passage at AN.I.223 expands on this:

> "Ānanda, if there were no element of sense-desire, and no action/karma to ripen [there], would any sense-desire-becoming be manifested?"
>
> "Surely not, Lord."
>
> "In this way, Ānanda, karma is the field, consciousness is the seed, craving is the moisture: for beings hindered by ignorance, fettered by craving, consciousness is supported in a lower element. Thus, in the future, there is re-becoming and production. Thus, Ānanda, there is becoming."

Parallel statements are then given for the "element of form," which is "middling," and the "formless element," which is "excellent." *Bhava*, then, seems to mean the continuation of the whole changing process of life, ongoing existence in one or other world of change – or perhaps the transition phase leading to a new rebirth in one of these.

The Theravādin Abhidhamma explains *bhava* as having two aspects: "karma-becoming" – i.e., karmically fruitful and harmful volitions – and "arising (*uppatti*)-becoming" – existence in some world as a result of grasping and karma (Vibh.137). Such a world is meant primarily as a new rebirth, but, arguably, it can also be seen as applying to a "world" in this life – i.e., a situation in which one finds oneself as a result of one's grasping and actions.

"Becoming" may also have been intended to refer to an "intermediary becoming" (*antarā-bhava*), a period of transition between rebirths. About half the pre-Mahāyāna schools, including the Theravādins, held that the moment of death was immediately followed by the moment of conception, with no intervening period. The other schools, and later the Mahāyāna, believed in such an existence. Some Pāli *sutta* passages seem to indicate that the earliest Buddhists believed in it. One refers to a time when a being has laid aside one body and has not yet arisen in another (SN.IV.399–400). Another refers to a subtle-bodied *gandhabba*, or spirit-being, as needing to be present if sexual intercourse is to lead to conception (MN.I.265–6). Further, *nirvāṇa*/arahatship may be attained "in between" (DN.III.237; SN.V.69–70; AN.IV.7–4) by the most advanced of the various types of Non-returners – Non-returners being those who are almost *arahats*, but die without attaining arahatship, not returning to "this shore" of the sense-desire world (of lower gods, humans, and others) but going on to attain arahatship beyond it. This probably meant they attained it between the end of one life and the start of the next rebirth. SN.II.67 also talks of:

> When consciousness is supported and growing, there is inclination (*nati*); inclination being, there is coming and going; coming and going being, there is falling away and arising; falling away and arising being, there is, in the future, birth, aging and death . . .

This suggests that the between-lives period has three phases: inclining to a further rebirth, seeking it here and there, and falling from one's previous identity into a new rebirth (Harvey 1995, 95–109).

*Birth (*jāti*) and Aging-and-Dying*

From "becoming" comes "birth" (*jāti*), in the sense of the very start of a rebirth, conception. It might additionally be interpreted, on a different time-scale, as referring to the constant rearising, during life, of the processes comprising the five *khandhas.* Once birth has arisen, "aging and death" and various other stressful experiences naturally follow, for the conditioned processes of life are in various ways painful, as explained in the teaching on the first True Reality for the Spiritually Ennobled. While saying that birth is the cause of death may sound rather simplistic, in Buddhism it is a very significant statement; for there is an alternative to being born. This is to attain *nirvāṇa*, so bringing an end to the process of rebirth and redeath. *Nirvāṇa* is not subject to time and change, and so is known as the "unborn"; as it is not born it cannot die, and so it is also known as the "deathless." To attain this state, all phenomena subject to birth – the *khandhas* and *nidānas* – must be transcended.

The round of rebirths is existence in time, the conditioned realm of impermanence. Each "birth" is a renewal of this. Confrontation with the *dukkha* of aging, sickness, and death is said to have been what set the Buddha off on his spiritual quest. In many accounts of the 12 links of Conditioned Co-arising, fathomed at his awakening, he starts at the final link, tantamount to *dukkha*, and keeps looking back to find what it is conditioned by, going back step by step until he comes to spiritual ignorance. Once the links are all understood, this ends spiritual ignorance, and so allows the whole chain to stop, to be transcended, such that the "unborn," "deathless" *Nirvāṇa* is experienced.

The Links Over Three Lives, and Over a Series of Moments

The above shows something of the details of the 12 links, but what kind of time sequence does this whole set of processes cover? The Theravāda and Sarvāstivāda traditions, while they sometimes sees the working of conditioned co-arising as occurring over one or a few moments (e.g., Vibh.147; AKB.III.24d), generally emphasize the twelvefold chain as an explanation of the working of personality over any three lives: past, present, and future (Patis.I.52; Vism.578–8I; AKB.III.21–4). Spiritual ignorance and constructing activities are karmically active states from one's past life which lead to the arising of karmically passive states in this life: consciousness, the sentient body, the sense-bases, stimulation, and feeling. In response to feeling, the karmically active states of craving, grasping, and (karma-)becoming arise, which then determine the karmically passive states of one's future life, namely birth, and aging and death. Of course, spiritual ignorance and constructing activities are present in this life as well as in one's last life, working in union with the other karmically active states; and consciousness, etc., arise in one's next life as well as in this. Note that it is never said that the last *nidāna*, aging and death, is a condition for the first, ignorance. Nevertheless, people may be led to this misapprehension by the fact that the Tibetan "Wheel of Life" has the 12 *nidānas* around its rim, so that the first and last are shown next to each other.

As regards the temporal relation of the links, among them, the sentient body is simultaneous with the sense organs it conditions, while birth comes prior to aging and death. It also makes sense to see spiritual ignorance as a dispositional state that precedes but is also simultaneous with the constructing activities it conditions. The Theravādin Abhidhamma goes into much detail on the kinds of causal links that can exist. The *Paṭṭhāna* discusses 24 kinds of conditional relations. Some involve temporal succession – e.g., "proximity" or "immediate succession" (*anantara*) conditions apply when a state of consciousness acts as a condition to whatever kind of consciousness immediately follows it, in the next moment. On the other hand, "conascent" condition applies when two states always arise together, simultaneously, as must also be the case with "object" condition, which concerns a sense-object acting as a condition for the consciousness which is aware of it.

Conditioned co-arising is about the fact that, when there has been or is "A" (among other conditions), B occurs. It is about the concomitance of phenomena and possible *patterns* in the arising of phenomena, whether over periods of lifetimes or as they flash in and out of existence, moment to moment. The point of focusing on this is in order to transform one's attitude to things and thus transform the pattern of conditions that is "you."

Fathoming, Stilling, and Transcending the Subtle Web of Conditions

While the process may be "profound," it can be gradually fathomed. This is partly by a person familiarizing themselves with teachings related to it, partly by thinking these ideas through in relation to experience, and partly (and most importantly) by mindful awareness of the flow of actions and experiences so as to observe patterns of relationship in these: conditioned co-arising at work.

Conditioned co-arising describes a complex of ever changing processes which is ever open to new influences, internal or external, at the cutting edge of the present moment. It describes an open, dynamic system, not a mechanical, rigidly determined one.

The chain's main weak points are primarily craving and spiritual ignorance (Vism.523–6), hence the Buddhist emphasis on calm/restraint and insight/understanding/awareness – respective counteractives to these two. The path aims to undermine craving by moral discipline and meditative calming and then destroy craving and ignorance by the development of wisdom. Thus AN.I.61 says of *samatha* (calm) and *vipassanā* (insight), which both "have a part in knowledge (*vijjā-*)": "*samatha* cultivates the heart-mind (*citta*) and this leads to the abandonment of attachment (*rāga*) . . . *vipassanā* cultivates wisdom (*paññā*) and this leads to the abandonment of ignorance (*avijjā*)." Thus:

> A mind defiled by attachment is not set free, nor can wisdom defiled by ignorance be cultivated. Indeed, monks, this fading away of attachment is mind-liberation (*ceto-vimutti*) and the fading away of ignorance is liberation-by-wisdom (*paññā-vimutti*).

Conditioned Co-arising as the Middle Way

As a general point on conditioned co-arising, it should be noted that it presents a "middle" way of understanding that echoes the Buddhist path as a "middle way" of practice. This idea was to be greatly influential on later forms of Buddhism (such as the Madhyamaka, or "Middle Way" school), all of which sought to best express the true "middle" way of understanding reality. In the early texts, the notion is seen in the idea of conditioned co-arising as avoiding the extremes of substantialism – seeing the experienced world as existing here and now in a solid, essential way – and nihilism – seeing it as purely an illusion, non-existent. Rather, the experienced world is a flow of constantly arising and passing away processes. This is seen in a passage explaining the deeper meaning of "right view" (*sammā-diṭṭhi*), the first factor of the Noble Eight-factored Path (*Kaccāyanagotta Sutta*; SN.II.17):

> Usually, Kaccāyana, the world depends on the pair "existence (*atthitā*)" and "non-existence."
>
> – But for one who sees, with right view, the origin of the world (*loka-samudaya*) as it actually is, there is no non-existence in regard to the world;
>
> – and for one who sees, with right view, the cessation of the world (*loka-nirodha*) as it actually is, there is no [solid] existence in regard to the world.
>
> – Usually the world is shackled by bias, clinging and insistence; but one such as this [with right view], instead of allowing bias, instead of allowing clinging, instead of affirming "my Self," with such bias, such clinging and such mental decision in the form of an underlying tendency to insist, he has no doubt or uncertainty that what arises is only arising *dukkha*, and that what ceases is only ceasing *dukkha*, and in this his knowledge is independent of others. This is what "right view" refers to.
>
> – "Everything exists" is one extreme; "nothing exists" is the other extreme. Instead of resorting to either extreme, the *Tathāgata* teaches *Dhamma* by the middle (*majjhena*): [The Buddha then enumerates the 12 factors of conditioned co-arising, each one conditioning the next, and then the cessation of one leading to the cessation of the next.]

It is also said that conditioned co-arising is a "middle" way of being that shows the error of the views that "all is a unity" (or "all is one") and "all is a diversity" (or "everything is separate") (SN.II.77). The first of these is exemplified by the Upaniṣadic idea that everything is *Brahman*, and indeed in some popular presentations of Buddhism. The second sees reality as a collection of separately existing, independent entities. Conditionally co-arising phenomena, though, are a network of processes which could not exist apart from one another, yet are not the same as one another.

Conditioned co-arising is also seen as a "middle" way of understanding that avoids the extremes expressed in the views "the life-principle (*jīva*) is the same as the mortal body (*sarīra*)" and "the life-principle is different from the mortal body" (SN.II.60–63). Mind and body are each seen as a set of interacting processes, which also interact with each other, and the enlivening factors are not seen as uniquely mental or physical (Harvey 1993). More broadly on the mind–body relationship, the Abhidhamma clearly differentiates between *dhammas* (basic process-events), which take objects and are thus part of mentality (*nāma*), and those which pertain to material form (*rūpa*). While *nāma* is centered on *citta*/consciousness and *rūpa* is centered on the "four great elements" of earth/solidity, water/cohesion, fire/heat, and wind/motion, there is no dualism of a mental "substance" versus a physical "substance": both *nāma* and *rūpa* refer to clusters of changing, interacting processes. Thus one can talk of a kind of "twin-category process-pluralism" rather than substance dualism. The processes of *nāma* and *rūpa* also interact with each other from the moment of conception, mutually supporting each other. For a life to begin, there must be the coming together, in the womb, of appropriate physical conditions and a flow of consciousness from a previous life. Life continues while there is "vitality, heat and consciousness" in a person, these comprising a conditioned, empirical life-principle (*jīva*) that is neither identical with nor entirely different from the mortal body (*sarīra*), but is (normally) dependent on and bound to such a body (Harvey 1993; 1995, 91–5). In the normal situation, mental processes are affected by physical ones in that the physical senses enable there to be types of consciousness that would not otherwise exist (the five sense-consciousnesses), and gives specific kinds of input-content to the mind; the physical support of mind (of unspecified identity, *Paṭṭhāna* I.5 and 72; Harvey 1993, 33–4) also supports the occurrence of the mind organ (*mano*) (that which is aware of mental objects) and mind-consciousness. In the normal situation, certain mental processes such as a sense of purpose and energy also lead to the origination of certain types of physical processes (which are also dependent on other physical processes), and some of these, in turn, may be modulated by other mental processes. These modulations (bodily intimation (*kāya-viññatti*) and vocal intimation (*vācī-viññatti*): *Dhammasaṅgaṇī* 596) lead to specific bodily movements or vocal articulations (Harvey 1993, 34–6). Death leads to the break-up of the normal mind–body interaction in such a way that consciousness, and certain accompaniments, flow on to another life. Four of the many forms of rebirth – the "formless" ones – are anomalous in that they remain totally free of material form; but, when there is thus *nāma* unaccompanied by *rūpa*, *nāma* itself occurs in a different way from normal, as seen in the names for these realms: the spheres of "infinite space," "infinite consciousness," "nothingness," and "neither-perception-nor-non-perception." The mind cannot simply be separated from the body without it undergoing change. Another anomalous state is that of "cessation," where there is temporarily a living body and yet – at least according to Theravādin Abhidhamma – no consciousness whatsoever. Again, when *nāma* restarts after cessation, it does so in a new way, with a deeper level of insight, leading to arahatship or becoming a Non-returner (AN.III.194). Other non-normal patterns of interaction between mind and body are found in the cases of development of the "mind-made" body (*manomaya kāya*; DN.I.77) and the exercise of psychic powers such as walking in the air or multiplying one's body (MN.I.494). As in the cases of the formless rebirths and cessation, these non-normal cases are dependent on the power of meditation to bring about transformations in the normal pattern of *nāma–rūpa* interaction.

Conditioned co-arising is also seen as a middle way between: "the one who does an action [a karma] is [identically] the same as the one who experiences [its karmic result]" and "the one who does an action is [completely] different from the one who experiences." This is seen at SN.II.18–22, where the Buddha does not accept that *dukkha* is created by oneself, by another, by both, or by neither. Elsewhere, the Buddha explains this by saying simply that *dukkha* arises conditioned by stimulation (*phassa*; SN.II.41). Here he explains it thus:

> Kassapa, [if one thinks,] "The one who does an action is the same as the one who experiences," [then one asserts] with reference to one existing from the beginning: "*dukkha* is created by oneself." When one asserts thus, this amounts to the eternalism. But, Kassapa, [if one thinks,] "The one who does an action is different from the one who experiences," [then one asserts] with reference to one stricken by feeling: "*dukkha* is created by another." When one asserts thus, this amounts to the annihilationism. Without veering to either of these extremes, the *Tathāgata* teaches *Dhamma* by the middle: Conditioned by ignorance are constructing activities [etc.].
>
> (SN.II.20)

"Eternalism" is taking oneself and one's world as containing eternal, fixed essences. This may take the form of ideas of some essential Self or I which will be untouched by death: an immortal soul, "me" forever. "Annihilationism" is identifying oneself totally with the present *khandhas*, especially just the body, taking oneself and one's world as being totally destroyed at death; more generally, it denies the continuity of cause and effect in life.

The above passage emphasizes that neither "eternalism" nor "annihilationism" applies as regards what happens to a being after death: rebirth is the continuation of a changing, conditioned process, not the continuation of an unchanging Self or a complete end of ongoing personal continuity. After death, a changing personality-flux flows on. Given long enough, this may become *very* different from how one is now: and yet what will be then will have developed out of how one is, and acts, now.

Of a person in two consecutive rebirths, it is said, "He is not the same and he is not different" (Miln.40): "he" neither retains any unchanging essence nor is wholly different. No unchanging "being" passes over from one life to another, but the death of a being leads to the continuation of the life process in another context, like the lighting of one lamp from another (Miln.71). One might put this by saying that a being in one life is a different "specific-being" than in the next, yet part of the same "continuity-being." The "later" being is a continuation, or mental evolute, of the "earlier" one on which he is causally dependent. They are linked by the flux of consciousness and the accompanying seeds of karmic results, so that the character of one is a development of the character of the "other." This principle of "not the same and not different" can be seen to apply equally within the present life.

All of this implies that, when the relationship of conditionality is properly understood, it makes one-sided views impossible. If one focuses too much on the "thingness" of things, one must attend to the conditions that make these things possible – and remember that final *nirvāṇa* brings the whole flow of conditions to an end. If one focuses too much on the ephemeral "thinglessness" of things, one must attend to the dynamic ongoingness of life that the flow of conditions makes possible.

The Type of Relationship Conditioned Co-arising Concerns

Apart from the specifics of how one *nidāna* ("ground", "foundation", "source" – i.e., conditioning link) is said to act as the condition (*paccaya*) for the arising of another, how is this kind of relationship conceived of in general? While the standard formula of 12 *nidānas* is most common, there are also variations on this, which emphasize the contribution of other conditions. These variations show that the "that" of the abstract formula is not a single determining cause but a major condition, one of several. It is clear that a *nidāna* is seen as a *necessary* condition for that which it conditions, but not as a necessary and *sufficient* condition, otherwise when a buddha or *arahat* experienced feeling they would inevitably experience craving, which they are beyond. Feeling can be seen as only *one* among the conditions for craving: a necessary condition, perhaps the predominant one, but not itself sufficient on its own to cause craving. What is also necessary, and is lacking in an enlightened person, is spiritual ignorance or misperception and the consequent lack of inner calm. Thus the Theravādin commentator Buddhaghosa says:

> Here there is no single or multiple fruit of any kind from a single cause (*kāraṇa*); nor a single fruit from multiple causes. . . . But one representative cause and fruit are given in this way, "with spiritual ignorance as condition are the constructing activities."
>
> (Vism.542)

The idea that nothing has a single cause is worth bearing in mind when reflecting on various differences of opinions in society, and sometimes in science: one side holds that "x causes y," the other that "no it doesn't, as there can be cases of x yet no y" (e.g., smoking for years yet no lung cancer), or "no, y is caused by z." It may be that y depends for its arising on both x and z (along with some other conditions), so the crucial question is not really "what is *the* cause of y?" – though it may be useful to focus attention on a particular condition, especially if it is a necessary (if not sufficient) condition for y, and is one that can be altered. In general, what is decided on as "the cause" of something is simply the last condition for it that falls into place. If one thing on its own could cause something else, then that thing would be producing that effect *continuously*, rather than only sometimes, dependent on other conditions.

Apart from this issue, how is the relationship of one *nidāna* acting as the key condition for the next conceived? Various kinds of similes for the process are given in the *suttas*:

- *hydraulic similes*: each of the *nidānas* is referred to as a "support" (*upanisa*) (SN.II.32) or "nutriment" (*āhāra*) (AN.V.113–14) for the next, just as, when tarns are filled up with rainwater, they then fill up lakes, which then fill up rivers (cf. SN.II.118). This suggests that, once a link is of sufficient strength, it causes the next to "swell" or "fill out" by "feeding" it.

- *organic similes*: SN.II.87–93 (cf. AN.V.4–5) compares the way in which looking for things to grasp at leads to craving, and on to *dukkha*, to the way in which a tree with a good root system, sending up sap, flourishes for a long time. This suggests that each link feeds and nurtures the next, enabling it to grow.
- *fire similes*: SN.II.86 uses a fire simile to illustrate the same process as at SN.II.87–93: a lamp supplied with fuel and having its wick regularly trimmed will burn for a long time. So, one link "fuels" the next.
- *mechanical similes*: SN.II.114–15 illustrates the mutual dependence of consciousness and name-and-form with the image of two sheaves of reeds which lean against each other. So one link lends support to another.

The General Nature of Conditioned Co-arising

At SN.II.25-7, it is said:

> What, monk, is Conditioned Co-arising? Aging-and-death, monks, are from birth as condition; whether *Tathāgatas* arise or not:
>
> this elemental fact (*dhātu*, or "principle") just stands (*ṭhitā*),
>
> (this) basic-pattern-stability (*dhamma-ṭṭhita-tā*),
>
> (this) basic-pattern-regularity (*dhamma-niyāma-tā*):
>
> specific conditionality (*ida-ppaccaya-tā*).
>
> A *Tathāgata* awakens to this and breaks through to it. Having done so, he teaches it, makes it known, establishes it, discloses it, analyses it, elucidates it. "See" he says, "Aging-and-death, monks, are from birth as condition" [this is then repeated for the relationship between each of the rest of the *nidānas*].

Elsewhere it is said: "First, Susīma, comes knowledge of *Dhamma*-stability (*dhamma-ṭṭhiti-ñāṇa*), afterwards knowledge of *nirvāṇa*" (SN.II.124; cf. SN.II.56 and 58). That is, the conditioned co-arising sequence is seen as a reality which a buddha simply discovers, then teaches others about. It is a principle of causal regularity, a Basic Pattern (*Dhamma*) of things that, once one has directly understood it, one can experience that which transcends it, *nirvāṇa*.

After discussing all the links in the twelvefold chain, the above SN.II.25–7 (cf. Vism.518) then says:

> So, monks, that herein which is:
>
> actuality (*tatha-tā* or "reality," "as-it-is-ness," "suchness," "thusness"),
>
> not unreality (*a-vitatha-tā*),
>
> invariability (*anañnatha-tā*, lit. not otherwiseness):

specific conditionality (*ida-ppaccaya-tā*) – this, monks, is called Conditioned Co-arising.

And what, monks, are conditionally co-arisen (*paṭicca-samuppanā*) *dhammas*? Aging-and-death, monks, is impermanent, constructed (*saṅkhata*), conditionally arisen, subject to (*-dhamma*) destruction, vanishing, fading away (*virāga-*), and cessation (*nirodha-*). Birth is impermanent . . . [and so on for the other *nidānas*].

(SN.II.26)

One might perhaps sum this up by saying that, within the overall Basic Pattern that is Dhamma, specific basic patterns (*dhammas*) flow into and nurture each other in complex, but set, regular patterns. They do not exist on their own, but arise in specific ways from the particular cluster of *dhammas* which sustain them.

Mahāyāna Developments

In the Mahāyāna movement, various uses were made of the idea of conditioned co-arising. The Madhyamaka school saw it as implying not only that phenomena were dependent on one another for their arising but also that their very nature was both causally and conceptually interwoven, such that they were empty of *svabhāva*: both inherent existence and inherent nature. The Yogācāra school saw the stream of dependent mental processes as generating the subject–object split and hence the idea of an inner "Self" and the "things" "it" craves. The Chinese Huayan school saw all phenomena in the entire universe, and of all times, as "interpenetrating" one another, with each one as the cause of the entire universe – i.e., without it, the universe would be different, not only in lacking this item but also in lacking all its influences. They did, though, also talk as if all phenomena were fluid forms of an underlying principle (Ch. *li*) that was empty of any fixed form, but not empty of the qualities of buddhahood: the "buddha-nature."

Notes

1 Note that around 1,000 words of this chapter overlap with part of chapter 3 in the author's *Introduction to Buddhism: Teachings, History and Practices*. Second edn. Cambridge: Cambridge University Press, 2013. This material is included here with permission.

2 Key sources for this doctrine are:

- the *Nidāna Saṃyutta* – twelfth *saṃyutta* of the *Saṃyutta Nikāya* (SN.12): vol. II, pp.1–133, of the Pali Text Society edition of the text in Pali and, in translation, Bodhi (2005, 533–620). Some of the 92 *suttas* are also found on the Access to Insight website: www.accesstoinsight.org/tipitaka/sn/index.html#sn12 [note that its volume and page references, as given here, are in square brackets, with volume number in small roman letters. The page numbers given are just that of the start of a *sutta*];
- the *Mahā-nidāna Sutta* – fifteenth *sutta* of the *Dīgha Nikāya* (DN.15): vol. II, pp. 55–71, of the Pali Text Society edition of the text in Pali and, in translation, Walshe (1996, 223–30), Bodhi (1995, which includes its commentary) and also on the Access to Insight website by Thanissaro Bhikkhu: www.accesstoinsight.org/tipitaka/dn/dn.15.0.than.html;

- the interpretation of the developed Theravāda tradition can be found at Vibh.135–92; Vibh-a.130–213; Vism.517–86, 98–605; and of the Sarvāstivāda tradition at AKB. III.21–36;
- contemporary books on the topic are Payutto (1994); Johansson (1979); Jones (2011); Kalupahana (1986). There are also various relevant articles in *Philosophy East and West*, many of which can be read online at: http://ccbs.ntu.edu.tw/FULLTEXT/cfb_phil.htm.

3 Though this misses the first two of the standard 12 links and replaces them with "name-and-form" as the condition for consciousness (which then, as in the standard version, is the condition for "name-and-form") and also does not explicitly mention the six sense-bases.

4 Plus in "imperturbable" constructing activities, leading to rebirth in the formless realms. These are listed separately from the karmically fruitful ones, as the latter lead to experiences of happiness, while the formless realms have a neutral feeling-tone.

5 At SN.II.73, this sequence then runs on from craving up to *dukkha*, as in the second half of the standard series of 12 links. This thus shows that the standard sequence of all 12 links is intended as just one talk-through of a complex situation.

6 Cf. MN.I.303, which says that neutral feeling is pleasant when there is understanding of it, but painful when this is lacking.

References

Bodhi, Bhikkhu (1995). *The Great Discourse on Causation: The Mahānidāna Sutta and its Commentaries.* Kandy: Buddhist Publication Society.

Bodhi, Bhikkhu (2005). *The Connected Discourses of the Buddha.* Boston: Wisdom.

Fuller, P. (2005). *The Notion of Diṭṭhi in Theravāda Buddhism.* London and New York: RoutledgeCurzon.

Harvey, P. (1993). The Mind–Body Relationship in Pali Buddhism: A Philosophical Investigation. In *Asian Philosophy* 3(1), 29–41.

Harvey, P. (1995). *The Selfless Mind: Personality, Consciousness and Nirvana in Early Buddhism.* London: Curzon Press.

Harvey, P. (2000). *An Introduction to Buddhist Ethics: Foundations, Values and Issues.* Cambridge: Cambridge University Press.

Harvey, P. (2007). "Freedom of the Will" in the Light of Theravāda Buddhist Teachings. In *Journal of Buddhist Ethics* 14, 35–98. At www.buddhistethics.org/14/harvey2-article.pdf.

Harvey, P. (2009). The Approach to Knowledge and Truth in the Theravāda Record of the Discourses of the Buddha; Theravāda Philosophy of Mind and the Person; Theravāda Texts on Ethics. In *Buddhist Philosophy: Essential Readings.* Ed. W. Edelglass and J. L. Garfield. Oxford: Oxford University Press, 175–85, 265–74, 375–87.

Johansson, R. E. A. (1979). *The Dynamic Psychology of Early Buddhism.* Oxford: Curzon Press.

Jones, D. T. (2011). *This Being, That Becomes: The Buddha's Teaching on Conditionality.* Cambridge: Windhorse.

Kalupahana, D. J. (1986). *Causality: The Central Philosophy of Buddhism.* Honolulu: University of Hawai'i Press.

Olivelle, P. (1996). *Upaniṣads: a New Translation.* Oxford: Oxford University Press.

Payutto, P. A. (1994). *Dependent Origination: the Buddhist Law of Causality.* Bangkok: Buddhadhamma Foundation.

Walshe, M. (1996). *Long Discourses of the Buddha.* Second rev. edn. Boston: Wisdom.

Part II

Major Schools of Buddhist Thought

4

Theravāda

ANDREW SKILTON

History and Context

The Theravāda monk is for many Westerners the iconic image of the Asian Buddhist. Theravāda is the tradition of Buddhism associated with South and South-East Asia.[1] Its monks, called *bhikkhus*, are shaven-headed and typically wear robes ranging in colour from a deep yellow, through ochre, to maroon, with minor variations in the details of how robes are worn. Non-monastic followers wishing to express this identity while at temples or during festivals wear white and are known as *upāsakas* (male) and *upāsikās* (female). The Theravāda nuns (*bhikkhuṇī*) order appears to have died out by the thirteenth century (Skilling 1994). There has been considerable resistance to the idea of its recent revival from the East Asian female ordination lineage in 1996, on the rationale that ordination is predicated on an assumption of an uninterrupted lineage of transmission. Women in Theravāda countries who wish to practice their Buddhism more intensively often undertake extra regulations and assume a recognized enhanced status somewhere between lay and full monastic – in Thailand, for example, such women are called *mae chi* and may have separate quarters within a temple.[2] Collectively, the Theravāda Buddhist community is designated by the term *saṅgha*. A widespread understanding of the term takes it to incorporate monastics only, although another that it includes both lay and monastic followers. A more restrictive term, *ariya-saṅgha*, "community of noble members," is understood to designate only those who have made specific progress on the path to awakening or enlightenment.

Theravāda is the majority religion in Sri Lanka, Burma (Myanmar), Thailand, Cambodia, and Laos. There are significant Theravāda Buddhist minorities in South Vietnam, Yunnan Province (People's Republic of China), and Bangladesh; and significant Theravāda Buddhist communities in countries such as Malaysia, Singapore, and the Buddhist homelands of India and Nepal. There are also widespread activities and representation of Theravāda in many Western countries serving both immigrant

A Companion to Buddhist Philosophy, First Edition. Edited by Steven M. Emmanuel.

communities and local converts. In the second half of the twentieth century significant representation of South-East Asian Theravāda Buddhists also appeared in relation to immigration from the region to the USA, Canada, and Australia. Important cultural and literary archives from Theravāda Buddhist countries are preserved in Western countries with former colonial influence in the region, notably France and the United Kingdom, as well as Denmark and Germany. New initiatives are under way to create film and/or digital archives of some national literatures, for example in Cambodia and Laos.[3]

The title "Theravāda" is Pāli language, meaning "doctrine (*vāda*) of the Elders (*thera*)," and is a self-assigned term expressing the belief that the tradition is continuous with and embodies the positions and values of the community of elders who were the personal disciples of the historical Buddha. In this sense the title implicitly dissociates its followers from perceived "divergences" from the Buddha's "original" teaching. Historically, such differentiation was actually between a range of other non- and pre-Mahāyāna schools of Buddhism that developed in India. Since none of these other schools have survived as such into the modern period, from the modern perspective Theravāda is to be distinguished from the Mahāyāna and Vajrayāna Buddhisms of Tibet, Mongolia, Nepal, China, Korea, Vietnam, and Japan. At present the title Theravāda is applied to Buddhist communities derived largely from the hegemonic influence of a single politically powerful temple tradition based at the Mahāvihāra Temple in Anuradhapura, Sri Lanka.

It seems likely that this title is used anachronistically, resulting from what might be seen as a strategic attempt by adherents of the Mahāvihāra temple (Sri Lanka) in the twelfth century to link it to this tradition, during a period of major reform under Parakramabāhu I (1123–1186) (see Bechert 1993; Collins 1990). Considerable historical confusion surrounds any such claims of identity due to the ambiguity of textual and inscriptional evidence for a *thera* community on the mainland of the subcontinent before this time. To understand this we need to know that the Pāli language is a close relative of the Sanskrit language, in which we find the parallel term *sthavira*, "elder." In any given occurrence of the term *sthavira/thera*, in text or epigraph, it can be difficult to determine whether this refers to one and the same or indeed any institutional entity.

This linguistic observation gains substance in connection with the broad narrative of historical development of the Buddhist community in India. Tradition records that, after the demise of the Buddha (*parinibbāna*), the community of his followers developed in harmony until a schism (*saṅgha-bheda*) occurred between two parties, one of which in the sources is entitled the *sthavira* or "elder" community. The other party was called by consensus the "great/large community" (*mahā-saṅgha*), implying, one reasonably assumes, that was the larger party. It should be understood that the sources for this division are not unanimous on the time, place, or basis for the split. It appears that the divergence could have been either doctrinally based, revolving around matters of disputed doxicological principle, or around matters of monastic regulation.[4]

Buddhist monastics, by definition, are bound by a comprehensive set of regulations that govern their personal and communal behavior. These regulae are codified in comprehensive monastic legal codes (*vinaya*) and enacted through precisely worded legal instruments known as *kammavācā*. This also combines with the principle of lineage, expressed by the term *nikāya*, which emphasizes the descent of monastic observance through rules inherited by every monk from the local and regional monastic community within which the individual monk takes ordination. Variations in the regulations observed makes communal life problematic. Individual monks or groups of monks cannot reside together, or necessarily co-own property, or manage collective resources if they observe divergent monastic legal codes that enjoin different, or differently worded, or even just differently interpreted, rules for the individual and community.

Our historical sources variously tell us that the Sthaviras were the group that sought either to adapt the monastic regulations or to preserve them unchanged, or that refuted various erroneous doctrinal positions (termed "heretical theses" in some secondary sources). The original Sthavira community thus constitutes, historically, a relatively intangible but religiously iconic identity that exerted a powerful appeal to incumbents at the Mahāvihāra who wished to assert their legitimacy and worthiness for patronage by activating more or less mythical links to these archetypal "elders."

The history of the Theravāda tradition as we know it is therefore properly pursued in relation to institutions in Sri Lanka and later South-East Asia. Theravāda identity is also therefore partly about the transmission and observation of distinctive monastic regulations, and indeed the field of monastic law (alongside Abhidhamma and Pāli grammar) has clearly absorbed considerable intellectual activity in Theravāda countries – as it did in medieval European Christian monasticism – as much as doctrinal matters.

The Pāli Canon

The claim of continuity made by the Mahāvihāra was not as arbitrary as this rather brief account of the historical background might suggest, for the same Mahāvihāra tradition was also an institution that was instrumental in the preservation and exegesis of a body of scripture that preserves some very early material that may indeed have been a part of the literary heritage of the Sthavira community. This brings us to the Pāli canon – i.e., the canon of scriptural literature preserved in the Pāli language by the Theravāda tradition. This canon was inherited and possibly partially formed by the Mahāvihāra tradition of Sri Lanka and, insofar as we can tell from limited manuscript remains and translations into Tibetan and Chinese, had its counterparts in other canons of scripture passed down by other Buddhist traditions of the subcontinent in other, albeit allied, languages, including Sanskrit and other Prakrits like Pāli. While these other canons survive only piecemeal, if at all, the canon in Pāli appears to survive intact and complete in its Indic language. It was allegedly put into writing late in the first century CE, although secure evidence for its content dates from comprehensive commentaries composed in the fifth century CE (see below).

Analytic descriptions of the Pāli canon are easy to locate, and so I shall survey the whole only briefly here (Hinüber 2000; Norman 1983). It consists of three major sections, the first of which is the *vinaya-piṭaka*, "the collection concerning discipline," containing a large body of case law on monastic regulations governing the conduct of individual monks and nuns and of the community at large, both in its internal arrangements and in its relations to secular society. The remaining two sections are usually of far greater interest to the general subject of the present volume, and are the *sutta-piṭaka*, "the collection of discourses," and the *abhidhamma-piṭaka*, "the collection of advanced teachings."

The *sutta-piṭaka* contains discourses on the teaching of the Buddha, commonly called the Dhamma, usually presented in the voice of the Buddha as a historical personality, in a more or less elaborate historical setting located in ancient North-East India. The content is varied in tone and genre, its focus on conduct or doctrine, and its age. Without doubt some parts of this collection, such as the *Thera-* and *Therīgāthā* or the *Sutta Nipāta*, are very ancient and may go back to the very time of the Buddha and his immediate disciples. Other parts, for example the *Khuddakapāṭha* ("*Short Texts*") or *Buddhavaṃsa* ("*Lineage of the Buddhas*"), are very likely of later compilation, post-dating the historical Buddha by several centuries. The *sutta-piṭaka* contains five subdivisions – also denominated *nikāya*, here in the sense of "collection" – each of which shows considerable signs of editorial activity, which suggests that, in general, in their present form these subdivisions postdate the time of the Buddha himself.

The final major section of the Pāli canon, the collection of advanced teachings (Abhidhamma), consists of seven substantial treatises that seek to abstract the doctrinal and philosophical principles enunciated piecemeal in the *sutta-piṭaka* and arrange them systematically (Potter 1996). While undoubtedly later compilations from an historical point of view, these, too, are regarded formally as the words of the Buddha and are otherwise anonymous (see below). This synthetic and abstracting agenda perhaps qualifies the Abhidhamma as a philosophical corpus proper. However, while being more explicitly "philosophical" in intent, it remains the least studied and least well understood of the three canonical collections in Western scholarship.

The canon is accompanied by important layers of additional para-canonical literature (see table 4.1). The *vinaya* is supported by legal instruments (*kammavācā*), by

Table 4.1 Canonical and para-canonical Pāli literature

	vinaya piṭaka	sutta-piṭaka	abhidhamma-piṭaka
Canonical	*Khandhaka* *Sutta-vibhaṅga* *Parivāra*	*dīgha-nikāya* "long texts" *majjhima-nikāya* "medium texts" *aṅguttara-nikāya* "numbered texts" *saṃyutta-nikāya* "thematic texts" *khuddaka-nikāya* "minor texts"	*Dhammasaṅgani* *Vibhaṅga* *Dhātukathā* *Puggalapaññatti* *Kathāvatthu* *Yamaka* *Paṭṭhāna*
Para-canonical	*kammavācā* commentaries and sub-commentaries manuals	commentaries and sub-commentaries to each *nikāya* compilations apocrypha	commentaries to each text sub-commentaries to each text treatises *"finger manuals"* *Visuddhimagga*

commentaries and sub-commentaries that include revisions and amendments to monastic legislation found in the *vinaya*, and by manuals that compile regulations in more systematic and practical arrangements useful for the functioning of the monastic legal system (see Hinüber 2000; Crosby 2006). The *sutta-piṭaka* is accompanied by layers of commentary and sub-commentary that elucidate context, locutions, grammar, and doctrine in the *sutta* texts, as well as by so-called apocryphal *sutta* materials and compilations of *suttas*, extracts, and so on, that serve to facilitate teaching and delivery of sermons. The Abhidhamma is supported by commentaries and sub-commentaries on the primary treatises, as well as by secondary treatises that elucidate specialist areas of thought and doctrine and summaries of the Buddhist path as a whole, of which the most famous is the *Visuddhimagga* of Buddhaghosa. With the exception of two parts of the *sutta-piṭaka* and two of the *abhidhamma-piṭaka*, the whole of the canon proper has been translated into English in volumes published by the Pali Text Society, as well as individual parts by other translators and publishers.[5] Translation of the supporting literature is much less advanced and at present its investigation requires a working knowledge of Pāli language at least.

It should also be noted that, while the above discussion focuses on canonical and related materials, there has also been a tradition of composition in Pāli and vernacular languages across a very wide range of literary genre, including those that overlap with philosophical interests, over the period between the redaction of the canon itself – probably complete by the beginning of the Common Era – and the twentieth century.

The history of the tradition that preserves this literature is poorly understood for the medieval period. The Mahāvihāra tradition was exported from Sri Lanka throughout South-East Asia during the first half of the second millennium of the Common Era. More recent centuries show a picture of complex interactions between South-East Asian countries and Sri Lanka, which is formally regarded as the source of orthodox Theravāda lineages throughout the region. In the modern period this picture is modulated by reform activities, usually implemented by centralizing governments, which promote particularly the Dhammayuttika Nikāya (founded in 1833 in Thailand) and standardized editions of the *tipiṭaka*. However, recent research is beginning to shed light on other influences at work in the region. These can be seen in residual traces of the Sarvāstivāda school in northern Thailand, and in other non-normative or pre-reform practices throughout the region preserved in peripheral areas that have resisted or been missed by centralizing reform processes which have otherwise created a relatively uniform Theravāda culture. At this stage of our understanding these differences appear most clearly expressed in practices (liturgy and meditation), although it is also clear that the ideological and cultural background to these features are of interest philosophically (Crosby 2000).

It has also become apparent that Western assumptions about the primacy of the Pāli canonical texts may not hold true for pre-reform establishments. The evidence of local libraries (where they have survived) suggests that local communities used textual resources in which canonical texts were relatively poorly represented (McDaniel 2008).

In the light of this account of its history, it should be apparent that claims that Theravāda represents the Buddhism of the personal disciples of the Buddha must be treated with considerable circumspection. It is, however, a regrettable feature of at least the so-called Anglo-German school of Buddhist studies (Conze 1967, 2) that Theravāda literature and doctrine have been treated as just that, with a significant amount of early Western scholarship assuming that they are an authentic witness to what the authors wish to see as "original" Buddhism. This is perhaps the inevitable outcome of a cultural concern with origins and foundational texts rather than what might be called the "developed church," and this is reflected in our existing histories of Theravāda, which offer considerable material on "origins" and the contemporary period but leave an uncomfortable gap for the intervening two millennia.

Theravāda Doctrine

The major philosophical work of the Theravāda is expressed through the *sutta-* and *abhidhamma-piṭakas* and the literature and ongoing traditions that developed in particular from the latter. In the first of these, this is expressed as doctrinal statements authoritatively uttered by the Buddha as a result of his insight into the nature of reality. In broad terms we can summarize the major areas of distinctive Buddhist doctrine expressed in *suttas* under four related heads. They are overwhelmingly concerned to demonstrate the Buddhist "truth" (*sacca*) of impermanence (*anicca*) and its corollary:

1 *anattā* (Skt *anātman*) "non-self" – i.e., the absence of an eternal unchanging essence within the individual person or indeed the external world. This is typically demonstrated both analogically and reductively. The classic analogy takes a manufactured object, such as a carriage, or a plant, such as a banana "tree," and by taking it apart asks an interlocutor to identify an enduring essence apart from the constituent components. The reductive strategy takes us to the next heads, where we encounter two types of reductive analysis employed:

2 diachronic analyses of causal relations involved in the experienced world (Karunadasa 2010). The term for this is *paticcasamuppāda*, "conditional arising."[6] The developed account of this doctrine describes a process of mutual conditioning across time of 12 *nidāna* or "links." These are most famously known from the outermost "rim" of the popular Buddhist image known as "the wheel of life." Here each component acts as the condition upon the presence of which the next link arises. Old-age and death (12) are seen as the determining condition for further arising of ignorance (1), and thus a vicious cycle is established. The links are shown in table 4.2. From a soteriological viewpoint, this "causal mechanism" is seen as the process by which unenlightened beings remain embroiled in suffering, and it is interpreted as operating both between lives (Buddhism assuming rebirth after death) and within a single lifetime, even momentarily within moments of consciousness. While it appears to be deterministic, exegetes identify an opportunity to opt out of this cycle between craving and attachment (links 7 and 8).

3 Three synchronic – i.e., non-causal – analyses of the experienced world are also frequently discussed and rehearsed in the *suttas*. These are the *khandhas*, "aggregates," *āyatanas*, "sense fields," or *dhātus*, "elements." The *khandhas* are five groups or aggregates of ultimates: materiality (*rūpa*), hedonic feeling (*vedanā*), apperception (*saññā*), volition (*saṅkhāra*), and consciousness (*viññāna*). The *āyatanas* are 12:

Table 4.2 The twelve *nidāna* or "links"

1	*avijjā*	ignorance
2	*saṅkhāra*	[mental] formations
3	*viññāna*	consciousness
4	*nāmarūpa*	mental and physical [aggregates]
5	*saḷāyatana*	six sense fields
6	*phassa*	contact
7	*vedanā*	hedonic feeling/sensation
8	*taṇhā*	craving
9	*upādāna*	attachment
10	*bhava*	becoming
11	*jāti*	birth
12	*jarā-maraṇa*	old age and death

the six senses plus their corresponding sense bases: the eye and visible objects, the ear and sounds; nose and odor, the tongue and tastes, the skin and touchable objects, and the mind and mental objects. The *dhātus*, in this context, comprise the 12 *āyatana* plus a corresponding consciousness, *viññāna*, for each sense. Each of these analyses is considered to account exhaustively for experienced phenomena, their application demonstrating the lack of need to posit fictional essences to explain identity and continuity.

4 The outcome of these processes of analysis is the identification of various ultimate constituents, which come to be known as *dhammas*. The function of *dhammas* is to provide the impersonal building blocks that demonstrate the absence of "self" or essence by accounting sufficiently for mental and physical phenomena and the process of conditional causality. The organization and accounting of *dhammas*, the way they interrelate, in particular in relation to pursuing the path to enlightenment and omniscience, become the primary concern of Theravāda Abhidhamma.

Aside of these concerns, *suttas* address a range of doctrinal and philosophical subjects: from psychological and practice dimensions of the Buddhist message, to accounts of the Buddhist path, to discussions of more recognizably philosophical subject areas such as *kamma* – i.e., action – in, for example, the *Mahā-* and *Cūla-kammavibhaṅga-suttas*: *The Great and Lesser Expositions of Kamma* (MN.III.248ff. and 254ff.), or epistemological issues, as in the *Caṅki-sutta* (MN.II.354ff.).

While the didactic stance of Theravāda is thus profoundly committed to positive statements about the nature of "the way things truly are," we should note that there appear to have been issues on which the Buddha chose to remain silent. These "unanswered questions" (*avyākata-pañha*) concerned whether or not the world is eternal or finite, the relationship of the body to the self, and whether or not the Buddha "exists" after death.[7] Also noteworthy is the untypical radical apophasis recommended in the *Aṭṭhakavagga*, "Section of Eights," one of the very earliest canonical texts of the *Sutta Nipāta* (Norman 2001, 90–111).

Focus of the Theravāda Abhidhamma

In that the Abhidhamma is an anonymous technical literature, it has yielded to chronological analysis largely through doctrinal and structural investigation. In this respect it is generally agreed that the core of these texts are the *mātikā* – i.e., bare lists of items – presented in the *Dhammasaṅgani*, the first volume of the seven. There are two *abhidhamma-mātikā*, one consisting of 100 dyads – i.e., pairs of opposites – and the other of 22 triads – i.e., sets of threes – giving a total of 122 categories. (A third *mātikā* lists 42 miscellaneous terms from the *suttas*.) These *mātikā* are elaborated through successive discussion to create the canonical volumes of Abhidhamma. Each of the Abhidhamma treatises is therefore constructed from the "matrix" which is the essential embodiment of the subject of the treatise. We can of course speculate that, in origin, these *mātikā* functioned as mnemonic devices for retaining a body of doctrinal information but evolved into a methodology for its investigation.

The Canonical Abhidhamma

The most immediately interesting (although not necessarily the most important) of the Abhidhamma treatises is the *Kathāvatthu*, or "subjects of debate." This is the only Abhidhamma text associated with a human author, Tissa (active 218 years post *parinibbāna*), who, however, supposedly only expanded a list of subjects compiled by the historical Buddha. Thus 217 topics of dispute with other Buddhist traditions are raised and refuted from a Theravāda point of view. The decisive and final consideration is sometimes the citation of authoritative scripture, but arguments are also resolved on the basis of consistency with general principles and categories, rectification of terms, and the universal validity of statements. The *Kathāvatthu* is therefore a major resource for understanding how the Theravāda differentiated itself from other Buddhist traditions. The points, all matters of doctrine, cover a broad range of topics, but a review shows that the following areas, some partly overlapping, were particularly fruitful for the process of mutual differentiation:

1. how to understand the doctrine of the absence of a "self," *anattā*
2. action, *kamma*, and its outcomes
3. the nature of the Buddha and the *arahat*
4. the nature of enlightenment
5. the nature of consciousness (*viññāna*) and the mind
6. meditation states (*jhāna*)
7. analyses of the experienced world
8. perception and the senses and their organs
9. the nature of matter
10. the nature of the Buddhist path and of specific points of attainment on it
11. volition
12. cosmology.

Nor is *Kathāvatthu* without more ephemeral interest. For example, Tissa recorded the Theravāda refutations of claims by other Buddhists that the Buddha's faeces smelt of

Table 4.3 The canonical Abhidhamma texts and their translations

Pāli titles	Pali Text Society translations
Dhammasaṅgani	*Buddhist Psychological Ethics*[i]
Vibhaṅga	*The Book of Analysis*[ii]
Dhātukathā	*Discourse on Elements*[iii]
Puggalapaññatti	*A Designation of Human Types*[iv]
Kathāvatthu	*Points of Controversy*[v]
Yamaka	"The Pairs"
Paṭṭhāna	*Conditional Relations* (incomplete)[vi]

i Rhys Davids (1993).
ii Thittila (1969).
iii Nārada (1962).
iv Law (1922).
v Aung and Rhys Davids (1915).
vi Nārada (1969–81).

perfume (xviii 4); that animals go to heaven (xx 4); and that non-human beings perform sexual intercourse while disguised as *arahants* (xxiii 2). The *Kathāvatthu* thus helps us build a rich and nuanced picture of the issues over which the Theravāda considered itself a distinctive tradition.

Also of more immediate interest, in that it illustrates the contrasting approaches to understanding topics according to the *sutta* and Abhidhamma methods, is the *Vibhaṅga*. This treatise reviews 18 topics – aggregates (*khandha*), sense bases (*āyatana*), elements (*dhātu*), etc. – firstly giving a discursive explanation, often by quoting from the *sutta piṭaka*; secondly by applying synonyms and numerical formulae; and finally through an interrogative format which incorporates the matrix of the *Dhammasaṅgani*. The last two treatments exemplify the Abhidhamma method, both by definition and by integrating the topics considered with the overall structure of the Abhidhamma through the *mātikā*.

The *Dhātukathā* considers all *dhammas* (ultimate constituents) in the light of whether or not each is or is not included in, or associated with, the three analytic structures of the aggregates (*khandhas*), sense bases (*āyatanas*), and elements (*dhātus*).

The *Puggalapaññatti* classifies types of person according to an ascending numerical structure: chapter 1 looks at types of single persons; chapter 2 at types of pairs of persons; chapter 3 at types of triads of persons; and so on.

The *Yamaka* gets its name from its strategy of contrasting paired questions, as in the dyad *mātikā* of the *Dhammasaṅgani*, usually in the form: "Is it the case that A is B?" and "Is it the case that B is A?" Through this method it seeks to establish conceptual precision in relation to Abhidhamma terminology.

The *Paṭṭhāna* is probably the latest and certainly the largest of the canonical Abhidhamma works and is also held in the highest esteem.[8] It achieves both of these through systematically applying each of 24 types of conditionality to every component of the *abhidhamma mātikā* from the *Dhammasaṅgini*. Since, however, the *mātikā* can be combined in six different ways, and, furthermore, that conditionality itself can be reviewed from four formally different perspectives (positive, negative, positive-negative, negative-positive), we thereby have another set of 24 categories. The *Paṭṭhāna* applies the 24 types of conditionality, in these 24 modes, to each of the 122 components of the *mātikā*. The result is a spectacularly complex account of reality from a causal point of view.

The written and printed texts of the *Paṭṭhāna* are always abbreviated because of the high numbers involved.

These last two texts illustrate well the observation "the Abhidhamma Pitaka is intended to divulge as starkly and directly as possible the totalistic system that underlies the Suttanta expositions and upon which the individual discourses draw" (Rewata Dhamma and Bodhi 1995–2011), although this was surely a system constructed retrospectively. However, the *Paṭṭhāna*, despite its daunting level of abstraction, has considerable popularity in Burma and is the content of devout recitation. There are several traditions of interpretation, and specialist study retreats are a popular venue for Burmese lay Buddhists. Perhaps it should not be forgotten that widespread Buddhist tradition maintains that the *abhidhamma-piṭaka* was taught by the Buddha directly to his mother (by this point in his career she is residing in a lower heavenly realm). It is a cliché of Western scholarly tradition that doctrinally "rich" texts and traditions are the preserve of (male) monastic specialists, but more recent research in Theravāda countries has revealed that lay people of both sexes can be creatively involved in the transmission and elaboration of this type of material.[9]

Abhidhamma Commentaries

These last observations bring us neatly to the issue of commentary. As already indicated, there is a suite of commentaries on the canonical Abhidhamma texts. These are all attributed to Buddhaghosa (fifth century), a highly educated brahmanical convert who travelled to Sri Lanka from India to draw on its rich and renowned commentarial archives. His method involved the synthesis and critical selection from a wide range of commentarial sources available to him at the Anuradhapura Mahāvihāra and the composition of his exegesis in the Pāli language. Such was his brilliance and authority that alternative commentarial voices were effectively silenced, and his writings, with occasional reference to or quotation of earlier commentators, are now all we have for the texts concerned. His work covered commentary on *vinaya-*, *sutta-*, and *abhidhamma-piṭakas*, although gaps in his coverage were filled largely by another exegete by the name of Dhammapāla (eighth–ninth century). Buddhaghosa's works thus represent a commentarial horizon beyond which it is very difficult to see. His best-known and possibly most important work, entitled *Visuddhimagga*, "The Path of Purification," was not so much a commentary as a summary of the Buddhist path. In this he constructs a succinct yet comprehensive survey of the Buddhist path under the traditional rubric of *sīla*, *samādhi*, and *paññā*, "morality, meditation, and understanding." These are distributed across four sections, the extra section being placed between meditation and understanding and consisting of a remarkable summary of Theravāda analyses of phenomena and conditionality, under the title "the soil in which understanding grows." A comprehensive manual of Theravāda doctrine and path, the *Visuddhimagga* has subsequently exerted an extraordinary influence over Theravāda scholarship, being widely cited, quoted, and extracted by later authors.

Less individually influential, but constituting a definitive and authoritative lens through which the canonical texts are understood, are Buddhaghosa's commentaries proper (see table 4.4).

Table 4.4 Commentaries on the Abhidhamma books and their translations

Canonical Abhidhamma texts	Buddhaghosa's commentaries	Translation
Dhammasaṅgani	*Atthasālinī*	*The Expositor*[i]
Vibhaṅga	*Sammohavinodani*	*Dispeller of Delusion*[ii]
Dhātukathā *Puggalapaññatti* *Kathāvatthu* *Yamaka* *Paṭṭhāna*	*Pañcappakaraṇa*	"Exposition of the Five [Books]"

i Pe (1920–1).
ii Ñāṇamoli (1987–91).

Inevitably the commentarial traditions synthesized by Buddhaghosa made distinctive contributions to Theravāda doctrinal development beyond that in the *sutta-* and *abhidhamma-piṭakas*. Distinctive contributions include developing the concept of the momentary character of *dhammas* (ultimate constituents), designated by the term *khaṇa*, and a detailed account of the momentary process of consciousness – i.e., the arising, sustaining, and decay of moments of awareness, designated *cittavithi*. These doctrines are the ultimate expression of the principle of impermanence, *anicca*, in Theravāda philosophy. The commentaries also complete an exhaustive classification of *cittas*, "mental states," and of the components of the material world (*rūpa*) in primary and secondary forms. Crucially also the commentaries work up a definition of *dhamma* (ultimate constituent) as "that which bears its own-nature" (*Atthasālinī* 39; Ronkin 2005, 112).

While there is evidence from inscriptional and textual sources that scholarly monks specialized in the memorization of specific sections of the canon, or indeed the whole of it, including the Abhidhamma (which in the form of its *mātikā* seems to bear the traces of such mnemonic necessity) (see Adikaram 1946), it is also apparent that the canonical texts are themselves somewhat intractable and over the centuries were displaced in favor of shorter treatises that performed the same work as the canonical texts but in a more digestible format. In the Burmese tradition, which has maintained an active engagement with Abhidhamma into the contemporary period, nine such texts are known as the "*little finger manuals*" (*let than*), the most important of these being the *Abhidhammatthasaṅgaha* (tenth–eleventh century).

The *Abhidhammatthasaṅgaha* is praised for its succinct and elegant summary of the entire Abhidhamma and as such is the foundation text by which Burmese monks are trained in the subject. Before looking at the canonical texts proper, trainees must first memorize Anuruddha's work in its entirety (see Carbine 2011, 147). Once the *Abhidhammatthasaṅgaha* is mastered, student monks move on to study the *Dhammasaṅganī*, *Dhātukathā*, *Yamaka*, and *Paṭṭhāna* in partial qualification for the national Dhammācāriya degree.[10] Although for the majority of studious monks the *Abhidhammatthasaṅgaha* is sufficient, and those who sit for the Dhammācāriya degree tackle only four of the *abhidhamma-piṭaka* texts, memorization of considerably larger quantities of material is not only possible but also a highly revered achievement. In the last 60 years a small

Table 4.5 The *"little finger manuals"*

	Title	Author	Translation
1	*Abhidhammatthasaṅgaha*	Anuruddha	*A Manual of Abhidhamma*[i]
2	*Nāmarūpaparicceheda*	Anuruddha	"The Determination of the Mental and Physical [Aggregates]"
3	*Paramatthavinicchaya*	Anuruddha	"The Discrimination of Ultimate Meaning"
4	*Abhidhammāvatara*	Buddhadatta	"Introduction to Abhidhamma"
5	*Rūpārūpavibhāga*	Buddhadatta	*The Classification of Forms and Formless Things*[ii]
6	*Saccasaṅkhepa*	Dhammapala	"Brief Account of the Truths"
7	*Mohavicchedanī*	Kassapa	"Destroyer of Doubt"
8	*Nāmarūpasamāsa*	Khema	*The Summary of Mind and Matter* [iii]
9	*Nāmācāradīpaka*	Saddhamma-jotipala	"Illuminating the Action of the Mind"

i Nārada (1980).
ii Exell (1992).
iii Saddhatissa (1987).

number of monks have managed to memorize the entire *vinaya-* and *abhidhamma-piṭakas* plus a significant portion of the *sutta-piṭaka*, thus qualifying for the advanced degree (and title) "Tipiṭaka-dhara." There are currently seven holders of this remarkable achievement, and there have been only 12 since the examination procedure was introduced in 1948. The examinations take place annually in December.[11] We should bear in mind that, while such study involves the mastery of a large body of complex Abhidhamma material that we would describe as philosophical in character, the character of the engagement that is thus cultivated does not map easily onto the critical training pursued for a philosophy degree in Western universities. Yet this kind of learning by heart is regarded as a precursor both to philosophical engagement and to meditation practice in much living Abhidhamma practice.

The *Abhidhammatthasaṅgaha* is concise and has as a result inspired numerous commentaries from the twelfth century through to the twentieth (Rewata Dhamma and Bodhi 1995–2011).

If the texts just discussed are the tools by which Asian Theravāda educational traditions access Abhidhamma, and in this sense constitute the curriculum for Buddhist philosophy in Theravāda countries, we should also note that Western engagement with philosophical dimensions of Theravāda have taken a different route. There are at least two contemporary Theravādas: the Theravāda of Asian countries, which of course varies regionally and locally, and the Theravāda of the Western imaginaire. The latter is a construct of Western scholars working with the textual materials of the Theravāda tradition as they have become available in critical editions (themselves a product of Western scholarship), and focusing not necessarily on the materials that are used in Asia but on those which they have identified as closest to the Buddha (this being reflected in the publishing history of the Pāli canon in Europe). The construction of this Western Theravāda Buddhism is therefore a handmaid (or should it be niece?)

of the essentially nineteenth-century search for Buddhist origins and the "historical Buddha." Peter Skilling suggests that

> The centering of "Theravāda" in the Pāli canon, above all in the "four main Nikāyas," is a child of the late nineteenth and the twentieth centuries. It has grown up to become what we might call a "new Theravāda," largely anglophonic but increasingly international in influence and outreach. This new trend should be respected and recognized as one of the Buddhisms active today. But should it be read back into the past?
>
> (Skilling 2009, 72)

It seems to the present author that a proportion of Western scholarship on Theravāda doctrine and philosophy participates in this transnational, anglophone, *sutta*-based Theravāda insofar as it focuses on selected *sutta* texts, rather than on the developed systematic philosophical literature of Abhidhamma, and also insofar as it imports into the materials terms and concepts that originate in the Western philosophical context. This makes such essays neither illegitimate nor uninteresting, but we should be aware that such debates as are raised on this basis may not be recognizable or relevant to traditional Theravāda scholars and cannot automatically be said to represent the actual or historical philosophical concerns of the Theravāda tradition.

Notes

1 Theravāda Buddhism has been known in Western scholarship under a number of designations: Ceylonese Buddhism, Southern Buddhism, Hīnayāna, and, in more politically correct times, *śrāvaka* or "mainstream" Buddhism.

2 Functionally similar statuses are observed in Sri Lanka, where such women are known as *dasa sil mātayo* ("10 precept mothers"); in Burma, where they are known as *thilashin* "having moral standing"; and in Cambodia, where they are *don chi*. The re-establishment of the *bhikkhuṇi saṅgha* is a subject of ongoing progress and controversy, the latest most notable development being the ordination by Ajahn Brahmavaṃso of *bhikkhuṇī* in Australia and the subsequent reaction of the Thai Saṅgha hierarchy.

3 The Cambodian Edition Manuscripts Fund (FEMC) at http://khmermanuscripts.org/; and the Digital Library of Lao Manuscripts at www.laomanuscripts.net/.

4 Much attention has been paid to determining the character and causes of such splits. See Bareau (1955); Nattier and Prebish (1977); Cousins (1991); and Skilton (1994) as useful introductions to this debate.

5 See the Pali Text Society website: www.palitext.com/.

6 Also translated as "conditioned co-production," "dependent origination," "dependent arising."

7 *Cūla-Māluṅkhyaputta Sutta* (MN.II.97ff.).

8 The *Paṭṭhāna* fills 2,500 pages of the 1957 Burmese tipiṭaka edition.

9 For example, chapter 4 of the *Abhidhammatthasaṅgaha* (see below), dealing in detail with the cognitive process (*cittavithi*), is elaborated as a Shan *lik long* verse text entitled *Abhidhamma Kammatthān*. See Scott Collection, Cambridge University Library, in which there are several copies of this text. See Crosby and Khur-Yearn (2010) on the *lik long* texts of Shan State (North-East Burma). My knowledge of the living traditions of *Paṭṭhāna* practice comes primarily from the current PhD research of Pyi Phyo Kyaw at the School of Oriental and African Studies, London, under the supervision of Kate Crosby.

10 Jotika Khur-Yearn (personal communication, 10 November 2011).

11 Printed English-language sources on the Tipiṭakadhara system are scarce. See Kyaw (nd.).

References

Adikaram, E. (1946). *Early History of Buddhism in Ceylon*. Colombo: M. D. Gunasena.

Aung, S. Z., and Rhys Davids, C. (trans.) (1915). *Points of Controversy*. London: PTS.

Bareau, André (1955). *Les Sectes bouddhique du Petit Véhicule*. Paris: École française d'Extrême-Orient. Eng. trans. forthcoming as *The Buddhist Schools of the Small Vehicle*. Trans. S. Boin-Webb, ed. A. Skilton. Honolulu: University of Hawai'i Press.

Bechert, Heinz (1993). The Nikāyas of Medieval Sri Lanka and the Unification of the Saṅgha by Parākramabāhu I. In *Studies on Buddhism in Honour of Professor A. K. Warder*. Ed. N. K. Wagle and F. Watanabe. Toronto: University of Toronto, Centre for South Asian Studies, 11–21.

Carbine, Jason A. (2011). *Sons of the Buddha: Continuities and Ruptures in a Burmese Monastic Tradition*. Berlin and New York: Walter de Gruyter.

Collins, Steven (1990). On the very idea of the Pāli canon. *Journal of the Pali Text Society* 15, 89–126.

Conze, Edward (1967). Recent Progress in Buddhist Studies. In *Thirty Years of Buddhist Studies*. London: Faber.

Cousins, Lance S. (1991). The "Five Points" and the Origins of the Buddhist Schools. *The Buddhist Forum*, Vol. 2: *Seminar Papers* 1988–1990. Ed. T. Skorupski. London: School of Oriental and African Studies, 27–60.

Crosby, Kate (2000). Tantric Theravāda: A Bibliographic Essay on the Writings of François Bizot and other Literature on the *Yogāvacara* Tradition. *Contemporary Buddhism* 2, 141–98.

Crosby, Kate (2006). Sāriputta's Three Works on the *Samantapāsādikā*. *Journal of the Pali Text Society* 28, 49–59.

Crosby, Kate, and Khur-Yearn, Jotika (2010). Poetic *Dhamma* and the *Zare*: Traditional Styles of Teaching Theravāda amongst the Shan of Northern Thailand. *Contemporary Buddhism* 11, 1–26.

Exell, R. (1992). The Classification of Forms and Formless Things. *Journal of the Pali Text Society* 16, 1–12.

Hinüber, Oskar von (2000). *A Handbook of Pāli Literature*. Berlin: Walter de Gruyter.

Karunadasa, Y. (2010). *The Theravāda Abhidhamma: Its Inquiry into the Nature of Conditioned Reality*. Hong Kong: Centre of Buddhist Studies, University of Hong Kong.

Kyaw, Pyi Phyo (nd.). The Centennial Commemorative Inscription of the Most Venerable Mingun Tipiṭakadhara Sayadaw U Vicittasārābhivaṃsa. Unpublished paper.

Law, B. C. (trans.) (1922). *A Designation of Human Types*. London: Luzac.

McDaniel, Justin Thomas (2008). *Gathering Leaves & Lifting Words: Histories of Buddhist Monastic Education in Laos and Thailand*. Seattle: University of Washington Press.

Ñāṇamoli, Bhikkhu (trans.) (1987–91) *The Dispeller of Delusion*. 2 vols. Henley on Thames: PTS.

Nārada, Ven. U. (trans.) (1962). *Discourse on Elements*. London: PTS.

Nārada, Ven. U. (trans.) (1969–81). *Conditional Relations*. 2 vols. London: PTS.

Nārada, Ven. U. (1980). *A Comprehensive Manual of Abhidhamma: Being Abhidhammattha Sangaha of Bhadanta Acariya Anuruddha*. Fourth edn. Colombo: Buddhist Publication Society.

Nattier, Jan, and Prebish, Charles S. (1977). Mahāsaṅghika Origins: The Beginnings of Buddhist Sectarianism. *History of Religions* 16, 237–72.

Norman, Kenneth R. (1983). *Pāli Literature, including the Canonical Literature in Prakrit and Sanskrit of All the Hīnayāna Schools of Buddhism*. Wiesbaden: Otto Harrassowitz.

Norman, Kenneth R. (2001). *The Group of Discourses*. Oxford: PTS.

Pe, Maung Tin (1920–1). *The Expositor*. London: PTS.

Potter, Karl (1996). *Encyclopedia of Indian Philosophies*, Vol. VII: Abhidharma Buddhism to 150 A.D. Ed. Robert E. Buswell, Jr., Padmanabh S. Jaini, and Noble Ross Reat. Delhi: Motilal Banarsidass.

Rewata Dhamma, U., and Bodhi, B. (1995–2011). *Introduction to Narada Mahathera's A Comprehensive Manual of Abhidhamma*. At www.accesstoinsight.org/lib/authors/bodhi/abhiman.html (accessed 18 October 2011).

Rhys Davids, Caroline (trans.) (1993 [1900]). *A Buddhist Manual of Psychological Ethics*. Third edn. London: PTS.

Ronkin, Noa (2005). *Early Buddhist Metaphysics: The Making of a Philosophical Tradition*. London: Routledge.

Saddhatissa, H. (1987). The Summary of Mind and Matter. *Journal of the Pali Text Society* 11, 5–31.

Skilling, Peter (1994). A Note on the History of the Bhikkhuni-sangha (II): The Order of Nuns after the Parinirvana. *World Fellowship of Buddhist Review* 31, 29–49.

Skilling, Peter (2009). Theravāda in History. *Pacific World: Journal of the Institute of Buddhist Studies* 11, 61–93.

Skilton, Andrew (1994). *A Concise History of Buddhism*. Birmingham: Windhorse.

Thittila, Ven. U. (trans.) (1969). *The Book of Analysis*. London: PTS.

5

Indian Mahāyāna Buddhism

JAMES BLUMENTHAL

Background

The ideas, topics, and parameters of Indian Mahāyāna philosophy are immense and diverse. The overarching label covers a wide range of issues, thinkers, and methodological approaches to the philosophical enterprise. And yet, within this breadth and diversity, Mahāyāna philosophies, like all Buddhist approaches to philosophy, have at their foundation a common soteriological aim. The Buddha described the fundamental cause of our suffering as a basic ignorance (*avidyā*) about the way things are and how they function. Due to our ignorance we create dysfunctional habits of mind that inevitably lead to further patterns of thinking, speaking, and acting that result in dissatisfaction and suffering. Because the seeds of these afflictions are uprooted only when one is able to replace the ignorance with insight, a primary purpose of the Buddhist philosophical enterprise is to point out as precisely as possible the nature of our misconceptions which keep us in bondage and suffering. Such conceptual presentations can serve as foundations for meditative exercises leading to a direct, unmediated experience of insight that is the basic requirement for liberating oneself from suffering and its causes – the achievement of *nirvāṇa*. Thus the soteriological goal of achieving the liberative state of *nirvāṇa* provides the basic aim and orientation of all Buddhist philosophy, including the Indian Mahāyāna.

Nevertheless, what distinguishes Mahāyāna when compared with non-Mahāyāna is that the achievement of one's own liberation is seen as a penultimate goal. Driven by great compassion for the suffering of all living beings and the altruistic wish to do all that is possible to be of maximum benefit to others in their pursuit of freedom from suffering, Mahāyānists aspire to become full-fledged buddhas rather than mere *arhats* because it is as buddhas that they can be of greatest benefit.

This fundamental motivation for all Mahāyāna is referred to by the term *bodhicitta*. Perhaps the most classic description of *bodhicitta*, the altruistic and compassionate

A Companion to Buddhist Philosophy, First Edition. Edited by Steven M. Emmanuel.

motivation of the bodhisattva, is found in Śāntideva's famous treatise *A Guide to the Bodhisattva's Way of Life* (*Bodhisattvacaryāvatāra*).[1] The path leading to buddhahood with this motivation is the path of a bodhisattva. Discussions of this altruistic motivation of a bodhisattva are contrasted in Mahāyāna literature with the motivations and paths of Hearers (*śrāvakas*) and the Solitary Realizers (*pratyekabuddhas*). These two ideal figures discussed in early mainstream Buddhism describe the achievement of arhatship as their final goal. As such, upon achievement of arhatship they enjoy the bliss of *nirvāṇa* and cease to take rebirth among the suffering beings of *saṃsāra*. Mahāyānists describe this as a somewhat selfish goal that lacks compassion for the welfare of others. In contrast, the bodhisattva commits to continue to be reborn among the suffering beings of the world until every last living being has achieved liberation. This bodhisattva sentiment is summed up in the famous stanza from *A Guide to the Bodhisattva's Way of Life* by Śāntideva:

> As long as space endures
> And as long as sentient beings remain
> May I, too, abide
> To dispel the miseries of the world.[2]

The particulars of the distinguishing characteristics of the bodhisattva progressing on the Mahāyāna path and the so-called Hīnayānists[3] (Solitary Realizers and Hearers) progressing on their paths find their foundational presentation in Mahāyāna literature in a text attributed to Maitreya called *The Ornament of Clear Realizations* (*Abhisamayālaṃkāra*). This path system literature consists of map-like descriptions of the various states of consciousness of practitioners as they ascend the path from its beginning until the achievement of buddhahood. Commentaries give detailed descriptions of the types of obstacles present in consciousnesses at various stages and the means by which they are removed (see below).

In addition to the critical role of compassion and *bodhicitta* in Mahāyāna thought and practice is the prominence of the related idea of skillful means (*upāya*). Generally the idea refers to the multitude of skillful methods a buddha might employ to lead disciples effectively on the path. This sentiment is presented on numerous occasions in the 8,000 stanza *Perfection of Wisdom Sūtra*, where, for example, it is explained that, though the Buddha's teachings all are of the taste of great compassion, they take a variety of forms to most effectively address the needs of particular individuals and situations (Conze 2001 [1973]). In addition, the idea of skillful means is succinctly addressed in the *Flower Ornament Sūtra*, when the Buddha says, "In this world there are four quadrillion names to express the four Holy Truths in accord with the mentalities of beings, to cause them all to be harmonized and pacified" (Cleary 1993, 276).

Probably the most famous account of skillful means drawn from a *sūtra* source is that found in the *Lotus Sūtra*, where the Buddha employs a parable. The enormous home of a very wealthy man has caught fire. The home has only one door. The wealthy man has three sons, who are engrossed in playing games inside the burning house and are unaware of the fire. The father first tells them they are in grave danger from the fire and must leave the house at once. Not understanding the fire or the danger, they ignore him and continue to play their games. Then he decides to try another tactic. He entices them with promises of deer carts, ox carts, and goat carts outside, objects with which he knows they enjoy playing as they customarily have enjoyed them in the past. This promise of gifts motivates them to run out of the burning house as quickly as possible. When they get out of the burning house, the father gives each a carriage drawn by a white ox and covered in jewels. The Buddha explains that the father was not guilty of misleading his sons by enticing them with three different types of carts to suit their present mentalities. He was using skillful means. In a similar way, the Buddha teaches three different vehicles, but all culminate in the bodhisattva vehicle leading to buddhahood. He could have taught the bodhisattva path originally to them all, but not everybody was inclined to the bodhisattva path at the time. Some would benefit more from the Hearer's path or Solitary Realizer's path. Thus, according to the *Lotus Sūtra*, he used skillful means at appropriate times to offer a variety of teachings including also the Hearer's path and the Solitary Realizer's path – those best suited to each type of person – while knowing that, in the end, all culminate in the bodhisattva path leading to buddhahood.

In the Mahāyāna tradition, the notion of skillful means has been employed in a variety of contexts to provide a theoretical justification for hierarchically organizing varying and competing Buddhist philosophical systems. In these settings the common argument is that the Buddha offered a spectrum of explanations with varying degrees of philosophical subtlety to accord with the predispositions and mentalities (karma) of the variety of Buddhist disciples. Thus, in one context or to one group of disciples, he may have taught that things exist and, in another, that all phenomena lack inherent existence. It is argued that, over the centuries, a variety of Buddhist philosophical systems emerged (e.g., Vaibhāṣika, Sautrāntika, Yogācāra, and Madhyamaka) in response to his varied descriptions of reality to different disciples. Later Buddhist inheritors of this diversity needed to make sense of it all, including what seemed like internal inconsistencies. Understanding the variations as a byproduct of skillful means has been a useful hermeneutical tool. Often these hierarchical presentations valorize the pedagogical utility of engagement with "lower" systems of thought as philosophical stepping-stones that ripen the mind for understanding the higher systems, and ultimately the highest (whichever that may be according to the individual or school presenting the hierarchy at hand). There are many examples of variations on this theme, from the P'an-Chiao systems of China to the various tenet-system texts (*siddhānta, grub mtha'*) or doxographies of India and Tibet.

Though the notion of "schools" of Mahāyāna philosophy can mistakenly lead one to infer a relative homogeneity among thinkers and systems of ideas, the description of Mahāyāna as largely falling into two main schools, Madhyamaka and Yogācāra (with numerous sub-schools and/or varying interpretations within those schools), does provide a taxonomy that is useful in approaching Mahāyāna systems of thought. This is how many Indian Mahāyānists, including doxography authors such as Bhāviveka,[4] Śāntarakṣita,[5] and Bodhibhadra,[6] go about organizing the Indian systems of thought in their presentations of Indian philosophical views.

Mahāyāna teachings rely on *sūtras* attributed to the Buddha that most likely were not publicly known until centuries after the historical Buddha's passing and are generally not accepted by non-Mahāyānists as authentic scriptures in the sense of having actually been taught by the historical Buddha. Such *sūtras*, including the corpus of the

Perfection of Wisdom Sūtras (*Prajñāpāramitāsūtra*), *The Sūtra Unraveling the Thought* (*Saṃdhinirmocanasūtra*), and the *Entrance to Lanka Sūtra* (*Laṅkāvatārasūtra*), among others, are the primary canonical sources for Mahāyāna philosophers such as Nāgārjuna (c. 150 CE) and Asaṇga (c. 325 CE).

Moreover, there are several key ideas that signal a Buddhist philosophical system as belonging to the Mahāyāna. Perhaps foremost among these, and the central subject of the *sūtras* mentioned above, is the notion that all persons and phenomena are properly characterized by the term "emptiness" (*śūnyatā*). Different Mahāyāna thinkers will describe the contours of emptiness in varying ways (discussed below), but the basic idea that persons and phenomena are empty of an enduring essence, or an independent, absolute way of existing, is an idea common to all. Though emptiness is interpreted variously by different Mahāyāna philosophers, it is nonetheless a key marker that distinguishes Mahāyāna from non-Mahāyāna. Rather than simply use the term "selflessness" (*anātman*), Mahāyānists argue that emptiness, with all that that term means and implies, is a much more subtle description of the nature of reality. In addition, emptiness or "essencelessness" is said to be an apt descriptor not only for persons but for all phenomena, whereas Mahāyānists contend that non-Mahāyānists generally discuss non-Self only as it applies to persons.

Some argue that this is simply a more subtle and refined rendering or development of basic pan-Buddhist ideas that trace back to Buddhism's earliest period, namely ideas such as impermanence (*anitya, annica*), dependent-arising (*pratītyasamutpāda, praticcasamuppāda*), and selflessness. However, the Mahāyāna characterization of all entities as being empty of essences is contrasted with non-Mahāyāna depictions of the world of saṃsāra, which is populated by suffering sentient beings as being fundamentally constituted by irreducible *dharmas*, infinitesimally small particles that are the real building blocks of the phenomenal world. Mahāyānists reject the notion of irreducible *dharmas* that are true and real. By rejecting the real or essential existence of even the supposed building blocks of the phenomenal world, Mahāyāna thought began to look like a quite radical departure from earlier mainline Buddhist thought. By denying the essential reality of the *dharmas*, Mahāyānists are left to explain the everyday experience of the unenlightened. In other words, they need to explain conventional reality. This is done in a variety of ways by Mahāyāna philosophers, including by way of variations of schema such as the two truths – ultimate truth (*paramārtha-satya*) and conventional truth (*saṃvṛti-satya*) – and the three natures – constructed nature (*parikalpitasvabhāva*), the dependent nature (*paratantrasvabhāva*), and the perfected nature (*pariniṣpannasvabhāva*) – as well as by way of epistemological schemas and systems of analysis advocated in the *pramāṇa* tradition.[7]

Historically two major "schools" of Mahāyāna philosophy emerged in the early centuries of the Common Era and continued to be commented upon, interpreted, and revised for roughly a millennium in India, not to mention further interpretations from Tibet and East Asia. The earlier of the two, the Madhyamaka, was first articulated and systematized by Nāgārjuna on the basis of his interpretation of the *Perfection of Wisdom Sūtras* in the second century. His thought and its proper interpretation has been the topic of extensive and ongoing commentary, analysis, and debate across Asia and beyond for nearly two millennia. Among the notable Indian Madhyamaka thinkers were Āryadeva (c. third century CE), Buddhapālita (470–540 CE), Bhāviveka

(500–570 CE),[8] Candrakīrti (600–650 CE), Śāntarakṣita (725–788 CE) and Kamalaśīla (740–795 CE).

The second of the Mahāyāna schools to emerge, Yogācāra/Cittamātra, was first systematically presented by Asaṇga and his half-brother Vasubandhu in the fourth century on the basis of more recently publicly known *sūtras* such as *The Sūtra Unraveling the Thought* (*Saṃdhinirmocanasūtra*) and *The Descent into Lanka Sūtra* (*Laṅkāvatārasūtra*). Subsequent thinkers associated with the Yogācāra school include the groundbreaking Buddhist logician-epistemologists (*pramāṇa* thinkers) Dignāga (c. 450 CE) and Dharmakīrti (c. 625 CE), as well as subsequent commentators such as Devendrabuddhi (c. 650 CE), Śākyabuddhi (c. 675 CE), Sthiramati (c. sixth century CE) and Dharmapala (d. 561 CE).

Madhyamaka

The foremost thinker and so-called founder of the Madhyamaka school of Māhāyana philosophy was Nāgārjuna, who authored several important philosophical treatises, the most famous of which is *The Fundamental Verses of the Middle Way* (*Mūla madhyamakakārikā*). The central idea in Madhyamaka philosophy is the notion that all persons and phenomena are empty of essence (literally "own existence," *svabhāva*) of any enduring or independent nature. On first glance this does not seem like a particularly radical idea for a Buddhist to posit, since in the earliest teachings the Buddha taught impermanence and dependent-arising, two ideas which when considered together seem to imply the emptiness (*śūnyata*) of all things. However, early Buddhist attempts to systematize the view focused on reducing the gross phenomena of the world to irreducible particles, which were described as the ultimately real building blocks of the phenomenal world. Thus, according to early systematization of Buddhist thought into schools such as the Vaibhāṣika, while gross, dependently arisen phenomena such as books and so forth are mere conventional truths and do not ultimately exist as books, the partless particles of which books are constituted do ultimately exist, have essences or *svabhāva*, and are ultimate truths. Nāgārjuna's Madhyamaka thought puts forth a new way of describing ultimate and conventional truths. He goes to great lengths to reject the existence of *svabhāvas* entirely, thus undermining the ultimate reality of even the building blocks of the phenomenal world as described by earlier Buddhist thinkers. It is the rejection of *svabhāvas* that is the recurring theme and guiding insight of his (and the Madhyamaka tradition's) most important treatise, *The Fundamental Verses of the Middle Way*.

Nāgārjuna frames much of his thought as coursing a philosophical middle way between two extremes. On the one hand, he rejects eternalism, the idea that anything endures for more than a moment. On the other, he rejects nihilism in the sense of an absolute nothingness where phenomena do not exist at all. Ultimately phenomena have no essences. Conventionally they do exist merely as momentary, dependently arisen phenomena. Thus the rejection of essences, while unsettling from a Vaibhāṣika perspective, does not entail full-fledged nihilism, according to Nāgārjuna. It is the middle way between these two extremes from which the Madhyamaka ("Middle Way") school derives its name.

The critical link between ultimate and conventional truths for Nāgārjuna is the idea of dependent-arising (*pratītyasamutpāda*). The central role of dependent-arising as a bridge between conventional and ultimate truths and Nāgārjuna's rejection of essences means that his rejection of essences is fundamentally a rejection of the independent existence of anything. All existent phenomena exist in dependent relationships with other phenomena. Because entities are fleeting and depend for that fleeting existence on other momentary entities that cause them to arise, they must *not* have essences. Nāgārjuna thought that the Vaibhāṣika idea that there could exist irreducible particles that were not dependently arisen or dependent upon relations with other entities and therefore had essences was absurd. According to Nāgārjuna, entities depend on fleeting causes for their momentary existence and/or on relations to other entities for their conventional identity. All entities exist in dependence upon relationships. Conventional truths are those dependent entities upon which those who are ignorant of the way in which they actually exist superimpose essences and fixed identities. They exist merely as dependent entities but without the essences that ignorant persons habitually impute to them.

All Buddhist schools agree that the removal of ignorance and the cultivation of experiential insight are the necessary conditions for the elimination of suffering. The details about how this ignorance and insight are described lies at the heart of the differences between Buddhist philosophical schools. The Vaibhāṣikas argue that the basic ignorance one must overcome is the mistaken belief that there exists a truly existent self (*ātman*), an essential or enduring and independent personal identity. According to Nāgārjuna and the Mādhyamikas, all entities, not just persons, lack an enduring independent essence or identity. To see things as they really are – the basic insight required to uproot the afflictions that keep people bound in suffering – is to see the emptiness of all persons and phenomena.

Nāgārjuna's first commentator, Āryadeva (c. third century CE), was universally accepted as an authoritative interpreter of Nāgārjuna's thought by all subsequent Madhyamaka philosophers, but consensus seems to have ended there. Disagreements and debates about the proper understanding of Nāgārjuna's thought and insights by later Madhyamaka commentators continued until the end of the Buddhist era in India. Perhaps the most noteworthy disagreement, one that became particularly prominent for Tibetan inheritors of Indian Madhyamaka but certainly one that is grounded in Indian Madhyamaka debates, concerns the role of "independent inferences" (*svatantrānumāna*) in Madhyamaka discourse. Since Dignāga (c. 450 CE) developed the earliest systematic form of Buddhist logic, his method became the standard among most Buddhist philosophers, including most Mādhyamikas. Yet a heated debate over the appropriateness of the use of independent inferences commenced soon afterwards in the writings of some early Madhyamaka philosophers. Though the debate lay dormant for several centuries in India, the issue arose again towards the end of Buddhism there and became a critical point of contention among Tibetan interpreters of Indian Madhyamaka.

Buddhapālita (c. 500 CE) was the first Mādhyamika after Dignāga to comment on Nāgārjuna. He did not employ independent inferences, but rather used a method of reasoning he believed to be consistent with Nāgārjuna's own, one which drew out the consequences (*prasaṅga*) or logical absurdities entailed in asserting the existence of essences. It does not appear that Buddhapālita saw himself as doing anything radical. However, the next Madhyamaka commentator, Bhāviveka (c. sixth century CE), took great exception to Buddhapālita's failure to use independent inference to establish the view of emptiness. He argued that it was alright for Nāgārjuna, as a "root text" or treatise author, to use only consequences, but that it was the duty of a Madhyamaka commentator to establish the view of emptiness with independent inference. Without establishing the view, he argued, one runs the risk of falling into the extreme of nihilism. In response, Candrakīrti (c. 625 CE) came to Buddhapālita's defense, arguing that he was exactly correct in his methodology of using only consequentialist reasoning. Moreover, Candrakīrti argued that Bhāviveka was making a fundamental methodological error in utilizing independent inferences to establish the view of emptiness. In an argument further developed by Tsongkhapa (1357–1419 CE) in Tibet, Candrakīrti argued that the utilization of independent inferences was actually incompatible with holding Madhyamaka tenets, because the very use of this method of reasoning would entail acceptance of the absolute, independent existence of those entities whose emptiness of independent existence a Mādhyamika is ostensibly attempting to establish. The reason is that independent inferences require valid establishment by both the proponent and the opponent of a commonly appearing subject of an argument. To use an example, if the book is the subject about which one is trying to establish the emptiness of an inherent nature in the book, that subject (the book) must be commonly known to both participants in the debate. It must appear in precisely the same way to both the proponent and the opponent of the argument if the argument is to make sense. In order for such a criterion to be met, Candrakīrti argues that the book must have some absolute independent mode of existence such that it can appear in precisely the same way to the advocates of each side of the argument.

According to the textual record that remains, it seems that for several centuries the vast majority of Madhyamaka philosophers utilized independent inferences and seem to have ignored Candrakīrti's argument. There is evidence that in the late period (eleventh–thirteenth centuries) in India, particularly in Kashmir, Candrakīrti's interpretation and methodology began to gain support. Discussions of the role of logic and conceptual thinking were central issues of debate among Tibetan authors (some of whom studied in Kashmir with late Indian followers of Candrakīrti) from the eleventh to fifteenth centuries (see Vose 2009). In fact the issue became so prominent among Tibetan doxographers that sub-schools of Madhyamaka are commonly distinguished according to the type of reasoning they employ.[9] Followers of Bhāviveka generally who utilize independent inference are categorized as "Svātantrika-Mādhyamikas" (*dbU ma rang rgyud pa*) and followers of Candrakīrti who favor the use of consequentialist reasoning are categorized as "Prāsaṇgika-Mādhyamikas" (*dbU ma thal 'gyur ba*).

Yogācāra/Cittamātra

The Yogācāra school (also known as Cittamātra) of Mahāyāna philosophy also makes use of the technical term "emptiness" (*śūnyatā*) in its descriptions of the essenceless way in which things are said to exist, yet the details of the way this is explained are strikingly different from those of their Madhyamaka counterparts. Early Yogācāra thinkers, such as Asaṇga and Vasubandhu, place a much greater emphasis on the mind (*citta*) or consciousness (*vijñāna*) and its role both in the way in which entities are mistakenly perceived under the sway of ignorance and in the descriptions of how entities exist. While Nāgārjuna described entities as empty of essences (*svabhāva*, literally "own nature") in and of themselves, early Yogācārins described entities as empty of essences that are utterly distinct from the consciousness perceiving them. Entities are empty of subject–object duality.

A marked emphasis is placed on the role of consciousness and the subjectivity implicit in the perception of all entities. Put another way, Nāgārjuna describes emptiness in terms of a lack of independence from relationships with causes, parts, others, and so forth. Asaṇga and Vasubandhu describe emptiness in terms of a lack of independence in the relationship between an object and the consciousness perceiving it.

Perhaps the most important source for this emergent school of thought was *The Sūtra Unraveling the Thought*. In the *sūtra*, a disciple named Paramārthasamudgata respectfully asks the Buddha to explain the apparent contradictions between his explanation of entities in earlier discourses (those referenced by Vaibhāṣikas), in which he describes entities as existent, and those in later discourses such as *The Perfection of Wisdom Sūtras* (those utilized by Nāgārjuna and subsequent Mādhyamikas), in which he says all entities are empty of real essences. The Buddha's response details what will later be systematized by Asaṇga and Vasubandhu as a Yogācāra theory of three natures (*svabhāva*) and corresponding non-natures (*asvabhāva*), or elements that the three natures lack.[10] The Buddha explains that when he said all phenomena have a nature he meant that they have these three natures, and when he said they were empty of having natures he meant that for each of those three there is a corresponding lack of nature. The three natures are: the constructed nature (*parikalpitasvabhāva*), the dependent nature (*paratantrasvabhāva*), and the perfected nature (*pariniṣpannasvabhāva*).

The theory of the three natures is the centerpiece of Yogācāra thought. All entities are said to be of three natures. In keeping with the critical role played by consciousness in Yogācāra thinking, each of the three natures describes entities in part in terms of their relationship with the subjects perceiving them. The dependent nature plays a critical role in the three-nature theory because it serves as the basis for explaining the other two natures. The notion of entities being dependently arisen is an idea basic to all Buddhist thought and is incorporated into Yogācāra thought here. All phenomena are characterized by their dependent natures in that they all depend on consciousness. Such phenomena are said to be empty of self-production. Independent self-production entails eternalism because an object's nature would be to (re)produce itself continually as itself with a nature to reproduce itself again, and so on. A constructed nature is ignorantly imagined to be utterly distinct from the consciousness perceiving it. In other words, it is mistakenly taken to exist independent of its relationship with the consciousness in which it appears. In that sense, the notion of an object existing in a dualistic relation to consciousness is an ignorant mental construction not reflecting the reality of the situation. According to the Yogācārins, this is the ignorance that needs to be purged and replaced with insight in order to uproot suffering and its causes. It also happens to be our ordinary way of experiencing the world. Since no entity actually exists this way in the world, its corresponding non-nature is its lack of existence by way of its own characteristics. The perfect nature is the nature of entities reflective of this insight about how they actually exist, as empty of independence from consciousness, empty of subject–object duality. Its corresponding non-nature is its lack of any of the qualities of the constructed nature.

Given the three-nature theory, Asaṅga and Vasubandhu need to explain what it is that causes these experiences of objects in the first place. Nāgārjuna explains the experience of conventional truths, the objects of the phenomenal world, in terms of their dependently arisen nature and a causal relationship between objects of consciousness and the perception of those by consciousness. For the Yogācāra thinkers, this all really begins and ends with consciousness itself. Buddhist philosophers other than Yogācārins all describe humans as having six types of consciousness, the five sense consciousnesses and the mental consciousness. Yogācārins describe two additional consciousnesses: the afflicted mentation (*kliṣṭmanas*) and the storehouse consciousness (*ālayavijñāna*). The cause of our perception of a phenomenal world is not material objects, but the ripening of karmic seeds (*bīja*) that are all maintained in our storehouse consciousness. When the karmic seed for seeing a particular book comes to fruition, I experience that book. The cause is the seed in the consciousness, and the experience of the object is a projection that, under the sway of ignorance, mistakenly conceives of its objects as distinct. The seventh consciousness, afflicted mentation, is simply that consciousness that wrongly imputes a notion of self (*ātman*) to the storehouse consciousness, mistakenly considering it to be a real self.

Later Yogācāra thinkers, for example Dignāga and Dharmakīrti, in conversation with non-Buddhist philosophers of language, epistemologists, and logicians, developed sophisticated theories of perception that went on to influence later Madhyamaka thinkers such as Bhāviveka (c. 500–570 CE) and Śāntarakṣita (725–788 CE), among others. These developments included formal methods for logical argumentation that not only enabled Buddhist philosophers to posit criteria for establishing the validity of their own theories but also gave them the basic structures for debating with other Buddhists and their non-Buddhist counterparts. Public debates among representative philosophers from rival schools were a relatively frequent occurrence in India during this period, and royal patronage of monasteries and traditions was often at stake in the more celebrated encounters.

Related to the increasingly sophisticated treatments of theories of perception were varying accounts of what it means when early Yogācārins claim that subject–object duality is a function of ignorance. Some argued that the ignorance refers to the perception of duality but does not impact the contents of perception. Figures such as Devendrabuddhi argued along these lines and were categorized by later Indian and Tibetan doxographers as "Proponents of True Representations" (*satyākāravāda, rnam bden pa*). The opposing stance on this issue, advocated by Yogācārins such as Śākyabuddhi, held that the representations in the experience, the contents of perception, were mistakenly construed due to ignorance in addition to the basic misconception of subject–object duality. Such figures argued that the contents of the perception of an ignorant being are false, and are thus referred to as Yogācāra "Proponents of False Representations" (*alīkākāravāda, rnam brdzun pa*).

Yogācāra-Madhyamaka

Several later Mahāyāna thinkers in India, such as Āryavimuktsena (c. 450 CE), Kamalaśīla (c. eighth century CE), Ratnākaraśānti (c. eleventh century CE), attempted to construct ways of reconciling the major streams of Mahāyāna philosophy. Perhaps the most prominent among those attempting to reconcile the two streams of thought came from Kamalaśīla's teacher, Śāntarakṣita. He was a syncretic philosopher who attempted to bring early Yogācāra thinking along with the logico-epistemological insights of Dignāga and Dharmakīrti into a fundamentally Madhyamaka framework.

Śāntarakṣita's approach was to incorporate Yogācāra ideas into a Madhyamaka two truths framework at the stage of conventional truth, and a fundamentally Madhyamaka analysis was employed in presentations of ultimate truth. At the same time he integrates many of the elements of Dharmakīrti's epistemology, including his theories of perception, use of inferential reasoning, acceptance of the reflexive awareness (*svasaṃvedana*) of consciousness, and rejection of objects that are utterly distinct from consciousness. In fact the last of these is incorporated into Śāntarakṣita's presentation of the two truths.

Śāntarakṣita describes conventional truths in ways that clearly borrow from his Yogācāra predecessors. He claims that conventional truths are not utterly separate from consciousness perceiving them and should be understood properly in this way by relying on the Yogācāra system. However, while he urges reliance upon Yogācāra ways of describing the ultimate, the perfected nature, he does so by explaining this to be merely an appropriate way of describing the conventional in his fundamentally Madhyamaka system. The incorporation of Yogācāra insights at the level of conventional truths is used as a stepping-stone for Śāntarakṣita. One can begin with conventional analysis to realize that objects are not distinct from consciousness, and then go on to an ultimate Madhyamaka analysis through which *yogīs* know there is no essence or nature at all, even in consciousness. In his further elaboration, Śāntarakṣita describes conventional truths as dependently arisen, impermanent, and causally efficacious. He particularly stresses functionality and causal abilities of conventional truths, leading the reader to categorize his particular type of Yogācāra advocacy (if one must, since he himself refrained from describing himself as anything other than a Mādhyamika) in doxographical terms as a "Proponent of True Representations." By bringing together the Madhyamaka thought of Nāgārjuna, the Yogācāra thought of Asaṅga and Vasubandhu, and the *pramāṇa* thought of Dignāga and Dharmakīrti into a single coherent philosophical system, Śāntarakṣita may be seen as representative of the final major development in Indian Mahāyāna philosophical thought.[11]

Mahāyāna Path System

It is frequently explained in commentaries that the explicit teaching of the *Perfection of Wisdom Sūtras* was the emptiness of inherent existence or own natures in entities and that the implicit teachings were the teachings on the Mahāyāna path system. The path system was said to have been explicitly taught first in a text attributed to Maitreya entitled *The Ornament of Clear Realization*. There were 21 Indian commentaries written directly on *The Ornament of Clear Realization* in addition to other treatises dealing with the topic of the Mahāyāna path system, such as Kamalaśīla's three treatises referred to as *Stages of Meditation I, II, and III* (*Bhāvanākrama*). The Mahāyāna path system is a description of states of consciousness and the obstacles to liberation and buddhahood one encounters as one ascends from the beginnings of the path to complete buddhahood. The details are dizzying in their complexity.

The system is structured around five paths, ten bodhisattva grounds (*bhūmi*), three realms,[12] and two types of obstacles to be removed. There are, of course, differences in interpretation of the details. Here we will present a basic outline of the structure with the caveat that, for individual thinkers, the devil, so to speak, is in the details.

The text describes two general categories of obstacles that need to be removed in order to achieve the primary types of Buddhist soteriological goals. In order to achieve arhatship and liberation from *saṃsāra*, the practitioner needs to remove all of the afflictions or afflictive obstacles (*kleśāvaraṇa*) from the root. These are disturbing emotions such as greed, anger, jealousy, and so forth. In order to achieve buddhahood, not only do all the afflictions need to be removed, but also all of the knowledge obstacles (*jñeyāvaraṇa*) or obstacles to omniscience need to be removed from the root. These are variously described as the subtle stains of karmic residue, the mistaken appearance of inherent existence in the perception of a bodhisattva after rising from meditative equipoise on emptiness, and so forth.

The fundamental structure of the Mahāyāna path system rests on five hierarchically organized paths: the path of accumulation (*saṃbhāra-mārga, tshogs lam*), the path of preparation (*prayoga-mārga, sbyor lam*), the path of seeing (*darśana-mārga, mthong lam*), the path of meditation (*bhāvanā-mārga, sgom lam*), and the path of no more learning (*aśaikṣā-mārga, mi slob pa'i lam*). *Path* in this context should be understood as a state of consciousness. Their descriptions revolve around the types of realizations and the details of the removal of the two types of obstacles on the ascent from the beginning to the state of buddhahood. The path of accumulation marks the entrance to the Buddhist path. In the Mahāyāna context it is said to be indicated by the achievement of *śamatha* concurrent with aspiring *bodhicitta*. Mahāyānists mark the beginning of the path for a Hīnāyanist as the achievement of *śamatha* concurrent with the generation of renunciation. The culmination of the second path, the path of preparation, is distinguished by the individual's first accurate conceptual understanding of emptiness. The beginning of the path of seeing is indicated by the practitioner's first direct realization of emptiness in meditative equipoise. This also marks the first of the ten bodhisattva grounds. Prior to the cultivation of a direct realization of emptiness it is said that the practitioner can merely temporarily subdue the afflictions, but that on the basis of a direct realization one can begin to remove them from consciousness entirely, or from the root such that they will not reappear.

From the beginnings of the path of seeing, which is concurrent with the first bodhisattva ground up through the end of the seventh bodhisattva ground, the afflictions that keep a person bound in *saṃsāra* are systematically removed. Thus at the beginning of the eighth bodhisattva ground, which occurs on the path of meditation, the individual achieves arhatship and thus liberation from *saṃsāra*. This is described in Mahāyāna literature as still short of the achievement of buddhahood. The difference between the achievement of arhatship and the achievement of buddhahood is the removal of the knowledge obstacles. This takes place on the eighth through tenth bodhisattva grounds, concurrent with the path of meditation. Though there are some debates regarding the descriptions and means by which the knowledge obstacles are removed, a standard position is that they are removed or purified by the immense merits a bodhisattva generates from their great compassion and the actions they take on that basis. Thus it is compassion that distinguishes the Mahāyāna path leading to buddhahood from the non-Mahāyāna paths culminating in arhatship. The path of no more learning, sometimes referred to as the eleventh ground, is the state of buddhahood, which is marked by the thorough eradication of all the afflictions and knowledge obstacles.

The Māhāyana traditions are distinguished by their soteriological goals, their metaphysics, and their methods. These are worked out in a long and detailed history of philosophical argumentation, polemics, and scholasticism. As such, Indian Māhāyana continues today, as it has for nearly two thousand years, to inspire the critical inquiry of some of the world's greatest philosophical minds and the contemplative investigations of some of the tradition's greatest adepts.

Notes

1 For an English translation, see śāntideva, *A Guide to the Bodhisattva's Way of Life*. Trans. Vesna Wallace and B. Alan Wallace. Ithaca, NY: Snow Lion, 1997.

2 Translation by Jeffrey Hopkins: www.bodhicitta.net/The%20Teaching%20on%20Aspirational%20Bodhicitta.htm.

3 Hīnayāna is a pejorative term that began to be employed in India several centuries after the early public emergence of Mahāyāna. It is not a label that applies to any living school of Buddhism but is most profitably used as a marker indicating a theoretical type of Buddhist with no compassion or concern for the welfare of others. It is used in Mahāyāna literature as a pedagogical device to contrast with non-Mahāyāna thought.

4 Bhāviveka, *Blaze of Reasoning* (*Tarkajvālā*).

5 Śāntarakṣita, *Compendium on Reality* (*Tattvasaṃgraha*).

6 Bodhibhadra, *Treatise Assembling the Essence of Knowledge* (*Jñānasārasamuccayanibandhana*).

7 The pramāṇa tradition was initially closely related to the Yogācāra school and was soon embraced by most Mādhyamikas as well. See the sections in this volume on EPISTEMOLOGY (Part IIIb) and LANGUAGE AND LOGIC (Part IIIc) for further discussion of the pramāṇa tradition.

8 Following Ruegg's dating (1981, 61).

9 Recent evidence has come to light to suggest the origins of the terms "Svātantrika-Mādhyamika" and "Prāsaṅgika-Mādhyamika" may actually trace back to the late period of Indian Madhyamaka in Kashmir. See Drefus and Tsering (2009–10).

10 This scene in this *sūtra* represents a critical juncture in the emergence of Buddhist hermeneutics. For Buddhists, hermeneutics largely revolves around theories and methods for discerning which discourses of the Buddha are to be considered definitive (and what that means) and which require interpretation from among the enormous body of discourses attributed to the Buddha. We also find in the *Sūtra Unraveling the Thought* the first mention in Buddhist canonical literature of a framework of "three turnings of the wheel" as a hermeneutical strategy for interpreting the apparent contradictions in the Buddha's

teachings. "First turning" teachings are those early discourses that are made most use of by philosophical schools such as the Vaibhāṣikas and Sautrāntikas. "Second turning" teachings are associated primarily with the corpus of *Perfection of Wisdom Sūtras* that formed the canonical basis for the Madhyamaka school. "Third turning" *sūtras* are those used primarily as canonical sources for the Yogācāra school. A wide variety of interpretive schemas have been employed for interpreting these teachings and concepts.

11 For more on Śāntarakṣita and his syncretic approach to Mahāyāna, see Blumenthal (2004, 2009).

12 The three realms are the desire realm, the form realm, and the formless realm.

References

Blumenthal, J. (2004). *The Ornament of the Middle Way: A Study of the Madhyamaka Thought of Śāntarakṣita*. Ithaca, NY: Snow Lion.

Blumenthal, J. (2009). śāntarakṣita. In *The Stanford Encyclopedia of Philosophy*. Ed. Edward N. Zalta. At http://plato.stanford.edu/entries/saantarak-sita/.

Cleary, T. (trans.) (1993). *The Flower Ornament Scripture*. Boston: Shambhala.

Conze, E. (trans.) (2001 [1973]). *The Perfection of Wisdom in Eight Thousand Lines & its Verse Summary*. San Francisco: Grey Fox Press.

Dreyfus, G., and Tsering, Drongbu (2009–10). Pa tshab and the Origin of the Prāsaṅgika. In *Journal of the International Association of Buddhist Studies* 32(1–2).

Ruegg, David Seyforth (1981). *The Literature of the Madhyamaka School of Philosophy in India*. Wiesbaden: Otto Harrassowitz.

Vose, K. (2009). *Resurrecting Candrakīrti: Disputes in the Tibetan Creation of Prāsaṅgika*. Boston: Wisdom.

6

Tibetan Mahāyāna and Vajrayāna

DOUGLAS DUCKWORTH

Introduction

The culminating philosophy and practice for Buddhist traditions in Tibet is what is found in tantra, or Vajrayāna. Yet Tibet is unique in the Buddhist world in that it is a place where not only the traditions of tantra (for which it is widely known) are practiced, but where the epistemological traditions of valid cognition (*pramāṇa*) and what came to be known as Prāsaṅgika-Madhyamaka also took root. It is hard to underestimate the significance of this fact, and the enormous influence this convergence had upon the distinctive forms of philosophical and contemplative practices that flourished in this culture.

In particular, the intersection of valid cognition (inspired by Dharmakīrti) and Prāsaṅgika-Madhyamaka (inspired by Candrakīrti) led to a vibrant philosophical tradition in Tibet. The deconstructive critiques of Madhyamaka and the systematic phenomenology of Yogācāra had already come to a synthesis in India, in the works of Śāntarakṣita in the eighth century. As one of the first Buddhist scholars to visit Tibet, Śāntarakṣita was particularly influential in the early transmission of Buddhism in "the Land of Snow." His tradition of Yogācāra-Madhyamaka – which presents the conventional truth in accord with Yogācāra and the ultimate truth in accord with the Madhyamaka – was a powerful synthesis that he brought to Tibet in the formative era of the assimilation of Buddhism there.

The systematic philosophy of Yogācāra-Madhyamaka contrasts sharply with Prāsaṅgika-Madhyamaka. Candrakīrti, who was renowned in Tibet as a proponent of Prāsaṅgika, had argued against central positions of Yogācāra, namely, that there could be minds without objects and that awareness was reflexive (self-aware) by nature. Since Candrakīrti came to be widely accepted in Tibet as the definitive interpreter of Nāgārjuna after the twelfth century, Yogācāra, despite its importance, tended to take a back seat

---

A Companion to Buddhist Philosophy, First Edition. Edited by Steven M. Emmanuel.

to Prāsaṅgika in most Tibetan representations of philosophical systems. However, the philosophical view of Yogācāra by and large can be seen in Tibet to be transposed into Vajrāyāna, and it is Vajrayāna that is held as supreme among all Buddhist paths in the traditions there.

Vajrayāna takes bodily presence as fundamental to the path of awakening, since the body is seen to contain wisdom. Also, bodily processes become central loci of meaning – processes such as birth, sex, and death are inscribed with resonances and significance as they structure worlds and correlate with a grand cosmological narrative. As opposed to the reductive conceptual analyses of abstract, propositional thought, tantra is a philosophy rooted in the body. It is (embodied) "philosophy in the flesh" in the way that Lakoff and Johnson (1999) use the term; or, better yet, a philosophy of "flesh" in a Merleau-Pontian sense – that is, (enminded) bodily flesh interpenetrating with the sensing flesh of the world (see Merleau-Ponty 1968). It is thus perhaps futile to *make sense* out of the Vajrayāna out of context, for it is first and foremost an embodied philosophy, a topic that does not lend itself easily to armchair theorizing, for it calls for a participatory orientation – part and parcel with lived (yet dying), unspoken (yet speaking), and unacknowledged (yet knowing) *performative* dimensions. But with this in mind (and body), we can perhaps here get *a feel* for some of the features that come to define Buddhist philosophy in Tibet.

Philosophical Vajrayāna (that is, Vajrayāna as philosophically articulated) shares a strong continuity with the Mahāyāna and also represents a clear break from it. The constructive role of mind (Yogācāra) and the universality of emptiness (Madhyamaka) both play predominant roles in Vajrayāna. Yet with Madhyamaka there can be a tendency to reify emptiness (at the expense of appearance), and there is a tendency in Yogācāra to reify the mind (and disregard body, which is also a denigration of appearance). Philosophical Vajrayāna professes a system that serves as a corrective to both of these tendencies: by applying the unity of appearance and emptiness (appearing–emptiness) and body–mind in an integrated theory–practice.

Philosophical Vajrayāna

The "resultant vehicle" of Vajrayāna is called such due to taking the effect as the path (Tsongkhapa 1995, 15–16). In the "causal vehicle" of *sūtra* one relates to the Buddha as the goal of a causal process of transformation. However, in the resultant vehicle of tantra the approach is different; one does not see a separate Buddha "out there" to be attained in a distant future, but the Buddha is approached as an immanently present reality accessible *right now*.

One of the most important themes that extends into Vajrayāna from Mahāyāna is buddha-nature (*bde gshegs snying po, tathāgatagarbha*). While many of the practices of the Vajrayāna are also shared with Mahāyāna, and are not different from simply ritual Mahāyāna,[1] the practical application of the theory of buddha-nature in Vajrayāna takes on a distinctive form. According to Tsongkhapa (1357–1419), the renowned forefather of the Geluk (*dge lugs*) tradition, what distinguishes Vajrayāna is the practice of deity yoga (Tsongkhapa 1995, 21) – that is, identifying with the Buddha, or the appearing aspects of the divine (or buddha-) nature.

According to Longchenpa (1308–1364), an important figure in the Nyingma (*rnying ma*) tradition (the "old school" of translations in Tibet), in the causal vehicle one sees buddha-nature as a future event of a causal process, while in the resultant vehicle one sees buddha-nature as the immanently present reality, qualitatively indivisible from its effect, the Buddha (Longchenpa 1996, 1169–70). Not all Buddhist sects in Tibet follow Longchenpa's formulation *vis-à-vis* buddha-nature, but perceiving the qualities of the Buddha here and now is an essential part of the practice of tantra, not only in his tradition but across all major Buddhist sects in Tibet. Arguably, the underlying philosophy behind the practice of deity yoga is the presence of buddha-nature within being(s). That is, buddha-nature can be seen as the philosophical underpinning for the practices of tantra.[2]

In any case, the descriptions of the world in certain (Highest Yoga) tantras radically differ from the negative appraisals of the aggregates, causality, and consciousness that we see in early Buddhists *sūtras*. In particular, these tantras invert the categories that are commonly expressed as negative in *sūtras* and form the basis of a distinctive Vajrayāna philosophy and practice. For instance, in Vajrayāna the truth of suffering arises as the essence of the truth of cessation, and the truth of origin (that is, afflictions and karma) likewise becomes the truth of the path (Mipam 2000, 443). Also, the five afflictions are described as the nature of the five wisdoms in tantra; they are the unceasing display of awareness. And in certain traditions, such as *Kālacakra* and the Great Perfection (*rdzogs chen*), the world is seen at its core not as a product of karma but as, more fundamentally, an expression of wisdom (Kongtrül 2002, 120–35). In this way, the dominant categories of early Abhidharma, such as the five aggregates, are completely overturned and creatively inscribed with positive meanings. This directly parallels how the permanence and purity of buddha-nature in *sūtras* that are classified in Tibet as the last "wheel of doctrine" (*dharmacakra*) overturns the descriptions of impermanence, suffering, and so on, in the first wheel of doctrine. Yet while Vajrayāna is commonly mistaken for the content of the Buddha's third turning of the wheel of doctrine, the content of the three turnings is *sūtra*, not tantra.

Before saying more about Vajrayāna and the nature of the relationship between *sūtra* and tantra, we will first briefly survey a range of ways in which Madhyamaka is represented in Tibet. Madhyamaka takes the place of the highest philosophical view (in the causal vehicle) among Tibetan Buddhist sects, and seeing how different traditions formulate the view of Madhyamaka is an important part of understanding how these traditions relate to tantra and negotiate the relationship between Madhyamaka and Vajrayāna.

Variations of Madhyamaka

An influential representation of Madhyamaka is found in the claim of "other-emptiness" (*gzhan stong*) made famous by the Jonang (*jo nang*) school. In the Jonang tradition, to affirm that the ordinary objects of relative truth exist in reality – such as tables and chairs that exist merely in ignorant, dualistic perspectives – is to fall into the extreme of essentialism. On the other hand, to say that the ultimate truth does not exist and is devoid of its own essence is to stray to the other extreme, the extreme of nihilism.

Avoiding these two extremes is the Middle Way in the Jonang tradition. Followers of this school claim to avoid the extreme of essentialism by maintaining that relative phenomena do not exist in reality, and to avoid the extreme of nihilism by affirming that the ultimate truth really exists.

Dölpopa (1292–1361) is known as the forefather of the Jonang tradition. He famously claimed that the ultimate truth is not empty of itself, but is "other-empty." For Dölpopa, what is other-empty exists within reality; it is real and empty of what is other – the unreal. In this way, the ultimate truth is not empty because it is the true ground of reality; it is "empty" only in the sense that it lacks all relative phenomena. He went on to claim that all phenomena of the relative truth are "self-empty" – that is, they are utterly absent in reality (Dölpopa 1976, 300–3). Relative phenomena are self-empty because they are empty of their own respective essences and not because they are lacking with reference to something extrinsic to themselves.

Tsongkhapa, who came to be known as the forefather of the Geluk tradition, criticized Dölpopa's interpretation as realist by arguing that it misrepresented the genuine meaning of the ultimate truth of emptiness. He said that the ultimate truth is not to be understood as one thing being empty of another, but must be known as a mere absence of true existence. Significantly, Tsongkhapa laid out a distinctive interpretation of Prāsaṅgika and distanced himself from Yogācāra.[3] He said that Prāsaṅgika alone has the correct interpretation of Madhyamaka, and argued that other Buddhist philosophies fall short of the authentic view. Tsongkhapa marks an important line between the old and new schools of interpretation of Madhyamaka in Tibet.

In the Geluk tradition, the genuine ultimate truth is always emptiness and appearance is always the relative truth; emptiness and only emptiness is the ultimate truth. In this tradition, to undermine the reality of ordinary appearances, such as tables and chairs, is to stray to the extreme of nihilism. Yet to say that the genuine ultimate truth is anything other than emptiness (that is, that the ultimate truth is anything other than *a lack* of true existence) is to stray to the extreme of essentialism. Madhyamaka according to this tradition is in between these two extremes.

The Geluk tradition's formulation of Madhyamaka emphasizes how the two truths are experienced from the perspective of an ordinary sentient being. The Jonang tradition, on the other hand, describes the two truths by emphasizing how they are experienced from the perspective of a buddha. In contrast to these two influential traditions, the Nyingma tradition represented by Mipam (1846–1912) asserts the Middle Way as *unity* (*zung 'jug*). In unity, there is no duality, so the duality of sentient beings and buddhas has also dissolved. In the Nyingma presentation of the Middle Way as unity, to claim that anything stands up to ultimate analysis is to fall to the extreme of essentialism. Wisdom or even a divine maṇḍala cannot be found when its true nature is sought by analysis. Thus, for Mipam, there is no true essence in anything, and the position that nothing ultimately exists is the claim of "self-emptiness" (Mipam 1987, 450). With this, his Nyingma tradition claims to avoid the extreme of essentialism. On the other hand, to deny the reality of what does indeed exist conventionally – for example, saying that tables and chairs do not exist in ordinary perspectives, or that wisdom and divine maṇḍalas do not exist in the perspectives of sublime beings (*'phags pa, ārya*) – is to fall to the extreme of nihilism. By asserting the conventional existence of these phenomena, his tradition claims to avoid this extreme (Mipam 1990, 420).

A late Nyingma commentator, Bötrül (1898–1959), regards the Nyingma position above as "self-emptiness" (*rang stong*) in contrast to the (Geluk) claim of "emptiness of true existence" (*bden stong*) and the (Jonang) claim of "other-emptiness" (*gzhan stong*). He makes this distinction based on three different ways of identifying the object of negation among three different representations of Madhyamaka in Tibet: (1) other-emptiness (Jonang/Yogācāra), (2) emptiness of true existence (Geluk/Svātantrika), and (3) self-emptiness (Nyingma/Prāsaṅgika) (Bötrül 2011, 37). He states that the primary object of negation in (Jonang) "other-emptiness" is inauthentic experience, the primary object of negation for the (Geluk) "Svātantrika" is true existence, and the primary object of negation in (Nyingma) "self-emptiness" is any conceptual reference. Accordingly, he says that the two truths can be said to be (1) different in the sense of "negating that they are one" (*gcig pa bkag pa*) in the context of other-emptiness, (2) "the same with different contradistinctions" (*ngo bo gcig la ldog pa tha dad*) in the contexts of (Geluk) Svātantrika discourse, and (3) "neither one nor many" (*gcig du bral*) in (Nyingma) Prāsaṅgika discourse (ibid., 149–50). In this way, he outlines three different approaches to Madhyamaka.

Despite the differences on the surface between these three traditional representations of Madhyamaka, we find a lot in common within their interpretations. Aside from a varied degree of emphasis upon certain aspects of a Buddhist worldview, we do not necessarily find a substantial difference between the Jonang, Geluk, and Nyingma interpretations. We can see this when we look beyond the language of self-emptiness and other-emptiness to see that all three traditions accept a fundamental appearance/reality distinction – the Buddhist doctrine of two truths – whereby it is held that (1) phenomena do not exist in the way they appear to an ordinary being (in which case appearances do not accord with reality), and (2) appearance and reality accord without conflict in the undistorted perception of a buddha.

Also, all these traditions accept that: (1) the undistorted perception of ultimate truth is not the distorted appearance of relative truth (other-emptiness), (2) relative phenomena are not found when their ultimate nature is analyzed (emptiness of true existence), and (3) emptiness in essence is inexpressible (the ultimate of Prāsaṅgika-Madhyamaka). Furthermore, in none of these traditions is emptiness the utter negation of everything – it is not utter nihilism because some type of *presence* remains. It is presence that becomes the primary subject matter of tantra, a topic to which we now turn.

Tantric Distinction

Madhyamaka holds the top place in a hierarchy of four philosophical systems (*grub mtha', siddhānta*) – Vaibhāṣika, Sautrāntika, Mind-Only, Madhyamaka – and each school can be seen in an ascending scale as transcending the limitations of the previous one. The hierarchy of views can also be seen to extend through to tantra, whereby Vajrayāna offers the next philosophical paradigm that resolves the shortcomings of the preceding level of the system (Madhyamaka), while incorporating its insight. In this light, tantra marks a distinct philosophical horizon.

The hierarchy of views in the four philosophical systems of *sūtra* appears to be based upon an internal principle of emptiness – the higher the view, the more increasingly ineffable, indeterminate, or essenceless ultimate reality is acknowledged to be. That is, the philosophical systems of *sūtra* can be seen to depict a hierarchy based upon the empty quality of reality – the higher the view, the more comprehensive is the explanation of emptiness. The increasingly immanent *presence* of the divine (Buddha), however, better represents the internal logic guiding the hierarchy of views within Vajrayāna, the vehicle of tantra. In the context of the four or six classes of tantras,[4] we see how the hierarchy shifts from the principle of increasing *transcendence* (emptiness) – as it is in *sūtra* – to the principle of *immanence*. That is, the higher the view, the more the wisdom and body of the Buddha become accessible as an *immanent presence* in reality.

We can see how the discourses of Madhyamaka deal explicitly with ontology and its deconstruction, *what is and what is not*, whereas a unique subject matter of tantra is a particular type of experience or *subjectivity*. In the philosophical systems represented within the "causal vehicle" of non-tantric Mahāyāna, the *empty* aspect of luminous clarity (*'od gsal*), the fundamental nature of mind, is emphasized, and, in the "resultant vehicle" of Vajrayāna (i.e., tantric Mahāyāna), the emphasis is on the aspect of *clarity* (*gsal cha*). Although luminous clarity is addressed in *sūtra*, the aspect of clarity is not as fully developed as it is in tantra (Bötrül 2011, 96–9).

Emptiness is a quality of objects, as well as a quality of subjective minds, whereas the aspect of clarity concerns the aspect of appearance, and specifically subjectivity, or awareness. By *subjectivity*, I do not mean a mode of consciousness that necessarily relates to a world as a subject encapsulated in a world partitioned into a metaphysical subject–object dualism. Rather, I use subjectivity simply to refer to phenomenological awareness, "being aware." In Vajrayāna, this interior space of subjectivity exhibits modes of awareness (ways of relating to experience) that are coarse and modes that are subtle. Rather than representing the habitual patterns of the coarse (dim and dull) registers of consciousness, the emphasis of Vajrayāna is to elicit a direct encounter with the most subtle nature of awareness. This nature of mind, the fundamental intelligence that is "bright" and "clear," is disclosed in tantra more directly and extensively than in *sūtra*. Thus, the primary distinction between *sūtra* and tantra is made in terms of the subject – or, in other words, the shift from *sūtra* to tantra can be seen as a move from ontology to subjectivity, from substance to spirit.

We see a parallel shift in Hegel's critique of Spinoza's pantheistic ontology, in what he calls "Spinozism." In his *Lectures on the Philosophy of Religion* he says: "God is the absolute substance. If we cling to this declaration in its abstract form, then it is certainly Spinozism or pantheism. But the fact that God is *substance* does not exclude *subjectivity*" (Hegel 1984 [1827], 370). Likewise, the nature of deity in Vajrayāna is not a substance; rather, it is a dynamic subjectivity, the awareness of emptiness and appearance in unity. Deity (Buddha) is not an abstract intellectual category that is a simple metaphysical absence or negation, for it is an experiential presence that is known – actualized and embodied. The mind of the deity is wisdom's subjectivity and appearance is the divine body (and sound is divine speech – mantra). That is, the universe – inside and out – is the (speaking) mind–body of the Buddha, the *dharmakāya*. The subject in tantra is empty (while aware), beyond words (while expressive), and transcendent (while embodied).

The philosophy of Vajrayāna maintains that the subject is wisdom (*yul can ye shes*) and that appearances are divine (*snang ba lha*) (Mipam 2000, 443–57). In *sūtra*, appearances are seen to be illusory; in tantra, however, appearances are also seen as divine. Thus, a "correct relative" (*yang dag pa'i kun rdzob, samyaksaṃvṛti*) of *sūtra* is the "incorrect relative" (*log pa'i kun rdzob, mithyāsaṃvṛti*) in tantra. As for the ultimate truth, while there is some disagreement in Tibet about a distinction in view between *sūtra* and tantra concerning the realized object (emptiness free from constructs), there seems to be no disagreement about the realizing subject being a more subtle awareness in tantra.[5]

For the Geluk school, Prāsaṅgika-Madhyamaka is the highest view, and thus, for this school, there is no difference between the view of *sūtra* (i.e., Prāsaṅgika-Madhyamaka) and that of tantra (Tsongkhapa 1995, 18). While the dominant Geluk tradition makes the tantric distinction based solely on method, this is not the case for Tibetan traditions that assert what we may call "philosophical Vajrayāna" and make an explicit distinction between *sūtra* and tantra based on a *philosophical* view as well. In such cases, we see more of a role for Yogācāra analyses, such as the phenomenological reduction (*snang ba sems su bsgrub*), both in coming to terms with emptiness in Madhyamaka and in the philosophical formulation of Vajrayāna.

In the case of the Nyingma school, "unity" is the key. For Mipam, for example, unity functions both to integrate the discourses of *sūtra* and tantra and to bring together the discourses on emptiness and appearance in the second and third turnings of the *dharmacakra* as representative of the "definitive meaning" (*nges don, nithārtha*). For this tradition, the world of tantra is also reflected within the presentation of Madhyamaka, as opposed to the Geluk and Sakya traditions, which maintain a more strict separation between these two discourses.[6]

In the Jonang tradition, Prāsaṅgika-Madhyamaka is not the highest view even within the philosophical systems of the causal vehicle. We can see with "other-emptiness" how a view of emptiness in *sūtra* (and emptiness articulated as an implicative negation) yields to a view of tantra, one that is not bounded by the constraints that delimit ultimate truth to a negative referent. An implicative negation (*ma yin dgag, paryudāsa-pratiṣedha*) plays an important role in Vajrayāna, where emptiness, or openness, becomes "emptiness endowed with all supreme aspects" (*rnam kun mchog ldan gyi stong pa nyid*). With the Jonang tradition, other-emptiness in Madhyamaka reflects directly the pregnant (fullness of) emptiness in the *Kālacakratantra*. This suggests how, in [Highest Yoga] Tantra, terms come to be charged with exalted values (*sgra mthun don spags*), values that tend to overturn their meanings within the *sūtra* system, as in the case with the afflictions.

Vajrayāna as Pantheism

Vajrayāna in Tibet is *pantheist* to the core, for, in its most profound expressions (e.g., Highest Yoga tantra), all dualities between the divine and the world are radically undone. Although there may be a variety of pantheisms, in *Concepts of Deity*, H. P. Owen characterizes "pantheists" in general as follows: "'Pantheism' (which is derived from the Greek words for 'all' and 'God') signifies the belief that every existing entity is, in some sense, divine" (Owen 1971, 65). A definition of pantheism from the *Encyclopedia of Philosophy* states: "Pantheism essentially involves two assertions: that everything that exists constitutes a unity and that this all-inclusive unity is divine" (MacIntyre 1971, 34). Both of these definitions reflect the view of philosophical Vajrayāna.

In his depiction of the "goal" of pantheism, Michael Levine, in *Pantheism: A Non-Theistic Concept of Deity*, echoes a characteristic of the "resultant vehicle" of Vajrayāna (and Mahāyāna more generally): "The pantheist eschews any notion of their [*sic*] being further goals; for example, the theist's beatific vision; personal immortality; *nirvāṇa*; and even Spinoza's 'blessedness,' interpreted as something other-worldly" (Levine 1997, 347). Levine apparently has in mind a *nirvāṇa* that is conceived as separate in space (i.e., non-Mahāyāna *nirvāṇa*) and time (i.e., non-tantric *nirvāṇa*), not the integral vision of the Buddha in Vajrayāna as an immanent, perfected reality that can be accessed in this body right now.[7]

Rather than being conceived as a separate transcendent world, in Vajrayāna the divine is seen within the world, and the infinite within the finite, as is characteristic of pantheism. As Hegel states: "The real infinite, far from being a mere transcendence of the finite, always involves the absorption of the finite into its own fuller nature" (Hegel 1873, 78). Compare this sense of the infinite with the ("bad") infinite of classical theism in Owen's statement: "The 'in' in 'infinite' is to be taken as a negative prefix. It means that God is non-finite. In order to arrive at a true notion of him we must deny to him all those limitations that affect created being" (Owen 1971, 13). Such a notion of the infinity of God negates the world and makes God an imagined "other" that is separate from the finite world. Such a dualism has the consequence that God becomes valorized at the expense of a devalued world. With Vajrayāna, by contrast, (ultimate) value is not forged at the expense of the (relative) world. Rather, the realm of the Buddha is discovered no place other than in this world and in this body.

A devaluation of finite being is not limited to the modern world, or even to classical theism. We can see similar instances of devaluation of body and world in other forms of South Asian monastic traditions, including medieval Mahāyāna and modern Theravāda. Śaṅkara's (c. eighth century) brand of Advaita Vedānta also shares this feature of world denial, where the world is an illusion that does not exist in reality. In the case of Śaṅkara, union with Brahman entails the dissolution of appearances – an end to the realm of *māyā* along with the world of plurality and difference. In contrast to the acosmism exemplified by Śaṅkara, we see a close parallel with the pantheism of Tibetan Vajrayāna in the non-dual tantric synthesis of Abhinavagupta's (975–1025) Kashmiri Śaivism, where appearance (*ābhāsa*) is a modality of the divine. A principal difference seems to lie in the fundamental role played by compassion in Buddhist Vajrayāna, which is the staple of all Mahāyāna practices.

Notes

1 Indeed, if we had access to living communities of Buddhist Mahāyāna practice in India, as we have in Tibet, we can reasonably speculate that we would find many rituals (e.g., *buddhānusmṛti*) that resemble Vajrayāna practices.

2 The importance of buddha-nature in tantra is reflected in the words of Tenzin Gyatso, the Fourteenth Dalai Lama:

> The substance of all these paths [*Guhyasamāja*, *Kālacakra*, Great Perfection] comes down to the fundamental innate mind of clear light. Even the sūtras which serve as the basis for Maitreya's commentary in his *Sublime Continuum of the Great Vehicle* [*Uttaratantra*] have this same fundamental mind as the basis of their thought in their discussion of the Buddha nature, or essence of a One Gone Thus (*Tathāgatagarbha*, *De bzhin gshegs pa'i snying po*), *although the full mode of its practice* is not described as it is in the systems of Highest Yoga Tantra.
>
> (Dalai Lama 1984, 224; emphasis added)

In the context of explaining a Geluk view, Jeffrey Hopkins affirms: "The fact that emptiness (and the mind fused with it in realization) is called a deity is similar to calling the emptiness of the mind Buddha nature" (Hopkins 2009, 51).

3 At least two of Tsongkhapa's eight unique assertions of Prāsaṅgika are rejections of central tenets of Yogācāra: (1) the unique manner of refuting reflexive awareness and (2) the necessity of asserting external objects as one asserts cognitions (Tsongkhapa 1998, 226).

4 The four classes of tantra are Action Tantra (*bya rgyud*, *kriyātantra*), Performance Tantra (*spyod rgyud*, *caryātantra*), Yoga Tantra (*rnal 'byor rgyud*, *yogatantra*), and Highest Yoga Tantra (*bla na med pa'i rgyud*, *anuttaratantra*). In the Nyingma tradition, there are six: the first three are the same as above, but in place of Highest Yoga Tantra there are the three "inner-tantras" (*nang rgyud*): Mahāyoga, Anuyoga, and Atiyoga (the Great Perfection).

5 Kongtrül stated that proponents of "self-emptiness" claim that the only difference in tantra is the subject (*yul can*), and not the object that is free from conceptual constructs; on the other hand, proponents of "other-emptiness" claim that there is a difference in the object (*yul*) as well (Kongtrül 2002, 716). Sakya Paṇḍita (1182–1251) stated that there is no view higher than the freedom of constructs taught in the "perfection vehicle" of *sūtra*: "If there were a view superior to the freedom from constructs of the perfection [vehicle], then that view would possess constructs; if free from constructs, then there is no difference [in view between tantra and the perfection vehicle]" (translation mine) (Sakya Paṇḍita 2002, 308).

6 In the Geluk tradition, the strict *sūtra*–tantra distinction is textually enshrined in Tsongkhapa's two great works: *The Great Exposition of the Stages of the Path* and *The Great Exposition of the Stages of Mantra*, which deal respectively with topics of *sūtra* and tantra.

7 Pantheism in North-West European traditions has historically been rejected and seen as horrible, not because it is irrational, but because it is pagan. Pantheism does not buy into the metaphysical assumptions of classical theism; there is no separation into a God/world duality. Hegel and Spinoza were labeled "pantheists" and even atheists, although they themselves did not describe their own views with those terms. Hegel even denied that Spinoza was an atheist; rather, he said that Spinoza had "too much God." We see an interesting point of departure in the works of Hegel for considering the relationship between the divine and the world in Buddhist thought. In particular, we can see this within Hegel's insight into the nature of the infinite. Hegel distinguishes between a "bad infinite," which is a series of finite things, and a true infinite that encompasses the finite. Charles Taylor describes Hegel's infinite as follows:

> The true infinite for Hegel thus unites finite and infinite ... he refuses to see the finite and the infinite as separate and over and against each other ... The infinite must englobe the finite. At its most basic level this reflects Hegel's option for an absolute which is not separate from or beyond the world but includes it as its embodiment.
>
> (Taylor 1975, 240)

References

Bötrül (2011). *Distinguishing the Views and Philosophers: Illuminating Emptiness in a Twentieth-Century Tibetan Buddhist Classic.* Introduced, translated and annotated by Douglas S. Duckworth. Albany: State University of New York Press.

Dalai Lama, the Fourteenth, Tenzin Gyatso (1984). *Kindness, Clarity, and Insight.* Trans. and ed. Jeffrey Hopkins. Ithaca, NY: Snow Lion.

Dölpopa (*dol po pa shes rab rgyal mtshan,* 1292–1361) (1976). *ri chos nges don rgya mtsho* [The Mountain Doctrine: Ocean of Definitive Meaning]. Gangtok: Dodrup Sangyey Lama; Eng. trans. in Jeffrey Hopkins, *Mountain Doctrine: Tibet's Fundamental Treatise on Other-Emptiness and the Buddha-Matrix.* Ithaca, NY: Snow Lion, 2006.

Hegel, G. W. F. (1873). *The Logic of Hegel: Translated From the Encyclopedia of the Philosophical Sciences.* Trans. William Wallace. Oxford: Clarendon Press.

Hegel, G. W. F. (1984 [1827]). *Lectures on the Philosophy of Religion.* Trans. R. F. Brown et al., Vol. 1. Berkeley: University of California Press.

Hopkins, Jeffrey (2009). *Tantric Techniques.* Ithaca, NY: Snow Lion.

Kongtrül (*kong sprul blo gros mtha' yas,* 1813–1899) (2002). *shes bya kun khyab* [Encyclopedia of Knowledge]. Beijing, China: Nationalities Press.

Lakoff, George, and Johnson, Mark (1999). *Philosophy in the Flesh: The Embodied Mind and its Challenge to Western Thought.* New York: Basic Books.

Levine, Michael P. (1997). *Pantheism: A Non-Theistic Concept of Deity.* London: Routledge.

Longchenpa (*klong chen rab 'byams,* 1308–1364) (1996). *theg pa chen po'i man ngag gi bstan bcos yid bzhin rin po che'i mdzod kyi 'grel pa padma dkar po* [White Lotus: Autocommentary of the Precious Wish-Fulfilling Treasury]. Published in *mdzod bdun* [Seven Treasuries]. Ed. Tarthang Tulku, Vol. 7, 139–1544. Sichuan, China.

MacIntyre, Alasdair (1971). Pantheism. In *Encyclopedia of Philosophy.* New York: Macmillan.

Merleau-Ponty, Maurice (1968). *The Visible and the Invisible.* Trans. Alfanso Lingis. Evanston, IL: Northwestern University Press [this is Merleau-Ponty's last and unfinished work where he introduces the vital notion of "flesh" (*fr. chair*), which is a subject matter that can speak to the mind–body integration in Vajrayāna].

Mipam (*'ju mi pham rgya mtsho,* 1846–1912) (1987). *dbu ma sogs gzhung spyi'i dka' gnad skor gyi gsung sgros sna tshogs phyogs gcig tu bsdus pa rin po che'i za ma tog* [Difficult Points of Scriptures in General]. In *Mipam's Collected Works* (Dilgo Khyentsé's expanded redaction of *sde dge* edn), Vol. 22, 427–710. Kathmandu, Nepal: Zhechen Monastery.

Mipam (*'ju mi pham rgya mtsho,* 1846–1912) (1990). *dbu ma rgyan gyi rnam bshad 'jam byangs bla ma dgyes pa'i zhal lung* [Words that Delight Guru Mañjughoṣa: Commentary on the Madhyamakālaṃkāra]. In *dbu ma rgyan rtsa 'grel.* Chengdu, China: Nationalities Press; Eng. trans. in Thomas Doctor (trans.), *Speech of Delight: Mipham's Commentary on Śāntarakṣita's Ornament of the Middle Way.* Ithaca, NY: Snow Lion, 2004.

Mipam (*'ju mi pham rgya mtsho,* 1846–1912) (2000). *spyi don 'od gsal snying po* [Overview: Essential Nature of Luminous Clarity]. Chengdu, China: Nationalities Press; Eng. trans. in Dharmachakra Translation Group, *Luminous Essence: A Guide to the Guhyagarbha Tantra.* Ithaca, NY: Snow Lion, 2009.

Owen, H. P. (1971). *Concepts of Deity.* New York: Herder & Herder.

Sakya Paṇḍita (*sa skya paṇḍita,* 1182–1251) (2002). *sdom gsum rab dbye* [Clear Differentiation of the Three Vows]. In Jared Douglas Rhoton, trans., *A Clear Differentiation of the Three Codes.* Albany: State University of New York Press.

Taylor, Charles (1975). *Hegel.* Cambridge: Cambridge University Press.

Tsongkhapa (*tsong kha pa blo bzang grags pa*, 1357–1419) (1995). *sngags rim chen mo* [The Great Exposition of the Stages of Mantra]. Qinghai, China: Nationalities Press. Eng. trans., *Tantra in Tibet.* Trans. and ed. Jeffrey Hopkins. London: George Allen & Unwin, 1977.
Tsongkhapa (*tsong kha pa blo bzang grags pa*, 1357–1419) (1998). *dgongs pa rab gsal* [Thoroughly Illuminating the Viewpoint]. Sarnath, India: Central Institute of Higher Tibetan Studies.
Tsongkhapa (*tsong kha pa blo bzang grags pa*, 1357–1419) (2000 [1985]). *lam rim chen mo* [The Great Exposition of the Stages of the Path]. Qinghai, China: Nationalities Press. Eng. trans. in *The Great Treatise on the Stages of the Path to Enlightenment*. 3 vols. Ed. Guy Newland. Ithaca, NY: Snow Lion, 2000–4.

7

East Asian Buddhism

RONALD S. GREEN

Historical Context

It is unclear exactly when and how Buddhism first entered China. Traditionally it was believed to have arrived with the translators Kāśyapamātaṇga and Dharmarakṣa, who came to Luoyang from Central Asia in 266 CE. However, early records indicate Buddhists were already in the country between the first century BCE and the first century CE. By the late Han dynasty (206 BCE–220 CE) Chinese intellectuals had developed sophisticated literary and philosophical traditions. They legitimized and maintained their aristocratic positions by instituting Confucian-based theoretical and bureaucratic systems of governing. Over time, however, greed and nepotism contributed to the corruption of the Han bureaucracy, which became a factor in widespread peasant revolts. This internal chaos was fertile ground for cultivating alternative views on social and metaphysical reality. The most successful of these were associated with the development of East Asian Buddhist philosophy.

Various historical events around this time had long-term consequences for this development. In the late Han period, a group of Chinese intellectual dissidents left the capital for the provinces. They were attracted to philosophical Daoism (which rejected the social philosophy of Confucianism), observed meditative practices to attain release from attachment to mundane circumstances, and hoped to realize their place in the natural world. Subsequently, in the late Six Dynasties period (222–589), a time of disunity in China, others who were influenced by this group established a movement to discuss metaphysics and other philosophical issues in ways we might compare with later Zen *kōans*. Developing a type of philosophical discourse called "pure conversation" (清談 *qingtan*), participants criticized the socio-political establishment from the standpoint of insightful wisdom (*prajñā*) and practiced Buddhist meditation (*dhyāna*). By the fourth and fifth centuries, Buddhist priests were actively involved. This Daoist–Buddhist syncretism movement helped popularize Buddhism, which in turn enabled monks to

A Companion to Buddhist Philosophy, First Edition. Edited by Steven M. Emmanuel.

exercise social influence. Such influence eventually contributed to the four major Buddhist persecutions in China and further shaped the development of Buddhist philosophy in East Asia.

Another important factor in this development is that linguistic and cultural differences made it difficult to compose accurate translations from Sanskrit. Buddhist philosophical terms such as *śūnyatā* ("emptiness") were unfamiliar to the Chinese. To deal with this, early translators used a style known as "matching meanings" (格義 *geyi*) that assigned what they considered rough Daoist equivalents to troublesome Buddhist concepts. Emptiness was translated as "original nothingness" (本無 *benwu*), a term used by neo-Daoists such as Wang Bi (226–249 CE) to describe cosmology and cosmogony. Other terms, including "*nirvāṇa*" and "buddha," were transliterated much as they are in English. It took nearly 500 years for Chinese Buddhists to abandon *geyi*, and its remnants remain at the heart of much of East Asian Buddhist thinking. Later translators, among them Daoan (312–385) and Kumārajīva (344–413), used different strategies that sent East Asian Buddhism in yet another direction. Kumārajīva's translations were in a polished literary style that increased their popularity. But his translations were not always precise. For example, he did not distinguish between a stupa (mounds where Śākyamuni's and other sages' ashes were allegedly buried) and a chaitya (a site for worship).

The Sui dynasty (589–618) reunified China and honored Buddhism. But because of the persecutions of the previous period, Sui Buddhists wanted to create an original Chinese Buddhism that was equal, if not superior, to that of India. Three features distinguished the native schools that developed during the Sui and early Tang (618–907) periods.

1 There was a shift from the identification of Indian and Central Asian founders to native Chinese founders. This was facilitated by the establishment of a Confucian-based patriarchal system consisting of Chinese monks.
2 Doctrinal classification systems (*panjaio*) were developed to evaluate the relative merits of various Buddhist philosophical teachings. These were designed to prove the superiority of Chinese Buddhist traditions compared to one another and to Indian Buddhism.
3 What has been called a positive worldview developed in contrast with the Indian notion of *duḥkha*, suffering or perpetual dissatisfaction. This was in line with centuries of Chinese predilection for viewing our natural state in positive terms, as seen in diverse writings by Daoists and Mencius.

In the seventh century a new translation tradition emerged with the potential of supplanting the Chinese developments with the philosophy of Indian Buddhism. This was epitomized by the style of Xuanzang (600–664), who had traveled to India to break away from Chinese interpretations and learn native Buddhist philosophy. Even though Xuanzang's translations may have been closer to the originals in many respects, a large number of Chinese Buddhists preferred the meanings they had grown up with, in the old-style translations of Kumārajīva and others. Very soon after his time, philosophical and political conflict arose over Xuanzang's interpretations and eventually the old Chinese understandings prevailed and developed further.

Table 7.1 outlines the Chinese patriarchal system. It indicates the shift from Indian and Central Asian to Chinese founders, which is not only an ethnic change but a doctrinal one. The philosophies of these East Asian Mahāyāna schools and the Zhenyan tradition are described below.[1]

Table 7.1 Buddhist philosophical traditions and founders/systematizers

Six Dynasties period	Sui-Tang period
Weishi (Yogācāra): Vasubandhu (fourth century)	Faxiang: Kuiji (632–682)
Sanlun (Madhyamaka): Kumārajīva (350–409)	New Sanlun: Jizang (549–623)
Niepan: Dharmarakṣa (231–308)	Tiantai: Huiwen (sixth century)
Huayan: Buddhabhadra (359–429)	Huayan: Dushun (557–640)
	Pure Land: Tanluan (476–542)
	Chan: Bodhidharma (c. fifth–sixth century)

Faxiang (法相; Jp. Hossō; K. Beopsang)

Faxiang is the Chinese version of Yogācāra, systematized in India by the brothers Asaṅga and Vasubandhu. The two had many gifted students, including Dignāga (c. 480–540), famous for developing Indian formal logic. Dignāga was followed by Dharmapāla (530–561) and his disciple Śīlabhadra (529–645). The Chinese monk Xuanzang risked his life by violating an imperial ban on traveling abroad so he could study Yogācāra in India. Arriving in 629, he studied under Śīlabhadra and other masters. He returned to China in 645 with many Sanskrit manuscripts, most related to Abhidharma and Yogācāra.

Xuanzang became engrossed in his assignment by the emperor to head a massive scripture translation project at the newly built Cien temple. Meanwhile, one of his top students, Kuiji (632–682), set about systematizing what would be the controversial first Chinese developments of Faxiang. One of his detractors was another student of Xuanzang, the influential Korean monk Woncheuk (613–696). Woncheuk left Cien temple and wrote his commentaries on the Yogācāra texts, which eventually became standard in China and throughout East Asia. In contrast, the Japanese monk Dōshō (629–700) studied closely under Xuanzang and Kuiji. In 660 he introduced Kuiji's version of Faxiang to Japan under the name Hossō. However, Hossō's doctrinal foundation was soon changed to Woncheuk's version by other Japanese monks who subsequently returned from China and by Korean monks living in Japan.

The words Faxiang, Hossō and Beopsang literally mean "*dharma* marks" or "*dharma* characteristics" (Skt *dharma lakṣaṇa*). In this case, as in the *Abhidharmakośa*, *dharma* means the elements of existence. That is, *dharma* is what we might cautiously call phenomenal reality. However, how the elements of existence are cognized is described differently in the *Abhidharmakośa* and the later Faxiang tradition. The *Abhidharmakośa* identifies the mind (*citta*) as the source which produces sensations. Its detailed analysis of the process of cognition is in terms of sight, hearing, smell, taste, and touch-consciousnesses, what we can logically and empirically verify about reality. Again noting the anachronism and cultural differences, we could conditionally see this approach as "psychological" in that it attempts to understand the mind by analyzing its functions. In contrast and with the same qualifiers, we can call Yogācāra's approach to mind "phenomenological." While Yogācāra is as logical and empirically oriented as the *Abhidharmakośa*, its methodology and assumptions are different, based in part on meditative insights. In a sense, then, the *Abhidharmakośa* maps the mind in terms of elements of existence, from the outside in; Yogācāra does the same from the inside out. Yogācāra analysis proceeds by indentifying and observing eight components of mind or "consciousnesses" (Skt *vijñāna*) and their interactions. One point of contention among adherents to Yogācāra theory that gave rise to East Asian strains is the interpretation of the cognitive function of the eighth of these, the *ālāyavijñāna* or storehouse consciousness.

The *ālāyavijñāna* is considered the repository of our past actions or karma. In short, it is the part of the mind that takes sights, sounds, etc., and interprets them according to present circumstances. Perception is conditioned by memories of past experiences deposited in the *ālaya*. For Faxiang, cognition involves four elements: (l) the perceived, (2) the perceiver, (3) awareness of the perceiver perceiving, and (4) awareness of that awareness. Other Yogācāra commentators disagree. Of these four elements of cognition, Sthiramati (c. 420–550) acknowledged only the first, Nanda (c. sixth century) the first two, Dignāga the first three, and, finally, Dharmapāla all four. Faxiang follows Dharmapāla's interpretation.

Faxiang traditionally relies on six *sūtras* and eleven *śāstras* for theoretical grounding. Foremost is the *Treatise on Consciousness-Only* (Ch. *Cheng Weishi Lun*) sometimes called by its Sanskrit equivalent name *Vijñaptimātratāsiddhi-śāstra*.[2] The text was composed by Xuanzang, translating Vasubandhu's *Thirty Verses on Consciousness-Only* (Skt *Triṃśikā-vijñaptimātratā*) and incorporating three of ten commentaries on it that Xuanzang discovered in India, including that of Dharmapāla. The *Treatise on Consciousness-Only* gives the details of the four elements of cognition based on Dharmapāla's tradition and different from the Yogācāra traditions developed by other Indians. Like other Yogācāra traditions, however, Faxiang finds that the world as we ordinarily know it is a mental fabrication.

Another important factor in Faxiang's eventual philosophical divergence from Indian traditions is Yogācāra's adherence to *gotra* theory. Accordingly, sentient beings are predestined by karma to be born into one of five lineages. These are śrāvakas, pratyekabuddhas, bodhisattvas, indeterminate beings, and icchantikas with no aptitude for awakening. These five *gotras* are first described in the *Sūtra of the Explanation of the Profound Secrets* (*Saṃdhinirmocana-sūtra*),[3] a prominent Yogācāra text. Like Indian Yogācāra, the early Faxiang tradition of Xuanzang and Kuiji adhered to this understanding. *Gotra* explains five basic dispositions, addressing, for example, why some people have no interest in Buddhism or any ability to understand it. However, there was a large problem in this for some Buddhists. *Gotra* theory appears contrary to the deeply held Chinese belief that all sentient beings have buddha-nature, meaning they are innately enlightened. This is the key ingredient to the positive worldview of East Asian Buddhism. Buddha-nature is accepted by the large and influential Ekayāna traditions, including Tiantai and Huayan. For this reason, some of the *panjiao* schemes of Chinese

Buddhist traditions classified Faxiang as only quasi-Mahāyāna. Likewise, Woncheuk rejected *gotra* theory in his version of Faxiang that was adopted as orthodoxy in China, Korea, and Japan soon after Xuanzang's time, and to the dismay of Kuiji. Another departure came when Chinese Buddhists decided to rewrite the section on bodhisattva ethics found in the Indian *Discourse on the Stages of Yogic Practice* (*Yogācārabhūmi-śāstra*) dated to the fourth century. Referring to *gotra*, the original text says those who are bodhisattvas must acknowledge this and act accordingly. Among the acts described as appropriate for those of the bodhisattva *gotra* are those opposing an unjust ruler and offering material support to the politically oppressed. This may have been the policy of early East Asian Yogācāra, influencing the social projects of Dōshō and his alleged disciple Gyōki (668–749), who was called a bodhisattva in Japan. However, the Chinese apocryphal text *Fawang-jing*,[4] while almost certainly based on the *Yogācārabhūmi-śāstra*, omits references to *gotra* and opposition to unjust civil authority. Given the Chinese partiality for Confucian morality and buddha-nature, as well as the direction of support from the court, it is perhaps unsurprising that the bodhisattva vows of the *Fawang-jing* soon eclipsed those of the *Yogācārabhūmi-śāstra*. The latter became obsolete throughout East Asia.

Sanlun (三論; Jp. Sanron; K. Samnon)

The name Sanlun means "three treatises." The three treatises that serve as main texts for the tradition are the *Fundamental Verses on the Middle Way* (Skt *Mūlamadhyamaka-kārikā*; Ch. *Zhong lun*),[5] the *Twelve Gate Treatise* (Skt *Dvādaśadvāra-śāstra*; Ch. *Shier men lun*),[6] and the *One Hundred Verses Treatise* (Skt *Śata-śāstra*, Ch. *Bai lun*).[7] The first two were written by Nāgārjuna (c. 150–250 CE) and the third by his disciple Aryadeva (c. 170–270). Sometimes another text is added, the *Treatise on the Prajñāpāramitā Sūtra* (Skt *Mahāprajñāpāramitā-śāstra*; Ch. *Da zhi du lun*), attributed to Nāgārjuna and translated by Kumārajīva.[8] Then the tradition is called Silun, "four treatises." Because three of these four texts were translated by Kumārajīva, he is considered the founder of what is called old Sanlun. Later, the monk Jizang (549–623) systematized the ideas and contributed to the methodology of the tradition. He thereby came to be known as the founder of new Sanlun. The philosophy of old and new Sunlun is grounded in Indian Mādhyamaka philosophy. However, there are distinct differences between these traditions.

In the sixth century, Indian Madhyamaka split into two schools: Prāsaṅgika, founded by Buddhapālita (c. 470–540), and Svātantrika, founded by Bhāviveka (c. 500–570). Prāsaṅgika attacked the claims of all schools of thought, revealing their internal contradictions and false premises. Like Nāgārjuna, it held that the truth of non-substantiality (Skt *śūnyatā*) can be revealed by refuting all assumptions about the nature of reality. Svātantrika criticized this method and argued for using Buddhist logic rather than criticism to reveal truth. Whereas Prāsaṅgika made no assertions about the nature of reality, Svātantrika did.[9] Sanlun takes a different approach. Although it also seeks to reveal truth by criticizing claims about reality, it makes more use of other ideas in its three treatises. It employs the two-truth theory expounded in the *Mūlamadhyamaka-kārikā*. That is, there are provisional or conventional truths about reality that are valuable for dealing with day-to-day life. However, there is also ultimate truth we can realize through meditative training, and this truth does not accord with what we ordinarily assume about the world. Similarly, from the *Twelve Gate Treatise*, Sanlun adopts the idea that wisdom has two levels, ordinary knowledge and extraordinary wisdom (*prajñā*). From the *One Hundred Verses Treatise*, Sanlun uses a cognitive argument about the realm of the knower and that of the known. Essentially, although we conventionally believe there is a distinction between these as subject and object, our assumptions are incorrect. The truth of the emptiness of such categories is revealed to us through *prajñā*.

Like Madhyamaka generally, Sanlun believes suffering is caused by attachment to objects, theories and ideas. It constructed a classification system of four categories: (1) non-Buddhists who believe in a self that is the agent that interprets the world; (2) adherents of the Abhidharma teachings who reject the reality of self but believe the elements of existence are substantial and permanent; (3) Satyasiddhi followers who reject the ontological existence of elements; and (4) the Śūnyavādins, who cling to the notion of emptiness as an absolute, including some followers of Madhyamaka itself. Sanlun argued that non-attachment can be achieved through a reorientation of consciousness so that there is achievement of *wuxin* (無心 Jp. *mushin*), no-mind. *Wuxin* is a state of consciousness free of the ordinary identification of self and mind, in which there is actualization of all sentient beings as interrelated and possessing buddha-nature. In these ways, new Sanlun diverges from both the attack-method of the Prāsaṅgika tradition and the logic of Svātantrika. Instead, it develops what can be seen as a devotional theme in the unconditional acceptance of and reverence for buddha-nature. This is the basis for its system of practical ethics.

Old Sanlun was essentially a projection of Indian Madhyamaka. Because new Sanlun emphasizes conventional reality, the idea of dependent co-arising (Skt *pratītyasamutpāda*) becomes more important than that of emptiness. Old Sanlun does not speak of buddha-nature but new Sanlun makes it a focus. The latter identifies buddha-nature with the *dharmadhātu*, the undifferentiated realm of reality experienced when there is no attachment. Thus, Jizang argued, both sentient beings and inanimate objects have buddha-nature. Through these ideas, new Sanlun helped shaped native traditions of Chinese Buddhism in the Sui-Tang period, especially Tiantai.

Tiantai (天台; Jp. Tendai; K. Cheontae)

This prominent East Asian Buddhist tradition takes its name from Mount Tiantai, where the renowned master Zhiyi (538–597) meditated and trained disciples. Zhiyi retreated to the solitude of the mountain after abandoning a prestigious post at the national academy in Nanjing when he realized the depth of student apathy there. Although he is considered the third patriarch of Tiantai, he is thought to have systematized its philosophy and practices. Zhiyi's ideas are preserved mainly in works compiled by his disciples from their lecture notes. Of these, the most important are the *Great Calming and Contemplating* (Ch. *Mohe zhiguan*),[10] *The Profound Meaning of the Lotus Sūtra* (Ch. *Miao fa lian hua jing xuan yi*),[11] and *Language and Phrases of the Lotus Sūtra* (Ch. *Miao fa lian hua jing wen ju*).[12]

Tiantai doctrine is based primarily on the *Lotus Sūtra*, the *Nirvāṇa Sūtra*, the *Prajñāpāramitā-sūtra*, and the *Treatise on the Prajñāpāramitā Sūtra* (Ch. *Da zhi du lun*).[13] These texts describe buddha-nature and explain the grounds for it. For Tiantai, buddha-nature refers to insight into emptiness. Unlike Indian Buddhist logicians, Tiantai masters do not attempt to understand emptiness through dialectical reasoning. Instead, like the Sanlun masters, they emphasize the ethical aspect of emptiness. Accordingly, insight into emptiness is insight into dependent co-arising which brings about the awareness that all sentient beings are interrelated and interdependent. Compassion springs from this realization. In the context of Tiantai, buddha-nature is compassion and it is *tathatā*.

Zhiyi describes ten aspects of *tathatā*: (1) its form, (2) the properties of its form, (3) the underlying essence of its form, (4) its potential function, (5) the manifestation of that function, (6) its cause, (7) its condition, (8) its result, (9) its retribution, and (10) the sum of the above. The ten aspects are meant not to define *tathatā* but to describe features related to it. Tiantai names the *Lotus Sūtra* as the canonical source for the ten aspects. However, its detractors have pointed out that the ten aspects appear only in Kumārajīva's translation and cannot be found in the Sanskrit version, Dharmarakṣa's Chinese translation, or the Tibetan translation. Just as Sanlun equated buddha-nature with *dharmadhātu*, Tiantai sees *tathatā* as *dharmadhātu*. For Tiantai, awareness of *tathatā* is Buddhist awakening. While meditation is required to gain insight into *tathatā*, Tiantai maintains that doctrinal study is of equal importance. Even though meditation may focus on subjective realization and doctrinal study on objective truth, these and all seeming dualities coexist and are inseparable. This is described in Tiantai's concepts of "3,000 realms in an instant of thought" (一念三千 Ch. *yi nian an qian*; Jp. *ichinen sanzen*) and "the threefold contemplation in a single mind" (一心三観 Ch. *yixin san guan*; Jp. *isshin sangan*). The former is Tiantai's central doctrine; the latter is the method for experiencing it.

The "3,000 realms in an instant of thought" doctrine begins with the idea of "ten realms" described in numerous Buddhist texts and illustrated in "wheel of life" paintings. These are the realms of (1) hell, (2) hungry spirits, (3) animals, (4) *asuras*, (5) human beings, (6) heavenly beings, (7) voice-hearers, (8) cause-awakened ones, (9) bodhisattvas, and (10) buddhas. At first these may have been thought of as physical realms where one is reborn according to karmic retribution. Later, however, and according to the *Lotus Sūtra*, these realms can be seen as psychological states, all present in each person in different proportions at different times. For Tiantai, in any one realm, the other nine are present in some capacity. The number 3,000 was arrived at by first considering that each of the ten realms is involved with each of the other realms, so that 100 realms exist. The ten aspects of *tathatā* are involved in each of these 100 realms, so that 1,000 realms exist. We are said to experience each of these 1,000 realms in three aspects, called three realms of existence. We experience them according to (1) the five aggregates that the Buddha said compose a human being (form, feeling, perception, impulse, and consciousness), (2) temporal conditions, and (3) our environment. Taking this into account, there are said to be a total of 3,000 realms in an instant of thought. Although this may be overly complex and unnecessarily divisive, it is meant to imply the unity and co-dependent nature of the universe.

Tiantai devised "the threefold contemplation in a single mind" as a means of experiencing this universal oneness, which is *dharmadhātu* and *tathatā*. This is a meditative practice aimed at examining one's own mind through the "threefold truth" mentioned by Nāgārjuna in the *Fundamental Verses on the Middle Way*. Accordingly, all things are empty (Skt *śunyatā*); all things are temporary (continually dependently co-arising and going out of existence); all things compose the Middle Path between these. The Middle Path may appear to imply the rejection of the first two as extremes, but Tiantai's understanding is that truth has three aspects that are really one. In *The Profound Meaning of the Lotus Sūtra*, Zhiyi describes this as the "round threefold truth," as opposed to a conceptualization of these as three opposing entities or a linear continuum. Accordingly, the ultimate truth of emptiness, which is the *dharmadhātu*, is not opposed to provisional truth experienced as *tathatā*. Indeed, *saṃsāra* is *nirvāṇa*. Zhiyi also calls this practice the "Round and Abrupt Contemplation." Depending on their aptitudes and level of understandings, practitioners may abruptly begin focusing on any point in the round truth: emptiness, dependent co-arising, or the Middle Path. They would then follow corresponding gradated steps for calming (*śamatha*) and contemplating (*vipaśyanâ*) described by Zhiyi. Since this process is seen as a circle, the beginner's practice is considered no less profound than that of advanced students.

Although Tiantai affirms phenomenal reality, this is not the same as the affirmation by the *Abhidharmakośa*. The *Abhidharmakośa* interprets reality in terms of the elements of existence, which are permanent and unchanging. Tiantai interprets it as emptiness, dependent co-arising, and the Middle Path all in one. As seen above, Zhiyi's conception of calming and contemplating is also different from that of Indian Buddhism. Indian *śamatha-vipaśyanā* practitioners observed calming and contemplation in sequential order, assuming calming produces contemplation. Tiantai sees them as inseparable and as a circle. While calming produces contemplation, contemplation brings calm.

Huayan (華嚴; Jp. Kegon; K. Hwaeom)

The name "Huayan" means "flower garland." It is the Chinese name of the tradition's most important text, the *Flower Garland Sūtra* (Skt *Avataṃsaka-sūtra*). The flower garland is symbolic of the *dharmadhātu*. Huayan conceptualized this as a multiverse composed of an infinite variety of universes, all of which reflect one another. Like Tiantai, Huayan is a native Chinese tradition that became culturally influential and politically powerful during the Tang dynasty. Likely because of this affluence, it was transmitted to Korea and Japan, where it was embraced and financially promoted by rulers and clergy alike. In Korea, as Hwaeom, it is still the most prominent Buddhist doctrinal system alongside Seon (Zen), which is the most popular tradition for Buddhist practice. In Japan during the Nara period (710–794), as Kegon, it was the most dominant among the Buddhist traditions and was the principal school of thought behind the imperial construction of the large statue of Vairocana Buddha in the capital.

The *Flower Garland Sūtra* appears to be made up of a number of books that were likely independent scriptures in India. It is unknown when and where they were assembled as one unit. In China there were various translations of it made between the fifth and eighth century, each of different length and content. Because of its strangeness in tone and themes, Tiantai and other *panjaio* systems classified it as a text expressing the Buddha's ideas within the first seven days of his awakening. Accordingly, at that time the Buddha entered sea-state *samādhi* (海印三昧 Ch. *hai yin san mei*; Jp. *kaiin sanmai*; Skt *sāgara-mudrā samādhi*), a condition wherein one experiences reality directly, without interpretation and evaluation. His thoughts and perceptions are said to have been extraordinarily peculiar and therefore incomprehensible through ordinary patterns of thought. The implication is that the multidimensional and ever evolving nature of reality defies the boundaries of static theories and can best be spoken of through creative ambiguity and uncertainty in language. Proceeding in this way, the central character in the scripture is not the historical Buddha, as in most *sūtras*, but the Buddha Vairocana, a symbolic personification of the *dharmadhātu*. This and other symbols are used to convey the Buddha's experience of awakening.

Huayan describes four patterns of thinking corresponding to four stages of development towards awakening. In each stage, one perceives a particular aspect of the *dharmadhātu*:

1 perceiving the *dharmadhātu* as fragmentary phenomena. This is the ordinary view of the world in which elements of existence are accepted as real and independent. We might call this a naïve realist view. The metaphor used to describe it is of one perceiving each wave in the ocean as a separate entity.
2 perceiving the *dharmadhātu* as empty. In this state, the world is viewed through intuition. It appears that an undifferentiated reality sustains phenomena. The metaphor is of one perceiving the water of an ocean but not seeing the waves.
3 perceiving the *dharmadhātu* as the unity of phenomena and emptiness. In this stage one sees phenomena and emptiness as identical. Only awakened beings can see the world in this way. The metaphor is of seeing the interdependence of the water and the waves.
4 perceiving the *dharmadhātu* as perfect harmony among all phenomena. In this state, all phenomenal existents are seen as individual but mutually interpenetrating to form a whole. That is, one perceives dependent co-arising in empirical reality. The metaphor says one sees that waves are manifestations of water working in harmony with one another as well as the whole.

While the first three stages are found in other Mahāyāna traditions, the fourth is an innovation by Chengguan (738–839), regarded as the fourth patriarch of Huayan. Huayan claims that it is the most complete teaching because the fourth stage goes beyond theoretical understandings of emptiness and perceives the world as an organic unit. The *Flower Garland Sūtra* describes this ecology, wherein each element interacts harmoniously with all others, with the metaphor of Indra's Net. The universe is likened to a divine fishing net of infinite expanse. In each of its knots is a shining jewel like the stars in the heavens. While each jewel shines uniquely and with change, it simultaneously reflects each and every other jewel. The metaphor illustrates the ideas of emptiness, dependent co-arising, and interpenetration central to the tradition.

Huayan developed two theories of causation: *dharmadhātu* dependent co-arising (法界縁起 Ch. *fa jie yuan qi*; Jp. *hōkkai-engi*) and *tathāgatagarbha* dependent co-arising (如来縁起 Ch. *ru lai yuan qi*; Jp. *nyoraizō engi*). Indian Buddhist traditions and Tiantai had referred to the ten realms causation theory wherein karma was thought to play out diachronically and on an individual scale. In contrast, *dharmadhātu* dependent co-arising theory conceptualized causation as occurring synchronically, trans-individually, and on a cosmic scale.

Tathāgatagarbha dependent co-arising sees causation in relation to buddha-nature, the potential for awakening in all beings. Accordingly, we are all innately awakened but suffer because of our ignorance of this. That being the premise, causation is seen as occurring due to the combination of these two factors, human and buddha action. *Dharmadhātu* dependent co-arising is a vision of cosmic harmony. *Tathāgatagarbha* dependent co-arising is about interrelational harmony among beings. Both causation theories were expounded by Fazang (643–712), the famous third patriarch of Huayan. Huayan's emphasis on interconnectedness and universal accord had strong appeal to East Asian sensibilities. Interestingly, and perhaps predictably, its popular message of harmony was seized upon as a means of expanding political influence. Rulers in China, Japan, and Korea sponsored construction projects for large statues of Huayan's universal Buddha Vairocana, seeking to be associated with its power. The face of the Vairocana at China's Longmen grottoes is said to have been modeled in the likeness of Empress Wu Zetian (reigned 690–705).

For some time, Chinese Buddhists debated over two storehouse-consciousness theories that seemed to be opposites. While Faxiang's *ālāyavijñāna* theory said there is a repository for defilement at the base of human consciousness, *tathāgatagarbha* theorists claimed the foundation of all beings is the innate womb of buddhahood. The argument harkened back to the time of Mencius and classical debates over whether human nature is good or evil. The solution seemed to be found in a text known as the *Awakening of Faith in the Mahāyāna* (大乘起信論 Ch. *Dasheng qixin lun*).[14] The text is attributed to the renowned Indian writer Aśvaghoṣa (c. 80–150 CE). It was said to have been translated into Chinese first by Paramārtha (499–569) and subsequently by Śikṣānanda (652–710). However, many scholars today believe it is an apocryphal text composed in China, perhaps by Paramārtha. The text claims that consciousness contains both *tathatā* and *ālaya*, that *tathatā* has a potential "perfuming" power to cleanse defilement stored in the *ālaya*, and that we should have faith in this power of *tathatā*. Commented on and embraced by Fazang, this explanation and the text itself became extremely influential in shaping East Asian Buddhism, even among theorists who acknowledged its likely Chinese origin.

Zhenyan (真言; Jp. Shingon)

The name Zhenyan means "true word," in this case referring to mantra. Mantra is a sound or series of sounds chanted in the belief that so doing will bring transformation of consciousness or other desired benefits. Mantra is typically associated with tantric practices, and Zhenyan is the Chinese version of Tantric Buddhism. Zhenyan seeks realization of oneness with the universe. To achieve this, it uses the "three mysteries," mudrā (hand gestures that are physical symbols), mantra (symbolic vocal sounds), and maṇḍala (visual symbols). These are thought of as mysteries in that the existence of language, for example, is astonishing, as is its potential to transform consciousness. Practitioners conceptualize ultimate reality symbolically personified as the perfect cosmic being, the Buddha Mahāvairocana. Then, by these three means involving the body, speech, and mind, they visualize being that perfect Buddha, imitating the Buddha with the hand gestures and mantra sounds associated with it, as well as by meditating on its image on the maṇḍala. Thereby, "Becoming the Buddha in this Body" (即身成佛; Jp. *sokushin jōbutsu*), a concept popularized by the Japanese patriarch Kūkai (774–835), means both to dwell in the *dharmadhātu* and to realize that reality in the world of *saṃsāra*.

Zhenyan was transmitted to China by the Indian master Śubhakarasiṃha in 716 and again by Vajrabodhi (671–741) and his disciple Amoghavajra (705–777) in 719. China received these teachings just as they were developing in India. Of the two main scriptures for Zhenyan, the tradition holds that the *Mahāvairocana-sūtra* represents the northern Indian Tantric Buddhist tradition, while the *Vajraśekhara-sūtra* represents the southern Indian tradition. The two are believed to have been united in China as one tradition. While this may be, there were additional tantric traditions in India not transmitted to China. The Chinese monk Huiguo (746–805) mastered the *Mahāvairocana-sūtra* under the supervision of Śubhakarasiṃha and the *Vajraśekhara-sūtra* under Amoghavajra. Afterwards, he rose to prominence in the service of the Chinese court, giving tantric lay initiations and instructions to three emperors; however, after Huiguo's death, the short-lived tradition faded to obscurity in China and lingered in fragments in Korea. In Japan, however, the Japanese monk Kūkai, who studied under Huiguo, introduced the tradition under the name Shingon, where it became the most affluent school of thought during the early Heian period, perhaps due in no small part to the force of Kūkai's personality and literary skills. It remains a vital tradition there today.

Shingon does not use the term "tantra" because of the word's association with sexual and other practices outside its tradition. The tradition prefers it be called *mikkyō* (密教), the mysterious or esoteric teachings. Shingon considers itself the most philosophical school of Buddhist thought, while qualifying that its system is experiential philosophy. The tradition interprets *tathatā* as the creative force that is the *dharmadhātu*. Based on Mahāyāna *trikāya* doctrine, Shingon views *dharmakāya* as the personification of *dharmadhātu*, which is called Dharmakāya Mahāvairocana. Vairocana Buddha in Huayan and Mahāvairocana in Shingon are both *dharmakāya* buddhas. However, in the Huayan conception, integration with Vairocana is based on causality. This is dramatized in Huayan's *Flower Garland Sūtra* as the seeker Suddhana passing through 53 causal stages in order to actualize the resultant *dharmadhātu*. Shingon speaks of buddha-mind (*bodhicitta*) as a quality sentient beings share with Mahāvairocana. From the perspective of sentient beings, *bodhicitta* is buddha-potential, just like *tathāgatagarbha*. But, while Huayan requires practice to realize buddha-potential, Shingon believes potential itself has the power to destroy delusion. Practice is considered the means through which the potential is manifested. That is to say, one manifests buddhahood bodily (*sokushin-jōbutsu*), by cultivating the merit of *Dharmakāya* Mahāvairocana with body (mudrā), speech (mantra), and mental visualization (maṇḍala). Thus, Shingon does not speak of causality as Huayan does. It deals directly with the resultant realm.

Shingon agrees with the *Awakening of Mahāyāna Faith* in its analysis of *tathatā* in three categories: its body or essence, its marks or attributes, and its function or practices for cultivating and manifesting its merits. The body of *tathatā*, of *Dharmakāya* Mahāvairocana, which is also the universe, is composed of six physical elements. Its attributes are expressed in the iconography of two maṇḍalas. Its function is manifested through the three mysteries practices.

While Empedocles conceived of four elements composing the world, Pythagoreans, Aristotle, the *Upaniṣads*, Sāṃkhya, and Vaiśeṣika philosophers saw five. Shingon regards *tathatā* as being comprised of six elements: space, wind, fire, water, earth, and mind. All things arise in combinations of these and disassemble again as them. Mahāvairocana and our identity as universal combinations of the six elements are realized through highly symbolic sets of ideas, sounds, and actions. The elements themselves become symbolic. Each also has a corresponding mantrā sound, a shape, a direction, and an associated image of a buddha or bodhisattva representative. The unity of these elements is, again, the *dharmadhātu*, the universe, Mahāvairocana, and human beings. Actualizing the realization of this is the goal.

While the *Mahāvairocana-sūtra* proceeds within the Madhyamaka contexts of emptiness and dependent co-arising, the *Vajraśekhara-sūtra* deals with the mind in reference to transformation, as in Yogācāra. Shingon blends Yogācāra and Madhyamaka theory by referring to awakening buddha-mind together with the emptiness and dependent co-arising of the six elements. Since our bodies are comprised of the temporary associations of these elements and after death will dissipate into new associations of them, Shingon grave markers or stupas (Jp. *gorin hōtō*) reflect this process in various symbols. The six elements are also variously illustrated in Shingon's two maṇḍala, which included intricate relationships among these elements, buddhas, directions, colors, mudrās, and mantras. The Garbhakośadhātu Maṇḍala or Womb Realm Maṇḍala is also known as the Truth Maṇḍala. The Vajradhātu Maṇḍala or Diamond Realm Maṇḍala is known as the Wisdom Maṇḍala. These represent two aspects of Mahāvairocana in numerous ways. The Truth Maṇḍala is female; the Wisdom Maṇḍala is male. The former represents the first five of the six elements; the latter represents the sixth. Truth is the known; Wisdom is the knower. Receiving initiations into the two maṇḍala realms and uniting these through the practice of three mysteries, Shingon followers realize the oneness of the universe.

Pure Land (净土 Ch. *Jìngtǔzōng*; Jp. *Jōdo*; K. *Jeongtojong*)

Pure Land was systematized as a separate tradition of Buddhism in China. While most of its scriptures were written in India, commentaries on them were written in China and rival schools of Pure Land developed throughout East Asia. The True Pure Land Tradition (Jōdo Shinshū) is the most popular form of Buddhism in Japan today. It is a devotional type of Buddhism concerned with a person's salvation in paradise after death and sometimes with creating a utopian society in the here and now. Other devotional types of Buddhism existed in East Asia before the development of Pure Land, which eventually replaced them. It may be that the Pure Land was first conceived not as a final heavenly paradise, but as a Land of Purification where one could temporarily live away from the degenerate world in order to work towards *nirvāṇa*.

Gyōnen (1240–1321) and other historians divided Japanese Buddhist traditions into two broad groups. Those that advocate meditation, the study of *sūtras* or engagement in other practices for awakening are classified as traditions of *jiriki*, self-power. Those that focus on devotion to a savior are called traditions of *tariki*, other-power. The other-power in the case of Pure Land is that of the Buddha Amitābha. Although it may seem at first glance that this defies the spirit of Buddhism, Pure Land Buddhists point out that belief in one's own power is egotistical. Accordingly, if Buddhists truly want to destroy their false image of the self, they must give up the notion that it is powerful and capable of salvation. For Pure Land Buddhists, letting go of attachment to the ego by giving oneself up to fate is key. They believe our actions are guided in the main by past karma, which determines the direction of our lives to a large degree.

Pure Land traditions rely chiefly on three texts for their doctrinal basis. These are the *Larger Sūtra of Immeasurable Life* (*Sukhāvatīvyūha Sūtra*), the *Smaller Sūtra of Immeasurable Life* (*Amitābha Sūtra*), and the *Amitāyurdhyāna Sūtra*, also called the *Meditation Sūtra* because it describes a series of contemplations on the Buddha Amitāyus. In the *Larger Sūtra of Immeasurable Life*, a bodhisattva named Dharmākara makes various vows to help all sentient beings realize salvation from suffering. Afterwards he transforms into a buddha called Amitāyus and also named Amitābha, representing two aspects of the Buddha. Amitāyus means "immeasurable life" and represents the Buddha in *nirvāṇa*. Amitābha means "immeasurable wisdom," symbolizing the Buddha's focus on sentient beings. Amitāyus is seated in meditation while Amitābha stands and communicates with others. The *Smaller Sūtra of Immeasurable Life* describes Pure Land as a physical place filled with jewels and ruled by a huge buddha. In this way, these two *sūtras* can be seen as a pair, one describing the savior Buddha and the other focusing on his kingdom.

Two major Pure Land traditions developed in China based on interpretations of scriptures. The monk Tanluan (476–542) claimed that birth in the Pure Land is achieved through faith in the vow of Amitābha to save all sentient beings. He is credited with having created the expression that is believed to lead to salvation when chanted: "Praise to Amitābha Buddha" (南無阿彌陀佛, Ch. *Namo Emituofo*; Jp. *Namu Amida Butsu*; K. *Namu Amita Bul*). Known as the *nianfo* (Jp. *Nembutsu*; K. *yeombul*), use of this phrase became standard among Pure Land traditions, although interpretations of how properly to employ it vary. Later, Shandao (613–681) claimed that even wicked beings can enter the Pure Land by repeating the *nianfo*.

In Japan, the first major figure to promote Pure Land Buddhism was Hōnen (1133–1212). The decline of aristocratic culture in his time brought a corresponding loss of interest in Buddhist doctrine, its unwieldy rituals, and corrupt priests behind the scenes at court. There was a widespread belief that the world had entered the degenerative era (末法 Ch. *mofa*; Jp. *mappō*), described in Pure Land and other *sūtras* as a time when people can no longer understand or practice the teachings of the Buddha. Accordingly, in this age one can rely only on the vow of a savior buddha for salvation from suffering. In Hōnen's time, repeating the *nembutsu* gained popularity among ordinary people outside the religious establishments. This annoyed the priests of the traditional temples in Kyoto, who pressured the government to ban the practice and banish Hōnen from the city. Hōnen's most influential follower was Shinran (1173–1263), the founder of Jōdo Shinshū, "the True Pure Land Tradition," also called Shin or Shin Buddhism. Whereas Hōnen taught that a person should repeat the *nembutsu* endlessly as a way to call on the savior Buddha, Shinran believed it should be repeated as thanks to Amitābha, who inevitably saves all people on account of his vow to do so. Taking the belief to its logical extreme, Shinran taught that an individual's deeds and past misdeeds have nothing to do with going to the Pure Land, since Amitābha vowed to save all sentient beings.

In Korea today, most Buddhist temples have a Pure Land devotional area as well as places for meditation and doctrinal study.

Chan (禪 Jp. Zen; K. Seon)

Chan and Pure Land traditions are sometimes said to be anti-philosophical, emphasizing instead practices for different reasons respectively. The name Zen is well known outside of Asia, likely due to the disproportionate number of writings about the tradition in European languages in the twentieth century. The name "Zen" is the Japanese reading of the Chinese graph "Chan." Chan is an abbreviation of "Channa" (禪那), which is a transliteration of the Sanskrit term *dhyāna*, meaning meditation. Thus, Chan is the tradition of Mahāyāna Buddhism that points to meditation as its central tenet. Chan meditation is closely related to Indian *vipassana*. Although the name is derived from Sanskrit, Chan was systematized in East Asia, beginning in China. Tradition says the south Indian monk Bodhidharma (c. fifth–sixth century CE) first transmitted the Chan Dharma to Chinese Buddhists around the year 520. His principle disciple, Huike (487–593), may be responsible for first recording his master's teachings. Chan has a general disdain for textual study and seeks direct experience of *tathatā*. It therefore claims the historical Buddha transmitted the tradition from mind to mind without the use of words. That being the case, Chan does not make use of *sūtras* for doctrinal grounding as do others traditions of Buddhism. Instead, it alleges to be "a special transmission outside the scriptures" (教外別傳 Ch. *jiao wai bie zhuan*). However, adherents have found several *sūtras* satisfactory, most notably the *Laṅkāvatāra Sūtra*.

Chan meditation is not aimed at cutting off the empirical world, as some Indian yoga systems may be. On the contrary, it seeks to engage deeply in experience by minimizing mental analysis and evaluation. Because such internal chatter is identified typically as the "self," Chan seeks to destroy this self as a false construction of what we really are, to end the tyranny of self-reflection. Such thoughts, it is believed, remove us from a more direct experience of reality by imposing endless dualisms, to which we cling, therefore resulting in suffering. The famous Chan saying "If you meet the Buddha on the road, kill him," suggests we should destroy such dualistic evaluations when we come upon them. It is typical of Chan instructions to use shocking images in this way, thereby aiding us in the process of letting go of the cherished notion of self.

Chan does not acknowledge a dichotomy between "enlightenment" and non-enlightenment. Instead of speaking of enlightenment, Chan practitioners seek understanding (悟 Ch. *wu*; Jp. *satori*). Specifically, they hope to understand their own nature (見性 Ch. *jian xing*; Jp. *kenshō*) through direct experience. Because our nature is believed to be buddha-nature, seeing into one's own nature is realizing buddhahood.[15] Related to this emphasis is Chan's principle of "no dependence upon words and letters" (不立文字 Ch. *buli wenzi*; Jp. *furyū monji*). "No dependence upon words and letters" derives from the Madhyamaka notion of non-duality. Referring to the *Vimalakīrtinirdeśa-sūtra*, Chan finds a model in the layman Vimalakīrti who, through silence, conveys to learned monks that verbal fabrications can only communicate dichotomies. Chan's practical method for reaching understanding is most notably known in Japanese as *zazen* (座禅 Ch. *zuo chan*), seated meditation. According to the tradition, sitting in *zazen* is itself already reaching the goal, since we are innately buddhas. While seated, practitioners typically place bare attention on breathing while concentrating on a central spot below the navel called in Chinese the *dantian* (丹田; Jp. *tanden*; K. *danjeon*). Chan meditation in the absence of doctrine is said to be the method for "direct pointing to the human mind" (直指人心 Ch. *zhizhi renxin*). These four phrases together are said to encapsulate the Chan teachings: "a special transmission outside the scriptures; no dependence upon words and letters; direct pointing to the human mind; seeing into one's own nature is realizing Buddhahood."[16]

Many East Asian artists have been attracted to the Chan idea of direct experience, which was widely applied to their practices, among them Noh drama, the Tea Ceremony, and martial arts. Through their interest in Zen, a number of general Buddhist ideas have become important and enduring aesthetic concepts in Japan, including *mushin*, *mujō* (無常 Ch. *wuchang*; K. *musang*), impermanence, and *yūgen* (幽玄), profound mystery. Zen also appealed to Japanese samurai, who sought to lessen their fear of death through meditation. In China, Chan's emphasis on "no dependence upon words and letters" may have contributed to its eventual decline. The tradition's appearance as illogical and indifferent towards the Confucian classics was contrary to the neo-Confucianism of the Song dynasty (960–1279). In modern Korea, Seon practitioners have struggled with doctrinal Buddhists and fought against non-celibacy and meat-eating behaviors that were introduced into their order during the Japanese occupation period (1910–45). Contrary to Buddhist vows, those struggles frequently turned violent. Eventually, these conflicts resulted in the creation of the Jogye Order, which is based primarily on Seon practice. Jogye is the largest Buddhist order in Korea today.

Notes

1 This does not treat the ancillary academic traditions, which were once separate (Sattvasiddhi, Mahāyānasaṃgraha, Dilun, Nirvāṇa). The latter aided in the doctrinal formulation of other traditions and were eventually absorbed by them. Nor does it consider the Vinaya and Abhidharma, both having origins in "Hīnayāna" Buddhism.

2 *Taishō* (T) 31, No. 1585, 成唯識論.

3 Xuanzang's translation can be found as T 16, No. 676.

4 T 24, No. 1484 and T 85, No. 2283.

5 Kumārajīva's translation is T 30, No. 1564, 中論.

6 Kumārajīva's translation is T 30, No. 1568, 十二門.

7 Kumārajīva's translation is T 30, No. 1569, 百論.

8 Kumārajīva's translation is T 25, No. 1509, 大智度論.

9 Later, in the time of Śāntarakṣita (c. 725–c. 784) and Kamalaśīla (c. 740–c. 794), these two traditions reunited and focused their criticism instead on Yogācāra.

10 T 46, No. 1911.

11 T 33, No. 1716.

12 T 34 No. 1718.

13 Skt *Mahāprajñāpāramitopadeśa-śāstra* by Nāgārjuna. Kumarajiva's translation is preserved as T 25, No. 1509.

14 T 32, No.1666.

15 This is expressed in Chinese as *jian xing chengfo*, 見性成佛.

16 T. 48, No. 2008, 364c9.

Part III

Themes in Buddhist Philosophy

A. Metaphysics

8

Metaphysical Issues in Indian Buddhist Thought

JAN WESTERHOFF

In Tibetan monasteries we often find depictions of eight Indian Buddhist philosophers collectively referred to as the "six ornaments and two supreme ones" (*rgyan drug mchog gnyis*).[1] The "six ornaments" are Nāgārjuna, Āryadeva, Asaṅga, Vasubandhu, Dignāga, and Dharmakīrti. These paintings are usually grouped around a central representation of Buddha Śākyamuni. This iconographic set gives us a straightforward way of dividing Indian Buddhist philosophical thought into four intellectual streams: Abhidharma (represented by the Buddha), Madhyamaka (Nāgārjuna and Āryadeva), Yogācāra (Asaṅga and Vasubandhu), and what is often referred to as the epistemological-logical school of Dignāga and Dharmakīrti (sometimes also referred to by the name *pramāṇavāda*).

Each of these four schools constitutes a philosophical system of considerable complexity dealing with questions in metaphysics, epistemology, the philosophy of logic and language, ethics, and so forth. Even restricting ourselves to the metaphysical issues within the scope of this essay it will not be possible to discuss all the metaphysical problems addressed by the various schools. We will therefore confine ourselves here to a limited number of metaphysical topics discussed by the four schools, focusing on issues that are particularly characteristic of each school or that have a close connection with problems raised in the contemporary philosophical debate. These are the relation between part and whole and the theory of momentariness for Abhidharma, notions of ultimate and conventional truth, causation, and property-instantiation for Madhyamaka, the question whether everything is mental for Yogācāra, and the rejection of universals and its semantic consequences for the school of Dignāga and Dharmakīrti.

It should also be noted that none of the four philosophical schools speaks with one voice, but each exhibits internal disagreements and specific interpretations characteristic of particular authors or texts. Explicating these in detail would take us far beyond what is possible in the context of this essay. While I will be glossing over such internal differentiations to a large extent, the reader should be aware that the reference to

A Companion to Buddhist Philosophy, First Edition. Edited by Steven M. Emmanuel.

"schools," "systems," and their "views" involves a significant amount of simplifying expository unification that is, nevertheless, indispensable in a survey such as this.

Abhidharma

The Abhidharma, which forms one of the three "baskets" or collections of texts that constitute the Buddhist canon (the others being the Buddha's discourses and the rules for monks and nuns), contains the earliest attempt at a philosophical systematization of the Buddha's teaching. Over time different interpretative approaches and thus different Abhidharmas emerged, but they are all united by a common core of philosophical principles.

One particularly important principle concerns the distinction between statements which are ultimately true and those which are true only in a conventional or transactional sense. Conventional truths are truths that lead us to successful action, whereas ultimate truths are truths about how the world is at the most fundamental level, independent of human interests or concerns. This distinction is fairly familiar to us and rests on the idea that, in order to get around in daily life, we make a lot of assumptions that, strictly speaking, we know to be false but that prove to be pragmatically useful. According to our best physical theories, the space in which we live is not Euclidean, even though for most practical purposes (measuring a piece of land, calculating the trajectory of a baseball, using perspective in drawing) it is advantageous to assume that it is.

Abhidharma distinguishes between, on the one hand, primary existent objects, or *dharmas*, that are ultimately real and, on the other, secondary existent objects that are mere fictional superimpositions on collections of primary existents. Such superimpositions are only conventionally but not ultimately real. Merely conventionally real is anything that has parts, as well as human persons or selves. What is ultimately real? This includes the physical *dharmas*, which consist of four different kinds – earth, fire, water, and air – as well as the non-physical *dharmas* – such things as feelings, volitions, and cognitions. A good way of conceptualizing the *dharmas* is in terms of particularized properties (sometimes also called tropes) (Goodman 2004). Particularized properties differ from properties as ordinarily conceived (sometimes called universals) in not being present at multiple locations at the same time. While the same universal red can be present at the same time in a postbox in London and a flag in Beijing, the particularized property of redness of this postbox is present only here, at this place and time, and the particularized property of this flag is present only there, at that place and time. The two particularized properties might be very similar, but they are not the same, and they are distinguished by their respective space–time locations.

Each *dharma* has its specific characteristics (*svalakṣaṇa*) that distinguish it from every other *dharma*, and it has these characteristics as an intrinsic nature (*svabhāva*). This means that each *dharma* has the properties it has independent of anything else; they exist no matter what, without depending on the existence of any other *dharma* or on any conceptualizing mind.

The Abhidharma distinction between ultimate and conventional truth requires not only that some statements are ultimately true (and that the objects these statements are about – the *dharmas* – are ultimately real) but also that some statements are only conventionally true, and that the objects these statements are about are mere conceptual fictions superimposed on the ultimately real *dharmas*. These conceptual fictions comprise everything that has parts. The Abhidharma therefore endorses a form of mereological reductionism: no composite entity is real, only its (ultimate) parts are.

The Abhidharmikas argue for this conclusion by examining the four possible ways in which the real/unreal distinction can be distributed across parts and wholes. One could hold that

1 parts and wholes are both real, or that
2 only the whole is real, but the parts are not, or that
3 neither is real, or that
4 the parts are real but the whole is not.

The first possibility leaves us in the difficult position of having to accommodate in our ontology not just all the parts of, say, a mechanical clock in a specific way but, in addition, the whole which these parts constitute. (Note that in the present context our talk of parts should be understood as including the specific way the parts are put together.) It is difficult to regard the whole and the parts as the very same thing, since they have different properties. The whole is one, yet the parts are many; the whole is a physical thing, yet the way the parts are put together is not a physical thing, but best understood as a structure or procedure.

On the other hand, considering the whole and the arrangement of the parts as separate leads to a difficulty when trying to determine *where* exactly the whole that exists in addition to the parts would be located. Each part has a precise spatial location, so we would expect the distinct whole to have a similarly precise location. One possibility would be to say that the whole is present in each particular part of the clock. Yet this seems somewhat counter-intuitive, since, when inspecting a particular part, say, the spring, we never find anything that looks remotely like the whole clock. In addition, we would not want to say that we see the whole object if we see just a single part of it. So it would be better to argue that the whole clock occupies the same space as all the parts as they are put together to form the clock. But, since the whole occupies a part of space, we now have to deal not just with the parts of the clock but, in addition, with the parts of the whole. Not only does it now seem as if we have really multiplied entities beyond explanatory necessity, we have also landed ourselves in an infinite regress. For, in order to explain the relation between the clock, the spring, the screws, and so on, we introduced the idea of the whole and its parts (which are different from the parts of the clock). But now we have to explain the relation between the whole and *its* parts, for which purpose we have to introduce yet another whole, and so on, ad infinitum.

The second possibility is based on the idea that the whole, the clock, is real, and that all its parts are merely abstractions from that whole. As each part is usually part of some bigger whole (the clock is part of the house, the house part of the neighborhood, the neighborhood part of the city, the city part of the country, etc.), it can really accept the reality only of one thing, The Whole, also known as the universe, or the totality of all that exists. This position, usually referred to as monism, has attracted some recent supporters (Schaffer 2010) but faces the difficulty of accounting for the diversity of the world as we experience it. If all is one, and therefore shares the same nature, why does oxygen support human life while nitrogen does not? Why are chanterelles edible while the very similar looking jack-o'-lantern mushroom is poisonous? Why does the fruit of the bignay tree (*antidesma bunius*) taste sweet to most Asians but bitter to most Europeans?

Given the plausible assumption that everything is either a whole or a part, the third possibility entails that nothing at all is real. If we understand "not real" to mean "non-existent," this position reduces to ontological nihilism, the claim that nothing whatsoever exists. In addition to its initial lack of plausibility, nihilism entails the difficulty that, if true, it seems to be false, for it implies the existence of the truth "nothing exists," yet by its own standards this truth should not exist either. If we understand "not real" as "not real in any fundamental sense," the third possibility entails not nihilism, but the claim that nothing at all is fundamentally real. The difficulty an Abhidharmika might see with this is that the existence of anything non-fundamental or derived appears to presuppose (as a matter of conceptual necessity) the existence of something fundamental or non-derived.[2] This reading of the third possibility is therefore not much more satisfactory.

This leaves us with the fourth position, which is the one the Abhidharmikas eventually adopt. The only ultimately real things, and the domain of ultimate truths, are the *dharmas*. Everything else, including medium-sized dry goods, such as chariots, and objects with mental and material properties, such as persons, is conventionally real and merely borrows its existence from the ultimately real parts that underlie it. They do not exist by the force of some intrinsic nature (*svabhāva*), but are merely mental fictions superimposed on conglomerations of fundamental objects that do exist in this manner.

Suffering as described in the First Noble Truth is a result of mistaking the conventionally real for the ultimately real, of regarding the fictional mental construct that is our self and the world around us as substantially existent. The cessation of suffering is obtained as a result of seeing through the mistaken view of an enduring self in persons and things, by realizing that only the *dharmas* are ultimately real. To see the world correctly from the perspective of ultimate truth, understanding that we, as well as the things with which we interact, are nothing but a momentary sequence of causally linked *dharmas* arising and ceasing, will lead to cessation of clinging to them and thereby, ultimately, to liberation.

It is therefore clear that the Abhidharma notions of ultimate and conventional truth and of mereological reductionism can be understood as an attempt to explain the first and the third of the three "seals" or "marks" of existence taught by the Buddha: that all things are suffering (*dukkha*) and that they are without self (*anātman*). The Abhidharma has also developed an elaboration of the second seal, impermanence (*anityatva*). This is the theory of momentariness. As such this theory goes beyond the simple idea that nothing lasts, for even if nothing is permanent things could still last for extended periods of time. But the theory of momentariness claims that nothing lasts for more than a moment. On the face of it this theory is as difficult to reconcile with our everyday experience of the world as atomism is. We cannot see or touch the smallest constituents of matter, and everything we *can* see or touch is non-atomic. Similarly all experiences we actually have last for more than a moment, and some last for a considerable time. The atomist replies that our visual and tactile powers of discrimination are not fine-grained enough to distinguish the final constituents of matter. A similar answer will be provided by the defender of momentariness. Each *dharma* lasts only for a moment, but gives rise to a new *dharma* very much like it in the moment immediately after it, much like one frame in a film is succeeded by a very similar one. Our powers of temporal discrimination being what they are, they cannot distinguish the successive similar *dharmas* and experience them as a single, continuous phenomenon.

One important argument for the theory of momentariness is based on the examination of how things go out of existence. There are two basic possibilities: either things cease, because some other event causes them to go out of existence, or they disappear spontaneously. The first difficulty for the cessation of things being the effect of some distinct cause is that it fails to account for the inevitability of the cessation. For any cause–effect relationship we can imagine circumstances where the cause is present, but for some reason the effect does not arise. Yet, it is argued, we do not observe any things that do not cease sooner or later. So whatever accounts for this had better be an explanation that entails a stronger kind of necessity than mere causal necessity can provide (Dreyfus 1997, 63).

A second difficulty is that, for the Abhidharma, absences or instances of non-existence are not real things.[3] For this reason there is a *prima facie* difficulty having a causal relation between some existent event (the sun shining) and some absence (the non-existence of the snowman), since the place of the second relatum is not filled. Of course there are other, unproblematic causal chains associated with this supposed causation (the sun shining causing a puddle of water), and perhaps such associated chains can always be found, but they are cases of one existent thing causing the presence of another existent thing, not of one thing causing an absence of something else.

So the second possibility, that *dharmas* cease to exist spontaneously, seems more promising. If the necessity provided by external causes is not enough to explain the impermanence of all things, we should assume that it is part of the intrinsic nature of things to cease. They do not need any external influence in order to go out of existence, but their going out of existence is constitutive of their being the very kind of things they are, caused by nothing but what is already responsible for the arising of the thing. In this case, however, it becomes unclear why *dharmas* continue to exist for any extended amount of time. If an object persisted for a minute, say, and then ceased, we would want to assume that there is some cause responsible, bringing about its cessation after a minute. But we have seen above that the assumption of such a cause is problematic. If a *dharma* ceases spontaneously then this cessation is not brought about by anything outside of the *dharma*, but only by its inner nature (Perrett 2004).

But why could it not be the case that a *dharma* persists for a sequence of moments and then self-destructs, as a consequence of its inner nature, in the same way as an alarm-clock rings at a given time, caused only by the working of its inner mechanism? The reason is that, in this case, the *dharma* could not be an ultimately real existent by Abhidharma standards. The "delayed self-destruction" view has to account for an inner change in the *dharma*, in the same way as an inner change in the alarm-clock causes it to ring. Now it would make no sense to conceive of this change as taking place by a persisting substance acquiring different properties over time, for in this case it would not be the *dharma* itself that is fundamental, but only the substance underlying it. But if we think instead that there is nothing persisting through the change in the *dharma*, so that we have just a sequence of resembling but distinct agglomerations of properties, then it looks as if the original *dharma* was not a *dharma* at all, but merely a mental superimposition on more fundamental entities.

On the Abhidharma understanding of the fundamental reality of the *dharmas* as objects that bear all their causal powers as part of their intrinsic nature, it becomes difficult to see why these powers are not discharged immediately after the *dharma*'s arising, a discharge which would also entail the immediate vanishing of the *dharma* itself.

In addition to this argument based on the cessation of things (*vināśitvānumāna*), the later discussion introduces an argument based on their existence (*sattvānumāna*) or, more specifically, on the causal efficacy of what exists (causal efficacy being deemed to be the mark of existence). The argument sets out to show that any object that was temporally stretched out – i.e., non-momentary – would not be able to exert causal influence. Since the things we see around us are able to exert such influence, they must therefore be momentary.

Imagine some fundamental *dharma* and assume, *per impossibile*, that it lasted for three moments of time. Let's also assume this *dharma* was a quantity of heat that had the power to warm up a cup of water by 12 degrees. Suppose the *dharma* produced its effect (the rise of temperature) already after the first moment. What would happen in the next two moments? The *dharma* could either produce its effect again, in which case we would end up with a cup of water 36 degrees warmer than the one we started out from, which contradicts our initial assumption about its causal power to raise the temperature by 12 degrees, or it would just be sitting there doing nothing during moments 2 and 3. But in this case there would have to be some internal change in the *dharma* that accounts for this difference in activity. And we have just seen that it is problematic to assume the presence of internal change in *dharmas*. So it seems that the *dharma* cannot discharge its causal powers in one instant. Could it do so gradually – say, by raising the temperature by 4 degrees each moment? But in this case the *dharma* would not be able to discharge its full effect at the beginning of its existence, while it would be able to do so at the end. Again, it seems, an internal change has taken place. The defender of momentariness now concludes that, if a cause cannot discharge its effect either instantaneously or gradually, it is unclear how it can discharge it at all. Since we have seen that causes do discharge their effects, we have to reject one of the central premises that led us to this counter-intuitive conclusion – that is, the premise that *dharmas* can last for more than a moment (Rospatt 1995, 2–6, 162–3).

Madhyamaka

The fundamental claim of Madhyamaka is the thesis of universal emptiness – that is, the claim that everything, without exception, is empty. Emptiness is of course always the emptiness of something, and the something Mādhyamikas talk about is denoted by the Sanskrit term *svabhāva*, often translated as intrinsic existence, inherent existence, essence, or substance. To say that something exists by *svabhāva* or has a property by *svabhāva* is to say that it exists or has that property all by itself, due to its own nature, and independent of any other object existing or having a specific property.

Belief in the existence of this *svabhāva* – which in the case of persons equates to belief in the existence of a substantially existent self – is the main cause of grasping and thereby the main cause of the suffering of cyclic existence. The Madhyamaka theory of emptiness is therefore an essential component of the Fourth Noble Truth, that of the path leading to liberation.

If some object is dependent on some other object in a specific way, this is incompatible with the first object existing by *svabhāva*. As such, many of the Madhyamaka arguments consist of indicating such dependencies. Buddhist writers distinguish three kinds of dependence, ordered in increasing levels of subtlety. The first is the mereological dependence of an object on its parts, as in the case of a mechanical clock that depends on its various constituents. The second is the causal dependence on whatever cause brought it into existence (my causal dependence on my parents, for example). The third and most subtle dependence is the dependence on the conceptualizing mind, as, for example, Sherlock Holmes exists in dependence on the minds of the readers of Conan Doyle. Demonstrating that an object is dependent in such a way (in particular, demonstrating its dependence in the third sense) shows that it is empty of *svabhāva*.

Before investigating the Madhyamaka arguments for the thesis of universal emptiness in more detail, it is useful to discuss first what exactly this thesis means. We can distinguish three main interpretations. First of all, we could understand the Mādhyamika to argue that things require *svabhāva* or intrinsic nature to exist at all, while also demonstrating that nothing can have *svabhāva*. For this reason, nothing whatsoever exists. This nihilistic interpretation reflects how some non-Buddhist authors understood the conclusions of the Madhyamaka arguments. Nevertheless, it is explicitly rejected already in the earliest Madhyamaka sources. Not only did the Madhyamaka authors deny that *svabhāva* is a precondition for the existence of objects, it is also apparent that the ontological nihilism that would result from this interpretation is hardly a consistent position. For, if nothing exists, what about the theory asserting that nothing exists? For the theory to be true it would presumably have to exist, thereby rendering the theory false.

We are therefore left with two main interpretations, which constitute the main alternatives for interpreting the Madhyamaka philosophical project. The first may be labeled the noumenal interpretation. Madhyamaka analysis generally proceeds by a point-by-point investigation of an exhaustive set of alternatives among which the *svabhāva* of some object could be found. It is then shown that none of the alternatives is actually able to supply us with the desired *svabhāva*. Rather than concluding that this implies that there is no *svabhāva*, the noumenal interpretation argues that *svabhāva* does exist but is cognitively inaccessible to us. Like the Kantian noumenon, it exists behind the realm of appearances but does not exist anywhere among the appearances. The cause of suffering, according to this interpretation, is to search for *svabhāva*, for a substantially existent core of persons and objects in places where it cannot be found.

The second main interpretation is sometimes labeled the "semantic non-dualist interpretation." The concept of semantics is intricately connected with the concept of truth, and we cannot understand the role of truth in Buddhist thought without taking into account the notion of the two truths, already familiar to us from our discussion of Abhidharma. We remember that, for the Abhidharma, spatio-temporally extended objects were taken to exist only at the level of conventional truth, while the momentary *dharmas* exist at the level of ultimate truth. At a more general level, we can view the conventional truth as the everyday, transactional truth that allows us to get around in the world, while the ultimate truth is the result of astute philosophical investigation into the nature of reality. For the Madhyamaka, the appearance of *svabhāva* exists as long as we do not analyze the world around us too closely, but, once we have done so, employing the arguments provided by the Mādhyamikas, this appearance vanishes. The semantic non-dualist interpretation claims that this amounts to the assertion that all there is is the conventional truth. From the point of view of the ultimate truth there is no ultimate truth, or, to phrase this in a less paradoxical manner, from the point of view necessary to obtain liberation, only one truth, the conventional truth, appears. Contrast this with the noumenal interpretation, which equates the appearance of *svabhāva* in the world with the conventional truth and ineffable reality underlying this with the ultimate truth. For the semantic non-dualist, the assertion that there is any way the world is like at the ultimate level, any view of reality that can be considered as the final truth, implies a commitment to *svabhāva*, a commitment to an intrinsic, inherent nature of reality. The semantic non-dualist strives to accommodate the Madhyamaka claim that emptiness itself is empty by rejecting the idea that emptiness is what the world looks like at the ultimate level. Instead he argues that what the theory of emptiness amounts to is that there is nothing beneath or beyond the level of conventional reality.

This of course raises the interesting question how we can accept the view that conventional truth is all there is without being forced into an extreme kind of relativism that claims that any theory is as good as any other. How can we maintain the view that, of the various conventionally true theories of the world, some are better than others, without spelling out "better than" in terms of being closer to the ultimate truth? One way of addressing this would be to argue that the idea of an ultimately true theory is pragmatically useful. If we pretend that there is some objective standard to which our theories have to conform, we are more likely to improve on the theories we currently hold than if we believe there is no distinction to be made between conventionally true theories in terms of bestness. Of course what this amounts to is the adoption of a meta-theory (considered as conventionally true) that postulates the existence of a unique ultimate truth. This, in turn, would be justified not by its correspondence with an underlying reality but by its pragmatic efficacy: believing in such a meta-theory has good consequences in the long run. This then leaves us with the problem of what makes the good consequences good consequences. However, here we would have to assume not that there is some ultimate standard of goodness but rather that, by the standards of the conventional reality we inhabit, having the bodies and minds we have, certain consequences are better for us than others. On this basis, various theories could then be given a "better than" ranking, even though we would not have to assume that any one theory is better than all the others.

The theory of the emptiness of emptiness underlines the fact that emptiness itself is not the final, ultimately true theory of reality, but rather an antidote against the mistaken superimposition of *svabhāva* onto a world that in fact lacks it. This superimposition can come in many forms, which implies that there can be no "master argument" for the theory of emptiness. Because the ways in which *svabhāva* is projected onto the world vary, there cannot be a single argument that demonstrates the emptiness of *svabhāva* in all cases. Madhyamaka arguments have to be set out on a case-by-case basis. This being said, some concepts are particularly prone to the superimposition of *svabhāva* and therefore occupy a central place in Madhyamaka analysis. One especially important one is the concept of causation.

If there is a substantial concept of causation, the Mādhyamika argues, it has to entail that cause and effect are related in one of the following four ways:

a cause and effect are identical
b cause and effect are distinct
c cause and effect are both identical and distinct
d cause and effect are neither identical nor distinct.

If we cannot understand the relationship between cause and effect in any of these ways, it may be because there is something wrong with our underlying presupposition of causation as an objective, mind-independent, external relation.

We are reluctant to regard cause and effect as identical since it is the cause that brings about the effect in the first place. What this means is that the cause is there first, and the effect follows later, after the cessation of the cause. But if cause and effect exist at two distinct times they cannot be one and the same thing. The second possibility, the distinctness of cause and effect, is equally problematic, because cause and effect appear to depend on each other. The effect obviously depends on the cause for its existence, but the dependence also holds the other way round. This is because causes are generally not single objects (such as seeds or sparks) but collections of various items that have to come together to bring about the effect. Without water, soil, sun, etc., the seed is no cause of the sprout; without petrol, oxygen, the appropriate temperature, etc., the spark is no cause of the explosion. These collections jointly form the cause, but what determines what is and what is not part of such a collection is precisely the effect. It is not any random collection that constitutes a cause, but only those related to a specific event regarded as its effect. But, if cause and effect are related by dependence relations in this way, they cannot be distinct, as one could not exist without the other existing.

The third possibility might appear as obviously absurd, since no two things can be both identical and distinct. Yet we could give this a more nuanced reading by arguing that the cause consists of two types, one of which is the effect *in potentia* (like a marble statue inside a rock) while the other is what realizes this potential (the sculptor's hammering). In this way we could say that cause and effect are identical because the effect is just the potential made real, while they are distinct because mere potency does not amount to actuality. All of this is fine as far as it goes, but it leads to problems if we want to assert that the individual entities related by causation all exist by *svabhāva*.

These two types of cause could not be: nothing can be an unrealized potential all in itself, unless there is something to make the potential actual. Similarly, the actualizing cause cannot exist on its own, either; it needs some potential to actualize in the first place.

The final alternative is generally interpreted as amounting to the absence of causation because the preceding three possibilities of the relation between cause and effect are considered to be exhaustive. If the relata of some relation are neither identical nor distinct, nor some combination of the two, then it seems fair to say that there is no relation connecting them in the first place. But this is also not a position we would want to adopt. The world is not a single unregulated chaos of events happening with little apparent connection, but seems to follow distinct causal patterns.

So our attempts at accounting for causation as an objective, mind-independent, external relation have failed. How then can the Mādhyamika understand causation? If we keep in mind the theory of momentariness, the view that things exist only for a moment before they self-destruct, it becomes apparent that there is not enough time for a causal relation in the familiar sense to take place. This is because, once the effect has arisen in the moment following the cause, the cause has already ceased to exist. As there is no effect before the cause, this implies that one of the two items related by the causal relation must always be absent. But, as we cannot have a two-place relation without two relata, this means that one of the relata must be supplied by the mind, either by anticipation (when the effect does not exist yet) or by memory (when the cause no longer exists). As such, the relation of causation cannot be regarded as something that could take place in a world without us; it is something that essentially requires the existence of minds. This explains why, for the Mādhyamika, nothing related by causality can exist by *svabhāva*. If the notion of causation always requires appeal to minds, so that causal dependence entails dependence on a conceptualizing mind, then items related by causation cannot have their existence and properties in a purely intrinsic way, independent of anything else.

A second important area prone to the superimposition of *svabhāva* is the relation of properties and their bearers. It is often thought that, in the case of an individual instantiating a property, there is some kind of substantial core that has all the properties; the properties depend on it, yet it does not depend on them. Such a core would be a good candidate for something existing by *svabhāva*. Of course such a core could not itself instantiate any property, for if it did there would be yet another, more fundamental core lying behind it instantiating this property. It would have to be what is sometimes called a *bare particular*, an individual devoid of all attributes. Yet it is not entirely clear how much sense can be made of such a bare particular, since it must presumably have at least one property (bare-particular-ness) that distinguishes it from everything else. Yet, if it does, then there must be at least one even barer particular instantiating this property, in which case the original bare particular could not exist with *svabhāva*. Needless to say, the argument can be repeated for the even barer particular.

An alternative construal of the relation between properties and their bearers would be to argue that individual, particularized, spatio-temporally located properties that exist by *svabhāva* are ultimately real, and that the objects of our acquaintance are mere bundles of such properties.[4] The difficulty the Mādhyamika sees with this approach is that we cannot simply individuate the different properties by reference to their specific space–time locations without giving some account of what differentiates the spatial and temporal points, which have themselves to be conceived of as properties or bundles of properties. We rather have to individuate the properties in terms of the other properties with which they co-occur in different bundles, saying, for example, that this instance of red is different from that because it co-occurs in a bundle together with this spatial property rather than with this other one. However, if this is the case, then the different particularized properties cannot bear their nature and existence by *svabhāva*, as their very distinctness from other objects is not anything that flows from the intrinsic nature of the property itself, but something it possesses only in dependence on other objects.

Yogācāra

The alternative names of this school, *cittamātra* (consciousness only) and *vijñaptimātra* (impression only), already hint at one of its most fundamental ideas: the view that nothing outside of the mind exists, and that things that do not appear mental to us, such as shoes and ships and sealing-wax, are just cleverly disguised kinds of mental phenomena.[5] Yogācāra disagrees with Abhidharma insofar as it does not believe that what the Abhidharma regards as basic material things (the *rūpadharmas*) have an underived, fundamental existence.

Yogācāra arguments for the exclusive existence of the mental are based on a representationalist theory of perception already defended by one school of Abhidharma, the Sautrāntikas. According to this theory, when we perceive some material object, such as a rock, we are acquainted not directly with the rock but rather with a set of mental images or representations, and on the basis of these we *infer* that there is a rock out there that caused these images.

Now there are cases of perception where almost everybody agrees that there is nothing out there, behind the perception, which the perception represents. A man suffering from jaundice sees a white conch shell as yellow, yet he would be mistaken to infer that there is something yellow in the world in the same way in which there would be if there is the perception of a yellow buttercup. When a torch is wheeled in a circle we see a ring of fire, even if there is not a ring out there; when we see a mirage we experience the mental image of water, even though there is no water present. In all these cases it is intuitively convincing to assume that we are dealing with *cittamātra*, with something mental only, but not with anything non-mental (a yellow object, a ring of fire, water) standing behind it. The Yogācārin of course wants to go one step further, by arguing that this is the case for *all* our perceptions, not just for a limited set usually regarded as visual illusions. In all these cases, the Yogācārin claims, we are dealing with mental images only, without there being any non-mental correlates of which these images are images.

The chief argument for this generalization is a combination of a representationalist theory of perception with the principle of lightness. The Yogācārin's theory postulates fewer unobservable entities (remember that, for a representationalist, material things are not observable, hidden as they are behind the veil of mental representations) and is as such to be preferred to the opponent's heavier theoretical load that has to postulate a world of material things *out there* over and above the world of mental images *in here*. Yet the lightness of a theory can only be appealed to in this way if the competing accounts indeed manage to explain the same things, and explain them equally well. At the present stage it is not at all clear that the Yogācāra position is able to do this. Four difficulties are immediately apparent.

1 *Spatio-temporal regularity* Our experience of the world is ordered in space and time. We do not usually hear the sound of birds unless there are birds in the vicinity. We

do not live in a world of chaotic mental images where certain images (the birdsong) can just as well occur without any other ones (the sight of birds), or where images suddenly pop in and out of existence without rhyme or reason. Now the opponent who believes that there is something more than just the mental representation can easily explain this. Because auditory and visual properties of birds are two aspects of the very same material thing, it makes sense that we usually perceive one while also perceiving the other. Since these material things tend to persist through time, the mental images derived from them persist in a similar manner. Yet, from a Yogācāra perspective, it appears to be impossible to explain why, in the absence of some material object out there that "holds it all together," the world we experience is not a chaotic mess of rapidly changing mental episodes.

2 *Causal powers* A key difference between illusory, purely mental and "real" perceptions, the opponent argues, is the fact that only the latter have causal powers. If I see a real lake in the desert my visual impression of water is usually followed by a thirst-quenching impression later on upon drinking the water. But if what I see is a mirage there will be no such impression. Real water has the power to quench thirst, while water that is "impression only" can do no such thing. The reason real water can do so is because of the causal powers of the unobservable that lies beyond the representation. For the Yogācārin, it appears impossible to explain the difference between representations that are accompanied by causal powers and representations that are not, since there are no cases where anything *lies beyond* the representation.

3 *Interpersonal regularity* A further crucial distinction between visual illusions (where it might be plausible to say that all we perceive is a set of mental images) and the majority of perceptions we have, the critic of Yogācāra will point out, is that, in the case of the former, there is usually no intersubjective agreement. The conch shell appears yellow to the ill observer but not to his healthy contemporaries; the wheel of fire does not appear to an observer who is moving at the same speed as the torch; the mirage will not occur to one looking at the same scene from a very different position. For the opponent it is easy to explain why we all seem to experience the same world, simply because our perceptions are all caused by the same set of material objects. But for the Yogācārin it must appear as a miracle that people are able to interact at all. If your perception of a hammer and my perception of a nail are not unified by a set of material objects that cause them and which they thereby represent, how can we ever manage to put up a picture together?

4 *Control* If there is nothing beyond mental representation, it appears as if we cannot draw a sharp line between the parts of our mind that come from the outside (namely, perceptions of our surroundings) and parts that come from the inside (plans, imaginings, very vivid daydreaming). These do not appear to be on a par; we have considerable control over what we choose to daydream about, yet perceptions have the uncanny tendency of imposing themselves on us independent of and often contrary to our own wishes. It seems that the Yogācārin has no straightforward way of explaining this difference, as he is unable to say that some mental events are connected to something outside, and some are not. But if this is the case, then it does not seem as if the Yogācārin's theory really is as explanatorily successful as that of

his opponents, in which case an appeal to the principle of lightness would be inadmissible.

Needless to say, the Yogācārin has something to say on each of these points in order to defend the view that his impression-only theory has the same explanatory power as that of his opponent, who believes that there is something beyond the impressions.

1 *Spatio-temporal regularity* The spatial and temporal ordering of our perceptions cannot only be explained by the spatio-temporal existences of some set of objects beyond our perceptions. Despite the sometimes chaotic nature of our dreams, they cannot just be reduced a random sequence of mental images. Rather, the images are connected by temporal and spatial locations. Some images occur after others, thereby creating a dream-narrative stretched out in time, and the images that occur simultaneously are related by spatial relations such that one is next to the other, one on top of the other, etc. Yet it is clear that these relations are not in any way derived from the objects they represent. It is not the case that, when we dream of a lotus flower opening its petals, what is ultimately responsible for the temporal persistence of our lotus-flower-dream-impressions is the continued existence of the dream-lotus of which our impressions are impressions. There is no dream-lotus, and there is nothing more to our dream of the lotus flower than the sequence of impressions occurring in our mind. But if these can possess spatio-temporal regularity in the absence of objects beyond them, then the presence of the same kind of order in our waking perceptions cannot be used as an argument to show that there are objects beyond these.

2 *Causal powers* One way in which the Yogācārin can reply to the charge that impressions without corresponding objects have no causal powers (such as water in a mirage which cannot be drunk) is by subsuming the causal effects among the impressions. When you drink water in a dream your dream-thirst is quenched in the dream. So it appears as if the impression of water has some causal power in the dream, just as real water does in the waking world. But if that is the case, then causal efficiency cannot have anything to do with the existence of represented objects, since there is no dream-water that the dream-impressions represent. The defender of Yogācāra is not too worried that water in a mirage cannot be used to water a tree, since the picture of the world he wants to defend is not one in which there are some impressions with objects behind them, and some without objects behind them, which have somehow to be shown to be equally causally effective. Rather, all there is is impressions without objects behind them.

Yogācāra does not restrict itself to the view that cause–effect relations can take place only at one level of reality (such as in a dream, in a mirage, in a magical display, in an artificially simulated environment). Vasubandhu himself uses the example of an encounter with a beautiful woman in a dream and the physiological consequences this has for the dreamer's body that exists in the waking world. It represents a case of a cause in a dream (the impression of a sexual encounter) connected to an effect in the waking world (ejaculation). We might also mention Elias Howe's dream of being captured by savages wielding curious spears with holes near the tip which lead to the invention of the sewing machine. Again, the cause, the sight of the savages, exists exclusively in the dream, while its effect, the sewing machine, is part of the waking world. A new approach to the treatment of burn victims uses head-mounted displays to immerse them in a virtual world during painful treatments. In this simulated reality (called Snow World) the patient plays a simple game in which he has to throw snowballs at penguins and snowmen. Doing so reduces the pain felt by the patient during the treatment, as well as reducing the activity in some parts of the brain usually associated with the experience of pain.

If it is therefore the case that, if impressions that are impressions-only, lacking their presumed objects (the beautiful woman, savages with spears, penguins and snowmen), can be causally effective, then we cannot argue that, because our impressions are usually causally effective, there must be objects behind these that the impressions represent.

3 *Intersubjective regularity* If the world consists exclusively of mere impressions each perceiver has, how can we explain that we live in a shared world where we appear to perceive more or less the same things? Vasubandhu uses the example of the beings in the hell realms that collectively have the impression of being tortured by the guardians of the hell realms, even though these guardians do not exist outside of their own minds. Because of their collective bad karma, these beings experience similar surroundings of the hell realms, yet we do not have to assume that the hells have any kind of objective, as opposed to mere intersubjective, existence.

For a more contemporary example we could refer to conditions such as koro, a mass psychogenic disease that entails the belief that one's genitals are shrinking into one's body, thereby causing death. No such shrinkage is in fact taking place, yet during epidemics hundreds of patients report experiencing the symptoms of retracting genitals. Koro constitutes an example of groups of people sharing similar sensory impressions, though the objects that are supposed to give rise to such impressions do not exist. Note that, given the nature of the present dialectical exchange, the opponent's response that koro and other mass delusions are rare and isolated cases does not cause great difficulties for the proponent of Yogācāra. He set out to refute the opponent's argument that intersubjective regularity was possible only if there are external objects corresponding to internal impressions that would guarantee the similarity of impressions across a group of perceivers. Yet examples like koro show that intersubjective regularity can occur in the absence of objects. The opponent therefore cannot refer to the intersubjective regularity of our experience in order to show that external objects must correspond to it.[6]

4 *Control* This criticism identifies some event being purely mental in nature with its being under our control, claiming that any restriction in our ability to control it would have to have come from an external object perceived by the mental event. The Yogācārin assumes that our mental impressions are caused by the ripening of karmic seeds that have been deposited in our mental continuum by our previous actions. While we are free to choose how to act, and thereby free to plant the karmic seeds we wish, once the seeds have been planted experiencing the result is beyond

our control. It is therefore not the case that there has to be some recalcitrant object of our impressions out there to explain the fact that we cannot just change our impressions in any way we wish.

Yet, even independent of the theory of karma, it appears that a variety of features of our mental life are purely mental in nature, and are not accessible to conscious control. Consider the apparent uniformity and continuity of our visual field. It appears to us as if our visual field were equally fine-grained everywhere, and as if we perceived the whole of this field at any one time. Yet facts about the blind-spot, about different properties of different retinal cells and about saccades, tell us that the visual information coming in is diverse and discontinuous. The process that transforms that into an appearance of something uniform and continuous is purely mental, but this does not mean it is under our control so that we could, for example, just perceive the different degrees of resolution in the different parts of our retinas by merely deciding to do so. That some process is purely mental in nature does not imply that its results are all up to us.

When the Yogācārin claims that everything is mental in nature, what exactly is the conception of mind at issue here? Yogācāra distinguishes eight types of mind – the familiar five sense-consciousnesses (*indrīya-vijñānāni*), thought-consciouness (*mano-vijñāna*), the defiled mind (*kliṣṭamanas*), and the foundational consciousness (*ālayavijñāna*). Of these the final two deserve particular comment. The foundational consciousness, also sometimes referred to as the "storehouse consciousness," functions as a receptacle of karmic traces (or "seeds") generated by previous actions. Given the right conditions, these seeds ripen, thereby becoming the impressions and perceptions we experience. The defiled mind is responsible for superimposing the idea of an enduring, substantial self on the momentary flow of the foundational consciousness, thereby producing a mistaken subject/object and internal/external distinction, creating an inner perceiving subject and outer perceived objects as separate entities.

The different kinds of mind are integrated into a comprehensive picture of reality in the Yogācāra notion of the three natures (*trisvabhāva*). These are the imagined nature (*parakalpita-svabhāva*), the dependent nature (*paratantra-svabhāva*), and the perfected nature (*pariniṣpanna-svabhāva*). The imagined nature is the world as it is ordinarily experienced, divided into spatio-temporally distinct objects of perception out there and a perceiving subject in here. The dependent nature is what the external mental and the internal physical are erroneously superimposed on – a flow of momentary impressions arising due to prior causes and conditions. The perfected nature, finally, is not substantially distinct from the other two, but simply the dependent nature stripped bare of the superimpositions of the imagined nature.

It is important to realize that, in this picture, the concepts of the underlying nature and of the ultimate truth come apart. Note that in Abhidharma these are the very same thing. The *dharmas* constitute the fundamental level of reality underlying everything that exists, and what is true of these *dharmas* constitutes the ultimate truth about reality. In Yogācāra, on the other hand, the fundamental reality, the foundational consciousness, is not the perfected nature but the dependent nature. The ultimate truth about reality, what is to be realized for liberation, is the emptiness of the dependent nature of the imagined nature. This absence of the merely imagined division into subject and object from the flow of momentary impressions constitutes the final truth that has to be known directly in meditative experience.

The theory of the three natures occupies an equally important place in Yogācāra as the theory of the two truths (*satyadvaya*) does in Mādhyamaka. It allows the Yogācārin to provide an explication of the notion of emptiness mentioned in central works such as the *Prajñāpāramitā* texts that differs from the anti-foundational theory of Madhyamaka. The emptiness discussed there, the Yogācārin argues, is precisely the emptiness of the dependent nature of the erroneous subject/object superimpositions, created by the defiled mind, that bring about the imagined nature. The theory of the three natures can also be used to reinterpret the theory of the two truths by equating the dependent nature with the conventional truth and the perfected nature with the absolute truth. In this way Yogācāra strives to construct a theory of emptiness that does not have to reject the idea of a foundational level of reality.

The school of Dignāga and Dharmakīrti

The theoretical focus of this school concerns problems in the theory of knowledge and the theory of reasoning. As such it did not put great stress on developing a unique metaphysical position, as we find in the Abhidharma, Madhyamaka, and Yogācāra. We can rather understand the aim of this school as providing an epistemological and logical framework – a Buddhist equivalent to the Nyāya framework we find in Classical Indian philosophy – that can be employed by thinkers with a variety of different philosophical presuppositions.

Nevertheless, the school of Dignāga and Dharmakīrti defends interesting metaphysical views. Most importantly, it distinguishes between momentary particulars, apprehended by perception, which are ultimately real, and universals, apprehended by inference, which are conceptual fictions. Unlike Nyāya, which takes universals to be full members of the realm of existence, Dignāga and Dharmakīrti are nominalists: they believe that, at the fundamental level, there are only particulars that do not have any temporal extension.

The particulars are unique and therefore cannot be described by thought or language, for each such use implies the possibility of some repetition. Thought and language rely on the possibility of identifying recurring properties in things, either by specifying some property other things also have or by identifying a property that stays constant over time, so that it is had by the object as well as by its continuants. But if there are no such recurring properties, because each particular is unique and distinct from the others, and because there are no continuants, since each particular is momentary, our linguistic and conceptual resources appear to be unable to convey any information about these ultimately real objects.

The key argument for the nominalism of the school of Dignāga and Dharmakīrti is based on the fact that universals do not change. When the color of the banana changes from green to yellow, the universal green does not cease to exist, it just ceases to be instantiated by the banana. This is no change in the universal's inner nature, just a change in the way it is related to other objects.

Any putative change in a universal could not be a change of an accidental property, leaving its essential properties untouched, since universals are properties had by particulars, rather than bearers of properties themselves. A putative change would therefore have to affect the essential nature of a universal, and as such a changed universal would be an altogether different object from the unchanged one. Since we assume that red things are red because they instantiate the universal red, any change in this universal would entail that all red things instantaneously stopped being red and started to be, say, magenta. Such sweeping changes in the world of objects are never observed, and for this reason the theory of changing universals has to be treated with suspicion.

If we assume, as the school of Dignāga and Dharmakīrti does, that causal efficacy (*arthakriyākāritva*) is the mark of the real, it is difficult to see how universals could be real, given the tension between some thing being unchanging and its entering into causal relations. Anything that is a cause will discharge its effect at a given time. But if something does not change it is hard to see why it produces its effect now, rather than at another time. Given that its internal nature does not change, if it produces its effect at one time it should produce it at all times and thereby keep producing it ad infinitum. The assumption of universals therefore entails either that they do not fulfill any causal roles at all (in which case they are not real by the causal efficacy criterion) or that they never stop discharging their causal activity (which does not accord with our experience of the world).

On either account, universals could not be perceived in the way we seem to perceive them. They either could not enter into the causal process of perception at all or they would never stop producing perceptual effects, so that a universal that was perceived once would continue to be perceived at all times. The lack of causal efficacy of universals entails that, despite being inexpressible in thought and language, particulars are the only things that can be perceived. Perception is a causal process, and only particulars have any causal powers, so only these can enter into a causal process involving a sense organ.

We should also note that the nominalism defended here does not cover just synchronic universals as ordinarily conceived (redness occurring at several distinct locations at the same time) but also diachronic universals (redness occurring at successive temporal stages of one thing). Not only is there no entity instantiated by all tomatoes, strawberries, postboxes, and so on, there is also no thing instantiated by the tomato now and in the next second. The theories of momentariness and nominalism support each other. If everything is momentary there cannot be any permanent universals (at least as long as universals are regarded as existing in time at all). And if there are no universals there cannot be any property that the tomato now and the tomato in the next second have in common. They are wholly distinct objects, so that it is justifiable to argue that no thing lasts for longer than a moment.

We sometimes find the theoretical presuppositions of the school of Dignāga and Dharmakīrti described as "Yogācāra-Sautrāntika." This might strike us as a curious classification, given that the two schools of thought joined here by a hyphen held mutually inconsistent beliefs. Sautrāntika, as one of the schools of Abhidharma, believed in the existence of extra-mental objects, whereas Yogācāra denied this. These difficulties are reconciled by a device sometimes called the "sliding scale of analysis."[7] This allows a philosopher to move between different mutually inconsistent philosophical theories that are ordered by theoretical accuracy, framing his exposition in terms of a less accurate theory if expository purposes demand it. There is no need to bring in relativistic mechanics to explain some physical phenomenon if it can be satisfactorily explained in Newtonian mechanics, even though Newtonian mechanics is the less accurate theory. Its descriptive disadvantages are compensated by the fact that it is more readily comprehended by the audience.

In this context it is helpful to distinguish three levels of theoretical description.

1 *The common-sense position* This position constitutes the epistemic default, the view ordinary (that is, unenlightened) beings have. It is characterized in particular by the assumption that wholes exist over and above their constituents and also that there is a self that exists over and above the collection of psycho-physical aggregates.
2 *The Sautrāntika position* According to this view there are no wholes over and above their parts; all that exists are particulars without any spatial or temporal extension. All particulars are unique; there are no universals that are instantiated by a variety of particulars. Particulars do not just fail to be distributed in space and in time, they also fail to be, so to speak, "conceptually distributed," by being co-instantiators of the same universal.
3 *The Yogācāra position* This position denies that any of the particles have any non-mental existence. As such the subject–object distinction implied by the view that momentary extra-mental particles are accurately represented in perception has to be given up.

Dharmakīrti's exposition moves between levels 2 and 3 in order to refute level 1. The move upwards in this hierarchy reflects not just a more accurate understanding of reality but also, as it moves further away from the common-sense position, a move closer to liberation from suffering. Ascent from level 1 to level 3 results in a more accurate view of reality, since entities regarded as ultimately real at a lower level are shown to be problematic at higher levels. They are rejected as ultimately real but retained as conventional appearances. The familiar Abhidharma critique shows that wholes regarded as real over and above their constituents (as assumed by common sense) cannot be given a satisfactory ontological analysis. We therefore have to conclude that, while the spatio-temporally extended objects are not ultimately real, their most fundamental constituents, the momentary particulars, are. Spatio-temporally extended objects are merely conventionally real, mind-made artifacts superimposed on the ultimate reality of particulars but nothing that could exist in and of itself. As we reach the higher level the same fate befalls notions such as objectively existent universals and mind-independent momentary particulars. They, too, will be shown to be inherently contradictory (much in the same manner in which spatio-temporally extended objects were)[8] and will be retained at higher levels, not as ultimately real objects but as mere transactional, conventional existents.

The move through the levels is a move closer to liberation from suffering because, for the Buddhist, the prime cause of suffering is grasping, in particular grasping at a self that is regarded as existent over and above the individual aggregates that make up a person. Yet grasping can be more subtle than this attachment to a self characteristic of level 1. Even though the world is now conceived of as split up into momentary particulars, once the understanding of level 1 has been replaced by the more accurate understanding of Abhidharma, there might still be the idea of a set of universals distributed across them, a set of properties shared by collections of individuals. While we may no longer be attached to a particular sweet object, such as a melon, since we know that the melon is nothing but a collection of particulars, we might now be attached to the property the melon exemplifies, and which it shares with various other sweet objects: the universal of sweetness. In a word, we do not become attached to the melon as an object, but to a quality or universal we regard as shared, unchanging, and permanent. The aim of the Sautrāntika analysis of level 2 is to remove this subtler object of grasping once the coarser grasping at a substantial self has been cleared away.

Yet even level 2 contains the possibility of grasping at an even subtler level. According to the Sautrāntika understanding, we still have the dichotomy of momentary particulars "out there" and their representation by sensory perception "in here." We are therefore still likely to react with attraction and aversion towards what we regard as external, drawing the distinction between external objects grasped and an internal grasper. In order to dissolve this dichotomy, the Yogācāra position introduces the theory that the assumption of an extra-mental world is erroneous, and that because there is no substantial external world there is no substantial internal recipient of such a world either.

A particularly interesting feature of Dharmakīrti's exposition is that most of the philosophical discussion takes place at level 2 – that is, at a level that Dharmakīrti does not regard as the most accurate description of the world. This is interesting insofar as we would expect a philosopher to defend what he regards as the final description of the world, rather than developing his system against a background theory he believes to be false. We can imagine two reasons for this, one pragmatic and one soteriological. Firstly, the level 2 analysis, with its belief in a world of external, though momentary particulars, would have been the highest level still acceptable to the majority of Dharmakīrti's Buddhist interlocutors. In order to debate with them it is sensible for pragmatic reasons to select a background theory one's co-debaters do not immediately regard as deficient. Secondly, it is evident that, as we ascend through the levels of analysis, the theories become more and more counter-intuitive. Since the aim of philosophical analysis is taken to be the removal of suffering, it is soteriologically important that we use a level of analysis for our exposition that is as high as possible (in order to eliminate as many potential objects of grasping as possible), while at the same time not so high as to go beyond the powers of comprehension of our audience. Dharmakīrti may have thought that level 2 is the level of analysis that fulfills both these conflicting demands.

The strict nominalism of the school of Dignāga and Dharmakīrti raises problems both for semantics and for logic. On the one hand, it has to explain how we can manage to speak successfully about a world using predicates if there are no similarities out there in the world to which these predicates refer. On the other hand, it is problematic how we could have a theory of inference that spells out entailment in terms of relations between universals (that fire can be inferred from smoke is due to the fact that the property of having smoke and the property of having fire are related in a certain way) if there are no universals to be so related.

In order to solve these problems a specific theory of "exclusion" (*apoha*) has been developed. According to this theory, predicates are linked to the world not via characteristics shared by certain groups of objects, but via the exclusion of their opposites. The predicate sweet does not latch on to some thing that is common to all the sweet things in the world (such as the universal sweetness) but acquires its meaning via exclusion of objects that are not sweet.

Two questions immediately arise concerning this account. Does talk about non-sweetness not just involve reference to the universal non-sweet, thereby failing to eliminate reference to universals? And why is saying that the predicate "sweet" means not non-sweet any more informative than saying that "sweet" means sweet?

In reply to the first point, note that we seem to be considerably more inclined to ascribe existence to the universal sweet than to the universal non-sweet. This is because the set of things that are non-sweet is so diverse (including lemons, symphonies, battles, prime numbers, and so forth) that it is hard to see how there could be anything "out there" that is shared by all these objects. Rather, what is common to all these objects is that our mind attaches the label "non-sweet" to all of them, rather than any property they have in and of themselves.

Secondly, absences (such as the absence of sweetness indicated by the term "non-sweet") are not properties "out there" in the world and therefore cannot be considered to be universal. Perception of an absence is not a perception of a universal, but rather the perception of a particular combined with the expectation of some other perception, and the realization that the former perception excludes the latter perception. Perceiving the non-sweetness of the lemon is not the perception of the property non-sweet inherent in the lemon, but rather a particular lemon-perception, combined with the expectation for the perception of another particular, such as honey, and the realization that one excludes the other. Absences are, to put it briefly, mind-made, since the perception of them involves reference to purely mental entities such as expectations at a crucial stage.

A third response is based on the distinction between two kinds of negation. The first, implicative negation is a negation that implies the presence of a property other than the negated one. If we say that a certain vase is non-blue, we imply that it has some other color, such as red or green. Non-implicative negations do not generate such entailments. They are pure rejections of certain properties but do not imply the presence of another property. If we say that the number five is not blue we do not mean to imply that it has some other color instead.

In the expression "not non-sweet" we now understand "not" as a non-implicative negation and "non" as an implicative one. This tells us why "not non-sweet" cannot just be reduced to "sweet." This elimination of two consecutive negations is allowed (at least according to the framework of classical logic) only if we have two instances of the same negation operator following each other. In this case we are dealing with different kinds of negation so that this reduction is not applicable.

In addition, the characterization "not non-sweet" is a pure rejection of the class of things that are non-sweet (and therefore have some other taste) but does not make any assertion about the kind of properties the things so characterized do have. This construction allows us to characterize a class of objects without committing us to subscribing to some property they all share.[9]

Neither the collection of things that falls under "sweet" nor that falling under "non-sweet" comes with some specific thing shared by all members. Each member of these collections is a unique particular, utterly distinct from anything else. Grouping them together does not have its roots in ontology, but in epistemology. We overlook the differences between the individual items we are going to call sweet, such as honey and sugar, by focusing on their differences with another, excluded group (the group of non-sweet things) and thereby collect together the honey and the sugar into one group.

The groups are collected together because they are all instrumental in satisfying a specific desire. We have specific wishes to acquire certain things and to avoid others, and our concepts are formed in accordance with these wishes. We have a specific desire, and this is satisfied by honey, for example. Later we realize that a different thing, sugar, also satisfies this desire. Honey and sugar are very different in various respects but distinct from all things that do not satisfy this specific desire (such as vinegar, charcoal, or the number five). We can therefore group honey and sugar together as what excludes the things that do not satisfy our specific desire, and refer to this group by the predicate "sweet." The theory of exclusion saves us from the unwelcome consequence of having to ascribe a common property such as "fulfilling this specific desire" to honey and sugar. For we define it as the exclusion of the collection of things that do not fulfill this desire, and, as we have just seen, such exclusions do not correspond to universals.

Notes

1 For some images, see www.himalayanart.org/pages/sixornaments/index.html.
2 As we will see later, the Mādhyamikas disagree with this assessment of the view that *everything* could be derived or non-fundamental.
3 It differs in this respect from the position of Nyāya, which accords absences (*abhāva*) the status of a proper category.
4 Such particularized properties are commonly called *tropes* in the contemporary philosophical discussion. It is sometimes argued that they provide a good model for the Abhidharma theory of dharmas. See Goodman (2004).
5 The questions whether this makes Yogācāra a form of idealism and whether the Yogācārin endorses an ontological position have recently attracted renewed attention. See Lusthaus (2002).
6 For more discussion of collective hallucinations, see Wood (1991, 171–90); Bartholomew (2001).
7 McClintock (2010, 12); Dunne (2004, 53–64).
8 See Dunne (2004, 62–3).
9 Siderits (1985, 142–3); see also Siderits (1982).

References

Bartholomew, Robert E. (2001). *Little Green Men, Meowing Nuns, and Head-Hunting Panics: A Study of Mass Psychogenic Illnesses and Social Delusion*. Jefferson, NC: McFarland.

Dreyfus, Georges (1997). *Recognizing Reality: Dharmakīrti's Philosophy and its Tibetan Interpretations*. Albany: State University of New York Press.

Dunne, John (2004). *Foundations of Dharmakīrti's Philosophy*. Boston: Wisdom.

Goodman, Charles (2004). The Treasury of Metaphysics and the Physical World. *Philosophical Quarterly* 54/216, 389–401.

Lusthaus, Dan (2002). *Buddhist Phenomenology: A Philosophical Investigation of Yogācāra Buddhism and the Ch'eng Wei-shih lun*. London: Routledge.

McClintock, Sara (2010). *Omniscience and the Rhetoric of Reason: Śāntarakṣita and Kamalaśīla on Rationality, Argumentation, & Religious Authority*. Boston: Wisdom.

Perrett, Roy W. (2004). The Momentariness of Simples. *Philosophy* 79/3, 435–45.

Rospatt, Alexander von (1995). *The Buddhist Doctrine of Momentariness: A Survey of the Origins and Early Phase of this Doctrine up to Vasubandhu*. Stuttgart: Franz Steiner.

Schaffer, Jonathan (2010). Monism: The Priority of the Whole. *Philosophical Review* 119/1, 31–76.

Siderits, Mark (1982). More Things in Heaven and Earth. *Journal of Indian Philosophy* 10, 187–208.

Siderits, Mark (1985). Word Meaning, Sentence Meaning, and Apoha. *Journal of Indian Philosophy* 13, 133–51.

Wood, Thomas E. (1991). *Mind Only: A Philosophical and Doctrinal Analysis of the Vijñānavāda*. Honolulu: University of Hawai'i Press.

9

Emptiness in Mahāyāna Buddhism

Interpretations and Comparisons

DAVID BURTON

Emptiness (*śūnyatā*) is a central concept in Mahāyāna Buddhist philosophy; however, it has multiple meanings. Many Mahāyāna Buddhist philosophers use the term "emptiness" but often in divergent ways. Moreover, there is considerable disagreement among contemporary scholars of Buddhism about the interpretation of emptiness. This is fueled in part by the hermeneutical challenges posed by Mahāyāna Buddhist philosophical works; different texts or portions of texts can suggest different readings, and often the same passage or verse can support more than one interpretation. There is also an understandable wish to relate teachings about emptiness to current philosophical trends and debates. When done without sensitivity to the original intellectual, linguistic, and social context of Mahāyāna Buddhism, this comparative thinking can lead to dubious readings (Tuck 1990). However, given the ambiguities and divergent views often present in the source material, even careful commentators reach different conclusions about the philosophical implications of emptiness. This rich polysemy provides an opportunity for vigorous debate about the relative philosophical merits of the variety of interpretations.

The purpose of this chapter is to identify the most prominent meanings of emptiness in Mahāyāna Buddhism and to highlight some important interpretive disputes. Given the complexity of the subject, there is no ambition to be comprehensive. Although there will be some discussion of statements about emptiness from relevant Buddhist sources, the focus will be on conceptual distinctions and their philosophical connotations rather than on in-depth investigation of texts. Attributions of particular interpretations of emptiness to individual Mahāyāna Buddhist philosophers will be intentionally avoided, as commentators often disagree about how specific Buddhist thinkers construe emptiness; engagement with these disputes is beyond the scope of this brief treatment of the topic. This chapter is also an exercise in comparative philosophizing; it discusses similarities between the emptiness concept and some Western philosophical ideas. However, it is naïve to think that similarity implies sameness; comparison becomes

A Companion to Buddhist Philosophy, First Edition. Edited by Steven M. Emmanuel.

insightful when interesting points of cross-cultural affinity are balanced by inevitable differences.

Madhyamaka: Emptiness as Absence of Intrinsic Existence

The Madhyamaka assertion that all things are empty means that they are all dependently originating (*pratītyasamutpāda*); they lack or are empty of autonomous existence because they are reliant on causes to bring them into and sustain their existence. The manifold entities that make up the world are related to one another in complex patterns of interdependence. Some contemporary Buddhists see this teaching as entailing the ethical responsibility to respond to the sufferings of other people. They also perceive similarities between the Buddhist focus on interconnectedness and contemporary environmental theories that stress our duties to the natural world (Edelglass and Garfield 2009, 420, 428–30). Moreover, parallels are sometimes drawn between the Buddhist teaching of dependent origination and trends in the philosophy of science such as cybernetics, which sees humans and the environment as irrevocably intertwined in symbiotic relationships within vastly intricate systems (Macy 1990).

However, the Madhyamaka concept of emptiness entails more than an assertion of interconnectedness; in addition, it means that all phenomena are empty in the sense that they lack existence independent of the conceptualizing activity of the mind. Dependent origination in the Madhyamaka context entails that all entities are mental constructions.

This Madhyamaka claim should be understood in the context of Abhidharma Buddhism, which, in its Vaibhāṣika form, distinguishes between fundamental or primary existence (*dravyasat*) and conceptual existence (*prajñaptisat*). This distinction corresponds to that between ultimate truths (*paramārthasatya*) and conventional truths (*saṃvṛtisatya*). Entities such as mountains and tables have conceptual existence and are conventional truths because they can be analyzed into their component parts. Their existence is the result of conceptual synthesis on the basis of their constituents. Entities have fundamental existence and are ultimate truths if they cannot be further analyzed into parts. Abhidharma philosophy refers to these partless components of all mental and material things as *dharmas*, each of which is said to have its own defining characteristic (*svalakṣaṇa*) and intrinsic existence (*svabhāva*). The *dharmas* are in most cases radically impermanent and causally produced by preceding *dharmas* in a chain of dependent origination. Nevertheless, they are ultimate truths and have intrinsic existence because they are the basic components into which all other things can be analyzed. Their existence is not the result of conceptual reification.

Mādhyamikas contend that this two-tier Abhidharma ontology does not go far enough. All things are empty of intrinsic existence. Even the *dharmas* have conceptual existence and are conventional truths. Mādhyamikas present a host of detailed arguments intended to refute the intrinsic existence of all things. But the key Madhyamaka contention is that *dharmas* would have to be independent and permanent in order to have their own, autonomous defining characteristics; however, nothing has that type of existence. All things originate dependently, and dependently originating existence entails conceptual existence; entities are reifications on the basis of their manifold causes. These causes are themselves always reifications on the basis of their own causes. There is just conceptual construction without exception. There are no ultimately true entities that function as an ontological bedrock on which conceptual construction takes place.

This means that, for Mādhyamikas, the ultimate truth is that there are no ultimate truths. This apparent paradox can be resolved by identifying two senses in which Madhyamaka philosophy uses the term "ultimate truth": ultimate truth (1) refers to the way things really are, while ultimate truth (2) is used in the plural to refer to entities that have intrinsic existence. The Madhyamaka claim is that the ultimate truth (1) is that there are no ultimate truths (2).

Mādhyamikas are insistent that emptiness has genuinely universal scope; emptiness is itself empty. Emptiness is not an independently existing Absolute Reality like Brahman in Advaita Vedānta, for example. On the contrary, emptiness is itself a characteristic of the entities of which it is the emptiness – it is the emptiness of the tree, the emptiness of the chair, and so forth. Emptiness is itself dependently originated. Without entities there would be no emptiness. The emptiness of emptiness does not mean that emptiness is not ultimately true (1) but it does entail that emptiness is not an ultimate truth (2). The ultimate truth (1) is that all things, including emptiness itself, are empty of intrinsic existence.

This account prompts interesting questions about the status of conventional truths which can be raised but not answered here (see The Cowherds 2011). Given that conventional truths are conceptual constructs, in what sense are they true? Mādhyamikas claim that unenlightened people fail to see that the conventional truths are merely conventional; the spiritually ignorant give such truths an ontological status they do not in fact have. Conventional truths are deceptive in the sense that they appear in a manner that conceals their true nature as empty of intrinsic existence. Nevertheless, can the Mādhyamikas provide an account of conventional truth that acknowledges that it is in some sense true that my book is sitting on the desk and false that I am a world-class violinist? Evidently some things are not even conventionally true – for example, square circles and winged horses. And there are presumably some serious constraints on the conventional truths that are possible – for example, we are not able conceptually to construct a world in which a picture of a cup of water can quench thirst. Are the Mādhyamikas required simply to accept whatever the consensus or the majority of people take to be true with the caveat that this conventional truth is merely conventional, unbeknown to most people? Or can Mādhyamikas accommodate a more demanding understanding of conventional truth as something that can be reformed and improved by, for example, scientific inquiry irrespective of the opinions of the (often scientifically uninformed) majority? Presumably Mādhyamikas consider some conventional truths – for example, the ethical and religious truths espoused by Buddhism – to be superior to others even when most people do not accept the Buddhist teachings. Finally, there are debates about whether the Madhyamaka account of conventional truths is compatible with a correspondence, coherence, or pragmatic theory of truth, the dominant theories of truth in contemporary philosophy. The Mādhyamikas do not all give the same responses to these questions concerning conventional truth, and in many cases it is debatable what their answers would be.

The Madhyamaka concept of emptiness invites comparison with contemporary currents in philosophy that attack ontological realism – that is, the philosophical view that there is a reality which is not conceptually constructed. The similarity is most pronounced in forms of ontological constructivism that claim that even physical and biological phenomena – such as race, sex, trees, chairs, and atoms – are human constructions rather than having existence independent of our interests and concerns. Thinkers such as Jacques Derrida, Terry Winograd, J. R. Wheeler, and Humberto Maturana have made such constructivist claims (Searle 1995, 157–60). There is clearly an affinity between this recent trend in Western thought and the Madhyamaka philosophy of emptiness. Nevertheless, there are notable differences. For instance, Mādhyamikas would highlight the influence of karma on the way the world is constructed, whereas contemporary constructivists often emphasize the impact of social conditioning.

When the contemporary constructivist thesis is taken to mean that the world is *entirely* a human construction, it has attracted stern opposition. For example, Searle acknowledges that many aspects of our social reality are constructed and that the socially conditioned mind is very active in creating the world that we inhabit (Searle 1995, 1–30). However, he finds unintelligible the notion that *everything* is a human construct; there must be some unconstructed "brute facts" on the basis of which such construction takes place. Similar doubts occur about the intellectual coherence of the Madhyamaka claim that all entities are entirely conceptually created.

Critics of Madhyamaka dismiss the philosophy of universal emptiness as a form of ontological nihilism; the claim that everything is empty means that nothing exists at all. The standard Madhyamaka reply is that this objection rests on a misunderstanding of emptiness. Emptiness means that entities exist without intrinsic existence but not that they do not exist at all. Emptiness is the ontological middle way between non-existence and intrinsic existence. Mādhyamikas claim that it is emptiness properly understood which explains and makes possible the existence of all things. Far from entailing ontological nihilism, it is because things are empty that they can exist in a dependently originating way (Nāgārjuna 1995, 67–72). However, it is not clear that the Mādhyamikas' explanation is entirely convincing, because they do not say only that all things are dependently originated; they also contend that all entities are caused completely by conceptual construction. It is this latter claim that many opponents find particularly problematic.

Yogācāra: Emptiness of the Subject–Object Duality

The Yogācāra concept of emptiness can be viewed as a reaction against the Madhyamaka contention that all things lack intrinsic existence. It also represents a return to the Abhidharma position that there must be an unconstructed ontological foundation for conceptual construction. For both Yogācāra and Abhidharma philosophy, the Madhyamaka claim that everything is conceptually constructed amounts to ontological nihilism. For the Abhidharma, the unconstructed substratum is the *dharmas*, which include the fundamental material constituents of the world. By contrast, the Yogācāra substratum is the dependently originating stream of consciousness. Hence, the Yogācāra ontology is described as "mind-only" (*cittamātra*). Emptiness for Yogācāra does not mean universal absence of intrinsic existence. On the contrary, there is something that has intrinsic existence, namely, the flow of cognitive events (*vijñapti*). It is this substratum which is erroneously bifurcated into the duality of subject and object. Unenlightened people fabricate a world of external objects and selves. However, in reality the objects and selves are nothing more than a flow of experiences. Emptiness in Yogācāra Buddhism means the emptiness of the subject–object duality.

Central to the Yogācāra philosophy is the teaching of the three aspects (*trisvabhāva*). The first of the three aspects is the "constructed aspect" (*parikalpitasvabhāva*). This is the world of subject–object duality which unenlightened people wrongly think intrinsically exists; in fact, it is a fabrication. The second aspect is the "dependent aspect" (*paratantrasvabhāva*). This is the intrinsically existing, dependently originating stream of cognitive events. It is the dependent aspect which is the way things really are and which functions as the substratum for the erroneous conceptual construction of reified subjects and objects. If the constructed aspect were removed, then only the non-dual dependent aspect would remain. The third aspect is the "perfected aspect" (*pariniṣpannasvabhāva*). It is what needs to be known for enlightenment to occur – namely, emptiness – understood here as the fact that the dependent aspect is empty of the constructed aspect. The perfected aspect is seeing the dependent aspect as it really is, devoid of the conceptual fabrications ordinarily superimposed on the non-dual stream of cognitive events. Enlightened people achieve human perfection by seeing this emptiness with perfect clarity. They overcome craving by fully understanding that the subjects and objects that most people grasp are merely conceptual constructions (Vasubandhu 2009).

The Yogācāra concept of emptiness does not go as far as the Madhyamaka assertion that everything lacks intrinsic existence; nevertheless, it is a radical and controversial position. The Yogācāra denial of the mind-independent existence of objects certainly contradicts the contemporary view of scientific realism that consciousness is dependent and evolves out of the material world. It has more in common with forms of Western ontological idealism which make the claim that nothing exists independent of the mind. The most famous Western proponent of this position is George Berkeley (see Berkeley 1998). The Yogācāra philosophers would agree with Berkeley's contention that the mind-independent existence of the world is unobservable; all that we perceive is cognitive experiences that we falsely believe to be caused by objects that exist independent of the mind. The existence of these cognitive experiences can be explained without recourse to an unobservable world of external objects.

However, there are also significant differences. For example, Berkeley considers the mind to be a thinking substance with ideas (including sensory images) as its qualities. By contrast, for Yogācāra philosophers the notion of an unchanging substance is anathema; their view is that the mind is a causally conditioned series of events. This is in accordance with the prevalent Buddhist rejection of an enduring self. The difference might be summed up as that between substance and process ontological idealism. Furthermore, one of the principal objections to ontological idealism is that it is difficult to explain the shared nature of sensory experiences. The ontological realists can claim that people have similar sensory experiences because there are mind-independent objects that cause these similar sensory experiences in different people. We have a shared experience of a river in the park because there really is a river in the park. If the ontological idealists are right, this explanation of shared sensory experience is not acceptable. Berkeley resorts to the explanation that God coordinates the experiences in different individual minds and ensures the regularities in our perceptions of nature. Yogācāra philosophers would have no truck with this theistic form of ontological idealism; instead they claim that shared sensory experiences are the result of similar karma. We are all able to perceive the river in the park because as humans we have broadly similar karmic backgrounds. Different karma leads to different sensory experiences. The stock example is that the bad karma of hungry ghosts (*preta*) causes them to experience rivers of pus rather than rivers of water (Siderits 2007, 152–8). However, it might be objected that the Yogācāra philosophers have simply replaced the ontological realists' assumption that there is an external world with the unverifiable belief in karma.

There is also the danger of solipsism – that is, the philosophical position that only the cognitive events that make up one's own mind exist or can be proven to exist. Many Yogācāra philosophers reject solipsism and assert the existence of a plurality of streams of consciousness; however, it is not evident how one would know that there must be streams of consciousness other than one's own. They might, after all, be nothing more than the product of one's own conceptual activity. Some Yogācāra thinkers demonstrate that they are aware of this difficulty and seek to prove the existence of other minds (Williams 2009, 309–10). Of course, solipsism is a challenging philosophical problem that is not peculiar to Yogācāra Buddhism.

Whether ontological idealism provides a better account of reality than ontological realism is a topic of perennial debate. The ontological idealists' denial of the existence of the external world is a counter-intuitive affront to common sense. However, this does not make it wrong, because intuition and common sense are not always reliable guides to truth. Moreover, Yogācāra philosophers do provide some arguments in support of their position. For instance, they claim that the perception of physical objects is analogous to the experience of apparently external objects in dream experiences. The fact that many people have similar perceptions of external objects is likened to a collective hallucination. Finally, the Yogācāra philosophers claim that it is impossible to make sense of the existence of external, physical objects. They provide detailed refutations of the notion that such objects can exist as whole entities or that they can exist as constructs out of indivisible atoms. Given that these are the only possibilities, the conclusion the Yogācāra thinkers wish us to draw is that physical objects do not really exist (Siderits 2007, 146–79). It is a moot point whether these Yogācāra arguments are convincing.

Buddha-Nature: Emptiness as Absence of Defilements

Another concept of emptiness occurs in the buddha-nature (*tathāgatagarbha*) teaching, which claims that sentient beings each have within them something that enables them to become a fully enlightened buddha. While this is sometimes interpreted as meaning that sentient beings have the potential to become buddhas, there is also a common view that the buddha-nature is an actual fully formed, primeval reality already present within sentient beings, who are therefore already enlightened. This buddha-nature is obscured by various adventitious moral and cognitive defilements (*kleśa*) – primarily greed, hatred, and delusion – which afflict the unenlightened. However, this nature is intrinsically pure and undefiled. The purpose of Buddhism is thus to remove the defilements and recognize that one has always been enlightened; this is sometimes likened to removing the layers of dust from a mirror or discovering a precious jewel hidden within one's clothing. This buddha-nature is referred to as empty in the sense that it is empty of the defilements. But it is also not empty because it has all of the pure characteristics of enlightenment, such as wisdom and compassion. A key interpretive question is whether this buddha-nature itself lacks intrinsic existence in accordance with Madhyamaka ontology or is identifiable with the Yogācāra non-dual stream of consciousness, purified of the conceptual constructions that constitute the imagined nature.

An alternative view, prevalent in East Asian Buddhism and also present in some forms of Tibetan Buddhism, is that the buddha-nature is an unchanging, intrinsically existing Absolute Reality. This latter understanding of the emptiness of the buddha-nature denies the universal scope of the Madhyamaka claim that things lack intrinsic existence. It also departs from the Yogācāra claim that the ultimate truth is an ever-changing flow of consciousness. It affirms what the earlier Madhyamaka and Yogācāra ontologies deny. Nevertheless, this belief in an Absolute Reality is sometimes conjoined with modified forms of the Madhyamaka and Yogācāra philosophies. Mādhyamikas who accept the existence of an Absolute Reality might claim that everything except this Absolute Reality is empty of intrinsic existence; an adapted form of Yogācāra would identify the Absolute Reality as a pure level of the mind unaffected by change (Williams 2009, 103–19).

This version of the buddha-nature teaching has been contentious. For example, the recent Critical Buddhism movement in Japan acknowledges that the buddha-nature doctrine has been widespread in East Asian Buddhism, partly as a result of its similarity to indigenous Chinese teachings concerning the Dao as a mysterious, ineffable Absolute Reality. However, the Critical Buddhists claim that this is a departure from the authentic Buddhist teachings of universal dependent origination and non-self. The views of the Critical Buddhist movement have been the subject of considerable interest and scrutiny (Hubbard and Swanson 1997). Their judgments concerning authenticity are controversial given the shear variety of forms that Buddhist thought has taken, each with its own claim to be genuine.

One of the defilements said to be absent from the buddha-nature is that of conceptuality. This means that the Absolute Reality is ineffable and can be apprehended by a special non-conceptual gnosis which is achieved by enlightened people. There has been detailed discussion in recent scholarship about comparative mysticism and the possibility of non-conceptual or inexpressible experience (King 1999, 161–86). Defenders of ineffability sometimes see the pure, unmediated apprehension of reality as lying at the heart of diverse forms of mystical experience, which then gets interpreted differently in different cultural and religious contexts. Critics argue that experience is necessarily mediated by concepts and language. Mystical experience is always already informed by conceptuality, and "ineffable knowledge" is an oxymoron. Furthermore, there is an apparent contradiction in the claim that reality is ineffable, given that this statement itself appears to be a description of reality. In response, it might be argued that, even if the claim that reality is indescribable is itself a description of reality, it is a negative description with minimal content.

What is clear is that the notion of non-conceptual knowledge is widely present in Mahāyāna Buddhist philosophy and not just in the context of the buddha-nature teaching. Mahāyāna Buddhist philosophy thus presents an alternative epistemology to that of many recent thinkers who claim that experience is always imbued with conceptualization. The classical Yogācāra philosophers who do not accept the existence of an unchanging Absolute Reality nevertheless identify language and conceptualization with the imagined aspect; this means that the enlightened knowledge of the non-dual flow of dependently originating consciousness is ineffable. The dependent aspect devoid of the imagined aspect is beyond the reach of concepts and words. Furthermore, those Mādhyamikas who deny that emptiness is an Absolute Reality nevertheless often claim that meditative techniques can be employed to induce a direct and focused awareness of emptiness in which the proliferation of conventional conceptually constructed entities subsides. Admittedly, this claim is puzzling if it is interpreted to mean that conceptuality is entirely absent. In this case, it would seem that even emptiness would not appear to the meditator given that emptiness, as a property of conceptually constructed things, itself has only conceptual existence. It would seem that, for these Mādhyamikas, a literally non-conceptual experience might be a blank state of mind, an experience of nothing at all.

The Emptiness of Views

A famous claim of Mādhyamikas is that they assert no views (*dṛṣṭi*) of their own and that emptiness is not itself a view (Nāgārjuna 1995, 26). This statement is perplexing. Isn't the emptiness of intrinsic existence a view about the way things really are that the Mādhyamikas wish to assert? One possible solution to this conundrum is to offer a non-literal reading of the Madhyamaka claim to have no views. The Mādhyamikas have no views in the sense that they have no views that assert the intrinsic existence of anything; however, they do assert the view that nothing has intrinsic existence, including emptiness itself. Their chastisement of those who take emptiness to be a view is directed at those who misconstrue emptiness as intrinsically existent. The Mādhyamikas do think that it is ultimately true that all things lack intrinsic existence; they do assert that emptiness is the way things really are, and in this sense they do have a view. In addition, the Madhyamaka aversion to views might be interpreted as a warning against a merely theoretical understanding of emptiness; the intellectual grasp of the ultimate truth that things lack intrinsic existence needs to be matured through meditative techniques into a perception of emptiness. In modern philosophical parlance this is akin to the distinction between propositional knowledge and knowledge by acquaintance. The latter has a potency which the former often lacks. For example, knowledge about a tiger does not have the same impact as an encounter with a tiger. A view is not the same as a vision; those who rest content with the theoretical understanding of emptiness will not achieve the direct insight that has powerful transformative effects on one's character. The unmediated perception of oneself and the objects one craves as empty of intrinsic existence is liable to undermine the psychological proclivity to crave and be attached.

However, it is also possible to take the Madhyamaka "no views" claim at face value. Mādhyamikas literally hold no position about the true nature of things and simply refute those who have such positions. In this case, emptiness is not the ultimate truth (1) in the sense identified earlier; it is not how things really are and is only a conventional truth. Mādhyamikas are not doing ontology when they teach emptiness; on the contrary, emptiness is a warning against all attempts to formulate views about the nature of reality.

The philosophical implications of this interpretation of emptiness are not clear. Some Mādhyamikas might think that all views should be abandoned because there simply is no way things really are. The emptiness teaching is intended to dispel all ontological speculation because the true nature of reality simply does not exist. Truth and reality are always contextual and relative. It can be objected that this is paradoxical because the claim that there is no way things really are is itself a claim about how things really are. The claim that truth and reality is always contextual and relative is not itself contextual and relative. However, the Mādhyamika might respond that this paradox does not demonstrate a fault in their teaching; on the contrary, it indicates that the misguided need for there to be ultimate truth is deeply rooted in the structures of our language and thought. There is no way things really are even if our minds struggle to make sense of this claim. This is arguably a risky move for the Mādhyamika to make because it seemingly neglects the constraints of rationality.

Another possibility is that the Madhyamaka abandonment of views is intended to be a critique of all knowledge claims about the true nature of things. Emptiness in this case is an epistemological rather than an ontological (or anti-ontological) teaching. It is not a claim about how things really are or even that there is no way things really are. On the contrary, the emptiness of all views means that we do not know the nature of the world as it exists independently of human interest and concerns. The world that we experience is without intrinsic existence in the sense that it is suffused with the conceptual constructs that originate from our minds. How the world exists in itself is beyond our comprehension, as we experience the world from behind the veil of conceptuality. The world as experienced is conventionally true in that it is the world as it appears to human beings; the Mādhyamika can accept this world as conventional but rejects any assertions that our perceptions correspond to the mind-independent world. The Madhyamaka focus on the emptiness of all views can be seen as an encouragement to let go of all pretensions to knowledge about the true nature of reality; hankering after knowledge of the true nature of things, as well as the misguided conviction that one has achieved such knowledge, fuels so much of the attachment, conflict, and suffering which Buddhism is dedicated to eradicating. The enlightened Mādhyamika is one who recognizes the futility of the search for knowledge of things as they really are.

Doubts about the reliability of truth claims concerning the world as it is, independent of our perceptions, have also been an important feature of Western philosophy. This has sometimes led to a thoroughgoing knowledge skepticism, which does not accept any knowledge about things as they really are, although in modern philosophy the arguments for such skepticism are often raised only in order to be refuted. A common objection to universal knowledge skepticism is that such skeptics must at least claim to know that they have no knowledge of the true nature of things. In the Madhyamaka context, this would mean that they must claim to know that all views are empty, in which case they still have one view about things as they actually are. One response is for knowledge skeptics to accept that this is the one exception to the general claim that we have no knowledge of things in their true nature. However, critics might object that this is a case of special pleading. Alternatively, the knowledge skeptics might choose to bite the bullet and contend that they do not even know that they have no knowledge. This is not necessarily paradoxical. For example, the knowledge skeptics might believe that they have no knowledge without attributing the status of knowledge to this belief. For Mādhyamikas, this would mean that they believe but do not know that all knowledge claims are empty. However, the paradox re-emerges if the assertion that all views are empty is interpreted as universal belief skepticism. That is, the Madhyamaka refutation of views is a refutation of all beliefs about things in their true nature and not just of all knowledge claims. In this case, it would seem that the paradox can be resolved only if the Mādhyamika can passively accept the claim that all views are empty without this acquiescence requiring the level of assent associated with a belief. The view that all views are empty is simply how matters appear to them without its having the status of a belief about how things really are.

The attempt to undermine beliefs and knowledge claims about things in their true nature is a feature of Pyrrhonian Skepticism in ancient Greece and Rome (Hankinson 1995, 21). Moreover, some of the arguments employed in Pyrrhonian Skepticism to undermine ontological assertions have quite close parallels in Madhyamaka texts. For instance, the Pyrrhonian Skeptics contend that attempts to make truth claims credible lead to circularity or an infinite regress (Empiricus 1994, 40–3). The Mādhyamikas also argue that circularity and an infinite regress occur when efforts are made to establish the instruments of knowledge (*pramāṇa*) as reliable (Nāgārjuna 2010, 30–5). Furthermore, Mādhyamikas liken emptiness to a drug that is expelled from the body once its curative work has been done (Candrakīrti 1979, 150–1). A similar metaphor is employed by the Pyrrhonian Skeptics; their skeptical arguments are said to be like purgative medicines which are not to be retained once their task has been accomplished (Empiricus 1994, 118).

There are scholarly disagreements about the nature and precise extent of the various forms of Classical Skepticism. However, it is clear that Pyrrhonian Skepticism aims to produce suspension of judgment (*epochē*) about competing beliefs concerning the true nature of things. The result is said to be a state of tranquillity (*ataraxia*), in which the mind gives up its restless search for what is really the case. The turmoil associated with the search for truth is removed. Nevertheless, the Pyrrhonians claim that they are still able to function in the world; they follow the appearances without making the mistake of believing that the ways things appear correspond to what is really the case. This is arguably similar to the Mādhyamika, who might accept conventional truths while recognizing that they are merely conventional (Hankinson 1995; The Cowherds 2011, 89–130).

While some Mādhyamikas contend that all knowledge claims are empty, others might claim that their skepticism extends only as far as conceptual knowledge claims; this does not appear to have any parallels in Pyrrhonian Skepticism. Such Mādhyamikas would maintain that there is a special non-conceptual form of knowledge which apprehends the true nature of things without any distorting mental impositions. The veil of conceptuality can be pierced but only by the enlightened consciousness. These Mādhyamikas would contend that knowledge is possible but hold no ontological views because the true nature of things cannot be captured in concepts.

The Yogācāra concept of emptiness is sometimes interpreted in a manner similar to this reading of Madhyamaka. This chapter has presented Yogācāra as a form of ontological idealism, which claims that the external world of objects is actually a creation of the mind. The alternative reading (see Lusthaus 2002) considers Yogācāra to be a form of epistemological idealism which contends that unenlightened minds are unable to distinguish the world as it actually is from the conceptual constructions which we place upon it. The unenlightened mind is thus unable to gain knowledge of things as they really are because it is trapped within a web of conceptual fabrications. The world as we experience it is a projection of our own minds to the extent that it is always a product of our own interpretive categories. These impositions are fueled by ignorance and craving. For example, objects of desire are imbued with a substantiality, an attractiveness, and a permanence which they do not have independent of the desiring mind. The mind thus interprets the world in an appropriative way; objects are there to be grasped by a grasping self. The true nature of things is empty of the conceptual mistakes, such as the duality of grasping subject and grasped objects, which permeate unenlightened experience. The Yogācāra philosophy is a mind-only teaching in the sense that the world as we experience it is a construct of consciousness; however, this does not mean that no mind-independent world exists. The world as it really exists independent of the conceptualizing mind is the dependent aspect understood as the complex causal flux; this is what the enlightened mind sees shorn of the false imaginings that are a feature of unenlightened experience. Contrary to ontological idealism, Yogācāra Buddhism is not making the claim that this causal flux is reducible to a flow of exclusively mental events. However, some scholars have criticized this alternative interpretation of Yogācāra as unsupported by the textual sources, no matter what its philosophical merits might be (Williams 2009, 302–4).

Emptiness as Therapeutic

Buddhist philosophy is inherently therapeutic in intent. It tries to correct mistaken mental attitudes and convictions that lead to suffering (Burton 2010). This characteristic of Buddhism has led to comparisons with and influences on contemporary psychological techniques for improving mental health, such as mindfulness-based cognitive therapy (Williams and Kabat-Zinn 2011).

A similar therapeutic attitude to philosophy is evident in the Hellenistic traditions of Stoicism, Epicureanism, and Skepticism, where philosophy is understood in its original etymological sense as "the love of wisdom." Philosophy treats the diseases of belief that cause people misery. Moreover, philosophical reflection is often complemented by less discursive therapeutic techniques such as self-control, ethical precepts, and meditation. The philosopher is envisaged as a compassionate doctor who endeavors to cure the world's ills by teaching people to live wisely (Hadot 1995). This contrasts with the attitude that philosophy is an abstruse and professional academic activity with little obvious relevance to the individual's own life.

This chapter has explained that the concept of emptiness in Mahāyāna Buddhism is contested and open to a variety of interpretations. However, these diverse readings are united in recognizing that emptiness, as a central part of Mahāyāna Buddhist philosophy, has a therapeutic purpose. Understanding emptiness removes the psychological impediments to enlightenment. Emptiness is likened to a medicine because it cures the mind of the causes of suffering, namely, the mental ailments of craving and ignorance. While emptiness might seem abstract, the concept is intended to have an existential impact. Moreover, emptiness is meaningful only in the context of Buddhist praxis; insight into emptiness is part of a broader Buddhist path of ethical training and meditation. Philosophical reflection on emptiness is not intended to be simply an intellectual and theoretical exercise; it is also meant to induce a profound change in one's psychological dispositions and motivations.

References

Berkeley, George (1998). *A Treatise Concerning the Principles of Human Knowledge*. New York: Oxford University Press.

Burton, David (2010). Curing Diseases of Belief and Desire: Buddhist Philosophical Therapy. In *Philosophy as Therapeia: Royal Institute of Philosophy Supplement: 66*. Ed. Clare Carlisle and Jonardon Ganeri. Cambridge: Cambridge University Press, 187–218.

Candrakīrti (1979). *Lucid Exposition of the Middle Way: The Essential Chapters from the Prasannapadā of Candrakīrti*. Trans. Mervyn Sprung. London: Routledge & Kegan Paul.

The Cowherds (2011). *Moonshadows: Conventional Truth in Buddhist Philosophy*. New York: Oxford University Press.

Edelglass, William, and Garfield, Jay L. (2009). *Buddhist Philosophy: Essential Readings*. New York: Oxford University Press.

Empiricus, Sextus (1994). *Sextus Empiricus: Outlines of Scepticism*. Trans. Julia Annas and Jonathan Barnes. Cambridge: Cambridge University Press.

Hadot, Pierre (1995). *Philosophy as a Way of Life: Spiritual Exercises from Socrates to Foucault*. Trans. Michael Chase. Oxford, and Malden, MA: Blackwell.

Hankinson, R. J. (1995). *The Sceptics*. New York: Routledge.

Hubbard, J., and Swanson, Paul L. (eds) (1997). *Pruning the Bodhi Tree: The Storm over Critical Buddhism*. Honolulu: University of Hawai'i Press.

King, Richard (1999). *Orientalism and Religion: Postcolonial Theory, India and "the Mystic East."* London: Routledge.

Lusthaus, Dan (2002). *Buddhist Phenomenology: A Philosophical Investigation of Yogācāra Buddhism and the Ch'eng Wei-shih lun*. London: Routledge Curzon.

Macy, Joanna (1990). The Ecological Self: Post-Modern Ground for Right Action. In *Sacred Interconnections: Postmodern Spirituality, Political Economy, and Art*. Ed. David Ray Griffin. Albany: State University of New York Press, 35–48.

Nāgārjuna (1995). *The Fundamental Wisdom of the Middle Way: Nāgārjuna's Mūlamadhyamakakārikā*. Trans. Jay L. Garfield. Oxford: Oxford University Press.

Nāgārjuna (2010). *Nāgārjuna's Vigrahavyāvartanī: The Dispeller of Disputes*. Trans. Jan Westerhoff. Oxford: Oxford University Press.

Searle, John R. (1995). *The Construction of Social Reality*. London: Penguin.

Siderits, Mark (2007). *Buddhism as Philosophy: An Introduction.* Farnham: Ashgate.
Tuck, Andrew P. (1990). *Comparative Philosophy and the Philosophy of Scholarship: On the Western Interpretation of Nāgārjuna.* New York: Oxford University Press.
Vasubandhu (2009). Vasubandhu's Trisvabhāvanirdeśa: Treatise on the Three Natures. Trans. Jay L. Garfield. In William Edelglass and Jay L. Garfield (eds), *Buddhist Philosophy: Essential Readings.* New York: Oxford University Press, 35–45.
Williams, J. Mark G., and Kabat-Zinn, J. (eds) (2011). *Contemporary Buddhism: An Interdisciplinary Journal,* 12/1, special issue: *Mindfulness: Diverse Perspectives on its Meaning, Origins and Multiple Applications at the Intersection of Science and Dharma.*
Williams, Paul (2009). *Mahāyāna Buddhism: The Doctrinal Foundations.* Second edn. New York: Routledge.

10

Practical Applications of the *Perfection of Wisdom Sūtra* and Madhyamaka in the Kālacakra Tantric Tradition

VESNA A. WALLACE

As a synthesis of the system of perfections (*pāramitā-naya*) and the system of mantras (*mantra-naya*), the Indian Kālacakra tantric tradition bases its tantric method of achieving buddhahood on a set of doctrinal and philosophical perspectives expressed in the Perfection of Wisdom literature and in the later treatises of Indian Mahāyāna authors. The *Kālacakratantra*'s system of perfections, characterized as a causal system, upholds the doctrine of the emptiness of all phenomena, which lies at the core of tantric practice, providing a basis for the application of tantric methods. Its system of mantras, which provides a method for the realization of the clear light of mind and imperishable bliss, is characterized as a resultant system. The integration of these two systems of wisdom (cause) and method (result) corresponds to the wisdom and method aspects constituting the path and the goal of the *Kālacakratantra* tradition.

The Kālacakra tradition positions itself in the philosophical system of Madhyamaka, from whose perspective it criticizes the doctrinal tenets of Hindu philosophical schools and of Buddhist schools other than Madhyamaka.[1] Its modes of reasoning are clearly based on those of Madhyamaka. It exalts Madhyamaka's soteriological potency as exceeding that of other Buddhist schools in the following manner:

> Vaibhāṣikas, Sautrāntikas, and Yogācārins have a *nirvāṇa* with remainder (*sopadhinirvāṇa*), and Mādhyamikas have a non-established (*apratiṣṭhita*) *nirvāṇa* without remainder. Due to the cessation of causes and effects, it [*nirvāṇa*] is free from the waking state and deep sleep, and it is similar to a dream and to the fourth state (*turyā*). Hence, devoid of grasping onto a dogmatic position, a full and perfect Buddha has a *nirvāṇa* without remainder.[2]

As will be shown later, the proponents of the Kālacakra tradition in India sought various ways to illustrate the manner in which the ultimate reality is free from dogmatic positions and the ways in which the *yogī* achieves that freedom from any dogmatic

A Companion to Buddhist Philosophy, First Edition. Edited by Steven M. Emmanuel.

position and thereby a non-established *nirvāṇa* without remainder. According to Puṇḍarīka's *Vimalaprabhā* commentary on the *Kālacakratantra*, one reason for the difference between the final attainments of the various Buddhist schools is found in the Buddha's teaching of different types of meditation to the followers of different Buddhist schools. The Buddha, we are told, taught to the Pudgalavādins a meditation on the impermanent person (*anitya-pudgala*); to the Arthavādins, he taught a meditation on the totality (*kṛtsnā*) of the earth and the like; to the Vijñānavādins, he taught a *samādhi* on making-known only (*vijñaptimātra*); and, to the Mādhyamikas, he taught a meditation on the imperishable, non-dual gnosis that is similar to a dream (*svapnopamakṣarā dvayajñāna*). The Mādhyamikas' meditation on the supreme, imperishable gnosis is seen as the means for the accumulation of gnosis. Its soteriological potency consists in being a *sādhana* of one's own mind that is practiced through the yoga of the supreme, imperishable *mahāmudrā*.[3] The *mahāmudrā*, whose greatness is a non-localized reality (*tattva*) that is endowed with the best of all aspects, is both a contributing condition (*pratyaya*) and a result (*phala*). As a contributing condition, it is free of conceptual fabrications (*parikalpanā*) and is the luminosity of the *yogī*'s mind. As a result, the *mahāmudrā* is characterized by the supreme, imperishable gnosis of bliss.[4]

In Indian sources of the Kālacakra tantric tradition, particularly in the *Vimalaprabhā* commentary on the *Kālacakratantra*, the expositions on emptiness and the methods of realizing it are often supported by citations from the *Eight Thousand-Lined Perfection of Wisdom Sūtra* (*Aṣṭasāhasrikā Prajñāpāramitāmahāyānasūtra*) and from the works of Nāgārjuna. In other sources, such as Nāropā's *Sekoddeśaṭīkā*, the *Kālacakratantra*'s views and practices are also supported by statements of Candragomin, known to be a Yogācārin, in addition to those of Mādhyamikas such as Nāgārjuna and Āryadeva.

As previously mentioned, the concept of emptiness is the most essential tenet of the *Kālacakratantra* practice. Before analyzing the practical applications of the doctrine of emptiness in the Kālacakra tantric tradition, it may be useful to examine first the ways in which emptiness is defined and explained in this tantric system. Diverse manners of explaining emptiness result from the various contexts in which this tradition applies and actualizes the doctrine of emptiness.

The buddhas are said to abide in emptiness for the sake of establishing superb bodhisattvas like Subhūti, Maitreya, and others in the highest, full, and perfect awakening (*paramasamyaksaṃbodhi*). That emptiness is defined as follows:

> Empty nature (*śūnya-svabhāva*) is emptiness (*śūnyatā*). Here, the past and future object of gnosis is empty. A perception of this [empty object of cognition] is a condition that is the profound and vast emptiness. It is profound because of the absence of the past and future, and it is vast due to seeing the past and future.[5]

As the state of the object of cognition and as the state of the perception of that object, emptiness is understood as the basis for the non-duality of both the object and the subject of gnosis. This non-duality is repeatedly emphasized in a variety of ways throughout the Kālacakra literature. In his *Sekoddeśaṭīkā*, Nāropā repeats the definition of emptiness given in the *Vimalaprabhā*, explaining further that a gnosis which is an apprehender (*grāhaka*) of that emptiness is a liberation through emptiness (*śūnyatā-vimokṣa*).[6]

Emptiness is further interpreted as the absence of obscurations (*nirāvaraṇatā*) of the psychophysical aggregates, elements, sense faculties, sense objects, and faculties of action, as their quality of being of the same taste (*samarasatva*), and as their state of unification (*ekalolībhūtatva*).[7] As the absence of obscurations appearing as subtle atomic particles of the mind–body complex, emptiness is referred to as the Buddha's body (*śarīra*), which is brought into manifestation through the experience of the moments of sublime, imperishable bliss. This personal emptiness is classified into three main categories, which comprise sixteen types of emptiness: (1) the emptiness of the five psychophysical aggregates, (2) the great emptiness (*mahāśūnyatā*) of the five elements, (3) the ultimate emptiness (*paramārthaśūnyatā*) of the five sense faculties, and the sixteenth type of emptiness that has all aspects (*sarvākāraśūnyatā*).[8] As the consequence of actualizing this type of emptiness, the body whose obscurations are eradicated becomes transparent (*svaccha*) like space, and the entire world appears transparent to the mind like a dream.[9]

In accordance with this interpretation of emptiness, a meditation on the gnosis with five aspects (*pañcākārajñāna*) – namely, on the mirror-like gnosis, the gnosis of equality, discriminating gnosis, all-accomplishing gnosis, and the gnosis of realm of phenomena (*dharmadhātujñāna*) – which are manifestations of the psychophysical aggregates purified from their obscurations, takes on the following form:

> This collection of phenomena in space, which has abandoned the nature of conceptual fabrication, is seen like an image in a maiden's prognostic mirror.
>
> (mirror-like gnosis)
>
> A single phenomenon, having become equal with all phenomena, remains imperishable. Being the imperishable gnosis, it is without cessation and without eternity.
>
> (gnosis of equality)
>
> Syllables consisting of all designations have arisen from the family of the letter "a." Having reached the sublime, imperishable state, they are neither designations nor the designated.
>
> (discriminating gnosis)
>
> In non-arisen phenomena devoid of mental formations there is neither awakening nor buddhahood, neither a sentient being nor life.
>
> Phenomena that have transcended the reality of consciousness, that are purified by gnosis, that are clear and luminous by nature, have entered the scope of the realm of phenomena.[10]
>
> (the all-accomplishing gnosis)

By meditating on the five aspects of gnosis in this Mādhyamika manner, the *yogī* is to cultivate the habitual propensities (*vāsanā*) of ultimate reality that is characterized by non-duality and is free from all dogmatic positions owing to the absence of conceptual fabrication. In the final analysis, ultimate reality is said to be nothing other than an appearance of the habitual propensities of one's own mind (*svacittavāsanāpr atibhāsa*).[11]

At times, emptiness is also said to be similar to space, since it is indestructible and without parts, indivisible, omnipresent, and all-pervading; at other times, it is identified with space directly. The Buddha's lion-seat from which he taught the *Kālacakratantra* is identified as the space element (*ākāśa-dhātu*) having all aspects.[12] Like space, emptiness is a source of phenomena (*dharmodaya*). It has conventional reality as its form, and it is also a form of conventional reality.[13] In this way, it is endowed with all aspects.

Because of the similarity of space and emptiness, in the first phase of the *Kālacakratantra*'s six-phased yoga (*ṣaḍaṅgayoga*), the retraction phase (*pratyāhāra*), a non-conceptual meditation on emptiness, or on the absence of phenomena, is practiced with open eyes gazing at the cloudless sky. Due to the repeated practice of this daytime yoga with a steady gaze, a great, self-arisen fire of the wisdom of gnosis arises in space.

According to Vajrapāṇi's "The Six-phased Yoga of the *Abbreviated Wheel of Time Tantra*," this meditation on emptiness was also taught in the *Perfection of Wisdom Sūtra*, where this is stated: "Then, Śakra, the lord of gods, said this to Venerable Subhūti: 'Noble Subhūti, whoever will attain yoga (*samādhi*) on this perfection of wisdom, on what will he attain yoga?' Subhūti replied: 'Kauśika, he who will attain yoga on the perfection of wisdom will attain yoga on space. Kauśika, he who desires to attain yoga on space will be considered as the one who is to be instructed in the perfection of wisdom.'"[14]

During the six-phased yoga, in a single-pointed meditation on space, the *yogī* perceives a form of the triple world in space in the sequence of ten non-conceptualized signs (*nimitta*), the six daytime signs, and four nighttime signs. The ten signs, which are appearances of the *yogī*'s mind, are referred to as images, or forms, of emptiness (*śūnyatābimba*), also called the "forms of wisdom" (*prajñābimba*), that are similar to space. According to Sādhuputra's *Sekoddeśa-ṭippaṇī*, these signs are aspects (*ākāra*) of the appearance of non-conceptualizing wisdom, which are indivisible from wisdom itself, like moon rays are indivisible from the moon.[15] The wisdom of emptiness is an apprehending mind (*grāhakacitta*), and the ten signs are appearances in the mirror of the apprehended mind (*grāhyacitta*). That apprehended mind is gnosis. According to the *Sekoddeśaṭīkā*, it is like an image of one's own eyes in a mirror, where one's own eye is an apprehended object. When the apprehending mind merges into the apprehended mind, the engagement with external sense objects ceases. From the immersion of those two minds arises the bliss of *nirvāṇa*, the fourth, innate, imperishable bliss. Since this arisen bliss does not have the actual or imagined consort as its cause, it is characterized by the appearance of all the aspects of emptiness (*śūnyatāsarvākārapratibhāsa*).[16]

At the time when the *yogī* completes the final, sixth phase of yoga, known as *samādhi*, the unity of the apprehending mind and the apprehended mind takes place. On account of the unbounded power of luminous gnosis, motionlessness (*acalana*) takes place, due to which there is an absence of obscurations and an understanding of the non-duality of the two realities (*satya-dvaya*).[17]

Since a form of emptiness, also known as emptiness having all aspects, is not conceptualized by the *yogī*, for the mind in meditation there is neither existence nor non-existence in that form. A form (*bimba*) that has arisen from emptiness, or from the absence of inherent existence, is a cause (*hetu*), and a bliss that has arisen from the imperishable, non-conceptual gnosis of *mahāmudrā* having all aspects is a result (*phala*). Being embraced by each other, these two constitute a non-dual yoga, a union of the conventional and ultimate realities that is without eternity and cessation. According to the *Sekoddeśaṭīkā*, what is meant by cessation here is an absence (*abhāva*) of the empty form, which is an appearance of the *yogī*'s mind that has all aspects.[18] According to the *Sekoddeśa*, a reason why the empty form is free from eternity and cessation lies in the fact that the form of emptiness is devoid of *nirvāṇa*, but the imperishable gnosis of bliss transcends *saṃsāra*. The faults of eternalism and nihilism do not apply to it for the following reasons. An empty form is not imbued with non-existence (*abhāva*) because it is characterized as that which has arisen from non-existence (*abhāvodbhūta*); or, to put it in terms of the *yogī*'s experience, it is not imbued with non-existence because of the appearance of the *yogī*'s self-awareness, which has all aspects arisen from the absence of inherent existence.[19] According to the *Sekoddeśaṭīkā*, an empty form is not imbued with non-existence because there is an arising of the appearance of the three worlds within the three times from an empty, stainless sky.[20] On the other hand, the imperishable gnosis does not have existence (*bhāva*) because it is characterized as that which has arisen from existence, or because it has arisen with all aspects that are primordially non-arisen.[21] For these reasons, this non-dual reality consisting of empty form and imperishable gnosis, which is a union of existence and non-existence and devoid of form (*rūpa*) and non-form (*arūpa*), is compared to an image in a prognostic mirror. Like an image in a prognostic mirror, an empty form does not have the characteristic of form (*rūpa*) because of the absence of materiality, but it is also without form (*arūpa*) because it is perceived. Thus, an image in a prognostic mirror serves as an example of the *yogī*'s direct perception (*pratyakṣa*), which is non-arisen due to the absence of its inherent existence. The *yogī*, who is like a virgin girl as a result of firmly holding his *bodhicitta* (seminal fluid), has a direct perception of transcendent reality, as he does not see it with his own eyes or through someone else's eyes because of the absence of seeing (*adarśana*).[22]

Although the relationship between emptiness having all aspects and imperishable gnosis is spoken of in terms of cause and effect, their non-duality, referred to as the gnosis of wisdom (*prajñājñāna*) free from grasping onto both existence and non-existence, referred to form and non-form, and so on, is not a gnosis born from the wisdom of emptiness as its cause. A reason for this is that the wisdom characterized by the emptiness of all phenomena is not born (*ajāta*) and cannot be designated as existent or non-existent, nor can it be described as both existent-and-non-existent, nor as that which is neither existent-nor-non-existent. Since the existence of a cause is not established, a result cannot be said to arise from a cause. Emptiness is conventionally spoken of as a cause only in terms of being the first, and a result, or the imperishable gnosis, consisting of compassion without an object, as being later; ultimately, though, the gnosis of wisdom is devoid of the conceptualizations of cause, effect, and the like. Since from the conventional point of view cause and effect are dependently arisen and from the ultimate point of view they are without beginning and end, an empty form, also called the *yuganaddha*, which is a unity of both cause and effect, is neither arisen nor ceased. The wisdom aspect of the empty form is perpetually non-arisen since it is primordially peaceful, and its method aspect is always arisen due to being knowable to itself. For this reason, the unity of wisdom and the gnosis of bliss is neither cause nor effect, nor is it a state of the mutual sealing of both cause and effect.[23]

If one wonders how it is possible for emptiness and gnosis, which are neither born nor ceased, to be conventionally established in terms of being gnosis and the object of gnosis, respectively, the answer is given in the *Sekoddeśa* in this way:

> Here a perception of the object of gnosis that is neither born nor ceased is the perception of one's own mind and not of something else because of its differentiation from an external object of gnosis.[24]

According to the *Sekoddeśa-ṭippaṇī*, one is not to understand this appearance of the object of gnosis, which is not inherently arisen and is similar to a dream, in terms of the Vijñānavādins' interpretation of consciousness characterized as an ultimate thing (*paramārtha-vastu*).[25] A reason for this is stated in the *Sekoddeśa*: "Hence, nowhere can the self be sealed by itself. Can a great sword cut itself with its own blade?"[26]

Although the form of emptiness is invisible to ordinary sense faculties but is visible to ephemeral sense faculties, or to the mind that is devoid of mental fabrications (*parikalpanā*), it is not to be understood as a complete non-existence on account of the presence of the tantric *yogī*'s self-awareness (*svasaṃvedyatva*).[27] However, this self-awareness is not to be seen like that of the *yogī* who is a beginner in practice, and who, having gotten up from non-conceptual meditation with a realization of his personal self (*pratyātma*), says, "My bliss arose." On the contrary, the bliss of the *yogī* who achieves the stage of completion in tantric practice is a bliss that has all aspects (*sarvākārasukha*) with which its emptiness is endowed.

Although mental impurities (*cittamala*) vanish due to the mind's union with emptiness, the mind's condition of being gnosis (*jñānatā*) does not vanish.[28] Similar to a person who experiences happiness when encountering in a dream his wife or his daughter, who are inherently non-arisen, the *yogī* experiences the non-conceptualized, sublime bliss (*avikalpitamahāsukha*) that has become unified with empty form, which is not inherently arisen in space, which is without conceptualizations, and which is endowed with all aspects.[29]

As the habitat of the gnosis of sublime bliss, emptiness is indivisible from the mind that is purified from the habitual propensities of *saṃsāra* and that has abandoned conceptual fabrications. Therefore, it is called a "conscious emptiness" (*ajaḍaśūnyatā*). A conscious emptiness is said to be a realm of phenomena (*dharmdhātu*) that has the characteristic of space (*ākāśa-lakṣaṇa*). In fact, emptiness is space, in which an unmediated perception (*pratyakṣa*) of emptiness, devoid of the fabrications of the *yogī*'s mind, manifests as the luminosity of his own mind that is similar to an image in a prognostic mirror and that cannot be perceived through meditation with conceptualizations. It is perceivable only to a non-conceptual mind (*nirvikalpa-citta*).

The clear light of the *yogī*'s mind belongs to the mind of gnosis (*jñāna-citta*) having imperishable bliss (*akṣarasukha*) as its result. The unity of these two minds – the clear light of mind that manifests in space as emptiness and the blissful mind of gnosis – is referred to as a *vajra-yoga* consisting of wisdom (emptiness) and method (gnosis of imperishable bliss). Due to its union with emptiness, gnosis cannot have cessation nor can it be eternal. Since the gnosis of supreme, imperishable bliss is a cause of the eradication of all obscurations, it is designated as the method aspect, while wisdom is the entire world, which is the object of gnosis. Since wisdom (*prajñā*) that consists of emptiness is an object of gnosis, ultimate reality is also known as the gnosis of wisdom (*prajñā-jñāna*), which, being without eternity and cessation, has abandoned the notions of existence and non-existence as well as logical reasons (*hetu*) and examples (*dṛṣṭānta*). When perceived through a *yogī*'s direct perception, it becomes an object of confidence. Since it represents the identity of existence and non-existence, it serves as an example for *yogīs* to eliminate grasping onto all dogmatic positions (*pakṣa*). In that regard it cannot be compared to the world, in which existence and non-existence are mutually exclusive, and worldly examples (*laukika-dṛṣṭānta*) such as these are the basis of logical reasoning:

> Due to its contrariety to a clay pot, a sky flower does not exist because it is entirely non-existent. Likewise, due to its contrariety to a sky flower, a clay pot does exist because it is entirely existent. Thus, due to the mutual contradiction of these two there is this example. Similarly, due to its contrariety with cessation [or *nirvāṇa*], a cyclic existence exists because it is [conventionally] entirely existent; and due to its contrariety to cyclic existence, a cessation does not exist because it is [conventionally] entirely non-existent.[30]

In contrast, an example of transcendent reality (*lokottara-dṛṣṭānta*) is said to be the identity of a sky flower and a clay pot, which are mutually contradictory from the conventional point of view, because transcendent reality is heterogeneous. Furthermore, in terms of conventional truth, what characterizes the mind as existent, that does not characterize it as non-existent; what characterizes the mind as non-existent, that does not characterize it as existent. However, an empty form of a purified mind that is similar to an image in a prognostic mirror is not characterized by form owing to its lack of atomic particles, nor is it characterized by formlessness, for it is found in space. As previously stated, it is free from the four dogmatic perspectives or extremes (*koṭi*), as it is neither existent nor non-existent, nor is it both existent-and-non-existent, nor is it neither existent-nor-non-existent.[31] Moreover, it can be said that the wisdom (*prajñā*) of emptiness has all aspects (*sarvākāra*) and is also without any aspects (*nirākāra*) whatsoever.[32]

A statement given by Śāriputra to Subhūti in the *Eight Thousand-Lined Perfection of Wisdom Sūtra*, which reads, "this mind which is a mind is a non-mind," is seen by Puṇḍarīka as applicable to the gnosis of wisdom in this way: "the mind which is a mind is a non-mind that is devoid of the characteristics of a phenomenon that has eternity or cessation and that is indivisible emptiness and compassion."[33] From the ultimate point of view, due to its heterogeneity, the reality (*tattva*) called "*vajra-yoga*," which consists of indivisible emptiness and gnosis of bliss, evades classifications such as "it exists" and "it does not exist," because, for it, the notions of existence and non-existence have vanished. This supreme, non-dual yoga, which is beyond existence and non-existence, does not abide in *nirvāṇa* or in cyclic existence, nor does it abide in both because these two are mutually contradictory. This ultimate reality of the buddhas, known also as the *mahāmudrā-siddhi*, is devoid of the appearances of a momentary mind. "The mind that is free from momentary phenomena is said to be without inherent existence (*niḥsvabhāva*)."[34] Since a dogmatic position of the absence of inherent existence (*niḥsvabhāva-pakṣa*) is not a dogmatic position, such a mind is free from all dogmatic positions. For this mind, phenomena do not arise, abide, or perish because their arising, abiding, and perishing takes place in sequence, and the simultaneity of their arising, abiding, and perishing is impossible, since the moments of their arising, abiding, and perishing are not identical. Although one may argue that each of these moments arises sequentially from the moment that precedes it, in terms of ultimate reality, this type of reasoning is considered inappropriate on the grounds that another moment does not arise from a previous moment that has ceased, nor does it arise from a non-ceased moment, in the same way that a sprout does not arise from a perished seed or from a non-perished seed.[35]

The mind that is a non-mind is free from the habitual propensities (*vāsanā*) of cyclic existence and is luminous by nature (*prakṛti-prabhāsvara*); it is designated as a buddha or buddhahood.[36] Puṇḍarīka informs us that, since this mind is a non-conceptual gnosis having all aspects, it is attainable only by a non-conceptual mind trained in the perfection of wisdom (*prajñāpāramitā*), for it is in the *Perfection of Wisdom Sūtra* that the Tathāgata stated:

> All phenomena are without conceptualizations, all phenomena are empty, all phenomena are signless, all phenomena are desireless, all phenomena are free from karmic formations, all phenomena are without origination, all phenomena are inexpressible, all phenomena are devoid of causes, and all phenomena are inconceivable.
>
> Therefore, at the attainment of the result of all-knowledge, a Bodhisattva, Mahāsattva, who is indifferent to all phenomena, should contemplate [in this way]: "One should not dwell on the aggregate of form nor on the [aggregates of] feeling, discernment, mental factors, and consciousness. One should not dwell on the earth element, nor should one dwell on the water element, on the fire element, on the wind element, nor on the space element. One should not dwell on the eye element, on the form element, nor on the element of visual consciousness, on the ear element, on the sound element, on the element of auditory consciousness, on the nose element, on the smell element, on the element of olfactory consciousness, on the element of tongue, on the taste element, on the element of gustatory consciousness, on the body element, on the touch element, on the element of tactile awareness, on the element of the mind, on the mental object, nor on the element of mental consciousness.[37]

These passages from the *Eight Thousand-Lined Perfection of Wisdom Sūtra* show that the perfection of wisdom is the inconceivable gnosis of the Tathāgata due to being of the nature of attachment and non-attachment. According to Puṇḍarīka, unintelligent people who desire unthinking (*niścintana*) gnosis will misinterpret the above-cited passages. They will say that in the case of ordinary beings, when thinking takes place, attachment to a desirable object arises and aversion to the undesirable object takes place. The two, attachment and aversion, are known to be the causes of transmigratory existence. But when the Tathāgata's unthinking (*niścintana*) gnosis takes place, attachment to desirable things does not arise, nor does aversion towards undesirable things occur. Through the absence of these two, there is an absence of *saṃsāra* and there is full and perfect buddhahood. Therefore, a *sādhana* on the Buddha is the Tathāgata's unthinking gnosis, and not some other *samādhi* with conceptualizations. Puṇḍarīka argues against this view, asserting the following:

> If this non-thinking gnosis gives Buddhahood, then why have all sentient beings not already become full and perfect Buddhas? When non-thinking gnosis arises in their deep sleep, there is neither attachment to desirable things nor is there aversion toward undesirable things. Thus, although attachment and aversion are absent in the state of deep sleep, no sentient beings have become full and perfect Buddhas due to non-thinking gnosis. Hence, a non-thinking gnosis of the Tathāgata is not possible because in the "Chapter on Samādhi" of the *Perfection of Wisdom*, the Lord's *samādhis* are described. Among them, there is a *samādhi* called "jewel lamp." Here, if there is no thinking in a jewel lamp [*samādhi*] nor is there luminosity, then why is the *samādhi* called a "jewel lamp?" Likewise, there are not other *samādhis* that are non-thinking because they are characterized by self-awareness and because of the absence of inanimate emptiness.[38]

To his Buddhist opponents, who say: "If this gnosis of the Tathāgata is self-aware, then why did the Tathāgata teach that all phenomena lack inherent nature," Puṇḍarīka responds, saying:

> The Tathāgata's gnosis, called "the understanding (*avabodhana*) of the lack of inherent nature of all phenomena," is not a mind of deep sleep characterized by the absence of everything. It is stated in the *Perfection of Wisdom*, "The mind that is a mind is a non-mind." If the Tathāgata's gnosis is not self-awareness called "luminous by nature," then there would not be the Tathāgata's teaching of Dharma in accordance with the dispositions of sentient beings. All phenomena are unaware (*aprabodha*) because they are not self-aware. If self-awareness would have sense faculties as its gates, then due to all obscurations, it would not be partless, free from obscurations, omnipresent, and all-pervading. Being completely undividable like space, it dwells in all sentient beings. The Tathāgata's gnosis is self-awareness that knows the nature of all phenomena and that is devoid of conceptualizations and sense faculties.[39]

In support of his assertion of the Tathāgata's gnosis as self-awareness, Puṇḍarīka points to the *Mañjuśrīnāmasaṃgīti*, in which Vajradhara is lauded as the knower of himself (*ātmavid*) and as the knower of others (*paravid*), who is all to all, partless, and all-pervading, omniscient, and universally knowing (*sarvavid*).[40] In the *Amṛtakaṇikā-ṭippaṇī* commentary on the *Mañjuśrīnāmasaṃgīti*, he is said to be the knower of himself because he is of the nature of space and has transcended all conceptual elaborations (*prapañca*); but he is also a knower of others due to his awakening to the non-duality of self and others.[41]

The *Kālacakratantra*'s interpretation of emptiness as the absence of the material nature of the psychophysical aggregates, elements, and sense-bases, in relation to the self-aware gnosis of bliss, from which it is indivisible, challenged the assumptions of those adhering to different Buddhist tantric views and practices, which were seen by the author of the *Vimalaprabhā* as corrupted. In the *Vimalaprabhā*, Puṇḍarīka presents a series of qualms and refutations concerning the feasibility of self-awareness in the absence of the sense faculties, which, according to his admission, are grounded on the Buddha's statements contained in various Buddhist kings of tantras (*rājatantra*). One such refutation holds that, in the absence of the psychophysical aggregates, the gnosis of wisdom cannot be attained because its attainment entails a sexual union, and the gnosis of sublime bliss that arises at the time of the flow of *bodhicitta* in between the experiences of innate joy (*sahajānanda*) and special joy (*viramānanda*) is self-awareness. Some others argue, questioning whether a drop of *bodhicitta*, which is devoid of *nirvāṇa*, can become the gnosis of sublime bliss that is separate from the sense faculties. To them, this is meaningless in a way in which a sky flower smelled by the son of a barren woman is meaningless. Puṇḍarīka addresses these criticisms, asserting that a drop of *bodhicitta* that is characterized by perishable bliss, by the bliss of seminal emission, is not the gnosis of wisdom that is all good (*samantabhadra*) and that has sublime bliss. He points to the statement ascribed to the Tathāgata in the *Guhyasamājatantra* (18, 113),[42] which suggests that there is the fourth [sublime bliss] in this way, "likewise there is that fourth." "That fourth" is interpreted by Puṇḍarīka to be the gnosis of wisdom that is different from the third perishable bliss. He argues that, if the third perishable bliss were the fourth sublime bliss, it would mean that "the fourth" is a designation for that which has been already designated. But this is logically unacceptable on account of the fallacy of repetition. According to Puṇḍarīka, it is fools who engage in non-virtue, desiring a perishable bliss that is contingent on sexual intercourse, and who stray away from the gnosis of sublime, imperishable bliss, who will argue that the third perishable bliss characterized by seminal emission is the fourth.[43] Since without that fourth moment of innate joy (*sahajānanda*), one could not become a buddha, the Tathāgata's self-aware gnosis is separate from the sense faculties. "For this reason, *yogīs* should firmly hold and protect [their] *bodhicitta* and should not release it."[44]

To those who mistake the final moment of innate bliss, by which the realization of buddhahood is achieved, with the third moment of bliss, and who ask what the gnosis of wisdom would be if it were the fourth moment of imperishable bliss, Puṇḍarīka responds in this way:

> Here, in the Vajrayāna, resorting to the mundane and transcendent truths, the Venerable One said that wisdom is of three kinds: the action *mudrā* (actual consort), gnosis *mudrā* (imagined, divine consort), and *mahāmudrā* (sublime consort). Among these, the bliss from the action *mudrā* and gnosis *mudrā* is characterized by vibration (*spanda*), whereas the bliss of *mahāmudrā* is characterized by the *yogī*'s non-vibration (*niḥspanda*). If the gnosis of wisdom that is characterized by seminal emission is a gnosis that belongs to wisdom (female consort), then it is a result that has arisen from wisdom; if, however, the gnosis of wisdom belongs to method (male consort), then method's gnosis of wisdom is a result arisen from method. Thus, due to their mutual consideration there are two kinds of gnosis. If each has its own individual gnosis, then there is an absence a non-dual gnosis; and due to this absence of non-dual gnosis, there is the absence of Buddhahood because of the absence of the pure, supreme, imperishable gnosis. If the wisdom of gnosis were a gnosis that belongs to wisdom, then the gnosis of method would be the gnosis that belongs to method; thus, there is a fault as in the previous case.[45]

Therefore, the bliss that comes from an action *mudrā* or from a gnosis *mudrā* is not the all-good, supreme, imperishable bliss. Those who stray away from the gnosis of *mahāmudrā* because of the instruction of corrupt spiritual mentors are said to engage in bestiality and to be unable to attain buddhahood, since they lack the gnosis of *mahāmudrā*.

However, Puṇḍarīka acknowledges that the Buddha taught meditation on sublime bliss with sexual intercourse, by means of which one can achieve buddhahood in this very life. In accordance with the *Kālacakratantra*'s teaching, he emphasizes that meditation on bliss by means of sexual union is to be understood as a state of non-emission of *bodhicitta*. Sentient beings' habitual propensity for seminal emission is of the nature of the mind's incidental stain (*āgantuka-mala*) since beginningless time and is a cause of transmigratory existence. Union with a consort that gives rise to the habitual propensity for seminal emission also provides the condition for the arising of the habitual propensity of non-emission. Just as mercury escapes due to its contact with fire, so also it is controlled with fire through the same method. Similarly, *bodhicitta* that escapes as a result of sexual contact with a consort can be also controlled by means of that sexual contact. Just as mercury that is controlled by fire transforms all metals into gold, so *bodhicitta* that is controlled through sexual union with a consort purifies the mind–body complex from all of its obscurations. Therefore, even in sexual union with an actual consort, a deity as a meditative object is taught for the sake of making the *yogī*'s *bodhicitta* motionless. By means of sexual yoga, the *yogī* should meditate on the *mahāmudrā*, which is an extent of the mind's luminosity generated within the *yogī*'s own mind. This *mahāmudrā* is the fire of gnosis that incinerates all stains and gives rise to bliss in the body.

Puṇḍarīka also introduces us to another reservation raised by certain Buddhists, which is the following.

> The Tathāgata said that in the absence of the psychophysical aggregates, elements, and sense bases, the gnosis of wisdom that is separate from sexual union does not become self-awareness due to [seminal] non-emission. How can the *yogī* liberate his mind from obscuration after coming into union with his own mind at the appearance of his own mind, and how can he experience the gnosis of sublime, imperishable bliss due to the absence of the body of atomic agglomerates? This is wrong, [just as is this statement:] "Having mounted his own shoulders, Devadatta goes to town."[46]

To them, Puṇḍarīka asserts that it is not necessary to have the psychophysical aggregates for the sake of experiencing sublime bliss due to the efficacy of the incidental habitual propensities of the mind (*āgantukacittavāsanā*). The psychophysical aggregates, elements, and sense basis are nothing other than incidental habitual propensities of the mind. Owing to these habitual propensities, feelings of suffering and happiness enter the mind when the body is injured or when it experiences pleasures. But, in the final analysis, these feelings do not enter the mind as a result of bodily injury or pleasure. While dreaming, suffering enters the mind when a different, dream body, which consists of the habitual propensities of the mind and which is devoid of physicality, seems to be injured by robbers and the like. Similarly, on account of experiencing sensual pleasures in dreams, happiness enters the mind. Hence, the mind's self-aware gnosis of suffering or happiness takes place in the absence of a physical body. The self-aware gnosis of sublime and imperishable bliss that is arisen from the habitual propensity of *nirvāṇa* is difficult to comprehend even by the wise.[47] There is no other *saṃsāra* apart from the habitual propensity of one's own mind. The habitual propensity of *saṃsāra* is a moment characterized by seminal emission. In contrast, the habitual propensity of *nirvāṇa* is a moment characterized by seminal non-emission. Therefore, the gnosis of wisdom is self-aware because of the power of the mind's habitual propensities and not due to the experiences of a physical body.

Puṇḍarīka also seeks to discredit those opponents who uphold the view of the reality of the wind of *prāṇa*, and for whom the power of in-breath and out-breath in the physical body is responsible for waking, dreaming, and the mind's deep sleep. He argues against their view in the following manner. If the sleeping state is impossible without in-breaths and out-breaths, then why in death or in a coma, without the in-breaths and out-breaths, is there an appearance of the mind for up to three hours (one *prahara*)? To a dead person led by the messengers of Yama, the city of Yama appears by the command of the king Yama himself. There in the city of Yama, even the king Yama, who examines the sins and virtues of that body, appears. Upon his investigation, Yama says: "Since the life of this one has not been exhausted, take him swiftly back to the world of mortals so that his body may not perish." When the messengers of Yama return the dead body to the world of mortals, then due to the power of the mind's habitual propensities, the in-breath and out-breath reappear in that dead body. After regaining consciousness in the waking state, that person informs his relatives about the king Yama. Therefore, without a physical body and without the in-breath and out-breath, the incidental and beginningless habitual propensity of the mind arises through the power of rebirth. This habitual propensity of *saṃsāra* is not inherent (*svābhāvikī*) to the mind. If it were inherent to the mind, then buddhahood would be impossible.[48]

There are also those who assert that, when a sexual act takes place in a dream, seminal emission occurs in the physical body and not in the dream body consisting of the mind's habitual propensities. For this reason, they argue, it is due to the power of this physical body that sublime bliss becomes self-awareness. In Puṇḍarīka's view this is invalid cognition on the grounds that seminal emission takes place also in the formless realm. His point is this: If emission does not take place in the absence of a physical body, if there is no *saṃsāra* without emission, and if without *saṃsāra* there is no attainment of sublime bliss, then why do beings with formless, non-physical bodies and without seminal emission undergo rebirth for the sake of buddhahood?[49]

Finally, there are also those who assert that the bodies of formless beings, which do not sustain themselves on food, do not have seminal emission owing to the absence of a physical body, and therefore have neither bliss nor *saṃsāra*. To them, Puṇḍarīka offers the following perspective. Although the elements in the body are due to consumption of food and drink that have the six tastes, the bodily elements do not further become the six tastes. The elements arise from the space element – that is, from the empty nature of the space element. All phenomena arise from emptiness, and empty phenomena are without origination and cessation and are an appearance of one's own mind. In the *yogī*'s experience, gnosis merges into that emptiness, or into the appearance of his own mind, in which origination and cessation are absent. In this way, gnosis becomes of the same taste as the appearance of his mind and not because of the connection between gnosis and its object.

As we have seen, in this tantric system, it is due to a non-conceptualized emptiness of gnosis that the Buddha's gnosis is peaceful, or blissful, as it is free from conceptualizations and of any point of view such as I and mine, beginning and end, subject and object, and so on. Through its union with emptiness, it knows the nature of all phenomena and is free from the habitual propensities of *saṃsāra*. Owing to its emptiness, it is similar to a dream, an illusion, an echo, and an image in a prognostic mirror.

Therefore, the highest possible accomplishment in this tantric tradition is said to be possible only due to *samādhi* on emptiness that has all aspects and that is indivisible from compassion without an object (*nirālambana-karuṇā*).[50]

In conclusion, one can say that the sole purpose of the intricate system of the *Kālacakratantra*'s yogic practices is to awaken the *yogī* to the gnosis of emptiness. The tantra's expositions on emptiness are adopted from the Perfection of Wisdom literature and from Madyamaka, and they are further elaborated in new ways that illuminate the relationship between emptiness and the self-aware imperishable gnosis of sublime bliss from both the conventional and ultimate points of view.

Despite the fact that the Kālacakra tradition emphasizes the self-aware aspect of the gnosis of wisdom, it has not been criticized by later Prāsaṅgika Mādhyamikas, whose refutations of self-awareness are based on Candrakīrti's *Madhyamakāvatāra* and Śāntideva's *Bodhicaryāvatāra*. A reason for this is that their refutation of self-awareness is pertinent to their critique of the Vijñānavādins' presentation of self-awareness as being inherently existent. Tibetan Prāsaṅgika Mādhyamikas such as Tsongkhapa and mKhas grub rje, who wrote commentaries on the *Kālacakratantra*, never refute the tantra's assertions of self-awareness because of its indivisibility from emptiness. In general, in the view of these Mādhyamikas, inconsistencies between the Prāsaṅgika Mādhyamika views and those presented in the *Kālacakratantra* are ultimately not to be found.

Notes

1 The *Kālacakratantra*'s criticism of philosophical systems from the Mādhyamika perspective is found in the seventh section of the *Kālacakratantra*'s "Chapter on Individual," verses 161–76, and in the accompanying *Vimalaprabhā commentary*. See Wallace (2004).

2 *Vimalaprabhāṭīkā of Kalkin Śrīpuṇḍarīka on Śrīlaghukālacakratantrarāja by Śrīmañjuśrīyaśas*. Vol. 3. (1994, 87).

3 Ibid., pp. 87, 90. We are further told by Puṇḍarīka that, to the Mādhyamikas, the Buddha also taught both personal identitylessness (*pudgala-nairātmya*) and phenomenal identitylessness (*dharma-nairātmya*), a meditation on the Four Noble Truths, and a *samādhi* on the emptiness of the inherent existence and non-existence of all phenomena. See the *Vimalaprabhāṭīkā of Kalkin Śrīpuṇḍarīka on Śrīlaghukālacakratantrarāja by Śrīmañjuśrīyaśas*. Vol. 3. (1994, 87, 93). Cf. *Vimalaprabhāṭīkā of Kalkī Śrī Puṇḍarīka on Śrīlaghukālacakratantrarāja by Śrī Mañjuśrīyaśas*. Vol. 1. (1986, 256, v. 161).

4 See *Sekoddeśaṭīkā of Nāropā* (1941, 56).

5 The *Vimalaprabhā commentary* on the *Kālacakratantra*. Vol. 3. (1994, 48, v. 92): *śūnyasvabhāvaḥ śūnyatā | ihātītānāgataṃ jñeyaṃ śūnyam | tasya darśanaṃ bhāvaḥ śūnyatā | gambhīrodārā atītānāgatābhāvād gambhīrā | atītānāgatadarśanād udārā*. This explicit assertion of the emptiness of the past and future object of cognition implicitly asserts the emptiness of the present object of cognition, as the beginning of the present moment of cognition has already passed and its end has not yet come.

6 *Sekoddeśaṭīka* of Nāropā (1941, 5).

7 *Vimalaprabhāṭīkā of Kalkī Śrī Puṇḍarīka on Śrīlaghukālacakratantrarāja by Śrī Mañjuśrīyaśas*. Vol. 1. (1986, 47–50, v. 2).

8 Ibid., p. 21. The three categories of emptiness are related to the three types of compassion: compassion that has sentient beings as its object (*sattvālamabinī*), compassion that has

phenomena as its object (*dharmālambinī*), and compassion that is without an object (*anavalambinī*).

9 *Vimalaprabhāṭīkā of Kalkin Śrīpuṇḍarīka on Śrīlaghukālacakratantrarāja by Śrīmañjuśrīyaśas*. Vol. 3. (1994, v. 164, and the commentary, p. 118).

10 The root tantra (mūlatantra), cited in the *Vimalaprabhāṭīkā of Kalkī Śrī Puṇḍarīka on Śrīlaghukālacakratantrarāja by Śrī Mañjuśrīyaśas*, Vol. 3. (1994, 101):

> *śūnye bhāvasamūho 'yaṃ kalpanārūpavarjitaḥ |*
> *dṛśyate pratiseneva kumāryā darpaṇe yathā ||*
> *sarvabhāvasamo bhūtvā eko bhāvo 'kṣaraḥ sthitaḥ |*
> *akṣarajñānasambhūto nocchedo na ca śāśvataḥ ||*
> *sarvasaṃjñātmakā varṇā akārakulasambhavāḥ |*
> *mahākṣarapadaprāptā na saṃjñā na ca saṃjñinaḥ ||*
> *anuptanneṣu dharmeṣu saṃskārarahiteṣu ca |*
> *na bodhir naiva buddhatvaṃ na sattvo naiava jīvitam ||*
> *vijñānadharmātītā jñānaśuddhā hyanāvilāḥ |*
> *prakṛtiprabhāsvarā dharmā dharmadhātugatiṃ gatāḥ ||*

11 *Vimalaprabhāṭīkā of Kalkin Śrīpuṇḍarīka on Śrīlaghukālacakratantrarāja by Śrīmañjuśrīyaśas*. Vol. 3. (1994, 100).

12 See *Vimalaprabhāṭīkā of Kalkī Śrī Puṇḍarīka on Śrīlaghukālacakratantrarāja by Śrī Mañjuśrīyaśas*. Vol. 1. (1986, 37).

13 Ibid., p. 43: "*saṃvṛtiḥ śūnyatā-rūpiṇī śūnyatā saṃvṛti-rūpiṇī*."

14 See *The Sekoddeśaṭīkā by Nāropā (Paramārthasaṃgraha)* (2006, 127–8).

15 See La Sekoddeśa-ṭippaṇī di Sadhuputra Śrīdharānanda (1996, v. 15 and commentary, p. 122, or p. 8).

16 *Sekoddeśaṭīkā* of Nāropā (1941, 46).

17 Ibid., p. 34.

18 Ibid., p. 70.

19 *Sekoddeśa: A Critical Edition of the Tibetan Translations* (1994, 148).

20 *Sekoddeśaṭīkā* of Nāropā (1941, 70).

21 *Sekoddeśa* (1994, 148, vv. 148–9) and La Sekoddeśa-ṭippaṇī di Sadhuputra Śrīdharānanda (1996, 141–2, or 28–9]).

22 *Sekoddeśaṭīkā* of Nāropā (1941, 49, 70–1).

23 Ibid., p. 71.

24 *Sekoddeśa* (1994, 149, v. 156):

> *ajātasya niruddhasya yaj jñeyeha darśanam |*
> *tat svacittasya nānyasya bāhyajñeyavibhāgataḥ ||*

25 La Sekoddeśa-ṭippaṇī di Sadhuputra Śrīdharānanda (1996, 143, or 29, commentary on v. 157).

26 *Sekoddeśa* (1994, 149, v. 157):

> *ato na cātmātmānaṃ mudritum śakyate kvacit |*
> *kiṃ chinnati mahākhaḍga ātmānam ātmadhārayā ||*

27 *Vimalaprabhāṭīkā of Kalkī Śrī Puṇḍarīka on Śrīlaghukālacakratantrarāja by Śrī Mañjuśrīyaśas*, Vol. 1 (1986, 47).

28 La Sekoddeśa-ṭippaṇī di Sadhuputra Śrīdharānanda (1996, 138–9, or 24–5, v. 119 with commentary, and v. 133).

29 Ibid., p. 143, or p. 29, commentary on v. 158.

30 *Vimalaprabhāṭīkā of Kalkī Śrī Puṇḍarīka on Śrīlaghukālacakratantrarāja by Śrī Mañjuśrīyaśas.* Vol. 1. (1986, 43).

31 *Vimalaprabhāṭīkā of Kalkī Śrī Puṇḍarīka on Śrīlaghukālacakratantrarāja by Śrī Mañjuśrīyaśas.* Vol. 3. (1994, 45, v. 89):

na sannāsanna sadasanna cāpyanubhayātmakam |
catuṣkoṭinivirmuktaṃ natvā kāyaṃ mahāsukham ||

32 *Vimalaprabhāṭīkā of Kalkī Śrī Puṇḍarīka on Śrīlaghukālacakratantrarāja by Śrī Mañjuśrīyaśas.* Vol. 1. (1986, 1).

33 Ibid., p. 43: "*asti taccitaṃ yaccitam acittaṃ śāśvatocchedadharmalakaṣaṇāpagataṃ śūnyatākaruṇābhinnam iti.*"

34 Ibid., p. 44.

35 Ibid.

36 Ibid., p. 23.

37 Cited in the *Vimalaprabhāṭīkā of Kalkī Śrī Puṇḍarīka on Śrīlaghukālacakratantrarāja by Śrī Mañjuśrīyaśas.* Vol. 3. (1994, 77).

38 Ibid.

39 Ibid.

40 See the *Āryamañjuśrīnāmasaṃgīti with Amṛtakaṇikā-ṭippaṇī* (1994, ch. 8, vv. 20–2, ch. 10, v. 13). In Ronald Davidson's (1981) *Litany of the Names of Mañjuśrī*, the verses are numbered as 96–8, 155.

41 *Āryamañjuśrīnāmasaṃgīti with Amṛtakaṇikā-ṭippaṇī* (1994, 93).

42 *The Guhyasam>ja Tantra.* Ed. Yukei Matsunaga. Osaka: Toho Shupan, 1978, p. 121.

43 *Vimalaprabhāṭīkā of Kalkī Śrī Puṇḍarīka on Śrīlaghukālacakratantrarāja by Śrī Mañjuśrīyaśas.* Vol. 3. (1994, 77–8).

44 Ibid., p. 79.

45 Ibid., pp. 79–80).

46 Ibid., p. 82.

47 Ibid.

48 Ibid., p. 83.

49 Ibid., p. 84.

50 La Sekoddeśa-ṭippaṇī di Sadhuputra Śrīdharānanda (1996, 140, or 26]); *Sekoddeśaṭīkā of Nāropā* (1941, 118, or 4]); *Vimalaprabhāṭīkā of Kalkī Śrī Puṇḍarīka on Śrīlaghukālacakratantrarāja by Śrī Mañjuśrīyaśas.* Vol. 3. (1994, 102).

References

Āryamañjuśrīnāmasaṃgīti with Amṛtakaṇikā-Ṭippaṇī by Bhikṣu Raviśrījñāna and Amṛtakaṇikodyota-Nibandha of Vibhūticandra (1994). Ed. Banarsi Lal. Bibliotheca Indo-Tibetica, Vol. 30. Sarnath, Varanasi: Central Institute of Higher Tibetan Studies.

Davidson, Ronald (1981). The Litany of Names of Mañjuśrī: Text and Translation of the Mañju śrīnnāmasaṃgīti. In *Tantric and Taoist Studies in Honour of R. A. Stein.* Ed. Michel Strickman. Vol. 1. Brussels: Institute Belge des Hautes Études Chinoises.

La Sekoddeśa-ṭippaṇī de Sādhuputra Śrīdharānanda: Il testo Sanscrito (1996). Ed. Raniero Gnoli. In *Rivista degli Studi Orientali* 70 (1–2), 115–46.

Sekoddeśa: A Critical Edition of the Tibetan Translations with an Appendix by Raniero Gnoli on the Sanskrit Text (1994). Ed. Giacomella Orofino. Serie Orientale Roma, Vol. 72. Rome: Istituto Italiano per il Medio ed Estremo Oriente.

Sekoddeśaṭīkā of Naḍapāda (Nāropā) (1941). *Being a Commentary of the Sekoddeśa of the Kālacakra Tantra*. Ed. Mario E. Carelli. Baroda: Oriental Institute.

The Sekoddeśaṭīkā by Nāropā (Paramārthasaṃgraha) (2006). Ed. Francesco Sferra and Stefania Merzagora. Serie Orientale Roma, Vol. 99. Rome: Istituto Italiano per L'Africa e L'Oriente.

Vimalaprabhāṭīkā of Kalkī Śrī Puṇḍarīka on Śrīlaghukālacakratantrarāja by Śrī Mañjuśrīyaśas. Vol. 1. (1986). Ed. Jagannatha Upadhyaya. Bibliotheca Indo-Tibetica Series, no. 11. Sarnath, Varanasi: Central Institute of Higher Tibetan Studies.

Vimalaprabhāṭīkā of Kalkin Śrīpuṇḍarīka on Śrīlaghukālacakratantrarāja by Śrīmañjuśrīyaśas. Vol. 2. (1994). Ed. Vajravallabh Dwivedi and S. S. Bahulkar. Rare Buddhist Texts Series, vol. 12. Sarnath, Varanasi: Central Institute of Higher Tibetan Studies.

Vimalaprabhāṭīkā of Kalkin Śrīpuṇḍarīka on Śrīlaghukālacakratantrarāja by Śrīmañjuśrīyaśas. Vol. 3. (1994). Ed. Vajravallabh Dwivedi and S. S. Bahulkar. *Rare* Buddhist Texts Series, vol. 13. Sarnath, Varanasi: Central Institute of Higher Tibetan Studies.

Wallace, Vesna (2004). *The Kālacakratantra: The Chapter on Individual together with the Vimalaprabhā*. Tanjur Translation Initiative, Treasury of the Buddhist Sciences series. New York: American Institute of Buddhist Studies at Columbia University and Columbia's University's Center for Buddhist Studies and Tibet House.

11

The Huayan Metaphysics of Totality

ALAN FOX

The story of Huayan Buddhism intertwines in many ways with many other more well-known forms of Buddhist thought. Even though there is nothing like a Huayan School in India at any point, the textual basis of Huayan includes materials clearly derived from Sanskrit sources. Huayan also stands at the crossroads of the sinicization of Buddhism, the process by means of which indigenously Chinese forms of Buddhism came into existence. In fact, some scholars have suggested that Huayan is the philosophy behind Chan 禪 (Jp. Zen) Buddhism and that Chan is the practice of Huayan, but it can be argued that, although Huayan is clearly more willing than Chan to engage in what might be seen as speculative metaphysics, it has its own meditative practice.

Of course, given the context of Buddhist thought, especially as the variety of Buddhist traditions proliferated in India and subsequently in China and elsewhere, all metaphysics is circumscribed by a pragmatic lack of dogmatism. There does not seem to be a necessary claim that this is actually how things are, but rather that this is a practical way to look at things if one wants to end existential disease or suffering. It is clear from the examination of scriptural texts that Buddhist soteriology has always been extremely pragmatic in its approach to truth. The notion of a single absolute truth is replaced by the idea of functional utility, known in the Sanskrit as *upāya*. The Buddhist tradition thus contains a wide assortment of soteriological approaches.

The Buddhist concepts of *upāya* (Ch. 方便 *fangbian*) or "skillful means," *prajnapti* ("convenient designation") from Yogācāra and *paramārtha satya* ("liberating discourse") from Madhyamaka, justify a range of pragmatic propositions which represent a healthy way of viewing the world, regardless of what the world is actually like. In some sense, *upāya* refers to the diagnostic and prescriptive skill of a buddha or bodhisattva, who is ostensibly able to discern a particular person's problem and recommend a helpful strategy for solving it. This is a completely contextual approach, though, because different problems lead to different strategies. Given the limitations of possible human experience, and ruling out revelation and knowledge by virtue of authority, there is no way

A Companion to Buddhist Philosophy, First Edition. Edited by Steven M. Emmanuel.

finally to know the answers to metaphysical questions. Therefore the goal is simply to find a metaphysical stance that contributes to the ending of suffering.

Since suffering is traced to attachment to the idea of a permanent self and eternal, fundamental realities, Buddhist metaphysics seems to seek alternative ways of understanding our experiences of self and reality which do not require us to posit permanent selves and fundamental realities. One early model along these lines involves breaking the personality down into five aggregates or *skandhas*. The model suggests that the person is like a fist, in the sense that a fist is nothing but the arrangement of five fingers. There is no fist other than that composed of the five fingers; the fist does not "have" five fingers, and the five fingers do not "have" the fist. When all five fingers are arranged in a certain fashion, we call it a fist, but it is not correct to say that the fist has independent existence, or that a fist comes into being or ceases to be. Similarly, the "self" is composed of five factors, which gives us a way of understanding the experience of selfhood without having to posit a permanent self. In the Abhidharma traditions, this analysis yields many more factors of experience, as many as 75 or 100.

We also find in the Buddhist traditions a way of understanding the experience of reality without having to posit a fundamental reality. The metaphysics underlying Huayan's philosophy of totality is based on the central Buddhist model of interdependent causality known as *prātityasamutpāda* (Ch. *yinyuan* (因緣), or "dependent origination." In earlier models, *pratītyasamutpāda* was described as a 12-link chain of causation, in which each link causes the next in a linear fashion, with the twelfth link causing the first link. In some sense, then, each link is causally connected to all of the other links. In Mahāyāna thought, particularly Huayan, it comes to be understood as an all-embracing web of causal relations defining reality: to say that something is real is to say that it participates in causal relations with everything else that can be said to be real. This changes the model from a primarily linear one to a "holographic" one, in which, at every moment, everything that can be said to be real is, in some sense, simultaneously the cause and effect of everything else that can be said to be real. This approach acknowledges reality, but not fundamental reality, and acknowledges causality, but not first cause, thus avoiding the kind of ontological commitment which Buddhism generally takes to be the most proximate cause of suffering.

This is expressed most clearly in several Huayan texts and images. Historically, Huayan draws much of its inspiration from a variety of textual sources. We might identify in this regard the *Huayan Jing* (華嚴 *Avataṃsaka* or *"Flower Garland" Sūtra*), the *Mahayana Awakening of Faith Treatise* (*Dasheng Qixin Lun* 大乘起信論), and a number of texts attributed to an early Chinese Buddhist thaumaturge, Dushun, including *Meditative Perspectives on the Huayan Dharmadhātu* (華嚴法界觀門) and *Cessation and Contemplation in the Five Teachings of Huayan* (*Huayan wujiao zhiguan* 華嚴五教止觀).

The *Huayan Jing* itself is a voluminous hodgepodge of diverse and controversial composition. Parts of it seem to be Chinese translations of Sanskrit texts, such as the *Gandavyūha Sūtra*; parts seem to be translations of other Sanskrit texts; and much of it seems to be of native Chinese composition. It presents a view of reality that can be described as fractal, or even psychedelic, with worlds within worlds within worlds, ad infinitum. In the *sūtra*, this macro/microcosmic "omniverse" is shaken periodically by earthquakes which might be seen as reminders to shake up and loosen or deconstruct fixed ontological commitments, as in the following passage from Thomas Cleary's translation: "Then the ocean of worlds of arrays of flower banks, by the power of the Buddha, all shook in six ways in eighteen manners, that is, they trembled, trembled all over, trembled all over in all directions . . ." (Cleary 1993, 148). Famous and powerful metaphors illustrating this insight include the famous "jeweled net of Indra." Indra is one of the Vedic gods, mentioned in the *Huayan Jing* as one of an indeterminate number of Indras residing in an indeterminate number of Sumeru Palaces. Book I opens with a vivid description of the site of the Buddha's awakening, representative of many such descriptions:

> Thus have I heard. At one time the Buddha was in the land of Magadha, in a state of purity, at the site of enlightenment, having just realized true awareness. The ground was solid and firm, made of diamond, adorned with exquisite jewel discs and myriad precious flowers, with pure clear crystals. . . . There were banners of precious stones, constantly emitting shining light and producing beautiful sounds. Nets of myriad gems and garlands of exquisitely scented flowers hung all around. . . . There were rows of jewel trees, their branches and foliage lustrous and luxuriant. By the Buddha's spiritual power, he caused all the adornments of this enlightenment site to be reflected therein. . . . By means of the ability to manifest the lights and inconceivable sounds of the Buddhas, they fashioned nets of the finest jewels, from which came forth all the realms of action of the spiritual powers of the Buddhas, and in which were reflected images of the abodes of all beings. . . . Clouds of radiance of jewels reflected each other.
>
> (Ibid., 55–6)

Dushun seems to extend this idea in his *Calming and Contemplation in the Five Teachings of Huayan* (*Huayan wujiao zhiguan* 華嚴五教止觀; T.1867) into the more elaborate one of a net which contains a multifaceted jewel at each vertex, which reflects and is reflected in every other jewel. In this sense, every "*dharma*" or "quanta of experience" is contained within every other *dharma*, even as it contains every other *dharma* and in fact contains itself as contained within every other *dharma*. This is what is referred to in the Huayan literature as "mutual containment" and "mutual penetration." As Dushun puts it:

> The manner in which all *dharmas* interpenetrate is like an imperial net of celestial jewels extending in all directions infinitely, without limit. . . . Because of the clarity of the jewels, they are all reflected in and enter into each other, ad infinitum. Within each jewel, simultaneously, is reflected the whole net. Ultimately, nothing comes or goes. If we now turn to the southwest, we can pick one particular jewel and examine it closely. This individual jewel can immediately reflect the image of every other jewel. As is the case with this jewel, this is furthermore the case with all the rest of the jewels – each and every jewel simultaneously and immediately reflects each and every other jewel, ad infinitum. The image of each of these limitless jewels is within one jewel, appearing brilliantly. None of the other jewels interfere with this. When one sits within one jewel, one is simultaneously sitting in all the infinite jewels in all ten directions. How is this so? Because within each jewel are present all jewels. If all jewels are present within each jewel, it is also the case that if you sit in one jewel you sit in all jewels at the same time. The inverse is also understood in the same way. Just as one goes into one jewel and thus enters every other jewel while never leaving this one jewel, so too one enters any jewel while never leaving this particular jewel. Question: Since you said that one enters into all jewels in one jewel without leaving this jewel, then

how can one enter into all other jewels [without ever leaving the one jewel]? Answer: It is only because one does not leave this one jewel that one can enter into all jewels. If one left one jewel to enter into all jewels, it would not be possible to enter into all the jewels. Why? Because outside of this one jewel there are no other jewels. Question: If outside of this jewel there are no other jewels, then the net is made of only one jewel. How can you say that it is strung out of many jewels? Answer: It is only because there are no separate jewels that many can be fashioned into a net. How is this so? Because only this one jewel alone constitutes the whole net. If this one jewel were removed, there wouldn't be any net at all. Question: If there is only one jewel, how can you say that they are woven into a net? Answer: A net woven of many jewels is itself a single jewel. Why is this so? The whole is constituted by its many parts. If there were no whole, the plurality of parts would also be absent. Therefore this net is constituted by each jewel. All entering into each – this is the way to understand this.

Typical of Chinese and especially Daoist rhetoric, there is a fair amount of equivocation at work in these rhetorical paradoxes – to say that things are and are not is to say that things are what they are in one sense, and they are not in another sense. Each jewel is identical to every other jewel in some sense and unique in another sense, and this is what makes these formulations seem so bizarre and oxymoronic. We consistently see language in the Huayan literature which reconciles identity and difference, or part and whole. The whole is identical to the part in the sense that the whole is nothing but its parts, and the parts are identical to the whole in the sense that they wouldn't be parts if not for the whole. This mutual definition – that the parts and wholes are defined by each other – is what is meant by these rhetorical paradoxes.

As Garma Chang describes the *Huayan* worldview: "the 'larger' universes include the 'smaller' ones as a solar system contains its planets, or a planet contains its atoms. This system of higher realms embracing the lower ones is pictured in a structure extending *ad infinitum* in both directions to the infinitely large or the infinitely small. This is called in the *Huayan* vocabulary the view of 'realms-embracing-realms.'" (Chang 1971, 12). This metaphor, though, illustrates only the familiar model of the macrocosmic containing the microcosmic. It seems the Huayan model goes further and suggests that "containment" works in both directions: just as the large contains the small, so does the small contain the large.

The *Huayan Jing* also contains many chapters whose titles invoke lists of ten qualities or aspects of some subject, such as "Ten Abodes," "Ten Practices," "Ten Inexhaustible Treasuries," "Ten Dedications," "Ten Stages," and others, which have greatly influenced the rhetoric of Huayan literature. For example, among the idiosyncratic formulations of the Huayan school are many lists of metaphors or ways of looking at things, such as the "Ten Mysteries," the "Perfect Interpenetration of Six Forms," and so on, but it is the idea of the "fourfold *dharmadhātu*" that arguably serves as the most central doctrine. The term "*dharmadhātu*" has been used in many ways throughout the history of Buddhist thought in India and China.

In the Pāli Nikāyas, there are passages which suggest that meditation or contemplation of *dharmadhātu* is the most profound method of attaining higher-order perspectives. For example, in the *Samyutta Nikāya*, *dharmadhātu* is one of the 18 *dhātus*. These *dhātus* represent the perceptual manifold, analyzed into subjective, objective, and mediational "realms." They are, using the visual sense as an example: the physical eye itself, the sensory organ; the ostensible sensory object, such as "color," which is seen; and the visual perceptive consciousness which mediates this sensory event. There are six such senses in this formulation, and in the *Samyutta Nikāya dharmadhātu* is treated as the object of the cognitive sense (*manovijñāna*). It is this understanding of *dharmadhātu* which is found most commonly in the Pāli Abhidharma materials, and is also dominant in the Theravāda and Sarvāstivāda Abhidharma traditions.

In the *Prajñāpāramitā* literature, the term *dharmadhātu* is expressed in apparently negative formulations such as *śūnyata* or "emptiness." Such expressions seem intended to deconstruct ontological fixation on *dharmadhātu* as one more thing among other things. The Madhyamaka school, also, because of its deconstructive approach to the problem of contextual dissonance, focused on more cognitive, epistemological concerns. To the Madhyamaka tradition, terms such as *dhātu* (realm, sphere, context) or *dharmadhātu* are too easily ontologized. Actually, the Huayan notion of an interpenetrative *dharmadhātu* is completely synonymous with the equation of *sunyata* and *pratītyasamutpāda*. *Dharmadhātu* is a contextual interpretation of interdependent co-origination.

The term *dharmadhātu* (Ch. *fa jie* 法界) occurs with great frequency In the *Huayan Sūtra* itself. At no point, however, is it "explained" or analyzed. Rather, it represents the goal of the bodhisattva practice, the end of Sudhana's journey in the final chapter. In most cases, the term *ru* (入 : "to enter") is used as the functional qualifier, suggesting that the nature of *dharmadhātu* is such that it must be entered. It is not necessary to ontologize *dharmadhātu* as any kind of mystical or "spiritual world" when it seems more likely to refer to a particular way of looking at the world, a particular perspective on reality. This understanding seems reflected in early Huayan literature, and especially in one of the most basic models of meditation found in Huayan, that of the "four *dharmadhātus*." This might be mistaken for a metaphysical model if *dharmadhātu* is understood as "world," as it often is, and so this notion might seem to suggest that there are four separate worlds into which one might enter. This is true in an existential, though not an ontological, sense. In Buddhism, a "world" or *dhātu* has no independent status apart from a consciousness which apprehends it, and vice versa. To paraphrase the opening lines of the *Dhammapada*, the world is a thought, and to change your thoughts is to change the world. In that sense, then, the "four *dharmadhātus*" are not four separate worlds but four cognitive approaches to the world, four ways of apprehending reality.

Although it was really Chengguan (738–839), the fourth Huayan patriarch, who first clearly articulated the "fourfold *dharmadhātu*" analysis, the idea is clearly visible in a work attributed to Dushun (557–640), the acknowledged initial patriarch of the orthodox Huayan tradition, entitled *Meditative Approaches to the Huayan Dharmadhātu*. It has become a hallmark of the Huayan tradition and the centerpiece of its theoretical structure. This work was basically a meditation manual, outlining three approaches to (or "layers" of) meditation on the *dharmadhātu*. The three levels of meditation are: (1) meditation on "True Emptiness"; (2) illuminating the non-obstruction of principle and phenomena; and (3) meditation on "universal pervasion and complete accommodation."

It is in Chengguan's commentary to the *Meditative Approaches* that we first find a clear description of the fourfold *dharmadhātu*. Here, the three layers of meditation on *dharmadhātu* found in the *Meditative Approaches* are interpreted as the second, third, and fourth *dharmadhātu*: the first layer becomes the second *dharmadhātu* – that of "principle" (*li* 理); the second layer becomes the third *dharmadhātu* – that of the "non-obstruction of principle and phenomena" (*lishi wuai* 理事無礙); and the third layer becomes the fourth *dharmadhātu* – that of the "non-obstruction of phenomena with other phenomena" (*shishi wuai* 事事無礙). The first *dharmadhātu* – that of "phenomena" (*shi* 事) – refers to our ordinary, tacit, superficial interpretation of experience, and so Dushun did not consider it a meditative approach. It is important to emphasize that these *dharmadhātus* are not separate worlds – they are actually increasingly more holographic perspectives on a single phenomenological manifold.

In some sense, then, similar to certain interpretations of quantum mechanics, *dharmadhātu* refers to the virtually infinite manifold of possibilities, which coalesces into an actual reality through the cognitive approach or perspective adopted by a conscious mind. A convenient metaphor is one of those "magic eye" pictures, which seems like visual noise until you focus your eyes to the correct depth into the picture, at which point the image appears. *Dharmadhātu* or "reality" is like that, except that, instead of only one image being available, an infinite number of different images is available depending on the depth and angle of viewing. Since, for the Huayan tradition, "principle" is equated with "emptiness," we might say that, in contextual terms, "principle" can be interpreted as "contextuality," while "phenomenon" can be interpreted as the particular significance of an event or ostensible thing. Specific significance is thus determined relativistically by context, or principle.

When Huayan speaks of the "interpenetration of principle and phenomena," it could be said that what is being described is the fact that, on the one hand, context is nothing other than the product of the interrelationships of its constituent significance events, and that, on the other hand, the significance of these events is determined by the context of which they are constitutive. "Interpenetration of phenomena with other phenomena" refers to the fact that all possible contextually determined significances of particular events overlap and coexist simultaneously and at all times, without conflict or obstruction.

What we think are the essences of objects are really therefore nothing but mere names, mere functional designations, and none of these contextual definitions need necessarily interfere with any of the others. The significance of an object, and in fact its very reality, at any given moment is a function of the contextual perspective from which it is approached. At rest, all of these potential contextual perspectives interpenetrate, in that each context is at that point still merely a possible approach to functional significance. Functional designations are actualized when the moment of their use for some practical purpose is at hand and a particular perspective is adopted.

This model correlates again with modern quantum mechanical views of the universe. Basically a statistical model of reality, quantum mechanics suggests that the occurrence of events can be described mathematically by a series of wave functions. As the occurrence of an event approaches, wave functions describe the probabilities of all particular possible outcomes of the event. These probability functions do not interfere with one another, and exist side by side until the event actually occurs. Until the event occurs, it is all of them and none of them. At that moment, one of the wave functions, that which describes the actual outcome, expands to 100 percent probability, while the others collapse to zero probability. The point is that, until the wave functions collapse and the event actually occurs, all possible outcomes are equally inherent, and it is only when the moment of actualization is at hand that one possible outcome becomes dominant.

This "all-in-one and one-in-all" philosophy pervades Huayan thought and rhetoric. Perhaps its most effective expositor was the seventh-century Huayan patriarch Fazang, who is famous for the demonstrations and metaphors which enabled him to explain Buddhist metaphysics to, among others, the Empress Wu, securing imperial support for his translation movement and for Buddhist institutions affiliated with his form of Huayan thought, often described as "orthodox." Among his most well-known demonstrations were the "Hall of Mirrors" and the "Golden Lion."

In the first instance, Fazang used ten mirrors to conform to the "tenfold" precedent established in the *Huayan Jing* itself. Eight large mirrors were arranged in an octagon, with additional mirrors placed on the floor and ceiling. In the center of this space was placed a statue of the Buddha. Fazang then ignited a torch in the center, and the room was filled with reflections within reflections of the torch and the Buddha. This effectively demonstrated the Huayan view of reality as a web of causal relations, each "node" or interstices of which lacks any essential identity, and each of which is in some sense contained within everything else even as it contains everything else.

In the second case, Fazang used a meticulously carved statue of a lion made out of solid gold he saw at the Imperial Palace. Every detail of the lion was represented on the statue – every hair, every tooth, every claw, etc. While all of these parts seemed distinct and unique, in fact they were all gold. The goldness of the lion did not interfere with the details of the lion and vice versa. In this sense the golden substance represents the empty (*śūnya*) nature of all things, which does not interfere with the ostensible individuality of all things. Things are unique and similar simultaneously, such that their uniqueness and similarity do not obstruct each other.

Of course, the metaphor illustrates that Fazang was willing and perhaps eager to reduce the world to a fundamental ontology, contrary to the premises of early Buddhism. The suggestion of an essential substance of which everything is a transformation seems to threaten to re-enter Buddhist tradition periodically. Certainly, Fazang championed that interpretation of Yogācāra thought and the *Awakening of Faith*, as opposed to his rival translator Xuanzang, whose understanding was shaped by the years he spent studying at the Sanskrit Buddhist institutions in India.

One last metaphor or teaching device for which Fazang is famous is his description of the universe as a house or building. Each part of the house is in some sense the whole house, and the whole house is in each part. As above, so below – because the house is nothing but the rafters and joists, etc., each rafter is necessary for the whole to exist and, in that sense, each rafter is the whole building. It is true that such an omni-causal model conflates the various types of causal relations that Aristotle, for example, distinguishes, such as efficient, material, final, contiguous, and other types of causal relations. On the other hand, the purpose of the model is not to distinguish causal subtleties but to stimulate contextual and perspectival flexibility.

The influence of other forms of Chinese thought on Huayan is clear. The emphasis on non-dogmatic contextual flexibility and perspectivalism sounds strikingly like ideas found in the writings of Zhuangzi (莊子). Various ideas introduced into Chinese thought by Zhuangzi encourage the soteriological transcendence of perspectival fixation through cultivation of higher order, more omni-perspectival viewpoints. We see what the *Zhuangzi* means by a "partial view" in Burton Watson's (1968) translation of chapter 17: "Jo of the North Sea said, 'You can't discuss the ocean with a well frog – he's limited by the space he lives in. You can't discuss ice with a summer insect – he's bound to a single season. You can't discuss the Way with a cramped scholar – he's shackled by his doctrines.'" Because of the limitations of perspective, significance cannot universally apply across contexts. Particular doctrines and ideological approaches are "shackles" or "blinders" which accommodate only the narrowest range of experience. To paraphrase Hans-Georg Gadamer, there can be no truth through method: method presupposes specific categories of result. Even the merest formulation of a question, by orienting the point of view, determines the nature of the response. By limiting perspective, we are limiting significance, and contextual fixation of this kind restricts what Zhuangzi calls "carefree meandering."

Most notable is the influence of the paradigmatic Chinese text known as the *Dasheng Qixin Lun* 大聲起信論 or *Mahayana Awakening of Faith*. According to Buddhist tradition, this text was written in Sanskrit by Asvagosa and translated into Chinese in the year 550 by the famous Central Asian translator Paramartha. This is disputed, however, by many scholars who believe that the text was actually Chinese in origin. According to its translator:

> The work is a comprehensive summary of the essentials of Mahayana Buddhism, the product of a mind extraordinarily apt at synthesis. . . . The *Awakening of Faith* has exerted a strong influence upon other schools of Buddhism as well. Fa-tsang, the third patriarch and the greatest systematizer of the Hua-yen school of Buddhism, wrote what was regarded as the definitive commentary on the *Awakening of Faith*, and moreover used this text as a foundation in creating his systematization of Hua-yen doctrine, and for this reason the text has often been thought of as peculiarly the property of the Hua-yen School. For example, Tsung-mi, the fifth patriarch of the Hua-yen School, also wrote a commentary on the *Awakening of Faith* and used its doctrines as a foundation in his attempts to synthesize the three religions of China, Confucianism, Taoism, and Buddhism.
>
> (Hakeda 2005, 3–10)

The core metaphor or model in the *Awakening of Faith* is the idea of the "One Mind" (*yi xin* 一心). For Zongmi, fifth patriarch of Huayan, this "One Mind" refers to the closure and unity of experience itself, which he characterizes as "intrinsic awareness" or "sentience," among other things. From a phenomenological point of view, Zongmi sees awareness as the "bottom line." It is pre-perspectival, and in that respect is identical to the *dharmadhātu* in its most comprehensive aspect. In the *Awakening of Faith*, two meditative approaches to the One Mind are adopted: those of Suchness (*tathata, zhen ru* 真如) and *saṃsāra*. It must be kept in mind, however, that these refer to two different perspectives on the One Mind, and do not describe two different entities or realities. According to the *Awakening of Faith*, One Mind includes both the one and the many.

Thus it would appear that such designations as "Suchness," "Dharmadhātu," "One Mind," and so on, all represent various perspectives towards the so-called omni-context or phenomenological manifold, which is itself identified with pre-perspectival, predualistic "awareness." As far as Zongmi's own formulation is concerned, the key to the unity of theory and practice lay in the idea of "immediate awakening followed by gradual cultivation." This also serves as Zongmi's attempt to reconcile the ongoing controversy within the Chan tradition of his time over the sudden or gradual nature of practice and awakening. As Zongmi himself says in the Chan Preface:

> The words "awakening," "cultivation," "immediate," and "gradual" seem to be very far apart [in meaning], and yet they are complementary. This means that [among] the various Sutras and sastras and the various Chan gates, some say that one must first attain success by means of gradual cultivation, and then immediately awaken. Others say that one must first immediately awaken, and then one can practice gradual cultivation. Others say that by means of immediate cultivation, one awakens gradually. Others say that the Dharma is neither gradual nor immediate, and that both gradual and immediate refer to the capabilities [of various individuals]. Each has its intended meaning. To say that they [only] seem to conflict is to say that, since awakening is the accomplishment of Buddhahood, fundamentally there never were any *klesas*: this is why it is called "immediate," because one need not practice cultivation in order to eliminate [*klesas*]. Then why continue to speak of gradual cultivation? Gradual cultivation is for when the *klesas* are not yet exhausted. The causal practice is not yet complete, so the resultant virtue is not yet ripe. How could it be called "immediate"? Immediate is that which is not gradual; gradual is that which is not immediate. Therefore they are said to be in conflict. By reconciling them in the following discussion, I will show that immediate and gradual are not only not contradictory, but are actually complementary.
>
> (T.2015)

Later on in the text, Zongmi specifies what he means by "immediate awakening followed by gradual cultivation":

> There are those who say that one must first suddenly awaken and then one can gradually [practice] cultivation. This refers to awakening as "insight." (In terms of the elimination of hindrances, it is like when the sun immediately comes out, yet the frost melts gradually. With respect to the perfection of virtue, it is like a child which, when born, immediately possesses four limbs and six senses. As it grows, it gradually develops control over its actions.) Therefore, the *Hua Yen* [*Jing*] says that when the *bodhicitta* is first aroused, this is already the accomplishment of perfect enlightenment.

The idea of immediate awakening followed by gradual cultivation rests upon a particular understanding of the nature of "enlightenment," an understanding which is first formulated in the *Awakening of Faith*. Here, "enlightenment" is looked at from several different perspectives. To begin with, all sentient beings are regarded as fundamentally already enlightened. As the result of what is termed "beginningless ignorance," this primordial awakening is forgotten, and the individual finds herself in *saṃsāra*. At some point, one experiences an "initial" awakening, which then matures into a "final" or "ultimate" awakening which is identical to the awakening of the buddhas. As Zongmi formulates it in the Chan Preface, the so-called initial awakening is termed "immediate insight awakening" and refers to the initial sudden insight into "One Mind" and the contextual nature of experience. However, what is being called "insight-awakening" involves more than merely intellectual understanding. In contextual terms, it refers rather to an existential realization of contextuality, or, in other words, to the fact that lived experience is indeed a complex of contextual closures. However, even though such insight-awakening has taken place, the habitual energies produced by conditioned fixations have generated a powerful momentum, accruing over the course of, perhaps, an uncountable multitude of lifetimes. Therefore the purpose of "post-insight" practice of gradual cultivation is gradually to break these habits. When this gradual cultivation results in the elimination of habitual, neurotic obsessions and fixations, this is what Zongmi calls "authenticated awakening." Together, "insight-awakening" and "authenticated awakening" constitute "comprehensive enlightenment." Indeed, in the final chapter of the *Hua Yen Sūtra*, it is suggested that, although the bodhisattva path consists of 52 distinct stages, as soon as one begins at the initial stage, one has already, in a sense, completed all 52 stages. Nevertheless, one must still proceed through the stages one at a time, much like a baseball player who hits a home run, and yet still has to run around and touch all of the bases to score a run. Thus, faced with the radical iconoclasm of some of the Chan traditions of his time, Zongmi manages to reconcile the spontaneous nature of awakening as emphasized in Chan with the need for textual study and meditation practice as emphasized in other, more classical forms of Buddhist tradition.

Although Huayan eventually ceased to function as an autonomous school of Chinese Buddhism, its thought had a significant influence on the development of later forms of East Asian Mahāyāna Buddhism. As indicated, many scholars have linked Huayan to Chinese Chan Buddhism. Zongmi, in fact, claimed lineage credentials in both the Huayan and the Chan traditions. The important Korean Son Buddhist thinker Wonhyo also commented on Huayan, Zongmi, and the *Awakening of Faith*. Although in many cases the link to Huayan is not explicitly stated, nevertheless the rhetoric and categories of later East Asian Mahāyāna are indebted to the Huayan thinkers and texts.

References

Chang, Garma C. C. (1971). *The Buddhist Teaching of Totality: The Philosophy of Hwa Yen Buddhism.* University Park: Pennsylvania State University Press.

Cleary, Thomas (trans.) (1993). *The Flower Ornament Scripture: A Translation of the Avatamsaka Sutra.* Boulder, CO: Shambhala.

Dushun. *Calming and Contemplation in the Five Teachings of Huayan (Huayan wujiao zhiguan* 華嚴五教止觀, Taisho 1867.

Hakeda, Yoshito (trans.) (2005). *The Awakening of Faith.* New York: Columbia University Press.

Watson, Burton (trans.) (1968). *The Complete Works of Chuang Tzu.* New York: Columbia University Press.

12

Forms of Emptiness in Zen

BRET W. DAVIS

Zen is a practice of awakening.[1] Who does one awaken as? What does one awaken to? The answer to both of these questions is, in a word, "emptiness" (Skt *śūnyatā*; Ch. *kong*; Jp. *kū*). One awakens as one's "true self" (Jp. *shin no jiko*), and yet the true self is selfless, not only in the sense of compassionate, but also in the sense of empty of a determinate and substantial ego. The true self is thus a "non-self" (Skt *anātman*; Jp. *muga*) that awakens to its "formlessness" (Jp. *musō*), its "self-nature which is no-nature" (Jp. *jishō sunawachi mushō*), as Hakuin puts it in his *Praise of Zazen* (Hakuin 1998, 101). At the same time, one awakens to the nature of reality – that is, one becomes capable of "seeing things as they really are" (Skt *yathābhūtadarśana*). How are things? They are "empty of own-being" (Skt *svabhāva-śūnya*) – that is, they do not have their being on their own but exist rather as impermanent events of dependent origination (Skt *pratītya-samutpāda*; Jp. *engi*). One thus awakens as the "formless self" underlying the formations of the ego, and one awakens to the emptiness of all the phenomenal forms that one encounters in the world. And these are not separate matters since, according to Zen, one also awakens to the non-duality of self and world.

Moreover, one awakens to the non-duality of form and emptiness. On the one hand, the formless true self creatively and compassionately expresses itself in personal form, and, on the other hand, the emptiness of things does not deny but rather characterizes the existence of things with concrete form. As is reflected in such adages as "true emptiness, wondrous being" (Jp. *shinkū myōu*) (Tagami and Ishii 2008, 291–2), East Asian Mahāyāna Buddhism speaks of emptiness, not only as what negates a falsely attributed substantiality to things, but also as what enables the forms of reality to be such as they really are, to be in their "suchness" (Skt *tathatā*; Jp. *shinnyo*).[2]

The pivotal line of the *Heart Sūtra* is well known: "Form is emptiness, and emptiness is form" (Nakamura and Kino 1960, 8). According to the Madhyamaka school, which philosophically develops the insights of the *Prajñāpāramitā Sūtras* such as the *Heart Sūtra*, this means that, once we see that things are empty of own-being or independent

A Companion to Buddhist Philosophy, First Edition. Edited by Steven M. Emmanuel.

substantiality, we can see them such as they are in their interrelational existence. Nāgārjuna even equates emptiness with dependent origination.[3] All beings are thus at once form and emptiness; indeed they are "forms of emptiness" in that it is their lack of independence and substantiality that allows them to be the interrelated processes that they are. Hence the first meaning of the title of this chapter – but only the first.

However significant Madhyamaka philosophy is for Zen, there are other forms that the teaching of emptiness takes in Zen besides the mere lack of own-being.[4] The *Prajñāpāramitā Sūtras* themselves make reference to 18 or 20 types of emptiness (Nakamura 2001, 778; Komazawa Daigaku 1985, 240). Indeed, frustrated readers of texts on Zen that seem to use the term "emptiness" in a bewildering variety of senses and contexts may not be surprised to hear Dōgen's claim that there are at least 84,000 kinds of emptiness (Dōgen 1990, 3: 406)! How can we begin to approach the great many forms the teaching of emptiness takes in the Zen tradition? Based on my own understanding of the texts and practice of Zen, rather than strictly following any traditional schema, I think we can schematize this manifold into six rubrics, six basic ways in which the notion of emptiness is used in the Zen tradition. These are: (1) lack of own-being; (2) formlessness of ultimate reality; (3) distinctionless state of meditative consciousness; (4) no-mind in the action of non-action; (5) emptiness (or emptying) of emptiness; and (6) emptiness of words.

Let me begin with a preliminary sketch of these six forms or rubrics of emptiness. First of all there are two ontological – or, better, "meontological" (from the Greek word for "non-being, *mēon*) or, best, "kenological" (from the Greek word for "emptiness," *kenotēs*) – senses of emptiness: (1) phenomenal beings' lack of own-being – i.e., absence of independent substantiality (which also, as we shall see, implies the fullness of "interbeing"); and (2) the formlessness of ultimate reality – i.e., the purity and essential indeterminacy of the "water" underlying the "waves" of the discriminations of phenomenal form. Next, there are two psychological senses of emptiness: (3) *samādhi* (Jp. *zenjō*) as a state of meditative concentration which reaches a deep level of consciousness beyond or beneath the waves of mental activity, a state which is empty in the sense of being pure or free from delusory discriminations; and (4) no-mind (Jp. *mushin*) as a radical openness of mind and heart which is not withdrawn from the world but rather non-dually involved in it by means of the "action of non-action" (Ch. *wei-wu-wei*; Jp. *mu-i no i*), a non-willful, spontaneously natural engagement with persons and things. The last two rubrics involve the self-negating nature of emptiness: (5) the emptiness (or emptying) of emptiness (Skt *śūnyatā-śūnyatā*; Jp. *kū-kū*) is an antidote to one or another type of "emptiness sickness" (Jp. *kū-byō*).[5] While emptiness negates our delusory reifications of reality, it is not itself an alternative reality in which we should dwell. Its thoroughly negating activity applies also to itself. This is understood either in ontological or, rather, kenological terms, as the constant self-emptying of emptiness into form, or in semantically deconstructive terms, as the emptiness (i.e., lack of independent existence) of the notion of emptiness itself. Finally, (6) the longstanding critique in Buddhism of the dualistically reifying effects of language, a critique which reaches an apex in Zen's claim that awakening is "not founded on words and letters," is reflected in the teaching of the emptiness of words, a teaching that points beyond all teachings, including itself, to a practice that issues in direct realization. As we shall see, each of the six rubrics contains a cluster of closely related teachings. Moreover, there are certainly many interconnections, and arguably some tensions, among the rubrics. For the sake of clarity, however, each of the six sections of this chapter will focus in turn on each of the six rubrics.

Before beginning to examine these six forms that the teaching of emptiness takes in Zen, let me comment briefly on Zen's relation to the doctrinal sources upon which it critically and creatively draws. The Zen tradition understands itself to be based on Śākyamuni Buddha's profoundest teaching, which has been passed down not through texts and doctrines but by way of face-to-face acknowledgment of awakening. Insofar as this is a "special transmission outside the scriptures," Zen cannot ultimately be understood in terms of doctrinal or philosophical teachings, but must be directly experienced by way of meditative practice, in stillness and in action, with one's "whole body and spirit" (Jp. *zenshin-zenrei*). Nevertheless, on the way to and from the meditation cushion, and indeed as an integral part of its holistic practice of realization, Zen frequently employs various teachings and texts of the Mahāyāna Buddhist tradition. The concept of emptiness, we shall see, is used in different ways in different *sūtras* and philosophical schools of the Mahāyāna tradition, and these differences are reflected in the forms in which emptiness appears directly or indirectly in Zen teachings. As is well known, the Zen tradition is also strongly influenced by Daoism, from which it inherits the key term "nothingness" (Ch. *wu*; Jp. *mu*). This Daoist term was initially used by early Buddhists in China to translate *śūnyatā*, before being replaced by the character meaning "sky" as well as "emptiness" (Ch. *kong*; Jp. *kū*). While most other Buddhist schools ceased to use *wu* in this sense, the Zen tradition has continued to use *wu/mu*, often synonymously with *kong/kū*. One can detect some Daoist influence in particular in our rubrics 2, 4, and 6. Let us, however, begin our exploration of the forms of emptiness in Zen with rubric 1, a foundational teaching of Mahāyāna Buddhism.

Lack of Own-Being

If one looks up "emptiness" in a Buddhist or a Zen dictionary, the main definition given is generally the lack of own-being or independent substantiality (Nakamura 2001, 312; Komazawa Daigaku 1985, 240). This teaching can be traced back to the early Buddhist teaching of non-self (P. *anattā*) as one of the three marks of existence, the other two being impermanence (P. *anicca*) and suffering or unsatifactoriness (P. *dukkha*). While suffering applies only to sentient beings, non-self applies to all existents, in the sense that everything is without permanent and independent substantiality. Nothing exists forever or on its own. Rather, the temporary existence of everything is due to causes and conditions, and, as is stressed in East Asian Mahāyāna, everything exists in a web of interconnectedness with all other things. Hence, the teaching of non-self is the other side of the teaching of dependent origination. It is in accord with these oldest of Buddhist teachings that Nāgārjuna identifies emptiness with dependent origination.

However, Nāgārjuna also criticizes earlier interpretations of these foundational Buddhist teachings, namely the Abhidharma doctrines of the so-called Hīnayāna schools, which sought to explain the self's lack of independent substantiality by means of breaking the self down into its components. The second century BCE Buddhist monk Nāgasena famously argued that, just as a chariot can be broken down into the wheels, axles, chassis, etc., a person can be broken down into its constituent parts (Dumoulin 1994, 32–3). The Abhidharma philosophers understood themselves to be taking up where the Buddha left off when he analyzed the self into five "heaps" (P. *khandha*; Skt *skandha*), namely: material form, feeling, perception, volitional mental formations, and consciousness. They broke each of these down further until they reached what they considered to be the ultimate physical and mental constituents of reality, which they called *dharmas*. Whether these *dharmas* were understood to be permanent (as in the Sārvastivāda Abhidharma) or momentary (as in the Sautrāntika Abhidharma), they were taken to be real existents, the atomistic building blocks of the universe, so to speak. The emptiness of the self was thus explained on the basis of its being analyzable as an ever changing conglomeration of these *dharmas*.

When the *Heart Sūtra* says that "form is emptiness," it is taking the non-self doctrine one revolutionary step further: even "the five *skandhas* are empty," indeed, "all *dharmas* are characterized by emptiness" (Nakamura and Kino 1960, 8). (It should be noted that "form" [Skt *rūpa*; Jp. *shiki*] in such phrases as "form is emptiness" is subsequently often used in the Mahāyāna tradition to refer not just to the first *skandha* of material form, but, as shorthand for all *dharmas*, to all material and mental phenomena with delimited form.) The critical point being made is that not only is the self empty of substantial selfhood (Skt *pudgala-nairātmya*; Jp. *ninkū*), *dharmas*, too, are empty of substantial selfhood (Skt *dharma-nairātmya*; Jp. *hokkū*). There are no substantial building blocks of the universe; nothing has independent existence; everything depends for its existence on causes and conditions; and everything is essentially interconnected. This radical teaching of the emptiness of own-being lies at the core of the *Prajñāpāramitā Sūtras* and Nāgārjuna's Madhyamaka school of thought, which established the initial philosophical basis of the Mahāyāna tradition.

Crucially, this radical negation enables an equally radical reaffirmation. Whereas the Abhidharma's analytical reductionism saw only that *the self is empty*, this new Mahāyāna teaching could also turn the coin over to see that *emptiness is the self*. Not only is form emptiness, but *emptiness is also form*. In China, Tiantai (Jp. Tendai) philosopher Zhiyi developed the Madhyamaka notion of the Two Truths (i.e., the conventional truth of provisionally designated forms and the ultimate truth of emptiness) into the Three Truths of "the provisional, the empty, and the middle" (Swanson 1995). The "middle" truth entails a reaffirmation of provisional forms *as provisional* – that is, as empty of independent substantiality but fully real as provisionally designated events of dependent origination.

The contemporary Vietnamese Zen master Thich Nhat Hanh beautifully expresses the sense in which, paradoxically, emptiness entails fullness. To begin with, he points out that to be "empty" is always to be empty *of something*. In this case, to be empty means to be "empty of a separate self." So, when we say for example that a sheet of paper is empty, this means that

> it is empty of a separate, independent existence. It cannot just be by itself. It has to inter-be with the sunshine, the cloud, the forest, the logger, the mind, and everything else. It is empty of a separate self. But empty of a separate self means to be full of everything.
>
> (Thich Nhat Hanh 2009, 6–7)

Emptiness of own-being thus implies fullness of interbeing.

The school of Buddhism that developed this teaching of interconnectedness furthest is the Huayan school, which has strongly influenced Zen. Huayan draws upon the *Avataṃsaka Sūtra*'s image of the "jewel net of Indra," a massive net representing the universe, in each knot of which lies a jewel reflecting all the others (Cook 1977, 2; Chang 1992, 165). In this sense, each phenomenon of the universe contains, and is contained in, all the others. No phenomenon could be what it is without the support of every other, and the universe could not be what it is without the support of each phenomenon. Fazang demonstrates much the same point with a hall of mirrors, where each mirror reflects an image of the Buddha as it is reflected in all the others (Chang 1992, 24).

Thich Nhat Hanh also stresses, as did Nāgārjuna, that emptiness implies openness to change. Indeed, in her interpretation of Nāgārjuna's philosophy, Nancy McCagney makes a good case for translating *śūnyatā* as "openness" rather than "emptiness," since it implies "the open-endedness of events, their openness to change, their nonfixedness, their impermanence" (McCagney 1997, 62). After all, if things had unchanging essences there would essentially be no growth and development, and thus no possibility for liberation from delusion and suffering. (Later we will see that, psychologically speaking, emptiness in Buddhism also implies open-mindedness and open-heartedness.)

Formlessness of Ultimate Reality

In the course of his explanation of the relation between emptiness and form in his commentary on the *Heart Sūtra*, Thich Nhat Hanh also employs a famous analogy: "Form is the wave and emptiness is the water. . . . So 'form is emptiness, and emptiness is form' is like wave is water, water is wave" (2009, 13). While used in Huayan (Tu Shun 1992, 214–18) as well as in Zen, this simile of water and waves does not in fact derive from the *Heart Sūtra* or indeed from any of the *Prajñāpāramitā Sūtras*, but rather from the *Laṅkāvatāra Sūtra* (Suzuki 1932, 42) and the *Awakening of Faith in Mahāyāna* (Hakeda 1990 [1967], 41, 55).

In his treatise on "Oriental Nothingness," the twentieth-century philosopher and Zen teacher Hisamatsu Shin'ichi uses this image of water and waves to explain the relation between the "nothingness" of the "one mind" and the multiple forms of the phenomenal world. He writes:

> In Buddhism there is the expression, "All is created by alone-mind." . . . Buddhism frequently employs the analogy of water and waves in order to illustrate . . . the creative nature of this mind. . . . Waves are produced by the water but are never separated from the water. . . . While the water in the wave is one with the wave and not two, the water does not come into being and disappear, increase or decrease, according to the coming into being and disappearing of the wave. . . . The mind of "all things are created by the mind alone" is like this water. The assertions of the Sixth Patriarch [of Zen], Huineng, that "self-nature, in its origin constant and without commotion, produces the ten thousand things" and that "all things are never separated from self-nature" . . . express just this creative feature of the mind.
>
> (Hisamatsu 2011, 225-6)

Other related analogies used in Mahāyāna Buddhist texts include the *Śūraṅgama Sūtra*'s one handkerchief with many knots (Low 2000, 137–40), and the Huayan thinker Fazang's statue of a golden lion, where the figure of the lion represents phenomenal forms or "aspects" (Ch. *xiang*; Jp. *sō*) and the gold represents the underlying essence or "body" (Ch. *ti*; Jp. *tai*) (See Fa Tsang 1992).

Such analogies have invited severe criticism lately from the proponents of so-called Critical Buddhism, who accuse Zen – along with most schools of East Asian Buddhism – of failing to uphold the most fundamental Buddhist teaching of emptiness understood as synonymous with dependent origination. Speaking of emptiness in terms of an innate "buddha-nature" (Jp. *busshō*) is said to conflate emptiness with precisely what it negates, namely an underlying substratum, and thereby to fall back into the "Ātman = Brahman" metaphysics that the Buddha rejected (Matsumoto 1994; Hakamaya 1990). As we shall see in the following section of this chapter, this criticism is in fact nothing new, but rather echoes longstanding debates *within* the Buddhist tradition between Madhyamaka thought, on the one hand, and Yogācāra and Tathāgatagarbha thought, on the other. Critical responses to the Critical Buddhists have ranged from accusations of promoting an exclusionary sectarian fundamentalism that does not take into account the evolving plurality of interwoven strands of the Buddhist tradition(s) (Gregory 1997) to pointing out that the doctrines they deem problematic should be read as "skillful means" (Skt *upāya*) (King 1997; see also Ogawa 1982). Of course, for Zen, all doctrinal teachings are, at best, skillful means. Yet, even on a doctrinal level, Zen thinkers would certainly deny that they understand emptiness or the buddha-nature in terms of an independent substantiality that is incompatible with other central Buddhist teachings such as dependent origination.

Hisamatsu does indeed claim that the nothingness (Jp. *mu*) of buddha-nature is "deeper than dependent origination," since it is the absolute One – or, as Nishitani Keiji puts it, "the None beyond the One" (Nishitani 1987a, 243) – whereas dependent origination is a relation between two or more things (Hisamatsu and Yagi 1980, 68).[6] As Hisamatsu's student Abe Masao puts the point, when we say there is "nothing" behind this world of thoroughgoing dependent origination, this "nothing" should not be understood merely as a "relative nothingness" or privation of being, but rather as an "absolute nothingness." The latter is a radical formlessness which is free even of the "form of formlessness," and so, "being formless in itself, true *śūnyatā* does not exclude forms, but freely and unrestrictedly takes any form as its own expression." According to Abe, this "formless *śūnyatā*, in Mahāyāna Buddhism, best describes the nature of ultimate reality" (Abe 2011, 752, 755–6).

Insofar as Zen thinkers understand emptiness in this manner as a formless, "non-objectifiable, ultimate reality," they can be said to have been influenced not only by such Buddhist texts as the *Awakening of Faith* but also by Daoist writings, which suggest that the multiplicity of phenomenal beings arise out of and return to an aboriginal nothingness.[7] Yet it is important to bear in mind that the Zen tradition has always understood this to be compatible with the principle of dependent origination and so with the idea that individual beings lack own-being – in other words, that they are empty in the sense of our first rubric.

Fazang in fact lists as the first reason for using the analogy of the golden lion:

> *To understand the principle of dependent-arising.* That is to say that gold has no inherent nature of its own [i.e., no *svabhāva*]. It is owing to the artistry of the craftsman that the form of the lion arises. This arising is the result solely of the cause-conditioning; therefore is called the arising through dependent-arising.
>
> (Fa Tsang 1992, 225)

He goes on to say, "Emptiness does not have any mark of its own; it is through forms that [Emptiness] is revealed." The "gold" is thus not some thing independent of the interdependent aspects of its form; it is the emptiness which allows those forms to be what they are. Insofar as we understand "emptiness" in what Hakeda Yoshito refers to as the two senses in which it is usually used in Buddhism, namely: in the sense of "empty or devoid of a distinct, absolute, independent, permanent, individual entity or being as an irreducible component in a pluralistic world," and in the sense of "empty of all predications" (Hakeda 1990 [1967], 36), then what the "gold" is meant to symbolize is indeed empty.

If emptiness in Zen is a metaphysical substratum, it is a peculiar one indeed, for it is essentially indeterminate and non-dually inseparable from phenomenal forms, which arise by means of its self-emptying – that is, by means of its self-negation as self-determination or self-delimitation. The modern Zen master Yamada Kōun speaks of emptiness in mathematical terms as an "empty-limitlessness" which is the "denominator" of all things of the phenomenal world, which are its "numerators" (Yamada 2004, 46). Moreover, since the zero of this empty-infinite is none other than one's true self, or, as Linji puts it, "the true person of no rank who goes in and out of the gates of your senses" (Iriya 1989, 20), Yamada states:

> We cannot locate our essential nature because it is a zero, yet it has infinite capabilities. It can see with eyes, walk with legs, think with a brain, and digest food with a stomach. It weeps when it is sad and laughs when it is happy. Though it is zero, no one can deny its existence. It is one with phenomena. The essential nature and phenomena are one from the very beginning. That is why the [*Heart Sūtra*] can say, "Form is nothing but emptiness; emptiness is nothing but form."
>
> (Yamada 2004, 28–9)

In Sanskrit *śūnya* means not only "empty" but also "zero" (Tachikawa 2003, 51), which here implies not just ultimate privation but also infinite potential.

Since the beginning of Mahāyāna thought, *śūnyatā* has also been closely related to the unlimitedness of space and the open sky. The translation of *śūnyatā* with the Chinese character that literally means "sky" as well as "emptiness" (Ch. *kong*; Jp. *kū*) is thus quite apposite, as is the link with "space" (Skt *ākāśa*) that is further reinforced by the translation of this term as "vacant sky" (Ch. *xukong*; Jp. *kokū*). In the earliest of the *Prajñāpāramitā Sūtras*, the sky and space were used as metaphors for emptiness and purity, as well as for the bodhisattva's unattached and unobstructed freedom and limitless depth of wisdom (Conze 1973, 11, 14, 25, 46, 57, 60). McCagney writes the following regarding sky and space as primal metaphors in the earliest Mahāyāna sources.

> The symbols in the early *Prajñāpāramitā* texts show that the Mahāyāna notion of *ākāśa* [i.e., "space" understood as "a luminous ether, filled with light"] derives from meditation

> (*dhyāna*) on the sky, which is experienced as vast, luminous and without boundaries. This use is consistent with early Buddhist *dhyānas* on the *arūpadhātus* (formless realms) as well as the close connection drawn between *ākāśa* and *nirvāṇa* as *asaṃskṛta* (unconditioned) events (*dharmas*) by six of the early schools.
>
> (McCagney 1997, xx)

We will take up the issue of meditative states in a moment, but here let us note that, alongside *nirvāṇa*, space was considered by most early Buddhist schools to be an "unconditioned *dharma*," unaffected by the conditioned events of dependent origination that took place within it.

The Zen philosopher Nishitani Keiji writes that the "sky is an eternally constant empty space with unlimited depth and endless width. It is the only 'eternal thing' we can see with our eyes," and so the "sky of the visible world has been used in scriptures as an image (*Bild*) to indicate . . . [this] eternal limitlessness" (Nishitani 2011, 728). Elsewhere Nishitani speaks of "a void of infinite space" and an infinite sphere with "its circumference nowhere and its center everywhere" (Nishitani 1982, 146). In many Mahāyāna texts, including those of Zen, space or the open expanse of a clear sky symbolizes the ultimate Dharma realm of non-obstruction which makes room for all, letting everything within it coexist in harmonious interaction (Komazawa Daigaku 1985, 332; Tagami and Ishii 2008, 199).[8] In the *Ten Oxherding Pictures*, after both the ox and the ox herder disappear in the eighth picture, leaving only an empty circle, a river and a tree and then an interpersonal encounter are depicted in the ninth and tenth pictures. The emptiness of the eighth picture is thus not an end state, but rather can be understood, at least in part, as an awakening to the open place in which the events of all the other pictures have always already been taking place (Ueda 2003, 175).

And yet, the sky or empty space analogy, however useful it is for understanding how emptiness lets things be without interference, does not work as well for explaining how emptiness is somehow the source of forms, unless, that is, we understand "space" as dynamically self-delimiting itself into the shapes and colors of things (Akizuki 1990, 55–6; 2002, 34). As Brook Ziporyn points out, in the *Platform Sūtra*, "Huineng is made to compare the 'self-nature' of all beings to empty space, which here both contains and produces all the particular objects within it" (Ziporyn 2011, 78). Ikkyū speaks of emptiness as a formless "original field" from which everything arises and to which everything returns. "All the forms, of plants and grasses, states and lands, issue invariably from emptiness, so we use a metaphorical figure and speak of the original field" (Ikkyū 2011, 172, 176–7). Nishitani also speaks of "the field of emptiness," and of this – in a manner that resonates well with contemporary physics – as a "field of force." He writes: "If we call nature a force that gathers all things into one and arranges them into an order to bring about a 'world,' then this force belongs to the field of emptiness, which renders possible a circulating interpenetration among all things" (Nishitani 1982, 163, translation modified). Drawing deeply on Huayan philosophy while also alluding to Heidegger's later thought, Nishitani says that, on this field of emptiness, all things are in the process of reflecting and being reflected in, supporting and being supported by one another, such that "when a thing *is*, the world *worlds*" (ibid., 150, 159). In his later period, Nishida Kitarō – Nishitani's teacher and the founder of the Kyoto school – understood the "self-determination of the place of absolute nothingness" in terms of the dialectically mutual determination of individual persons, things, and concrete universals such as languages and cultures (Nishida 1987–9, 7: 163). The self-emptying of emptiness occurs as the interdependent origination of all things.

In line with this self-determining field-like understanding of *śūnyatā*, the modern Zen master Yasutani Hakuun (1966, 74) has said, "[*Kū*] is not mere emptiness. It is that which is living, dynamic, devoid of mass, unfixed, beyond individuality or personality – the matrix of all phenomena." Albert Low comments, "The closest we can come to this in modern thought is the notion of a magnetic field. Even so, the field is an abstraction from life, Buddha nature is life itself" (Low 2000, 124). While the quantum electromagnetic field may indeed approximate the "objective" aspect of what Nishitani calls the "field of emptiness" (Jp. *kū no ba*), Low is right to point out the need to stress the "subjective" aspect of this field. Nishitani calls this the "radical subjectivity" (Jp. *kongen-teki shutaisei*) which, having transcended or, rather, "trans-descended" both the field of reified being and the field of vacuous nihility, realizes – i.e., awakens to and actualizes – the field of emptiness as the "standpoint of emptiness" (Jp. *kū no tachiba*) (Davis 2004b). As Nishida puts it, the true self is aware of itself as a "focal point" of the expressive self-determination of the place of absolute nothingness (Nishida 1987–9, 10: 437, 441; 11: 378). Or as Dōgen, in the "Empty Space" (Jp. *Kokū*) fascicle of the *Shōbōgenzō*, quotes his teacher Rujing as saying, "My entire embodied self is like the mouth [of a bell] hanging in empty space" (Dōgen 1990, 3: 411).

Distinctionless State of Meditative Consciousness

Thich Nhat Hanh tells us that, if we learn to identify ourselves with the ubiquitous emptiness of the "water" rather than with the finite form of a particular "wave," we will no longer fear death and will be able to live life to the fullest (2009, 24). Yet how can we do this? The Zen tradition has always stressed the efficacy of meditation; indeed the very word Zen derives from the Sanskrit word *dhyāna*, signifying a state of meditative concentration.

The association of emptiness with meditation in fact goes back to the beginnings of Buddhism. Indeed the earliest references to emptiness are the Buddha's instructions on meditation, such as verse 373 in the *Dhammapada*, which speaks of "entering the empty room [P. *suññāgāraṃ*] and quieting one's mind." In addition to referring to a vacant place for meditation, the "empty room" is presumably a reference to a meditative state of consciousness that is free of distractions and attachments. This psychological sense of emptiness is explicitly developed in such texts as the *Smaller Emptiness Sūtra* and the *Larger Emptiness Sūtra*, a development which culminates in what are called the three states of *samādhi* (meditative concentration): emptiness *samādhi* (Skt *śūnyatā-samādhi*), signless *samādhi*, and wishless *samādhi* (Tachikawa 2003, 87–97; Tagami and Ishii 2008, 225; Harvey 1990, 256). Also related here is the so-called formless realm, which is experienced in the meditative states of "the sphere of infinite space, the sphere of infinite consciousness, the sphere of nothingness, and the sphere of neither-cognition-nor-non-cognition" (Tagami and Ishii 2008, 247, 464; Harvey 1990, 251).

To be sure, these rarified states of meditative concentration are still considered to be but the highest abodes in *saṃsāra*, even if it was generally maintained that one passes through them on the way to *nirvāṇa*.[9] The Theravāda tradition has maintained that such states of meditative concentration (P. *samatha*) are merely preparatory to the more analytical forms of insight meditation (P. *vipassanā*) which lead to liberating wisdom (P. *paññā*). The Zen tradition, by contrast, holds there to be a more direct relation between non-discursive meditative concentration and enlightenment. Huineng in fact explicitly links – even identifies – meditative concentration (Skt *dhyāna*; Ch. *ding*; Jp. *jō*) with liberating wisdom (Skt *prajñā*; Ch. *hui*; Jp. *e*) (Yampolsky 1967, V, 135).

We will turn to Huineng's dynamic understanding of meditation in the next section of this chapter. Here, to begin with, we could apply the water/wave analogy to say that by quieting the mind one can experience the stillness of the water beneath the turbulence of the waves. This formless quietude discovered through meditation as the deepest layer of consciousness was frequently understood in the Yogācāra and Tathāgatagarbha traditions – especially as these were synthesized in the *Laṅkāvatāra Sūtra* and the *Awakening of Faith* – as "the original purity of the mind" (Jp. *honrai-shōjō-shin*). Whereas the Madhyamaka school has maintained the notion of "intrinsic emptiness" (Tb. *rang stong*; Jp. *jishō-kūshō*), meaning that something is in and of itself empty, these texts and traditions have frequently advanced the idea of "extrinsic emptiness" (Tb. *gzhan stong*; Jp. *tashō kūshō*), meaning that something is empty of something else. For example, it is thought that the phenomenal flow of experience is *empty of subject–object duality* but nevertheless real, or that the *tathāgatagarbha* or buddha-nature is *empty of defilements* but full of positive virtues (Williams 1989, 85, 101, 105–8; Harvey 1990, 111, 113, 116–17). Paul Williams writes that

> the tension between the two approaches to [emptiness] can be traced to an opposition between the Madhyamaka view of emptiness as an absence of inherent existence in the object under investigation, and the *tathāgatagarbha* perspective on emptiness, so influential in Chinese Buddhism including Chan, which sees emptiness as radiant pure mind empty of its conceptual accretions.
>
> (Williams 1989, 195)

The *Śrīmālā Sūtra* and the *Awakening of Faith* suggest that, by means of "cutting discursive activity, the mind is 'returned' to the state it was already really in, that of a pure, mirror-like, radiant stillness" (ibid., 111).

There have been centuries of debates, which continue among scholars today, over the extent to which, and the sense in which, Madhyamaka and Yogācāra's Cittamātra or "mind only" philosophy are compatible. One solution, that of the Yogācāra-Svātantrika Madhyamaka school, was to see Cittamātra as a provisional teaching which enables one to see objects as empty, insofar as they are dependent on the mind, but which in the end gives way to the Madhyamaka insight that the mind, too, is inherently empty (Williams 1989, 59, 280; Tachikawa 2003, 177–89). Despite the differences between sudden and gradual approaches to enlightenment foregrounded in the legendary debate in Tibet between a proponent of this school (Kamalaśīla) and a proponent of Zen (Moheyan), something similar might be said of the provisional treatment of Cittamātra in the Zen tradition.[10]

To be sure, the analogy of the enlightened mind as a "mirror" that is pure – i.e., empty of defilements – so that it reflects things as they are without imposing on them egocentric prejudices – in other words, what the Cittamātra tradition calls the "great perfect mirror wisdom" – has been widely used in the Zen tradition, especially in its early stages of development. The famous episode in *The Platform Sūtra of the Sixth Patriarch*, where Huineng trumps Shenxiu in a competition of verses, revolves around this analogy. Shenxiu had written, "The body is the Bodhi tree. / The mind is like the stand of a clear mirror. / At all times we must strive to polish it, / And must not let the dust collect" (Yampolsky 1967, III, 130, translation slightly modified). Shenxiu's view corresponds to that of Yogācāra insofar as he understands meditation as a means of "emptying" the mind in the sense of "purifying" it of defilements (Yokoyama 1982, 562–4). According to the earliest version of the text, Huineng responds, "Bodhi originally has no tree, / The mirror also has no stand. / Buddha nature is always clean and pure; / Where is there room for dust?" (Yampolsky 1967, IV, 132). Note that here Huineng does not directly question the aptness of the analogy of the mind as a mirror, only that its essential purity could ever be defiled. In a later version of the text, however, which became the standard in the tradition, the third line of Huineng's verse is changed to the famous phrase "Originally there is not a single thing" (Ch. *benlai wu yi wu*; Jp. *honrai mu ichi motsu*). This canonical line can be understood to entail that even the remnant of an ontological duality between a pure and unchanging mirror and the impure and changing images reflected in it needs to be let go of; even the empty mirror needs to be emptied out into the world.

As Yanagida Seizan explains, after Huineng the teaching of the mirror mind increasingly gave way to the teaching that the mind – or rather the "no-mind," as will be discussed in the following section of this chapter – is inseparable from the things and events of the world (Yanagida 1975, 81–106). Indeed, Xuedou (Jp. Setchō) strikingly says, in *The Blue Cliff Records* (Ch. *Biyanlu*; Jp. *Hekiganroku*), "mountains and rivers do not exist within the vision of a mirror." Yuanwu (Jp. Engo) adds the comment, "Don't view mountains and rivers . . . with a mirror. To do so produces a dualism. It's just that mountains are mountains, waters are waters, each dharma abides in its dharma position, and the features of the mundane world constantly abide as they are" (Iriya et al. 1994, 2: 104–5).

Later in life Huineng is said to have come across two monks arguing about whether a flag or the wind was moving, to which he remarked, "It is neither . . . It is your mind that is moving." And yet, in case we are tempted to think that Huineng's Cittamātra-like response is the ultimate truth rather than a skillful means, Wumen comments: "It is neither the wind nor the flag nor the mind that is moving. . . . All of them missed it" (Nishimura 1994, 122; Shibayama 2000, 209). What is the "it" that they missed? Two *mondō*[11] involving Mazu are also pertinent here. In the first one, in response to the question "What is Buddha?" Mazu replies, "This very mind is Buddha." However, in the second one, in response to the same question, Mazu now answers, "No mind, no Buddha" (Nishimura 1994, 125, 135; Shibayama 2000, 214, 235, translation modified). What then is "it"? This is where our demand for a philosophical theory is overridden by Zen's insistence on direct realization through holistic practice.

Zen practice is first and foremost *zazen*, seated meditation. Dōgen bluntly states, "The practice of Zen (*sanzen*) is zazen," which he describes as "the Dharma gate of great repose and bliss" (Dōgen 2002, 109–10). On the one hand, he says that this requires a "total commitment to immovable sitting," and yet, on the other hand, he also says that "the practice of Zen has nothing whatsoever to do with the four bodily attitudes of moving, standing, sitting, or lying down." "As you proceed along the Way," he tells us, "you will attain a state of everydayness" in all of these postures (ibid., 3, 5). Following Dōgen's lead, the Sōtō school has stressed the practice of bringing the meditative mindfulness cultivated in *zazen* into one's daily activities.

By comparison, the Rinzai school, with its use of *kōans*, teaches a more dramatic route through an intense state of meditative concentration back to the "everyday mind." Hakuin urges practitioners initially to use *kōans* such as "the sound of one hand" or the *Mu kōan* in order to cultivate the "great ball of doubt." He writes:

> When a person faces the great doubt, before him there is in all directions only a vast and empty land without birth and without death, like a huge plain of ice extending ten thousand miles. As though seated within a vase of lapis lazuli surrounded by absolute purity, without his senses he sits and forgets to stand, stands and forgets to sit. Within his heart there is not the slightest thought or emotion, only the single word *mu* (no!). It is as though he were standing in complete emptiness.
>
> (Hakuin 2011, 208)

When one "advances single-mindedly" into this state of frozen emptiness, Hakuin goes on to say, one will eventually achieve a breakthrough: "suddenly it will be as though a sheet of ice were broken or a jade tower had fallen," and one will "experience a great joy."

An entrance to the world of Hakuin's Rinzai Zen requires one first to break through all dualistic oppositions, of subject/object, inner/outer, pure/defiled, being/nothingness, speech/silence, etc. The entire world of relativities in which we live must be transcended, or rather trans-descended, before it can be reaffirmed (Hirata 1982, 2: 213). The sacred/secular duality must also be transcended, which means that even the transcendence/immanence duality must be relinquished. As the opening *kōan* in the *Blue Cliff Records* relates, when Bodhidharma was asked for "the first principle of the holy truth," he responded, "vast emptiness, nothing holy" (Ch. *kuoran wusheng*; Jp. *kakunen mushō*) (Iriya et al. 1994, 1: 36). The relation between emptiness and form must itself be understood non-dually. Zen affirms the *Vimalakīrti Sūtra*'s teaching that the relation of emptiness and form can be understood only by way of passing through the ultimate Dharma gate of non-duality (Watson 1997, 26, 29–30). Even the duality between duality and non-duality must be let go of. To attempt to do this by means of analytical reason, however, only produces yet further dualities. This Gordian knot cannot be teased apart with the fingers of the intellect; it must be cut directly and holistically with the sword of intuitive wisdom. The practice of meditation and *kōan* training is meant to unsheathe this sword.

"Not thinking of good or evil, what is your original face?" or "What is your original face before your father and mother were born?" is sometimes used as a first *kōan* in Zen training. Most often, however, the "initial barrier" through which Zen practitioners in the Rinzai tradition are required to pass is the first *kōan* in *The Gateless Barrier* (Ch. *Wumenguan*; Jp. *Mumonkan*), which could also be translated as *The Barrier (or Checkpoint) with the Gate of Mu*. This is the so-called *Mu* or "the one letter *Mu*" (Jp. *mu no ichiji*) *kōan*, in which Zhaozhou (Jp. Jōshū) answers "no!" (Ch. *wu*; Jp. *mu*) to a monk's question regarding whether or not a dog has buddha-nature.[12] Wumen instructs us not to "attempt nihilistic or dualistic interpretations"; in other words, *Mu* is neither a sheer vacuity nor is it the mere opposite of being; it is neither a "no" as opposed to a "yes" nor a "has" as opposed to a "has not." Rather than attempt to understand *Mu* intellectually from a distance, you must wholeheartedly "rouse the word *Mu*" by "concentrating yourself into this *Mu* with your 360 bones and 84,000 pores, making your whole body one great ball of doubt." Yet Wumen does not simply tell us to become *Mu* on the meditation cushion and stay there. This would be a form of emptiness sickness. Rather, like Hakuin, he says that, after "inside and outside have naturally become welded into a single block . . . all of a sudden it will break open, and you will astonish heaven and shake the earth" (Nishimura 1994, 21–3; Shibayama 2000, 19–20, translation modified).

No-Mind in the Action of Non-Action

Huineng tells us that only "the deluded man" thinks "that straightforward mind is sitting without moving and casting aside delusions without letting things arise in the mind"; in truth, "the *samādhi* of oneness is a straightforward mind at all times, walking, staying, sitting, and lying" (Yampolsky 1967, VI, 136). The true *samādhi* of oneness does not exclude an engagement with the plurality of things in the world, but entails a non-duality of equality and differentiation and a stillness in the midst of movement. What Huineng calls "no-thought" (Ch. *wunian*; Jp. *munen*), and what later is often referred to as "no-mind" (Ch. *wuxin*; Jp. *mushin*), does not exclude thinking; rather, "No-thought is not to think even when involved in thought" (ibid., VII, 138). The problematic kind of thought involves "the dualism that produces the passions" – in other words, we separate ourselves from things and reify them, and then we react to these illusory reifications with attachment or revulsion. However, Huineng says, "If you give rise to thoughts from your self-nature, then, although you see, hear, perceive, and know, you are not stained by the manifold environments, and are always free" (ibid., VII, 139).

This capacity of the formless self to engage freely with things, precisely because it does not attach itself to or rigidly identify itself with – i.e., "linger in" – any of their forms, is what is meant by no-mind. As Bankei puts it, "The unborn Buddha-mind deals freely and spontaneously with anything that presents itself to it" (Bankei 2011, 195). Peter Harvey depicts this as follows.

> When a person is in such a state he is aware of his surroundings in a total, all-round way, without getting caught up and fixed on any particular. The mind does not pick and choose or reflect on itself, but is serenely free-flowing, innocent and direct, not encumbered by thought-forms. When the need arises, the "mind of no-mind" can instantly react in an appropriate way.
>
> (Harvey 1990, 272)

The fact that the no-mind is "non-lingering" or "non-abiding" (Ch. *wuzhu*; Jp. *mujū*) does indeed mean that it does not get stuck on anything; but it does not mean that it cannot be intensely focused on something. Quite to the contrary, no-mind is akin to what athletes or musicians experience when they are "in the zone," utterly absorbed in an activity of the here and now (including when the "here and now" involves remembering, planning, or otherwise thinking of the "there and then"). A Zen master, however, would live all of life in the zone, whether listening or laughing, crying or dying, and would be able to shift effortlessly between different activities, at once absorbed in and yet unattached to any of them.

In his book on the subject, D. T. Suzuki unfortunately translates no-mind as "the Unconscious." What he meant by this, in any case, was not a coma-like state of unconsciousness or what psychoanalysts mean by the subconscious, but rather non-dualistic-consciousness or unselfconsciousness. In this sense he speaks of "everyday acts . . . done naturally, instinctively, effortlessly, and unconsciously" (Suzuki 1958, 106–7). Thomas Kasulis points out that no-mind or no-thought is "not an unconscious state at all" but rather a heightened state of non-dualistic awareness "in which the dichotomy between subject and object . . . is overcome" (Kasulis 1981, 47–8). As he goes on to say, it is "an active responsive awareness of the contents of experience as directly experienced," and, although he adds the phrase, "before the intervention of complex intellectual activity," I see no reason why it could not take place, as we have seen Huineng suggest, and as Nishida says of "pure experience" (Nishida 1990, 13), in the midst of complex intellectual activity. Not only when one is absorbed in a train of thought, but also when one effortlessly switches one's focus from one train of thought to another, this too is an instance of no-mind. No-mind is thus not thoughtlessness or unconsciousness but rather a purified consciousness; it is pure *not* in the sense that it is without content or oblivious to the complexity of interrelated distinctions, but rather in the sense that it is free from the distortions of this manifold by egocentric discrimination and dualistic reification.

To think and act in a state of no-mind is to be at once free and natural; it is to exist in a state of natural freedom (Davis 2011). In Zen, as in Daoism, such naturally free action is referred to as "non-action" or as "the action of non-action" (Ch. *wei-wu-wei*; Jp. *mu-i no i*), which indicates not a lack of action but rather pure activity, in other words, activity that is empty of willfulness and artificiality (see chapters 2, 3, 43, 48, and 64 of the *Daodejing*; Nakajima 1982; and Davis 2004a, 99–101). Suzuki cites several classical texts where Zen masters describe their state of awakening as follows: "When I feel sleepy, I sleep; when I want to sit, I sit"; or: "In summer we seek a cool place; when it is cold we sit by a fire." When a monk asks, "That is what other people do; is their way the same as yours?" the master replies that it is not the same, for "when they eat, they do not just eat, they conjure up all kinds of imagination; when they sleep, they do not just sleep, they are given up to varieties of idle thoughts" (Suzuki 1996, 207). Linji (Jp. Rinzai) says that "the Buddha Dharma is without artifice: just act naturally in your ordinary life, as you defecate and urinate, wear clothes and eat food" (Iriya 1989, 50; Cleary 1999, 20, translation modified). The term translated as "naturally" could be rendered more literally as "without ado" (Ch. *wushi*; Jp. *buji*), and, as with the term translated "without artifice" (Ch. *wuyonggong*; Jp. *muyōkō*), it begins with the character *wu*/*mu*, which means no, not, non, nothing, or does not have.

As we have seen, Zen often employs terms that begin with *wu*/*mu*: no-mind, no-thought, no-form, non-abiding, non-action, and so on. Along with "emptiness" and "nothingness," such terms may strike our ears as negative. Indeed they should, insofar as they do imply a radical negation of all the subtle and gross forms of our egocentric impulses, such as greed and hate, as well as delusions, such as the idea of own-being, all of which shapes our habitual manners of perceiving, thinking, feeling, and acting. However, these terms ultimately also indicate, as the other side of this radical negation, the affirmation of a liberated and liberating way of life. Perhaps we can begin to understand the affirmative aspect of such expressions as "emptiness" and "no-mind" if on occasion we substitute for them nearly synonymous words to which we are more attracted – words such as "freedom" and "openness."

We are not sure if we want to be "empty," but everyone wants to be "free." We are not sure if we want to be in a state of "no-mind," but everyone wants to be open-minded and open-hearted.[13] In German, "the open," in the sense of "outdoors," is called *das Freie*. In English we speak of "going out into the open to get some fresh air" and "the freedom of the outdoors." Also in English, "Is this seat free?" means "Is this seat empty?" which in turn means "May I potentially sit in it?" Emptiness thus implies the freedom not just of vacancy, but of potentiality, just as impermanence implies the ability to change. Change can of course be for the better or for the worse, depending on how we respond to an open-ended situation. We can respond with a closed mind, attaching ourselves to an illusory sense of permanent possession, or we can respond "freely," with an open mind attuned to its ever changing circumstances. Emptiness implies, then, freedom from attachment, from fixating on one place, and in this sense non-lingering or non-abiding. This term was employed by Huineng, who was initially enlightened upon hearing the *Diamond Sūtra*'s teaching to "arouse the mind that does not abide anywhere" (Tagami and Ishii 2008, 139; Nakamura and Kino 1960, 80). Not abiding or lingering anywhere, the open mind is able to take in and respond freely to the ever changing world, and the open heart is able to acknowledge and respond – i.e., is response-able – to the needs of others. In short, the realization of emptiness opens the door to wisdom and compassion, insofar as "emptiness is the 'nonduality of self and other' (Jp. *ji-ta funi*)" and the "oneness of thing and self" (Jp. *motsu-ga ichinyo*) realized by the "formless self" (Akizuki 1990, 48, 51).[14]

Emptiness (or Emptying) of Emptiness

Just as emptiness implies non-attachment to things, be they falsely apprehended substances or dogmatic "views," it also implies a non-attachment to emptiness itself. Emptiness too is empty, or must be emptied, or constantly empties itself. Among the 20 types of emptiness listed in traditional accounts, along with "the emptiness of ultimate reality" and "the absolute emptiness," we find "the emptiness of emptiness" (Skt *śūnyatā-śūnyatā*; Jp. *kū-kū*) (Nakamura 2001, 778; Komazawa Daigaku 1985, 240; Chang 1992, 119).

Garma Chang suggests that this teaching marks the difference between Mahāyāna Buddhism's emptiness and the absolute Being of the Upanishads. "The Upanishads affirm the *ultimate substratum, the Great One*; whereas Buddhism stresses the *Thorough Emptiness* without attachment to any Self-being or Sva-bhāva." The distinctive feature of absolute emptiness in Buddhism is thus said to be its "self-negating or thorough-transcending aspect" (Chang 1992, 93, 90). Also writing from a Huayan perspective,

Kaginushi Ryōkei explains that there are two interrelated meanings of the "emptiness of emptiness." On the one hand, along with the negation of the own-being of everything else, emptiness is itself emptied; emptiness itself is no-thing. On the other hand, "true emptiness . . . constantly negates its own emptiness and necessarily takes concrete form as the beings of dependent origination" (Kaginushi 1982, 743, 750).

The contemporary Zen philosopher Ueda Shizuteru writes of this twofold emptying of emptiness, or self-negation absolute nothingness, as follows:

> Now absolute nothingness, the nothingness that dissolves substance-thinking, must not be clung to as nothingness. It must not be taken as a substance, or even as the nihilum of a kind of "minus substance." The important thing is the de-substantializating dynamic of nothingness, the nothingness of nothingness. Put in philosophical terms, it refers to the negation of negation, which entails a pure movement in two directions at the same time: (1) the negation of negation in the sense of a further denial of negation that does not come back around to affirmation but opens up into an endlessly open nothingness; and (2) the negation of negation in the sense of a return to affirmation without any trace of mediation. Absolute nothingness, which first of all functions as radical negation, is maintained as this dynamic coincidence of infinite negation and straightforward affirmation.
>
> (Ueda 1982, 161–2)

Ueda warns that we must not confuse the first direction with a negative theology that would employ the *via negativa* in order to approach the ineffable "being" of an absolutely transcendent God. "Emptiness" or "nothingness" is not a negative theological finger pointing at an otherworldly moon. Furthermore, the second direction is said to distinguish the this-worldly orientation of Zen from a mysticism that would leave the everyday world of plurality behind in a *unio mystica* with the transcendent divine (Davis 2008). Emptiness constantly empties itself into form; absolute nothingness ceaselessly delimits itself as relative beings. While Ueda thus distinguishes Zen from negative theology and mysticism, other Kyoto school thinkers have drawn parallels between the second direction of the self-negation of absolute nothingness (or emptying of emptiness) and a radical interpretation – or a radicalization – of the Christian notion of *kenosis* as the "self-emptying" of God into the world (Nishida 1987–9, 11: 398–9; Nishitani 1982, 26, 58–9; Abe 1990; Davis 2005).

The following *mondō* from *The Book of Equanimity* (Ch. *Congronglu*; Jp. *Shōyōroku*) can be understood to convey both senses or directions of the emptying of emptiness.

> Yanyang (Jp. Gonyō) asked Zhaozhou (Jp. Jōshū): How about when one arrives carrying not a single thing? Zhaozhou responded: Cast that down! The monk then asked: Since there is nothing at all to carry, what should I cast down? Zhaozhou responded: In that case, pick it up and go!
>
> (Yasutani 1973, 321)

Chang comments, "cast that down" means "lay down your so-called Emptiness" (Chang 1992, 99). Elsewhere Wumen drives this point home: "Even vast emptiness does not yet accord with my principal teaching. Why don't you completely cast down emptiness too?" (Nishimura 1994, 109). Zhaozhou's "In that case, pick it up and go!" is generally understood to be an ironic reprimand to Yanyang which points out his contradictory attachment to emptiness; he is captive to his sense of liberation. Yet Chang suggests that it can also be understood to imply that, "by freeing oneself from clinging to the dead-emptiness, one can participate in every activity in life without losing the *śūnyatā* insight" (Chang 1992, 99). Only with empty hands, after all, is one free to pick things up.

Nishitani writes that the "absolute negativity" of emptiness does not entail a nihilistic annihilation of beings, but is rather the "force" or "place" that lets them be as they are in their interrelatedness (Nishitani 1987b, 92–3). It is ultimately a force not just of "nullification" (Jp. *muka*) but of "beification" (Jp. *uka*) (Nishitani 1982, 124, 146). The Zen philosophers of the Kyoto school have thus understood the self-emptying of emptiness in terms of what we might call a topological kenology or even a kenotic panentheism (Nishida 1987–9, 11: 399).

Other philosophers of Zen may prefer to restrict their understanding of the emptiness of emptiness to a deconstruction of any hypostatizing "view" of emptiness as a self-sufficient entity or state of being. As Candrakīrti puts it, the teaching of the emptiness of emptiness is "for the purpose of controverting any understanding of emptiness as an [ontological reference to] 'being'" (Candrakīrti 1989, 180). Candrakīrti is echoing his Madhyamaka predecessor Nāgārjuna, for whom the "emptiness of emptiness" means that we should not reify emptiness, turning the means of freeing us from conceptualized objects of attachment into another conceptualized object of attachment. On the one hand, if we were to misunderstand emptiness as an ultimate reality beyond the fray of this world of plurality and change, Nāgārjuna would say that we would fall back into the extreme of eternalism. On the other hand, if we were to misunderstand emptiness as sheer non-existence or as a nihilistic void, we would fall into the opposite extreme of annihilationism (Williams 1989, 62–3; Garfield 1995, 280–1, 299–321). Rather, Nāgārjuna's "middle way" understands emptiness as empty in the sense that, as the negation of own-being, it has itself no own-being. And so Nāgārjuna writes, "Emptiness is proclaimed by the victorious ones (Buddhas) as the refutation of all views; but those who hold 'emptiness' as a view are called incurable" (*Mūlamadhyamakakāri kā*, chapter 13, verse 8; Harvey 1990, 102). In other words, the teaching of emptiness does not exist on its own, but rather originates in relation to – i.e., as a negation of – the false idea of own-being. Once we have seen into the falsehood of the idea of own-being, we should also discard the idea of emptiness, like a thorn that has been used to remove another thorn.

Emptiness of Words

Nāgārjuna himself claims to have no view (Skt *dṛṣṭi*), but rather merely to refute – today we might say deconstruct – the inherently self-contradictory views of others. Language inevitably entails the proliferation of discriminatory conceptual fabrication (Skt *prapañca*). Specifically, words artificially separate what is interconnected and solidify what is ever in flux; language re-presents interrelated events and fluid processes as discrete independent substances. Seeing the world through language in this way leads us to mistake the map for the territory (McCagney 1997, xx, 29–30, 80, 99; Kasulis 1981, 21–8; Kajiyama 1992, 90–9). Here again we see connections with the Daoist tradition, especially with Zhuangzi's claim that language, with its dualistic reifications, imposes rigid boundaries (Ch. *zhen*) on an originally fluid world of interrelated processes (Ziporyn 2009, 9–20, esp. 16). Zhuangzi not only speaks of a practice of "sitting and forgetting" and of a "fasting of the mind" that makes way for a "vital energy that is an emptiness" (ibid., 49, 26–7), he also playfully uses humor, irony, paradox, and metaphor in ways that loosen up the logical rigidity of language. Nāgārjuna, on the other hand, through his more terse and sober deconstructive argumentation, aims to lead us to liberation by way of a "quieting of the proliferation of discriminatory conceptual fabrication" (Skt *prapañcopasamaḥ*) (*Mūlamadhyamakakārikā*, dedication and chapter 25, verse 24).

Harvey takes Nāgārjuna to be saying that "the ultimate truth, then, is that reality is inconceivable and inexpressible." Hence the final finger that can be used to point to the moon of reality is *tathatā*, "thusness" or "suchness," tautologically indicating that things are such as they are. "The thusness of something, equivalent to its emptiness, is its very as-it-is-ness . . . without adding anything to it or taking anything away from it" (Harvey 1990, 102). As the *Awakening of Faith* puts it, "all things are incapable of being verbally explained or thought of; hence, the name Suchness." The term "suchness" itself is "the limit of verbalization wherein a word is used to put an end to words." Regarding the emptiness of emptiness, the text goes on to say that, since unenlightened persons are alienated from suchness through our deluded use of words and concepts, "the definition 'empty' is used" to free them from these; "but once they are free from their deluded minds, they will find that there is nothing to be negated" (Hakeda 1990 [1967], 33, 35). Through realizing the emptiness of words, we are awakened to the suchness of reality.

When we see things as they really are, we realize that they are "empty of all the [egocentric and reifying] concepts by which we grasp them and fit them into our world, empty of all we project upon them" (Bercholz and Kohn 2003, 153). That this ultimately applies even to the doctrines of Buddhism themselves is impressed upon us in the *Heart Sūtra*, which not only proclaims the emptiness of all *dharmas* but also negates such fundamental doctrines as the Four Noble Truths when it says that there is "no suffering, no cause [of suffering], no end [of suffering], and no path [leading to the end of suffering]" (Nakamura and Kino 1960, 10). After all, Śākyamuni himself said that his teachings are like a raft used to get to the other shore, not a set of dogmas to be clung to (Rahula 1974, 11–12).

Zen stands out even among Buddhist traditions in its stress on the emptiness of words, especially words purporting to indicate ultimate truth. Wumen admonishes the pious adherent: "Don't you know that one has to rinse out his mouth for three days if he has uttered the word 'Buddha'?" (Nishimura 1994, 125; Shibayama 2000, 214). According to the motto attributed to Bodhidharma, Zen is "not founded on words and letters" (Ch. *buli wenzi*; Jp. *furyū monji*), but involves rather "directly pointing at the human heart-mind, seeing into one's nature and becoming a Buddha" (Ch. *zhizhi renxin jianxing chengfo*; Jp. *jikishi ninshin kenshō jōbutsu*). The direct (i.e., linguistically unmediated) "mind to mind" transmission that forms the core of the Zen tradition is said to have begun with Śākyamuni Buddha's Flower Sermon, when Mahākāśyapa smiled in response to the Buddha's holding up a flower in silence (Nishimura 1994, 43; Shibayama 2000, 58). This "special transmission outside the scriptures" (Ch. *jiaowai biezhuan*; Jp. *kyōge betsuden*) is said to have been subsequently passed down from one patriarch to the next, such as when Bodhidharma recognized his successor in Huike (Jp. Eka), who demonstrated his understanding by means of bowing and standing in silence. Other canonical references to the transcendence of language include the *Vimalakīrti Sūtra*, a much revered *sūtra* in the Zen tradition, the climax of which is generally held to be the layman Vimalakīrti's "thunderous silence," which is presented as the "entrance into nonduality" where "there is no use for syllables, sounds, and ideas" (Thurman 1976, 77).

And yet, as the modern Zen master Shibayama Zenkei warns, Vimalakīrti's silence should not be misunderstood as silence in opposition to speech (Shibayama 2000, 230–1, 255–6), a point made by a number of *kōans* (e.g., cases 24, 25, 32, and 36 of the *Gateless Barrier* and cases 70 to 73 of *The Blue Cliff Records*). Victor Sōgen Hori points out that elsewhere in the *Vimalakīrti Sūtra* itself we are told: "do not point to liberation by abandoning speech!" (Thurman 1976, 59; quoted in Hori 2000, 299). Furthermore, Dōgen suggests that other responses to Bodhidharma besides Huike's silence were also appropriate, such as that of Daofu, who said: "I neither cling to nor abandon words and letters; I use them as a means of the Way" (Dōgen 1990, 2: 359). While Dōgen affirms the potential of speech as well as silence to express an understanding of the matter of Zen, Wumen warns against the pitfalls of both: "If you open your mouth, you will lose 'it'. If you shut your mouth, you will also miss 'it'. Even if you neither open nor shut your mouth, you are a hundred and eight thousand miles away" (Nishimura 1994, 106; Shibayama 2000, 182). For Zen, silence can be just as problematic as speech, and speech just as effective as silence.

Recalling the emptying of emptiness, we could say, with Ueda, that the point is not to abide in silence any more than it is to get stuck in language. Rather, the point is to participate in a circulating movement between the emptying of language into silence and the emptying of silence back into language, an incessant dynamic of "exiting language and then exiting into language" (Davis 2013). The filters of language, after all, not only distort reality, they also render it intelligible and thus livable. The point is to see into the emptiness of words, not merely to annihilate them; the point is not to be free from the use of language, but rather to be free in one's use of language. After all, Huineng is not just depicted as tearing up the *sūtras*; he is also said to have dictated a new one. There can be words of silence, just as there are forms of emptiness. And there can be words of silence about the forms of emptiness.

Notes

1 Zen is pronounced Chan in Chinese. For the sake of consistency and to avoid confusion, the transliteration of terms in quoted passages will occasionally be silently modified. Chinese and Japanese names are written in the traditional order of family name first. Unless otherwise noted, translations from Chinese and Japanese are my own.

2 Tachikawa Musashi (2003, esp. 6, 324–9) traces how, during the course of the development of Mahāyāna Buddhism in India and then in East Asia, the positive, world-reaffirming aspects of the teaching of emptiness became ever more pronounced. According to Tachikawa, whereas the notion that "form is emptiness" was initially understood mainly as a warning not to cling to impermanent phenomena, later, and especially in East Asia, it came

to be understood to mean that phenomenal forms are as such the true face of reality (Jp. *shohō-jissō*).

3 Nāgārjuna, *Mūlamadhyamakakārikā*, chapter 24, verse 18. Translations of this influential text include Inada (1970) and McCagney (1997) (from the Sanskrit) and Garfield (from the Tibetan). The last includes an illuminating chapter-by-chapter philosophical commentary.

4 Paul Williams writes: "There is a tendency among modern scholars to reduce all Mahāyāna philosophy to a series of footnotes to Nāgārjuna. This tendency should, I think, be firmly resisted. Mahāyāna thought is not so monolithic" (Williams 1989, 132). As we shall see, Zen draws not only on Madhyamaka but also on the Cittamātra and Tathāgatagarbha strands of Indian Mahāyāna thought, as well as the way these get taken up and synthesized in China, especially in the Huayan school.

5 In his essay on "emptiness sickness," Yanagida Seizan writes, "Zen has developed thorough repeatedly criticizing false views of emptiness and purifying the thought of emptiness" (Yanagida 1982, 778).

6 Compare this with a passage from an early *Prajñāpāramitā Sūtra*, which says that emptiness is a synonym for "depth," and that, "Where there is no form, etc., that is the depth of form, etc." (Conze 1973, 209).

7 See the *Daodejing*, chapters 16, 25, 40, 42 (translations include Ivanhoe 2003). For a lucid interpretation of Zen as a synthesis and practical development of Nāgārjuna's emptiness and Daoist nothingness, see Kasulis (1981).

8 Garma Chang cites a traditional Chinese list of similes of emptiness, the first seven of which compare emptiness to "space or the Void," which "embraces everything everywhere" and yet "never hinders or obstructs anything" (Chang 1992, 100–1). Incidentally, the last two entries on the list, "the negation of negation" and "ungraspability," correspond to our last two rubrics of emptiness. For a recent philosophy of Zen that develops the metaphor of "empty space" as a "hollow expanse" that envelops the delimited horizons of our worlds of meaning, see Ueda (2002) and Ueda (2011).

9 In early Buddhism, *nirvāṇa* itself is at times described positively, as for example "the highest bliss" and "permanent and eternal," but is more often indicated *via negativa* with terms that include "emptiness" (P. *suññatā*), in the "extrinsic emptiness" (see below) senses of "empty of attachment, hatred and delusion" and "empty of a substantial self" (Harvey 1990, 62–3).

10 See Nishitani (2009) for an illuminating discussion of Fayan (Jp. Hōgen) and his decisive conversion from Cittamātra to Zen.

11 *Mondō* are recorded dialogues, generally between a master and a disciple, which are often used as *kōans* – that is, "cases" assigned to a Zen practitioner in order to trigger and cultivate enlightenment.

12 For a collection of teachings on Zen practice using this *kōan*, see Ford and Blacker (2011).

13 It is worthwhile noting that, in Chinese and Japanese, "heart" and "mind" are written with the same character (Ch. *xin*; Jp. *shin* or *kokoro*). In other words, these languages do not separate the seat of the intellect and the seat of the emotions, suggesting that a truly open mind entails an open heart, and vice versa.

14 Yamada Mumon Rōshi thus teaches that the realization of emptiness is a means to the ultimate goal of Buddhism, namely the wisdom and compassion entailed in the realization of one's non-duality with the world and with others (Yamada and Takahashi 1999, 49–50). See also Tamaki (1982), who argues that the teaching of emptiness is a means to wisdom and compassion, not vice versa; and Hirata Seikō Rōshi, who teaches that "emptiness" is a metaphor which works well to convey the open-space-like quality of the Buddha-nature, but not as well for conveying its content of wisdom and compassion (Hirata 1982, 2: 133–6).

References

Abe, Masao (1990). Kenotic God and Dynamic Sunyata. In *The Emptying God: A Buddhist–Jewish–Christian Conversation*. Ed. John B. Cobb, Jr., and Christopher Ives. Maryknoll, NY: Orbis Books, 3–65.

Abe, Masao (2011). Śūnyatā as Formless Form. In *Japanese Philosophy: A Sourcebook*. Ed. James W. Heisig, Thomas P. Kasulis, and John C. Maraldo. Honolulu: University of Hawai'i Press, 750–7.

Akizuki, Ryōmin (1990). *Zen bukkyō to wa nanika* [What is Zen Buddhism?]. Kyoto: Hōzōkan.

Akizuki, Ryōmin (2002). *Mumonkan o yomu* [Reading the Gateless Barrier]. Tokyo: Kōdansha.

Bankei, Yōtaku (2011). The Unborn. Trans. Norman Waddell. In *Japanese Philosophy: A Sourcebook*. Ed. James W. Heisig, Thomas P. Kasulis, and John C. Maraldo. Honolulu: University of Hawai'i Press, 195–9.

Bercholz, Samuel, and Kohn, Sherab Chödzin (eds.) (2003). *The Buddha and His Teachings*. Boston: Shambhala.

Candrakīrti (1989). The Entry into the Middle Way. Trans. C. W. Huntington, Jr., and Geshé Namgyal Wangchen. In *The Emptiness of Emptiness: An Introduction to Early Mādhyamika*. Honolulu: University of Hawai'i Press, 143–96.

Chang, Garma C. C. (1992). *The Buddhist Teaching of Totality: The Philosophy of Hwa Yen Buddhism*. Delhi: Motilal Banarsidass.

Cleary, J. C. (trans.) (1999). The Recorded Sayings of Linji. In *Three Chan Classics*. Berkeley, CA: Numata Center for Buddhist Translation and Research.

Conze, Edward (trans.) (1973). *The Perfection of Wisdom in Eight Thousand Lines & its Verse Summary*. San Francisco: City Lights.

Cook, Francis H. (1977). *Hua-yen Buddhism: The Jeweled Net of Indra*. University Park: Pennsylvania State University Press.

Davis, Bret W. (2004a). Zen after Zarathustra: The Problem of the Will in the Confrontation between Nietzsche and Buddhism. In *Journal of Nietzsche Studies* 28, 89–138.

Davis, Bret W. (2004b). The Step Back through Nihilism: The Radical Orientation of Nishitani Keiji's Philosophy of Zen. In *Synthesis Philosophica* 37, 139–59.

Davis, Bret W. (2005). Kami wa doko made jiko o kūzuru ka – Abe Masao no kenōshisu-ron o meguru giron [How Far Does God Empty Himself? On the Debate Surrounding Masao Abe's Theory of Kenosis]. In *Sekai no naka no Nihon no tetsugaku* [Japanese Philosophy in the World]. Ed. Fujita Masakatsu and Bret Davis. Kyoto: Shōwadō, 245–59.

Davis, Bret W. (2008). Letting Go of God for Nothing: Ueda Shizuteru's Non-Mysticism and the Question of Ethics in Zen Buddhism. In *Frontiers of Japanese Philosophy 2*. Ed. Victor Sōgen Hori and Melissa Anne-Marie Curley. Nagoya: Nanzan Institute for Religion and Culture, 226–55.

Davis, Bret W. (2011). Natural Freedom: Human/Nature Non-Dualism in Japanese Thought. In *The Oxford Handbook of World Philosophy*. Ed. Jay Garfield and William Edelglass. Oxford and New York: Oxford University Press, 334–47.

Davis, Bret W. (2013). Expressing Experience: Language in Ueda Shizuteru's Philosophy of Zen. In *Dao Companion to Japanese Buddhist Philosophy*. Ed. Gereon Kopf. New York: Springer.

Dōgen (1990). *Shōbōgenzō*. 4 vols. Ed. Mizuno Yaoko. Tokyo: Iwanami.

Dōgen (2002). *The Heart of Dōgen's Shōbōgenzō*. Trans. Norman Waddell and Masao Abe. Albany: State University of New York Press.

Dumoulin, Heinrich (1994). *Understanding Buddhism*. New York: Weatherhill.

Fa Tsang [Fazang] (1992). On the Golden Lion. In *The Buddhist Teaching of Totality: The Philosophy of Hwa Yen Buddhism*. Ed. Garma C. C. Chang. Delhi: Motilal Banarsidass, 224–30.

Ford, James Ishmael, and Blacker, Melissa Myozen (eds) (2011). *The Book of Mu: Essential Writings on Zen's Most Important Koan.* Boston: Wisdom.

Garfield, Jay L. (1995). *The Fundamental Wisdom of the Middle Way.* Oxford and New York: Oxford University Press.

Gregory, Peter N. (1997). Is Critical Buddhism Really Critical? In *Pruning the Bodhi Tree: The Storm over Critical Buddhism.* Ed. Jamie Hubbard and Paul L. Swanson. Honolulu: University of Hawai'i Press, 287–97.

Hakamaya, Noriaki (1990). *Hihanbukkyō* [Critical Buddhism]. Tokyo: Daizō Shuppan.

Hakeda, Yoshito S. (1990 [1967]). *The Awakening of Faith.* New York: Columbia University Press.

Hakuin, Ekaku (1998). Zazenwasan [Praise of Zazen]. In *Zenshū nikka seiten* [Daily Scriptures for the Zen Sect]. Kyoto: Baiyō Shoin.

Hakuin, Ekaku (2011). Kōan and the Great Doubt. Trans. Norman Waddell and Phillip B. Yampolsky. In *Japanese Philosophy: A Sourcebook.* Ed. James W. Heisig, Thomas P. Kasulis, and John C. Maraldo. Honolulu: University of Hawai'i Press, 207–10.

Harvey, Peter (1990). *An Introduction to Buddhism: Teachings, History, and Practices.* Cambridge: Cambridge University Press.

Hirata, Seikō (1982). *Mumonkan o yomu* [Reading the Gateless Barrier]. 3 vols. Tokyo: Hakujusha.

Hisamatsu, Shin'ichi (2011). Oriental Nothingness. Trans. Richard DeMartino. In *Japanese Philosophy: A Sourcebook.* Ed. James W. Heisig, Thomas P. Kasulis, and John C. Maraldo. Honolulu: University of Hawai'i Press, 221–6.

Hisamatsu, Shin'ichi, and Yagi, Sei'ichi (1980). *Kaku no shūkyō* [Religion of Awakening]. Tokyo: Shunjūsha.

Hori, G. Victor Sōgen (2000). Kōan and *Kenshō* in the Rinzai Zen Curriculum. In *The Kōan: Texts and Contexts in Zen Buddhism.* Ed. Steven Heine and Dale S. Wright. Oxford and New York: Oxford University Press, 280–315.

Ikkyū, Sōjun (2011). Skeletons. Trans. R. H. Blyth and Norman Waddell. In *Japanese Philosophy: A Sourcebook.* Ed. James W. Heisig, Thomas P. Kasulis, and John C. Maraldo. Honolulu: University of Hawai'i Press, 172–9.

Inada, Kenneth K. (1970). *Nāgārjuna: A Translation of his Mūlamadhyamakakārikā with an Introductory Essay.* Tokyo: Hokuseido Press.

Iriya, Yoshitaka (ed.) (1989). *Rinzairoku* [Ch. *Linjilu;* The Record of Linji]. Tokyo: Iwanami.

Iriya, Yoshitaka, et al. (eds) (1994). *Hekiganroku* [Ch. *Biyanlu;* The Blue Cliff Records]. 3 vols. Tokyo: Iwanami.

Ivanhoe, Philip J. (trans.) (2003). *The Daodejing of Laozi.* Indianapolis: Hackett.

Kaginushi, Ryōkei (1982). Kegon gakuha no kū shisō [The Thought of Emptiness in the Huayan School]. In *Kū* [Emptiness] (part 2), *Bukkyō shisō* [Buddhist Thought]. Vol. 7. Ed. Bukkyō shisō kenkyūkai [Research Group for the Study of Buddhist Thought]. Kyoto: Byōrakuji Shoten, 735–54.

Kajiyama, Yūichi (1992). *Kū nyūmon* [An Introduction to Emptiness]. Tokyo: Shunjūsha.

Kasulis, Thomas (1981). *Zen Action/Zen Person.* Honolulu: University of Hawai'i Press.

King, Sallie (1997). The Doctrine of Buddha-Nature is Impeccably Buddhist. In *Pruning the Bodhi Tree: The Storm over Critical Buddhism.* Ed. Jamie Hubbard and Paul L. Swanson. Honolulu: University of Hawai'i Press, 174–92.

Komazawa Daigaku Zengaku Daijiten Hensansho [Komazawa Editorial Institute for the Large Dictionary of Zen Studies] (1985). *Zengaku daijiten* [Large Dictionary of Zen Studies]. New edn. Tokyo: Daishūkan Shoten.

Low, Albert (2000). *Zen and the Sutras.* Boston: Tuttle.

Matsumoto, Shirō (1994). *Zen shisō no hihan-teki kenkyū* [Critical Studies of Zen Thought]. Tokyo: Daizō Shuppan.

McCagney, Nancy (1997). *Nāgārjuna and the Philosophy of Openness.* Lanham, MD: Rowman & Littlefield.

Nakajima, Ryūzo (1982). Rokuchō-jidai ni okeru mui no shisō [The Thought of Non-Doing in the Six Dynasties Period]. In *Kū* [Emptiness] (part 2), *Bukkyō shisō* [Buddhist Thought]. Vol. 7. Ed. Bukkyō shisō kenkyūkai [Research Group for the Study of Buddhist Thought]. Kyoto: Byōrakuji Shoten, 669–94.

Nakamura, Hajime (2001). *Kōsetsu bukkyōgo daijiten* [Large Dictionary of Extensive Explanations of Buddhist Terminology]. 2 vols. Tokyo: Iwanami.

Nakamura, Hajime, and Kino, Kazuichi (eds) (1960). *Hannyashingyō, Kongōhannyakyō* [The Heart Sūtra, The Diamond Sūtra]. Tokyo: Iwanami.

Nishida, Kitarō (1987–9). *Nishida Kitarō zenshū* [Complete Works of Nishida Kitarō]. 19 vols. Tokyo: Iwanami.

Nishida, Kitarō (1990). *An Inquiry into the Good.* Trans. Masao Abe and Christopher Ives. New Haven, CT: Yale University Press.

Nishimura, Eshin (1994). *Mumonkan* [Ch. *Wumenguan;* The Gateless Barrier]. Tokyo: Iwanami.

Nishitani, Keiji (1982). *Religion and Nothingness.* Trans. Jan Van Bragt. Berkeley: University of California Press.

Nishitani, Keiji (1987a). *Zen no tachiba* [The Standpoint of Zen], *Nishitani Keiji chosakushū* [Collected Works of Nishitani Keiji]. Vol. 11. Tokyo: Sōbunsha.

Nishitani, Keiji (1987b). Hannya to risei [Prajñā and Reason]. In *Nishitani Keiji chosakushū* [Collected Works of Nishitani Keiji]. Vol. 13. Tokyo: Sōbunsha, 31–95.

Nishitani, Keiji (2009). Nishitani Keiji's "The Standpoint of Zen: Directly Pointing to the Mind." Ed. and intro. Bret W. Davis. Trans. John C. Maraldo. In *Buddhist Philosophy: Essential Readings.* Ed. Jay Garfield and William Edelglass. New York: Oxford University Press, 93–102.

Nishitani, Keiji (2011). Emptiness and Sameness. In *Japanese Philosophy: A Sourcebook.* Ed. James W. Heisig, Thomas P. Kasulis, and John C. Maraldo. Honolulu: University of Hawai'i Press, 728–32.

Ogawa, Ichijō (1982). Nyoraizō shisō to kū [Tathāgatagarbha Thought and Emptiness]. In *Kū* [Emptiness] (part 2), *Bukkyō shisō* [Buddhist Thought]. Vol. 7. Ed. Bukkyō shisō kenkyūkai [Research Group for the Study of Buddhist Thought]. Kyoto: Byōrakuji Shoten, 579–605.

Rahula, Walpola (1974). *What the Buddha Taught.* Second enlarged edn. New York: Grove Press.

Shibayama, Zenkei (2000). *The Gateless Barrier: Zen Comments on the Mumonkan.* Boston: Shambhala.

Suzuki, Daisetz Teitaro (trans.) (1932). *The Lankavatara Sutra.* London: Routledge & Kegan Paul.

Suzuki, Daisetz Teitaro (1958). *The Zen Doctrine of No-Mind.* London: Rider.

Suzuki, Daisetz Teitaro (1996). *Zen Buddhism: Selected Writings of D. T. Suzuki.* Ed. William Barrett. New York: Doubleday.

Swanson, Paul (1995). *Foundations of T'ien-T'ai Philosophy: The Flowering of the Two Truths Theory in Chinese Buddhism.* Berkeley, CA: Asian Humanities Press.

Tachikawa, Musashi (2003). *Kū no shisōshi: Genshibukkyō kara Nihon kindai e* [A History of the Thought of Emptiness: From Early Buddhism to Modern Japan]. Tokyo: Kōdansha.

Tagami, Taishū, and Ishii, Shūdō (eds) (2008) *Zen no shisō jiten* [Dictionary of Zen Thought]. Tokyo: Tōkyō Shoseki.

Tamaki, Kōshirō (1982). Kū shisō e no hansei [Reflections on the Thought of Emptiness]. In *Kū* [Emptiness] (part 2), *Bukkyō shisō* [Buddhist Thought]. Vol. 7. Ed. Bukkyō shisō kenkyūkai [Research Group for the Study of Buddhist Thought]. Kyoto: Byōrakuji Shoten, 907–1015.

Thich Nhat Hanh (2009). *The Heart of Understanding: Commentaries on the Prajñāpāramitā Heart Sūtra.* Rev. edn. Berkeley, CA: Parallax Press.

Thurman, Robert A. F. (trans.) (1976). *The Holy Teaching of Vimalakirti: A Mahayana Scripture.* University Park: Pennsylvania State University Press.

Tu Shun [Dushun] (1992). On the Meditation of Dharmadhātu. In *The Buddhist Teaching of Totality: The Philosophy of Hwa Yen Buddhism*. Ed. Garma C. C. Chang. Delhi: Motilal Banarsidass, 208–23.

Ueda, Shizuteru (1982). "Nothingness" in Meister Eckhart and Zen Buddhism. Trans. James W. Heisig. In *The Buddha Eye: An Anthology of the Kyoto School*. Ed. Frederick Frank. New York: Crossroad, 157–69.

Ueda, Shizuteru (2002). *Kokū/sekai* [Hollow-Expanse/World], *Ueda Shizuteru shū* [Ueda Shizuteru Collection]. Vol. 9. Tokyo: Iwanami.

Ueda, Shizuteru (2003). *Jūgyūzu o ayumu* [Walking the Ten Oxherding Pictures]. Tokyo: Daihōrinkaku.

Ueda, Shizuteru (2011). Language in a Twofold World. Trans. Bret W. Davis. In *Japanese Philosophy: A Sourcebook*. Ed. James W. Heisig, Thomas P. Kasulis, and John C. Maraldo. Honolulu: University of Hawai'i Press, 766–84.

Watson, Burton (trans.) (1997). *The Vimalakirti Sūtra*. New York: Columbia University Press.

Williams, Paul (1989). *Mahāyāna Buddhism: The Doctrinal Foundations*. London and New York: Routledge.

Yamada, Kōun (2004). *The Gateless Gate*. Boston: Wisdom.

Yamada, Mumon, and Takahashi, Shinkichi (1999). *Mumonkan* [The Gateless Barrier]. Kyoto: Hōzōkan.

Yampolsky, Philip B. (trans.) (1967). *The Platform Sūtra of the Sixth Patriarch*. New York: Columbia University Press [Note that I have used capital roman numerals to refer to pages of the original text included at the back of this book].

Yanagida, Seizan (1975). *Zen shisō* [Zen Thought]. Tokyo: Chūkō Shinshō.

Yanagida, Seizan (1982). Kūbyō no mondai [The Problem of Emptiness Sickness]. In *Kū* [Emptiness] (part 2), *Bukkyō shisō* [Buddhist Thought]. Vol. 7. Ed. Bukkyō Shisō kenkyūkai [Research Group for the Study of Buddhist Thought]. Kyoto: Byōrakuji Shoten, 755–98.

Yasutani, Hakuun (1966). *The Three Pillars of Zen*. Ed. Philip Kapleau. New York: Harper & Row.

Yasutani, Hakuun (ed.) (1973). *Shōyōroku* [Ch. *Congronglu*; The Book of Equanimity]. Tokyo: Shunjūsha.

Yokoyama, Kōitsu (1982). Yuishiki shisō no kū [Emptiness in Cittamātra Thought]. In *Kū* [Emptiness] (part 2), *Bukkyō shisō* [Buddhist Thought]. Vol. 7. Ed. Bukkyō shisō kenkyūkai [Research Group for the Study of Buddhist Thought]. Kyoto: Byōrakuji Shoten, 559–78.

Ziporyn, Brook (trans.) (2009). *Zhuangzi: The Essential Writings*. Indianapolis: Hackett.

Ziporyn, Brook (2011). Chinese Buddhist Philosophy. In *The Oxford Handbook of World Philosophy*. Ed. Jay Garfield and William Edelglass. New York: Oxford University Press, 68–81.

13

Between the Horns of Idealism and Realism

The Middle Way of Madhyamaka

GRAHAM PRIEST

Introduction

When one travels to a foreign culture, one may find all kinds of new things. Take food, for example. All cultures have food, and food is food. But different cultures do different things with it, prepare it in different ways, use different ingredients, and so on. The product may be quite surprising and unlike anything one has experienced before.

So it is with philosophy. When Western-trained philosophers venture into the cultures of the great Asian traditions, India and China, they find philosophy. (Well, if they bother to go there at all. Some never even consider it worth looking. That's their loss.) Not only that, but they find philosophical problems with which they are familiar: what is the nature of reality, how should one live, how should one run the state, how does one know any of these things? But these questions may be approached in ways quite unfamiliar, and this may result in the traveler obtaining a whole new perspective on matters. That is what I hope to demonstrate in this chapter.[1]

The topic I choose to illustrate this is realism vs. idealism. Debates concerning these "*isms*" are legion in Western philosophy. For a start, one can be an idealist or a realist about many different kinds of things: abstract objects, the future, social dynamics, etc. The topic with which we will be concerned is the natural/physical world. In what follows, I will refer to this simply as *the world*.

A number of Western philosophers have held that the world exists and has its nature(s) quite independently of thought. It would have been there even had sentience never evolved. The view (in various forms) was held by Aristotle, Locke, Marx – to name but a few. These are the realists. On the other side of the debate have been those who held that the world does not have a mind-independent existence. In some sense, it depends on thought. The view (in various forms) was held by Berkeley, Kant, Hegel – to name but a few.

A Companion to Buddhist Philosophy, First Edition. Edited by Steven M. Emmanuel.

In Western philosophy in the twentieth century, dominated as it was by the philosophy of language, the contrast between the two positions was usually drawn in terms of whether or not the world is independent of language. Some, such as Foucault and, arguably, Derrida, were linguistic idealists. Language "constructs" the world. Others, such as most contemporary analytic physicalists, take the world to be constituted by what physics tells us to be out there, which is quite independent of what we say about it.

Now, language and thought are not the same thing. But the earlier debates and the twentieth-century debates are pretty much the same in important ways. Both kinds of debate can be captured under the rubric of the relationship between the world and our concepts – even if the notion of a concept in the two cases is not exactly the same. The difference, at any rate, is not one that is important for what follows. In particular, I will frame the debate between realists and idealists simply in terms of the conceptual dependence or independence of the world.

The debate between idealists and realists about the world is well known in the Asian philosophical traditions. The one that will concern us here is the Indian Buddhist tradition. In this, there were realists and idealists; but there was also one very important and influential school of Buddhists – Madhyamaka – which was neither realist nor idealist, but which went between the horns of the two positions. There is, as far as I am aware, no view similar to the Madhyamaka view in Western philosophy.[2]

I will not be concerned to evaluate the Madhyamaka view here. My aim is simply to explain it, putting a whole new kind of dish before Western philosophers who have never eaten in India.[3]

Buddhist Realists

Before I do this, it will be necessary to talk about the Buddhist realists and idealists. Let us start with the realists.[4]

Buddhist philosophy started with the ideas of the historical Buddha, Siddhārtha Gautama (exact dates uncertain, but roughly 563 to 483 BCE). Most aspects of his thought need not concern us here, but a central one was that there is no such thing as the self – something that persists through a person's existence and defines them as one and the same person during that time.[5]

What, then, is a person? Matters were debated in the ensuing centuries. Philosophical debates on this and other matters came to constitute the Abhidharma (roughly, "higher teachings") literature.[6] The view of what a person is that emerged was as follows. Consider your car, which has lots of bits. They came together under certain conditions, interact with each other and with other things; some wear out and are replaced. In the end they will all fall apart. We can think of the car as a single thing, and even give it a name (such as XYZ 123), but this is a purely conventional label for a *relatively* stable and self-contained aggregate of components. Now, a person is just like the car. The parts of which they are composed (the *skandhas*) are psycho-biological; but otherwise the story is much the same.

Of course, it is not just a person who has parts. Lots of things do: chairs, trees, countries, etc. The Abhidharmika could see no reason to treat other partite things in any different way. They are all conceptual constructions out of their parts.

But must there then be ultimate impartite things? The answer would seem to be *yes*. To have conceptual constructions, one must, it would seem, have something out of which to construct them. So, the Abhidharmika said, there are ultimate constituents of the world, which they called *dharmas*. These have *svabhāva*. That is, they exist, and are what they are intrinsically, independently of any process of mental construction. There were different views about what, exactly, the *dharmas* were: there were, in fact, a number of different Abhidharma schools, which disagreed about various matters.[7] But all agreed that *dharmas* were the ultimate constituents of the world and were not mental constructions. In this way, they were realists about the *dharmas*.[8]

At about this time emerged the doctrine of two truths.[9] In Sanskrit, one and the same word means "truth" and "reality": *satya*. The doctrine is of two *satyas*. Which of the two meanings does the word have in this context? Unfortunately, both – not always clearly distinguished. Let us start with the view as it applies to reality.

There are two realities, an ultimate reality and a conventional reality. Ultimate reality is constituted by the *dharmas*. As I have said, the Abhidharmika were realist about ultimate reality. Conventional reality (which is the way the world appears to most people) is constituted by the objects which are conceptual constructions out of these. How to understand the nature of their reality is a nice point. Exactly how should one understand the nature of the reality of conceptual constructions? This is a vexed question, even in the West. How should one understand the nature of the objects of fiction, social objects such as the Equator, institutions such as Parliament? Fortunately, we do not need to resolve this question. The important point is that, for the Abhidharma schools, whatever reality conceptual constructions have supervenes on that of the *dharmas*. The relationship, moreover, is asymmetric. The *dharmas* do not in any way depend for their reality on the things conceptually constructed out of them.

And what of truth? Truth is a relationship between propositions – things composed of concepts (whatever one takes these to be), and the world. This is not a profound claim; it is a quite banal one. No one is going to deny that the proposition that I am sitting on a chair is true if and only if I am indeed sitting on a chair (something concerning the world). What is not banal is how, exactly, to understand this relationship.

Though there is little explicit discussion of this relationship in the Buddhist canon, it is natural enough to take the notion of truth for ultimate reality to be a robust correspondence theory. What renders propositions ultimately true are facts about the *dharmas*. What to say about truth for conventional reality is less clear. There are various options, but perhaps the simplest is to say that truths about conventional reality, such as that I am sitting on a chair, are not truths at all, *in stricto sensu*. What are true are these statements prefixed by an appropriate modifier, such as "It appears that . . ." This modifier behaves like modifiers such as "In the Holmes stories of Conan Doyle . . ." In particular, "It appears that p" does not entail p – if anything, in this context, it entails that $\neg p$. Call this the *modifier theory* of truth.

So much for the Buddhist realists. Next to the idealists.

Buddhist Idealists

Around the turn of the Common Era, a new kind of Buddhism emerged: Mahāyāna Buddhism. This occasioned changes in ethics, metaphysics, and a number of other things. Our only concern here will be with the metaphysics. The core idea was to reject the Abhidharma understanding of the two realities. In particular, *all* things in the world were argued to have the same sort of reality.

There are several ways that one can articulate this idea, however. Different ways were articulated by the two main schools of Indian Mahāyāna Buddhism which developed – the Madhyamaka school and the Yogācāra school. The second of these arose historically later than the first, but the idea is articulated in a more straightforward way there. So let us take this first.[10]

The Yogācāra school is traditionally taken to have been founded by the brothers Asaṅga and Vasubandhu in about the fourth century CE. For the Abhidharma philosophers, partite things are not real, simply conceptual constructions. For Yogācāra, everything is like that.[11]

The view was spelled out by Vasubandhu in a text *Trisvabhāvanirdeśa* ("Treatise on Three Natures"),[12] with a doctrine called the *three natures*. Every object has "three natures." What these are is best explained by an example. Take a tree. One naively thinks of this as an object that exists "out there" in a mind-independent way. But it does not. This is the tree's *imagined nature*. All that there is, is a mental representation of a tree, which exists purely in the mind (as one might have a mental representation of water in a mirage). The only kind of existence the tree has depends on the mind, and so this is called its *dependent nature*. The mental representation is formed by deploying conceptual categories, such as *tree*, *branches*, *green*. If one strips these away, one arrives at the ultimate reality of the object, its *consummate* nature. And what is this like? It is impossible to say, since one can do so only by applying conceptual categories, but the consummate nature of something is what is left, once all concepts are stripped off. This does not mean that it is a nothing. One can have a direct acquaintance with it – in various meditative states, for example. But it is a simple *tathātā*, "thatness."

In Yogācāra Buddhism there are still two realities. Conventional reality is the world, the illusion. This is the tree with its dependent and imagined natures.

Ultimate reality obviously cannot be the same as the ultimate reality of the Abhidharma. It can only be *tathātā* itself. What theories of truth is one to apply when talking about these two realities? When talking about conventional reality, the appropriate theory is, presumably, whatever it was for conventional reality in the Abhidharma case. Yogācāra, after all, just generalizes what was said there about partite things to the world in general. What about ultimate reality? Since one can say nothing at all about this – true or false – the question of truth does not even arise.

At any rate, the Yogācāra philosophers are obviously idealists about the world: it is all just a conceptual construction. The world is dependent on the mind. Moreover, the relationship of dependence is asymmetric. The mind does not depend on the extra-mental world: there isn't one.

One does need to take a little care here. In Western idealisms (such as Kant's) there is a self (subject) that makes the conceptual constructions (objects). In Yogācāra, the duality between subject and object is just as much a conceptual construction as any other distinction (duality). In the end, therefore, the picture of a self and its constructs itself has no ultimate reality. Nonetheless, the view is clearly an idealism.

Between the Horns: Madhyamaka

We see, then, that there are realisms and idealisms in Buddhist philosophy. They have a distinctively Buddhist spin – just as Western idealisms have their own distinctive spins. But they are recognizable as of their kinds. Let us now turn to the view that goes between the horns.

This is the view of the other Mahāyāna school: Madhyamaka. The school grew out of the profound but elusive writings of Nāgārjuna, and especially his *Mūlamadhyamakakārikā* ("Fundamental Verses of the Middle Way").[13] His dates are uncertain, except that they are some time in the first or second century of the Common Era. Nāgārjuna's thought was articulated by subsequent commentators, such as Candrakīrti (seventh century, India) and Tsongkhapa (fourteenth century, Tibet).

Like the Yogacārin, the Mādhyamika rejected the picture of the Abhidharmika. But while Yogācāra universalized the Abhidharma picture of conventional reality, Madhyamaka launched an attack on its notion of ultimate reality. The two approaches, it turned out, did not result in the same picture.

According to Abhidharma, there are *dharmas*, things with *svabhāva* (self-being, intrinsic nature). That is, they exist and have their nature in and of themselves. The Mādhyamika argued that there is nothing of this kind. Everything is empty (*śūnya*) – that is, empty of self-being.

If this is so, in what way do things have their being? Not intrinsically, but only in relation to other things. To give an example from Western philosophy, consider the year 1066. According to Newton, this date refers to an objective thing, a time. The time is independent of the events in time, and would indeed have existed even had there been no such events. On the other hand, according to Leibniz, 1066 has no self-standing reality of this kind. 1066 is merely a locus in a set of events ordered by the before/after relation. Thus, 1066 is just the place in this ordering that applies to things after Caesar's invasion of Britain, before the British colonization of Australia, etc. Had there been no events in time, there would have been no 1066. 1066 has its being only in relationship to other things.[14]

According to the Mādhyamika, *everything* has its being in this relational way. The partite objects of the Abhidharmika have their being in this way. A partite object has whatever sort of being it has only in relationship to its parts. The Madhyamaka network of being–constitutive relations included this part–whole relation – though, it would be wrong to think now that the parts are real in a way that the whole they compose is not. Both have exactly the same kind of reality – relational.

But the web of relations that were relevant for the Mādhyamika were wider than mereological ones. (Some objects may have no physical parts.) Two others were particularly significant for them. One was the relation to causes and effects. Thus, you are the thing that you are (including existing) because of your relationship to your genetic inheritance (I update the picture a bit here), the way your parents treated you, the school you went to, and so on. The other – which is of particular concern to us here – is the relation to concepts. Again, the Abhidharmika held that an object of conventional reality is what it is, to the extent that, and only to the extent that, we conceptualize it in a certain way. This view is also subsumed in the more general Madhyamaka picture.

We can now see how the Madhyamaka position goes between the horns of idealism and realism. It should be immediately clear that it is not a realism. Its very rationale is a critique of the realism of Abhidharma. Each object in the world depends for its reality on many other things. Some of these are other objects in the material world, such as their causes; but some of these are concepts. The world is not concept-independent.

In virtue of this, it might be thought that this is simply another species of idealism. It is not. The world, it is true, depends for its nature on concepts. But in Madhyamaka the relationship is symmetric. In Yogācāra, concepts do not depend for their nature on the world; in Madhyamaka, they do. Concepts are just as empty of intrinsic nature as anything else. Some of the things a concept depends on are other concepts. Thus, the concept *stray dog* depends on the concept *dog*. But some of them are in the world. The concept *dog* is what it is in virtue of its relationship to dogs. Thus, concepts depend for their nature on the world, just as much as the world depends for its nature on concepts. The natures of each are mutually dependent.

Madhyamaka is, therefore, neither a realism nor an idealism. The dependence relation of Abhidharma and Yogācāra is incorporated into a larger "middle way" picture. ("Madhyamaka" means, in fact, "middle way.") Each of these other schools was right in seeing some of the dependence relations. Each was wrong in seeing only some of them.

The Two Truths Again

The main point of this essay is now made, but we should not leave the matter at this point: we have had the main course, but there is dessert to come. For this, let us return to the question of conventional and ultimate reality. What did the Mādhyamika say about this? That there are two truths was affirmed by the Mādhyamika just as much as the Abhidharmika and the Yogacārin. However, according to them, there was only one reality. How to understand the situation is a vexed question, which is – and was – open to dispute.[15]

As for the other two schools, conventional reality is the reality of the world around us. This is a world where things *appear* to be substantial and independent objects. Thus, it would appear to be the case that, if *everything else* in the entire cosmos went out of existence, the chair on which I sit could remain, and be exactly the same object as it is now. If the Mādhyamikas are right, this appearance is a deep mistake. How things *really* are is empty. There is nothing, then, with ultimate reality. There is, then, no ultimate reality.

It would be tempting to think of the emptiness of things as a self-standing ultimate reality behind appearances (rather like a Kantian noumenal realm). But that would be a mistake. When the Mādhyamikas argued that everything was empty, they meant *everything*; emptiness is just as empty as everything else. In particular, it exists only in relation to the empty things of conventional reality.

If, then, there is only one reality, how is one to make sense of the thought that there are two truths? One approach – that of Candrakīrti in chapter 6 of his *Madhyamakāvatāra* ("Introduction to the Middle Way")[16] – is to say that the reality has two aspects, or dispositions to be perceived, corresponding to the two ways it can be seen. In virtue of one disposition it can be seen as what it really is: empty. In virtue of the other, it can be seen as what it is not: composed of objects with *svabhāva*. (In the same way, an objective optical illusion, such as the configuration of the Müller–Lyer illusion, has a disposition to be seen as what it is not.) The two truths correspond to these two aspects.

But what notions of truth are involved here? One option would be to tell the same story as was told about Yogācāra. Conventional truth is to be handled by the modifier theory; and there are no ultimate truths. There are heavy downsides to this strategy, however. First, conventional truth – and there is no other, since there are no ultimate truths on this view – turns out to be literal falsity. One cannot say anything true! Maybe that's okay if you are a Yogācārin who thinks that everything is an illusion; but the Mādhyamikas were not idealists. Secondly, we not only find the Mādhyamikas affirming things they appear to take as true, we find them affirming that some things are ultimate truths but not conventional truths, such as that everything is empty.

In virtue of this, there would appear to be a better way to go: a simple deflationist view of truth. There is no more to truth than satisfying the *T*-schema. This allows for conventional truths to be true, without any realist reification. What of those things that are said to be ultimate truths but not conventional truths? Perhaps the simplest policy is to mark the ultimate truths with a modifier, "Ultimately." So it is not the case that everything is empty, but ultimately everything is. At this point, one is forced to make a choice concerning the principle that "Ultimately *p*" entails *p* – and, in particular, its instance when *p* is "everything is empty." The principle looks very natural; and, indeed, a cost of rejecting it is that, when Mādhyamikas say that it is ultimately true that everything is empty, what they say to be ultimately true is literally false! The other is to accept the principle, and so the consequence that everything is empty and not: Madhyamaka trespasses into the paradoxical.

This is not the place to pursue that matter further.[17] Let us assume it to be resolved in some way or other. However one does this, on this deflationist option it is the case that we have just the one language to describe the one reality. Now what of this language? Its propositions (the things that language expresses), like all things, are empty. That is, they are what they are only in relation to other things. It follows that, whatever propositions are, they cannot be self-standing entities like Fregean senses. This does not mean that there are no such things. That would be an idealist mistake at the opposite extreme. But propositions, like the concepts that comprise them, have an existence interdependent with other things.[18]

Of course, attacks on self-standing senses are well known in the West, from Saussure, Quine, (the later) Wittgenstein, and Derrida – to name just some of the more notable critics. So the conclusion, in this case, is not new. But the Madhyamaka route to it certainly is.

Conclusion

None of this is, of course, to argue for (or against) the Madhyamaka position. That is an interesting and important matter; but it is not the matter at hand. Travel, it is said, broadens the mind. What we have been engaged with here is simply a bit of mind-broadening for Western philosophers who know nothing of Asian philosophical cuisines.[19]

Notes

1 Not that illumination need be only one way: it can be mutual, as we will see.

2 Positivists, from Hume on, have held that answers to questions concerning the existence and nature of the external world are not verifiable – hence, that the questions are meaningless. In some sense, this view is neither an idealism nor a realism, but of a kind quite distinct from the Madhyamaka view, as we will see.

3 For a general introduction to Asian philosophies, see Koller (2002). For a general introduction to Buddhism (including Chinese and Japanese Buddhism), see Mitchell (2002). A good collection of Buddhist primary texts in English translation, with some commentary, can be found in Edelglass and Garfield (2009). For a discussion of Indian epistemology and metaphysics in general, see Ganeri (2001).

4 A word of terminology. We are going to meet three schools (or kinds of school) of Buddhist philosophy: Abhidharma, Yogācāra, and Madhyamaka. The members of these schools are called, respectively: Abhidharmikas, Yogācārins, and Mādhyamikas.

5 For an account of early Buddhism, see Koller (2002, ch. 12); Mitchell (2002, ch. 1); and Siderits (2007, ch. 2).

6 This is one part of the early canon, the other two being the *Sūtras* (discourses attributed to the historical Buddha) and the *Vinaya* (the rules for monastic living).

7 Perhaps the most common view was that they are tropes (property instances).

8 For a discussion of the early Buddhist view of the self and, more generally, the Abhidharma tradition, see Siderits (2007, chs. 3, 6).

9 For a general introduction to the notion of the two truths in Buddhism, see The Cowherds (2011, chs 1, 8).

10 For general accounts of Mahāyāna, Yogācāra, and Madhyamaka, see Siderits (2007, chs 7–9).

11 There are different ways of interpreting the Yogācāra thinkers. It is possible, for example, to see them as concerned only with a phenomenological analysis, which brackets the existence of the external world. However, I will concern myself here with the ideas of Vasubandhu, who is clear that the external world is a mental projection.

12 The text can be found in Anacker (1998, ch. 9). A commentary is provided in Garfield (2002, ch. 7).

13 The text and commentary can be found in Garfield (1995). Another discussion of Nāgārjuna and Madhyamaka can be found in Westerhoff (2009).

14 The connection between the Madhyamaka view and the Newton/Leibniz dispute about space and time is discussed further in Priest (2009).

15 Further discussion can be found in The Cowherds (2011).

16 The text can be found in Huntington (1989, 157–83). The chapter also contains a critique of the Yogācāra view.

17 Further discussion can be found in Garfield and Priest (2003) and The Cowherds (2011, ch. 8).

18 The matter is addressed in detail by Nāgārjuna in his *Vigrahavyāvartanī* (Dispeller of Disputes). See Westerhoff (2010).

19 Many thanks go to Jay Garfield for comments on an earlier draft of this essay.

References

Anacker, S. (1998). *Seven Works of Vasubandhu.* Delhi: Motilal Barnarsidass.

The Cowherds (2011). *Moonshadows: Conventional Truth in Buddhist Philosophy.* New York: Oxford University Press.

Edelglass, W., and Garfield, J. (2009). *Buddhist Philosophy: Essential Readings.* Oxford: Oxford University Press.

Ganeri, J. (2001). *Philosophy in Classical India.* London: Routledge.

Garfield, J. (1995). *The Fundamental Wisdom of the Middle Way: Nāgārjuna's Mūlamadhyamakakārikā.* New York: Oxford University Press.

Garfield, J. (2002). *Empty Words: Buddhist Philosophy and Cross-Cultural Interpretation.* New York: Oxford University Press.

Garfield, J., and Priest, G. (2003). Nāgārjuna and the limits of thought. In *Philosophy East and West 53, 1–21* [This essay also appears as ch. 5 of Garfield's *Empty Words* and as ch.16 of Priest's *Beyond the Limits of Thought.* Second edn. Oxford: Oxford University Press, 2002].

Huntington, C. W. (1989). *The Emptiness of Emptiness: An Introduction to Early Indian Mādhyamika.* Honolulu: University of Hawai'i Press.

Koller, J. M. (2002). *Asian Philosophies.* Fourth edn. Upper Saddle River, NJ: Prentice-Hall.

Mitchell, D. W. (2002). *Buddhism: Introducing the Buddhist Experience.* New York: Oxford University Press.

Priest, G. (2009). The Structure of Emptiness. In *Philosophy East and West* 59, 467–80.

Siderits, M. (2007) *Buddhism as Philosophy: An Introduction.* Aldershot: Ashgate.

Westerhoff, J. (2009). *Nāgārjuna's Madhyamaka: a Philosophical Introduction.* Oxford: Oxford University Press.

Westerhoff, J. (2010). *The Dispeller of Disputes: Nāgārjuna's Vigrahavyāvartanī.* Oxford: Oxford University Press.

B. Epistemology

14

A Survey of Early Buddhist Epistemology

JOHN J. HOLDER

The Historical Context of the Early Buddhist View of Knowledge

The quest for knowledge has played a central role in the religious philosophies of India from the earliest times. The ancient Vedas, which form the canonical foundation for Brahmanical (and, later, Hindu) traditions, are focused on the spiritual power of knowledge. Indeed, the very word "*veda*" means "knowledge." In the earliest portions of the Vedas, knowledge of complex cosmological analogies and identities revealed the divine forces that lay behind mundane appearances; knowledge thus gave control over these forces to the extent that both earthly and transcendent goals might be achieved. The Upaniṣads went even further in this direction and promised full spiritual liberation upon the realization of the ultimate cosmological analogy: that the true essence and identity of the person is none other than the source of all Reality (that *ātman* – the eternal self – is Brahman – the Ultimate Reality; that I am this All!).[1] Thus, at the high-point of Brahmanical philosophy, *to know is to be* and to be is to realize fully a metaphysical truth that is the key to spiritual liberation (*mokṣa*).

The early Buddhist view of knowledge arose against this Brahmanist background. In Buddhism's earliest texts, collected as the Pāli canon,[2] knowledge is likewise philosophically and spiritually central. And yet the salvific role of knowledge in early Buddhism is not conceived as an insight into a transcendent, metaphysical reality. Early Buddhist epistemology is distinguished from that of its Indian predecessors by the fact that the Buddha's Dhamma (teaching) does not focus on realizing grand cosmological analogies or uncovering Ultimate Realities, because, from the perspective of early Buddhism, these pursuits are useless as a means for achieving the ultimate goal of religious liberation. Instead, it is the knowledge of the origins and cessation of human suffering (*dukkha*)[3] – an understanding and control over the human mind – that leads to spiritual liberation. Thus, it is psychology, not metaphysics or theology, that guides early Buddhism. Spiritual liberation requires knowledge of the causal factors that shape human

A Companion to Buddhist Philosophy, First Edition. Edited by Steven M. Emmanuel.

experience. For this reason, the early Buddhist texts, specifically the Pāli Nikāyas,[4] provide a detailed account of the way human beings perceive and grasp the sensory world. Even at the highest levels of knowledge, the Buddha claimed only the psychological knowledge that leads to the destruction of the factors that corrupt the human mind. As we will see below, such knowledge is an essential factor in the achievement of *nibbāna* (Skt *nirvāṇa*) – Buddhism's highest goal.

This chapter attempts to cover in broad outline the Buddha's views on knowledge – his "epistemology" – as they are expressed in the Pāli Nikāyas. The Buddha avowed many times over that the one and only reason for teaching was to show the way to religious liberation – that is, to help others free themselves, as he had freed himself, from the profound suffering (*dukkha*) that permeates human existence. Hence, the Buddha's views on knowledge are developed for the specific purpose of understanding and eliminating the causes of suffering. It is very important to keep in mind that the Buddha's Dhamma should always be understood in the context of this religious purpose. Whereas epistemology in modern Western philosophy has been in large part a reaction to the developments of modern science (which has its origins in the physics, astronomy, and chemistry of the seventeenth century), the Buddha was trying to solve what he saw as the fundamental spiritual/existential problem. Early Buddhism declares a way to spiritual liberation and happiness by means of a this-worldly knowledge of how the changing nature of the world and the response of the human mind to that world can be controlled and reorganized to avoid suffering. Knowledge, in short, is a crucial factor in early Buddhism because it is an essential component of the threefold training (*tisikkhā*) that leads to final liberation: moral conduct (*silā*), mental culture (*samādhi*), and wisdom (*paññā*).

Early Buddhist Epistemology: A Broad and Rich form of Empiricism

No doubt, any attempt to place a contemporary philosophical label on an ancient religious tradition such as early Buddhism has limited value. But, so long as we make the requisite qualifications, it does no lasting harm to use modern labels to characterize the Buddha's epistemological philosophy. In fact, it may well be useful in bringing the Buddha's ideas into the contemporary philosophical conversation. In this light – and recognizing that further qualifications are in order – we can say that the Buddha was an *empiricist* in the sense that his religious philosophy was grounded on *experience*. Experience figures prominently in the Buddha's teaching in at least three ways: first, he taught that experience is the proper way to justify claims to knowledge – this is the heart of modern empiricism; second, the experience of suffering is the motivation for seeking a religious path in life; and, third, he provided a highly sophisticated psychological account of experience as a way of explaining how suffering arises, and how one might gain control over the causes of suffering so as to bring about the cessation of suffering. This account of human experience has a remarkably modern ring to it. Because of the Buddha's sophisticated analysis of human experience, early Buddhist epistemology can make a significant contribution to contemporary philosophy.

The Buddha's empiricism is also evident, perhaps uniquely so for a religious tradition, in the way he handled metaphysically speculative issues and the claims of religious authority. Whereas most religious traditions are based on metaphysically speculative doctrines – doctrines for which there is little empirical evidence (e.g., the existence of a soul or the reality of heaven) – the Buddha told his disciples that one should believe only those doctrines that can be personally verified in experience. The Buddha reasoned that what cannot be verified in experience has little to contribute to the resolution of the religious issues that confront a person. Furthermore, the urge to speculate beyond what can be empirically verified usually derives from the ego's demands for security and self-aggrandizement. Reliance on religious or sacred traditions, or the mere authority of a teacher, is not an appropriate way to develop or justify a belief, suggested the Buddha, not even in spiritual matters where other religious traditions call upon "faith" (see MN.I.26.5).

Some scholars resist calling early Buddhism a form of empiricism because the Buddha's view of experience does not conform to the simple sensation-oriented empiricism of seventeenth- and eighteenth-century European philosophers (such as John Locke and David Hume). But there is no reason to limit the conception of empiricism so narrowly. The Pāli canon contains a remarkably rich and detailed psychological theory of experience. The Buddha's view of experience is much richer than the cognitivist views of experience that formed the basis of early modern epistemology in Western philosophy. In the early Buddhist view of experience, experience is more than just knowledge, more than cognition, and certainly much more than an aggregation of data points impressed on the mind by the processes of sensation. As we will see below, noncognitive or affective dimensions of experience, such as feelings, dispositions, and habits, play an essential role in human experience, according to the Buddha's account in the Pāli discourses. But the fact that the Buddha held such a richer view of experience is not a good reason to reject calling early Buddhism a form of empiricism.

Knowledge Claims Require Personal Verification

Today, as in ancient India, there are many different religious traditions and philosophical systems. These various traditions or systems of thought offer very different views on the nature of reality, human nature, the goals of religious/philosophical life, and the means of achieving the goals of such a life. Unless a person is completely absorbed by a stubbornly blind attachment to a particular religious or philosophical tradition, questions will arise about which of the claims of the many religions (or philosophies) are true and which are false. Surely, the vastly different claims of the world's many religions cannot all be true. So, which religious traditions should be believed? What are the proper criteria for determining the truth in such matters? Compounding the problem is the tendency of most religious traditions to claim to have exclusive ownership of the highest religious truth. No doubt, this issue remains a problem for any person who takes religion or philosophy seriously.

The "Discourse to the Kālāmas" focuses precisely on this issue, framing the problem in terms that apply just as much today as they did over two millennia ago. In this text, a group referred to as the Kālāmas approach the Buddha for help in sorting out the different religious claims professed by the various religious teachers who visit them. These teachers and sages make vastly different claims about religious truth and the practices necessary to achieve religious goals. Furthermore, the religious teachers not only promote their views as the only truth, but they disparage and heap scorn on the views of others who disagree with them. So, ask the Kālāmas, how does one know which one is right? What criteria can one use to determine who is telling the truth? Whom should one believe? On this the Buddha instructed the Kālāmas:

> [The Buddha said:] In such cases, Kālāmas, do not accept a thing by recollection, by tradition, by mere report, because it is based on the authority of scriptures, by mere logic or inference, by reflection on conditions, because of reflection on or fondness for a certain theory, because it merely seems suitable, nor thinking: "The religious wanderer is respected by us." But when you know for yourselves: "These things are unwholesome, blameworthy, reproached by the wise, when undertaken and performed lead to harm and suffering" – these you should reject.
>
> But, Kālāmas, when you know for yourselves: "These things are wholesome, not blameworthy, commended by the wise, when undertaken and performed lead to one's benefit and happiness" – you should live undertaking these.
>
> (AN.I.191–2)

In this response to the Kālāmas, the Buddha demonstrated very clearly that his approach to knowledge is empirical (at least insofar as knowledge is considered as a *guiding belief*). The Buddha is making two important points here: first, that there should be proper *reasons* for accepting any religious or philosophical doctrine; and, second, what counts as a proper reason derives from verification in one's own personal experience. Most religious traditions, of course, hold that their scriptures or the pronouncements of their spiritual leaders are ultimate truths and should be accepted unquestioningly by the faithful. But the Buddha's approach is quite different. The Buddha disagreed with traditions that require unquestioning faith in scriptures or spiritual leaders.

In "The Discourse on Threefold Knowledge," the Buddha gave a scathing appraisal of the Brahmans who claim to have a higher spiritual status based on specialized religious knowledge (DN.I.235–53). This discourse opens with two Brahmans arguing about which teacher knows the best way to "union with Brahmā."[5] To settle their dispute, they consult the Buddha, who, surprisingly, claims to know a path to "union with Brahmā." Using arguments that could apply to many other religious traditions, the Buddha counters the Brahmans' claims to religious knowledge by emphasizing the fact that none of them has the requisite personal experience necessary to justify their claims. Precisely where many religions invoke a leap of faith, the Buddha stressed that one should use personal experience to verify claims to knowledge. So the gist of the Buddha's argument in this discourse is that, because neither these Brahmans nor their teachers going back seven generations have ever seen Brahmā face to face, they should not make claims about religious matters that they have not experienced for themselves. By means of a number of similes, the Buddha led his Brahman interlocutors to the conclusion that, without empirical support, the boasts of many Brahmanical teachers are no more than foolish talk. From the Buddha's perspective, knowledge claims that rely on faith without the support of good experiential evidence are biased by one's likes/dislikes and cannot adapt to new evidence or situations. The Buddha insisted that such standards of empirical evidence apply as well to his own teaching, the Dhamma – a position that is highly unusual for a religious teacher. As Richard Gombrich put it, "the Buddha stressed that what gave him the right to preach his doctrine as the truth was that he had *experienced* its truth himself, not just learnt it from others or even reasoned it out" (Gombrich 1996, 5). Thus, although it is permissible within the framework of the Buddha's teaching that the authority of the Buddha and the Buddhist texts may be taken as a starting point in the quest for knowledge, one should not attach authority to the Buddha's teachings as a matter of blind faith.

In another famous passage, the Buddha stressed the need for *personal* verification of claims about religious truth:

> "Monks, do you only speak that which is known by yourselves seen by yourselves, found by yourselves?"
>
> "Yes, we do, sir."
>
> "Good, monks, That is how you have been instructed by me in this timeless doctrine which can be realized and verified, that leads to the goal and can be understood by those who are intelligent."
>
> (MN.I.265)

In this way, the Buddha's disciples were told not to take anyone's (even the Buddha's) word for a belief, but they should "come and see" (*ehipassiko*) for themselves.

The Buddha was critical of dogmatism of any sort. The intelligent person remains open to new facts and never considers the achievement of belief as final, unassailable, knowledge. This anti-dogmatic sentiment is clearly indicated by the Buddha in the following passage:

> [The Buddha said:] Even if I claim to know something on the basis of best faith, [or likes or tradition or reflection on form or delight in views] that [claim to knowledge] may be empty, hollow, and confused, while what I do not know on the best faith [or by any other method] may be factual, true, and not otherwise. It is not proper for an intelligent person, safeguarding the truth, to come categorically to the conclusion in a given matter that such alone is true and whatever else is false.
>
> (MN.II.170–1)

This is a remarkable approach for a renowned religious teacher who offers his own highly developed path to spiritual liberation. The Buddha stands out (perhaps, even alone) among religious teachers for his *anti-dogmatic* treatment of knowledge, including even religious doctrines.

But what standard should one use to verify personally a knowledge claim? Here the Buddha instructed his disciples that a belief should be evaluated in regard to its consequences in actual practice. A belief counts as knowledge only if the belief guides action successfully in practice, more specifically, in one's *own* practice. This pragmatic maxim is stressed not only in the "Discourse to the Kālāmas" but also elsewhere in the texts, such as in the "Discourse to Prince Abhaya" (MN.I.392–4). In this discourse, the Buddha convinces Prince Abhaya that a doctrine should be measured by its usefulness (even if the doctrine seems unpalatable or disagreeable in the near term).[6] One should look carefully at what sort of results are likely if one were to act in accordance with a belief or doctrine. A belief should be accepted only to the extent that it leads to wholesome and happy consequences. This has significant implications for contemporary Buddhist practice. The canonical Buddhist texts are certainly revered by Buddhists, but, if one takes the Buddha at his word, the texts are to be read critically and the teachings contained in them subjected to reflection and empirical assessment in practice.

The Buddha's insistence on personal empirical verification is welcomed by many in the present day, especially given the influence of the empirical methods of the modern sciences on contemporary epistemology. But the Buddha's position raises several important philosophical questions. For example, are all aspects of the Buddha's teaching consistent with this anti-dogmatic, empirical attitude? Some might argue that the doctrines of karma and rebirth that are central to the Buddha's teaching are difficult or impossible to verify in one's own personal experience. The Buddha himself claims to have verified such doctrines using certain supersensory powers (the *abhiññā*, which are discussed further below), thus he fully intended to offer an empirical verification of these doctrines even if the normal sensory faculties are not involved. Furthermore, do we really want a less dogmatic approach to our religious beliefs if such an approach diminishes a person's degree of religious conviction? An opponent might well argue that a dogmatic faith is required to motivate good choices under morally difficult circumstances or in a morally ambiguous world. The Buddha would surely find such a faith to be an impediment to the exercise of intelligence – that is, to the flexible and creative response demanded by a precarious and changing world.

Limitations on Human Knowledge: The Unexplained Questions (*avyākatā*)

Unwavering certitude about core metaphysical issues is essential for salvation in most religious systems. Most religions hold doctrinal positions on such questions as: "Does God exist?," "Is there an afterlife?," "Does the world have a beginning?," "Will the world end?," "Do human beings possess an immortal soul?," etc. In many religions, *knowledge* of the deepest truths about Reality, or about God, is itself the goal of the religious life. But this is not the case in early Buddhism. Early Buddhism is perhaps the only religious tradition that explicitly avoids taking a stance on speculative metaphysical issues.

There are many passages in the Pāli Nikāyas where the Buddha is challenged to give his view on ten metaphysical questions. In each case, he refrains from giving an answer to such questions. These ten speculative views (*diṭṭhi*) are referred to collectively as the "unexplained" views (*avyākatā*). In the "Discourse to Vacchagotta on Fire," these ten views are presented as five pairs:

1 Is the world eternal or is the world not eternal?
2 Is the world finite or is the world infinite?

3 Are the life principle (soul) and the body identical or are the life principle and the body not identical?
4 Does the *Tathāgata* (Buddha) exist after death or does the *Tathāgata* not exist after death?
5 Does the *Tathāgata* both exist and not exist after death or does the *Tathāgata* neither exist nor not exist after death? (MN.I.484)

These and many other metaphysical questions seem to be the staple of religious life for most religions. But when Vaccha asks the Buddha whether he holds one of these views, he replies: "I do not hold the speculative view that 'The world is eternal; this alone is true, and any other view is false'" [and likewise for each of the other nine views] (MN.I.485).

A very important question thus arises: why did the Buddha refrain from attempting answers to these metaphysical questions? Are these questions answerable (in principle) and the Buddha simply did not know the answers? Or is it the case that the questions may be answerable, but just not relevant to the spiritual path? Or was the Buddha's refusal to give answers an indication that the questions themselves are meaningless? Scholars have debated for more than a century the various interpretations of the Buddha's reasons for leaving these speculative questions unexplained.[7] Based on this debate, and from a careful reading of the texts, it seems likely that the Buddha had several reasons for leaving these questions unexplained. First, and most important, the Buddha states that such issues are irrelevant to living the religious life. He said to Vaccha: "These questions are not connected with the goal, with the Dhamma, nor with the fundamentals of the religious life. They do not lead to aversion, dispassion, cessation, calmness, higher knowledge, and *nibbāna*" (MN.I.485). Second, as an empiricist, the Buddha recognized that the scope of human knowledge is very limited and such metaphysical questions fall outside that scope. As we saw above, knowledge claims must be justified by experience, but these ten views are beyond any possible justification in experience. Human beings, with our limited means of knowledge, are simply not in a good position to know whether the world is eternal or not, finite or infinite, etc. Thus, attempts at answering such metaphysical questions involve a kind of overreaching, even hubris, on the part of the one who dogmatically clings to particular speculative views. Lastly, the *motives* for raising metaphysical questions often involve ego-driven grasping and thus are a cause of suffering (see, e.g., AN.I.83). If one thinks of the reasons *why* one wants to know answers to questions about the finitude of the world or about the afterlife, one realizes that in most (if not all) cases it is the ego that wants to know, either to satisfy its own aggrandizement or to quell its fears of annihilation. Thus, attempts to answer the unexplained views reinforce the obstacles to spiritual progress.

The very famous "Parable of the Arrow" (in the "Shorter Discourse to Mālunkyaputta") illustrates this last point vividly. In this discourse, a monk named Mālunkya refuses to live the monastic life under the Buddha unless the Buddha gives him answers to the ten unexplained views – the very same metaphysically speculative views raised by Vaccha. The Buddha replies to Mālunkya's request by saying that he never promised to answer such questions. The Buddha then explains to Mālunkya the famous "Parable of the Arrow":

> Just as a person – having been pierced by an arrow thickly smeared with poison, and his friends and relatives having procured a surgeon – might speak thus: "I will not have this arrow withdrawn until I know whether the person who wounded me is either a nobleman, a Brahman, a merchant or a worker." – or might speak thus: "I will not have this arrow withdrawn until I know whether the person who wounded me has a certain name and a certain clan." . . . Mālunkyaputta, this person would still be ignorant of those things and then that person would die. So, too, were any person to speak thus: "I will not live the religious life under the Exalted One [Buddha], unless the Exalted One will declare these speculative views to me." And still these would be unexplained by the Tathāgata [Buddha], and then that person would die.
>
> (MN.I.429–30)

The parable demonstrates by analogy that, just as the first priority for a person shot by an arrow is medical attention, not speculation about much less urgent details of the situation, so, too, the unenlightened person does not have the luxury to ask such frivolous metaphysical questions when the urgent task is the elimination of suffering. The Buddha's point is that a person should focus his or her attention on matters proper to the path that leads to liberation and not on these metaphysically speculative issues.

At this point, we can address the question whether the Buddha claimed omniscience, as some later Buddhist traditions hold. In the Pāli Nikāyas, the Buddha denied that he was omniscient (all-knowing) (see MN.I.482 and II.127). In fact, the Buddha claimed to teach only two things: suffering and the elimination of suffering. The Buddha, as a person, is subject to the same empirical limitations of knowledge as everyone else. He was a perfected human being, according to the texts, not a god. The Buddha did not claim to have knowledge of a transcendent reality that stands behind the world of sense experience. Even liberating knowledge, an essential factor in the achievement of *nibbāna* – discussed below in the final section of the chapter – is not a god-like knowledge of everything. It is the knowledge of how to transform the mind in a world that is fundamentally changing – nothing more, nothing less. This conception of highest knowledge does not require anything like omniscience, and this point indicates a clear contrast between early Buddhism and the Brahmanist quest for knowledge of an Absolute Reality.

A critic of the Buddha's teaching may point out that the Buddha himself held certain views that cannot be empirically verified. For example, some might argue that the early Buddhist views on karma and rebirth are theories that cannot be empirically verified. This is not the place to sort out an answer to this criticism, but it is worthwhile to raise the question of the Buddha's consistency on this issue, since it goes to the heart of the claim that the Buddha was genuinely an empiricist. One might also raise the objection to the Buddha's handling of core metaphysical issues that holding speculative (empirically unverifiable) views is, in fact, required to live a religious life. No doubt, those who practice most of the world's other major religions would want to argue that the religious life cannot be lived without such metaphysical commitments.

The All: Senses and Their Objects Define Reality

Because most religions and philosophies teach that the highest reality is transcendent (e.g., Brahman, the Forms, or God), they must posit a mode of knowledge that goes beyond sense experience. But the Buddha tied his view of reality to his conception of human experience. For the Buddha, normal human experience is limited to what we can sense with the six sensory modes of experience (*āyatanā*) – namely, seeing, hearing, smelling, tasting, touching, and "minding."[8] These modes of experience are processes that involve both the sense organ and the sensory object. It is for this reason that the early Buddhist texts refer to sense experience as having twelve "doors" – the six senses together with their objects. The importance of this point will become clearer below when we see that the Buddha denied the self-subsistence of both the sense organs and their objects. Furthermore, such an account of sense experience is a functional or integrated account of experience that gives neither the sensory organ nor its object ontological priority.

The Buddha held that the senses and their objects exhaust the entirety of existence. This is a very bold claim when it is viewed against the Brahmanical background of the Buddha's day. In the short text entitled the "Discourse on the All," the Buddha said that sense organs and their objects are the "All," or everything that exists. No doubt, the Buddha's use of the word "All" was a deliberate attempt to parody the Upaniṣadic claim that the All is identical to the transcendent reality Brahman. In this very short text, the Buddha stated his position thus:

> [The Buddha:] "*Bhikkhus*, I will teach you the all [that exists]. Do listen to this.
>
> "And what is the all? It is eye and visible objects, ear and sounds, nose and smells, tongue and tastes, body and tangible objects, mind and mental objects. This is called 'the all.'
>
> "Whoever would speak in this way: 'Rejecting this all, I will declare another all' – would be engaging in mere talk on his part. One would not be able to reply to a question and, further, would come to vexation. What is the reason for this? Because that which one claims would be beyond the scope of (sense) experience."
>
> (SN.IV.15)

And so sensory perception (together with the supersensory modes of perception discussed below) is the basis for knowledge even in religious matters. Given this approach, there can be little doubt that early Buddhist epistemology is a form of empiricism. Here, the Buddha transforms the metaphysical conception of the "All" in the Upaniṣadic tradition ("All" = "Brahman") into an epistemological concept, an empirical limitation on experience and knowledge. The "All" is not Reality (in the absolute, metaphysical sense) but the comprehensive range of possible human experience. As David Kalupahana put it, "to posit anything more than [this All] is a metaphysically speculative position that is engendered by a corrupt mind grasping after a self and ultimately leads to vexation and worry . . . because such views can never be justified; they are 'beyond the sphere of experience' (*avisaya*)" (Kalupahana 1976, 23).

It must be kept in mind that the Buddha did not offer such an analysis of experience and reality for its own sake; rather, his epistemology serves his ethical and religious concerns. So later in the same text the Buddha explains that, in a mind defiled by lust, hatred and delusion, the "All" is burning – a metaphor for the fact that sensory experiences typically instigate a chain of addictive behaviors that inevitably leads to suffering. The alternative, suggested by the Buddha, is to abandon all attachment to sense experiences.

Given the Buddha's account of suffering and his call to abandon sense experience, it may appear that his general attitude towards sense experience is completely negative. To some scholars of Buddhism, the Buddha is recommending that a person abandon all sense experience. But a careful look at how suffering arises shows that sense experience in itself is not bad. In fact, a good case could be made that sense experience in itself is neutral – sometimes it leads to craving and attachment (quite often in the case of the normal, unenlightened mind) and at other times it can lead to wholesome experiences and actions (when the moral corruptions are absent). The senses are dangerous, specifically when craving (*taṇhā*, literally "thirst") is present in the mind. In the corrupted mind, then, the operation of the senses can mislead us both intellectually and morally. The senses give us a wrong picture of the world, and we are prone to act immorally because we do not fully comprehend how a desire for (or aversion towards) a thing will play out. We do not see a thing's true value. Thus, it is not sense experience that is abandoned – it really could not be – but only the unwholesome *attachment* to sense experience that often occurs in the corrupted mind.

An Empirical Account of Experience as a Natural Process

One might ask why the Buddha thought that the scope of human knowledge is so limited as compared to other religious traditions. The reason for this lies in his detailed analysis of human experience. The Buddha offered a remarkably detailed analysis of human experience because his spiritual purpose was to understand completely suffering and its elimination. This requires an understanding of the processes of experience that lead to suffering and the knowledge of how to transform experience so that suffering no longer arises. This is not metaphysical knowledge – although a view of the changing nature of humanly experienced reality plays a part; rather, such knowledge is ethical or religious psychology. For such reasons, early Buddhist epistemology focuses not only on the justification of knowledge claims but on the psychological processes that comprise human experience.

To understand the Buddha's view of experience, one must first take account of his view of the human person. Early Buddhism's most famous analysis of the person is the five aggregates (*khandhas*). In this account, a human being is comprised of five changing factors (or processes): the body (*rūpa*), feeling (*vedanā*), apperception (*saññā*), dispositions to action (*saṅkhārā*), and consciousness (*viññāna*). None of these five aggregates forms a static, permanent essence (a soul or Hindu *ātman*). A person, then, is a complex arrangement of mental and physical/biological processes. It is clear that the Buddha was not a mind–body dualist – he did not claim that the mind and the body are metaphysically distinct parts of a person. Instead, he held that the person is an integrated, psycho-physical process. Although the Buddha spoke of the human person as a psychophysical personality (*nāmarūpa*), yet the psychological and the physical aspects of a person were never discussed in isolation, which is to say that he did not treat the mind and the body as distinct, self-subsistent entities.

The Buddha's analysis of experience must explain how experience arises and functions without reference to a permanent self. In the "Discourse of the Honeyball," consciousness and experience generally are explained as a naturally emergent process:

> Visual consciousness arises dependent on the eye and visible objects. The meeting of the three is contact. Dependent on contact, there is feeling. What one feels, that one perceives. What one perceives, that one reasons about. What one reasons about, that one mentally proliferates.[9] What one mentally proliferates, that is the cause by which mentally proliferated perceptions and (obsessive) notions assail a person in regard to visible objects cognizable by the eye, in the past, future, and present.
>
> (MN.I.111–12; cf. SN.IV.86)

This emergentist view of consciousness can be represented as follows:

Visual consciousness

↑

Contact

↗↖

Eye ↔ Visual object

The same pattern holds for the other five modes of consciousness (auditory consciousness, olfactory consciousness, tactile consciousness, gustatory consciousness, and mental consciousness). Each mode of consciousness arises because of the complex interactions of sensory organ and sensory objects. Conscious experience, then, is an organic/integrated process that can be analyzed into a coordination of both a sensory organ and the sensory object. But it is very important to realize that neither the sense organ nor the sensory object is given a more fundamental status – they are functions delineated within an experience that is integrated as a unitary process.

This passage explains consciousness as a reflexive function that emerges from the complexities of human–world interaction. In other words, consciousness involves self-awareness. Consciousness, therefore, gives experience its continuity, but it does so without appealing to a permanent or transcendent *subject* of experience. Many would argue against the early Buddhist position here, saying that such a view cannot account for a personal identity that endures through time. But this is why the Buddha used the metaphor of a "*stream* of consciousness" (*viññāna-sota*) to illustrate how a changing process can maintain continuity and identity despite ongoing change.[10]

Although the Buddha claimed that all knowledge is based on sense experience (or inferences based on sense experience), he did not claim that sense experience is infallible. The Buddha realized that sense data can lead to errors of fact and judgment. This is not due to a defect in perception, per se, but to the way that a corrupt (unenlightened) mind processes sense perception. The Buddha recognized the fact that subjective attitudes such as likes and dislikes, attachments, aversions, confusion, and fears prevent one from perceiving things as they are. Here we see how subjective or affective factors, such as likes and dislikes, enter directly into the character of objects of sensory experience (and have the effect of distorting them). It is precisely because of the way the mind distorts experience in unwholesome ways that we need to transform our minds in radical ways through the development of mental culture and insight.

The Role of Affective Modes of Experience in Cognition

The Pāli Nikāyas show clearly that the Buddha held a sophisticated and rich view of human experience in which non-cognitive or affective dimensions of experience are given a central place. According to the Buddha, all experience is shaped or constructed by mediating factors, many of which are affective. Put differently, human beings inhabit the world through such non-cognitive dimensions of experience as feeling (*vedanā*) and various underlying tendencies (*anusaya*) that operate on the affective levels of experience. This has important implications for the discussion of knowledge (or any form of cognition). The Buddha saw the cognitive and affective dimensions of experience not as opposed but as integrated aspects of all experience. This position is remarkably similar to mainstream cognitive science today and thus is an aspect of early Buddhism that bears on current research in the field of epistemology.

In the passage quoted above from the "Discourse of the Honeyball," it is said that "what one feels, that one perceives." Such a statement shows that there can be no purely cognitive experience because all experience is necessarily conditioned by affective factors such as feelings, dispositions, habits, and selective biases that are built into the very process of human experience. These affective factors color and shape and evaluate the objects of sense experience. All percepts are filtered or mediated objects dependent at least in part on human experience for what they are. In short, the world in which we live is shaped by the *way* we experience it. Sue Hamilton sums up this important aspect of early Buddhist epistemology in the following way:

> all of the factors of our experience, whatever they may be, are dependent for their existence *as that* on our cognitive apparatus. This explains the famous early Buddhist expression "In this fathom-long living body, along with its apperceptions and thoughts, lies the world, the arising of the world, and the cessation of the world." [*Aṇguttara Nikāya*, II.48] And this is why the factors of experience are referred to as "conditioned things" – *saṃkhārā*. They are conditioned *by us*. . . . all of the factors of experience are constructed or made *like that* by our cognitive processes. It is we ourselves who construct the world as we know it from the mass of sensory data we continually receive.
>
> (Hamilton 2000, 109)

The fact that all experience is mediated by affective factors in the human mind makes it impossible that any human experience can provide us with a completely objective and unbiased view of reality. To some, namely speculative metaphysicians, this comes as bad news. However, the good news, from a Buddhist point of view, is that such absolute objectivity regarding reality is not necessary to achieve religious liberation. The Buddha was simply not interested in speculative metaphysics. He sought only a model of human knowledge and experience that would explain suffering and the elimination of suffering.

Although the Buddha's analysis of *saṃkhārā* accounts for how we construct a world within our experience, the Buddha considered feeling (*vedanā*)[11] as the most critical link in the unfolding of experience for the purpose of diagnosing and curing suffering. Feeling is *the key link* (*nidāna*) in the twelvefold formula of dependent arising because it is precisely where experience turns from a neutral process into an unwholesome one.

According to the twelvefold formula of dependent arising, feeling causes craving (*taṇhā*). This is a shift from a morally neutral aspect of experience to a decidedly unwholesome aspect of experience that in the normal (unenlightened) mind eventually gives rise to suffering.

In the structure of experience, feeling signifies the affective quality that permeates a given experience. Feeling colors all the constituents within an experiential event or situation. Feelings are *not* so much localizable *things* as pervasive qualities that bind together the constituents of an experience and mark one experience off from other experiences. And, in the ongoing process of experience, such underlying aesthetic factors regulate the vector or direction of an experience. That is, feelings of pleasantness often engender pursuit of the objects tinged with pleasantness, while painful feelings typically engender aversion to objects tinged with painfulness.

The Pāli sources emphasize that feeling, perception, and other cognitive functions are closely connected or intertwined. In the "Greater Discourse on Questions and Answers," the Buddha said: "feeling, perception, and consciousness – these factors are conjoined, not disjoined, and it is impossible to separate each of these factors from the others in order to describe the difference between them" (MN.I.293). Thus, in regard to seeing, hearing, and the other modes of perception, there is no such thing as perception or cognition *plus* feeling. The perceived object or thought is pervaded with the qualities of feeling. Here, the texts recognize that, even under normal circumstances, affective factors of experience play an essential role in determining our perceptions and other cognitive experiences. One might even say that feelings are neither exclusively *in* the experiencing subject nor exclusively *in* the experienced objects; they are as much a part of the things experienced as of the experiencer. In his translation of the *Majjhima Nikāya*, Bhikkhu Bodhi emphasizes this crucial point in a note about feeling: In the Pāli texts, feeling is "simultaneously a quality of the object as well as an affective tone of the experience by which it is apprehended" (Ñānamoli and Bodhi 1995, 1236).

In response to such a view of experience, some might argue that the mediating factors involved in human experience obviate the possibility of genuine knowledge. Genuine knowledge, according to some philosophers, must be purely cognitive and achieve a high standard of objectivity. But all of the filters and complexities of experience on the Buddha's model of experience might seem to make knowledge claims highly subjective so that the requisite standards for objectivity required by knowledge would be unachievable on the Buddha's view of experience. Thus, the critic of early Buddhism might argue that the Buddha's view of experience inevitably (if unintentionally) leads to skepticism. And yet the Buddha clearly tried to carve out a middle way on the issue of knowledge by avoiding the extremes of both absolute certainty and complete skepticism.

The Role of Knowledge in Achieving Spiritual Liberation (*nibbāna*)

Knowledge is an essential part of the path to spiritual liberation in early Buddhism. But, given the restrictions and limitations placed on claims to knowledge within the Buddha's empiricist epistemology, one might wonder what role liberating knowledge plays and whether it can be achieved in a way that is consistent with the Buddha's epistemological outlook. Put another way, what part does knowledge have in the achievement of *nibbāna* in early Buddhism?

When the Buddha spoke of the kind of knowledge that is relevant to spiritual achievement, he regularly used the phrase "knowing and seeing" (*ñāṇa-dassana* or *jānāti passati*). This phrase has a special meaning because it is a cognitive state that is caused by the development of "mental culture" (*samādhi*) that forms the second stage of the threefold training. When "knowing and seeing" is achieved fully, one attains a level of knowledge that is described as *paññā*, "wisdom" or "insight." This is the third and final stage of training. The texts make it clear that "knowing and seeing" refers to knowledge gained both by sense perception and by supersensory powers (*abhiññā*). Thus, the Pāli Nikāyas do not treat *paññā* as wholly distinct from knowledge gained through mundane perception. There is no mystical or transcendental mode of liberating knowledge, according to early Buddhism. This differs significantly from the Brahmanical forms of spiritual knowledge depicted in the Upaniṣads. In the Upaniṣads, liberating knowledge arises mysteriously and requires the intervention of transcendent realities or divinities. Whereas liberating knowledge in the Brahmanical tradition is a kind of grace bestowed on the meditator, the early Buddhist texts tell us that all spiritual knowledge is a product of one's training, and therefore depends entirely on one's own efforts.

But what is the nature of liberating knowledge in early Buddhism? Liberating (or "highest") knowledge is presented in two modes in the early Buddhist texts: knowledge *how* and knowledge *that*. Liberating knowledge, according to the Buddha, is achieved by mastering the knowledge (*how*) that transforms the way the mind processes experience so that suffering does not arise and also by knowing *that* everything that exists is a dependently arisen (and so an impermanent) process.

Consistent with the order of the threefold training, the texts usually say that the knowledge that eliminates the corruptions of the mind is a prerequisite for the "final" knowledge or *paññā* that involves the realization of dependent arising. Not all of the discourses in the Pāli Nikāyas agree on this, however. And scholars themselves have debated whether the knowledge *how* or the knowledge *that* is the knowledge that leads directly to liberation from suffering.

Knowing how fully to eliminate the factors that corrupt a person's mind is the fruit, the highest benefit, of mental culture (*samādhi*). Mental culture, in turn, is achieved through the practice of meditation. According to the early Buddhist texts, one who meditates can develop powers that extend the normal six sensory modalities. Along with the six sensory modes discussed earlier, the Buddha recognized six supersensory modes of perception (*abhiññā*): psychokinesis, clairaudience, telepathy, retrocognition, clairvoyance, and the knowledge that leads to the destruction of the defilements (*āsavakkhayañāṇa*). These are powers available to anyone who becomes adept at meditation. In this way, the Buddha recognized that each person has the potential to develop powers of perception and knowledge that go beyond the ordinary senses. Thus, these supersensory powers are not supernatural powers, but best thought of as extensions of ordinary human sensory powers that can be achieved by someone who has a mind that is developed by meditative practices.

The supersensory modes of knowledge were used by the Buddha to probe deeper into the sources of human suffering. In particular, the Buddha used them to develop direct knowledge about the universality of dependent arising, impermanence, suffering, and the lack of a permanent essence (Self) in all things. The most important of the supersensory powers is the knowledge that leads to the destruction of the defilements. The defilements (*āsavas*) are the psychological factors of greed, hatred, and delusion that pervade the unenlightened mind. They distort our perceptions in unwholesome ways that lead ultimately to suffering. Eliminating the defilements has a positive effect on the mind as well. By purifying the mind in this way, the mind becomes supple, flexible, steady, and undisturbed (DN.I.76).

But just as normal sensory experience does not always produce true knowledge, likewise any experience based on the supersensory modes of perception is fallible to the extent that they may be filtered through a corrupted mind. In fact, the Buddha thought that just such a misuse of these powers led the sages of the Brahmanical tradition to their erroneous beliefs about a permanent Reality (Brahman) and permanent Self (*ātman*). For the Buddha's purposes, the practice of meditation and the development of the supersensory powers have nothing to do with perceiving a transcendent reality. Rather, such powers of knowledge are aimed at eliminating the corrupting filters (the defilements) that distort our valuation of percepts in all forms of sensory experience.

In "The Discourse to Vacchagotta on the Threefold Knowledge," the Buddha said that the most important of these supersensory modes of perception were retrocognition (knowledge of one's former rebirths), clairvoyance (the power to see the rebirths of others as product of their karma), and the knowledge that leads to the destruction of the defilements (MN.I.482). These three higher modes of knowledge are referred to as the "threefold knowledge" (*tevijjā*) (DN.I.235ff. and MN.I.481ff.). The use of the term "threefold knowledge" was no accident. In ritual practice and in later Vedic theology, "Brahman" came to be conceived as the god Brahmā, creator of the universe and among the highest *devas* in the Hindu pantheon. A theological form of salvation thus became available, namely, "union with Brahmā," a kind of beatific relationship with this highest deity. According to the Vedic tradition, one achieves "union with Brahmā" through the study and mastery of the "threefold knowledge," which referred to knowledge of the three Vedas.[12] This is another example of the Buddha using a term borrowed from the Brahmanical tradition but reconstructing it in a radically different way. By redefining the "threefold knowledge" as powers that aid in the cleansing of the mind, the Buddha was rejecting theology in favor of psychology. Thus, according to this discourse, the knowledge that is central to the achievement of spiritual liberation is how to transform a person's mind by removing from it the corrupting factors that lead inexorably to suffering.

Some scholars reject the claim that early Buddhism is a form of empiricism because of these supersensory powers. Empiricism, some might argue, requires that all knowledge be derived only from the normal five senses. But there seems to be no good reason to stipulate such a narrow definition of empiricism. If empiricism is the claim that all knowledge is based on experience, and if the supersensory powers only extend normal sense modalities, there's no compelling reason to reject calling early Buddhism a form of empiricism. After all, the Buddha's discussion of these supersensory powers is not an abandonment of sense experience for a higher kind of experience. Furthermore, such powers do not reveal any ultimate truths about a transcendent reality.

The fact that the removal of the corrupting factors of the mind paves a path to such higher knowledge about the dependently arisen nature of existence is reinforced in the "Discourse on Right View," where the Buddha said:

> When a noble disciple knows what is unwholesome, and the root of the unwholesome – and he knows also, the wholesome and the root of the wholesome – because of this knowledge the noble disciple abandons completely the tendency for lust, the tendency for anger (or aversion) and he removes the tendency to deceive himself into believing "I am." By removing this ignorance and developing such knowledge, a noble disciple here and now brings suffering to an end.
>
> (MN.I.47)

The early Buddhist texts tell us that the catalyst for the Buddha's achievement of enlightenment was his knowledge of *things as they really are* (*yathābhūta*). This is what it means to be "freed by insight" (*paññā-vimutto*). Such is not an insight into a permanent or mystical reality, but the realization that everything (including each person) is a dependently arisen phenomenon (*paṭiccasamuppanna*), an unfolding process, and not a substantial entity.

As the Buddha said to the monks (*bhikkhus*) in "The Shorter Discourse on the Lion's Roar":

> Whenever, bhikkhus, a bhikkhu has abandoned ignorance and knowledge has arisen in him, then, through this abandonment of ignorance and the arising of knowledge, he no longer clings to sensual pleasures, nor to speculative views, nor to customary practices, nor to the doctrine that there is a permanent self.
>
> (MN.I.67)

This is a knowledge *that* (not a knowledge *how*), because it arises based on a deeper understanding of the changing world in which we live. Such liberating knowledge in early Buddhism does not stand opposed to normal everyday knowledge or perception but, rather, builds on it. When one sees things as they truly are, as processes and not as permanent things, one realizes the futility of grasping onto personal possessions, sensual pleasures, and the fiction of a permanent self. Such knowledge leads to spiritual freedom, *nibbāna*, through non-grasping (*anupādā vimutti*) because, when one truly knows that there is nothing permanent anywhere, one realizes that one must "let go." Given this, one thing is abundantly clear in the early Buddhist texts: *nibbāna* is not knowledge of a transcendent or highest reality, but a transformed way of living in this world. Even the highest kind of knowledge in early Buddhism is not an end itself, but simply a key factor in bringing about the needed transformation of the person.

The Buddha said that "when one dwells with one's mind obsessed with craving and one does not truly know and see the elimination of such craving that has arisen, it is a cause of one's failure to know and see . . . [likewise] ill-will, sloth and indolence, excitement and perplexity, and doubt are causes of one's failure to know and to see" (SN.V.127). One could argue from this, and the previous two passages quoted from the texts, that there is a reciprocal relationship between the corrupting factors of the mind and the lack of higher knowledge about the way things really are. As we have seen, knowledge about the dependently arisen nature of the world and the person is required to remove the corrupting factors in the mind, but these same corrupting factors are part of the reason why a person fails to achieve higher knowledge. A person who is fully liberated is one who has achieved *both* the knowledge of how to eliminate the defilements *and* the penetrative knowledge of the dependently arisen nature of the world. Whatever their sequence or connection, both modes of knowledge are required to achieve *nibbāna*, according to early Buddhism.

Notes

1 See the *Bṛhadāraṇyaka Upaniṣad*, I.4.10.

2 The present chapter considers early Buddhism as the views expressed in the texts of the Pāli Canon, more specifically, the discourses (*suttas*) collected in the Pāli Nikāyas.

3 *Dukkha* includes physical pain; but it is much more than that. This word is typically translated as "suffering," although "unsatisfactoriness" may be more apt. *Dukkha* refers to the psychological and existential anxieties that taint normal human experience.

4 In the narrowest sense of the term, "epistemology" focuses on the justification of knowledge claims. But here (and often in Western philosophy, too) the term applies more broadly to include a psychological account of human *experience*.

5 The Brahmanical goal of "union with Brahmā" is a beatific relationship with this highest deity, Brahmā, which can be achieved by someone who masters the threefold knowledge – namely, the knowledge contained in the three Vedas.

6 The Buddha drives home his point by getting Prince Abhaya to admit that he would stick his finger down the throat of a choking child. Such an action is disagreeable to the child in the near term, but would surely be for the child's good in the long term. The truth the Buddha preaches is sometimes like that.

7 For a full account of all the possible interpretations of the unexplained questions and the views of some the more notable scholars on this matter, see Jayatilleke (1963, 471ff.).

8 Early Buddhism, along with other ancient Indian traditions, refers to six senses, rather than the normal five. The sixth sensory mode, "minding," refers to the way objects (*dhammā*) appear before the mind. This sixth sensory mode is an attempt to explain how the data from the other five senses must appear before the mind in order for us to be aware of them at all. See, for example, DN.I.63 and SN.II.218 for more on the six sensory modes.

9 *Pāpañceti*. This is a curious word that means "to mentally proliferate," but clearly in a pejorative or negative sense. The term is rendered in some translations as "to become obsessed with."

10 David Kalupahana (1987) connects the Buddha's metaphor of consciousness as a stream with the conception of a "stream of consciousness" that is developed in William James's *Principles of Psychology*.

11 The term *vedanā* is usually rendered as "feeling" in English, but it also can be translated as "sensation" or, more generally, as "experience." A related verb, *vediyati*, means "to feel or experience a sensation." In the texts, feeling is described repeatedly by a stock formula: "*tisso vedanā, sukkhā, dukkhā, adukkhamasukhā*," which means "there are these three kinds of feeling: pleasant, painful, and neither-painful-nor-pleasant." But *vedanā* seems to be a term that covers a fairly broad spectrum of the affective factors in human experience.

12 The original three Vedas are: the *Rig Veda*, the *Sāma Veda*, and the *Yajur Veda*.

References

Ñāṇamoli, Bhikkhu, and Bodhi, Bhikkhu (ed. and trans.) (1995). *The Middle Length Discourses of the Buddha: A New Translation of the Majjhima Nikaya.* Boston: Wisdom.

Gombrich, Richard (1996). *How Buddhism Began: The Conditioned Genesis of the Early Teachings.* London: Athlone Press.

Hamilton, Sue (2000). *Early Buddhism: A New Approach: The I of the Beholder.* Richmond, Surrey: Curzon Press.

Jayatilleke, K. N. (1963). *Early Buddhist Theory of Knowledge.* London: Allen & Unwin.

Kalupahana, David (1976). *Buddhist Philosophy: A Historical Introduction.* Honolulu: University of Hawai'i Press.

Kalupahana, David (1987). *The Principles of Buddhist Psychology.* New York: State University of New York Press.

15

Reason and Experience in Buddhist Epistemology

CHRISTIAN COSERU

Introductory Remarks

As a specific domain of inquiry, "Buddhist epistemology" (sometimes designated in the specialist literature by the Sanskrit neologism *pramāṇavāda*, or the "theory of reliable sources of knowledge") stands primarily for the dialogical-disputational context in which Buddhists advance their empirical claims to knowledge and articulate the principles of reason on the basis of which such claims may be defended. The main questions that we shall pursue here concern the tension between the notion that knowledge is ultimately a matter of direct experience – which the Buddhist considers as more normative than other, more indirect, modes of knowing – and the largely discursive and argumentative ways in which such experiential claims are advanced.

The Sanskrit philosophical idiom, in which Buddhist epistemology finds its first and perhaps most elaborate expression, contains one distinctive term, *anubhava*, for the concept of "experience" and several terms that closely approximate the concept of "reason." For instance, *tarka* captures the notion of speculative or logical inquiry; *nyāya* stands for the notion of rule or method for investigating objects by reliable means; *yukti* for the notion of ground, proof, or motive, or for something that is right, fit, or appropriate; and *hetu* for the notion of means by which what was hitherto unproved is now proven. From this cursory terminological survey one may hastily conclude that, whereas the epistemic notion of experience is universal, reason and the corresponding notion of rationality (with their roots in the Latin *ratio*, which conveys the sense of "reckoning" or "giving an account of judgment," as one might do in court) as a distinctive epistemic faculty or process is not. Of course, this observation assumes a Western frame of reference for examining the relation between reason and experience. An alternative project would be to explore the relation between experience and whatever it is that Buddhists mean when they examine, reflect upon, or seek to prove a given thesis without any reference to Western concepts and ways of thinking. Given that this second

A Companion to Buddhist Philosophy, First Edition. Edited by Steven M. Emmanuel.

project is well nigh impossible if carried out in a language such as English, whose philosophical vocabulary has been shaped by a longstanding tradition of Western thought, we face a dilemma: can Buddhist philosophy be written in English without losing the explanatory force of its original concepts and categories?

Perhaps setting the problem in terms that are alien to the ways in which the Buddhists have pursued their epistemological reflections showcases a limitation that the tradition in fact does not possess. Since analyses of experience, argumentation, and debate are ubiquitous features of Buddhist thought – barring all caveats about translatability – it should be possible to offer an account of the role that reason and experience play in Buddhist epistemology that is neither inauthentic nor mere reportage. It may also be the case that this distinction between reason and experience is too sharply drawn, and that there are ways of conceiving of what it is like to perceive and reflect that regard them as complementary rather than opposite practices. Indeed, the recent recognition that the exercise of reason varies both over history and across cultures (see Weinberg et al. 2001; Machery et al. 2004; Huebner et al. 2010) should suffice to call into question any attempt to see both practical and theoretical reason as removed from the embodied patterns of conduct that characterize our specific ways of being in the world. As will be argued at length in this chapter, epistemological inquiries in India, particularly with regard to examining the sources of reliable cognition, have never displayed the sort of non-naturalism distinctive to the Cartesian and Kantian traditions in Western philosophy and their characteristically abstract epistemic notions of experience and rationality. Thus, with the return to naturalism in epistemology, hence to understanding cognition in embodied and causal terms, we may now be in a better position to appreciate the contributions of Buddhist philosophers to epistemology.

This chapter explores how the relation between direct experience and discursive modes of knowing is articulated in Indian Buddhism. The first account of this relation, as is well known, originates with Siddhārtha Gautama's experience of enlightenment. This experience becomes at once the source of the Buddhist metaphysical picture of reality and the culmination of all aspiration for genuine knowledge (the kind that guarantees the successful accomplishment of such practical ends as freedom from suffering). Key to this metaphysical picture is the causal principle of dependent arising and a thoroughly psychological account of persons, which takes experience and rational deliberation to be but two of the many contributing factors that shape human identity and agency. Indeed, at the foundation of this Buddhist inquiry into the sources of knowledge is the notion that awakened knowledge has existential consequences, and can effect the removal not only of such afflictions as ignorance and deception but also of the reifying tendencies inherent in common-sense beliefs. It is not surprising, therefore, that epistemological inquiry is central to Buddhist philosophy, and that understanding the nature of knowledge, its sources, and its conditions of possibility are constitutive of its main thrust.

We will start with a brief overview of canonical and Abhidharma perspectives on the scope of epistemological reflection, then evaluate the well-known Madhyamaka skepticism about the possibility of conceptually articulating our specific modes of being in the world, and conclude with an examination of Dignāga and Dharmakīrti's accounts of the relation between observation and inferential reasoning. Lastly, given the modern audience for this essay (and, indeed, for this volume), adopting a constructive, rather than merely critical and exegetical approach seems not only appropriate but also timely. If our efforts to reclaim the legacy of non-Western traditions of philosophical inquiry are to have more than a historical or broadly exegetical value (and thus appeal to those outside Buddhist scholarly circles) we must necessarily consider whether Buddhist epistemology can provide a basis for analytic and constructive engagements of the sort typically found in contemporary philosophical debates.

Doubting, Knowing, and Seeing

In one of his best-known discourses, the Buddha endorses doubt as a legitimate epistemic attitude, telling his disciples that it is fitting to doubt and be perplexed. Enjoining his followers not to accept oral and scriptural tradition, but to rely on personal experience and discernment, the Buddha appears to challenge even such widely accepted modes of inquiry as logical and inferential reasoning: "Do not go by . . . logical reasoning, by inferential reasoning, by consideration of reasons, by the reflective acceptance of a view" (*Kālāma Sutta*). Rather, the Buddha urges, one is to discriminate between wholesome and unwholesome states of mind and use that discrimination as a guide to undertaking only those particular tasks, and following only those specific practices, that are conducive to welfare and happiness. It is nonetheless obvious that, despite such apparent disclaimers of reason, an endorsement of the notion that liberating insight demands careful empirical scrutiny can be clearly gleaned from the canonical literature. Furthermore, the knowledge one gains from such scrutiny must be ascertained on the basis of its effectiveness in removing both afflictive and cognitive obscurations, as well as in overcoming the kind of hindrances typically associated with conditioned phenomena. This emphasis on direct experience as a preferred mode of knowing is one of the reasons why some authors have interpreted the quest for truth in early Buddhism as akin to Western forms of empiricism, even though the Buddhist operates with a wider notion of "experience" than empiricist accounts of knowledge (as derived solely from sense experience) would allow. Thus, contrary to what might seem from afar like a Buddhist endorsement of misology, canonical sources make quite clear that several distinct factors play a crucial role in the acquisition of knowledge. These are variously identified with the testimony of sense experience, introspective or intuitive experience, inferences drawn from these two types of experience, and some form of coherentism, which demands that truth claims remain consistent across the entire corpus of doctrine. Thus, to the extent that Buddhists employ reason, they do so primarily in order further to advance the empirical investigation of phenomena. It is principally for this reason that early Buddhism presents us with a causal account of cognition and takes theories of causation to play a central role in any theory of knowledge. As K. N. Jayatilleke, one of the first proponents of a Buddhist sort of empiricism, notes, "inductive inferences in Buddhism are based on a theory of causation. These inferences are made on the data of perception . . . What is considered to constitute knowledge are direct inferences made on the basis of such perceptions" (Jayatilleke 1963, 457).

But there are matters that are simply not amenable to rational inquiry (and justification), and cannot be offered the sort of categorical answer one would expect of more straightforward issues such as the difference between true and false belief or between wholesome and unwholesome mental and affective states. Perhaps the best-known examples of such matters are the so-called unexplained or undetermined (*avyākṛta*) questions: whether the self and the world are eternal or not, whether they are finite or infinite, whether the soul and the body are identical or different, and whether one who has thus gone or come (a *tathāgata*: one who has realized that the real nature of things is just "thus," free from any conceptual imputations) continues, does not continue, both continues and does not continue, or neither continues nor does not continue to exist after death. Modern scholars have proposed different interpretations of the Buddha's apparent non-committal on these crucial metaphysical and epistemological questions. Some claim a philosophical basis for the Buddha's silence, asserting either that he wished to leave the matter open for further inquiry and debate or that he did have answers but refused to reveal them as a deterrent to those seeking to make progress along the path. The canonical literature makes amply obvious that those who are able to follow in the Buddha's footsteps will likewise come to realize that all views are merely conventions established upon common practice, and, as a result, will forgo all philosophical disputation: the adept "agrees with no-one, disputes with no-one, and makes use of philosophical terms without erring" (*Dīghanakha Sutta*).

We can easily recognize in one of these questions the well-known mind–body problem. Are we to conclude that the Buddha does not consider this to be a real problem, deserving of a careful and measured answer? Or, is it rather the case that our conceptual resources are simply inadequate and cannot provide an answer to these questions in unambiguous and uncontroversial terms? If the knowledge project in Buddhism is about overcoming adherence to mistaken views, then it may well be the case that these questions are simply verbally and conceptually ill-formed, typical examples of pointless speculation (cf. Collins 1982, 132). Phenomena, including the five aggregates that are constitutive of human existence and/or experience (form, feeling, apperception, dispositions, and consciousness), come together as a product of multiple causes and conditions and cease with the removal of these causal and conditioning factors. None of these elements and factors in the web of interdependent arising, however, has causal priority. Any attempt to understand them in terms of permanence or complete dissolution disregards the fundamental causal principle of dependent arising, and therefore is not worthy of serious consideration.

Abhidharma traditions – essentially comprising a large body of literature concerned with examining the received teachings that emerged roughly three centuries after the death of the Buddha – do concede that there are specific principles of reason for why causal chains display patterns of regularity. But even here the assumption is that the descriptive framework of analysis is intended to serve not as a complete metaphysical picture of reality, but as a primer for identifying those elements (thoughts, desires, habitual tendencies) that are unwholesome, with the ultimate aim of overcoming them. The goal is thus pragmatic rather than speculative: unwholesome thoughts and desires must be properly identified and eradicated if liberation from suffering is to be achieved. Attempts to identify specific principles of reason, and indeed to employ them for the purpose of achieving greater clarity about controversial issues, become formalized in such representative works as the *Points of Controversy* (*Kathāvatthu*), where we come across issues of doctrinal conflict that warrant serious critical discussion and debate. Whether works such as the *Points of Controversy* anticipate something like a logical system of deductive principles and propositional laws, as early interpreters have claimed (Aung and Rhys Davids 1915; Schayer 2001 [1933]; Bochenski 1961; and Matilal 1998), is less significant for our purpose here than their pragmatic valuation of rational modes of inquiry.

It is true that, in terms of both structure and strategy, these methods aim to codify specific rules of debate, by means of which controversial issues can be addressed and arguments (adduced by both parties) properly weighed and considered. Typically, the debate revolves around such issues as whether all knowledge is analytic, whether one can know the minds of others, whether sensations follow one another continuously, and whether continuity of awareness is genuinely achieved only in meditative equipoise. These debates, which involve a back-and-forth exchange concerning statements of the sort "Is *a b*? ("Is knowledge analytic?"), most certainly appeal to principles that are discerningly like forms of material implication, contraposition, and some version of *reductio ad absurdum*. We may thus recognize these philosophically non-eristic dialogues as "reasoned examinations" (*yukti*) of controversial points.

The pattern of argumentation at work in *Points of Controversy*, as Jonardon Ganeri has convincingly shown, is presumptive rather than demonstrative, since the burden of proof switches from one party to the next, neither of which offers any positive thesis (Ganeri 2001, 487). It is precisely this preference for *argumentum ad ignorantiam* (of the sort: "I am right because not proven wrong") that gains prestige with Nāgārjuna's development of the radical thesis that it is not just that some controversial (or difficult) issues must be rigorously debated, but rather that reality itself in some sense is beyond the reach of conception. Nāgārjuna's skepticism about the possibility of positive argumentation hinges on a crucial insight: that our ordinary ways of conceiving – which depend on such standard concepts and categories as origin, motion, sensation, physical objects and their properties, past, present, and future, and the idea that objects in the class of what J. L. Austin calls "medium-sized dry goods" have a self-standing nature or essence – are seriously flawed. That is, they are the result of a pervasive and systemic ignorance that afflicts the unenlightened human condition.

Before we turn briefly to consider Nāgārjuna's challenge to rationality as a method for establishing positive views, and its implications for Buddhist epistemology, let us first consider the causal aspects of the principles of reason formulated by Abhidharma philosophers.

In the context of addressing such basic doctrinal issues as the nature and scope of Buddhist teachings, Asaṅga, for instance, identifies four widely shared "reasons" (*yukti*) for which one may proceed to inquire into the nature of things. The assumption is that such inquiries are indispensable for all who seek knowledge, however it may be defined. The issue under debate is not whether the desire to know itself needs to be called into question – presumably by those who might see it as an affliction, and thus doubt its inherently positive value – but how one who has realized that there are good and perhaps many reasons to examine things is to carry out such examinations. In the *Collection on Higher Knowledge* (*Abhidharmasamuccaya* II) (see Tatia 1976), Asaṅga lists four such reasons. First, there is the principle of dependence (*apekṣāyukti*), which takes into account the fact that conditioned things necessarily arise in dependence upon conditions: it is a principle of reason, for instance, that sprouts depend on seeds. Second, there is the principle of causal efficacy (*kāryakāraṇayukti*), which accounts for the difference between things in terms of the different causal conditions for their apprehension: it is a principle of reason, thus, that, in dependence upon form, a faculty of vision, and visual awareness, one has visual rather than, say, auditory or tactile experiences (of course, the phenomenon of synesthesia, which Buddhist philosophers did not consider, poses a challenge to this principle). The requirement that any sort of instruction about what must be established as a matter of principle is not contrary to the means by which it can be established captures the sense of the third principle of reason: the realization of evidence from experience (*sākṣātkriyāsādhanayukti*). We realize the presence of water from moisture and of fire from smoke. Lastly, there is the principle of natural reasoning, or the principle of reality (*dharmatāyukti*), which concerns the phenomenal character of things as perceived (for instance, the wetness and fluidity of water). These four principles of reason become a near permanent fixture with later Indian Buddhist philosophers, and come close to embodying internalist and externalist accounts of rationality for the purpose of justifying certain claims to knowledge (or for appealing to causal explanation). That is, the principles of reason (*yukti*) capture both the notion of "her reason for doing *x*" and "the reason *x* happened" (cf. Kapstein 1988, 153).

This account of the principles of reason could be read in at least two ways: first, as a causal theory of natural fitness, which would postulate that the world is such that it is reasonable to assert that things arise due to specific causes and conditions (for instance, that sprouts come from seeds). Such a theory would share common ground with views expressed by Sanskrit grammarians such as Bhartṛhari, who claim that the manner in which words are capable of capturing objects in the empirical domain – such that the thing cognized is in some sense indistinguishable from the word (or expression) by which it is thus cognized – reflects the latter's natural fitness (cf. Iyer 1969, 204). Second, we may understand this account in Kantian terms as describing the *a priori* conditions for knowledge, since it is reasonable to assume that causal laws justify claims about the order of the objective and subjective domains of experience.

What we have here are examples of natural reasoning or of reasoning from experience, rather than attempts to use deliberative modes of reasoning for the purpose of justifying a given thesis or arguing for its conditions of satisfaction. With Dignāga and Dharmakīrti, such uses of reason, as we shall argue below, develop in what may be best described as a system of pragmatic or context-based reasoning.

Emptiness, Rationality, and the Impossibility of Proof

The expansive taxonomies of Abhidharma traditions, and their long and detailed lists of the elements of existence and/or experience (*dharmas*), stand as testimony to the central role that descriptive accounts of experience play in the Buddhist epistemological project. But these descriptive accounts rely on observation, and observation leads to the old philosophical problem of the difference between "seeing" and "seeing as." Recent developments in epistemology, in particular those centered around the project of naturalism, have challenged the empiricist claim that observation is in some sense a type of "seeing" that is always dissociated from "seeing as." As Jerry Fodor, for instance, puts it, letting psychology settle what an observation is, or just letting the observations be the data, is legitimate; but "it's sheer Empiricist dogmatism to take it for granted that you can do both at once. In fact, there is no good reason to suppose that the psychological notion of perception – or, indeed, *any* psychological notion – will reconstruct the epistemological notion of a datum" (Fodor 1991, 200).

For the Buddhist epistemologists, however, this distinction between "seeing" and "seeing as" is instrumental in discriminating conception-free from conception-laden cognitive states, and, indeed, for claiming that only the former warrant the proper label of veridical perception. Typically, the Buddhist points to such examples as being able to attend to perceptual input while thinking of something else, as proof that there is an epistemic gap between direct observation and perceptual judgment. It is this distinction that philosophers such as Nāgārjuna and Candrakīrti challenge, and those such as Dignāga and Dharmakīrti defend as normative for any epistemological project. To say that there is a way that things are that is separate from how they show up to us, and that it is possible to have something like a pure, undiscriminating awareness of phenomena that is implicitly (thought non-discursively) cognitive, is to endorse the view that reality is in effect accessible to thought. The Buddhist epistemologists are not unaware that our cognitive capacities are constrained in some aspects. However, their emphasis is not on the internal and external constraints imposed upon our cognitive systems, but on what can be known and by what means. For Nāgārjuna, though, it is not just that some aspects of reality might escape our discerning capacities, but rather that reality itself is beyond the reach of thought. As he famously puts it in his *Stanzas on the Middle Way* (*Mūlamadhyamakakārikā*):

> Where the reach of thought turns back, language turns back. The nature of things is, like complete cessation, without origin and without decay.
>
> (MMK.18.7)

> For that reason, namely that the truth is deep and difficult to understand, the Buddha's mind despaired of being able to teach it.
>
> (MMK.24.12)

Though at first glance this position might be suggestive of skepticism, it has elicited a wide range of interpretations (some reiterating criticism leveled against Nāgārjuna by his historical rivals, both Buddhist and non-Buddhist, and some reflecting novel and constructive engagements with his philosophy). His position has been variously described as skepticism, nihilism, irrationalism, misology, agnosticism, criticism, dialectic, mysticism, acosmism, absolutism, nominalism, relativism, Wittgenstenian linguistic analysis, philosophical therapy, anti-realism, and deconstructionism, and as articulating a version of paraconsistent logic (see Ruegg 1981; Siderits 1988; Huntington 2007; and Garfield 2008). As these widely divergent readings suggest, the exegetical question about how best to interpret Nāgārjuna's Madhyamaka is yet to be settled. What is indisputable, however, is Nāgārjuna's unambiguous stance *vis-à-vis* reliance on the common-sense conceptual schema that takes the world to be constituted of enduring, self-sustaining objects.

For the purpose of our analysis, Nāgārjuna appears to raise serious concerns not only about the very notion that there is such a faculty as reason, one attributable to a stable and enduring agent, but also about what it is like to be undergoing an experience. Indeed, his dialectical stance calls into question the very notion that our modes of being in the world (and the activities we typically associate with what it is like to see, hear, or verbally comprehend) have something like an inherent existence or character or their own (a *svabhāva*). The Madhyamaka dialectical project is thus anchored in a deconstructive analysis of key concepts such as causation, essence, and the self. But, for this deconstructive analysis to be effective, Nāgārjuna needs to establish the view of universal emptiness and supply arguments in defense of such a view.

Now, Nāgārjuna does discuss the four modes or sources of knowledge admitted by the Naiyāyikas (perception, inference, cognition of similarity, and verbal testimony), but it seems he is reluctant to commit to the view that such modes of knowing constitute effective epistemic guides. That is, while he recognizes that, say, objects in the empirical domain are established in dependence upon perception, he is less disposed to credit perception with the capacity to disclose entities as ultimately lacking inherent existence. Perception, at best, may be able to establish that objects exist as they appear (though, given the possibility of perceptual illusion, it cannot establish that what has thus appeared has its conditions of ascertainment intrinsically). That is, perception cannot establish by itself whether its contents are veridical or not.

What, then, are some of the ways in which we may explain what our modes of knowing can, if at all, accomplish? Addressing this issue with respect to Nāgārjuna's account, Jan Westerhoff identifies at least three such ways: (1) establishment by mutual coherence; (2) self-establishment; and (3) mutual establishment (Westerhoff 2009, 166). In the first instance, the testimony of experience is corroborated by other means, such as inference. I know that my perception of a blue sky is non-deceptive because I can infer its presence from the absence of clouds or the presence of the sun's warm radiance (given causal relations, or relations of entailment between clouds, sky, and sunlight). Second, it may be that perceptions are in some sense self-revealing. In perceiving I am aware not merely of the object, in this case of the blue sky, but also of my act of perceiving. This view of perception relies on the notion that there is something it is like to see that requires no further corroboration. Finally, it may be the case that perception and object perceived are mutually established: vision discloses a world of visible objects, touch a world of textures, and so on.

Most of Nāgārjuna's efforts are aimed at refuting the self-establishment thesis (though he also briefly considers, and rejects, the mutual coherence thesis) and at justifying the mutual establishment thesis. For Nāgārjuna's opponents, chiefly the Naiyāyikas, the sources of knowledge cooperate in disclosing a world of self-standing, enduring objects, something that, of course, is antithetical to the emptiness thesis. Taking fire, and its capacity to illuminate, as a metaphor for the revealing nature of cognition, Nāgārjuna advances the thesis that phenomena of this sort cannot be established either by perception or by inference. To claim that cognitions are intrinsically self-revealing (just as fire is inherently self-illuminating) is effectively to say that everything knowable is established by some source of knowledge: visible objects are established as such by a faculty of vision. At least in the case of empirical awareness, to know something is to bring it forth and make it manifest to conscious awareness. But Nāgārjuna is not content merely to refute the thesis that, like fire, a mode of knowing, such as perception, discloses both itself and other objects. Rather, he deploys his dialectical method to argue that, in effect, a mode of knowing discloses neither itself nor other objects (a double refutation of the opponent's thesis). It is here that Nāgārjuna's conceptual schema, which places objects in mutually exclusive classes, leads to an epistemological impasse: that is, he presents us with an analysis of experience that ignores the difference between what one might deem to be case (on the basis of assumptions about the nature of experience) and what seems actually to be the case in the occurrence of a perceptual event:

> A lamp cannot illuminate when it is connected with darkness since their connection does not exist. Why are the lamp and darkness not connected? Because they are opposed. Where the lamp is, darkness is not. How can the lamp remove or illuminate darkness?
>
> (*Auto-Commentary to Refutation of Logic* (*Vaidalyaprakaraṇa-Svavṛtti*), 24.2–8; in Tola and Dragonetti 1995)

In postulating darkness as something that has the power to conceal, Nāgārjuna in effect appears to reify a phenomenon that is established only negatively: darkness is not something that can be defined as the possessor of some (concealing) capacity in the same way that light is defined by its capacity to illuminate. The phenomenological picture at work here is somewhat inadequate, given that it contains a description of darkness that assumes its discrete existence. Thus, Nāgārjuna's refutation of the capacity of light to illuminate (or, by analogy, of perception to reveal) is problematic, since light and darkness are not independent objects but phenomena within the horizon of intentional awareness. The mutual exclusion of light and darkness, however, is used here not simply to justify the impossibility of light to illuminate what was hitherto concealed; rather, the argument is intended to demonstrate that fire cannot be self-established as a source of illumination for other objects (presumably because it is itself dependent on other things, such as fuel). Such self-establishment of illumination in its dual role would require that light and object illuminated stand in a relation of causality. Though Nāgārjuna does admit that darkness is merely the absence of light, he nonetheless appears to argue that absence itself has some kind of positive existence (which perforce prevents it from entering into any causal relationship with light, its opposite).

Against the self-illumination theorist, who postulates that our modes of knowing have a revealing character, the Mādhyamika advances the argument that no mode of knowing has its characteristics intrinsically. Just as a knife cannot cut itself, so also any given mode of knowing cannot know itself in the process of revealing an object. Two principles seem to underlie the Mādhyamika's argument: (i) the anti-reflexivity principle, which postulates that vision does not see itself; and (ii) the doctrine of emptiness, which postulates that vision lacks intrinsic existence (viz., *seeing*) (cf. Siderits 2003, 32). The argument goes as follows: if seeing is the intrinsic nature of vision, then vision must have seeing intrinsically. Thus, vision must see even in the absence of a visible object, because seeing would otherwise be dependent on external visible objects. But seeing (by definition) requires that there is something that is seen. Hence, in the absence of a visible object, vision itself is what vision sees. But vision cannot see itself (as per the anti-reflexivity principle). Hence, seeing is not the intrinsic nature of vision. Conclusion: it is not true that vision sees visible objects.

What, then, is it like to have veridical visual experiences, and how might one meaningfully articulate their epistemic status? Neither Nāgārjuna nor his followers offer us a positive answer. For these Buddhist philosophers of the Middle Way, the true nature of reality is such that it is beyond the limits of thought. But we may ask: is it also beyond the reach of experience? And, if it is, by what means may this thesis be ascertained? It is worth noting that Nāgārjuna's categorical stance on the limits of knowledge is decidedly different from such paradoxical inquiry into the possibility of knowledge one comes across, for instance, in Plato's *Meno* (80d-e). We are dealing here not with the impossibility of inquiring into that which we do not know, but with the impossibility of reaching beyond what inquiry itself can deliver. What we have here is a rejection of the notion that (ultimate) reality can form an object of rational inquiry.

Not all followers of Nāgārjuna are satisfied with his uncompromising stance about the possibility of making assertions about the ultimate nature of reality. As Bhāviveka (who takes seriously the virtues of positive argumentation in discriminating between true and false beliefs) claims, *there is* something it is like to see the nature of reality, even though only buddhas have such abilities: "Buddhas, without seeing, see all objects of knowledge just as they are, with minds like space and with nonconceptual knowledge" (*Verses on the Heart of the Middle Way* (*Madhyamakahṛdayakārikā*), 5.106; in Eckel 2008). The terminology used here includes terms such as *āloka* (light) and *locana* (illuminating), both of which convey the sense of vision as having a revealing and disclosing capacity. For the ordinary individual, the clouds that obscure their vision exist only in their minds, since reality is as clear as the autumn sky. Even the experience of enlightenment itself is in some sense associated with a specific type of vision that is effortless in revealing the nature of reality. Such reality cannot be merely the postulate of reason. But Bhāviveka is not only willing to rehabilitate empirical awareness; he also comes to the rescue of reason (even though he admits that inferential knowledge does not possess the kind of vividness that alone qualifies direct experience as a true source of knowledge): "It is impossible to understand reality as an object of inference, but inference can rule out the opposite of the knowledge of reality" (ibid., 5.107). It is this rehabilitation of a reason that is firmly grounded in experience that informs the spartan epistemology of Dignāga and Dharmakīrti, who, as will be examined below, will come to recognize that epistemological inquiries cannot be properly undertaken (or disputes settled) without taking into account that cognitive events are grounded in all aspects of an individual's conscious experience.

Cognitive Events, Logical Reasons, and Causal Explanation

That reason may be more readily (and effectively) deployed to exclude unwarranted beliefs, rather than to make warranted assertions, marks an important shift in attitude towards the role of rational inquiry. Indeed, the development of Buddhist epistemology as a distinct type of discourse is marked by the gradual acceptance of certain canons of logic and argumentation by those Buddhist philosophers who would come to regard polemical engagement with their Brahmanical opponents as vital to influencing their standing in a wider philosophical community. But there are more than simply sociological reasons at work in this novel orientation towards the scope of rational inquiry. We may see this engagement as reflecting a certain eagerness on the part of (at least) some Buddhists to guarantee that their modes of argumentation are commensurable with the widely accepted methods of reasoning formulated by the Naiyāyikas. What seems to concern philosophers such as Dignāga, Dharmakīrti, and their successors is precisely this need to withstand the criticism that core doctrinal principles such as those of momentariness and dependent arising can neither be defended on rational grounds nor find any sort of empirical support.

Debates about the proper way to conduct epistemic inquiries, and about the kind of sources that can provide evidential ground for knowledge, form an integral part of the Indian philosophical traditions. Though there is no universal agreement on what should count as an "accredited" source of knowledge, perception is often singled out as the exception: most philosophers agree that the testimony of direct experience ought to play a central role in any theory of knowledge. For inference and verbal testimony to play the sort of epistemic role that is typically attributed to them, the content of one's mental states (or propositional attitudes) must be grounded in veridical experiences. Indeed, what use would inference have if, in trying to infer the presence of fire from an observation of smoke, one were to mistake dust (or mist) for smoke? But grounding knowledge on a foundation of empirical experience is not without its challenges: perceptual ambiguities are often experienced even under the best conditions of observation, and there is always the possibility of less than optimal perceptual functioning.

How, then, do the Buddhist epistemologists resolve the tension between experience and reasoning? In the first instance, they take perception to function not only as a psychological process, to be understood within the framework of classical Abhidharma phenomenology, but also as an epistemic modality for establishing a cognitive event as knowledge. Secondly, they do not make a radical distinction between epistemology and the psychological processes of cognition, at least not in the Western sense in which modern normative epistemology eschews naturalist explanations. This understanding of epistemology as cognitive theory is most clearly illustrated in Dignāga's formulation of the method of reasoning known as the triple inferential mark (*trairūpya*), which relies on empirical observation as the most authentic criterion for establishing the validity of inferential cognitions.

What interests us here is not Dignāga's method or its theoretical underpinnings, but the specific way in which he conceives of the relation between reason and experience. For Dignāga (and all subsequent Buddhist epistemologists), cognition operates in two distinct domains: that of particulars, which are only available to empirical awareness, and that of universals, which can only form an object of inferential reasoning:

> The sources of knowledge are perception and inference, because the object of cognition has only two characteristics. There is no object of cognition other than the particular characteristic and the universal characteristic, because perception has as its object the particular and inference the universal characteristic of the thing.
>
> (*Collection on the Sources of Knowledge* (*Pramāṇasamuccaya*), I. 1; in Hattori 1968)

First, unlike Nāgārjuna and his Madhyamaka followers, Dignāga is quite categorical in his assertion that *there are* reliable sources of knowledge. Furthermore, by offering a phenomenological (thus descriptive) account of cognition, Dignāga makes obvious that these two sources of knowledge (roughly equivalent to experience and the exercise of reason) are distinguished not only on the basis of the sort of objects they intend but also in terms of their functional role (cf. Dreyfus 1997, 49). In other words, perception apprehends real individuals by virtue of its constitution (its cognitive architecture and organization: seeing occurs only in organisms endowed with a visual system), whereas inference can apprehend only what are essentially conceptual constructs. This co-presence of perception and object *as perceived* explains why only perception can enter in a direct causal–cognitive coupling with phenomena in the empirical domain.

Thus, the Buddhist epistemologist comes to regard conception as a secondary, rather than a higher-order cognition: the chasm between the world *as experienced* and its conceptual apprehension can only be bridged in cognitive events that are pragmatically efficacious. What makes such pragmatic cognitive events "indubitable" is precisely their efficacy, the fact that they attain their object. If the Buddhist epistemologists come to conceive of the relation between reason and experience in context-specific terms, then their epistemology may well be described as a system of pragmatic or context-dependent reasoning. Unlike the deductive systems of semantic reasoning, which are context-free, pragmatic reasoning is generally inductive and encompasses the types of logic (non-monotonic and paraconsistent) that represent reasoning from premises that are context specific (cf. Bell 2001). On this model of pragmatic reasoning, we reason by first observing the occurrence of certain properties in an object or class of objects and the non-occurrence of those same properties when the object is absent. This model of reasoning operates by deriving hypothetical statements from past observations of the inductive domain. Take the example of empirical objects: these are understood to come into existence due to causes and conditions, and thus to be impermanent, for whatever is produced must necessarily cease. Conversely, a permanent object cannot be produced. Propositions of the type "Sound is impermanent, because it is a product," are then true so long as we do not come across an example of permanent (or indestructible) sounds. Shoryu Katsura has defined this type of logic as "hypothetical reasoning based on induction" (Katsura 2007, 76). Assuming this system of reasoning, which is based on the observation and non-observation of evidence, is open to revision so as to accommodate cases where there is a violation of the linguistic convention, we may describe it as a system of context-specific reasoning.

Such appeals to empirical observation tie logical reasoning to the ability to establish causal connections between the things we directly experience. Consequently, exploring the limits of our ability to establish various causal connections between the elements of experience has less to do with principles of logical entailment and more with psychological inquiries into the nature of our perceptual and cognitive systems.

Thus, Dharmakīrti's attempt to ground reasoning on a stronger principle than mere observation and non-observation of the evidence would lead him to postulate that there must be some "natural connection" (*svabhāvapratibandha*) between the thesis and what is to be demonstrated in order to provide a stronger basis for reasoning. This essential connection is meant to overcome the challenge posed by reliance on hypothetical reasoning. However, since Dharmakīrti's ultimate criterion for truth is the causal efficacy of cognitions, this essential relation cannot be viewed as pragmatically neutral. Reasoning from the empirical data, so the argument goes, must be grounded on more than the simple observation and non-observation of occurring associations and dissociations. In Dharmakīrti's technical vocabulary, the notions of identity (*tādātmya*) and causal generation (*tadutpatti*) thus come to represent two essential conditions on the basis of which we distinguish between theories of meaning and theories of reference. Whereas the truth of the former is contingent upon the semantic content of the sentence, the truth of the latter requires additional empirical knowledge of the causal relation that obtains between the designated objects (cf. Hayes 1988, 254; Arnold 2008, 421).

In order to establish the sort of evidence that can serve as a warrant for sound inference (and to rule out instances of erratic attribution of an essential connection between premises in an argument), Dharmakīrti provides various examples of things that are ordinarily thought of in conjunction: the act of speaking and passion, a living body and breathing, perceptual awareness and the senses, and the stock example of fire and smoke.

But this mode of understanding pragmatic reasoning must explain what sort of properties, whether observed or unobserved, in similar or dissimilar cases, can be counted as evidence for asserting a given thesis? Furthermore, it must also explain how such properties are ascertained. In the case of the act of speaking and passion, for instance, observation of their occurring association is just a case of erratic evidence, for at most the act of speaking can serve as ground for inferring the presence of a speech organ and a capacity to communicate, not of passion. In this example, we see Dharmakīrti indirectly rejecting the notion that speech requires passion – seen as an affliction – for its cause. Obviously, in delivering speeches, buddhas cannot be seen to act from passion or impulse (conditions that afflict only the unenlightened).

Given that observation of one occurring relation does not guarantee the same relation will obtain at a different place and time, how can one escape the risk that there may be unobserved instances to the contrary? For Dharmakīrti, appeal to rules of reasoning that best reflect the nature of causally efficient entities (that is, to the so-called natural relation between the properties of an inference) offers the best solution to this conundrum. As he explains, one cannot infer from a cause to its effect, or from a causal totality (*kāraṇasāmagrī*) to an effect, because there is always the chance of impending factors preventing the arising of the given effect. One can infer, however, from the effect to the cause, though only in a restricted case. Thus, "only an immediate effect enables the inference of a cause, because it is dependent on it" (*Auto-Commentary* to *Commentary on the Sources of Knowledge* (*Pramāṇavārttika-svavṛtti*), II 12.4; In Pandeya 1989). In this effort to tie reason to causal explanation (and thus view reasons as causes of a certain type), we see the Buddhist epistemologist's concern with maximizing our predictive capacity to make sound inferences, the ultimate goal of which is achieving desired ends.

We have now come full circle in our account of how specific concerns with identifying and formulating principles of reason come to inform the Buddhist epistemological relation between reason and experience. What does it mean, then, to say that there is a natural relation between the properties of an inference, or that the truth of the major premise can be known by perception? It is to put forth a particular view of perception – one that regards empirical awareness as a form of embodied action. To perceive is to understand how we cope with the environment we inhabit.

Conclusion: Knowledge as Enactive Transformation

All Indian Buddhist philosophers argue in one way or another for preserving the canonical teachings as conveying a vision of reality that requires constant actualization through a dynamic praxis of interpretation and enactment. This praxis is essentially epistemic in character, marking a gradual progression from the act of listening to, and reflecting upon, a set of statements, to actualizing their significance in an enactive manner. Such dynamic integration of disciplined observation and rational deliberation provides both a pragmatic context and the phenomenological orientation necessary in order to map out the cognitive domain. It is this praxis that leads a representative thinker such as Dharmakīrti to claim that the Buddha, whose view he and his successors claim to propound, is a true embodiment of the sources of knowledge. Thus, far from seeing a tension between empirical scrutiny and the exercise of reason, the Buddhist epistemological enterprise positions itself not merely as a dialogical-disputational method for avoiding unwarranted beliefs, but as a practice aimed at achieving concrete, pragmatic ends. As Dharmakīrti reminds his fellow Buddhists, the successful accomplishment of any human goal is wholly dependent on having correct knowledge.

Appealing to the Buddha's extraordinary cognitive abilities, therefore, is a case not of the abdication of reason in the face of authority, but of showcasing the embodied and enactive character of enlightened knowledge. Against the dialectical method of Nāgārjuna, whose ultimate aim is the relinquishing of all views, the Buddhist epistemologists emphasize the critical and positive role of perspicacious reasoning. Indeed, with Dignāga, Dharmakīrti, and their successors, epistemology comes to be regarded as an effective discipline that brings about real results. This is a new epistemology, one that is constrained by the phenomenology of first-person experience rather than by *a priori* notions about the operations of reason or metaphysical assumptions about the nature of reality.

References

Arnold, Dan (2008). Transcendental Arguments and Practical Reason in Indian Philosophy. In *Argumentation* 22, 135–47.

Aung, S. Z., and Rhys Davids, C. A. F. (1915). *Points of Controversy, or, Subjects of Discourse: Being a Translation of the Kathāvatthu from the Abhidhammapiṭaka*. PTS translation series no. 5. London: Luzac.

Bell, John (2001). Pragmatic Reasoning: Pragmatic Semantics and Semantic Pragmatics. In *Modeling and Using Context: Proceedings of the Third International and Interdisciplinary Conference*. Berlin: Springer, 45–58.

Bochenski, J. M. (1961). *A History of Formal Logic*. Notre Dame, IN: University of Notre Dame Press.

Collins, Steven (1982). *Selfless Persons: Imagery and Thought in Theravāda Buddhism*. Cambridge: Cambridge University Press.

Dreyfus, Georges (1997). *Recognizing Reality: Dharmakīrti's Philosophy and its Tibetan Interpretations*. Albany: State University of New York Press.

Eckel, Malcolm D. (2008). *Bhāviveka and His Buddhist Opponents*. Cambridge, MA: Harvard University Press.

Fodor, Jerry A. (1991). The Dogma that Didn't Bark (A Fragment of a Naturalized Epistemology). In *Mind* 100, 201–20.

Ganeri, Jonardon (2001). Argumentation, Dialogue, and the *Kathāvatthu*. In *Journal of Indian Philosophy* 29, 485–93.

Garfield, Jay L. (2008). Turning a Madhyamaka Trick: Reply to Huntington. In *Journal of Indian Philosophy* 36, 507–27.

Hattori, Masaaki (1968). *Dignāga, On Perception*. Cambridge, MA: Harvard University Press,.

Hayes, Richard (1988). *Dignāga on the Interpretation of Signs*. Dordrecht: Kluwer Academic.

Huebner, B., Sarkissian, H., and Bruno, M. (2010). What Does the Nation of China think about Phenomenal States? In *European Review of Philosophy* 1, 225–43.

Huntington, C. (2007). The Nature of the Mādhyamika Trick. In *Journal of Indian Philosophy* 35, 103–31.

Iyer, K. A. Subramania (1969). *Bhartṛhari: A Study of the Vākyapadīya in the Light of the Ancient Commentaries*. Poona: Deccan College Postgraduate and Research Institute.

Jayatilleke, K. N. (1963). *Early Buddhist Theory of Knowledge*. London: George Allen & Unwin.

Kapstein, Matthew (1988). Mi-pham's Theory of Interpretation. In *Buddhist Hermeneutics*. Ed. Donald S. Lopez. Honolulu: University of Hawai'i Press, 149–74.

Katsura, Shoryu (2007). How Did Buddhists Prove Something? The Nature of Buddhist Logic. In *Pacific World Journal* 3(9), 63–84.

Machery, E., Mallon, R., Nichols, S., and Stich, S. (2004). Semantics, Cross-Cultural Style. In *Cognition* 92, B1–B12.

Matilal, Bimal K. (1998). *The Character of Logic in India*. Ed. J. Ganeri and H. Tiwari. Oxford: Oxford University Press.

Pandeya, Ram Chandra (ed.) (1989). *The Pramāṇavārttikam of Ācārya Dharmakīrti with The Commentaries "Svopajñavṛtti" of the Author and "Pramāṇavārttikavṛtti" of Manorathanandin*. Delhi: Motilal Banarsidass.

Ruegg, David S. (1981). *The Literature of the Madhyamaka School of Philosophy in India*. Wiesbaden: Otto Harrassowitz.

Schayer, S. (2001 [1933]) Studies in Indian Logic. Trans. Joerg Tuske. In *Indian Logic: A Reader*. Ed. J. Ganeri. London: Curzon Press; orig. pubd as Altindische Antizipationen der Aussagenlogik. In *Bulletin International de l'Academie Polonaise des Sciences et des Lettres*, classe de philologies, 90–6.

Siderits, Mark (1988). Nāgārjuna as Anti-Realist. In *Journal of Indian Philosophy* 16, 311–25.

Siderits, Mark (2003). *Personal Identity and Buddhist Philosophy*. Aldershot: Ashgate.

Tatia, Nathman (1976). *Abhidharmasamuccaya-bhāṣyaṃ*. Patna: K. P Jayaswal Research Institute.

Tola, Ferdando, and Dragonetti, Carmen (1995). *Nāgārjuna's Refutation of Logic*. Delhi: Matilal Banarsidass.

Weinberg, J., Nichols, S., and Stich, S. (2001). Normativity and Epistemic Intuitions. In *Philosophical Topics* 29, 429–60.

Westerhoff, Jan (2009). *Nāgārjuna's Madhyamaka: A Philosophical Introduction*. New York: Oxford University Press.

16

The Three Truths in Tiantai Buddhism

BROOK ZIPORYN

The idea that the term "truth" is a univocal descriptor, that there is one consistent meaning of the word "truth," that when propositions are described as "true" this is meant always in a single unambiguous sense, and that therefore all true propositions must be consistent with one another, such that there are no self-contradictions in the total body of truths – let's call this the "One Truth" Position. Such seems to be the default assumption of mainstream European philosophy and religion, indeed one that is assumed to be essential to preventing utter chaos, both epistemologically and ethically.[1]

A very different position appears in the Buddhist tradition, where we find, from a very early period, many ways of distinguishing and admitting multiple forms of validity. This can be seen clearly already in the Parable of the Raft and in the Abidhammic distinction between *nītattha* (statements which are to be taken literally) and *neyyattha* (statements which must be interpreted indirectly, or not at face value). In Mahayana Buddhism, following Nāgārjuna, this tendency reaches full flowering in the distinction between *samvritti satya* and *paramārtha satya* – respectively, "conventional" and "ultimate" truths – constituting the so-called Two Truths theory. All Mahayana schools adopt some version of the Two Truths theory, with one exception: the Tiantai school, which alone among all Buddhist schools moves from the *Two Truths* epistemology to a *Three Truths* model of truth. This has enormous consequences, which it is our purpose in this chapter to explore.

The Buddhist tendency to distinguish multiple forms of legitimacy can be traced in part to the purely pragmatic (i.e., soteriological) orientation of the Buddhist tradition, which proclaims openly that its one and only purpose is *to end suffering*. This premise allows all elements in the tradition, both propositions and procedures, to be evaluated in terms of their instrumental value towards achieving this goal. Buddhism is, in other words, completely *pragmatic* in its approach to truth. The question of what kinds of statements may count as *legitimate* is the only standard of "truth" in Buddhism, the

---

A Companion to Buddhist Philosophy, First Edition. Edited by Steven M. Emmanuel.

only sense in which *any* proposition can be said to be "true," and this legitimacy is measured solely in terms of effectiveness in furthering the overriding Buddhist soteriological aims. Every statement and every practice is justified *solely* in terms of its utility for the goal of *diminishing suffering*. Those statements are *valid* which are conducive to ending suffering, and those actions are *good* which are conducive to ending suffering. "True" here does not mean "accurately describing in words an extra-verbal reality": it means only "valid in the sense of conducive to behaviors that lead to the end of suffering."

We may understand this in terms of the Parable of the Raft, attested already in the earliest written stratum of the tradition: what helps one get across is good, is useful, is valid, is to be clung to for the duration of one's journey. Strictly speaking, whatever may be on the other shore is neither "true" nor "untrue," neither "good" nor "bad"; all such terms pertain only to the intermediate realm of what is relevant for the goal of ending suffering – and, of course, this means mainly Buddhist doctrines and practices. True is different from false, as clinging to the raft is different from sinking. But this has nothing to do with contradiction or with the description of facts divorced from specific courses of action and the human motivations that endorse them;[2] it has to do with utility in the goal of ending suffering, which is accomplished by ending attachment to desire and definitive views about reality.

When this model develops beyond in the hands of Nāgārjuna to the full-fledged Two Truths model, we have the same structure expanded and articulated with greater precision. Here, too, "conduciveness to ending suffering" is the *sole* criterion for "truth." But, under conventional truth, Nāgārjuna includes two things: ordinary speech (terms such as "I," "you," "cause," "effect," "world," "time," "entities," etc.) and specifically Buddhist doctrines ("non-self," "nirvana," "suffering," "dependent co-arising," etc.). The criterion for including both of these under the heading of "truth" is exactly the same: *not* that they correspond to an external reality or can be consistently unpacked without self-contradiction, but that speaking and acting in accordance with them is conducive to the ending of suffering. Without ordinary language, it is impossible to give instructions on how to end suffering, to point out the problem of suffering, to point out the doctrines and practices of Buddhism. Hence Nāgārjuna tells us (MMK.18.6) that the Buddha preached both self (ordinary speech) and non-self (Buddhist teachings), both for the same reason: they are necessary for giving instructions on how to end suffering and are skillfully deployed in such a way as to lead one to do so.

Both of these belong to conventional truth, which is "truth" only in that it leads beyond itself to "ultimate truth." Ultimate truth cannot be spoken or conceptualized. In fact it is not a "truth" at all, in the usual sense of some true proposition providing cognitive information about the world. The designation "truth" is just a placeholder indicating the experience of the end of suffering itself, liberation of mind. Liberation of mind is not allegiance to any picture of how the world is. In fact, it is described only negatively, precisely as the lack of any identifiable predicates and of the holding of any views about how the world is at all. The possibility of a definitive right view about reality, the bare "being so" of any state of affairs, disappears together with the belief in self-nature (*svabhāva*). For "being-so" would have to be something that is warranted by the state of affairs itself, acting as a cause which has efficacy in creating and ensuring this "being so" by its own power, and this is just what the most basic of all Buddhist ideas, the doctrine of dependent co-arising, and the concomitant denial of self-nature, excludes. The state of affairs would be the cause; the fact that the state of affairs is thus and so, is unambiguously one way or another, would be the effect – a one-to-one causality that is definitely excluded by all Buddhist theory from the Abidhamma on. "This cup is red" means "this cup alone is the cause of the redness attributed to the cup." This is what it would mean to have a "self-nature" – i.e., a self-determining essence. But every view about "the way things are," on any level of abstraction, means that it is the self-determining essence for the world to be this way and no other. The essence alone acts as a cause that makes certain determinations and not others the case. Emptiness of self-nature, then, really means simply *ontological ambiguity*: not the usual epistemological ambiguity, where we assume that *in itself* each thing is simply what it is, but our perception of it is vague or admits of multiple readings; rather, *ontological* ambiguity, where any possible something is in and of itself incapable of simply being one way or another to the exclusion of other ways – to be is to be ambiguous. Definitive views about reality – that any given thing simply *is* one way or another, is this or that, in isolation from a relation to other things – are shown to be incoherent and actually meaningless.

Nāgārjuna also tells us that the teaching of emptiness is dangerous if grasped wrongly, like a snake (MMK.24.11). "Grasped wrongly" seems to mean "taken as a definitive view about what is so," as if "empty" were a property that belongs to things in a single-cause, self-nature way. Emptiness is also empty, and those who cling to the view of emptiness are declared incurable. The absence of self-determining essence should not itself be viewed as a self-determining essence. This means that the view that things are "empty," and all propositions to that effect, is only the highest (i.e., most powerfully effective) conventional truth. Ultimate truth is itself not a description of any facts, and regarded as a description it is merely a conventional truth. Ultimate truth is neither "emptiness" nor "not-emptiness." These are, as they say, mere "concepts." But a concept is precisely what we normally call a *truth*: a proposition about what predicates *actually, unambiguously, in all contexts, from all perspectives*, apply to a particular entity – the essence or marks of that thing, which it alone, simply by being what it is, makes it so. This is what "objective" means: that things are so *on their own*, without the participation of some *other*, some observer, some perspective. Clinging to emptiness, *attachment* to emptiness, means no more and no less than *regarding emptiness as objectively true*. "Clinging" and "assuming something to be objectively true" are synonyms.

There is of course an obvious self-contradiction *here*, the usual relativism paradox: is it *true* that there is no truth? The answer is that it is true only in the way in which truth is defined in Buddhism: saying so is conducive to the liberation of living beings from suffering. Contradiction is no objection to this kind of truth. Another contradiction: is it *always* true that this way of talking and viewing is conducive to ending suffering? This is where, as we shall see shortly, Tiantai provides a further insight.

To understand this, we must be clear on the exact criterion for conventional truth. Conventional truth is what is conducive to the end of suffering. The end of suffering is the end of all statements and views. So conventional truth is precisely *those views that are conducive to ending all views*. Like the raft, they are self-transcending, and *this alone* is the *criterion* of what makes any statement *count* as a truth at all. If it did *not* contradict itself, it would not be a truth. That is, if, when taken literally and fully unpacked, it allowed one to continue to cling to it as a consistent statement about how the world really is, it would *ipso facto* not be a truth – i.e., a conventional truth, a statement or belief that leads to its own overcoming. And conventional truth is the only kind of truth that is describable or speakable *at all*. Hence, *only* those statements and beliefs that lead to their own self-cancellation are true. *Only* self-contradictions are true.

Note that, on this Two Truths theory, not all statements are included in conventional truth. What is excluded are cosmological theories, statements meant to be taken *literally* about how the world is, how the world began, what the world is made of. These are *not* conventional truths, much less ultimate truths, because they do *not* lead to their own self-overcoming, they do not encode their own demise. They claim to be literal representations of how the world really is, without qualification. Precisely because they do not contradict themselves, they cannot be truths. They are, for Nāgārjuna, just plain falsehoods or errors.

This changes decisively in Tiantai Buddhism, which takes its clue from Nāgārjuna, but as read through the lens of the *upāya* theory of the *Lotus Sūtra*. Simply stated, if we assume Nāgārjuna's model of truth, the distinction between the *three* categories of his Two Truth system falls apart. Again, those three are: (1) *just plain false* statements, such as the metaphysical and theological-religious theories of non-Buddhists, absolutist claims of science, etc. – all theory, in short, which is not inherently self-transcending; (2) conventional truths such as untheorized common-sensical everyday language, which says "I" and "you" and "cause and effect" but without claiming a theory or systematic objective worldview to unpack them consistently, fuzzy around the edges; and (3) further conventional truths of Buddhist rhetoric, including the concept of emptiness. Above and beyond all of these is ultimate truth, which has no cognitive content at all, but is determined precisely as the leaving behind of all conventional truth. The criterion of truth, recall, was "what is conducive to liberation from suffering" – which means, what will, if given full play, contradict and cancel itself, serving as a vehicle by which to pass beyond itself, like a raft. So (2) and (3) are both truths (conventional truth), while (1) is just false. Ultimate truth, on the other hand, *is* the end of suffering, and thus also given the honorific name of truth, though it has no propositional content. The negation of all the propositional content of the other categories, falsehood and conventional truth, is not to be viewed as a propositional content in its own right. So it stands for Nāgārjuna (on most but not all readings of MMK.18.6).

In Tiantai, however, this same criterion of truth is now applied across the board. Category 1 also *can* serve as a raft – and, in fact, all purported metaphysical systems, while claiming to arrive at a consistent, non-self-contradictory complete objective view of the universe, can *all* be shown to fail *in their own terms*: they can be shown to contradict themselves when taken absolutely seriously and when their key theoretical terms are absolutized. Even purportedly unsurpassable absolute claims are truths, for precisely their claims to absoluteness is what undermines their absoluteness and allows them to serve as a raft beyond themselves. Tiantai theory uses Nāgārjuna's method to perform these instances of *reductio ad absurdum* on all existing theories. But the demonstration that they contradict themselves is not meant to show that they are false; rather, it is precisely what shows that they are *true*! For "true," as we have seen, simply means "capable of leading beyond itself, capable of destroying itself, conducive to the move beyond all clinging to fixed views, conducive to ending suffering." When a metaphysical view is shown to involve contradictions, it is shown to be a conventional truth rather than a mere falsehood: it serves as a raft to the abandoning of views. Furthermore, categories (2) and (3) are also not *always* effective as rafts. There are infinite sentient beings with infinite differing needs, and in some circumstances one view will work (to transcend itself and all views) while in other circumstances others will work. Even "ordinary speech" and "emptiness" are not *always* true (for "true" means only "conducive to . . ."). All three categories *can* serve as rafts leading beyond themselves, while none of them *always* does so. So the buddhas preach both self and non-self, not because one is conventional and the other is ultimate truth (as MMK.18.6, might lend itself to being read, both pointing to the higher neither-self-nor-non-self of experienced ultimate truth): *both* are conventional truths, meaning that both can, in given circumstances, lead to the dropping of both views. Neither is intrinsically more true than the other (for to be "intrinsically" anything would be to have a self-nature). Hence we have the other enormous change in Tiantai: ultimate truth is no longer "beyond" conventional truth, no longer a "higher" truth. They are equal, and in fact the very idea of "ultimate truth" is itself a conventional truth. However, they are not only equal. The most radical Tiantai move is that conventional and ultimate truth are *identical*. They have *exactly the same content*. Whatever is conventional truth is also ultimate truth, and vice versa. Indeed, this is the only kind of truth there is.

This point is illustrated nicely in the interpretation of the story of the lost son from chapter 4 of the *Saddharmapundarikasūtra* (known in Chinese as *Miaofalianhuajing* and in English usually as *The Lotus Sūtra*), offered by Zhiyi, the founder of Tiantai Buddhism. *The Lotus Sūtra* has just announced that all the Buddha's disciples are bodhisattvas – buddhas-to-be, nascent buddhas – even those who are not aware of being so or in fact explicitly deny that they are so (namely the disciples, called Śrāvakas, of what is polemically called here the "Lesser Vehicle" – the teaching aimed at achieving arhatship, at transcending forever the suffering of the wheel of samsara, instead of remaining lifetime after lifetime in the world as bodhisattvas and eventually becoming buddhas, as is aspired to by the disciples of the "Great Vehicle," or "Mahayana"). In this story, Śāriputra offers a parable to explain the impact of this news for himself and his fellow Śrāvakas. Now that we have heard this *Lotus Sūtra*, which proclaims that all along, unbeknown to ourselves, we have been working towards buddhahood, he says, we realize that we are like a son who, while still a youth, had been separated from his father, went off on his own, and became lost. The father searches all over for him, but finally gives up in despair; he can find him nowhere. Instead he settles in a certain town and becomes very rich. Meanwhile the son has to fend for himself and lives hand to mouth in extreme poverty, taking whatever odd jobs come his way. In his wanderings, quite by chance, he eventually comes to the gate of his father's opulent mansion. He is greatly intimidated by the splendor of this palatial estate, seeing nothing there that seems remotely relatable to his own condition; this is someone as different from himself as imaginable, someone with whom he has nothing at all in common. Indeed, he fears this must be a king of some sort, a person of great authority and might who will force him into military service or corvée labor if he doesn't flee as quickly as possible. The father, instantly recognizing this broken impoverished man at the gate as his own long lost son, is overjoyed. He sends his servants to apprehend him – but the son is terrified and falls into a faint. Realizing that his son has forgotten his own identity and is in no condition to take in the news, he devises a "skillful means": the son is allowed to return to the poor part of town, and two ragged-looking messengers are sent, pretending to be searching randomly for cheap day laborers, paid at the minimum wage. This the son can accept; it accords with his own concept of himself and his worth. He takes the job, and works shoveling out manure for 20 years.

The father, of course, represents the Buddha. The son represents Śāriputra and the other Śrāvakas disciples. Though the text is a little vague on this point, it makes sense to assume that the father was not yet rich at the time of the estrangement: the Buddha and all sentient beings began together as sentient beings, bound by consanguinity, in the same state of samsara. During their separation, the father gets rich – the Buddha becomes enlightened. But his bond with all beings from before that time, as one deluded suffering being among them, remains. Shoveling the manure is a metaphor for the practice of the Śrāvaka path – cleaning out delusion, just trying to get pure, with no greater purpose or positive goal beyond that – a rather shocking critique of earlier Buddhism!

Sometimes the father himself dresses in ragged clothes, impersonating a foreman, and goads the son to work hard or compliments his diligence. Sometime later, the father tells the son that, because he's been such a good laborer, he's being promoted to a "house" servant, no longer having to labor in the muck.

The irony here, of course, is that the real reason the son gets promoted has nothing to do with the quality of his work. He was a blood son from the beginning; he is just gradually coming into his own patrimony. Similarly, the Śrāvakas think that their progress on the path is due to their good work, that they have attained something new, that their state of relative peace and small enlightenment is achieved by their practices; actually, it is a meager first taste of what was always already theirs, which they are only gradually getting mentally prepared to accept as their own.

In fact, the son is made treasurer of the estate. His job will be to oversee all the business transactions, to know exactly what the father owns, and all his expenditures and income.

This is a metaphor for the Śrāvakas' knowledge of the Bodhisattva Way and the glory of the buddhas, and even their retelling of it to others: they were "counting someone else's treasure," could enumerate all these qualities, but thought that it all pertained to another, not realizing they were enumerating things about themselves, about their own possessions, their own destiny.

The father tells his trusty accountant that he is "like a son" to him – just as the Buddha "metaphorically" describes his students as his children. But then, on his deathbed, the father calls a meeting of all sorts of kings and dignitaries and officially announces the truth: this man is my own blood son, and always has been. All that I have, I leave to him: all these treasures he's been counting belong to him! And always have!

The key point to note here, in the context of our present discussion, is, as Zhiyi points out, that the status of the "skillful means" is configured here very differently than it is in the Two Truths schema of emptiness theory, the "raft" model, where the means are transcended and discarded once the goal is reached. The resources of the estate are what the father uses as a skillful means to draw his son to the final recognition of his own status, to his final enlightenment – the servants, the buildings, the treasury. But these are not abandoned when the son finally does come into his inheritance. On the contrary, these *are* the inheritance! This means that what one is enlightened to when one is enlightened is not the dropping away of all skillful means, the letting go of the raft, the transcendence of all determinate phenomenal concepts, ideas, practices, forms. Rather, these things are the very content of enlightenment. Enlightenment is not the renunciation of skillful means. Enlightenment is the *mastery* of all skillful means, the integration of skillful means, the more thorough possession of them, rather than the discarding or elimination of them. Conventional truth is not what you renounce when you reach ultimate truth, as in the parable of the raft and the Two Truths theory. Conventional truth is what you *get* when you reach ultimate truth. The content of the two is the same. Ultimate truth is simply a name for the totality of conventional truths and the virtuosic mastery of being able to move unobstructed from one conventional truth to another, as the situation demands, to the comprehension of the way they fit together or can function together, or the way in which they are each, as it were, "versions" of the other. Ultimate truth is the non-obstruction between conventional truths, the fact that they all interpenetrate, that in their non-absoluteness each is simply a different way of saying what the others say. Ultimate truth is the free flow of conventional truths, their co-presence in spite of their apparent oppositeness (e.g., you are a worker, you are a son).

For Tiantai, "conventional truth" means "anything that *can* be conducive to the elimination of suffering – which is clinging, attachment, desire, and fixed views of objectivity." Not "will" or "must," but "can." For no idea, not even "emptiness," *always* conduces thereto. It is situational, and this is the *sole* criterion and meaning of truth. Now, given this definition, anything and everything is a conventional truth: anything *can*, under the right conditions, dislodge an attachment and lead to less suffering. Nothing always does so, but everything, without exception, in the right context, can do so. Everything, without exception, is therefore a conventional truth. But conventional truth, as we just saw, is in Tiantai not merely a means to ultimate truth, but is ultimate truth itself. Ultimate truth is just the coexistence and maximally skillful application of any and all conventional truths. Since everything is conventional truth, everything is ultimate truth. But they are ultimate truth because of their interpenetration and mutual non-obstruction, because what would be mutually exclusive if taken as "truths," in the sense of "corresponding to how things really are *simpliciter*, independently of any other factors, including experiencers of them as such," are now seen to be true in the sense of "conducive to liberation from suffering sometimes." This renders their coexistence not only possible but *necessary* for ultimate truth. Ultimate truth *is* the co-presence of what would, on the naïve "objective" definition of truth, be contradictory (self/non-self, son/worker, suffering/bliss, permanence/impermanence, samsara/nirvana, etc.), the *interchangeability* of the two apparently contradictory forms of conventional truth. This is the Mean, the Center – the Third Truth.

In the Tiantai "Three Truths" theory, in contrast to the Two Truths model, instead of concluding that every particular view and proposition and thing is ultimately false, we conclude that all is, ultimately, true. Every possible view is equally a truth. There is no longer a hierarchy between the levels and no category of plain falsehood. Zhiyi, the *de facto* founder of the Tiantai school, teases out the transition from Two to Three Truths in his *Fahuaxuanyi* by delineating seven distinct modes of understanding the Two Truths model:

1 The Conventional Truth is that there exist real entities.
The Ultimate Truth is [what is revealed when] these real entities cease to exist.

2 The Conventional Truth is that all that exists is illusory.
The Ultimate Truth is that these illusory existences are [already] devoid of a self-determining essence [i.e., "empty"].

3 The Conventional Truth is that all that exists is illusory.
The Ultimate Truth is that these illusory existences are at once both devoid of self-determining essence and not devoid of self-determining essence ["empty and non-empty"].

4 The Conventional Truth is that all that exists is illusory.
The Ultimate Truth is that these illusory existences are all at once both devoid of self-determining essence and not devoid of self-determining essence at once, and that for something to be at once both devoid and not devoid of self-determining essence is to have all possible phenomena converge into [and discoverable within] it.

5 The Conventional Truth is that all that exists is illusory and that all these illusory existences are devoid of self-determining essence.
The Ultimate Truth is that all this illusory existence is neither devoid of self-determining essence nor existent as some particular essence.

6 The Conventional Truth is that all that exists is illusory and that all these illusory existences are devoid of self-determining essence.
The Ultimate Truth is that all this illusory existence is neither devoid of self-determining essence nor existent as some particular essence, and that for something to be neither devoid of self-determining essence nor as some particular essence is to have all possible phenomena converge into [and discoverable within] it.

7 The Conventional Truth is that all that exists as some particular essence is illusory and that all these illusory existences are devoid of self-determining essence.
The Ultimate Truth is that all this illusory existence is neither devoid of self-determining essence nor existent as some particular essence, and that for something to be devoid of self-determining essence is to have all phenomena converge into [and findable within] it; and that for something to exist as some particular essence is to have all phenomena converge into [and findable within] it; and that for something to be neither devoid of self-determining essence nor existent as some particular essence is to have all phenomena converge into [and findable within] it.[3]

From number 4 onwards, we find two new ideas being added to the traditional Two Truths. First is the idea of a third thing which is neither one extreme nor the other, neither an affirmation nor a negation of how things appear within a particular conventional framework, or which is both simultaneously: a "neither/nor" or "both/and" judgment on what had previously been opposed as conventional and ultimate truth (and thus as means and ends) in the previous levels. This is the Third Truth, which in Tiantai is called "the Center" or "Middle." And second is the idea that somehow this implies that "all possible phenomena converge into [and are discoverable within] something": first this "Center" alone, but finally, in the seventh level, as in the mature Tiantai Three Truth theory, in *all three* of the other determinations, and indeed in all determinations without exception. This is the derivation of the idea of mutual penetration and interfusion, the idea that all possible entities interpervade that is so distinctive to the Tiantai and Huayan schools of Chinese Buddhism.

The Center is said to denote "the identity" between conventional truth and ultimate truth – the idea that they are synonyms, that "conventional" and "empty" are alternate words for one and the same meaning. But this is a peculiar type of "sameness," and we cannot understand in what sense this sameness implies "all possible entities converge into and are findable in" the Center, the second of the new ideas in Tiantai Three Truths theory, unless we understand in just what sense these two are "the same." This peculiar mode of sameness is explained in the Tiantai doctrine of "opening the provisional to reveal the real" (開權顯實 *kaiquan xianshi*). This is a means of further specifying the relation between local coherence and global incoherence, illustrating the way in which these are not only synonymous but also irrevocably opposed, and indeed identical only by means of their opposition. Provisional truth is the antecedent, the premise, and indeed in a distinctive sense the *cause* of ultimate truth, but only because it is the strict exclusion of ultimate truth.

The clearest way to explain this structure is to compare it to the contrasting relation between the setup and the punch line of a joke. To use a suitably silly example:

Setup: It takes money to make money.
Punch line: Because you have to copy it really exactly.

Let's talk about that structure. When I said, "It takes money to make money," it seemed as if, and it was interpreted as, a serious remark, a real piece of information, perhaps about investment strategies or the like. It had the quality of seriousness, of factuality, of non-ironic information. It does not strike anyone as funny; there is nothing funny about that statement. But, when the punch line comes, retrospectively, that setup is funny. That setup is funny because it has been recontextualized by the pun on the word "make," which is made to have more than one identity when put into a new context.

The interesting thing here, most closely relevant to relation of identity between conventional and ultimate in the Tiantai Three Truths, is that it is precisely by *not* being funny that the setup was funny. In other words, if it were already funny, if you didn't take it seriously for at least a moment, the contrast between the two different meanings of this thing could never have clashed in the way that is necessary to make the laughter, to create the actual effect of humorousness. We have a setup, which is serious, and a punch line, which is funny, but, when you look back at the setup from the vantage point of having heard the punch line, *that setup is also funny*. After all, we don't say that just the punch line is funny. We say the whole joke is funny. The setup is funny, however, in the very strange mode of "not being funny yet." It is only funny because it wasn't funny. This is the sense in which the Third Truth, the Mean, reveals the "identity" between provisional positing and emptiness. Provisional positing *is* emptiness only inasmuch as it is the very opposite of emptiness, the temporary exclusion of emptiness. It is by being non-empty (i.e., something in particular) that it is emptiness (i.e., devoid of any unambiguous or unconditionally self-determining self-nature). It is only because it is locally coherent that it is globally incoherent. Its global incoherence is present *as* local coherence, just as humor is present in the deadpan setup *as* seriousness. This same form of "identity" – really neither identity nor difference, or both identity and difference – then applies at the meta-level between the Center itself and the other Two Truths: they "are" the Center precisely because they are not the Center, because they are the two opposed extremes.

The same structure is applied in the Tiantai reading of *The Lotus Sūtra*. You're enlightened! That is what Mahayana Buddhism says – everyone is enlightened! Everybody is a buddha! But the way in which you are a buddha is the way in which the setup of a joke is funny: you are a buddha precisely by *not* being a buddha. By desiring and struggling to become something you are not – whether buddhahood or something else – but in addition by revisualizing or recontextualizing or expanding awareness of that struggle, the details of dealing with conditions and suffering which constitute that struggle are not just a means to buddhahood, they are buddhahood itself. They are themselves buddhahood qua the life of a sentient being, expressing itself in the form of the life of a sentient being, as the funniness of a joke is expressed in, present in, the serious unfunniness of its setup.

The "provisional," conventional truth, local coherence, is the setup. The "ultimate truth," emptiness, global incoherence, ontological ambiguity, is the punch line. What is important here is to preserve *both* the contrast between the two *and* their ultimate identity in sharing the quality of humorousness that belongs to every atom of the joke considered as a whole, once the punch line has been revealed. The setup is serious, while the punch line is funny. The funniness of the punch line depends on the seriousness of the setup and on the contrast and difference between the two. However, once the punch line has occurred, it is also the case that the setup is, retrospectively, funny. This also means that the original contrast between the two is both preserved and annulled: neither funniness nor seriousness means the same thing after the punch line dawns, for their original meanings depended on the mutually exclusive nature of their defining contrast. Is the setup serious or funny? It is both: it is funny *as* serious and serious *as* funny. Is the punch line serious or funny? It is both, but in an interestingly different way. It is obviously funny, but is it also serious? Yes. Why? Because now that the setup has occurred, both "funny" and "serious" have different meanings. Originally, we thought that "funny" meant "what is laughed at when heard," or something like that, and "serious" meant "what gives me non-funny information," or something similar. But now we see that "funny" can also mean: "What I take to be serious, what I am *not* laughing about, what I am earnestly considering, or crying over, or bewailing even." But this means also that "serious" means "what can turn out to be either funny or serious." So both "funny" and "serious" now both mean "funny-and-serious, what can appear as both funny and serious." Each is now a center that subsumes the other; they are intersubsumptive. As a consequence, the old pragmatic standard of truth is applied more liberally here: all claims, statements, and positions are true in the sense that all *can*, if properly recontextualized, lead to liberation – which is to say, to their own self-overcoming. Conversely, none will lead to liberation if not properly contextualized.

We can restate the above somewhat more formulaically as follows.

Every phenomenal object is a coherence: that is, it is a joining (cohering) of disparate elements – (1) the factors that comprise it, its internal parts, or (2) its temporal antecedents, or (3) its contrasting conceptual contexts (i.e., its qualitative contrast to whatever it is "not," which is regarded as essential to its determination as this particular entity). Context and content are in the same boat on this view, in that, for this object to appear phenomenally – to be "coherent" or legible, discernible – requires the coming together of multiple factors: figure and ground, elements in a structure, causal conditions. What is crucial here is that these factors are heterogeneous and differ phenomenally in some discernible way from the object they come to constitute.

Every coherence is a local coherence: it remains coherent as such and such only within a limited horizon of relevance. That is, its legibility depends on the fixing of a certain scale, frame, or focal orientation; its identity as this precise thing depends phenomenally on restricting the ways in which it is viewed or the number of other factors which are viewed in tandem with it.

Every local coherence is globally incoherent. When all contexts are taken into account at once, and all applications and aspects are brought to bear, the original coherence vanishes into ambiguity.

Every globally incoherent local coherence subsumes all other local coherences.

Every subsuming is an intersubsumption. Each entity is readable as every other entity, as part of every other entity, and as the whole that subsumes all other entities as its parts. Each entity is identifiable, ontologically ambiguous, and all-pervaded as all-pervading.

In the story of the lost son from chapter 4 of *The Lotus Sūtra*, the "skillful means" (the resources of the father's estate) were not just what gets the son to the realization of enlightenment but also what he actually received when he got there. In the same way, "conventional truth" in Tiantai is not something to be left behind when we reach enlightenment, but rather what is obtained and mastered there. Moreover, nothing is left out of it – all possible statements, viewpoints, ideas, concepts, positions are conventional truths. The criterion is still the same: all things can be used as "skillful means" to lead to buddhahood, just as even Śrāvakahood and the behavior of Devadatta, the extreme rejection of the Buddha, were in fact causes and antecedents to the attainment of buddhahood. So now we have Three Truths, which are not a raft-like instrument to get beyond all statements and concepts, and a final higher truth that allows us to have no biased and particular view of things, but rather three true ways of viewing any particular thing. However you may be viewing a particular part of the world or the world as a whole, it is "conventionally" true. There are not just a few conventional truths but an infinite number of them, even when they are directly opposed and contradictory. So, in Two Truths theory, we would say that "This is a cup" is conventionally true and that "This cup is empty" is a higher conventional truth, which finally leads us to a direct inconceivable experience of the emptiness of this cup and the liberation from all suffering. If I were to point to this "cup" and say, "This is an elephant," however, that would not even be a conventional truth, because that is not how most people think of it. That would be a plain error. And if I said, "This is an expression of the will of God," that would also be an error, not even a conventional truth, since it tried to make a claim beyond that of conventional usage to an ultimate, universally applicable, absolute truth. But, in Tiantai Three Truths theory, it is just as true to say, "This is an elephant," as to say, "This is a cup." And neither of these is less true than saying, "This is empty," or indeed any less true than "experiencing" the emptiness of this cup/elephant.

In both cases, what I have is a *locally coherent* way of viewing this thing – it just means that it *looks that way* from some perspective, within some set of parameters, for some length of time. It doesn't matter any more whether those parameters are shared by the common sense of a particular community or speech group; all that matters is that it is possible to make it look that way, that it looks that way *from anywhere*, for *even one moment*. In Two Truths and emptiness theory, nothing is really true. In Tiantai Three Truths theory, *everything* is true. We don't need an extra "emptiness" outside of this locally coherent way of seeing things; emptiness just means that whatever is *locally* coherent is also, *ipso facto, globally in*coherent. That is, when all factors are taken into consideration, the original way any thing appears is no longer unambiguously present.

To understand this, consider the following. What is this symbol?

O

What is it now?

−1 −2 O 1 2

What is it now?

M
N
−1 −2 O 1 2
P
Q

When we looked at the original symbol together with only *one* context, it had a clear identity: it was the number zero. But when we added another context at the same time, the figure became ambiguous: it could now be read as either a zero or the letter O. As we keep adding more contexts, its identity becomes more and more ambiguous. And when we consider all things in the universe at the same time, the initial identities we assigned to them are supplemented by more and more ambiguity. Looking at just the single series of letters, it was a zero: this is local coherence. When I see this cup simply as a cup, I am doing the same thing: ignoring a lot of other factors, contexts, points of view, ways of viewing, and narrowing down the relevant factors to allow it to appear as a single unambiguous something: a cup. If I consider the molecules of which it is made, or the energy it expresses, or the uses to which it might be put in the context of various narratives, or its deep past and deep future, its "cupness" becomes ambiguous: it is simultaneously lots of other things, part of many different stories. It is a blip on the screen of energy transformations, or a murder weapon, or an art object, or a doorstop. The same is true of yourself, and your actions right now. They are unambiguous only to the extent that we narrow our vision around them. This is the meaning of emptiness in Tiantai: ontological ambiguity. The term "ambiguity" usually refers only to how we see things. We assume that, in themselves, all things are simply what they are; but we may have an unclear view of something; we can't *yet* tell if it's this or that. We assume that, at least in principle, it must be one or the other. The idea of emptiness is the idea that this is true "ontologically": that is, it pertains to the very being of things. To say they are empty does not mean they are a blank – for that would be a definite something. It means that they are, in themselves, *ambiguous*. Put another way, everything is *more* than it seems to be, or than it *can* seem to be, no matter from what angles it is seen, no matter how thoroughly it is known, no matter how comprehensive a sum of information is gathered about it. It has the character of being a "something" (a cup, a chair, an elephant), with a number of specifiable characteristics, but every "something," just to be there as something, has the additional characteristic of "moretoitivity" – of always overflowing whatever is determined about it, of being *more* than what can be seen from any angle.

This "more," however, does not leave the original "known" part unchanged. Rather, it recontextualizes it. We are always seeing the tip of an iceberg. But even the "tip" is no longer what we thought it was before we knew it was a tip *of* something more. Imagine that you come upon what looks like a white marble lying on the ground. You experience it as round, as small, as white, and immediately you construct a lived attitude towards it – something that can be picked up, rolled, played with, pocketed. But then you go to pick it up and find that it is stuck to the ground. You cannot lift it. You try to dig it out and find that it extends downwards, further than you can dig: it is the tip of a larger item. It appears to be a long rod or cylindrical pipe of some kind. But, as you dig further, you find that after about 5 inches of narrow thinness it starts to expand outwards; it is a spire on top of a cone. This cone expands outwards as you keep digging down. When you get about 20 feet down, the cone ends, embedded in a soft, scaly material. Then the earth rumbles and an enormous two-horned monster emerges from underground; it is 500 feet tall, and each of its horns is 20 feet high, with a long sharp tip. You had been digging out one of the horns. What you had seen as a marble on the ground was in fact the very tip of one of the horns. Now look again at that tip. You had experienced it as round. But it turns out it was not round at all: it is sharp. Yet it has not changed at all: you are still seeing what you saw. It is not white, either: the tip had looked white against the ground, but now, looking at the monster's horn as whole, you see it as a pattern of mostly green spots interspersed here and there with white: looked at as a whole, the horn, including its tip, looks green. Nor is it movable, pocketable, playwithable – it is rather dangerous, razor sharp, to be avoided. And yet nothing of what you saw was taken away: it was just supplemented with further information, with its larger context.

Tiantai views all things this way. To see something is to see "not-all" of it. We are always seeing a little fragment of the world, but every bit of the world is changed by the fact that it is a part of the world, is recontextualized by the rest of the world, by the rest of space and the rest of time. In fact, if we ever saw all, we would see nothing. For to see, to take something as "there," as "real," is to place it within a context, to contrast it to something outside of itself, something which is not it. To see all is to see nothing. If I were to say that the entire universe is "round," this would make no sense. This round would not be round: for round requires a non-round *outside it* to be round. It would have to be bordered by something to shape it into roundness, but the universe would also include that outside-the-roundness part. If I were to say the entire universe is sharp, this would also make no sense. This sharp would not be sharp; for sharp requires a non-sharp *outside it* to be sharp. To say the whole universe is sharp, then, means no more and no less than saying the whole universe is round. We can make no specific determinations about the whole, about the entire universe, for that outside of which nothing exists; for all particular specifications require a contrast to something outside of them. Everything we can say or think comes from the realm of the finite and cannot be applied to the infinite. But the Tiantai point is that we cannot speak of anything finite without also involving some determination of the Whole, of the infinite. If I were to say this thing is sharp, I would have to be assuming that "the whole universe is such that this thing is sharp." I cannot say that the whole universe cannot be "such that this marble is sharp" any more than the whole universe can be "sharp." But this also means I cannot say the whole universe is "such that this marble is not-sharp." Either is equally legitimate, either is equally illegitimate. What I can say, then, is that "this marble appears to be round, but round is such that it is always turning out also to be more than round, to be non-round, and vice versa. Roundness is moretoitive. Round and non-round intersubsume each other."

The Three Truths, then, are actually three different ways of looking at any object or state. Each implies the other two, and each is one way to describe the *whole* of that object, including its other two aspects. This cup is *a cup*: that is provisional truth, conventional truth, local coherence. This cup is *not a cup*: that is ultimate truth, its emptiness, its global incoherence. To be a cup is not to be a cup: that is its Centrality, its Non-duality, its Absoluteness. To be a cup is to be any other locally coherent thing or state: a non-cup, an elephant, a superhighway, a chair, perfect enlightenment: that is the further implication of Centrality, the intersubsumption of all coherences, the presence of all in and as each. This cup is all things, all possible ways of being, all universes, *as* this cup. You are the entire world and all states of all things seen from all possible angles *as* you.

Notes

1 Although quite a few European systems, beginning with Plato, admit the permissibility of a kind of "pious fraud" – the promulgation of doctrines and ideas that are not strictly true but which are of value for the education or control of masses of people who are unequipped to access philosophical truth – this is presented not, strictly speaking, as an alternate type of truth, but as falsehood which is nonetheless morally good to propagate in certain situations. It may be true that it is good to propagate this falsehood, but this is not the same as saying that this falsehood is itself a kind of truth.

2 It should be noted as well that the endeavor to end suffering is itself something one may choose to embark upon or not; Buddhism is good and true only to the extent that this is one's goal. It may be that all goals can be (not "must be") reduced to this goal – all human activity can be seen (not "must be seen") as various attempts to reduce suffering in one way or another. But this is different from asserting that something that is useful for this goal is true or good outside of the context of having adopted this goal explicitly.

3 Zhiyi, *Miaofalianhuajing xuan yi*, in *Taisho Tripitaka* [T] 33.702c.

17

"Spiritual Exercise" and Buddhist Epistemologists in India and Tibet

MATTHEW T. KAPSTEIN

I

Why do we practice philosophy? An ancient tradition in Western thought regards philosophical reflection as a necessary element in the quest for a life well lived. In contemporary European and American philosophy, however, the actual relationship between the concrete life of the individual and the abstract conceptual spheres in which philosophy most often stakes its claims is seen as a problematic one. If some, such as the French philosopher Vladimir Jankélévitch or the American Robert Nozick, have sought to affirm a role, albeit a modest one, for philosophy in their conceptions of the good life,[1] others, such as the historian of analytic philosophy Scott Soames, have preferred to remain circumspect in regard to philosophy's practical entailments. As Soames writes:

> In general, philosophy done in the analytic tradition aims at truth and knowledge, as opposed to moral or spiritual improvement. There is very little in the way of practical or inspirational guides in the art of living to be found, and very much in the way of philosophical theories that purport to reveal the truth about a given domain of inquiry. In general, the goal in analytic philosophy is to discover what is true, not to provide a useful recipe for living one's life.[2]

Although there is a fair consensus that Buddhism overall has always been very much concerned with the way in which we choose to live, whether or not this concern extends to Buddhist philosophy in all its departments has been much contested. Certainly, there are some philosophical currents within Buddhism – the Madhyamaka tradition of Nāgārjuna and his successors offers perhaps the most striking example – in which the underlying harmony of practical soteriology and philosophical reflection is entirely

A Companion to Buddhist Philosophy, First Edition. Edited by Steven M. Emmanuel.

evident: Madhyamaka thought seeks to guide us to insight into the relationship between appearance and reality, and holds, moreover, that this insight, when cultivated in contemplation in the course of the ethically disciplined life, proves to be liberating. Some of the greatest masterpieces of the Madhyamaka thinkers – works such as Candrakīrti's *Introduction to the Madhyamaka* (*Madhyamakāvatāra*) and Śāntideva's *Introduction to Enlightened Conduct* (*Bodhicaryāvatāra*) – explicity situate their philosophical concerns in the context of advancement on the Mahāyāna path.[3] There can be no doubt that, for these thinkers, among many others, philosophy was of interest primarily in so much as it contributed to progress towards enlightenment. The precise link between philosophical reason and contemplative insight was in these cases sometimes expressed in terms of three grades of wisdom, or discernment (*prajñā*): that born of audition (*śrutamayī*) – i.e., learning the Buddhist doctrine from one's teachers; that born of reasoned reflection (*cintāmayī*); and that born of the cultivation of insight through meditation (*bhāvanāmayī*). Madhyamaka thought regarded this sequence to represent the cause for the realization of the emptiness (*śūnyatā*) of all conditioned things, specifically described in the later tradition not as vacuity, but as "endowed with the excellence of all phenomenal forms" (*sarvākāravaropetā*).[4]

Despite the clear connections between philosophy and spiritual discipline we find in this case, when we turn our attention to those areas in which Buddhist philosophy has most insisted upon the rigorous investigation of knowledge and argument – the areas that most closely correspond with philosophical practice as we find it in the Anglo-American analytic tradition – some scholars maintain that, as Soames says of analytic philosophy, Buddhist philosophy offers "very little in the way of practical or inspirational guides . . . and very much in the way of philosophical theories that purport to reveal the truth about a given domain of inquiry." While not denying that Buddhist thinkers, particularly in India and Tibet, were often much concerned with the technical aspects of the analysis of truth and knowledge, in the present chapter I wish to suggest that their efforts in this regard were often nevertheless tied to the overarching Buddhist interest in the contours of the good life – that is, the life directed to realizing the peace, insight, and compassion whose highest exemplar was always considered to be the Buddha himself.

II

Throughout much of a millennium, from the fifth century until the decline of Indian Buddhism in the twelfth, one of the primary subjects in the curricula of the monastic universities was *pramāṇaśāstra*, the "science of the measure of knowledge," or "criteriology," to borrow the felicitous expression of Cardinal Mercier (1851–1926), a domain corresponding roughly to logic and epistemology taken together.[5] *Pramāṇaśāstra* – I will use *pramāṇa*, the "measure of knowledge," for short in what follows – embraces the investigation of the criteria of knowing, the means whereby knowledge is achieved, especially perception and inference, and also the practice of debate. Within these broad areas, topics such as universals and particulars, the logic of relations, and the theory of meaning were among the focal points of research. The achievements of Indian Buddhist thinkers with respect to these problems have been appreciated, at least among specialists, since the early twentieth century, when the Russian academician Theodore Stcherbatsky (1866–1942) published his monumental *Buddhist Logic*, the first major synthesis of learning in this field. Though it has been superseded over the past few decades with respect to many of the particulars it treats, and thanks to the recovery of numerous textual sources that were unavailable when Stcherbatsky wrote, our understanding of the general history and subject matter of the Buddhist *pramāṇa* tradition in India has not changed fundamentally since the revised and expanded English edition of Stcherbatsky's work first appeared in Leningrad in 1930.[6]

Among the outstanding questions about which only modest progress is to be seen in scholarship since Stcherbatsky's time is this: to what ends, given their religious commitment to the Buddha's teaching, did Indian Buddhist scholars devote so much attention to the ostensibly mundane philosophy of *pramāṇa*? The problem, as Stcherbatsky conceived of it, was clearly set out in the introduction to *Buddhist Logic*, in these words:

> In the intention of its promoters the system had apparently no special connection with Buddhism as a religion, i.e., as the teaching of a path towards Salvation. It claims to be the natural and general logic of the human understanding. However, it claims also to be critical. Entities whose existence is not sufficiently warranted by the laws of logic are mercilessly repudiated, and in this point Buddhist logic only keeps faithful to the ideas with which Buddhism started. . . . The ultimate aim of Buddhist logic is to explain the relation between a moving reality and the static constructions of thought.[7]

The tension that is in evidence here, between a description of "Buddhist logic" as a system that "had apparently no special connection with Buddhism as a religion" and one that is nevertheless "faithful to the ideas with which Buddhism started," remains in some sense part of Stcherbatsky's legacy to the field. But it is important to note that, though it is true that Stcherbatsky was eager to present Buddhist logic as broadly consistent with an early twentieth-century European vision of philosophical research as critical reason unbridled by the presuppositions of religion, this was certainly not the sole source of the tension we find in his words. For it is already intimated in the Indian sources themselves, and made fully explicit in Tibetan scholastic traditions that were among the main inheritors of Indian Buddhist philosophical learning (and of which Stcherbatsky was to an impressive extent aware). In fact, there were at least three major trends in relation to this problematic that we can identify within Buddhist textual traditions:

1. some maintained that, although *pramāṇa* did not embrace the whole of the spiritual path, it was nevertheless an essential component thereof – that is to say, it had at least a propædeutic role with respect to soteriology;
2. there were those who regarded *pramāṇa* as a simple organon, applicable in many spheres of human activity, but with no necessary connection with possibilities of spiritual growth; and
3. the sharpest critics held that the project of *pramāṇa* was fundamentally misguided, at best warranted in some narrowly defined, worldly contexts, but still either obstructive or altogether irrelevant in regard to spiritual development.[8]

Here, I would like to explore somewhat the elaboration of these alternatives, both in traditional Buddhist and in contemporary academic writings. Among the latter, something of a dispute has emerged in recent years, dividing those who, like the present writer, have proposed to explore the relevance of the late Pierre Hadot's interpretations of Hellenistic philosophy in terms of the concept of "spiritual exercise" for our investigations of Indian Buddhist thought, from those who have expressed reservations in regard to any such project.[9]

Hadot's discussion of philosophy as a spiritual exercise for the Stoics may be taken as a useful introduction to his approach:

> The Stoics . . . declared explicitly that philosophy . . . was an "exercise." In their view, philosophy did not consist in teaching an abstract theory – much less in the exegesis of texts – but rather in the art of living. It is a concrete attitude and determinate life-style, which engages the whole of existence. The philosophical act is not situated merely on the cognitive level, but on that of the self and of being. It is a progress which causes us to *be* more fully, and makes us better. It is a conversion which turns our entire life upside down, changing the life of the person who goes through it. It raises the individual from an inauthentic condition of life, darkened by unconsciousness and harassed by worry, to an authentic state of life, in which he attains self-consciousness, an exact vision of the world, inner peace, and freedom.[10]

In short, to adopt a way of speaking that is more customary in the study of religion than it is in contemporary philosophy, Hadot directs us to envision philosophy itself in this context as a soteriological practice.

In the study of Buddhism, by contrast, the overall soteriological orientations of the tradition are generally recognized and taken for granted; what has proven more difficult is to investigate the relation between its philosophical and soteriological dimensions. Certainly, there are aspects of Hadot's description of Stoic philosophical practice that do not at all fit the Buddhist case: Buddhist traditions in India and Tibet, for instance, were always deeply concerned with the exegesis of texts. But at the same time, as was true for the Stoics and other Hellenistic schools, the prerequisite of a "determinate life style" provided the ineluctable foundation for all philosophical education: Buddhist philosophy was typically the domain solely of novices and fully ordained monks living and studying in monastic colleges, and occasionally, too, for householder scholars who had received the Buddhist layman's ordination.[11] And, as we have suggested above in referring to the three degrees of wisdom, some schools of Buddhist philosophy, much like Hadot's Stoics, sought to raise "the individual from an inauthentic condition of life [to] an exact vision of the world, inner peace, and freedom."

But how is the study of *pramāṇa* – the study of logic, epistemology, and the rules of debate – to be squared with this perspective?

III

The Buddhist discipline of *pramāṇaśāstra* was in some respects a response to the rise, within non-Buddhist Indian traditions, of the specialized domain of Nyāya, both as a general field embracing epistemology and debate and as a distinct Brahmanical school of thought, staking its claims on its particular mastery of this area.[12] But, at the same time, Buddhists were interested in debate practice almost from the beginnings of the Buddhist order, so that the later *pramāṇa* tradition was also in part an outgrowth of important early trends within Buddhism itself.

Indeed, the Buddha is depicted as having participated on some occasions in the ancient Indian custom of holding debates among rival sages and teachers in the royal court, success in which might guarantee the sovereign's protection and patronage, perhaps even his conversion. A scripture inspired by one such debate, preserved in the Pāli Buddhist canon under the title *Fruits of the Homeless Life* (*Sāmaññaphala Sutta*), provides capsule summaries of the discourses of six of the Buddha's rivals, who are depicted as embracing the extremes of determinism or skepticism, and is regarded as an important source for the study of the early history of Indian thought.[13]

Later, following the Buddha's passing, his successors took to debating among themselves, in their attempt to find reasoned means to settle their differences concerning the understanding of his doctrine. Several early texts present themselves as transcripts of Buddhist intramural debates that were said to have been sponsored by the famed emperor Aśoka (reigned 269–232 BCE) and, though they were no doubt set down in the form in which they have been preserved some centuries following the events they report, they clearly demonstrate a close attention to rule-governed principles of argument.[14] The earliest Buddhist writings that deal explicitly with the rules of debate are known from the writings of the Yogācāra school and belong to the late fourth and early fifth centuries CE.[15] This was the matrix from which *pramāṇa* arose, so that early Yogācāra attitudes with respect to debate practice and allied disciplines offer important evidence in regard to any putative relationship between these disciplines and properly spiritual concerns.

A major Yogācāra proof-text cited by those who argue for the clear separation of *pramāṇa* from Buddhist religious practice is the *Ornament of the Mahāyāna Scriptures* (*Mahāyānasūtrālaṃkāra*), a fourth-century treatise on the path of Mahāyāna Buddhism that, in a verse (11.60) consecrated to the classification of the departments of learning, states that:

> Without immersing himself in the five sciences, the superior person cannot advance to omniscience;
>
> Hence, to correct and to attract others, and for the sake of his own knowledge, he thus devotes himself to them.

The commentary, attributed to the great fifth-century master Vasubandhu, explains these laconic words as indicating that, among the five sciences, the major branches of learning recognized in Indian Buddhism, two – grammar and logic – are studied primarily to correct others; two other sciences – medicine and the arts – to attract others; and the inner, spiritual science of Buddhism for the sake of one's own knowledge.[16]

Many interpreters (including some within medieval Buddhist traditions) have understood "logic" (*hetuvidyā*) in this context to refer to *pramāṇa* generally. As the text seems to insist that "logic" served merely to correct and criticize non-Buddhists, and because the "inner science" (*adhyātmavidyā*) of Buddhism was treated separately therefrom, it has been concluded that *pramāṇa* had no interesting role to play in connection with

Buddhist practices of spiritual cultivation.[17] In my view, however, there are several important difficulties with this reading of the text.

First, the *Ornament of the Mahāyāna Scriptures* quite clearly presents itself as a general manual of the Mahāyāna Buddhist path. Within this context, a very important place is accorded to the aspirant's "seeking the Dharma," his search for the truth revealed in the Buddha's teaching, which is the overall topic of the chapter in which our verse occurs. As the first line of the verse indicates, and as the commentaries make clear, at issue here is the requirement that the "superior person," that is, the aspiring bodhisattva, immerse himself in the five sciences in order to achieve "omniscience." We need not dwell on the vexed question of just how "omniscience" is to be understood here; what is clear is that, at a minimum, this is conceived to be the mastery of the essential learning that was deemed characteristic of the "superior person," the bodhisattva, who was striving to attain the enlightenment of the Buddha, at once the source and goal of Mahāyāna Buddhist teaching.[18] Furthermore, in accordance with the Mahāyāna conception of spiritual awakening's fulfilling at once the interests of the individual who awakens and the world at large, the five sciences are here regarded as operating in the service of both self and other. In their latter role, they both correct and attract, and are thereby employed to bring order and well-being to the world. The concern of our text, therefore, is with the formation of a particular type of person, one who is oriented to the ideal presented by the Buddha, and *all* of the particular elements of its discussion are subservient to that end. In short, the conception of logic as intended primarily to correct errant reason by no means contradicts its role in the formation of an individual *capable to correct*, not solely to win debating points, but to advance the salvific project that is the very heart of Buddhist spirituality itself. In this connection, it may be stressed, too, that the correction of false views, though presented here as directed to others, was in some contexts also related to the rectification of one's own views, and hence explicitly tied to the discipline of self-cultivation.[19]

Moreover, although the *Ornament of the Mahāyāna Scriptures* specifies a primary role for logic in the context of disputations with Buddhism's rivals, it is clear that, for the text's commentator, Vasubandhu, the role of logic was by no means limited *only* to this. In another of his celebrated works, *Principles of Commentary* (*Vyākhyāyukti*), a manual for the interpretation of Buddhist scriptures, he devotes a major section to the role of reasoned argument in hermeneutics. The task of argument here is to help us to get clear about how the *sūtras* are to be understood, by resolving apparent contradictions and answering objections. As such, argument is conclusive among the five procedures required to ensure the correct transmission of the *sūtras* (the four preceding being statement of purpose, summarization, word-by-word exegesis, and contextualization). The proper transmission of the scriptures, in turn, conduces to the disciple's achievement of the three degrees of discernment, among other benefits.[20]

Lastly, we must note an important historical transformation that occurred within Buddhist thought during the fifth and sixth centuries. When the *Ornament of the Mahāyāna Scriptures* speaks of "logic," it uses the term *hetuvidyā*, the "science of reasons," which was primarily understood to be the art of debate. The text was composed some generations before the rise of *pramāṇa* as a broadly conceived discipline that embraced, but went considerably beyond, the older discipline of the "science of reasons." The philosopher responsible for the paradigm shift that this involved was the great fifth-century thinker, and disciple of Vasubandhu, Dignāga, whose contributions amounted to, as Stcherbatsky already well understood, a genuine *Novum Organum*, in some respects supplanting, for the later history of Indian Buddhist philosophy, the older Buddhist systematic dogmatics known as Abhidharma, and putting in its place a remarkably sophisticated edifice integrating logic, epistemology, philosophy of language, and more.[21] Although this new science did replace the earlier "science of reasons" in later discussions of the "five sciences," we would be in error to assume that its purview was considered as limited to correcting the errant opinions of Buddhism's opponents. On the contrary, the aim of *pramāṇa*, as affirmed in the works of Dignāga and his successors, was now explicitly held to be the elucidation of the conditions for the achievement of "genuine knowledge," *samyag-jñāna*, knowledge whose supreme exemplar was, once more, the Buddha, the consummate Sage, now declared to be the very embodiment of *pramāṇa* (*pramāṇabhūta*).[22] "Genuine knowledge" was in its turn defined as instrumental to the attainment of "all human ends," or, as one of the figures in the Buddhist epistemological tradition, Dharmottara, put it: "genuine knowledge is that whereby one may achieve well-being and abandon pain."[23]

IV

Dignāga's assimilation of the figure of the Buddha to the criterion of reason, *pramāṇa*, provoked remarkable developments in subsequent Buddhist philosophy, particularly thanks to the achievements of his greatest follower, Dharmakīrti (c. 600). Dignāga, in fact, explores but thinly the implications of his own idea. Though he uses the phrase *pramāṇabhūta*, "who embodies the criterion," as an epithet of the Buddha in the opening verse of his major treatise, the *Summation of Pramāṇa* (*Pramāṇasamuccaya*), he explains it in his commentary by saying only that it signifies "the Lord's perfection of cause and result," adding that, by "cause," he means both intention – the aspiration to benefit the whole world – and practice – the practice of the teacher who instructs the world – while "result" refers to the achievement of highest ends of self and other.[24] Dharmakīrti, on the other hand, devotes an entire, lengthy chapter, entitled "Proof of the [Buddha as] Criterion" (*pramāṇasiddhi*), to unpacking the entailments of Dignāga's brief words.[25]

For Dharmakīrti, the Buddha's epistemic authority, his status as a criterion, follows from his satisfying certain conditions, to adopt Cardinal Mercier's terms (see note 5 below). Accordingly, Dharmakīrti is concerned first to set forth the conditions that constitute the criterion of truth and then to ask how this applies in the case of the Buddha. The cardinal's proposals, in fact, may help us to clarify those of Dharmakīrti.

Let us recall that three conditions were specified: the criterion should be "*internal*, *objective*, and *immediate*." The first is required because "the mind cannot attain to certainty [with regard to an external authority] until it has found *within itself* a sufficient reason for adhering to the testimony of such an authority."[26] The difficult second condition, objectivity, was usefully dissected by Roderick Chisholm, who equated it with what he termed "epistemic preferability": "If a state of mind A is to be preferred to a state of mind B, if it is, as I would like to say, intrinsically preferable to B, then anyone who prefers B to A is *mistaken* in his preference."[27] Finally, the condition of immediacy is required, as Cardinal Mercier says, because, "if we are to avoid an infinite regress, we must find a ground of assent that presupposes no other."

Dharmakīrti, of course, does not address the issue in quite the same terms. It will be apparent, however, that he is concerned to identify some closely similar conditions. His first definition of the criterion reads: "The criterion (*pramāṇa*) is uncontradicted knowledge entailing efficiency."[28] At the outset, we should note that the stipulation that the criterion is a cognitive act (*jñāna*) clearly expresses the internality of this condition; it is one which the mind finds within itself.[29] Its objectivity is denoted in saying that it is "uncontradicted" (*avisaṃvādī*) and "entailing efficiency" (*arthakriyāsthiti*). The first of these qualifications may perhaps be related to Chisholm's concept of "epistemic preferability." It is not apodictic certainty, by any means, but conforms, rather, to a more modest epistemic standard. That which has no known evidence counting against it is "uncontradicted" and, hence, clearly preferable to accept than its opposite.[30]

Pertaining, too, to the objectivity of the knowledge in question is the condition that it entails "efficiency." This is a difficult concept that Dharmakīrti frequently employs and that has aroused considerable discussion both in traditional commentaries and in contemporary scholarship. The former sometimes explain it by taking as an example fire, which both burns and cooks.[31] This has led recent interpreters to suggest that "efficiency" for Dharmakīrti covers at least two different ideas: that of *causal* efficiency (e.g., burning); and that of efficiency in the achievement of *human aims* (e.g., cooking). (Some writers have taken to calling this latter sort of efficiency "telic function.") Significantly, as suggested in the final lines of section III above, the latter sense of efficiency seems to have taken precedence in the tradition of Dharmakīrti and his successors.[32]

The commentators suggest, moreover, that the absence of contradiction and the presence of efficiency be taken together, that they are the two faces of one and the same condition, which we have related to the notion of objectivity among Western epistemologists. What this tells us is, I think, something like this: when (i) one is subject to an apparent act of knowledge ("here's a fire," for instance), without evidence contradicting this ("no, it's just a holographic projection of fire," for instance), and (ii) the apparent object of the cognition may be reasonably supposed to function coherently in the chains of causality (burning) and/or action (cooking) in which we characteristically believe it to be enmeshed (this is the condition of "efficiency"), then (iii) the act in question satisfies the criterion of genuine knowledge.

There are, of course, many problems to be raised about all this, and Dharmakīrti and his successors do treat them in much detail. In the present brief introduction, in which we must be content with a quick survey, one such issue nevertheless seems particularly pertinent to note: it was well appreciated that the condition of efficiency could not be actually tested in every case. It serves largely to flesh out the sense of "uncontradicted" – that is, to call it to our attention that failure to satisfy the condition of efficiency (as in the case of the holographic fire, which does not burn) is a condition of defeat for a candidate cognition.

What, now, of Cardinal Mercier's final condition, immediacy? This appears to me to be entailed by two qualifications Dharmakīrti adds to his discussion of the definition of *pramāṇa*, one an exclusion and the second a further condition. The first pertains to discursive thought born of memory and past dispositions, which, being unrelated to obtaining objects, fail to fulfill the condition of efficiency. The second, sometimes regarded as an entirely distinct definition of the criterion, is the disclosure of what was previously unknown – the knowledge of a truth is conceived here as a sort of "aha!" moment. Together with the exclusion of discursive thought, this seems strongly suggestive of a concept of immediacy.

Given this characterization of *pramāṇa*, where Dharmakīrti surpasses the demands of a critical epistemology alone is in his additional assertion that the Buddha (an *external authority*, as Cardinal Mercier would have it) in some sense embodies *pramāṇa*. This is due to his teaching's instantiation of the two defining properties of the criterion: truthfulness and discovery. These may both be demonstrated with reference to the Four Noble Truths, the chief elements of which are within the purview of natural reason and thus may be verified by one who reasons carefully about them. The second is seen in the novelty of this teaching, which reveals what was not fully revealed elsewhere and, in particular, what must be renounced and what must be undertaken in order to achieve the goal of liberation from suffering, *nirvāṇa*.[33]

Detailed consideration of Dharmakīrti's arguments cannot be undertaken in the space available here; in the course of the chapter on the "Proof of the Criterion," he treats knowledge of the chain of rebirth, rebuts the notion of a divine creator, establishes the sixteen aspects of the Four Noble Truths, and demonstrates the Buddha's compassion as the motive of his awakening and teaching.[34] In the course of these discussions, he takes up and criticizes the views of several non-Buddhist schools: his arguments in favor of rebirth, for instance, counter the Lokāyata, the skeptical, worldly tradition of Indian thought;[35] while those against theism are addressed primarily to the views of the Nyāya and Vaiśeṣika schools.[36] Owing to Dharmakīrti's sustained concern to address himself here to Buddhism's opponents, some have embraced the conclusion that this is virtually his sole concern, and that his work therefore accords with the model in which "logic" for medieval Indian Buddhism applies above all to the refutation of others' wrong views.

Nevertheless, it is by no means apparent, to this reader at least, that disputation with non-Buddhists is in fact the pre-eminent interest of the "Proof of the Criterion," despite its evident engagement in aspects of non-Buddhist thought. The remarkable emphasis one finds therein on the Buddha's compassion and love, for example, which could have hardly garnered debating points with those ill-disposed to Buddhism in Dharmakīrti's day,[37] suggests to me rather that Dharmakīrti's chief concern is to clarify on behalf of his co-religionists what he believed to be a rational model through which to comprehend the Buddha and his teaching. Even more, one might say that the investigation of the arguments of the "Proof of the Criterion" is intended to provoke a transformation whereby reason finds its proper orientation in a progressively refined engagement in the meaning and message of the ideal sage. As such, among the three degrees of discernment introduced earlier, Dharmakīrti's project conforms notably with the second, discernment born of critical reflection upon the teaching. Though it is not by any means clear that this perspective would have been unanimously affirmed by his successors, it is certain at least that a prominent trend in later Indian Buddhism – the "religious" school of Buddhist logic, as Stcherbatsky termed it – did adopt such a view.[38] Among Dharmakīrti's later commentators, it was primarily the influential Prajñākaragupta and his many later followers who emphasized the spiritual dimensions latent in Dharmakīrti's text. Their views, as we shall see, would have a considerable legacy in Tibet.

V

The project of harmonizing the preoccupations of *pramāṇa* with the orientations of the Buddhist spiritual quest found a culmination of sorts in the *Gathering of the Quiddities* (*Tattvasaṃgraha*), the masterwork of the great eighth-century philosopher Śāntarakṣita. In some 3,600 verses in 26 chapters, Śāntarakṣita dissects the world of Indian philosophy in his time, examining the full range of topics that had been disputed between Buddhists and their opponents over the preceding centuries:

1 the Sāṃkhya doctrine of "nature" (*prakṛti*) – that is, prime matter (*pradhāna*);
2 the Nyāya-Vaiśeṣika conception of God as creator;
3 whether nature and God are "co-creators" of the world;
4 the notion that the world is a chance occurrence;
5 the linguistic philosopher Bhartṛhari's theory of *śabdabrahma* – that is, the absolute as Word;
6 the Vedic myth of the primordial Cosmic Man (*Puruṣa*);
7 the nature of the self (*ātman*) and the Buddhist "non-self" (*anātman*) doctrine;
8 whether there are persisting entities;
9 the relationship between act and result;
10–15 the six Vaiśeṣika categories of substance (*dravya*), quality (*guṇa*), act (*kriyā*), universal (*sāmānya*), particular (*viśeṣa*), and inherence (e.g., of quality in substance, *samāvāya*);
16 the relationship between word and meaning;
17 perception (*pratyakṣa*);
18 inference (*anumāna*);
19 whether there are other means of knowledge besides perception and inference;
20 the Jain logic of "may be" (*syādvāda*);
21 past, present, and future time;
22 materialism;
23 the existence of an external world corresponding to the objects of sensory perception;
24 scriptural authority;
25 the self-validation of religious claims;
26 the seer's extrasensory perception.

The sustained focus throughout the work on the refutation of non-Buddhist positions corresponds closely with the description we have seen earlier of logic as intended primarily for the "correction" of others. But Śāntarakṣita, who was inspired by Nāgārjuna's Madhyamaka teaching no less than by Dharmakīrti's approach to *pramāṇa*, gives this a novel twist; for the grand tour on which he guides us through the myriad pathways of Indian thought has as its stated theme the proper characterization of the compassionate and omniscient Buddha's cardinal teaching of "conditioned origination" (*pratītyasamutpāda*).[39]

The intentions and aims informing Śāntarakṣita's work are explored in the detailed introduction to the commentary authored by his prominent disciple Kamalaśīla.[40] Several of the points he underscores here have a direct bearing on our understanding of the relationship between philosophy and spiritual cultivation for medieval Indian Buddhists.

In accord with a broadly accepted understanding of the hierarchy of values, Kamalaśīla affirms that it is freedom, or liberation (*mokṣa*), that is the "supreme value for persons" (*paramapuruṣārtha*).[41] For Mahāyāna Buddhists, such as Śāntarakṣita and Kamalaśīla, this is normally conceived, as the latter makes quite explicit, as embracing the two ends of "elevation" (*abhyudaya*) – that is, birth as a human being or divinity, who is free from the torments of infernal, ghostly, or animal realms – and the *summum bonum* (*niḥśreyasa*), *nirvāṇa*, complete emancipation from the painful round of rebirth, or *saṃsāra*. Above all, as it is understood here, *nirvāṇa* is valued as no mere extinction, but is characterized by the compassion and omniscience of the Buddha. Of course, no one pretends that the immediate aim of studying Śāntarakṣita's book is the attainment of these lofty ends. The purpose of the work, rather, is to facilitate easy understanding of the "quiddities" (*tattva*), the nature of things as set forth in the various philosophical systems and, in particular, the manner in which these contribute to comprehending the key Buddhist teaching of conditioned origination. By achieving such comprehension, one is freed from error with respect to the Buddha's teachings, and this carries two cardinal entailments: (1) because conflicting emotions (*kleśa*) are rooted in error, one may abandon them and the self-defeating patterns of action they provoke, thereby ensuring one's "elevation";[42] and, (2), because freedom from error involves insight into the two aspects of "selflessness" (*nairātmya*) – that of persons (*pudgala*) and that of fundamental phenomena (*dharma*) – one thus approaches the realization constituting the highest good. Though these ends are not achieved just by mastering the contents of Śāntarakṣita's work, they may be won through the progressive cultivation of that mastery in accord with the three degrees of discernment. These supreme values, therefore, are the final aims (*prayojananiṣṭhā*) to which the immediate purpose of the work – namely, the achievement of a philosophical understanding of the teaching of conditioned origination – is itself directed.[43]

In summarizing the individual chapters of his master's text, Kamalaśīla reinforces this perspective by regularly pointing to relations between the philosophical topics treated and themes pertaining to conditioned origination as they are encountered in the discourses attributed to the Buddha. Thus, for example, the first seven chapters, in which Śāntarakṣita investigates a range of metaphysical concepts from the Sāṃkhya notion of prime matter to the notion of an enduring self, are referred to the critique of causation offered by the Buddha in the *Śālistambha Sūtra*: "This shoot is neither self-produced, nor produced by another, nor produced by both, nor emanated by God, nor sprung from nature; it is neither dependent upon a single cause, nor causeless."[44] In this manner, Kamalaśīla affirms that the *Gathering of the Quiddities* offers not just refutations of the erroneous beliefs and opinions of non-Buddhists but, much as Vasubandhu had urged in his *Principles of Commentary*, also a hermeneutical use of dialectics as a means to get clear about the meaning of the Buddha's teaching. Philosophical refinement is here intimately tied to demands of spiritual cultivation on the Buddhist path – the path, that is, as characterized by one's progressive development of the three degrees of discernment.

VI

But if this much is so, how was it that anyone *within* the Buddhist tradition ever entertained the idea that *pramāṇa* was to all intents and purposes devoid of spiritual import? In order to clarify now the tension that Buddhist thinkers themselves expressed here, I will focus upon two later masters, both of whom address the issue explicitly. The first, Dīpaṃkaraśrījñāna, better known as Atiśa, was an eleventh-century Indian teacher who played an exceptional role in the promulgation of Buddhism in Tibet. The second, Tsongkhapa Lozang Drakpa (1357–1419), is generally recognized as one of the most powerful thinkers throughout Tibetan history and is considered the founder of the Gelukpa order, which came to dominate Tibetan religious and political life in tandem with the rise of the Dalai Lamas during the sixteenth and seventeenth centuries.

Atiśa's standpoint was that of the skeptics; he held that the study of *pramāṇa* was all but a waste of time. His words about this read:

> Perception and inference are both upheld [as means of knowledge] by the Buddhist [logicians], but superficial persons ignorantly affirm that "emptiness [the universal relativity of things] may be realized by both." This entails that the non-Buddhists and adherents of the inferior vehicles of Buddhism [may both] realize reality, as do, even more, the proponents of [Buddhist] Idealism. It follows from this that they have no disagreement with the Madhyamaka [teaching of emptiness], and hence that all the philosophical systems are in agreement in their application of the criteria of knowledge. However, because all the dialecticians are in fact in disagreement, would not the reality to which these criteria are applied then have to be manifold? [This follows because, if we assume perception and inference as such to be valid means of knowledge, the genuine criteria, then all the conflicting systems born of these means of knowledge would have an equal claim to truth.]
>
> [Philosophical doctrines of] perception and inference are unnecessary. They have been formulated by the learned in order to refute the disputations of the non-Buddhists. But it is clearly stated by the learned master Bhavya that [reality] is not realized by means of either perception or inference.[45]

Atiśa's position is indebted above all to that of Nāgārjuna and several of his leading successors, notably Candrakīrti. For these thinkers the true task of critical reasoning was neither system-building nor the establishment of a well-founded, definitive method; it was rather a deconstructive process aimed at clearing away all hypostases of system and method in order to achieve an opening in which the direct realization of the Buddha's message might be disclosed. This was to be achieved by the twin movement of the deconstructive dialectic of Nāgārjuna's Madhyamaka teaching together with a well-formed program of spiritual discipline that aimed to build an individual who embodied the ethical qualities of the bodhisattva: compassion, generosity, forebearance, etc., as well as tranquility born of profound meditation. In Atiśa's view, because Buddhism's dialectically savvy Brahmanical opponents were a product of the Indian cultural sphere, and not at all present in Tibet, the study of *pramāṇa*, for the Tibetans, was a mere distraction that served no good purpose at all.

Although some of Atiśa's Tibetan successors accordingly steered clear of the whole business of logic and epistemology, this was perhaps the sole area in which the counsels of this much admired master came to be quietly ignored, and it was the nephew of one of his leading disciples who in fact established *pramāṇa* as the foundational discipline for all subsequent monastic education in Tibet.[46] Nevertheless, Atiśa's misgivings ensured that one of the topics that would be routinely debated in the monastery courtyards was this: why do we bother with *pramāṇa* at all? While many thinkers addressed this question, the remarks of Tsongkhapa are notable for the clarity with which he set forth the conflicting positions and his own resolution to them. In the passage cited here, he presents his understanding of Dharmakīrti's project in the "Proof of *Pramāṇa*" chapter we have examined briefly above:

> In order that persons seeking freedom may enter into liberation, having well differentiated the true path from the false, their sole eye is the science of reason formulated by the peerless *mahātma* Dignāga, together with his successors [. . .] [Concerning the reasons for which the science of *pramāṇa* developed among Buddhists,] there are two topics: (1) removing misconceptions about the purpose, and (2) the actual true purpose. In the first are three subtopics: (1.1) refuting misconceptions with reference to those seeking liberation; (1.2) refuting them with reference to the particular features of the object; and (1.3) refuting the assertion that, though there is some purpose [to *pramāṇa*], it is a base one.
>
> (1.1) As for the first, some say: the *pramāṇa* treatises are useless for those seeking liberation, for they are treatises of speculative reason, and so form a science of logic external to the treatises of inner significance.
>
> To that, it must be explained: the so-called doctrines of speculative reason that are the teachings of the non-Buddhists have been set forth imaginatively by such teachers as the sage Dvaipāyana [Vyāsa], to whom the whole truth was not disclosed, and hence the treatises following their [teaching] are called "treatises of speculative reason." But, on the other hand, as it has been explained that "immature persons must rely upon speculative reason, though uncertain . . . ," accordingly it is necessary that [such persons] understand the reality of things by first apprehending it under a general description, though it has not yet been disclosed to them. So this too is called "speculative reason." Of the two, the first, it is true, is of no use for those aspiring for liberation. Nevertheless, we do not affirm that these treatises of logic [that were composed by Dignāga and his successors] are to be included therein, nor is it reasonable to do so, for they [unlike the authors of the non-Buddhist logic treatises] were followers of our root-teacher [the Buddha] who did directly perceive all that can be known. And as for the second, [it is true] they are useless for aspirants who have already attained [the higher stages of the path], because they treat reality as a conceptual object [while for those at the heights of the path reality is directly disclosed], but, nevertheless, it would be unreasonable to hold them to be external to the treatises of inner science. For these treatises of reason establish, by inerrant reason, that emptiness that is the insubstantiality of self and of phenomena, and so teach, as their foremost meaning, the lesson of superior discernment. Because, in this textual

tradition [of *pramāṇa*] the construction and deconstruction of *saṃsāra* are established in detail, thereby terminating errancy in the mind within, what is taught here is the unerring means whereby one enters the genuine path. Hence, you who affirm the "inner science" [to be quite distinct from the teaching of the *pramāṇa* tradition] must explain in what respect that science is [thought to be] superior to this. [. . .]

(1.2) Second, some say that these treatises are merely useful in order to refute the misconceptions of the non-Buddhists, so that, in places where non-Buddhists are not present there is no reason to study and to reflect upon them. But this is to undermine the teaching, and is merely erroneous thought that leads to abandonment of the holy Dharma. For these texts establish in full the means to refute such inflated opinions as those which hold there to be no former or past lives, no liberation or omniscience, and which hold the aggregates [constituting the body and mind of a living being] to be pure, happy, enduring, self, etc. Therefore, even in this place [Tibet], where non-Buddhists are not present, you must consider introspectively whether or not you need to eliminate inflated opinions whereby you grasp your own aggregates as pure, happy, enduring, self, etc., and whether or not you need to achieve certainty in regard to past and future lives, liberation, omniscience, etc. And, if those be needed, you must indicate whether, to achieve them, there is any other means superior to these treatises on reason.

(1.3) Third, it is unreasonable to hold that these treatises have a base purpose, comparable to salt, which is not of foremost necessity but merely useful for seasoning other foodstuffs, which are foremost. For there is no other basis that one can obtain that is superior to this insomuch as it establishes the ground of the three [degrees of discernment, to wit] study, reflection, and contemplation.

(2) Second, as for the matter of the genuine purpose: here, there are both those whose minds have been refined by exposure to philosophical systems and [those whose minds] have not. The latter, following the elders of this world, make efforts solely with respect to the means of this life, while not primarily occupying themselves with the next life and beyond. The Lokāyata [worldly philosophers], though their minds have been touched by a philosophical system, do not hold there to be past or future lives. The other non-Buddhists do hold there to be a need to achieve the ends of future lives. The Mīmāṃsaka-s hold heaven to be the sole objective of future lives, and that there are neither liberation nor omniscience; and they say that the mind is by nature tainted, so that there is no prospect for separation [from taint]. Except for those two, the other [non-Buddhists] as well as our co-religionists think as follows: is there a means or not to stop this suffering that continues through birth and death, one to the next? Assuming there is, if one does not strive for it, one fails to achieve a great end and hence we must make efforts for the means to seek it.

In this context, generally speaking, one who is said to be possessed of understanding is one who, having engaged for himself in the investigation of such topics, questions whether there is or is not understanding [to be found in the various systems], and seeks out teachers who, when one enters into their following, teach without error the distinction between that which deceives and that which is undeceptive for those desiring freedom. Seeking in this way, having met with a spiritual mentor, that person who aspires to liberation takes in the distinctive features of his thought, remains unbiased, and strives energetically [. . .].

Accordingly, though one depends upon a spiritual mentor at the outset, one must attain certainty by one's own power. Hence, when you investigate which system is proven in what

> respect, and conclude that the teaching of the Sage, Lord Buddha alone, is flawless, you will adhere to him as your teacher. And so it is that these treatises of reason, which demonstrate the Three Precious Jewels by means of unerring reason – to wit, that the Dharma comprised of scripture and reason is flawless, that its teacher is the embodiment of *pramāṇa*, and that the saṅgha are those who have achieved the significance of what he has taught – conduce to incorrigible certainty about this; and *that* is the purpose of this science [. . .]. One should not merely practice it to engage in disputations, for one thereby diminishes oneself and hinders the growth of others' respect for this science.[47]

The study of *pramāṇa*, therefore, on this account serves not merely, or even primarily, as a method to be deployed in polemical engagements with Buddhism's opponents. It is, rather, a method whereby one may come to know what it is to know, whereby one may come to discern which objects of knowledge are to be most highly valued, and how it is that one may orient oneself to them. The objects in question include the ideal sage, the Buddha, and the truths that he taught, including the path culminating in Buddhism's highest goal, that of enlightenment. Traversing that path requires more than the study of *pramāṇa* alone, however, so that "spiritual exercise" in this context cannot be restricted to this domain. But, by refining the individual in relation to his or her rational orientation to Buddhism's ends and means, *pramāṇaśāstra* surely came to find a place for itself among the tradition's foremost systems of spiritual exercise.

Nevertheless, as we have seen, this view of the matter was a contested one. Against those who have held, however, that the available evidence does not permit us to conclude that there was any interesting relationship between the Buddhist *pramāṇa* tradition and those Buddhist intellectual practices that we might characterize as "spiritual exercise," I would argue that the very presence of contestation about this within the tradition itself sufficiently demonstrates that the possibilities of such a relationship were well understood. And there is good reason to maintain that these possibilities were actualized, at the very least in that branch of the Indian *pramāṇa* school that Stcherbatsky long ago characterized as "religious," despite his reservations about this with respect to the school as a whole, and to a very high degree of certainty among their successors in Tibet.

Notes

1 "On peut, après tout, vivre sans le je-ne-sais-quoi. Comme on peut vivre sans philosophie, sans musique, sans joie et sans amour. Mais pas si bien." Jankélévitch (1953, 266). Cf. Nozick (1990, 15): "I do not say with Socrates that the unexamined life is not worth living – that is unnecessarily harsh. However, when we guide our lives by our own pondered thoughts, it then is *our* life that we are living, not someone else's. In this sense, the unexamined life is not lived as fully."

2 Soames (2005, xiv). Soames's use here of the phrase "as opposed to" is telling: is the search for truth really "opposed to" moral refinement? One imagines that even some analytic philosophers have considered their commitment to the philosophical pursuit of knowledge to be at least in part a moral one.

3 These two works are translated in Huntington (1989) and Crosby and Skilton (1995), respectively. On the interrelationships between Madhyamaka philosophy and Buddhist soteriology, see, too, Eckel (1992).

4 Refer to Prajñākaramati's commentary on the *Bodhicaryāvatāra* in Vaidya (1960, 169–70).

5 Chisholm (1982, 63) quotes Mercier as saying: "*If* there *is* a criterion of truth, then this criterion should satisfy three conditions: it should be *internal, objective*, and *immediate*" (emphasis in the original). Mercier's words very well capture the problem of *pramāṇa* as it was often understood in medieval Indian philosophy.

6 Stcherbatsky (1962 [1930]). The initial Russian version, in fact Stcherbatsky's doctoral dissertation, had been published in 1904.

7 Ibid., 1: 2.

8 The first Buddhist philosopher to adopt an explicitly skeptical stance with respect to the claims of epistemology to ground the formation of knowledge was Nāgārjuna, in his *Dispeller of Disputes* (*Vigrahavyāvartanī*), on which see now Westerhoff (2010). For an excellent study of the legacy of Nāgārjuna's epistemological skepticism, refer to Arnold (2005).

9 Kapstein (2001, "Introduction: What is Buddhist Philosophy?") proposes an Hadotian approach to Buddhist philosophy. Eltschinger (2008) critiques this undertaking; some of his arguments are mentioned herein. McClintock (2010, 14–22) offers a rebuttal to Eltschinger. Gowans (2003), though not specifically engaging the work of Hadot, argues robustly for a comparative approach to Buddhist and Hellenistic philosophies.

10 Hadot (1995, 82–3).

11 On philosophical education in the Tibetan monastic system, see Dreyfus (2003).

12 An excellent historical survey and introduction may be found in Matilal (1977).

13 Translated in Walshe (1995, 91–109). On the implications of the teachings of the six rivals for the early history of Indian thought, refer to Basham (1951, 10–26) and Vogel (1970).

14 Refer to Brendan Gillon, LOGIC AND LANGUAGE IN INDIAN BUDDHIST THOUGHT, in the present volume and to Kapstein (2001, 81–8).

15 The most recent contribution to the study of debate in early Yogācāra, with abundant references to both the major primary texts and previous scholarship, may be found in Todeschini (2011).

16 The Sanskrit text, including Vasubandhu's commentary, is edited in Lévi (1907–11, 1: 70–1, with French translation in 2: 127–8). A full English translation is now available; for the present passage, see Jamspal et al. (2004, 141).

17 Eltschinger (2008, 522–7) adopts just this view and writes: "les quatre premières disciplines assument des fonctions essentialements mondaines" (ibid., 523).

18 McClintock (2010) offers a detailed study of the question of "omniscience" in medieval Indian Buddhism.

19 As Krasser (2004, 137) rightly argues: "Here the division of the four *vidyāsthānas* [i.e., logic, grammar, medicine, and the technical arts] into external and mundane is not applied, and it is also clearly stated that a Bodhisattva has to master all five sciences in order to obtain omniscience, that is to say, in order to obtain liberation."

20 The Tibetan text of the *Vyākhyāyukti* is edited in Lee (2001). Refer to Skilling (2000) for an introduction to and survey of the *Vyākhyāyukti* and related literature, and Nance (2012, 129–52), for a translation of Book I, which concerns the first three of the five procedures mentioned. On Vasubandhu's contributions to Buddhist logic, refer to chapter 18 in this volume, by Brendan Gillon.

21 Though much valuable scholarship on Dignāga has appeared during the decades since it was published, Hattori (1968) provides a still useful introduction to this major figure.

22 Refer to Jackson (1988) and, for later Tibetan developments, Tillemans (1993).

23 Dharmottara, *Pramāṇaviniścayaṭīkā*, in Rdo-rje-rgyal-po (1990, vol. 4: 8). Note, too, that the phrase "all human ends" (*sarvapuruṣārtha*) generally implies the four aims traditionally affirmed in classical Indian thought: wealth (*artha*), pleasure (*kāma*), righteousness (*dharma*), and the "supreme end" of liberation (*mokṣa*).

24 For the reconstructed Sanskrit text of Dignāga, see Steinkellner (2005, 1), and for Jinendrabuddhi's commentary thereupon, Steinkellner et al. (2005, 2–19).

25 Aspects of Dharmakīrti's *Pramāṇasiddhi* chapter are studied in Vetter (1990), Franco (1997), and van Bijlert (1989). The same text as interpreted by a prominent Tibetan commentator is studied in Jackson (1993). Eltschinger (2007) investigates further aspects of Dharmakīrti's religious thought. See, too, Richard P. Hayes's PHILOSOPHY OF MIND IN BUDDHISM in this volume.

26 Mercier, in Chisholm (1982, 63; emphasis in original).

27 Chisholm (1982, 70; emphasis in original).

28 Dharmakīrti, *Pramāṇavārttika, Pramāṇasiddhi* 3ab, in Pandeya (1989, 2).

29 The use of a word meaning "knowledge" (*jñāna*) in this context may lead to the suspicion of circularity. This is not the case, however, as *jñāna*, without further qualification, may refer to apparent acts of knowledge as well as to genuine ones.

30 The commentator Manorathanandin glosses this as meaning that the cognitive act in question is without deception or dillusion (*vañcanam*). Pandeya (1989, 2).

31 This example is given in the commentary of Prajñākaragupta.

32 Refer to Dunne (2004, 252–98), for a useful discussion of Dharmakīrti's conception of *arthakriyā*, summarizing *inter alia* the scholarship on this question to date.

33 Dharmakīrti, *Pramāṇavārttika, Pramāṇasiddhi* 9, with the commentary of Manorathanandin, in Pandeya (1989, 5).

34 Refer to Richard Hayes's contribution to this volume (chapter 25) for a discussion of Dharmakīrti's arguments in regard to the Buddha's compassion.

35 See, especially, Franco (1997).

36 See Patil (2009) for detailed consideration of the rejection of theism in Dharmakīrti's tradition.

37 The celebrated Vaiṣṇava poet Jayadeva (twelfth century) did extol the Buddha for his message of love and for the prohibition of the sacrificial slaughter of animals that this entailed. See Siegel (2009, 9). But Jayadeva lived more than half a millennium after Dharmakīrti's time; and the latter's Brahmanical opponents would have been for the most part committed upholders of the sacrificial cults of the Veda.

38 Stcherbatsky (1960 [1930], 1: 42–7).

39 Cf. Kapstein (2001, 11–15).

40 On this introductory part of the work, refer to Funayama (1995).

41 Shastri (1968, 1: 6). It may be noted that Krishna (1991) argues at length that the affirmation of *mokṣa* that one often sees in the introductions to Sanskrit philosophical and scientific writings is to all intents and purposes a vacuous gesture. Although a thorough discussion of his thesis in connection with Indian learned culture in general would be beside the point of the present essay, and far outstrip the space available, it should be stressed that Buddhist authors, at least, did take the goal of spiritual freedom seriously.

42 Buddha's thinkers seem generally to have accepted what we might term the "Socratic assumption" – that is, that genuine knowledge of the good entails living accordingly.

43 Shastri (1968, 1: 12).

44 Ibid., 1: 13.

45 Atiśa's text is studied, edited, and translated in Lindtner (1981). The translation given here, however, is my own. The "Bhavya" to whom Atiśa refers here is perhaps the author of a

late treatise entitled *Madhyamakaratnapradīpa* and not the renowned sixth-century philosopher Bhāviveka.

46 The nephew was the prolific translator Ngok Loden Sherap (1059–1109), who founded the philosophical college at his uncle's monastery at Sangpu. The tradition stemming from Atiśa's foremost disciple, Dromtön Gyelwé Jungné (1004–1064), remained circumspect in regard to *pramāṇa* studies.

47 Rgyal-tshab (1987, 679–83). Translated by the present author.

References

Arnold, Daniel (2005). *Buddhists, Brahmins, and Belief: Epistemology in South Asian Philosophy of Religion*. New York: Columbia University Press.

Basham, Arthur L. (1951). *History and Doctrines of the Ājīvikas*. London: Luzac.

Chisholm, Roderick M. (1982). *The Foundations of Knowing*. Minneapolis: University of Minnesota Press.

Crosby, Kate, and Skilton, Andrew (trans.) (1995). *The Bodhicaryāvatāra*. Oxford and New York: Oxford University Press.

Dreyfus, Georges B. J. (2003). *The Sound of Two Hands Clapping: The Education of a Tibetan Buddhist Monk*. Berkeley, Los Angeles and London: University of California Press.

Dunne, John D. (2004). *Foundations of Dharmakīrti's Philosophy*. Boston: Wisdom.

Eckel, Malcolm David (1992). *To See the Buddha: A Philosopher's Quest for the Meaning of Emptiness*. Princeton, NJ: Princeton University Press.

Eltschinger, Vincent (2007). *Penser l'autorité des écritures: la polémique de Dharmakīrti contre la notion brahmanique orthodoxe d'un Veda sans auteur*. Vienna: Austrian Academy of Sciences.

Eltschinger, Vincent (2008). Pierre Hadot et les "exercices spirituels": quel modèle pour la philosophie bouddhique tardive? In *Asiatische Studien* 62, 485–544.

Franco, Eli (1997). *Dharmakīrti on Compassion and Rebirth*. Wiener Studien zur Tibetologie und Buddhismuskunde 38. Vienna: ATBS.

Funayama, Toru (1995). Arcaṭa, Śāntarakṣita, Jinendrabuddhi, and Kamalaśīla on the Aim of a Treatise (prayojana). In *Wiener Zeitschrift für die Kunde Südasiens* 39, 181–203.

Gowans, Christopher W. (2003). *Philosophy of the Buddha: An Introduction*. London and New York: Routledge.

Hadot, Pierre (1995). *Philosophy as a Way of Life*. Ed. Arnold I. Davidson. Trans. Michael Chase. Oxford: Blackwell.

Hattori, Masaaki (1968). *Dignāga, On Perception*. Harvard Oriental Series, vol. 47. Cambridge, MA: Harvard University Press.

Huntington, C. W., Jr., with Geshé Namgyal Wangchen (1989). *The Emptiness of Emptiness: An Introduction to Early Indian Mādhyamika*. Honolulu: University of Hawai'i Press.

Jackson, Roger R. (1988). The Buddha as 'Pramāṇabhūta': Epithets and Arguments in the Buddhist "Logical" Tradition. In *Journal of Indian Philosophy* 16, 335–65.

Jackson, Roger R. (1993). *Is Enlightenment Possible? Dharmakīrti and rGyal tshab rje on Knowledge, Rebirth, No-Self and Liberation*. Ithaca, NY: Snow Lion.

Jamspal, L., Clark, R., Wilson, J., Zwilling, L., Sweet, M., and Thurman, R. (trans.) (2004). *The Universal Vehicle Discourse Literature (Mahāyānasūtrālaṃkāra)*. New York: American Institute of Buddhist Studies.

Jankélévitch, Vladimir (1953). *Philosophie première*. Paris: P.U.F.

Kapstein, Matthew T. (2001). *Reason's Traces: Identity and Interpretation in Indian and Tibetan Buddhist Thought*. Boston: Wisdom.

Krasser, Helmut (2004). Are Buddhist Pramāṇavādins non-Buddhistic? Dignāga and Dharmakīrti on the Impact of Logic and Epistemology on Emancipation. In *Hōrin: Vergleichende Studien zur japanischen Kultur* 11, 129–46.

Krishna, Daya (1991). *Indian Philosophy: A Counter-Perspective*. New Delhi: Oxford University Press.

Lee, Jong Cheol (ed.) (2001). *The Tibetan Text of the Vyākhyāyukti of Vasubandhu*. Bibliotheca Indologica et Buddhologica 8. Tokyo: Sankibo Press.

Lévi, Sylvain (1907–11). *Mahāyāna-sūtrālaṃkāra: Exposé de la doctrine du grand véhicule*. Paris: Honoré Champion.

Lindtner, Christian (1981). Atiśa's "Introduction to the Two Truths," and its Sources. In *Journal of Indian Philosophy* 9, 161–214.

Matilal, Bimal K. (1977). *Nyāya-Vaiśeṣika. A History of Indian literature*, Vol. 6: Scientific and technical literature, pt. 3, fasc. 2. Wiesbaden: Harrassowitz.

McClintock, Sara L. (2010). *Omniscience and the Rhetoric of Reason: Śāntarakṣita and Kamalaśīla on Rationality, Argumentation, and Religious Authority*. Boston: Wisdom.

Nance, Richard F. (2012). *Speaking for Buddhas: Scriptural Commentary in Indian Buddhism*. New York: Columbia University Press.

Nozick, Robert (1990). *The Examined Life: Philosophical Meditations*. New York: Simon & Schuster.

Pandeya, Ram Chandra (1989). *The Pramāṇavārttikam of Ācārya Dharmakīrti*. Delhi: Motilal Banarsidass.

Patil, Parimal (2009). *Against a Hindu God: Buddhist Philosophy of Religion in India*. New York: Columbia University Press.

Rdo-rje-rgyal-po (ed.) (1990). *Tshad ma rig pa'i rgya gzhung rtsa 'grel bdam bsgrigs*. Beijing: Nationalities Press.

Rgyal-tshab Dar-ma-rin-chen (1987). *Rgyal tshab chos rjes Rje'i drung du gsan pa'i tshad ma'i brjed byang chen mo*, in *Rje Tsong kha pa chen po'i gsung 'bum*, vol. 14 (*pha*). Xining: Qinghai Nationalities Press, 677–749.

Shastri, Swami Dwarikadas (ed.) (1968). Śāntarakṣita, *Tattvasaṃgraha*, with the Pañjikā commentary of Kamalaśīla, 2 vols. Varanasi: Bauddha Bharati.

Siegel, Lee (trans.) (2009). *Gita·govínda: Love Songs of Radha and Krishna*. Clay Sanskrit Library. New York: New York University Press.

Skilling, Peter (2000). Vasubandhu and the *Vyākhyāyukti* Literature. In *Journal of the International Association of Buddhist Studies* 23, 297–350.

Soames, Scott (2005). *Philosophical Analysis in the Twentieth Century*, Vol. 1: *The Dawn of Analysis*. Princeton, NJ: Princeton University Press.

Stcherbatsky, Theodore (1960 [1930]). *Buddhist Logic*, 2 vols. Repr. New York: Dover.

Steinkellner, Ernst (ed.) (2005). *Dignāga's Pramāṇāsamuccaya, Chapter 1: A Hypothetical Reconstruction of the Sanskrit Text*. At http://ikga.oeaw.ac.at/Mat/dignaga_PS_1.pdf.

Steinkellner, Ernst, Krasser, Helmut, and Lasic, Horst (eds) (2005). *Jinendrabuddhi's Viśālāmalavatī Pramāṇasamuccayaṭīkā, Chapter 1, Part I: Critical Edition*. Beijing: China Tibetology Publishing House.

Tillemans, Tom J. F. (1993). *Persons of Authority*. Wiesbaden: Franz Steiner.

Todeschini, Alberto (2011). On the Ideal Debater: *Yogācārabhūmi, Abhidharmasamuccaya and Abhidharmasamuccayabhāṣya*. In *Journal of Indian and Tibetan Studies* 15, 244–72.

Vaidya, P. L. (ed.) (1960). *Śāntideva, Bodhicaryāvatāra*. Buddhist Sanskrit Texts Series 12. Darbhanga: Mithila Institute.

van Bijlert, Victor (1989). *Epistemology and Spiritual Authority*. Wiener Studien zur Tibetologie und Buddhismuskunde 20. Vienna: ATBS.

Vetter, Tilmann (1990). *Der Buddha und seine Lehre in Dharmakīrtis Pramāṇavārttika*. Vienna: ATBS.

Vogel, Claus (1970). *The Teachings of the Six Heretics according to the Pravrajyāvastu of the Tibetan Mūlasarvāstivāda Vinaya*. Wiesbaden: Franz Steiner.

Walshe, Maurice (1995). *The Long Discourses of the Buddha: A Translation of the Dīgha Nikāya*. Boston: Wisdom.

Westerhoff, Jan (2010). *Nāgārjuna's Vigrahavyāvartanī: The Dispeller of Disputes*. New York: Oxford University Press.

18

Yogic Perception, Meditation, and Enlightenment

The Epistemological Issues in a Key Debate

TOM J. F. TILLEMANS

I

Towards the end of the eighth century CE there occurred a debate over the future direction of Buddhism in Tibet. It happened in Samyé (*bsam yas*), in the Brahmaputra valley not far from Lhasa, and pitted an Indian side, with their Tibetan sympathizers, against a Chinese side, with their Tibetan and perhaps even some Indian sympathizers too. The debate may have gone on for about a year in one way or another – one cannot but speculate on the formidable linguistic challenges of managing and somehow translating the polemical exchanges in Sanskrit, Tibetan, and Chinese – but the actual details of the procedure are obscure. In any case, it was not long until things took a disastrous turn. Some members of the Chinese entourage despaired of losing and committed suicide; one of the prominent Tibetans allied with the Indians also committed suicide by starving to death; and the debate finally concluded with the murder of the leader of the Indian side, Kamalaśīla, at the hands of hired assassins, who supposedly "crushed his kidneys." The Chinese leader, who was known simply as "Monk" (Tb. *hva shang*; Ch. *he shang* 和尙) or, often, "Monk of the Great Vehicle/Mahāyāna" (*hva shang mo ho yen*) – henceforth simply "Heshang" – was ignominiously expelled from Tibet, unfairly as his side claimed. Details of the debate and its historical context, as well as a French translation of the memoir of Wang Xi (王錫) in defense of Heshang and excerpts from the *Bhāvanākrama* by Kamalaśīla, are found in the classic work of the Sinologist Paul Demiéville, *Le Concile de Lhasa* (Demiéville 1987 [1952]).[1] Colourful details aside, the debate, which superficially might seem to be no more than political rivalry, jealousies, and their brutally violent outcomes, is also about questions that regularly arise among Buddhists, past and present. It is in part about the efficacy of various types of meditation, but, more broadly, it is about the respective *worth* of analysis and meditation as approaches to knowledge and enlightenment. The debate, as we shall see shortly, is fundamentally about epistemological issues, problems of knowledge.

A Companion to Buddhist Philosophy, First Edition. Edited by Steven M. Emmanuel.

II

Here is the background. Kamalaśīla, in his work "Stages of Meditation" (*Bhāvanākrama*), speaks of two aspects of meditation: "calmness" (*śamatha*) and "insight" (*vipaśyanā; prajñā*), the conjunction of the two being the means through which Buddhist liberation/enlightenment is achieved. As the way to develop this conjunction he advocated that one first alternate between philosophical analysis and concentrated fixation on the conclusions of that analysis. Meditation was thus, for him, a back and forth between analytical reasoning – i.e., a kind of subtle internal debate over metaphysical issues – and concentrated absorption (*samādhi*). This is in effect the alternation between the so-called analytic meditation (*dpyad sgom*) and fixed meditation (*'jog sgom*) that would become important for later Tibetan thinkers in their theoretical account of meditation, as we see, for example, in the extensive endorsement it received in the "insight" chapter of the *Lam rim chen mo* of Tsong kha pa (1357–1419) (see Newland 2002, 351ff; see Tillemans 1998 on the debate in Tibet). The essential point of the method was – and is still conceived to be – that the practitioner continues this process of alternation until he can finally conjoin calmness with insight and the object of meditation (e.g., moment by moment change, the painfulness of phenomena, selflessness, the uncleanliness of the body, etc.) appears clearly without the intermediary of conceptual representation. The goal is thus the development, via a series of analyses and intense concentration, of *yogipratyakṣa*, a yogin's direct perception of higher and thus liberating features about reality, features that appear to him as vividly as in a sense perception.

Such a position on meditation and the resultant yogic perception (*yogipratyakṣa*) was not at all unique to Kamalaśīla. His philosophy on yogins' knowledge and almost all other matters epistemological was derived largely from Dharmakīrti, a seventh-century thinker who had an extraordinary influence on later Indian and Tibetan Buddhism.[2] Kamalaśīla's philosophy of meditation and *yogipratyakṣa* thus concords by and large with mainstream Indo-Tibetan Buddhist *theoretical* accounts. Not only did Buddhists from Dharmakīrti to Śāntarakṣita, Kamalaśīla, and Ratnakīrti promote it, but it was what non-Buddhists, such as Vācaspatimiśra, took to be the main Buddhist theory and criticized (see Taber 2009). And in Tibet, too, it was by and large the received theory of meditation and yogic knowledge, promoted especially intensely by the Geluk (*dge lugs*) and Sakya (*sa skya*) schools. Indeed, prominent twentieth-century Geluk teachers would regularly stress the importance of Kamalaśīla-style meditation, and would often repeat verbatim the formulae Kamalaśīla used to ridicule the followers of Heshang.

Kamalaśīla's opponent, Heshang, on the other hand, dismissed philosophical analysis as antithetical to meditation and utterly unable to lead to liberating insight; instead he advocated a non-conceptual approach. While it is not precisely settled who his doctrinal ancestors were, it is apparent that he subscribed to major Chan (Zen) ideas and advocated a certain variant, prevalent in the Dunhuang Buddhist circles that he frequented, on *kan xin* 看心 "[non-conceptually] looking at the mind." His formulations of recurring Chan ideas are often provocative, as we see in a description of his views in the Dunhuang text entitled *Cig char yang dag pa'i phyi mo'i tshor ba* ("The Sudden Awakening to the Originally Real"). In this old Tibetan translation of an eighth-century Chinese Chan text, one is counseled to observe repeatedly the nature of thought until all appearances disappear, so that one dwells "perpetually in the source of [their] non-existence" (*brtag tu myed pa'i gnas*) (see Tanaka and Robertson 1992).

The details of Heshang's position on "appearances disappearing," etc., are perhaps somewhat odd and may even seem philosophically unsophisticated – interestingly enough, Heshang himself admitted to Kamalaśīla that he was no match for him, lacking scholarship and skill in debate. However, the broad outline of the position is certainly discernible from Wang Xi's memoir:

> "Looking at the mind" (*kan xin* 看心) means turning one's focus inward to the "source of the mind" (*xin yuan* 心源) and abstaining from all thought and examination (*bu si bu guan* 不思不觀), whether notions arise or not and whether they are pure, impure, empty or non-empty.[3]

There is thus no use for alternation between philosophical analysis and concentrated absorption and equally no place for a Dharmakīrtian version of yogic perception gained by strenuous effort and development of concentration; when a person directly sees the innately present nature of mind, he or she is suddenly and fully enlightened.

What do we know about the pair of key terms that Heshang used to designate this abstention from thought? As Demiéville pointed out (Demiéville 1987 [1952], 78–9, n. 3), the possible Sanskrit equivalents for the terms *bu si* 不思 and *bu guan* 不觀 are many depending on the periods and the translators; among others he gives *avicāra-avitarka* (no analysis, no rational deliberation) (ibid., 15, n. 1). Elsewhere, in related Tibetan or Chinese contexts treating of Heshang's views, we find terms such as *mi/myi rtog pa* and *wu fen bie* 無分別 (= *avikalpa*), which can be rendered as "no(n) conceptualization," although the Chinese quite clearly adds the nuance of "no differentiation" (see ibid., 128). Finally, when Kamalaśīla depicts Heshang's position in *Bhāvanākrama* III, he almost always uses the Sanskrit terms *asmṛti* (not bringing to mind, no remembrance) and *amanasikāra* (not focusing upon, not thinking about) (Tucci 1971, 15–17), which seems to be his attempt to use essentially Abhidharmic notions to translate the usual Chan terms "no-thinking" (*wu nian* 無念) and "no-mind" (*wu xin* 無心) (Demiéville 1987 [1952], 80 n.).

Given the plethora of terms, it may thus seem that the potential was extremely high for a debate at cross purposes. Such indeed seems to have been the conviction of Paul Demiéville who warned:

> The protagonists of the Council of Lhasa [= the Samyé debate] must have constantly ended up in impasses because they did not attribute the same sense to the words that were always coming back again and again in the debate.[4]

If this were right, then understanding the debate would be largely a matter for philological and historical analysis where one sought above all to sort out the (perhaps deliberate) semantic confusions; one might even eventually find (as Demiéville seems to attempt to do) a significant degree of reconciliation and common ground between the parties once the terminological misunderstandings had been cleared away.

I would venture that, fortunately, things are not quite as badly confused terminologically as Paul Demiéville seems to have thought them to be. Even though the terms are varied across three languages, sympathetically understanding this debate is not essentially or only a matter of untangling a series of misunderstandings by detailed philological and historical analyses. The various terms can be seen as attempts to express a relatively constant idea about not thinking, not analyzing, not representing things conceptually. Indeed, the records of this debate bring out the parties' markedly different philosophical and religious stances; those differences are real and not simply explicable as due to "a text that is rife with terminological misunderstandings" (*un texte qui fourmille de malentendus terminologiques*; Demiéville 1987 [1952], 22). Perhaps the most basic formulation that is used to represent Heshang's views is Kamalaśīla's *na kiṃcic cintayitavyam* (Tucci 1971, 14), "one shouldn't think about anything at all." The formula is obviously very blunt and simple, but it is not fundamentally wrong, confused, or unfair to Heshang. The enemy of insight is conceptualization *simpliciter*; understanding the world via the intermediary of any concepts and representations – be they true, pure, impure, false, what have you – is thus an obstacle to spiritual insight.

III

The exchange between Kamalaśīla and Heshang was heatedly polemical. Kamalaśīla argued repeatedly in the third book of the *Bhāvanākrama* that the Chinese path, whereby a practitioner does away with all conceptual thought, results in nothing more than voluntary stupefaction; being in a state of "no thinking" (*amanasikāra*) as Heshang understands it[5] – i.e., without any dependence upon analysis or reasoning – is thus nothing noble or enlightening as the practitioner simply does not know anything at all, *period*.

Kamalaśīla, however, went much further, and here is where things did arguably become unfair. For him, practicing Heshang's non-conceptualization would mean that all moral observances and other basic Buddhist practices would go by the wayside and that, in sum, the Buddhist path would be utterly destroyed. Let me translate a substantial representative passage from Kamalaśīla's *Bhāvanākrama* III to convey the issues and the tone of the debate.

> What [Heshang] thought, however, was the following: When sentient beings experience karmic results like rebirths in heavens, [hells] and so forth due to the virtuous and unvirtuous karma that they produce through their conceptual thinking, they transmigrate in *saṃsāra*. But on the other hand, whosoever thinks about nothing at all and does no action (*karma*) at all will be thoroughly liberated from *saṃsāra*. Thus, one should not think about anything at all (*na kiṃcic cintayitavyam*). Nor should one practice virtues such as giving and the like. Giving and other such practices were only taught for foolish people (*mūrkhajanam adhikṛtya*).
>
> [We reply:] That is tantamount to rejecting the whole of the "Great Vehicle" (*mahāyāna*). Now, the most fundamental of all the [Buddhist] vehicles is the Great Vehicle, so that if one rejects it, then one would end up rejecting absolutely all vehicles. Indeed, by saying that one should not think about anything, one would reject any insight (*prajñā*) that can be characterized as being a "correct examination" (*bhūtapratyavekṣālakṣaṇā*). Because the root of all correct understanding is correct examination, then by rejecting the latter one

> would reject [all], even transcendental, insight. And because one rejects that, one would reject omniscience (*sarvākārajñatā*). And by saying that one should not practice giving and the like either, then it is utterly obvious that one would reject "methods" (*upāya*) [of Buddhist morality] like giving and so forth. Now, this is precisely how one can summarize the Great Vehicle, i.e., insight and methods. [. . .]. So therefore, one who does not respect scholars, has not learned the ways of the Tathāgata's teaching, is himself lost and makes others lost too, will violate both scripture and reasoning, and thus his discourse, contaminated as it is with poison, should be cast out very far away by anyone intelligent who desires [the best] for himself, just as if it were toxic food.[6]

Woe to the heretic! Heshang is, in short, depicted not just as a misguided promulgator of some ineffectual methods of meditation; he is an enemy of the faith putting forth theories that are supposedly toxic to anyone who consumes them.

Kamalaśīla was no doubt irritated by what he perceived as Heshang's anti-intellectualism and disrespect for scholars, and hence the somewhat petulant remark that Heshang was "one who does not respect scholars, has not learned the ways of the Tathāgata's teaching, is himself lost and makes others lost too." Probably a good deal of Kamalaśīla's motivation was plain conservatism. He sought to defend the Buddhist institutions of learning as found in the later Indian monastic universities, while Heshang, with his professed rejection of all conceptual thinking, at least indirectly threatened those institutions and their hierarchy. That said, it is hardly surprising to find such politicized exchanges. The Indian party was surely *not* trying to be charitable towards Heshang or a Heshang-like position, and the Samyé debate was never destined to be collaborative. The mistake would be to think that, because it was strongly politicized, it was only politics and never philosophy.

IV

Let's leave aside the vested political interests of conservative religious institutions and their defenders. What could we say if we took the charitable high road? In Kamalaśīla's favor, we could certainly grant that observing moral precepts and making ethical decisions would involve thinking and intentions, the latter being (according to basic Buddhism) responsible for *karma*, with good intentions leading to good karmic results and good rebirths. But did Heshang mean only that a practitioner should not think conceptually when engaged in meditation, or did he actually advocate no conceptual thought *across the board*, even in more ordinary contexts where decisions, intentions, and analyses *do* undoubtedly matter? If the latter were what he meant, then Heshang would not just be a bad Buddhist, as Kamalaśīla alleges, but it is hard to see how he could function at all in most of the complex affairs of daily life and human society. Reading Wang Xi's memoir, however, gives the distinct impression that it is the former that Heshang advocated, and certainly the principle of charity would be against an *across the board* and total abstention from thinking. The provocative phrase "Giving and other such practices were only taught for foolish people," if it were interpreted more charitably than it is by Kamalaśīla, would not mean that Heshang actually advocated that the wise behave in a thoroughly antinomian fashion and reject all Buddhist morality as just "conceptual distinctions," but only that the wise would not take moral practices and the conceptual discriminations that they involve as the way to enlightenment. It would be only fools who make *that* mistake. In short, moral concepts and actions might be important in life, but moralizing fools go wrong in holding that they are also enlightening.

We will not pursue the passionate, but seemingly confused, polemic about the ethical implications of Heshang's philosophy. Instead we'll take the main issue in Samyé as whether not-thinking *in meditation* can lead to enlightenment or whether such meditation invariably results in voluntarily induced stupefaction. Kamalaśīla, of course, says that it does invariably result in stupefaction, and he repeatedly characterizes this meditative state of mind as being like the absence of thinking that occurs when someone simply faints (*saṃmūrchita*), is bereft of memory/awareness (*muṣitasmṛti*), or is utterly stupid (*atyantamūḍha*) (Tucci 1971, 16). Such a *reductio ad absurdum* of the Chinese position figures repeatedly in the *Bhāvanākrama* and in the subsequent chronicles of the Samyé debate, and it is regularly cited approvingly by later Tibetan writers, such as Tsong kha pa and others, who saw themselves as building on the victorious eighth-century dialectics of Kamalaśīla. It is, undoubtedly, at the heart of the debate.

Now, one might easily (and in the end wrongly, I think) say that this *reductio* too was no more than rhetorical intimidation because Kamalaśīla simply begged the question as to whether there is a significant difference between the not-thinking of an unconscious individual – e.g., someone who has fainted or is comatose – and the not-thinking of someone who is perfectly conscious and lucid. An intelligent follower of Heshang could of course insist that there is such a significant difference and that Kamalaśīla was deliberately being uncharitable by disregarding it.[7] Indeed, Heshang himself seems to have allowed that the non-conceptual state he was advocating was not one of complete absence of concepts – a type of perfectly blank mind or *tabula rasa* – but one in which notions, "whether they operate or not" (see note 3), are not thought about – i.e., not *pursued by conceptual thought*. We find roughly comparable methods of not pursuing thoughts in several schools, including Tibetan Mahāmudrā and Great Perfection (*rdzogs chen*) philosophies, which also develop the idea of "directly becoming acquainted with the nature of the mind" (*sems kyi ngo sprod*) without the intermediary of conceptual thoughts, and in the "insight meditation" (*vipassanā* = *vipaśyanā*) of certain Theravāda traditions as well. There is no doubt a big difference between simply having a dull thoughtless *tabula rasa* and lucidly abstaining from pursuing the thoughts that arise.

Was *that* kind of distorted argumentation all there was to the debate? I do not think so. There *were* serious issues – and not just repeated question begging – about whether non-thinking leads to meditative self-stultification. As I think it will become clear, these issues won't simply go away if we take Heshang's "not-thinking" as meaning "lucidly not pursuing thoughts." Kamalaśīla's arguments can very well be seen as undermining that position too. So let's take up two serious issues in the debate.

V

First, the Samyé debate turned in part on rival metaphysical accounts of the buddhahood, or the buddha-nature, that is supposedly present in all sentient beings so that they *can* become enlightened.[8] Heshang's view was that people are and have been all along a buddha, fully and *ab initio*. The innately present enlightened mind is thus to be directly disclosed or manifested; enlightenment is not something newly gained by a series of conceptual steps leading to better and more vivid understandings of metaphysical principles, such as emptiness, suffering, impermanence, etc. In reply to the objection "How does one obtain omniscience [i.e., enlightenment] if one has no notions, reflection or analysis?," Heshang supposedly said: "If thoughts don't arise and one abstains from all notions, the true nature that exists in us and omniscience manifest by themselves."[9] The connection Heshang wishes to make between non-conceptualization and realizing innate enlightenment is thus the following: concepts distort or even preclude our understanding of that nature; it is only by avoiding them that the true innate enlightened nature – the buddha-nature – can manifest.

To this, Yeshé wang po (*ye shes dbang po*), a prominent Tibetan monk in Kamalaśīla's entourage, supposedly argued as follows, according to the sixteenth-century chronicle *mKhas pa'i dga' ston*:

> If you [Heshang] accede suddenly [to enlightenment] then why are you still doing anything? If you are a buddha from the beginning (*dang po nas sangs rgyas*), what then is wrong? (*mKhas pa'i dga' ston* 1986, 389; see Tillemans 1998, 406)[10]

And elsewhere on the same page in this Tibetan history, Yeshé wang po is said to have insisted upon the absurdity of "being enlightened without having done anything at all" (*ci yang ma byas par 'tshang rgya ba*) (Tillemans 1998, 406). A similar charge also figures in the *Bhāvanākrama* itself: the Suddenist's passive, non-conceptual state could not possibly constitute enlightenment, "because it would follow absurdly that everyone everywhere would be liberated" (*sarvatra sarveṣāṃ muktiprasaṅgāt*) (Tucci 1971, 16). The arguments against Heshang's view on the buddha-nature and sudden enlightenment are, in effect, a kind of appeal to gradualist common sense.

Such rival metaphysical accounts on how one is innately, or "from the beginning (*dang po nas*)," do impact significantly on the main question of whether non-conceptualization leads to spiritual progress or ever greater stupefaction. Kamalaśīla (like many mainstream Indian paṇḍits of his time) probably had a relatively "thin" description of the buddha-nature as a mere potential for enlightenment, so that the practitioner is not actually enlightened but can become enlightened by following a certain step-by-step path. Heshang, on the other hand, had a very "thick" description of that nature as an enlightened state that is actual and fully present "from the beginning." For Kamalaśīla, then, simply abiding in a non-conceptual state is an obstacle to progress. One does not "see" anything soteriologically relevant – just more of the same dullness and confusion – and thus one would remain as ignorant as one is or regress even further.

With a thick description of the buddha-nature, on the other hand, there is something very important to be disclosed. It is not clear how Heshang himself answered the specific objection of Kamalaśīla's entourage that, if sentient beings had innate (full) buddhahood, any effort and practice would be redundant. But in one way or another the problem comes up repeatedly in traditions – such as the Great Perfection (*rdzogs chen*) – that advocate such innate enlightenment and a disclosive path by which it is actualized without artifice or effort. These thinkers – often polemically tarred in later literature as close to Heshang – then had to develop their respective versions of what constituted ignorance and the path to overcome it, all the while recognizing that enlightenment was innately present all along as a type of innate awareness (*rig pa*). Disclosive artifice-less paths are no doubt more elusive than their gradualist counterparts. It is not possible to take them up here in any detail.[11] Suffice it to say that Tibetan thinkers devoted deep thought to this matter and seem to have been aware of the gross absurdities to be avoided. It is hard to see that all such accounts are *a priori* precluded by "common-sense" charges of redundancy like those leveled by Kamalaśīla and his entourage.

VI

The other serious difference between the parties is on the *epistemological value* of not thinking about things and not pursuing notions analytically. Kamalaśīla repeatedly speaks of the necessity for the meditator to engage in rigorous philosophical analysis, "correct examination" (*bhūtapratyavekṣā*), without which he or she falls into the trap of stupefaction (Tucci 1971, 16–17). Why would Heshang – or anyone like him – fall into that trap if he or they consciously abstained from rigorous analytic thinking and simply remained meditatively lucid?

In fact, what is in the background is once again a key theme in Dharmakīrtian epistemology, namely, the proper way in which knowledge can be reached by "non-apprehension" (*anupalabdhi*). Kamalaśīla, as a Mādhyamika, held that no things have intrinsic natures (*svabhāva*) – natures that they would have purely "in themselves" independently of other things. This "absence of intrinsic nature" (*niḥsvabhāvatā*), which constitutes ultimate and hence liberating truth, is to be understand by means of a Dharmakīrtian non-apprehension (see Keira 2004). The meditator thus uses Madhyamaka-like reasonings – typically four or sometimes five major "reasons" (see Tillemans 1984, 361, 371 n. 16) – to convince himself that such natures are in fact impossible, and thus that they cannot be found or apprehended (*upalabdhi*) anywhere under "correct examination" (*bhūtapratyavekṣā*).

Now, there is, for Kamalaśīla (as for most people), a crucial difference between *concluding* rationally that something does not exist and simply not thinking about its existence. This is the difference between a rationally founded "non-apprehension" or "non-perception" (*anupalabdhi*; *anupalambha*; *adarśana*) of something and a "mere [rationally unfounded] absence" (*abhāvamātra*) of thinking or apprehension. In the former case, one examines the notion of X and shows it to be incoherent and hence that it cannot exist, or one searches physically for X under conditions where it would normally be visible if it were there. When one does not apprehend it for appropriate reasons (e.g., that it is impossible, or that it is not observed where it should be observed), one concludes rightly that it does not exist. In the latter case, however, one does not conclude anything at all: one just does not think about the matter. The former then leads to knowledge (i.e., true understanding reached by a reliable procedure), whereas the latter does not, and indeed, so Kamalaśīla would argue, is conducive to dullness: the more it is "practiced" the less one would know. It is this latter type of meditation – i.e., mere absence of awareness and thinking (*smṛtimanasikārābhāvamātra*; Tucci

1971, 15) – that Heshang supposedly advocated and that was, for Kamalaśīla, a method conducive to indifference and neglect, but nothing more.[12]

The issue is thus the epistemic worth of meditative states. Kamalaśīla's central point could be reformulated as follows: the debate is not about whether Heshang-style meditation would likely make one *become* semi-comatose or have other such damaging psychological effects. Instead, the debate is about the *value* of the Heshang-style meditative state of mind. The charge would be that, even if it were psychologically possible to be non-conceptually lucid and not pursue notions further, this would yield no knowledge. "Stultification" would then refer to the lack of knowledge that occurs when people, for one bad reason or another, fail to think things through rigorously and seek to understand by another means – i.e., a meditation that bypasses or avoids analysis.

VII

The debate thus formulated has larger philosophical implications. What generally is the epistemic worth or epistemic contribution of a meditative state of mind when it is based upon good philosophical thinking about real states of affairs? And what is its worth if it is not? There are, broadly speaking, two recurring traditional Buddhist, as well as modern, orientations on the relationship between meditative and philosophical approaches. Roughly, the two are: (1) a "continuity thesis" – viz., that meditative understanding leads to knowledge of objects but is continuous with and dependent upon philosophical thinking; or (2) an "independence thesis" – i.e., the position that meditative states of mind are independent of philosophy. This latter thesis has it variants: it is sometimes held that meditation is "aphilosophical," only a practical matter that does not need to be assessed philosophically; or it can be thought that meditation is radically different from, or opposed to, philosophical evaluation. In the final part of this chapter, we will consider the prospects for both these theses and their variants.

First, to take up the continuity thesis, this view is clearly what Dharmakīrti, Kamalaśīla, and other later mainstream Indian Buddhist thinkers held. So, if we take the Indian discussions as instructive – as I think we should, given that these later Indian Buddhists developed the details of their position in almost unparalleled depth and subtlety – what then are the philosophical prospects for this view on meditation? The prospects would appear to be quite mixed. Of course, as we have seen, there is little doubt that meditative understanding as depicted in Kamalaśīla-style Indian accounts is indeed somehow interwoven with philosophy, but the key question is whether that version of meditative understanding could make any contribution to knowledge *distinct from or over and above* the contributions of philosophical thinking. If we look at the textual accounts on this, I do not think it would.

Let us, then, look briefly at the mainstream Indian Buddhist discussions of the "direct perception of the yogin" (*yogipratyakṣa*) that is supposedly the goal of meditation. Kamalaśīla's philosophical mentor, Dharmakīrti, had recognized that the direct perception of the yogin is engendered by the power of the yogin's concentration, and is not caused or directly linked to an object in the world. Instead of arising *because* of the object (as in the case of sense perception) it arises because of previously developed mental powers. It seems then that the would-be "direct perception" is not very direct at all, as it is caused by factors quite different from the properties of the object – primarily by the subject's extraordinary powers of visualization.

Indians were rightly worried that, as there would be no direct causal connection with real objects (contrary to the case of sense perception, where there is such a connection), the possibility of error would loom large. What makes the would-be yogic perception more than a subjective state unanchored in reality, a *mere auto-suggestion*, and hence quite possibly wrong? This doubt was also formulated by non-Buddhist thinkers such as Vācaspatimiśra and is to be taken seriously.[13]

Indeed Kamalaśīla and Dharmakīrti themselves recognized that seeming "direct perceptions" engendered by previous thought processes could well turn out to be merely auto-induced hallucinations, as is the case when a man, overpowered by his intense desires, has vivid obsessive fantasies.[14] The test for Dharmakīrti, Devendrabuddhi, Dharmottara, and others as to whether a putative yogic perception is a mere hallucination or not is to see whether it can be vindicated by philosophical analysis.[15] It is to be examined by reason (*yukti*) and determined to be in accordance with other reliable means of knowledge (*pramāṇa*). In short, genuine yogic perception must apprehend matters that have already been confirmed rationally or will subsequently pass the tests of philosophical thinking (see Eltschinger 2009, 195ff.) This may sound ingenious, but it is surprising how little autonomy it accords meditation. It is clear that all the epistemic weight is once again on philosophical thinking and that yogic perception adds no new discoveries of truths.

One could of course just bite the bullet and agree that the yogic perception promoted by Kamalaśīla and Dharmakīrti *is* nothing more than a vivid presentation of conclusions reached by prior correct rational analysis. It could arguably still be important and transformative, at least psychologically. Indeed, yogic perception of a real object might well be comparable to a fictional or cinematographic re-creation of a real historical event; such re-creations, when done well, certainly do affect individuals' emotional lives and ways of understanding events. Nonetheless, it seems clear that it would not provide any new *information* from what had been given by philosophy (just as a modern cinematographic dramatization of a historical event by itself adds nothing new to the historian's knowledge of the details of the event). Kamalaśīla's yogic perception, in effect, appears to be neither a genuine direct perception nor a source of new knowledge, but rather a type of amplification or integration of the contents of philosophical thought. Philosophy would be doing the significant epistemic work of discovering truths. This version of the continuity thesis, in effect, would relegate meditation to the status of a powerful accessory.

Second, what are the prospects for the independence thesis? There is, at the outset, a confused variant of this position that has wide currency in modern circles that promote Buddhist meditation. It is more or less the following: Buddhist meditative states are better not assessed philosophically; meditation is "aphilosophical" in that it is practical in orientation and seeks primarily improvement of the mind rather than knowledge of truths. In brief, what counts is the therapy, the cultivation of beneficial states; meditation *need not* aim for knowledge of real objects. Thus, for example, some modern applications of Buddhist "mindfulness meditation" largely pass over Buddhist philosophical positions on metaphysical issues in favor of techniques to develop calmness, increased concentration, improvement of memory, happiness, stress management, harm reduction, better decision-making, and other benefits.[16]

Whatever the efficacy of these Buddhist-based techniques might be – and I'm not putting their therapeutic efficacy into question – interpreting Buddhist meditation in terms of psychological, physiological, or neurological effects largely to the exclusion of two thousand years of rich philosophical, religious, and ethical thought is uncomfortably close to trivialization. It is very doubtful that an emphasis on psychological techniques could be taken as reflecting the essentials of Buddhist meditation. Buddhists generally hold that accomplishing the religious goal of enlightenment involves knowledge of how things are and not just psychological techniques for developing desirable states of mind and traits of character.

There is, however, a more sophisticated variant of the idea of Buddhist meditation, and Buddhism in general, as a form of therapy. People familiar with philosophies such as those of the American thinkers William James, Thomas Dewey, Richard Rorty, and others, sometimes argue that Buddhism is *not* indifferent to getting things right and knowing reality, but that it is essentially a form of philosophical pragmatism.[17] The criterion for any state of mind being (or leading to) knowledge of real things, then, is just that it will result in maximally useful/beneficial effects, or the long-term accomplishment of such human goals as liberation from the realm of suffering. In short, Buddhists are not purely practical therapists disregarding issues of knowledge; they pursue soteriological goals as *pragmatists* in their philosophies of truth and knowledge.

It has sometimes been argued that Dharmakīrti's philosophy, with its emphasis on *arthakriyā* – i.e., effective action, sometimes interpreted as "the accomplishment of human goals" – did indeed focus on a pragmatic theory of truth, and that this is even one of its more attractive features (see Powers 1994; Cabezón 2000). I have on occasion argued against this interpretation of Dharmakīrtian thought, seeing his philosophy as involving instead a rather specific type of correspondence theory (Tillemans 1999, 6–12). Be that as it may, we need not try to settle that debate over truth theories: even if we agreed that Dharmakīrti and Kamalaśīla were somehow amenable to philosophical pragmatism, it is doubtful that they, as pragmatists, could agree that not thinking about things, or any other meditative technique, results in maximal utility *unless they had some plausible account of how it could accomplish that end.* Alas, mere unexplained data on success rates shows precious little about genuine efficacy.[18] At some point we need to fill in the gaps and account for why such and such a technique is likely to succeed when practiced in such and such circumstances, etc., and another is not. One way to see Kamalaśīla's arguments is that, for him, no such account will be forthcoming in the case of a purely non-conceptual meditation. Kamalaśīla may perhaps have been wrong on the specific matter of whether such meditation could work, but he was surely on the right track in putting the onus on an advocate of non-conceptual meditation to show that the explanatory gap could be bridged.

Finally, are there more promising defenses of the independence thesis in traditional Indo-Tibetan Buddhism that do address that gap? Already from the time of the *Madhyamakārthasaṃgraha* (attributed rightly or wrongly to the sixth-century author Bhāviveka), some Indian Buddhists promote the idea that a propositional philosophical understanding of the ultimate differs radically from an understanding of the ultimate as it is. The former, termed *paryāya* (expedient, approximative), is a kind of philosophers' version of the ultimate; the latter – i.e., *aparyāya* (not expedient, not approximative) – is genuine and beyond propositional thought. And indeed many are the Indo-Tibetan thinkers that would emphasize in one way or another the transcendence and inconceivability of genuine Buddhist knowledge of the ultimate. That said, in the present context, a mere appeal to inconceivability is very short on explanation. We would need much more to address Kamalaśīla's explanatory demands.

One of the more audacious defenses of the independence thesis is that of the Tibetan polymath Long chen pa (klong chen rab 'byams pa, 1308–1364), who made a wide-ranging distinction between "dualistic mind," or "dichotomizing thought" (*sems*), and "primordial gnosis" (*ye shes*). Propositional, philosophical knowledge is in the domain of the former and non-objective, non-dual, ultimate understanding in the latter. Enlightenment is taken to be the disclosure of this primordial gnosis itself – dualistic mind is in fact something samsaric to be eliminated[19] – and is a special type of understanding free from all objects (*yul*). The aim of a meditative approach would thus be knowledge of deep features of reality, but not knowledge that could be said to be *of* any objects, states of affairs, or true propositions.[20]

The question will rightly arise, too, as to why one should value this "intransitive" type of meditation[21] as leading to genuine knowledge, for clearly, once philosophy has been dismissed as "dualistic thought" and is regarded as something to be eliminated, the usual epistemological ways of evaluating reliability are not available. The reasoning Long chen pa develops for the value and trustworthiness of such meditative states and gnosis does not, indeed, follow usual Buddhist epistemological strategies. Instead they appear to be essentially transcendental arguments, seeking to show that, if we accept that enlightenment is possible, then a primordial gnosis must be presupposed as underlying all samsaric thought. There is a sense in which Long chen pa stands Kamalaśīla's arguments on their head. Whereas Kamalaśīla had argued that non-conceptualization leads to stultification and that we therefore need to rely on concepts, Long chen pa begins with the premise that conceptualization and all other forms of "dualistic thinking" must be abandoned if we are to become enlightened – this he takes to be the basic recurring message of Buddhist canonical literature. However, he does not accept that enlightenment could consist in a *mere* abandonment of concepts and dualistic thinking, as this *would* lead to a stupor (*mun pa*), just as Kamalaśīla had argued. There must therefore be a more fundamental underlying understanding, a ground (*gzhi*) or innate awareness (*rig pa*), that is always present and whose disclosure is enlightenment.[22] The arguments, although they can and will be challenged at several places, would seem to turn on intriguing intuitions: that if one was not somehow actually enlightened all along, one never could become so; that the state of *saṃsāra* and its ignorance would seem to be a form of intelligent self-deception, rather than just darkness or absence of understanding.[23] It may well be that this approach – or one broadly along these lines – would hold the most promise for the independence theorist.

Notes

1 Some of the other important publications in the considerable literature on the subject are Gomez (1983); Tucci (1986 [1956], 1971); Seyfort Ruegg (1989); and Williams (1992).

2 On yogic perception in Dharmakīrti, see, e.g., Eltschinger (2009, 2010); Taber (2009); Woo (2003); and Dunne (2006). In Kamalaśīla's defense of yogic perception in his work the *Madhyamakāloka*, we see him regularly quoting the major definitions and ideas of Dharmakīrti; see Keira (2004, 5: 101ff.). On Dharmakīrti's philosophy and biography, see Tillemans (2011); Eltschinger (2010); and the references therein.

3 See the translation of Wang Xi's memoir in Demiéville (1987 [1952], 78–80): *Question ancienne* – Qu'entendez-vous par « regarder l'esprit » [i.e., *kan xin*]? *Réponse* – Retourner la vision vers la source de l'esprit, c'est « regarder l'esprit »; c'est s'abstenir absolument de toute réflexion et de tout examen, que les notions se mettent en mouvement ou non, qu'elles soient pures ou impures, qu'elles soient vides ou ne le soient pas, etc.; c'est ne pas réfléchir sur la non-réflexion. C'est pourquoi il est dit dans le *Vimalakīrti-sūtra:* « Le non-examen, c'est la *bodhi* ».

4 Our translation of Demiéville (1987 [1952], 22): "Les protagonistes du concile de Lhasa durent constamment tomber dans les impasses parce qu'ils n'attribuaient pas le même sens aux mots qui revenaient sans cesse dans le débat."

5 Kamalaśīla does in fact accept a *certain* kind of *amanasikāra* – i.e., not thinking about such and such things when one has understood through analysis that they don't/can't exist. See note 12 below. But *that* of course is *not* what Heshang meant by the term. Hence the critique.

6 Sanskrit text in Tucci (1971, 13–15): *yas tu manyate / cittavikalpasamutthāpitaśubhāśubhakarmavaśena sattvāḥ svargādikarmaphalam anubhavantaḥ saṃsāre saṃsaranti/ ye punar na kiṃcic cintayanti nāpi kiṃcit karma kurvanti te parimucyante saṃsārāt / tasmān na kiṃcic cintayitavyam / nāpi dānādikuśalacaryā kartavyā / kevalaṃ mūrkhajanam adhikṛtya dānādikuśalacaryā nirdiṣteti / tena sakalamahāyānaṃ pratikṣiptaṃ bhavet / mahāyānamūlatvāc ca sarvayānānāṃ tatpratikṣepeṇa sarvam eva yānaṃ pratikṣiptaṃ syāt / tathā hi na kiṃcic cintayitavyam iti bruvatā bhūtapratyavekṣālakṣaṇā prajñā pratikṣiptā bhavet / bhūtapratyavekṣāmūlatvāt samyagjñānasya / tatpratikṣepāl lokottarāpi prajñā pratikṣiptā bhavet / tatpratikṣepāt sarvākārajñatā pratikṣiptā bhavet / nāpi dānādicaryā kartavyeti vadatā copāyo dānādiḥ sphuṭataram eva pratikṣiptaḥ / etāvad eva ca saṃkṣiptaṃ mahāyānaṃ yaduta prajñopāyaś ca / [. . .] tasmād asyānupāsitavidvajjanasyānavadhāritatathāgatapravacananīteḥ svayaṃ vinaṣṭasya parān api nāśayato yuktyāgamadūṣitatvāt viṣasaṃsṛṣṭavacanaṃ saviṣabhojanam ivātmakāmena dhīmatā dūrata eva parihartavyam / .*

7 There is evidence that Chan meditators were indeed confronted with the objection that their "no thought" would make them similar to wood and stones; they reply that their type of no thought has to be distinguished from the no thought of brute matter. The objection and reply figures in a Chan text attributed to Bodhidharma. See Demiéville (1987 [1952], 99, n. 2).

8 By and large, metaphysics is *not* a secondary speculation that subsequent scholastic thinkers impose upon an otherwise essentially practical activity, or upon an exclusively experiential state of mind. That it *is* secondary or derivative in this way is a longstanding view that has been argued by many major figures in Buddhist Studies, e.g., *inter alia* Constantin Regamey, Lambert Schmithausen, and Edward Conze. For critiques of this view of the derivative nature of Buddhist philosophy and the primacy of experience, see Sharf (1995) and Franco (2009). In much the same spirit as Franco (who discusses the positions of Regamey, Schmithausen, et al. in detail), I would suggest that accounts of what one should meditate upon, how one should do it, and what one will experience do vary notably with ontologies adopted about what is real, ultimate, and hence conducive to liberating experience. The Samyé debate on meditation seems to be no exception.

9 Cf. Demiéville (1987 [1952], 94–5): *Question ancienne* – Si l'on est sans notion, sans réflexion, sans examen, comment obtiendra-t-on l'omniscience? *Réponse* – Si les fausses pensées

ne se produisent pas et qu'on s'abstienne de toute fausse notion, la vraie nature qui existe au fond de nous-mêmes et l'omniscience se révèlent d'elles-mêmes. Note, however, that Demiéville's translation "fausses pensées" for *wang xin* 妄心 or "fausse notion" for *wang xiang* 妄想, while literally faithful to the Chinese, might lead one to think that Heshang is advocating that one just avoid false thoughts and instead seek true ones. The point is rather that *all* thoughts or notions are, in the important sense for Heshang, fundamentally false.

10 *mKhas pa'i dga' ston = Dam pa'i chos kyi 'khor lo bsgyur ba rnams kyi byung ba gsal bar byed pa mkhas pa'i dga' ston* of the sixteenth-century scholar dPa' bo gtsug lag phreng ba (Tsuklak Trengwa). Ed. rDo rje rgyal po. Beijing: Minzu chubanshe,1986.

11 I owe the term "disclosive path" to my student David Higgins. Higgins (2012) is a study on Long chen pa's key difference between conceptualizing *dualistic mind* (*sems*) and *primordial gnosis* (*ye shes*). See also Read (2009) on such disclosive Buddhist paths and Wittgenstein's famous ladders (or rather appearances of ladders) that are to be set aside.

12 Cf. *Bhāvanākrama* I (Tucci 1986 [1956], 211–13): . . . *tathā coktaṃ sūtre katamaṃ paramārthadarśanam / sarvadharmāṇām adarśanam iti / atredṛṣam evādarśanam abhipretam / na tu nimīlitākṣajātyandhānām iva pratyayavaikalyād amanasikārato vā yad adarśanam / . . . yat punar uktam avikalpapraveśadhāraṇyām amanasikārato rūpādinimittaṃ varjayatīti / tatrāpi prajñayā nirūpayato yo 'nupalambhaḥ sa tatrāmanasikāro 'bhipreto na manasikārābhāvamātram* /. "As it was said in the [Prajñāpāramitā]sūtra, 'What is the perception of the ultimate? It is the non-perception of any dharmas.' Here what is meant is just this kind of [analytical] non-perception, but not a non-perception that is due to causal circumstances being incomplete or due to lack of thought, as when, e.g., people close their eyes or are blind from birth." . . . "Moreover it was said in the Avikalpapraveśadhāraṇī, 'One eliminates characteristics of form and so forth, by not thinking [of them].' Here too, not thinking about them means the non-perception when one analyzes by means of insight, and not the mere absence of thinking."

13 Cf. Deleanu (2010, 61), who rightly underlines how autosuggestion is a serious problem *whenever* knowledge claims are made for meditation: "To put it bluntly, how can we be certain that at least part of the cognitive content gained through, or associated with, advanced meditative states is not the result of autosuggestion rather than of genuine knowledge?"

14 The comparison between yogic perception and such hallucinations had already figured in Dharmakīrti's *Pramāṇavārttika* (III.282), and regularly recurs in later writers, including Kamalaśīla, to serve as a supposedly comprehensible worldly analogy of how yogic perception proceeds. See Eltschinger (2009, 193–4); Keira (2004, 112–15).

15 See *Pramāṇavārttika* III.286: *tatra pramāṇaṃ saṃvādi yat prāṅnirṇītavastuvat / tad bhāvanājaṃ pratyakṣam iṣṭaṃ śeṣā upaplavāḥ* // "Amongst these [yogic understandings] we accept as a means of knowledge the meditation-induced direct perception that is reliable, like the entities that we had ascertained earlier. The rest are deluded."

16 Clear examples of such predominantly therapeutic use of aspects of Buddhist mindfulness meditation are what we find promoted by Elizabeth Stanley, at www.mind-fitness-training.org, or by Jon Kabat-Zinn in his Mindfulness Based Stress Reduction program at the University of Massachusetts. Cf. also the endorsements of these approaches by the Mind and Life Institute (www.mindandlife.org). Now, there were visualizations, concentration exercises, ways to pacify the mind by focusing on the breath, and several other such techniques. Probably the most notorious example in the scholastic literature is the so-called meditation on the loathsome (*aśubhābhāvanā*), in which the practitioner visualizes corpses "turning blue and rotting" or skeletons; another is visualizing the whole world as earth or water. Buddhist writers concerned with epistemological issues, as well as authors of other schools, recognized fully well that the corpses and water "seen" or visualized were unreal – the point of

doing such practices was thus certainly not knowledge of the real objects on which one meditated, but the psychological effects – non-attachment – that result. That said, I think that it does not need much textual exegesis – of either Hīnayāna or Mahāyāna texts – to show that the importance of such a psychological or purely therapeutic approach is quite limited if it is indifferent to questions of knowledge and reality.

17 As William James notoriously summarized his version of pragmatism: "an idea is 'true' so long as to believe it is profitable to our lives" (see Goodman 1995, 63).

18 The situation is not unlike people citing suggestive data on homeopathic cure rates without having an inkling as to how homeopathy could conceivably work given its use of minuscule doses of pharmacological agents.

19 Cf. *Sems dang ye shes kyi dris lan* of Long chen pa (klong chen rab 'byams pa), *gSung thor bu*, p. 384. *mdor bsdu na khams gsum pa'i sems sems byung cha dang bcas pa thog ma med pa nas brgyud pa'i bag chags can sgrib pa gnyis kyi ngo bo 'dzin cing / bskyed par brten pas spang bya yin zhing dgag dgos par bshad pa yin no /*. "In short, the three realms' dualistic minds (*sems* = *citta*), mental factors (*sems byung* = *caitta*), and their qualities are subject to imprints coming down from beginningless [time], have as nature the two obscurations and rely on production. As such, it is explained that they are to be eliminated and should be stopped."

20 In this respect, Long chen pa and other Great Perfection thinkers could be favorably compared with thinkers such as Heidegger, for whom discursive understanding and manipulation of things and propositions – the ontic – is parasitical upon a more fundamental understanding of Being.

21 I owe this classification of meditations into transitive and intransitive to D. Higgins.

22 *Theg mchog rin po che'i mdzod* of Long chen pa (p. 1041):*'dir mi shes pa kha cig / sems med na bems po'am mun pa ltar 'gyur ro zhes pa'ang thos pa chung ba yin te / sems med kyang ye shes yod pas rig pa 'gag pa ma yin pa'i phyir ro / de'ang ma rig pa 'khrul pa'i sems 'gags pas / ye shes gsal ba'i nyi ma 'char te / mtshan mo sangs pas nyin mo shar ba bzhin no /*. "Some ignorant people argue as follows: 'If there is no dualistic mind (*sems*), it is similar to being inanimate (*bems po*) or in a stupor (*mun pa*).' But these people have studied little. Even in the absence of dualistic mind, since primordial gnosis (*ye shes*) is present, it is not the so that awareness (*rig pa*) ceases. Moreover, through the cessation of ignorance, i.e., one's deluded dualistic mind, the sun of radiantly clear primordial gnosis dawns just as with the fading of night comes the dawning of day."

23 On ignorance, self-deception, and epistemic versions of *akrasia* in Buddhism, see Tillemans (2008).

References

Bhāviveka. *Madhyamakārthasaṃgraha.* Peking Tibetan Tripiṭaka 5258. Trans. in C. Lindtner (1981). Atiśa's Introduction to the Two Truths, and its Sources. In *Journal of Indian Philosophy* 9 (1981), 161–214, at 200–1, n. 14.

Cabezón, José I. (2000). Truth in Buddhist Theology. In *Buddhist Theology: Critical Reflections by Contemporary Buddhist Scholars*. Ed. R. Jackson and J. Makransky. London: Curzon, 136–54.

Deleanu, Florin (2010). Agnostic Meditations on Buddhist Meditation. In *Zygon: Journal of Religion and Science* 45, 605–26. www.zygonjournal.org.

Demiéville, Paul (1987 [1952]). Le Concile de Lhasa: une controverse sur le quiétisme entre bouddhistes de l'Inde et de la Chine au VIIIe siècle de l'ère chrétienne. Paris: Collège de France, Institut de Hautes Etudes Chinoises.

Dharmakīrti (1972). *Pramāṇavārttika.* Sanskrit and Tibetan ed. Y. Miyasaka. *Acta Indologica* 2, 1–206.

Dunne, John D. (2006). Realizing the Unreal: Dharmakīrti's Theory of Yogic Perception. In *Journal of Indian Philosophy* 34, 497–519.

Eltschinger, Vincent (2009). On the Career and Cognition of Yogins. In *Yogic Perception, Meditation and Altered States of Consciousness.* Ed. Eli Franco. Vienna: Verlag der Österreichischen Akademie der Wissenschaften, 169–213.

Eltschinger, Vincent (2010). Dharmakīrti. In *Revue internationale de philosophie* 64(3), 397–440.

Franco, Eli (ed.) (2009). *Yogic Perception, Meditation and Altered States of Consciousness.* Vienna: Verlag der Österreichischen Akademie der Wissenschaften.

Gomez, Luis O. (1983). Indian Materials on the Doctrine of Sudden Enlightenment. In *Early Ch'an in China and Tibet.* Ed. W. Lai and L. Lancaster. Berkeley Buddhist Studies Series. Berkeley: Asian Humanities Press, 393–434.

Goodman, Russell B. (1995). *Pragmatism: A Contemporary Reader.* New York and London: Routledge.

Higgins, David (2012). The Philosophical Foundations of Classical *rDzogs chen* in Tibet: Investigating the Distinction between Dualistic Mind (*sems*) and Primordial knowing (*ye shes*). Doctoral thesis, University of Lausanne.

Kamalaśīla. *Bhāvanākrama.* Sanskrit and Tibetan texts of chapters I and II in Tucci (1986); texts of chapter III in Tucci (1971). French translation of chapter III by E. Lamotte in Demiéville (1987). English summary of I and II in Tucci (1986).

Keira, Ryusei (2004). *Mādhyamika and Epistemology: A Study of Kamalaśīla's Method for Proving the voidness of all Dharmas.* Introduction, annotated translations, and Tibetan texts of selected sections of the second chapter of the *Madhyamakāloka.* Vienna: Arbeitskreis für Tibetische und Buddhistische Studien Universität Wien.

Long chen pa (klong chen rab 'byams pa). *Sems dang ye shes kyi dris lan* of Klong chen rab 'byams pa. In *Kun mkhyen klong chen pa dri med 'od zer gyi gsung thor bu.* Reproduced from xylographic prints from A 'dzom 'brug pa chos sgar blocks. 2 vols. Pema Thinley, Gangtok.

Long chen pa (klong chen rab 'byams pa). *Theg pa'i mchog rin po che'i mdzod* of Klong chen rab 'byams pa. Oddiyana Institute edition published by Tarthang Rinpoche based on blockprints from Khreng tu'u. [Available from Tibetan Buddhist Resource Center, www.tbrc.org]

Newland, G. (ed.) (2002). Tsong-ka-pa, *The Great Treatise on the Stages of the Path to Enlightenment.* Vol. 3. Ithaca, NY: Snow Lion.

Powers, John (1994). Empiricism and Pragmatism in the Thought of Dharmakīrti and William James. In *American Journal of Theology and Philosophy* 15(1), 59–85.

Read, Rupert (2009). Wittgenstein and Zen Buddhism: One Practice, No Dogma. In *Pointing at the Moon: Buddhism, Logic, Analytic Philosophy.* Ed. Jay L. Garfield, Tom J. F. Tillemans, and Mario D'Amato. New York: Oxford University Press, 13–23.

Seyfort Ruegg, David (1989). *Buddha-Nature, Mind and the Problem of Gradualism in a Comparative Perspective: On the Transmission and Reception of Buddhism in India and Tibet.* London: School of Oriental and African Studies.

Sharf, Robert (1995). Buddhist Modernism and the Rhetoric of Meditative Experience. In *Numen* 42(3), 228–83.

Taber, John (2009). Yoga and our Epistemic Predicament. In *Yogic Perception, Meditation and Altered States of Consciousness.* Ed. Eli Franco. Vienna: Verlag der Österreichischen Akademie der Wissenschaften, 71–92.

Tanaka, K. T., and Robertson, R. E. (1992). A Ch'an Text from Tun-huang: Implications for Ch'an Influence on Tibetan Buddhism. In *Tibetan Buddhism: Reason and Revelation.* Ed. S. D. Goodman and R. M. Davidson. Albany: State University of New York Press, 57–78.

Tillemans, Tom J. F. (1984). Two Tibetan Texts on the "Neither One nor Many" Argument for śūnyatā. In *Journal of Indian Philosophy* 12. 357–88.

Tillemans, Tom J. F. (1998). Issues in Tibetan Philosophy. In *Routledge Encyclopedia of Philosophy*. Ed. E. Craig. Vol. 9. London: Routledge, 402–9.

Tillemans, Tom J. F. (1999). *Scripture, Logic, Language: Essays on Dharmakīrti and his Tibetan Successors*. Studies in Indian and Tibetan Buddhism. Boston: Wisdom.

Tillemans, Tom J. F. (2008). Reason, Irrationality and Akrasia (Weakness of the Will) in Buddhism: Reflections upon Śāntideva's Arguments with Himself. In *Argumentation* 22, 149–63.

Tillemans, Tom J. F. (2011). Dharmakīrti. In *Stanford Encyclopedia of Philosophy*. At http://plato.stanford.edu/archives/fall2011/entries/dharmakiirti/.

Tsong kha pa Blo bzang grags pa. *Byang chub lam rim chen mo*. Trans. in Newland (2002).

Tucci, Giuseppe (1971). *Minor Buddhist Texts*, Pt. III. Serie Orientale Roma. Roma: Istituto Italiano per il Medio ed Estremo Oriente.

Tucci, Giuseppe (1986 [1956]). *Minor Buddhist Texts*, Pt. II. Containing the first *Bhāvanākrama* of Kamalaśīla. Sanskrit and Tibetan texts with introduction and English summary. Delhi: Motilal Banarsidass.

Wang Xi 王錫. *Dun wu da cheng zheng li jue* 頓悟大乘正理決 [= "Wang Xi's memoir"]. See Demiéville (1987).

Williams, Paul (1992). Non-Conceptuality, Critical Reasoning and Religious Experience: Some Tibetan Buddhist Discussions. In *Philosophy, Religion, and the Spiritual Life*. Ed. M. McGhee. Cambridge: Cambridge University Press, 189–210.

Woo, Jeson (2003). Dharmakīrti and his Commentators on Yogipratyakṣa. In *Journal of Indian Philosophy* 31, 439–48.

C. Language and Logic

19

Language and Logic in Indian Buddhist Thought

BRENDAN S. GILLON

Introduction

The study of human reasoning and the study of human language have been closely connected in European philosophical thought reaching all the way back to Aristotle (384–322 BCE). Except for the Buddhist thinker Dignāga (fifth century CE), these two areas of study have not been connected in classical India. However, the connection which Dignāga made between inference (*anumāna*) and meaning (*artha*) in his theory of exclusion (*apoha*) is a distinguishing feature of Buddhist philosophical thought in classical India and, for that reason, it is useful to treat the Indian Buddhist views of reasoning and meaning together. Yet, before we turn to Indian Buddhist reflections on these two topics, let us first bear in mind some very general things about language and reason.

Humans use language. Humans also reason: that is, taking some things to be true, humans conclude that other things are true. Now, the fact that a human uses a language does not mean that the person using the language can formulate the rules whereby its acceptable expressions are distinguished from its unacceptable ones. Similarly, the fact that a human reasons does not mean that the person reasoning can formulate the rules whereby good reasoning is to be distinguished from bad. Clearly, then, just as the fact that humans use language is no guarantee that those who do so reflect on which expressions are acceptable and which are not, so also the fact that humans reason is no guarantee that those who do so reflect on which reasoning is good and which is bad. Thus, just as the activity of using a language and the activity of reflecting on a language are distinct, so the activity of reasoning and the activity of reflecting on reasoning are distinct. And thus, too, just as the formulation of the grammar of a language results from reflection on the use of language, so the formulation of the rules of reasoning results from reflection on the use of reason.

A Companion to Buddhist Philosophy, First Edition. Edited by Steven M. Emmanuel.

Not every classical civilization tried to formulate rules to identify which expressions are part of the civilization's classical language and which are not. The classical Greek and Indian civilizations did, however. The earliest extant grammar to give the rules of Greek is the *Technē grammatikē* of Dionysius Thrax (c. 100 BCE), while the earliest extant grammar to give the rules of Sanskrit is the *Aṣṭādhyāyī* ("Eight Chapters") of Pāṇini, the great Sanskrit grammarian of early classical India (c. sixth–fifth century BCE). Nor did every classical civilization try to formulate rules whereby to distinguish good from bad reasoning. But, again, the classical Greek and Indian civilizations did. The earliest known formulation of rules of reasoning in classical Europe is that due to Aristotle; the earliest known formulation of rules of reasoning in classical India is not clear, but works attempting to do so date from at least the beginning of the common era.

Logic, at least as traditionally conceived, seeks to distinguish good reasoning from bad. More particularly, it seeks to identify the general conditions under which what one concludes is true, having taken other things to be true. This raises the questions of what it is which is true and what it is which is false. In contemporary philosophy, truth and falsity are usually taken to apply to linguistic expressions, declarative sentences, for example. But they can also be taken to apply to cognitive entities, such as thoughts or beliefs. Indeed, Aristotle (*De Interpretatione*, ch. 1) took truth and falsity to apply primarily to thoughts or beliefs and, by extension, to the sentences expressing thoughts or beliefs. After all, one can use a sentence to express a thought. If a thought is true and a sentence accurately expresses it, then the sentence expressing the thought is true.

This, in turn, suggests that reasoning can be seen as a sequence of thoughts, wherein, taking some thoughts to be true, one concludes that some other thought is true. Let us call such sequences of thoughts inferences. At the same time, Aristotle's observation suggests equally that reasoning can be seen as a sequence of sentences, where, taking some sentences to be true, one concludes that some other sentence is true. Let us call such sequences of sentences arguments. In this way, inference and argument are but two sides of the same coin: an argument can be thought, and hence become an inference; an inference can be expressed, and hence become an argument.

In addition to seeing reasoning cognitively and linguistically, one can view it symbolically, as contemporary logic does. Contemporary logic formulates rules whereby, when certain strings of symbols in a notation are taken to be true, another string of symbols in that notation is also taken to be true. The inspiration is clearly linguistic, for it seeks to put into a notation what is expressed in language, namely to specify that a sentence is true, if certain other sentences are true.

We see, then, that there are three perspectives on reasoning: the symbolic, the linguistic, and the cognitive. These perspectives differ according to what each takes the locus of truth to be: a thought, a sentence, or a string of symbols in a notation. However, they all share the idea of characterizing reasoning as, when some things are true, something else is true.

The linguistic perspective on reasoning suggests still a fourth perspective. A shared language makes it possible for one person to communicate his or her thoughts to anyone else who speaks the same language. More specifically, a shared language makes it possible to formulate arguments to communicate inferences. Indeed, humans often do so with the express aim of persuading other humans that something is true. Thus, reasoning, insofar as it is formulated as an argument, can also be viewed as a sequence of sentences where, accepting some sentences as true, one should accept another as true. Such is the dialectical perspective on reasoning.

Finally, there is the ontic perspective on reasoning. While, in one sense of the word "express," sentences may express one's thoughts, in another sense, sentences express the state of affairs which the corresponding thought takes to be its object. Thus, instead of asking, under what circumstances do certain thoughts being true require another thought to be true, one can ask under what circumstances do certain states of affairs, the ones corresponding to the true thoughts, require other states of affairs, the ones corresponding to the other true thought.

While we find in Aristotle all five perspectives, in classical India we find only the ontic, the epistemic, and the dialectic, and neither the linguistic nor the symbolic.

It is perhaps useful to illustrate the distinction between a linguistic approach and an ontic approach to logic with examples of how Aristotle, on the one hand, and various classical Indian thinkers, on the other, formulated the three laws of logic: the law of non-contradiction, the law of excluded middle, and the law of double negation. Let us begin with the law of non-contradiction. Here is an example of Aristotle's ontic formulation: "that a thing cannot at the same time be and not be" (*Metaphysics*, bk 3, ch. 2, 996b29–30). However, he also provides linguistic formulations, as exemplified by the following: "Contradictory statements are not at the same time true" (*Metaphysics*, bk. 4, ch. 6, 1011b13). Classical Indian thinkers, too, formulated the law of non-contradiction, but its formulation is always ontic. Thus, for example, the Buddhist philosopher Āryadeva (third century CE) asks the rhetorical question: "Moreover, how can one property be existent and also non-existent?" (Tucci 1929, 51, l. 7).

The law of excluded middle is formulated ontically by the classical Indian philosopher and grammarian Bhartṛhari (sixth century CE), who says in his work the *Vākyapadīya* ("On Sentences and Words") (bk 3, ch. 9, verse 85): "A thing is either existent or non-existent. There is no third." In contrast, the formulations by Aristotle tend to be linguistic: "One side of the contradiction must be true. Again, if it is necessary with regard to everything either to assert or to deny it, it is impossible that both should be false" (*Metaphysics*, bk. 4, ch. 8, 1012b10–12).

And, finally, the classical Indian thinkers also formulated the law of double negation ontically. This is how the Buddhist philosopher Dharmakīrti (seventh century CE) puts it in his *Pramāṇa-vārttika* ("Gloss on the Means of Epistemic Cognition"): "What other than affirmation is the negation of a negation?" (ch. 4, verse 221).

Logic in Indian Buddhism

Logic, as said above, seeks to distinguish good reasoning from bad. Since reasoning is often communicated and, to that extent, expressed in a language, it is natural to use the forms of language to identify the forms of reasoning. Aristotle, for example, devoted much effort to the analysis of language with a view to identifying forms of argument known as syllogisms and to distinguish among them those whose forms preserve truth and those which do not. Classical Indian thinkers were also sensitive to the fact that some forms of language give expression to good arguments and others to bad, though, unlike Aristotle, they never availed themselves of variables to describe the forms of the arguments which were their object of study. Their sensitivity is well illustrated by the arguments recorded in a Buddhist work of the third century BCE, Moggaliputta Tissa's *Kathā-vatthu* ("Points of Controversy"). This work contains the refutation by Sthaviravādins, one of the Buddhist schools, of some two hundred propositions held by other schools of Buddhism. The refutation of a proposition turns on demonstrating its inconsistency. In the passage below, for example, the Sthaviravādin questions his opponent, a Pudgalavādin, about whether or not the soul is known truly and ultimately.

STHAVIRAVĀDIN:	Is the soul known truly and ultimately?
PUDGALAVĀDIN:	Yes.
STHAVIRAVĀDIN:	Is the soul known truly and ultimately just like any ultimate fact?
PUDGALAVĀDIN:	No.
STHAVIRAVĀDIN:	Acknowledge your refutation. If the soul is known truly and ultimately, then indeed, good sir, you should also say that the soul is known truly and ultimately just like any ultimate fact. What you say here is wrong: namely, that we ought to say (a) that the soul is known truly and ultimately; but we ought not to say (b) that the soul is known truly and ultimately just like any ultimate fact. If the latter statement (b) cannot be admitted, then indeed the former statement (a) should not be admitted. It is wrong to affirm the former statement (a) and to deny the latter (b).

One easily abstracts from this the following form, which is repeatedly instantiated throughout Book 1, Chapter 1:

STHAVIRAVĀDIN:	Is A B?
PUDGALAVĀDIN:	Yes.
STHAVIRAVĀDIN:	Is C D?
PUDGALAVĀDIN:	No.
STHAVIRAVĀDIN:	Acknowledge your refutation. If A is B, then C is D. What you say here is wrong: namely, (a) that A is B but that C is not D. If C is not D, then A is not B. It is wrong that A is B and C is not D.

Clearly, the author takes for granted the following: first, that the propositions assented to are inconsistent, satisfying the following inconsistent propositional schemata of α, $\neg\beta$, $\alpha \rightarrow \beta$; second, that it is wrong to hold inconsistent propositions; and, third, that if $\alpha \rightarrow \beta$, then $\neg\beta \rightarrow \neg\alpha$ – that is, half of the equivalence of the principle of contraposition.

Over the following 500 years, Buddhist, Jain, and Brahmanical thinkers explicitly addressed the problem of distinguishing good arguments from bad. The earliest examples of arguments which are precursors to the canonical classical Indian syllogism are found in a commentary to a Brahmanical treatise on rational inquiry. The treatise, attributed to Gautama, who is also known as Akṣapāda (c. second century CE), is entitled the *Nyāya-sūtra* ("Aphorisms on Logic"); the commentary, written by Vātsyāyana (fifth century CE), also known as Pakṣalisvāmin, is entitled the *Nyāya-bhāṣya* ("Commentary on Logic"). Here is one of the arguments found in the commentary:

PROPOSITION (*pratijñā*):	sound is non-eternal
GROUND (*hetu*):	because of having the property of arising
CORROBORATION (*udāharaṇa*):	a substance, such as a pot, having the property of arising, is non-eternal
APPLICATION (*upanaya*):	and, likewise, sound has the property of arising
CONCLUSION (*nigamana*):	therefore, sound is non-eternal because of having the property of arising

This argument has the following form:

PROPOSITION (*pratijñā*):	p has S
GROUND (*hetu*):	p has H
CORROBORATION (*udāharaṇa*):	*d* has H and *d* has S
APPLICATION (*upanaya*):	As *d* has H and has S, so p has H and has S
CONCLUSION (*nigamana*):	p has S

Many other examples of arguments with essentially the same form are found in the commentary.

As noted by Randle (1930, ch. 3, sec. 4), the argument is clearly an argument from analogy. However, there soon emerged an argument of a similar form, which we would classify as a deductively valid argument. The earliest extant works which attempt to specify a related deductively valid argument are those of the Buddhist philosopher Vasubandhu (fifth century CE). Vasubandhu is thought to have written three works on logic, only two of which have survived and neither of them in their original Sanskrit. One is the *Vāda-vidhi* ("Rules of Debate"), extant only in Tibetan fragments, which were collected by Frauwallner (1957) and translated into English by Anacker (1984, ch. 3). Another is extant only in Chinese. This text, whose title in Chinese is *Rú shí lùn* ("Treatise on Truth"), is best known under the Sanskrit title *Tarka-śāstra* ("Treatise on Reasoning") given to it by Tucci (1929), who translated the Chinese translation back into Sanskrit. The third is the lost text entitled *Vāda-vidhāna* ("Precepts of Debate").

In the *Vāda-vidhi*, Vasubandu identifies the various parts of an argument as well as defines and illustrates the technical terms he uses. First, he identifies the argument's thesis (*pratijñā*), which comprises a term denoting the argument's subject (*pakṣa*) and a term denoting the property to be established (*sādhya*) in the subject. He also identifies the term for the ground (*hetu*), which, in the argument, is ascribed to its subject. He explains that the ground bears the relation of *indispensability* (*a-vinā-bhāva*, literally, not being without, or being *sine qua non*) with respect to the property to be established. Finally, he identifies a term denoting a corroborating instance (*dṛṣṭānta*) which illustrates the indispensability relation borne by the ground to the property to be established.

From the illustrations of the various parts of an argument, one can glean the following complete argument:

THESIS (*pratijñā*):	sound is non-eternal
GROUND (*hetu*):	because of resulting from effort
CORROBORATION (*dṛṣṭānta*):	whatever results from effort is observed to be non-eternal, like a pot

From this, one easily abstracts the following clearly valid form of argument:

THESIS (*pratijñā*):	p has S
GROUND (*hetu*):	p has H
CORROBORATION (*dṛṣṭānta*):	whatever has H is observed to have S, like *d*

(where *d* is an instance of something recognized to have both H and S).

In his *Tarka-śāstra* (T 1633, 30c, l. 20), Vasubandhu deploys an idea whose precise origins are presently unknown but which proves to be central to all subsequent treatments of the classical Indian syllogism, the so-called *tri-rūpa-hetu* (three-formed ground) – that is, the three conditions of a ground (*hetu*). The first condition is that the ground (*hetu*), or H, should occur in the subject of an argument (*pakṣa*), or p. The second is that the ground (*hetu*), or H, should occur in things similar to the subject (*pakṣa*). And the third is that the ground (*hetu*), or H, should not occur in things dissimilar from the subject (*pakṣa*) (Katsura 1986a, 165).

While these last two conditions are clearly intended to define when the property to be established is indispensable for the ground, they are stated rather imprecisely. First, similarity and dissimilarity are stated with two relata, though these relations are not binary relations but, rather, ternary relations. After all, it is not contradictory for one thing to be both similar and dissimilar to another. Thus, for example, two things are similar insofar as both are leaves, yet they are dissimilar from one another insofar as one is an oak leaf and one is a maple leaf. Nothing in the statement of the three conditions specifies in what respect things are to be similar to the subject of an argument and in what respect they are to be dissimilar. Second, it is made precise neither whether or not the ground occurs in some or all of the things which are similar to the subject of the argument, nor whether or not the ground does not occur in some or all of the things which are dissimilar to the subject of the argument.

Dignāga (c. fifth–sixth century CE), building on the insights of Vasubandhu, played a decisive role in the development of the canonical classical Indian syllogism (Steinkellner 1993). His ideas are set out in his three extant works, his *magnum opus*, the *Pramāṇa-samuccaya* ("Compendium on Epistemic Cognition"), *Hetu-cakra-ḍamaru* ("The Drum Wheel of Reason") and *Nyāya-mukha* ("Introduction to Logic"). Unfortunately, again, the original Sanskrit texts have been lost, all three texts surviving in Tibetan translation and the last alone surviving also in Chinese translation.

Dignāga's first contribution is to make explicit the intimate connection between inference and argument, calling the former inference for oneself (*sva-artha-anumāna*)

Table 19.1 Wheel of grounds

H occurs in:	all S	all S	all S
	all S′	no S′	some S′
H occurs in:	no S	no S	no S
	all S′	no S′	some S′
H occurs in:	some S	some S	some S
	all S′	no S′	some S′

and the latter inference for another (*para-artha-anumāna*). Second, Dignāga addressed the shortcomings of the three conditions of a ground mentioned above. He made clear that things are similar or dissimilar to the subject of an argument with respect to the property to be established. In addition, he reformulated in a more rigorous way the three conditions of a ground (*tri-rūpa-hetu*), pressing into service the Sanskrit particle *eva* (only) (Katsura 1986a, 163; 1986b, 6–10; see also Randle 1930, 180–9) to ensure that it characterized more accurately the form of the syllogism.

Lastly, and most strikingly, Dignāga gave an alternative and an essentially equivalent characterization of the truth conditions of his syllogism, which he called the *wheel of grounds* (*hetu-cakra*). The so-called wheel of grounds is a three by three matrix, which distinguishes a proper from an improper ground, and is equivalent to the last two forms of the three conditions of a ground (*tri-rūpa-hetu*). It comprises, on the one hand, the three cases of the ground (H) occurring in some, none, or all of the property-possessors where the property to be established (S) occurs, and, on the other, three cases of the ground (H) occurring in some, none, or all of the property-possessors where the property to be established (S) does not occur. Letting S be the property-possessors in which S occurs and S′ be the property-possessors in which S does not occur, one arrives at what is set out in table 19.1.

Dignāga identified the arguments corresponding to the top and bottom cases of the middle column as good arguments and those corresponding to the other cases as bad.

The view of Dignāga's work as an attempt to identify a formally valid syllogism raises two questions. First, why did Dignāga hold that the major premise, or statement of corroboration (*dṛṣṭānta*), must have associated with it an example, even though examples are irrelevant to the validity of an argument? Second, why did Dignāga regard as a bad argument any argument corresponding to one whose major premise, or statement of corroboration (*dṛṣṭānta*), corresponds to the middle case of the middle column, which is, in fact, a valid argument?

Some scholars think that these questions arise from a misunderstanding of what Dignāga was striving to do. According to some, such as Oetke (1994, 1996), Dignāga and some of his predecessors and contemporaries were striving to spell out a defeasible form of argument (see Taber 2004 for a critical assessment of Oetke's view). According to others, such as Hayes (1980; 1988 ch. 4.2), Dignāga was striving to work out not a deductively valid form of argument, but rather a good inductivist form of argument. A third view – my own – is that Dignāga was indeed trying to pin down what we today would call a deductively valid argument, but that he had not managed to disentangle fully the purely logical features of an argument from its dialectical features.

However much scholars may disagree about Dignāga's aim in the formulation of the syllogism, all agree that his works set the framework within which subsequent Buddhist thinkers addressed philosophical issues pertaining to inference and debate. Thus, Śankarasvāmin (c. sixth century CE) wrote a brief manual on inference and argument for Buddhists called the *Nyāya-praveśa* ("Beginning Logic"), based directly on Dignāga's work. Not long thereafter, Dharmakīrti (c. seventh century CE), the great Buddhist metaphysician, also elaborated his views on inference and debate within the framework found in Dignāga. At the same time, these same ideas came to be adopted by Jain and Brahmanical thinkers. Whether or not the ideas were arrived at independently or were borrowed from the Buddhists is not clear.

Of course, Buddhist, Jain, and Brahmanical thinkers had different views, both epistemological and ontological, yet they all came to adopt the classical Indian syllogism and the specification of its validity in terms of the three conditions of a ground. Part of the attraction is that the underlying concepts are easily construed in terms of common-sense realism. Let us see how this is so.

The three terms used to specify the three parts of the three conditions on a ground – namely, "subject of an argument" ("*pakṣa*"), "ground" ("*hetu*"), and "property to be established" ("*sādhya*") – draw on three basic kinds of entities: the relation of possession and its two relata of property (*dharma*) and property-possessor (*dharmin*). An argument's subject is a property-possessor, while the ground and what is to be established are properties. A converse equivalent of the possession relation is the relation of occurrence: a property-possessor possesses a property just in case the property occurs in the property-possessor.

These entities are easily construed in terms of the common-sense ontology of Indian realists such as the Naiyāyikas. According to their view, the world consists of individual substances, or things (*dravya*), universals (*sāmānya*), and relations between them. They thought that the relation of occurrence (*vṛtti*) is of two kinds: contact (*saṃyoga*) and inherence (*samavāya*). So, for example, one individual substance, a pot, may occur on another, say the ground, by the relation of contact. In this case, the pot is the property and the ground is the property-possessor. Or, a universal, say treeness, may occur in an individual substance, say an individual tree, by the relation of inherence. Here, treeness, the property, inheres in the individual tree, the property-possessor.

As we saw above, essential to the formulation of the three conditions of a ground are the relations of similarity and dissimilarity. Realists, such as the Naiyāyikas, have a ready explanation of what these relations consist in. What accounts for two things being similar to each other in some respect is that they share an entity known as a universal (*sāmānya*). Thus, for example, two things which are both leaves share the universal of being a leaf and they thereby are similar to each other in that respect. If one is a maple leaf and the other an oak leaf, then they are also dissimilar to each other insofar as one has the universal of being a maple leaf and the other does not, while the other has the universal of being an oak leaf and the one does not.

However, Buddhists cannot appeal to universals as part of an account of similarity and dissimilarity, since universals are eternal and the Buddha taught that everything is impermanent. However, the Buddhists did not content themselves just with relying on scripture. Starting with the Abhidharmika thinkers, they formulated arguments to support this teaching of the Buddha. One argument has been succinctly stated by Mark Siderits as follows.

1 Only what is causally efficacious is real.
2 To be causally efficacious is to produce an effect at a particular time.
3 Something eternal would be unchanging.
4 There would be no reason for an unchanging thing to produce an effect at any one time and not another.
5 Hence nothing eternal could be causally efficacious. Therefore no existing things are eternal.

(Siderits 2007, 214)

In addition, Dignāga himself formulated an argument to show that universals do not exist (see Hayes 1988, ch. 5.2.3.). The argument is based on two principles: first, that nothing can wholly exist in two places at once; and, second, that all entities are partless. Since all entities are partless, universals are partless. Since no entity can exist wholly in two places at once, no universal can. Yet, universals are entities which exist wholly in more than one location at a time. Furthermore, Dignāga argued that, even if universals exist, they are unknowable. To know a universal one must know all the things in which the universal has inhered. But there are many things outside of the ken of any person in which universals inhere. Therefore, any person of limited knowledge cannot know a universal.

So, if Dignāga could not draw upon universals to account for similarity and dissimilarity, crucial to the formulation of the three conditions of a ground, how could he make sense of the second and third conditions of a ground (*hetu*)? The answer is that Dignāga drew upon the notion of exclusion (*apoha*). Unlike realists, such as the Naiyāyikas, who take the fundamental relation to be explained to be that of similarity and who then explain similarity as two things sharing a universal, Dignāga takes similarity and dissimilarity to be by-products of our use of words, and he seeks to explain how humans come to use words correctly through exclusion (*apoha*).

To appreciate better Dignāga's appeal to exclusion in connection with the application of words to things, let us consider briefly the background to the fundamental linguistic issue, which has its origin, if not in grammatical thought preceding Pāṇini, then in his *Aṣṭādhyāyī*. The basic idea underlying Pāṇini's grammar is this: each Sanskrit sentence can be analyzed into minimal constituents, and the sense of each minimal constituent contributes to the sense of the entire sentence. Thus, a grammar of a natural language should not only generate all and only its acceptable constituents, it should also make clear how the meanings of the constituents comprising a more complex constituent determine its meaning. In his *Aṣṭādhyāyī*, the meanings associated with minimal constituents comprise, among other things, the constituents of situations, namely, actions (*kriyā*) and their participants (*kāraka*) (for details, see Gillon 2007).

Consider the sentence "Devadatta is milking a cow." The activity is milking. This activity has two participants (*kāraka*): Devadatta and a cow. The question arises: how do the words get correlated with the individual Devadatta, the activity of milking, and the individual cow? In the case of proper nouns such as "Devadatta," nothing much needs to be said: one simply has to associate, for each proper noun, the single thing to which it applies. However, in the case of a common noun, there is, in general, no single thing to which it applies, and hence there is, in general, no single thing with which to associate a common noun.

Let us consider an example of the contrast between proper nouns and common nouns. If one person points out Devadatta to a second and tells the second person that Devadatta's name is "Devadatta," the second person knows all he or she needs to know to apply Devadatta's name correctly to him. No one who, having had Devadatta correctly identified and having been told that the name of that person is "Devadatta," would apply that name to any stranger which he or she could clearly distinguish from Devadatta, nor would that same person withhold the application of the name "Devadatta" when presented with Devadatta and fully recognizing him as Devadatta. But this is not surprising; after all, what else does one need to know to apply the name correctly, once one knows to whom the name applies? In contrast, suppose that one person points out an animal to a second and says correctly to the second person that the animal pointed out is called a "gayal." If all that the second person knows is that "gayal" applies to the object pointed out, he or she does not know enough to apply it correctly to other animals. After all, what prevents the second person from applying it incorrectly to a horse and what guarantees that the second person will not, incorrectly, withhold applying it to a domesticated ox, indigenous to India. Clearly, unlike in the case of a proper noun, just knowing a single thing to which the common noun applies does not provide an adequate basis for its application (*pravṛtti-nimitta*) to things he or she may not have previously encountered.

The question arises: is there perhaps some other entity, different from things to which a common noun applies, which could provide a basis whereby one would be in a position to apply it to things other than the ones which have been identified as those to which the common noun applies? For realists, universals provide a basis for the application of a common noun. Once one associates the single entity, a universal, with a common noun, then one has a basis for the application of the common noun: it applies to all and only those things which have the associated universal. But, as we saw, Dignāga rejected the existence of universals, and so he could not appeal to them to explain how one knows to apply a word to the things to which it applies. Instead, Dignāga turned to exclusion (*apoha*). What one learns, according to Dignāga, is what a word does not apply to, and, through exclusion, one comes to use the word correctly.

It is easy to see that exclusion does not seem to bring us any closer to a satisfactory account of how one learns to apply a word to things. Just as we saw above, being told that a word applies to a thing provides no basis for its correct subsequent application, so too being told that a word does not apply to a thing provides no basis for what else not to apply it to subsequently. Thus, for example, just as when one person points out some animal to another person and tells the second person that the animal pointed out is called a "gayal," the second person will have no idea of how to apply the word subsequently, so too should the first person, in pointing out the animal to the second person, tell the second person that it is not called a "gayal," the second person will have no idea of what else it might not apply to subsequently. Rather, just as one must associate with the word "gayal" some characteristic whose possession is both a necessary and a sufficient condition for the word's application, so one must associate with the word "gayal" some characteristic whose failure to be possessed is both a necessary and a sufficient condition for the word not to apply. But what characteristic is there which all things not called "gayal" fail to have in common? For the realist, all things which are not called "gayal" fail to have the universal of being a gayal in common. This answer, of course, is not available to Dignāga (for discussion, see Hayes 1988, ch. 5; and Pind 2011).

Dignāga's theory of exclusion was widely criticized. Non-Buddhist thinkers, most prominent among them the Naiyāyika Uddyotakara (c. late sixth century CE) and the Mīmāṃsāka Kumārila Bhaṭṭa (c. early seventh century CE), and even some Buddhist thinkers, for example, Bhāvaviveka (c. early sixth century CE), raised many objections to the theory of exclusion, including ones similar to the one raised above. Uddyotakara and Kumārila Bhaṭṭa, for example, both argued that the theory of exclusion is circular (for discussion, see Hugon 2011).

Dharmakīrti, in his *Pramāṇa-vārttika*'s first chapter, *Svārtha-anumāna* ("Inference for Oneself"), emended Dignāga's exclusion theory to circumvent the criticisms it had encountered (for details, see Dunne 2011; Hugon 2011; and Tillemans 2011). The essence of his proposal is to shift question of the similarity of things to the similarity of the images to which they give rise (see Dunne 2011). But this merely shifts the problem of explaining similarity among things to explaining similarity among mental images.

The theory of exclusion (*apoha*) was a peculiarly Buddhist theory, and it remained central to Buddhist thought in India, so long as Buddhist thought survived on the subcontinent. Important contributors to the theory were Śantarakṣita (c. late eighth century CE), Kamalaśīla (c. late eighth century CE), Karṇakagomin (c. late tenth century CE), Jñānaśrīmitra (c. eleventh century CE), Ratnakīrti (c. late eleventh century CE), and Mokṣākaragupta (c. twelfth century CE) (see Siderits 2007, 35–7, for discussion of the views of Śantarakṣita and of Kamalaśīla; see Patil 2011 for discussion of those of Jñānaśrīmitra and of Ratnakīrti).

One other aspect of the relation of words to the things to which they apply should be mentioned. Buddhists maintain that there are only two means by which to learn about things in the world: perception (*pratyakṣa*) and inference (*anumāna*). Yet, Buddhists also recognize that one learns about the world from what one is told by others. It seems to have been Dignāga who first suggested that what one learns about the world from others can be reduced to a form of inference. As part of this reduction, Dignāga maintained that words bear an inferential relationship to the things to which they apply. He seems to have been encouraged in this view by the following parallel. First, just as the ground should occur in the subject of an argument, so a word used in a discourse should apply to the subject of the discourse. Second, just as the ground should occur in things similar to the subject insofar as they have the property to be established, so the word must be applicable to objects similar to the subject of discourse. Third, just as the ground should not occur in things dissimilar from the subject, so the word must be restricted in application to that which is to be learned through it (for further details, see Hayes 1988, ch. 5.2.5; and Pind 2011).

Conclusion

We have seen that Buddhist thinkers played a central role in the development of logic in early classical India. In their earliest texts, there are copious examples of canonical forms of reasoning. Later, Buddhist thinkers helped to transform a canonical form of analogical reasoning into a form of deductive reasoning, not only settling the form of what became the canonical classical Indian syllogism but also setting out its truth conditions. In addition, driven by ontological concerns, Buddhist thinkers tried to develop a theory of meaning for words which eschewed universals by appealing to exclusion. Finally, eager to maintain that there are only two sources of knowledge, inference (*anumāna*) and perception (*pratyakṣa*), they sought to use the notion of exclusion to include knowledge of the meaning of words in inference.

References

Anacker, Stefan (1984). *Seven Works of Vasubandhu: The Buddhist Psychological Doctor.* New Delhi: Motilal Banarsidass.

Dunne, John (2011). Key Features of Dharmakīrti's apoha Theory. In *Apoha: Buddhist Nominalism and Human Cognition.* Ed. Mark Siderits, Tom Tillemans, and Arindam Chakrabarti. New York: Columbia University Press, 84–108.

Frauwallner, Erich (1957). Vasubandhu's Vādavidhiḥ. In *Wiener Zeitschrift für die Kunde Süd- und Ostasiens und Archiv für Indische Philosophie* 1, 104–46.

Gillon, Brendan S. (2007). Pāṇini's Aṣṭādhyāyī and Linguistic Theory. In *Journal of Indian Philosophy* 35, 445–68.

Hayes, Richard P. (1980). Dignāga's Views on Reasoning (svārthānumāna). In *Journal of Indian Philosophy* 8, 219–77.

Hayes, Richard P. (1988). *Dignāga on the Interpretation of Signs.* Studies of Classical India, Vol. 9. Dordrecht: D. Reidel.

Hugon, Pascale (2011). Dharmakīrti's Discussion of Circularity. In *Apoha: Buddhist Nominalism and Human Cognition.* Ed. Mark Siderits, Tom Tillemans, and Arindam Chakrabarti. New York: Columbia University Press, 109–24.

Katsura, Shoryu (1986a). On Trairūpya Formulae. In *Buddhism and its Relation to Other Religions: Essays in Honour of Dr. Shozen Kumoi on His Seventieth Birthday.* Kyoto: Heirakuji Shoten, 161–72.

Katsura, Shoryu (1986b). On the Origin and Development of the Concept of Vyāpti in Indian Logic. In *Hiroshima Tetsugakkai* 38, 1–16.

Oetke, Claus (1994). *Studies on the Doctrine of Trairūpya.* Wiener Studien zur Tibetologie und Buddhismuskunde, 33. Vienna: Arbeitskreis für Tibetische und Buddhistische Studien.

Oetke, Claus (1996) Ancient Indian Logic as a Theory of Non-Monotonic Reasoning. In *Journal of Indian Philosophy* 24, 447–539.

Patil, Parimal (2011). Constructing the Content of Awareness Events. In *Apoha: Buddhist Nominalism and Human Cognition.* Ed. Mark Siderits, Tom Tillemans, and Arindam Chakrabarti. New York: Columbia University Press, 149–69.

Pind, Ole (2011). Dignāga's apoha Theory: Its Presuppositions and Main Theoretical Implications. In *Apoha: Buddhist Nominalism and Human Cognition.* Ed. Mark Siderits, Tom Tillemans, and Arindam Chakrabarti. New York: Columbia University Press, 64–83.

Randle, Herbert Niel (1930). *Indian Logic in the Early Schools: A Study of the Nyāyadarśana in its Relation to the Early Logic of Other Schools.* Oxford: Oxford University Press.

Siderits, Mark (2007). *Buddhism as Philosophy: An Introduction.* Indianopolis: Hackett.

Steinkellner, Ernst (1993). Buddhist Logic: The Search for Certainty. In *Buddhist Spirituality: Indian, Southeast Asian, Tibetan, and Early Chinese*. Ed. Takeuchi Yoshinori. New York: Crossroad, 171–87.

Taber, John (2004). Is Indian Logic Nonmonotonic? In *Philosophy East and West* 54, 143–70.

Tillemans, Tom (2011). How to Talk about Ineffable Things: Dignāga and Dharmakīrti on apoha. In *Apoha: Buddhist Nominalism and Human Cognition*. Ed. Mark Siderits, Tom Tillemans, and Arindam Chakrabarti. New York: Columbia University Press, 50–63.

Tucci, Giuseppe (1929). *Pre-Dinnāga Texts on Logic from Chinese Sources.* Gaekwad's Oriental Series, 49. Baroda: Oriental Institute.

20

Buddhist Philosophy of Logic[1]

KOJI TANAKA

Logic in Buddhist Philosophy

Logic in Buddhist philosophy, as we understand it in this chapter, concerns the systematic study of *anumāna* (often translated as inference) as developed by Dignāga (480–540 CE) and Dharmakīrti (600–660 CE). Buddhist logicians think of inference as an instrument of knowledge (*pramāṇa*) and, thus, logic is considered to constitute part of epistemology in the Buddhist tradition. The focus of this chapter is on the tradition of Buddhist philosophy called *pramāṇavāda*, which is concerned mainly with epistemology and logic. Thus, we are not concerned with various reasoning patterns that can be discerned in the writings of Buddhist philosophers – for example, when the Mādhyamika philosopher Nāgārjuna presents an argument in terms of *catuṣkoṭi* (four "corners": true, false, both, neither).[2] Nor are we concerned with lists of "rules" for debates, such as the ones contained in the Indian *vāda* (debate) literature and Tibetan *bsdus grwa* (collected topics), though debates are important aspects of Indo-Tibetan Buddhist intellectual life.[3]

This chapter contains a discussion of the philosophy of logic that is attributable to Buddhist logicians. I will attempt to make sense of the Buddhist *conception* of the nature of logic by weaving together the main threads of thought that are salient in Dignāga's *Pramāṇasamuccaya* (and his auto-commentary *Pramāṇasamuccayavṛtti*) and Dharmakīrti's *Pramāṇaviniścaya* and *Pramāṇavārttika*. The exegetical studies of these texts and other texts recognized as belonging to the *pramāṇavāda* tradition are extensive but not exhaustive. The collection of historical data and the close reading of these texts are important tasks. In this chapter, however, we step back from the texts and examine (or re-examine) what "inference" or "logic" might mean for Buddhist logicians.[4] I will sketch the Buddhist conception of the nature of logic by uncovering some of the presuppositions that underlie the thoughts expressed in Buddhist logic texts.

A Companion to Buddhist Philosophy, First Edition. Edited by Steven M. Emmanuel.

The Role of Inference in Epistemology

Epistemology in the Buddhist philosophical tradition is generally concerned with instruments or sources of knowledge. *What* we know is considered to depend on *how* we know. That is, what we are warranted to be aware of depends on how we come to be aware of it. So, in order to understand what we know, Buddhist philosophers investigate the sources which give rise to warranted awareness (*pramā*).

Buddhist logicians identify two sources of knowledge: perception (*pratyakśa*) and inference (*anumāna*). Perception is said to be an immediate contact with particulars without any mediation of conception (which is considered to involve universals). There are two standard examples used to illustrate inference. In one standard example, when we are aware that there is smoke on a mountain, we may infer that there is fire on that mountain. When we become aware of the presence of fire on the mountain in this way, that awareness is said to be warranted by inference, and, thus, it counts as knowledge. In another example, we may become aware of the presence of a tree by inferring from our awareness that there is rosewood (*śiṃśapā*). Such awareness of the presence of a tree that is brought about by inferential cognition is said to be warranted and, thus, it is ascribed the status of knowledge.

Dignāga explains that the purpose of his texts – the foundational texts for the Buddhist epistemological and logical tradition – is to refute his opponents' views on the instruments of knowledge as well as to establish his own view as correct.[5] Once inference is shown to be an instrument of knowledge, it is also shown to serve as an instrument for producing a cognition that can be ascribed the status of knowledge. Hence, inference can be thought to result not only in awareness that inference is an instrument of knowledge, but also in awareness of the truths of Buddhist thought.

Buddhist logicians recognize two contexts in which inference can be used as an instrument of knowledge. On the one hand, it can be used as an instrument for becoming aware of soteriological truths, such as the Four Noble Truths, by themselves. This is called "inference for oneself" (*svārthānumāna*). On the other hand, inference can be used as an instrument in dialectical engagements with opponents. In this context, it serves as a tool for showing that the opponents' views are mistaken and to demonstrate that Buddhists' own views are correct in dialectic practice. This is called "inference for others" (*parārthānumāna*). Thus, inference has a function directed at oneself and a function directed at others.[6]

Logic or Epistemology?

If we understand inference as a source of knowledge, it must be assumed that a certain relationship holds between inference and knowledge. In particular, it must be assumed that inference has a direct impact on one's knowledge state. As is implicit in the standard examples, inference subsumes three elements, which might be thought to be distinct. One element of inference in the standard examples is the awareness of smoke or rosewood. This is the cognitive state prior to the involvement of the inferential cognitive process. The second element is the inferential cognitive process, which moves cognition from awareness of smoke or rosewood to awareness of fire or tree. The third element is the resulting cognitive state – that is, awareness of fire or tree. These elements of Buddhist logic may strike some as problematic given that "inference" (or logic in general) is often understood as not having any bearing on knowledge. Some may even consider them to show that there is no logic in the Buddhist tradition (as we will see below). I will consider this issue before going on to explicate how Buddhist logicians understand inference in the context of epistemology.

According to the "Western" conception of logic prevalent since the twentieth century, logical study is the *formal* study of *arguments*. An argument consists of premises and a conclusion (or conclusions). A study of logic is considered to be a study of the (syntactic) *form* of the relationship between the premises and a conclusion. If an argument has the form: A and $A \supset B$ (if A then B), therefore B (*modus ponens*), for example, then the argument which instantiates this form is said to be valid. The form that an argument instantiates may also capture a sub-sentential (sub-propositional) structure. For example, an argument may have the following form: $\exists x \forall y Rxy$ (Something Rs everything), therefore $\exists x Rxx$ (Something Rs itself). Any argument which has this (sub-sentential) form is also said to be valid.

Western logicians disagree about which forms of argument should count as valid. Strict Aristotelian logicians regard the above sub-sentential structure (first-order structure) invalid as it is not one of the syllogisms that Aristotle identified. Intuitionistic logicians reject as invalid the form: $\neg\neg A$ (it is not the case that A is not the case), therefore A, as they interpret negation in terms of the failure to find a proof, and, thus, a failure to find a negative proof does not amount to a success of finding a positive proof. Paraconsistent logicians – whose logics have recently been applied to the study of reasoning involving *catuṣkoṭi* – may regard *modus ponens* invalid. If A were both true and false, then A and $A \supset B$ would be true (since A would also be false) while B might be only false.[7]

Which forms of argument should count as valid is evidently a contentious matter. Nonetheless, there is one thing that contemporary (Western) logicians share in common – namely, the idea that logic is concerned with the forms of arguments. An argument is said to be valid if it instantiates a valid argument form. It is important to notice that, for contemporary logicians, the specific contents of the premises and the conclusion are irrelevant to logical study. The main focus of logical study is with the mathematical structures that satisfy valid argument forms rather than a concern with what the argument is about.[8]

If we understand the nature of logic to be *formal* in this way, it is difficult to see what bearing logic has on cognitions that result in knowledge. Consider the following argument: there is smoke on a mountain, and if there is smoke on a mountain then there is fire on that mountain, therefore there is fire on that mountain. This argument has the form of *modus ponens* and, thus, is formally valid. Now, assume that we know that there is smoke on the mountain and that where there is smoke there is fire, but we do not know that there is fire on the mountain. It seems that we *ought to* come to reason so that we know that there is fire on the mountain. However, what is the role of the validity of *modus ponens* in this reasoning? In order to think of *modus ponens* itself as having an impact on our cognitive activity, it would not be sufficient for *modus ponens* to be, in fact, valid: we would have to be *aware* of the validity of *modus ponens*. We would also have to be aware that, if an argument has a valid form, then we would have to infer the conclusion of the argument. But, in order to have this awareness, we would also have to be aware that, if we are aware that "if an argument has a valid form, then we have to infer the conclusion of the argument," then we would have to infer the conclusion. But, then, we would also have to be aware that . . . *ad infinitum*. It seems that the form of the argument is not sufficient for thinking that there is fire on the mountain.[9]

The difficulty of accounting for the relationship between valid forms of arguments and knowledge can also be illustrated by examining what kind of cognitions are, in fact, involved in order to acquire new knowledge. We most likely infer that there is fire on a mountain if we are aware that there is smoke on that mountain and that where there is smoke there is fire. But that is because awareness that there is fire on a mountain is consistent or coherent with what we already know, and not because cognitive activity involved in inferring that there is fire on a mountain has the form of *modus ponens*. When we acquire new knowledge by means of inferential cognitions, it is not the form of an argument (or reasoning) that forces us to infer the conclusion but the consistency (or coherency) of what we are aware of that moves us to cognize in a certain way.[10] Hence, it seems that knowledge of the validity of an argument form is not even a necessary condition for knowing that there is fire on a mountain based on what we already know.

Faced with these difficulties in accounting for the significance of epistemology in *formal* logic, we have (at least) two options in our attempt to understand the role that inference (*anumāna*) plays in Buddhist epistemology. One is to suggest that the study of *anumāna* is not a study of logic at all (and, thus, it is misleading to translate it as "inference"). After all, *anumāna* is an instrument for acquiring knowledge and, as such, is an epistemological, not a formal, apparatus. Thus, according to this suggestion, there is no logic in Buddhist epistemology; there is just epistemology (see Siderits 2003). It would follow that, strictly speaking, there is no Buddhist philosophy of *logic*.

This is not the only way in which we can respond to the above difficulties, however. Alternatively, we can reconceive the nature of *logic* in the context of epistemology and demarcate the logical part of epistemology which can be recognized as *logic*.[11] To think of an inference simply as a formal matter is to think of it as having logical significance independent of the cognitive act, which can be characterized as inferential. If we think that logic is only about argument forms, it is difficult to understand the impact of inference on cognitive activities. However, we can understand inference as having logical significance within certain cognitive acts of inferring (or cognition which acts inferentially). Thus, according to this suggestion, we can focus on the nature of the role that inferential *cognition* plays. This is not to say that the form in which such cognition takes place cannot be ascertained. It does suggest, however, that the form of the cognition is not what is at issue for Buddhist logicians.

Which of these two suggestions is most faithful to the Buddhist tradition is a controversial matter that I shall not attempt to settle in this chapter. If we are to elucidate Buddhist philosophy of *logic*, however, we must assume that we can recognize logic as part of the Buddhist study of *anumāna* (inference). Based on this (defeasible) assumption, I present what I take to be the conception of *logic* assumed by Buddhist logicians. Since logic is conceived in the context of epistemology, the Buddhist conception of logic must be unique (at least in comparison with twentieth- and early twenty-first-century Western orthodoxy). If so, this chapter does not merely present the way in which Buddhist logicians understand the nature of the object of their study, it also makes an important contribution to the philosophy of logic in general in that it develops an alternative to the conception of logic as purely formal in nature.[12]

The Elements of Inference

Buddhist logicians hold that, by inference, one seeks to establish for oneself or for others the presence of what is to be proven (*sādhya*) in a particular locus (*pakṣa*) on the basis of the presence of an inferential reason (*hetu*) at that locus. For example, to use a standard example, when one sees smoke (inferential reason) on a particular mountain (locus), one may infer that there is fire (what is to be proven) on that mountain.

For an inference to count as "valid" or as an instrument of knowledge, the inferential reason must satisfy the triple conditions (*trairūpya*). There are mainly two interpretations of these triple conditions: ontological and epistemological. According to the ontological interpretation (which seems the more common interpretation), they can be presented as follows. (1) What is identified as the inferential reason must be present in the locus in question. This means, in our example, that smoke must be present on the mountain in question. This implies that a cognizer is, in fact, in a situation where there is smoke on the mountain. The second and third conditions are called pervasion (*vyāpti*). (2) The inferential reason must be present in at least one similar case (*sapakṣa*) – a locus where what is to be proven is present.[13] For example, smoke must be present in a kitchen with a wood-burning stove. (3) The inferential reason must not be present in any dissimilar case (*vipakṣa*) – a locus where what is to be proven is absent. For example, smoke must not be present in a misty lake. The reason given for a thesis to be proven by inference must satisfy these triple conditions to count as an instrument of warranted awareness (i.e., knowledge).

According to (a strong form of) the epistemic interpretation, the triple conditions can be presented as follows: (1) the inferential reason must be *known* to occur in the locus; (2) the inferential reason must be *known* to occur in a similar case; and (3) the inferential reason must be *known* not to occur in dissimilar cases.[14]

The difficulty of reconciling the ontological and epistemological interpretations is due to the epistemic context in which inference must be understood. In order properly to understand inference in epistemic contexts, we cannot think of these two interpretations as mutually exclusive. According to the ontological interpretation, it is a *fact* that the triple conditions are satisfied. This fact can be appealed to as evidence for *justifying* one's awareness of the presence of fire on a mountain, for example. That is, if it can be demonstrated that one's awareness of fire can be characterized by the triple conditions, then that awareness, not its form but its content, can be given the status of knowledge by appealing to the fact about the satisfaction of triple conditions. This means that the triple conditions function as the standard of evaluation for what counts as knowledge. If one accepts this ontological interpretation, however, it is difficult to understand how the triple conditions have bearing on the *acquisition* of knowledge. Just as the validity of an argument form is not sufficient for coming to have knowledge, the *fact* that there is a justification does not seem to be enough for one to *acquire* knowledge.[15] If we are to think that the triple conditions serve as a means of knowledge, they must contain the epistemic fact about one's having knowledge. Hence, if we are to understand the role that inference plays in epistemological contexts, we need to accommodate both interpretations.[16]

Buddhist Conception of Logic

Our discussion in the previous section suggests that inference is both ontological and epistemological. As an *instrument* of *warranted* awareness, inference must warrant or justify one's awareness but must also be instrumental in moving one's cognitive state to another cognitive state.

Consider, again, our example of smoke and fire on a mountain. Suppose that one is in a situation where there is smoke on a particular mountain. In order for awareness of fire on that mountain to be warranted, smoke must co-occur or must be co-located with fire on the mountain in the same way that smoke co-occurs with fire in a kitchen. However, smoke on a mountain must never co-occur with fire in a misty lake despite the fact that it may look as though there is smoke on the lake and, thus, there may be a mistaken "appearance" of fire in the lake. Supposedly, these are the facts about the elements of inference. It may be difficult to establish that these facts actually obtain. Nonetheless, if they are presented as facts, one can appeal to them in order to justify the inferential awareness of the presence of fire on the mountain based on the awareness of the presence of smoke on that mountain.

For pervasion between inferential reason and what is to be proven to have any cognitive grip, however, it has to be expressed to us in an intelligible manner. For example, I would not be cognitively moved at all by the mere fact that there is fire where there is smoke, unless that fact places some demand on my cognition. Nor would my cognition be stimulated to produce awareness of the presence of fire if I were simply perceiving smoke on a mountain. An immediate, perceptual awareness of smoke is not, of itself, enough for warranted awareness of the presence of fire to occur. In order for cognition to be warranted and a cognitive process required such that certain awareness is brought about, we must connect the concept *smoke* with *fire* in a cognitively robust relation. By making a conceptual commitment to invoke *fire* together with *smoke*, we can *act* appropriately in the presence of fire when we become aware of smoke. The resulting awareness is dependent upon the warrantable relation of the elements in the inference becoming cognitively significant.[17]

The concepts invoked in making a conceptual commitment are not fully formed independent of their use in cognition. Instead, the contents of concepts are shaped by the commitment one undertakes through inferential cognition. It is by making a conceptual commitment that we acquire knowledge. In turn, the triple conditions which hold among the elements of inference become incorporated into cognition.

As the content of a concept becomes more determinate, it is assumed that one may come to recognize more robust relations between *smoke* and *fire*. The more one learns about smoke (its chemical constitution, etc.), the better one ascertains its relation to fire. Of course, there may be a situation where we may have to revise our commitment about smoke and fire. If one thought that smoke is just something caused by cooking, for example, then one might have to revise one's epistemic commitment so that one would now be aware that smoke is something caused by fire. So an inferential cognition may defeat the inferential cognition that forms the content of *smoke* in its premature form (when one was not aware that smoke is caused by fire and not by cooking as such).[18] In this way, as the content of concepts becomes more determinate through inferential cognitions, one attains more *certainty* as well as *truth* of the matter and, thus, acquires warranted awareness.

Now, it is true that an inferential cognition requires an awareness of triple conditions that can be given a formal treatment:

Inferential reason (*hetu*) must be (known to be) present in the locus in question (*sapakṣa*).
Inferential reason must be (known to be) present in at least one similar case (*sapakṣa*).
Inferential reason must not be (known to be) present in any dissimilar case (*vipakṣa*).

One can provide mathematical structures that satisfy these triple conditions as a study of Buddhist "logic."[19] Buddhist logicians may express the forms that inferential cognition may take. Nonetheless, for them, inference is considered to be important insofar as it shapes the contents of our awareness. That is, the importance of inference lies not in ascertaining forms of knowledge but in their contribution to the content of knowledge. It is in this way that we can see an understanding of the nature of *inferential* cognition as a crucial aspect of Buddhist epistemology, as well as the conception of inference (and logic more generally) that can be attributed to Buddhist logicians.

Logic in Buddhist Logic

If we thought that logic was essentially formal, the notions of inference and inferential cognitions must be assumed to come apart in a certain way. An inference might be said to *underwrite* the validity of an inferential cognition. Yet it would not impel one to *undergo* an inferential cognitive process. According to the formal conception of logic, an inference expresses the fact about the validity of an inferential cognition, but it does not express the *norm* by means of which an inferential cognition ought to take place. Thus, under the formal conception of logic, an inferential cognition must be understood as independent of inferences. Buddhist logicians, by contrast, do not think of inferential cognitions as independent of inferences. An inference expresses an epistemic commitment that forms the content of a warranted awareness. This means that Buddhist logicians do not think of inference as *underwriting* an inferential cognition. Rather, an inference is considered to express an epistemic commitment – more specifically a conceptual commitment – that is *undertaken* in an inferential cognitive process. For Buddhist logicians, the significance of inference lies within the context of inferential cognitions.

Thus, the Buddhist study of inference (*anumāna*) is not a formal study of arguments. Buddhist logicians are not concerned with abstracting forms of arguments and studying the (mathematical) properties of these forms. While one might take this as evidence for the thought that there is no Buddhist logic, one might alternatively attempt to understand the role of inference according to a conception of logic that does not abstract from the contents of knowledge.[20] As I have attempted to show, we can recognize the logical significance of inference as understood by Buddhist logicians, despite the fact that its logical significance lies within the context of cognition and its contents.

Notes

1 Many thanks go to Parimal Patil and Tom Tillemans for their extensive comments on an earlier version of this chapter.

2 There is a large amount of secondary literature written about *catuṣkoṭi*. See, for example, Robinson (1957) and Ruegg (1977). For treatments of *catuṣkoṭi* using contemporary logical machinery, see Garfield and Priest (2003); Priest (2010); Tillemans (1999, ch. 9); and Tillemans (2009).

3 For a discussion of *bsdus grwa* logic, see Tillemans (1999, ch. 6).

4 For studies of Dignāga's works, see, for example, Hattori (1968) and Hayes (1988). For book-length studies of Dharmakīrti's works, see, for example, Dreyfus (1997) and Dunne (2004). For brief accounts of Dharmakīrti's life and works, see Steinkellner (1998) and Tillemans (2011). See also Gillon (2011) for a brief discussion of Buddhist logic in a larger historical context.

5 See *Pramāṇasamuccayavṛtti* 1.10–1.13, translated in Hattori (1968, 23–4).

6 See Kellner (2004); Krasser (2001); and Patil (2009, ch. 6).

7 Paraconsistent logicians reject *modus ponens*, which is formulated in terms of the "material conditional" $\supset$. $A \supset B$ is said to be true if and only if A is false or B is true. Some paraconsistent logicians introduce different accounts of the conditional, usually *relevant* conditionals, which validate *modus ponens*. For an introduction to paraconsistent logics, see, for example, Priest and Tanaka (2009).

8 This "orthodox" conception of logic is, in fact, a combination of the views on the nature of logic held by several logicians. It was Kant who argued for the view of logic according to which logic is abstracted from the objects of cognition. It is this view that became the main stream in the modern development of logic. See his *Lectures on Logic*. Translations of some of Kant's lectures on logic can be found in Young (1992). However, the account presented here is largely a model-theoretic account due to Tarski. See, for example, Tarski (1983 [1936]).

9 For the difficulty of this kind, see Carroll (1895), though the point of Carroll's discussion is moot.

10 For a discussion of this kind, see Harman (1986).

11 I believe that this is the option taken by, for example, Matilal (1998), Mohanty (1992), and Tillemans (1999).

12 In fact, despite the fact that logic is standardly understood to be formal in the sense that it does not have any bearing on knowledge, a study of the history of logic reveals that epistemological considerations often framed the development of logic. See, for example, Macbeth (2005) and Hylton (2005) for discussions of logical development by Frege and Russell – two of the founding figures of modern logic – respectively. Generally, the (Western) history of logic is much more complicated than what many scholars of Buddhist logic assume. In fact, it lacks the uniformity that is often assumed when they appeal to (Western) logical apparatus. See, for example, Goldfarb (1979); MacFarlane (2000); and van Heijenoort (1967).

13 This is the formulation of Dignāga. Dharmakīrti modifies the second condition as: the inferential reason must be present in at least one similar case *and only in similar cases*. See Potter (1969).

14 The secondary literature on the triple conditions is extensive. See, for example, Franco (1990); Katsura (1983, 1984); Oetke (1994a); Patil (2010): Tillemans (1999, ch. 5); as well as several papers in Katsura and Steinkellner (2004). The majority of the secondary literature seems to present ontological interpretations. For epistemological interpretations, see Oetke (1994b, 846) and Patil (2009, 66ff.).

15 For a discussion of the need for the epistemologization of the triple conditions, see Tillemans (2004).

16 One way to reconcile these two interpretations is to think of Buddhist logicians as being internalists about justification. That is to say that, for Buddhist logicians, the basis for the justification lies within one's cognition. This internalist characterization of Buddhist epistemology is given in Arnold (2005, ch. 2). I shall put aside this internalist interpretation of Buddhist epistemology. In this chapter, I attempt to accommodate both ontological and epistemological interpretations without resorting to internalist epistemology. For a discussion of internalist/externalist epistemology as applied to Buddhists (and Nyaiyāyikas), see Patil (2009).

17 The Buddhist theory of concepts and concept formation is what is known as the theory of *apoha*. For the most recent study of *apoha*, see Siderits et al. (2011).

18 For a discussion of the defeasible nature of triple conditions, see Oetke (1996).

19 For a book-length study of Buddhist logic in terms of mathematical structures, see Chi (1969).

20 After a careful investigation into the (Western) history of logic, one becomes aware that it is a mistake to think that there is only one way to understand the nature of logic. See, for example, MacFarlane (2000). It is equally mistaken to think that there is no Buddhist logic simply because Buddhist logicians are not concerned with the forms of arguments independent of what the arguments are about.

References

Arnold, Dan (2005). *Buddhists, Brahmins, and Belief: Epistemology in South Asian Philosophy of Religion.* New York: Columbia University Press.

Carroll, Lewis (1895). What the Tortoise Said to Achilles. In *Mind* 4, 278–80.

Chi, R. S. Y. (1969). *Buddhist Formal Logic.* London: Royal Asiatic Society of Great Britain.

Dreyfus, Georges B. J. (1997). *Recognizing Reality: Dharmakīrti's Philosophy and its Tibetan Interpretations.* Albany: State University of New York Press.

Dunne, John D. (2004). *Foundations of Dharmakīrti's Philosophy.* Boston: Wisdom.

Franco, Eli (1990). Valid Reason, True Sign. In *Wiener Zeitschrift für die Kunde Südasiens* 34, 189–208.

Garfield, Jay, and Priest, Graham (2003). Nāgārjuna and the Limits of Thought. In *Philosophy East and West* 53, 1–21.

Gillon, Brendan (2011). Logic in Classical Indian Philosophy. In *The Stanford Encyclopedia of Philosophy*. Ed. Edward N. Zalta. At http://plato.stanford.edu/archives/sum2011/entries/logic-india/.

Goldfarb, Warren (1979). Logic in the Twenties: The Nature of the Quantifier. In *Journal of Symbolic Logic* 44, 351–68.

Harman, Gilbert (1986). *Change in View.* Cambridge, MA: MIT Press.

Hattori, Massaki (1968). *Dignāga, On Perception.* Cambridge, MA: Harvard University Press.
Hayes, Richard (1988). *Dignāga on the Interpretation of Signs.* Dordrecht: Kluwer Academic.
Hylton, Peter (2005). *Propositions, Functions, and Analysis.* Oxford: Clarendon Press.
Katsura, Shoryu (1983). Dignāga on Trairūpya. In *Journal of Indian and Buddhist Studies* 32, 15–21.
Katsura, Shoryu (1984). Dharmakīrti's Theory of Truth. In *Journal of Indian Philosophy* 12, 215–35.
Katsura, Shoryu, and Steinkellner, Ernst (eds) (2004). *The Role of the Example (Dṛṣṭānta) in Classical Indian Logic.* Vienna: Arbeitskreis für Tibetische und Buddhistische Studien, Universität Wien.
Kellner, Birgit (2004). First logic, Then the Buddha? In *Hōrin* 11, 147–67.
Krasser, Helmut (2001). On Dharmakīrti's Understanding of Pramāṇa-bhūta and His Definition of Pramāṇa. In *Wiener Zeitschrift für die Kunde Südasiens* 45, 173–99.
Macbeth, Danielle (2005). *Frege's Logic.* Cambridge, MA: Harvard University Press.
MacFarlane, John G. (2000). *What Does it Mean to Say That Logic Is Formal?* PhD dissertation, University of Pittsburgh.
Matilal, Bimal Krishna (1998). *The Character of Logic in India.* Ed. Jonardon Ganeri and Heeraman Tiwari. Albany: State University of New York Press.
Mohanty, Jitendranath (1992). *Reason and Tradition in Indian Thought: An Essay on the Nature of Indian Philosophical Thinking.* Oxford: Clarendon Press.
Oetke, Claus (1994a). *Studies on the Doctrine of Trairūpya. Wiener Studien zur Tibetologie und Buddhismuskunde,* Vol. 33. Vienna: Arbeitskreis für Tibetische und Buddhistische Studien, Universität Wien.
Oetke, Claus (1994b). Praśastapāda's Views on the "Antinomic Reason" and Their Consequences for a Theory of Default Reasoning. In *Asiatische Studien/Études asiatiques* 48, 845–66.
Oetke, Claus (1996). Ancient Indian Logic as a Theory of Non-Monotonic Reasoning. In *Journal of Indian Philosophy* 24, 447–539.
Patil, Parimal G. (2009). *Against a Hindu God: Buddhist Philosophy of Religion in India.* New York: Columbia University Press.
Patil, Parimal G. (2010). History, Philology, and the Philosophical Study of Sanskrit Texts. In *Journal of Indian Philosophy* 38. 163–202.
Potter, Karl (1969). Dignāga and the Development of Indian Logic. In *Buddhist Formal Logic.* Ed. R. S. Y. Chi. London: Royal Asiatic Society of Great Britain, xliii–xlviii.
Priest, Graham (2010). The Logic of the catuṣkoṭi. In *Comparative Philosophy* 1, 24–54.
Priest, Graham, and Tanaka, Koji (2009). Paraconsistent Logic. In *The Stanford Encyclopedia of Philosophy*. Ed. Edward N. Zalta. At http://plato.stanford.edu/archives/sum2009/entries/logic-paraconsistent/.
Robinson, Richard (1957). Some Logical Aspects of Nāgārjuna's System. In *Philosophy East and West* 6, 291–308.
Ruegg, D. Seyfort (1977). The Uses of the Four Positions of the catuṣkoṭi and the Problem of the Description of Reality in Mahāyāna Buddhism. In *Journal of Indian Philosophy* 5, 1–71.
Siderits, Mark (2003). Deductive, Inductive, Both or Neither? In *Journal of Indian Philosophy* 31, 303–21.
Siderits, Mark, Tillemans, Tom, and Chakrabarti, Arindam (eds) (2011). *Apoha: Buddhist Nominalism and Human Cognition.* New York: Columbia University Press.
Steinkellner, Ernst (1998). Dharmakīrti. In *The Routledge Encyclopedia of Philosophy*. Ed. E. Craig. London: Routledge, 51–3.
Tarski, Alfred (1983 [1936]). On the Concept of Logical Consequence. Trans. J. H. Woodger. In *Logic, Semantics, Metamathematics.* Second edn. Ed. John Corcoran. Indianapolis: Hackett. Orig. pubd as O pojeciu wynikania logicznego. In *Przeglad Filozoficzny* 39, 58–68.

Tillemans, Tom J. F. (1999). *Scripture, Logic, Language: Essays on Dharmakīrti and His Tibetan Successors.* Boston: Wisdom.

Tillemans, Tom J. F. (2004). The Slow Death of the trairūpya in Buddhist Logic: a propos of Sa skya Paṇḍita. In *Hōrin* 11, 83–93.

Tillemans, Tom J. F. (2009). How Do Mādhyamikas Think? Notes on Jay Garfield, Graham Priest, and Paraconsistency. In *Pointing at the Moon: Buddhism, Logic, Analytic Philosophy*. Ed. M. D'Amato, J. Garfield, and T. Tillemans. Oxford: Oxford University Press, 83–99.

Tillemans, Tom J. F. (2011). Dharmakīrti. In *The Stanford Encyclopedia of Philosophy*. Ed. Edward N. Zalta. At http://plato.stanford.edu/archives/fall2011/entries/dharmaki-rti/.

van Heijenoort, Jean (1967). Logic as Calculus and Logic as Language. In *Synthese* 17, 324–30.

Young, J. Michael (1992). *Lectures on Logic.* Cambridge: Cambridge University Press.

21

Candrakīrti on the Limits of Language and Logic

KAREN C. LANG

Candrakīrti (c. 570–650) is known for his commentaries on the major works of Nāgārjuna and Āryadeva. In addition to his commentaries on Nāgārjuna's *Mūlamadhyamakakārikāḥ* (MMK), *Yuktiṣaṣṭikā*, and *Śūnyatāsaptati*, and on Āryadeva's *Catuḥśataka* (CŚ), he wrote an auto-commentary on his independent work, the *Madhyamakāvatāra*, which depicts the ten "perfect virtues" (*pāramitā*) associated with the bodhisattva's ten-stage path to buddhahood.[1] His quotations from the *Madhyamakāvatāra* (MĀ) in his commentaries on MMK and CŚ suggest it may be his first work.

According to medieval Tibetan accounts of his life, Candrakīrti was born in South India, entered a monastery where he studied Nāgārjuna's and Āryadeva's writings, and defended Buddhapālita's interpretations of Madhyamaka teachings against the Yogācāra partisan Candragomin.[2] These accounts of his life and evidence from his own writings depict Candrakīrti criticizing the innovations of Bhāviveka (c.500–570) and the epistemologist Dignāga (c. 480–540).

Despite its descriptive inadequacies, language has a certain pragmatic value for Candrakīrti. Language is the means by which the path leading to buddhahood can be pointed out. Words have practical value inasmuch as they indicate the direction in which we must travel to attain the final goal. The implications of language are often subject to varied interpretations; and Candrakīrti, like others before him, differentiates Buddha's direct discourse from indirect discourse. Candrakīrti classifies those *sūtras* concerned with the teachings about emptiness and ultimate reality as direct (*nītārtha*) and those *sūtras* that are not as indirect (*neyārtha*) (MĀ.199). He cites a passage from the *Akṣayamatisūtra*, which defines indirect *sūtras* as those that introduce disciples to the path and direct *sūtras* as those that introduce them to the fruit. The former indicate the means; the latter, the goal. The two truths, the conventional or surface truth (*saṃvṛti satya*) and the ultimate truth (*paramārtha satya*), are classified in a similar fashion. Candrakīrti's rejection of his opponents' philosophical propositions does not

A Companion to Buddhist Philosophy, First Edition. Edited by Steven M. Emmanuel.

indicate his ignorance of the rules that determine whether one side or another prevails in debate. He knows the formal criteria set down in the works of the Buddhist logicians and in the manuals of the Nyāya school for judging the validity of an argument. He uses these criteria to demonstrate the technical flaws in his opponents' inferences and arguments. In this chapter I will examine how Candrakīrti uses language and logic to undermine people's confidence in cherished beliefs about a self and point them towards the Buddha's path and its goal – the peace of nirvana – that transcends the limitations of language and logic.

The Doctrine of Two Truths

Candrakīrti's explanations of the relation between ultimate and conventional truth have produced debate over the nature of these truths among Madhyamaka proponents in India from the fifth century onwards. Echoes of these debates recur in the writings of both medieval Tibetan monastics and contemporary scholars.[3]

Candrakīrti first sets out his view on the two truths in the *Madhyamakāvatāra* (MĀ. VI.80, 175):

> Those outside the path of Nāgārjuna
> Have no means of achieving peace.
> They are misled about conventional and ultimate truth,
> And because they are misled they do not attain liberation.
> Conventional truth is the means
> And ultimate truth is the result of that means.
> Whoever does not know the difference between these two
> Enters the wrong path because of that false conception.

He associates both truths with the soteriological goal of Nāgārjuna's path: the peaceful state of nirvana. In his *Prasannapadā* commentary (PP.492–4)[4] on the MMK, Candrakīrti analyzes the compound "worldly convention" (*lokasaṃvṛti*). The first member of the compound is synonymous with the word "person" (*pudgala*), which conventionally designates the five aggregates. The second member is explained in three ways: (1) as ignorance (*ajñāna*), because it covers completely the true nature of things; (2) as mutually originating (*parasparasaṃbhava*) through reciprocal dependence; and (3) as a convention (*saṃketa*), corresponding to an ordinary person's speech and behavior patterns (*lokavyavahāra*). In contrast, the compound ultimate truth is explained as signifying both the goal (*artha*) and the ultimate (*parama*). Conventional truth, according to Candrakīrti, conforms to the commonplace experience of ordinary people who are ignorant of the true nature of things; ultimate truth transcends the limits of ordinary language and thought (Huntington 1983).

The distinction between two truths parallels the distinction made between two kinds of people: ordinary people, the cowherds out in the field, and extraordinary people, the Āryas, who experience the world differently as a result of putting the Buddha's teachings into practice. Ordinary language is essential for explaining the Buddha's teachings to ordinary people, for, as Āryadeva points out: "Just as it's impossible to make a barbarian understand in a foreign language, it's impossible to make people of this world understand without reference to worldly things" (CŚ.VIII.19). In *Bodhisattvayogāracatuḥśatakaṭīkā*, Candrakīrti comments:

> Without understanding conventional truth, even intelligent people can't grasp that the self and things resemble magical illusions and have an essence that is inexpressible. But by understanding conventional truth as it really is, they recognize that things resemble magical illusions, and by understanding them as being like magical illusions, they can realize that an ultimate thing's essence is inexpressible.
>
> (CŚṬ D f.141a)[5]

The language used here – recognizing, understanding, realizing – builds upon the conception of conventional truth as concealing reality. Extraordinary people uncover the veil that hides the real nature of things from ordinary people. But communication of the Buddha's message requires that people first be taught in language that they can understand. The use of ordinary language and conventional truth prepares the way for intelligent people to comprehend the Buddha's teachings about mistaken belief in a self, an "I" that appropriates things as "mine," and about the empty and insubstantial nature of things they desire. But understanding conventional truth as it really is (*yathābhūtam*) involves recognition of the limitations of language when describing an ultimate characterized as inexpressible (*avācya*).

Metaphoric language is often used in Buddhist scriptures to express profound teachings about the nature of reality. Candrakīrti cites both from some mainstream version of the *Saṃyutta Nikāya* and from the Mahāyāna *Samādhirajasūtra* (SR):[6]

> Form is like a mass of foam, feeling is like a bubble.
> Constructed dispositions are like a banana tree's core.
> And consciousness is like an illusion.
> Thus, the energetic monk, fully aware and mindful,
> While he investigates things day and night,
> Should enter the tranquil state, the bliss
> Which is the calming of karmically constructed forces.
>
> (SN.III.141–2)

> A large lump of foam is carried away by the current and, after investigating it, one sees no solid substance. Know all things in this way.
>
> Just as the rain god lets it rain and the rain bubbles arise one by one. On arising they burst, then there are no bubbles. Know all things in this way.
>
> Just as, in the hot season at noon, a person tormented by thirst might wander about and see a mirage as a pool of water. Know all things in this way.
>
> Just as a person in search of the core might split in two a banana tree's green trunk and there is no core inside or outside. Know all things in this way.
>
> A magician conjures up visible forms, Wonderful elephant chariots and Horse chariots. Under these circumstances, nothing exists the way it appears there. Know all things in this way.
>
> (SR.IX.1–3, 5–6)

The *Saṃyutta Nikāya* passage makes the point that the five aggregates are as insubstantial and impermanent as foam on the sea's shore. The *Samādhirajasūtra* passage extends that image even further. The Abhidharma scholiasts consider the self and most other things ordinary people speak about as conceptual fictions; their Mahāyāna critics regard even the things (*dharma*) these scholiasts identify and classify as real as conceptual fictions.

To get people to the point where they realize the fabricated and fictitious nature of all things requires careful and calibrated instruction. To the question "Why not just teach meditation if nirvana is the goal?," Candrakīrti responds (CŚṬ D f.137b) that people have different capabilities. The Buddha spoke to some people about generosity; to others, he spoke about moral conduct, but he recommended meditation only to people of superior capabilities. His instruction, moreover, is gradual: people are taught first to reject immoral behavior, then to reject speculative views about the self, and, finally, they are taught to reject attachment to the things the Abhidharmists believe are real: the aggregates, the elements, and the sense bases.

Cessation, Nirvana, and Nihilism

The gradual nature of the path to nirvana is also the reason for two types of religious practice: activity (*pravṛtti*) in the world that leads to a good and a cessation of worldly activity (*nivṛtti*) and realization of nirvana. Why teach about the world at all? "Surely, only the emptiness of intrinsic nature should be taught," someone says, "because that is ultimate in nature." In response, Candrakīrti (CŚṬ D f.140b–141a) defends the practice of giving preliminary teachings since they are "the gateway for entry into the truth." "It is impossible to reveal the truth that has the emptiness of intrinsic nature as its defining characteristic," he says, "without discussing the nature of worldly activity before the ultimate." All discourse about worldly activity will show how people become involved in the world and how ignorance motivates their actions. As the student's capacity for understanding increases, the instruction given will change. Advice on turning away from activity and disengaging from the world is coupled with discourse about the emptiness of intrinsic nature and dependent origination. Craving ceases when the attachment to sensations ceases; and, from the realization of the ultimate emptiness of intrinsic nature, birth, old age, and death cease.

"His mind was liberated like the extinguishing of a lamp," the monk Anuruddha says of the Buddha's nirvana. Vasubandhu quotes this verse in the *Abhidharmakośabhāṣya* (Hwang 2006, 98) to make his point that nirvana should be described as a non-existent thing (*nirvanam abhāvam*). Candrakīrti (PP.525) quotes the verse and Vasubandhu's remarks to refute another Abhidharma position that nirvana is an existent thing. Nāgārjuna refuses to attribute existence, non-existence, both, or neither to nirvana. Candrakīrti's commentary criticizes the Abhidharmists' concept of *nirvāṇa* as the cessation of the afflictions and the mind–body continuum. He denies that cessation could occur as long as the aggregates still exist, and once the aggregates cease there is nothing left to apprehend the cessation.

Abhidharma interpretations describe *nirvāṇa* as an unconditioned entity distinct from the world of *saṃsāra*, but according to Nāgārjuna, in MMK 25:19: "Nothing distinguishes *saṃsāra* from nirvana; and nothing distinguishes nirvana from *saṃsāra*." Candrakīrti notes (PP.536) that both have the same nature of being peaceful. Āryadeva, in CŚ.V.22, implies that the distinction between the two is epistemological not ontological: "Even in this world no harm comes to those who have powerful minds. For that reason, there's no difference for them between *saṃsāra* and nirvana." Candrakīrti (CŚṬ D f.103b) explains that, because bodhisattvas have powerful minds incapable of regressing from their aspirations for enlightenment, they are not troubled by the afflictions of desire, anger, and delusion. Using a well-known analogy, he compares the bodhisattva in *saṃsāra* to a lotus that remains unstained by the muddy water in which it grows.

A familiar objection is raised. If all things are empty, nothing exists, no action is necessary, and no liberation is possible. Madhyamaka teaching amounts to nihilism. Candrakīrti responds (CŚṬ D f.136a) that the charge of nihilism is wrong because there is no repudiation of moral actions. In the *Prasannapadā* (368–9) he has much more to say. The Madhyamaka belief in dependent origination of all things is a repudiation of intrinsic nature or an unchanging essence (*svabhāva*). Nihilism, as Candrakīrti understands it, is not equivalent to the simple statement that things do not exist; the charge of nihilism is accurate only when this assertion is associated with an ontological belief in an unchanging essence. Emptiness when properly understood is not nihilism, because neither moral behavior nor the soteriological goal of nirvana is denied.

The Doctrine of Emptiness

If afflictions cease through rational inquiry (*vicārāt*), why, more often than not, do we see people whose afflictions are not controlled? Candrakīrti replies (CŚṬ D f.134a–b) that it is because people lack conviction in the profound teaching of emptiness. Different ways of seeing the world separate the learned from the ignorant. He defines an ignorant person as someone whose deluded vision has become accustomed to the beginningless cycle of death and rebirth and is convinced that things that resemble reflections are real. This ignorant person's belief in the reality of familiar things prevents the possibility of seeing the world in another way. Any teaching about emptiness seems as dangerous as a steep cliff; any misstep could lead to a terrifying fall into a dark abyss. But where does this fear come from? Candrakīrti argues that this present fear of the profound teaching of emptiness is rooted in the habitual actions of the past. A frightened person's mental stream lacks the good roots that are the reason for conviction in emptiness (*śūnyatādhimukti*). Past mental states and actions failed to generate enough merit to yield an open mind in the present. "Even doubt (*saṃśaya*) about this teaching of emptiness – Is this so or not – does not occur to such a person." "But if for some reason doubt develops when the teaching of emptiness is explained, and someone wonders 'Is this teaching so or not?,'" Candrakīrti says, "this mere doubt surely breaks the cycle of existence." Why does this happen? He has two answers. First, when the process of skeptical inquiry begins with the doubt – Is this so? – it sets in motion a series of actions that gradually lead to the cessation of the afflictions. But in his second explanation we have a determined skeptic seeking certainty (*saṃśayito niścayenārthī*). Because of the power of rational scriptures (*sopapattikāgama*), this skeptic becomes certain of the correct vision. The cycle of death and rebirth is seen as broken even at the moment of doubt. Candrakīrti seems to be making the case here that skepticism is not interminable and that there are grounds, the reasons set forth in Buddhist scriptures, for removing doubt. His skepticism concerns ordinary people having the cognitive and meditative skills required to understand any discourse about emptiness. But it is not radical skepticism. Doubting is an everyday practice that is useful but also has its limits. Candrakīrti envisions doubt as part of critical inquiry into the teaching of emptiness that, if used skillfully, will lead to liberation.

In MMK.XIII.8, Nāgārjuna refers to an early Mahāyāna scripture, the *Kāśyapaparivarta*, in which the Buddha speaks of the therapeutic role of emptiness. In this text the Buddha asks Kāśyapa to determine if a patient would be cured under these circumstances: a doctor gives medicine to a patient, but, after it cures his symptoms, it remains in his bowels without being expelled. If it remains, Kāśyapa replies, the patient's problems would become worse. The Buddha encourages him to regard emptiness in the same way. Drawing on this story, Nāgārjuna similarly describes emptiness as a therapeutic antidote to the ill effects of attachment to views: "The buddhas have said that emptiness is a purgative for all views. But they have said that those who hold emptiness as a view are incurable" (MMK.XIII.8). Emptiness here works like a laxative to free mental blockages. After it has accomplished its purpose, there is no reason to continue using it. Nāgārjuna caustically suggests that people who hold on to emptiness will be no better off than the formerly constipated fool who fails to understand the proper use of his medication. Candrakīrti's commentary on the verse (PP.24) criticizes those who make emptiness, which is just the cessation (*nivṛttimātra*) of views, into an existent thing. That is analogous, he says, to one person saying to another, "I'll give you no wages at all," and the other responding, "Give me those wages you referred to as 'none at all.' " This is an example of his use of a non-implicative negative (*prasajyapratiṣedha*). The statement of one man that he will not give another wages does not imply that there is any real thing that corresponds to the negation "no wages at all." Like the Buddha's raft or Wittgenstein's ladder, emptiness should be discarded after it has served its purpose.

Paradoxical Language

The question arises: is emptiness itself empty? Emptiness when used as a therapeutic antidote to the ill effects of attachment to views is dependent upon specific factors – e.g., ignorance – that function as the target for its operation. And, like all things that operate in dependence upon others, emptiness, too, is empty. Emptiness, however, is also related to the concept of intrinsic nature, and Candrakīrti uses this term in more than one sense. He defines it as "that property which a thing invariably has because that property is not dependent upon anything else. In ordinary language, heat is called the intrinsic nature of fire because fire invariably has heat" (PP.241.7–9). Heat as the unchanging essence of fire is rejected, since a fire's heat can be shown to be dependent on other things, such as fuel. An empty thing has no essence in this sense. But Candrakīrti also says (MĀ.108): "Ultimate reality for the Buddhas is intrinsic nature itself. That, moreover, because it is nondeceptive is the truth of ultimate reality. It is known through personal experience."

William Ames identifies two apparent contradictions in Candrakīrti's use of the term:

> The first is that between the statement in the *Madhyamakāvatāra* that *svabhāva* exists and the statement in the *Prasannapadā* that "it neither exists, nor does it not exist, by intrinsic nature." In the *Prasannapadā* Candrakīrti adds that, through imputation it is said to exist. Thus we can reconcile the two statements if we suppose that, in the *Madhyamakāva-tāra*, Candrakīrti is speaking on the level of imputation and conventional reality (*saṃvṛtyā samāropya*).
>
> (Ames 1982, 172–3)

In the *Madhyamakāvatāra*, Candrakīrti sets out the stages of the Buddhist path. So that his audience won't reach the nihilistic conclusion that the spiritual path is worthless, he equates intrinsic nature with ultimate reality. But also he denies in his commentaries on the works of Nāgārjuna and Āryadeva that things have an intrinsic nature:

> Things are empty of inherent existence because they have arisen in dependence like a magic illusion. Āryas, whose mental streams are purified through perceiving accurately the truth about things and untainted conceptualizing the extremes of imputation and negation (*samāropāpavādakalpanā*), understand these things as empty of intrinsic nature.
>
> (CŚṬ D f.135b)

The contradiction is resolved through understanding the context of the message and the audience it is directed towards. People on the beginning stages of the path need the encouragement of positive descriptions of reality, while those who have progressed much further along understand that positive and negative descriptions of reality are inaccurate.

Ames identifies a second apparent contradiction that occurs in the *Prasannapadā* when, after stating that *svabhāva* exists, Candrakīrti explicitly states that it does not exist. This apparent contradiction cannot simply be resolved by appealing to two levels of truth. However, Ames argues convincingly that the two statements are not contradictory because the meaning of *svabhāva* differs in each context. A thing's essential nature is generally assumed to be some positive property rather than its absence. Candrakīrti's statement that *svabhāva* does not exist means that none of a thing's properties can be a *svabhāva*, since all things and their properties are contingent and dependent on causes and conditions. Indeed, as Ames notes,

> The fact that things lack *svabhāva* follows from their being dependent on causes and conditions; but it does not depend on the presence of some particular conditions, rather than others. Thus the fact of the absence of *svabhāva* satisfies the explicit part of the definition of *svabhāva*!

But it differs from the example given of heat as the intrinsic nature of fire in two ways: (1) it does not satisfy the implicit condition that *svabhāva* be a positive property; and (2) it is not a property of things but a fact about the properties of things – namely, that none of them are a *svabhāva*. We can speak of the absence of *svabhāva* in things as their *svabhāva*, but there is no existent thing that corresponds to the absence of *svabhāva*. If the lack of *svabhāva* is the *svabhāva* of things, then it seems that things have *svabhāva* if they do not have it and vice versa. Ames concludes that the paradox can be resolved by observing that the *svabhāva* which is affirmed belongs to a higher level of abstraction than the *svabhāva* which is negated. Since what is being negated is not the same as what is being affirmed, there is no paradox (Ames 1982, 173–4).

Jay Garfield and Graham Priest take a different line of argument. They find the dialetheist's approach of accepting true contradictions a useful strategy for talking about Madhyamaka concepts of essence and emptiness. "When people are driven to contradictions in charting the limits of thought," they write, "it is precisely because those limits are themselves contradictory" (Garfield and Priest 2003, 3). Any description of ultimate reality will be contradictory. That emptiness is an essential property of things is a paradox about what can be expressed.

> We can think (and characterize) reality only subject to language, which is conventional, so the ontology of that reality is all conventional. It follows that the conventional objects of reality do not ultimately (nonconventionally) exist. It also follows that nothing we say of them is ultimately true. That is, all things are empty of ultimate existence, and this is their ultimate nature and is an ultimate truth about them. They hence cannot be thought to have that nature, nor can we say that they do. But we have just done so.
>
> (Ibid., 13)

Garfield and Priest find another more fundamental ontological contradiction concerning emptiness itself underlying the limits of language:

> Emptiness is the nature of all things; by virtue of this they have no nature, not even emptiness. . . . Nāgārjuna's enterprise is one of fundamental ontology, and the conclusion he comes to is that fundamental ontology is impossible. But that is a fundamentally ontological conclusion – and that is the paradox. . . . Reality has no nature. Ultimately, it is not in any way at all. So nothing can be said about it. Essencelessness thus induces noncharacterizability. But, on the other side of the street, emptiness is an ultimate character of things.
>
> (Ibid., 15)

They conclude that the contradictory notion of emptiness shows that paradoxical linguistic utterances are "grounded in the contradictory nature of reality" (ibid.). This conclusion, though it may well be true, seems to go farther than what the Mādhyamikas argue. If I interpret them correctly, it's not that they set out to prove that conventional reality is incoherent, but only that it is incoherent if the assumption is made that things exist by intrinsic nature.

Garfield and Priest take what Mark Siderits calls a semantic approach to the interpretation of emptiness. In contrast to metaphysical interpretations that take the doctrine of emptiness to be a metaphysical theory about the ultimate nature of reality, a semantic interpretation of emptiness takes the doctrine to concern not the nature of reality, but the nature of truth. Siderits advocates a semantic interpretation of emptiness that says that truth is non-dual (Siderits 2007, 202). According to this view, "the point of establishing emptiness is to show the very idea of an ultimate truth to be incoherent," to show "that the ultimate truth is that there is no ultimate truth" – there is only conventional truth. But this is not an interpretation that Candrakīrti (or the Buddha) would recognize, for he says (MĀ.119): "The Buddha said: 'Monks, this is the unique ultimate truth, namely, nirvana which is non-deceptive.' Because conventional truth is deceptive it is not absolutely true."

The possibility that someone might collapse both truths into conventional truth is anticipated in a passage from the *Satyadvayāvatārasūtra*, which Candrakīrti quotes (MĀ.110–11):

> Devaputra, if the ultimate truth in reality were to be the object of body, speech, and mind, it would not be counted as ultimate truth. It would just be conventional truth. But Devaputra, the ultimate truth surpasses all convention, is without qualities, unborn, unceasing, free from the namable, and the name and the knowable and the knowledge [of it].

The anonymous author of this passage describes a conception of ultimate truth that transcends the limits of ordinary language and the limits of dualistic thought. But the passage does not necessarily point towards a mind-independent reality. Candrakīrti cites *Samādhirājasūtra* (D f. 103b) in support of the idea that nirvana is not some alternative reality outside of this world:

> Through insight I know that the aggregates are empty;
> And knowing that, I am not accompanied by afflictions.
> I speak using just ordinary language;
> And in this world I have entered nirvana.
>
> (SR.VI.12)

This citation implies that nirvana is not a mind-independent reality but rather involves the power of the mind to realize that anything that could be considered a self – even the five aggregates – is empty of any intrinsic nature. This liberating insight eliminates the attachment that motivates desire, and the aversion motivates anger and the ignorance that underlies them both. Without the suffering that these three afflictions cause, "There is," Candrakīrti says (CŚṬ D f.103b), "no difference between saṃsāra and nirvana."

The Soteriological Value of Emptiness: The Peace of Nirvana

Nāgārjuna and Āryadeva note that people who say "Nirvana will be mine" (MMK.16.9b) and "Let me attain nirvana" (CŚ.VIII.7b) won't attain it. According to Candrakīrti (PP.295), people who make such statements reveal their strong attachment to a view of a reified self (*satkāyadṛṣti*) and will not attain the peace of nirvana.

Candrakīrti's further rejection of his opponents' methods follows also from his unwillingness to support philosophical systems whose assertions categorize things in dualistic terms. Debate produces in its participants the proponent's attachment to his own thesis and his aversion to that of his opponent. On CŚ.VIII.10d: "There is no peace for someone who engages in quarreling," Candrakīrti comments:

> If you are partial to your position and think that the position of emptiness is superior and you dislike the opponent's position and think that it is wrong, you will not attain nirvana. There is no nirvana for someone who engages in quarreling and is damaged by attachment and anger. Impartial people always attain peace, the unique taste of bliss that never ceases, because they have eradicated attachment.
>
> (CŚṬ D f.136)

Candrakīrti uses ordinary language and rational arguments to undermine confidence in cherished beliefs about a self, but neither language nor logic adequately conveys the peace of nirvana. When both the realm of thought (*cittagocāra*) and the objective referents of language (*abhidhātavya*) have ceased, he asks (PP.493), how can words or knowledge operate? He describes the ultimate as peace, transcendent to all conceptual development and accessible only to Āryas through their own personal experience (*pratyātmvedya*). It is not necessary to interpret his words as referring to an ineffable state of being that transcends the capabilities of ordinary language and conceptual thinking. His words seem rather to point towards a meditative experience that cannot be adequately described after the fact. The nature of the truths, he explains, is realized through the perfection of meditation, on the fifth stage of the bodhisattva path (MĀ.69–71).

In his commentary on CŚ.XIIc: "Emptiness is nirvana (*śūnyatām eva nirvāṇam*)," Candrakīrti says, "What we have explained as emptiness the buddhas have stated to be nirvana. The calming of all suffering that takes the form of the five aggregates is nirvana" (CŚṬ D f.194a). This perception of nirvana follows from realizing that nothing, not even suffering, has arisen essentially. Candrakīrti never explicitly mentions the details of this or any specific spiritual or meditative experience. His claim (CŚṬ D f.142a) that nirvana is realized through an accurate perception of the ultimate and through gnosis of the ultimate (*paramārthajñāna*), and therefore that intelligent people should direct their minds towards contemplation, indicates that he advocates some type of meditative practice. The relationship between what meditative experience is and what Buddhist literature says about it is, as Robert Sharf notes, "tenuous." But the assumption that Buddhist philosophical literature was intended to constitute "a detailed map of inner space, charted with the aid of sophisticated meditation techniques that allowed Buddhist yogis to travel the breadth of psychic terrain," is mistaken (Scharf 1995, 230–1). Candrakīrti's *Madhyamakāvatara* describes the ten-stage path towards nirvana and buddhahood, but he provides no topographical details.

The Four Positions (*catuṣkoṭi*)

Garfield and Priest suggest that the contradiction at the limits of expressibility can be approached through looking at Mādhyamikas' use of both positive and negative forms of the Indian tetralemma (*catuṣkoṭi*). Classical Indian logic and rhetoric regards any proposition as defining a logical space involving four positions, or corners (*koṭi*), in contrast to most Western logical traditions, which consider only two possibilities – truth and falsity (Garfield and Priest 2003, 13).

The *catuṣkoṭi*, sometimes referred to as "the four logical alternatives" or when each one of its four members is successively negated, as "the principle of four-corned negation," contains a set of four alternative positions which were debated in the philosophical discussions of ancient India. The tetralemma encompasses these four propositions: (1) x exists/is true, (2) x does not exist/is false, (3) x both exists and does not exist/is both true and false, and (4) x neither exists nor does not exist/is neither true nor false.

Most Mādhyamika uses of the tetralemma are negative in form. Nāgārjuna (in MMK. XXII.11) rejects the applicability of each of the four positions to the Buddha: " 'Empty' should not be asserted. 'Nonempty' should not be asserted. Neither both nor neither should be asserted. These [expressions], however, are used in a nominal sense (*prajñaptyartham*)." The last line clarifies Nāgārjuna's view that these alternative positions are asserted only in a nominal sense. Candrakīrti (PP.444) denies that the intent of Nāgārjuna's use of a negative tetralemma here is to attribute non-existence to Tathāgatas, since positing non-existence would incur the fault of negation (*apavāda*). The intention of Nāgārjuna, whom he describes as an "insightful yogin," is to explain that Tathāgata lacks *svabhāva*. He explains that it is impossible to explain *svabhāva* when nothing at all is said; and, for that reason, Mādhyamikas resort to using imputation (*āropa*) and conventional truth (*vyavahārasatya*) in a way that is appropriate for students. Moreover, he says (PP.446), just as it is irrational to describe the complexion of a barren woman's son as either light or dark, it is irrational to apply any of the four positions to the Tathāgata.

Candrakīrti uses the same analogy of the barren woman's son earlier in his commentary on MMK.XVII.8, an example of a tetralemma stated in positive terms: "Everything is real, non-real, both real and not real, neither real nor not real – this is the Buddha's teaching." His lengthy commentary on this verse (PP.370–2) makes it clear that the gradual nature of his teachings is the context in which the Buddha's remarks were made. First the Buddha teaches that the aggregates, elements, and bases are "real" to students who have the desire to learn the distinct nature of various commonly accepted things in order to gain their trust. He teaches students who know that he is omniscient that things are "unreal" and impermanent, since they perish each moment. He teaches others that "everything is both real and not real" to show that what seems real from an ordinary person's perspective is in fact unreal from the perspective of Āryas. Finally, to those who have eliminated most of the afflictions and wrong views that obstruct the path to buddhahood, he teaches that things cannot be characterized as either real or unreal, just as the complexion of a barren woman's son cannot be described as light or dark. Candrakīrti concludes his commentary by quoting Āryadeva (CŚ.VIII.20): "Existence, non-existence, both existence and non-existence, and neither existence nor non-existence are taught. Surely, isn't it in accordance with the illness that the medicine becomes beneficial?" In his commentary on this verse he says:

> "Existence" is taught for the purpose of cleansing the stain of the view that everything is nonexistent. "Nonexistence" is taught for the purpose of eliminating attachment to existent things. Both

> "Existence and nonexistence" are taught for the purpose of refuting views that have aspects of both. "Neither existence nor nonexistence" is revealed for the purpose of destroying conceptual proliferation in its all aspects.
>
> (CŚṬ D f.141b)

Candrakīrti compares the Dharma to treatment for an illness and, since illnesses have different symptoms, many medicines need to be employed, not just one medicine for all cases. The analogy made to illness and treatment suggests that he regards the use of the tetralemma as therapeutic, but not in the sense of "pseudo-propositions" used as a psychological technique designed to induce a certain meditative state (Tillemans 1999, 190). As Candrakīrti explains, each of the positions is intended to refute specific philosophical stances.

The first verse of Nāgārjuna's MMK.I.1 states: "There exists nowhere at all, any existent things, arisen either from themselves or from something else, either from both or without cause." "There is nothing whatsoever anywhere which has arisen from itself, from others, from both, or from no cause." Shoryu Katsura notes that these positions successively negate views on causality held by other schools: the Sāṃkhya view of causation that every result inheres in its cause; the Vaiśeṣika view that a completely new result emerges out of its causes; the Abhidharma view that everything arises out of its cause and conditions; the *syādvāda* of the Jainas, who claim that a result occurs from itself in one sense and from others in another sense; and the view of those who deny causation altogether, such as that of the Lokāyata, according to whom everything occurs naturally and without any particular cause (Katsura 2007, 68–9).

Candrakīrti on Bhāviveka's Use of Inferences and Syllogisms

The Svātantrika–Prāsaṅgika distinction, often used in discussing the views of Buddhapālita (c. 470–550), Bhāviveka, and Candrakīrti developed late in Buddhist textual history, perhaps not until the eleventh century. Their commentaries on Nāgārjuna's MMK.I.1 reflect differing strategies on how to defend Madhyamaka ideas. The Svātantrika strategy of Bhāviveka uses formal independent (*svatantra*) syllogistic inferences and adds the qualifier "ultimately" to Nāgārjuna's negative statements. The Prāsaṅgika strategy of Buddhapālita and Candrakīrti involves primarily identifying errors and unwanted conclusions (*prasaṅga*) that result from inconsistencies in their opponents' arguments. Bhāviveka criticized Buddhapālita's use of *prasaṅga* arguments as inadequate to prove that things have no intrinsic nature and for or his failure to use formal syllogisms. His thesis is a more restrictive version of Nāgārjuna's claim and adds a reason and an example. Bhāviveka believes that syllogistic logic is implicit in the MMK verses and that Nāgārjuna's negation of origination is non-implicative (*prasajyapratiṣedhisa*) and cannot be interpreted as implying an affirmation of non-origination. Ames concludes that Bhāviveka's differences with Buddhapālita were primarily methodological.[7]

He argues (PP.15–24) that the Sāṃkhya opponent interprets "from themselves" to mean that the effect pre-exists in its cause, which Mādhyamikas consider equivalent to saying that an already existent thing is produced a second time. This logic is faulty, they argue, because a repeated production serves no purpose and would lead to an infinite regress. Buddhapālita's use of *prasaṅga* arguments that force the self-contradiction implicit in the Sāṃkhya doctrines are sufficient for refutation. If this line of argument advanced does not sway the opponent, neither will the autonomous inferences with their additions of a reason and an example.

Candrakīrti quotes Bhāviveka's restatement of Nāgārjuna's claim that things do not arise from themselves:

[THESIS:]	The sense organs ultimately do not originate from themselves;
[REASON:]	because they exist [already]
[EXAMPLE:]	like consciousness (*caitanya*).

(PP.25–6)

He criticizes Bhāviveka's use of autonomous inferences as inappropriate for Mādhyamikas – regardless of whether the inference is formulated with the intent of refuting an opponent's position or establishing one's own.

Candrakīrti also finds Bhāviveka's use of the qualification "ultimately" problematic (PP.26–35). If it is applied to the whole proposition, then it could imply an acceptance of self-causation on the conventional level; and if it is restricted to Sāṃkhya and other non-Buddhist theories of causality, then it is unnecessary, since people do not accept their theories even on the level of conventional truth. Since Mādhyamikas don't accept things, such sense organs, as being ultimately existent or real (*dravya*), unlike the Sāṃkhya opponent, the thesis would be defective either because, for Bhāviveka, the subject term is unproven (*āśrayśiddha*) or the reason would have no real locus (*asiddha*). These defects of subjects and reasons apply only to those who formulate independent inferences and not to his use of inference, which is intended only to negate the opponent's thesis. His negation of the opponent's arguments does not imply the affirmation of a counter-position, and in that sense he denies that Mādhyamikas hold a thesis.

Moreover, both parties in the debate need to agree on the terms of inference; an inference is not valid if it is based only on the opponent's assumptions (PP.35). Candrakīrti returns to the point again in CŚṬ D f.104a–b, criticizing a Mīmāṃsa opponent whose syllogistic argument he formulates in this way:

[THESIS:]	The Tathāgata is not omniscient
[REASON:]	because he is a human being
[EXAMPLE:]	like other human beings.

According to Mīmāṃsikas, there are no omniscient beings, and so a Buddhist who argues that the Buddha is omniscient violates the logical rule that all elements in the argument must have members. Candrakīrti responds by questioning his opponent: "Do the proposition's two terms express the same thing or a different thing? If it is the same thing, then the fault of redundancy (*vīpsā*) would ensue. If it is a different thing, then it would not communicate the speaker's intention." His first point seems to be that, if the subject "Tathāgata" and its qualifying predicate "omniscient" are the same (and, for a Buddhist, "Tathāgata" and "Omniscient One" both refer to the Buddha) – the proposition's two terms are redundant. His second point seems to be that, if the two are totally different, then the relation of qualified (the subject) and qualifier (the predicate) can never exist between them and there is a failure to communicate what the opponent wants to say (*vivakṣā*). While the opponent privileges inference, inferential arguments find little support among ordinary people. Then, in rapid-fire succession, he throws out three syllogisms that ridicule the opponent's wife, his religious beliefs, and his caste status:

[THESIS:]	Mothers, etc., are not off limits sexually[8]
[REASON:]	because they are women,
[EXAMPLE:]	just like your own wife.
[THESIS:]	The word of the Vedas is not eternal, uncreated, self-arisen and valid,
[REASON:]	because it is speech
[EXAMPLE:]	just like the speech of a lunatic.
[THESIS:]	This man is not a brahmin priest,
[REASON:]	because he has hands, etc.,
[EXAMPLE:]	just like a fisherman.

Candrakīrti's rejection of Bhāviveka's autonomous inferences and use of syllogisms is a matter primarily of style rather than of substance. Both Mādhyamikas reject the various positions alluded to in Nāgārjuna's verse. But Candrakīrti regards the use of syllogisms an unnecessary innovation that adds nothing to the arguments needed to refute opponents' positions.

Candrakīrti on the Function of Valid Means of Knowledge

Candrakīrti (PP.75) concedes that inference is a means of valid cognition (*pramāṇa*) that is useful for establishing worldly knowledge, along with direct perception, scripture, and analogy, the knowledge derived from comparing unknown things (the wild gayal) to known things (the domestic cow). He follows Nāgārjuna's critique in the *Vigrahavyāvartanī*: these four means of valid cognition are all in fact dependent upon the propositions they ostensibly justify. Inference can be used in cases where things are not directly perceptible, and, when perception and inference fail to give certain knowledge about things that are beyond the scope of the senses, the scriptural authority of the Buddha should be relied upon (CŚṬ D f.186b–187a). These four *pramāṇas* are known primarily from Nyāya sources, but Eli Franco's work on a third-century CE Buddhist manuscript suggests that some Buddhists – likely of the Sarvāstivādins – also accepted them (Vose 2010, 556).

Anne MacDonald argues persuasively that the opponent Candrakīrti refutes in PP.55.11–58.13 is not Dignāga but a Naiyāyika. The Naiyāyika objects that, if the Mādhyamika admits *pramānas* exist, they will contradict his view that nothing exists; if, however, the Mādhyamika does not admit *pramāṇas* exist, his conviction that things do not exist is as good as any other unjustified imaginary thing. If the Mādhyamika makes conclusions about the ontological status of the world without the epistemological tools that would validate them, then opponents are also free to assert whatever they wish without reliance on *pramāṇas*. The assertion that all things exist and the corroboration of their existence through common-sense experience accords with Naiyāyikas' realist views. MacDonald identifies similar versions of the arguments in Uddyotakara's *Nyāyavārttika* and speculates that Candrakīrti may have also used a no longer extant Nyāya text that the PP partially preserves (MacDonald 2011).

Candrakīrti denies that Mādhyamikas make any judgments based on *pramāṇas* that would affirm a counter-position. When challenged by the opponent that the sentences in MMK.I.1 do appear to be judgments, he concedes that they function in that way for ordinary people but not for Āryas, for whom ultimate reality is silence. They resort to ordinary language and advance the appropriate arguments only to enlighten ordinary people, who, under the influence of ignorance, erroneously impute essences to things.

Candrakīrti then (PP.58.14–74) criticizes Dignāga's views that there are just two means of valid cognition: direct perception, which apprehends only unique characteristics or particulars (*svalakṣaṇa*), and inference, which apprehends the conceptually constructed and conventionally existent common characteristics or universals (*sāmānyalakṣana*). Dignāga privileges the non-conceptual perception of these unique particulars, which are the foundation for his conceptually constructed world. Candrakīrti's line of attack on these two *lakṣana* follows Nāgārjuna's similar treatment in MMK.V of the mutual dependence of character and characterized (*lakṣana/lakṣya*). The opponent then counters that pramāṇas are self-validating and introduces the notion of self-reflexive awareness (*svasaṃviti*), which Candrakīrti rejects on the grounds that it would lead to an infinite regress of self-validating cognitions.

In the CŚṬ (CŚṬ D f.196a–197b) Candrakīrti rejects Dignāga's definition of perception as non-conceptual (*kalpanāpoḍha*) and restricted to the apprehension of inexpressible and momentary particulars. He questions how one momentary instant of a sense consciousness could be a perception, since the momentary instants of sense organs and consciousness cease as soon as they arise. He rejects Dignāga's denial of pots as the proper object of perception, since these are conceptually constructed. Candrakīrti takes the common-sense approach and supports the position that pots and crescent moons are perceptible because this agrees with the way ordinary people see and describe the world. On a conventional level, it is unreasonable to reject ordinary people's experience. But he cautions that there should be no assertion of any essence for pots, since in no way can the pot's essence be perceived. Candrakīrti does not hesitate here to use conservative realist positions on perception to undermine Dignāga's epistemological innovations.

Candrakīrti's views on the perception of the ultimate, however, may have been influenced by Dignāga's conception of yogic perception. In his *Yuktiṣaṣṭikā* commentary on verse eight's characterization of the Buddhist Vaibhāṣika and the Sautrāntika opponents' *nirvāṇa* as a real cessation, he denies that perception of cessation could occur while the aggregates still exist; and, as the verse says, once the aggregates cease, there is no subject left to apprehend the cessation. Candrakīrti then paraphrases Dignāga's views (*Pramāṇasamuccaya* I.6cd and its auto-commentary) on yogic perception and presents it as the yogins' non-conceptual perception of the ultimate, but disagrees with their explanations of the meditative process:

> Candrakīrti initiates the presentation of his Madhyamaka view by rhetorically asking how, even if the meditative process posited by the epistemologists would be correct, there could be the direct perception of the consciousness of cessation (*'gog pa, *nirodha*) when in cessation there does not exist even a trace of an entity having the form of the cessation of suffering. Next, in reliance on scriptural testimony which states that awareness of the non-arising of suffering is direct perception, he argues that it would, in fact, be impossible for consciousness to arise when its objective support (*dmigs pa; *ālambana*) has the form of non-arising; in such a case consciousness would definitely assume the mode of non-arising, that is, it would not arise at all. . . . In Candrakīrti's words: If consciousness, like its object, has the form of non-arising, it is proper to maintain that it has proceeded by way of the object just as it is. And given its proceeding by way of its object, its conforming to its object, it is proper to designate it direct perception.
>
> (MacDonald 2009, 156)

He offers an example of a situation where people speak of "direct perception" in regard to non-existent things. A traveler sees water off in the distance and asks a local farmer about it, who explains that what looks like water is actually a mirage. He adds that, if the traveler doesn't believe him, he should go and look for himself; then he will directly perceive what he has just been told. Candrakīrti concludes that, from the point of view of conventional truth, it is not contradictory to call a consciousness of non-perception, which for Candrakīrti is no consciousness at all, a "direct perception" (ibid.).

Why does he describe the Mādhyamika yogin's lack of consciousness as direct perception? MacDonald suggests that it was necessary that Candrakīrti acknowledge direct perception of nirvana, for not to have done so would have left him open to attack regarding the Mādhyamika's and Buddha's direct realization of nirvana and the Buddha's establishment as an authority. MacDonald concludes that Candrakīrti's assertion that consciousness does not arise when the object is the ultimate is secondarily intended to point to the fact that, for him, all perceptual activity – as well as all conceptual and linguistic activity – ceases in the experience of nirvana (MacDonald 2009, 159).

That the authority of the Buddha was important to Candrakīrti is evident from the frequency of his use of scriptural testimony as "proof texts" that supplement the reasoned arguments he presents in his commentaries. When arguing against the positions of fellow Buddhists, he employs the scriptural authority of Buddhist texts to prove that their views are incompatible with the Buddha's own word. He also frequently quotes the authority of Nāgārjuna and Āryadeva in support of his arguments. He refers to Nāgārjuna as an "authoritative person who has realized the profound nature of things" (MĀ.75).

Conclusion

More than one hundred years have passed since Louis de La Vallée Poussin edited Candrakīrti's *Prasannapadā* commentary on Nāgārjuna's MMK and his independent work, the *Madhyamakāvatārabhāṣya*; an edition of his third major work, the *Bodhisattvayogāracatuḥśatakaṭīkā*, has yet to be published. There are no complete translations of any of these works and there is no consensus on what Candrakīrti means when he speaks about Nāgārjuna's realization of the profound nature of things. It is not surprising that contemporary scholars cannot agree on how to interpret Madhyamaka, since interscholastic debate on how to understand Nāgārjuna commences in India by the fifth century and in Tibet in the eleventh century. Speculation about the metaphysical nature of Madhyamaka thought has now given way to various semantic interpretations. Garfield interprets Nāgārjuna's arguments as employing skeptical methods; Dan Arnold, in contrast, sees them as transcendental arguments working against skeptical challenges by showing that the challenges are only intelligible given the truth of the claim being challenged (see Arnold 2005, 135–40). Many of these interpretations focus on the philosophical import of the language and logic used in Nāgārjuna's works, and there is little doubt that Nāgārjuna is a compelling philosopher; but for Candrakīrti he is a religious authority, like the Buddha himself.

Two of Candrakīrti's works, his independent *Madhyamakāvatāra* and his *Bodhisattvayogāracatuḥśatakaṭīkā* commentary on Āryadeva's *Catuḥśataka*, have as their central focus the soteriological goal of attaining buddhahood. Both discuss the Buddhist tradition's recognition of the different abilities of ordinary practitioners and extraordinary practitioners, the Āryas. Corresponding to this distinction of differing abilities is a system of gradual and hierarchical practice, beginning with the cultivation of virtues of generosity and moral behavior. Only people of superior ability cultivate meditation and the insight into the empty nature of all things. Despite its inadequacies, ordinary language and conventional truth have pragmatic value for Candrakīrti, since they point towards the ultimate truth, the peace of nirvana. The logic of tetralemma similarly reflects a hierarchical system that has a certain pragmatic value. Some beliefs are useful on beginning stages of the path, even though other more refined beliefs can supersede them. As Candrakīrti explains, the position of "existence" is advanced to counteract the nihilist belief that everything is non-existent, and the position "neither existence nor non-existence" is advanced to destroy conceptual proliferation in all its aspects. He implies that nothing whatsoever can describe the ultimate; it is at this point the silence of the Āryas intervenes.

Notes

1 For references to MMK and MĀ, see La Vallée Poussin (1970a) and (1970b) respectively. For references to CŚ, see Lang (1986).

2 See Cabezón (2008). Cabezón summarizes Tārānātha's account of the debate and discusses whether his Jonang pa sectarian affilation and its antipathy to the Geluk school, which championed Candrakīrti's version of the Madhyamaka, might have influenced his depiction of the debate.

3 See, for example, the articles in Dreyfus and McClintock (2003) and The Cowherds (2011).

4 For references to PP, see La Vallée Poussin (1970a).

5 References to *Bodhisattvayogāracatuḥśatakatīkā* correspond to vol. Ya, 30b–239a (here abbreviated as CŚṬ D) in *Sde dge Tibetan tripiṭaka bstan 'gyur*. Ed. K. Hayashima et al. 17 vols. Tokyo: Sekai Kanko Kyokai, 1977–9.

6 For references to SR, see Vaidya (1961).

7 W. Ames, "Bhāvaviveka's Own View of His Differences with Buddhapālita," in Dreyfus and McClintock (2003, 41–57).

8 The expression *agamya* (literally: not to be approached) when used to describe a woman implies that she ought not to be approached sexually because she is of low caste or because any relationship with mothers and daughters would be incestuous.

References

Ames, W. (1982). "The Notion of Svabhāva in the Thought of Candrakīrti." In *Journal of Indian Philosophy* 10, 161–77.

Arnold, D. (2005). *Buddhists, Brahmins, and Belief: Epistemology in South Asian Philosophy of Religion*. New York: Columbia University Press.

Cabezón, J. (2008). "Buddhist Narratives of the Great Debates." In *Argumentation* 22, 71–92.

The Cowherds (2011). *Moonshadows: Conventional Truth in Buddhist Philosophy*. New York: Oxford University Press.

Dreyfus, G., and McClintock, S. (eds) (2003). *The Svātantrika–Prāsaṅgika Distinction: What Difference Does a Difference Make?* Boston: Wisdom.

Garfield, J., and Priest, G. (2003). "Nāgārjuna and the Limits of Logic." In *Philosophy East and West* 53, 1–13.

Huntington, C. W. (1983). "The System of the Two Truths in the Prasannapadā and the Madhyamakāvatāra: A Study in Mādhyamika Soteriology." In *Journal of Indian Philosophy* 11, 77–106.

Hwang, Soonil (2006). *Metaphor and Literalism in Buddhism: The Doctrinal History of Nirvana*. New York: Routledge.

Katsura, S. (2007). "How Did the Buddhists Prove Something? The Nature of Buddhist Logic." In *Pacific World* 3(9), 63–84.

La Vallée Poussin, Louis de (1970a). *Mūlamadhyamakakārikās de Nāgārjuna avec la Prasannapadā commentaire de Candrakīrti*. Osnabrück: Biblio Verlag [reprint].

La Vallée Poussin, Louis de (1970b). *Madhyamakāvatāra par Candrakīrti*. Osnabrück: Biblio Verlag [reprint].

Lang, K. (1986). *Āryadeva's Catuḥśataka: On the Bodhisattva's Cultivation of Merit and Knowledge*. Copenhagen: Akademisk Forlag.

MacDonald, A. (2009). "Knowing Nothing: Candrakīrti and Yogic Perception." In *Yogic Perception, Meditation and Altered States of Consciousness*. Ed. E. Franco and D. Eigner. Vienna: Verlag der Österreichischen Akademie der Wissenschaften, 133–69.

MacDonald, A. (2011). "Who is that Masked Man? Candrakīrti's Opponent in Prasannapadā I 55.11–58.13." In *Journal of Indian Philosophy* 39, 677–94.

Scharf, R. (1995). "Buddhist Modernism and the Rhetoric of Meditative Experience." In *Numen* 42, 230–1.

Siderits, M. (2007). *Buddhism as Philosophy: An Introduction*. Aldershot: Ashgate.

Suzuki, K. (1994). *Sanskrit Fragments and Tibetan Translation of Candrakīrti's Bodhisattvayogācāra catuḥśatakaṭīkā*. Tokyo: Sanibo Press.

Tillemans, T. (1999). "Is Buddhist Logic Non-Classical or Deviant." In *Scripture, Logic, Language*. Boston: Wisdom, 187–205.

Vaidya, P. L. (ed.) (1961). *Samādhirajasūtra*. Darbangha: Mithila Institute of Post-Graduate Studies and Research in Sanskrit Learning.

Vose, Kevin (2010). "Authority in Early Prāsaṇgika Madhyamaka." In *Journal of Indian Philosophy* 38, 553–82.

22

On the Value of Speaking and Not Speaking

Philosophy of Language in Zen Buddhism

STEVEN HEINE

Language Versus Silence

In considering the role of language in Zen Buddhism, a basic conundrum is immediately confronted. Given the school's self-proclaimed emphasis on serving as a "special transmission outside the scriptures / without a reliance on words and letters" (Ch. *jiaowai biechuan/buli wenzi*; Jp. *kyōge betsuden/furyū monji*), perhaps what we would expect to hear at a Zen temple would be not language that is spoken but rather the eloquent sounds of silence.[1] This might include, for example, the murmur of rustling leaves or whispering pines, the hush of falling snow, or the gurgle of rushing streams that are considered to evoke the voice of Śākyamuni.[2] In addition to these natural resonances, temple life would encompass non-verbal sounds generated by monks, such as by sweeping floors or cooking and doing other chores, or through the ritual ringing of the temple bell at key intervals during the daily round of activities and the reciting or chanting (though not necessarily delivering explanations) of the *sūtras*.

However, historical studies demonstrate that in Zen there has always been a very large and fundamental role for verbal communication via poetry and prose narratives included in commentaries on enigmatic *kōans*, such as "Does the dog have buddha-nature?," with the answer being the one-syllable transcendental negation "Mu" (literally "No," suggesting nothingness) yet accompanied by extensive, generally paradoxical, exegesis. During Song dynasty China, Zen masters produced an abundant volume of writings that originally were based on the spontaneous and deliberately eccentric oral teachings of Tang dynasty patriarchs. This literature forms the heart of the modes of textual study and ritual practice used in Zen today.

Does this apparent discrepancy between highlighting the use of language while also stressing its transcendence point to a basic contradiction in the tradition, or does the prevalence of literary production mean that our understanding of what constitutes Zen transmission in relation to rhetorical discourse must be reconfigured? It has been said

A Companion to Buddhist Philosophy, First Edition. Edited by Steven M. Emmanuel.

that nobody writes or talks more about the need to refrain and desist from writing or speaking than mystics. In advocating the path of silence as key to realizing an ultimately interior and inexpressible truth, mystics produce, often at an accelerated or even feverish pace, lengthy and complex texts filled with poetic and prose compositions, as well as the records of oral discourse.[3] If it seems that mystics are violating their sacred principles, is this a product of some basic confusion or inconsistency held in the mystical viewpoint? Or, should we instead focus on the positive side – that is, the eloquence of mystical literature that is very much celebrated, ranging from the exalted verse of the *Song of Songs* and creativity of the Sufi and Taoist poetic traditions to the metaphysical musings of Neo-Platonic, Kabbalistic, and Advaita Vedantic thinkers? In that vein, perhaps the role of language in Zen involving various sorts of writings used in pursuit of the aims of religious practice to liberate the mind from fixation and attachment seeks a middle path between ineffability that abandons words and the view that verbal expression and speech is central to the seeker's quest for enlightenment.

The Zen philosophical view of language claims to be consistent through using devices such as the Mu *kōan* or the image of masters Huineng and Deshan ripping, burning, or defiling the *sūtras* in bringing to a culmination a basic trend in Buddhist thought towards a grave suspicion and transcendence of words. This tendency is indicated in the Buddha's refusal to respond to questions about the afterlife or eternity that "tend not to edification," the Madhyamika refutation of partial viewpoints (e.g., Jizang's "the denial of all false views is the correct view"), and the *Vimalakīrti Sūtra*'s highlighting the significance of "no words about no words." Zen also borrows heavily from Taoist critiques of the limitations of conventional language and logic, as in Laozi's opening line, "The Dao that can be talked about is not the real Dao," or Zhuangzi's emphasis on "forgetting" ordinary patterns of thought in order to achieve a higher level of spiritual realization.

The Zen approach to reticence was perhaps given its first forceful assertion in the early transmission of the lamp record from around 710, the *Chuan fabao ji* (Jp. *Den hōbōki*), which argues, "This transcendent enlightenment is transmitted by the mind [in a process that] cannot be described. What spoken or written words could possibly apply?"[4] This outlook is extended by Linji's proclamation that he "discarded" all the texts he had studied after having "realized that they were medicine for curing illness that otherwise displayed [one-sided] opinions" (T.47: 502c), and by similar examples of disdain for the written word in Zen sayings and anecdotes far too numerous to mention. However, Zen is perhaps best known not so much for the negation of speech, which would represent an extreme view, but for inventing a creative new style of expression that uses language in unusual and ingenious fashion to surpass a reliance on everyday words and letters.

Zen "encounter dialogues" (Ch. *jiyuan wenda*; Jp. *kien-mondō*) serving as the literary root of *kōan* case records demonstrate radical irreverence and iconoclasm in evoking "extraordinary words and strange deeds" – a phrase used to characterize the Tang dynasty Hongzhou school, which includes such luminaries as Mazu, the founder, and disciples Baizhang, Huangbo, and Linji. In this style, paradox, irony, non sequitur, and absurdity mingled with sarcastic put-downs and devastating one-upmanship are linked to extreme physical – that is, non-verbal – gestures and body language, including grunts and shouts, or striking and slapping as ways of moving beyond conventional speech. Moreover, Dongshan Shouchu, a disciple of Yunmen, makes the distinction between living words, which surpass reason, and dead words, which are limited in reflecting a reliance on logical thinking that results in "speaking all day long without having said a thing." For Zen, living words have usefulness in that they are deployed to expose the futility and to bring to an end the use of dead words, or as a poison to counteract poison or an example of fighting fire with fire.

As the prime example, *kōan* (Ch. *gongan*) literature is based on puzzling dialogues attributed to eccentric, quixotic, and irreverent patriarchs culled from the vast storehouses of transmission of the lamp records, including the *Jingde chuandeng lu* (Jp. *Keitoku dentōroku*) of 1004 and the *Tiansheng guangdeng lu* (Jp. *Tenshō dentōroku*) of 1036. These dialogues became the subject of extensive, multi-layered prose and verse commentaries containing philosophical and biographical elements replete with complex wordplay and allusions. According to Heinrich Dumoulin's assessment of the creative ingenuity evident in the most prominent *kōan* collection, the *Biyan lu* (Jp. *Hekiganroku*), or *Blue Cliff Record*, compiled in the twelfth century, "The selection of one hundred cases is exquisite. In the rich variety of their content and expression the [*kōan* cases] present the essence of Zen," making this text rank as "one of the foremost examples of religious world literature" (Dumoulin 1987, 249).

It is clear, based on modern historical studies, that the radical iconoclasm of the early patriarchs in the Hongzhou lineage was a Song dynasty invention applied retrospectively to the exploits that supposedly took place in the Tang dynasty. First making their appearance in transmission of the lamp records, the rhetorical devices of dialogues and *kōan* cases were designed to support the autonomous identity of Zen in an era of competition with Neo-Confucianism, and are not to be regarded as accurate expressions of the period they are said to represent.[5] A close examination of sources reveals that Tang masters with a reputation for irreverence and blasphemy were often actually quite conservative in their approach to doctrine by citing (instead of rejecting) Mahāyāna *sūtras* in support of teachings that were not so distinct from, and were actually very much in accord with, contemporary Chinese Buddhist schools (see Poceski 2007). For example, the famous *kōan* about Mahākāśyapa's receiving the flower after Śākyamuni's wordless sermon, as well as slogans such as "special transmission outside the teaching" and "no reliance on words and letters" – originally separate items that came to be linked in a famous Zen motto attributed to the first patriarch Bodhidharma – were created not in the seventh or eighth but rather in the eleventh and twelfth centuries.[6]

Zen Literature Seen through the Shift to the Dharma Hall

The debate concerning ineffability versus speech, or of the role of language and verbal discourse in a tradition that has produced voluminous texts, despite an emphasis on being a silent transmission independent of words and letters, needs to be oriented in terms of the origins and historical context for the articulation of Zen teachings. This can be seen in terms of the shift of emphasis in the Zen monastic setting from the ritualistic role of the Buddha Hall, as was used in the majority of Chinese Buddhist schools, to the literary role of the Dharma Hall and Abbot's Quarter, chambers where the temple's master held forth through delivering a variety of formal and informal sermons.

One of the main ideas of the first Zen monastic code attributed to Baizhang is that a spiritually insightful and morally superior Abbot becomes the center of religious life as the living representative of the Buddha. Thus, the development of Zen literature is directly linked to the ascendancy and authority of the charisma and wisdom of the Abbot as a substitute or replacement for Śākyamuni, and to his manner and content of expression. As Griffith Foulk notes, "In effect, Zen patriarchs *were* Buddhas." Furthermore, whereas the teachers in other Buddhist schools at the time had only second-hand or hearsay knowledge of awakening, Zen masters "derived their spiritual authority from a direct experience of the Buddha-mind." Therefore, "their words and deeds [of each generation of living buddhas] were at least equivalent to the *sūtras*, which recorded the words and deeds of Śākyamuni and the other Indian Buddhas, and perhaps even superior in that they were the records of native Chinese Buddhas."[7]

Several well-known literary conventions quickly emanated from the distinguished masters, including refined poetry commemorating transmission and death experiences and the dialogical style of interaction encompassing seemingly absurd, nonsensical remarks considered revelatory of the enlightened state beyond reason (Welter 2006, 126). These discourses were recorded in the hagiographical transmission of the lamp texts. From that set of materials, arranged according to the sequence of masters in a lineage, there were created two additional genres with different arrangements: recorded sayings texts, which contained all relevant biographical anecdotes and utterances of an individual master; and *kōan* collections, or extensive prose and verse commentaries on prominent encounter dialogues:

> Baizhang's text also specifies that a primary requirement for the Abbot is the delivery of public sermons, and furthermore, this innovation is related to the function of the temple halls: The entire assembly meets in the Dharma Hall twice a day for morning and evening convocations. On these occasions, the Abbot enters the hall (Ch. *shangtang*, Jp. *jōdō*) and ascends the high seat. The head monks and rank-and-file disciples line up on either side of the hall to listen attentively to the Abbot's sermon. The sermon is followed by an opportunity for a stimulating debate about the essential meaning of Zen doctrines, which discloses how one must live in accord with the Dharma.
>
> (T.51: 251a)

This passage indicates that twice-daily sermons were delivered by the Abbot, who "enters the hall" as a demonstration of his wisdom and guidance. Dale Wright remarks of Tang master Huangbo, "Like other Zen masters of his time, he was perhaps first and foremost a skilled speaker, both on the lecture dais and in personal encounter" (Wright 1998, 17n.41). Wright also points out that Zen "priests of this time either gained fame, or failed to do so, primarily based upon their mastery in these domains. The master spoke from the position in the Dharma Hall traditionally given to the image of the Buddha and, therefore, spoke as an instantiation of enlightenment" (ibid.).

The style of sermon known as entering the hall became synonymous with the location of the Dharma Hall, which was generally a two-story structure that had an aura of grandeur much like the Buddha Hall, which it was supposed to replace. One of the innovations of Zen was that this building became the central site on the compound:

> Dharma halls in Sung Zen monasteries were large structures with architectural features and appointments identical to Buddha halls, with the exception that their Sumeru altars had no Buddha images on them. Instead, dharma hall altars bore high lecture seats that were used by abbots for preaching the dharma, engaging the assembled monks and laity in debate, and other services. The association of an abbot with the Buddhas in this context was unmistakable.[8]

The Baizhang monastic rules text mentions another key aspect of the style of discourse provided by Zen masters, which is also associated with one of the temple halls: "Monks may request or be invited for personal interviews or instruction by entering into the Abbot's Quarter. Otherwise, each disciple is primarily responsible for regulating his own diligence or indolence [in making an effort at meditation], whether he is of senior or junior status." According to this passage, the practice of meditation is less important – or at least less organized and regularized – than the individual, private teachings provided by the Abbot to motivated disciples. The procedures required for requesting permission to "enter the [Abbot's] room" are prescribed in later texts, especially the *Chanyuan chingquei* (Jp. *Zen'en shingi*), a comprehensive rules text compiled in 1103 and used as the basis for Japanese monasteries of the Rinzai and Sōtō sects. This text mentions how the master is to give informal private sermons known as "small convocation" in his room, which are distinguished from the formal public sermons provided in the Dharma Hall known as "large convocation." However, exact requirements and methods of implementation probably varied with the particular temple and its Abbot.

Although technically not part of the seven-hall temple layout which was followed as the core of the monastic construction of Zen temples, the Abbot's Quarter was generally of great importance in the rituals of the compound, and it is usually situated above (north) and a little to the left (western) side of the Dharma Hall – hence, off center from the central axis. The chamber is a central area of the temple where the master gives oral sermons and other instructions, some of which have been transcribed and made part of the Buddhist canon. One of the main reasons why Dōgen admired his Chinese mentor Rujing, he reports, is that at Mount Tiantong temple the master often spontaneously initiated the entering the room ceremony, even by waking up the assembly during the night to call a special session.[9]

For the most part in China, however, the informal sermons of Zen masters were not recorded, whereas careful records were kept of the formal sermons, although these records do not generally contain the open discussions and sometimes freewheeling debates held during the public sessions. Perhaps inspired by his teacher, Dōgen collected his own informal sermons, some of which were later heavily edited, in the *Shōbōgenzō*, which is one of the few texts in the history of the tradition that captures a master's entering-the-room style of sermon. The appeal of the *Shōbōgenzō* is largely due to this unusual quality, but the collection of Dōgen's formal sermons, the *Eihei kōroku*, while often overlooked, is equally important for an understanding of his complete writings (see Leighton and Okumura 2004).

The Abbot's Quarter is also known as the "ten-foot square hut," following a passage in the *Vimalakīrti Sūtra* in which an informed layman holding forth in a humble abode demonstrates the ability to outsmart bodhisattvas. This chamber also seems to have roots in the layout of Taoist temples, which did not have the equivalent of a Dharma Hall or Buddha Hall and where the room for the Abbot was more of an all-purpose area used not only for residential and instructional purposes, but also for administration and cultural demonstrations. As time went by, the function of the Abbot's Quarter as a center of cultural activities began developing in Zen, as well. Also, for both Taoist and Chinese Zen temples, the term *fangzhang* (Jp. *hōjō*) was used to refer both to the facility and to the person residing therein, much as Zen masters often took their moniker from the name of the mountain where they abided (or vice versa).

This basic pattern of linking the two structures (Dharma Hall and Abbot's Quarter) with the two styles of sermons (entering the hall by the master and entering the room of the master) initiated in Song dynasty Chinese Zen temples is also found in Japanese temples established in the mid-thirteenth century, when Zen was being imported from the mainland. These include such prominent examples as Tōfukuji, founded in Kyoto by Enni Ben'en, Eiheiji, founded in Echizen province by Dōgen, and Kenchōji, founded in Kamakura by Lanxi (Jp. Rankei). Enni and Dōgen both traveled and trained at temples in the Chinese Five Mountains monastic system, including Mount Jing, the lead temple in the system where Enni spent six years, and Mount Tiantong, where Dōgen studied for a few years, and brought back the Sung style. Lanxi came to Japan from Mount Jing at the invitation of the shogun.[10] However, the scale of the Chinese temples was considerably larger and grander, with the monastery becoming a sizable administrative unit with many divisions and departments, whereas Japanese temples functioned on a more minimalist and simplified scale.

Recent scholars have noted several problems with the traditional account of the Dharma Hall and Abbot's Quarter. First, Zen temples in both China and Japan were much more complex and diverse in their practices, so that relics, repentance, chanting, and incense burning, among many other functions, led to the establishment of multiple structures for administration, ceremonies, labor, and outreach. Indeed, Zen temples in China "had spacious compounds encompassing over fifty major and minor structures, facilities for a rich variety of religious practices and ceremonies, and sometimes more than a thousand persons in residence, including monastic officers, ordinary monks and nuns, lay postulants and laborers."[11] Furthermore, the emphasis on the Abbot's public functions in the Dharma Hall is supposed to obviate the need for a Buddha Hall, but this structure apparently did remain the centerpiece of many Zen temples in China and Japan as a place to enshrine and display images and icons as objects of worship.

Sense or Nonsense?

Zen discourse as found in the collections of *kōans* and the sermons of masters is deliberately opaque and mysterious, sphinx-like and perplexing, elusive and enigmatic. Ambiguity, incongruity, and contradiction are blended with tautology and assertions of the obvious in order to throw the disciple/reader off guard or catch him by surprise so as to overturn idle assumptions and preoccupations. Who can say for sure what any of this really means, or if it means anything at all? Dale Wright comments on a quixotic event in which Huangbo drove monks away from the Dharma Hall with his staff, and when they were leaving he called to them to say, "The crescent is like a bent bow, very little rain but only strong winds." Wright wonders about the relevance of the master's seemingly random remark: "Perhaps, like us, no one [in the audience at the time] had the slightest idea what Huang Po was talking about. Or perhaps there were clues, present only in that immediate context or decipherable only to an exclusive few" (Wright 1998, 10).

Some skeptics, including Western missionaries and other modern cultural observers and commentators, have suggested that monks in meditation are nothing but zombies, an attack that cannot avoid being considered Orientalist in its one-sided, dismissive disregard of trying to understand Zen sympathetically and on its own terms. A prime example is the comment by the Jesuit Leon Wieger, who wrote in 1927 that the "immense literature" of the Zen school was "a quantity of folios filled with incoherent, meaningless answers, made to any kind of question, and carefully registered, without any commentary or explanation. They are not, as has been supposed, allusions to interior affairs of the convent unknown to us. They are exclamations which escaped from the stultified ones, momentarily drawn from their coma."[12] Furthermore, Arthur Koestler, in *The Lotus and the Robot*, a critique of Asian mysticism more generally, dismisses the "mumbo jumbo" or "hocus pocus" of Zen rhetoric (Koestler 1960a, 245, 246). For Koestler, the contradictory quality in Zen rhetoric is an example of "double-think" put forth by the "only school which has made a philosophy out of [inarticulateness], whose exponents burst into verbal diarrhea to prove constipation."[13]

However, forceful criticism comes not only from the West but also from the Orient. In an example of what can be referred to as inverted Orientalism, Mishima Yukio ponders the question: if Zen dialogues are so open-ended as to allow for constant shifting between multiple perspectives, on what basis can standards of evaluation and guidance be established without self-contradiction or hypocrisy? In *The Temple of the Golden Pavilion*, a scathing critique of Zen monastic life in postwar Japan by an author known for his pro-imperial and anti-Buddhist political leanings, Mishima exposes a potentially fatal flaw of *kōan* cases used in Zen training when given idiosyncratic and seemingly capricious, distorted readings by key characters to justify their questionable motives.

In this novel, based on a true incident in which a disturbed acolyte torched one of the famous Zen temples, the Father Superior of the temple uses the "Nanquan kills the cat" *kōan* to explain away the tragedy of war as well as his own lack of leadership during times of hardship. Also, the disabled social misfit Kashiwagi evokes the same case to defend his exploitation of beautiful women. Mishima further contrasts Father Zenkai, who exhibits "the gentleness of the harsh roots of some great tree that grows outside a village and gives shelter to the passing traveler" with more typical Zen priests. These are depicted as being

> apt to fall into the sin of never giving a positive judgment on anything for fear of being laughed at later in case they have been wrong. [They are] the type of Zen priest who will instantly hand down his arbitrary decision on anything that is discussed, but who will be careful to phrase his reply in such a way that it can be taken to mean two opposite things.
>
> (Mishima 1959, 244, 245)

In contrast to various sorts of critics, defenders who argue that Zen masters do in fact make sense beyond the dichotomy of sense and nonsense show that the school's rhetoric derives in part from a variety of East Asian literary games, which have the effect of making discourse seem mysterious, or even pointless, as uninitiated readers grasp in vain to discern unidentified resonances. Typical techniques include:

1 the extensive use of allusions, which create a feeling of disconnection with the main theme;
2 indirect references, such as tilting a poem with one topic and composing a verse that seems on the surface to be totally unrelated;
3 inventive wordplay based on the fact that kanji are homophonic and convey multiple, often complementary or contradictory meanings;
4 linking the verses in a sustained string based on hidden points of connection or continuity, such as seasonal imagery or references to myths and legends.

As Victor Hori points out, "In Chinese literature, the generally dominant place given to allusion and analogy means that language is often used to say one thing and mean another. Indeed, the game is at its best when the opponent-partners are so well matched that each understands the other's use of images, allusions, or turns of phrase without requiring anything to be explained or deciphered" (Hori 2003).

At the same time, Zen also has a great affinity with, and in some cases a direct impact on, a variety of intellectual, artistic, and literary movements in the modern West, a significant point overlooked by the skeptics. These connections range from American transcendentalism and French impressionism in the nineteenth century, when America and Europe were first being exposed to Asian thought, to phenomenology in the twentieth century, along with Dadaism, expressionism, surrealism, stream of consciousness, beat poetry, and postmodernism, as well as the zany comedy of the Marx Brothers and the experimental music and writings of John Cage. In these diverse examples we find thinkers, writers, or artists moving away from factual discussions or realistic portrayals towards a form of expression that allows the inner truth of subjectivity to prevail in a de-centered universe in which the lines separating subject and object, reality and illusion, or truth and untruth, have broken down.

The recent trend in the West has been away from language used for the sake of signification, assertion, and insistence on logical argumentation, which is invariably partial and one-sided, towards endlessly playful uses of words and interplay with silence. Contemporary philosophical, literary, and other kinds of artistic works may not seem to make much sense, but harbor other levels of meaning. This, too, has a resonance with Zen rhetoric. As Mark Taylor suggests, Western discourse recognizes presence pervaded by absence and evokes notions of liminality, marginality, transgression, or the carnivalesque to cause the disappearance of fixed notions and presuppositions and the erasure of differences between falsely imposed categories (Taylor 1987, 103). This bears a striking resemblance to Dongshan's living words, which may appear senseless or disruptive of common sense, but, in revealing that all words have only relative validity and are therefore ultimately meaningless, actually point to a higher truth or uncommon sense beyond speech and silence.

One of the most aggressively anti-logocentric movements at the beginning of the twentieth century was Dadaism, which sought an overturning of logic and reason brought about by eccentric expressions of poetry and art. At the first public soiree at a cabaret on July 14, 1916, the manifesto for the Dada movement was recited, calling for a reading of poems meant to dispense with conventional language. Dadaists claimed to have lost confidence in modern culture and wanted to "shock common sense, public opinion, education, institutions, museums, good taste, in short, the whole prevailing order."[14]

Another interesting modern Western example is Lewis Carroll's two "Alice in Wonderland" books, which raise a series of interesting questions regarding the nature of language, selfhood, and time that challenge conventional views and point towards a Zen-like realm of understanding. Carroll was a don at Oxford who published hundreds of books and pamphlets on mathematics and logic, among other topics, in addition to the parody nonsense epic *The Hunting of the Snark*. Hugh Haughton points out that, throughout the two Alice books, there are "persistent puzzles, paradoxes and riddles, which haunt the apparently stable mirror theories of language which have dominated the philosophy of the West."[15]

Logical reasoning is used in Alice's conversations to prove nonsensical assertions, suggesting that conventional logic happens to be upside-down or that, in snubbing, contradicting, and ordering Alice about quite callously, characters who are pseudo-logicians can prove themselves superior by arguments which are nonsense but nevertheless seem to satisfy them. The effect is to show the innately absurd and futile nature of language and logic. According to Humpty Dumpty, called "the most belligerently radical of the many philosophers of language who haunt their pages" and demonstrate "linguistic aberration and disorder,"[16] "When I use a word, it means just what I choose it to mean – neither more nor less." He adds, "The question is, which is to be master – that is all."[17] Wordplay in the Alice books includes the deformation of words, such as, "We called him Tortoise because he taught us" (Carroll 1998, 83). Time is given similar treatment by the Mad Hatter, who refers to this dimension not as an "it" but as a "him," of whom he asks favors such as speeding up the clock. Time and how it serves as a tool for organizing human affairs is not what it seems, and it is pointed out in *Alice* that an "un-birthday" is celebrated much more frequently than a birthday.

In another example, T. S. Eliot's *The Waste Land* is a poem of anguish, desperation, and collapse on both personal and cultural levels amid a "crazy, fragmented"[18] world that is so obtuse it requires a set of notes by the author to illumine some of the more obscure references. Eliot's writing confronts the first-time reader with the question of "how to read the poem: how to assimilate it and make sense of it." The "apparent chaos of the work, the difficulty, the excess," which in a way captures "the dazzling and sometimes incoherent world outside," discloses not meaninglessness but a multiplicity of layers of meaning and levels of allusion that make it endlessly rich and thought-provoking.

Similarly, in a foreword to the 1961 book *Silence: Lectures and Writings*, which collects a variety of works concerning the basis of musical composition and performance from a twenty-year period (1939–1958), John Cage cites influences from Zen and the *Book of Changes* as well as Western mysticism and psychology. For example, Cage is known for his composition *4:33* (which refers to 4 minutes and 33 seconds of silence), in which the pianist sits at and opens the instrument but makes no sound. In the book he experiments with various stylistic features in terms of format, fonts, layout, etc., to show the limits of written discourse and the avenue to understanding the true meaning of the title. Responding to disparagement by Alan Watts that he had not studied Zen properly, Cage issues the disclaimer, "What I do, I do not wish blamed on Zen, though without my engagement with Zen . . . I doubt whether I would have done what I have done. . . . I mention this in order to free Zen of any responsibility for my actions" (Cage 1961, xi). The Zen quality in Cage, regardless of whether he was immersed in studies of the classical Zen tradition (which critics would argue Watts himself knew only superficially), is continually to cast aside conventional notions of what art and literature are supposed to be and continually to reinvent uses of language even if seemingly incomprehensible or absurd.

The light shed on Zen writings by making comparisons with examples of modern Western thought and art can be summed up with a paraphrase of a double-edged Bob Dylan lyric, "There's no sense like nonsense, and nonsense makes no sense at all." On the one hand, the point is that one must delve between the lines or beneath the surface to appreciate writings that on the surface do not make much sense. But the real point is that there is no point, and isn't that really the point? Or is it? Once sense itself is challenged as a legitimate category, the next question asks, what is the sense of all this nonsense? That is, are words useful as an instrument for surpassing words, as claimed by some traditionalist commentators on Zen rhetoric? Or, is it because nonsensicality opens up a completely new meaning of sense evoked not by the abandonment but rather through the use of words, as argued by another wave of observers emphasizing a hermeneutic approach to language used in Zen?

Silence has always been highlighted in Zen. However, there has also been a long-standing controversy about whether silence should be seen as the goal, with language serving as a means like the finger pointing to the moon or the polishing of glass to make a mirror bright, or whether the inverse is the case and silence is to be seen as a means with creative uses of language understood as the goal. The emperor's preface to the transmission of the lamp record, the *Tiansheng guangdeng lu*, maintains that language is a form of illusion and bondage: "Those who achieve understanding will thereupon dispel illusion. Those with transcendent realization will thereupon discard the cage of scriptural teaching" (Welter 2006, 186). At best, he suggests, language is an expedient means that enables one to "peacefully dwell on snowy mountains," but only after its use has been transcended. Yet, in contrast to this, many *kōan* texts, such as the *Wumenguan*, argue that it is false to speak of transmission yet equally false to deny or to refrain from speaking of it.

How to reconcile these seemingly contradictory approaches and find a resolution to the double-bind implied by the *Wumenguan*? True realization of the Dharma invariably transcends the words that convey it, and leads to an awareness that this process of going beyond is the real meaning of the phrase "a special transmission outside the *sūtras*," which does not imply a literal rejection of scripture or other forms of language. Rather, the phrase refers to a "superior ability to penetrate to the deepest meaning of the *sūtras*, a penetration that follows words as far as they can go and then, at the extreme limit of conceptualization, leaves them behind."[19] According to this outlook, the way of verbal expression is to be cut off (*yanyu taoduan*), as exemplified by Huiko's silent bow to Bodhidharma which won him the transmission as the second patriarch. Language, as the basis of mental activity, is detrimental to the attainment of enlightenment, but it can function as a provisional tool leading beyond itself.

The valorization of silence reduces discourse to a mere instrument, but this can be corrected by a contrasting upgrade of the role of language used extensively by Zen masters, such that words and letters are considered not as an obstacle but rather as a great reservoir of resources for communicating shades of truth.[20] For example, the passage in which Zhuangzi uses the fish trap analogy ends with the query, "Where can I find a man who has forgotten words so I can have a word with him?", which suggests that, once the true value of words are understood, they can be used in an ongoing creative dialogue. In another passage, Zhuangzi puts an emphasis on using "goblet words" or "no words," which stand in contrast to Dongshan's dead words. "With words that are no words," Zhuangzi writes, "you may speak all your life long and you will never have said anything. Or you may go through your whole life *without* speaking them, in which case you will never have stopped speaking" (Watson 1968, 304).

Another way to look at the Zen philosophy of language is to note that the aim of straightforward, systematic writings is to create a manner of exposition that strives for clarity, precision, and persuasion. However, the point of an indirect communication in religious discourse is to be deliberately cryptic, ironic, and obscure, if necessary, in order to stimulate a "leap" into the realm of pure subjectivity. This leap of Zen awakening (rather than a leap of faith in the Kierkegaardian Christian sense) is symbolized by case no. 46 in the *Wumenguan kōan* collection, which urgently demands that, when climbing to the top of a 100-foot pole, one must immediately jump or leap forward in order "to manifest the whole body throughout the ten directions of the universe." Straightforward analysis, however intellectually appealing, may fall short of inspiring an awakening of genuine wisdom, or it may even go a long way towards subverting and obstructing the goal of Zen. The opacity of indirect discourse is illuminative because it invites and remains open to the active participation of the audience/reader in the process of thought and expression.

This frequently stimulates what Roland Barthes refers to as the "pleasure of the text," a process of ec-static reading whereby the reader enters into and becomes as important for the creation of the text as the author. From that vantage point, there is an erasure of difference between reader and author. A parallel to Barthes's view is Dōgen's notion that the fertile, eminently engaged imagination contributes to, and indeed is ultimately responsible for, all expressions of enlightenment. In the *Shōbōgenzō* "Gabyō" fascicle, Dōgen interprets the term for painted rice cake (*gabyō*), which conventionally referred to false or illusory conceptions in contrast to reality, as an image for self-reflection and self-understanding:

> If there is no painted rice cake, there is no remedy to satisfy hunger. If there is no painted hunger, there is no satisfaction for people. If there is no painted satisfaction, there is no capacity [to satisfy]. Furthermore, satisfying hunger, satisfying no-hunger, not satisfying hunger, and not satisfying no-hunger can be neither attained nor expressed without painted hunger.
>
> (Kawamura 1993, 1: 287)

Thus, the painting of the rice cake as well as the hunger for it, which are both aspects of creative expression, are more satisfying or fulfilling than the tangible rice cake or physical sensation of hunger.

Kōans, in general, represent a highly imaginative, poetic form of indirect expression that has absorbed the influence of the anecdotal, aphoristic, and epigrammatic style of edifying instruction typical of indigenous Chinese religions. Judith Berling remarks that, in comparing the role of encounter dialogues in Song works with Tang texts, including the *Platform Sūtra* in addition to the collected sayings of Baizhang and Huangbo, "we see that a shift has occurred in the presentation of Zen teachings for posterity. . . . A master was judged by his prowess in the paradoxical, intuitive interchanges of Zen dialogues . . . rather than homilies or more straightforward doctrinal statements" (Berling 1987, 75). John McRae further notes, "Where early Zen texts contain a wide variety of doctrinal formulations, practical exhortations, and ritual procedures, the texts of classical Zen [Mazu dialogues] are more uniform in their dedication to the transcription of encounter dialogue incidents, and they delight in baffling paradoxes, patent absurdities, and instructive vignettes of nonconformist behavior . . . [and] are alternately charming, informative, and baffling."[21]

Kōan as Monastic Narrative: Actions Speak Louder

The key element to interpreting the function of Zen discourse is not the issue of whether language is a means or an end, but the message of the *kōan* cases with regard to their role as monastic narratives. In contrast to Leon Wieger's comment cited above that *kōans* are not allusions to "interior affairs of the convent unknown to us," in many instances that is exactly what they are. But the message is at once hidden and revealed in a kind of code that provides a metaphor of, and at the same time obscures, the kinds of conflicts and decisions that take place in a monastic setting. As Bernard Faure suggests in his performative approach to Zen writings:

> Perhaps [*kōans*] do not intend to express a meaning, but to impress an interlocutor, to gain the upper hand in a contest where all moves are allowed. Like any ritual or language game, they work simultaneously on several levels – the semantic, the syntactic, and, more important, the semiotic or pragmatic levels. They are essentially performative. Their function is, to use Austin's terminology, illocutionary (insofar as they create an "event" and necessitate some kind of social ceremonial) and perlocutionary (insofar as they produce effects that are not always perceived by the interlocutors).[22]

The political factor of contestation – in a twofold sense of turf battles within the monastic institutional system set against the background of the larger socio-political context of Chinese society – is quite evident in the literature of encounter dialogues depicting the interpersonal exchanges of Zen masters. Although often appearing in the guise of presenting a historical account, Zen writings do not stick to the task of precise historiography. This is partly because they were products of the pre-modern Chinese worldview, which was fanciful and mythological in taking magic seriously, but it is also because their aim was not factuality but persuading the selected audience of the significance of master–disciple relations in terms of legitimating lineages and establishing the authority and hierarchy of transmission.

We can consider how the enigmatic concluding line of *Biyan lu* case 73 on "Mazu's Four Affirmations and Hundred Negations" underscores the merit of a comprehensive interpretation of *kōan* literature, including the element of monastic politics.[23] The final line of the case at first seems to epitomize nonsensicality in bearing no logical relation to the main narrative, but, in the final analysis, it highlights the monastic model of interpretation. The case record's pointer opens with characteristic paradoxicality: "In explaining the Dharma, there is neither explanation nor teaching; in listening to the Dharma, there is neither hearing nor attainment. Since explanation neither explains nor teaches, how can it compare to not explaining? Since listening neither hears nor attains, how can it compare to not listening? Still, not explaining and not listening will amount to something." The pointer sets up the question: where does one go from the double-bind regarding sense and nonsense evoked here, other than to an even greater sense of senselessness?

In the main case narrative, a disciple asks Mazu, "Beyond the four assertions and hundred denials, what is the meaning of Bodhidharma coming from the west?" Saying that he is too tired to explain, Mazu directs the disciple Zang to see one of his primary followers, Hai, who says he has a headache and cannot explain it and recommends that the disciple visit Baizhang, Mazu's most famous follower, who carries on the Hongzhou school lineage. Baizhang also bows out by saying that he does not understand the question. The frustrated disciple returns to and tells what happened to the teacher, who declares, "Zang's head is white, Hai's head is black."

In this case, the disciple prefaces an unanswerable question used in many Zen dialogues with a reference to transcending the polarity of assertion and denial. After getting the runaround from Mazu and his important followers, he receives the teacher's final statement, which could be interpreted as a non sequitur that does away once and for all with the question–answer process. The disciple, who did not get the message the first three times, is informed in no uncertain terms that it is time to cease and desist his pestering. Or perhaps the last line is an ironic affirmation of everyday existence akin to the Zen sayings "Willows are green, flowers are red," or "My eyes lie horizontally and my nose is vertical" (Sekida 1977, 338). This arbitrariness of the actual words makes the statement seem nonsensical, but it makes sense on a meta-level by pointing beyond verbiage to a higher truth. Either reading of the final line, as a thorough negation of the inquiry or as a deceptively simple affirmation of everyday reality, would seem to support an instrumentalist interpretation of the *kōan* as a kind of verbal stop sign to the questioner, and this method of analysis appears complete and without the need for exploring additional levels of meaning.

However, further probing of the concluding line indicates a more complex pattern that tends to support a more comprehensive view of *kōan* rhetoric. Ogawa Takashi shows that, in Chinese pronunciation at the time (Sung dynasty), the character for "head" was pronounced the same as another character for "marquis" (Ogawa 2003, 23-31). Ogawa suggests that a reading of the final sentence should be seen in light of

Congrong lu (Jp. *Shōyōroku*), or *Record of Serenity* case 40, Yunmen's "White and Black," which uses the character for marquis in evoking an old story of two robbers. According to the case, Yunmen responds to a monk who outsmarts him by saying, "I thought I was Marquis White, but I find that here is Marquise Black." Marquis White and Marquise Black are noted thieves in Chinese folklore. Marquise Black, a female robber, seems to have been the cleverer of the two who, by a foxy ruse, took away everything the male thief had gained in his efforts.

This apparently is why John Wu translates the line in *Biyan lu* case 73 as "Xizang (or Zang) wears a white cap, while Huaihai (or Hai) wears a black cap." By combining the allusion to the thieves with the reference in the case to the word "head," he comes up with a hybrid rendering. Wu remarks that, in the legend, the black-capped thief (or perhaps it should be Marquise Black) was "more ruthless and radical than" the white-capped thief (or Marquis White). For Wu, this shows that Baizhang was more "ruthless" than Zang in the sense of being unsparing in his treatment of the junior figure's irrelevant query. While both monks dismiss the disciple, the latter's put-down carried a greater sense of authority and finality (Wu 1975, 103).

So far, this has not moved beyond an instrumentalist approach, which would find a creative use of literary game-style allusions as a key to understanding the *kōan* but would also agree that the point of the case refers to spiritual attainment, with Mazu giving praise to one of his main disciples for evoking silence. However, without denying this interpretation, a crucial factor to be added to the analysis is that the compilers of Zen encounter dialogues were trying to make a case for the superiority of Baizhang, who became the heir to Mazu's lineage, over the other two followers, Xizang and the inquirer. This interpretation stressing the politics of lineal transmission is reinforced by the *Biyan lu*'s capping phrase comment on the concluding line: "Within the realm the emperor rules, but past the gates it is the general who gives orders." This implies that the masters and monks resemble warlords in establishing their domains of hegemony and battling over protected terrain.

By making a rather bold declaration comparing his followers to thieves (and, by extending the theme of combat, to generals), Mazu demonstrates the kind of attitude exhibited in many *kōan* dialogues that combines elements of a conventional, regulation-based adherence to institutional structure with an unconventional line-crossing and tables-turning anti-structuralism. Anti-structure evident in such extreme acts as "killing the Buddha" or "jumping from a 100-foot pole," to cite a couple of prominent cases, is transgressive in challenging any and all levels of the status quo. Exchanges in dialogues featuring role reversals and one-upmanship, violent outbursts and physical blows, insults and the undermining of authority show that truth is revealed through the process of contest and confrontation.

This creativity is the basis for Zen's seeking to go beyond conventional words and letters, rather than holding to an exclusive focus on silence, and the reason why *kōan* literature is much celebrated for its classical literary and historical roles as well as contemporary philosophical significance in cross-cultural significance. Zen's language of non-language, or vice versa, leaves open the possibility for inventive expression and productive silence to intermingle and to be alternatively used or discarded, as appropriate for particular discursive contexts and pedagogical situations.

Notes

1 Some of the material in this section of the chapter is drawn from my book *Zen Skin, Zen Marrow: Will the Real Zen Buddhism Please Stand Up?* (Heine 2008), especially the chapter on "Zen Writes."

2 For instance, see Dōgen's group of five poems on the *Lotus Sūtra*, which includes "Colors of the mountains / Streams in the valleys / One in all, all in one / The voice and body of / Our Sakyamuni Buddha," in Heine (2005, 109). This is based on a traditional verse cited in *Shōbōgenzō* "Keisei sanshoku," by the noted Buddhist lay poet Su Shi, "The sounds of the valley stream his long tongue / The changing colors of the mountains his blissful body / Since last night I have heard 84,000 hymns / But how can I explain them all to people the following day?"

3 See Katz (1978). Katz begins on p. 1 by considering, "Mystics do not say what they mean and do not mean what they say," and then cites Rumi: "When you say, 'words are of no account,' you negate your own assertion through your words. If words are of no account, why do we hear you say that words are of no account? After all, you are saying this in words."

4 McRae (1986, 257). See also Welter (2006).

5 See Albert Welter, "Mahakasyapa's Smile: Silent Transmission and the Kung-an (Kōan) Tradition," in Heine and Wright (2000, 75–109). Also, according to Welter, "In the early Song, the meaning of Bodhidharma's coming from the west increasingly came to be understood also in terms of 'a separate transmission outside the teaching' (*kyōge betsuden*)" (Welter 2006, 201).

6 This is included as the sixth case of the *Wumenguan* (T 48: 293c). The third and fourth lines of the motto are "Pointing directly to the human mind / Seeing into one's own nature and becoming a Buddha." According to T. Griffith Foulk, these words were even put into the mouth of Śākyamuni Buddha in some texts; see "Sung Controversies Concerning the 'Separate Transmission' of Chan," in Gregory and Getz (1999, 268).

7 T. Griffith Foulk, "Myth, Ritual, and Monastic Practice in Sung Zen Buddhism," in Ebrey and Gregory (1993, 180).

8 Ibid., p. 176. See also Collcutt (1981, 195).

9 Dōgen mentions this in several places, including *Shōbōgenzō zuimonki* fascicle 3 (in the traditional edition), *Shōbōgenzō* "Shohō jissō," and *Eihei kōroku* 2.128. Although it is difficult to determine whether this practice was as unique and extraordinary as he claims, Dōgen had traveled to several of the Chinese Five Mountains temples and therefore had a comparative perspective.

10 The Japanese Zen version was somewhat different from the earlier "seven-hall" style dating back to the period of Nara Buddhism, which included the pagoda (*tō*), golden Buddha hall (*kondō*), lecture hall (*kōdō*), bell tower (*shōrō*), *sūtra* repository (*kyōzō*), monks' dormitories (*sōbō*), and refectory (*jikidō*). This was because of a new emphasis on several key facilities, among them the Dharma Hall and Sangha Hall, as well as the Abbot's Quarter (although this was not considered one of the seven main halls), and the elimination of the pagoda, bell tower, and *sūtra* repository as main buildings – although the latter two were often included. Also, Dōgen was apparently offered by Hōjō Tokiyori the opportunity to lead Kenchōji in the then capital city of Kamakura, but he declined, preferring instead to stay at Eiheiji in the remote mountains.

11 T. Griffith Foulk, "Myth, Ritual, and Monastic Practice in Sung Zen Buddhism," in Ebrey and Gregory (1993, 163–4). Also, "The elite ranks of Zen masters in the Sung included not only meditation specialists but also Pure Land devotees, Tantric ritualists, experts on

monastic discipline, exegetes of *sūtra* and philosophical literature, poets, artists, and even monks with leanings toward Neo-Confucianism" (ibid., 161).

12 Cited from *A History of the Religious Beliefs and Philosophical Opinions in China from the Beginning to the Present Time*, in Faure (1993, 42). Faure notes that Wieger was a former Protestant turned Jesuit who showed contempt for Chinese "paganism" and saw Chan as an offshoot of Vedantism citing the oracles of Brahman.

13 Koestler (1960b, 58). Cited in Fader (1980, 48).

14 See http://en.wikipedia.org/wiki/Dadaism (accessed August 28, 2006).

15 Carroll (1998, xiv). Haughton points out that Alice, who asks, "Who in the world am I? That's the great puzzle!" while the Cheshire Cat grins, "We're all mad here," consistently and matter-of-factly dismisses her interlocutors as nonsensical, but this does not mean their wild disorder has no impact or intrusion on her.

16 Haughton, "Introduction," ibid.

17 Ibid., p. 186. Humpty also says he "pays" words to work for him and that he can "explain all the poems that were invented – and a good many that haven't been invented just yet" (ibid., 187).

18 Quotes in this paragraph are cited from Eliot (2005, xxi).

19 T. Griffith Foulk, "Sung Controversies Concerning the 'Separate Transmission' of Chan," in Gregory and Getz (1999, 260).

20 Victor Hori adopts and applies a term first used by Hee-Jin Kim regarding Dōgen's use of the kōan, which was employed in many ways in contrast to the Lin-chi/Rinzai school approach, to the Rinzai Zen monastic curriculum. Both Hori and Kim agree in their critique of "the instrumentalist idea that a kōan is merely a nonrational instrument for a breakthrough to a noncognitive pure consciousness," according to "Kōan and *Kenshō* in the Rinzai Zen Curriculum" (Heine and Wright 2000, 281). Hori cites Hee-Jin Kim, "The Reason of Words and Letters: Dōgen and *Kōan* Language," in LaFleur (1985, 54–82).

21 John R. McRae, "Shen-hui and the Teaching of Sudden Enlightenment," in Gregory (1991, 229).

22 Bernard Faure, "Fair and Unfair Language Games in Chan/Zen," in Katz (1992, 173).

23 *Biyan lu* case 73 (T 48: 200c–201c).

References

Berling, Judith A. (1987). Bringing the Buddha Down to Earth: Notes on the Emergence of Yü-lu as a Buddhist Genre. In *History of Religions* 27, 56–88.

Cage, John (1961). *Silence: Lectures and Writings*. Middletown, CT: Wesleyan University Press.

Carroll, Lewis (1998). *Alice's Adventures in Wonderland and Through the Looking-Glass*. Ed. with an Introduction and Notes by Hugh Haughton. New York: Penguin.

Collcutt, Martin (1981). *Five Mountains: The Rinzai Zen Institution in Medieval Japan*. Cambridge, MA: Harvard University Press.

Ebrey, Patricia B., and Gregory, Peter N. (eds) (1993). *Religion and Society in T'ang and Sung China*. Honolulu: University of Hawai'i Press.

Eliot, T. S. (2005). *The Waste Land and Other Poems*. Introduction and Notes by Randy Malamed. New York: Barnes & Noble.

Dumoulin, Heinrich (1987). *Zen Buddhism: A History*, Vol. I: *India and China*. New York: Macmillan.

Fader, Larry A. (1980). Arthur Koestler's Critique of D. T. Suzuki's Interpretation of Zen. In *Eastern Buddhist* 13(2), 48.

Faure, Bernard (1993). *Chan Insights and Oversights*. Princeton, NJ: Princeton University Press.

Gregory, Peter N. (ed.) (1991). *Sudden and Gradual: Approaches to Enlightenment in Chinese Thought*. India: Motilal Books.

Gregory, Peter N., and Getz, Daniel A. (eds) (1999). *Buddhism in the Sung*. Honolulu: University of Hawai'i Press.

Heine, Steven (trans.) (2005). *The Zen Poetry of Dōgen: Verses from the Mountain of Eternal Peace*. Mount Tremper, NY: Dharma Communications.

Heine, Steven (2008). *Zen Skin, Zen Marrow: Will the Real Zen Buddhism Please Stand Up?* New York: Oxford University Press.

Heine, Steven, and Wright, Dale S. (eds) (2000). *The Kōan: Text and Context in Zen Buddhism*. New York: Oxford University Press.

Hori, Victor Sōgen (2003). *Zen Sand: The Book of Capping Phrases for Kōan Practice*. Honolulu: University of Hawai'i Press.

Katz, Steven (1978). *Mysticism and Philosophical Analysis*. New York: Oxford University Press.

Katz, Steven (ed.) (1992). *Mysticism and Language*. New York: Oxford University Press.

Kawamura, Kōdō (ed.) (1993). *Dōgen zenji zenshū*. Tokyo: Shunjūsha.

Koestler, Arthur (1960a). *The Lotus and the Robot*. New York: Harper Colophon Books.

Koestler, Arthur (1960b). Neither Lotus nor Robot. In *Encounter* 16, 58.

LaFleur, William R. (ed.) (1985). *Dōgen Studies*. Honolulu: University of Hawai'i Press.

Leighton, Dan, and Okumura, Shohaku (trans.) (2004). *Dōgen's Extended Record: A Translation of the Eihei Kōroku*. Boston: Wisdom.

McRae, John R. (1986). *The Northern School and the Formation of Early Ch'an Buddhism*. Honolulu: University of Hawai'i Press.

Mishima, Yukio (1959). *The Temple of the Golden Pavilion*. New York: Perigee.

Ogawa, Takashi (2003). Hekiganroku zōkō (5). In *Zen bunka* 179, 23–31.

Poceski, Mario (2007). *The Hongzhou School and the Development of Tang Dynasty Chan*. New York: Oxford University Press.

Sekida, Katsuki (trans.) (1977). *Two Zen Classics: Mumonkan and Hekiganroku*. New York: Weatherhill.

Taylor, Mark C. (1987). *Erring: A Postmodern A/theology*. Chicago: University of Chicago Press.

Watson, Burton (trans.) (1968). *The Complete Works of Chuang Tzu*. New York: Columbia University Press.

Welter, Albert (2006). *Monks, Rulers, and Literati: The Political Ascendancy of Chan Buddhism*. New York: Oxford University Press.

Wright, Dale S. (1998). *Philosophical Meditations on Zen Buddhism*. New York: Cambridge University Press.

Wu, John C. H. (1975). *The Golden Age of Zen*. Taipei: United Publishing Center.

23

The Voice of Another

Speech, Responsiveness, and Buddhist Philosophy[1]

RICHARD F. NANCE

> *Friend, there are two conditions for the arising of right view: the voice of another and wise attention* (parato ca ghoso, yoniso ca manasikāro)*. These are the two conditions for the arising of right view.*
>
> Mahāvedallasutta[2]

> *Philosophy does not speak first . . . philosophy's first virtue, as it matters most to me, is responsiveness.*
>
> Stanley Cavell, *Cities of Words*

The term "Buddhist philosophy" can fruitfully be understood as naming those practices that aim at the cultivation of what has traditionally been called "right view" – one component of a multi-componential path whereby human beings are brought closer to an ideal of perfection that is articulated in and by the figure of a buddha. As one approaches this ideal, one comes to view things more and more accurately; buddhas, for their part, see things just as they are. To say this does not, of course, tell us very much about how things in fact are. They may be composed of irreducible and essentially existent *dharmas* or be empty of essence; they may transform in three ways, be nothing more than mind, or be permanent or impermanent; they may have, or be, a buddha-nature. Likewise, it does not tell us very much about the phenomenal properties (if any) that characterize such seeing. Seeing things just as they are may or may not seem like something determinate to those who engage in it, and what it seems like (if it seems like anything) may or may not be something that non-buddhas are capable of conceptualizing.

Debates over what it might be, and how it might seem, to see things rightly have been elaborated by Buddhists across the history of Buddhist thought. There is, however, remarkable consensus regarding the formal claim that buddhas do indeed see things just as they are. There is also broad consensus that, in doing so, buddhas

---

A Companion to Buddhist Philosophy, First Edition. Edited by Steven M. Emmanuel.

see things as they are not merely *presently* and *locally*, but *tenselessly* and *universally*. Thus, buddhas who endeavor to speak of what they see (to the extent that this is counted as a possibility)[3] are traditionally understood to speak in very general terms. For example, a buddha who offers a teaching expressible in English as *suffering is of three kinds* is understood to characterize not only the present sufferings of his or her immediate audience, but also the past and future sufferings of any sentient being (cf. SN.V.56). At the same time, buddhas are traditionally held to be perfected rhetors. "Supreme among speakers" (*pavadataṃ varoti*), they are presumed to be equipped with the unfailing ability to suit their speech to the needs and interests of particular audiences (SN.I.42).

Occasions thus simultaneously matter, and do not matter, to what a buddha says. One way of beginning to make sense of this *prima facie* paradoxical claim is by distinguishing a teaching's form from its content and to say that, although the *form* in which a buddha's claims are phrased on this or that occasion of utterance may not be universally *intelligible*, the *content* of those claims is traditionally presumed to be universally *applicable*. Something like the distinction between form and content is marked by Indian Buddhist authors in their discussions of a teaching's phrasing (*vyañjana*, *ruta*) versus its meaning (or aim: *artha*). As Vasubandhu notes explicitly, a single meaning may be phrased in many different ways, and a single phrase may bear multiple meanings (Nance 2012, 138). The distinction between phrasing and meaning makes room for synonymy (one meaning, many phrasings) and ambiguity (one phrasing, many meanings). Once these possibilities are opened up, paraphrase likewise becomes possible: the *artha* of a given teaching need not be tied to any single *vyañjana* but can instead be expressed in many different ways.

The language of Buddhist teaching is thus Janus-faced. One face looks towards the local and responds to shifting historical, institutional, cultural, and personal conditions. The other face looks towards the translocal: to that which is stable and persists across time.[4] To date, scholarly work on Buddhist philosophy has tended to focus on the latter face, and to view the former as a matter of dispensable (usually rhetorical) ornament.[5] In this brief contribution, I want to invite reconsideration of the comparatively neglected former face, by asking after the ways in which Buddhist intellectuals have historically thematized the contribution to philosophy of what I will be calling *responsiveness*. As used here, the term *responsiveness* will mark a variety of actions of body, speech, and mind that range from complex formulations of judgment involving a fine-grained appraisal of unfolding events to swift reactions that may seem to those who engage in them to involve no judgments at all. Responsiveness is a contingent feature of action; particular acts (e.g., the act of saying "suffering is of three kinds") may manifest, or fail to manifest, this quality, depending on how things stand at the time they are performed. Context is thus crucial: responsive actions are ineluctably shaped by the circumstances under which they are undertaken.[6]

In reading the texts that usually figure in contemporary discussions of Buddhist philosophy, one may be tempted to ignore responsiveness altogether. Buddhist Abhidharmic literature, for example, does not appear to lend itself readily to an analysis in terms of responsiveness. Its summary lists of doctrine, unmoored from specific contexts of teaching, comprise free-floating vocabularies of very general application. A comparable emphasis on generality is visible also in the epistemological literature. Texts on *pramāṇa* offer detailed accounts of – among other things – how language may be used (and misused) in debate and the means by which warrant is secured. They are thus plausibly read as articulating grammars of argument, providing principles of reasoning held to be applicable across a wide variety of contexts.

These texts make it easy to neglect the contributions made by responsiveness to the success of the forms of practice they advocate. Reading them as paradigms for Buddhist philosophy, one might easily conclude that responsiveness is a marginal concern among Buddhist philosophers. This conclusion is, it seems to me, mistaken. The mistake does not lie in seeing Abhidharmic and epistemological texts as eminently philosophical; it lies, rather, in neglecting the fact that "philosophy," in Buddhist contexts, cannot be understood apart from certain forms of practice: those presumed to facilitate, and to be facilitated by, the achievement of right view. Just as knowledge of vocabulary and grammar does not guarantee oratorical success, knowledge of Abhidharmic categories or epistemological principles does not guarantee that those categories and principles will be applied effectively. A set of additional skills is needed: among them, the ability to orient oneself to the shifting demands of circumstance and the ability to apply one's knowledge to meet those demands.

Skills of orientation and application take different forms. Here, I will be concerned with those that Indian Buddhists have understood as applying to – or as manifesting in – speech acts undertaken by buddhas (or *arhats*), and by those who would be buddhas (or *arhats*). These speech acts are dramatically depicted in Buddhist texts, particularly in passages that recount dialogical – and pedagogical – encounters between figures of authority (often, but not always, buddhas) and their students (often, but not always, monks). In such encounters, authorities are prompted to teach, and to clarify their teachings, by requests from students; students, in turn, are prodded to learn, and to recognize the limits of their learning, by attending to what their teachers say. Responsiveness is thus mutual and, for each party, alternates between listening and speaking. It is within this responsive give and take that "right view" is both expressed and cultivated; it is within this responsive give and take, therefore, that philosophical work is done.

If these points are granted, certain questions naturally arise. How did Indian Buddhist authors conceptualize this interplay of instruction and insight? And how might attention to forms of responsiveness elucidated in and by Buddhist texts impact what we might count as Buddhist philosophy?

A common presupposition unites the otherwise widely varied traditional accounts of what buddhas can and cannot do: whatever other actions they may engage in, buddhas teach. Their teaching is traditionally presumed to be perfected, and one of the hallmarks of this perfection is an unfailing ability to tailor speech to the interests and aptitudes of an audience. Such a notion firmly embeds buddhas in space and time, even if what they know by virtue of becoming buddhas is traditionally understood to be timeless.[7]

To be a buddha is to know, among other things, what others need and to respond to others on the basis of such knowledge. These points are explicitly acknowledged in verses from the *Śatapañcāśatka*, a famed work composed as a direct address to a buddha by the poet Mātṛceṭa (c. second century CE):

> Sometimes you, a knower of times and hearts,
> did not speak even though questioned;
> Sometimes [you] approached others and fashioned a discourse.
> Elsewhere, having excited interest, you spoke . . .
> There is no method or power by which you did not try
> To rescue the miserable world
> From the terrible hell of saṃsāra.[8]

Here, Mātṛceṭa stresses that a buddha is "a knower of times and hearts" (*kālāśayavid*). This knowledge provides the Buddha with insight into the demands of specific speech situations – demands that shift from person to person and from moment to moment. A buddha's speech acts, tailored to these shifting demands, are correspondingly various.

Underlying the variety of methods and powers (*upāya, śakti*) a buddha may employ is a single aim: "to rescue the miserable world from the terrible hell of saṃsāra" (*ghorāt saṃsārapātālād uddhartuṃ kṛpaṇaṃ jagat*). In ascribing a determinate intention to a buddha, Mātṛceṭa raises an issue that goes on to be the subject of considerable debate among Indian Buddhists: the issue of whether buddhas possess determinate intentions. Here, I want to opt for less loaded language: a way of phrasing things not in terms of intentions, but in terms of effects. Of course, it is one thing to say that *x* always intends *e* in saying *p*, and quite another to say that *x*'s saying *p* always brings about *e* – but the reformulation proposed here arguably remains consonant with a position articulated elsewhere in the *Śatapañcāśatka*.[9] The reformulation is this: regardless of the form taken by a buddha's speech, the *effect* of that speech is uniform; a buddha's speech inevitably *benefits* those fortunate enough to encounter it. In terms made famous by J. L. Austin, we may say that, although a buddha's locutions are various, they are united in producing a common perlocutionary effect.

In *How to Do Things with Words*, Austin distinguishes perlocutions (roughly, what is accomplished *by* the saying of something) from both locutions (the saying of something) and illocutions (what is accomplished *in* the saying of something).[10] Perlocutionary verbs, as a class, are distinguished from illocutionary verbs by what has been called "second-person dependency."[11] The success of a perlocution will be a matter not only of how things stand with an action's agent but also of how things stand with the target of the action. Consider, for example, the perlocutionary verb *convince* as opposed to the illocutionary verb *argue*. Whether I am able to *argue* for something will depend on certain things about *me*; but whether I am able to *convince* you of something will depend also, and crucially, on certain things about *you*: whether you are disposed to listen to me, whether you have the capacity to understand my claims, whether you happen to attend to them (or fail to attend to them), and so on. Beyond their second-person dependency, perlocutions are a mixed bag and differ considerably in what they require of their addressees.[12] Some – e.g., *shaming* – would seem to require that an auditor have some comprehension of the content of a locution (and perhaps the nature of the illocution performed in uttering the locution). Others – e.g., *bewildering* – demand no such comprehension (indeed, the effect of bewildering may be impeded by an auditor's recognition of the content or illocutionary force of the locution). Both *shaming* and *bewildering* do, however, appear to share a quality that is distinct from second-person dependency per se: the target of both actions stands in a privileged position to judge whether the actions have occurred. Call this characteristic *transparency*. Many perlocutionary effects are transparent in this way. If a target has been annoyed by a particular locution, she will be aware that she has been annoyed (so too with being offended, alarmed, inspired, shamed, bewildered, and so on). We should, however, resist the temptation to suppose that transparency is a necessary feature of perlocution. Consider, for example, the action of *lulling*. A baby need not recognize that she is being lulled to sleep in order for the action to be successfully brought off; what is required is simply that she be lulled to sleep.

The action of *benefiting* clearly manifests second-person dependency: whether one benefits, or fails to benefit, another is a matter that will depend crucially on how things stand for the putative recipient of the benefit. Interestingly, however, the action of benefiting is not presumed by Indian Buddhist authors to be transparent in every case. Even if those who listen to a teaching do not recognize that they are being benefited thereby – even if they are completely unable to make sense of what is going on – benefit (*hita, saṃhita*) can still be conferred. This idea is suggested in several texts. In his *Śālistambasūtraṭīkā*, for example, the great eighth-century Buddhist author Kamalaśīla attempts to explain an occasion on which Śākyamuni, rather than offering an extensive teaching, is said simply to have uttered a terse and cryptic pronouncement and fallen silent. Kamalaśīla suggests that we are to understand the Buddha's silence as aimed at removing the pride of monks who think that they are able to understand a profound teaching swiftly. He does not elaborate further, but his point seems to be that the Buddha's silence is intended to allow these monks room both to reflect on how little they actually understand and to spur them on to greater efforts in the future (cf. Nance 2012, 126–7).

Other Buddhist texts suggest that even this minimal level of recognition – understanding that one does not understand – is not required for benefit to be conferred. The *Suvarṇa(pra)bhāsottamā*, for example, relates the story of a group of fish who are reborn as gods as a consequence of hearing Buddhist teachings (see Bagchi 1967, 98–104). Their fortunate rebirth is presented as occurring not because the fish have engaged in deep piscine reflections on the nature of dependent arising (or on their own failure to understand the nature of dependent arising), but simply because they have been treated to the sonic contours of the teaching. Mere exposure to the sounds of the teaching conveys benefit, even for those who lack the ability to recognize those sounds as words bearing meanings.[13]

To claim that benefit – with or without transparency – is an ineluctable perlocutionary effect of a buddha's speech need not commit one to the view that it is the *only* perlocutionary effect of such speech. Indian Buddhist texts acknowledge this point as well, depicting teachings as gladdening, irritating, boring, alarming, and confusing (and, on at least one occasion, killing) those to whom they are offered.[14] Teachings can clearly strike different sentient beings in different ways – but each of these ways is supplementary to the perlocutionary effect of benefit: the Dharma's "single taste" (*ekarasa*) of liberation from suffering.

The ability of a buddha to respond verbally in ways that unerringly maximize benefit comes to be associated (especially, though not exclusively, in Mahāyāna texts) with his perfection of skillful means (*upāya, upāyakauśalya*; Tb. *thabs mkhas*).[15] It is as a consequence, or as an expression, of a buddha's perfected skillful means that he is able to tailor his utterances so as to benefit those of diverse needs, aptitudes, and interests. As

Bielefeldt has pointed out, the notion of skillful means is presented in conflicting terms in Buddhist *sūtras* – even within a single *sūtra* (Bielefeldt 2009). The *Saddharmapuṇḍarīka*, for example, vacillates between presenting *upāya* as a constitutive feature and as a contingent feature of a buddha's utterances. A view of skillful means as constitutive surfaces in the chapter on the lifespan of the Tathāgata, which strongly suggests that all the utterances (and, indeed, all the actions) of all buddhas are rightly seen as nothing other than skillful means. Consider, for example, the following passage. The translation is by Leon Hurvitz, from Kumārajīva's Chinese translation of the text. Hurvitz has adopted "expedient device" as a translation for the Chinese *fangbian* – i.e., *upāya* (*kauśalya*):

> For a hundred thousand myriads of millions of *nayuta*s of *asamkhyeyakalpas* I have been constantly dwelling in this Sahā world sphere, preaching the dharma, teaching and converting . . . I preached of the buddha Torch Burner and others, and I also said of them that they had entered into nirvāṇa. Things like this are all discriminations made as an expedient device.[16]

Passages such as this suggest that all the teachings of all buddhas are informed by *upāya* (*kauśalya*) in some way. Whether skillful means is applied in this or that case is thus not a contingent matter. What *is* contingent is *how* the application of skillful means plays itself out in the specifics of the utterance: what a buddha opts to say, and how he opts to say it.

There are, however, passages in the *Saddharmapuṇḍarīka* that suggest a rather different view, according to which buddhas can refrain from exercising skillful means. In the second chapter, the Buddha is portrayed as saying (again in Hurvitz's translation from the Chinese):

> Now I, joyfully and fearlessly,
> In the midst of the bodhisattvas
> Frankly casting aside my expedient devices
> Merely preach the unexcelled path.[17]

This passage suggests a view according to which skillful means is dispensable. A Buddhist teaching that lacks *upāya* – and here the *Saddharmapuṇḍarīka* positions itself as just such a teaching – is superior to a Buddhist teaching in which *upāya* is present.[18]

Remarks consonant with a contingency view occasionally surface in other Buddhist texts extant in Sanskrit and Tibetan. In the *Upāyakauśalyasūtra*, for example, the Buddha counsels his hearers to refrain from propagating the *sūtra* among *śrāvakas*, *pratyekabuddhas*, and foolish common persons, "since no one but a bodhisattva-mahāsattva is a fit vessel for this teaching of skillful means; no one else is to be trained in this teaching."[19] And in the first chapter of the *Mahāyānasūtrālaṅkāra* – a text probably composed sometime around the fourth century CE and attributed to Asaṅga/Maitreya – we are told that "the hearers' vehicle is not called a teaching of the Mahāyāna . . . because of [its] non-*upāya*ness."[20] These passages may be read to suggest that skillful means is a dispensable feature of a buddha's utterances. They need, however, to be read very carefully. The passage from the *Upāyakauśalya* does not require that a buddha refrain from *employing* skill when teaching to non-bodhisattvas. Rather, the passage advises that, when teaching to such persons, skillful means should not be *discussed*. And although the passage from the *Mahāyānasūtrālaṅkāra* could be read to suggest that skillful means is absent either from the hearers' vehicle or from the Mahāyāna (a claim that, in turn, could mean either that skillful means is not employed, or that it is not discussed, in certain Buddhist teachings), an early prose commentary on the passage reads it differently: as claiming that the hearers' vehicle is not a means (*upāya*) by which buddhahood can be attained.[21]

Regardless of a text's specific take on skillful means, *responsiveness* would appear to be an indispensable characteristic of a buddha's utterances; I know of no Buddhist text that suggests that a buddha's speech is to be understood as intermittently *unresponsive* to the needs of sentient beings. Even the second chapter of Kumārajīva's translation of the *Saddharmapuṇḍarīka* – where skillful means is explicitly stated to be dispensable – suggests that it is dispensable in certain circumstances and not others, and that the Buddha opts to dispense with skillful means precisely because he recognizes that his present audience of bodhisattvas is well suited to receive a teaching in which skillful means is absent. In short, Kumārajīva's Buddha responds to circumstances, even as he claims to be discarding skillful means.

If skillful means is understood to be a contingent (i.e., dispensable) feature of a buddha's utterances, then it marks not responsiveness per se, but rather certain *ways* of responding. If, on the other hand, skillful means is understood to be a constitutive feature of a buddha's utterances, then it becomes plausible to read it as marking responsiveness per se. The extant texts do not speak in a single voice on this issue, though they do tend to agree on the point that a buddha inevitably responds to others in ways productive of benefit for them. The latter view is compatible with either understanding of skillful means. If one takes the view that skillful means is a contingent feature of a buddha's utterances, then one need simply assume that a buddha withholds skillful means in just those cases in which benefit will follow from doing so. If, on the other hand, one takes the view that skillful means is a constitutive feature of a buddha's utterances, then one can understand the notion as an explanatory device – one that accounts for the fact that benefit ineluctably follows from the speech of buddhas.

A striking fact about both the *Saddharmapuṇḍarīka* and the *Upāyakauśalyasūtra* is that both texts present skillful means as a capacity that is not restricted to buddhas. It may also be possessed by *bodhisattva-mahāsattvas* – i.e., practitioners of the Mahāyāna who have not yet achieved full-fledged buddhahood. The move to associate skillful means with the figure of the bodhisattva is an intriguing conceptual shift. A bodhisattva may now respond to others with the compassion of buddhas, though he lacks the perfected knowledge traditionally associated with the attainment of buddhahood. At a point short of buddhahood – though well beyond the level of a beginner – a bodhisattva acquires perfected skillful means. According to the system of stages or levels (*bhūmi*) propounded in the *Daśabhūmikasūtra* (a system correlated with the traditional system of ten perfections), this occurs on the seventh bodhisattva stage (see Vaidya 1967, 36–41; Honda 1968, 199–213). Although his knowledge may not yet be that of a buddha, a bodhisattva's possession of skillful means assures that his speech will bring benefit to sentient beings, whether or not they recognize it as beneficial. This makes room for the idea that to respond as a buddha would respond does not require a buddha's capacity for knowing times and hearts: perfected responsiveness does not presuppose perfected knowledge.

Perfected responsiveness does, however, presuppose extensive training – training that normatively encompasses activities of listening, reflection, and cultivation that are traditionally associated with the production of insight (see Dayal 2004 [1932], 270–91). While "listening," "reflection," and "cultivation" may appear to suggest essentially private activities, undertaken in seclusion, to read them in this way is to risk missing the way in which each draws from, and gives rise to, social practice. The idealized practitioners presented in Buddhist *sūtras* listen to the voices of others; they reflect on what they hear using tools acquired from others; they subject their reflections to the critical assessment of others; and they cultivate themselves by applying meditative techniques learned from others.[22] Over time, through engaging in forms of personal and interpersonal practice, they develop their ability to attend to, internalize, comprehend, and apply Buddhist teachings in various circumstances.

They may also begin to teach – a skill that, like the other skills cultivated on the path, is developed over time. The activity of teaching begins well before it is perfected, and Buddhist texts explicitly acknowledge that one need not be a buddha to teach effectively. Indeed, one need not even have achieved perfected skillful means. According to the *Daśabhūmikasūtra*, bodhisattvas begin to teach on the fifth bodhisattva level, prior to obtaining perfected skillful means. They attain a full complement of pedagogic skills only later, on the ninth bodhisattva level – the very cusp of buddhahood (see Vaidya 1967, 29; Honda 1968, 180). Bodhisattvas who abide on the fifth through the ninth levels are thus portrayed as at once teachers and students. As they respond to the shifting demands of pedagogy, they refine their responsiveness to the voices of countless others: to those who have taught them the Dharma, to their own students, and to an ever widening circle of sentient beings whom they work to benefit. They must strive to hear many teachings, to retain what they have heard, and to fix a vast treasury of Buddhist teaching in memory (see Nance 2012, 103, 130). They must also cultivate forms of responsiveness that enable them to recognize occasions for learning and teaching (and learning via teaching), and to tailor what they say and how they say it – whether as students or as teachers – to the fluid opportunities and demands presented by teaching occasions.

The transmission of tradition and the development of right view occur in this interplay between fixity and fluidity. The distinction between fixity and fluidity does not, however, neatly track the distinction between a teaching's *artha* and its *vyañjana*. In their attempts to determine what to say, what has been said, and what to say regarding what has been said, teachers and students may struggle to find the appropriate words to express what they have in mind (thus viewing *artha* as fixed and *vyañjana* as fluid), or they may struggle to make sense of a specific phrase attributed to a buddha (thus viewing *vyañjana* as fixed and *artha* as fluid). In both cases, the association of a specific *artha* with a specific *vyañjana* is facilitated by responsiveness to context: to (a) real and imagined audience(s) in the present, past, and future and to the possibilities and limitations of vocabulary, style, register, genre, and content.

These multiple contextual considerations influence both what is said and how it is said. Their impacts may vary from occasion to occasion, and are as open-ended as our use of language itself. Although it is surely possible to overstate their importance, we cannot afford to ignore them. Responsiveness to context ineluctably shapes the forms of speech that we study, as well as the forms of speech that we ourselves use. To deny this shaping role in either domain is to opt for a needlessly shuttered vision of what Buddhist philosophy has been – and what it might yet be.

Notes

1 Thanks are due to Jeremy Biles and Kathryn Graber for helpful comments on previous drafts of this paper, and to Heather Blair for her assistance with Kumārajīva's translation of the *Saddharmapuṇḍarīka*.

2 MN.I.294; AN.I.87. Translation in Ñāṇamoli and Bodhi (1995, 390).

3 Buddhist texts diverge on the issue of whether buddhas in fact speak. On this point, see D'Amato (2009); Lugli (2010).

4 As will become apparent below, this distinction does not neatly track the distinction between form and content: a teaching's form may be treated as either fixed or fluid, as may its content.

5 For an elaboration and defense of this perspective, see Griffiths (1990).

6 This way of putting the point raises questions. What does it mean, exactly, to be "shaped by" circumstances? Does responsive action require explicit acknowledgment of what those circumstances are on the part of the one who engages in it? Or can the impacts of context operate in the absence of such acknowledgment? For the purposes of this chapter, I will leave these questions aside, in order to preserve sufficient vagueness in the notion of responsiveness to allow for the notion to apply to the actions of buddhas, regardless of the position one takes on the extent or nature of their cognitive activity. On the latter point, see Dunne (1996).

7 See Collins (2010).

8 On the popularity of the *Śatapañcāśatka* among Indian monastics, see Li (2000, 141–2). The translation above has been modified from Bailey (1951, 175). The Sanskrit (ibid., 131–3) reads: *pṛṣṭenāpi kvacin noktam upetyāpi kathā kṛtā / tarṣayitvā paratroktaṃ kālāśayavidā tvayā // . . . na so 'sty upāyaḥ śaktir vā yena na vyāvataṃ tava / ghorāt saṃsārapātālād uddhartuṃ kṛpaṇaṃ jagat //*

9 See ibid., pp. 99, 169; cf. MN.III.47–9; MN.I.394–5.

10 For a more elaborated account of perlocution, see Austin (1975 [1962], 101–4).

11 The language of "second-person dependency" is borrowed from Cavell (2006, 180).

12 For a recent attempt to elaborate general conditions for perlocutions, see ibid., pp. 155–91.

13 So long as one understands benefit as admitting of degrees, this view is compatible with the idea – voiced repeatedly in the works of Atiśa (see Sherburne 2000, 196–7, 454–5) – that, although beings may benefit to some degree merely by hearing the Dharma, they benefit still more when they reflect carefully on its meaning.

14 See AN.IV.128–35. Cf. Miln.164–8 (Horner 1969 [1963], 1: 231–5).

15 As Nattier has noted, these terms are subject to rather different uses in different texts (Nattier 2003, 154–6). The most detailed study of skillful means remains Pye (1978).

16 Trans. Hurvitz (2009, 220).

17 Ibid., p. 42.

18 Intriguingly, however, the extant Sanskrit and the Tibetan diverge from the Chinese here – and from each other. The Sanskrit reads *saṃlīyanāṃ sarva vivarjayitvā* – i.e., "casting aside all timidity." The Tibetan (at D mdo sde *ja* 37b1) is closer to the Sanskrit than it is to the

Chinese, though *yang dag nang 'jog* suggests that the translators may have read *saṃlayana* – i.e., that what is cast aside is not timidity, but concealment. All three versions of the verse emphasize a reflexive point regarding the *Saddharmapuṇḍarīka*: that it represents a superior teaching, distinct from other teachings. Kumārajīva's Chinese text, however, contrasts the *sūtra* with teachings that manifest *upāya*; the Sanskrit and Tibetan texts do not draw the same opposition.

19 Translation slightly modified from Tatz (2001 [1994], 87). D dkon brtsegs *cha* 70a1–2: *thabs la mkhas pa bstan pa 'di'i snod du 'gyur ba dang / gang dag gis bstan pa 'di la bslab par bya ba ni byang chub sems dpa' sems dpa' chen po rnams ma gtogs par gzhan 'ga' yang med pa'i phyir ro /*

20 Lévi (1907, 4): *anupāyatvāt . . . na śrāvakayānam idaṃ bhavati mahāyānadharmākhyaṃ*. Cf. Jamspal et al. (2004, 9).

21 Ibid.

22 On interpersonal corrections to reflection, see the *Pāsādikasutta* (DN.29), translated in Walshe (1995 [1987], 427–39). On techniques of cultivation, see Griffiths (1993).

References

Austin, J. L. (1975 [1962]). *How to Do Things with Words*. Oxford: Oxford University Press.

Bagchi, S. (1967). *Suvarṇaprabhāsasūtra*. Darbhanga, India: Mithila Institute of Post-Graduate Studies and Research in Sanskrit Learning.

Bailey, D. R. S. (1951). *The Śatapañcāśatka of Mātṛceṭa: Sanskrit Text, Tibetan Translation & Commentary, and Chinese Translation, with an Introduction, English Translation, and Notes*. Cambridge: Cambridge University Press.

Bielefeldt, C. (2009). Expedient Devices, the One Vehicle, and the Life Span of the Buddha. In *Readings of the Lotus Sūtra*. Ed. S. Teiser and J. Stone.New York: Columbia University Press, 62–82.

Cavell, S. (2004). *Cities of Words: Pedagogical Letters on a Register of the Moral Life*. Cambridge: Belknap Press of Harvard University Press.

Cavell, S. (2006). *Philosophy the Day after Tomorrow*. Cambridge: Belknap Press of Harvard University Press.

Collins, S. (2010). *Nirvana: Concept, Imagery, Narrative*. Cambridge: Cambridge University Press.

D'Amato, M. (2009). Why the Buddha Never Uttered a Word. In *Pointing at the Moon: Buddhism, Logic, Analytic Philosophy*. Ed. M. D'Amato, J. Garfield, and T. Tillemans. Oxford: Oxford University Press, 41–55.

Dayal, H. (2004 [1932]). *The Bodhisattva Doctrine in Buddhist Sanskrit Literature*. Delhi: Motilal Banarsidass.

Dunne, J. (1996). Thoughtless Buddha, Passionate Buddha. In *Journal of the American Academy of Religion* 64, 525–56.

Griffiths, P. (1990). Denaturalizing Discourse: Ābhidhārmikas, Propositionalists, and the Comparative Philosophy of Religion. In *Myth and Philosophy*. Ed. F. Reynolds and D. Tracy. Albany: State University of New York Press, 57–91.

Griffiths, P. (1993). Indian Buddhist Meditation. In *Buddhist Spirituality: Indian, Southeast Asian, Tibetan, and Early Chinese*. Ed. Y. Takeuchi. New York: Crossroad, 34–66.

Honda, M. (1968). Annotated Translation of the Daśabhūmikasūtra. In *Studies in South, East, and Central Asia*. Ed. D. Sinor. New Delhi: International Academy of Indian Culture, 115–276.

Horner, I. B. (trans.) (1969 [1963]). *Milinda's Questions*. 2 vols. London: Luzac.

Hurvitz, L. (trans.) (2009). *Scripture of the Lotus Blossom of the Fine Dharma: The Lotus Sūtra*. New York: Columbia University Press.

Jamspal, L., et al. (trans.) (2004). *The Universal Vehicle Discourse Literature (Mahāyānasūtrālaākāra) by Maitreyanātha/Asaṅga*. New York: American Institute of Buddhist Studies.

Lévi, S. (1907). *Mahāyānasūtrālaṃkāra: Exposé de la doctrine du grand véhicule selon le système Yogācāra*. Vol. 1. Paris: Bibliothèque de l'École des Hautes Études.

Li, R. (trans.) (2000). *Buddhist Monastic Traditions of Southern Asia: A Record of the Inner Law Sent Home from the South Seas*. Berkeley, CA: Numata Center for Buddhist Translation and Research.

Lugli, L. (2010). Meaning without Words: The Contrast between Artha and Ruta in Mahāyāna Sūtras. In *Buddhist Studies Review* 27, 139–76.

Ñāṇamoli, B., and Bodhi, B. (trans.) (1995). *The Middle Length Discourses of the Buddha*. Boston: Wisdom.

Nance, R. (2012). *Speaking for Buddhas: Scriptural Commentary in Indian Buddhism*. New York: Columbia University Press.

Nattier, J. (2003). *A Few Good Men: The Bodhisattva Path According to the Inquiry of Ugra (Ugraparipṛcchā)*. Honolulu: University of Hawai'i Press.

Pye, M. (1978). *Skilful Means: a Concept in Mahāyāna Buddhism*. London: Duckworth.

Sherburne, R. (2000). *The Complete Works of Atīśa Śrī Dīpaṃkara Jñāna, Jo-bo-rje*. New Delhi: Aditya Prakashan.

Tatz, M. (trans.) (2001 [1994]). *The Skill in Means (Upāyakauśalya) Sūtra*. Delhi: Motilal Banarsidass.

Vaidya, P. L. (1967). *Daśabhūmikasūtra*. Darbhanga, India: Mithila Institute of Post-Graduate Studies and Research in Sanskrit Learning.

Walshe, M. (trans.) (1995 [1987]). *The Long Discourses of the Buddha: A Translation of the Dīgha Nikāya*. Boston: Wisdom.

D. Philosophy of Mind

24

Mind in Theravāda Buddhism

MARIA HEIM

The most precise and intricate model of mind from the tradition we now refer to as the Theravāda[1] is developed in the Abhidhamma. The term "*abhidhamma*" can be said to have several referents. It refers, first, to one of the three branches of canonical texts and, second, to the post-canonical tradition of commentary and compendia that interpreted and developed further this canonical material. But perhaps most importantly, "*abhidhamma*" refers to a distinctive *method* (*naya*) said to have been deployed by the Buddha to elucidate and expand the essentials of the Dhamma. The Abhidhamma method entails discerning phenomena from an ultimate sense (*paramattha*) and classifying them into various categories that show how they work. Buddhaghosa, regarded by the Mahāvihāra authorities as the translator and editor of the main Abhidhamma commentaries, says that classifications of phenomena are incomplete in the Suttanta, but the Abhidhamma provides them in detail; in this respect the Abhidhamma can be said to "exceed and surpass" the Dhamma as articulated in the Suttanta (Dhs-a.3–4).[2]

In keeping with these ideas, my approach to mind in the Pāli intellectual tradition is particularly attentive to method, aiming to introduce a method for thinking about the mind as much as a theory or system of it. As important as it is to discern *what* the basic features of consciousness are, our knowledge of them will be undeveloped unless we can understand *how* this system works by training us to see the mind differently than we do ordinarily. It does so through lists of phenomena and classifications that define and elaborate what those phenomena do. While the first book of the canonical Abhidhamma provides a useful schema to enter into this method, its phenomenology, consisting mostly of lists with little comment on how to interpret them, is rather spare. We can turn to the early commentarial tradition on it (represented primarily by Buddhaghosa)[3] for a sophisticated approach on how to read and interpret these lists and for its development of them into a rich and complex psychology. My analysis will center mostly on this early commentarial layer of Abhidhamma reflection. Modern scholars

A Companion to Buddhist Philosophy, First Edition. Edited by Steven M. Emmanuel.

have sometimes leapt quickly to the medieval compendium the *Abhidhammatthasaṅgaṇī*, which, useful as it is as a distillation or summary, does not display the same attentiveness to the possibilities of method as Buddhaghosa provides.

The basic Abhidhamma analysis of human experience proceeds through breaking it down into its smallest components, regrouping them into various functional classifications and exploring their interrelations. In its analysis there are 82 factors or phenomena (*dhammas*) classified into a fourfold division of reality: 28 *dhammas* are material (*rūpa*), 52 are mental (*cetasika*), one is conscious awareness (*citta*), and one is unconditioned and enduring (*nibbāna*). Our concerns will center on the two kinds of mental phenomena (*cetasika* and *citta*) and, to a lesser degree, on material phenomena (*rūpa*) when we consider the relationships between mind and matter. (*Nibbāna* is unconditioned, exists outside space and time, is not characterized by the many kinds of processes we will consider here, and remains largely outside of our purview.) The conditioned *dhammas* are momentary events rather than things or states. Though in some sense these factors cannot be further reduced or broken down, they are not essences or discrete, isolated particles of reality. Rather, while each *dhamma* has a definition, it is also conditioned by and "open," as Nyanaponika puts it, to other factors in the relational system in which it occurs (1998, 40). The qualities and intensity of a factor vary according to which other factors occur with it in any given moment. The Abhidhamma's various classificatory schemas aim at depicting how these complex interrelations yield almost infinite possibilities for experience.

Much of the first book of the canonical Abhidhamma, the *Dhammasaṅgaṇī* ("The Enumeration of Factors"), breaks down conscious awareness into its constitutive mental factors. Consciousness or mind (*citta*) is not an enduring entity but rather a momentary unit of conscious awareness that, when analyzed at the closest level possible, is seen to be made up of any number of the 52 mental factors (*cetasikas*). What we normally experience as a continuous stream of awareness can be parsed into these very tiny momentary events, fractions of a second in duration. As evanescent as these conscious events are, they are comprised of many factors in complex relationships with one another.

The Abhidhamma's dissection of thoughts is the product of meditative introspection and a tool for meditative cultivation. The Buddha is said to have attained this knowledge through his enlightened introspection. His ability to analyze mental experience in this way is regarded as extremely difficult, likened to a person at sea scooping up a handful of water and determining which drops in it came from which rivers (Dhs-a.142; Miln.87). The analytical insight he provided is then put to the service of meditative practice (practiced today in Burma, for instance), which aims at fundamentally restructuring ordinary mental experience to bring about happiness and freedom. The Buddha was very interested in how much the mind can change through moral and meditational practice and how intractable minds are when not developed: "Monks, I know nothing so supple and malleable as the mind when highly cultivated" and "nothing so intractable as the untamed mind" (AN.I.9; AN.I.6).

Buddhaghosa says that the Abhidhamma method destroys latent defilements because its wisdom opposes them (Dhs-a.22). Shedding light on how the mind works is the key to freeing it from bad experience. The first chapter of the *Dhammasaṅgaṇī* begins with an opening question that frames its inquiries into mind. It asks: "what factors are good?" (Dhs.8). By "good" (*kusala*), the text signals an important designation operative throughout its treatment of mind. Mental experience can be good, bad, or neutral, a classification crucial to a system aimed at manipulating psychological experience. But what is meant by "good"? Buddhaghosa defines *kusala* as fourfold: healthy, faultless, productive of happy results, and skillful, with the first three senses operative in this particular context (Dhs-a.38). The term often has moral value. *Akusala* or bad factors are described as the opposite of *kusala*, and there are also "neutral" factors (Dhs-a.39).

The *Dhammasaṅgaṇī* goes on to supply a list of 56 mental factors (*cetasika*) that can occur in one kind of a good moment of conscious awareness (*citta*). Although there are only 52 mental factors in the system as a whole, certain of them are repeated under different subheadings and classifications in this listing. This particular list describes a type of conscious awareness associated with happiness and connected to knowledge and that occurs in the realm of desire. In other words, this first list depicts relatively ordinary conscious experience, not that known to those residing in the heavenly spheres or in advanced stages of meditation that correspond to those spheres. The 56 factors that can occur in this moment of good conscious awareness are given in table 24.1, along with additional factors added by the commentary; in separate columns are lists of representative bad and neutral thoughts. First in each column are five factors present in every moment of conscious awareness, understood as a distinct grouping by the commentary: contact, feeling, perception, intention, and consciousness itself. These five operations of the mind, since they are ever present and fundamental to all mental experience, will occupy much of our attention below and will serve as our chief schema for interpreting mind. But some constellation of the 56 factors will occur in every instance of this particular kind of good conscious experience, though not all of them will appear in any given moment. The *Dhammasaṅgaṇī* provides many lists for other types of good, bad, and neutral conscious awareness in their many varieties. We can examine these three lists, following closely Buddhaghosa's commentary on them, to begin to appreciate the types of mental experience possible, and to discern how the entire relational model works.

The First Five Factors: Contact, Feeling, Perception, Intention, Consciousness

Conscious experience is always intentional in the phenomenological sense of intentionality: mental phenomena are characterized by an essential or immanent relation to their objects. As Buddhaghosa puts it, consciousness arises with its sensory or mental object (*ārammaṇa*) (Dhs-a.107); there is no "bare" consciousness. While consciousness is fundamentally *about* its object, we can refer to sensory contact or stimulation (*phassa*), the first factor on the *Dhammasaṅgaṇī's* list, when we want to state more precisely *how* it is that consciousness arises. *Phassa* refers to the contact of conscious experience with the objects of the six senses – that is, the five sensory organs and the mind sense.

Using the commentator's standard interpretative device of naming a phenomenon's characteristic, function, manifestation, and proximate cause, Buddhaghosa defines sensory contact as follows: "Contact means 'it touches.' Its characteristic is 'touching';

Table 24.1 Lists of mental factors

Good mental factors (Dhs.8)	Bad mental factors (Dhs.75)	Neutral mental factors (Dhs.87)
Contact (*phassa*)	Contact (*phassa*)	Contact (*phassa*)
Feeling (*vedanā*)	Feeling (*vedanā*)	Feeling (*vedanā*)
Perception (*saññā*)	Perception (*saññā*)	Perception (*saññā*)
Intention (*cetanā*)	Intention (*cetanā*)	Intention (*cetanā*)
Conscious awareness (*citta*)	Conscious awareness (*citta*)	Conscious awareness (*citta*)
Initial thinking (*vitakka*)	Initial thinking (*vitakka*)	
Sustained thinking (*vicāra*)	Sustained thinking (*vicāra*)	
Joy (*pīti*)	Joy (*pīti*)	Equanimity (*upekkhā*)
Pleasure (*sukha*)	Pleasure (*sukha*)	
Oneness of mind (*cittassekaggatā*)	Oneness of mind (*cittassekaggatā*)	Oneness of mind (*cittassekaggatā*)
Faculty of faith (*saddhindriya*)		
Faculty of energy (*vīriyindriya*)	Faculty of energy (*vīriyindriya*)	
Faculty of mindfulness (*satindriya*)		
Faculty of concentration (*samādhindriya*)	Faculty of concentration (*samādhindriya*)	
Faculty of wisdom (*paññindriya*)		
Mental faculty (*manindriya*)	Mental faculty (*manindriya*)	Mental faculty (*manindriya*)
Faculty of happiness (*somanassindriya*)	Faculty of happiness (*somanassindriya*)	Faculty of equanimity (*upekkhindriya*)
Faculty of vitality (*jīvitindriya*)	Faculty of vitality (*jīvitindriya*)	Faculty of vitality (*jīvitindriya*)
Right view (*sammādiṭṭhi*)	Wrong view (*micchādiṭṭhi*)	
Right thought (*sammāsaṅkappa*)	Wrong thought (*micchāsaṅkappa*)	
Right effort (*sammāvāyāma*)	Wrong effort (*micchāvāyama*)	
Right mindfulness (*sammāsati*)		
Right concentration (*sammāsamādhi*)	Wrong concentration (*micchāsamādhi*)	
Power of faith (*saddhābāla*)		
Power of energy (*vīriyabāla*)	Power of energy (*vīriyabāla*)	
Power of mindfulness (*satibāla*)		
Power of concentration (*samādhibāla*)	Power of concentration (*samādhibāla*)	
Power of wisdom (*paññābāla*)		
Power of shame (*hiribāla*)	Power of shamelessness (*ahiribāla*)	
Power of apprehension (*ottappabāla*)	Power of brazenness (*anottappabāla*)	
Non-greed (*alobha*)	Greed (*lobha*)	
Non-hatred (*adosa*)		
Non-delusion (*amoho*)	Delusion (*moha*)	
Non-covetousness (*anabhijjhā*)	Covetousness (*abhijjhā*)	
Non-malice (*abyāpādo*)		
Right view (*sammādiṭṭhi*)	Wrong view (*micchādiṭṭhi*)	

Table 24.1 *Continued*

Good mental factors (Dhs.8)	Bad mental factors (Dhs.75)	Neutral mental factors (Dhs.87)
Shame (*hiri*)	Shamelessness (*ahirika*)	
Apprehension (*ottappa*)	Brazenness (*anottappa*)	
Tranquility of body (*kāyapassadhi*)		
Tranquility of mind (*cittapassadhi*)		
Lightness of body (*kāyalahutā*)		
Lightness of mind (*cittalahutā*)		
Softness of body (*kāyamudutā*)		
Softness of mind (*cittamudutā*)		
Workableness of body (*kāyakammaññatā*)		
Workableness of mind (*cittakammaññatā*)		
Proficiency of body (*kāyapāguññatā*)		
Proficiency of mind (*cittapāguññatā*)		
Uprightness of body (*kāyujukatā*)		
Uprightness of mind (*cittujukatā*)		
Mindfulness (*sati*)		
Meta-attention (*sampajañña*)		
Calmness (*samatha*)	Calmness (*samatha*)	
Insight (*vipassanā*)		
Exertion (*paggāha*)	Exertion (*paggāha*)	
Balance (*avikkhepa*)	Balance (*avikkhepa*)	
"and other factors" (Dhs-a.131)	*"and other factors"* (Dhs-a.250)	*"and other factors"* (Dhs-a.264)
Attention (*manasikāra*)	Attention (*manasikāra*)	Attention (*manasikāra*)
Initiative (*chanda*)	Initiative (*chanda*)	
Resolve (*adhimokkha*)	Resolve (*adhimokkha*)	Resolve (*adhimokkha*)
Impartiality (*tatramajjhattatā*)		
Compassion (*karuṇā*)		
Sympathetic joy (*muditā*)		
Abstention from bodily misconduct (*kāyaduccaritavirati*)		
Abstention from verbal misconduct (*vacīduccaritavirati*)		
Abstention from wrong livelihood (*micchājīvavirati*)		
	Conceit (*māna*)	
	Envy (*issā*)	
	Avarice (*macchariya*)	
	Rigidity (*thīna*)	
	Sluggishness (*middha*)	
	Agitation (*uddhacca*)	
	Remorse (*kukkucca*)	

its function is 'impact'; its manifestation is 'coinciding'; and its proximate cause is the object coming into the field of experience" (Dhs-a.108). We learn from this and from Buddhaghosa's further discussion that there is a kind of "touching" and "impact" that describes the contact of consciousness with its object. He mentions the theory of doorways, a metaphorical way of referring to where contact takes place in each of the thresholds of the six senses. "Coinciding" can be said to be contact's manifestation, the way it presents itself in experience, "because it is known through its own cause which is said to be the coinciding of three things" – that is, external object, sensory organ, and consciousness, according to the *Majjhima* (MN.I.111, which he cites here). And finally, its proximate cause is the (sensory or mental) object that has come into the field of awareness (Dhs-a.108–9).

Feeling (*vedanā*) is the next of the five universally present mental factors. Upon contact there is a basic response to the object which is the feeling or affective experience of it, whether painful, pleasurable, or neutral. Feeling is the "hedonic tone" in the consciousness of an object. Buddhaghosa says, "its characteristic is 'what is felt', its function is 'enjoying,' or, alternatively, its function is enjoying what is desirable in it; its manifestation is 'tasting' [other] mental factors; and its proximate cause is 'tranquility' " (Dhs-a.110). Like a king who gets to relish the delicacies prepared for him (unlike the cook, who merely prepares them), *vedanā* is the direct affective experience or tasting of the mental or sensory object and its coinciding consciousness. Buddhaghosa does not offer much explanation of why "tranquility" is the proximate cause of feeling; he says only that "a tranquil body causes the feeling of pleasure," suggesting that some element of calmness or relaxation in the body must be present for feeling (or at least pleasurable feeling) to occur (Dhs-a.110).

The third factor in all moments of conscious awareness is *saññā*, perceptual judgment or conception. This refers not to a passive perceiving of an object but to the "recognizing (or naming) of an object, such as 'blue' " (Dhs-a.110). This mental factor has various processes associated with it, including selecting out an object's salient property and labeling it ("blue"). Buddhaghosa defines *saññā*'s characteristic as "perceiving" and its function as "recognizing that which had been noted before." This occurs, he suggests by way of example, when a carpenter recognizes particular pieces of wood he earlier tagged or when a person recognizes a man by the dark mole on his face observed previously. Buddhaghosa suggests a possible alternative interpretation: its characteristic is "perceiving by way of general inclusion," while its function is making marks that are the ground for later perception (Dhs-a.110). He defines its manifestation as the fixing on the object according to how its distinguishing mark has been grasped. Perception or forming a conception about an object is thus a matter of noticing, labeling, and memory, or, as Nyanaponika puts it, "the taking up, the making, and the remembering of the object's distinctive marks" (1998, 121).

Buddhaghosa offers another account of *saññā*'s manifestation: "alternatively it has briefness as its manifestation, like lightning, because of its manner of not plunging deeply into its object" (Dhs-a.110). Perception so defined is not a matter of probing analysis into things, but rather the all too quick (and often false) labeling of the things in our experience and recalling them. Its proximate cause is whatever is present to the field of perception, illustrated by the example of a young deer having the conception "man" arise when presented with a scarecrow.

The fourth universally present factor, intention (*cetanā*), is the most constructive and creative of these five processes. Buddhaghosa defines it as what "puts together (*abhisandahati*) with itself accompanying factors as objects" (Dhs-a.111). That is, intention brings together some arrangement of other mental factors to construct the objects of experience. Recall our list of 56 *cetasikas* that can occur in this particular kind of *citta*. Intention is the dynamic process of arranging or coordinating which of these potential factors will be present in the experience of the object. In this effort it is an active volitional force: "exceedingly energetic, exceedingly striving, it does double effort, double striving" (Dhs-a.111). Buddhaghosa proposes several similes to illustrate its activity. Like a head carpenter who works and makes the other workers work on a project, intention marshals the other mental factors to their tasks and toils alongside them. Similarly, it is like a head student who sees the teacher coming and learns his lesson and rallies the other students to theirs. It rallies accompanying mental factors to their efforts by "recollecting urgent work," thus connecting up present experience with past experience.

Above all, intention "produces its object by its own work, and makes the other associated factors produce it with their own actions" (Dhs-a.111). This assertion refers to the very active role the mind plays in creating and constructing the objects of experience. Intention, by pulling together and animating particular arrangements of mental factors "produces its object." Just as the head carpenter together with his subcontractors produce an object of their labors, such as a building, intention, with the other mental factors, produces the objects of all experience. Objects do not arrive unmediated and unprocessed in consciousness but are fashioned by intentional activity. This is not idealism; the reality of external objects is presupposed (though perhaps not philosophically defended) in the Theravāda; moreover, Buddhaghosa is here making phenomenological rather than epistemological or ontological claims. Though we might wish he had worked out more precisely how this works, it is clear that, for him, the mind has a large role in constructing the world we experience, and the factor of intention plays the leading part in this construction.

The overlaps of this Buddhist notion of intention and the modern phenomenological sense of intentionality should not go unnoticed: *cetanā* names the particular ways the mind is related to its objects (that is, it constructs them). But also like the English word "intention" in one of its other meanings relating to purposeful action, *cetanā* is also inherently linked with karma. This is evident when Buddhaghosa identifies intention's function as "accumulating" (*āyūhana*). He says that, in good and bad thoughts, intention "accumulates good and bad karma" (Dhs-a.111). This can be understood in reference to the linking of karma and intention, a formulation in the *suttas* that has garnered much modern scholarly notice. The Buddha was said to have identified the interior dimensions of karma with intention: "it is intention (*cetanā*) that I call action (*kamma*); intending, one acts by body, speech, and mind" (AN.III.415). The significance of this identifying intention as the principal part of action has been interpreted variously, but, from an Abhidhammic perspective, what is being said is that *cetanā*, in its process of putting together conscious experience by assembling and activating other *cetasikas*, is karma, and karma is the accumulating of further karma that keeps us trapped in *saṃsāra*. Intention is the mental side of morally relevant action that gathers and causes, karmically, present and future experience.

This sense of accumulating that connects intention to karma also links it to the important category of "constructions" or "formations" (*saṅkhāra*), though on this point we go outside the *Atthasālinī* to the *Sammohavinodanī*, where "*cetanā* is the principal *saṅkhāra*" because "of its well-known sense of accumulation" (Vibh-a.20). *Cetanā* is frequently regarded as foremost of this broad category of constructed and constructing processes and phenomena known as *saṅkhāras*, the mental factors, temperaments, dispositions, and habits that condition the nature and quality of all conscious experience. *Saṅkhāras* are the past psychological constructions we bring to all (unawakened) experience as well as the active, creative ways we make present and future experience. *Cetanā*, intentional activity, is at the forefront of them and sometimes stands in for this entire category.

When we assemble all of these interrelated aspects of intention – its arranging and rallying of other mental factors in the construction of the objects of sensory and mental awareness, its identification with karma and karma's logic of accumulating conditions, and its link with the constructing and constructed activity of *saṅkhāra* – we locate intention's centrality to a range of ethical and soteriological doctrines. When modern scholars have tried to interpret intention's role in karma by pairing it with English words for will, choice, rational decision-making, and so on, they have missed this basic *sutta* and Abhidhamma sense of the creative activity of the mental construction of experience. The subjective or internal aspect of karma is not moral choice, but a much more elementary putting together of the mental factors that shape our present and future experience. This is not to deny agency, but rather to define it as the very basic process by which the mind puts together its processes to construct the world of experience; this activity is, at bottom, what karmic action is all about.

Finally, conscious awareness (*citta*) is the fifth factor of the pentad: all conscious awareness is defined by *citta*, which Buddhaghosa glosses as that which thinks of (*cinteti*) or cognizes (*vijānāti*) its object. The identifying of consciousness (*citta*) as a distinct factor in a moment of conscious awareness (*citta*) is not as redundant as it may seem. The Abhidhamma method names various items in lists that can be taken in several ways and under different headings; *citta* is both one of the four divisions of reality (*citta, cetasika, rūpa, and nibbāna*) and itself a *cetasika*. Buddhaghosa argues that, though *citta* in the first sense is derivative of or constituted by the first four *cetasikas* just described, it is in another sense (as a *cetasika*) distinct from them or even prior to them (Dhs-a.113–14). (This suggestion may not have been ultimately persuasive to later scholastics, as we will see, since *citta* is eventually dropped in listings of *cetasikas*).

Buddhaghosa says that, as a *cetasika*, *citta* has "cognizing" as its characteristic, "preceding" as its function, "connecting" as its manifestation, and "mind and body" (*nāmarūpa*) as its proximate cause (Dhs-a.112). It is "preceding" in that it is prior to or a condition for sensory contact, and it manifests as "connecting" because it is connected to the immediately preceding moment. The temporal aspects of the pentad are subtle: even though listed first, contact is not really first in that it initiates conscious experience. Rather, *cetasikas* occur concurrently in a given moment of conscious thought, even while sometimes it is deemed useful to try to understand how one might be viewed as the condition for the other or how two (or more) might be mutually conditioning. Because contact is the impact of consciousness and the object or the coinciding of the object, sense organ, and consciousness, consciousness is in this sense conceived as prior.

However, the quality and nature of consciousness will be determined by its object, which, as we have begun to see, rests on all of the other mental factors that occur with and construct it.

When Buddhaghosa defines the manifestation of consciousness as "connecting," he is assigning it a role in effecting continuity across time. Nyanaponika shows how each moment of consciousness has "depth in time": it is founded on energies from the past and it functions as a potentiality for the future (1998, 97, 105). As we have seen, Buddhaghosa defines *saññā* (perception) in temporal terms as involving *memory* of the past and a "tagging" of an item for future reference, and he defines intention as "*recollecting* urgent work" in its activity of arranging and marshalling mental factors. These elements of memory attempt to show how thought moments are connected to one another within the flow of experience. Though Abhidhamma analysis is focused on the contents of discrete momentary events, it interprets these events with an eye for how they work in time.

Citta is frequently used interchangeably with other terms for mind and consciousness, and the *Dhammasaṅgaṇī* lists several terms overlapping or related to *citta* (*mano mānasaṃ hadayaṃ paṇḍaraṃ mano manāyatanaṃ manindriyaṃ viññāṇaṃ viññāṇakkhandho*; Dhs.10). Glossing these, Buddhaghosa says that "*citta* is so called because of its being variegated (*vicitta*)" (Dhs-a.140), an etymology which picks up on the constantly changing and variable nature of conscious awareness. Mind (*mano*), a synonym for *citta*, is so called "because it knows by measuring (*minamāno*) the object," which means, he says, that it exercises a kind of governing role over mental factors as it sizes up the object (Dhs-a.123, 140). This notion of governing other factors goes some distance in explaining *mano*'s role also as the "mental faculty" (*manindriya*), listed as a *cetasika*, since faculties govern other factors. *Mānasa*, mental action, is the same as mind (*mano*). There is also *mano* as sense sphere (*āyatana*), which is like the other five senses, except its objects are ideas or mental experiences, not external objects. Sense sphere (*āyatana*) covers much ground, referring simultaneously to the sense organ (the "origin," *sañjāti*), the sense object (the "cause," *karaṇa*), and the "meeting" of them (*samosaraṇa*) (Dhs-a.141).

A further overlap with *citta* is heart (*hadaya*). *Citta* is "said to be the heart in the sense of being the interior part," not the actual physical organ (Dhs-a.140). As with English "heart," the physical organ is but just one of the senses of *hadaya*. "White" (*paṇḍara*) means "clear" in connection to the *bhavaṅga*, the life continuum, in accordance with the Buddha's claim that "this consciousness is very bright but it is defiled by added depravities" (Dhs-a.140, quoting AN.I.10). Though morally bad, a *citta* may be said to be "white" because it issues forth from the *bhavaṅga*, like a tributary of the Ganges issues forth from the River Ganges (Dhs-a.140). This reference to *bhavaṅga* posits a clear and luminous mind that underlies other forms of consciousness which are contaminated by external taints, a doctrine suggested (though not fully elaborated) in the Suttanta and somewhat incompletely treated even in the Abhidhamma.[4] Finally, in its list of terms related to or interchangeable with *citta*, the *Dhammasaṅgaṇī* mentions *viññāṇa*, consciousness, and *viññāṇakkhandha*, the aggregate of consciousness. *Viññāṇa* means cognizing, while the aggregate of consciousness (one of the five aggregates, as we have seen) refers to a "heap" or group of conscious processes. But here, Buddhaghosa says, since *citta* means only one momentary event of consciousness, just part of the aggregate, the word "aggregate" is said only conventionally (Dhs-a.141). Both *viññāṇa* and *mano* are often used as synonyms of *citta* (Dhs.10; Dhs-a.123; Vism.452), referring to the momentary element or phenomenon (*dhātu*) in the fivefold group (Dhs-a.141).

This group of five provides the rudimentary operations always present in the making of our experience. Post-canonical Abhidhamma texts became more explicit and precise in specifying a finite list of factors described as present universally (*sabbacittasādhāraṇa*) and arrived at a list of seven such factors: contact, feeling, perception, intention, bringing-to-mind, the faculty of vitality, and attention (*manasikāra*), dropping *citta*, and replacing it with three factors, the first two of which are, in fact, present in all of the *Dhammasaṅgaṇī*'s lists (Nārada and Bodhi 1993, 77); the other addition, attention, will be discussed below. In any case, these five elementary factors of all conscious experience given in the *Dhammasaṅgaṇī* provide a useful introduction to mind in this early stratum of the tradition. As Nyanaponika points out, they are "the briefest formulation, by way of representatives, of the four mental aggregates," which together with material phenomena (*rūpa*) comprise all human experience: feeling and perception are represented by themselves, sense contact and intention together represent the aggregate of the *saṅkhāras*, and *citta* represents the consciousness aggregate (*viññāṇakhandha*).[5] Insofar as these five processes constitute the immaterial aggregates, they are at the bottom of all human psychological experience. The five aggregates doctrine is used to delineate the possibilities for human experience as much as to undermine our sense of their substantiality, as evident in an extended analogy given in the *Samyutta*: physical reality is like a lump of foam, feeling, like a bubble, perception, a mirage, constructions (*saṅkhāra*), a plantain stem, and consciousness, an illusion (SN.III.140; discussed in Vibh-a.32–4). All of these images reinforce the cardinal Buddhist doctrine that at the core of our experience are processes that are fundamentally impermanent, insubstantial, and deluded.

These first five mental factors also occur either directly or by way of categories they represent in the formula of dependent origination, a formula that, like the five aggregates, could have served equally well as an organizational schema for entering into the larger system. Lists function as matrices that imbricate, subsume, and suggest further lists, which in turn develop ideas in different directions. No matter with which list one begins, one will, eventually, be brought round to other lists and to the doctrines they convey. The doctrine of five aggregates serves to dismantle human experience in such a way that no stable self can be posited, while dependent origination serves to refine our understanding of the conditionality that creates human experience.[6]

The Other Factors

The remaining factors present in each of the three good, bad, and neutral *cittas* in table 24.1 are variable in that they may or may not appear in any particular thought; they are thus not as essential to our study of the basic workings of mind as the first five. Many of them, however, have much to offer the study of moral phenomenology, which we can only touch on here. Each of them is classified into various groupings by Buddhaghosa and we can treat them according to their groups. The next five items on the lists of both good and bad factors, called "factors of absorption" (*jhānaṅga*) in the commentary, intensify and differentiate awareness in ways that are cognitive (initial and sustained thinking), affective (joy – that is, both rapture and interest, and pleasure), and focusing (oneness of mind with the object).[7] These items, like the first five, can be either good or bad depending upon which other factors are present. Similarly, other functions are shared by both lists: certain varieties of energy (and effort and exertion) and concentration (and balance), stated in different ways, are part of both good and bad consciousness. Good and bad thoughts alike require an energy towards their object, as well as a focus on or directedness towards it.

The remaining items on the list of good factors belong to groups of morally and soteriologically valuable mental activities familiar from other contexts, such as elements of the Eightfold Path, certain faculties, the seven powers, and the moral sentiments of shame and apprehension. The several instances of repetition of items on the list may seem unsatisfactory given the precision with which the topic is approached: why should concentration, for example, occur four times, as a faculty, a power, a path factor, and separately? Buddhaghosa takes up this problem and argues that, by repeating items in their membership in different groupings, attention is drawn to their functions and aspects in those groupings; just as a king hires an artisan who may be able to offer several kinds of crafts and belong to several different guilds, so the same factor can perform different functions according to its membership in groups. Since classification is a key instrument for the development of meaning and possibility, seeing to which groups each item belongs suggests important variations in its qualities and intensities.[8] Here Buddhaghosa teaches us to read Abhidhamma as a *method*: its method is to consider factors in their functionally classificatory roles, which will entail diverse roles for many of them.

The motivational roots or causes (*mūla* or *hetu*) are of particular importance in Buddhist psychology. Among the good factors, three motivational roots are listed – non-greed, non-hatred, non-delusion – together with their intensified states, non-covetousness, non-malice, and right view. The significance of these factors of mind is hard to overstate. They are largely the criteria by which a thought is good, bad, or neutral. Except for "right view," all the good factors are described in the negative – that is, they are the opposites of the bad roots (greed, malice, delusion) and the abstentions from the bad mental actions (covetousness, malice, and wrong view). Their statement in the negative is significant; chiefly they are the abstinence from the bad motivations and bad mental actions. The bad motivations listed are greed, delusion, covetousness, and wrong view, opposites of the good motivations; greed and delusion are two of the three roots at the heart of all entrapment and woe in *saṃsāra*. Notably absent in the table are the motivational roots hatred and malice; this is because this particular listing is for bad thoughts that occur accompanied by joy (*somanassa*). The *Dhammasaṅgaṇī* gives another list of bad factors that occur in the presence of distress (*domanassa*): many of the same items are listed but, instead of elements of joy, pleasure, happiness, greed, and covetousness, we find suffering, distress, and the motivational roots hatred and malice (Dhs.83). It is in the eradication of the three deeply seated roots greed, hatred, and delusion (not to speak of their three amplifications – covetousness, malice, and wrong view) that *nibbāna* is attained (Vibh-a.53).

The list of good factors includes six pairs of qualities that can describe both body and mind, for a total of 12 qualities which always arise together: tranquility (being quiet and composed), lightness (agility and buoyancy), softness (being pliable, resilient, and adaptable), workableness (the right balance of softness and firmness "which makes the gold – that is, the mind – workable"), fitness (health and competence), and uprightness (sincerity and straightforwardness) (Dhs-a.150-1; see Nyanaponika 1998, 71–81). These dispositions are not treated in much detail, but they suggest attributes that dispose one to good action through mental and physical composure, malleability, health, readiness, and rectitude. Following them we have several potentialities: mindfulness, mental clarity, and insight, which refer to distinctive aptitudes in the development of mental culture. Lastly, calmness, exertion, and balance (present in both good and bad thoughts) overlap with some of the earlier items and provide elements of steadiness, energy, and concentration necessary for good and bad action.

A full description of the factors will also depend upon understanding their relations to one another and external conditions (the primary concern of the Abhidhamma book the *Paṭṭhāna*). The richness of this moral psychology suggests that scholars of Buddhist ethics might fruitfully train their attention on a phenomenological treatment of Buddhist moral thought. For our purposes, we have gained a glimpse of the factors that make up the varieties of conscious experience.

Additional Factors

At the end of its lists of the factors that may be present in every type of thought, the *Dhammasaṅgaṇī* leaves open the possibility that there may be more factors present than it has listed, concluding each list by gesturing to "whatever other factors" might be present (as, for example, Dhs.9, 75, 87). This detail is highly significant for our interpretation of what the canonical Abhidhamma is up to. While sometimes mistakenly taken to be a reductive account of mind, the lists – and the glimpse of mind that they offer – are not intended to be exhaustive or complete. While perhaps the later tradition lost sight of this early resistance to closure and came to treat the lists more like catechisms, this early canonical and commentarial period was importantly open.

Buddhaghosa makes much of the idea that the Abhidhamma is not closed. Since the Dhamma itself, in the sense of "the teaching as thought out in the mind," is endless and immeasurable, the Abhidhamma – "that which exceeds (*abhi*) the Dhamma" – goes even further (Dhs-a.15, 2). He suggests that, although the Abhidhamma texts are finite in how long it takes to recite them, they are in fact "endless and immeasurable when expanded" (Dhs-a.7). Even though the Abhidhamma was taught straight through without stopping in three months' time, which must have seemed like a single moment to its audience, the Dhamma that was taught is endless and immeasurable (Dhs-a.15). To ponder the depth and reach of the Abhidhamma method one should picture the ocean. As vast and seemingly endless is the sea for one drifting in a lonely boat upon it, one knows that it is still bordered by land below and on all sides. But the limits of the Abhidhamma cannot be known (Dhs-a.10–12).

When we place the Abhidhamma in the context of meditative practice we can also discern its open and dynamic nature. Rupert Gethin advises that the Abhidhamma's method is, in the end, practical. Its breaking up of wholes into parts undermines our constant and fruitless tendency to grasp and fix the world of experience. The restless re-examination of these arrangements through proliferating lists is itself a method for destabilizing our yearning for a fixed and stable sense of the world: "the indefinite expansions based on the *mātikās* continually remind those using them that it is of the nature of things that no single way of breaking up and analyzing the world can ever be final" (Gethin 1992, 165). As much as Abhidhamma phenomenology advances a *model of* mind – and we do come to know what the elemental components of mental life are and how they interact – its very method destabilizes an overly fixed or final version of it. It is not an ontology designating the smallest "reals" that constitute experience, but rather a method for shaking up and reconsidering experience from new vantage points; chiefly it penetrates things from an ultimate sense (*paramattha*) to seek factors of experience that cannot be broken down further, even while the relations between them can extend and vary almost infinitely. Buddhaghosa says that the Abhidhamma is taught expressly for those who falsely hold onto a sense of self in what is really just a heap of changing factors (Dhs-a.21). Dismantling that heap in diverse ways provides a dynamic *model* for mind that facilitates new ways of exploring human experience.

When the canonical list suggests that there may be additional factors present in this kind of good conscious experience that it has not named, Buddhaghosa readily offers, on the basis, he claims, of knowledge of the *suttas*, nine additional factors. In particular he adds attention (*manasikāra*), a factor that increasingly gained traction in lists of universally present factors as the Abhidhamma tradition developed. Here its presence in all three types of thought suggests that Buddhaghosa saw it as a universally present factor, and indeed, as we have seen, it was taken to be so in other texts (Miln.56; Vism.589; Nārada and Bodhi 1993, 77–81). Attention is, according to Buddhaghosa, what "makes the mind different from how it was before." He sees it in this context as the process which can make the mind advert or shift to a different object. It has the characteristic of "driving," the function of "yoking associated mental factors to the object," the manifestation of "facing the object," and it belongs to the *saṅkhāra* aggregate (together, we recall, with contact and intention). It "should be seen like a coachman driving the associated factors to the object" (Dhs-a.133; Vism.466). Attention, like others among the basic factors, shows how the mind changes over time; it is that distinctive process of shifting from one object to another.

Buddhaghosa also adds "resolve" (*adhimokkha*) to the lists of good, bad, and neutral thoughts, and, though, unlike attention, it does not make it into later lists of universally present factors (where *ekaggatā*, one-pointedness of mind, may, in effect, assume its basic duties), he sees it present in every list that he provides. Its "characteristic is 'ascertainment,' its function is 'not wandering,' its manifestation is 'steadfastness,' and its proximate cause is 'a factor that should be ascertained.' It should be seen like a doorstop in its fixedness to the object" (Dhs-a.133). When we take resolve and attention together we see two counter aspects of mind, both present in the mind grasping an object: one keeps the mind focused on it and the other makes it possible for it to shift from it. A third important process, initiative or desire-to-act (*chando*), absent in neutral thought moments, is a movement of the mind reaching towards an object that results in action. The remaining factors added by the commentary are further good and bad sentiments that need not detain us here.

Mind and Cosmos

Mind can be supple, but it is also highly conditioned. Intentional processes that construct reality are conditioned by previous karma. Thus mind is not what it is just for the willing of it, but rather is shaped – though not determined – by past experience: the dispositions, latent tendencies, and the forces of habit implicit in the term *saṅkhāra* influence all moments of unawakened experience. At the same time, key to understanding the fundamentally dynamic nature of mind is to recognize all the factors just described as "possibilities" or "potentialities," to employ Nyanaponika's interpretation (1998, 55, 90). Mind is not mechanical, with factors simply operating according to their working definitions, factory-style, in the manufacturing of conscious awareness. Rather, factors represent potentialities for both present and future. The presence or exclusion of a given factor in a particular moment of conscious awareness affects the strength and quality of the other factors (ibid., 112–13). Moreover, they shape the quality of mind in the immediate future as well as distant future lives. A mind habituated to moments of mindfulness and insight, for example, can increasingly perpetuate these experiences in this human life, as well as create the quality of consciousness in the formless realms that may be experienced in a future rebirth.

Nyanaponika refers to some of these factors as "seeds of 'another world' " present in ordinary human mental experience, "where they are waiting to be nursed to full growth and fruition" (1998, 56). The factors of absorption (*jhānaṅga*), in particular, when strong and accompanied by mindfulness, are also the key ingredients of advanced stages of meditation (*jhāna*) that correspond to spheres in the cosmos where celestial beings inhabit increasingly rarified experiences of joy and equanimity. "On the other hand," as Nyanaponika shows,

> the possibilities latent in average human consciousness may also lead downward to rebirth in the animal realm . . . If human consciousness did not share certain features in common with the lower and higher worlds, rebirth as an animal or in the celestial spheres would not be possible.
>
> (Ibid., 57)

This insight that factors are open to upward and downward trajectories for future experience suggests the range in quality that human minds are capable of experiencing, from the basest processes of sense gratification common to animals to the most sublime encounters with joy and equanimity that characterize the experience of celestial beings. These trajectories are a matter of karmic processes; since karma is about how we make and construe the world of experience, we are creating our experience – and the types of beings we become – in present and future.

Rupert Gethin has shown that there is a "general principle of an equivalence or parallel in Buddhist thought between psychology on the one hand and cosmology on the other" (Gethin 1997, 189). We can discern a hierarchy in the 56 states we have considered, beginning with rudimentary sense consciousness and moving upward to various capacities for mindfulness, calmness, and insight.[9] The cosmos, too, is hierarchically ordered, from the lowest realms of *saṃsāra*, in which hell beings, animals, humans, and lower deities function mostly (but not entirely) from within the realm of sense experience, to higher realities of pure form, and thence to the highest formless echelons. The mind can "inhabit" these various realms either by perpetuating base, lustful, and violent thoughts, which are the abodes of hell beings and animals, or by journeying through the celestial realms in advanced stages of meditation (*jhānas*). In this sense, the mind is a microcosm of the cosmos. The shift of scale is a primarily a temporal one:

> the mind [of certain beings] might range through the possible levels of consciousness in a relatively short period – possibly in moments. A being, in contrast, exists at a particular level in the cosmos for rather longer – 84,000 aeons in the case of a being in the realm of "neither consciousness nor unconsciousness" – and to range through all the possible levels of being is going to take a very long time indeed.
>
> (Ibid., 195)

The same shift of scale, Gethin points out, is implicit in the model for change articulated by dependent origination: it provides a model for momentary conscious experience as well as the process of rebirth over large spans of time.

Mind and Matter

One of the aims of the Abhidhamma method is to teach the distinctions between mind and matter (Dhs-a.21), which, as we have seen, are often paired in a single formulation: *nāma-rūpa*. Buddhaghosa treats *nāma-rūpa* as a fundamental topic of wisdom in the *Visuddhimagga*, and focuses on it in several chapters that explain the refinement and fortification of wisdom. *Nāma-rūpa* is easily dismantled into its smaller components. *Nāma* refers to the four immaterial aggregates (feeling, perception, *saṅkhāra*, and consciousness) which, as we have seen, collectively comprise all mental processes;[10] it also is known "by the grouping of the five starting with contact," bringing us full circle back to our initial schema of mind (Vism.626). The four aggregates are all "*nāma*" (literally "name") because they are "name-making"; each names its experience spontaneously as it arises (Dhs-a.392). This means, I extrapolate, that when we feel, say, pain, it arises announcing itself as "pain" in our awareness, or when we perceive (*saññā*) blue there arises a conception labeled as "blue." To have these experiences is to *name* them at some level. They are also called *nāma* in the sense of "bending" (*namana*) and causing to bend (*nāmana*), "because they bend towards their objects and because they cause one another to bend towards the object," which is another way of stating their intentionality, their relatedness to objects (Dhs-a.392; Vibh-a.135). Buddhaghosa also says that *nāma*'s "characteristic is bending, its function is association, its manifestation is not being separated into components, and its proximate cause is consciousness (*viññāṇa*)" (Vbh-a.136). We can take it as the experience of "mentality" manifested as a whole, in effect, the four aggregates (or first five factors) operating as a functional unity rather than dismantled, for the sake of analysis, into its parts.

Rūpa, materiality or form, is familiar from other listings: it serves as one of the four divisions of reality (*rūpa*, *citta*, *cetasika*, and *nibbāna*), and it serves as one of the five aggregates. *Rūpa* "has the characteristic of being molested (*ruppana*), its function is dispersing, its manifestation is undeclared" (that is, it manifests variously depending on the particular material form), and its proximate cause is, as with *nāma*, consciousness (Vibh-a.136). It is "molested" – that is, changed or destroyed by other things such as cold (Vism.443). We can break it down into its four component elements (earth, water, fire, air) or into its 28 *dhammas* (the four elements and 24 additional classifications of materiality) (Vism.443–50).

Thus, while *nāma-rūpa* itself and both parts of it can be readily dissembled into smaller bits, the pair often functions in this coarser grouping of "mind–body" (more precisely "mentality–materiality"). Though much of Abhidhamma analysis is based on resolving wholes into parts, the categories of *nāma* and *nāma-rūpa* are retained as useful precisely in contexts in which further resolution is not helpful. In one of his chapters on the refinement of wisdom, Buddhaghosa says that there are several different kinds of understanding: one involves analysis of the specific characteristics of particular factors, and another involves "comprehension by groups," which is recognizing general characteristics shared among factors.[11] The value of the method of "comprehension by groups" is sometimes overlooked, but in this chapter Buddhaghosa argues forcefully for it, since there is a kind of understanding possible only by general inclusion rather than by reductive analysis. He applies it to *nāma-rūpa* with considerable creativity, examining all the ways that groupings shed light on it.

For our interest in the relationship of mind and body this is significant. The Abhidhamma method dismantles them very effectively to show their insubstantiality and separateness, but at the same time treats them as a psycho-physical complex that functions in certain respects as a unity. *Nāma-rūpa* is featured most prominently as a single link in dependent origination (though some of the components of *nāma* occur as distinct links themselves), where it is conditioned by consciousness[12] and is the condition for sensory experience. It is useful, indeed indispensible at times, to conceive of mind and body as a dynamic, mutually constitutive pair that has a certain causal agency. Several metaphors for their interrelatedness are helpful: like a drum and sound, they occur together but are not mixed up; like two sheaths of reeds holding each other up, they depend on one another to stand; and like a ship with its crew they can journey only together (Dhs-a.595–6). There is no person over and beyond them, but there is also no person without them in their complex interdependence.

The Buddha is remembered for being, among other epithets, the "Knower of Worlds" (*lokavidu*), because he is said to know "the world in all ways." There is the geographic world which can be known through travel, but this the Buddha does not describe. Rather, it is in "this fathom-long carcass with its conceptions and mind" that he makes the world known (Vism.204). Here again we encounter the logic of microcosm: the human entity is, in potential, the cosmic reality, and it is by exploring possibilities for human psychology that the vastness of the world can be known. Buddhaghosa goes on to say that Buddha is "Knower of Worlds" in that he knows the worlds of mental constructions (*saṅkhāras*), of beings (that is, all possible psychologies), and of cosmic space. The world of constructions can be known by groupings: "one world: all beings subsist by sustenance; two worlds: *nāma-rūpa*; three worlds: three kinds of feeling; four worlds: four kinds of sustenance; five worlds: the five aggregates; six worlds: the internal sense spheres," and so on. Each classification, each grouping, is a "world," a reality or mode of existence that the Buddha knows fully. The Buddha's facility with enumerated teachings and grouping phenomena, extended potentially endlessly, is the method by which one creates models of and for interpreting mind in an ultimate sense.

Notes

1 As Peter Skilling has observed, the widespread use of the term "Theravāda" is a modern development and does not serve us well if conceived of as a historical identity which premodern Buddhists in South and South-East Asia used to describe themselves, though, given its ubiquity in contemporary usage, it is a term difficult to do without (Skilling 2009). The intellectual tradition discussed in this chapter might more accurately be referred to as the Mahāvihāra lineage or the Pāli tradition.

2 All abbreviations follow the conventions of the Pali Text Society. Translations from Pāli texts are my own, unless otherwise specified, from the editions in the *Chaṭṭha Saṅgāyana*: Vipassana Research Institute, 1995.

3 While aware of historical scholarship that casts doubt on Buddhaghosa's involvement with some of the commentaries ascribed to him (the *Atthasālinī* in particular), I follow the Mahāvihāra authorities who attributed these texts to him because they saw (as I do) a systematic and conceptual coherence in the body of material he is said to have edited. Buddhaghosa refers here to the implied authorial voice of the *Atthasālinī*, the *Sammohavinodanī*, and the *Visuddhimagga*, the main commentaries explored in this chapter.

4 The best treatment of *bhavaṅga* is Gethin (1994). *Bhavaṅga* refers to a type of consciousness that is present between moments of conscious thought (in dreamless sleep, but also in between *cittas* in ordinary wakeful experience), is operative following death in linking to another rebirth, functions as a kind of steady consciousness that is a key aspect of one's distinctive nature, and, as here, posits a radiant and clear "mind" that underlies sullied conscious thought (AN.I.10; AN.I.60).

5 Nyanaponika (1998, 48). The *Sammohavinodanī* defines the *saṅkhāra* aggregate as consisting of sense contact, intention, and attention (Vibh-a.169).

6 We might also have begun our study of mind with a classification schema of 89 classes of consciousness, a post-canonical formulation of the *Dhammasaṅgaṇī*'s chapter on *cittas* (Dhs-a.6; Vism.XIV.81–110; Nārada and Bodhi 1993, 1–5). While useful, this schema involves multiplying a number of variables to increase the number of classes of *citta*, but the basic elements used in its systematization are presented by the *Dhammasaṅgaṇī*. See Gethin (1994, 16, 24–8).

7 Nyanaponika (1998, 53–5). He notes that these *jhānaṅgas* are here presented as rudimentary aspects of mind, but they can also be developed "upward" into the highly advanced meditative stages (*jhānas*).

8 Dhs-a.135–6. Nyanaponika offers a very helpful and sympathetic amplification on Buddhaghosa's treatment of factors according to function or application or degree of intensity among these factors (1998, 37–42, 88–92).

9 More often the 89 classes of conscious experience are mapped onto the 31 realms of *saṃsāric* existence, but the basic parallel can be shown in the lists of table 24.1. See Gethin (1997, in particular his table on p. 194; 1998, 121–3).

10 There are different parsings of this, however: in some places the texts say that *nāma* is three aggregates – *vedanā, saññā, saṅkhāra* (which includes *phassa, cetanā, and manasikāra*). The difficulty is consciousness: in the sense in which consciousness is a condition (*paccaya*) for *nāma-rūpa*, it should not be considered one of the aggregates in *nāma*, but, in the sense of it as a *cetasika*, it is assumed to be present (Vibh-a.169; Vism.558). In most analyses

nāma-rūpa comprises the five aggregates, with *rūpa* corresponding to the material aggregate and *nāma* to the immaterial aggregates (Dhs. §1314, which also includes "the uncompounded element" (*nibbāna*) in *nāma*; Dhs-a.392; Vism.452; Vibh-a.254, 265).

11 There are three kinds of worldly understanding: full understanding of what is known (analysis of specific characteristics of *dhammas*), full understanding as investigation (i.e., comprehension by groups), and full understanding as abandoning (the wisdom achieved by recognizing the insubstantiality and transience of all things) (Vism.606–7, ch. 20).

12 Its relationships with consciousness, as suggested above, are complex in part because *nāma-rūpa* includes consciousness in an important sense; yet, as we have seen elsewhere, sometimes it is still useful to conceive of *nāma-rūpa* as the "proximate cause" of consciousness and, conversely, with consciousness as the condition (*paccaya*) for *nāma-rūpa* in dependent origination. Here descriptions of various kinds of interrelationships in the *Paṭṭhāna* are helpful; theirs is a kind of "mutual arousing and consolidating" relation (see Ronkin 2005, 217).

References

Gethin, Rupert (1992). The Mātikās: Memorization, Mindfulness, and the List. In *In the Mirror of Memory*. Ed. J. Gyatso. Albany: State University of New York Press, 149–72.

Gethin, Rupert (1994). Bhavaṅga and Rebirth according to the Abhidhamma. In *The Buddhist Forum*. Vol. 3. Ed. T. Skorupski and U. Pagel. London: School of Oriental and African Studies, 11–35.

Gethin, Rupert (1997). Cosmology and Meditation: From the Aggañña-Sutta to the Mahāyāna. In *History of Religions* 36, 183–217.

Gethin, Rupert (1998). *The Foundations of Buddhism*. Oxford: Oxford University Press.

Nārada, Mahāthera, and Bodhi, Bhikkhu (trans.) (1993). *A Comprehensive Manual of Abhidhamma: The Abhidhammattha Sangaha of Ācariya Anuruddha*. Kandy, Sri Lanka: Buddhist Publication Society.

Nyanaponika, Thera (1998). *Abhidhamma Studies: Buddhist Explorations of Consciousness and Time*. Boston: Wisdom.

Ronkin, Noa (2005). *Early Buddhist Metaphysics*. New York: RoutledgeCurzon.

Skilling, Peter (2009). Theravāda in History. In *Pacific World* 11, 61–93.

25

Philosophy of Mind in Buddhism

RICHARD P. HAYES

Why is Philosophy of Mind an Issue in Buddhism?

The entire project of Buddhist theory and practice is aimed at bringing an end to the root causes of unpleasantness (*duḥkha*), which is usually portrayed as being tied up with the beginningless cycle of births into various kinds of body and the eventual deaths of those bodies. The kind of body with which a mentality becomes associated in any given rebirth is determined by the kinds of decisions habitually made with that mentality. For this doctrine of rebirth to make sense, it must be supposed that the mentality is separate from the physical body and can therefore be associated now with one physical body and now with another. Without some version of mind–body dualism, in other words, the majority of Buddhist doctrines that presuppose rebirth would be largely incoherent. Indeed, in those versions of Buddhism that identify misunderstanding (*avidyā*) or delusion (*moha*) as the principal cause of all forms of unsatisfactory experience, the main form that misunderstanding is said to take is a denial of the principle of karma – that is, a denial that wholesome actions pave the way for pleasant experiences and that unwholesome actions result in unpleasant experiences, and a denial that this karmic process reaches so far into the future that not all the actions of the present life can possibly be experienced in this life but will come to fruition in the next life and in lives beyond that. Not to accept that scenario is to be vitiated by wrong view (*mithyādṛṣṭi*) in the train of which comes all manner of unpleasantness. So it could be said that all success in the enterprise of Buddhism depends on right view (*samyagdṛṣṭi*), and that right view must include, among other things, a conviction of the truth of mind–body dualism. As we shall see, however, mind–body dualism is not the only view acceptable to Buddhists, for some Buddhists argued that the physical world is nothing but an idea within consciousness. So the views available to Buddhists are mind–body dualism and mind-only monism. What seems not to be available to

A Companion to Buddhist Philosophy, First Edition. Edited by Steven M. Emmanuel.

most Buddhists is physicalism – the view that what we call mind is nothing but matter described in a particular way.

Canonical Views on the Relation of Physical and Mental Events

In the *Brahmajālasutta*, the first *sutta* of the *Dīgha Nikāya* (see Walshe, 1987), there is a catalogue of 64 views that are considered defective in some way and that are contrasted with the truth proclaimed by the Buddha. Among those views, there is one saying that the faculties of vision, hearing, smelling, and so forth are all material objects and transitory, while awareness or consciousness is non-material and eternal; this view is one among several that have in common a conviction that some parts of the world are transitory while other parts are eternal. Another among the views that fail to measure up to the standard of Buddhist teachings is the conviction that the self is material in nature, is created through the union of mother and father, and continues from conception until the dissolution of the material body, and, upon the disintegration of the physical body, the self passes out of existence. This view is one of several known collectively as cessationism (*ucchedavāda*), the view that a self exists for a while, when the conditions of its existence are right, and then ceases to exist when those conditions no longer obtain. Given just the rejection of these two views, one can conclude that the canonical Buddhist position is that consciousness and mental events are not regarded as permanent and unchanging, but neither are they regarded as dependent upon the series of events that collectively may be called the physical body.

In the second *sutta* of the *Dīgha Nikāya*, the *Samaññaphalasutta*, six ethical stances are presented, each of them associated with an ascetic teacher whose views were reportedly being practiced by the Buddha's contemporaries, and again each one is set aside as somehow defective when measured against the standard of the Buddha's teachings. The views that are described in this text are (1) that there is no moral causality – that is, no connection between the actions that one does and the happiness or unhappiness that one subsequently experiences; (2) that there is no personal responsibility, since all that happens is determined by fate, as is all the happiness and unhappiness that one experiences; (3) that there is a moral causality, but it is purely material in nature and therefore ceases to operate when the physical body ceases to be alive, which means that there is no afterlife; (4) that the soul or self is eternal and unchanging and therefore has no interaction with the constantly changing material world and the emotional states associated therewith; (5) that karma is a material force that continues to produce consequences until one liberates oneself from the process by fasting, avoiding pleasures, living in solitude, and denying the normal physical cravings of the body; and (6) that there is no truth to the matter of moral claims and counterclaims, perhaps because no such claims can be either verified or falsified and so are nothing more than assertions. That all six views are found somehow substandard suggests that the canonical Buddhist position is that there are moral facts, that there is responsibility and accountability, that the causality that links actions with their consequences is taking place both in the material world and in non-material events, and that there is an interplay between the material and non-material sides of reality. Thinking about ethics in the proper way, in other words, entails thinking about material and non-material causality in the proper way. Thus ethics and the mind–body problem are best treated as so interconnected that trying to tease them apart would amount to a distorted way of thinking. But what exactly is the right way to think about all these matters? That question preoccupied Buddhists, at least in India, for as long as Buddhism was a vital force in the Indian subcontinent.

Nāgārjuna

The question of the causal relation between mental events and physical events is handled by the second-century philosopher Nāgārjuna by delving into the very idea of causality itself. In the first chapter of his *Mūlamadhyamikakārikā* ("Fundamental Verses on Centrism," hereafter abbreviated MMK), Nāgārjuna begins with the startling claim that nothing whatsoever arises from anything. There are only four logically possible relations between a putative cause and a putative effect: (a) an effect is identical with its cause, (b) an effect is different from its cause, (c) an effect is both identical and different from its cause, or (d) an effect arises from nothing at all. If one says an effect arises from itself, one is really denying that an effect has arisen and is saying instead that a thing (whether it is called cause or effect) remains unchanged. If one says an effect can be different from its cause, then one is saying that anything can arise from anything. A bowling ball is different from a laptop computer, so either could be the cause of the other if all that is required is that effect be different from cause. If one says that an effect is both identical to and different from its cause, one is speaking nonsense, since identity and difference are mutually exclusive. If one says a thing can arise without any cause at all, then one is denying causality altogether. There are several ways of interpreting just what Nāgārjuna's agenda was in analyzing causality this way. Suffice it to say here that throughout his work he calls into question the most basic categories of thinking: identity and difference, unity and plurality, priority and posteriority.

In the third chapter of MMK, Nāgārjuna turns to the specific topic of the relation between the physical sense faculties and the awareness of various kinds of sense data. He begins by saying that there are six types of sense faculties (the instruments by which seeing, hearing, smelling, tasting, touching, and mentating are done) and each faculty has a field of data upon which it operates. Then Nāgārjuna makes the puzzling claim that, since the faculty of vision cannot see itself, it cannot see anything other than itself. The commentators Bhāviveka and Candrakīrti explain that a flower that has the capacity to perfume other objects must first perfume itself, an explanation that is as puzzling as the claim being explained, since it is not clear why a very specific capacity that is found in flowers should be taken as a paradigm for all things with any kind of capacity. Nāgārjuna moves from his claim that the faculty of seeing sees nothing to the uncontroversial claim that no other sense faculty has the capacity to see. Therefore, there is no vision, and without vision there can be neither an agent of the act of seeing nor a direct object of the act of seeing. At the end of this chapter, Nāgārjuna says that everything that has been said about vision can be said *mutatis mutandis* about all the other faculties. Nāgārjuna's account of the significance of all these claims is that, according to the traditional doctrine of dependent origination, consciousness gives rise to evaluative feelings (approval, disapproval, and neutrality), and these feelings give rise to the desire to acquire what is approved or to avoid what is disapproved or to disregard what is evaluated neutrally. Desire in turn evolves into clinging, which leads to having the desires necessary for continued existence, and continued existence leads to unsatisfactory experiences. If there is no consciousness, however, the disaster of unsatisfactory experiences can be averted.

As was said above, there are various accounts of what Nāgārjuna was trying to achieve by presenting these arguments, such as they are. What Nāgārjuna himself says is that he admires the Buddha for having found a way to bring an end to conceptual prolixity (*prapañca*) and opinions (*dṛṣṭi*). If these reasons for admiring the Buddha are taken seriously, then the conviction on which Nāgārjuna is operating could be that thinking about exactly how everything works gets in the way of anything actually working. He could be convinced that people, rather than taking the doctor's orders and reducing their frustration-producing desires, become engrossed in pointless speculation and theorizing. If Nāgārjuna's agenda is to produce deliberately sophomoric argumentation as a way of making the satirical point that all theorizing really amounts to nothing much but specious argumentation, then his contribution to the discussion of whether mental events cause physical events or vice versa might be to suggest that we realize the futility of such discussions and get on to more important tasks. According to all his major commentators, the most important task is the cultivation of *bodhicitta*, the resolve to become awakened for the sake of relieving the suffering of all sentient beings. About that task, the central task of the bodhisattva, more will be said below.

Vasubandhu

Writing in the fourth or fifth century, Vasubandhu articulated the positions of at least three major schools of Buddhism in his various writings. In his *Abhidharmakośam* (see Vasubandhu 1988), both in the verses and in his prose commentary to the verses, Vasubandhu presents the doctrines of two canonical schools that wrestled with questions of the nature of karma and the relation of mental events and material events. The Vaibhāṣika school, whose position is articulated in the verses of the *Abhidharmakośam*, held the view that all karma is initiated in the non-material aggregate of mental formations (*saṃskāra*) as intentions. This initial mental action may then be followed by a bodily or verbal action that is perceptible and thus belongs to the material world. Immediately following this material manifestation of an intention, there is an unmanifested trace of the action that also belongs to the material aggregate (*rūpaskandha*). All things being momentary, this unmanifested material trace begins a series of momentary unmanifested material traces that continues until the original karma ripens as a palpable pleasant or unpleasant result. So we find in this account of karma the notion that non-physical events – intentions – can create a particular kind of matter. Moreover, it is claimed in this text that the mental events can influence the sense faculties and therefore can help determine the sorts of phenomena the physical sense faculties can register.

This notion that non-material intentions shape the material body of an individual have a cosmological counterpart in the claim, made at the beginning of the fourth chapter of the *Abhidharmakośam*, that all the physical worlds are the result of the ripening of the karma of countless sentient beings. The idea seems to be that the physical worlds take the form they take so as to provide the kinds of experiences that the sentient beings living in them are qualified by their mentalities to have. While the totality of the karma of countless beings shapes the various world-systems, the individual karma of a sentient being determines which of the various world-systems he will be reborn into after dying. In turn, the experiences that are delivered up to a sentient being in a particular world-system shape the mentality of the sentient being. Given that this cycle of mental events shaping material events and material events shaping mental events has no beginning, it is not strictly speaking possible to determine whether mental events are the cause of material events or vice versa. Each kind of event causes the other kind through a complex interaction that has no beginning.

In works that are usually assumed to have been written later than the *Abhidharmakośam*, Vasubandhu follows a line of argumentation that strongly gives primacy to mental events as the predominant cause in all experiences. In a text variously called *Viṃsikā* or *Viṃśatikākārikā* ("Set of 20 Verses", see Vasubandhu 1984), for example, Vasubandhu argues that the traditional hell realms cannot physically exist as they are described in Buddhist texts. The hell realms are described as places of unbearable unpleasantness. They are also described as places where hell guards lead people around to various places of torment and administer punishments to them. If, says Vasubandhu, the environments in the hell realms were truly unbearably hot or unbearably cold as they are said to be, then the guardians would be unable to perform their appointed tasks. This suggests that at least the guardians, if not the hell realms themselves, do not physically exist but instead are the projections of a mentality that is so depraved as to be capable of having none but the worst kinds of experience. Vasubandhu gives other examples of the mind creating experiences that are experienced by it alone rather than being shared by other experiencers; the phenomena of dreams and hallucinations and strong fantasies attest to there being experiences that are almost surely caused by the experiencing mind itself, rather than by an external physical world that enters awareness through the physical bodily sense faculties. This claim is consistent with the claim in the *Abhidharmakośam* that the physical world is the product of the collective ripening of the karma of countless sentient beings.

Dharmakīrti

According to biographical texts written many centuries after the time of the lives described in them, Vasubandhu had a disciple named Dignāga, who began a school of thought that placed an emphasis on personal experience and reasoning as our most reliable guides to knowing the true nature of things. Unlike previous Buddhist thinkers, members of this school of thought rarely quoted the words of the Buddha and tended not to try to offer systematic accounts of all the realms described in Buddhist scriptures. Arguably the most influential member of this new approach was Dharmakīrti, usually said to be the disciple of Dignāga. Dharmakīrti probably lived at the beginning of the seventh century CE and is remembered for writing several works on the art of clear thinking and communicating one's thoughts convincingly to others. By far his most ambitious work was entitled *Pramāṇavārttikam* ("Comments on Sources of Knowledge"), which takes as its point of departure several ideas in Dignāga's *Pramāṇasamuccaya* ("Collected Writings on Sources of Knowledge"). Whereas Dignāga had limited himself to talking about direct sensory experience and reasoning as two sources of knowledge, Dharmakīrti was concerned to show that the corpus of teachings of the Buddha, while not being a source of knowledge that is different in kind from other sources of knowledge, is nevertheless a source of knowledge in that it is a species of reasoning. His claim, in brief, is that, if one were to collect direct experiences carefully and mindfully, and if one were to apply properly restrained reasoning in those matters beyond the range of one's collected experiences, then one would arrive at exactly the same conclusions that the Buddha had arrived at. In the meantime, said Dharmakīrti, it is not unreasonable to accept the teachings of the Buddha, at least provisionally, until one has experienced for oneself the realities that the Buddha had experienced. While one should not believe anything solely on the grounds that the Buddha had taught it, one would be well advised to regard the teachings of the Buddha as trustworthy, since by placing confidence in them one is more likely to arrive at the goal of eradicating the root causes of human discontent.

A question that naturally arises for Dharmakīrti is why one should place any more confidence in the teachings of the Buddha than those of any other teacher who claims to have identified the root causes of unhappiness and to have found a way of eliminating them. After all, the world is filled with people who offer promises of salvation to those who will but place trust in them, and many such people turn out to be charlatans and cheats. Why, then, trust the Buddha? Once this question arises, Dharmakīrti expends considerable energy arguing that the Buddha is not like others who promise salvation, for he has an entirely different character from ordinary men and women. The Buddha, Dharmakīrti points out, has spent countless eons purifying his mentality and cultivating compassion. The purification of his mentality has resulted in the Buddha's having eliminated prejudices and fantasies of the sort that distort perception, and so he sees things just as they are, without the warping influences of wishful thinking. The cultivation of compassion has resulted in a mentality that has no other motivation than to remove the root causes of suffering in all beings. In short, the Buddha knows what he is talking about, and he has no vested interests that would tempt him into misleading others for his own personal gain. One can trust such a man and take him at his word.

Dharmakīrti's account of what makes the Buddha's teaching reliable raises a further question, since his claim of what made the Buddha special was that he cultivated virtues over the course of countless lifetimes. This claim may be plausible to one who believes that consciousness and personality can survive the death of the physical body and somehow become associated with another physical body. Not everyone, however, holds that belief. In Dharmakīrti's time (as in the twenty-first century) there were physicalists who held the view that consciousness and all other aspects of mentality are entirely dependent on the physical body. When matter becomes organized to a sufficient degree of complexity, they claimed, something that we can call consciousness or mind arises, but, when its nature is properly understood, one sees that what we call mind is really nothing but complex material under a conveniently simplified description. If mind is an emergent property of highly structured matter, it cannot survive when matter loses the structure necessary to support it. When the physical body dies, it loses the consciousness-supporting structures, said the physicalists. There can be no continuity of mind and mentality from one living body to another, so it is impossible that the Buddha continued to cultivate compassion over the course of uncountable lifetimes.

Dharmakīrti also has his physicalist opponent raise the challenge of the ancient counterpart to biochemistry. According to the principles of *āyurveda*, a person's emotions and moods are influenced by humors in the body. A person with an abundance of bile, for example, is more prone to anger than a person with an abundance of phlegm, and people with an abundance of wind are more likely to be distracted. Maintaining a balanced temperament, said the physicalists, is aided by keeping the humors in a state of balance, and this in turn is achieved by a combination of diet and exercise. These principles are well established and widely followed, says Dharmakīrti's materialist opponent, and it would make little sense for people to be careful about their diet and the general health of their physical bodies if physical health did not promote a sense of psychological well-being, and, if physical chemistry does indeed influence psychology, then it is difficult to deny that physical events are the cause of mental events and not vice versa.

Once the question arises as to whether physical events cause mental events or vice versa, Dharmakīrti acknowledges that it is impossible to know for certain which causes which. One can know that one thing, *x*, is the cause of another thing, *y*, only if one has observed that *y* arises when *x* is present and one has never observed *y* in the absence of *x*. Given that both physical events and mental events have always been present, everyone has observed the two kinds of event together, and no one has ever observed one in the absence of the other. Therefore, one could just as reasonably conclude that mental events cause physical events as that physical events cause mental events. That being so, the physicalist cannot prove that his theory that mind arises from highly organized matter is true. Nor can the Buddhist prove that mental events are causally independent of physical events. As for the argument from the physical humors, says Dharmakīrti, it may be granted that the humors play a role in the kinds of moods and emotions that a person experiences, but the humors themselves could arise as a result of karma and thus be an example of a physical event being caused by a mental event. It could be, for example, that a person who chooses to act on anger produces an abundance of bile, which in turn conduces to further anger. All we know for sure is that there is a correlation between an abundance of bile in the physical body and a tendency to anger in the mentality. Given that people who do certain types of meditative exercises can change the extent to which they are prone to anger, it is reasonable to conclude that one mental event (meditation) is causing another (patience) and that the physical event (achieving a balance of the humors) is also a consequence of the mental event.

In his dialogue with the physicalist, Dharmakīrti at best shows that the physicalist cannot prove his hypothesis, but neither can the Buddhist prove his hypothesis. In other parts of his *Pramāṇvārttikam*, Dharmakīrti follows a line of thinking that Vasubandhu and Dignāga had both pursued. The principal strategy is to argue that the physical world turns out to be unintelligible. Dignāga had argued that the principal theory of the nature of the physical world is that it is made up of particles. If that is so, then there must be an ultimately small particle that is a building block of all larger physical masses. Any particle that has any dimension at all, however, has sides and is therefore composed of geographical parts. Anything that is composed of parts is not ultimately small. So the ultimately small particle must have no dimension whatsoever. Something that has no dimension occupies zero space, and, no matter how many particles of zero dimension one puts together, the resultant mass will have zero dimension. The conclusion of this line of reasoning is that the material world is really just an idea – a bad idea at that, given that it cannot possibly have a counterpart in anything outside the realm of ideas.

Like other philosophers who can be read as idealists, Dharmakīrti was liable to be accused of being a solipsist. If the material world is but an idea in the mind, then why would one not, in addition, hold that other minds are also nothing but ideas in one's own mind? Dharmakīrti addresses this question in a separate work entitled *Saṃtānāntarasiddhi* ("Establishing Other Sequences [of mental events than one's own]"). In this work he makes the remarkable claim that there is no need to posit the existence of physical bodies in space, for two mentalities could communicate with each other directly, each projecting the image of a physical body into the other's stream of consciousness. Whether he is pitching his discussion from the perspective of a mind–body dualist or a mind-only monist, Dharmakīrti is consistent in his insistence that the mental events are not the product of the solely physical events. Ontologically speaking, mind is for Dharmakīrti independent of matter, and matter is either dependent on mind or a figment of imagination.

Śāntideva

It was mentioned above that the principal commentators on Nāgārjuna's work placed Madhyamaka philosophy within the context of the career of the bodhisattva – that is, a person who has undertaken to cultivate and then act upon the resolve to alleviate the suffering of all sentient beings. Given that the most effective way to alleviate the suffering of all beings is to become awakened, the bodhisattva's resolve is to become awakened in order to lead others to awakening. Śāntideva's *Bodhicaryāvatāra* ("Introduction to the Practice of Awakening," hereafter BCA; see Śāntideva 1996) is written as a sort of a manual for those undertaking the bodhisattva's resolve. As such, the text devotes chapters to each of the virtues that a bodhisattva is encouraged to cultivate, one of those virtues being patience (*kṣanti*).

Patience is the antidote to anger, and one moment of anger, says Śāntideva, has the power to destroy the benefits of thousands of eons of good practice. Convinced that anger is to be avoided at all costs, Śāntideva offers numerous strategies for avoiding anger when the irritation of unpleasant feelings arises. In the context of presenting ways in which one might talk oneself out of letting an incipient angry impulse become the motivation of a destructive physical action or a verbal comment designed to make another feel diminished, Śāntideva mentions the humors (which were discussed above in the section on Dharmakīrti). He makes the observation at BCA.6.22 that he has no anger towards bile and the other biological humors, so why should he feel anger towards conscious beings whose anger is caused by their bile? A modern counterpart to this line of thinking would be that it makes no sense to feel angry towards biochemistry, since it simply is what it is and does not make conscious decisions to be as it is. That being the case, it also makes no sense to feel angry towards the obnoxious behavior of a person whose emotional states are the product of a biochemistry over which he has no control. To talk oneself out of anger by using this line of thinking, one would have to believe (if only a for a few moments) that conscious beings have no control over their emotions and the behavior motivated by them, since they are caused by underlying physical states. In other words, one would have to subscribe, if not to physicalism, at least to a view in which the physical body drives the mind and not vice versa. On the other hand, to take seriously the advice to make an effort to talk oneself out of anger in the first place requires that one believe (if only for a few moments) that mental states (decisions to think in a particular way) give rise to other mental states (patience). Perhaps what is required is to believe in the primacy of mind long enough to make the decision to talk oneself out of anger and then quickly change to a belief that sentient beings are hapless victims of indomitable facts of physiology. The implications of all this for a Buddhist philosophy of mind are unclear.

Another of the virtues that a bodhisattva is encouraged to cultivate is wisdom, a correct understanding of how things are. At the outset of his discussion on the perfection of wisdom, Śāntideva makes the claim at BCA.9.2 that there are two truths, a concealing truth (*saṃvṛtisatya*) and a truth connected to the highest goal (*paramārthasatya*). Reality, he goes on to say, is not within the intellect's range; the intellect is that which conceals. In the next verse, Śāntideva says that there are two kinds of people, *yogīs* and ordinary people. The truths accepted by ordinary people are overturned by the *yogīs*. Ordinary people observe beings and deem them to be real rather than illusory. Ordinary people observe the objects apprehended by the senses and accept them at face value, and yet things apprehended by the senses are not established through reliable sources of knowledge. Up to this point, it sounds as though Śāntideva might be heading in the direction of Dharmakīrti in calling into question the reality of the physical world but affirming the reality of consciousness – that is, denying body while affirming mind. For most of the rest of the chapter on wisdom, however, Śāntideva argues against the affirmation of mind at the expense of the physical world, insisting that they are *both* incapable, in the final analysis, of being established. And so it appears that one can say of Śāntideva what was said above of Nāgārjuna, namely, that he was wary of the entire enterprise of what we call philosophy of mind, seeing it as an intellectual distraction from the more pressing task of alleviating the world's suffering.

Conclusion

Over the course of the first fifteen centuries of Buddhist philosophy one finds several positions taken on the relation of mental events to physical events. In some quarters one finds a robust mind–body dualism in which the physical world and consciousness are ontologically independent of one another but interactive; in other quarters one finds a view that consciousness is the ultimate source of the physical world; in other quarters one finds a tendency to reject the reality of the physical world as anything other than a figment of imagination; and in yet other quarters one finds an anti-intellectual tendency to regard this very problem as a distraction from more important tasks.

References

Śāntideva (1996). *Bodhicaryāvatāra*. Trans. Kate Crosby and Andrew Skilton. Oxford and New York: Oxford University Press.

Vasubandhu (1984). *Seven Works of Vasubandhu: The Buddhist Psychological Doctor*. Trans. Stefan Anacker. Vol. 4. Religions of Asia Series. Delhi: Motilal Banarsidass.

Vasubandhu (1988). *Abhidharmakośabhāṣyam*. Trans. Leo M. Pruden from La Vallée Poussin's 1923 French translation. Vol. 1. Berkeley, CA: Asian Humanities Press.

Walshe, Maurice (1987). *Thus Have I Heard: The Long Discourses of the Buddha: Dīgha Nikāya*. London: Wisdom.

26

Cognition, Phenomenal Character, and Intentionality in Tibetan Buddhism

JONATHAN STOLTZ

On a non-philosophical, naïve understanding of the mind, when I look out my window at a tree, I take myself to have a direct experience of the tree itself. (And, even after turning away from the window, the naïve view tells me that I can still think about that tree. I can still direct my mind towards the very same tree that I earlier perceived with my eyes.) The history of philosophy, both East and West, is full of arguments claiming that this naïve understanding of the mind's acquaintance with external objects is deeply mistaken. In the Indian epistemological tradition, the Buddhist theory of perception associated with Dignāga and Dharmakīrti is seen as rejecting the direct realist understanding of perception found in the Nyāya school of Indian philosophy.[1]

Not all Buddhist epistemologists follow Dignāga and Dharmakīrti's lead in rejecting direct realism. In the eleventh and twelfth centuries a group of Tibetan Buddhists residing principally at Sangpu Monastery in central Tibet articulated an epistemological program that endorses a direct realist understanding of perception. This is so despite the fact that these Tibetans take themselves to be clarifying and refining the views of Dignāga and Dharmakīrti. The thinkers associated with this philosophical movement at Sangpu Monastery are generally classified as members of the Kadam school of Tibetan Buddhism. Thus, I shall speak of these thinkers as "Kadam Tibetans." The two most significant figures writing on epistemology within the Kadam school – thinkers whose views impacted much of the future trajectory of Buddhist philosophy in Tibet – were Ngog Loden Sherab (1059–1109) and Chaba Chokyi Senge (1109–1169). These philosophers, and Chaba in particular, produced epistemological treatises that formed the polemical basis for many future philosophical works in Tibet and helped usher into that land profound developments within the fields of epistemology and the philosophy of mind (among others).

In this chapter I will elucidate just one small sliver of these developments within the philosophy of mind. Among many other contributions, Chaba articulates a complex typology of cognition that serves as the foundation for many subsequent Tibetan

A Companion to Buddhist Philosophy, First Edition. Edited by Steven M. Emmanuel.

discussions of the mind and knowledge. This essay has the dual aim of (a) clarifying Chaba's account of cognition and its objects and (b) examining some of the more profound philosophical consequences that flow from this Kadam Tibetan understanding of cognition. The first half of the chapter elucidates the Kadam understanding of the phenomenology of cognition. In that section I will argue that Chaba and his followers should be seen as endorsing a *disjunctive theory of perception*. The second half takes up the issue of intentionality and how cognition engages objects that are not directly present to it. In that section I will show that Chaba's categorization of cognitive states forces him to adopt a strong form of *cognitive externalism*.

The Phenomenal Character of Cognition

Within the Indian and Tibetan epistemological traditions it is widely accepted that, for something to count as a cognition at all, it must be a cognition *of* something. For every cognition there must be a cognitive object. But there are several different ways in which philosophers can explicate the thesis that it is constitutive of cognition that it be of something. In this section, I will look at one way of understanding this thesis by focusing on the so-called phenomenal character of cognition.

For each cognitive episode, there is a certain feel or way things seem. Kadam Tibetans grapple with the phenomenal character of cognition not by emphasizing *how* things seem, but by identifying *what* appears to the mind. The objects that appear directly to the mind are called *phenomenal objects* (*gzung yul*).[2] Chaba and his followers claim that there are three different kinds of phenomenal objects: (1) real particulars, (2) concepts, and (3) hallucinations/illusions.[3] This threefold typology is held to be exhaustive of the different kinds of entities that can appear in cognition.

Chaba and his Kadam followers maintain that in cases of perception we experience real particulars.[4] That is, what appears to the mind is the particular object itself. Moreover, Chaba contends that these perceived objects appear directly, without sense-impressions or representations as intermediaries (Phywa pa 2006, 8a.7). In ordinary circumstances, these particular entities will be external objects, but his account allows for mental items as objects of perceptual experience as well. The key point is that, in cases where someone is having a genuine perceptual episode, what appears to the person's mind is held to be a real particular. Concepts, by contrast, are the phenomenal objects that are experienced in any and all conceptual mental episodes – that is, in all episodes of thought (*rtog pa*). Chaba maintains that concepts are unreal and functionally impotent. (The concept of water, for example, cannot quench your thirst.) Concepts differ from real particulars inasmuch as the latter entities are said to be determinate with respect to time and location and have functional powers, whereas concepts are indeterminate and functionally impotent.

The third type of phenomenal object is that associated with non-conceptual cognitions that are erroneous. These entities appear as though they are real particulars but are not real objects at all. Importantly, this category includes both what contemporary analytic philosophers call *hallucinations* – cases in which a phenomenal object appears despite there being no real, external object that is the cause for it – and *illusions* – cases where there *is* a real object, but where the phenomenal entity that appears to the mind

Table 26.1 Phenomenal objects of cognition

Cognitive episode (*shes pa*)	Phenomenal object (*gzung yul*)
Conceptual thought (*rtog pa*)	Concept (*don spyi*)
Non-conceptual, non-erroneous cognition (*rtog med ma 'khrul ba'i shes pa*)	Real particular (*don rang gi mtshan nyid*)
Non-conceptual, erroneous cognition (*rtog med 'khrul ba'i shes pa*)	Hallucination/Illusion (*med pa gsal ba*)

does not match up with reality. A common example of a hallucination given in the Buddhist epistemological tradition is that of a person having a vivid dream of something. The dreamt object does not exist in reality, but the mind has nevertheless given rise to a certain experience. Illusions, by contrast, are tied to objects in the real world. A frequently used example of an illusion in the Buddhist tradition is that of a white conch shell appearing yellow (to a person with jaundice). There is a real object, a real conch shell, but the way it appears to the person does not match up with reality. Another frequently employed example is that of stationary trees appearing to be moving (to a person travelling on a boat). There really are trees, but those trees are misperceived as though they are moving.

It is very important keep in mind that Kadam Tibetan philosophers characterize both hallucinations and illusions as being the same kind of phenomenal object. The most common Tibetan names for this class of phenomenal objects[5] are more naturally translated with the term "hallucination," but in practice the majority of the examples that Tibetans give of these phenomenal objects are in fact instances of illusion. I will explain more fully below why it can be valuable to distinguish hallucinations from illusions.

Like concepts, hallucinations/illusions are held to be functionally impotent, but, unlike concepts, hallucinations/illusions are determinate with respect to time and location in a way that concepts are not. Hallucinations/illusions are said, by definition, to differ from real particulars insofar as real things possess functional powers, whereas hallucinations/illusions are functionally impotent. (A hallucination of a fire cannot burn you.)

Having briefly introduced these three types of phenomenal objects, it is now useful to make a couple of points about the relations between these objects and the mental episodes wherein these phenomena manifest. Concepts are the phenomenal objects encountered in conceptual thought. As for non-conceptual cognition, if it is non-erroneous, the cognition is an instance of perception and the phenomenal object is a real particular. If the non-conceptual cognition is erroneous, then its phenomenal object is a hallucination/illusion (see table 26.1). The first important point to make is that the kind of cognitive episode a person has depends on the kind of object that appears to that person. Put another way, it is the phenomenal objects that are taken as *primitive*, and the cognitive episodes as *derivative*. Kadam Tibetans maintain that the reason for delineating three types of cognitions is precisely because there are (antecedently) these three types of phenomenal objects.[6]

Disjunctivism

The point made above may not seem very important, but it actually has quite dramatic consequences for Kadam Tibetan theories of cognition and mental content. Specifically, Chaba and his followers are committed to a form of *experiential* and *phenomenal disjunctivism*.[7] To understand fully what experiential and phenomenal disjunctivism are, I will first describe some of the basic consequences of this Tibetan account as they relate to the phenomenology of experience, and then show how different their account is from certain, more "traditional" accounts of perception.

It is surely possible, at least in principle if not in practice, that a genuine case of perceiving an external object could be phenomenally indistinguishable from a vivid hallucination or illusion. So, for example, a person's perception of a tree might be phenomenally indistinguishable from the experience that person has as of a tree in the midst of a hallucination. Matters could appear the same in these two different situations. Yet, even though phenomenally indistinguishable, on the Kadam Tibetan account, what appears to the mind is *different* in the two situations. What is experienced in instances of perception is something completely different from what is experienced when hallucinating, even though the experiences appear to be the same. Moreover, because the phenomenal objects are different in kind – one is a real particular and one is a hallucination – the kind of mental episodes the person is having in these two cases are different as well. The experiences are introspectively indistinguishable, but what kind of experience the person is really having is different in the two cases.

This example brings into focus the two related forms of disjunctivism to which these Tibetan epistemologists find themselves committed. *Phenomenal disjunctivism* is the view that the phenomenal character of an experience does not decisively determine the object that is experienced. Because a genuine perception of a tree and a hallucination as of a tree can be phenomenally indistinguishable, according to the disjunctivist, all a person knows is that she is experiencing *either* a real tree *or* a hallucination of a tree (hence, the term "disjunctivism"). The key point is that, in terms of the phenomenology of experience, *there is no single object that is common to perceptual and hallucinatory experiences*. Kadam Tibetan epistemologists implicitly endorse phenomenal disjunctivism insofar as they accept that the objects experienced in perception and hallucination could be indistinguishable and yet two completely different kinds of phenomenal objects.

Experiential disjunctivism maintains a roughly analogous thesis about the experiences (cognitive episodes) that a person has. According to experiential disjunctivism, the kind of experience a person is having is not determined by the phenomenal character of their experience, for the phenomenal character is consistent with the mental episode being one *either* of perception *or* of hallucination. Using the previous example of a person having an experience as of a tree, the (experiential) disjunctivist would maintain that the person perceiving a real tree is having a radically different experience – i.e., is having a completely different cognitive event – than what she would have if hallucinating. As can be seen from the above description, just as these Kadam epistemologists are committed to phenomenal disjunctivism, they are also committed to experiential disjunctivism.

Not a Sense-Datum Theory

It needs to be appreciated that this commitment to disjunctivism puts Chaba and his followers at odds with most traditional Western accounts of perception. To see more clearly how different the disjunctivist account is, let us put it in contrast with both (1) the sense-datum theory of perception that was propounded by both modern British empiricists and twentieth-century logical empiricists and (2) the intentionalist theory of perception that has grown in popularity since the second half of the twentieth century. On the sense-datum theory, in granting that a person's perception of a tree may be phenomenally indistinguishable from a hallucination of a tree, it is maintained that we should account for this indistinguishability by positing the existence of a sense-datum (or set of sense-data) that is shared in common between the two experiences. The reason why a genuine perception of a real tree may be indistinguishable from a hallucination is because we only ever experience the world *indirectly*, by way of sense-data, and the sense-data experienced in cases of perception can be the same as the sense-data encountered in certain hallucinations and illusions. More simply, the idea is that we can explain the sameness of phenomenal character found in perception and hallucination by claiming that the objects (the sense-data) experienced in both cases are the same. In addition, because the sense-data experienced are the same in cases of perception and hallucination, it is also open to the sense-datum theorist to uphold the view that a person perceiving a real tree is *in the very same state of mind* as a person who is merely experiencing a hallucination of a tree.

The account endorsed by Chaba is quite different from this. Whereas the sense-datum theory holds that there is a single object common to both perception and hallucination, Chaba and other Kadam Tibetans reject this view and instead maintain that perception and hallucination share no object in common. Nor are the mental episodes the same. Because two different kinds of objects are experienced, these Tibetan philosophers can and do hold the view that the cognitive episodes are fundamentally different as well.

Not an Intentionalist Theory

In contrast to the sense-datum theory, the intentionalist theory of perception claims that we can account for the similarities between perception and hallucination without positing the existence of an intermediary object (such as a sense-datum) that is directly experienced in both cases. Intentionalism maintains that in perception (but not in hallucinations) we do *directly* encounter real (external) objects themselves. Yet, because there can be certain cases in which perception and hallucination would have the same phenomenal character, the intentionalist contends that what perception and hallucination share is *a common intentional element*. In both cases (when a person perceives a tree and when a person has a hallucination as of a tree) the *representational content* – the way reality is represented – is held to be the same. The world can appear the same way when perceiving a tree as it does when hallucinating a tree, and this commonality is explained by proposing that the contents of the two experiences are the same. In addition, because both perception and hallucination can have the same content, and the mental episode is essentially determined by its content, the intentionalist is committed to the view that the person could have the same kind of mental event when perceiving a tree as she has when hallucinating a tree.

This intentionalist account comes closer to the Kadam Tibetan presentation, inasmuch as it grants that persons perceive objects directly and not by means of intermediary entities such as sense-data. But there are several critical differences. As explained above, on Chaba's account, in order for a given cognitive episode to be a perception at all, it is *essential* that the cognition bear a relation to the object perceived. But this is not the case on the intentionalist account of perception, for on that account it is the representational contents and not real objects in the world that are essential to experiences. Thus, when a perception and a hallucination have the same phenomenal characters, intentionalists maintain that the two mental events are of the same kind, even though in the perception (but not in the hallucination) there is a real object. In short, on the intentionalist theory of perception, standing in a relation to a real object is *not essential* to the kind of experience a person is having (it is the representational content that is held to be essential), whereas, on the Kadam Tibetan account of perception, standing in a relation to a real object *is* essential to that experience.[8]

Disjunctivism Again

It should be clear from the preceding that the account put forward by Chaba and his followers is a version of disjunctivism – and, in fact, a version of disjunctivism that is meant to complement a direct realist account of perception. Disjunctivism is not without its problems, however. One of the more commonly cited difficulties with the theory revolves around the status of illusion.[9] Recall that illusions differ from hallucinations insofar as in illusions (but not in hallucinations) there is a real, external object that is responsible for the phenomenal character of the experience. There is disagreement among disjunctivists about the status of illusions. Some disjunctivists claim that illusions are similar or identical in kind to perception, whereas others maintain that illusions are alike in kind with hallucinations. (As was noted at the outset, Chaba and his followers lump illusions together with hallucinations, and put them in contrast to perception.) This disagreement about illusions stems from the fact that, in an illusion, a person is *perceiving* a real object *inaccurately*. Thus, some philosophers maintain that illusion should be bundled together with perceptual knowledge, for both are cases of (in some sense) perceiving a real thing. Other philosophers claim that illusion should be bundled together with hallucination, as both are cases in which the cognitive event is inaccurate.

I raise this disagreement because, if Kadam Tibetan epistemologists do adopt a form of disjunctivism, we should expect them to address the peculiar status of illusion. By the same token, if these Tibetan philosophers do debate the classificatory status of illusions, that would lend additional credence in support of the view that these thinkers do, in fact, propound a version of disjunctivism.

Early Kadam Tibetan epistemologists do grapple with the problem of illusion, and there is recognition of the problem of determining whether or not occurrences of illusion are to be classified as instances of perception. Consider a hypothetical case of a person (with jaundice) experiencing a white conch shell as being yellow. On the one hand, we might anticipate a temptation on the part of Kadam thinkers to say that this experience is genuinely perceptual – and constitutes knowledge – because, as direct realists, what is experienced is *a real conch shell*. On the other hand, because the experience is *erroneous* – a white shell is experienced as yellow – there is also a temptation to maintain that the cognitive episode is quite unlike one of perception. Now, as we have seen above, Chaba and other Kadam Tibetans classify illusions such as these together with hallucinations, and as fundamentally different from perceptions.

This is a somewhat delicate position to defend, however, for how, as direct realists, can it be denied that a real conch shell is perceived? Naturally, the person cannot be said to perceive a *yellow* conch shell, for her cognition is erroneous with regard to the shell's color. But can't it be said that the person still perceives a right-turning conch shell, since, with respect to the shape, the cognition is non-erroneous? Kadam Tibetans contend that the answer is "No." Because the person's visual experience does not match up with the actual state of affairs, it cannot meet the conditions required for perception. These Tibetans also acknowledge that their position here runs counter to that held by "some students" of the Indian Buddhist epistemologist Dignāga, who held that such a person can have partial knowledge (via perception) of the shape of the conch shell (Rngog 2006, 10a.3–4; Klong chen 2000, 119).[10]

The late eleventh-century Kadam figure Loden Sherab argues that these students of Dignāga are only partially incorrect, however. Because the experience of a white conch shell as yellow is erroneous, one cannot be said *visually* to perceive the conch shell, even when the experience of the shell's shape is non-erroneous. But, Loden Sherab maintains, the conch shell can still be validly perceived via other sense faculties, such as touch. As he puts the point, "Although there is no knowledge with respect to a [visual] sense object wherein a white conch shell appears yellow, a tactile sensation, etc., simultaneous to that [visual experience] is itself [an instance of perceptual] knowledge" (Rngog 2006, 10b.3–5). That said, subsequent Tibetans, even epistemologists within his own Kadam tradition, disagree with Loden Sherab's position on this issue (see, for example, Klong chen 2000, 119–20, and Go rams 1998, 239–40). They contend that the fact that illusory experiences are erroneous automatically rules out their objects being perceptually knowable, and thus puts those experiences in the same general category as instances of hallucination.

Without going further into the details of these debates, the point is that illusions generate a special problem for disjunctivism. And, as A. D. Smith notes, "The reason why illusion poses a problem for such a view is that illusions can be, indeed almost always are, partial" (2010, 388). This is precisely the problem that Kadam Tibetans must deal with in the conch shell case. Now, this question of what to say about a white shell appearing yellow to a person with jaundice has historical precedent in the Indian tradition (see Dreyfus 1997, 348–50), but the issue is all the more pressing once one adopts a disjunctivist understanding of experience as these Kadam Tibetans do.

Epistemically Engaged Objects and Intentionality

There is more to cognition than its phenomenology, however. Tibetan philosophers realize this, and also realize that a fully adequate theory of knowledge cannot be captured with just the three kinds of phenomenal entities and three types of cognitive episodes that are described in the first half of this chapter. A more robust typology of cognitive episodes is needed to account for our knowledge of reality, which will in turn require more than just the phenomenology of experience. The key move made by Kadam Tibetan philosophers is to realize that the mind can be related to objects in ways other than just by having objects appear to it. The mind can play an active role by *aiming towards* or *desiring* real objects, even though those objects do not appear to the mind.[11]

In saying that the mind aims at or is directed towards objects, a clear appeal is being made to intentionality. The intentional capacity of the mind is captured in the Tibetan notion of an *intentional object* (*zhen yul*).[12] It is understood as the object that is sought or desired in conceptual thought (*rtog pa*). During episodes of thought the mind has concepts appear to it, but those thoughts typically aim towards (or are *about*) objects in the external world. So, for example, upon seeing smoke rising from a hilltop, I might reason that there is a fire on that hilltop. When reasoning in this way, what appears directly to my mind, the phenomenal object, is the concept of fire. But when I form the thought that there is a fire on the hill, my thought is not about the concept of fire. Rather, my thought is about a real fire on the hilltop. My thoughts are directed towards a real fire, even though that fire does not appear to me at all. In cases like this, Kadam philosophers maintain that my cognition of a fire on the hilltop relates to both a phenomenal object and an intentional object. The phenomenal object is the concept of fire (on the hill), but the intentional object, the object that my thought is about, is a real fire (on the hill).

Allowing for the existence of intentional objects helps Tibetan epistemologists grapple with more than the phenomenology of experience, which is essential for developing a more refined typology of cognitions. What is additionally needed, however, is a way by which to identify and distinguish cognitive episodes that is not grounded (merely) in differences between their cognitive objects. As we saw in the first half of this chapter, the three different kinds of cognitive episodes are delineated by their having different phenomenal objects. For the purposes of a rigorous epistemology, however, there is a value in focusing on more than a cognition's objects – whether its phenomenal object or its intentional object. Beyond looking at the phenomenal and intentional objects associated with a type of cognition, one can also focus on features of the cognitive process itself as a means by which to delineate cognitions. More simply, cognitions can be partitioned not just by what kind of objects are associated with them but also by *how* cognitions engage their phenomenal or intentional objects.

By focusing on the processes by which objects are engaged in a cognition, Chaba and (most of) his successors conclude that seven different kinds of cognitive episodes are possible.[13] The seven differ in the precise ways in which they engage their objects, and these processes can be isolated via six criteria that any given cognition may or may not meet.[14]

1 *The uniqueness criterion* Some cognitive episodes waiver or vacillate, without definitively engaging a single object. For example, a person might have a mental episode wherein she wonders whether there is or is not a cow in front of her. Cognitions that vacillate in this way are considered to be episodes of *doubt* (Tb. *the tsom*).

2 *The correspondence criterion* Of those cognitions that do not vacillate – that is, of those that unhesitatingly engage their object – some are in accord with reality and some are not. Those cognitions in which there is a *lack* of accord with reality are episodes of *false cognition* (*log shes*).

3 *The elimination of superimpositions criterion* Those cognitions that satisfy these first two criteria can be further subdivided between (a) cognitions that are consistent with the presence of superimpositions and (b) those that are inconsistent with the presence of superimpositions. Here, by a "superimposition," what is meant is any feature or quality ascribed to an object that does not in fact have that quality. Chaba and his followers believe that some cognitive episodes can meet the correspondence criterion while at the same time being unable to preclude the presence of superimpositions. This could happen, for example, when a person, without sufficient attention, glances at a silver bowl. Though a real silver bowl appears to the person, such a person, because of a lack of attention, would be unable to rule out the false superimposition of the bowl being non-silver.[15] When (in addition to meeting criteria (1) and (2) above) the presence of superimpositions of this sort is possible, the cognition is said to be an instance of *unascertained appearing* (*snang la ma nges pa*).

4 *The novelty criterion* Ideally, however, one's cognition should be able to rule out superimpositions. When all of the first three criteria are met, it may or may not further be the case that the cognition's object has been previously realized. If the object has been previously realized, the cognitive episode is said to be one of *subsequent cognition* (*gcad pa'i yul can*).

5 *The manifestation criterion* If there is no previous realization of the object, the object that is engaged may be directly manifest in the cognition, or it may be "hidden." When its object is directly manifest, the cognitive episode is an instance of *perceptual knowledge* (*mngon sum tshad ma*).

6 *The evidential criterion* If the object is not directly manifest – i.e., when it is "hidden" – then it is either engaged via an appeal to good evidence or it is not. When the object is engaged as a result of proper evidential reasoning, the episode is classified as one of *inferential knowledge* (*rjes dpag*). If, on the other hand, the object is not engaged through an appeal to good evidence, the episode is one of *factive assessment* (*yid dpyod*).

In this way, Chaba and many of his followers conclude that there are seven different kinds of cognitive episodes: doubt, false cognition, unascertained appearing, subsequent cognition, perceptual knowledge, inference, and factive assessment. Only two of these cognitions – perceptual knowledge and inference – provide us with knowledge, however. The other five are all deemed to fall short of yielding knowledge for one reason or another. What I want to draw attention to in the following pages are some of the important philosophical consequences flowing from this way of delineating cognitions.

Correspondence and Perception

In looking at this sevenfold typology of cognition, it is not surprising that these Tibetan thinkers would regard the cognitive episodes as different in kind when the mental processes underlying those cognitions are different. In an episode of doubt, for example, a person has a different attitude towards the cognition's object than she would have in a non-doubting cognition. As this attitudinal difference quite plausibly constitutes a cognitive difference, it is not at all surprising that Chaba would identify doubt as a different kind of cognitive episode from the other six cognitions that all satisfy the uniqueness condition. Putting this in contemporary philosophical terms, philosophers accept that *believing that p* is a different kind of mental state from *wondering whether p*, inasmuch as these are two fundamentally different kinds of attitudes a person can have towards proposition *p*. It is, thus, quite sensible that Kadam Tibetans classify a hesitating cognitive attitude such as *doubt* as different in kind from cognitions that definitively engage a unique object.

Not all six of the criteria are obviously cognitively significant, however. Whether the *correspondence criterion* is satisfied depends (in many cases) on what the external world is like. It is not straightforwardly obvious, however, that a person's cognition corresponding to the way things are in the external world should make it a fundamentally different kind of mental episode from what they would have experienced had their cognition not corresponded to the external world. To make this clear, I will provide an example that highlights this philosophical concern.[16] First, consider two situations, call them α and β, in which the following is the case. In both α and β I am walking through a desert when I nonchalantly glance at the flat expanse to my left. It appears to me that there is a lake in the distance. In case α, there really is a lake in the distance, and so my cognition meets the correspondence criterion. In case β, there is no lake at all. Instead, my visual experience came about as a result of a mirage. Nevertheless, in both cases the phenomenal experience I have is the same. Let us further stipulate that in neither case does my cognition meet the "elimination of superimpositions criterion" described above.

Because case α satisfies the correspondence criterion whereas case β does not, Chaba and his followers are committed to the view that I would be having fundamentally different kinds of cognitive episodes in these two cases. (Case α yields an episode of unascertained appearing, whereas β yields an episode of false cognition.) Yet, because the only difference between the two cases is one involving the presence or absence of an object (a lake) in the external world, it is not immediately obvious that an *objective* difference like this should have any effect on my *subjective* state of mind. The phenomenology of the two experiences is the same, after all. And, because of this, many contemporary philosophers would maintain that I am having the same kind of cognitive episode in α as I am having in β.

Chaba and his followers do have a solid philosophical response, however. As direct realists and disjunctivists about perception, these Kadam Tibetan thinkers maintain that, in cases of perception, the mind directly experiences (external) objects themselves, whereas this is not the case when someone is having a false cognition. This means that, in a case like α above, the real lake itself is a constitutive element of my cognition. Since there is no lake present in case β it must follow (on the direct realist's account) that the cognitive episode is different as well.

Now, what all of this goes to show is that, while it may initially appear that "the correspondence criterion" can play no role in distinguishing cognitions – because that criterion does not bear on the way in which the mind engages its objects – we can now see that this is not the whole story. As direct realists and disjunctivists, Kadam Tibetans are in a position to maintain that what kind of experience a person is having does depend on whether the correspondence criterion is met. At least, this is the case with non-conceptual cognitions.

Correspondence and Conception

Given Kadam Tibetan views on perception, the correspondence criterion makes sense as a device for distinguishing between different kinds of non-conceptual cognitions, for that criterion fits together well with their direct realist understanding of perception. I will now argue, however, that the correspondence criterion makes much less sense when applied to conceptual cognitions. Let us keep in mind that, on the Tibetan account, all episodes of conceptual thought take concepts as their *phenomenal objects*, and that these cognitions are (typically) directed towards objects – their *intentional objects* – in the external world. When we apply the correspondence criterion to cases of conceptual thought, what matters is not the status of the phenomenal objects, but the status of these thoughts' intentional objects. With regard to a given conceptual cognition, it meets or does not meet the correspondence criterion depending on whether the cognition's intentional object accords with reality – i.e., depending on whether the object that the cognition is about is truly there. What I now want to argue is that it is not clear that a conceptual cognition's meeting or failing to meet the correspondence criterion should have any impact on what kind of mental episode a person is having.

To make this point, let us again consider two cases, γ and δ. In case γ I am standing outside looking at a mountain in front of me. On the mountain's peak I catch a glimpse of what I think is smoke rising. In reality, I'm mistaken, for there is no smoke there – it is actually a storm on the mountain top that has caused a plume of dust to bellow into the air. Nevertheless, as a result of thinking that there is smoke on the peak, I judge that there is a fire on the peak of the mountain. In addition, let us suppose that in case γ there actually is a fire there. Thus, in this case, my cognition accords with reality. It meets the correspondence criterion, inasmuch as the cognition's intentional object accords with reality. I judge that there is a fire on the mountain top, and that judgment is correct.

Let us suppose that case δ is exactly the same as in case γ, except that there is no fire on the mountain at all. In this case, my cognition does not accord with reality. Given that case γ satisfies the correspondence criterion whereas case δ does not, Kadam Tibetan philosophers are committed to the view that I must be having different kinds of cognitive episodes in the two cases. (Chaba would maintain that in case γ I am having an episode of *factive assessment*, whereas in δ it is an episode of *false cognition*.) Yet, in these two cases, there is no underlying difference in the cognitive process that occurs. The only difference stems from whether there is or is not actually a fire on top of the mountain. But it is not at all clear that this sort of difference should have any impact on what kind of mental episode I am having.

It should be clear that in these two cases, γ and δ, the actual mental activities – the thought processes – that I undergo are the same. The phenomenal objects are the same as well. Moreover, in both cases my thought takes a fire on the mountain as its intentional object. Why should it be that the presence or absence of an actual fire has any bearing on what kind of mental event I am having? Unlike the perceptual cases where my mind is taken to have direct awareness of a real object, there is no comparable access to the real fire in these conceptual cases. Yet, Chaba and his followers still maintain that my thought's corresponding or not corresponding to reality plays a decisive role in determining what kind of cognitive experience I am having.

This example goes to show, as I have argued elsewhere (Stoltz 2009), that Kadam Tibetan epistemologists adopt a form of externalism about the mind. In short, the kind of mental episode a person is having can depend on features of the world that are external to the person's mind. Externalism is an increasingly respectable philosophical position, but this particular Tibetan version should still be regarded as highly controversial.[17] To see why, let us briefly expand upon cases γ and δ described above. Recall that the only difference between the two cases is that, in γ, but not in δ, there really is a fire on the mountain top. Let's further suppose that in both cases there is a person at the summit with a pile of firewood and a match. In case γ, this person has decided to light the match and start a fire. In case δ, he has decided not to start a fire. It is very odd to think that the decision this person makes about whether to light the firewood should have any impact on what kind of cognitive experience I, at the bottom of the mountain, am having. After all, the mountain top person's actions have no causal (let alone perceptual) impact on me.[18] My judgment is formed due to my having confused billowing dust with smoke, and this would have occurred regardless of whether the person on the mountain top started the fire or not. Yet, according to Kadam Tibetan views on the matter, what kind of cognitive event I am having does depend on whether a causally irrelevant fire is or is not burning on the mountain top. Now, this does not mean that the Tibetan account here is philosophically untenable. It means only that its tenability requires endorsing a strongly externalist account of cognition.

Conclusion

In the preceding pages I have tried to make clear some of the central features of the Kadam Tibetan account of cognition as that account is developed by Chaba and his followers. In part, my aim has also been to show readers that these Tibetan discussions of cognition mirror ongoing debates in contemporary philosophy. In particular, by elucidating the theory developed by Chaba and other Kadam Tibetans, we can see that these thinkers accept (a) a direct realist understanding of perception coupled with (b) an implicit commitment to phenomenal and experiential disjunctivism, as well as (c) a strong form of externalism about the mind. It should also be recognized that these three features all fit together, mutually supporting one another. It is up to the reader to decide whether these features of the Kadam Tibetan account of cognition have philosophical merit.

Notes

1 For a fuller discussion of this, see Dreyfus (1997, chs 19, 20) and Arnold (2005, chs 1, 2).
2 Most literally, *gzung yul* means "object to be held/grasped."
3 In Tibetan, the first two categories are labeled *don rang gi mtshan nyid* (particular) and *don spyi* (concept). The third category, while having a consistent meaning, is named in a variety of ways. Chaba calls these objects *rtog med 'khrul pa'i dmigs pa* (the observed object of a non-conceptual, erroneous cognition). Dorje Öser (c. late twelfth century) calls the same entities *dngos med gsal snang* (vivid appearance but not a real thing). Sakya Paṇḍita (1182–1251) terms these entities *med pa gsal ba* (vivid non-existent).
4 Within the context of this chapter, to say that a cognition is an instance of perception does not imply that it yields knowledge. In the typology of cognitions that Chaba and his followers endorse, perception as a general category includes three subtypes: (a) perceptual knowledge, (b) unascertained appearing, and (c) subsequent cognition.
5 See note 3 above.
6 This point is expressed clearly by the thinker Dorje Öser, who writes, "The reason for dividing these (cognitive episodes) in this way is because there are three phenomenal objects to be taken as one's basis. As such, the cognitions apprehending them are also divided into three." [*gang gis 'byed pa'i rgyu mtshan ni snang yul tsam gzhir byas pa la 3 yod pas de 'dzin pa'i shes pa yang 3 du phye'o /*] (Gtsang 2007, 4b.8).
7 For more on disjunctivism and the contrast between perception and hallucination, see Fish (2008).
8 The foregoing discussion should also have made it clear to those familiar with earlier Indian Buddhist accounts of perception that this Kadam Tibetan understanding of perceptual experience is quite different from the Sautrāntika theory that is developed (if not fully endorsed) by Dignāga and Dharmakīrti. For more on their accounts, see the references in note 1 above.
9 For more on this, see Brewer (2008) and Smith (2010).
10 The author of the *Tshad ma'i de kho na nyid bsdus pa* identifies one of the "students" of Dignāga holding this view to be the late eighth-century Indian philosopher Jinendrabuddhi. There is good reason to think that this attribution is correct (see Franco 2006). Given that Jinendrabuddhi lived more than 200 years after Dignāga's death, however, we should not regard the former as an actual student of Dignāga. Rather, he is considered to be a "disciple" of Dignāga insofar as he wrote a commentary on Dignāga's *Pramāṇasamuccaya*.
11 I certainly do not mean to imply that this is a Tibetan invention. It is quite clear that Buddhist appeals to this intentional activity of the mind go back at least to the Indian philosopher Dharmakīrti in the seventh century.
12 The term "intentional object" is generally associated with the tradition following Franz Brentano. By translating the Tibetan term *zhen yul* in that way, I am suggesting that there are some similarities between the Tibetan notion and that of Brentano. A prolonged discussion of this notion will have to wait for a future publication, however. For more on intentional objects, see Crane (2001).
13 This typology has been discussed in various scholarly works. The earliest discussion of the typology is found in van der Kuijp (1978).
14 See Phywa pa (2006, 9a.5–7); Klong chen (2000, 52–3); or Gtsang (2007, 9b.2–4). In my presentation, I am most closely following the breakdown given in Gtsang.
15 For an excellent discussion of this issue, please see Hugon (2011).
16 The following examples follow the model I employ in Stoltz (2007, 2009).

17 Classic discussions of externalism in the philosophy of mind can be found in Putnam (1973) and Burge (1979), and also in developments by Clark and Chalmers (1998).

18 In a genuine case of inference, the person's actions would be relevant, but not in the cases (γ and δ) described here.

References

Arnold, D. (2005). *Buddhists, Brahmins, and Belief: Epistemology in South Asian Philosophy of Religion*. New York: Columbia University Press.

Brewer, B. (2008). How to Account for Illusion. In *Disjunctivism: Perception, Action, Knowledge*. Ed. A. Haddock and F. Macpherson. Oxford: Oxford University Press, 168–80.

Burge, T. (1979). Individualism and the Mental. In *Midwest Studies in Philosophy* 4, 73–121.

Clark, A., and Chalmers, D. (1998). The Extended Mind. In *Analysis* 58, 7–19.

Crane, T. (2001). Intentional Objects. In *Ratio* 14, 336–49.

Dreyfus, G. (1997). *Recognizing Reality: Dharmakīrti's Philosophy and its Tibetan Interpretations*. Albany: State University of New York Press.

Fish, W. (2008). Disjunctivism, Indistinguishability, and the Nature of Hallucination. In *Disjunctivism: Perception, Action, Knowledge*. Ed. A. Haddock and F. Macpherson. Oxford: Oxford University Press, 144–67.

Franco, E. (2006). A New Era in the Study of Buddhist Philosophy. In *Journal of Indian Philosophy* 34, 221–7.

Go rams pa bsod nams seng ge (1998). *Tshad ma'i rigs pa'i gter gyi don gsal bar byed pa* [Clarifying the Meaning of the Treasury of Knowledge]. In *Tshad ma rigs gter rtsa ba dang 'grel pa*. Chengdu: Sichuan People's Press.

Gtsang drug pa rdo rje 'od zer (2007). *Yang dag rigs pa'i gsal byed sgron ma* [The Lamp that is the Illuminator of Pure Reason]. In *bka' gdams gsung 'bum phyogs bsgrigs*, Vol. 47. Chengdu: Sichuan People's Press.

Hugon, P. (2011). Phya pa Chos kyi seng ge's views on perception. In *Religion and Logic in Buddhist Philosophical Analysis*. Ed. H. Krasser, Helmut, H. Lasic, E. Franco, and B. Kellner. Vienna: Verlag Der Österreichischen Akademie der Wissenschaften, 159–76.

Klong chen rab 'byams (attributed) (2000). *Tshad ma'i de kho na nyid bsdus pa* [Summary of the Essence of Knowledge]. Chengdu: Sichuan People's Press.

van der Kuijp, L. (1978). Phya pa Chos kyi seng ge's Impact on Tibetan Epistemological Theory. In *Journal of Indian Philosophy* 5, 366–79.

Phywa pa chos kyi seng ge (2006). Tshad ma yid kyi mun sel [Knowledge: Clearing Away the Darkness of Mind]. In *bka' gdams gsung 'bum phyogs bsgrigs*, Vol. 8. Chengdu: Sichuan People's Press.

Putnam, H. (1973). Meaning and Reference. In *Journal of Philosophy* 70, 699–711.

Rngog blo ldan shes rab (2006). Tshad ma rnam nges kyi 'grel ba [Commentary on the *Pramāṇaviniścaya*]. In *bka' gdams gsung 'bum phyogs bsgrigs*, Vol. 1. Chengdu: Sichuan People's Press.

Smith, A. D. (2010). Disjunctivism and Illusion. In *Philosophy and Phenomenological Research* 80, 384–410.

Stoltz, J. (2007). Gettier and Factivity in Indo-Tibetan Epistemology. In *Philosophical Quarterly* 57, 394–415.

Stoltz, J. (2009). Phywa pa's Argumentative Analogy between Factive Assessment (*yid dpyod*) and Conceptual Thought (rtog pa). In *Journal of the International Association of Buddhist Studies* 32, 369–86.

27

The Non-Self Theory and Problems in Philosophy of Mind

JOERG TUSKE

The non-self theory is one of the cornerstones of Buddhist philosophy. In this chapter, I examine this theory and discuss some of the issues it raises for Western philosophy of mind, in particular for the problem of free will. In the first part, I trace the non-self theory through several formulations, focusing on different Buddhist texts. In the second part, I analyze some of the similarities and dissimilarities of the non-self theory with discussions of the mind–body problem and the free will problem in Western philosophy.

The Buddhist Non-Self Theory

At the heart of the Buddhist non-self theory is the claim that what we call the "self" is nothing over and above the five psycho-physical aggregates: physical form (*rūpa*), feeling or sensation (*vedanā*), cognition or perception (*saṃjñā*), mental formations or volition (*saṃskāra*) and consciousness (*vijñāna*). These aggregates are changing and impermanent and they are all that is required to explain the concept of "self." Every self is made up of these aggregates. This non-self theory stands in opposition to the ideas of Brahmanical philosophers, who view the self as an unchanging, non-physical, and eternal entity called *ātman*.

The term "non-self theory" is problematic because it suggests that there is one theory that can be traced through all the Buddhist texts. However, as Oetke (1988) points out, what we call the non-self theory continued to develop from the earliest Buddhist texts through the writings of later Buddhist philosophers in India and other countries to which Buddhism spread. In order to trace the development of this theory in Buddhist thought, Oetke frames the discussion in a way that relates it to arguments about the self in Western philosophy. I believe that Oetke's approach is very useful, and I will follow his framework.

A Companion to Buddhist Philosophy, First Edition. Edited by Steven M. Emmanuel.

According to Oetke, there are several ways in which the idea of "non-self" can be taken. Of particular philosophical interest is the question whether the non-self theory is a "no ownership" theory of the sort that P. F. Strawson (1959) contrasts with the Cartesian view of the person. According to the Cartesian view, we ascribe states of consciousness to a non-material self. Thus, the self exists over and above the states of consciousness that a person possesses. One of the problems with this view is that it is difficult to provide an account of what this Cartesian self is. Hume (1978, 252) famously argued that there is no evidence for the existence of such a self. Introspection reveals only states of consciousness, not a self that possesses these states. If we deny the existence of a Cartesian self we are left with the "no ownership" view, according to which states of consciousness exist without belonging to any particular person. This view, according to Strawson, is as problematic as the Cartesian view because it would allow, for example, for a pain to exist without a subject to whom we could attribute the state of being in pain. The pain would not have an "owner." The notion of pain or any other state of consciousness seems to presuppose the existence of a subject who is in pain. Strawson argues that this subject is a person and provides an account that does not require the existence of a Cartesian self. He also shows that the Cartesian view of the self is logically independent of the no-ownership theory because the falsity of one does not imply the truth of the other.

The reason why Strawson's view is relevant to a discussion of the non-self theory is that the Buddhist view has been interpreted as a "no ownership" view that rejects the Brahmanical idea of an *ātman* – i.e., a non-physical, unchanging and eternal self that acts, among other things, as the possessor of states of consciousness. According to some interpretations, the debate between Brahmanical philosophers defending the existence of an *ātman* and Buddhist philosophers denying its existence mirrors the "debate" between Descartes and Hume. Hume, of course, holds a bundle theory of the self, according to which the self reduces to a bundle of perceptions or states of consciousness. One of the main differences between Descartes and Hume is that the latter denies the existence of a subject that exists over and above its qualities (states of consciousness, perceptions).

Oetke makes the important point that, just as the view of the Cartesian self is logically independent of the "no ownership" theory, in the same way the Brahmanical view that the self is an *ātman* is logically independent of the Buddhist non-self theory, unless the *ātman* is defined as the owner of states of consciousness. However, not all Brahmanical schools define the *ātman* in this way. Oetke identifies four distinct theses:

1 Experiences and states of consciousness do not inhere in anything – i.e., there is no subject that they exist in.
2 Experiences and states of consciousness inhere in some thing.
3 Experiences and states of consciousness inhere in an immaterial substance.
4 The assertion or non-denial of the existence of an *ātman*.

(Oetke 1988, 65; my translation)

He points out that only thesis 1 and thesis 2 contradict each other. Thesis 1 and thesis 3 are contraries, so they cannot both be true but they can both be false. If in addition to thesis 4 we postulate that an *ātman* has to have the property of being that in which states of consciousness inhere, then this thesis becomes equivalent to thesis 3 and hence a contrary of thesis 1.

It is important to clarify which theses Buddhists endorse and which they deny. Not surprisingly, the answer depends on the particular Buddhist text under discussion. It is certainly true that later Buddhist authors reject the existence of an *ātman*. However, what exactly is meant by "*ātman*" depends on the author and the position he argues against. Oetke argues very persuasively that we cannot find the explicit denial of the existence of the self as a subject in the Pāli canon. All we can find is the rejection of an *ātman* as an eternally existing entity that could account for personal identity. In particular, we find various arguments showing that none of the five aggregates (*skandhas*) by themselves or as a collection can account for the self. From this, however, it does not follow that the early Buddhist authors did not believe in a self as a subject. While Oetke does not explicitly draw this comparison, one could think of the Buddhist view along the lines of Strawson's analysis, which rejected the notion of a Cartesian self without thereby endorsing a no-ownership view of mental states. Oetke argues that the sources leave open the possibility that Buddhist authors held a "common-sense" view of the self, according to which the self is that to which we attribute personhood and moral agency without the commitment that this self is eternal. Oetke emphasizes, however, that the texts of the Pāli canon are unclear about their commitment to or rejection of a self. All we can say is that we find a rejection of thesis 4 in the Pāli canon. But, as long as the *ātman* whose existence is denied in this thesis is not connected with any term in one of the other three theses, we cannot conclude that the authors of the texts of the Pāli canon argued for the non-existence of the self.

The Questions of King Milinda

Perhaps the best-known Buddhist text referred to in discussions of the non-self theory is the *Milindapañha*, which supposedly records a discussion between King Milinda and the monk Nāgasena.

The *Milindapañha* begins with King Milinda asking the monk what his name is. The monk answers that he is called Nāgasena but that he could have been named differently, and that this name certainly does not refer to a self (he uses the term *pudgala* rather than *ātman* for "self"). The king then becomes slightly irritated and replies that, if there is no self to which the name Nāgasena refers, then Nāgasena does not exist, because Nāgasena cannot be identified with any of the five *skandhas* or even with the combination of these *skandhas*. Nāgasena agrees that none of these *skandhas* are the self, but he argues that it does not follow that Nāgasena does not exist. He asks King Milinda whether he came to visit him on foot or by chariot, knowing of course that the king always travels by chariot. When the king confirms this, Nāgasena asks him if there is anything over and above the parts of the chariot (e.g., the axle, the wheels, etc.) to which the word "chariot" refers. When the king denies this, Nāgasena points out that, by the king's own reasoning, it would have to follow that the chariot does not exist. Of course the king objects and replies that conventionally we use the term "chariot" when confronted with the individual parts of it, provided they are assembled in the right way. Nāgasena tells him that the same applies to names such as Nāgasena, and that it does not follow from this convention that a self exists over and above the parts that we designate with a name.

The main problem with interpreting the *Milindapañha*, according to Oetke, is that it is not clear what exactly is meant by the term *pudgala*. The interpretation is not helped by the fact that we have a Pāli version as well as a Chinese version of the story, and that these differ in certain details. Oetke argues that the most plausible interpretation of both of the versions of the *Milindapañha* is that the *pudgala* consists of parts, namely the *skandhas*, and is therefore comparable to terms such as "house," "tree," or "army," which also consist of parts (1988, 184). According to the *Milindapañha*, these terms do not exist in "true reality" but are merely used conventionally. Unfortunately, it is not clear what the relationship is between conventional language and the language of true reality. Therefore we cannot say that the *Milindapañha* rejects the notion of a subject, only that it rejects its existence in "true reality."

So, even in what is perhaps the most famous Buddhist text with regard to the non-self theory, we do not have an explicit rejection of the self, merely the claim that the existence of the self is different from the existence of its parts.

Vasubandhu's Rejection of the Self

We can, however, find an explicit rejection of the existence of a self or subject in "The Refutation of the Theory of a Self," which forms a part of Vasubandhu's *Abhidharmakośa* (see Duerlinger 2003). Vasubandhu begins his discussion by pointing out that only Buddhism can lead to salvation because only Buddhism has the right concept of the *pudgala* or *ātman*. According to Vasubandhu, the *pudgala* does not exist over and above the five *skandhas* that make up human beings. By this he means that the *pudgala* is not an entity that exists as an independent substance apart from the *skandhas*. Vasubandhu admits that what we call the "self" is the conjunction of the *skandhas*. However, he denies that the *pudgala* is real. For this reason, his view has been characterized by some commentators as a reductionist view of the self. Vasubandhu does not deny that it makes sense to talk about a self in certain contexts, but he argues that the self reduces to the collection of the five *skandhas*.

During the course of this discussion, Vasubandhu argues with an imaginary opponent who is a fellow Buddhist from the Pudgalavādin school. The Pudgalavādins or Vātsīputrīyas ("followers of Vātsīputra"), as Vasubandhu calls them, are Buddhists who believe that a *pudgala* does exist and that it is neither identical to nor different from the five *skandhas*. According to their view, the *pudgala* is based on the *skandhas*. Vasubandhu argues against this view by pointing out that it is not clear what it means to say that the *pudgala* is based on the *skandhas*. He offers two possible interpretations. First, the *skandhas* form an object, which we call *pudgala*. But, if this is the case, then our concept of a *pudgala* actually refers to the collection of *skandhas* and not to an independent object called the *pudgala*. Second, the existence of a *pudgala* is caused by the *skandhas*. But Vasubandhu claims that, if this were the case, then again the concept of a *pudgala* would refer only to the *skandhas*. This would not establish the existence of an independent substance called *pudgala*. Instead, Vasubandhu argues that the *pudgala* is identical with the collection of *skandhas*. His two main arguments are as follows.

Vasubandhu's first argument is that we can perceive the *pudgala* either by perceiving the *skandhas* or by perceiving the *pudgala* directly. In the first case, Vasubandhu claims that the term "*pudgala*" simply refers to the *skandhas* and not to an entity called the *pudgala*. In the second case, the question is how we can account for the relationship between the *skandhas* and the *pudgala*. After all, the Vātsīputrīyas claim that the *pudgala* is based on the *skandhas* and "being based on" is relational. Vasubandhu, however, argues that, if we could perceive a *pudgala* directly, the *skandhas* would be based on the *pudgala*. Thus, the relation of "being based on" would be turned around. However, according to the Vātsīputrīyas, the relation of "being based on" simply means that the *pudgala* can only be perceived if there are *skandhas* in the first place. Vasubandhu objects to this view because, according to him, it would lead to the absurd claim that color "is based on" the existence of eyes because the eyes are necessary for the perception of color. The general format of this argument is that everybody has to agree that there is a relation between the *pudgala* and the *skandhas*, and the Vātsīputrīyas, who argue for the existence of an entity called *pudgala*, have problems accounting for this relation.

The problem with Vasubandhu's argument is that he construes the following two possibilities as mutually exclusive: first, that our knowledge of the *pudgala* is based on the perception of the *skandhas* and, second, that the knowledge of the *pudgala* is gained through direct perception. However, it is not clear why we cannot simultaneously have a perception of the *skandhas* and a perception of the *pudgala*. Consider as an example the perception of a moving train. We perceive the train and at the same time we perceive the movement. There is no problem with perceiving both, even though in order to perceive the movement of the train we have to perceive the train.

Vasubandhu's second argument is more straightforward. He asks how it is we perceive the *pudgala*. What sense is used in order to perceive it? By "sense" Vasubandhu means the five senses plus the "sense of thought" – i.e., the mind (*manas*). The Vātsīputrīyas claim that we gain knowledge of the *pudgala* through all six senses. Vasubandhu replies that, if the *pudgala* is perceived through the six senses, then this shows that the *pudgala* is in fact nothing over and above the *skandhas*. He argues that whenever one perceives something that is made up of certain qualities, such as sound, smell, touch, taste, etc., the resulting "object" that one perceives is nothing over and above these qualities. So, when you perceive an apple, you perceive a certain color, shape, taste, and smell, and the apple is nothing over and above these qualities. The apple is not a substance in which these qualities inhere. The same is true of the *pudgala*. All we perceive are the *skandhas*, not the *pudgala* itself. Hence the *pudgala* does not have an existence over and above the *skandhas*.

The problem with this argument is that it treats inference analogously to the other five senses. If one allows that inference can be a source of knowledge, then it is not clear why one cannot gain knowledge of the existence of a *pudgala* through the perception of the *skandhas*. The idea is that I perceive certain processes and infer from them the existence of an entity called *pudgala*. Vasubandhu thinks of perception as primary to inference. He relies on two assumptions: (i) the external world can only be apprehended through the five external senses and (ii) a *pudgala* is part of the external world. If one does not allow these presuppositions, then it is not clear why one cannot infer that there is a *pudgala* or *ātman* from the perception of the *skandhas*.

Vasubandhu maintains that the self is a causal chain made up of the *skandhas* and that this is all we need in order to account for the self. This view was also shared by Śāntarakṣita, who in his work *Tattvasaṃgraha* (hereafter TS) defends it against several criticisms by Brahmanical philosophers. The two criticisms that I want to focus on are (i) that our sense of self, the I-consciousness, makes sense only if it refers to an unchanging entity and (ii) that we would be unable to account for the relationship between actions and their results without the notion of an unchanging subject which is the "Doer" of the action.

Agent and I-Consciousness

Śāntarakṣita discusses the first of the above-mentioned criticisms in TS.229–84. The criticism, which is presented in the context of the Mīmāṃsa view of the *ātman*, refers to the undeniable experience of the self as something that exists over time. For example, when I recognize the fig tree in my garden as the same tree that I saw yesterday, I postulate the existence of a self that saw the fig tree yesterday and sees it again today. Furthermore, the self that saw the tree yesterday is the same self as the one that looks at it today. In addition, this self has to have the sense that it is the same self; it has to have I-consciousness. According to several Brahmanical philosophers, this shows that the self has to exist unchanging over time and therefore cannot be a chain of *skandhas*.

Śāntarakṣita dismisses this argument on the grounds that an unchanging self would have to have unchanging cognitions (TS.241), and this does not make sense because thinking, which means "re-cognizing," entails the constant change of cognitions. In addition, Śāntarakṣita argues that the sense of I-consciousness that refers to an unchanging entity is an illusion and that the change in our cognitions can only be explained by a self that consists of these changing cognitions and other momentary states.

The second objection, which concerns the relationship between actions and their results, is discussed by Śāntarakṣita in TS.476–546. If there is no self that persists through time, then the good or bad results of my action are not going to have any effect on me because the "I" that performs these actions would no longer exist. Hence there would be no "Doer" or agent of the action who would reap the benefits or suffer the consequences of the action. However, if there are no "karmic consequences," it is not clear why anybody would bother to perform an action in the first place.

Śāntarakṣita replies to this argument by appealing to causation, particularly the causal effects we observe in nature – for example, the relation between a seed and a sprout (TS.505–6). The seed causes the sprout but the seed does not continue once it has caused the sprout. In the same way, the action is the cause of its result and does not require an agent that persists through time. In fact, Śāntarakṣita claims that the notion of the agent is an illusion that exists only because of the unity we perceive in the causal chains of momentary states. Thus the notion of a self only makes sense on the background of the *skandhas* being related causally to one another. The important point for Śāntarakṣita and other Buddhist philosophers is not to let this perceived unity deceive us into thinking that there is more to the self than this causal chain.

The purpose of this brief summary of some of the main Buddhist positions on the self has been to show (a) that the non-self theory is not one theory but has undergone many developments and (b) that some of the later formulations of the theory can be interpreted as a reductive view of the self. By reductive I mean that the existence of a self over and above the five *skandhas* is rejected and that the five *skandhas* explain everything there is to explain about the self. In the next section, I would like to highlight one problem for this view: the problem of free will.

The Non-Self Theory and Free Will

The Buddhist non-self theory raises several issues that are relevant to contemporary Western discussions in philosophy of mind and metaphysics. However, it is important to be mindful of the intellectual contexts in which these discussions occur. The Buddhist non-self theory is a response to the Brahmanical postulation of an eternal, unchanging, and non-physical self (*ātman*). As such, it appears to share some similarities with the "debate" about the concept of self in Western philosophy, particularly in the seventeenth century. This debate also influenced views about the metaphysics of the mind. Descartes' view of the self (see Descartes 1985) was a way to establish the existence not only of a subject, but a subject of a very particular kind, namely a non-physical substance that is the subject of mental states. While nowadays Descartes' view is often regarded as a foil to materialism, this does not capture the positions of philosophers in the early modern period. For example, Hume's view that the self is nothing but a bundle of perceptions allows for the idea that perceptions are mental rather than physical. The debate between the Buddhists and Brahmanical philosophers is similar in this respect because, while the Buddhists deny the existence of an unchanging, non-physical, and eternal substance called the self, they do not advocate a form of materialism. In fact, they advocate a "middle way" between the view that the self is an *ātman* and materialism. So the self is nothing over and above the five *skandhas* and some of the *skandhas* are non-physical.

One of the most significant issues for the Buddhist non-self theory is the status of free will. Clearly, Buddhist philosophers believe that humans have free will. They account for it by including it among the five *skandhas*. Will or volition is included in the *skandha saṃskāra* among other "mental formations," such as habits or opinions. The problem is that the Buddhist non-self theory does not allow for an entity that functions as the subject of the will. In addition, the non-self theory relies on the view that the *skandhas* are causally related. So, if the will does not exist in isolation from previous causal influences, and there is no subject that is independent of this causal influence, then it is not clear to what extent Buddhist philosophers can legitimately claim that we have free will. This problem has led to recent scholarly attempts to analyze the Buddhist position on free will by comparing it to theories of the will in Western philosophy.

In Western philosophy, the two main positions in the free will debate are compatibilism and incompatibilism. Compatibilists hold that free will is compatible with determinism (the view that all events have causes and that they are determined by those causes). Incompatibilists hold that free will and determinism are incompatible.

Incompatibilists fall into two camps: "hard determinists" believe that determinism is true and free will is an illusion, while "libertarians" hold that determinism is false and that we have free will. For libertarians, free will requires the absence of a cause, because they believe that causes determine their effects and we do not have control over causes. Thus, many libertarians reject materialism because they believe that within the material world determinism holds, and thus there is no room for free will. Instead, they believe in a non-material self that is partially causally independent, insofar as it is not affected by causes but is able to act as a cause for effects within the world. Recent discoveries in quantum physics have opened up a way for libertarians to formulate their view without having to reject materialism. The fact that there are certain events at the quantum level that do not seem to have a cause but appear randomly has led some philosophers to the view that free will could be an expression of these random events. However, the argument against this view is that a random event would not be able to account for what we ordinarily mean by free will. After all, we do not have any influence on the occurrence of a random event, and this would seem to undermine our ideas about moral agency.

When we compare these positions with the discussion about the nature of the self in Indian philosophy it seems that the Brahmanical view (that there is an *ātman* that is the subject of our experience) bears some resemblance to the libertarian view. I believe there are significant differences between these views, but they need not concern us at present. The important question is whether the Buddhist non-self theory allows for the existence of free will and, if it does, whether this view has any parallel in Western thought.

Buddhist philosophers embrace the notion of dependent origination, or conditioned co-arising, which says that nothing exists independently of causal conditions, not even psycho-physical events. This view suggests an affinity with determinism, the view that every event is determined by its causes. However, Buddhism also advocates liberation – i.e., a state in which we extinguish, among other things, our cravings. The liberated state is characterized by mental freedom in the sense that we are no longer the "slaves of our passions." Thus, Buddhism distinguishes between states that are free and states that are not free. The question then is whether this freedom is compatible with the determinist nature of dependent origination.

As Repetti (2010a) points out, there is a significant difference between the Western concept of "free will" and the Buddhist notion of mental freedom (see Repetti 2010b for a good overview of the Buddhist positions). Western ideas of free will usually involve the notion of "autonomy," which requires the existence of an autonomous self that is the author of its own actions. This means that, in the final analysis, the self or subject must have been free to choose an action without being determined by causes over which it has no control.

However, according to Repetti, Harry Frankfurt's discussion of free will provides a model for the synthesis of determinism and free will in Buddhist thought. Frankfurt (1969) argues that the traditional definition of a free agent as someone who "could have done otherwise" does not capture what free will is. He develops a series of ("Frankfurt-style") cases in which an individual could not have done otherwise, but in which she nevertheless acted freely. The most famous example involves taking control of someone's brain and being able to tell how this person is going to vote. If the subject decides to vote Democrat, then the person in control will not intervene. However, if the subject decides to vote Republican, then the person in control will stimulate the subject's brain in such a way that causes her to vote Democrat. The latter case is clearly not a free act, but what about the former case? The subject decided to vote Democrat of her own accord, even though, unbeknown to her, she was not able to vote otherwise. It would appear that her decision was free. However, according to the definition that free will requires the ability to do otherwise, her action should not count as free. For this reason, Frankfurt argues that this definition of free will does not capture what it means to be free, and hence determinism does not necessarily prevent me from making free choices. In the example the subject is determined to vote Democrat but at the same time her action is free.

A better way to think about free will, according to Frankfurt (1971), is that, for an action to be free, the desire to perform it has to be in accord with our higher-order desires (meta-volitions). So, even though our actions are determined by our desires, an action is free if our first-order desire to perform the action is in line with a higher-order desire to have the desire to perform the action. Consider the example of a drug addict who takes heroin but does not want to take heroin: on one level the addict desires to take the heroin, but she does not desire to have that desire. Because her first-order desire is not in line with her higher-order desire, the action is not free. For the action to be free, the higher-order desire has to be the same as the first-order desire, as in the case when I eat a piece of chocolate because I want to eat it and I want to have the desire to eat it. This means that determinism and free will are compatible and that actions are free as long as they do not run counter to our higher-order desires.

Repetti (2010a) argues that Buddhism can use Frankfurt's argument in order to account for a sense of free will in the context of dependent origination. Buddhists believe that it is possible for us be able to control our mental states through concentration and meditation, and that being able to do so is liberation. This would allow for the idea that human existence is determined by causes, while allowing for the ability to free ourselves from them. It does not require a sense of free will that involves the absence of causes. Free will for Buddhism, then, can be understood as bringing more and more of our actions in line with our higher-order desires. The path to enlightenment is the attainment of increasing levels of freedom culminating in *nirvāṇa*, complete liberation from the causes of suffering. According to some Buddhist traditions, we can even have momentary experiences of *nirvāṇa* on the path to final enlightenment.

While Frankfurt's argument provides a way for Buddhism to reconcile the ideas of dependent origination and free will, it does not address the question of whether free will or free mental states require the existence of a self that possesses these states. Western libertarianism proposes the existence of a non-physical self that has mental states, because this allows for an autonomous self that is unaffected by causes but that can act as a cause to bring about effects in the physical and non-physical realm. However, Buddhism does not require a strong sense of free will that entails the absence of causes. As we have seen, free will in the Buddhist sense may be understood as bringing the causes of our actions into alignment with our higher-order desires and to exercise control in this way. The problem for the Buddhist non-self theory is to make plausible the idea that a higher-order desire counts as my desire rather than just a "subjectless" desire.

The reason why this issue arises specifically in the context of free will and not in the context of other mental states is that free will seems to require the existence of agency and therefore of an agent. The concept of an agent in turn seems to presuppose the notion of an enduring self. The non-self theory allows only for volitional states that do not form a self, but the question is how these volitional states can be said to form a will that is mine. Frankfurt's view is often criticized by way of the infinite regress objection. Briefly stated, if an action is free to the extent that the desire to perform that action is in accord with a higher-order desire, then this higher-order desire must be in accord with a desire of the next-highest order, and so on. As Repetti points out, one way to block the infinite regress would be to say that someone exhibits free will if she is "an agent whose relevant, highest-level metavolition causes, causally controls, or counterfactually controls her volitional action" (Repetti 2010a, 190–1). It is not clear, however, how Buddhist philosophers, such as Vasubandhu or Śāntarakṣita, who argue for the non-self theory, can make use of this reply. The problem here is the notion of an "agent." For these Buddhist philosophers, the agent or self is nothing over and above the aggregates that make up the agent, including volitions and meta-volitions. However, this theory of the "non-self" does not stop the regress. There would have to be an ultimate level of agency in order to stop the regress, and this agency cannot be simply more meta-volitions.

Buddhist philosophers were confronted with this problem by philosophers from Brahmanical schools, and it is not clear that they had a good response to it. Of course, they could (and did) counter by asking what such an agent (i.e., one that exists over and above volitional states) would be like, thereby shifting the burden of proof back to the Brahmanical philosophers. In many cases, the best arguments in this "*ātman* controversy" are the ones made against the "other side."

References

Descartes, R. (1985). Meditations on First Philosophy. In *The Philosophical Writings of Descartes*, Vol. 2. Trans. J. Cottingham, R. Stoothoff, and D. Murdoch. Cambridge: Cambridge University Press, 1–62.

Duerlinger, J. (2003). *Indian Buddhist Theories of Persons: Vasubandhu's "Refutation of the Theory of a Self."* New York: RoutledgeCurzon.

Frankfurt, H. (1969). Alternate Possibilities and Moral Responsibility. In *Journal of Philosophy* 66, 829–39.

Frankfurt, H. (1971). Freedom of the Will and the Concept of a Person. In *Journal of Philosophy* 68, 5–20.

Hume, D. (1978). *A Treatise of Human Nature*. Ed. L. A. Selby-Bigge. Second edn, rev. P. H. Nidditch. Oxford: Oxford University Press.

Oetke, C. (1988). *"Ich" und das Ich: Analytische Untersuchungen zur buddhistisch–brahmanischen Ātmankontroverse* ["I" and the I: analytical investigations regarding the Buddhist–Brahmanical *ātman* controversy]. Stuttgart: Franz Steiner.

Repetti, R. (2010a). Meditation and Mental Freedom: A Buddhist Theory of Free Will. In *Journal of Buddhist Ethics* 17, 166–212.

Repetti, R. (2010b). Earlier Buddhist Theories of Free Will. In *Journal of Buddhist Ethics* 17, 279–309.

Strawson, P. F. (1959). *Individuals: An Essay in Descriptive Metaphysics*. London: Routledge.

E. Ethics and Moral Philosophy

28

Ethical Thought in Indian Buddhism

CHRISTOPHER W. GOWANS

Buddhist thought flourished in India for well over a thousand years after the life of the Buddha around the fifth century BCE. During this time there were many diverse developments, but for the purpose of the overview in this chapter two central traditions will be featured. The first centers on the original teaching of the Buddha as represented in a set of texts written in Pāli called the "Three Baskets" (*Tipiṭaka/Tripiṭaka*).[1] These are the canonical texts of Theravāda Buddhism, the most ancient Buddhist tradition that survives in the contemporary world (mainly in Sri Lanka and parts of South-East Asia). The second tradition is rooted in a set of texts written in Sanskrit called the "Perfection of Wisdom Sūtras" (*Prajñāpāramitā Sūtras*) that began to emerge a few centuries later, around the beginning of the new millennium. These texts constitute the historical heart of Mahāyāna Buddhism, a multifaceted tradition that transformed the original teaching of the Buddha in important ways and has influenced diverse forms of Buddhism in many parts of Asia until the present day. As will be seen, it is obvious that in both traditions Buddhist thought in India was fundamentally concerned with ethical values. But it is less obvious to what extent this thought presupposed or was in some way committed to a moral philosophy.

The Ethical Themes in Brief

In order to see this, let us begin with a brief summary of some central ideas. In the standard biography handed down by the tradition, it is said that at age 29 Siddhattha Gotama (Siddhārtha Gautama) underwent some kind of existential crisis upon realizing that aging, illness, and death were inescapable features of human life, and that this prompted him to leave his wife and young son in order to understand and overcome human suffering. After searching for six years, first with others and then on his own, he entered an intense period of mental concentration that brought about an

A Companion to Buddhist Philosophy, First Edition. Edited by Steven M. Emmanuel.

enlightenment experience. He was now a Buddha – an Awakened One – and he devoted his remaining 45 years to teaching what he had discovered.

Part of the Buddha's message was a threefold set of beliefs that were similar to what many people in India accepted at the time. First, a natural feature of the world is that actions have consequences – in particular, for the Buddha, morally good actions tend to produce happiness for the person who performs them, while morally bad actions tend to produce unhappiness. This is the doctrine of karma. Second, each person undergoes a series of lives, without an apparent beginning, and the degree of happiness in each life depends on the morality of the person's past actions, including those in previous lives. This is the extension of karma to the doctrine of rebirth. Finally, although some lives are happier than others, the entire cycle of rebirth is fundamentally problematic, but fortunately it is possible to achieve a form of wisdom that enables us to escape this cycle in some sense and attain a blissful state that exceeds anything possible within the cycle. This is the doctrine of liberation.

One of the most distinctive features of the Buddha's thought is his understanding of liberation as enunciated in the "Four Noble Truths" (the most prominent of several brief summaries of the Buddha's teaching). The First Noble Truth says that human life is pervaded by suffering. This refers to a wide range of ways in which human life regularly lacks contentment, fulfillment, satisfaction, security, and the like. The Second Noble Truth states that suffering results from craving. This includes a variety of phenomena, such as clinging, attachment, greed, lust, hatred, etc., which are said to have their origin in a basic misunderstanding of human life. The heart of this misunderstanding is that we think that we are selves when in fact, on account of the impermanent and dependent nature of all things, we are not selves. The Third Noble Truth declares that there is a state of freedom from suffering – nirvana – that we can all attain by realizing that we are not selves and thereby abandoning craving. The most important characterizations of someone who has attained nirvana are wisdom, compassion for all persons, and unsurpassed peace or tranquility. The Fourth Noble Truth says that anyone can attain nirvana by following the Eightfold Path. This has three sections: wisdom (right view and intention), morality (right speech, action, and livelihood), and concentration (right effort, mindfulness, and concentration – the mental disciplines frequently referred to as meditation). The eight steps of the path outline the basic program of personal transformation advocated by the Buddha, and many aspects of the path have ethical dimensions.

In Mahāyāna Buddhism, the original teaching of the Buddha was modified in several important respects. Three of these are especially pertinent to ethics. The first is the assertion of the ideal of the bodhisattva, a figure of extraordinary compassion who is said to seek enlightenment in order not simply to overcome his or her own suffering (as was alleged to be the case for followers of the earlier tradition), but to enable all persons – indeed, all sentient beings – to overcome suffering. Second, those committed to pursuing the journey of a bodhisattva should do so by fulfilling Six Perfections: generosity, morality, patience, vigor, meditation, and wisdom. In many respects, striving to attain the Six Perfections is similar to following the Eightfold Path, but there are significant differences in detail and emphasis. From the Mahāyāna perspective, the Six Perfections are distinctive in being put in service of the purportedly superior bodhisattva ideal. In any case, the bodhisattva ideal and the Six Perfections together provide the basic ethical framework of Mahāyāna Buddhism. In order to understand this framework, however, it is essential to consider a third feature of Mahāyāna Buddhism, the contention that the perfection of wisdom to which a person on the bodhisattva path aspires is the realization of the emptiness of all things. To say that all things are empty is to say that they lack "own being" – that is, they have no inherent existence or essential nature of their own. Understanding the emptiness of all things is thought to be the key to achieving the universal compassion of a bodhisattva.

Was There a Moral Philosophy in Indian Buddhism?

It is evident from this brief summary that ethical concerns are at the heart of Indian Buddhist thought and practice. But do these concerns involve anything that could be called a moral philosophy? If we understand philosophy in a very broad way – for example, as consisting of some general ideas about how we ought to live our lives – then the answer is clearly yes. However, this is not a very useful sense of the term, since almost any ethical outlook would include a moral philosophy in this sense. By contrast, if we understand philosophy in a more specific way, in particular as relating closely to the intellectual enterprise developed by Socrates, Plato, and Aristotle, and to the teaching and research activities common in philosophy departments today, then the answer is basically no. Philosophy in this second, more strict sense is usually thought to concern rather abstract topics in fields such as metaphysics, epistemology, and ethics, and the proper form of philosophical reflection and discourse is believed to consist in paying close attention to consistency, carefully drawing distinctions, responding to objections, and above all rigorously and systematically formulating arguments in which premises are clearly articulated, and valid inferences from these premises are explicitly drawn to establish conclusions that are also clearly articulated. By this standard, a good deal of philosophy developed in Indian Buddhist thought, especially in fields such as metaphysics, epistemology, the philosophy of language, and the philosophy of mind. Though the texts of the Pāli canon and the *Perfection of Wisdom Sūtras* express philosophical positions and (sometimes) the rudiments of supporting arguments concerning central Buddhist ideas such as non-self and emptiness, it is only in works by later authors rooted in these texts – such as Nāgārjuna, Vasubandhu, and Dignāga – that these positions and arguments are developed and debated in a detailed, systematic, and careful way. There is no question that there were Buddhist philosophers in the Indian tradition who were quite capable of explicit, abstract, and rigorous reflection on philosophical topics.

It is often observed, however, that, though this tradition did generate systematic theoretical works in the fields of philosophy just noted, it did not generate such works in moral philosophy (e.g., Dreyfus 1995, 29). There are no texts in the Indian Buddhist tradition that resemble the classic moral philosophical treatises of Aristotle, Kant, and Sidgwick that are often taken to be paradigmatic of moral philosophy in the Western tradition. This is not to say that there is nothing in Indian Buddhism that contains philosophical reasoning on ethical topics. But this does not take the form of a systematic theoretical investigation into the nature of ethical concepts and principles that is common in the Western philosophical tradition.

A partial explanation of the absence of such investigation is that Buddhist thought was always oriented towards a practical aim, overcoming suffering, and the wisdom that was thought to be necessary for achieving this aim was primarily a metaphysical rather than an explicitly practical wisdom: the realization that there is no self or that all things are empty of inherent existence. However, the practical orientation of Buddhist thought does have one especially interesting parallel in the Western tradition: the Hellenistic schools of Epicureanism, Stoicism, and Pyrrhonian Skepticism.[2] A classic statement of this orientation in the Hellenistic schools comes from Epicurus: "Empty are the words of that philosopher who offers therapy for no human suffering (*pathos*). For just as there is no use in medical expertise if it does not give therapy for bodily diseases, so too there is no use in philosophy if it does not expel the suffering of the soul" (Long and Sedley 1987, 155). All three of the Hellenistic schools embraced a similar medical analogy to the effect that philosophy cures diseases of the soul just as medicine cures diseases of the body. This analogy has several implications. First, there are diseases of the soul (*psuchē* in Greek and *anima* Latin). These diseases were understood to be such things as anxiety, distress, fear, anger, and grief. Second, these diseases can be cured. Hence, a healthy soul was taken to be a soul that is mostly or wholly free of these diseases, a soul that has attained well-being (*eudaimonia*), understood to be an especially tranquil state. Third, philosophy has the expertise (art or skill) to effect this cure. A primary point of making the analogy was obviously to affirm this expertise. And, fourth, given the understanding of philosophy inherited from Socrates, Plato, and Aristotle, this expertise consists, at least in part, in the use of explicit philosophical argument in some sense. The Epicureans and Stoics can be read as maintaining that we can properly understand nature (both human nature and the world as a whole) on the basis of rational argument, and that this understanding will enable us to overcome the diseases of the soul and thus to achieve a peaceful form of well-being. The approach of the Skeptics was quite different, but they too can be read as claiming that rational argument brings about this well-being, except that it does so via suspension of belief.

One of the striking similarities between Hellenistic philosophy and Indian Buddhist thought is that Buddhists also made widespread use of a medical analogy (see Gowans 2010). For example, the Buddha is portrayed as a kind of physician, and his teaching is said to be akin to a medical analysis and treatment (see Ñāṇamoli and Bodhi 1995, 615–16, 867). In the most precise formulation of the analogy in Buddhism, the Four Noble Truths were said to be similar to a medical diagnosis. According to the great Theravāda commentator Buddhaghosa, "the truth of suffering is like a disease, the truth of origin is like the cause of the disease, the truth of cessation is like the cure of the disease, and truth of the path is like the medicine" (Ñāṇamoli 1999 [1975], 520). This appears to have some significant features in common with the medical analogy employed by the Hellenistic philosophers. First, the diseases of the soul – suffering in the First Noble Truth – are nearly identical. They refer to such things as anxiety, fear, anger, grief, and the like. Second, the claim that it is possible to attain a healthy state of being in which these diseases are overcome is also made in both cases. Though this healthy state is not understood in exactly the same way in the two traditions, there is significant overlap, in particular in the assertion that this state – *eudaimonia* in the Hellenistic tradition and nirvana in the Buddhist tradition – is a tranquil state. It should be added that there is also a similarity and a difference in the understanding of the cause of the disease: that it depends on craving and related phenomena (the Second Noble Truth) is substantially endorsed by both the Epicureans and the Stoics, but that this depends on the mistaken belief that one is a self or that things have inherent existence, the central Buddhist claims, is not accepted by any of the Hellenistic philosophers. The content of the wisdom needed to attain the healthy state is very different in Indian Buddhism and Hellenistic philosophy.

However, in both cases it was supposed that rigorous philosophical argument played an important role in attaining this wisdom. This does not mean that such argument by itself was sufficient for attaining *eudaimonia* or nirvana, respectively. The Stoics and Epicureans believed that, in addition to strictly rational considerations, a variety of therapeutic or spiritual exercises were required to reach the ideal state.[3] Prominent among these exercises were various efforts to bring about moral transformation. These included the use of imagination and narrative as well as techniques such as memorization and the examination of conscience. Philosophy in the sense of explicit rational argument was not a mere academic exercise: not only did it have a practical aim, it was one instrument among others for achieving this aim.

Something similar can be said about Indian Buddhism. In both the Theravāda and Mahāyāna traditions, wisdom is central to attaining nirvana and explicit philosophical argument plays a role in attaining wisdom. However, it is evident from both the Eightfold Path and the Six Perfections that the intellectual pursuit of wisdom so understood is one instrument among many for pursuing nirvana. Both programs of development emphasize moral training, and both involve exercises rather like those employed by the Hellenistic philosophers (albeit with the important difference that, for the most part, the meditative disciplines in Buddhism have no correlates in Hellenistic philosophy).

Though the affinities between Indian Buddhist thought and Hellenistic philosophy certainly suggest one significant way in which the aspirations and approaches of Buddhism were comparable to a familiar strand of Western philosophical thought, they also highlight the fact that Indian Buddhist philosophers were not inclined to develop a systematic moral philosophy. The ancient Greek Stoics and Epicureans such as Chrysippus and Epicurus wrote systematic theoretical works in moral philosophy rather similar in ambition to those of Aristotle.[4] They did not suppose that their practical aim and their employment of an array of means to attain it implied that it was inappropriate or pointless to do this. They were moral philosophers just as much as they were metaphysicians and epistemologists. The situation was rather different in Indian Buddhism. Though there were some philosophical considerations of ethical topics, these occurred primarily in practical contexts, especially in discussions of the path to enlightenment, usually alongside a good deal of moralizing and exhortation for moral improvement. There was virtually no aspiration to a general, systematic account of these topics. The main perspective was typically concern for moral training with a view to our overall spiritual progress. Moreover, many questions that Western philosophers have often found it natural to ask about moral philosophy were not directly addressed by Indian Buddhist philosophers. As a result, discussions of ethics in Indian Buddhism can often seem incomplete to those with Western philosophical expectations.

In the remainder of this chapter, we will survey the central ethical themes, first in the original teaching of the Buddha and then in subsequent developments in Mahāyāna

Buddhism. At the end, we will briefly discuss different interpretive responses that have been given to the absence of an explicit moral philosophy in Indian Buddhism.

Ethical Themes in the Original Teaching of the Buddha

The original teaching of the Buddha is said (by the Theravāda tradition) to be represented in the Pāli canon, especially in the collection of texts called the *Sutta Piṭaka* (one of the "Three Baskets") that include works such as the *Middle Length Discourses* (Ñāṇamoli and Bodhi 1995). Ethical themes are developed throughout these texts, and they are emphasized in particular in discourses such as "Effacement," "The Brahmins of Sālā," "To Potaliya," and "The Shorter Exposition of Action" (ibid., chs. 8, 41, 54, and 135). In addition, there are important discussions of ethical ideas in the Pāli canon in later non-Mahāyāna works such as *The Questions of King Milinda* (Mendis 2007) and Buddhaghosa's *The Path of Purification* (Ñāṇamoli 1999 [1975]).

An account of the original ethical teaching of the Buddha should begin with the doctrines of karma (*kamma/karma*) and rebirth. It is significant that a fundamental part of the Buddha's enlightenment experience was said to be the acquisition of an understanding of these doctrines. On the night of his enlightenment, the Buddha is said to have attained three kinds of "true knowledge." The third was knowledge of the Four Noble Truths. But the first two were knowledge of his past lives and knowledge that the cycle of rebirth is governed by the law of karma: those whose lives were "ill-conducted" were reborn "in a state of depravation," while those whose lives were "well-conducted" were reborn "in a good destination" (Ñāṇamoli and Bodhi 1995, 105–6). Karma and rebirth are fundamental features of the Buddha's ethical teaching: understanding them is a crucial part of right view, one step in the Eightfold Path. In discussions of Buddhism in the West in recent years, it has sometimes been suggested that karma and rebirth, as traditionally understood, may not be essential to what is important in the Buddha's message. Whatever might be said about the plausibility of this suggestion from a contemporary philosophical perspective, it is likely that the Buddha himself would have found it quite incredible. After all, his doctrine of liberation, as explained in the Four Noble Truths, is precisely liberation from the cycle of rebirth.

The concepts of karma and rebirth, as understood by the Buddha, are both influenced by and a critique of beliefs that were already widely held in India. In Brahmanism, the dominant religious tradition in India during the Buddha's lifetime, a form of rebirth had come to be accepted (and perhaps was accepted early on). However, what governed the quality of a person's rebirth was not ethical conduct but the proper performance of ritual. A distinctive feature of the Buddha's approach was to reject the importance of ritual and to emphasize that how well or badly we lived our lives, morally speaking, was the factor that determined how happy or unhappy we would be in future lives (the Jains' understanding of rebirth also emphasized ethics over ritual).

The Buddha understood karma and rebirth as natural causal processes in the universe. A basic feature of his teaching is that all things are causally conditioned or dependently arisen (*paṭicca samuppāda/pratītya-samutpāda*). Karma and rebirth are an instance of this general phenomenon. There is no suggestion that karma and rebirth should be understood as a system of cosmic justice in which a just God administers rewards and punishments. Karma is not presented as a form of desert: it is not claimed that morally good (bad) people deserve happiness (unhappiness). All that is claimed is that this is what happens as a natural part of the causal order of the universe. Karma is more akin to a principle of biology, such as the depiction of the process of photosynthesis, than the intervention of a divine being. A common metaphor is that morally good and bad actions are like seeds that will bear fruit in the future, either in this life or in a future life.

The cycle of rebirth is presented as part of a cosmology in which there are 31 planes of existence arranged from lower to higher levels of well-being. Human beings are situated below various gods (*devas*) at the upper levels of the hierarchy and above animals, ghosts, and others at the lower levels (non-sentient living things such as plants are not included). Depending on how we human beings live, we might be reborn as another human being, perhaps with more or less happiness than we enjoy in this life, or possibly as a god or an animal (similarly, an animal might be reborn as a human being or a god as an animal). All these beings are caught up in an ongoing process of rebirth called *saṃsāra* (meaning perpetual wandering). The entire process is governed by karma, but there is no indication that it has either a beginning or an overall purpose – though of course it is claimed that we can be liberated from it by attaining nirvana (if all beings were liberated, presumably the process would come to an end).

The word "karma" means action, and the doctrine of karma is an account of the consequences of an agent's actions for that agent. A full understanding of this doctrine requires a specification of what makes an agent's actions morally good or bad and what constitutes positive and negative consequences of those actions for the agent's happiness. The order of explanation is clear: good actions are not good because it turns out that they have positive consequences for the agent; rather, they have positive consequences for the agent because they are good actions. Hence, there must be some specification of what makes an action morally good or bad that is independent of the positive or negative karmic consequences of the action for the agent who performs it.

Many examples of morally good and bad actions are commonplaces and standard features of the Buddha's moral teaching. For instance, killing, lying, and being covetous are bad actions that generate negative consequences for the agent (these are respective instances of the three parts of a standard Buddhist classification of morally relevant actions into those which are bodily, verbal, and mental). Two pairs of terms are especially relevant to understanding the connotations of (what is rendered here in English as) good and bad actions. The first pair is *puñña* (*puṇya*) and *apuñña* (*apuṇya*). A *puñña* action is one that is purifying, or meritorious, and hence a source of positive fortune. An *apuñña* action is the opposite. The second and more important pair of terms is *kusala* (Skt *kuśala*) and *akusala* (Skt *akuśala*). A *kusala* action is one that is wholesome or healthy. It is also a skillful action, suggesting that good actions require some kind of skill. An *akusala* action is the opposite. The three roots of *akusala* actions are said to be greed (*lobha*), hatred (*dosa/dveṣa*), and delusion (*moha*), and the three roots of *kusala* actions are the opposite states of non-greed, non-hatred, and non-delusion. In more positive Buddhist terms, the last might be described as generosity (*dāna*), lovingkindness (*metta/maitrī*), and wisdom (*paññā/prajñā*). This is because what is fundamental to determining whether actions are good or bad is the mental state of the agent – in particular, his or her intention and motivation. It is primarily these that are said to be wholesome or unwholesome. Though it is common to speak of the karmic effects of particular actions, this is in some ways misleading. What matters most are actions as manifestations of good or bad moral character.

The positive and negative consequences of good and bad actions are usually portrayed in unsurprising terms. Morally good actions are said to result in such commonly recognized goods as wealth, social status and influence, good reputation, health, long life, beauty, wisdom, etc., as well as a happy or heavenly destination after death. Negative consequences are the opposite of these and are often portrayed in somewhat graphic terms rather similar to some traditional depictions of hell in Christianity. Another kind of consequence of actions is their influence on the development of a person's character. For example, a generous action makes another generous action more likely, and this in turn can lead to the development of generosity in a person (and similarly for a vice such as greed). Insofar as virtue is a constitutive feature of happiness or well-being and vice is a constitutive feature of the opposite – and there is reason to suppose that the Buddha thought that they were – the doctrine of karma can be seen as part of the Buddhist understanding of moral training.

Though the basic idea of karma is rather simple, a number of complexities were recognized in the ways in which the law of karma manifested itself. For example, better effects come from giving to persons who are more virtuous or spiritually advanced rather than less so, and especially good effects come from giving to the Sangha, the Buddhist monastic community. In addition, meditation – in particular, meditation on the "divine abode" of lovingkindness (about which there is more below) – can be a source of positive benefits. On the side of effects, the effects of good and bad actions can take place at any point in the future, and it appears rather indeterminate whether these will be soon, in this life, or in some future life. Moreover, the kinds of effects of our actions can also vary.

Several philosophical questions are raised by the doctrines of karma and rebirth. At the heart of these doctrines is the notion that we live in a morally ordered universe in which morality and happiness are intelligibly correlated in ongoing cycles of lives. An obvious question is whether or not the Buddha, or early followers of the Buddha, provided any compelling reason to believe that this is true, and the basic answer is that they did not. The Buddha spoke as if it were evident that these doctrines are true, presumably on the strength of his enlightenment experience, and his followers accepted the testimony of this experience or perhaps had what they took to be their own confirmation of it in meditative experience. Nothing that could be considered a philosophical argument, or ordinary empirical evidence, was presented in favor of these doctrines.

On occasion, the Buddha or one of his followers does respond to objections. For example, it might be claimed that a morally bad life does not always result in unhappiness for that person. The Buddha's response was that there must have been some moral goodness in the life or eventually there will have to be some unhappiness (Ñāṇamoli and Bodhi 1995, 1064). However, since these assertions refer to past and future lives, they are not verifiable in any ordinary way. A related objection, which to my knowledge was not discussed in the Pāli canon, is that it is morally problematic – unjust or unfair – to suppose that a very young child with cancer suffers on account of something he or she has done, presumably in a past life. It might be said in response that the objection begs the question: this is likely to appear problematic only if it is assumed that the child had no past life in which he or she performed morally wrong actions. However, even if this is true, it is also true that the belief that the child does suffer for this reason presupposes the truth of the Buddha's teaching about karma and rebirth. It might be thought to be unfair to the child to maintain this belief in the absence of undeniable evidence to support it. In response, a follower of the Buddha might claim that meditative experience does support it, and that, in any case, out of compassion we should always try to help the child overcome suffering. The use of the doctrine of karma was often (though not always) more forward-looking, to encourage morally good behavior, than backward-looking, to explain the good or bad fortune of people.

There are other more metaphysical issues raised by the doctrines of karma and rebirth. An obvious question is whether or not these doctrines are consistent with the non-self teaching: if there is no self, then what is reborn and bears the karmic fruits of the past? This question was considered by the Buddha and his early followers (Ñāṇamoli and Bodhi 1995, 350; see also Mendis 2007). Rebirth was understood in terms of a causal sequence of mental events from one life to the next that often creates the illusion, but does not require the actual existence, of a distinct self with identity through time. Another question that might seem equally pressing was not discussed in Indian Buddhism: does karma (and in general the doctrine of causal conditioning) involve some form of determinism, and are these compatible with freedom of the will? Some contemporary interpreters have argued that determinism is an implication of Buddhist teaching, and some have maintained that a doctrine of free will is presupposed in this teaching. In recent discussions, different views have been put forward about whether or not these would be compatible. But these issues did not engage the tradition.

The heart of the remainder of the Buddha's teaching is briefly outlined in the Four Noble Truths. The first of these declares that all human lives – and indeed all lives in the cycle of rebirth – are characterized by suffering, no matter how happy or unhappy they might be. The term "suffering" is the most common translation of *dukkha* (*duḥkha*). A better translation might be "unsatisfactoriness," but it is probably best to stay with the less cumbersome term "suffering" and remain aware of its limitations. The Buddha thought that there is something fundamentally unsatisfactory or problematic about unenlightened human life. But he did not suppose that we are always miserable, and he did not think that the First Noble Truth means that no form of happiness is possible for the unenlightened. Various familiar features of our lives are associated with suffering. These include aging, illness, and death as well as experiencing what is unpleasant and not getting what we want. A frequent characterization is that "what is impermanent is suffering" (Bodhi 2000, 2: 1133). That all things are impermanent is a central aspect of the Buddha's teaching, and it is not difficult to see the connection with suffering. If we have things we want or find pleasing, we fear that we might lose them, and if we have avoided what we do not want or find displeasing, we fear that these things may eventually overcome us. The Buddha drew attention to common anxieties about these prospects. However, what matters most for suffering is not simply what happens to us but our mental attitude towards what happens.

This is evident in what the Buddha says about pain: though he associates pain with suffering, persons who are enlightened, and hence have overcome suffering, are portrayed as sometimes having pain (the Buddha himself is reported to have suffered great pains just before his death). According to the Buddha, when an unenlightened person feels pain, "he sorrows, grieves, and laments; he weeps beating his breast and becomes distraught. He feels two feelings – a bodily one and a mental one." By contrast, when an enlightened person feels pain, he does not sorrow and grieve: "he feels one feeling – a bodily one, not a mental one" (Bodhi 2000, 2: 1264). The difference between the unenlightened and enlightened person is a mental attitude: while the first person feels aversion to the pain, the second person does not. The Buddha's teaching is analogous to medical treatment, not a replacement of it. A medical doctor might alleviate our pain. What the Buddha purports to alleviate is our distress about the pain.

This is made clearer in the Second Noble Truth, the assertion that the origin of suffering is craving. The term "craving" is a translation of *taṇhā* (*tṛṣṇā*). This connotes powerful and incessant desires that are difficult or impossible to satisfy fully. Closely related terms include greed, lust (*rāga*), hatred, and clinging (*upādāna*). Some texts seem to suggest that all forms of desire are sources of suffering. This would imply that an enlightened person, having overcome suffering, has no desires. However, the word "desire" in English encompasses a great deal. In one familiar sense, a desire is a disposition to bring something about (to the extent that this is in one's power). For example, my desire for food is a disposition to bring it about that I eat. In the Pāli canon, enlightened persons are regularly portrayed as having dispositions to bring things about. In particular, the Buddha is depicted as being compassionate, as being disposed to bring it about that people attain enlightenment. He appears to desire this. Hence, it does not seem plausible to suppose that all forms of desire are a source of suffering. However, it is clear that many desires that are especially urgent and disruptive, both to attain what we think would be pleasing and to avoid what we think would be displeasing, are at the root of suffering for the Buddha. Suffering is the dissatisfaction that accompanies these cravings.

There is more to the story of craving and suffering. The deeper source of these is a specific form of delusion, namely the false belief that one is a self. The craving that my pain must end, and the suffering that goes with this craving, originates in the connection of the pain with the perspective of "I," "me," and "mine," – as, for example, in the thought that "this pain is mine." Likewise, the realization that one is not a self, the key to enlightenment, undermines this thought (there is no "me" to whom this pain belongs) and hence eliminates the craving that this pain must end. Enlightenment does not eliminate the pain, but it does eliminate the suffering, the dissatisfaction that is associated with the urgent desire that my pain must end. The Buddha, as compassionate, appeared to desire that the pain of all living beings end. But he did not experience any of these pains as his own – as, from his perspective, *mine* – and so he did not crave that they end. The realization of one's selflessness is the crucial element in overcoming suffering.

The Third Noble Truth tells us that it is possible to attain this state, a state that is often referred to as nirvana (*nibbāna*/*nirvāṇa*). The Buddha said that he taught the Four Noble Truths so that people could attain nirvana: it is obviously the focal point of his practical teaching. In view of this, it might be thought that he would have a great deal to say about it. However, the Buddha's depictions of nirvana are infrequent, sometimes perplexing, and usually in terms of what it is not rather than what it is. He appeared to think that the unenlightened would find it difficult to understand nirvana while the enlightened would have no need for an account of it. Nonetheless, the Buddha did give some indication of what it would mean to attain nirvana.

A person who has reached the state of nirvana is called an *arahant* (*arhat*). A distinction is drawn between an *arahant* who is still alive and an *arahant* who has died. Almost nothing is said about an *arahant* who has died except that he or she has escaped the cycle of rebirth. More is said about an *arahant* who is still alive. Accounts of this, alongside accounts of the Buddha's own life after his enlightenment, reveal a great deal about the ethical character of the Buddha's teaching. In line with what has been said above, we are told that an enlightened person who is alive "still experiences what is agreeable and disagreeable and feels pleasure and pain" just as an unenlightened person does (Ireland 1997, 181). The difference is that, in an enlightened person, the three roots of unwholesome actions – greed, hatred, and delusion – have been destroyed. The delusion that has been destroyed is the false belief that one is a self. This puts an end to troublesome desires and aversions – nirvana is sometimes depicted simply as the destruction of craving – and this brings suffering to an end. However, this characterization leaves out an important dimension of nirvana. It is portrayed not merely as the absence of craving or suffering but, in much more positive terms, as a state of supreme peace or tranquility, indeed as a blissful state. It appears to be the ultimate state of happiness or well-being.

Since a living *arahant* is destined to escape the cycle of rebirth at death, he or she is no longer generating positive and negative future consequences through morally good and bad actions. In light of this, it can sometimes appear that an *arahant* is beyond morality altogether. But this is a misleading characterization. It would be more accurate to say that an *arahant* is supremely virtuous. One of way seeing this is in connection with the four divine abodes (sometimes called the immeasurable deliverances of the mind): lovingkindness, compassion, appreciative joy, and equanimity. These are presented in a variety of contexts. They are both forms of ethical training, typically involving meditation, and ethical states of being to which this training is directed, states that are perfected in an *arahant*. According to Buddhaghosa, the divine abodes "bring to perfection all the good states" and "are the best in being the right attitude towards beings" (Ñāṇamoli 1999 [1975], 325, 320).

Lovingkindness (*mettā*/*maitrī*) means wishing for the happiness or welfare of all beings. This enables us to overcome ill-will. Compassion (*karuṇā*) means striving to eliminate the suffering of others. This allows us to overcome cruelty. Compassion has great importance in the Buddha's teaching. He decided to teach out of compassion for all persons, and he instructed his first followers to do the same. Appreciative joy (*muditā*) is taking pleasure in persons who are happy and doing well. This enables us to overcome envy or aversion. Equanimity (*upekkhā*/*upekṣā*) is a peaceful state of neutrality that is neither glad nor sad. It implies regarding different kinds of persons – including those who are dear, neutral, and hostile – with impartiality. This is said to allow us to overcome greed or resentment.

In short, an *arahant* who is alive still feels pleasure and pain, but has overcome suffering insofar as he or she has realized the absence of self, destroyed greed, hatred, and delusion, attained a tranquil and blissful state, and acquired the supreme virtues of lovingkindness, compassion, appreciative joy, and equanimity. According to the Fourth Noble Truth, the way to become an *arahant* is to follow the Eightfold Path, the most prominent of several summaries of how to attain enlightenment. This was presented as a "middle way" between "the pursuit of sensual happiness" and "the pursuit of self-mortification" (Bodhi 2000, 2: 1844). The eight steps of the path concern eight right or correct (*sammā*/*samyak*) ways of doing things. These were divided into three groups: wisdom (*paññā*), morality (*sīla*/*śīla*), and concentration (*samādhi*). However, all three of these groups have ethical dimensions. They are clearly intended to be mutually supportive. For example, we are told that wisdom and morality purify one another. It appears that the eight steps are to be pursued not in strict sequence, but more or less together, though at any given time some parts may receive more attention than others.

The wisdom section includes right view and right intention. Right view is usually said to be knowledge of the Four Noble Truths, but it clearly involves knowledge of the Buddha's teaching as a whole. Hence, a person needs to understand karma and rebirth as well as the basic metaphysical doctrines of impermanence, dependent origination, and, especially, non-self. Since craving and suffering are said to depend on ignorance or delusion, it is not surprising that overcoming these is thought to require knowledge. Right intention means "intention of renunciation, intention of non-ill will, and intention of non-cruelty" (Ñāṇamoli and Bodhi 1995, 1100). Renunciation is renunciation of sensual desire. If we convert right intention into more affirmative Buddhist language, we could think of it as a commitment to being free of sensual desire as well as living in accord with the values of lovingkindness and compassion. Though included in the wisdom section, right intention has obvious moral content.

Right speech, right action, and right livelihood are three steps of the Eightfold Path classified under *sīla*, a term that is variously translated as morality, ethics, moral virtue, or moral discipline. Right speech is not engaging in speech that is false, malicious, harsh, or idle, and right action is not "killing living beings," not "taking what is not given," and not engaging in "misconduct in sensual pleasures" (Ñāṇamoli and Bodhi 1995, 1100). The primary reference of the last is sexual misconduct (for monastics, this would be any departure from strict celibacy; for others, it would include such things as adultery). Together these look rather similar to some of the Ten Commandments. The Buddha also prohibited, though not explicitly as part of the Eightfold Path, the consumption of intoxicants such as alcohol. When combined with right speech and action, we have the five moral precepts that are sometimes said to be the minimal standards of Buddhist ethics: prohibitions on improper speech, killing, stealing, sexual misconduct, and consuming alcohol.[5] The Buddha had little to say about right livelihood, but its general meaning is obviously that we are not to earn our living in a way that involves violation of the other parts of the ethical code – for example, by trading weapons or alcoholic beverages. It is somewhat surprising that right livelihood is featured in the Eightfold Path, at least insofar as this path was intended primarily for monastics: since they lived on alms, they did not earn a livelihood in the ordinary sense. The Buddha spoke mostly to monastics because he thought that a monastic life was the primary way to attain enlightenment. But he allowed that it was possible for laypersons to gain enlightenment, and sometimes his teaching was directed to these persons. For example, he described ethically proper ways for husbands and wives to treat one another.[6]

The Buddha clearly thought that moral rules were very important. All Buddhists were expected to follow the five precepts in some form, and the monastic community was governed by over 200 rules (more for women than for men). Divine abodes such as lovingkindness and compassion, and other important attributes such as generosity and patience, are best thought of as moral virtues. They are morally admirable character traits that cannot helpfully be put in the form of rules. There is also a rich array of terms for moral vices such as envy, avarice, arrogance, and vanity (among many others). It is evident that both moral rules, typically in the form of prohibitions, and character traits are emphasized in the Buddha's original moral teaching.

The concentration section of the Eightfold Path includes right effort, right mindfulness, and right concentration. The first of these concerns, once again, is ethical training: we are to make great effort to eliminate and prevent unwholesome states and to bring about and develop wholesome states. Unwholesome states are based on the three unwholesome roots – greed, hatred, and delusion – and wholesome states are based on the opposites of these. This is an important preparation for the meditative disciplines that constitute the remaining two aspects of the path. Right mindfulness involves various contemplations (of the body, feelings, mind, and mind-objects) and right concentration concerns the attainment of four progressively higher meditative states (*jhānas/dhyānas*). These disciplines are fundamental to Buddhist training. They may not seem to be forms of ethical development, but from a Buddhist perspective they are closely related to it. For example, as preparation for right concentration, it is necessary to overcome "the five hindrances," namely covetousness for the world, ill will and hatred, sloth and torpor, restlessness and remorse, and doubt (Ñāṇamoli and Bodhi 1995, 275).

The early Buddhist tradition envisioned many forms of meditation. A basic distinction is between serenity meditation (*samatha-bhāvanā/śamatha-bhāvanā*), meditative practices that aim to purify and calm the mind (sometimes correlated with right concentration), and insight meditation (*vipassanā-bhāvanā/vipaśyanā-bhāvanā*), meditative disciplines that bring about direct knowledge or wisdom (sometimes correlated with right mindfulness). Some forms of meditation have clear ethical content. Central examples of these are the meditations on the divine abodes mentioned earlier (lovingkindness, compassion, appreciative joy, and equanimity). In connection with these, Buddhaghosa describes a variety of meditation practices such as a technique in which a person extends lovingkindness first to himself, then to a friend, then to a neutral person, and finally to an enemy. These meditations are directly concerned with the development of moral character.

Ethical Themes in Mahāyāna Buddhism

The origins of Mahāyāna Buddhism are not well understood. However, it is generally agreed that, in the period from about the first century BCE to the first century CE, texts in Sanskrit began to appear in India – most importantly, the *Perfection of Wisdom Sūtras* – that purported to be, in some sense, the word of the Buddha and yet contained a teaching that was said to be superior to the teaching of earlier forms of Buddhism (pejoratively called the Hīnayāna, "Lesser Vehicle," in contrast to the Mahāyāna, "Great Vehicle," that was the new teaching). The new teaching did not repudiate most of the fundamentals of the old teaching, but it did expand, reinterpret, and revise it in some important ways. It was sometimes said that the Buddha inaugurated this new teaching because people at that time, but not earlier, were ready to receive it. There are numerous practical and theoretical features of Mahāyāna Buddhism that distinguish it from the earlier forms of Buddhism. For the purpose of this chapter, what is primarily important are the bodhisattva ideal, the Six Perfections, an understanding of "skillful means" that pertains to morality, and the paradoxical nature of some Mahāyāna moral discourse. These themes make it evident that morality is fundamental to the Mahāyāna tradition, arguably more so than it is in the Buddha's original teaching.

Though many *Perfection of Wisdom Sūtras* have significant ethical content – for example, *The Perfection of Wisdom in Eight Thousand Lines* (Conze 2006 [1973]) and *The Large Sūtra on Perfect Wisdom* (Conze 1975) – there are several other important sources of ethical teaching in the Indian Mahāyāna Buddhist tradition. These include Nāgārjuna's *Precious Garland* (Hopkins 1998), Āryadeva's *Four Hundred Verses* (Lang 1986), Ārya-Śūra's *Compendium of the Perfections* (Meadows 1986), Asaṅga's "The Chapter on Ethics" in the *Bodhisattva Stage* (Tatz 1986), Candrakīrti's *Advice for Travelers on the Bodhisattva Path* (Lang 2003), and Śāntideva's *Understanding the Way to Awakening* (Crosby and Skilton 1995) and *A Compendium of Buddhist Doctrine* (Bendall and Rouse 1971 [1922]). Though these texts are in some respects more philosophical than the *sūtras*, they are far from being systematic treatises in moral philosophy. Taken together, these classic Indian works – the *sūtras* and the more philosophical texts – were composed over a period of nearly a thousand years (the latest, those of Śāntideva, were probably written in the eighth century CE). Though they are unified in many respects, there are important differences in emphasis and approach. But we will focus on some common themes.

To a large extent, the ideal of the bodhisattva is the heart of Mahāyāna Buddhism. The two most fundamental characteristics of a bodhisattva are the mutually supportive traits of universal compassion, the commitment to enable all beings to overcome suffering, and wisdom, the realization of the emptiness (*suññatā*/*śūnyatā*) of all things. Each of these signifies an important modification of the earlier tradition. In that tradition, the Buddha was said to be a bodhisattva (P. *bodhisatta*) in previous lives, but this was not presented as a model for others to follow. By contrast, in Mahāyāna Buddhism the bodhisattva becomes a universal ideal. In the earlier tradition, each of us is encouraged to become an *arahant*, an enlightened being. But, in Mahāyāna Buddhism, each of us is encouraged to become a bodhisattva, a being who is committed to attaining perfect buddhahood for the sake of the enlightenment of all sentient beings.

Mahāyāna texts repeatedly proclaim the superiority of their teaching over previous forms of Buddhism. According to Nāgārjuna: "The subjects concerned with the Bodhisattva deeds were not mentioned in the [Hearers' Vehicle] sūtras but were explained in the Great Vehicle. Hence, the wise should accept it [as Buddha's word]."[7] One of the most common motifs in these texts is a contrast between the *arahant*, who is said to be inferior because he sought enlightenment only for himself, and the bodhisattva, who is said to be superior because he sought enlightenment, not just for himself but for the sake of all sentient beings. This contrast might seem surprising insofar as the *arahant* is portrayed in the Pāli canon as possessing universal compassion and other altruistic traits. How could such a figure be thought of as rather selfish? At least two kinds of philosophical answer to this question might be given. One has to do with the initial motivation for seeking enlightenment. In the earlier tradition, it sometimes appears that the reason for seeking enlightenment is that it is in one's self-interest, that it is good for a person to be enlightened. Mahāyāna Buddhism does not deny that enlightenment is good for a person, but it is committed to removing self-interest from the entire motivational structure of the bodhisattva path. Self-interest has no place on this path, even as an initial motivation for undertaking it. The other answer has to do with what is said to happen to the respective figures at death. In the Pāli canon, the *arahant* is portrayed as escaping the cycle of rebirth and attaining final nirvana. It is difficult to know exactly what this might mean, but it can look as if the *arahant*, even if compassionate as an enlightened being in this life, chooses at death to depart for the promised land with no concern for the rest of us, caught up as we are in the inevitable suffering of the cycle of rebirth. This can appear selfish in comparison with the bodhisattva, who is committed to remaining in the cycle of rebirth as long as it takes in order to help those who are not yet enlightened. There might also be a sociological explanation of the critique: it might be that, when the Mahāyāna tradition arose, some actual Buddhist monastics who were seeking enlightenment appeared as if they were basically seeking it for themselves. Perhaps, despite Buddhist teaching about compassion, they did not show much concern for anyone else. The Mahāyāna critique might have been a critique of practice on the ground as much as doctrine.

The rationales for the purported contrast between the bodhisattva and the *arahant* are evident in the central claim that the path of the bodhisattva begins with the aspiration to seek enlightenment, not just for oneself but for the sake of all sentient beings (one aspect of *bodhicitta*, the thought of enlightenment, a key Mahāyāna concept). Hence, from beginning to end, the bodhisattva path is characterized by an extraordinary altruistic commitment. However, it was recognized that this aspiration is itself a significant achievement that typically requires a process of moral development in past and present lives. For instance, there are meditative disciplines intended to promote the aspiration.

Bodhisattvas are often presented as cosmic beings, more godlike than human, and hence as subjects of devotion and addressees of prayer. As such, bodhisattvas are especially noteworthy for their extraordinary powers and ingenious skills as well as for their unlimited compassion. However, becoming an advanced bodhisattva over a multitude of lifetimes is commonly presented as a possibility for each human being on account of our buddha-nature (*buddha-dhātu*), our capacity for enlightenment, and indeed this is regarded as our highest calling: readers – at least those who are sufficiently advanced – are constantly urged to undertake and persist in the long and arduous bodhisattva path. This is the primary context in which the morality of Mahāyāna Buddhism finds expression. The substance of this morality takes a variety of forms, including prohibitions as well as virtues, and it is depicted in different systems of classification. The most prominent of these is the Six Perfections (*Pāramitās*): generosity, morality, patience, vigor, meditation, and wisdom. These perfections are discussed in numerous Mahāyāna texts.

The full bodhisattva path actually requires the attainment of ten perfections. The last four of these pertain to the cosmic development of the bodhisattva in future lives. The first six are the aforementioned Six Perfections, and these perfections chart a course of moral training in a human life (more or less) as we know it. In many respects, the

Six Perfections are a reworking of the Eightfold Path of the earlier tradition. Much of the content is substantially the same. However, there are important differences. Right livelihood is not featured in the Six Perfections, and generosity and patience, though certainly affirmed as virtues in the Pāli canon, are given increased importance in the Six Perfections. In addition, though wisdom is important on both lists, it is understood quite differently. The Six Perfections are usually presented in a standard sequence, the order followed below. This might suggest that they are to be undertaken and achieved one after the other, just as a person climbs the steps on a ladder. Sometimes they are associated with a series of temporal stages in spiritual progress. On this model, it is important to begin with generosity and to culminate with wisdom. But often it seems that the Six Perfections are to be pursued more or less simultaneously, the development of each reinforcing the development of the others. On this approach, it is only with the completion of the perfection of wisdom that the other perfections can be fulfilled.

The first perfection is generosity (*dāna*). Since the fundamental commitment of the bodhisattva is compassion, it is not surprising that generosity is featured at the beginning of the list. Generosity is sometimes understood in familiar ways – for example, as giving material goods – but what is more important is dispensing spiritual goods such as Buddhist teachings that will enable recipients to progress towards enlightenment. A distinctive feature of generosity emphasized in Mahāyāna Buddhism is the transfer of karmic merit from an advanced bodhisattva, who is thought to have accumulated a great deal, to other sentient beings (an apparent departure from an earlier understanding of karma in which, as it were, each person had his or her own karmic account, and there were no transfers from person to person). An important element of generosity is the mental state of the giver: in purer forms, generosity is selfless, involving no thought of reciprocation, rooted in an impartial concern for the well-being of all sentient beings. Sometimes the generosity of a bodhisattva is depicted as a form of extraordinary self-sacrifice – for example, giving up not only one's life but one's wife and children as well. In the perfected form of generosity, grounded in the realization of the emptiness of all things, what might ordinarily seem to be essential to generosity – the basic distinctions between giver, recipient, and gift – are seen as illusory. This is an example of what, from the standpoint of common sense, might appear to be the deeply paradoxical nature of much Mahāyāna Buddhist moral discourse (more about this below).

Morality (*śīla*), the second perfection, consists of a set of rules or precepts, often in the form of prohibitions. The related Pāli term *sīla* is employed in the threefold division of the Eightfold Path to refer to the section that encompasses right speech, action, and livelihood. Much of the content of the second perfection is substantially similar. For example, there are precepts proscribing lying or using harsh speech, stealing, harming or killing sentient beings, inappropriate sexual activity, etc. Beyond this there are numerous and often extensive lists of precepts in the tradition. This might suggest that morality in Mahāyāna Buddhism is at least to a large extent a matter of following a set of moral rules. This is not entirely wrong: persons on the bodhisattva path are ordinarily expected to follow the precepts. But this may be misleading. Adhering to the moral precepts is part of a program of the development of moral character. Hence, what is important is not merely outer actions such as not killing, but states of mind involving motive and intention. In addition, as will be seen below, there are circumstances in which it is envisioned that a bodhisattva would violate the rules out of compassion.

The third perfection is patience (*kṣānti*), sometimes translated as tolerance or forbearance. The main concern of patience is different kinds of adversity: suffering in general, but especially actions by others that are typically taken to be harmful, abusive, insulting, unjust, and the like. People usually respond to such actions with anger and sometimes hatred. Patience means overcoming these common reactions. Instead of anger, we are to respond with equanimity and calm. Instead of hatred, we are to respond with compassion. According to Śāntideva, "even if people are extremely malignant, all that is skillful should be done for them" (Crosby and Skilton 1995, 61). It was recognized that this is quite difficult to do – that, in effect, it requires a distinctive form of courage. Various explanations were offered as to why patience makes sense (for instance, anger has bad consequences, the harmful actions of others are conditioned by various factors, and the harms we suffer are due to our past actions on account of karma), and various techniques were put forward for developing this perfection. It might be thought that patience involves an objectionable passivity. But it is better understood as rejecting common reactions, such as trying to get back at someone, and replacing them with different forms of action rooted in compassion, including especially compassion for the wrongdoer. This differs from the moral outlook commonly presupposed in anger, but it is not sheer inaction.

The first three perfections have obvious moral content: generosity, various moral precepts, and patience. The remaining perfections are rather different. They do not specify additional moral virtues or principles as such. Rather, they concern activities that, in the context of the bodhisattva path, are considered essential to full moral development. The fourth perfection is vigor (*vīrya*). It is sometimes translated as energy, striving, or strength. This perfection concerns motivation and it relates closely to the concerns of right effort in the Eightfold Path, both in its opposition to unwholesome states and in its promotion of wholesome states. The unwholesome states are such things as sloth, despondency, and discouragement. Since the bodhisattva path is long and difficult, these are obstacles to pursuing it successfully. What is needed is determination, perseverance, and enthusiasm. In his discussion of this perfection, Śāntideva says that "desire for what is good must be created" (Crosby and Skilton 1995, 71).

The fifth perfection is meditation (*dhyāna*). As noted in the discussion of the concentration section of the Eightfold Path, there are various forms of meditation in the early Buddhist tradition. Many of these are incorporated into the Mahāyāna meditative disciplines, interpreted as part of the bodhisattva path rather than the journey to becoming an *arahant*. As in the earlier tradition, these disciplines often aim at serenity or wisdom. However, as before, some of them are concerned more directly with the development of moral character. Two of the best known of these are two meditations described by Śāntideva (Crosby and Skilton 1995, ch. 8). The first is a meditation on the equality of oneself and others. The second is a meditation focusing on an exchange of oneself and others. Each of these is intended to bring about a vivid realization that suffering as such is bad, not merely one's own suffering, and hence that overcoming the suffering of all beings is equally important.

The final perfection is wisdom (*prajñā*). In Mahāyāna Buddhism, the heart of wisdom is the realization of the emptiness of all things. To say that all things are empty is to say that they lack "own-being" (*svabhāva*) – that is, that they have no inherent existence or essential nature of their own. This is often thought to be an extension of the Buddha's non-self teaching and in particular an implication of his claim that all things are causally conditioned by other things. But the recognition of this implication, and of its full meaning and significance, is thought to come only in the Mahāyāna tradition. In addition, it is ordinarily supposed that the other five perfections may be truly perfected only with the realization of emptiness. More important, this realization is thought to go hand in glove with the universal compassion that animates the bodhisattva path: a person who fully grasps emptiness, and only such a person, will spontaneously work to liberate all beings from suffering.

Though the Six Perfections are clearly at the heart of Mahāyāna Buddhist ethics, there are two other topics that deserve attention here. First, an important difference between Mahāyāna Buddhism and earlier forms of Buddhism is an ethical application of the concept of skillful means (or skill in means, translations of *upāya-kauśalya*). This concept has great importance in Mahāyāna Buddhism and is employed in diverse ways. A central use is the contention that buddhas and bodhisattvas may teach in a variety of different ways – employ different skillful means – depending on their audience and context. From this perspective, Buddhist teachings are sometimes regarded as provisional claims, justified by their efficacy in promoting the aims of Buddhism, rather than as statements of straightforward doctrines. The ethical use of the concept of skillful means that is important here is the notion that the compassion and wisdom of a bodhisattva may sometimes justify violating the central Buddhist moral precepts. This can seem a surprising suggestion, since Mahāyāna texts commonly state that the moral precepts must not be broken. Yet a number of texts declare the contrary. For example, in the "Chapter on Ethics," it is said that a bodhisattva may perform acts that are "reprehensible by nature" if they are done with a good intention and have good results. For instance, a bodhisattva may overthrow an oppressive king for this reason. Other examples involve killing, stealing, sexual intercourse, and lying. In each of these cases, it is said, "there is no fault, but a spread of much merit" (Tatz 1986, 70–2). This understanding of skillful means might also shed light on the assertions of Vajrayāna or Tantric Buddhism (a prominent tradition in the later phases of Buddhism in India) to the effect that ordinarily forbidden actions involving such things as sexual intercourse or consumption of alcohol might sometimes be efficacious in attaining enlightenment. In both cases, violations of moral rules are sanctioned by more fundamental Buddhist aspirations.

These claims appear to diverge from the ethical outlook of earlier forms of Buddhism, for example, as enunciated in the Eightfold Path. Moreover, a number of questions are raised by these contentions. One is whether they can be reconciled with the intent of the rigorist passages within Mahāyāna Buddhism that appear to insist on a strict following of the precepts. Related to this is the issue whether, as sometimes seems to be the case, it makes sense for a bodhisattva who violates moral precepts out of compassion to be prepared to suffer negative karmic consequences on account of acting in this way (even if this does not happen). Are these violations still wrong or are they no longer wrong in these cases? Another question is whether such actions are merely morally permissible, as they sometimes appear to be, or are more like moral obligations (at least for some persons). Finally, there is an issue about whether breaking moral precepts out of compassion is reserved for advanced bodhisattvas, as typically seems to be the case, or whether this has implications for others who are less advanced, but have good intentions and know that breaking a precept will have the best results.

The texts that sanction violations of the moral precepts by bodhisattvas might be thought to suggest that they are on occasion beyond morality. But they are probably better interpreted as stating that sometimes bodhisattvas may transgress ordinary moral precepts in the name of a more fundamental moral commitment to compassion (and similarly in the examples from Vajrayāna Buddhism). However, there are other texts that seem to imply that bodhisattvas may be beyond morality in a different sense. Though advanced bodhisattvas (and buddhas) are often presented as ideal moral agents, as saintly figures we are invited to emulate, sometimes they appear more as forces of nature from which goodness spontaneously emanates than as anything that looks like a moral agent who has goals, makes judgments, forms intentions, and performs actions. For example, Nāgārjuna says: "In liberation there is no self and are no aggregates" (Hopkins 1998, 99). But, without aggregates, there would be no perceptions, volitions, or consciousness – each of which would seem to be essential for moral character. Since these liberated figures function in light of the full implications of selflessness and emptiness, they do not think of themselves as moral agents as these are ordinarily understood (indeed, they do not think of *themselves* at all). Hence, though much Buddhist moral teaching is manifestly about the development of moral character, there is a sense in which the ultimate goal of this development is a state that cannot be correctly described as a state of character as usually understood. This is one of the many paradoxical features of Mahāyāna Buddhism. Other paradoxes stem from the non-dualist implications of emptiness. For example, since nothing has an essential nature, there is no real difference between nirvana and the cycle of rebirth or between following the precepts and breaking them. Again, according to Nāgārjuna, "here long and short, subtle and coarse, virtue and non-virtue, and here names and forms, all are ceased" (ibid.). In Mahāyāna Buddhism, these paradoxical formulations are not only tolerated, they are often eagerly embraced (by contrast, in earlier forms of Buddhism, paradoxical statements are hardly unknown, but their assertion is more limited and cautious). In this mode of discourse, rooted in an understanding of ultimate truth as emptiness, the staples of ordinary moral thought (such as the attributes of moral character and the elements of basic moral distinctions) are said to lack inherent existence. Morality as typically understood might seem to disappear altogether. However, the discourse of ultimate truth is complemented by another mode of discourse, that of conventional truth, the pragmatically useful speech of common sense, in which our customary ways of speaking about moral character and moral distinctions are preserved, now understood for what they are in light of the insight of emptiness. This is also a common way of speaking about ethics in Mahāyāna Buddhism. Indeed, it is an indispensable way of speaking. But its use is thought to be unproblematic so long as its status as conventional truth is understood.

Buddhist Moral Philosophy

We have now surveyed the main features of Indian Buddhist ethical thought. Let us now return to the fact that Indian Buddhists, though deeply committed to a set of ethical values, did not develop an explicit systematic moral philosophy to understand these values. For the most part, the customary concerns and issues of Western moral philosophers were not directly addressed by Indian Buddhists. Broadly speaking, there are two basic interpretive responses that may be taken to this absence. First, it might be argued that Indian Buddhists tacitly presupposed a systematic moral philosophy, or perhaps more than one moral philosophy (since they sometimes disagreed with one another), but did not fully and directly articulate it. On this approach, various aspects of Buddhist ethical thought may be seen as indications of a general moral philosophy that, for whatever reasons, was never completely stated and developed. Hence, such a moral philosophy could properly be attributed to Indian Buddhists, as something they implicitly accepted, even though they did not spell it out. An attempt to explain this moral philosophy may be called a *reconstructive* approach. Second, by contrast, it might be maintained that Indian Buddhists thought that the development of a systematic, theoretical moral philosophy was pointless or perhaps even contrary to the pursuit, or nature, of Buddhist enlightenment. On this view, it is no accident that no such moral philosophy was developed: it was a conscious decision firmly rooted in Buddhist perspectives. An argument along this line may be called an *antithetical* approach.

As illustrations of these divergent lines of interpretation, we may conclude by briefly considering two central examples of the reconstructive approach, one from meta-ethics and one from normative ethics, along with the responses of their antithetical critics. First, it has been claimed that a passage from Śāntideva, in which he discusses the meditation on the equality of oneself and others, implicitly contains an argument for an obligation to prevent all pain or suffering.[8] According to this argument, the non-self teaching shows that there is no real distinction between one's own pain and the pain of others (pain is impersonal). Hence, either all pain is ultimately bad or no pain is ultimately bad. But it is absurd to say that no pain is ultimately bad. Hence, all pain is ultimately bad, and so there is an obligation to end it (and not merely one's own pain). However, it has been claimed that it is not obvious that Śāntideva is endorsing this argument, and that the text should be understood simply as a description of a meditation technique rather than as an argument for Buddhist altruism (Harris 2011). Moreover, it has also been argued that the Madhyamaka school of Mahāyāna Buddhism, of which Śāntideva is a part, is concerned basically with practice rather than with the justification of its ultimate moral commitments (Finnigan and Tanaka 2011).

Second, some interpreters have maintained that Indian Buddhism, especially in the Mahāyāna tradition, is committed to a form of ethical consequentialism, the view that the moral rightness of an action depends entirely on the fact that it has the best overall consequences for all sentient beings. The centrality of overcoming all suffering, and the occasional willingness to violate moral precepts to achieve this, has been thought to lend credence to this interpretation.[9] However, others have rejected this consequentialist reading and have argued that Buddhism is best understood as similar to virtue theory – the view that the moral rightness of an action depends entirely on what a virtuous agent would characteristically do.[10] The great emphasis on the importance of mental states such as intention and motivation, as well as on the centrality of virtues such as generosity and compassion, has been supposed to give support to this interpretation. Both the consequentialist and the virtue interpretations are reconstructive approaches.[11] However, against both of these, it may be said that it is not obvious that Indian Buddhists had any interest in establishing whether consequences or virtues are the most fundamental moral concept, and some commentators have argued that they were not committed to any normative ethical theory.[12] In this view, the ethical concerns of Indian Buddhists were mainly practical, and they addressed particular cases, not on the basis of a unified theoretical structure but through discussions of stories, exemplars, and the like.

Notes

1 The primary languages of Indian Buddhism are Pāli and Sanskrit. For key terms, the Pāli and/or Sanskrit originals are in parentheses (where these differ, the Pāli comes first).

2 For an early statement of this parallel, see Dreyfus (1995). See also Cooper and James (2005).

3 For discussion of these, see Hadot (1995), Nussbaum (1994), and Sorabji (2000).

4 These works survive only in fragments, but we have good reason to think that they were written.

5 For discussion of these, see Harvey (2000, 66–79).

6 Moral precepts for laypersons are presented in "To Sigālaka: Advice to Lay People," in Walshe (1987, ch. 31).

7 Hopkins (1998, 147). The expression "Hearers' Vehicle" refers to the original teaching of the Buddha.

8 See Siderits (2003, 102–3). The passage from Śāntideva is found in Crosby and Skilton (1995, 96–7).

9 For example, see Goodman (2009, 2010) and Siderits (2003, 2007).

10 For instance, see Cooper and James (2005); also Keown (1992).

11 They are sometimes combined; see Clayton (2006).

12 For example, see Garfield (2010 and nd.) and Hallisey (1996).

References

Bendall, Cecil, and Rouse, W. H. D. (trans.) (1971 [1922]). *Śikṣā-Samuccaya: A Compendium of Buddhist Doctrine, Compiled by Śāntideva Chiefly from the Earlier Mahāyāna Sūtras*. Delhi: Motilal Banarsidass.

Bodhi, Bhikkhu (trans.) (2000). *The Connected Discourses of the Buddha*. 2 vols. Boston: Wisdom.

Clayton, Barbra (2006). *Moral Theory in Śāntideva's Śikṣāssamuccaya: Cultivating the Fruits of Virtue*. New York: Routledge.

Conze, Edward (trans.) (1975). *The Large Sutra on Perfect Wisdom with the Divisions of the Abhisamayālaṅkāra*. Berkeley: University of California Press.

Conze, Edward (trans.) (2006 [1973]). *The Perfection of Wisdom in Eight Thousand Lines and its Verse Summary*. San Francisco: City Lights.

Cooper, David E., and James, Simon P. (2005). *Buddhism, Virtue and Environment*. Burlington, VT: Ashgate.

Crosby, Kate, and Skilton, Andrew (trans.) (1995). *Śāntideva: The Bodhicaryāvatāra*. Oxford: Oxford University Press.

Dreyfus, Georges (1995). Meditation as Ethical Activity. In *Journal of Buddhist Ethics* 2, 28–54.

Finnigan, Bronwyn, and Tanaka, Koji (2011). Ethics for Mādhyamikas. In *Moonshadows: Conventional Truth in Buddhist Philosophy*. Ed. The Cowherds. New York: Oxford University Press, 221–31.

Garfield, Jay L. (2010). What is it Like to be a Bodhisattva? Moral Phenomenology in Śāntideva's *Bodhicaryāvatāra*. In *Journal of the International Association of Buddhist Studies* 33, 333–57.

Garfield, Jay L. (nd.). Buddhist Ethics. Unpublished paper.

Goodman, Charles (2009). *Consequences of Compassion: An Interpretation and Defense of Buddhist Ethics*. New York: Oxford University Press.

Goodman, Charles (2010). Ethics in Indian and Tibetan Buddhism. In *The Stanford Encyclopedia of Philosophy*. Ed. Edward N. Zalta. At: http://plato.stanford.edu/archives/fall2010/entries/ethics-indian-buddhism/.

Gowans, Christopher W. (2010). Medical Analogies in Buddhist and Hellenistic Thought: Tranquility and Anger. In *Philosophy as Therapeia*. Ed. Clare Carlisle and Jonardon Ganeri. Cambridge: Cambridge University Press, 11–33.

Hadot, Pierre (1995). Spiritual Exercises. In *Philosophy as a Way of Life: Spiritual Exercises from Socrates to Foucault*. Trans. Michael Chase. Oxford, and Cambridge, MA: Blackwell, 81–125.

Hallisey, Charles (1996). Ethical Particularism in Theravada Buddhism. In *Journal of Buddhist Ethics* 3, 32–43.

Harris, Stephen (2011). Does *Anātman* Rationally Entail Altruism? On *Bodhicaryāvatāra* 8:101–103. In *Journal of Buddhist Ethics* 18, 93–123.

Harvey, Peter (2000). *An Introduction to Buddhist Ethics: Foundations, Values and Issues*. Cambridge: Cambridge University Press.

Hopkins, Jeffrey (trans.) (1998). *Buddhist Advice for Living and Liberation: Nāgārjuna's Precious Garland*. Ithaca, NY: Snow Lion.

Ireland, John D. (trans.) (1997) *The Udāna & The Itivuttaka: Two Classics from the Pāli Canon*. Kandy, Sri Lanka: Buddhist Publication Society.

Keown, Damien (1992). *The Nature of Buddhist Ethics*. New York: St Martin's Press.

Lang, Karen C. (trans.) (1986). *Āryadeva's Catuḥśataka: On the Bodhisattva's Cultivation of Merit and Knowledge*. Copenhagen: Akademisk Forlag.

Lang, Karen C. (trans.) (2003). *Four Illusions: Candrakīrti's Advice for Travelers on the Bodhisattva Path*. New York: Oxford University Press.

Long, A. A., and Sedley, D. N. (eds) (1987). *The Hellenistic Philosophers*, Vol. 1: *Translations of the Principal Sources, with Philosophical Commentary*. Cambridge: Cambridge University Press.

Meadows, Carol (trans. and ed.) (1986). *Ārya-Śūra's Compendium of the Perfections: Text, Translation and Analysis of the Pāramitāsamāsa*. Bonn: Indica et Tibetica Verlag.

Mendis, N. K. G. (trans. and ed.) (2007). *The Questions of King Milinda: An Abridgement of the Milindapañha*. Kandy, Sri Lanka: Buddhist Publication Society.

Ñāṇamoli, Bhikkhu (trans.) (1999 [1975]). *The Path of Purification (Visuddhimagga) by Bhadantācariya Buddhaghosa*. Seattle: Buddhist Publication Society Pariyatta Editions.

Ñāṇamoli, Bhikkhu, and Bodhi, Bhikkhu (ed. and trans.) (1995). *The Middle Length Discourses of the Buddha (Majjhima Nikāya)*. Boston: Wisdom.

Nussbaum, Martha (1994). *The Therapy of Desire: Theory and Practice in Hellenistic Ethics*. Princeton, NJ: Princeton University Press.

Siderits, Mark (2003). *Personal Identity and Buddhist Philosophy: Empty Persons*. Burlington, VT: Ashgate.

Siderits, Mark (2007). Buddhist Reductionism and the Structure of Buddhist Ethics. In *Indian Ethics: Classical Traditions and Contemporary Challenges*, Vol. 1. Ed. Purushottama Bilimoria, Joseph Prabhu, and Renuka Sharma. Burlington, VT: Ashgate, 283–95.

Sorabji, Richard (2000). *Emotion and Peace of Mind: From Stoic Agitation to Christian Temptation.* New York: Oxford University Press.

Tatz, Mark (1986). *Asanga's Chapter on Ethics with the Commentary of Tsong-Kha-Pa, The Basic Path to Awakening, The Complete Bodhisattva.* Studies in Asian Thought and Religion, Vol. 4. Lewiston, NY: Edwin Mellen Press.

Walshe, Maurice (trans.) (1987). *The Long Discourses of the Buddha.* Boston: Wisdom.

29

Character, Disposition, and the Qualities of the *Arahats* as a Means of Communicating Buddhist Philosophy in the *Suttas*

SARAH SHAW

A popular protective chant in South-East Asia and Sri Lanka salutes eight *arahats*, companions of Gotama Buddha, thought to guard the four directions and their median points (Skilling 2000; Shaw 2009, 134–8). Their stories are described in the earliest Buddhist texts and would be well known to Southern Buddhists, told such narratives from childhood. In the East is Kondañña, who, at the boy's birth, foresaw that he would become a fully awakened buddha, and went to wait until that event occurred. He is the "first to see," becoming enlightened immediately after the Buddha's first teaching, and is of quick wisdom and apprehension: having spent many past lives preparing for the advent of a buddha, he is immediately ready to attain his final goal. In the West, in direct contrast, is Ānanda, the Buddha's attendant, whose personal path is slow: he attains enlightenment only after resigning himself to failure in this the day before the First Council after the Buddha's death, to which only enlightened followers are invited. He achieves arahatship however, between standing up and lying down, just as he is getting into bed to go to sleep after apparently fruitless effort. It is because of his copious memory that the entire Buddhist corpus of texts was remembered and developed for recitation. In the South is Sāriputta. Of quick progress in the path, he masters the meditations on calm (*samatha*), but is known primarily as the teacher pre-eminent in wisdom, whose golden-colored image frequently appears in art as, literally, the Buddha's right-hand man. Opposite, in the North, is (Mahā)Moggallāna, whose body is the color of the blue lotus or the rain cloud, master of psychic powers and exponent of *samatha* meditation, usually depicted on the Buddha's left. Less interested in doctrinal analysis, he is enabled by his psychic abilities to visit beings in many realms and to exercise great feats of psychic skill. At the intermediate directions are, in the South-East, (Mahā)Kassapa, a lover of austerity, ascetic practices, and solitary rural retreats, who is opposed to Gavampati, in the North-West, whose great power is demonstrated only occasionally, at times of crisis, as, according to the stories, he prefers to rest in heaven realms on most afternoons. In the South-West is Upāli, a low-caste barber who became

---

A Companion to Buddhist Philosophy, First Edition. Edited by Steven M. Emmanuel.

pre-eminent in upholding and explaining the monks' monastic rules, and, in the North-East, opposite him, is Rāhula, the well-born and gifted son of the Buddha, who became an *arahat* shortly after taking ordination with his father.

The chant says that these *arahats* "sit," in the present tense, to protect the person who chants to them, with the Buddha at the center.[1] Their importance in modern practice is testimony to the way followers of the Buddha, such as these, of such great diversity of caste, type of person, and temperamental disposition, have played a central role in Southern Buddhism.[2] Their life stories, and "past" life stories, are constantly told to children and recounted through narratives from the *Jātakas* and the *Dhammapada* commentary.[3] They are regarded with affection and respect by Southern Buddhists, and are frequently depicted in murals, tableaux, and statues around Buddhist temples, as well as in manuscripts, comics, and children's books. These *arahats* have also accompanied the Buddha through the many lives in which he is said to have developed the ten perfections in his preparation for his final life, a testimony to the central role the early *saṅgha* played and still plays in Southern Buddhist practice. If the nuns, such as the chief female disciples of Khemā and Upalavaṇṇā, and chief lay disciples, Citta among men and Visākhā among women, are included, a sense of the great diversity of modes of practice, from all four assemblies of monks, nuns, laymen, and laywomen, is communicated. Other important characters in the Buddha's life, such as his wife, are also frequently cited, with their stories often recounted at festivals and talks on the teaching (*Dhamma*).[4]

In practice, it is stories of the progress of these figures that have provided the principal source of information to lay Buddhists about meditative practice, the variety of approaches possible in the development of meditation and wisdom, and an underlying understanding that, after enlightenment, character does not disappear. Indeed, the most popular chant in Southern Buddhist countries, the *iti pi so*, is to the Buddha, the teaching, and the *ariyasaṅgha* – those who have attained any stage of path. The qualities of each are enumerated according to the formulae associated with recollections of each of these three elements, and both chanted in a eulogy as a daily homage and used as a meditation practice (*anussati*; see Shaw 2006b, 112–23). The *arahats* exhibit behavior that is idiosyncratic, non-formulaic, and in accordance with their disposition, but which nonetheless demonstrates their enlightened status in different ways, as they manifest disparate powers and abilities in their teaching and guiding of others around them. In the recent and welcome reawakening of respect for the Buddhist narrative traditions for their enactment of Buddhist principle over the last two decades, the feature that has been most popular among practicing Southern Buddhists, the nature of the various characters who embody the path and the manner of their participation and intercessions in the embodied discourses of the Buddha, is starting to receive the attention it deserves.[5] Indeed, appreciation of the full intention of the texts in communicating an eightfold path enacted by varied individuals is possible only with some sense of their diverse roles and distinctions. These figures are not typological characters, personifications, or even allegorical presentations of particular paths: they are described through their interactions as genuine people who have attained awakening. Over a period of many lives, as the stories show, they follow a complete eightfold path, of right view, right intention, right speech, right action, right livelihood, right effort, right mindfulness, and right concentration. They enact, however, different meditative approaches, which they demonstrate in their actions and teachings up to enlightenment and after. They exhibit great compassion and care in their teachings and dealings with others; they also offer a community to one another, the laity, and newcomers. Information about these figures, part of growing up in a Buddhist context, provides animated and diverse layers of psychological narrative that accompany what has been termed by Steven Collins the Pāli *imaginaire*, the imaginative landscape that forms the background of Buddhist discourse and teaching (see Collins 1998).

What is an *Arahat*?

The first issue that needs to be addressed is the nature of arahatship. In an early Buddhist Abhidhamma root chant (*mātikā*), three kinds of states are described: those of beings not in training, those of beings in training, and those of beings who are neither in nor not in training (*sekkhā dhammā, asekkhā dhammā, neva sekkhā nāsekkhā dhammā*).[6] The first category of being has not yet attained any stages of path, the second has attained one or more stages on the way to enlightenment, and the third has attained arahatship, or awakening. The second includes stream-enterers, who will achieve enlightenment in seven lifetimes; once-returners, who will achieve enlightenment within one lifetime; and non-returners, who will attain enlightenment by the end of their present lifetime. The last heading, however, covers three kinds of being who attain awakening: a buddha, who through countless lives has developed the ten perfections; a *paccekabuddha*, sometimes called a "silent" buddha, who has also developed great knowledge and many perfections but does not teach a complete path to awakening; and an *arahat*, who has attained enlightenment on hearing the words of a buddha or in the dispensation of a buddha's teaching.[7] It is commonly thought that the latter two of the three "lineages" do not involve teaching, but, in early Buddhism, awakened beings from all frequently teach and encourage others, exhibiting compassion and sympathetic joy in their interactions with others. In early Buddhism, *paccekabuddhas*, a later addition to the types of enlightenment, feature frequently in *Jātaka* stories, even though they do not teach a full path to others. They can arise at any time, as they do not need the word of the Buddha to become enlightened, but are usually associated with finding awakening through a surprise event in the outside world that acts as a supporting condition (*upanissaya*) for this process to occur. Within *Jātaka* literature, where the aspirant buddha, the bodhisatta, often has no teaching guidance, they provide reminders of the possibility of awakening and teach through practice – through, for example, silence, riddles, and elliptic verses that encourage and point the way (J.529). They form a central part of *Jātaka* literature and are notable for their mysterious methods in the absence of enlightened beings to teach a full path (see Shaw 2006a: 222–6).[8] In one story a *paccekabuddha* rebukes the bodhisatta for his arrogance, directing him in the appropriate manner as he seeks to develop the perfections (J.490); in others they also encourage and teach (J.378, J.421; see Jones 1979, 169). Throughout early Buddhist texts, *arahats* also instruct, encourage, offer discourses, and train those following the Buddhist path: they often employ similes "never heard before" and offer advice to others and to one another (see Nyanaponika and Hecker 2003, 59–65, 125–33). According to the Abhidhamma, at the moment of awakening, for those following any of the three lineages, all of the ten fetters that bind the mind are finally destroyed.[9] After this, those from all three are in a position to help others, in accordance with their predisposition and the strengths of their chosen path. Many of the followers of the Buddha have made "*arahat*" vows, often eons ago, of a specific kind – to be pre-eminent in wisdom or psychic powers, for instance. So, in *Jātaka* stories and *Dhammapada* stories, vows made lifetimes before sustain the continued existence in the struggle in *saṃsāra*; vows of this kind come to fruition in their final life and teaching.

It is against this background that their differing approaches to meditation need to be seen, embodying doctrinal points, made frequently by the Buddha, that his tradition should accommodate a variety of attitudes to meditative practice, ascetic life, and appropriateness to different conditions (see *Mahāsakuludāyi Sutta*, MN.II.1–22).

Sāriputta and Moggallāna: Two Strands of Meditative Practice

Two figures tower over early Buddhism: Sāriputta and Moggallāna, the chief disciples of the Buddha. When Alexander Cunningham excavated Bharhut in India in the nineteenth century, the antiquity of the axis they embody in the chant quoted at the beginning of this chapter was revealed: a casket was found in the North, with the initials Ma, and another in the South, with the initials Sa. In Buddhist temple art the two are shown flanking the Buddha, with Sāriputta on the right and Moggallāna on the left. They are mentioned in the late canonical *Chronicle of Buddhas* (*Buddhavaṃsa*) as the Buddha's chief disciples (Horner 1975, 95): all buddhas – and according to this work there were 24 before Gotama – have two chief monk disciples and two chief nun disciples.[10]

The two, closely connected with each other and with the Buddha through many past lives, are born in neighboring families. They agree to tell each other when they meet a suitable teaching, and join the Buddha's order at the same time. Both become "both ways liberated": while all *arahats* achieve liberation from ignorance and suffering, some also cultivate proficiency in higher meditations, which this category describes. Sāriputta obtains liberation through quick penetration, with smooth progress; Moggallāna is also quick – taking a week – but with difficult progress (AN.II.154–5).

Sāriputta

Although skilled in *samatha* meditation, Sāriputta has no wish to cultivate the psychic powers liked by his partner, Moggallāna. He enjoys meditative practice, however, after his enlightenment: in the *Piṇḍapātapārisuddhi Sutta* the Buddha asked him the reason for the radiance of appearance, which he explains as the result of cultivation of the *suññatāvihāra*, abiding in no-thingness (MN.III.293–7). This state is associated with the attainment of the fruit of arahatship, focusing on the aspect of emptiness. Equally important, however, is the stress the *sutta* and narrative literature constantly place on Sāriputta's humaneness, humility, kindliness when rebuked, and careful dealings with others (Nyanaponika and Hecker 2003, 16–39).

Sāriputta's interest and disposition are towards insight and the discriminatory knowledges (*paṭisambhidā*): like other followers of the Buddha, he also teaches, and his discourses bear the stamp of powerful analysis and investigation, including examination of the five aggregates (*khandhas*) and the nature of right view (see *Mahāhatthipadopama Sutta*, MN.I.184–91 and *Sammādiṭṭhi Sutta*, MN.I.46–55; see Nyanaponika and Hecker 2003, 59–66 for a full list). He has a farsighted sense of the future perpetuation of the tradition: in the *Saṅgīti Sutta* (DN.III.207–71), he presents a tabulated series of Buddhist lists, organized by groupings of ones, twos, threes, and so on, with the stated intention of collection for memorization in the event of the Buddha's death. Sāriputta, however, predeceases the Buddha, who warmly compliments his career. Several canonical and post-canonical works are, perhaps apocryphally, attributed to him: his particular method, the commentaries say, is seen in the ordering and style of the books of the Abhidhamma. "The one by one as they occurred teaching" (*Anupada Sutta*, MN.III.25–9) gives us an example of his particular method. Other *arahats* simply "emerge" from meditation. Sāriputta labels every aspect of this process, anticipating the Abhidhamma mode of scrupulous classification and investigation.

That this precision of observation, characteristic of what is known as the "dry" insight approach, accompanies a character renowned for his kindliness and care seems no accident. In an age somewhat immunized to hagiography, eulogistic description of his character might seem excessive, but important points are being made not just about the man, whom we really see only in the texts after his enlightenment, and hence without many of the usual human foibles, but his method, too. The analytical approach based primarily on right view, the first factor of the Eightfold Path, is articulated through a character who has also a profound development of other path factors and the divine abidings of lovingkindness and compassion. Sāriputta's excellencies associate him with the strand of meditative practice known today as *vipassanā*: it is embodied through a kindly, protective, and humble teacher.

Moggallāna

In contrast to Sāriputta, his counterpart Moggallāna, born on the same day, develops a path based primarily on *samatha* meditation, though as an *arahat* he also cultivates wisdom and great morality (*sīla*). At each stage of his development of the four *jhānas* and the formless attainments, he suffers from great drowsiness, a hindrance sometimes associated with concentrative methods (AN.IV.85–8). On his attainment of arahatship, however, he demonstrates their extraordinary capacities, too: he is cited by the Buddha as pre-eminent in psychic powers (*iddhi*: see AN.I.23). He can create shapes and transfer himself at will. He visits Sakka, for instance, king of the *Tāvatiṃsa* heaven, and, finding him arrogant, shakes his palace so that the god trembles. A proud *nāga*, Nandopananda, a mythical serpent, is quelled by his powers. His death is violent and sudden, the result of his attacking his parents in an earlier life. It was his habit to visit beings in many realms, and he reported back that those who followed the Buddha were reborn in happy states, those who rejected him in bad. As a consequence, some teachers from other traditions apparently paid assassins to kill him. For six days he exercised his psychic powers and escaped through the keyhole. On the seventh, accepting his kammic fruit, he was attacked, and died in the Buddha's presence. He was renowned as a teacher, particularly for those with more experience, and his friendliness towards Sāriputta and other monks is also stressed in the texts. His path was essentially *samatha* based, but his powers are used for the service of the teaching; his wisdom, teaching expertise, and respect for others are constantly emphasized (see Nyanaponika and Hecker 2003, 86–96).

The other *arahats* in the chant each have comparable distinctions, if not as great. Appropriately the Buddha faces in the East the seer who foretold at his birth his destiny and who is the first to understand his teaching. Behind the Buddha is his attendant Ānanda, his greatly humane and fallible guide and companion, who protects him throughout his teaching career. Unable to attain enlightenment in the Buddha's lifetime, Ānanda is nonetheless described by the Buddha as pre-eminent in five ways, as his carer, and as one with wide knowledge, memory, good conduct, and resolve. He provides also the voice and presence of the "common man" in the *suttas*, weeping at the onset of the Buddha's death and interceding on behalf of women wishing to become nuns: as an exemplar of slow progress he seems eminently suited to sit opposite Kondañña. His enlightenment, only after the "sunset" of the Buddha's life, when he has fulfilled all his duties, seems apt.

The *arahats* at the four median points appear to operate on comparable axes: the strict ascetic Kassapa, pre-eminent in observing rules, is opposite the relaxed Gavampati, who, through his psychic powers, nonetheless averts a flood when the order is threatened. Upāli, the great interpreter of the form and code of the monastic rules (*vinaya*), sits opposite the Buddha's son, perhaps representative of the innovative and the fresh in Buddhist teaching.

Nuns, Laymen, and Laywomen

The sense of a whole community is not complete without reference to other categories of followers, however. The very presence and description of female *arahats* is a testament to the Buddha's rejection of caste, gender, or status as an impediment to meditation and the attainment of enlightenment. According to the Abhidhamma, women take rebirth with the faculty of femininity rather than masculinity as the underlying basis of the body (*rūpa*) with which they are born. No doctrinal differentiation, however, is made between the mental state that constitutes the underlying continuum (*bhavaṅga*) of any given rebirth and that present in men: women are also usually reborn with a *bhavaṅga* consciousness that is the result of one of eight skillful sense-sphere consciousnesses – that is, with two or three skillful roots, as men are, according to their kammic inheritance. So, like other humans, they have latent tendencies towards unskillfulness but also usually have the two roots of non-greed (generosity), non-hatred (lovingkindness). A third root, non-delusion, or wisdom, also usually accompanies the passive *citta* that forms the basis of most human rebirths (Gethin 1998, 215–18). The Buddha, in contrast to most other Indic traditions, asserted the possibility of enlightenment for women. In the *Buddhavaṃsa*, all buddhas are said to have four assemblies – of monks, nuns, laymen, and laywomen. All are described as having particular attainments and strengths (see AN.I.23ff. and note 4). It is important to explore these figures, too, as without the perspective they offer of varied paths within a lay and monastic life a radically important element of Southern Buddhist practice and doctrine can be neglected.

The foremost nuns are Khemā and Uppalavaṇṇā, counterparts to Sāriputta and Moggallāna, and the chief female disciples of the Buddha. They reflect and mirror the axis suggested by the two chief male disciples, with Khemā renowned for her mastery of insight and Uppalavaṇṇā for her abilities in the psychic powers.

Khemā

In her final existence Khemā was the strikingly beautiful chief consort of King Bimbisāra, with, like Sāriputta, "golden skin." She refused to visit the Buddha because she thought he would criticize bodily beauty and attachment to the sense pleasures. Her husband, however, tricked her by hiring a singing troupe to extol the natural beauties of the Bamboo Grove monastery, knowing that, as a nature lover, she would want to visit. Dressed in silk and perfumed with sandalwood, she entered the monastery and the hall where the Buddha was teaching. The Buddha, reading her concerns through his psychic powers, created a divinely beautiful figure beside him, fanning him while he speaks. Khemā had never seen such bodily loveliness, and reflected that the teacher who has an attendant like that could not be a disparager of physical beauty. The Buddha then made this figure age, so that her teeth yellowed, her skin wrinkled, and her hair became gray, until, in the last extremities of old age, she fell down dead. The Buddha asks Khemā to consider the nature of the body and the impermanence of its features, and she becomes a stream-enterer, on the first stage of the path. He then spoke the following verse to her:

> Those who are attached to passion follow a stream
> They have made for themselves, as a spider follows its web.
> But, cutting even this, the wise go on, without longing, leaving all suffering behind.
>
> (Dhp.347/Roebuck, 68)

On hearing this, Khemā becomes an *arahat* and joins the Buddhist order. She is named as the female nun pre-eminent for wisdom. Since she had, it is suggested, practiced extensively in past lives, hers is a rapid and painless path to awakening.

Khemā is mentioned frequently in *Jātaka* and other stories in her earlier births, often in a royal connection and often as generous, like Sāriputta demonstrating kindness as well as wisdom: she had made a vow eons ago to be the disciple of this buddha, and frequently makes donations, thus accruing fortunate and beneficial kamma, building monasteries when living as a laywoman. Her past lives presage and anticipate her last: in the time of an earlier buddha, she apparently understood dependent origination as it was described by him and recited it. In one birth she is even the wife of the bodhisatta, a rare occurrence for a role occupied almost exclusively by Yasodharā in earlier lives (J.354). In this tale, also in anticipation of the insight of her final life, Khemā is able to practice equanimity on the untimely death of their son and see the impermanence of conditioned phenomena. "Past-life" identities often suggest resonance, affinities, or, indeed, sometimes enmities between characters: Khemā's association with Sāriputta, the *arahat* renowned for his wisdom, is suggested by the *Jātaka* in which, when he is king, she is his wife: she encourages him in the virtues of good kingship (J.534).

In the *Mahājanaka-Jātaka* (J.539) she teaches the bodhisatta as he takes his renunciation. A little girl, shaking a winnowing basket, she has one bangle on one hand, two on the other, jangling together: she explains that the solitary one is associated with happiness, as it makes no noise. Her sentiments are true to the atmosphere of a *Jātaka* that throughout deploys the enigmatically riddling imagery and tropes of *paccekabuddhas*: it is worth stressing, however, that these sentiments are particularly appropriate to the *pacceka* path constantly evoked throughout the *Mahājanaka-Jātaka* and are not those followed by these characters in their last life, where companionship and teaching become strong elements in most of the *arahats*' interactions with others. After Khemā's awakening, her analytical approach is evinced in her teaching to King Pasenādi about the subtle doctrines concerned with whether the Buddha exists or does not exist after death. Just as monks are encouraged to aspire to be like Sāriputta and Moggallāna, nuns are constantly encouraged to emulate Khemā and Uppalavaṇṇā (e.g., AN.I.88).

Uppalavaṇṇā

The other chief female disciple, whose skin was the "colour of a blue lotus" and who, like her male counterpart Moggallāna, is paramount in psychic powers, is Uppalavaṇṇā. Also strikingly beautiful, she received so many offers of marriage that her father, a banker, became concerned he would offend too many families by accepting any one of them. He suggested she become a nun, to which she willingly agreed. When it was her turn to tend the meeting hall, she swept the floor and lit a lamp; on the basis of this she developed the calm (*samatha*) practice based on the fire device (*kasiṇa*). She attained to arahatship, with discriminatory knowledges and abilities to transform herself at will (*iddhivikubbana*). Uppalavaṇṇā was declared by the Buddha the foremost nun in psychic powers. She features a number of times in *suttas* and commentarial stories, but it is her "past-life" history, anticipating her range of command over mental states in her final life, that is so extraordinarily rich and adventurous. Khemā, as we have seen, exhibits wisdom and generosity in earlier lifetimes, which are almost exclusively human, in maternal, wifely, or ascetic roles. Uppalavaṇṇā, however, has an exotic and dramatically wide range of "past-life" experience. She is often born as a goddess: in the *Temiya-Jātaka*, she lives inside the royal parasol, giving advice to the bodhisatta (J.538), while in the *Mahājanaka-Jātaka* she rescues the bodhisatta from drowning (J.539). She is a courtesan in one story (J.276) and a femme fatale in another (J.527). She is the bodhisatta's daughter in his life as Vessantara, but, after being given to the wicked brahmin, she is not reborn in that family again (J.547). Like Moggallāna, Uppalavaṇṇā experiences violent attack in her last life after becoming an *arahat*, when she is raped by her cousin. The Buddha insists that her virtue in her last life is unimpeachable. Like Khemā, she is regarded as exemplary and frequently complimented by the Buddha.

Wife and Nun: Yasodharā

Another figure who is most popular today in South-East Asia oddly enough rarely earns a mention in books on chief disciples, though her presence threads in and out of *Jātakas* and is central to modern Southern Buddhism: Yasodharā, or, as she is called in

Jātakas, Rāhulamātā, the mother of Rāhula, the Buddha's wife and partner for many eons in rebirths before. According to the traditional understanding of the life stories of *arahats*, Yasodharā/Rāhulamātā made a vow to assume this role many eons ago, and so Gotama's renunciation and enlightenment would have been anticipated by her – an element of the background to the life story that it is useful to know if the frequently depicted scene of Gotama's leaving her and his son in the palace is to be placed in its context: his intention is to seek a path to liberate them as well as himself, and both his wife and his son would have been considered to have made vows to undertake this role in their final lives.

Although not mentioned in the *Nikāyas*, the public discourses of the Buddha, Yasodharā's presence throughout the *Jātakas* is significant for its assertion of sexual happiness and marriage as part of a spiritual path: she appears in 32 stories, always as the bodhisatta's spouse. *Jātaka* verses date from the earliest level of the texts, and in these a wife, attributed by the commentary to Rāhulamātā, features frequently. She is described as wise, resourceful, and accomplished (J.539, J.424). She rarely breaks the precepts, and, indeed, just as her rebirths are perhaps less varied than those of the bodhisatta – she is not reborn as a smaller, landbound animal like a mouse or a hare, for instance – her behavior in this regard is also more straightforwardly consistent. She tends to prefer the lay life to the monastic. She sometimes makes eloquent denunciations against asceticism (J.411, J.525, J.539) and occasionally, where she does not follow him as an ascetic, tries to seduce her husband away from the ascetic path (J.539, J.459). Despite this, one does not find elaborate descriptions of her as the abandoned wife, which inform, for instance, the depiction of Saundarī when her husband renounces in Aśvaghoṣa's poem *Saundarananda*. The bodhisatta rarely leaves her to become an ascetic: in only four *stories* does she not accompany him when he adopts this path. In the *Mahājanaka-Jātaka* (J.539) she also becomes a solitary ascetic, and this tale is distinguished by her attainment of *jhāna* after the bodhisatta has left the palace.[11] In three tales they live as ascetics together. In the *Kumbhakāra-Jātaka* (J.408), Rāhulamātā takes the first step to renunciation. In this tale, the bodhisatta, a potter, discusses the superiority of the holy life. His wife rises and leaves through the back door to become an ascetic herself, leaving him to look after the children until such time as they are independent and he can assume an ascetic life too (J.408). But while there are also a very few stories where they live together chastely, usually in accordance with both their wishes, in 24 they exist as a normal "married" couple, whether as brahmani ducks (J.434, J.451), deer (J.328), or *nāgas* (J.506), or in various human castes. In the *Mahāsudassana-Jātaka*, at her husband's instigation, Rāhulamātā encourages him, before death, to renounce his palaces and riches (J.95).

The multiple identifications of various rebirths in *Jātaka*s provide a subtle language for the manifold possibilities of a character's identity and relationships with others in his/her final life: they offer varied perspectives contributing to a psychological and metaphoric individual "history" that allows the perspective of the laws of *kamma* to be seen operating over many lifetimes: identities over many lifetimes change, as do names, conditions, and species, an important aspect of the workings of the theory of non-self over many lifetimes. This kammic inheritance finds fruition in the disciples' last life with the Buddha. In the *Jātakas*, Yasodharā's virtue, rather like the Western medieval *vertu*, is figured as a natural vitality or goodness that produces an answering resonance in the world around her. While the bodhisatta searches for the perfections, Yasodharā lives harmoniously and appropriately in the environment in which she finds herself. Through her trust in and alignment with the beings that inhabit the physical environment around her, she can, at times of crisis, assume a proactive, initiatory role, invoking protective deities or behaving in such a manner that the spirits identified with that locality come to her aid. So, in the *Candakinnara-Jātaka*, a story supposedly told by the Buddha when he returns after the enlightenment to see her, his son, and his family, she saves the day by an act of truth (*sacca-kiriya*), which can be a statement of one's own virtue or, sometimes, as in this case, an eloquent declaration of the differentiated virtues that inhere within the immediate locality, such as the hills, mountains, lakes, and skies (J.485). King Sakka, stirred by Yasodharā's evocation of the "truth" of the environment, revives the bodhisatta; in the preamble, the Buddha expresses his gratitude to her.

In South-East Asia and Sri Lanka, Yasodharā is a folk heroine, either in her last life guise as Yasodharā – in Sri Lanka in particular, songs, poems, and dramas are composed about her as an exemplar of a loyal and kindly wife (Obeyesekere 2009) – or as Maddī, in the *Vessantara-Jātaka*, the wife of the king who gives away everything, to have it all returned – a life in which the bodhisatta is said to perfect generosity (Cone and Gombrich 1977). This *Jātaka* is the most popular story in South-East Asia and in some regions is known, recounted, and dramatized at festivals with far more fervor than the last life of the Buddha. In this regard, Maddī, the mother of the bodhisatta's two children, whose courage, patience, and uncompromising integrity never falters, is quite simply the most popular heroine in the Southern Buddhist world.[12] South-East Asian and Sri Lankan Buddhism has historically depended on strong lay support and interchange between the monastic orders and the laity, and the domestic sphere has traditionally offered the principal way of doing this: perhaps because of this, Yasodharā's story has resonated strongly with women in these regions. According to the *Apadāna*, her autobiographical verses, in her final life she eventually also becomes a nun. Although *Jātaka* stories give only one "life" where she practices meditation, her strengths usually consisting in leadership, generosity, and loyalty; she masters the various psychic powers (*iddhis*) on the basis of *jhāna* in her final existence. Finally, she visits the Buddha before her death, demonstrating a spectacular display of psychic powers, in which her bodily form assumes the guise of Mount Meru and the universe, before dissolving into emptiness, and then reassuming her natural form and speaking of enlightenment. She is then complimented with deep gratitude by Gotama, before dying at the age of 78.

In Pāli texts, once people become *arahats* they join the *saṅgha*. Many laypeople, however, develop other stages of path. The householder Citta practices the four *jhānas* and formless meditations, teaches others, and is a stream-enterer. On death the gods try to persuade him to take his next rebirth as a universal monarch: he chooses the path to enlightenment instead (see note 4). Another *arahat* whose virtues are primarily those of the lay life, in her generosity, fertility, beauty, and keeping of the precepts, is Visākhā, who constantly offers hospitality to the monastic orders and intercedes on their behalf: she becomes a stream-enterer, proficient in some meditations and wisdom (see note 4).

In a way perhaps analogous to Ānanda's lack of arahatship in his final life, the active role in the Buddha's life of lay followers, or those who become monks or nuns only later in life, accords merit and auspiciousness to activities not directly salvific but contributing to the perpetuation of the teaching. The presence of such figures in such a central role is suggestive: *nibbāna* is not presented as a goalpost with only a linear path that finds it. Any moment of skillful *citta*, according to the Abhidhamma, has path factors that may be less developed but nonetheless give a glimpse of the path itself (Dhs.1–145): such moments are accessible even in the animal kingdom, though they will be very weak. The lay life, and what we could term life "in the world," has, according to the earliest texts, plentiful possibilities for acquiring good *kamma* and setting the practitioner on the way to enlightenment.

Diversity of path, an endorsement of lay and domestic life as well as the monastic, and the possibility of the three lineages also emerge from these narratives, in which a complex vocabulary of possibilities within Buddhist practice is enacted: the doctrine of non-self needs to be seen in this multiple life perspective. Awakening is not the only criterion for accomplishment, ability to teach, or auspiciousness: the *arahats* have varied paths, over many lifetimes, in which they develop in varied ways, and they teach in accordance with experience and practice derived from their earlier lives.

The Buddhist Understanding of Character

According to the early Buddhist tradition, all human beings are composed of the five aggregates or "heaps" (*khandhas*): bodily form, feeling, perception (identification), volitional activities, and consciousness. The manner in which this doctrine is taught is not through abstraction, except where it is a helpful tool for debate, but through examination of what the pupil or querent experiences for him or herself. An extensive system of character and temperament is developed in commentarial literature, based on canonical precedent, which provides an important element in the assignment of meditations and the teaching of individuals (see Shaw 2006b, 6–12). As Sue Hamilton notes, the Buddha explores through his teachings in the canon, and the early *saṅgha* presents through their accounts of these teachings, not the ontological concerns of an abstract concept of the human being but an epistemic path for humans through which they can find release from suffering. In this light, the famous doctrine of "non-self," the third mark of the three marks of all existence (the other two are "impermanence" and "suffering"), does not apply to the negation of a self or a denial that it exists at all: rather, as Sue Hamilton says,

> there is no independently existing or permanent entity which one might call a self or a soul . . . Nirvana is selfless both because it is the experience of ceasing to project the separateness of selfhood onto oneself and everything else and also in the sense that it is an epistemic experience. This means that thinking in terms of self *or of there being no self* is making a category mistake. None of the Buddha's teachings is actually concerned with what is, *or with what is not*. The fundamental error is simply thinking in any such terms since they are all missing the point that the way things (really) exist does not correspond to the notion of separateness that is implicit in the confirmation *and in the denial* of selfhood.
>
> (Hamilton 1996, 195–6)

This underlying attitude permeates early Buddhist texts, in which distinct and varied characterization animates the discourse through the presentation of highly differentiated individuals, who voice and enact their own perceptions and discoveries, to the Buddha and, in friendship, to one another, in sometimes colorful and idiosyncratic ways. In an early twentieth-century account of character in fiction, E. M. Forster made the distinction between "flat" and "rounded" characters: those that are typological, such as personifications of particular qualities, and those that demonstrate some development or change in the way they are presented in a literary work (Forster 1927, 93–112). In a fundamental sense, the *arahats* experience a dramatic change: they become enlightened. In other senses, too, their dispositions and temperaments color their meditative practice and teaching in ways that should not be neglected if their role in early Buddhist texts is to be fully appreciated. They are described over many lifetimes, and a fluid sense of change and transformed identities accompanies a path where character is the product of many factors for beings described as "heirs to their *kamma*."

In the study of Buddhist texts it is inevitably the doctrinal and philosophical expositions that have received the most attention. The isolation of these from the texts in which they are expressed, however, can miss much of the approachability and straightforward interest of early discourses. The *suttas* and the narrative tradition offer specific situations and characters who embody and articulate particular paths, approaches, and differentiated perspectives as they themselves undergo changes from one life to the next, providing a sense of moving points for different loci of consciousness over an extended period of time. Their contribution provides a richly diverse, humane, and occasionally humorous account of Buddhist practice: most Buddhists historically would have been familiar with many issues of doctrine through their life events and behavior, and the significance of the vivid drama of these narratives, recounted within a tradition designed to be memorized and learned for oral recitation, should not be underestimated. Doctrines of non-self and the workings of *kamma* are demonstrated through the interdependency and mutual friendliness of a network of beings described as working within the Buddhist path, interacting with one another, and the teaching, at different stages of development and practice, over many lives, leading up to and including awakening itself. Narrative is a central element in early Buddhist texts: *sutta*, *Jātaka*, and (auto)biographical *Apadāna* form three of the nine limbs (*aṅga*) of the teaching from the earliest times.[13] Listening to such stories, in a non-literate culture, would have aroused understanding, concentration (*samādhi*), and interest: at the end of most *Jātakas* listeners are described as attaining enlightenment after hearing in addition the teaching on insight that brings their minds to final awakening, a feature indicative of their significance in Buddhist practice. The meditation on the community of those who have attained various stages of the path (*saṅghānussati*) is constantly advised in early texts and practiced today, as a means of arousing confidence, happiness, and freedom from fear. The stories of those who have pursued such various routes to enlightenment, which nonetheless follow each element of an eightfold path, often over many lifetimes, provides a rich vocabulary of transformation and diverse illustration of Buddhist principle.

Notes

1 For a translation of the chant that is of unknown antiquity, see Shaw (2009, 134). It starts: "Among two footed beings, the Fully Awakened One is best, sitting in the centre / Kondañña sits in front of the Buddha, Kassapa to the Southeast / Sāriputta at the Buddha's right-hand, Upāli to the Southwest / Ānanda behind the Buddha, Gavampati to the Northwest, Moggallāna at the Buddha's left-hand, and Rāhula to the Northeast / These Buddhas are indeed auspicious, all well established here." "Buddha" is here a generic term for an enlightened being. For the chant, see *Buddhamaṅgalagāthā*, in the *Samatha Chanting Book*. At www.samatha.org/images/stories.samatha-chantingbook.pdf, p. 9.

2 The term "Southern Buddhism" refers to the traditions of Sri Lanka, Thailand, Burma, Cambodia, and Laos.

3 For a translation of all 547 *Jātakas*, see Cowell's edition (1972 [1895–1907]), still accessible, if occasionally a little archaic in style, after more than a century. In this chapter, *Jātakas* are cited by the number of each story as given there. For discussion of the stories as a collection, see Shaw (2006a) and Appleton (2010). Burlingame's translation of the stories of the *Dhammapada* commentary, also now nearly a century old, communicates well the narrative momentum of a readable and entertaining primary source recounting many of the interrelated life stories of the *arahats* (Burlingame 1980 [1921]).

4 Sources used for this article have been too varied and extensive to cite in full. Works which have been invaluable are Malalasekera (1960 [1937–8]), which gives extensive references for each figure, and, for wide-ranging discussion of Sāriputta, (Mahā)Moggallāna, (Mahā)Kassapa, Ānanda, Citta, and Visākhā, Nyanaponika and Hecker (2003, 1–66; 67–105; 107–36; 139–82; 365–72; 247–55, respectively). A good short account of the Buddha's contacts with his disciples is given in Strong (2001, 77–99, 163–6). A key section in writing this article is AN.I.23–7 (Woodward 1932, 16–25), which gives the disciples' pre-eminences.

5 See, for example, Nyanaponika and Hecker (2003), Murcott (1993), Obeyesekere (2009), and Strong (2001, 77–99).

6 "Root" chants open the *Dhammasaṅgani*, the first book of the *Abhidhammapiṭika*. "The higher teaching," the third of three "baskets" of the Buddha's teaching, also includes the monastic code (*Vinayapiṭika*) and teachings in specific situations (*Suttapiṭika*). The first book delineates on a moment-by-moment basis each moment of consciousness – skillful, unskillful, and under other categories – as it arises and passes away, labeling each of the features present and describing the ways consciousness (*citta*) and matter (*rūpa*) interact (See Rhys Davids 1974, M 1–9).

7 For the *arahat*'s consciousness, see Dhs.277–364 (Rhys Davids 1974, 74–89).

8 For an account of *Jātakas* that contain *paccekabuddhas*, see Jones (1979, 166–70).

9 The ten fetters (*saṃyojana*) are views identifying various features as "self," skeptical doubt, attachment to precepts and rituals, sense-desire, ill will, desire for form, desire for formlessness, conceit, restlessness, and ignorance.

10 Sāriputta and Moggallāna are called Upatissa and Kolita in this work. Ānanda is also mentioned as the Buddha's attendant, and Khemā and Uppalavaṇṇā as the chief nuns.

11 The meditation state described as *jhāna* is considered essential for the attainment of the path. It is remembered by the Buddha as the state he had experienced in childhood that dissuades him from self-mortificatory practices (MN.I.246–8). He then practices all four *jhānas*, before insight, to attain enlightenment.

12 See Cone and Gombrich (1977, x–xxvi).

13 For further discussion of Buddhist biographical and autobiographical expression, see Covill et al. (2010).

References

Appleton, Naomi (2010). *Jātaka Stories in Theravāda Buddhism*. Farnham: Ashgate.

Burlingame, E. W. (1990 [1921]). *Buddhist Legends: Translated from the Original Pāli text of the Dhammapada Commentary*. Harvard Oriental Series 28–30. Cambridge, MA: Harvard University Press.

Collins, S. (1998). *Nirvana and other Buddhist Felicities of the Pali Imaginaire*. Cambridge: Cambridge University Press.

Cone, M., and Gombrich, R. F. (1977). *The Perfect Generosity of Prince Vessantara: A Buddhist Epic Translated from the Pali and Illustrated by Unpublished Paintings from Sinhalese Temples*. Oxford: Clarendon Press.

Covill, L., Roesler, U., and Shaw, S. (2010). *Lives Lived, Lives Imagined: Buddhist Biographies of Awakening*. Boston: Wisdom.

Cowell, E. B. (ed.) (1972 [1895–1907]). *The Jātaka, or Stories of the Buddha's Former Births*. 7 vols. London: Pali Text Society [*Jātakas* cited by number].

Forster, E. M. (1927). *Aspects of the Novel*. London: Edward Arnold.

Gethin, R. (1998). *Foundations of Buddhism*. Oxford: Oxford University Press.

Hamilton, S. (1996). *Identity and Experience: The Constitution of the Human Being According to Early Buddhism*. London: Luzac Oriental.

Horner, I. B. (trans.) (1975). Chronicle of the Buddhas (Buddhavaṃsa). In *The Minor Anthologies of the Pali Canon*, Part III. London and Boston: Pali Text Society.

Jones, J. G. (1979). *Tales and Teachings of the Buddha: The Jātaka Stories in Relation to the Pāli Canon*. London: George Allen & Unwin.

Malalasekera, G. P. (1960 [1937–8]). *Dictionary of Pali Proper Names*. 2 vols. London: Pali Text Society.

Murcott, S. (1993). *The First Buddhist Women*. London: Parallax.

Nyanaponika, Thera, and Hecker, H. (2003). *Great Disciples of the Buddha: Their Lives, their Works, their Legacy*. Ed. Bhikkhu Bodhi. Boston: Wisdom.

Obeyesekere, R. (trans.) (2009). *Yasodharā, the Wife of the Bodhisattva: The Sinhala Yasodharāvata (The Story of Yasodharā) and the Sinhala Yasodharapadanaya (The Sacred Biography of Yasodharā)*. New York: State University of New York Press.

Rhys Davids, C. A. F. (trans.) (1974). *A Buddhist Manual of Psychological Ethics (translation of the Dhammasaṇgani)*. Third edn. London and Boston: Pali Text Society.

Shaw, S. (2006a). *The Jātakas: Birth Stories of the Bodhisatta*. Delhi: Penguin.

Shaw, S. (2006b). *Buddhist Meditation: An Anthology of Texts*. London: Routledge.

Shaw, S. (2009). *An Introduction to Buddhist Meditation*. London: Routledge.

Skilling, P. (2000). The Arahats of the Eight Directions. In *Fragile Palm Leaves for the Preservation of Buddhist Literature* 6, 12 and 22.

Strong, J. S. (2001). *The Buddha: a Short Biography*. Oxford: Oneworld.

Woodward, F. L. (trans.) (1932). *The Book of the Gradual Sayings: Translation of the Aṇguttaranikāya*, Vol. I. London: Pali Text Society.

30

Compassion and the Ethics of Violence

STEPHEN JENKINS

Definitions

Buddhaghosa, the great Theravāda commentator, defined compassion in a way that might be acceptable to all Buddhists: "When others suffer it makes the heart of good people tremble (*kampa*), thus it is *karuṇā*; it demolishes others' suffering, attacks and banishes it, thus it is *karuṇā*; or it is dispersed over the suffering, is spread out through pervasion, thus it is *karuṇā*" (Jenkins 1999, 31; Warren 1950, 263; cf. Ñāṇamoli 1956, 343). Compassion is part of a complex of interrelated concepts that express empathetic attitudes. Many terms indicating helpfulness, kindness, affection, caring, and empathy are employed to enrich its meaning. Sometimes it is described with negative terms, such as *ahiṃsā*, non-harm, or *akrodha*, the absence of anger, but should not be understood as purely negative. The language of erotic attachment, so important to Hindu *bhakti* traditions, is avoided. However, the most common metaphor is parental affection. This fundamental human attachment, generally seen as a psychological obstacle, is idealized when it is expanded to include all sentient beings. The meditation practices for generating compassion often begin with self-cherishing, perhaps the most basic combination of attachment and ignorance – i.e., passion and self-conception. Self-cherishing is expanded to incorporate ever greater areas, from villages to nations, or ever more difficult types of relationships, from loved ones to enemies. In the formula of the four "immeasurables," friendliness, compassion, and sympathetic joy are amplified to immeasurability, and balanced by the fourth, equanimity, which eliminates discriminating attachment. The passions and attachments regarded as basic problems, rather than simply being extinguished, as in some forms of asceticism, or redirected to a perfect object, as in Hindu devotion, are transformed through expansion into universal and impartial qualities. Compassion practices suggest an evolution or transformation of *tṛṣṇā*, the fundamental "thirst" for life that

A Companion to Buddhist Philosophy, First Edition. Edited by Steven M. Emmanuel.

drives the wheel of *saṃsāra*, into the compassion that ultimately turns the wheel of Dharma (Jenkins 1999).

Compassion and the Rhetoric of Superiority

Both Mahāyāna and mainstream Buddhism agree that a buddha's compassion is "great" when compared with ordinary compassion. For mainstream Buddhism, this distinguishes the Buddha as a unique being worthy of extraordinary reverence. Meditation on the qualities of the Buddha, including great compassion, was a general practice. But Mahāyānists take buddhahood as a general goal. What was a supererogatory ethic became one of imitation. Language that hyperbolically expressed the superiority of the Buddha's compassion served to express the Mahāyāna's superiority. Buddhists who did not aspire to great compassion were denigrated as inferior, "*hīna*." However, in the early canon and Abhidharma schools, the valorization of compassion for all sentient beings, often with identical phrasing to the Mahāyāna, is pervasive. Here, *mettā*, "lovingkindness," and *anukampā*, empathy, are more common terms than *karuṇā*. *Anukampā* should inform every relationship, from employer and employee to ruler and subject. *Metta-citta*, a "loving mind" for all sentient beings, may be a model for the Mahāyāna's *bodhicitta*. *Metta-citta* is idealized as the essential quality for both monastics and laity. It motivates every aspect of practice, from meditation to philanthropy. Modern characterizations of mainstream Buddhists as concerned only with individual liberation are merely appropriations of the Mahāyāna rhetoric of superiority.

There is one salient difference in the Mahāyāna's conception, a massive relative preponderance of exhortations to social action (Jenkins 2003). Mainstream sources emphasize making merit by giving to monks (Aronson 1980, 37). These are the richest "fields" of merit, and generosity towards them produces the most merit. This instinct does not disappear in Mahāyāna, but here the poor, homeless, disabled, sick, and defenseless are proclaimed as worthy a merit field as the buddhas. Sentient beings in general are regarded as merit fields through which an aspirant attains the massive amounts of merit necessary for buddhahood. Rather than the ideal practitioner being the optimal recipient of generosity, the bodhisattva is conceived as the perfect source of generosity. Mahāyāna *sūtras* clearly differentiated and prioritized material and spiritual giving. The needy should be supplied with basic material needs before they are offered the Dharma. These beliefs, understood through narrative more than philosophical argumentation, were a massive stimulus to charitable works throughout Asia, including hospitals, famine relief, and all kinds of public works, such as road and bridge building (Jenkins 2003).

The Benefit of Self and Other

Stories of incredible generosity, such as the Buddha giving his life for a hungry tigress, resonate strongly with Christian sacrificial concepts. However, Buddhists of all traditions recognized a reciprocal interrelation between altruism and self-benefit. The trope *svaparārtha*, "the benefit of self and other," broadly pervades Buddhist texts. Mahāyāna and mainstream sources elucidate *svaparārtha* with a formula of four types of persons (Jenkins 1999, 55–62). First are those interested only in self-benefit. Second are those uninterested in benefiting anyone. Third are those interested only in benefiting others. This seems to be the Buddhist ideal; however, this too is rejected. The ideal is interest in benefiting both oneself and others. One who fails to benefit herself is less capable of benefiting others. Someone who does not love herself cannot even begin the meditations for generating love. Compassion for all includes oneself. When the Buddha enters the jungle to sacrifice his life to a tigress, he declares that this is a vast opportunity, and the story ends by describing his dramatic acceleration towards buddhahood. Such behavior should be understood from a multiple life perspective rather than as self-termination. Pursuit of one's highest empowerment is motivated by the intention to benefit others, and benefiting others leads to one's highest empowerment. As Śāntideva famously put it:

> Upon afflicting oneself for the sake of others, one has success in everything. The desire for self-aggrandizement leads to a miserable state of existence, low status, and stupidity. By transferring that same desire to someone else, one attains a fortunate state of existence, respect, and wisdom. . . . All those who are unhappy in the world are so as a result of their desire for their own happiness. All those who are happy in the world are so as a result of their desire for the happiness of others.
>
> (Wallace and Wallace 1997, 105–6)

This circularity is expressed in the bodhisattva vow, sometimes misunderstood as a self-abnegating renunciation of enlightenment. A bodhisattva vows to attain the supreme self-benefit, buddhahood, for the sake of benefiting others. At the same time, actions that benefit others generate the merit required to achieve that supreme self-benefit. Neither self-interested nor self-abnegating altruism fit as definitions here. If self-interested pursuit of merit becomes the motivation, then no merit is attained. The circularity here is similar to the capitalist conception that individualistic pursuit of self-interest ultimately benefits all; however, the energy in this circuit runs in the opposite direction. Instead, pursuit of others' interests ultimately benefits the individual and the general pursuit of self-interest leads to common misery. To relieve both our own suffering and that of others, we should dedicate ourselves to others (Wallace and Wallace 1997, 106).

Compassion benefits the compassionate. Although compassion that actually benefits others generates more merit, even compassion that benefits no one else generates merit for those who have it. Similarly, anger is damaging to the angry, whether others are harmed by it or not. Lists of the benefits of compassion cover everything from prosperity to a good night's sleep. The *Mettā Sutta*, which advocates compassion for all creatures as if they were your children, is recited today by Theravādins to ward off snakebites. Compassion can even make one bulletproof. There are tales of arrows bouncing off their compassionate target, only to strike home when the victim became enraged, or of kings who could not be struck by an arrow until the precise moment their compassion lapsed. This explains why Mahāyāna scriptures exhort bodhisattvas to take up the "armor" of compassion.

Compassion and Ontology

Buddhist deconstructions of the self raise doubts about the status of the object of compassion. Abhidharma thinkers recognized this problem, but quickly dismissed it. They deconstructed the naïvely conceived self, but affirmed a causal continuity of incessantly self-renewing, ephemeral, and microscopic elements referred to as *dharmas*. The strength of that karmic continuity, *santana*, is the basic challenge of the Buddhist path and the basis for conventional references to persons. They do not, however, resort to ideas of interconnection or interdependence. Compassion is conventional; the *dharmas* revealed as ultimate truth are not an adequate object of compassion (Jenkins 1999, 165–83, 247).

The standpoint of emptiness makes this problem more challenging, since even the evanescent elements of the psychophysical continuum dissolve under analysis. This problem is well recognized in Mahāyāna sources. The *Perfection of Wisdom Sūtras* repeatedly declare that the single most difficult thing for bodhisattvas is that they vow to save beings, even though those beings do not ultimately exist (Jenkins 1999, 165; Conze 1973, 259). In the Madhyamaka school, this problem takes its strongest form. Whereas Abhidharma thinkers found referents for language in the basic components of reality, for the Madhyamaka the process of deconstructing referents for language is bottomless. The instinct to pursue ultimate referents for language, and thus validate "reifying thought," is the fundamental problem. Linguistic designations, such as self or *dharma*, reduce their referents to a simple static objectivity that obtains only in language itself. We think in linguistic concepts and we see as we think. Thus we are bound to the illusion that reality is composed of a field of objective phenomena that can be labeled. The Madhyamaka's insistence that all things dissolve under analysis means that the objective structures of language do not ultimately have referents. Objects are a mode of thinking, not the way things are. Simple static objectivity itself is a human fantasy, a mere mental construction. This is the *sūtra*'s meaning in saying that, ultimately, no sentient beings exist. This is nihilism only if we insist that, if reality does not exist according to linguistic rules, it must not exist at all, a remarkably anthropocentric conceit. The fact that reality is ultimately empty of objective entities does not mean that the world as such does not exist, nor does it negate the value of conventional language. Although Buddhist thinkers debunk various levels of objectivity, they regard objective language as necessary and useful. Though they may be ultimately deconstructed, the objects of compassion are conventionally meaningful. The continued appearance of sentient beings and other objects for an enlightened person is often compared to the continued appearance of an illusion to the magician who produces it. The appearance remains, but without being mistaken for something objective.

The Western study of Buddhist ethics has focused on how selflessness, emptiness, interconnection, or a matrix of interrelativity serve as more compelling ontological perspectives for compassion. However, dependent origination is not used as a basis for personal interrelation, and is only problematically interpreted as interconnection. Indian Buddhist texts do not make ethical arguments based on a matrix of interrelativity or webs of interrelations, and yet this view is even projected on the Madhyamaka.

Compassion is the basis of the aspiration to realize higher truths, and so must precede them and be strong enough from the start to be the foundation of the path. Compassion is more a cause of enlightenment than its result. The question becomes how compassion can continue, or be developed, in the light of those realizations. It was recognized that only an elect few understood such ideas. A Buddhist ethics based on elite philosophical perspectives would be challenged to motivate cultures and polities. Central concepts, such as the benefit of self and other, far from dissolving the distinction between self and other, take that distinction as a basic predicate for ethical thought. A related trope, the sameness of self and other, refers not to ontological sameness but to psychological sameness – i.e., that all beings dread suffering. Suffering is the fundamental presumption of Buddhism, and it is commonly assumed that the key to generating compassion is recognizing that all beings dread it just as we do.

The Western sense of moral selflessness is often conflated with the Buddhist sense of ontological selflessness, but the meanings are completely different and are not necessarily correlated. One cannot attain selflessness or become selfless as often stated; selflessness is simply the way things are. From a Mahāyāna perspective, the *arhats*, who are identified with realizing selflessness (and often emptiness), are specifically faulted for their lack of compassion. As noted below, their failure in regard to compassion is often attributed to a premature realization of emptiness.

A possible exception is found in a touchstone for Western readings of Buddhist ethics, Śāntideva's *Bodhicaryāvatāra*. The eighth chapter, much of which is of uncertain origin (Ishida 2010), offers a meditation for generating compassion based on abhidharmic contemplation of sufferings as ownerless phenomena. Because there is no self, no sufferings have an owner. So bias towards one's own suffering makes no sense, and all suffering should be treated equally. Interestingly, Śāntideva does not apply emptiness analysis by taking the next step and deconstructing the ownerless sufferings as nonexistent. As a meditation practice, the Mahāyānist utilizes an abhidharmic perspective of ownerless phenomena in a way that Abhidharmists had ruled out. It is a mistake to read this as a typical Buddhist argument. In contrast, Buddhaghosa's elaboration of compassion meditation never refers to deconstructive perspectives until he uses them (after trying several other things first) as an antidote to overcome anger that arises when attempting to generate compassion for an enemy. The point here, though, is not to advocate interconnection, but to show that attitudes such as anger make no sense once they are seen to have no meaningful object. He playfully asks: are we angry with the hairs, nails, or perhaps the urine? (Ñāṇamoli 1956, 331–2; Warren 1950, 253–4; Jenkins 1999, 169). The same argument would also eliminate an object for compassion, and Abhidharma sources generally agree that impersonal *dharmas* cannot function as the object of compassion (Jenkins 1999, 165–83). Compassion requires a conventional perspective. Śāntideva's argument here is the subject of rich debate, with Gómez, Williams, and Siderits concluding for different reasons that it is unsound (Gómez 1973, 365; Williams 1998; Siderits 2007, 83). No doubt this is why Buddhists generally do not use it. It may be important to recognize the context as a chapter on meditation practices, in which Buddhists often creatively visualize things that are not true for a specific purpose.

In the next chapter on wisdom, the commentator, Prajñākaramati, offers a rich discussion of the question for whom there can be compassion, if sentient beings do not exist (Gómez 1973, 363–6; Jenkins 1999, 219–31). To explain Śāntideva's answer that compassion is for illusory beings, he resorts to the common theme of the three objects, *ālambana*, of compassion. Each object of compassion is correlated with a different stage of the bodhisattva path. At the outset of the path, compassion is for undeconstructed sentient beings. Compassion is the means, *sādhana*, of realizing ultimate truth and precedes the realizations that negate sentient beings. Compassion is not a response to selflessness; it is a prerequisite for acquiring such wisdom. Compassion must be compelling without being based on the deconstruction of the self. In his own treatment, Candrakīrti praises this type of compassion most highly of all as the basis for the entire Buddhist path (Jenkins 1999, 210).

The second basis, *dharma-ālambana*, deconstructs beings into streaming masses of components. This is correlated with advanced bodhisattvas at stages prior to the realization of emptiness and is the perspective used in Śāntideva's meditation. Prajñākaramati does not say that this is a vision that supports compassion but states, as in Abhidharma, that the components serve as a basis for the conventional designation of a self that functions as the object of compassion.

The last, *nirālambana*, or no basis, is correlated with the full realization of emptiness. This does not mean compassion for a void; each perspective is associated with the appearance of sentient beings. In this case, sentient beings are perceived as empty of inherent existence. As Candrakīrti put it elsewhere, their appearance is like a reflection of the moon on shimmering water (Jenkins 1999, 209–15). Conventional appearances do not disappear and conventional designations are accepted for practical purposes. This perspective is correlated only with the highest-level bodhisattvas. For many *sūtras*, the realization of emptiness is connected to *nirvāṇa* and is thus a dangerous moment for compassion. It is precisely the mistake of *arhats* to terminate the path to full buddhahood by realizing emptiness. The *sūtras* are pervaded with exhortations not to realize emptiness prematurely. According to the *Daśabhūmika Sūtra*, which laid out stages of the bodhisattva path, at the moment of realizing emptiness, were it not for the exhortations of the buddhas and the power of former vows, all activity for sentient beings would cease (ibid., 142). There is no automatic relationship between emptiness and compassion here. Compassion, through the power of the vow and the intercession of the buddhas, assures that the bodhisattva continues on to attain all the empowerments and omniscience of a buddha. Prajñākaramati never resorts to the idea that emptiness or non-self actually provides a rationale for compassion, particularly not through a conventional perspective of interconnection, interdependence, or interrelation (ibid., 225). If this were the connection, it would present itself broadly and explicitly in the literature. However, Mahāyāna and Abhidharma sources agree that higher philosophical perspectives contribute to compassion by revealing more subtle types of suffering, providing the wisdom necessary to relieve suffering, and enabling the ability to remain in *saṃsāra*. Concepts such as the universal desire to avoid suffering, *svaparārtha*, and merit-making, richly elaborated in narrative literature, are the primary bases of Buddhist ethics.

The Ethics of Violence

There is increasing awareness of a dissonance between historical practices and perceived Buddhist values. Buddhist polities generally had horrific penal codes that included capital punishment, and Buddhist kings went to war ostensibly for the sake of the Dharma with relics in their scepters and carrying buddha images into battle. In many cases, monks themselves were warriors and even fought with other monasteries. To some degree this merely shows that Buddhist cultures are as human as any other, none of whom have lived up to their religious ideals. However, there is also a sense in which the historical record is at odds only with Western fantasies of Buddhist pacifism. The power of those fantasies has obscured a far more nuanced ethics of violence than has yet been explicated.

In the *Cūḷasaccaka Sutta*, we find the Buddha making an argument based on the fact that kings have the right and are worthy to execute criminals. When his non-Buddhist interlocutor refuses to concede this, the Buddha's bodyguard threatens to kill him by smashing his head with his hand-weapon, a *vajra*. The debater is described as visibly terrified (Ñāṇamoli and Bodhi 1995, 322–31). This armed bodyguard, Vajrapāṇi, is understood in both mainstream and Mahāyāna scriptures to follow the Buddha everywhere and often appears in artwork. He is identified with the Vedic deity Indra, who represents the ideal king and models royal behavior towards the Buddha. Vajrapāṇi came to be increasingly important throughout Buddhist history, and his sidearm became, in addition to body armor, the most important symbol of the power of compassion. Other protector deities in Abhidharma traditions smash mountains down on the enemies of Buddhism or wipe out entire armies. In *Jātaka* tales, the most important source for Buddhist ethics, the Buddha is portrayed in past lives as a minister who cleverly lures a siege into a crocodile moat, a weapons-master, a warhorse, a battle elephant's mahout, etc. Killing evil ascetics, vicious animals, and unjust kings is praised. In a Mahāyāna *Jātaka*, the Buddha is born as Indra himself and leads a bloody battle against demonic beings, once again modeling ideal kingship (Jenkins 2011). In the narrative literature, Śākyamuni himself occasionally manifests fire *samādhis* to drive away unwanted peoples or subdue demonic beings.

These examples do not contradict the general Buddhist concern to avoid harm. But, when read together with passages that seem to suggest unqualified pacifism, they reveal a more complex picture. The Buddha notably denied that warriors who die in battle automatically go to heaven. Instead, warriors with the intention to kill will go to hell. But, the intentions are the key here. Military heroes are glamorized in narrative literature, but only in a few cases do they deliberately set out with the intention to kill (Jenkins 2011). Accounts of the Buddha's past lives as a war hero glorify winning through trickery or diplomacy rather than violence, capturing the enemy alive, the decent treatment of abusive captives, and avoidance of unnecessary killing. The importance of intention can lead to the common misinterpretation that karma is merely based on intention. If this were true, then the mere intention to kill would suffice for the karma of murder. However, the analysis of killing generally presents the belief that killing must include an actual death; even a failed attempt to kill does not produce the karma of killing. On the other hand, unintentionally killing or, in

Mahāyāna contexts, killing with a compassionate intention does not produce the karma of killing (ibid.).

In the famous case of King Duṭṭhagāmaṇi from the Theravādin epics, a gathering of saints relieved the king of his remorse for killing many thousands in his war to spread the Dharma. They tell him he has actually killed only one and a half persons, the rest are no more than animals. The one and a half are counted according to their commitment to Buddhism. This is an unusual example, but it shows that the moral status of the victim is as crucial as the intentions of the killer. Killing a saint is a far different matter from killing an enemy of Buddhism or executing a murderer. The "quasi-canonical" *Milindapañha* advocates torture, death, and dismemberment as punishments for criminals, arguing that these are the result of the victims' karma (Rhys Davids 1963, 254–7; Jenkins 2011). However, Theravādin tradition does not offer the logic of compassionate killing found in the Mahāyāna. Even in the case of a king who apparently relishes executing a criminal, there must be some subtle level of revulsion and therefore negative karma (Gethin 2004).

Mahāyāna sources emphasize that compassionate killing, including warfare and animal euthanasia, can produce great merit. The touchstone for this idea, known throughout contemporary Mahāyāna cultures and cited by many great classical thinkers, is the *Upāyakauśalya Sūtra's* tale of the Buddha's past life as the ship captain "Greatly Compassionate." Captain Compassionate stabbed to death a thief who intended to murder his passengers. Everyone, including the thief, benefited. Captain Compassionate saved the thief from suffering in the hell realms for murder. He saved the passengers from either angrily killing in self-defense or suffering murder. Because of his compassionate intentions, he himself made great merit and enormous progress towards buddhahood. The story is double edged in employing compassionate murder to protect someone from the karma of murder. This logic validated everything from mercy sex to prevent a suicide to unseating vicious rulers. The analogy of amputation by a physician showed that sometimes violently inflicting pain may bring benefit. An antecedent is found in the early canon, where the Buddha's use of harsh speech, technically a form of violence, is compared to clearing a choking child's throat, even if it draws blood (Jenkins 2011).

The broadly cited *Satyakaparivarta Sūtra* advises a fierce king on compassionate violence (Zimmerman 2000). He may imprison and torture criminals, but he should not maim or execute them. He may go to war to protect his family and his people. But he should systematically attempt to avoid war by first using bribes, diplomacy, and intimidation. He must carefully consider how his policies are responsible for the arising of enemies. A king is protected by his benevolent cultivation of the well-being of his subjects, vassals, and neighbors. If they are happy and secure then, instead of becoming enemies, they will be allies when enemies do arise. A benevolent king will enrich his treasury through gifts and the general prosperity of his realm, while a rapacious king will engender a culture of tax evasion and become poor. A king should go to war with three intentions: to care for life, to win, and to capture the enemy alive. Even if he kills the enemy, as long as he avoids the destruction of life, infrastructure, and nature, he will be blameless and produce great merit. The concern to care for life involves the well-being of all innocents, including animals and the spirits that dwell in trees and water. Burning homes or cities, destroying reservoirs or orchards, confiscating the harvest – i.e., harming infrastructure or the environment – is forbidden. There is no sense that the king, his warriors, or law-enforcement officials must be bodhisattvas, quite the opposite (Jenkins 2010).

In general, compassionate killing is a supererogatory ethic, not one of imitation. It is double edged in opening the possibility for murder precisely to prevent its horrific karmic outcome. The everyday examples also suggest something commonsensical about compassionate violence. They draw on issues and choices that doctors, leaders, parents, or pilots may face in everyday life and derive their force from the fact that they appeal to natural human responses to protect children and companions. In regard to power politics, compassion serves the purposes of domination, pacification, national security, and enrichment. Compassionate policy, rather than being an awkward extension of ascetic idealism into practical political realities, was understood to support the acquisition and retention of power.

References

Aronson, H. (1980). *Love and Sympathy in Theravada Buddhism*. Delhi: Motilal Banarsidass.

Conze, E. (trans.) (1973). *The Perfection of Wisdom in Eight Thousand Lines*. Bolinas, CA: Four Seasons.

Gethin, R. (2004). Can Killing a Living Being Ever Be an Act of Compassion? The Analysis of the Act of Killing in the Abhidhamma and Pali Commentaries. In *Journal of Buddhist Ethics* 11, 166–202.

Gómez, L. (1973). Emptiness and Moral Perfection. In *Philosophy East and West* 23, 361–73.

Ishida, C. (2010). Relocation of the Verses on "the Equality of Self and Others" in the *Bodhicaryāvatāra*. In *Journal of Institute for the Comprehensive Study of Lotus Sutra* 36, 1–16.

Jenkins, S. (1999). The Circle of Compassion: An Interpretive Study of Karuṇā in Indian Buddhist Literature. PhD Dissertation. Harvard University. Ann Arbor, MI: University Microfilms International.

Jenkins, S. (2003). Do Bodhisattvas Relieve Poverty? The Distinction Between Economic and Spiritual Development and their Interrelation in Indian Buddhist Texts. In *Action Dharma: New Studies in Engaged Buddhism*. Ed. C. Queen, C. Prebish, and D. Keown. London: RutledgeCurzon, 38–49.

Jenkins, S. (2010). Making Merit through Warfare according to the Ārya-Bodhisattva-gocara-upāyaviṣaya-vikurvaṇa-nirdeśa Sūtra. In *Buddhist Warfare*. Ed. M. Juergensmeyer and M. Jerryson. Oxford: Oxford University Press, 59–75.

Jenkins, S. (2011). On the Auspiciousness of Compassionate Violence. In *Journal of the International Association of Buddhist Studies* 33, 299–331.

Ñāṇamoli, Bhikkhu (trans.) (1956). *The Path of Purification: Visuddhimagga*. Kandy, Sri Lanka: Buddhist Publication Society.

Ñāṇamoli, Bhikkhu, and Bodhi, Bhikkhu (trans.) (1995). *The Middle Length Discourses of the Buddha*. Boston: Wisdom.

Rhys Davids, T. W. (trans.) (1963). *The Questions of King Milinda*. Vol. 1. New York: Dover.

Siderits, M. (2007). *Buddhism as Philosophy*. Indianapolis: Hackett.

Wallace, V., and Wallace, A. (trans.) (1997). *A Guide to the Bodhisattva's Way of Life*. Ithaca, NY: Snow Lion.

Warren, Henry Clarke (ed.) (1950). *Visuddhimagga of Buddhaghosācariya*. Rev. Dharmananda Kosambi. Harvard Oriental Series vol. 41. Cambridge, MA: Harvard University Press.
Williams, P. (1998). *Altruism and Reality*, Richmond, Surrey: Curzon Press.
Zimmermann, M. (2000). A Mahāyānist Criticism of *Arthaśāstra*, the Chapter on Royal Ethics in the *Bodhisattva-gocaropāya-viṣaya-vikurvaṇa-nirdeśa-sūtra*. In *Annual Report of the International Research Institute for Advanced Buddhology at Soka University for the Academic Year 1999*, 177–211.

31

Buddhist Ethics and Western Moral Philosophy

WILLIAM EDELGLASS

Introduction

Following his enlightenment under the Bodhi tree, in what is regarded as his first sermon to his former companions, Gautama Buddha taught the Four Noble Truths (*ārya-satyāni*) that were taken to be the foundation of Buddhist traditions: the truth that life is characterized by dissatisfaction, unease, or suffering (*duḥka*); that the cause or origin (*samudaya*) of suffering is attachment, especially to self; that a cessation (*nirodha*) of suffering is possible; and the practices that constitute the path (*mārga*) to the cessation of suffering. The Buddhist path, as articulated in the fourth truth, is constituted by three kinds of activity: *prajñā* (insight or wisdom), *śīla* (moral discipline or moral conduct), and *samādhi* (mental discipline). Because the Buddha argued that lack of wisdom and mental discipline results in behavior that leads to suffering of both self and others, Buddhist traditions have understood *prajñā* – the wisdom and insight of understanding the nature of reality – and *samādhi* – the mental discipline and capacity for attention that enables equanimity – to be morally significant. Without wisdom or mental discipline I cannot attend to the needs of others or, indeed, my own needs. Moral concerns, then, are at the heart of Buddhist theory and practice, and every aspect of the Buddhist path is morally relevant.

While there is no precise equivalent for the English term "ethics" in Buddhist canonical languages, Buddhist traditions have devoted much attention to the moral significance of thoughts and feelings, intentions and actions, consequences and character, duties and commitments. There are works with extensive lists of appropriate and inappropriate actions and texts that detail psychologically desirable and undesirable qualities. There are texts presented as guidebooks to cultivating the virtues necessary to become a bodhisattva. And there are numerous works that address the proper conduct of specific kinds of beings, such as kings, monks, nuns, and laypersons. In marked contrast, though, to the kinds of theorizing pursued in some Buddhist traditions in

A Companion to Buddhist Philosophy, First Edition. Edited by Steven M. Emmanuel.

areas of metaphysics, epistemology, and philosophy of language, Buddhist thinkers rarely pursued the sort of systematic ethical theorizing that would justify moral principles or inquired into the source and meaning of morality as such. Buddhist writers do employ sophisticated moral concepts – for example, the distinction between artificial precepts (such as culturally relevant monastic practices that are not inherently morally significant) and natural precepts (such as killing or stealing) – but these concepts are not the focus of theoretical inquiry or philosophical debate. For the most part, Buddhists were not engaged in the kind of philosophical theorizing on the nature and justification of moral principles that has characterized much Western moral thought. In the terminology of contemporary Western moral philosophy, then, Buddhist thinkers focused a great deal on normative and applied ethics but very little on meta-ethics.

Meta-ethics is the branch of moral philosophy that inquires into the source and justification of moral principles. It is concerned with foundational issues in ethical theory – for example, demonstrating how morality is grounded in human nature, or the nature of reality – rather than focusing on specific rules of right conduct. This latter task, articulating standards of moral action, is the province of normative ethics. Normative ethics provides rules of conduct to distinguish between morally acceptable and unacceptable behavior. Employing the results of meta-ethics and normative ethics to specific areas of moral concern, such as medicine, business, the environment, sexuality, poverty, or war, applied ethics recommends right behavior for particular situations or roles. Normative and applied ethics, implicitly or explicitly, are seen as grounded in meta-ethics. Justified by three different meta-ethical accounts, Aristotle's virtue ethics, Kant's deontology, and Mill's consequentialism may result in three different morally appropriate responses to a particular situation. Meta-ethics, then, is of great significance in Western philosophy because, as many philosophers believe, morality, including the rightness of specific moral rules, is ultimately justified at the meta-ethical level.

Perhaps because meta-ethics is so important in Western moral traditions, in recent decades academic scholars of Buddhist philosophy have sought to provide theoretical frameworks to understand Buddhist moral teachings as components of coherent ethical systems. However, scholars of Buddhist ethics are faced with different challenges from those who work on Buddhist philosophy of language, epistemology, or metaphysics. Buddhist and Western philosophers have asked similar kinds of questions about the relations of words and things, the conditions for knowledge, and the sorts of beings that constitute the world. But the approach to thinking about morality in Buddhist traditions is very different from Western moral thought. Thus, scholars working in moral philosophy must first analyze prescriptions, descriptions, narratives, and meditations on appropriate behaviors and then construct the meta-ethical framework they deem necessary to justify Buddhist normative and applied ethics.

In what follows I show how some forms of Buddhist ethics share features with Western moral philosophies, especially virtue ethics and consequentialism. Interpreting various forms of Buddhist ethics with the aid of diverse Western moral theories can, I believe, increase our understanding. In the end, though, I suggest that no one Western meta-ethical theory provides an adequate theoretical framework for grasping moral thinking in any of the major traditions of Buddhism and, *a fortiori*, the vast and heterogeneously diverse tradition of Buddhism as a whole. Instead of translating Buddhist moral thinking into Western categories, scholars will understand Buddhist ethics better if approached, in the end, on its own terms, an approach that leads to a richer and more fertile philosophical dialogue.

Buddhist Ethics as Virtue Ethics

Interpreting Buddhist texts through the hermeneutic frameworks of contemporary European philosophy is as old a practice as the European study of Buddhist thought (Tuck 1990; Droit 2003). The interest in constructing theoretical frameworks for Buddhist ethics or drawing on Western moral categories to systematically order Buddhist approaches to moral life, however, is relatively recent.[1] Before the 1990s, academic scholars made only modest efforts to understand Buddhist ethics according to Western theoretical reflections. Most of the scholars who did draw on Western categories characterized Buddhist ethics as a form of consequentialism.[2] But with the revival of virtue ethics in Anglo-American moral philosophy in the 1980s, some scholars began interpreting Buddhist moral thought as a form of Aristotelian virtue ethics. The most prominent interpretation of Buddhist morality as virtue ethics is that of Damien Keown, who argues that "Aristotelianism provides a useful Western analogue . . . [for] . . . elucidating the foundations and conceptual structure of Buddhist ethics" (Keown 1992, 196).[3] In particular, Keown claims that Buddhist ethics is structurally similar to Aristotelian virtue ethics because both systems are oriented towards a supreme goal that is understood as the perfecting of human nature, because the path to achieve this goal is through the cultivation of moral and intellectual virtues, and because the virtues are cultivated through a faculty of making relevant choices. Drawing primarily from Theravāda texts – as had much of the previous philosophical work on Buddhist ethics – and to a lesser degree on Indian Mahāyāna works, Keown's *The Nature of Buddhist Ethics* became one of the most important studies of Buddhist moral theory.

In the *Nichomachean Ethics*, Aristotle argues that all human beings pursue the good as they conceive it and the highest human good is *eudaimonia*, translated variously as "human flourishing," "well-being," or "happiness." According to Aristotle, all other goods, such as health, friendship, political power, or riches, are not desirable for their own sake but are pursued because we believe they will contribute to our well-being. In contrast, *eudaimonia* is that for the sake of which we pursue other goods; it is pursued for its own sake. Aristotle argues that *eudaimonia* is the fulfilling of our function with *aretē* (excellence or virtue). Because, according to Aristotle, reason is distinctively human, the human function is the exercise of reason with excellence. *Eudaimonia* is thus rational activity in accord with virtue over the course of a life. Grounded in an account of human nature, then, Aristotle presents *eudaimonia* as the goal of human life, the telos towards which the wise person orients her choices (Aristotle 1999, 1–18).

Achieving *eudaimonia*, according to Aristotle, requires the good luck of being properly educated and trained to cultivate appropriate habits, as well as external goods which enable us to exercise our capacities for virtue. However, he believes, we are ultimately responsible for cultivating and exercising virtues through making choices which over time form our character. Making the choice to act the way a virtuous person would act is necessary to become virtuous but is not itself an indication of virtue; it may be a sign of continence, that one's will overrides one's desires. The virtuous person transforms herself through appropriate choices over time and takes pleasure in virtuous activity. She is not motivated primarily by duty, then, but enjoys and desires virtuous activity and finds vicious action repugnant. Thus, the virtuous think, feel, and act differently from the vicious. As Aristotle claims in the *Nichomachean Ethics*, *eudaimonia* requires the cultivation of both intellectual and moral virtues. Intellectual virtues include the activity of both theoretical reason, understanding the nature of reality, and practical reason, the prudence to successfully accomplish one's goals. In order to develop moral character, one also needs to cultivate intellectual virtues so that one can properly understand appropriate goals and how to pursue them. Thus, virtues are cognitive, affective, embodied dispositions that lead us to feel, act, and think in ways that are beneficial to ourselves and those we care about.

Aretē, the Greek word Aristotle uses to refer to "excellence," is translated into English as "virtue," through the Latin *virtus*. In Asian Buddhist languages there is no one word that can straightforwardly be translated as virtue. Perhaps the closest Sanskrit equivalents are *pāramitā*, typically translated as "perfection," and *śīla*, but other terms cover a wide range of affective, cognitive, and embodied moral qualities and attributes. And Buddhist texts include descriptions and analyses of particular virtues, such as generosity (*dāna*), compassion (*karuṇā*), patience (*kṣānti*), humility (*nirmāna*), mindfulness (*smṛti*), meditative contemplation (*dhyāna*), wisdom (*prajñā*), and reverence (*ādara*). While *śīla* may best be translated as moral discipline, it can also refer to the moral precepts that lay people and monastics vow to uphold. Practicing the five precepts – refraining from killing, stealing, lying, sexual misconduct, and intoxication – requires the cultivation of virtues that constitute the Buddhist path. Thus, there is much discussion of the precepts and the ways in which they lead to the goal of freedom from ignorance, attachment, and aversion, the three mental defilements that cause suffering. These descriptions and analyses of virtues, as well as the many narratives that portray exemplary moral characters, permeate Buddhist moral thought and lend themselves to an interpretive framework of virtue ethics.

According to Keown's interpretation of Buddhist morality as virtue ethics, particularly in Theravāda traditions, *nirvāṇa* constitutes a telos analogous to *eudaimonia* in Aristotle. For Theravādins, as the cessation of suffering, *nirvāṇa* is the *summum bonum*, the final goal towards which all activities on the Buddhist path aim (Keown 1992, 196–203). Like *eudaimonia*, *nirvāṇa* is desired for its own sake. And, as with *eudaimonia*, all other activities on the Buddhist path are chosen because they contribute to *nirvāṇa*. *Nirvāṇa* is never chosen instrumentally to achieve a further goal; it is the source of value that nourishes Buddhist practice. Moreover, the path to *nirvāṇa* is realized through the cultivation of cognitive, affective, embodied dispositions, including both moral and intellectual virtues, not unlike the path to *eudaimonia*. Intellectual virtues remove the ignorance that leads sentient beings to act in ways that are counterproductive to the telos of *nirvāṇa*. And moral virtues dissolve the attachment and aversion that are obstacles to compassion for the needs and sufferings of others. One can only fully achieve wisdom, moral discipline, and mental discipline through simultaneously cultivating all three. Thus, insight into the lack of a substantial self may be superficial, but is deepened through overcoming attachments to things and giving generously. Not succumbing to hatred may, in some situations, require both the mental discipline of stepping back and observing one's own mind and the insight that someone else's behavior is dependent on causes and conditions beyond her control. Thus, Keown characterizes non-hatred (*adosa*), non-passion (*arāga*), and non-delusion (*amoha*) as the "three Buddhist Cardinal Virtues" (ibid., 62–3). Because these virtues lead to and embody the *summum bonum*, he argues, from a Buddhist perspective they are objectively good.

All three kinds of activity that constitute the path to the cessation of suffering – wisdom, moral discipline, and mental discipline – are not only necessary as means to achieve *nirvāṇa*, but are perfected in *nirvāṇa*. Keown understands *nirvāṇa* in two ways: first, as the enlightenment achieved in life – for example, the Buddha's *nirvāṇa* at the age of thirty-five – and, second, the final *nirvāṇa* upon the death of one who has already achieved enlightenment. Thus, *nirvāṇa* does not surpass ethics as a preliminary stage but naturally embodies and expresses moral behavior. Indeed, Keown emphasizes, *nirvāṇa* is precisely the realization of moral discipline intertwined with insight and mental discipline.[4] While there may be important differences between nirvāṇa and *eudaimonia* – for example, *nirvāṇa* is the kind of perfection that Aristotle does not believe humans can achieve – both Buddhist and Aristotelian ethics share a structure in which all activity is oriented towards a telos achieved through virtue.

In many Mahāyāna texts, where the telos is generally understood not as *nirvāṇa* but as *bodhicitta*, the awakened mind characterized by great compassion (*mahākaruṇā*) and the perfection of wisdom (*prajñāpāramitā*), it is especially clear that practicing virtue constitutes the path and perfecting the virtues constitutes the goal. According to some Mahāyāna thinkers, *bodhicitta* is precisely the perfection of the virtues that constitute the path to becoming a bodhisattva: generosity (*dānapāramitā*), moral discipline (*śīlapāramitā*), patience (*kṣāntipāramitā*), vigor (*vīryapāramitā*), meditative contemplation (*dhyānapāramitā*), and wisdom (*prajñāpāramitā*). (Sometimes this list is expanded to include skill in means [*upāya kauśalya*], vow or commitment [*praṇidhāna*], strength [*bala*], and knowledge [*jñāna*].) Cultivating generosity, moral discipline, patience, and the other perfections is the cultivation of *bodhicitta*. The telos, whether *nirvāṇa* or *bodhicitta*, then, is not the transcendence of morality; it is a completion of, but still continuous with, the path of cultivation of virtue.

The virtuous character of the enlightened being is embodied without struggle, according to Keown. Thus, "it is unnecessary for him to guard against misdeeds of body, speech and mind" (Keown 1992, 114). Moreover, Mahāyāna thinkers insist that, as one cultivates the perfections, one takes pleasure in serving the needs of others; advanced practitioners are said to delight even in extreme acts of generosity. In this sense, *nirvāṇa*, or achieving *bodhicitta*, is similar to Aristotelian *eudaimonia*, which is itself constituted by virtuous activity, and to achieve *eudaimonia* is to delight in virtuous action. Not only does practicing a virtue – say, generosity – bring the aspiring bodhisattva happiness; practicing the virtues is precisely what allows the practitioner to make progress on the path. As Śāntideva writes, "since he helps me on the path to Awakening, I should long for an enemy like a treasure discovered in the home, acquired without effort" (Crosby and Skilton 1995, 59). The needy, those who frustrate me, my enemies, are not obstacles on the path but are necessary for my progress. Thus, a virtue ethics interpretation allows us to understand how Buddhists subvert a radical distinction between altruism and egoism.

As Keown interprets Buddhist ethics, then, like Aristotelian ethics, it is teleological – with the goal of *nirvāṇa*; naturalist – it is grounded in human nature; and objective – there are precepts and perfections which are inherently good insofar as they are necessary conditions for achieving the goal.

While the interpretation of Buddhist ethics as a virtue ethics is now widespread, not everyone has been convinced by Keown's interpretation of Buddhist ethics as sharing essential characteristics with Aristotelian moral philosophy. Some scholars, such as Georges Dreyfus, suggest that Keown went too far in searching for similarities between Buddhist and Aristotelian ethics and that a better correspondence is the eudaimonistic virtue ethics as articulated by one or another of the later Hellenistic philosophers, such as the Epicureans, Stoics, or Skeptics. In contrast with Aristotle, who possessed a more complex metaphysics and psychology and regarded pursuing common pursuits with friends and political communities as a significant component of the telos of human life, the Hellenistic schools were more interested in achieving self-sufficiency, equanimity, and liberation from perturbations. Like Buddhism, then, these schools provide a kind of therapy, overcoming the afflictions that characterize human life, achieved through cognitive, affective, embodied moral and intellectual virtues (Dreyfus 1995, 35–7). Other scholars have suggested that, while Theravāda ethics, for example, may be a kind of virtue ethics, Keown overstates the significance of intention and neglects the moral relevance of consequences. According to Abraham Velez de Cea, for example, Theravāda Buddhism is indeed a kind of virtue ethics, but one that is different from any found in Western moral philosophy because it includes features of moral realism and utilitarianism (Velez de Cea 2004, 139).

Buddhist Ethics as Consequentialism

The ethical significance of the consequences of actions and the universalist goal of Mahāyāna Buddhism to liberate all sentient beings from suffering has led some scholars to reject the analogy of Buddhist thought with any form of virtue ethics, which is focused more on the self and its choices, and instead to suggest that Buddhist ethics is a form of consequentialism. "Consequentialism" covers a range of ethical theories which share the common view that the moral value of an act should be assessed by the goodness of its consequences. The most famous consequentialist moral theory, utilitarianism, in its classic form took up the Epicurean idea that pleasure and happiness alone are inherently good, and pain and unhappiness, alone, inherently bad. According to the principle of utility – the greatest good for the greatest number – proposed by Jeremy Bentham, an act is good to the degree that it promotes as much good as possible for as many as possible. Because pleasure was taken to be the sole intrinsic good for sentient beings, classic utilitarianism argues that an act is good if it results in the greatest pleasure or happiness for the greatest number.

Today there are numerous varieties of consequentialism, all rooted, to some degree, in classic utilitarianism. In retrospect, we can see Bentham's consequentialism as a form of act utilitarianism (in contrast to rule utilitarianism). That is, the moral focus is on acts: an act is right if it results in the greatest net good – in this case, happiness

– compared with other possible acts. In contrast to Kantians, classic utilitarians do not believe acts are intrinsically right or wrong; there is nothing inherently bad about telling a lie, stealing, or even killing. And there is nothing inherently right about telling the truth or being generous. Moreover, the moral value of an act does not depend on the agent's intention. Instead, the rightness of an act is determined solely by its results. An act utilitarian may accept that there are rules of conduct we should follow as guides because they generally result in acts that lead to greater happiness. If, however, such a rule conflicted with the principle of utility, it should be overridden. In contrast, rule utilitarians argue that an act is morally wrong if it conflicts with a rule such that if the rule were enforced it would lead to the greatest good.

Because according to classic utilitarianism pleasure, or happiness, is the sole inherent good, we can further distinguish it from other forms of consequentialism. For example, one could believe that, instead of pleasure, the satisfaction of any preference is the only inherently good thing. An act, then, would be good to the degree that it promotes the greatest satisfaction of desires. Or, one could articulate and defend a plurality of features of a life – for example, a list of virtues that are objectively good. In this kind of Objective List theory, an act is good if it results in the greatest realization of these features for the greatest number of sentient beings. Character consequentialism, for example, regards both happiness and a list of virtues that are thought to make our lives better as intrinsically good. What classic utilitarianism shares with Objective List theory is the view that intrinsic value is necessarily value – or welfare – for a sentient being. Pleasure, or the degree to which the features on the list of goods are realized, constitutes a sentient being's welfare. Thus, these forms of consequentialism which root moral value in the welfare of sentient beings are called "welfarist." Because classic utilitarianism considers the welfare of all sentient beings, in contrast to some moral theories, which may give greater consideration to the agent or those who are nearest and dearest, it is a form of universal consequentialism. Thus, classic utilitarianism is agent neutral. That is, the moral value of the consequence is not relative to the agent but can be assessed equally from any perspective.

According to Charles Goodman, Theravāda, Mahāyāna, and Vajrayāna ethics in South Asia and Tibet are best understood as a form of universal, welfarist, character consequentialism. Thus, Goodman's consequentialism is more sophisticated than the utilitarianism Keown rejects as a candidate for the structure of Buddhist ethics. Goodman believes that there are differences between Theravāda and Indian Mahāyāna accounts. For example, he interprets Theravāda ethics, with its greater commitment to the precepts, as a form of rule consequentialism (Goodman 2009, 47–72) and Indian Mahāyāna ethics as a kind of act consequentialism (ibid., 89–107). Nevertheless, ethical theories in these traditions, he argues, share a fundamental commitment to the welfare of all sentient beings as the source and justification of moral norms and are committed to a list of virtues that are inherently good.

In contrast to virtue ethics, which, Goodman argues, is agent relative, Buddhist ethics often calls for meeting the needs of others by sacrificing one's own. Instead of pursuing my own good, or the good of those who are nearest and dearest to me, much Mahāyāna ethics exhorts us to take on the sufferings of all sentient beings. Some Buddhist narratives tell of bodhisattvas so compassionate they give even their own flesh to the hungry. For Goodman these are vivid examples of the ways in which Buddhist ethics is not agent relative, and therefore not an exemplification of virtue ethics. However, this is precisely the kind of immoderate demand we find frequently in consequentialism, which obligates us to give the resources that make our lives comfortable to those who are in greater need (Goodman 2009, 131–44). Indeed, as a good consequentialist, Śāntideva observes that we ought to sacrifice ourselves for another who is equally or more compassionate, but we should not sacrifice ourselves for someone who is less sensitive to the sufferings of others. "That way," he writes, "there is no overall loss" (Crosby and Skilton 1995, 42). This kind of self-sacrifice, Goodman argues, is alien to virtue ethics but at home in consequentialism.

Moreover, as Goodman points out, Buddhist thinkers are often quite clear in articulating universalist, welfarist views. Śāntideva famously asks, "When happiness is liked by me and others equally, what is so special about me that I strive after happiness only for myself? When fear and suffering are disliked by me and others equally, what is so special about me that I protect myself and not the other?" (Crosby and Skilton 1995, 96). For Śāntideva, freedom from suffering is clearly an inherent good. On occasion, Śāntideva does seem to acknowledge a positive aspect to suffering. However, what justifies this positive value is that it can help alleviate greater suffering – for example, when the aspiring bodhisattva is motivated by her own suffering or the suffering of others to practice the perfections (ibid., 97). But, as many Buddhists, including those Goodman discusses, believe that freedom from suffering is achieved through cultivating perfections such as generosity, moral discipline, wisdom, and compassion, this means that one can generate a list of virtues that are intrinsically good. Forms of consequentialism known as character or perfectionist consequentialism regard both happiness and virtuous states of character as intrinsically good. Thus, Goodman argues, we can see Buddhist ethics as a form of universal, welfarist, character consequentialism.

Another problem Goodman sees for those seeking to interpret Buddhist ethics as a form of virtue ethics is that Buddhist traditions are replete with stories of bodhisattvas performing acts which do not appear to be virtuous. The bodhisattva seeks to alleviate the sufferings of sentient beings. Thus, if motivated by compassion and guided by wisdom, Śāntideva argues, a bodhisattva is permitted to commit "even what is proscribed" (Crosby and Skilton 1995, 41). Indeed, to be skillful (*kauśalya*) in the method, strategy, or means (*upāya*) for alleviating the suffering of others, including transgressing the precepts, is often claimed by Mahāyāna authors to be the primary observable characteristic of a bodhisattva.

Practicing skillful means, it is said, in previous lives even the Buddha transgressed the precepts by killing, lying, stealing, and engaging in sexual misconduct. These compassionate deeds are presented as exemplary moral acts. For example, a bodhisattva may kill a person who is about to kill many others to save that person from the consequences of her own actions. Transgressing the precepts, then, is morally right if it benefits others, but not if it is intended to bring worldly benefit to oneself. From the perspective of virtue ethics, according to Goodman, these transgressions of the precepts don't make sense.[5] But in the context of a universal, character, welfarist, act consequentialism they are morally right.

Buddhist Ethics and Other Western Moral Theories

In addition to seeing structures of virtue ethics and consequentialism in Buddhist ethics, scholars have noted features of other Western moral philosophies in Buddhist thought. Some scholars discern contours of Derridean and Levinasian ethics, especially in East Asian Buddhist and Madhyamaka thought. For Jacques Derrida and Emmanuel Levinas, responding to the vulnerability and need of the other ruptures the totalizing thinking that justifies violence; heeding the call of the ethical means subverting the conceptual reification that is the cause of violence. If, as many Madhyamaka thinkers claim, accepting things as inherently existing is a kind of ignorance which leads to attachment and aversion, and therefore results in suffering, subverting conceptual reification is, then, of moral significance. This is why so many Mahāyāna Buddhists argue that even the precepts are ultimately empty of inherent existence. It is for this reason, according to Jin Park, that Wŏnhyo, the great Korean thinker, applies the concept of emptiness in such a way that it destabilizes conventional ethical discourse. "Wŏnhyo's discussion of bodhisattva precepts problematizes the basic assumptions of normative ethics. It problematizes ethical categories by showing the provisional nature of precepts and revealing the limits of binary oppositions commonly employed in ethical discourse" (Park 2009, 412). For Wŏnhyo and many other Mahāyāna Buddhists, especially in East Asia, but also Indian Mādhyamikas, conceptual reification, including the reification of moral precepts, is an obstacle to the ethical.[6] There is, then, a correspondence between some Buddhist texts and the ethical thinking of Derrida and Levinas.[7]

Other scholars have noted similarities between some Buddhist texts and Stoicism. Stoics argue that, because all external events are governed by natural law, they are necessary. As necessary, they happen according to reason and thus, ultimately, are good. Suffering arises, then, not because of anything external, but because of the judgments we make that external events are bad. The key to achieving the Stoic telos of freedom from perturbation is correctly distinguishing between that which we control – most importantly our judgments about things, and thus intentions, desires, and aversions – and what is not subject to our exclusive power. Thus, the Stoic sage acts appropriately but does not concern herself with external goods. Similarly, many Buddhists are committed to the idea of dependent origination (*pratītyasamutpāda*), that every event has multiple conditions and therefore that no one causal power, including an individual moral agent, could be held fully responsible for the consequences of an act. For this reason, like the Stoics, many Buddhists do not believe it is possible to control the external world and seek to tame the mind instead. As Śāntideva notes, in a Stoic vein, "since I cannot control external events, I will control my own mind" (Crosby and Skilton 1995, 35).

The Stoic view that the external world is not subject to our control is echoed in Immanuel Kant's moral philosophy. Kant agrees that, because the world is governed by natural laws, human beings cannot be fully responsible for the consequences of their actions. Thus, Kant argues, the locus of morality lies in intention, in the agent's motivation. Some scholars, then, have explored similarities between various forms of Buddhist ethics and Kantian morality. In *The Discipline of Freedom: A Kantian View of the Role of*

Moral Precepts in Zen Practice, for example, Philip Olson employs a Kantian framework to interpret Sōtō Zen Buddhist theory and practice. According to Olson, Kant's distinction between noumena and phenomena corresponds to the form and emptiness distinction central to Zen Buddhist teachings (Olson 1993, 44–8). Moreover, the idea of an original buddha-nature or original mind, Olson argues, corresponds to Kant's moral law (ibid., 84–9). Zazen, Zen sitting meditation, because it liberates the practitioner from the forces of emotions and the senses, corresponds to Kantian autonomy, which characterizes the moral will, in contrast with heteronomy, the power of psychological forces to motivate action (ibid., 59–68). Zazen, then, is interpreted as a discipline of freedom; the moral law is the basis of meditation, according to Olson, and meditation is the means for realizing the requirements of the Kantian moral law. Finally, the practice of sitting meditation in Zen, a practice which is not *essentially* dependent on any specific ritual or culturally limited practice, corresponds to the Kantian understanding of the moral law as universal (ibid., 125–52).

In contrast to attempts to employ a classic Western ethical framework to interpret Buddhist ethics, Charles Hallisey has argued that a contemporary Western category – particularism – is more appropriate for understanding at least some Theravāda ethics. According to Hallisey, the expectation, and search for, a meta-ethical structure that articulates and justifies the foundational principles of Buddhist ethics as a whole has obscured the ways in which Buddhist ethical thought does not conform easily to traditional Western conceptions of consequentialism, virtue ethics, deontology, or other theories. Why shouldn't Theravāda Buddhism, as with any other heterogeneous tradition, not include a multiplicity of moral theories, just as we may recognize deontological and virtue theories in Christianity? Thus, Hallisey claims, "we realize that there can be no answer to a question that asks us to discover which family of ethical theory underlies Buddhist ethics in general, simply because Buddhists availed themselves of and argued over a variety of moral theories" (Hallisey 1996, 37). According to Hallisey, the diversity of moral theories and approaches in some Theravāda texts is not arbitrary, but intentional. The underlying framework of these texts is ethical particularism, an inclusive approach to moral phenomena. According to particularists, there is no need for overarching moral principles. Instead, they argue, moral features arise in particular contexts. Hallisey notes that some Theravāda texts regard different prescriptions as appropriate, depending on the situation. In general, killing is proscribed; but kings are sometimes required to kill in order to uphold justice and preserve the safety of their people. Monks and nuns are required to be celibate but householders are required to care for their children. The task of moral agents, then, is to cultivate the discernment of how best to respond in contextualized, specific, moral landscapes.

Buddhist Ethics and Western Moral Philosophy in Dialogue

Attentive readers will have noticed that many of the correspondences contemporary scholars have made between Buddhist and Western ethics have actually been between South Asian or Tibetan ethics and Western ethics. This is because South Asian and Tibetan Buddhist thinkers have tended to ask questions and pursue philosophical investigations in a manner much more akin to that of Western philosophers than that of many Chinese and East Asian thinkers before the modern era. Thus, we are less likely to find features that correspond to Western ethical systems in Chinese and East Asian Buddhism. To take one example, the rejection of a gradual path in favor of the doctrine of sudden awakening in some Chinese traditions that became dominant in East Asia resulted in a very different framework of moral development than virtue ethics approaches. As Stephen J. Lewis and Galen Amstutz argue, in reference to Shin Buddhism, "if a Buddhist practitioner . . . cannot causally achieve his own ultimate soteriological end . . . it is impossible to refer to that end as teleological or as ultimately amenable to processes of rational organization, and thus as ethical or virtue-oriented in any normal English sense of the term" (Lewis and Amstutz 1997, 147–8). Thus, employing virtue ethics as an interpretive framework might work quite well for some Buddhist texts, but it does not work for all of them. And, as various scholars have pointed out, there is still a great deal to learn about the diversity of Mahāyāna ethics (Chappell 1996, 62).

The differences between South Asian and East Asian Buddhist moral theories, together with the differing accounts in this chapter, suggest that Buddhist traditions are vast and diverse. Principles that ground the monastic code appear alien to the principles that justify the narratives of antinomian behavior of enlightened teachers, whether the "divine madmen" of Tibet or Chan teachers who skillfully shock their students out of mundane consciousness. These differences, together with the results of many excellent anthropological, social and political, historical, and literary studies of Buddhist morality as lived in very different cultures, suggest that "Buddhist ethics" names a heterogeneous set of practices and moral concerns that ought not to be forced into one grand framework.

This does not mean that specific theories and practices of Buddhist ethics do not share features with traditional Western philosophies. Philosophical elements of Theravāda traditions, and Mahāyāna and Vajrayāna in South Asia and Tibet, are clearly similar in important respects to the Western moral theories of consequentialism and virtue ethics. And, as I noted above, some Buddhist texts correspond to conceptual strategies found in other Western approaches to ethics. Employing these Western philosophical terms to conceptualize aspects of Buddhist ethics can, I believe, illuminate structures of Buddhist moral views and practices. It allows scholars to draw on the resources of Western moral philosophy to analyze Buddhist ethics. And, importantly, understanding Buddhist ethics in the language employed by contemporary Western moral philosophers can help scholars draw on Buddhist resources to contribute to contemporary academic moral debates. Charles Goodman, for example, upon constructing a conceptual bridge between Buddhist ethics and consequentialism, draws on Indian Buddhist insights to critique penal policies in the United States (Goodman 2009, 165–81). Interpreting Buddhist ethics in terms of Western moral philosophy certainly makes some kinds of comparative analyses easier.

But projects that seek to give a global interpretation of a tradition of Buddhist ethics in terms of a particular Western meta-ethical framework force the texts to conform to a preferred interpretive schema. Goodman, for example, in order to argue that Buddhist ethics is a form of universal consequentialism, claims that acts that enable progression along the bodhisattva path do not necessarily benefit the practitioner. This is because, according to Goodman, the excessive demands on the bodhisattva, while benefiting the greatest number, do not necessarily benefit the agent. And, following virtuous acts, the aspiring bodhisattva generously gives whatever merit, happiness, and virtue are gained through cultivating the perfections of the bodhisattva. But the excessive demands are made only for those who are capable (Crosby and Skilton 1995, 69). The extraordinary examples of bodhisattvas who sacrifice their bodies for others illustrate how progress is made on the path to liberation from suffering. Moreover, if one is training appropriately, meritorious acts should not be a cause of suffering (ibid., 73). The donation of merit, which Goodman interprets as illustrating how Mahāyāna ethics does not benefit the self, lifts virtuous action outside the economy of exchange. If one performs a virtuous action in order to achieve some benefit in the future, the action is still motivated by attachment to self. Donating merit, then, perfects the action, and thereby allows further progress on the path. This is not an example of ethics demanding the aspiring bodhisattva to suffer for the general good.

Similarly, while much Buddhist moral thinking clearly shares features with one form or another of eudaimonistic virtue ethics, it would be a mistake to confuse Buddhist ethics with an Aristotelian virtue theory. As Goodman points out, the bodhisattva often performs acts which are not "virtuous" to benefit others, and those who are near and dear are not the only ones of concern. Moreover, Keown's emphasis on the self who cultivates virtue as analogous to an Aristotelian self is made possible by his suggestion that ethics is a field distinct from metaphysics and does not need to conform to metaphysical views. But this seems wrong, both for Aristotle and for Buddhist ethics. Aristotle's ethics is precisely grounded in a particular account of human nature in a larger metaphysical framework. Similarly, many of the Indian Buddhists Keown discusses ground their understanding of suffering and morality in an account of dependent origination and the problems that arise when we misunderstand the nature of the self.

While there may be some instances where Buddhist ethics might correspond to aspects of Kantian moral thought, Buddhist metaphysics undermines strong conceptions of moral responsibility and free will, and hence the understanding of a subject who could be responsible and free in a Kantian sense. Thus, as Peter Harvey notes, "the rich field of Buddhist ethics would be narrowed by wholly collapsing it into any single one of the Kantian, Aristotelian or Utilitarian models" (Harvey 2000, 51). In attempting to articulate the features of Buddhist ethics in Western philosophical terms, we risk privileging correspondences and downplaying differences that problematize the schema we happen to be using. Constructing meta-ethical theories "implicit" in Buddhist ethics may then obscure as much as disclose Buddhist moral traditions. When this happens, not only do we misunderstand the tradition we study by forcing it into an alien conceptual structure, but we miss out on the opportunity to learn from a different way of approaching moral questions.

What this different way of approaching moral questions would be depends on the specific text, practice, and tradition of Buddhist ethics we happen to be studying. In China and East Asia, for example, Buddhist traditions were profoundly influenced by Confucianism and Daoism, and thus relationships and social practices play more important roles than they do in South Asia. What would it mean for Western moral thinking, which in many instances is dominated by abstract, universal principles, to give more weight to the relationships and practices in which our lives are embedded?

And what could we learn from the Shin Buddhist "ethics" that Lewis and Amstutz describe in Japan, which eschews moral principles and even virtues cultivated on a path towards a telos? According to Lewis and Amstutz, Shin Buddhist moral teachings consist largely of narratives, especially of " 'rare followers' of Shin teachings. Rather than ethics or virtue, these sources report mere psychological and aesthetic features as the hallmarks of the ideal Shin consciousness: simplicity, an unselfconscious frugality, gratitude, worrilessness, joy, naturalness, disinvestment in personal ego, and concern for others" (Lewis and Amstutz 1997, 150). Lewis and Amstutz argue that, though these religious qualities do not constitute a coherent ethical framework, or even a virtue theory in any traditional sense, "they were substantial enough to create a moral foundation for one of the strongest and richest sectors of traditional Japanese society" (ibid.). What could Western philosophers learn about moral phenomena by attending to such an approach?

It should be clear that much Buddhist ethical thought is grounded in what is taken as a fact: that suffering is bad and should be reduced. Because reducing suffering involves every aspect of our lives, Buddhists often pursue multiple aspects of ethics at once. Rules of conduct, intentions, acts, consequences, virtues, feelings, desires, and character are all morally significant. And so are our thoughts, which color our feelings and intentions. Moreover, our capacity for attention is intertwined with morality, for attention and mindfulness free us from intellectual and affective defilements, such as jealousy, anxiety, anger, and hatred, that cause suffering both to ourselves and to others. For many Buddhist thinkers, all of these constitute spheres of moral significance, and they are understood within metaphysical frameworks of interdependence. According to these accounts, there is no autonomous self and no autonomous will, and our interests are always intertwined with the interests of others. What we have, then, is a descriptive morality that is sensitive to the ways we are situated in the world and the diverse spheres in which morality is relevant.

Western moral philosophers have much to learn from Buddhist traditions, with their broader sense of what belongs to the realm of ethics. And Buddhist ethics can benefit from Western moral theories, especially in areas that are underdeveloped in Buddhist traditions. I am thinking, here, particularly of sophisticated theories grounded in the autonomy of the individual that Western philosophers have developed since the Enlightenment. These theories have provided the intellectual foundation for the numerous liberation movements of the past several centuries. Buddhist and Western moral traditions can still engage each other in mutually productive dialogue, even if Buddhist ethics, or Buddhist ethical traditions, do not fit easily into any of the dominant Western moral philosophies. Today, this dialogue is perhaps most visible in the work of Buddhist teachers, activists, and scholars who have applied Buddhist ethics to a wide variety of contemporary concerns, including the environment; biomedical ethics; animals; human rights; violence, justice, and peace; and psychology and psychotherapy.

Notes

1 For overviews of the kind of work that academic scholars were doing on Buddhist ethics from the 1960s through the 1980s, see Reynolds (1979) and Hallisey (1992).

2 For an account of the ways in which previous scholars understood Buddhist ethics as a form of consequentialism, see Keown (1992, 14–17).

3 For other accounts of Buddhism and virtue ethics, see Cooper and James (2005); Whitehill (2000); Dreyfus (1995); and Mrozik (2007).

4 Keown devotes considerable attention to critiquing what he calls "the transcendency thesis," defended by Winston King and Melford Spiro. According to King and Spiro, there are really two forms of Buddhism. One is *kammatic* and concerned with accumulating merit through good actions. This, they say, is the goal of the laity. This goal, however, is transcended by the *nibbanic* goal of the monks, who are focused on *nirvāṇa*, or the transcendence of the world. Thus, according to King and Spiro, while moral concerns are dominant in *kammatic* Buddhism, they no longer apply in *nibbanic* Buddhism. For his presentation and critique of the transcendency thesis, see Keown (1992, 83–105).

5 Keown interprets such transgressions of the precepts as making "a symbolic as opposed to normative statement of the importance attached by the Mahāyāna to concern for others" (1992, 159).

6 This helps us understand teachers whose antinomian behavior becomes a method of teaching. Consider, for example, the famous *kōan* from the *Mumonkan*, the story of Nansen, who, when two halls of monks were fighting over a cat, cut the cat in half.

7 See, for example, the essays by Douglas Berger, Youru Wang, David Loy, Gereon Kopf, William Edelglass, Robert Magliola, Jin Y. Park, and Victor Forte in Wang (2007).

References

Aristotle (1999). *Nichomachean Ethics*. Trans. Terence Irwin. Indianapolis: Hackett.

Chappell, D. (1996). Are There Seventeen Mahāyāna Ethics? In *Journal of Buddhist Ethics* 3, 44–65.

Cooper, D. E., and James, S. P. (2005). *Buddhism, Virtue and Environment*. Aldershot: Ashgate.

Crosby, K., and Skilton, A. (1995). *Śāntideva: The Bodhicaryāvatāra*. New York: Oxford University Press.

Dreyfus, G. (1995). Meditation as Ethical Activity. In *Journal of Buddhist Ethics* 2 28–54.

Droit, R. P. (2003). *The Cult of Nothingness: The Philosophers and the Buddha*. Trans. David Streight and Pamela Vohnson. Chapel Hill: University of North Carolina Press.

Goodman, C. (2009). *Consequences of Compassion: An Interpretation and Defense of Buddhist Ethics*. New York: Oxford University Press.

Hallisey, C. (1992). Recent Work on Buddhist Ethics. *Religious Studies Review* 18, 276–85.

Hallisey, C. (1996). Ethical Particularism in Theravāda Ethics. In *Journal of Buddhist Ethics* 3, 32–43.

Harvey, P. (2000). *An Introduction to Buddhist Ethics*. Cambridge: Cambridge University Press.

Keown, D. (1992). *The Nature of Buddhist Ethics*. London: Macmillan.

Lewis, S. J., and Amstutz, G. (1997). Teleologized "Virtue" or Mere Religious "Character"? A Critique of Buddhist Ethics from the Shin Buddhist Point of View. In *Journal of Buddhist Ethics* 4, 138–59.

Mrozik, S. (2007). *Virtuous Bodies: The Physical Dimensions of Morality in Buddhist Ethics*. New York: Oxford University Press.

Olson, P. (1993). *The Discipline of Freedom: A Kantian View of the Role of Moral Precepts in Zen Practice*. Albany: State University of New York Press.

Park, J. Y. (2009). Essentials on Observing and Violating the Fundamentals of Bodhisattva Precepts: Wŏnhyo's Nonsubstantial Mahāyāna Ethics. In *Buddhist Philosophy: Essential Readings*. Ed. W. Edelglass and J. L. Garfield. New York: Oxford University Press, 409–18.

Reynolds, F. (1979). Buddhist Ethics: A Bibliographical Essay. In *Religious Studies Review* 5, 40–8.

Tuck, A. (1990). *Comparative Philosophy and the Philosophy of Scholarship: On the Western Interpretation of Nāgārjuna*. New York: Oxford University Press.

Velez de Cea, A. (2004). The Criteria of Goodness in the Pāli Nikāyas and the Nature of Buddhist Ethics. In *Journal of Buddhist Ethics* 11, 123–42.

Wang, Y. (ed.) (2007). *Deconstruction and the Ethical in Asian Thought*. London: Routledge.

Whitehill, J. (2000). Buddhism and the Virtues. In *Contemporary Buddhist Ethics*. Ed. D. Keown. Richmond, Surrey: Curzon Press, 17–36.

F. Social and Political Philosophy

32

The Enlightened Sovereign

Buddhism and Kingship in India and Tibet

GEORGIOS T. HALKIAS[1]

> *As the fame of some blameless king who, like a god, maintains justice; to whom the black earth brings forth wheat and barley; whose trees are bowed with fruit, and his sheep never fail to bear, and the sea gives him fish.*
>
> Homer, Ode XIX

All religions, insofar as they are championed by individuals and develop in communities and particular historical contexts, have shaped and been shaped by prevailing political ideas on how to arrange our collective life, social institutions, and practices, including our economy and systems of governorship. Buddhism is no exception, despite statements that it is fundamentally an "other-worldly" religion. In different parts of Asia – India, Sri Lanka, Thailand, Burma, Laos, Tibet, China, Japan, and Mongolia – and at different periods down to the present time, political, social, and legal structures have been influenced by Buddhist precepts (Dhamma) and sanctioned by monastic institutions (Sangha), while the historical spread of Buddhism in India and outside its borders might not have taken place were not for the patronage of sympathetic rulers who embraced it as a state religion. Many Buddhist rulers attained the cultic status of divinity as buddhas or celestial bodhisattvas and were expected to exercise their power in accord with Buddhist principles.

Conceptions of Kingship in Early Buddhism

The principal goal of Buddhism for monks and laymen alike has always been soteriological – the attainment of *nibbāna* (Skt *nirvāṇa*) – and, however this term is understood, it has never implied escape from the affairs of the world.[2] It is true that the Buddha never articulated a systematic theory of politics and government, such as Kauṭalya's *Arthaśāstra* – a well-known and frequently consulted Indian political treatise on

A Companion to Buddhist Philosophy, First Edition. Edited by Steven M. Emmanuel.

statecraft rejected by the Buddhist tradition for framing the "maximum advantage to the ruler and his polity" in Machiavellian terms (Tambiah 1976, 16). Nevertheless, a synthesis between Buddhist precepts and practice is fundamental to Buddhism (Gombrich 1971), and the Pāli canon contains numerous allusions to the ideal functioning of the state and society. These alleged prescriptions of the Buddha often come in the form of sermons, legends, or parables spread throughout the *Dīgha Nikāya* ("The Book of Long Sayings"), the *Aṅguttara Nikāya* ("The Book of Gradual Sayings"), and in *Jātaka* and *avadāna* stories of the Buddha's previous lives as a *bodhisatta* (Skt *bodhisattva*). In these rebirth stories, the bodhisatta is depicted as perfecting both the virtues of kingship and the virtues of renunciation, thus preparing the way for his supreme enlightenment in which the two strands of sovereignty and renunciation "receive their final synthesis and fulfilment" (Reynolds 1972, 14). These strands were modeled after Śākyamuni's life, and there is no shortage of instructive stories of Indian kings listening to the Buddhist teachings and renouncing the world along with their subjects (Collins 1998, 425–32). The centrality of *Jātaka* tales is attested in a plethora of sculptures and paintings at Buddhist monasteries and *catiyas* and *stūpas* (reliquaries) that depict scenes from the most popular stories, which were read carefully by the literati who translated them into various vernacular languages and utilized them in the legal systems of South-East Asia (Lewis 2003, 235).

While it is true that, for the most part, the monastic community, the Sangha, respected the autonomy of the political field, it did not hesitate to legitimize the political power of and idealize kingship in a Buddhist fashion (Tambiah 1976). The survival of the Buddhist movement required a transaction with the secular sphere, for, as put tersely by Houtart (1977, 209), "had it not been able to furnish the necessary justification to the political power, it would have been replaced by another religious system." However, there are important theoretical reasons for demarcating Buddhist soteriology and political expediency, for neither can be reduced to the inner logic of the other, since they are conditioned by a different set of assumptions and circumstances. At the same time we should be cautious not to treat them as two exclusively distinct categories of interpretation. It is commonly assumed that political matters are driven by concerns about how to exercise temporal power and authority over others, while Buddhist doctrines deal with a power over oneself for the purpose of attaining mastery of one's grosser levels of consciousness in pursuit of liberation from suffering (*dukkha*). In reality, of course, things are not one-sided, and a symbiotic relation between the Sangha and the king existed in India and manifested in overlapping conceptions of what constitutes Dhamma (Skt *Dharma*; duty, morality, law, truth, etc.) – articulated in Buddhism as *buddha-dhamma* and in the temporal sphere as *rāja-dhamma*.

For Buddhism, human suffering is caused, to a large extent, by unwholesome human actions and states of mind whose origin is greed (*lobha*), hatred (*dosa*), and confusion (*moha*). These "poisons" do not just affect individuals but contaminate institutions and society at large. The role of the Buddhist community, then, is to influence policy-making to ensure that it accords with the Dhamma, while an ideal ruler would be a righteous leader that works for the welfare and harmony of his subjects.

The relationship between state and religion was a subject of some concern in Manu's *dharmaśāstra*, one of the most widely discussed ancient Indian sources for litigation. If the *Manusmṛti* ("Laws of Manu") were in effect at the time of the Buddha, we may assume that the king was advised to support the regulations of religious associations in his state and that the Sangha enjoyed state recognition as one of the constituent communities in the body politic (Voyce 1986, 129). In the Vinaya, the Buddhist monastic code, the Buddha made it clear that the monastic body should never compete on issues of political authority with the state or disregard the laws of the land in any way, including accepting into the order those who have broken such laws (Lewis 2003, 237). Monks and nuns were expected to perform their duties in an environment of legal pluralism, for they were subject both to the Buddhist code, the general social expectations of mendicants concerning brahmanical concepts of purity and pollution, and to the *dharmaśāstra*, the laws of the state enforced by the king (Voyce 2007, 36).

While there are clear lines of demarcation between the role of the Buddha and his Sangha and the function of the king, there is often a blurring of these lines in the literary, practical, and cultural manifestations of Buddhism across Asia. Ambiguity is nowhere more evident than in the promotion and application of notions of "dual sovereignty" combined in a single person capable of arbitrating secular and spiritual power in this world and the world beyond.

The Ruler and the State

The Beloved by the Gods, King Aśoka speaks thus.

Having in view this very matter, I have set up pillars of morality, appointed Officers of morality, and issued proclamations on morality.

Delhi-Topra Pillar Edict

From what we know from the sources, Śākyamuni (lit. "sage of Śākya") was a prince who came from a tribal oligarchy. He abandoned his kingdom and his right to inherit the throne for a life in search of the ultimate truth that he characterized as *nibbāna* – the suppression of endless transmigrations and the unfailing, deathless, sorrowless, undefiled, and unexcelled security from bondage (AN.I.145). For pragmatic reasons, and because of his privileged upbringing, he had no difficulty in mingling in the courts of Indian monarchs and nobles. He advised them on religious matters, welcomed their patronage, and admitted scions of royal families to join his order of monks and nuns – many of whom played a leading part in "the propagation of the creed during its early critical years" (Gokhale 1966, 15). His close relationship with King Prasenajit of Kośala and King Bimbisāra of Magadha is well documented in Buddhist texts (Bareau 1993).

This period in Indian history featured a patchwork of small monarchies where the religious caste of the *brāhmana* priests was dominant and placed at the top of a hierarchical division of society according to four castes (*varnas*). It was followed by the class of warriors and kings, the *kṣatriyas*, then the *vaiśyas*, who engaged with agriculture and trade, and lastly the servants, the *śūdras*, at the bottom of the social ladder. The Buddha, who belonged to the *kṣatriya* class, voiced his reaction against the injustice of the caste system. In the *Aggañña Sutta* (DN.III.83), he proclaimed that dark and bright qualities are scattered indiscriminately among the four castes, and there is no reason to hold the *brāhmanas* as the highest. Furthermore, "not by birth is one an outcast; not by birth is one a brāhmana. By deeds one becomes an outcast, by deeds one becomes a brāhmana" (*Vassala Sutta*, SN.116.142).

There are political implications to these statements that parallel Plato's political thought – namely, that leadership in society should rest on individual talent and merit and not on the basis of its sanction by an elite class, by popular vote, or through primogeniture. Buddhism's greatest contribution to the social and political landscape of ancient India is the radical assumption that all men and women, regardless of their caste, origins, or status, have equal spiritual worth. This is especially pertinent concerning the status of women, who were traditionally prevented by the *brāhmanas* from performing religious rites and studying the sacred texts of the Vedas. Their oppression in society and religion is laid out in the "Laws of Manu" (V, 147–8, 155): "By a girl, by a young woman, or even by an aged one, nothing must be done independently, even in her own house. In childhood a female must be subject to her father, in youth to her husband, when her lord is dead to her sons; a woman must never be independent." And, "no sacrifice, no vow, no fast must be performed by women apart from their husbands; if a wife obeys her husband, she will for that [reason alone] be exalted in heaven." On the other hand, the pursuit of Buddhist practice and attainment is not bound by considerations of gender – "what difference does being a woman make when the mind's well-centred, when knowledge is progressing, seeing clearly, rightly, into the Dhamma. Anyone who thinks 'I am a woman' or 'a man' or 'Am I anything at all?' – that's who Mara's fit to address" (*Soma Sutta*, SN.I.129).[3]

In remarkable ways, the Buddha was a progressive and visionary leader whose understanding of the world was as relevant 2,500 years ago as it is today (Zsolnai 2011). Nevertheless, the Buddha was not a political reformer, and his philosophy on equality and social justice was part of his soteriological teachings. He admitted in his spiritual order everyone, regardless of caste or sex – or, rather, almost everyone. People with natural physical handicaps – cripples, eunuchs, hermaphrodites – or those bearing marks imposed by the state as punishment for crimes (branding, mutilation, scars) were not permitted to ordain as monks or nuns so that they might not disrupt the community. Those who had certain liabilities that fell outside the Sangha's jurisdiction were also excluded: debtors, slaves, members of the king's service, or anyone who had committed an offence, such as matricide, patricide, murder, theft, or who was in theory subject to the king's criminal jurisdiction (Voyce 1986, 137).

In the *Kūṭadanta Sutta* (DN.I.135–7) the Buddha acknowledges that crime in society cannot be reduced through executions and harsh punishments but ought to be based on sound plans of economic development, such as practicing moderation and modifying the nature of consumption. Similar sentiments resound in the *Cakkavattisīhanāda Sutta*, where poverty is identified as the origin of social vices and crime. Kings and governments may try to suppress crime through rigid laws, but it is futile to hope to eradicate society's ills by sheer force. There are more effective methods, such as introducing agricultural and rural reforms, providing state subsidies to entrepreneurs and businesses, and granting sufficient wages to workers, who may then uphold with dignity their duties and the interests of the state. An effective government ought to encourage the development of private enterprise and prosperity with the aim of alleviating poverty and providing basic material needs to its citizens – food, shelter, clothing, and medicine, which are necessary prerequisites for living with dignity and for spiritual advancement.

The generation of wealth, though not recommended for monastics and renunciants, is not disparaged in Buddhism, for it is often thought of as a sign of virtue and partly the result of good karma. The more important issue is whether wealth was acquired by means that do not bring harm to oneself and others, and ultimately how one relates with it.[4] As long as money doesn't become the cause for greed, attachment, and craving, there are five ways to utilize it with generosity and prudence that are equally satisfying and pleasant: (1) to provide for oneself and one's parents, spouse, children, and servants; (2) to share with one's friends and associates; (3) to save for hard times and emergencies; (4) to spend on performing oblations to relatives, guests, kings, the dead, and the gods; and (5) to offer for supreme aims to spiritual teachers and monks (AN.III.45).

Although it is not clearly laid out in the *suttas* how a ruler should actualize sound socio-economic policies, it is implicit in Buddhist discourse that reforms ought to disavow social and economic structures that rely on the exploitation of sentient beings. The generation and circulation of wealth is encouraged insofar as it is rightfully gained and does not rely on five kinds of trading activity: manufacturing or trading in weapons, and trading in living beings (the slave trade and prostitution), in meat, in intoxicants, and in poisons (AN.III.208). The aim of effective social policies and laws is society's inner transformation, the recognition that the Buddhist precepts of abstaining from taking life, stealing, sexual misconduct, lying, and the excessive consumption of intoxicants are important factors for healthy and harmonious communities.

A social philosophy framed by Buddhist principles is sufficiently pragmatic to allow for the enforcement, if it is justifiable, of laws through punishment, a stance commonly reiterated in Indian books on jurisprudence. The ruler of the land should possess certain qualities and rely on the advice of those accomplished in counselling, warfare, religion, and wealth on how best to perform the "true sacrifice," not by slaughtering animals and offering them to the gods, but by improving the conditions of his people (*Kūṭadanta*, DN.I.140–3). The *Cakkavattisīhanāda Sutta* warns against a feeble king whose failure properly to punish a thief leads to the deterioration of values in society. In the story, a thief is caught stealing and blames his poverty for his actions. The king decides to give him money instead of punishing him. This hasty action for a ruler served as the cause of an unfortunate chain of events. Thieves went on stealing, hoping to receive money for their deeds. Informed of this, the king decided to put an end to it by having a culprit executed. This incited robbers to kill their victims for fear that they should be reported to the authorities and share in the same fate. In due course, the whole social fabric was torn asunder by a vicious cycle of violence. The parable of the unwise king, without explicitly condoning violence as a form of reparation, warns against this idealistic monarch who was unable to be effective in the affairs of the world. Killing as a form of punishment goes against the very essence of Buddhist ethics and is not recommended for rulers. On the other hand, disregard for any form of punishment towards wrongdoing can cause social degradation and anarchy. This state of affairs, as we will see in the next section, prompted people to elect a ruler among them who would enforce the laws of the land, bring harmony, and protect the people.

There is a large body of Indian literature delineating the functions and duties of a king, and Buddhist notions of kingship draw largely from this legacy. In the Pāli sources the ruler should possess certain qualities (*dasa-rāja-dhamma*), singled out as "ten royal virtues":

1 liberality, generosity, and charity (*dāna*)
2 a high sense of morality (*sīla*)
3 self-sacrifice for the good of the people (*pariccāga*)
4 honesty and integrity (*ajjava*)
5 kindness and gentleness (*maddava*)
6 austerity and self-control (*tapas*)
7 to possess no ill will and enmity (*akkodha*)
8 to promote peace and non-violence (*avihiṃsā*)
9 forbearance, patience, and tolerance (*khanti*) and
10 to rule in harmony without giving offence and opposing the will of his people (*avirodha*).

(Rāhula 1985, 84–5)

These virtues serve as ethical guidelines for the rulers of states and have a powerful effect insofar as they trickle down to the ministers and the people. In "The Book of the Fours," the Buddha explains to his listeners:

> But, monks, when rājahs (kings) are righteous, the ministers of rājahs also are righteous. When ministers are righteous, brāhmins and householders are righteous. This being so, moon and sun go right in their courses. This being so, constellations and stars do likewise; days and nights, months and fortnights, seasons and years go on their courses regularly; winds blow regularly and in due season. Thus the devas (gods) are not annoyed and the sky-deva bestows sufficient rain. Rains falling seasonably, the crops ripen in due season. Monks, when crops ripen in due season, men who live on those crops are long-lived, well-favoured, strong and free from sickness.
>
> (AN.II.85)

The striking discovery of a Greek–Aramaic bilingual inscription in 1957 in Kandahar (present-day Afghanistan) reveals that the Greek part of the inscription, 14 lines in all, is based on King Aśoka's first minor edict and differs considerably from the Aramaic and Prākrit versions.[5] The fluent use of standard Hellenistic language and vocabulary (*koine*) shows that it was adapted to the cultural needs of a Greek audience. It informs us that, after ten years have passed since his consecration, King Aśoka, known by his title "benevolent-looking," *Piyadassi* (Skt *Priyadarśin*), showed the Dhamma (Gk *εὐσέβεια*) to men by personal example. He refrained from harming sentient beings (Gk *ἀπέχεται τῶν ἐμψύχων*), and so did others – those who were hunters and fishermen similarly refrained from taking life, ceased being intemperate, and obeyed their parents and elders. And from that time onwards he made men more pious and everything on earth (*κατὰ πᾶσαν γῆν*) prospered (*εὐθηνεῖ*).[6]

The doctrine of psycho-physical causation, or the "law of co-dependent origination" (*paṭiccasamuppāda*), suggests that people can have an effect on their environment not only by their physical actions but also through their moral conduct. This concept is worked out in both positive and negative terms. In the *Rājovāda-jātaka* there is a story of King Brahmadatta, who is offered a fig by a bodhisatta. The king praises its sweetness and the bodhisatta explains to him that, "in the time of unjust kings, oil, honey, molasses and the like, as well as wild roots and fruits, lose their sweetness and flavour . . . but when the rulers are just, these things become sweet and full of flavour, and the whole realm recovers its tone and flavour" (Cowell 1957, 3: 73). The moral of the story is clear: kings, like their subjects, are not exempt from ethical responsibility. Failure to act according to the Dhamma will bear karmic retributions to the kingdom, to the subjects, and to the king himself. On the other hand, spiritual merit (*puñña*) is accrued by those who act in conformity with the Buddhist teachings.

This point is reiterated in several stories. In the *Khantivādi-jātaka*, a wicked king who maltreats and kills an ascetic is cast into the Avīci hell, and in the *Culladhammapāla-jātaka* another one incurs the same punishment after committing murder out of jealousy. In the *Dhonasākha-jātaka*, a monarch is led by the immoral counsel of his evil priest and orders that 1,000 kings have their eyes removed. The violation of his moral duty to serve as a just ruler brings nature against him – personified by a *yakkha* and a vulture that blind him. Once blind, he recalls in remorse the words of the bodhisatta who spoke before his mind's eye: "These mortals experience results corresponding to their deeds, even as fruit corresponds with the seed" (Cowell 1957, 5: 106).

Examples like these underlie many *Jātaka* stories. The power of the state poses a threat of royal tyranny in the arbitrary abuse of a king's prerogatives. These fears are mitigated by the Buddhist ideals of compassion and non-injury, the power of Dhamma against crude selfishness that dwells at the heart of men. The *Tesakuṇa-jātaka* contains admonitions delivered by the Buddha to the King of Kośala and includes some revealing material on early Buddhist ideas, expressed as the duties and powers of a king and the basis for kingship: "First of all should a king put away all falsehood and anger and scorn; Let him do what a king has to do, or else to his vow be forsworn. By passion and sin led astray, should he err in the past, it is plain he will live to repent of the deed, and will learn not to do it again" (Cowell 1957, 5: 61).

Buddhist Accounts of Government: Elected Kings and Universal Monarchs

While Buddhism does not promote any specific form of government, our Pāli sources elaborate on two models of kingship which were familiar to the Buddha – namely, village republics and monarchies. We will start with the first model, which forms a part of the *Aggañña Sutta* narrative on Buddhist cosmogony.

The Buddhist origins of human society differ from the Vedic view that celebrates the creation of human society in positive terms as the self-reflective will of a demiurge and the participation of gods in shaping the physical and social reality. At different times the world and its inhabitants abide in a pristine state of undifferentiated perfection, a non-dual state of pure radiance, bliss, and consciousness. But the universe is in flux, subject to contraction and expansion. During the latter phase, an inexplicable coagulation of primal liquids occurred like a "skin that forms itself over hot milk as it cools," endowed with yellow color and sweet odor. A self-luminous being under the influence of residual karma from a previous world cycle comes to taste this savory formation and in time develops a craving for it. Soon after, other beings follow his lead, indulging greedily in material consumption. They continue like this for a long time, feeding and being nourished by the earth, eventually losing their formless luminosity as their bodies assume a growing coarseness that gives rise to mental concepts of beauty and ugliness, pride and envy. In due course, untruth, greed, theft, and savagery rule the lives of humans. Confronted with this anarchy, the people (*mahājana*) decide to elect a person from their community that has the most "perfect form" (*abhirūpa*), "appearance" (*dassanīya*), "grace" (*pāsādika*), and "great power" (*mahesakkha*). They confer upon him the power of kingship with the task of enforcing law and order in their community. He is thus called "the great chosen one," Mahāsammata, and is granted a share of their rice produce in return for protection. The elected ruler is also referred to as the "Lord of the Fields," but above all as the one who rules guided by Dhamma – a *dhammarājā*.[7]

According to the *sutta*, the state originates as a collective arrangement without an appeal to "divine right" or "divine appointment." It comes into operation as a "contract" between the electors and the elect, the Mahāsammata whose legend finds expression across South-East Asia granting sacred authority to the Mon-Pagan and Thai legal codes as their first institutor (Tambiah 1976, 93–5). Similarly, Lycophron, a disciple of the sophist Gorgias (483–375 BCE), formulated the idea of the social contract declaring that all men are equal and that nobility is a hollow sham. The philosopher Aristotle reports that Lycophron proclaimed that "law becomes a compact and 'a guarantor of mutual justice,' instead of being what makes the citizens good and just men" (*Politics* 1280, 10–12). Along the same lines, Plato, in the *Protagoras*, states that during the development of civilization it was the weakness of men that necessitated the need for laws and government. Though there is no explicit mention of any contract or agreement, for Protagoras, law and justice "find their origin in man's desire to escape from the insecurity of a lawless existence for reasons of individual self-protection," and it is "essentially similar to the contract theory of Epicurus" (Mulgan 1979, 124).

It is important to note that, although the ideal of the elected king was sanctioned by ancient Asian traditions, it does not seem to have been a method of selection that fared well in the Indian historical process that featured hereditary monarchies. The novelty of the democratically chosen ruler was overshadowed by other canonical formulations of kingship – namely, the "righteous king" (*dhammarājā*) and the "wheel-turning monarch" (P. *cakkavatti*; Skt *cakravartin*) – the latter being a counterpart of Buddha Śākyamuni in the temporal world.

The *Cakkavattisīhanāda* and *Mahāsudassana suttas* discourse on Buddhist governorship based on the *cakkavatti* model.[8] We can better appreciate the duties and functions of the universal wheel-turning monarch by looking at some stock epithets that describe him: (1) ruler of four quarters (*dhammiko, dhammarājā, cāturanto*); (2) conqueror (*vijitāvī*); (3) guardian of the people's good (*jana-padatthavāriyappatto*); and (4) possessor of seven treasures (*sattaratanasamannāgato*).[9] According to the *Cakkavattisīhanāda*, *Mahāsudassana* and *Ambaṭṭha suttas*, a *cakkavatti* comes to possess seven precious objects that manifest during his reign.[10] There is much we could say about the Indian symbolism and mythological references to these treasured items – especially the *cakka* (Skt *cakra*), which represents the greatest emblem of a monarch's conquering might over his dominions and one which has been appropriated by the Buddhists to indicate their teacher's first sermon in the deer park in Sarnath (*Dhamma-cakka-pavattana*).

The symbolism of the *dhammacakka*, the wheel of Dhamma, lies at the heart of Buddhist notions of kingship. The king's ability to rule is dependent not on his might but, ultimately, on whether he respects the principles of justice (Dhamma). The *Cakkavattisīhanāda Sutta* (§5) explains:

> But what, sire, is the duty of an Ariyan wheel-turning monarch? It is this my son: Yourself depending on the Dhamma, honouring it, revering it, cherishing it, doing homage to it and venerating it, having the Dhamma as your badge and banner, acknowledging the Dhamma as your master, you should establish guard, ward and protection according to Dhamma for your own household, your troops, your nobles and vassals, for Brahmins and householders, town and country folk, ascetics and Brahmins, for beasts and birds.

In the *Aṅguttara Nikāya*, the wheel of state (*āṇācakka*) cannot stand alone but depends on being attached to another wheel, the *dhammacakka*. The conception of the universal wheel-turning monarch is further developed in the fourth part of the *Dirghāgama* ("Long Treatise"), the earliest and most complete source of cosmological ideas in Buddhism translated into Chinese. Chapter 3 of Part 4, known as the *Shih chi ching* ("Sūtra of Cosmology"), is dedicated to the story of how a *cakkavatti* attained each of the seven treasured objects that mark his greatness. On the day of the full moon after cleansing his body with scented water, the king had retired to the upper rooms of his palace with his women when suddenly before him appeared a brilliantly lit thousand-spoked wheel, 14 feet in diameter. Following the golden wheel to the east with his four armies, he meets the kings of the eastern kingdoms and delivers the following Buddhist sermon to them:

> you should administer in the correct Law, you must not deviate from it. In your land there must be no activities against the Dharma. Do not kill living beings, teach others not to kill living beings, do not steal, do not commit adultery, do not engage in double talk, do not slander, do not lie, do not engage in exaggerated speech, do not covet, do not succumb to anger and do not hold biased views. These are the tenets by which I administer.
>
> (Howard 1986, 125)

The idea of the universal monarch superseded contractual models of the state, and may be framed as a response to the territorial extension and growing power of monarchies in India that subsumed in their fold smaller village republics. In the *cakkavatti* model, the king is not elected by the people but assumes power on the basis of being born a "Great Being" (*mahāpurisa*) who bears "thirty-two" major signs (*lakkhaṇāni*) and many accompanying minor marks in his body. However, his power is not automatically passed from one generation to the next, as is the case in Indian monarchies (Strong 1983, 47). Auspicious events and astrological configurations precede such extraordinary birth, and he who bears these marks[11] is destined to become either a universal monarch or a fully enlightened being (*sammāsambhuddha*), whose Dhamma bears universal implications, since "the welfare of the entire world is considered to depend on it" (Wiltshire 1990, 188). A "Great Being" once born is confronted by two options: he may remain a monarch and acquire the stature of a *cakkavatti* or, like Śākyamuni, abandon his kingdom and become a world renouncer (ibid., 191). These options share much in common. Just as there can be only one universal monarch at a time in the world, there can be only one Buddha. Buddhas and universal monarchs are two sides of the same coin. The funeral of a *cakkavatti* should be carried out in the same way as the funeral of a buddha, a Tathāgata. In the *Mahāparinibbāna Sutta* (DN.II.143), Śākyamuni tells his disciple Ānanda that, in a former life at Kuśinagar, he was the king Mahāsurdarśana and when he passed away he was given the funeral of a wheel-turning king. In memory of this tradition, buddhas and universal monarchs should have their remains disposed of in the same manner:

> But, Lord, what are we to do with the Tathāgata's remains? Ānanda, they should be dealt with like the remains of a wheel-turning monarch. And how is that, Lord? Ānanda, the remains of a wheel-turning monarch are wrapped in a new linen-doth. This they wrap in teased cotton wool, and this in a new doth. Having done this five hundred times each, they enclose the king's body in an oil-vat of iron, which is covered with another iron pot. Then having made a funeral-pyre of all manner of perfumes they cremate the king's body, and they raise a stupa at a crossroads. That, Ānanda, is what they do with the remains of a wheel-turning monarch, and they should deal with the Tathāgata's body in the same way.

The manner of disposing of the remains of the Buddha were known not just among Indians but also among the Indo-Greeks who settled in India after Alexander's campaigns in the Far East. It appears that it was not unusual for Indo-Greeks and Buddhists to engage in philosophical debates. The conversion to Buddhism of King Menander (Milinda, c.155–130 BCE), the greatest of all the Indo-Greek kings of the Euthydemid dynasty, who ruled over much of Afghanistan and Pakistan, is narrated in the *Milindapañha* ("Milinda's Questions"), a well-known philosophical dialogue between King Menander and the otherwise unknown Buddhist monk Nāgasena. For Nāgasena, a king and a buddha share a tradition of righteousness in common.

> A king is one who, in his turn proclaiming laws and regulations according to the instructions laid down in succession by righteous kings of ancient times, and thus carrying on his rule in righteousness, becomes beloved and dear to the people, desired in the world and, by the force of his righteousness, established his dynasty long in the land. The Blessed One, sire, proclaiming in his turn laws and regulations according to the instructions laid down in succession by the Buddhas of ancient times, and thus in righteousness being teacher of the world, is beloved and dear to both gods and humans, desired by them and, by the force of his righteousness, makes his teaching last long in the land. For this reason too the Blessed One is called a king.
>
> (Mendis 1993, 116)

King Menander not only served as a patron of Buddhism as the Indo-Greek Agathocles had done before him,[12] but, according to the *Milindapañha* and later traditions, he embraced the Buddhist teachings and attained arhatship (enlightenment). Even if

Menander's alleged devotion to Buddhism may be questioned as a pious reconstruction of a Buddhist legend, it is reinforced by Plutarch's account (*Moralia*, 52.28) – namely, that after Menander's death his relics were distributed, like those of a *cakravartin*, across his capitals in *stūpas* erected to enshrine them.

The similarities between a buddha and a *cakkavatti* reveal the ways in which Buddhism was preoccupied with temporal power as a parallel development to spiritual sovereignty. Across Buddhist literature, Sākyamuni's life is thoroughly fused with royal mythology and symbols of sacral kingship. He is often addressed with epithets of sovereignty – "the Conqueror," "the Vanquisher," "the Ruler of Rulers" – and even *stūpas* are referred to as repositories of the Buddha's "power of conquest" (Snodgrass 1985, 90). Furthermore, Buddhist monks are compared with the warriors of a king (AN. II.170). Max Moerman aptly suggested that there is a tension that lies within the earliest tradition in which the Buddha and the king are placed in a relationship of both identity and opposition.

> Sākyamuni abjured kingship in order to become a buddha and yet his hagiography, his iconography, and his ritual prerequisites are those of the cakravartin, the wheel turning universal king. By abdicating the throne he became the royal par excellence. One could thus say that the king is always already present in the figure of the Buddha and hence also the Buddha in the figure of the king.[13]

The powers of a *cakkavatti* are on a par with those of a buddha, while the office held by the latter is no longer regarded as a rational choice, much less contractual, but as subordinate to the Dhamma. The Dhamma bestows on the king a charisma by an agency higher than himself, which turns into an instrument for the legitimation of his political power. Ethics and politics are closely bound up with each other, and Wiltshire notes that if the monarch does not rule according to the Dhamma he loses the right to be king; hence, Buddhism absorbs the "notion of 'power' entirely into the notion of 'ethical justice,' so that the former cannot thrive without the latter" (Wiltshire 1990, 194). The role of the Sangha, then, is to function as the conscience-keeper of the state; it is equipped with sanctions far more subtle, and powerful in certain circumstances, than the state. In other words, whereas the king "commands," the Buddha "persuades through his spiritual authority," and should the king be opposed to the Dhamma he is no longer fit to rule. This balance of forces "limits the potential despotism of the state and its subordination to the dhamma makes it an instrument of morality"; hence, "the state becomes a moral institution" (Gokhale 1994, 130–1).

The Buddhist *cakkavatti*, like the philosopher-king in Plato's *The Republic*, draws his authority from the Platonic maxim: "the knowing is wise and the wise is good." This view is eloquently expressed by Socrates:

> Until philosophers are kings, or the kings and princes of this world have the spirit and power of philosophy, and political greatness and wisdom meet in one, and those commoner natures who pursue either to the exclusion of the other are compelled to stand aside, cities will never rest from their evils, – no, nor the human race, as I believe, – and then only will this our State have a possibility of life and behold the light of day.
>
> (Bk V, 737)

Notions of Kingship in Mahāyāna and Vajrayāna Buddhism

But now, I will speak of those among the twice-born laymen, virtuous in the Dharma, who, through their persistent employment in mantras and Tantras, will be engaged in the functions of the state.

Mañjuśrīmūlakalpa

Buddhism spread in India for a variety of reasons, not least because it gained support and patronage from the rulers who sought in Buddhism a powerful solvent to the brahmanical caste system and a means of reducing the political and economic power of traditional status groups. At the same time Buddhist notions of kingship were flexible enough to provide legitimation to rulers who arrogated the title of *cakravartin* to themselves. Others were referred to by the Buddhist tradition as "wheel-turning" monarchs, such as King Aśoka, who conveyed his political vision in religious terms using public inscriptions carved on polished cliffs or stone pillars. He respected other religions and creeds of faith, yet his conversion to Buddhism and open support of the Buddhist Sangha is evident by a careful study of all the major and minor edicts he issued. In order to propagate a rule based on morality and righteousness (Dhamma), he employed several official languages and scripts, namely Brāhmī, Kharoṣṭhī, Greek, and Aramaic. In what may have been the earliest of these inscriptions, issued in 258 BCE, Aśoka claims to have been a Buddhist lay disciple (*upāsaka*) for more than two and a half years, and by the eighth year of his reign he expresses remorse for the massacre in Kaliṇga and denounces taking life. In the twelfth year of his reign, he issued edicts that prescribed: (1) no votive offerings are to be made with living beings (i.e., animal sacrifice is prohibited), while the killing of animals for food has been restricted and will henceforth cease so far as the royal kitchen is concerned; (2) medical services for men and animals are to be established throughout the kingdom and medicinal herbs have been distributed and planted for this purpose (Warder 1970, 244).

The successful growth of Buddhism across the Indian subcontinent and its missionary spread in Central and East Asia is the result of complex forces and conditions that gave rise to unique interpretations of kingship, many of which elaborated on earlier conceptions, as well as others adopted according to local systems and institutions of power. Buddhism in Central Asia internalized and reaffirmed Greek and Iranian solar imagery, and in Tibet and East Asia it overlapped traditional concepts of divine kingship with Mahāyāna themes of incarnate bodhisattvas. From early on the identification of buddha and bodhisattva in the single person of Śākyamuni is attested in Mahāyāna art and literature, on the grounds that there is no essential difference between the actions of Buddha and the saving efforts of bodhisattvas who, having reached their final stage short of actual buddhahood, continue incarnating among living beings in order to assist them and convert them (Snellgrove 1987, 79). In the *Laṅkāvatāra* and *Daśabhūmika sūtras*, the ritual of coronation is firmly embedded in the narrative of a bodhisattva at the tenth stage of his spiritual evolution, gaining confirmation by the buddhas of the ten directions, who shower him with light (Davidson 2002, 125). More than ever before, there is a plethora of royal symbolism in Mahāyāna and Vajrayāna texts, rituals, and art – especially in the depiction of bodhisattvas in royal garments, jewellery, and crowns, in the iconography of the Buddha seated on a lion throne in a celestial palace or his own spiritual land (buddha-field), in the use of *maṇḍalas* as potent symbols for the ruler and his polity, and in the reproduction of images of *cakravartins* in Buddhist sculptures and *stūpas*.[14]

Following on earlier conceptions of kingship, many Mahāyāna texts elaborated on the notion of *cakravartin*, while the *Durgatipariśodhana Tantra* is noted for its overriding concern on how to achieve such a state.[15] The *Mahābherihāraka-parivarta-sūtra* calls a *cakravartin* a "dharmarājika dharmarakṣa, a righteous monarch protecting the dharma, who is the king of kings" (Ku 2001 [1991], 163). In the royal policy chapter of the *Ratnāvalī*, attributed to the second-century Indian philosopher Nāgārjuna, the king is counseled on how to rule his kingdom based on Buddhist principles (Zimmerman 2006, 228). The *Śrīmālādevī Siṃhanāda-sūtra* features Queen Śrīmālā empowered by the Buddha to teach the Buddhist doctrines, and the *Suvarṇabhāsa-sūtra* ("Sūtra of Golden Light") expands on the correlation between the king's duties and the stability in his realm. It states explicitly that calamities may befall a state because of the negligence of its king, and it therefore recommends that the *Sūtra of Golden Light* be recited for peace and prosperity, for the protection of the state from enemies, and for the well-being and long life of rulers. It became the standard model in China and Japan for "state protection *sūtras*" (Tanabe and Tanabe 1989, 16), along with the *Lotus Sūtra* (*Saddharma Puṇḍarīka*). The apocryphal Chinese *Renwang jing*, the "Sūtra of the Humane Kings," proposes that the benevolent king ought to provide "outer protection" and Buddhism "inner protection," hence serving and complementing each other.

With the advent of Vajrayāna Buddhism we discern the most politically involved form of Buddhism most acculturated to the socio-political landscape of medieval India.[16] Tantras featured the systematic use of consecration, coronation, and protection rituals, the deployment of powerful visualization techniques of oneself as a deity, the uttering of mantras and spells, and the construction of *maṇḍalas*. In the hands of ritual adepts, tantricas, and monastics, Buddhist tantras acquired political and military efficacy in promising effective ways of empowering individuals to assume the throne and acquire extraordinary powers. The following passage from the *Vajrapāṇi-abhiṣeka-mahātantra* illustrates the central position of imperial metaphors in tantric discourse:

> Now, O possessor of the vajra, this Dharma of vajra has been explained [for] you, and the vajra arisen from meditation has been actually placed in your hand by all the Buddhas. So, from today, all the magical ability of Vajrapāṇi in the world is just yours. It is yours to tame those insufferable beings harming the Dharma and to kill those afflicted with anger – that is why the guides of the world have given you the vajra. In the way a Universal Conqueror [*cakravartin*] is coronated that he might achieve dominion, in the same sense it is said that you have been consecrated Adamantine Intellect so as to be the King of the Dharma.
>
> (Davidson 2002, 126)

The appropriation of royal metaphors, symbols, and ritual acts played a vital role in mapping territorial and supra-regional claims corresponding to the Buddhist religious universe, legitimizing the consolidation of the state process, and sacralizing rule among the subject population. In fact it is only in tantric practice that we may identify a notion of kingship that is in some sense sacral or divine. In the early period the ethical goal of

Buddhism coincided with the aims of the state, but there was nothing regal in the make-up of an *arhat*. Later, with the development of Mahāyāna, the goal came to be conceived as a kind of potential altruistic activity in the persona of bodhisattvas, the princes of *Dharma*. These higher beings were conceived in regal terms in ways that appealed to the ruling classes who sought a model that corresponded with exalted and popular forms of worship. It is in the tantras that we learn of new practices that were able to turn the notion of kingship to practical account (Snellgrove 1959, 1).

The currency of Mahāyāna themes and Vajrayāna formulations of Buddhist kingship among the ruling classes was not confined to medieval India but had considerable impact in Central and East Asia. In Tibet and in culturally Tibetan areas, variant models of dual sovereignty (Tb. *chos-srid*) were adopted by the kings of Ladakh, Sikkim, Bhutan, and other principalities in the Himalayas, who were expected to support the Sangha and abide by Buddhist principles. The famous statement of the fourth Buddhist king of Bhutan, Jigme Sangye Wangchuk (b. 1954), that "gross national happiness" (Tb. *rgyal yongs dga' skyid dpal 'dzoms*), or GNH, is more important than gross national product (GNP), pronounces the impact of Buddhist ethics for the political philosophy of this last of Himalayan kingdoms.

The Bodhisattva-Emperors of Tibet

For the most part, Tibetans recount their history in terms of Buddhism (Tb. *nang-pa'i chos*; lit. "the religion of the insiders") and its introduction to Tibet in two major phases. They identify the early spread of the Buddhist doctrine (Tb. *bstan-pa snga-dar*) during the reign of the Tibetan emperors (Tb. *btsan-po*), followed by a later revival (Tb. *bstan-pa phyi-dar*) that coincides with the rise of monasticism in the early eleventh century. The institutionalization of Buddhism in Tibet is closely tied to the state that supported the spread of religion within the empire and beyond its borders. This was reinforced in a variety of ways, among them the public erection of Buddhist markers (i.e., pillars, temples, monasteries, *stūpas*, etc.); forging theophoric associations with the emperors; the importation, translation, reproduction, and study of Buddhist scriptures; the sponsorship of Buddhist crafts and art; and inviting and welcoming foreign Buddhist teachers to visit Tibet and attend to the spiritual needs of the royal court.

State sponsorship of the Buddhist creed was sanctioned by Emperor Srong-brtsan-sgam-po (c. 617–649/50), who was identified with the Indian bodhisattva of compassion Avalokiteśvara and was regarded by a later Tibetan polity as the first in a series of three incarnations of bodhisattva-*dharmarājas*. At the times of the Tibetan Empire, Buddhism was established in many borderland areas, and the model of the enlightened sovereign was successfully adopted by the neighboring kings of Khotan, who, according to the Khotanese religious history *Li yul lung bstan pa* ("Buddhism in Khotan"), were considered incarnations of the bodhisattva Maitreya.[17] Tibetan texts seem to suggest that the Tibetan sons of heaven (Tb. *lha-sras*) modeled themselves on the *cakravartin* ideal and were identified as celestial bodhisattvas before the collapse of the empire. There is a post-imperial interpolation of Srong-brtsan-sgam-po pleading with his parents to grant him power to rule on the grounds that he had vowed to Buddha Amitābha to discipline Tibet through the teachings of Buddhism.

According to the Yar-lung edicts, the royal pledging of monastic protection and sustenance goes back to 779, during the reign of sovereign Khri Srong-lde-btsan (756–c. 800), who was exalted in traditional narratives as the second Buddhist king (Skt *dharmarāja*; Tb. *chos-rgyal*) of Tibet – and for good reason: in the late eighth century he declared Buddhism the official religion of the Tibetan Empire by erecting inscriptions and issuing two royal edicts swearing to preserve the creed of the Buddha, and he actively supported the Tibetan Buddhist Sangha. He took a keen interest in the interpretation and dissemination of Buddhist literature and established the Buddhist Council (Tb. *mdun-sa*), an institution responsible for overseeing the official translations of Buddhist texts into Tibetan. Because of these activities, he is invariably referred to as an incarnation of Mañjuśrī, the celestial bodhisattva of wisdom and knowledge.

Much of the life of Khri Srong-lde-btsan is discussed in the Padma Kathang (*Padma bKa' thang*), a popular Tibetan biography of the Indian tantric *siddha* Padmasambhava, who was requested by the emperor to expel the factions opposed to the construction of Tibet's first Buddhist monastery, Samye. His skills at binding demons with oaths and eventually serving as the emperor's Vajrayāna teacher – that is, showing mastery in both religious and secular spheres – should not surprise us, given the political efficacy exhibited by esoteric discourses in India by that time. Their relationship, governed by the rules of conduct and an indissoluble bond between a Vajrayāna master and his disciple, presents an inversion of power, the secular domain succumbing to the spiritual instructions of the Tantric adept.

Khri gTsug-lde-brtsan (815–841), also known in Tibetan as Ral-pa-can, is the last glorified Dharma king of the empire and is traditionally identified with Vajrapāṇi, the celestial bodhisattva of powerful means. He vigorously enacted religious reforms, restoring Buddhist temples and initiating a major literary revision movement to standardize Tibet's Buddhist heritage. Before Buddhism, models of divine kingship played an important role in the political traditions of Tibet, as they did in Chinese and Eurasian contexts. Heavenly beliefs and mortuary rites in pre-Buddhist Tibet were probably shaped through contact with Central Eurasian peoples. Whatever the lines of transmission may have been, old Tibetan beliefs about the afterlife were not eclipsed by the advent of Buddhism in the Tibetan court. Early Indo-Tibetan forms of Buddhism would struggle and eventually succeed to build upon older notions of divine kingship refashioned in a new light through the doctrine of reincarnation and the conviction of an afterlife in a pure land. The monastic appropriation of the returning bodhisattva theme was one of a series of tropes that went into the creation of Tibet's socio-political system in service of a stable and non-hereditary process of political succession.[18]

> According to the indigenous belief, the Tibetan kings were direct descendants of the gods of Phyva. They . . . were gods like the Phyva themselves and so were imbued with supernatural qualities such as byin, "splendor" of body for the overpowering of political and military opponents and 'phrul, "magic sagacity" of mind enabling them to sustain the order of the world. Nevertheless, Buddhism seems to have adjusted itself, as it usually did in the countries where it spread, to the native beliefs by assimilating the indigenous conception of kingship and the notion of royal powers to its own notions: the term byin came to be used in conjunction with rlabs to form the word byin rlabs (adhisthāna) and 'phrul with rdzu, rdzu 'phrul (siddhi) or with other similar Buddhist terms. Both the terms subsequently almost entirely lost their original and early connotation. The kings

themselves became simply chos rgyal (dharmarāja) and were finally subjected to the Buddhist moral code.

(Karmay 1988, 2)

Rule by Incarnation Regimes

Following the collapse of the Tibetan Empire in the ninth century and the restoration of Buddhism from the tenth century onwards, Buddhism became the one unifying force in the whole region. A system of dual governance was adopted in Western Tibet by the ruling house of royal descendants, lHa-lde and his father lHa Lama Ye-shes-'od (royal lama and ex-king), who were instrumental in the second diffusion of Buddhist teachings during the latter part of the tenth century. In time, Tibetan political authority shifted from the *nirmāṇakāya* model of bodhisattvas emanating as emperors – and thus combining ultimate spiritual and temporal power in them – to charismatic monks entrenched in big monasteries serving as spiritual counselors for Mongolian and Chinese rulers. Chos-rgyal 'Phags-pa, of the Sa-skya school of Tibetan Buddhism, was appointed "imperial preceptor" (Tb. *dbu-bla*) by his patron-disciple (Tb. *yon-bdag*), the Yuan Emperor Kublai, who, upon becoming Khan at Karakorum in 1260, promoted his guru to "State Preceptor" and at the same time made Tibetan Buddhism the official religion of the whole eastern part of the Mongol Empire in China.[19]

For 91 years, nine Sa-skya hierarchs and 20 regional chief officials (Tb. *dpon-chen*) ruled over the whole of Tibet and became the leaders in charge of Tibetan secular and religious affairs. The fall of the Mongol power in China in the mid-fourteenth century and the political decline of the Sa-skya abbots left an ideological structure that remained the basis of subsequent political activity. Sa-skya succession was hereditary and did not go unchallenged by those who might have rightly thought that ability and heredity had no inherent connection to each other. They may have opted instead for a more democratic method of succession that would turn the Buddhist belief in incarnation into a chain of ecclesiastical legitimation. The Buddhist idea of rebirth provided enough prestige and flexibility to connect histories, people, and places across time and space.

The head of the bKa'-brgyud school of Tibetan Buddhism and founder of the lineage of the Karmapas, Dus-gsum mKhyen-pa (1110–1193), was reportedly the first to introduce incarnation as a means of succession by requesting that his foremost disciple find him 11 years after his death in Talung, Eastern Tibet. Karma Pak-shi (1204–1283), the second Karmapa, was very effective at spreading the doctrine and founding monasteries in Tibet, Mongolia, and China.[20] From the twelfth century onwards, all schools adopted the institution of incarnate lamas, which led to the emergence of numerous incarnations in nearly all Tibetan Buddhist monasteries.

The seventeenth century saw the consolidation of secular and religious power by the dGe-lugs-pa school of Tibetan Buddhism, founded by the reformist Tsong kha-pa Blo-bzang grags-pa (1357–1419). The order developed rapidly, gaining more force and leverage, which brought about a widespread reaction against them and led to a series of draining civil wars. Political ascendancy for this school did not come until 1642 – when Gu-shri Khan gained suzerainty over Tibet and the Fifth Dalai Lama, Ngag-dbang blo-bzang rgya-mtsho (1617–1682), received authority to reign over all Tibet, along with a "governor" (*sde-srid*) imposed on him by the Mongols. The stratification of incarnation-based power structures was glossed for domestic and international consumption with the marketing of the Fifth Dalai Lama as an incarnate emanation of the Mahāyāna deity Avalokiteśvara and patron deity of the whole of Tibet. The Lhasa government was aptly renamed the dGa'-ldan Pho-brang, (lit. "Tushita Palace"; Avalokiteśvara's pure-land). It unified Tibet under one sovereign ruler, the Dalai Lama, and one dominant state religion, of which the Dalai Lama was the head.

As we have seen, from the earliest times Buddhism had a political dimension. Without advocating a particular system of governance it placed its emphasis on Dhamma and social equality, applicable to the lives of monastics and householders and to democratic and autocratic systems of governance. This situation reflected both prevailing norms and a real opportunity for the Sangha both to educate leaders on matters of ethics, social policy, and political processes and to gain their patronage. Politics was realistically seen as an unavoidable exercise of power that can and ought to be used to promote righteousness, while the philosophical interpretation of Buddhist doctrines reflects the pragmatic nature of Buddhist ethics, which, unlike the deontological and absolutist ethical traditions, allows for the expression of multiple and variant attitudes towards the state and the role of religion in shaping and being shaped by social and political conditions.

Notes

1 I wish to thank the Käte Hamburger Kolleg, Center for Religious Studies, at the Ruhr-Universität Bochum for providing me with research facilities and generous support for the duration of the completion of this chapter.

2 The view that Buddhism is an "other-worldly" religion was promoted by the German sociologist Max Weber (1970, 213). Premasiri (2001 [1991], 46) has argued convincingly that "Buddhism does not see any opposition between an improvement of the conditions of this world and man's striving for salvation. It is a considerable distortion of Buddhism to interpret it as a religious idea which ignores the process of mankind in this world, to escape into a euphoric bliss in a mystical and metaphysical realm of transcendental being."

3 *Samyutta Nikaya: The Grouped Discourses*, ed. John T. Bullitt. At www.accesstoinsight.org/tipitaka/sn/index.html (accessed 30 December 2011).

4 Sivaraksa encapsulates these concerns when he writes that in Buddhism there are three poisons to be avoided, namely: greed, hatred, and delusion. "All three are manifestations of unhappiness, and the presence of any one poison breeds more of the same. Capitalism and consumerism are driven by these three poisons. Our greed is cultivated from a very young age. We are told that our desires will be satisfied by buying things, but, of course, consuming one thing just arouses us to want more. We all have these seeds of greed within ourselves, and consumerism encourages them to sprout and grow" (Sivaraksa 2000, 181–2).

5 Transcription and translation of the Greek text in Carratelli and Garbini (1964, 29–39). For a discussion and English translation of the Greek edicts of Aśoka, see Halkias (2013). Drawing from a mixture of legends and historical facts, the figure of Emperor Aśoka exerted enormous influence on a number of rulers in South and East Asia to pattern their states after his own. Though there is regrettably little written about Aśoka in traditional Indian literature such as the Purāṇas, perhaps on account of his preference for Buddhism, there are many sources in Pāli, Chinese, Sanskrit, and Tibetan where he figures as one of the

greatest patrons that Buddhism has ever known. His depiction of the *dharmacakra*, the symbol of the "righteous state," is found in a number of his edicts, only to be adopted nearly two millennia later by the independent Republic of India on its national flag.

6 Compare with Homer's ode XIX at the beginning of this chapter as also quoted in Plato's *The Republic*.

7 The Singhalese Buddhist scholar Buddhaghosa (c. fifth century CE) explains that the term *dhammarājā* applies to a king who has acquired his power not through violence or fraudulent means, but through rightful succession and faithful adherence to the precepts of "righteous kings" (Gokhale 1953, 162).

8 The origins of the *cakkavatti* are much debated by scholars. Although Babylonian influences have been posited, in India the concept goes back at least to the tenth century BCE, acquiring its own special significance in Buddhism but also retained in non-Buddhist circles (Strong 1983, 48). Early Buddhist and Jain sources distinguish three types of *cakkavtti*: (a) a king who rules over all four continents posited by ancient Indian cosmography (*cakkavāla-cakkavatti*); (b) he who governs only one of these continents (*dvīpa cakravartin*); and (c) the *pradeśa cakravartin*, who rules only a part of the continent and may be equivalent to a local king (Doniger 1999, 193).

9 For further occurrences and explanations of these terms, see *The Pali Text Society's Pali–English dictionary* (Davids and Stede 1959).

10 These seven treasures are the wheel (*cakka*); the treasure of the elephant (*hatthiratana*); the treasure of the gem (*maṇiratana*); the pearl among women (*ltthiratana*); the commoner (*ghapatiratana*); the treasurer (*gahapati*); and the treasure of the councillor (*parināyaka-ratana*).

11 The marks of a "Great Being" are mentioned in several places in the Pāli canon, and elsewhere in Buddhist literature, and there are variations in their order of presentation. For a list of the 32 signs of a *mahāpurisa*, see the *Mahāpadāna* and *Lakkhana suttas*.

12 For Narain (1989, 406), Agathocles was "the first Yavana king to possess Taxila and initiate a forward policy of extending patronage to Indian religions and cults, both Buddhist and Brahmanical." On a unique coin issued by him, there is a depiction of a Buddhist *stūpa* and the legend "Akathukreyasa"; on the reverse there is a depiction of a tree inside a railing with the legend "Hirañasame."

13 Quoted in Strong (2002, 38).

14 Archaeological reports show that many Indian and Central Asian kings, around the period from the fourth to the fifth century CE, adopted and sponsored representations of the *cakravartin* (Ku 2001 [1991], 164).

15 Snellgrove (1987, 266). Ku (2001 [1991], 164) notes that the *vaipulya sūtras* (extensive scriptures), the *Mahāvaipulya (vedalla) mahāsannipāta-sūtra*, the *Suvarṇaprabhāsa-sūtra*, and so forth, were particularly instrumental in promoting the idea of *cakravartin*, and many of these texts were retranslated and used by later Chinese emperors for the purpose of promoting identification. She cites the example of the Empress Wu-ze tian (fl. 662–705) of the Tang dynasty, who issued, in the first year of her reign, a decree to spread the text of the *Mahāmega-sūtra* in every state of her territory in order to advance the idea that she was a female *cakravartin*.

16 Davidson argues that "the evidence supports a position that is curiously both astonishing and reassuring: the Mantrayāna is simultaneously the most politically involved of Buddhist forms and the variety of Buddhism most acculturated to the medieval Indian landscape. Briefly the mature synthesis of esoteric Buddhism – the form defined as a separate method or vehicle employing mantras – is that which embodies the metaphor of the practitioner becoming the overlord (rājādhirāja). In this endeavour, the candidate is coronated and provided with ritual and metaphorical access to all the various systems that an overlord

controls: surrounded by professors of mantra, he performs activities to ensure the success of his spiritual 'state'" (2002, 114).

17 Emmerick (1967, 25). The idea expressed here – namely, that the secular ruler is an incarnation of a buddha or bodhisattva – was popular in China in 419 with the monk Fa-kuo, who was the first to formulate the idea when he claimed that his sovereign, the Emperor T'ai-tsung of the Northern Wei dynasty, was in fact the Tathāgata, a Buddha. Farquhar further explains that "the Manchu rulers, beginning with T'ai-tsung, were all regarded by the lamas as bodhisattvas, but paralleling the development of ecclesiastical reincarnations in Tibet and Mongolia, where the occupants of a particular monastic throne were always the same bodhisattva, the Manchu emperors were all reincarnations of Mañjuśrī. They managed their divinity in a very different way from the Yüan emperors of the fourteenth century: whereas the latter did not hesitate to proclaim their bodhisattvahood, the former never formally referred to it" (1978, 33).

18 Tucci (1955, 199–200), in his detailed study on Tibetan kingship before the advent of Buddhism, explains that Tibetan monarchs were endowed with four powers – namely, religious law (Tb. *chos*); dominion (Tb. *mnga'-thang*); government (Tb. *chab-srid*); and "helmet" (Tb. *dbu-rmog*) – signifying their majesty and rank. Kapstein notes that, "as the later Tibetan institution of an incarnate religious hierarchy demonstrates, the Buddhist teaching of transmigration would itself eventually be made to serve an ancient and autochthonous Tibetan interest in stable succession" (2000, 5).

19 Ruegg (1997, 866) distinguishes three theoretical models that shed light on the constitutional relationship between spiritual authority and temporal power in Tibet: (a) the dyarchic model of *dharmarāja-cakravartin* and *officiant-spiritual* preceptor; (b) the model of the *vajrayāna-lama* and his neophyte disciple; and (c) the hierocratic and *nirmānic* model of the bodhisattva-king combining in himself both spiritual and temporal power.

20 Franz reports: "There followed a period of political infighting during which the secular heads of government were strongly backed by the Karmapa incarnations, who did not assume open power but were deeply involved in politics. The new political role of the incarnations marked a decisive shift of power away from the ruling houses, and from now on, the incarnations were installed by the monks of a sect and monastery" (1982, 38).

References

Bareau, André (1993). Le Bouddha et les rois. In *Bulletin de l'Ecole Française d'Extrême-Orient* 80, 15–39.

Bühler, Georg (1964 [1886]). *The Laws of Manu*. Delhi: Motilal Banarsidass.

Carratelli, G. P., and Garbini, G. (1964). *A Bilingual Graeco-Aramaic Edict by Asoka: The First Greek Inscription Discovered in Afghanistan*. Serie Orientale Roma, XXIX. Rome: Instituto Italiano per il Medio ed Estermo Oriente.

Collins, Steven (1998). *Nirvana and Other Buddhist Felicities: Utopias of the Pali Imaginaire*. Cambridge: Cambridge University Press.

Cowell, Edward (1957). *The Jātaka, or the Stories of the Buddha's Former Births*. 7 vols. London: Pali Text Society.

Davids, Rhys, and Stede, William (1959). *The Pali Text Society's Pali–English Dictionary*. London: Luzac.

Davidson, Ronald (2002). *Indian Esoteric Buddhism: A Social History of the Tantric Movement*. New York: Columbia University Press.

Doniger, Wendy (ed.) (1999). *Merriam-Webster's Encyclopedia of World Religions*. Springfield, MA: Merriam-Webster.

Emmerick, R. E. (1967). *Tibetan Texts Concerning Khotan*. Oxford: Oxford University Press.

Farquhar, M. David (1978). Emperor as Bodhisattva in the Governance of the Ch'ing Empire. In *Harvard Journal of Asiatic Studies* 38, 5–34.

Franz, Michael (1982). *Rule by Incarnation: Tibetan Buddhism and its Role in Society and State*. Boulder, CO: Westview Press.

Gokhale, Balkrishna G. (1953). Dhammiko Dhammaraja: A Study in Buddhist Constitutional Concepts. In *Indica*, 161–5.

Gokhale, Balkrishna G. (1966). Early Buddhist Kingship. In *Journal of Asian Studies* 26, 15–22.

Gokhale, Balkrishna G. (1994). *New Light on Early Buddhism*. London: Sangam Books.

Gombrich, Richard (1971). *Precept and Practice: Traditional Buddhism in the Rural Highlands of Ceylon*. Oxford: Clarendon Press.

Halkias, Georgios (2013). When the Greeks Converted the Buddha: Asymmetrical Transfers of Knowledge among Indo-Greek Cultures. In *Trading Religions: Religious Formation, Transformation and Cross Cultural Exchange between East and West*. Ed. Volker Rabens. Leiden: E. J. Brill.

Houtart, François (1977). Theravada Buddhism and Political Power-Construction and Destructuration of its Ideological Function. In *Social Compass* 24, 207–46.

Howard, Angela Falco (1986). *The Imagery of the Cosmological Buddha*. Leiden: E. J. Brill.

Kapstein, T. Matthew (2000). *The Tibetan Assimilation of Buddhism: Conversion, Contestation, and Memory*. Oxford: Oxford University Press.

Karmay, Samten (1988). *The Great Perfection: A Philosophical and Meditative Teaching of Tibetan Buddhism*. Leiden: E. J. Brill.

Ku, cheng-mei (2001 [1991]). A Ritual of Mahāyāna Vinaya: Self-Sacrifice. In *Buddhist Thought and Ritual*. Ed. D. Kalupahana. Delhi: Motilal Banarsidass, 159–68.

Lewis, Todd (2003). Buddhism: The Politics of Compassionate Rule. In *God's Rule: The Politics of World Religions*. Ed. J. Neusner. Washington, DC: Georgetown University Press.

Mendis, N. G. K. (1993). *The Questions of King Milinda*. Kandy, Sri Lanka: Buddhist Publication Society.

Mulgan, R. G. (1979). Lycophron and Greek Theories of Social Contract. In *Journal of the History of Ideas* 40, 121–8.

Narrain, A. K. (1989). The Greeks of Bactria and India. In *The Cambridge Ancient History*, Vol. VIII. Cambridge: Cambridge University Press, 388–421.

Premasiri, P. D. (2001 [1991]). The Social Relevance of the Buddhist Nibbāna Ideal. In *Buddhist Thought and Ritual*. Ed. D. Kalupahana. Delhi: Motilal Banarsidass.

Rāhula, Walpole (1985). *What the Buddha Taught*. London: Gordon Fraser.

Reynolds, Frank (1972). The Two Wheels of Dhamma: A Study of Early Buddhism. In *The Two Wheels of Dhamma: Essays on the Theravada Tradition in India and Celylon*. Ed. G. Obeyesekere, F. Reynolds, and B. Smith. Chambersburg, PA: American Academy of Religion.

Ruegg, D. Seyfort (1997). The Preceptor–Donor (yon mchod) Relation in Thirteenth Century Tibetan Society and Polity, its Inner Asian Precursors and Indian Models. *PIATS 1995: Proceedings of the Seventh Seminar of the International Association for Tibetan Studies*, Vol. 2: *Tibetan Studies II*. Vienna: Verlag der Österreichischen Akademie der Wissenschaffen.

Sivaraksa, Sulak (2000). The Religion of Consumerism. In *Dharma Rain: Sources of Buddhist Environmentalism*. Ed. S. Kaza and K. Kraft. London: Shambhala.

Snellgrove, David (1959). The Notion of Divine Kingship in Tantric Buddhism. In *Studies in the History of Religions*. Leiden: E. J. Brill.

Snellgrove, David (1987). *Indo-Tibetan Buddhism: Indian Buddhists and their Tibetan Successors*. London: Serindia.

Snodgrass, Adrian (1985). *The Symbolism of the Stupa*. Ithaca, NY: Cornell University, Southeast Asia Program.

Strong, John (1983). *The Legend of King Aśoka: A Study and Translation of the Aśokāvadāna*. Princeton, NJ: Princeton University Press.

Strong, John (2002). Aśoka's Wives and the Ambiguities of Buddhist Kingship. In *Cahiers d'Extrême-Asie* 13, 35–54.

Tambiah, Stanley J. (1976). *World Conqueror and World Renouncer: A Study of Buddhism and Polity in Thailand against a Historical Background*. Cambridge: Cambridge University Press.

Tanabe, George, and Tanabe, Jane (1989). *The Lotus Sutra in Japanese Culture*. Honolulu: University of Hawai'i Press.

Tucci, Giuseppe (1955). The Secret Characters of the Kings of Ancient Tibet. In *East and West* 6(4), 197–205.

Voyce, Malcom (1986). Some Observations on the Relationship between the King and the Buddhist Order in Ancient India. In *Journal of Legal Pluralism* 24, 127–50.

Voyce, Malcom (2007). The Vinaya and the Dharmaśāstra: Monastic Law and Legal Pluralism in Ancient India. In *Journal of Legal Pluralism* 56, 33–65.

Warder, A. K. (1970). *Indian Buddhism*. Delhi: Motilal Banarsidass.

Weber, Max (1970). *The Religion of India*. Trans. H. Gerth and D. Martindale. New York: Free Press.

Wiltshire, Martin (1990). *Ascetic Figures Before and in Early Buddhism: The Emergence of Gautama as the Buddha*. Berlin: Mouton de Gruyter.

Zimmermann, Michael (2006). Only a Fool Becomes a King: Buddhist Stances on Punishment. In *Buddhism and Violence*. Ed. M. Zimmermann. Lumbini, Nepal: Lumbini International Research Institute.

Zsolnai, Laszlo (2011). *Ethical Principles and Economic Transformation: A Buddhist Approach*. New York: Springer.

33

Political Interpretations of the *Lotus Sūtra*

JAMES MARK SHIELDS

The *Sūtra on the White Lotus of the Sublime Dharma* (Skt *Saddharmapuṇḍarīka-sūtra*; Ch. *Miàofǎ liánhuá jīng*; Jp. *Myōhō renge kyō*), commonly known as the *Lotus Sūtra*, is arguably the most influential *sūtra* of Mahāyāna Buddhism, and certainly one of the most revered sacred texts in East Asia.[1] Via parables and short stories, the 28 chapters of the *Lotus Sūtra* indirectly present a number of core doctrines of the early Mahāyāna, the form of Buddhism that first emerged in India and West Asia roughly five centuries after the death of the historical Buddha Siddhartha Gautama (c. 563–486 BCE) and would eventually come to dominate East Asian Buddhism. The *Lotus Sūtra* is a devotional text rather than a philosophical one – i.e., it seems intended to work on the level of the emotions and the senses rather than the intellect. And yet, despite its otherworldly aspects, the *Lotus Sūtra* has been employed over the centuries as a political text, both as a tool for maintaining the status quo and – especially in the twentieth century but with a few historical precedents – as an inspiration and justification for political transformation or reform. This chapter explores some of the various ways in which the *Lotus Sūtra* has been understood and utilized as a political text.

Origins and Early Usage

Though its precise origins are obscure, the *Lotus Sūtra* is believed to have been composed between the first century BCE and the second century CE. The *sūtra*'s self-referential claims to transcendent authority and its insistence on the "one vehicle" of Dharma are indicative of some of the disputes and transformations taking place within Indian Buddhism at the time of its creation, particularly the origins of a diffuse movement that would eventually self-identify as the Mahāyāna, or "great vehicle." Monks associated with the Mahāyāna were generally critical of what they perceived as the "selfish" pursuit of individual *nirvāṇa* (lit. "extinction"), replacing the traditional monastic goal

A Companion to Buddhist Philosophy, First Edition. Edited by Steven M. Emmanuel.

of becoming an *arhat* with the other-directed practice of compassion as embodied in the figure of the bodhisattva. Given this context, we are compelled to read the *Lotus Sūtra* as part of a larger polemic by those affiliated with the broader Mahāyāna movement to establish their credentials *vis-à-vis* more traditional Buddhists. In other words, despite – or perhaps because of – its exaggerated cosmic tableaux and repeated assertions of otherworldly power, the *Lotus Sūtra* was, from its very origins, embedded in a sectarian struggle that we might reasonably call "political" in nature, as it turned upon competing claims to authority within the institutional structures of Buddhism (though this is not to suggest that the success of the *Lotus Sūtra* as an inspirational and transformative text throughout East Asian history can be reduced to this aspect alone).

Whatever its Indian (or possibly West Asian) origins, the oldest extant versions of the *Lotus Sūtra* are in Chinese, and it is these Chinese translations – particularly that of the Kuchean monk-translator Kumarajiva (344–413) – that became the standard versions of the text as it spread throughout East Asia. The *Lotus Sūtra* would eventually serve as the primary scripture for two important East Asian Buddhist sects: the sixth-century Tiantai (Jp. Tendai) sect, often called the first indigenous Chinese Buddhist school, and the twelfth-century Nichiren (also known as the Hokke, or Lotus Flower) sect, which makes a similar claim to being the first indigenous Japanese Buddhist sect. For followers of both these traditions, the *Lotus Sūtra* contains the highest stage of the teachings of Śākyamuni, the historical Buddha. All earlier teachings – i.e., the texts and doctrines of the so-called Hīnayāna (a pejorative term meaning "lesser vehicle"), but also competing Mahāyāna schools and sects and even non-Buddhist traditions – are considered provisional stages on the path towards the highest truth as revealed in the *Lotus Sūtra*. For all this, the *Lotus Sūtra* is notoriously vague about the actual content of this "highest law," to the extent that it has been called (and criticized as) an "empty text." This vagueness plays a role in the ability of modern devotees of the *Lotus Sūtra* to interpret it in manifold ways and employ it to various political ends.

Within its spectacular scenes and various parables, the *Lotus Sūtra* presents the following core ideas of Mahāyāna Buddhism: (1) the doctrine of *upāya* (Jp. *hōben*), or "skillful means," as the way in which buddhas and advanced bodhisattvas teach the Dharma to less advanced beings; (2) perfect awakening or buddhahood as a realizable goal for all beings; (3) the way of the bodhisattva and the practice of compassion as the highest goal of Buddhism; (4) the eternal and transcendent character of the Buddha. Though less immediately apparent, other significant Mahāyāna doctrines such as emptiness (Skt *śūnyāta*), buddha-nature (Skt *tathāgata-garbha*), and the three bodies of Buddha (Skt *trikāya*) have also been read into the text by later exegetes. The following section provides a historical and philosophical analysis of a few of the most significant political interpretations of the *Lotus Sūtra* throughout East Asian history, with reference to the four core teachings outlined above.

The *Lotus* as Protector of the Realm

In the last two decades of the sixth century, Chinese Tiantai sect founder Zhiyi (538–597) wrote two commentaries, *Fǎhuā wénjù* and *Fǎhuā xuányì*, interpreting the *Lotus*

Sūtra as the pinnacle of Buddhist teachings and as a basis for meditative practice. By focusing on the *sūtra*'s teaching of *ekayāna*, or the One Vehicle of Dharma, Zhiyi helped to centralize the text as a foundation for East Asian Buddhism, due in no small part to the fact that Tiantai would become – thanks to imperial patronage during the Sui dynasty (581–618 CE) – the most influential of all Chinese Buddhist schools. This influence would spread to Korea as well as Japan, where by the Heian period (794–1185) Tendai had become the dominant Buddhist institution, and would give birth in turn to the various popular new sects of the succeeding Kamukura period (1185–1333), including the Nichiren sect. In this respect, Japan's equivalent to Zhiyi was Saichō (767–822; posthumously known as Dengyō Daishi), who founded Japanese Tendai and gave lectures on the *Lotus Sūtra* before the Heian court.

At the time of the emergence of the Mahāyāna, if not even earlier, it was common for Buddhists to appeal to certain texts, artifacts, or rituals for their protective – thaumaturgical, or what we might call today "magical" – capacities. Indeed, the debates and disputes surrounding the acceptance of Buddhism on the part of the Japanese imperial court in the mid-sixth century were based entirely on whether or not these imported teachings and artifacts could help protect and preserve the realm. In Japan, several centuries before Saichō formally introduced Tendai, the *Lotus Sūtra* was already understood as a text that held the capacity to act as spiritual protector to the imperial family and the realm. One of the earliest commentaries is attributed to Shōtoku Taishi (573–621), the semi-legendary sixth-century regent and so-called father of Japanese Buddhism. From the early medieval period, monasteries were constructed throughout the nation with the express purpose of reciting the *Lotus Sūtra*, which had become established as one of several "nation-protecting *sūtras*" (*chingo kokka kyō*) (see Stone 2009, 217–19).

A significant appeal of the *Lotus Sūtra*, alluded to above, is its dual promise of (a) universality and (therefore) acceptance of various paths (see, e.g., Hurvitz 1976, 237) and (b) a single transcendent law that must (and will) eventually be attained, protecting and granting success (both worldly and otherworldly) to all those who subscribe to it (see, e.g., ibid., 262, 301), with harsh punishments for those who resist or malign the *Lotus* and/or its followers (see, e.g., ibid., 175). In other words, the *Lotus Sūtra* is both inclusivistic and (ultimately) exclusivistic, a dynamic that creates an extraordinary tension within the text itself, and presumably within many of its readers or hearers. This is also a combination that would no doubt appeal to rulers such as Shōtoku Taishi and his descendants in the Heian court, who were sufficiently versed in Daoist and Confucian principles to recognize the value of both "harmony" and "hierarchy" as stabilizing political forces. Again, this basic idea – of "protective power" – is not exclusive to the *Lotus Sūtra*, but it is associated with this text more often than with any other, due to the fact that this promise is made explicit in the *Lotus* itself. The exclusivistic quality of the One Law of the Lotus was picked up centuries later by the eponymous founder of the Nichiren sect, who, in works such as the influential *Risshō ankoku ron* (1260), explicitly correlates devotion to the *Lotus Sūtra* with the protection and pacification of the realm. As we shall see below, however, Nichiren's reading of this power has implications that extend well beyond the protection of those in positions of power, allowing for alternative interpretations of the *Lotus Sūtra* as a model and tool for resistance and socio-political reform.

By Any Means Necessary

Beginning in medieval China and extending to Japan, a number of so-called "miracle tales" focusing on the power of the *Lotus Sūtra* began to circulate. Though these were not necessarily intended for a popular audience, they no doubt contributed to the spread of devotion to the *Lotus* among the non-literate population in both countries. The parable of the Medicine King (Hurvitz 1976, 293–302), in which a bodhisattva burns himself to death as an offering to the Buddha, inspired a tradition of self-immolation among certain Chinese (and more recently Vietnamese) monks. In addition, the *Lotus Sūtra* played a role in spreading the cult of the bodhisattva Guanyin (Jp. Kannon), the most popular Buddhist figure in East Asia (ibid., 311–19). The miracle tales and stories of Guanyin express the "self-sacrificial" mandate of bodhisattvas – itself a subcategory of the larger theme of *upāya*, or "skillful means" – which most contemporary scholars see as the heart and soul of the *Lotus Sūtra*. Early on in the text, the Buddha claims to have employed a variety of parables and expedient measures in order to inspire his followers, who were not yet prepared for the higher, unifying wisdom of the *Lotus Sūtra*. Also of note in this regard is the *Lotus Sūtra's* repetition of the trope of the Buddha as a "father" to those he teaches (e.g., in the parables of the Burning House, the Prodigal Son, and the Medicinal Herbs), a concept that scholars such as Alan Cole have argued is fundamental to understanding the transformation brought about by the early Mahāyāna *sūtras* in general, and which may help account for the success of the *Lotus Sūtra* in East Asia, where culturally embedded notions of family and filial piety would otherwise seem to work against Indian Buddhist traditions of monasticism and asceticism (see Cole 2005).

The text also notes that buddhas appear in the world during times of chaos and pollution, an idea that would have a profound effect on the way later East Asian followers of the *Lotus Sūtra*, such as Nichiren, would interpret its message as a call to radical personal and collective transformation in a time of the "end of the law" (Jp. *mappō*). There is debate among scholars as to the precise implications of the doctrine of *upāya* – specifically with regard to how far the notion of "expedient means" extends, i.e., whether it has metaphysical and ontological in addition to its more obvious pedagogical implications. However, there is no question that it has been taken by some followers of the *Lotus Sūtra* to imply that, in exceptional circumstances, extreme measures may be justified in order to spread the Dharma for the purpose of saving beings and transforming this world into a "buddha land," an idea to which we will return below.

Hope for the Outcast

Though considered by contemporary scholars to be a relatively late addition to the *Lotus Sūtra*, chapter 12, "Devadatta," is both dense and of significant historical impact on account of its presentation of the concept of the universality of buddhahood for all beings. The chapter opens with the Buddha telling the assembly that, at one time in the distant past, he had been a king who sought "unexcelled awakening." One day he met a seer, who introduced the king to the Mahāyāna teachings as embodied in the *Lotus*

Sūtra. This wise seer, whom the king served faithfully for a thousand years and who was instrumental in leading the king towards full buddhahood was, we are told, none other than Śākayamuni's cousin Devadatta. The Buddha completes this short tale with a declaration to the assembly that Devadatta, too, will one day become a buddha (Hurvitz 1976, 195–8). Though the text does not make note of this, Devadatta was a figure notorious to early Buddhists as the epitome of evil.

The second half of the Devadatta chapter provides another well-known example of an unlikely buddha, though in this case one who has already achieved full awakening. Here Mañjuśrī, the bodhisattva of wisdom, relates the tale to a skeptical bodhisattva called Accumulated Wisdom. Mañjuśrī has just arrived from the palace of Sāgara, the dragon (Skt *nāga*) king, where he claims to have successfully converted innumerable beings via the teachings of the *Lotus Sūtra*. Mañjuśrī provides the remarkable example of the daughter of the dragon king, who, at just eight years old, achieved full buddhahood "in an instant." Accumulated Wisdom (as, we might expect, most hearers or readers of the text), finds this unbelievable, given the countless eons it took even Śākyamuni to achieve this same goal. The dragon princess duly appears before the assembly, and, in response to further skeptical and denigrating remarks by Śāriputra, immediately transforms herself into (a) a male, (b) a bodhisattva in a distant realm called Spotless, and (c) a fully awakened buddha, proclaiming the Dharma to all living beings. The entire assembly, including Accumulated Wisdom and Śāriputra, "silently believed and accepted [this]" (Hurvitz 1976, 198–201).

Once again, as with the example of Devadatta, the choice of the dragon princess as a fully awakened buddha undercuts traditional Buddhist understandings of the necessary conditions for awakening, including the various hindrances associated with being a child, a woman, and a non-human being. Later exegetes would interpret this chapter and similar promises of buddhahood in the *Lotus* in terms of the later Mahāyāna doctrine of "buddha-nature," whereby all beings are possessed of a "spark" or "seed" of buddhahood. Contemporary feminist readers have mixed feelings about its message for women: on one hand, it seems liberatory, given that the dragon princess is able to attain full buddhahood, and yet in order to do so she has had to transform herself, even if only for an instant, into a male.

Nichiren: The Personal is Political

As one of a number of popular new "reform" movements that arose during the tumultuous Kamakura period (1185–1333), the Nichiren sect developed a unique and influential interpretation of the relation between religious practice and social affairs, one that is intimately connected to the *Lotus Sūtra*. Nichiren (1222–1282), the founder of the sect, was, along with many of his day, convinced that the surrounding chaos could only mean that the world had reached its "latter days" – in Buddhist tradition, a period known as *mappō* (lit. "the end of the Dharma/Buddhist law"). Rather than seeking release in meditation (as in Zen) or in faith in an otherworldly saviour (as in the popular Pure Land sects), Nichiren posited that "salvation" could be found only within society itself – remade or rediscovered under the auspices of the *Lotus Sūtra*. According to this understanding, it is incumbent upon visionary leaders to work for social transformation, so that a "buddha land" can be realized in which there is both peace and prosperity. Such includes what we would today call politics, as well as economics, education, and various aspects of culture.[2] The underlying premise behind Nichiren's religio-political vision, spelled out in works such as *Kanjin honzon shō* ("On the Contemplation of the Mind as the Object of Worship"), is that "the self and society are mutually intertwined, and, together as one, shape reality. Thus, in conjunction with one's own transformation and salvation, the surrounding environment will also change and be saved, which in turn will again have an impact on one's own transformation" (Machacek and Wilson 2000, 103; also see Habito 2002, 315; Stone 2009, 221).

As Jacqueline Stone notes, this sense of microscosmic–macrocosmic unity was not by any means unique to Nichiren – it was an assumption shared by most Buddhists in medieval Japan, and was one that played a foundational role in the ritual praxis of the dominant Tendai and Shingon esoteric sects (Stone 2002, 262–3). Given Nichiren's debt to Tendai thought, it is hardly surprising that he would continue this theme. What is distinctive, however, is Nichiren's bold claim – albeit one also implied by the text itself – that it was *solely* by means of faith in the *Lotus Sūtra* that such a transformation could take place. This was a distinction that would come to make a huge difference in terms of socio-political attitudes. Whereas Tendai, with its doctrinal inclusivism and reliance on state patronage, was rarely involved in social conflict, Nichirenist exclusivism (and relative isolation) – based in the belief there exists a source for loyalty that transcends worldly obligations based on filial piety or traditional social hierarchies, and that those in power who decline to follow that source must be "admonished" – provides a solid basis for social critique and resistance to authority, something that is, as Stone understates, "rather rare in the history of Japanese Buddhism" (ibid., 280). The doctrinal basis for such critique would become institutionalized in the generations after Nichiren's death with the practice of *kokka kangyō* (lit. "admonishing the state").

Stone argues that Nichiren "transfigured" Confucian filial piety, as well as traditional East Asian concepts of loyalty to one's lord and the state, by raising the *Lotus Sūtra* above these as the primary locus for "loyalty." In practice, this meant that Nichiren's followers could (and frequently did) challenge their "superiors" if the latter failed to adhere to the Dharma as expressed in the *Lotus Sūtra*. As much as we moderns might frown upon "exclusivism" as a religious perspective that promotes intolerance and conflict, we would do well to note that, in this instance, it was precisely such exclusivism that provided the Nichiren sect with a foundation for social and political critique.

The Land of Ever Tranquil Light

The practice of *upāya*, or skillful means, is particularly embraced or embodied by bodhisattvas – those beings whose very marrow is compassion (Skt *karuṇā*; Jp. *jihi*). Again, though there is debate among scholars of the *Lotus Sūtra* as to whether the method of skillful means is one that can be put in practice by ordinary (i.e., unawakened) beings in daily (i.e., samsaric) life, Nichiren clearly understood the text as providing ample foundation for employing means and methods of compassion that might seem unorthodox in terms of tradition, but which are in fact best suited to the particular requirements of time and place.[3] In short, along with many modern practitioners inspired by the *Lotus Sūtra*, Nichiren found within it the grounds for an "*upāya*-inspired ethic," which "break[s] free from the code of laws passed on through tradition and approach[es] the situation of ethical decision-making . . . armed with a revised scale of values in which *karuṇā* is predominant" (Keown 2002, 188). Here we see the origins of a transgressive reading of the *Lotus Sūtra* – one that seeks to reinvent and overturn the existing order rather than to support or affirm it.

Again, there is some irony to this, given that the text – as with other early Mahāyāna works such as the *Avataṃsaka Sūtra* – revels in descriptions of otherworldly splendor that border on science fiction. Yet, as Gene Reeves argues, the reiteration of supernatural events and cosmic figures is intended not to disparage the temporal world but rather to affirm its "supreme importance." This is because the miraculous world envisoned in the text is not "other" than this very world in which we, like Śākyamuni, dwell. It is simply our world *as seen through the eyes of awakened beings*. Similarly, William LaFleur has argued that the *Lotus Sūtra* is a text that radically affirms the world without denying the reality of suffering: "within the sutra there is an umistakeable philosophical move opposite to that in Plato's *Republic*, a move to affirm the complete reality of the world of concrete phenomena in spite of the fact that they are impermanent" (LaFleur 1983, 87). This idea is summarized nicely in the phrase *shaba soku jakkōdo* – "the *sahā* world is the land of ever-tranquil light" (see Dolce 2002, 232–4; Reeves 2002, 185–6, 196). In short, although the *Lotus Sūtra* fails to provide an explicit model for society, it does hint at the promise of a better world to come. Chapter 3, for example, opens with Śāriputra's expression of ecstatic joy upon hearing the promise of universal buddhahood for all. Śākyamuni responds with a promise that Śāriputra himself will in the distant future assuredly become a buddha called Flower Light, and goes on to provide an elaborate description of the paradisiacal realm over which Śāriputra will preside (Hurvitz 1976, 49-56). This is just one example of the *Lotus Sūtra*'s envisioning of a "utopia," or "buddha land," as spatial (and temporal) equivalent of the soteriological promise of universal buddhahood.

An interpretation of the *Lotus Sūtra* as world-affirming is central to Nichiren's religio-political vision. "For Nichiren, [in contrast to Zhiyi,] there is only one *sahā* world. Vulture Peak, the place where the Lotus Sutra is taught, represents both this world of ours and the most perfect world, the only possible 'paradise.' There is no other reality, neither for humanity, nor for the Buddha" (Dolce 2002, 232–3). The point is not, for Nichiren, that we are presently living in the perfect world, but rather that we are living in a world that is, with faith, dedication, and great effort – "perfectible." As Linda Dolce puts it, his emphasis "is not on the absolute per se, but on the relative that has to become absolute" (ibid., 235). This, it can be argued, is the primary source for the ineluctable social dimension of Nichiren Buddhism from the Kamakura period through today. In this sense, the *Lotus Sūtra* can be seen as "primarily an ethical text, ethical not in the sense of offering a theory of morals, or in the sense of offering a set of commandments, but ethical in the sense of recommending a certain way of life, a way of life guided by a single overarching purpose . . . [i.e.,] nothing less than the salvation, the happiness of the entire world" (Reeves 2002, 178).

Though it would be stretching it a bit to suggest that mainstream Nichiren Buddhism has been mainly antagonistic to the state, this legacy of "prophetic criticism" runs deep, as can be seen in the case of the Fuju-fuse-ha, a Nichiren subsect founded by Nichiō

(1565–1630) in the early Edo period. The sect, whose name means "nothing received, nothing given," took a radically uncompromising stance on the issue of accommodation to other religious groups, based on a reading of a particular passage from a text attributed to Nichiren. This led to direct conflict with the Tokugawa shogunate. Officially outlawed in 1669 and subject to intense persecution for over two centuries, the sect somehow survived and was legalized in the early Meiji era (1876). Interestingly, in their defiance of secular authority and rejection of rival religious groups, and the consequences of these stances (persecution and the creation of an underground "church"), the Fuju-fuse sect is a Buddhist *Doppelgänger* to its *kakure* (i.e., hidden) Christian contemporaries (Kashiwahara 1990, 45–6).

And yet, for all this discussion of "prophetic critique," there is little in the writings of Nichiren or his sectarian heirs to suggest what moderns would call a historical consciousness regarding structural suffering and the need for socio-political change. The specific "problems" that he and his followers took to indicate the nation's misguided course were such things as natural disasters or impending invasions, while their "solution" was inevitably a call to eliminate all forms of Buddhist practice besides devotion to the *Lotus Sūtra* – something which the shoguns would not have been able to accomplish even had they wished to. Along these same lines, it is important to point out that, before modern interpretations of the *Lotus Sūtra* and Nichiren that arose in late nineteenth-century Japan in the context of the Meiji Buddhist Enlightenment, the protective and salvific power of the *Lotus* was deeply interfused with Buddhist thaumaturgy and ritual practice – including concern for the restless spirits of the dead (see Stone 2002, 261). In other words, the socio-political function of the *Lotus Sūtra* – including the use of such within the Nichiren sect – was very much beholden to the sort of "magical Buddhism" against which most Buddhist "modernists" were fighting (despite the fact that it was precisely this "magical" aspect that accounted for much of the text's historical political appeal; see Williams 2009, 158). In particular, modern Buddhists committed to Nichiren and the *Lotus Sūtra* are likely to dismiss the idea that the *daimoku* – i.e., ritual chanting of the title of the *Lotus Sūtra* – is in and of itself sufficient to bring earthly reward (see, e.g., Niwano 1976, 48). In short, it would take the emergence of the "modernist" understanding of Buddhism in Meiji-era Japan to allow for interpretations of the *Lotus Sūtra* that are (largely or fully) bereft of this magical component.

Modern(ist) Interpretations of the *Lotus Sūtra*

The modern (or modernist) interpretation of the *Lotus Sūtra* may be dated to the work of Tanaka Chigaku (1861–1939), who, along with Honda Nisshō (1867–1931), developed an influential sectarian ideology known as Nichirenism (*Nichirenshugi*), which flourished in Japan in the early decades of the twentieth century. While rooted in the traditional teachings of Nichiren – and thus in the *Lotus Sūtra* – Tanaka sought a form of Buddhist practice that was more socially and politically engaged. Increasingly skeptical of the institution of monasticism, he left the Nichiren priesthood at the age of 19, and soon emerged as a vocal and controversial proponent of Buddhist restoration (Jp. *fukko*). Here again, just as it did with Nichiren seven centuries previously, the rhetoric of decline, embedded within the *Lotus Sūtra* itself, provided Tanaka with a useful heuristic to promote a "restoration" of Lotus-inspired social practice (see Hubbard 2002, 212). Tanaka sought to create a modernized lay Buddhism, thus laying the foundations for later Nichiren lay movements such as Reiyūkai Kyōdan (1924), Sōka Gakkai (1930), and Risshō Kōseikai (1938) – and even, despite the obvious political differences, the socialistic Youth League for Revitalizing Buddhism (1931). Where Tanaka's views diverge from those of his more moderate peers – even his collaborator Honda – is with his assumption that, since Japan had *already* manifested the essence of the *Lotus Sūtra*, it was now up to Japan to bring peace to the world, even by use of force. Thus, he would go on to interpret the nation's imperialist aims as a (completely justified) form of national *shakubuku*.[4] This is more forcibly expressed in Tanaka's work *Shūmon no ishin* ("Restoration of Our Sect"), published in 1901.

Moving further along the path of interpretating the *Lotus Sūtra* in terms of nationalism, we find the figure of Inoue Nisshō (1887–1967). Inspired by both Honda Nisshō and Tanaka Chigaku, Inoue chose to spend his career as a lay advocate of radical Buddhist reform. Even Tanaka's firebrand version of Nichirenism was not "engaged" enough for Inoue's tastes, however, and in 1928 he left Tanaka's Kokuchūkai Academy to establish his own temple and training center, Risshō Gokokudō (Righteous National Defense Temple) (Kashiwahara 1990, 217). In 1932, with the support of a number of young military officers, Inoue founded the Ketsumeidan or Blood Pledge Corps, a radical right-wing movement whose goal was nothing less than a militarist revolution. The group would soon embark on a wave of assassinations of prominent political and economic figures, including the former finance minister Inoue Junnosuke (1869–1932), the Mitsui *zaibatsu* director Dan Takuma (1858–1932), and Prime Minister Inukai Tsuyoshi (1855–1932), for which Inoue was arrested and sentenced to life imprisonment. Released from prison in 1940, he was rehabilitated after the war and remained active in right-wing politics until his death in 1967.

At the other end of the political spectrum from both Tanaka and Inoue lies Seno'o Girō (1889–1961), founder of the Youth League for Revitalizing Buddhism (Jp. Shinkō Bukkyō Seinen Dōmei), an experiment in Nichiren-inspired Buddhist radicalism that set itself up as a vanguard of socialist protest against poverty, injustice, colonialism, and imperialism before being suppressed by the government in 1936. In his late twenties, Seno'o became increasingly attracted to Tanaka and Honda's Nichirenism, and in summer of 1918 he left his home in Okayama for Tokyo in order to put these new ideals into practice. The following year, under Honda's guidance, he established a group called the Greater Japan Nichirenist Youth Corps (Jp. Dainippon Nichirenshugi Seinendan). By the mid-1920s, however, Seno'o was also starting to entertain serious doubts about the justice of the capitalist system, and he began to consider socialism as a practical foundation for his thoughts on social and religious reform (Kashiwahara 1990, 214). In effect, socialism becomes the (new) "one vehicle" that will at long last establish the foundations for the promised attainment of buddhahood by all beings. Seno'o was particulary encouraged by the well-known passage "Such nonform [i.e., of the One Law] is formless and without form. Being without form, and formless, it is called the real aspect of things. The bodhisattva-mahāsattva realizes this, and, with compassion in his heart, dwells without fear" (see Inagaki 1974, 11). Just as it was for Nichiren, the way of the bodhisattva is central to Seno'o's progressive vision. It bears noting that

Seno'o was also open to the incorporation of ideas and influence from Christianity – more specifically, Christian socialism or the sort being developed simultaneously by Nakajima Shige (1888–1946).[5]

At almost exactly the same time that Seno'o Girō was establishing the Youth League for Revitalizing Buddhism, Makiguchi Tsunesaburō (1871–1944) and Toda Jōsei (1900–1958) were founding the Nichiren lay movement known as Sōka Gakkai. Like Seno'o, Inoue Nisshō, and Tanaka Chigaku, the founders of Sōka Gakkai were inspired by the *Lotus Sūtra* to create a broad-based movement that was both religious and socially engaged. Persecuted for resisting the state-sponsored imposition of Shinto in the late 1930s and early 1940s, Makiguchi died in prison in 1944, becoming a martyr figure for later followers of the movement, which flourished in the 1960s and 1970s under the leadership of Ikeda Daisaku (b. 1928). Sōka Gakkai gave birth to a political party in the 1960s known as Kōmeitō (Clean Government Party). Though Sōka Gakkai and Kōmeitō were formally separated in 1970, both continue to come under criticism in Japan for infringing laws regarding the separation of church and state. While it is not as popular as Sōka Gakkai, Risshō Kōseikai is another modern Nichiren lay movement that has flourished in the postwar period. Founded in 1938 by Niwano Nikkyō (1906–1999) and Naganuma Myōkō (1889–1957), this movement also emphasizes the practical, material benefits of Buddhist practice dedicated to the *Lotus Sūtra*.

Conclusions: Left, Right, or Everywhere?

In modern times, the *Lotus Sūtra* has played a significant role in a variety of Buddhist reform and activist movements in Japan, as well as, to a lesser extent, in China and Taiwan. This is due primarily to the fact that the *Lotus* can be understood as valorizing the phenomenal world, an interpretation that runs from Zhiyi through Nichiren down to modern lay Buddhist movements such as Sōka Gakkai and Risshō Kōseikai. Nichiren, in particular, interpreted the message of the *Lotus Sūtra* in a political and eschatological fashion, teaching that widespread devotion to the *Lotus* in an age of decline could transform this world into an ideal "buddha land" and that, contrariwise, a refusal to embrace the text would bring disaster upon the realm and its inhabitants (via, for instance, the Mongols). This message, combined with the inherent vagueness of the *sūtra* itself, has allowed for manifold political interpretations. In pre-war Japan alone, the *Lotus Sūtra* inspired figures as diverse as Seno'o Girō and Inoue Nisshō, discussed above; the philosopher Kita Ikki (1883–1937), whose unique brand of "pure socialism" influenced several ultranationalist factions of the military that attempted coups in the early 1930s; Miyazawa Kenji (1896–1933), the left-leaning poet, agronomist, and activist; and Ishiwara Kanji (1889–1949), the imperial army general famous for his role in fomenting the 1931 Manchurian Incident. Thus, while Whalen Lai suggests that "It would be no exaggeration to say that in the modern period the Lotus Sutra is firmly identified in the popular mind with the political right" (Lai 1984, 1), I believe Christopher Ives is closer to the mark when he notes that "Nichiren's dual commitment to constructing a 'Lotus land' in Japan and denouncing whatever he regarded as standing in the way of that construction, such as other Buddhist practices and institutions [and, I would add, the state], provided a template for radicalism – at either end of the political spectrum" (Ives 2009, 126-7). In ways similar to the Bible, the *Lotus Sūtra* is open to a multitude of interpretations, though compared with many sacred texts these interpretations tend to encourage direct (and often radical) engagement with this *sahā* world.

Notes

1 Some of what follows has been adapted (with permission) from my article on the *Lotus Sutra* published in *Milestone Documents of World Religions*. Ed. David M. Fahey. Dallas: Schlager Group, 2011, 372–89.

2 More controversially, it also involves a commitment to "breaking off" the false and erroneous views of others – a practice known within the Nichiren tradition as *shakubuku*, and one for which the new religious movement and the Nichiren offshoot Sōka Gakkai have been roundly criticized. Sōka Gakkai has of late – no doubt in response to public criticism – turned away from *shakubuku* towards a principle of *shōju*, which seeks unity between religions. Still, it is important to understand that *shakubuku* can work both ways – i.e., as a form of internal thought control and discrimination against others, but also, more positively, in relation to the notion of "admonishing the realm," as a vehicle for social critique. This dual effectiveness helps explain the polarized interpretations of Nichirenism that one sees during the 1930s.

3 See, e.g., Keown (1992, 151); Morgan (2002, 358); also Keown (2002, 377) vs. Tatz (1994, 16) on the issue of whether or not skillful means is "available" to non-bodhisattvas – a question which, as Keown notes, raises another important issue: *just who is a bodhisattva?*

4 It was Tanaka who came up with slogan *hakko ichi'u* ("All countries under one roof"), adopted in 1940 by the government to support and justify its creation of the so-called Greater East Asia Co-Prosperity Sphere (Dai-tō-a Kyōeiken).

5 In particular, Seno'o combined the bodhisattva commmitment to compassion for sentient beings with the Christian socialist passion for social justice and building a Kingdom of God here on earth – which Seno'o understood to be the meaning underlying their pledge to "carry the cross on [their] backs" (*jūjika o seō*). Indeed, this latter phrase made such an impression on Seno'o that he would borrow it, only slightly modified, as a motto for the League itself: "carry the buddha on [our] backs" (*budda o seō*).

References

Cole, Alan (2005). *Text as Father: Paternal Seductions in Early Mahayana Literature*. Berkeley and Los Angeles: University of California Press.

Dolce, Linda (2002). Between Duration and Eternity: Hermeneutics of the 'Ancient Buddha' of the Lotus Sutra in Chih-i and Nichiren. In *A Buddhist Kaleidoscope: Essays on the Lotus Sutra*. Ed. G. Reeves. Tokyo: Kōsei, 223–40.

Habito, Ruben (2002). Buddha-Body Theory and the Lotus Sutra: Implications for Practice. In *A Buddhist Kaleidoscope: Essays on the Lotus Sutra*. Ed. G. Reeves. Tokyo: Kōsei, 305–17.

Hubbard, Jamie (2002). A Tale of Two Times: Preaching in the Latter Age of the Dharma. In *A Buddhist Kaleidoscope: Essays on the Lotus Sutra*. Ed. G. Reeves. Tokyo: Kōsei, 201–21.

Hurvitz, Leon (trans.) (1976). *Scripture of the Lotus Blossom of the Fine Dharma (The Lotus Sūtra)*. New York: Columbia University Press.

Inagaki, Masami (1974). *Budda o seoite gaito e: Seno'o Girō to Shinkō Bukkyō Seinen Dōmei* [Out to the Streets and Villages, Carrying the Buddha on our Backs: Seno'o Girō and the Youth League for Revitalizing Buddhism]. Tokyo: Iwanami Shoten.

Ives, Christopher (2009). *Imperial-Way Zen: Ichikawa Hakugen's Critique and Lingering Questions for Buddhist Ethics.* Honolulu: University of Hawai'i Press.

Kashiwahara, Yūsen (1990). *Nihon bukkyōshi: kindai* [History of Japanese Buddhism: Modernity]. Tokyo: Yoshikawa Kōbunkan.

Keown, Damien (1992). *The Nature of Buddhist Ethics.* London: Macmillan.

Keown, Damien (2002). Paternalism in the Lotus Sutra. In *A Buddhist Kaleidoscope: Essays on the Lotus Sutra.* Ed. G. Reeves. Tokyo: Kōsei, 367–78.

LaFleur, William R. (1983). *The Karma of World: Buddhism and the Literary Arts in Medieval Japan.* Berkeley: University of California Press.

Lai, Whalen (1984). Seno'o Girō and the Dilemma of Modern Buddhism: Leftist Prophet of the Lotus Sutra. In *Japanese Journal of Religious Studies* 11(1), 7–42.

Machacek, David W., and Wilson, Bryan R. (eds) (2000). *Global Citizens: The Soka Gakkai Buddhist Movement in the World.* Oxford: Oxford University Press.

Morgan, Peggy (2002). Ethics and the Lotus Sutra. In *A Buddhist Kaleidoscope: Essays on the Lotus Sutra.* Ed. G. Reeves. Tokyo: Kōsei, 351–66.

Niwano, Nikkyō (1976). *Buddhism for Today: A Modern Interpretation of the Threefold Lotus Sutra.* Trans. Kōjirō Miyasaka. Tokyo: Kōsei.

Reeves, Gene (2002). The Lotus Sutra as radically world affirming. In *A Buddhist Kaleidoscope: Essays on the Lotus Sutra.* Ed. G. Reeves. Tokyo: Kōsei, 177–9.

Stone, Jacqueline (2002). When Disobedience is Filial and Resistance is Loyal: The Lotus Sutra and Social Obligations in Medieval Nichiren Tradition. In *A Buddhist Kaleidoscope: Essays on the Lotus Sutra.* Ed. G. Reeves. Tokyo: Kōsei, 261–81.

Stone, Jacqueline (2009). Realizing this World as the Buddha Land. In *Readings of the Lotus Sutra.* Ed. S. F. Teiser and J. I. Stone. New York: Columbia University Press, 209–36.

Tatz, Mark (trans.) (1994). *The Skill in Means (Upāyakauśalya) Sutra.* Delhi: Motilal Banarsidass.

Williams, Paul (2009). *Mahayana Buddhism: The Doctrinal Foundations.* Second edn. London and New York: Routledge.

34

Socially Engaged Buddhism

Emerging Patterns of Theory and Practice

CHRISTOPHER S. QUEEN

> *On the evening of October 13, Ambedkar held a press conference. He told newsmen that his Buddhism would cling to the tenets of the faith as preached by Lord Buddha himself, without involving his people in differences which had arisen on account of Hinayana and Mahayana. His Buddhism would be a sort of neo-Buddhism or Navayana.*
>
> (Keer 1987, 498)

So the biographer of B. R. Ambedkar (1891–1956) recalled the remarks that the celebrated Indian politician and scholar made on the night before his conversion to Buddhism in 1956. Nearly 400,000 of his Dalit or ex-untouchable followers had made their way to Nagpur to recite the Three Refuges and Five Precepts and thus signify their new identity as Buddhists. As a human rights activist, Dr. Ambedkar had announced decades earlier his intention to abandon Hinduism, which he viewed as the perennial source of caste violence and untouchability. He had studied comparative religion and collected hundreds of classical and modern Buddhist writings since his student years in New York and London. He had met with Buddhist leaders in five countries to explore what Buddhism might offer his fellow untouchables. And, having made history by drafting the Indian Constitution as a member of Nehru's first cabinet, Ambedkar had retired from politics to write his last book, *The Buddha and His Dhamma*.

What did Dr. Ambedkar mean by a "neo-Buddhism" or "a new vehicle" (*navayāna*), and how could that be consistent with "the faith as preached by Lord Buddha himself"? Inasmuch as Ambedkar died six weeks after the Nagpur *dīkṣā*, the answers must be sought in his book and in the legacy of the Buddhism practiced by his followers. Buddhism exploded more than 1,000 percent in India, from the 181,000 citizens claiming Buddhism as their religion in the 1951 census to the 3,250,000 who claimed it in 1961, as a result of Ambedkar's conversion. And, in the decades since, the Dalit Buddhists of India have increasingly resembled Buddhists from traditional Buddhist countries and the West in beliefs and practices that have come to be called "socially engaged Buddhism."

A Companion to Buddhist Philosophy, First Edition. Edited by Steven M. Emmanuel.

Our objective in this chapter is to examine a sampling of these beliefs and practices to ascertain whether there are emerging patterns that link the otherwise independent, globally dispersed movements of engaged Buddhism. To this end, we shall survey the scope of engaged Buddhism in Asia and the West and then examine three Buddhist teachings – the doctrines of suffering (*dukkha*), action-rebirth (*karma-saṃsāra*), and morality (*pañcasīla*) – as they are presented by preceptors of engaged Buddhism, Thich Nhat Hanh, B. R. Ambedkar, and Sulak Sivaraksa. But first we must ask whether a quest for "emerging patterns" may be taken as a preliminary stage in the formulation of a unifying philosophy, taken as the Navayana that Ambedkar announced in the 1950s, as the engaged Buddhism that Thich Nhat Hanh coined in the 1960s, or as a Fourth Yana that I have attempted to describe in recent years. As we shall see, the quest for emerging patterns, enduring essences, and unifying categories in the history of Buddhism is not new.

It would be tempting to see Ambedkar's coinage of the term Navayana as a conscious reference to the *ekayāna* or "one vehicle" preached in early Mahāyāna scriptures. Texts such as the *Laṅkāvatāra, Avataṃsaka,* and *Saddharmapuṇḍarīka sūtras* sought to consolidate or supersede the rapidly multiplying doctrines and practices of Indian Buddhism several hundred years after the founder's death. There is no doubt that Ambedkar was familiar with this stage in Buddhist history, as the critical markings of his copies of the literature attest.[1] Thus he knew how paradoxical the term "one vehicle" had been from the start, reflecting each text community's advocacy for a chosen formulation of the essence of the tradition: *dharmakāya* ("teaching-body"), *tathāgata-garbha* ("buddha-matrix"), *ālaya-vijñāna* ("store-consciousness"), and, most paradoxically, *śūnyatā* ("emptiness"), the teaching that there are no essences to be found. Surely this was not his intention. "Anyone who is not a Buddhist finds it extremely difficult to present the life and teachings of the Buddha in a manner which would make it a consistent whole," he wrote in the introduction to *The Buddha and His Dhamma*. "Depending on the Nikayas, not only the presentation of a consistent story of the life of the Buddha becomes a difficult thing, but the presentation of some parts of his teachings becomes much more so. . . . Is it not necessary that these problems should be solved and the path for the understanding of Buddhism be made clear?" (Ambedkar 1984, xli).

This has been the fervent wish of Buddhist practitioners and scholars from the beginning. My own mentors in the field, Donald Swearer, an authority in the traditions of South Asia, and Masatoshi Nagatomi, fluent in these as well as the traditions of Central and East Asia, warned students that the quest for a unifying philosophy of Buddhism was a fool's errand, and that anyone who spoke of "one Buddhism" had not done his homework. Nagatomi, in particular, would often begin his lectures with the proclamation that, "Today, we will finally discover *what Buddhism is all about*!" With that, his eyes would twinkle, he would smile to himself, and we would get to work – analyzing a particular word in a particular text from a particular time and place in the long history of the traditions we still call Buddhism, as if they were a single religion.[2]

Yet an alert graduate student will soon discover respected commentators who are ready to argue that a certain teaching, doctrine, or perspective is indeed what Buddhism is all about. In *What the Buddha Thought* (2009), Richard Gombrich writes of the doctrine of karma, "I believe that it is not only fundamental to the Buddha's whole view of life, but also a kind of lynchpin which holds the rest of the basic tenets together by providing the perfect example of what they mean." The law of karma (*kamma niyāma*) is akin to a "law of nature, analogous to a law of physics," and it is what the Buddha meant by "right view" (*sammā diṭṭhi*), the first step in the Noble Eightfold Path.[3]

Reading these lines may remind some of Junjiro Takakusu's *The Essentials of Buddhist Philosophy* (1947). Under the rubric "Fundamental Principles of Buddhist Philosophy," the author begins with the Principle of Causation. He avoids reference to karma "because it is often confused with the idea of soul and thus leads to misunderstanding of Buddhist Doctrine." Instead, Takakusu prefers to relate the idea of causation to the teaching of dependent co-origination, *pratītyasamutpāda*, and the twelvefold cycle of birth, death, and rebirth, the *nidānas* (1947, 23–4.) But what happened to the Buddha's first sermon, the Middle Path and the Four Noble Truths? Here, the modern Theravāda philosopher Buddhadāsa Bhikkhu pointed to the *Majjima-nikāya* passage that reads, "In the past, Bhikkhus, as well as now, I teach only *dukkha* and the utter quenching of *dukkha*." Anyone who calls himself "the servant of the Buddha" (a play on the author's name) must faithfully carry out the Buddha's word. "*Dukkha* and its quenching" is a summary of the Four Noble Truths, he asserts, which is, in turn, *the framework of all Buddhism*. Santikaro, a disciple of Buddhadāsa, comments: "Here we have the entire scope and range of the Buddha's teachings, although its heights and depths may not be immediately apparent" (Santikaro 1996, 156f.).

Buddhadāsa offers another candidate for Buddhism's "central teaching," however – that of *dhamma*, which is best translated "nature," including perceptible reality, the law that governs this reality, the duties that flow from this law, and the results that follow the performance or neglect of these duties (Santikaro 1996, 159). Here he is in agreement with the Russian Buddhologist Theodor Stcherbatsky, whose title *The Central Conception of Buddhism and the Meaning of the word "Dharma"* (1923) speaks for itself. But we cannot end this rehearsal of arguments for the *One True Idea* upon which all the other Buddhist ideas hang without reference to another famous work, T. V. R. Murti's *The Central Philosophy of Buddhism* (1955), which begins with the claim: "The entire Buddhist thought turned on the Śūnyatā doctrine of the Mādhyamika," which, we learn a few pages later, is Nāgārjuna's reinterpretation of our old friend *pratītyasamutpāda* (Murti 1955, vii, 7).

Are these competing arguments for the primacy of different core concepts in Buddhist philosophy complementary or mutually cancelling? In a world in which competing ideologies, markets, and political entities are increasingly irreconcilable or even violent, are we more inclined to heed the warnings of Swearer and Nagatomi than we were 40 years ago? The hazards of system-building seem clear in the history of philosophy and in Buddhist philosophy *a fortiori*. At the same time, the intuition of Ambedkar, Thich Nhat Hanh, and many other Buddhist thinkers since the middle of the last century is that a socially engaged Buddhism, increasingly manifested in mass movements, non-governmental organizations, and a distinctive literature, may be the common ground for a convergence of theories and practices in the Buddhism of the twenty-first century. The argument for such a convergence must be empirical and inductive, drawing upon a cumulative body of field reports, case studies, and published reflection by scholars and engaged Buddhists themselves. For while the turn to social ethics and activism may also be identified in the other great religions of the world during the twentieth century, there is no claim here that the internal dynamics of Buddhism would predict a common set of patterns by the turn of the twenty-first century.

The Scope of Engaged Buddhism

The rise of socially engaged Buddhism since the middle of the last century has been intensively documented and analyzed by scholars for more than 30 years. Widely identified with the anti-war activism of the Vietnamese Thien master Thich Nhat Hanh, who coined the expression engaged Buddhism in the 1960s; the decades-long struggle for Tibet led by the Fourteenth Dalai Lama; the Buddhist conversion of India's Dalits, led by Dr. B. R. Ambedkar; the Sarvodaya Shramadana village development and peace movement in Sri Lanka, founded by Dr. A. T. Ariyaratna in the 1950s; and the liberation movements for Cambodia and Burma led respectively by the late Maha Ghosananda and the Nobel Peace laureate Aung San Suu Kyi – the principles of engaged Buddhism have shaped thinkers, activists, and organizations throughout Asia and the West.[4]

To encompass the range and depth of this development in Buddhist precepts and practice, one must include the Pure Land Buddhists of China and Taiwan, who employ the term *Humanistic Buddhism* (*Rénjiān Fójiào*), notably Foguangshan, Ciji Gongdehui, and Fagushan in Taiwan, and temples affiliated with the Chinese Buddhist Association and Hong Kong Buddhist Association in the People's Republic of China, as well as the international peace groups inspired by the Nichiren traditions of Japan: Soka Gakkai, Rissho Kosei-kai, and Nipponzan Myohoji. In the West, engaged Buddhism is represented by the Buddhist Peace Fellowship, Zen Peacemakers, and Buddhist Global Relief (founded by the renowned scholar-monk Bhikkhu Bodhi), among many others in the United States, and by peace, justice, and service groups in the UK, Europe, Latin America, South Africa, and Australia. Finally, we make note of two organizations that represent engaged Buddhists from all the traditional *yānas* and sects: the International Network of Engaged Buddhists (INEB) and Sakyadhītā, "Daughters of the Buddha," devoted to the revival and support of nuns' Sanghas worldwide.

In addition to the international dispersion of Buddhist organizations explicitly devoted to social action and social service – both within the traditional branches of the tradition and linking them – we must consider a much larger phenomenon throughout the Buddhist world. This is the fact that local Buddhist Sanghas have spontaneously begun to include social outreach and service as an integral part of their spiritual practice – not to be mistaken for outreach for new members or public sponsorship of traditional Buddhist rituals and study. This outreach typically takes the form both of service or fundraising for the poor and needy and for victims of natural disasters, and of activism for progressive social change. Peace and justice work, environmental protection, and voluntary service in hospices and prisons are among the actions that rank-and-file Buddhists have taken up with greater determination and focus since the appearance of large-scale liberation movements and NGOs on the world stage.[5]

Overarching the variety of social challenges these groups confront in the world – war, poverty, caste, terrorism, environmental and natural disasters, to name only a few – and the widely divergent practice vehicles from which the practitioners come – Theravāda, Mahāyāna, Vajrayāna – there is growing evidence of a pattern of thought and action that uniquely transcends local Buddhist cultural and sectarian histories. The most salient example of this is the profound evolution of the very notion of "suffering," as it was presented in the Four Noble Truths of the earliest scriptures. Engaged Buddhists universally see the political, economic, and ecological causes of "social suffering," in addition to the psychological and spiritual suffering that Buddhist ritual and mental training traditionally addressed. Second, ancient conceptions such as karma, rebirth, interdependence, merit-making, and merit-transfer are seen in new ways that facilitate global Buddhist cooperation and alliances with other religious and civil-society associations. Finally, new methods of social action and interpretation inform many familiar formulations of the Dharma. The Eightfold Path, the Five Precepts, the *brahmavihāras*, and the *pāramitās* are now invested with social and collective meanings related to the rise of information technology and social networking, geopolitical and economic interdependence, and revolutions in healthcare and education. Let us consider an example from each of these categories.

Three Marks of Engaged Buddhist Philosophy

The doctrines of suffering (*dukkha*) and action-rebirth (*karma-saṃsāra*), and the moral guidelines known as Five Precepts (*pañcasīla*), may be taken as markers of the philosophical breadth and depth of the new Buddhism, and of its readiness to enter into dialogue with philosophies and theologies beyond its borders. Buddhism's evolving reflection on suffering is analogous to problems of evil and divine justice (*theodicy*) in the Abrahamic religions, while the significance of *karma-saṃsāra* parallels the importance of the philosophy of mind in Greek and European thought. The cornucopia of virtues and values reflected in such formulations as the Theravāda *brahmavihāras* and Mahāyāna *pāramitās* may be seen in the context of Western philosophy's perennial conversation on ethics. Here we will examine the Five Precepts (*pañcasīla*) as the Buddhist place-holder. Our texts are drawn from the writings of three of the most influential engaged Buddhists: Thich Nhat Hanh, B. R. Ambedkar, and Sulak Sivaraksa.

Suffering

A classic expression of socially engaged Buddhism is the poem "Please Call Me by My True Names," by Thich Nhat Hanh. Written in 1976 after the author heard that a 12-year-old girl, one of the boat people crossing the Gulf of Siam, had thrown herself into the sea after being raped by a sea pirate, the poem was eventually included in a collection of "writings on nonviolent social change" titled *Love in Action* (1993). Thich Nhat Hanh, already an international figure following his anti-war activism in the 1960s, confessed his anger at the story of the girl but realized, after meditating for several hours, that he could not "just take sides against the pirate. I saw that if I had been born in his village and brought up under the same conditions, I would be exactly like him. Taking sides is too easy. Out of my suffering, I wrote this poem."

In addition to the stanza telling of the girl's violent death and identifying with both the girl and the pirate, the poem contains these verses:

> I am the child in Uganda, all skin and bones,
> my legs as thin as bamboo sticks.
> And I am the arms merchant,
> selling deadly weapons to Uganda.
>
> I am a member of the politburo,
> with plenty of power in my hands,
> and I am the man who has to pay
> this "debt of blood" to my people,
> dying slowly in a forced-labor camp.
>
> My joy is like spring, so warm
> that it makes flowers bloom all over the Earth.
> My pain is like a river of tears,
> so vast that it fills all four oceans.
>
> Please call me by my true names,
> so I can wake up
> and open the door of my heart,
> the door of compassion.
>
> (Thich Nhat Hanh 1993, 107–9)

Here the teaching of "*dukkha* and its quenching" and the Four Noble Truths that it summarizes is subjected to profound transformation. Suffering is still presented as the universal lot of sentient beings. The poem begins with an evocation of life and death in the predatory cycles of nature, as the bird swoops down to swallow the mayfly and the grass-snake "silently feeds itself on the frog." But the causes of the suffering of the creatures and humans caught in webs of violence and death range far beyond the mental characteristics of sufferers themselves – called hatred, greed, and delusion in the canonical accounts. Instead we see the workings of Darwinian selection and of global marketing. We see personalities twisted by poverty and politics and we see children helpless to escape the conditions that have descended upon their families and countries. In a word, we see victims whose suffering is not attributed to their own blighted karma or their own willful cravings and ignorance. We see a world that is truly interdependent, not the world implied by the traditional formulation – where suffering and its quenching is the sole responsibility of the sufferer.

Finally, Thich Nhat Hanh calls the recognition of his "true names" – his identification with all who suffer and all who rejoice – an awakening. This is his interpretation of the third Noble Truth, the experience of *nirvāṇa*, the opening of the heart to compassion for all beings. It is a deep perception of interdependence, *pratītyasamutpāda*, and of *śūnyatā*, the absence of definitive essences (*svabhāva*) in the dramas of life: predator and prey, evil pirate and innocent girl, genocidal cartel and virtuous villager.

Action-Rebirth

In the introduction to *The Buddha and His Dhamma*, written in the final, turbulent years of his life and published posthumously in 1957, B. R. Ambedkar highlights four problems for modern readers of the life and teachings of the Buddha. Referencing Pāli sources, Ambedkar questions the story of the Buddha's "going forth" at the age of 29: the idea that a gifted young man would abandon his family and career after witnessing illness and death for the first time "is not plausible," he writes. He calls the Four Noble Truths "a great stumbling block in the way of non-Buddhists accepting the gospel of Buddhism," rooting universal suffering in the hearts and minds of sufferers but ignoring its social causes. He finds the teachings of non-self, karma, and rebirth to be contradictory, invoking the age-old question of how moral effects can be transmitted from moment to moment or life to life by a non-entity. Finally, Ambedkar questions the motivation and mission of the Buddhist clergy: are monks dedicated to their own perfection or to the service of others (Ambedkar 1984, xli–xlii)?

As the bible of millions of Dalits who followed Ambedkar into Buddhism, *The Buddha and His Dhamma* is not a rejection of the traditional jewels of Buddha, Dhamma, and Sangha, as it might sound from these initial queries. But, in his analysis of the central doctrines of the tradition, Ambedkar subjects the earliest records to what I have called a hermeneutics of Buddhist liberation. Each teaching is viewed through the subaltern eyes of those who, like Ambedkar, have experienced the social shunning, poverty, and violence of the Indian caste system. For these witnesses, the story of a young man of privilege who renounces family and social responsibilities is disturbing. A reading of human suffering that stresses the sufferer's ignorance and craving hits close to home: do not the poor crave education and the basic necessities of life? Teachings that dissolve or disparage the struggling, embodied self by reference to invisible forces and previous lives are mystifying, if not humiliating. And the luxurious lifestyle of the cloistered monks Ambedkar met in Sri Lanka, Burma, and Nepal seemed to him a travesty of the Buddha's injunction to wander "for the benefit and happiness of the many-folk, out of compassion for the world."[6]

The uneven texture of *The Buddha and His Dhamma* reveals Ambedkar's advancing illness in his final years. Indeed, it became necessary for him to marry his medical doctor in order for her to care for him without scandal; no other Brahman doctor would enter the house of an Untouchable. His principles of selection and analysis were stated clearly in a section of the work titled "Causes of Misunderstanding." Noting that the Pāli canon remained an oral tradition for hundreds of years before it was written down, and citing five *suttas* in which the Buddha is shown correcting his followers' memory slips or willful distortions in reporting his words, Ambedkar warns that "One has to be very careful in accepting what is said in the Buddhist canonical literature as being the word of the Buddha" (1984, 254–5).

Singled out for special mention in the section on misunderstandings are the teachings on karma and rebirth. Just as there are natural laws governing the movement of heavenly bodies and the growth of plants – *rutu niyāma* and *bija niyāma* – so there must be moral order in society. This is the meaning of *kamma niyāma*, the law of karma. Indeed, no one can fail to benefit from positive actions, *kusala kamma*, or escape the ill effects of negative ones, *akusala kamma*. But the effects of karmic intentions and actions are unpredictable: they may be immediately apparent, or they may be delayed, remotely discernible, too weak to operate, or counteracted by karma from another source. Karmic effects cannot be limited to the actor; sometimes actions affect others more demonstrably than they do the actor.

Here Ambedkar moves inexorably towards the collective or social perspective that he called Navayana or "new vehicle" Buddhism – and that we identify as engaged Buddhism. *Kusala kamma* will bring about a beneficial moral order for humanity, he argues, while *akusala kamma* will lead to a broken moral order. In the end, *kamma niyāma* has nothing to do with the fortunes or misfortunes of an individual. "Individuals come and individuals go, but the moral order of the universe remains." In this way, *kamma niyāma* takes the place of God in other religions, Ambedkar concludes (1984, 170–3).

What about *saṃsāra* – not only the notion of rebirth, but particularly the transmission of individual karmic effects from one life to the next? The Buddha believes in rebirth, Ambedkar acknowledges – *but of what or whom?* At death the body returns to its constituents, whether considered as the traditional earth, air, fire, and water or as the chemical elements and energy of modern science. Yet these elements and forces are not annihilated. Rather, they return to the pool of matter and energy from which new bodies and minds emerge. Only in this sense can the Buddha be said to have believed in rebirth. His analysis of the self into the *khandhas* or heaps of psycho-physical patterning is compelling and congruent with current psychological research, Ambedkar argues, but it does not provide a platform for personal reincarnation.

If one must look for a mechanism of transmission of influence from the past, we are better served by the sciences of genetics and embryology. After noting the biology of conception as understood today, Ambedkar cites a text in which the Buddha explains the facts of life to a woodsprite (*yakkha*) on Indra's Peak. Following the four stages of fetal development, nourished by the mother's diet, a child is born with characteristics inherited from the parents. Yet it was the Hindus that believed that the body is genetic but that the soul is implanted into the body from outside – from an unspecifiable source. Here Ambedkar lowers the gavel on the doctrine of transmigration: if a characteristic is neither inherited from parents nor acquired from experience – in the womb or after birth – then it cannot be detected by scientific means. It remains "an absurdity."

Why, then, did the teaching of *karma/saṃsāra* have such powerful currency at the Buddha's time and up to the present – even to the extent that it was imported into Buddhism by renegade editors? "The only purpose one can think of is to enable the state or society to escape responsibility for the condition of the poor and lowly. . . . It is impossible to imagine that the Buddha, who was known as the *Maha Karunika* [great compassionate one], could have supported such a doctrine" (Ambedkar 1984, 242–8).

The Five Precepts

Along with Thich Nhat Hanh and Dr. Ambedkar, who fought to end the ravages of war and caste in their respective societies, the Thai intellectual and activist Sulak Sivaraksa has earned international recognition as a crusader for human rights and environmental justice in his native Siam (as he insists on calling a country controlled by a military-industrial complex). Jailed more than once for exposing public corruption,

Sivaraksa is the founder and today the guiding spirit of the International Network of Engaged Buddhists.

In his most widely read work, *Seeds of Peace: A Buddhist Vision for Renewing Society* (1992), Sivaraksa addresses the "politics of greed," "the religion of consumerism," "development as if people mattered," "personal and societal transformation," and "Buddhism with a Small 'b.' " Perhaps the most memorable section of the book is his engaged Buddhist reading of the *pancaśīla* or Five Precepts of moral discipline, which constitute, along with the Three Refuges (*ti-saraṇam*), the central formulas of Buddhist identity in the Theravāda world. By "engaged Buddhist reading" I mean that in each case the admonition to refrain from *akusala kamma*, unskillful and unwholesome conduct, is related to a wider world of social and institutional relationships than the dyadic paradigm implied in the canonical texts. Now it is the ripple effects of violent speech and actions, of the abuse of sexuality and intoxicants, and of confiscatory behavior that comes into view. It is the institutions that cause mass killing through the manufacture of armaments and insecticides, and through industrial animal farming, that fall under the precept "to abstain from taking life." The second precept, "to abstain from stealing," is extended beyond petty theft or shoplifting. Sivaraksa writes:

> Economic justice is bound up with Right Livelihood. We must take great pains to be sure there are meaningful jobs for everyone able to work. And we must also take responsibility for the theft implicit in our economic systems. To live a life of Right Livelihood and voluntary simplicity out of compassion for all beings and to renounce fame, profit, and power as life goals are to set oneself against the structural violence of the oppressive status quo. But is it enough to live a life of voluntary simplicity without also working to overturn the structures that force so many people to live in involuntary poverty?
>
> (Sivaraksa 1992, 75)

The precept against sexual misconduct directs the practitioner "to look at the global structures of male dominance and the exploitation of women," while the precept against false speech is applied to abuses of "the mass media, education, and patterns of information that condition our understanding of the world. . . . The Quakers have a practice of 'speaking truth to power.' It will only be possible to break free of the systematic lying endemic in the status quo if we undertake this truth-speaking collectively." Finally, the precept against taking intoxicants is extended to the disastrous effects on Third World economies of the promotion of the cash crops of heroin, cocoa, coffee, and tobacco, when an agrarian system based on locally distributed food crops – rice and vegetables – is consistent with principles of economic justice and self-sufficiency. Citing the "unloading of excess surplus cigarette production onto Third World consumers through intensive advertising campaigns," Sivaraksa concludes that we must also "examine the whole beer, wine, spirit, and drug industries to identify their power base" (1992, 76–9).

Conclusion

Like Christianity and Islam, Buddhism has been a universal religion from the beginning – the Buddha's Dhamma was directed to all people, not only to members of a tribal or sectarian group. Yet the local variations of Buddhism that evolved in places such as Ceylon, Afghanistan, Tibet, Mongolia, Japan, Cambodia, and Indonesia remained largely isolated from one another following their introduction by itinerant merchants and missionaries. Local assimilations of Buddhist thought and practice advanced in a branching-coexisting fashion over the centuries, making it unreasonable throughout most of its history to speak of *Buddhism* in the singular. Even within countries as thoroughly "Buddhist" as Ceylon and Tibet, doctrinal and ceremonial differences among the local monastic orders and lineages engendered intense rivalries over the centuries.[7]

Today, these patterns of differentiation and diffusion continue. But, at the same time, with the rise of socially engaged Buddhism, we see the outlines of a counter-tendency. As a result of accelerating communication and travel, engaged Buddhism has been manifested as a global impulse, emerging from and interacting with all the sectarian and cultural expressions of the ancient tradition. A majority of engaged Buddhists in Asia and the West are not involved in political activism, as newsworthy as that has been since the self-immolation of the anti-war monk Thich Quang Duc on a Saigon street corner in 1963. Most engaged Buddhists practice what might be called "service *dharma*" – helping the poor and ministering to the incarcerated, the dying, and the socially marginalized. In this they are no different from the teaching and medical missionaries from the Christian denominations and secular organizations such as the International Red Cross, the Red Crescent, and Doctors Without Borders.

Yet the engaged Buddhists offer something not offered by the others. This is a philosophy of emptiness, impermanence, and connectedness that sees all people as equally subject to suffering and exploitation and equally capable of realizing freedom and dignity. They share conceptions of lovingkindness, compassion, altruistic joy, and equanimity which are supported by specific techniques of cultivation. *Mettā bhāvanā* (lovingkindness meditation), for example, begins by wishing oneself peace and well-being; then it extends this wish, successively, to loved ones, acquaintances, persons in general, and then to those who would harm you – your enemies. Jesus taught the love of enemies, too, but his teaching was rooted in a notion of divine community, not in the experience of spontaneous co-dependent origination.

Finally, there is unity among the engaged Buddhists at another point: the ubiquity of suffering in the world evokes in them a feeling of "universal responsibility," as the Dalai Lama has called it, and the traditional Mahāyāna vow to "save all beings." Engaged Buddhists are inclined to go beyond a vow, however, to initiate social actions on behalf of the "others" that are in jeopardy now. At a time when those who speak of "saving the world" can expect snide derision, if not social ostracism, engaged Buddhists seem uninhibited in their expression of universal compassion (*mahā karuṇā*). A slogan of the Dalit Buddhists, likely borrowed from the American labor movement by Ambedkar during his years at Columbia University, expresses the sense of collective urgency: "Educate, Agitate, Organize." And lest observers conclude that these imperatives arise merely from the material struggles of an insurgent social movement, their founder sought to set the record straight:

> My final word of advice to you is educate, agitate, and organize, have faith in yourself. With justice on our side, I do not see how we can lose our battle. The battle to me is a matter of

> joy. The battle is in the fullest sense spiritual. There is nothing material or social in it. For ours is a battle not for wealth or for power. It is a battle for freedom. It is a battle for the reclamation of human personality.
>
> (Keer 1987, 351)

For Ambedkar, Thich Nhat Hanh, the Dalai Lama and millions of Buddhists awakening today, the challenge of spiritual practice is to seek mindfulness, justice, and joy without abandoning the myriad battles that beckon.

Notes

1 For a discussion of Ambedkar's Buddhist library and research methods, see Queen (2004, 132–50).

2 Richard H. Robinson has written:

> *Buddhism* – as a term to denote the vast array of social and cultural phenomena that have clustered in the course of time around the teachings of a figure called the Buddha, the Awakened One – is a recent invention. It comes from the thinkers of the eighteenth-century European Enlightenment and their quest to subsume religion under comparative sociology and secular history. Only recently have Asian Buddhists come to adopt the term and the concept behind it. Previously, the terms they used to refer to their religion were much more limited in scope: *the Dharma, the Buddha's message*, or *the Buddha's way*. In other words, they conceived of their religion simply as the teaching of the Buddha, what the Buddha himself called *Dharma-Vinaya* (Doctrine and Discipline). Whereas Dharma-Vinaya is meant to be prescriptive, advocating a way of life and practice, *Buddhism* is descriptive in that it simply denotes the actions of people who follow a vision of Dharma-Vinaya without suggestion that the reader accept that vision or follow it, too.
>
> (Robinson and Johnson 1997, 1–2)

It is significant that the fifth edition (2004) of Robinson's text (co-authored by Willard Johnson and Thanissaro Bhikkhu) has been renamed *The Buddhist Religions* and treats the Theravāda, Mahāyāna, and Vajrayāna traditions as "separate religions."

3 Gombrich (2009, 11, 19, 27). It may be noted that Walpola Rahula (1959) makes no such claims, presenting "the Buddhist attitude of mind" and the range of early teachings as an organic and evolving whole, allowing for contemporary (some would say "modernist") interpretations that resonate for readers and practitioners today.

4 More than 40 scholars have contributed to the anthologies I have co-edited on the history and phenomenology of engaged Buddhism since 1996. See Queen (2000); Queen and King (1996); Queen et al. (2003).

5 These local initiatives are regularly documented in the pages of *Turning Wheel*, the quarterly journal of engaged Buddhism, published in print and online by the Buddhist Peace Fellowship, Berkeley, California. They may also be found increasingly in the more mainstream magazines of American Buddhism – *Tricycle, Shambhala Sun, and Buddhadharma* – each of which has an active online community.

6 Christopher S. Queen, Dr. Ambedkar and the Hermeneutics of Buddhist Liberation. In Queen and King (1996, 45–72).

7 Some scholars, such as the late Professor Masatoshi Nagatomi of Harvard, speak of *Buddhisms* in the plural, to disabuse students of the impression that a monolithic tradition with universal teachings and practices may be found.

References

Ambedkar, B. R. (1984). *The Buddha and His Dhamma*. Bombay: Siddharth.

Gombrich, Richard (2009). *What the Buddha Thought*. London: Equinox.

Keer, Dhananjay (1987). *Dr. Ambedkar Life and Mission*. Bombay: Popular Prakasan.

Murti, T. V. R. (1955). *The Central Philosophy of Buddhism: A Study of the Mādhyamika System*. London: George Allen & Unwin.

Queen, Christopher S. (ed.) (2000). *Engaged Buddhism in the West*. Somerville, MA: Wisdom.

Queen, Christopher S. (2004). Ambedkar's Dhamma and the Rise of Engaged Buddhism. In *Reconstructing the World: B. R. Ambedkar and Buddhism in India*. Ed. Surendra Jondhale and Johannes Beltz. New Delhi: Oxford University Press.

Queen, Christopher S. and Sallie B. King (1996). *Engaged Buddhism: Buddhist Liberation Movements in Asia*. Albany: State University of New York Press.

Queen, Christopher S., Prebish, Charles, and Keown, Damien (eds) (2003). *Action Dharma: New Studies in Engaged Buddhism*. London: RoutledgeCurzon.

Rahula, Walpola (1959). *What the Buddha Taught*. London: Gordon Fraser.

Robinson, Richard H., and Johnson, Willard L. (1997). *The Buddhist Religion: A Historical Introduction*. Fourth edn. Belmont, CA: Wadsworth.

Robinson, Richard H., Johnson, Willard L., and Thanissaro, Bhikkhu (2004). *The Buddhist Religions: A Historical Introduction*. Fifth edn. Belmont, CA: Wadsworth.

Santikaro, Bhikkhu (1996). Buddhadasa Bhikkhu: Life and Society through the Natural Eyes of Voidness. In *Engaged Buddhism: Buddhist Liberation Movements in Asia*. Ed. C. Queen and S. King. New York: State University of New York Press.

Sivaraksa, Sulak (1992). *Seeds of Peace: A Buddhist Vision for Renewing Society*. Berkeley, CA: Parallax Press.

Stcherbatsky, Theodor (1923).*The Central Conception of Buddhism and the Meaning of the word "Dharma"*. London: Royal Asiatic Society.

Takakusu, Junjiro (1947). *The Essentials of Buddhist Philosophy*. Delhi: Motilal Barnarsidass.

Thich Nhat Hanh (1993). Please Call Me by My True Names. In *Love in Action: Writings on Nonviolent Social Change*. Berkeley: Parallax Press.

35

Comparative Reflections on Buddhist Political Thought

Aśoka, Shambhala, and the General Will

DAVID CUMMISKEY

Historically and philosophically, there are two primary paradigms that capture much of Buddhist political thought. I will call these the Aśokan model and the Shambhalan model. The Aśokan model is deeply rooted in Buddhist history and has played a significant role in shaping Buddhist conceptions of political power, especially in South-East Asia, Bhutan, and Tibet.[1] King Aśoka is the first significant Buddhist king, and he represents the ideal Buddhist ruler and the normative standard for all future kings. The Aśokan model involves a balance between the ruler, the community of monks that constitute the Sangha, and the lay Buddhist people. The Aśokan king is a benevolent ruler who defends the Sangha and also maintains internal and national security. In a hostile and violent world, a powerful Aśokan king serves as the righteous protector of the Sangha, the Dharma, and the people. In contrast, the Shambhalan model is focused on creating a more enlightened populace and thus a more just political system. The Shambhalan approach, named after the mythical Buddhist kingdom of Shambhala where all people lived in profound harmony and peace (Midal 2006), aims for social change by increasing individual compassion and through non-violent social action. The Shambhalan paradigm is common in Buddhist Diaspora writings, and it is a model of political action embraced by some engaged Buddhists and Western Buddhists.[2] These two paradigms are not incompatible: the Shambhalan approach focuses on promoting justice by increasing enlightenment, the Aśokan approach on political legitimacy and a just basic structure for an unenlightened people. Aśokan and Shambhalan distinguish different approaches to political philosophy; one person can embrace both.

We will explore these two strands of Buddhist political thought and consider points of contrast and agreement with Western political philosophy, concentrating on Hobbes, Hume, and Rousseau. Buddhism provides the basis for a compelling critique of Hobbes's moral psychology, his individualism, and his account of social conflict. On the other hand, although many discussions of Buddhist politics focus on the need for greater virtue and a more enlightened people, the Aśokan Buddhist tradition, like Hobbes

A Companion to Buddhist Philosophy, First Edition. Edited by Steven M. Emmanuel.

and Hume, has always emphasized the problem of competitive individualism and recognized the essential role of political authority. The classical Aśokan approach, however, is too undemocratic for contemporary societies. I conclude by sketching an alternative Buddhist theory of justice that is inspired by Rousseau's conception of the general will.

Human Nature, the State of Nature, and the Nature of Peace

As John Rawls has emphasized, one of the most important features of Western political thought is its individualism. Indeed, the starting point for contractualist theories of justice is the moral importance of the distinctness and separateness of persons (Rawls 1971, 27). In contrast, Buddhism emphasizes the interdependence of persons and argues that the very idea of the independent autonomous self is rooted in ignorance and delusion. The conception of the person is the Archimedean point of a theory of justice. The distinct contours of Western and Buddhist political theory flow from their contrasting conceptions of the nature of persons.

In thinking about Western political thought, Hobbes's *Leviathan* (1651) sets the stage nicely. Hobbes starts his defense of government with the idea of the "State of Nature," which conceptually precedes the formation of civil society and political power.[3] Hobbes starts with a conception of human nature that is governed by the law of self-love. All voluntary actions are done for some perceived good, and the good is subjective and desire-based. What is good for a person is determined by the (rational and well-informed) desires of the person. Most importantly, Hobbes insists that the primary ends of human desire are self-preservation, pleasure, and power. Although Locke, Rousseau, Hume, Kant, and Rawls reject Hobbes's distinctive psychological egoism, they all share his basic individualism and the idea that a system of justice is necessary to solve social conflict. A social contract or convention justifies a system of law and government, which regulates our competitive instincts and resolves conflicts between individuals. Life, liberty, and the pursuit of happiness are secured under a system of justice. In defense of this contractualist conception of justice, Hobbes paints a picture of human relations without the restraint of civil law.

In addition to natural egoism, Hobbes defends the natural equality of all people by noting our common mortality and vulnerability. By nature, we are sufficiently equal in strength and intellect that the weakest can kill the strongest either by ganging up in combination with others or by secret machinations. Eventually we all must sleep, and a mere rock to the head can end a life. For Hobbes, the prime goal is continued life, and yet we are all equally vulnerable to death. There is thus no basis for one person to claim greater rights or social status. Instead, social rank, worth, and value are determined by one's value to others, which Hobbes sums up as the price of one's services in a market.

Natural egoism and equality combine to undermine social harmony. The natural state of humans is a natural and basic competition for goods and power. However, in a competition without a dominant power, individual power is needed to secure even a modest share. Since people fear death and harm, and since some individuals are sure to pursue glory and power, all must be ready to fight and defend themselves in any way necessary to survive. This is Hobbes's basic right of nature: a right (a natural liberty) to judge and to take whatever is necessary for self-preservation. The basic law of nature is that each must strive to protect himself or herself by *whatever means* necessary. This is both a rational requirement and a biological necessity of being a person.

As a result of the right of nature, there is in a state of nature perpetual insecurity and distrust because all are in a race for power. No matter how much power I have, someone is likely to pursue more. Competition, distrust, and the vainglory of some lead to perpetual insecurity and conflict. Hobbes famously concludes that the natural state of conflict justifies a state of war of all against all. In a state of war, self-interest rightly rules; there are no binding contracts; and there are no property rights. A promise or contract where there is no dominant power to back it up is worthless and foolhardy. There are no promises or contracts in the state of nature. Without promises and contracts there is no justice, and, as a result, people enjoy none of the advantages of social cooperation. In a state of nature, life is "solitary, poor, nasty, brutish, and short" (Hobbes 1994, 76).

This is the dilemma of the state of nature. Although we have a right to all things, we own nothing. In the pursuit of security, we all end up more insecure. In the pursuit of self-preservation, we end up more vulnerable. The solution for Hobbes is that we must seek peace and lay down our right to all things (provided others are willing to do so as well). The security and assurance of mutual agreements, however, requires a power to enforce it, and thus we must authorize a sovereign power, a government, to secure and enforce contracts and protect civil rights. For Hobbes, to avoid insecurity and death, the individual pursuit of self-interest must be restrained by civil law.

Buddhism, of course, recognizes the insecurity caused by the fear of death. However, Buddhism also emphasizes the inescapability of illness, aging, and death. This is the human condition. In addition, Buddhists argue that the pursuit of material gain and glory is based on delusion and does not lead to happiness. Desire satisfaction may temporarily distract us from our discontent, but it also undermines any possibility of inner peace. Buddhists agree with Hobbes that the pursuit of pleasure and power is a source of conflict and insecurity. But Buddhists emphasize that craving, the treadmill of desire after desire that defines so much of everyday life, never brings real satisfaction. It is instead the source of suffering and dissatisfaction. Like Hobbes, Buddhism tells us to "seek peace," but it is an *inner peace* that we must seek, not the artificial truce imposed by an external political power. Sovereign power brings civil peace, but what we really need is an inner transformation of desire itself.

External and internal conflicts are caused by the three *inner* poisons of greed, hatred, and ignorance. These three poisons are the root of all of our self-destructive emotions. It is easy to see that jealousy and anger are self-consuming; they wreak havoc on our health and peace of mind. The Dalai Lama describes these types of emotions as afflictions; it is "afflictive emotions" that are the real obstacle to both peace of mind and peaceful relationships (Dalai Lama 1999, 86–100). It is a core insight of Buddhism that, contra Hobbes, real peace comes from an inner peace of mind, which requires much more than external political security. Only a personal transformation, based on insight and wisdom, will end interpersonal conflict and lead to real happiness. If inner transformation is the key, what are the implications for the realm of politics?

The Shambhalan Paradigm

Monastic life is the classical path for Buddhists seeking enlightenment. The community of monks, the Sangha, is also a core social and political institution of Theravāda Buddhist societies. Before discussing the role and function of the Sangha, however, we will explore the non-monastic Shambhalan approach to politics. The limits of the Shambhalan approach set the stage for the political significance of the Sangha as a check on sovereign power.

There is an important common element in engaged Buddhism, Humanistic Buddhism, and many variations of Western Buddhism. In contrast to monastic Buddhism, these Buddhist teachings are addressed explicitly to lay Buddhists, and indeed to all people. This is one of the elements that distinguish what I call the Shambhalan approach – aptly called Shambhalan after the mythical Buddhist kingdom where all the people were enlightened and lived in profound harmony and peace (Midal 2006, 89). The mythological king of Shambhala asks the Buddha for a path to enlightenment that does not require renunciation of family life and civil society. For followers of Shambhala, as Chogyam Trungpa explains, "it is not necessary to renounce all material possessions and worldly pursuits . . . the basic message of Shambhala teaching is that the best of human life can be realized under ordinary circumstances. That is the basic wisdom of Shambhala: that in this world, as it is, we can find a good and meaningful life that will also serve others."[4] On the Shambhalan approach the entire Buddhist community, laity and monastic, constitutes the Buddhist Sangha. This broader conception of the Sangha contrasts with the idea of a monastic Sangha, which emphasizes the importance of a withdrawal from society, from economic activity and family life.

The Shambhalan non-monastic approach is also a more secular form of Buddhism. It emphasizes the psychological insights and universal moral truths of Buddhism, which are supposed to be sharable by secular humanists and people of all faiths. The idea is to provide a vision of enlightenment that does not presuppose controversial theological doctrines or metaphysics (Midal 2006, 96–7; Dalai Lama 1999, 234; see also Kiblinger 2005 and Flanagan 2011). Non-violence, compassion, generosity, forbearance, and self-restraint are universal values. These shared values provide an "Ethics for the New Millennium" based simply on a diagnosis of our discontents and an understanding of moral psychology that provides a path to inner peace, increased flourishing, and happiness (Dalai Lama 1999).

As a result, the non-theological Shambhalan vision offers a cosmopolitan conception of political philosophy. The goal is to reveal "a shared ethic to make our increasingly globalized world a more peaceful place" (Thich Nhat Hanh 2012). Although it also has a monastic following, the engaged Buddhism of Thich Nhat Hanh is especially influential because of its universal and global non-monastic teaching. Engaged Buddhism is focused on developing ever greater mindful awareness, non-violence, and compassion in all aspects of one's everyday life. Similarly, the Dalai Lama develops an inspiring conception of boundless compassion, equanimity, and universal responsibility that would surely transform the world for the better (Dalai Lama 1999, chs 8–11). The goal is to have "A Heart as Wide as the World," as Sharon Salzberg (1997) nicely puts it.

Like the monastic approach, the key to greater enlightenment is the practice of insight meditation. For engaged Buddhists, however, meditative practice is not distinct from other daily activities; it is instead a distinctive form of engagement with all daily activities: eating a meal, brushing one's teeth, answering the phone, working in a factory. Any form of work or activity can provide the basis for meditation and greater mindfulness. Engaged Buddhism is aimed at living every day in a more enlightened, non-aggressive, and compassionate way.

The Shambhalan approach has a clear socio-political dimension. Individual self-transformation itself promotes social justice. The emphasis, however, is on developing inner peace, seeing the interdependence of all beings, and thus expressing greater compassion in all aspects of one's daily life. We must be the change we want to see. The social and political priority of personal transformation is the characteristic that distinguishes the Shambhalan approach to political philosophy.

Although Chogyam Trungpa, Thich Nhat Hanh, and the Dalai Lama differ in emphasis and approach, they agree on the priority of personal transformation in effecting socio-political change. Thich Nhat Hanh (2006, 41–3) emphasizes that "Our daily lives have the most to do with the situation of the world. If we change our daily lives, we can change governments and the world." The Dalai Lama (1999, 19–33) also argues that the first step for any social transformation is an inner transformation, a spiritual revolution. Competition and consumerism must be replaced with compassion, forbearance, and simplicity. Addressing the United States Congress, Thich Nhat Hanh (2006, 132) explained that "all these acts of terrorism and violence come from wrong perceptions. Wrong perceptions are the ground for anger, violence, and hate. You cannot remove wrong perceptions with a gun."

Chogyam Trungpa, Thich Nhat Hanh, and the Dalai Lama clearly appreciate the problem of institutional injustice, but their main prescription for structural social change is through personal transformation. Of course, there is no reason why an engaged Buddhist cannot be equally concerned with the basic structure of society. Indeed, the engaged Buddhism of Sulak Sivaraksa centers on transforming the social and political structure of Thai society (Sivaraksa 1984, 1992; Hongladarom 1998).

To summarize, the Shambhalan paradigm has four core elements. First, it is a non-monastic approach that addresses all people, and as such it is adapted to everyday socio-economic needs and family life. Second, it offers a more secular and universal Buddhist vision, which is detached from more distinctively Buddhist concepts and metaphysics. The goal is to provide a basis for a shared ethic that brings together people from different theological perspectives. Third, it offers a cosmopolitan vision, and a conception of universal responsibility, for an interconnected global world. And, fourth, its prescription for social justice and world peace is cultivating compassion, generosity, and understanding. The goal is increased enlightenment and a collective awakening.

Recall that, for Hobbes, we are limited in our pursuit of desire by the desire of others, and our insecurity is caused by the threat that others pose. The Hobbesian problem is competitive individualism and the solution is the counter-balancing threat posed by a sovereign power. The sovereign ends the "war of all against all" so that we can pursue our desires without constant fear and insecurity. In contrast, for the Shambhalan, the key to peace is recognizing the self-defeating nature of competitive and selfish desires. The real obstacle to peace is our own delusional, misguided selfishness.

The doctrine of the priority of individual enlightenment, with the goal of the collective awakening of all people, is the essence of the political philosophy of the Shambhalan approach. Insight meditation, and the increased mindfulness this brings, is itself political action. While competitive individualism is rooted in the delusion of egoism, insight meditation is the transformative means for overcoming competitiveness, materialism, vainglory, anger, hatred, and all the delusions of selfish egoism. If we can overcome our afflictive emotions, then selfishness will be transformed into boundless compassion. With enlightenment and inner transformation, we end the treadmill of destructive materialism, and all the circumstances that give rise to the problems of justice dissolve. In a world where we all are deeply committed to nonviolence and compassion, there is no injustice and thus no need for rules of justice.

Unfortunately, this ideal Shambhalan world is not the one we inhabit. The point of Hobbes's social contract, or Hume's social conventions, is to respond to the problem of selfishness and partiality that defines too much of human interactions. Indeed, Hume agrees that the Shambhalan ideal renders rules of justice unnecessary. He writes:

> Suppose, that, though the necessities of the human race continue the same as present, yet the mind is so enlarged, so replete with friendship and generosity, that every man has the utmost tenderness for every man, and feels no more concern for his own interest than for that of his fellows: It seems that the USE of justice would, in this case, be suspended by such an extensive benevolence, nor would the divisions and barriers of property and obligation ever been thought of . . . Every man, upon this supposition, being a second self to another, would trust all his interests to the discretion of every man; without jealousy, without partition, without distinction. And the whole human race would form only one family.
>
> (Hume 1983, sect. III: 21–2)

The Shambhalan solution does render justice unnecessary, but it also assumes near universal enlightenment. Indeed, is this not why Shambhala is a mythical kingdom? Buddhists recognize and emphasize the three poisons, and afflictive emotions, that give rise to conflict and insecurity. In response to conflict and insecurity, laws that enforce rules of social justice are necessary. In short, all societies need rules of justice, enforcement mechanism for the rules, and political institutions.

It is noteworthy that the monastic Sangha (the community of monks dedicated to moral virtue, meditation, and increased enlightenment) is governed by over 200 rules that constitute the Vinaya Code of monastic discipline. The Sangha is also usually hierarchical in its social structures, and the monastic code is enforced with sanctions, among them expulsion from the Sangha for sexual intercourse, theft, homicide, or claiming knowledge that one does not have, including the heresy of propounding false doctrines.[5]

The Shambhalan vision does indeed provide an inspirational ideal, but it must be supplemented by an account of just laws and political structures that regulate imperfect social relations. Of course, this is not to deny that increased mindfulness and compassion will improve both one's own life and the lives of others. Indeed, the more enlightened and virtuous a people, the less they will need external laws to regulate their behavior. We will return to the importance of the Shambhalan vision after discussing the limits of the Aśokan model.

Political philosophy must address human nature as it is. Buddhism highlights and diagnoses the disordering and corrupting influence of the passions, and thus the need for rulers to maintain civil order. Indeed, Somboon Suksamran (1984, 25–6) extracts an analogy of Hobbes's conception of the state of nature (as the origin of political authority) from Buddhist creation myths. After the emergence of elements and then planets out of a primordial fire, life slowly evolves and differentiates into plants, animals, and then humans. When humans first evolved, there were unlimited amounts of clear-grained rice, there was abundance for all, and all property was communal. With time, however, some people became increasingly interested in sexual relationships, and as a result they were cut off and separated from the community. Others became greedy, despite having their needs satisfied, and hoarded rice. With the introduction of lust and greed, passions flared; and with shortages of rice and the jealousies of romantic passions, conflict, competition, and discontent inevitably followed. Competition for goods and unbridled passions also led to theft, fraud, and deception, and, in response to these retaliations, retribution and punishments. The need for a ruler to restore civil peace and order became clear to all. The best and most favored among the people was thus chosen to rule and regulate society. In Buddhist mythology, too, the origin of government is a solution to immorality and disorder, and its purpose is thus to create civil order and reintroduce security and morality.

A Buddhist theory of justice must also focus on the role of government and the basic civil and economic structure of society. As John Rawls has emphasized, the basic structure of society must be a central focus of any theory of justice (Rawls 1971, 9–11). The basic structure of society determines civil rights and responsibilities, powers and opportunities, property rights and control of the means of production, and, of course, income and the distribution of wealth. What then is the Buddhist model of government and of a just basic social structure? We will consider two possible answers to this question: the first is the Theravāda Aśokan model; the second, a Buddhist form of democratic socialism inspired by Rousseau's idea of the general will.

The Aśokan Paradigm

The Aśokan paradigm shaped political and social institutions in the Theravāda Buddhist countries of South-East Asia. From roughly 304 to 230 BCE, about 100 years after the death of Buddha, Aśoka conquered, unified, and ruled the northern territories of what is now contemporary India.[6] The rule of Aśoka, who converted to Buddhism after his triumphant, but horrific, conquest over Kalinga (modern Orissa), marked the first rise of Buddhism to a national religion on a grand scale. Overcome by the death and destruction of war, he committed himself to the benevolent and just rule of his subjects. As a Buddhist ruler, he adopted vegetarianism, dug wells for the people, provided free medical care for humans and animals, and, in general, supported the public welfare.

We are told that King Aśoka promoted religious toleration, but, even more important, as a Buddhist king he devoted his rule to spreading the Dharma, the teaching of the Buddha, and supporting the community of monks, the Sangha. Aśoka also convened the Third Buddhist Council, which ensured the accuracy and orthodoxy of the teaching and practice of Buddhism. The decisions and commentaries of the Third Council were widely disseminated by Aśoka and, according to tradition, they provided the basis for the Theravāda Buddhist tradition and the Pāli canon. It is hard to exaggerate the significance of the rule of Aśoka to Buddhism in South-East Asia.

As a just and compassionate ruler, Aśoka rejected war as a means of territorial expansion or as a tool of national interests. It is perhaps difficult today to appreciate the moral significance of this decision. It is now a commonplace that, although defensive war and humanitarian interventions are permissible, wars for national gain and glory are a violation of international norms. In contrast, world history is full of the deeds of conquerors. The ruthless conquests of Alexander the Great and the Roman legions are still glorified in film and fiction. Aśoka ruled in the historical epoch of the conquering hero during the Warring States period in China. He nonetheless rejected the heroic conception of aggressive war. As a Buddhist king, Aśoka was perhaps the first ruler of a hegemonic military power to reject unilaterally the realist view of war.

Aśoka, however, was no pacifist. His special role as king was to preserve the Dharma and protect the Sangha and the people. And, as sovereign, he used his power to secure the peace. He erected stone pillars throughout his kingdom, and on one of the pillars wrote:

> [Aśoka] Beloved-of-the-Gods thinks that even those who do wrong should be forgiven where forgiveness is possible. Even the forest people, who live in Beloved-of-the-Gods' domain, are entreated and reasoned with to act properly. They are told that despite his remorse [at the slaughter of innocents in his past] Beloved-of-the-Gods has the power to punish them if necessary, so that they should be ashamed of their wrong and not be killed. Truly, Beloved-of-the-Gods desires non-injury, restraint and impartiality to all beings, even where wrong has been done. Now it is conquest by Dharma that Beloved-of-the-Gods considers to be the best conquest . . . This conquest has been won everywhere, and it gives great joy – the joy which only conquest by Dharma can give.
>
> (Aśoka, *Fourteen Rock Edicts*, #13)

As the model Buddhist ruler, Aśoka insisted that he "desires non-injury, restraint and impartiality to all beings," but he also had "the power to punish if necessary." He did not disband his army; he remained the dominant superpower in his region.[7] Despite his hegemonic power, Aśoka strove to be merciful and compassionate towards criminals and other people within or beyond his borders. For Aśoka, the goal of sovereign power was to teach and encourage virtue and wisdom. Nevertheless, aggressors, whether internal or external, were not to be passively tolerated; criminals had to be punished and invaders repelled. In other edicts, Aśoka assured people on his borders that they need not fear conquest because he wished only to spread the Dharma. Although he had a missionary zeal, he also insisted on mutual respect among religions.

In short, these are the political lessons we can draw from the idealized rule of Aśoka: trust the people, provide social services that secure their basic needs, and treat them with compassion; support the Sangha, for it preserves and teaches the Dharma; defend the innocent against all transgressors (but never with hatred or malice); deter and prevent aggression when possible; recognize and acknowledge the harm to the victims of aggression; and punish but also forgive the transgressors.

The Theravāda Tripartite Political System

The essence of the Aśokan model of politics, and the basic structure of all future Aśokan societies, is a tripartite relationship between the Sangha, the ruler, and the people.[8] The monastic Sangha is one of the core institutions that make up the basic structure of Theravāda Buddhist societies. The Sangha is a central institution because monastic life is the primary path to enlightenment. However, monastic practice is about more than individual growth. In addition, this community of monks preserves and passes on the teachings of the Buddha. The people cherish and respect the Sangha. As a result, the endorsement of the Sangha is essential to the perceived legitimacy of sovereign power. A ruler may have *de facto* power, but the people look to the Sangha to affirm the legitimate authority of the ruler.

On the other hand, the Sangha also relies on the ruler for support, and its official social/political position is easily reinforced or undermined by the ruler. In addition to providing security for the people, the ruler is the protector of the Sangha. Although the Sangha serves as a check and balance on sovereign political power, its political power comes from both the ruler and the people. For its authority and prestige, the Sangha must represent Buddhist ideals and its monks must live a more meditative and virtuous life. If the people think that the monks are corrupt or unfaithful to their monastic vows, the Sangha loses the respect of the people and thus its moral authority. The people, the Sangha, and the ruler are thus all mutually dependent.

The Sangha preserves the Dharma and serves the religious needs of the people, but it also plays an essential role in checking and legitimizing the political power of the ruler. The Sangha is thus as much a part of the basic structure of society as the ministries of the government. Without the ministers there is no effective power, no *de facto* authority, but without the Sangha there is no moral, *de jure*, authority. According to Ian Harris, "it is perhaps not too much of an exaggeration to suggest that a healthy functioning Buddhist polity is one in which the respective powers of king and *Sangha* are held in a state of antagonistic symbiosis" (Harris 2007, 3).

It is also the case that the Aśokan ruler is often associated with a God or Buddha. In his Stone Edicts, Aśoka refers to himself as "Beloved-of-the Gods." It is natural to think that the ruler's position is dictated by superior karma and the Dharma [rightful] order of the world. A Buddhist king is supposed to be righteous and virtuous, and thus can be trusted by the people. Such an exalted being must be more enlightened and closer to Buddha than the people. The Aśokan ruler loves the people like a parent and the people trust their ruler to look after their interests. The king is the immediate source of civil order and security, but the king's authority is rooted in the Ten Kingly Virtues of charity, morality, self-sacrifice, rectitude, gentleness, self-restriction, non-anger, non-violence, forbearance, and non-obstruction (Stengs 2009, 36; Swearer 2010, 263 n. 9). The legitimate authority of the king is ultimately and essentially based on the virtues of the king.

In Tibetan Buddhism, the political ruler is elevated further to a direct emanation of the Buddha of Compassion. The Dalai Lama has achieved enlightenment but has taken a bodhisattva vow to protect and care for the Tibetan people. The Dalai Lama is both the religious and political leader, and the Tibetan people trust the Dalai Lama unconditionally *because* the Dalai Lama is an incarnation of the Buddha of Compassion. The association of buddha-nature with the political leader is a natural extension of the Aśokan political model (Jackson 1989). The ruler's status and dignity is rooted in his enlightened rule, and enlightened rule implies enlightenment. An Aśokan ruler is thus always close to a living buddha.

Absolute, but not unconditional, monarchy is the traditional corollary of the doctrine of Buddhist kingship. Although both Thailand and the Tibetan government in exile are now constitutional democracies, the people of these Buddhist lands have resisted the end of absolute monarchy. Even today, despite the official end of any constitutional political power, both the Thai king and the Dalai Lama have tremendous real power and influence with the people.

King Chulalongkorn, who ruled Siam/Thailand from 1868 to 1910, in response to petitions for the establishment of a constitutional monarchy, explains the status of a Buddhist king:

> [The king] must always practice moderation and justice . . . Contrary to what happened in Europe, Siamese kings have led the people so that both they and the country might be prosperous and happy . . . [The people] have more faith in the king than any members of parliament, because they believe the king more than anybody else practices justice and loves the people.
>
> (Stengs 2009, 12)

The people accept the elevated and special status of the king; they trust, and indeed worship, the Thai king as a living manifestation of the Buddha. Mere elected ministers can never have the same exalted status as a Buddhist king or Dalai Lama. It is no wonder that the Tibetan people have resisted replacing the rule of the Dalai Lama with democracy.

The current Dalai Lama, in particular, strongly supports democracy, and the rule of law (where no person, even the Dalai Lama, is above the law), but the Tibetan people have consistently resisted his introduction of democratic rule. As John Powers explains,

> After centuries of rule by lamas believed to be manifestations of Buddhas, the [the Dalai Lama's] proposal to grant effective power in merely human representatives struck many Tibetans as a misguided idea, since ordinary humans could be expected to pursue petty goals, engage in political maneuvering for themselves and their associates, and sometimes put their own welfare ahead of that of the people . . . The people's resistance to his initiative indicates how foreign democratic principles remain to many Tibetans.
>
> (Powers 1998, 193–6)

In response, Tibetan primary schools in Dharamsala, India, introduced courses on democratic theory and practice to help change attitudes of the next generations. The Tibetan exile government also sponsors "Democracy Days," where the schoolchildren join the community, listening to patriotic speeches on human rights and Buddhist principles, and sing songs in praise of democracy.

There are preconditions for democracy. Democracy presupposes a high level of civic trust, perhaps a robust civil society, and, since one cannot simply rely on the virtue of elected politicians, checks and balances on political power. Democratic sensibilities also involve a robust respect for minority rights and respect for freedom of conscience; otherwise majority rule is just a new form of tyranny.

Rousseau, Buddhism, and the General Will

Rousseau's account of the general will provides a theoretical framework for a Buddhist conception of democratic political legitimacy. Rousseau emphasizes how easily democratic elections can collapse into a mere factional battle of interest groups. Instead of a society with a shared general will and a shared sense of a common good, it is too easy to remain in a more or less constrained war of faction against faction. Rousseau argues that, for there to be a just society, first a collection of individuals must be transformed into a unified people – a people that share an identity and a common conception of the good. Rousseau distinguishes the mere aggregation of individual preferences, which he calls the "will of all," from a unifying and shared "general will": "There is often a great difference between the will of all and the general will. The latter considers only the general interest, whereas the former considers private interest and is merely the sum of private wills" (1987, Bk II, ch. III). Democratic elections often reflect "intrigues and partial associations" which actually undermine the general will. Laws based on majority power alone often undermine social unity and justice. For Rousseau, by definition, "the general will is always right and always tends toward the public utility. However, it does not follow that the deliberations of the people always have the same rectitude" (ibid.). If democratic elections function simply as tools of competing factional interests, there is no reason to assume that the results reflect a common good or a shared purpose. Indeed, a majority vote does not in any way check the potential tyranny of the majority. These are the same concerns about democracy expressed by the Thai and Tibetan peoples.

Rousseau argues that elections should not be a battle of competing preferences. The goal of elections should be the discovery of a shared general will. The citizen casting a vote should not ask, "What will serve my individual interests most?" Instead, the citizen should ask, "What policy choice advances the common good that we all share?"

> When a law is proposed in the people's assembly . . . what is asked of them is not whether they approve or reject, but whether or not it conforms with the general will that is theirs. Each man, in giving his vote, states his opinion on this matter, and the declaration of the general will is drawn from the counting of votes.
>
> (1987, Bk IV, ch. II)

The idea here is simple but easily lost. If laws obligate all citizens equally, political commitments and obligations must be mutual, must be equitable and promote a common and public good, and must apply to all equally (Ibid., Bk II, chs. IV and VI).

The shift of focus to the common good provides an apt model for a Buddhist democracy. The interconnectedness of our lives, and rejection of narrow self-interest, is at the core of the Buddhist worldview. Indeed, Rousseau's conception of the shared general will of the people is actually in conflict with Western individualism. For Rousseau, the key to turning individuals into a people is converting self-love and vanity into patriotism and nationalism. This is clearly a dangerous path; it replaces civil competition with international competition; it replaces interpersonal conflict with war. Buddhism offers an alternative vision of a general will that is based on a rejection of both delusional self-interest and militant nationalism. Buddhism also rejects preference satisfaction as the key to happiness. The key to happiness is instead the recognition of the centrality of relationships and the necessity of mutual support. The idea of the general will actually fits Buddhism better than it fits Western individualism. In fact, it is a natural corollary to the traditional Buddhist conception of political legitimacy. The righteous laws and just decrees of an Aśokan king must serve and reflect the good of the people, and as such reflect the general will of the people.

Rousseau also argues that significant economic inequality inevitably leads to social and political inequality. Inequality is thus one of the most significant obstacles to a shared sense of a common good and to laws rooted in a general will (1987, Bk II, ch. XI). Similarly, for Buddhists, basic material goods are necessary for health and life, but luxuries and ever increasing material consumption do not bring greater happiness. Social and political structures should secure a satisfactory minimum for all, and surpluses should be used to promote the common good.[9]

Creating, Sustaining, and Enforcing the General Will

Political institutions, political officials, and citizens (when enacting legislation) need to be guided by a general will that overrides our private interests. Of course, it is not easy for people to think of others before themselves and the common good instead of private gain. As a result, Rousseau emphasizes the need for an inspirational and charismatic leader (a great legislator) to inspire and unify individuals into a people (1987, Bk II, chs. VI and VII). In a similar vein, we have seen how the Dalai Lama instituted "Democracy Days" to inspire his people to be self-governing and identify with the common good.

Rousseau also defends the coercive authority of the general will: "whoever refuses to obey the general will will be forced to do so by the entire body. This means merely that he will be forced to be free" (1987, Bk I, ch. VII). Rousseau is concerned with the justification of sovereign power. Laws are enforced. If the laws are based on shared interests and a shared general will, then we also authorize the necessary coercive power of the state. Buddhism is not focused on liberty, but a similar logic applies to a Buddhist justification of coercive laws. If law is necessary for the common good and prevents serious harm, then disobeying the law harms others and is thus unwholesome. It is best, of course, to obey just laws because it is the just and virtuous thing to do. Nonetheless, the enforcement of justice promotes wholesome conduct. To quote Aśoka again, "it is conquest by Dharma that Beloved-of-the-Gods considers to be the best," but "Beloved-of-the-Gods has the power to punish [wrongdoers] if necessary, so that they should be ashamed of their wrong and not be killed" (Aśoka, *Fourteen Rock Edicts*, #13). Laws are justified because they are necessary for the common good, promote wholesome conduct, and protect innocents from harm. Since these are ends that we all share, we cannot object to the enforcement of law. Coercive law, authorized by a shared general will, forces us to do what we really will. "This means merely that [we] will be forced to be [good]" (Rousseau 1987, Bk I, ch. VII). More needs to be said to flesh out

Buddhist justifications of legal authority and police powers. The enforcement of law, however, is a commonplace of Buddhist societies. Indeed, monasteries have always enforced the Vinaya code, and large monastic communities have also exercised policing powers. A comprehensive account of Buddhist political theory would explore more fully Buddhist justifications of legal authority.

As the Shambhalan approach and Hume rightly emphasize, an enlightened people would not need a coercive legal system at all. The need for enforceable law is always a response and reaction that marks the need for progress. Nonetheless, if we focus on a theory of justice for the basic structure of society, we do not need to assume a fully enlightened citizenry. For a just society, people must care about justice, and they must appreciate that law and political institutions must reflect a general will. A just people, however, need not be fully virtuous or enlightened. It is much easier to recognize what is right, and vote for laws that serve the general will, than it is to act rightly on one's own. For example, it is easier to vote for a law that redistributes wealth, including one's own, than it is voluntarily to give away a substantial portion of one's wealth. It is easier for people to support comprehensive health-care reform than personally to fund health-care charities. Collective action through legislation is also often the most effective means of promoting the common good. Building social, economic, and political institutions on a conception of shared and equitable common good is especially congenial to Buddhist sensibilities.

Buddhism has always embraced a conception of government for the people, and, historically, the Sangha has served as a check on political power. Representative government, by means of free and fair elections, is another means of holding rulers accountable. In a Buddhist democracy, the people must fulfill the role of the Sangha as a political check on the legal power of the rulers. The monastic Sangha is replaced with the more expansive conception of the Sangha, which embraces the entire Buddhist community. Similarly, a Supreme Judicial Court (which limits legislative and executive power, protects minority rights, and enforces the constitution) is fully compatible with Buddhist principles and provides a contemporary analogue of the Aśokan Sangha council. The members of the court serve as a more enlightened special council, which limits the law to the boundary set by the idea of a just and equitable general will. Instead of the "antagonistic symbiosis" of the respective powers of king and Sangha, democratic elections and a constitutional court provide limits on political power.[10]

In this way, Buddhism can function like a "civil religion" that provides the foundation for a shared commitment to a common, equitable, and just society (Rousseau 1987, Bk IV, ch. VIII). The conception of Buddhism as a civil religion, however, does not provide an adequate model for a pluralistic society. An essential question, for future inquiry, is how this Rousseauian model of politics can be modified to incorporate Buddhist conceptions of toleration, inclusion, and pluralism (Fu and Wawrytko 1991; Kiblinger 2005; Hershock 2006).

Conclusion

The Shambhalan political vision emphasizes the necessity of individual enlightenment. The Aśokan tripartite system emphasizes the role of government in creating an environment where the unenlightened people, the Sangha and the laity, can pursue greater enlightenment. The monastic Sangha also serves as an essential check and balance on the political power of the king. Government is indeed necessary, but the idea of the Aśokan king is out of step with contemporary democratic sensibilities. On the other hand, democracy, understood as simple mechanisms for aggregating competing individual preferences, is also out of step with Buddhist sensibilities. Rousseau offers an alternative conception of democracy as the rule of law based on a shared general will. The idea of the general will fits especially well with the Buddhist rejection of individualism and its alternative relational conception of the self.

As the Shambhalan vision makes clear, individual growth towards collective enlightenment is important. In a just democratic society, the general will must override factional interests and individualism. It would thus seem that a just and equitable democracy presupposes a partially enlightened people. The general will is itself a partial realization of the Shambhalan ideal. People need political institutions, but just politics also needs good people. Like all else, social justice and virtue, the political and the personal, are thoroughly interdependent.

Notes

1 See, e.g., Harris (2007); Hongladarom (1998); Ratnapala (1997); Smith (1978); Suksamran (1976); Swearer (2010); Terwiel (1984).

2 In addition to scholarly and historical accounts of Buddhism, I am interested in the contemporary experience of Buddhism as reflected in more popular publications. For a discussion of Western Buddhism as supposedly opposed to authentic Asian Buddhism, see Quli (2009).

3 The summary of Hobbes's argument is extracted from *Leviathan*, especially chapters 6, 9–11, 13–15, and 17. My summary is also indebted to Peter Railton's political philosophy course (1982–6).

4 Trungpa (1995, 250). The Shambhala warrior must renounce and overcome inner obstacles to peace, especially fear, self-deception, and selfishness (ibid., 236–9). In addition, Chogyam Trungpa defends a more Confucian vision that focuses on the priority of family life, the importance of one's ancestors, and the history of one's social relationships (ibid., 148–51).

5 See Bhikkhu (2007–12).

6 My summary of Aśoka is based on Strong (1994, 1989).

7 For a discussion of Buddhist just war theory, see Cummiskey (2011); Jerryson and Juergensmeyer (2010); and Schliff (2011).

8 See references in note 1.

9 For Buddhist critiques of consumer capitalism, see Sivaraksa (1984); Hongladarom (1998); Thinley (2006); Loy (2003); and Sizemore and Swearer (1990). Focusing on overall production, as a corollary of consumption, does not indicate the well-being, contentment, or happiness of a people. Gross Domestic Product (GDP) is thus not a reliable index of national flourishing and greater well-being. From a Buddhist perspective, we must instead focus on increasing Gross National Happiness (GNH). Bhutan has led the way in developing a workable GNH index which measures nine domains of human life that capture key areas of overall and collective human flourishing, including psychological well-being, health, education, and good governance. For an explanation of the domains and the measurement tools

used to construct a GNH index, see www.grossnationalhappiness.com/9-domains/. Buddhist economics also emphasizes sustainable development and "right livelihood" (see Essen 2010; Loy 2008, 140–1). Although Buddhism rejects consumerism and the GDP standard of success, it need not reject capitalism and markets as such. European socialism has shown that markets can coexist with a substantial commitment to equity, social services, and social solidarity, and perhaps even maximize GNH.

10 For an interesting discussion of constitutional democracy in Thailand, see Connors (2003). Connors (ibid., 108) draws attention to the (mis)use of the concept of the general will in Thai discourse.

References

Bhikkhu, Thanissaro (trans.) (2007–12). *Bhikkhu Pāṭimokkha: The Bhikkhus' Code of Discipline.* At: www.accesstoinsight.org/tipitaka/vin/sv/bhikkhu-pati.html.

Connors, Michael Kelly (2003). *Democracy and National Identity in Thailand.* New York: RoutledgeCurzon.

Cummiskey, David (2011). The Law of Peoples. In *Global Justice Reader*. Ed. M. Boylan. Boulder, CO: Westview Press, 299–324.

Dalai Lama (1999). *Ethics for the New Millennium.* New York: Riverhead Books.

Essen, Juliana (2010). Sufficiency, Economy and Santi Asoke: Buddhist Economic Ethics for a Just and Sustainable World. In *Journal of Buddhist Ethics* 17, 70–99.

Flanagan, Owen (2011). *The Bodhisattva's Brain.* Cambridge, MA: MIT Press.

Fu, Charles, and Wawrytko, S. (eds) (1991). *Buddhist Ethics and Modern Society.* Westport, CT: Greenwood Press.

Harris, Ian (ed.) (2007). *Buddhism, Power, and Political Order.* New York: Routledge.

Hershock, Peter D. (2006). *Buddhism and the Public Sphere: Reorienting Global Interdependence.* New York: Routledge.

Hobbes, Thomas (1994). *Leviathan.* Ed. Edwin Curley. Indianapolis: Hackett.

Hongladarom, Soraj (1998). Buddhism and Human Rights in the Thoughts of Sulak Sivaraksa and Phra Dhammapidok (Prayudh Prayutto). In *Buddhism and Human Rights.* Ed. Damien Keown, C. Prebish, and W. Husted. Richmond, Surrey: Curzon Press, 97–109.

Hume, David (1983). *An Enquiry Concerning the Principles of Morals.* Ed. J. B. Schneewind. Indianapolis: Hackett.

Jackson, Peter (1989). *Buddhism, Legitimation, and Conflict: the Political Functions of Thai Urban Buddhism.* Singapore: Institute of South Asian Studies.

Jerryson, Michael, and Juergensmeyer, Mark (eds) (2010). *Buddhist Warfare.* New York: Oxford University Press.

Kiblinger, Kristin (2005). *Buddhist Inclusiveness.* Burlington: Ashgate.

Loy, David R. (2003). *The Great Awakening: A Buddhist Social Theory.* Boston: Wisdom.

Loy, David R. (2008). *Money, Sex, War, Karma: Notes for a Buddhist Revolution.* Boston: Wisdom.

Midal, Fabrice (2006). Creating Enlightened Society: The Shambhala Teachings of Chogyam Trungpa. In *Mindful Politics: A Buddhist Guide to Making the World a Better Place.* Ed. Melvin McLeod. Boston: Wisdom, 89–97.

Powers, John (1998). Human Rights and Cultural Values: The Political Philosophies of the Dalai Lama and the People's Republic of China. In *Buddhism and Human Rights.* Ed. Damien Keown, C. Prebish, and W. Husted. Richmond, Surrey: Curzon Press, 175–202.

Quli, Natalie E. (2009) Western Self, Asian Other: Modernity, Authenticity, and Nostalgia for "Tradition" in Buddhist Studies. In *Journal of Buddhist Ethics* 16, 1–38.

Ratnapala, Nandasena (1997). *Buddhist Democratic Political Theory and Practice*. Ratmalana, Sri Lanka: Sarvodha Vishva Leekha.

Rawls, John (1971). *A Theory of Justice*. Cambridge, MA: Harvard University Press.

Rousseau, Jean-Jacques (1987). *On the Social Contract*. In *The Basic Political Writings*. Trans. and ed. Donald A. Cress. Indianapolis: Hackett.

Salzberg, Sharon (1997). *A Heart as Wide as the World*. Boston: Shambhala.

Schliff, Henry M. (2011). A Review of *Buddhist Warfare*. In *Journal of Buddhist Ethics* 18, 170–6.

Sivaraksa, Sulak (1984). Buddhism and Society: Beyond the Present Horizon. In *Buddhism and Society in Thailand*. Ed. B. J. Terwiel. Gaya, Bihar, India: Centre for South-East Asian Studies, 97–119.

Sivaraksa, Sulak (1992). *Seeds of Peace: A Buddhist Vision for Renewing Society*. Berkeley, CA: Parallax Press.

Sizemore, Russell F., and Swearer, Donald K. (eds) (1990). *Ethics, Wealth, and Salvation: A Study of Buddhist Social Ethics*. Columbia: University of South Carolina Press.

Smith, Bardwell L. (ed.) (1978). *Religion and Legitimation of Power in Thailand, Laos, and Burma*. Chambersburg, PA: Anima Books.

Stengs, Irene (2009). *Worshiping the Great Modernizer: King Chulalongkorn, Patron Saint of the Thai Middle Class*. Singapore: NUS Press.

Strong, John (1989). *The Legend of Aśoka: A Study and Translation of the Aśokavadana*. Princeton, NJ: Princeton University Press.

Strong, John (1994). *King Aśoka and Buddhism: Historical and Literary Studies*. Ed. Anuradha Seneviratna. Kandy, Sri Lanka: Buddhist Publication Society.

Suksamran, Somboon (1976). *Political Buddhism in Southeast Asia: The Role of the Sangha in Modern Thailand*. New York: St Martin's Press.

Suksamran, Somboon (1984). Buddhism and Political Authority: A Symbiotic Relationship. In *Buddhism and Society in Thailand*. Ed. B. J. Terwiel. Gaya, Bihar, India: Centre for South-East Asian Studies, 25–42.

Swearer, Donald K. (2010).*The Buddhist World of Southeast Asia*. Albany: State University of New York Press.

Terwiel, B. J. (ed.) *Buddhism and Society in Thailand*. Gaya, Bihar, India: Centre for South-East Asian Studies.

Thich Nhat Hanh (2006). Call Me by My True Names; We Have the Compassion and Understanding Necessary to Heal the World; and Compassion is Our Best Protection. In *Mindful Politics: A Buddhist Guide to Making the World a Better Place*. Ed. Melvin McLeod. Boston: Wisdom, 39–43; 129–39; 273–83.

Thich Nhat Hanh (2012). *Good Citizens: Creating Enlightened Society*. Berkeley, CA: Parallax Press.

Thinley, Jigmi (2006). Gross National Happiness. In *Mindful Politics: A Buddhist Guide to Making the World a Better Place*. Ed. Melvin McLeod. Boston: Wisdom, 213–23.

Trungpa, Chogyam (1995). *Shambhala: The Sacred Path of the Warrior*. Boston: Shambhala Press.

Part IV

Buddhist Meditation

36

Buddhist Meditation

Theory and Practice

CHARLES GOODMAN

Introduction: The Place of Meditation in Buddhism

Meditative practices exist in many of the world's religious traditions. Sufi Muslims, monastic Catholics, and Vedāntist Hindus, among others, devote considerable time and effort to quiet, contemplative practices that involve directing the attention within and that lead, sometimes, to sublime peak experiences. Yet meditation is fairly marginal in the lives of most ordinary followers of Islam, Christianity, and Hinduism, and these religions teach several paths to salvation that do not depend on meditative experiences. Most lineages of Buddhism, by contrast, place meditative accomplishment at the center of their understanding of how to achieve liberation from suffering. In many contemporary Buddhist contexts, everyone – whether lay or monastic, man or woman – is expected to meditate and to gain some of the considerable benefits that practice can bring.

Buddhists lay great stress on a list called the Three Forms of Training (Skt *tri-śikṣā*). The three are moral discipline (Skt *śīla*), stable attention (Skt *samādhi*), and wisdom (Skt *prajñā*). The Three Forms of Training can be seen as three progressively higher stages of development, but they also reinforce one another. By producing a quiet, moderate life and reducing disturbing emotions, moral discipline creates appropriate conditions for the inner work needed to stabilize attention. Stable attention, which is cultivated through and attained in meditation practice, produces emotional health, making the practitioner much less likely to want to violate the commitments of moral discipline. Buddhists claim further that stable attention in meditation leads directly to wisdom. We will be examining in detail the plausibility of this claim and the grounds that could be offered for it. Wisdom, in turn, by making it possible to see how things are, overcomes temptations to break moral discipline and dissolves obstacles to stable attention. Together, the three forms of training are said to lead to an inner state of peace, clarity, freedom from suffering, kindness, compassion, and happiness.

A Companion to Buddhist Philosophy, First Edition. Edited by Steven M. Emmanuel.

Although the doctrines and ways of life of the Buddhist religion are heavily dependent on meditation practices, the converse typically does not hold. Most forms of Buddhist meditation do not require any particular doctrinal commitments, metaphysical assumptions, or leaps of faith in order to work as advertised. You need only sufficient confidence in the practice to invest the effort and time needed to make it work. Doing so may or may not lead a practitioner to gravitate towards a Buddhist worldview. Many Westerners have found that meditation can be helpful even when entirely separated from any doctrinal framework; this is the approach, for instance, of Jon Kabat-Zinn's Mindfulness-Based Stress Reduction programs.

According to Buddhists, then, meditation can be helpful to people in general, whether they currently find other aspects of Buddhist teaching plausible or not. But what is meant by the term "meditation" in Buddhism, and how do you actually practice it? What reason is there to believe that meditation actually offers any of the benefits claimed for it? This chapter will explain how to do three major forms of meditation widely practiced in Buddhism, being shared in common by a number of lineages, including both Theravāda and Tibetan Buddhism. Drawing on the basic texts of the Pāli canon, sacred to the Theravāda tradition, I will also try to offer some elements of an explanation of how meditation could work in the way Buddhists say it does.

Breathing Mindfulness Meditation

Across most Buddhist traditions, one of the most important practices available, and one of the foundational practices for any other kind of spiritual work, involves bringing attention to the experience of breathing. Known as breathing mindfulness meditation (P. *ānāpāna-sati*), this form of practice is quite simple – but not at all easy! While sitting in this way, there is no place to hide from your own emotional turmoil. In order to carry out the practice, you must face all the sensations, emotions, or thoughts that arise, without holding on to them or pushing them away. Through this demanding form of effort, patience and courage begin to grow: the patience to be present with the storm of chaos in your mind and the courage to face what is difficult for you to experience.

To do the actual practice, sit still with your back straight. Here "straight" does not mean like a ruler but, rather, without slumping or leaning, allowing your spine to have its natural S-shaped curvature. "Still" does not mean rigidly still; you should not try to use muscle tension to hold your body still by force. A sense of relaxation, of ease, will help this practice to work. On the other hand, if you feel a slight pain or itch, simply rest and do not do anything about it. This can be a highly valuable spiritual practice. If the pain becomes intense, you may move so as to relieve it.

Bring attention to the experience of breathing. Rest without trying to force the breath to take on any particular form. Do not try to make your breath deep or shallow, short or long, fast or slow. Simply allow the breath to be entirely natural, but watch it. Gradually, as you relax, your breathing may naturally become deeper and slower. Notice the details of how you are breathing, without trying to control them.

Inevitably, distractions will arise, and you will lose touch with the breath. If many distractions appear, and you do not feel peaceful at all, do not think that you are doing the practice incorrectly. To draw this conclusion is a common mistake. This is simply how breathing mindfulness meditation works. Instead, whenever you notice that you have become distracted, gently bring the attention back to the breath. The moment when you notice that you have become distracted is the most crucial point of this practice. By bringing attention back to the breath at this moment, you gradually build a greater capacity for clear, stable attention.

Many beginners find it helpful to count the breath. One complete cycle of inhalation and exhalation counts as one. Keep counting up to ten; if you reach ten, start counting again at one. If you become distracted and lose count, when you notice this, just start counting again at one.

If you are practicing alone, it is helpful to set a timer of some kind to chime when the meditation session ends, so that you do not have to keep looking at your watch. When you sit down with the intention to practice for a certain amount of time, make sure you continue to practice for the entire time you intended. If your legs cannot continue to hold your sitting posture, then stand up for a minute or two, keep bringing attention to the breath while standing, and then, once your legs are a bit refreshed, sit back down again.

Moving forward in this practice involves finding a middle point of attention that is neither agitated nor dull. If the mind is very agitated, with thoughts rushing this way and that way incessantly, simply return again and again to the breath. Gradually, it will become possible to rest in the experience of the coming and going of thoughts, while remaining vividly aware of them. On the other hand, you may find your mind becoming dull, so that you "space out" and there is no vividness to your attention. To prevent dullness, it is helpful to get enough sleep! Proper meditation posture can help counteract dullness. And many meditators discover that agitation and dullness are related to the angle of the gaze. If the direction of your gaze is too low, you may be more likely to encounter dullness, and if the direction is too high, you may have more of a problem with agitation. If your experience is similar, adjusting your gaze can help find a balance where neither extreme disrupts your attention.

Some people find that, at the beginning of a practice session, their minds are full of distractions, but that gradually, as they continue to sit still, agitated thoughts settle down and clarity begins to emerge. If your experience in meditation is like theirs, you should try to develop the capacity to sit for longer and longer periods of time, so as to deepen your engagement with the practice. By contrast, other people find that they begin a practice session with sufficient energy and strength of intention that their mind quickly settles down, and they can rest in the breath with few distractions for a while; but, over time, the mind loses its ability to rest, distractions become more frequent, and they are overwhelmed by agitation or dullness. If your experience is like theirs, it will be more helpful to sit for shorter periods of time – perhaps just 10 minutes – but aim to do several practice sessions a day.

When it comes to breathing mindfulness meditation, more is often better. At first, though, it is not necessary to commit a great deal of time in order to see the benefits. The most important quality is consistency – to practice every day, or as close to this as you are able. With consistent, sincere practice, even 10 or 15 minutes of breathing mindfulness a day is likely to bring about valuable and significant changes in your life.

Do not try to force your mind to become empty or quiet. The effort and strain expended to try to hold the mind still will simply lead to more mental disturbances. Your mind in meditation is like a jar of muddy water. If you stir it to try to force it to be clear, you will only arouse the mud. If you just let the jar sit for a while, the mud and dirt will naturally drift downwards, and the water will become clear by itself.

Do not get caught up in expectations about what you are supposed to experience while sitting. During meditation, very unpleasant thoughts or images may arise, revealing truths about the depths of your mind that injure your pride. Do not try to suppress these or push them away. Just let them go naturally, and return to the breath. Alternately, good and virtuous thoughts might arise. Do not tell stories about them or try to hold on to them. Just let them go naturally, and return to the breath. Try to be patient and accepting towards whatever arises in meditation. There is no need to rush. Just let your experience be whatever it naturally is, and keep coming back to the breath. (These and other valuable pieces of advice about the attitude to take while practicing meditation can be found in Gunaratana 2002, 39–43.)

In the *Discourse on Mindfulness of Breathing* (*ānāpāna-sati-sutta*), the Buddha said that, "when mindfulness of breathing is developed and cultivated, it is of great fruit and great benefit" (Ñāṇamoli and Bodhi 1995, 943). Today, many psychologists would agree: the cultivation of mindfulness is increasingly becoming recognized as a powerful way to alleviate and heal some kinds of psychological problems and the suffering they cause. But you do not necessarily need to take anyone else's word for this. The Buddha described his teaching as *ehipassiko* – "a come-and-see kind of thing." He encouraged those who would listen to try his path of practice for themselves and see its results in their own experience. He was confident that they would find, as he did, that practice of this kind is highly effective in relieving the suffering of human life and opening the door to joy and peace.

Walking Meditation

The most powerful forms of walking meditation usually involve dramatically slowing down the pace of walking. One effective method is to synchronize your steps with your breathing. Take one step on the in-breath and one step on the out-breath. Do not force your breathing to keep pace with your walking; instead, adjust the speed of walking to the natural flow of the breath. Do not leave your feet on the ground for long periods of time, occasionally taking a quick step. Instead, slow down the entire process of walking, so that one of your feet is off the ground most of the time. This way of walking requires you to bring attention into the subtle movements of your legs and feet, which is very much the intention of the practice. Make an effort to keep some of your attention continuously resting in the sensations you are experiencing in your feet. When you notice that you have lost touch with your feet, gently bring attention back to them.

Walking meditation can be done more quickly if you have somewhere to go. Just make sure to keep some attention in the sensations in your feet. You can move at a reasonable pace and still keep the breath and your steps together if you take two steps on the in-breath and two steps on the out-breath. Or you can take attention off the breath, and just make sure some attention is present in the sensations in your feet. In this way, you can include meditation practice in your everyday life without taking time away from other activities: just convert some of the walking you would need to do anyway, for practical purposes or for exercise, into meditation. This can be a major enhancement to your practice, but it is not exactly a free lunch: unless you are regularly doing sitting meditation as well, it will be very difficult to sustain your attention while walking, and your intention to do walking meditation will bring fewer benefits.

There are a number of variants on the basic practice of walking meditation. In one charming version, you imagine that the world, like a giant beach ball, is rolling underneath you as you walk. In other words, while paying attention to the sensations in your feet, you change your perspective such that you are not moving; the earth is turning under you, moved by your steps.

Though the practice of walking meditation requires keeping some attention in your feet, as well as the attention involved in bringing your feet and breath into the same rhythm, nothing prevents you from also noticing the scene around you. Objects that catch your eye may begin chains of thought that distract you. When you notice this, simply bring your attention back to the sensations in your feet. But, of course, you need to have your eyes open so that you can see where you are going! And if you can be aware of visual sensations without being distracted from your feet, then it is possible to develop a whole new level of appreciation of nature. Through this practice, you can cultivate mindfulness and stable attention while enjoying the vivid beauty of a world seen with less attachment and distortion.

Through resting meditation practices such as mindfulness of breathing, it is possible to nourish and strengthen the capacity for attention. The impact of meditation begins to be felt in daily life when clear, stable attention becomes available to improve the quality of engagement with other activities. One of the best ways to create the conditions for this change is walking meditation. Through walking meditation, we can learn to bring attention to a simple activity. In this way, we can gradually learn to be more mindful in all aspects of life.

Meditation on Lovingkindness (*metta-bhāvanā*)

Sit in a comfortable posture with your back straight, as before. Close your eyes and think of someone towards whom you have strong, uncomplicated positive feelings. Some people can use one of their parents for this purpose – but not all of us are so fortunate! A suitable person would be someone who has showed you genuine kindness at some point in the past, such as a teacher or very good friend. A young child would not be a good choice. A living person is a better choice than a deceased person. Do not choose someone towards whom you are sexually attracted.

Visualize this person in your mind and, with your thoughts, wish for this person to have every kind of good fortune and well-being you can think of, focusing on the wish for the person to be happy. So, for example, if this person's name is George, you might think:

> May George be happy. May George have health, good fortune, and long life. May he not have to be sick, or sad, or in pain, but may he be happy. May good things happen to George. May his dreams come true. May he live in harmony with all those around him. May George find peace. May he find joy. May he find real, lasting happiness. May George be happy.

Continue arousing this series of wishes for several minutes. This is the first stage of the meditation.

For the second stage of the meditation, choose a friend: someone towards whom you have positive feelings, but not as strong as those for the person you pictured in the first stage. Now, visualize your friend and, just as before, wish for this person to have every kind of good fortune and well-being, focusing on the wish for the person to be happy.

In the third stage, choose an acquaintance: someone whom you have met, and can picture, but towards whom you have no strong feelings one way or another. Proceed as before.

In the fourth stage, visualize someone you do not like, someone towards whom you have negative feelings. This could be either someone who has caused difficulties for you in your personal or professional life or a public figure of whom you do not approve. Wish for this person to have every kind of good fortune and well-being. This may sound quite difficult. But if you do the meditation properly, the emotional momentum built up during the earlier stages will make it remarkably easy for you to wish happiness even to your worst enemy.

In the fifth stage, visualize waves of lovingkindness emanating from your body and spreading out in all directions. Imagine that everyone touched by these waves will feel just a little bit happier. The waves gradually spread out to cover the whole earth. Visualize many different groups of people and animals from all over the planet and wish for all of them to live in peace and harmony, to be safe and happy. At the conclusion of this stage, imagine that the waves of lovingkindness spread out in all directions, throughout the entire universe. Think, "May all sentient beings, no matter how far away or strange, be happy."

In the sixth stage, bring the waves of lovingkindness back to the center and wish for yourself to be happy. Form the wish that you yourself will receive all types of good fortune and well-being. The practice concludes here.

The meditation on lovingkindness is not a prayer. You are not asking any being outside yourself to provide good fortune and well-being to others, but merely wishing for this to occur. Doing this meditation most likely will not magically cause others to become happy. What this practice does do is reduce the influence of anger and hatred in your personality, replacing these emotions with the immeasurable, non-reactive emotion of lovingkindness. Over time, the intensity of the negative feelings that you have towards others who have harmed or displeased you will diminish. If this practice is done consistently, then feelings of lovingkindness will begin to appear spontaneously, without effort, when you encounter other beings, such as birds flying through the sky. This is the primary benefit of the meditation: it gradually brings about a profound change in your emotional responses to others.

The meditation on lovingkindness has several other benefits as well. Many people report that the meditation on lovingkindness makes it easier to fall asleep. One reason for this benefit may be that intense anger can keep people awake; by weakening the anger, this form of practice may be able to alleviate insomnia. Many people also greatly enjoy the meditation on lovingkindness. The emotional state it produces, an opening to everything, is often wonderfully pleasurable and can have a powerful positive effect on one's mood.

Lovingkindness practice can also gradually improve your relationship with other people around you. Some Buddhist texts even claim that practitioners who radiate lovingkindness towards all living beings will be safe from attack by dangerous wild creatures (see Harvey 2000, 170–1). The fact that you approach a situation with lovingkindness does not guarantee that it will turn out as you expect or intend. But, over time, if you treat others with an attitude of lovingkindness, they will tend to reciprocate, and what may have seemed like intractable dislikes and disagreements can soften and become workable.

How Does Meditation Work?

Buddhists make many claims about the beneficial effects of meditation practice. Through what processes are these effects thought to be produced? I have already made some preliminary remarks in this direction. This section will explore in more detail the ways in which meditation may be able to provide the benefits claimed for it.

Ken McLeod draws a helpful distinction between the *effects* and the *results* of meditation practice. The short-term effects of meditation can vary quite dramatically from one session to another. Sometimes meditation produces wonderful feelings of peace, joy, and bliss. But it is also possible to emerge from a meditation session feeling drained by the effort to remain present with severe emotional pain, or buffeted by the waves of rapidly changing emotions. Over time, however, long-term results gradually emerge. In McLeod's formulation, "The results are an increase in the level of attention, the ability to stay in attention in both formal practice and daily life, and less reactivity in our lives" (McLeod 2002, 59).

Of the processes by which the long-term practice of meditation leads to results, one of the most important, both philosophically and practically, is disidentification. Meditation allows the practitioner to stop seeing what is not self as a self or as belonging to a self. The Buddha briefly described this process, and suggested its importance, in the *Discourse on the Simile of the Snake* (*alagaddūpama-sutta*). There we read:

> "Bhikkhus, what do you think? If people carried off the grass, sticks, branches, and leaves in this Jeta Grove, or burned them, or did what they liked with them, would you think: 'People are carrying us off or burning us or doing what they like with us'?" – "No, venerable sir. Why not? Because that is neither our self nor what belongs to our self." – "So too, bhikkhus, whatever is not yours, abandon it; when you have abandoned it, that will lead to your welfare and happiness for a long time. What is it that is not yours? Material form is not yours . . . Feeling is not yours . . . Perception is not yours . . . Formations are not yours . . . Consciousness is not yours. Abandon it. When you have abandoned it, that will lead to your welfare and happiness for a long time."
>
> (Ñāṇamoli and Bodhi 1995, 235)

Disidentification has many facets and often proceeds over an extended period of time. One aspect pertains to the psychological processes that produce our thoughts. Many people identify with these processes, regarding thinking as a form of volitional action. But the attempt to sit in meditation quickly discredits this view. If you tell the processes that produce your thoughts to stop doing so, they will not obey you. Over time, it is possible to recognize this very clearly; instead of seeing thoughts as actions or as manifestations of your true self, you can come to see them as more like the weather. They appear independently of your intention and disappear without the necessity for any active effort to get rid of them. Thoughts come and go; you do not make them, and you do not have to hold on to them.

Just as meditation helps you disidentify from the process of the production of thoughts, in the same way it can help you disidentify from recurrent patterns of thought and emotion. These habitual patterns are central to how we define character or personality, both in ourselves and in others; but, unfortunately, they can be destructive. Recurring greed makes us think that getting and holding on to things will make us happy, even though it will not. Recurring anger makes us think that the people around us are wicked and malevolent, even though they are not. Recurring fear makes us see perfectly harmless people and situations as posing terrible threats to us, even though they do not. If you think of the deluded perceptions generated by these patterns as *yours*, or as *just the way you are*, it will be extremely difficult to see through them. But if you recognize the patterns as not being who you are – if you disidentify from them – then it will be much easier simply to experience them without being taken in by them.

As the *Discourse on the Simile of the Snake* suggests, disidentification also weakens the tendency to anger and strengthens patient endurance and equanimity. Our bodies naturally deteriorate over time, becoming older and sicker. If you identify your body as your self, this process can be demoralizing and depressing in the extreme. But if you can disidentify from the body, a gentle, patient acceptance of the aging process becomes possible. Similarly, disagreement about beliefs and values is pervasive in today's complex world. If you identify with your beliefs, regarding them as part of who you are, then a challenge from others who disagree can feel like a threat to your survival. But if you can hold your beliefs easily, not identifying them as part of your self, it becomes possible to disagree gently and respectfully with others – and that, in turn, makes mutual understanding and mutual learning far more likely.

The simplest way in which serious, long-term practice helps bring about disidentification is that it leads to short periods of freedom from habitual patterns. If you are so used to reacting to experience in a certain way that you cannot imagine any other way to be, then it will be natural to identify that way of reacting as part of who you are. But if you know what it is like to relate to your experience in a different way, even for a brief period of time, then that identification will lose its seductive power. You will know and see: "This is not mine, this I am not, this is not my self" (Ñāṇamoli and Bodhi 1995, 232). This way of knowing and seeing is a form of freedom. The thoughts and emotions generated by the pattern keep telling you to do things, but you do not have to do them.

This entire process is encouraged and helped along by an unappealing-sounding power: simple boredom. You sit in meditation with nowhere to hide, while thoughts and emotions arise without restriction. The same thoughts appear again and again, some quite disturbing, others seemingly very normal – the fabric of your life. The mere fact of repetition gradually weakens the power these thoughts and emotions have over you. You are less likely to be taken in and more likely to think, "Oh, *that* again." Simply being present with the thoughts as they arise gradually dissipates their emotional energy. And the tediousness of the repetition reinforces the lesson: whatever it is that keeps bringing this boring, dreadful thought into my awareness, it certainly is not me!

Through disidentification and boredom, then, sitting meditation gradually and naturally weakens habitual, reactive patterns, reducing both their emotional intensity and their ability to take you over and control your actions. But is it possible actually to dismantle these patterns? Buddhists claim that this is possible, and there are a number of different methods taught in different lineages for accomplishing this goal. The most important of these depend entirely on mindfulness.

Mindfulness of body is the ability to maintain vivid, present-moment awareness of the state and position of the various parts of the body, and of the information coming in through the senses, while engaged in various kinds of activities. Breathing mindfulness meditation helps to develop this ability, since the heart of the practice is to let go, again and again, of thoughts, memories, and daydreams, coming back to the present moment. Moreover, clear awareness of the breath is itself one form of mindfulness of body. But a form of practice that is especially well suited to the cultivation of mindfulness of body is walking meditation. In this form of practice, the sensations in the feet are the focus of the meditation, but you also need to attend to visual sensations, so as not to bump into objects in your environment. Thus walking meditation effectively builds the capacity to get in touch with the details of what is actually happening now, in and around your body.

To many people, mindfulness of body may seem to be an obscure and not particularly important ability, not to mention one which is extremely difficult and demanding to develop. However, in the Pāli canon, the Buddha makes some remarkable claims about this capacity. For example, we read in the *Discourse on Mindfulness of the Body* (*kāyagatāsati-sutta*):

> "Bhikkhus, when anyone has developed and cultivated mindfulness of the body, Māra cannot find an opportunity or a support in him. Suppose a man were to throw a light ball of string at a door-panel made entirely of heartwood. What do you think, bhikkhus? Would that light ball of string find entry through that door-panel made entirely of heartwood?" – "No, venerable sir." "So too, bhikkhus, when anyone has developed and cultivated mindfulness of the body, Māra cannot find an opportunity or a support in him."
>
> (Ñāṇamoli and Bodhi 1995, 955)

In this passage, as often in Buddhist writings, Māra functions as a personification of the obstacles that interfere with the practitioner's path to freedom from suffering. So in this passage the Buddha is telling the monks, or bhikkhus, who form his audience that, if they can develop mindfulness of body, these obstacles will not be able to function, and their further spiritual progress will be unobstructed.

The discourse goes on to list ten benefits of the thorough and repeated practice of mindfulness of body, culminating in the complete liberation of a saint (P. *arahant*). One of the more preliminary benefits is particularly interesting:

> One bears cold and heat, hunger and thirst, and contact with gadflies, mosquitoes, wind, the sun, and creeping things; one endures ill-spoken, unwelcome words and arisen bodily feelings that are painful, racking, sharp, piercing, disagreeable, distressing, and menacing to life.
>
> (Ñāṇamoli and Bodhi 1995, 957)

How could it be that mindfulness of body would have these benefits?

Several contemporary spiritual teachers have discussed a framework within which it is possible to make sense of these remarkable claims. This framework involves the claim that there are complex and subtle connections between the position and sensations of the body and the thoughts and emotions of the mind. Mental disturbances also show up in the body, as when stress leads to muscular tension. And changes in bodily posture have mental effects, as when deliberately moving your mouth into a smile actually makes you feel better.

Another claim that is crucial to understanding this model is that the psychological processes that lead to suffering require distraction in order to function and cannot operate in the presence of stable, clear attention. (This thesis is central to McLeod 2002; see especially 207–13. The discussion that follows draws on this important work in several places.) Unfortunately, most people's lives are full to overflowing with distractions of various kinds. Moreover, emotional pain is mirrored in the body by intense physical sensations, which are activated when the relevant emotions are triggered. A mild but extremely common example of this would be butterflies in the stomach caused by nervousness. It is quite difficult to experience painful, psychologically induced sensations with full attention, and so various mental processes generate distractions to protect us from having to experience them. Unfortunately these distractions take us away from our actual experiences, lead to self-destructive avoidance behaviors, and also prevent us from healing the underlying emotional wounds. Such problems accumulate over time, making us more and more rigid and reactive and narrowing the range of situations we can deal with skillfully.

Mindfulness of body reverses this process. Walking or sitting in attention can put you in touch with bliss and beauty, but it also makes you aware of physical and emotional pain. Gradually, you develop the capacity to feel more and more intense sensations without having to distract yourself from them or find a way to avoid them. This is why the *Discourse on Mindfulness of Body* tells us that this capacity leads to the ability to bear unpleasant sensations. But when you can bear unpleasant sensations, you can bring attention into reactive patterns and the reactive emotions they generate. And if you can bring clear, vivid attention to bear on them, then eventually they will begin to dissolve. As the patterns dissolve and the associated emotions dissipate, it becomes possible for the mind to rest more stably than before.

Numerous canonical Buddhist texts describe stages of meditation practice in which the mind rests more and more deeply. One important framework of stages, discussed repeatedly in the Pāli canon, is the four *jhānas* (Skt *dhyānas*). The first *jhāna* is "accompanied by applied and sustained thought, with rapture and pleasure born of seclusion" (Ñāṇamoli and Bodhi 1995, 105). Unfortunately the terms *vitakka* and *vicāra*, translated here as "applied and sustained thought," are obscure, and their exact meaning is controversial among scholars. The second *jhāna* "has self-confidence and singleness of mind without applied and sustained thought, with rapture and pleasure born of concentration." In the transition to the third *jhāna*, rapture disappears, but bodily pleasure remains; the third *jhāna* is characterized by equanimity and mindfulness. According to the texts, the fourth *jhāna* "has neither-pain-nor-pleasure and purity of mindfulness due to equanimity." It is important to note that the disappearance of rapture and pleasure is an aspect of the transition to deeper, more advanced states of meditation. Buddhist teachers often emphasize the importance of not getting attached to the bliss that can arise from meditative stability. Such bliss is just an experience, nothing more; it may be wonderful but, like all experiences, it is impermanent. It is not a solution to the problem of suffering.

The fourth *jhāna* is not the highest state of meditation that can be attained. Canonical texts allude to four other states, even more advanced than the *jhānas*. In these states, often known as the formless absorptions, the mind rests so deeply that the practitioner is no longer even aware that she has a body. These states are known as the base of infinite space, the base of infinite consciousness, the base of nothingness, and the base of neither-perception-nor-non-perception (see Ñāṇamoli and Bodhi 1995, 85). Yet Buddhists claim that, although these states are exceptionally peaceful, subtle, and difficult to obtain, they do not constitute liberation.

The historical Buddha Śākyamuni did not invent meditation. In an important scriptural text, the *Noble Search* (*ariya-pariyesanā-sutta*), the Buddha describes how, while still a bodhisatta – someone seeking Awakening – he learned the practice of meditation from two teachers, known in Pāli as Āḷāra Kālāma and Uddaka Rāmaputta (Ñāṇamoli and Bodhi 1995, 256–9). Āḷāra Kālāma based his teachings on his personal experience of the base of nothingness, whereas Uddaka Rāmaputta took as his foundation his father's experience of the base of neither-perception-nor-non-perception. When the Buddha, following the teachings he was given, attained these formless absorptions, he was offered positions of leadership within these spiritual communities. But he was not satisfied: the meditative states he had attained, though peaceful and still, did not represent a definitive solution to the problem of cyclic existence. The peace and bliss they brought was impermanent and, when it ended, struggle and suffering would return. Leaving these teachers behind, the future Buddha sought for, and eventually attained, "the sorrowless supreme security from bondage, Nibbāna" (ibid., 260).

At the end of the *sutta*, the Buddha describes the path to liberation of a Buddhist saint. After reaching and surpassing all the stages of practice that the Buddha had learned from his teachers, the practitioner "enters upon and abides in the cessation of perception and feeling. And his taints are destroyed by his seeing with wisdom" (Ñāṇamoli and Bodhi 1995, 268).

Drawing on passages like this one, the Buddhist tradition came to draw a distinction between two different forms or aspects of meditation: resting (P. *samatha*; Skt *śamatha*) and insight (P. *vipassanā*; Skt *vipaśyanā*). Buddhists were happy to recognize that members of other religious traditions, such as followers of the various sects of Hinduism, could develop the ability to rest very deeply in meditation. This kind of resting would have many important benefits, both in this life and in future lives. But without insight, they claimed, it was not possible to become completely free from the suffering of cyclic existence.

Resting and insight are not independent of each other. One metaphor for their relationship, found in various Indic texts, both Buddhist and non-Buddhist, involves seeing by the light of an open lamp. If there is any significant wind, and especially if the wind is changing direction quickly, the lamp will waver and flicker, and it will not be possible to see much by its light. But if the air is still, the flame will be relatively stable, and those relying on its light will be able to see the details of objects. Here the rapidly shifting wind corresponds to the distractible, unsteady quality of untrained, ordinary awareness.

Clear, stable attention, the intended result of resting meditation practice, corresponds to the stillness that makes it possible to see.

It follows that there is an asymmetric relationship between these two qualities. First, the practitioner must cultivate the capacity to rest. Then, that capacity will make possible the genuine practice of insight. This picture was adopted not only by the Theravāda tradition but also by most other Buddhist lineages. However, I note in passing that the Zen tradition is unique in rejecting this picture and the distinction on which it rests. Hui-Neng, the Sixth Grand Master of Zen, taught his students:

> Do not make the mistake of considering stabilization [resting] and insight to be separate. Stabilization and insight are one entity, not two. Stabilization is the substance of insight, insight is the function of stabilization . . . Students of the Way, do not say there is a difference between stabilization coming first and then producing insight, and insight coming first and then producing stabilization. Those who entertain this view are dualistic in their doctrine.
>
> (Cleary 1998, 31)

In the Zen tradition, insight meditation practice often takes the form of enigmatic spiritual sayings and questions known as *kōans*. But the fundamental Zen sitting practice, zazen, is not classified as exclusively either resting or insight meditation; it could be said to be both, or perhaps neither.

Other practices besides resting meditation can help make insight possible. The cultivation of certain emotions can be an effective support for insight practice. These include the qualities known as the Four Divine Abidings (P. *brahma-vihāra*) or the Four Immeasurables: lovingkindness, compassion, joy, and equanimity. In the Theravāda tradition, lovingkindness is most commonly used for this purpose. Most of the time, strong emotions have a powerfully disturbing effect on the mind, like a storm on the ocean. With the buffeting of the winds and waves, the mind becomes very confused and cannot see deeply. But, although it is an emotion, lovingkindness does not have this kind of effect; it can become quite intense without disturbing the calm of the mind. This, in turn, means that the emotional energy of lovingkindness can make possible higher levels of attention that lead, in turn, to the ability to see. In the Tibetan tradition, not only the Four Immeasurables but also feelings of devotion to one's spiritual teacher are used to enhance the power of attention.

The point of insight practices is to know, through direct experience, the way things actually are. But how can we be confident that such knowing is actually possible? What, if any, is the epistemic value of meditative practice?

Does Meditation Lead to Knowledge?

Buddhists regularly claim that meditation produces certain kinds of knowledge that cannot be obtained in any other way. For instance, the *Discourse on Mindfulness of Body* tells us that "anyone who has developed and cultivated mindfulness of the body has included within himself whatever wholesome states there are that partake of true knowledge" (Ñāṇamoli and Bodhi 1995, 954). Referring to meditation, the *Discourse at Kīṭāgiri* says, "resolutely striving, he realises with the body the ultimate truth and sees it by penetrating it with wisdom" (ibid., 583). The *Discourse to Subha* defends the existence of "distinctions in knowledge and vision worthy of the noble ones" made possible by meditation, and compares those who lack such abilities to the blind (ibid., 811–12). Such citations could be multiplied at length; the message they express is one of the central truth claims of the Buddhist religion.

There are, however, important reasons why some would doubt Buddhist assertions about the epistemic value of meditation. Supporters of empiricism might argue that we cannot possibly gain knowledge simply by sitting on a cushion and watching the breath. In order to find out how things work, we need to be active in the world, devising controlled experiments that follow scientific procedures and using critical reasoning to evaluate the results of those experiments and integrate them into theories. Since Buddhist meditation apparently does not involve any of these kinds of activity, and meditation instructions encourage us to let go of conceptual thoughts as they arise, how could such a practice possibly lead to knowledge?

Insofar as this objection is motivated by a commitment to an epistemological view in the empiricist tradition, it becomes relevant to note that major figures in that tradition, such as Locke and Hume, believed that we could gain knowledge about the mind through a careful examination of inner experience. If it is true that meditation makes available certain kinds of inner experience that would not otherwise be possible, then those forms of experience might possibly result in new knowledge.

At the same time, many contemporary researchers in psychology may object to relying on a method of introspection to learn about the mind. In the past, philosophers and armchair psychologists, relying on introspection, have arrived at widely varying conclusions; they have also missed basic facts about how minds work that can be established by simple experiments. Psychologists might argue that introspection simply allows people to project their hypotheses and presuppositions onto their experience and does not help us learn new truths about how the mind works. Only careful experiments, carried out with scientific rigor and from a third-person point of view, can reveal such truths.

Buddhists could reply by drawing a distinction between trained and untrained introspection. In most people, they could argue, the faculty of attention is weak and undeveloped, and, as a result, attempts at serious introspection will typically be overwhelmed by various forms of distraction. But those who, through meditation practice, reduce the intensity and frequency of distractions and gradually develop their capacity for attention are eventually able to look at mental phenomena and see them as they actually are.

A canonical description of the development of an enhanced capacity for attention, and of the results this brings, is found in the *Discourse on Fear and Dread* (*bhaya-bherava-sutta*). Describing his own experience on the night of his Awakening, the Buddha says:

> When my concentrated mind was thus purified, bright, unblemished, rid of imperfection, malleable, wieldy, steady, and attained to imperturbability, I directed it to knowledge of the destruction of the taints. I directly knew as it actually is: "This is suffering"; I directly knew as it actually is: "This is the origin of suffering"; I directly knew as it actually is: "This is

> the cessation of suffering"; I directly knew as it actually is: "This is the way leading to the cessation of suffering." I directly knew as it actually is: "These are the taints"; I directly knew as it actually is: "This is the origin of the taints"; I directly knew as it actually is: "This is the cessation of the taints"; I directly knew as it actually is: "This is the way leading to the cessation of the taints."
>
> (Ñāṇamoli and Bodhi 1995, 106)

The first four elements of the list of what the Buddha claimed to have known are, of course, the Four Noble Truths, which constitute the most fundamental doctrine of Buddhism. This teaching is thus held to arise neither from rational analysis nor from divine revelation but, rather, from direct meditative experience.

The obvious question to ask now is whether Buddhists assert only that the discovery of the Four Noble Truths occurred in the context of meditative experience, or whether they go further to argue that the justification of these basic Buddhist claims also depends on meditative experience. Now, in the case of the First Noble Truth, no special kind of meditative expertise is necessary to become confident of its accuracy. The First Noble Truth, that all beings in cyclic existence undergo some form of suffering (P. *dukkha*), either manifest or subtle, is a pervasive feature of ordinary experience. This term *dukkha* is often translated as "suffering," but other aspects of its meaning can be captured by alternate translations such as "struggle" and "unsatisfactoriness." Now for those of us who are not buddhas or saints, even in our best moments, there is an underlying feeling of dissatisfaction: "Is this all there is?" Our daily lives are filled with greater or lesser degrees of stress, anxiety, worry, frustration, desire, anger, and other manifestations of *dukkha*. It is easy, then, to establish the existence of the problem diagnosed by the First Noble Truth. Moreover, the Second Noble Truth, that the cause of this suffering is craving, is plausible on an intellectual level: we struggle against and reject our experience because we want it to be different.

The Third Noble Truth is in a different category. It is the claim that the cessation of suffering is possible through the cessation of craving. Even if craving is indeed the cause of suffering, this does not imply the possibility of the cessation of suffering. Craving might be an ineliminable part of human life itself; it might be that we can cease to crave only through physical death. The only people who can know the Third Noble Truth with certainty are those who have actually experienced what it is like to live without suffering. This is possible only through very extensive meditation practice. The rest of us must infer, from the outward behavior of those who have realized the truth for themselves, the truth of their claim to be free – at least until we have found something similar in our own experience. Thus, in relation to this particular Buddhist truth claim, genuine knowledge of it is inseparable from the existence of meditators, at a minimum, and, more ambitiously, from the knower's own meditation practice.

More generally, Buddhist texts identify three levels of "wisdom" or "discernment" (P. *paññā*; Skt *prajñā*). Wisdom can be based on study, on reflection, or on meditation. It is possible to have accurate knowledge of some statement or description as a result of having heard it in a lecture or read it in a book. If the source of information on which you depend is reliable, and you have justified confidence in the information you have received, your belief would normally count as knowledge. But the level of your understanding may not be very high. If you have thought carefully about the topic, explored the evidence for and implications of a claim in detail, and made inferential connections between that claim and the rest of what you believe, then that claim will be a more secure and more useful part of your web of belief than if you accept the claim merely on the authority of another. This is what is meant by wisdom based on reflection.

One form of wisdom based on meditation is a thorough assimilation and incorporation of a truth into your entire way of relating to the world as a result of having rested the mind on that truth during meditation, letting it sink deeply into the lower levels of awareness. To understand what this process might involve, consider the fact of inevitable death. We all know that we are going to die. Yet it is widely recognized that many people go about their activities ignoring, more or less completely, the implications of this basic truth of life. (For a powerful Western presentation of this issue, see Tolstoy's famous novella *The Death of Ivan Ilyich*.) Buddhism teaches that genuinely recognizing the inevitability of death and allowing ourselves to appreciate its significance will have a major effect on our motivational structure and on what we consider important or worth doing. Such recognition and appreciation, in turn, can arise from practicing the meditation on death and impermanence. There are a number of techniques for this meditation, but the basic practice is to remind yourself, over and over, and in different ways, of the simple fact of impermanence in general and your own death in particular. Though you gain no additional information by this practice, the effect on your way of life could be quite dramatic. It is plausible, moreover, that, through a practice of this kind, your way of thinking can become more aligned with the way things actually are and, therefore, more realistic and accurate.

The wisdom that arises from Buddhist meditation can develop through a gradual process of maturation, as just described, but it can also appear through a sudden flash of insight. Both Theravāda and Mahāyāna traditions refer to a particularly significant type of experience that transforms a practitioner's entire approach to life, changing an ordinary person into a Noble One. The Theravāda tradition calls someone who undergoes this transformation a Stream-Winner (P. *sotāpanna*). When discussing Stream-Winners, texts in the Pāli canon typically describe them as having abandoned three fetters: the false view of a real self (*sak-kāya-diṭṭhi*), doubt (*vicikicchā*), and attachment to vows and moral discipline (*sīla-bbata-parāmāsa*) (see Walshe 1995, 291; and Rhys Davids and Stede 1997, 656). On the Mahāyāna path, these same three fetters are abandoned by attaining the first of the ten Bodhisattva Stages (Skt *bhūmi*) – again, through a transformative experience of insight. This experience involves directly seeing both the Four Noble Truths and the absence of any real self.

On reflection, it makes sense that an experience of this kind could overcome the cognitive problems known as the three fetters. Powerful and persuasive arguments can be given for the absence of any real, substantial self. Yet the innate tendency to believe in a self is so strong that even someone who has been convinced by these arguments is likely still to feel the nagging question "But must not I, somehow, really exist as a thing? Must not there be something that is me, after all?" A direct experience of *being no one* can accomplish what intellectual arguments cannot: it can bring about genuine confidence in the view of non-self and the actual abandonment of the false view of a real self. Since you cannot know what you do not even believe, this represents an advance in knowledge for someone who finds the view of non-self to be utterly persuasive intellectually and yet impossible to believe on an emotional level.

In the list of the three fetters, "doubt" refers primarily to doubt about the possibility of Awakening (*bodhi*). Indeed, Buddhists describe Awakening in such glowing and superlative terms that those with no relevant experience might have good reason to doubt that such a state is possible. But if you are suddenly catapulted into a very high level of consciousness that is even partly free from the illusion of self, then, even after the energy and vividness of that experience has faded, you will know that a profound transformation of consciousness can be achieved, since you have experienced such a transformation yourself. At this point, it makes sense that the practitioner would no longer have reason to doubt the possibility of Awakening.

Moreover, such an experience makes it clear to the one who has it that simply following some set of rules or practices is just not going to be sufficient to achieve true freedom. Self-discipline can be valuable in making spiritual progress possible, but by itself, without the ability to rest the mind deeply in meditation and without the cultivation of experiential insight, it cannot lead to the end of suffering. So direct experience of the power of seeing things as they are, free from the illusion of self, will lead to abandoning the third fetter as well, that of attachment to vows and moral discipline.

As practitioners progress through the stages of meditative experience, Buddhist texts claim that they gain extraordinary powers of various kinds, including the ability to know what is going on in the minds of others. We may want to dismiss some claims of this kind as relics of the pre-modern cultural context in which Buddhism developed. Yet the experience of many students is that advanced Buddhist meditators are often astonishingly perceptive. We do not need to assume any kind of magic in order to explain how this might be true. I have been attempting to describe how meditation leads, in various ways, to self-knowledge. Accompanying this self-knowledge is a heightened empathy that puts the practitioner in touch with what others are thinking and feeling. Mindfulness makes it possible to pick up small, subtle cues that distracted people would miss. And, since the process of suffering operates in the same general way in everyone, knowing how your own mind works can make it possible to perceive, intuitively and quickly, why someone else is reacting in a certain way. These skills take a long time and much effort to develop, but they are not mythology. They are real human possibilities that have been actualized by people we can meet and with whom we can talk.

Buddhist philosophers often defend their views with powerful and sophisticated arguments. Many actual Buddhists rely heavily on their own trust and faith in particular teachers who have gone far down the path. Yet, in the final analysis, the most important Buddhist truth claims depend neither on reason nor on authority. Any of us can know them directly in our own experience, if we are willing to invest the necessary time and effort in meditation practice. Many people have tried meditation, only to give it up quickly when they realize just how emotionally demanding the practice is. Yet, of those who have pursued meditation seriously for a long time, very few have regretted it. You do not need to rely on anyone else's testimony to know the benefits of meditation. After only a few sessions, you can experience some of the basic ones for yourself. And, if you pursue the practice over months or years, you can begin to see changes that you may not presently even be able to imagine. Some people are simply not ready to engage with meditation in a serious way. But if you have the courage, the perseverance, and the patience to meditate, nothing will do more to enrich your life. As the Buddha said,

> Your worst enemy cannot harm you
> As much as your own thoughts, unguarded.
> But once mastered,
> No one can help you as much,
> Not even your father or your mother.
>
> (Byrom 2001, 32)

References

Byrom, Thomas (2001). *The Dhammapada: The Sayings of the Buddha*. New York: Bell Tower.

Cleary, Thomas (1998). *The Sutra of Hui-Neng, Grand Master of Zen*. Boston: Shambhala.

Gunaratana, Bhante Henepola (2002). *Mindfulness in Plain English*. Boston: Wisdom.

Harvey, Peter (2000). *An Introduction to Buddhist Ethics*. Cambridge: Cambridge University Press.

McLeod, Kenneth (2002). *Wake Up to Your Life: Discovering the Buddhist Path of Attention*. San Francisco: HarperCollins.

Ñāṇamoli, Bhikkhu, and Bodhi, Bhikkhu (trans.) (1995). *The Middle Length Discourses of the Buddha*. Boston: Wisdom.

Rhys Davids, T. W., and Stede, William (1997). *The Pali–English Dictionary*. New Delhi: Asian Educational Services.

Tolstoy, Leo (2011). *The Death of Ivan Ilyich*. Trans. Robert Bain. New York: Tribeca Books.

Walshe, Maurice (1995). *The Long Discourses of the Buddha*. Boston: Wisdom.

37

Seeing Mind, Being Body

Contemplative Practice and Buddhist Epistemology

ANNE CAROLYN KLEIN

Overview

From the earliest days of Buddhist teachings, it was made clear that neither the teaching itself, nor the realization of it, was a matter simply of speaking words or of understanding them. Refuge, for example, is something Buddhists recite every day. Yet refuge is not just words. It is an experience born of learning, reflection, and the wisdom of meditation that these make possible. This wisdom, though widely described as inconceivable and inexpressible, is capable of becoming fully evident. The practices that make it evident go beyond texts to include posture, chanting, movement, imagination, the performing and visual arts, ethical orientation, and more. These are related not only with words or ideas but also with the felt sense of the body, touching on the shifts in energy that accompany even the most elementary practices.

The wisdom of meditation requires the movement of energy. This energy is the mount or steed of consciousness and experientially all but indistinguishable from knowing itself. These energies must be part of what we consider when we look into the living practices of Buddhist communities.

Body as Dynamic Mystery

Meditation practices are the revered heart of Buddhist culture, even if relatively few persons seriously engage them. Meditation is the culmination of the three wisdoms of listening, reflection, and meditation.[1] Our way of inquiring into meditation and meditators will focus not only on their texts and instructions or even on the practices themselves. We take interest in the multiple dimensions of learning that these practices are meant to foster: physical, aesthetic, psychological, emotional, energetic, sensory, intentional, and attentional.

A Companion to Buddhist Philosophy, First Edition. Edited by Steven M. Emmanuel.

Meditation engages the entire being, not just the intellect. Above all, it engages the body and the body's intrinsic dynamism. We want to see how this dynamism participates in Buddhist practice, how it is a category that suffuses mind as well as body, and how it offers a fresh way to organize what we know of Buddhist thought and culture in relation to meditation.

Often overlooked, especially in non-esoteric contexts, are the energetic flows of the body. Yet these have a role to play in each of the three main areas of Buddhist practice: the cultivation of attention, of loving compassion, and of wisdom. Knowing that the texts, images, chants, and practices of Buddhist traditions address this energetic sensibility, we can read texts differently and understand contemplative practice differently as well. This difference is our focus here.

Using this bodily dynamism or energy as an organizing principle, I will be pointing out three things. First, this often overlooked or under-analyzed category is important for a fuller picture of Buddhist religious life. Second, its importance by no means undermines, and in fact extends, the significance of the philosophical import of Buddhist literature. Third, the significance of "energy" is not limited to esoteric Buddhism. To aid this discussion, I am introducing and exploring the new term "energetic sensibility" as a way of referring to the cluster of important Buddhist terms associated with the viscerally energetic or dynamic dimension of persons and their practices.

Persons and Practice

A full picture of the human organism to whom practices and instructions are addressed will include these energies, and such a picture is vital to success, both in practice and in academic contemplative studies. These are a significant category in every classic Buddhist iteration of what a human being is. When the narrative of the five *skandhas*, or aggregates, is used, the consciousness *skandha* is described as riding a wind-horse of energy. When a person is described in terms of the five elements – earth, water, fire, wind, and space – each of these elements finds its most subtle expression in a particular type of dynamism, or energy. These energies are crucial for achieving the kind of stability, expansiveness, or receptivity associated with certain contemplative practices.

All practice also involves body, speech, and mind. These are referred to in Buddhist literature as the "three gates" by which one accumulates karma or moves along the path to transcending karma. It is a crucial cultural given that "speech" here refers not simply to verbal expression but also to energy (Tb. *rlung*; Skt *prāṇa*; Ch. *ch'i*). No less an authority than the eighteenth-century scholar-poet-visionary Jigme Lingpa states concisely in one of his *Wisdom Chats* that "The essence of speech is energy."[2] From this, as well as from the oral commentary of contemporary Tibetan luminaries such as Chögyal Namkhai Norbu Rinpoche, we see that "speech" (Tb. *ngag*) as a category includes the energy or wind upon which speech rides and upon which the mind directing speech also always rides.

Such energy is intimately conflated with knowing, such that attention to the sensation itself is sufficient for sense or meaning to be present. Direct awareness of it is the province of the energetic sensibility, which is not separate from the steed of energy itself. This energetic sensibility[3] is indispensible to our understanding of how contemplative practices – and the texts, rituals, music, or contexts in which they are embedded – engage human being.

In terms of the five senses, the energetic sensibility integrates a subtle sense of touch with an awareness which is not interpretive but which simply and immediately knows what that touch signifies. A common example is butterflies in the stomach: you know immediately how that feels and what it means about your psycho-emotional state. On the other hand, a sense of expansiveness, of opening like a flower or entering a vast and quiet ocean, immediately impacts your sense not only of your mood but, potentially, of your very being. Buddhist physiology takes the tactile sense to be the underlying basis for experiencing the other senses. That the sense of touch is said to be the last to dissolve in the process of dying tells us that Tibetan physiology also regards it as very, very basic. Recent studies of touch, which science labels hapticity, likewise conclude that "Touch is the first sense to develop and a critical means of information acquisition and environmental manipulation" (Ackerman et al. 2010). All five senses – and mind itself – ride steeds of wind, called wind-horses, which themselves are sensed by the body consciousness and whose meaning is present to the energetic sensibility.[4]

Even more interesting for our purposes, this same scientific study also concludes that physical touch may create an ontological scaffold for the development of intrapersonal and interpersonal conceptual and metaphorical knowledge as well as a springboard for the application of this knowledge. In these ways we can see that, at least in a general sense, tactile cues significantly alter one's interpretation of events and sense of self. Something as simple as holding a heavy clipboard while interviewing another person is likely to make interviewers feel that their observations are more important than those of persons with lighter clipboards. Heavy objects also made job candidates appear more important, rough objects made social interactions feel more difficult, and hard objects increased rigidity in negotiations. In these ways tactile sensations are seen to influence higher social cognitive processing in specific ways as well.

Science already sees that we move from touch to cognitive sensations. Buddhist meditators also have this experience. For example, bringing continuous attention to the body within a settled state of concentration yields in time the palpable sense that the body is nothing but a fluctuating mass of sensations. This is a visceral knowing of impermanence, of interdependence, and of the lack of a stable, independent self. This information comes directly to the energetic sensibility without an intervening conceptual latticework. The energetic sensibility is also associated with intuitive responsiveness, such as a nurse or friend knowing exactly what kind of touch to apply to a body in pain (Goleman 1995, 83). No wonder that the in-depth cultivation of meditation sometimes leads to an increase in intuitive capacities, even, according to many classic texts, of clairvoyance. All this, though profoundly related to the body sense and body intelligence, requires a more careful articulation and appreciation of what is usually referred to as "the somatic."

Buddhist texts and Asian cultures make very clear that body, energy, and mind are all crucial to understanding, training, and optimizing the human organism. The principle of impermanence, basic to Buddhist teachings, is not only an intellectual assessment of the world but a knowing available to the entirety of the practitioner's being. From the cultivation of mindfulness in the *Foundations of Mindfulness Sūtra* to the bestowing of consecrating initiations in tantra, practices explicitly address themselves to the transformation of body, speech-energy, and mind. In introducing the energetic sensibility as a central category for our reflections on contemplative texts and practices, we find that we can link it with the full spectrum of actual currents palpable in the body.

This is an exciting time in religious studies for those of us interested in contemplative matters. We are still in the business of reading texts and researching cultures, but we are reading and researching differently. We are freer than ever to see these not only as linguistic productions or as nested strictly in the epistemological nexus of European post-Enlightenment concerns. We are encouraged to take emic categories as serious and as central. Above all, we are invited to juxtapose nuanced analyses of cultural construction with what Jorge Ferrer calls in his introduction to *Participatory Turn* "the mystery." This last, combined with postmodern and feminist emphases on embodiment and sacred immanence, also noted by Ferrer (Ferrer and Sherman 2008, 7), are particularly relevant to the material I want to bring forward here. In particular I note his comment that

> it is becoming increasingly plausible that epistemological frameworks that take into account a wider – and perhaps *deeper* – engagement with human faculties (not only discursive reason, but also intuition, imagination, somatic knowing, empathetic discernment, moral awareness, aesthetic sensibility, meditation and contemplation) may be critical in the assessment of many religious knowledge claims.
>
> (Ibid., 11)

This heady brew of issues actually comes to rest and resolution in the body itself. How can this be? What do we even mean by "body"? Buddhist theories of knowing and Buddhist practices of contemplation require that we understand beings as possessing three interfusing dimensions: the physical body, the energy that fuels verbal speech and all other expression, and mind. Epistemologies that too graphically or stringently separate mind and body – as Western orientations typically have done – or that omit the energetic dimension altogether will not be able to see clearly what is occurring in Buddhist texts or practices.

Contemplatives who read texts for instructions, inspiration, or insight regarding meditation read those texts on fire with their own seeking and searching and open to an ongoing process of attunement, reading not simply the text but also their own experiences in light of it. They read not only with their minds but also with their energetic sensibilities. In order to see this more explicitly we turn briefly to a few well-known passages of Buddhist literature. What I see – and what I invite you to investigate – is that the interactive latticework of concepts relevant to the body, its energies, and the impact of these on our state of mind offers a way to extend what Ferrer calls "empathetic discernment" towards Buddhist texts, practices, and cultural context.

First, we can note that three types of sources help clarify the energetic domain in Indian- and Tibetan-based Buddhist traditions. These are (1) classic Buddhist texts, from the early Indian tradition (especially those with observations on posture, mindfulness, the *skandhas*, or elements composing the body) to the later tantric descriptions of death, rebirth, and the experiences of the four intermediate states; (2) Buddhist – in this case mainly Tibetan – medical texts, including physiological and embryological descriptions of the body and its formation; and (3) actual meditation instructions derived from either of the above. These latter not only describe and identify energetic systems in the body; they also address them with the intention of impacting them in any of a number of ways. For example, instructions on cultivating mindfulness show how to strengthen and stabilize the energy supporting attention; instructions on compassion teach how to expand energy to include others; and instructions to meditate on specific areas of the body, or to identify with specific images, shapes, or deities, show how to undermine patterns of energy associated with one's ordinary reaction patterns.

The categories of "energy" known to the energetic sensibility and relevant to meditation are not limited to the human body. We have already seen that the category of bodily dynamism confounds common Western notions of body and mind as separate. Mind rides and is experientially indistinguishable from these dynamic currents, and the entire body is suffused by them. There is no division in the energetic sensibility and, from this perspective, none between mind and body, either.

The life-vitality (*bla*) known ubiquitously in Tibetan culture and beyond (related to the Turkish word *qut*) is found in living beings as well as in the landscape, especially in mountains and lakes. The "soul lake" or "spirit lake" of Yeshe Tsogyal, for example, is the place associated with her life-vitality, or *bla* (pronounced "la," rhymes with "ma"). This tells us something important about the world a traditional practitioner inhabits: living persons are not "set against a contrasting background," as Clifford Geertz famously put it, but participate with mountains and rivers in the overall dynamic of their shared environment. In other words, there is a readily available cultural category that bears some analogy to certain fruitional experiences of meditation.

For example, *bla* bypasses the Cartesian dualism through emphasizing an important resonance between "internal" and "external," between Yeshe Tsogyal, for example, and the lake that sprang up at her birth. This holistic dynamism is integral to, for example, the way Kālacakra practice involves transforming personal energies by synchronizing them with larger, impersonal ones that are their intimate analogues.[5] Here the body is revealed as part of an alternative universe that gradually displaces the ordinary universe in the experience of the most advanced practitioner. Displacement comes about not through a shift in ideas or even a deepening of concentration but through an opening, refining, and actual rechanneling of the body's deepest energies. Scholars and meditators alike appreciate this best by acknowledging the felt dynamism at the heart of this entire process. The body itself does not simply symbolize but actually expresses, and also deeply knows, the very mystery the practitioner encounters. How does acknowledging this energetic component change how we know a text?

Seeing Being

Practice and human beings are both dynamic. This dynamism is referenced in many of the most essential communications about meditation. Here are a few select examples from three main areas of practice.

The *Foundations of Mindfulness Sūtra*, a classic of the early Theravāda tradition and studied also in Tibet, opens with a rhetorical question about how meditation is to be done:

> 1. There is the case where a monk – having gone to the wilderness, to the shade of a tree, or to an empty building – sits down folding his legs crosswise, holding his body erect and setting mindfulness to the fore [lit: the front of the chest]. Always mindful, he breathes in; mindful he breathes out.[6]

Why this emphasis on posture? At least as discussed in Tibetan traditions, it is clear that posture is emphasized because of the way it impacts the movement of energies in the body. "When the body is straight, the channels are straight. When the channels are straight, the energies flow well within them. When the energies flow well, the mind riding them moves well."[7]

Taking one's seat with awareness integrates body, mind, and energy in a single move. Maintaining a straight spine facilitates the smooth movement of energy along the central corridor of the body. Being aware of subtle energetic fluctuations makes one less likely to become lost in thought, caught in concepts. The conceptual mind, skittering back and forth, remembering the past, anticipating the future, is rarely in the present.

To cultivate attention is to develop an energy stream that supports it. Such cultivation also refines the energetic sensibility, allowing ongoing awareness of the feel and impact of that increased support. Recognizing this, we see that these are instructions for sensing, shifting, and releasing energy.

Even when it is focused on the idea or agenda of the moment, the totality of one's being cannot be present in an idea as such. Only an energetic system, not a cognitive one, can hold the present fully. Is this reading too much into a simple instruction? Perhaps not, when we consider other descriptions of what the cultivation of attention feels like. In a story made famous by Patrul Rinpoche in *Words of My Perfect Teacher*, Buddha counsels the musician Srona, who despairs at his inability to meditate, as follows:

> "When you were a layman, you were a good *vīṇā*-player, weren't you?"
>
> "Yes, I played very well."
>
> "Did your *vīṇā* sound best when the strings were very slack or when they were very taut?"
>
> "It sounded best when they were neither too taut nor too loose."
>
> "It is the same for your mind," said the Buddha; and by practicing with that advice Śroṇa attained his goal.
>
> (Patrul Rinpoche 1998, 14–15)

Clearly, the cultivation of attention is not a matter of forcing your mind to do something but rather of striking the right balance between tightness and looseness – in other words, working with one's energy system. Likewise, the tenth-century female adept Majig Lapdron, in one of the most famous instructions of the entire tradition, says: "Tighten with tightness, then loosen with looseness; the essence of the teaching is there" (see Khetsun Sangpo 1982, 40). This modification comes in large measure through a sensitivity to touch, along with allowing the natural settling that occurs as one learns to focus. But even in the ninth level of the calm state (Tb. *zhi gnas*; Skt *śamatha*), when no effort at all is required, the body is said to feel "light like cotton" and like "warm water on a shaved head." This is evidence of a shift in the energy patterns of the body.

In the Theravāda tradition, a feeling of extreme lightness akin to physical dissolution is associated with a stage known as "little stream winner."[8] These are indications that body is in service to one's practice (Tb. *shin sbyangs*; Skt *praśrabdhi*). Such serviceability is important in all nine levels of cultivating the calm state (the function of mindfulness as such is complete by the fourth of these levels), and the calm state itself is fully conjoined with a mental and physical serviceability (Lodrö 1992).

These too arise because of shifts in bodily energy. When mental serviceability occurs, it is because

> winds or currents of energy involved in unsalutary physical states are first calmed and leave the body through the top of the head, where a sense of bliss develops, like the touch of a hot hand after shaving the head. Immediately afterwards . . . a wind of serviceability that induces physical pliancy moves throughout the body, causing separation from unsalutary physical states of roughness and heaviness and affording an ability to use the body at will . . . [and later there arises] a physical pliancy of smoothness and lightness in which the body feels light like cotton.[9]

Let us return for a moment to the *Foundations of Mindfulness* practices and how our understanding of attention as an elemental expression of the energetic sensibility opens our understanding of what is actually occurring there. After contemplating the body, the practitioner is directed to shift the focus from body to feelings, later to mind with its spectrum of emotions, and finally to mental qualities, especially negative ones that obstruct further development. Foundations here might read as a simple list of objects to which attention will be directed, as if the point were simply to move from one to the other. Yet, given the lens of the energetic sensibility, we can see the importance of recognizing that this passage also sets in motion a developing transformation of energy and thus the capacity to remain stable in the face of increasingly challenging topics. As Ken McLeod, a highly insightful Western Buddhist teacher in the Kagyu tradition, puts it, "As you rest attention in the experience of sensory sensations, energy is transformed."[10] Less distracted by thoughts and more conscious of sensations, you become aware of subtle inner currents associated with each sensation.

This and related observations get to the heart of the matter: the energy shifts associated with the development of practice. These have been largely overlooked in the Western academic study of Buddhism, partly because "energy" or "energetic sensibility" has not yet become a robust category of analysis. Attention, as we have seen, cannot be primarily a function of will or intellectual acuity or psychological development, though all of these may have their place. It arises in the domain of a delicately detected energetic sensibility.

The *Foundations*' iconic articulation of progressive stages in the cultivation of attention can be read as a narrative of growing skill in maintaining awareness of increasingly deep-seated and potentially disruptive patterns of behavior. If the windhorse supporting attention is weaker than the distracting patterns, one is carried away by that distraction. If attention is the stronger of the two, one can observe even deeply conflictual states without the energy of attention becoming ensnared by them. As the great twentieth-century *yogī* Nyala Padma Dudul put it:

> The karmic wind is a prancing flying wild horse
> Ridden by the childish mind
> [When] demons of immediate conceptual thoughts stir it
> It runs into the plain of habituated laziness.
> Pull on the bridle of mindfulness.[11]

The term "bridle of mindfulness" conveys the energetic impact of cultivating attention. Less obviously, this cultivation involves increasingly intimate interactive communication between the energy flow, which is breath, and the energy steed carrying the mind observing breath.

This mirroring communication impacts many other energy flows within the body, including the increasingly subtle ones that arise as the supporting steed of attention itself. Attention comes into such close contact with the building blocks of identity that the reified sense of identity is viscerally challenged. Finally, attention coalesces with insight, so that one no longer senses what was until now experienced as one's material body or the usual sense of a more or less reified, independent identity. This letting go is isomorphic with the cultivation of both compassion and wisdom. Nāgārjuna says in one of the most frequently cited passages from his *Precious Garland* (verse 79):

> Beings are not earth, not water,
> Not fire, not wind, not space,
> Not consciousness and not all of them.
> What person is there other than these?

And what are these elements? In the *Eight Session Mind Training*[12] attributed to Atisha we see their identification with palpable properties of different dynamisms:

> This body, now transformed into the four elements of nature, serves the welfare of living beings – earth through its nature of solidity and firmness, water through its nature of moisture and fluidity, fire through its nature of heat and burning, and wind through its nature of lightness and motility.
>
> (Jinpa 2006, 232)

These descriptions of the elements, which in Tibetan are simply called "arisings" (*'byung ba*), are retained down to the present day. In Tibetan monastic training, they are memorized in the first years of study by every child enrolled.[13]

Emphasis on a visceral dissolving of the ordinary solidity of identity is found in many practices, from the type of insight practice alluded to above to the dissolving of one's body and arising as an enlightened being composed of colored light in Tibetan-style tantric mediation litanies, known as *sādhanas*. Practitioners of these and other methods describe a sense of dissolving, of immateriality, of expansion. And these occur at every level of practice, from the most foundational to the most secret. They are not just metaphors; they are visceral responses to the complex practices, ideas, and cultural categories of human being in which persons are engaged with body, speech, and mind.

What is dissolving, according to Buddhist sensibilities, is the holding on to self. The holding dissolves because one viscerally experiences the absence of that habitually held self. We grab and hold onto this self for dear life. It is not simply the idea of self that dissolves, it is the holding, the grasping. The choice of terms in Sanskrit and Tibetan here is telling. The Tibetan term for "hold," *'dzin*, is a translation of the Sanskrit term *grāhya*, which is cognate with the English "grab." As this dissolves, the various patterns, comprising the elemental energies involved in structuring, cohering, burning-devouring, moving, and allowing, also lose their ability to deploy the self in habitual ways.

This is how the genuine transformation of habits to which practice is directed can occur. It is supported powerfully by Buddhist discourse on how thought moves towards direct experience on the path, especially through the use of imagery. We can note that imagery impacts energy: reflecting on the fact that everything changes from one moment to the next can yield a visceral *and* highly articulate understanding of impermanence. Imagining that the body is composed of light maps well onto Buddhist philosophical discussions of all phenomena as illusory and also of all things as empty of true existence yet fully functional, and so on. The energetic sensibility is in fact deeply affected by words and images, and it also gives rise to words and images, as any writer or artist knows, perhaps calling it "inspiration" without even recognizing that there is both a visceral and a cognitive component. This coalescence accounts in part for the sense of zest and wholeness that comes when inspiration dawns, possibly in addition to a sense of the emptying out of some habitual pattern that until now obstructed that new vision from arising.

We opened by noting that the most fundamental Buddhist practices of refuge and the cultivation of attention involve components of dynamism. We have alluded also to the widely acknowledged importance of the energetic sensibility when it comes to the elemental energies and the steeds carrying awareness in habitual peregrination. All of this indicates the relevance of a dynamic sensibility for the basics of Buddhist thought and practice. Recognizing this, we can better appreciate that esoteric practices, wherein very subtle sensibilities are centrally featured, are actually a continuation of something embedded in the stream of Buddhist thought and practice from the very beginning, as well throughout the ancient Asian cultures in which Buddhism first emerged.

We point briefly to the esoteric significance of the energetic sensibility with one of the most widely recited expressions of refuge in the Tibetan tradition. This is Jigme Lingpa's famous prayer of refuge – itself arisen when he was in a deep and persistent visionary state – which encompasses all nine vehicles of the ancient Nyingma Buddhist tradition in Tibet. That is, it contains sutric, tantric, and Dzogchen-oriented pictures of refuge:

> In three real jewels, three root Bliss Filled Ones
> Channels, winds, bright orbs, this Bodhi Mind
> Essence, nature, moving-love mandal
> Until full Bodhi I seek refuge.[14]

The first line refers to the refuge common to virtually all Buddhist traditions: Buddha, Dharma, and Sangha. Their dynamics are the energies of Awakening, Holding, and

Gathering, respectively. The Sugatas, the refuge of the outer tantras, are the Guru, Deity, and Wisdom Woman (Guru, Deva, Dakini), whose special energies are beyond the scope of our discussion here. We move on to point briefly to the clear mention in the third line of the channels, which are the pathways for the body's subtle wind currents, as well as the winds themselves and the luminous orbs they carry. These are objects of refuge for the Inner Tantras. Jigme Lingpa could well be thinking of some pithy phrases from the *Blazing Lamp*, cited by the great Longchen Rabjam, whom Jigme Lingpa encountered in vision:

> At the very core of the bodies of all being
> sLies the precious immeasurable mansion of the heart center
> From which come many thousands of channels.
> In particular there are four supreme channels . . .
> Riding on subtle energy, awareness dwells particularly
> Within these four channels.
>
> (Longchenpa 2007, 342)

The channels, straightened by posture from the very outset of the path, now become so significant that they and the currents flowing through them are themselves refuge. And, finally, the last line expresses the refuge of the Secret Great Completeness. This line also introduces another important term of dynamism: the spontaneously compassionate responsiveness seen as the fruition of the practitioner's earlier cultivations of love and compassion. This aspect of awakening carries forward the core aspiration that animates the entire bodhisattva path, as expressed by Shantideva in *A Guide to the Bodhisattva Way of Life*: "Like the great elements such as earth and space, may I always serve as the basis of the various requisites of life for innumerable sentient beings" (Shantideva 1997, ch. 3, verse 20).[15] As experienced by the energetic sensibility, attention, love, and wisdom have one essential thing in common: they are all profoundly receptive. They receive what arrives without overlaying anything onto it and without subtracting anything, either. In this they are related to Dzogchen's enlightened expression of receptivity described by Jigme Lingpa above.

Attention rests with what is and does not judge the present as better or worse than what was anticipated, than what could be, or than what was. It is not lost in past or future. Love and compassion seek only to further the happiness and reduce the suffering of others, with no other agenda. They do not compare these beings or feel more or less inclined towards some of them because of anything they do or say. They take in the situation and respond. This responsive receptivity, just like any sense of receptivity with which we are familiar in our everyday life experience, is not just an idea, though it may be supported by a whole array of ideas. At its most alive, it is a visceral relaxation and resonant responsiveness in the body. Wisdom, which is nascent in both attention and compassion, is a naked embodied presence, a delicate matrix of energies in communication with everything around it, yet which any failure of recognition can obstruct. Wisdom is not impinged upon by anything it reflects or by anything that obstructs it. Like space, it is wholly receptive and wholly inviolable. Like the inspired artist or the fully present contemplative, it receives, mirrors, and displays.

For the scholar, categories such as wind-horse, elemental energies, or life force provide a lens through which we read texts and practices, allowing us to consider how they impact, manipulate, or refine energy. For the practitioner, it becomes a habit to notice whether the mind-steed is stable or unstable, whether it is focused or open, and how it feels in the body. This means, as we have suggested, sensing and attending to the flux of phenomena in which one's body and mind directly participate. Some energy impressions arise mainly in response to stimuli coming from within, such as feelings, memories, and body sensations. Others are felt as responses to events or objects impacting one's attention from "outside." These are never completely separate. Energies of interactive connection suggest the reciprocity of giving and sending associated with transmission, blessings, and the mutually impacting flows that occur whenever two or more persons are in contact. This category also applies to the relationship between the human organism and art, including the art of spiritual practice and ritual.

The Sufi sage Rumi, who grew up on the edges of Central Asian Buddhist culture and sometimes included Buddhist figures in his writing, tells a story about Chinese artists and Greek artists, each side claiming superiority. The king urged them to settle the matter by debate. The Chinese immediately began talking, but the Greeks left without saying anything. So each group was given a room in which to work their artistry. The Chinese requested hundreds of colors. The Greeks did not. "They are not part of our work."

The Greeks each day went to their room and polished it. "They made those walls as pure and clear as an open sky." When both groups had completed their work, the king came to pass judgment. Entering the Chinese room, he was "astonished by the gorgeous color and detail." Then the Greeks pulled the curtain to reveal their work:

> The Chinese figures and images shimmeringly reflected
> On the clear Greek walls. They lived there,
> Even more beautifully, and always
> Changing in the light. . . .
> They receive and reflect the images of every moment,
> From here, from the stars, from the void.
> They take them in
> As though they were seeing
> with the lighted clarity
> that sees them.
>
> (Rumi 1995, 121–3)

Such is the marvelous dynamic of sheer receptivity, expressed in attention, compassion, and wisdom.

Every practice, from the cultivation of stillness, to opening one's heart to others, to dissolving into the wisdom of unbounded wholeness, has its own way of training, opening, expanding, strengthening, or releasing some type of energy. Energies that distract from reality and the path are known as karmic energies, and those that can enter the central channel are known as the wisdom energies in a culminating phase of practice. But, as we have seen, dynamism and the energetic sensibility have been present from the beginning. Virtually every text, practice, and philosophical position is implicitly or explicitly addressing them and the way they do or do not express themselves through hanging onto, and thereby perpetuating, the mistaken sense of self that animates the karmic energies, instead gradually refining away obstructions so that an entirely different set of energies can emerge to support an entirely different way of being: the dynamism of an awakened life.

Notes

1 For a particularly rich account of these three wisdoms, see Dzogchen Ponlop (2006, 34–44).

2 *Collected Works of Jigme Lingpa* (gsung 'bum/ 'Jigs med gling pa, W7477 in Tibetan Buddhist Resource Center collection, 7:799.5. www.tbrc.org/#home).

3 I coined this term some years ago as a way of bringing together an important cluster of human experience having to do with "energy." I am in the process of writing several articles and a book that explore this important category more fully.

4 The Dalai Lama mentions the foundational nature of the tactile sense in a discussion with Paul Ekman (Ekman 2008, 42). For a detailed discussion of direct perception in the Indian and Tibetan traditions, see Klein (1998, introduction and chapter 3). For an especially succinct description of the stages of dying, see Lati Rinbochay and Hopkins (1985, 16–17).

5 This could be considered a Buddhist analogue to a reflection on the body that, in James Nelson's words, "is nothing less than our attempts to reflect on body experience as revelatory of God" (cited in Ferrer and Sherman 2008, 13).

6 *Māhasattiipathāna Sutta*. Many translations are available, including that by Nyanaponika (1998) and Rāhula (1974). For ease of access, a translation by Thanissaro Bhikkhu can be found at www.zhaxizhuoma.net/DHARMA/Tripitaka/Maha-satipatthanaSutta.htm.

7 I believe that every one of the ten or so Tibetan teachers with whom I have studied fairly closely has stated this principle in virtually identical words. I have taken some liberty with the translation. Technically the word "straight" (*drang po*) is used to describe body, channels, and winds as well as mind.

8 Sri Satya Narain Goenka, Bodhgaya, October 1971.

9 Adapted slightly from Hopkins (1996, 87). Lati Rinbochay is the oral source for description of energies departing through the practitioner's crown. The source for the statement that mental pliancy removes assumptions associated with negative mental states is Atisha's *Compendium of Evident Knowledge*, mentioned in Lodrö (1992, 191). For an extensive discussion of sources on the calm state, see ibid., 182 ff. See also Zahler 2009.

10 Ken McLeod, What to Do when Energy Runs Wild. In *Buddhadharma*, Winter 2011.

11 Adapted slightly from Anyen Rinpoche (2009, 99). Tibetan not cited.

12 Translated by Thupten Jinpa (Jinpa 2006, 225–37).

13 A practitioner's sensing into his or her constituent elements is not an intellectual process, even though memorization of the appropriate lists and definitions might have preceded, and now provide add cognitive support for, this kinesthetic exploration. It is not clear to me that Tibetans themselves articulate this kind of introspective sensing, but they do seem to take it for granted, much as the energy system is taken for granted, which is partly why it is so important for Western scholars, for whom this system is not a given, to take care to articulate it.

14 This is my chantable English translation, matching the number of syllables in the Tibetan so it can be sung to traditional Tibetan melody, thereby including the important dynamic of sound and rhythm that has always transmitted the energy of refuge practice. For the full

text of Jigme Lingpa's foundational practices in chantable English as well as free verse translation, see Klein (2009).

15 The translation given here is from the Tibetan. See Shantideva (1997, 35, n. 58).

References

Ackerman, Joshua M. et al. (2010). Incidental Haptic Sensations Influence Social Judgments and Decisions. In *Science* 328, 1712–16.

Anyen Rinpoche (2009). *Momentary Buddhahood: Mindfulness and the Vajrayana Path*. Trans. Allison Graboski. Boston: Wisdom.

Dzogchen Ponlop Rinpoche (2006). *Mind beyond Death*. Ithaca, NY: Snow Lion.

Ekman, Paul (ed.) (2008). *Emotional Awareness: Overcoming the Obstacles to Psychological Balance and Compassion: A Conversation between the Dalai Lama and Paul Ekman*. New York: Times Books.

Ferrer, Jorge N., and Jacob H Sherman, (eds) (2008). *The Participatory Turn: Spirituality, Mysticism, Religious Studies*. Albany: State University of New York Press.

Goleman, Daniel (1995). *Emotional intelligence*. New York: Bantam Books.

Hopkins, Jeffrey (1996). *Meditation on Emptiness*. Rev. edn. Boston: Wisdom.

'Jigs-med-gling-pa Rang-byung-rdo-rje (1729/30–1798) (2004). *The A-Dzom Chos-Sgar Redaction of the Collected Works of Kun-Mkhyen 'Jigs-Med-Gliṅ-Pa Raṅ-Byuṅ-Rdo-Rje-Mkhyen-Brtsei-Od-Zer*. New York: Tibetan Buddhist Resource Center.

Jinpa, Geshe Thupten (2006). *Mind Training: The Great Collection. Library of Tibetan Classics*, Vol. 1. Boston: Wisdom.

Khetsun Sangpo Rinbochay (1982). *Tantric Practice in Nying-ma*. Ed. and trans. Jeffrey Hopkins. Co-ed. Anne C. Klein. Ithaca, NY: Snow Lion.

Klein, Anne C. (1998). *Knowledge and Liberation: Tibetan Buddhist Epistemology in Support of Transformative Religious Experience*. Ithaca, NY: Snow Lion.

Klein, Anne C. (2009). *Heart Essence of the Vast Expanse: A Story of Transmission*. Ithaca, NY: Snow Lion.

Lati Rinbochay and Hopkins, Jeffrey (1985). *Death, Intermediate State and Rebirth in Tibetan Buddhism*. Ithaca, NY: Snow Lion.

Lodrö, Geshe Gedün (1992). *Walking through Walls: A Presentation of Tibetan Meditation*. Ed. Jeffrey Hopkins, Leah Zahler, and Anne C. Klein. Trans. Jeffrey Hopkins. Ithaca, NY: Snow Lion.

Longchenpa (Klong-chen-pa Dri-med-od-zer; 1308–1363) (2007). *The Precious Treasury of Philosophical Systems: A Treatise Elucidating the Meaning of the Entire Range of Spiritual Approaches*. Trans. Richard Barron. Junction City, CA: Padma.

Nyanaponika, Thera (1988). *The Heart of Buddhist Meditation (Satipaṭṭhāna): A Handbook of Mental Training Based on the Buddha's Way of Mindfulness, with an Anthology of Relevant Texts Translated from the Pali and Sanskrit*. York Beach, ME: Samuel Weiser.

Patrul Rinpoche (1998). *The Words of My Perfect Teacher*. Trans. Padmakara Translation Group. Second edn. Walnut Creek, CA: AltaMira Press.

Rāhula, Walpola (1974). *What the Buddha Taught*. New York: Grove Press.

Rumi (Jalal al-Din Rumi, Maulana) (1995). *The Essential Rumi*. Trans. Coleman Barks. San Francisco: Harper.

Shantideva (Śāntideva) (1997). *A Guide to the Bodhisattva Way of Life*. Trans. Vesna A. Wallace and B. Alan Wallace. Ithaca, NY: Snow Lion.

Zahler, Leah (2009). Tsoṅ-kha-pa Blo-bzaṅ-grags-pa, and Dkon-mchog 'Jigs-med-dbaṅ-po. *Study and Practice of Meditation: Tibetan Interpretations of the Concentrations and Formless Absorptions*. Ithaca, NY: Snow Lion.

38

From the Five Aggregates to Phenomenal Consciousness

Towards a Cross-Cultural Cognitive Science

JAKE H. DAVIS AND EVAN THOMPSON

Introduction

Buddhism originated and developed in an Indian cultural context that featured many first-person practices for producing and exploring states of consciousness through the systematic training of attention. In contrast, the dominant methods of investigating the mind in Western cognitive science have emphasized third-person observation of the brain and behavior. In this chapter, we explore how these two different projects might prove mutually beneficial. We lay the groundwork for a cross-cultural cognitive science by using one traditional Buddhist model of the mind – that of the five aggregates – as a lens for examining contemporary cognitive science conceptions of consciousness.

The model of consciousness and meditative transformations of consciousness that we offer in this chapter is inspired by the accounts found in the Pāli Nikāyas. For this reason and for the sake of simplicity, we make reference especially to Pāli textual sources and terminology. Nevertheless, it is important to note at the outset that these texts admit of multiple possible readings. Our reconstruction differs in certain respects from the traditional interpretation of the five aggregates in the Theravāda Buddhist commentaries on the Pāli Nikāyas. Our aim, however, is not to give an historical account of what these concepts meant at any point in the development of Buddhist thought; and we make no claim that anyone in the Buddhist tradition, early or late, actually understood this model in the way we suggest. The model of attention, consciousness, and mindfulness that we draw from the Nikāya account of the five aggregates is of interest to us because it suggests promising new directions for scientific investigations of the mind. Put another way, whatever value our model has lies not in any claim to historical authenticity but, rather, in its claim to being empirically accurate and productive of further research.

Situating Buddhist views within recent scientific debates about consciousness allows us to see how these views might be tested experimentally and thereby opens up new

A Companion to Buddhist Philosophy, First Edition. Edited by Steven M. Emmanuel.

understandings of what these ancient teachings mean for us today. At the same time, understanding the conceptual frameworks of the Buddhist teachings can help scientists to refine the theoretical frameworks they bring to research on meditation and consciousness. This opportunity is lost if we simply apply existing scientific frameworks to interpret data from experiments on Buddhist meditation practices.

The burgeoning scientific literature on "mindfulness" meditation offers a case in point. This form of meditation can be broadly characterized by the aim to cultivate a lucid awareness of one's own moment-to-moment bodily, emotional, perceptual, and cognitive processes. Seeing the potential for this technique in medical settings, Jon Kabat-Zinn pioneered in the 1980s the Mindfulness-Based Stress Reduction program (MBSR). MBSR is now offered in the secular context of hospitals and clinics around the world and has become the subject of a burgeoning scientific literature. Kabat-Zinn's approach was influenced by Korean Zen Buddhist teachings as well as by Advaita Vedanta, and the particular technique he incorporated into MBSR was directly inspired by Theravāda Buddhist teachers drawing on texts from the Pāli discourses such as the *Mahāsatipaṭṭhāna Sutta*, or "Longer Discourse on Mindfulness" (DN.II.290–315). Yet, attempts in the scientific literature to formulate what mindfulness is have often proceeded in almost total independence from theoretical formulations of mindfulness practice contained in Buddhist textual traditions. In the absence of references to such traditional canonical sources, there has been an inordinate focus on one particular phrase Kabat-Zinn used in his seminal introductory guide for practitioners to describe mindfulness – namely, "paying attention in a particular way: on purpose, in the present moment, and nonjudgmentally" (Kabat-Zinn 2004, 4).

When specific references occur in the scientific literature to the Buddhist textual sources, these references often consist in noting that the term "mindfulness" is a translation of the Pāli term *sati*. In Buddhist theory, however, the term *sati* carries connotations of memory and remembrance, making attempts to understand mindfulness as a present-centered, non-elaborative, and non-judgmental attention appear inaccurate and confused (see Bodhi 2011; Dreyfus 2011). Indeed, the term "mindfulness" seems to have been chosen by early translators of the Pāli texts because they saw parallels not with a notion of non-judgmental present-centered attention but, rather, between the Christian ethical notion of conscience and the textual usage of *sati* in the context of holding in mind and being inspired by certain truths, for the sake of improvement of one's ethical character (Gethin 2011). The broad usage of the term *sati* is perhaps best captured by the colloquial English notion of "minding." The Pāli texts employ *sati* in reference to everything from "minding" one's livestock (MN.I.117) to "minding" one's meditation object in practices such as lovingkindness (Sn.26), in addition to using *sati* specifically in the context of mindfulness meditation or, more literally, in the establishment of *sati* (*sati-upaṭṭhāna*).[1] In this general sense, *sati* clearly can involve elaborative and evaluative cognitive processes. In the role *sati* plays in the context of mindfulness meditation, however, the involvement of memory may be of a more limited and specific kind.

In order to investigate properly a given type of meditation practice, scientists must take account of the traditional theoretical frameworks used to conceptualize and teach that practice (Lutz et al. 2007). We outline here how the traditional theoretical context of mindfulness practice can offer important suggestions for scientific research. In particular, the five aggregates model draws distinctions that are not always clearly formulated in contemporary cognitive science, but that are crucial for a scientific understanding of the function of mindfulness meditation. We suggest below how empirical hypotheses about the role of memory and its relation to attention and consciousness in mindfulness meditation can be refined in light of distinctions suggested in the Buddhist five aggregates model.

A Buddhist Model of the Mind

The Buddhist five aggregates model parallels a number of distinctions drawn in cognitive science and therefore serves as a useful theoretical resource for developing a cross-cultural cognitive science of consciousness (Varela et al. 1991). In the Pāli texts the five aggregates (*khandhas*) are listed as *rūpa*, *vedanā*, *saññā*, *saṅkhāra*, and *viññāṇa*. Deciding what each of these words means, however, is not straightforward. Indeed, as we will see, interpreting the *khandhas* raises philosophical issues that directly connect with contemporary debates about consciousness.

The first aggregate, *rūpa*, is often understood as referring simply to the physical matter of the body. In the Pāli dialogues, however, this term connotes not only the body's solidity and extension but also its mobility, temperature regulation, fluid, and digestive systems, as well as its processes of decay. For this reason, some textual scholars suggest that *rūpa* is better understood as referring to the "lived body rather than simply its flesh" (Hamilton 2000, 29). On this reading, the conceptual framework of the five *khandhas* anticipates contemporary cognitive scientific and phenomenological accounts of the bodily basis of cognition, emotion, and consciousness (see Thompson 2007 for an overview).

Bodily changes such as the contraction of the gut and the flush of blood in anger have long been recognized as central to emotion. William James (1884) proposed that emotions essentially are such bodily reactions, an idea that still plays an important role in emotion theory today; for example, the neuroscientist Antonio Damasio (2000) and the philosopher Jesse Prinz (2004) have both argued that emotions are constituted in part by bodily reactions. But emotion theorists also recognize a second aspect of emotion, one that takes us from *rūpa* construed as the living body to *vedanā*, the second of the five *khandhas*. This second aspect is the specific feeling tone belonging to a given emotion. Some emotions feel pleasant and others feel unpleasant. When we consciously feel joyful, the experience is pleasant, and when we feel fearful, the experience is unpleasant. Psychologists call this aspect of emotion its affective valence or hedonic tone (see Colombetti 2005 for the complicated history behind this concept of "valence").

The notion of affect valence provides a close analogue to the Buddhist notion of *vedanā*. In the *Khajjaniya Sutta* (SN.III.86–7), *vedanā* is defined as feeling pleasure, feeling pain, or feeling neither-pleasure-nor-pain. In the case of both concepts, valence and *vedanā*, the feeling tone of pleasant versus unpleasant is closely related to action tendencies of approach versus avoidance. From the modern neuroscience perspective, the bodily responses constitutive of an emotion, including an emotion's valence and action tendency, can be activated even when we do not report consciously feeling the emotion

(LeDoux 2000). For example, we may exhibit bodily responses associated with fear, even though we do not report seeing anything fearsome or feeling fearful. Thus, like *vedanā*, valence motivates us at implicit as well as explicit levels. Moreover, recent work has shown that such implicit affect valence is not limited to emotional episodes and influences decision-making on everything from consumer choices to moral judgment (Loewenstein and Lerner 2003). This understanding of the pervasive role of affect valence in human psychology finds a parallel in the Buddhist suggestion that *vedanā* is present with every mental state, not just those Western psychology includes under the emotions.

In understanding the function of meditative training in bringing about personal transformation, the habits of mind that dispose an individual to perceive and react to the world in certain distinctive ways are of obvious importance. These habits of mind fall under the fourth of the five aggregates, *saṅkhāra*. This category can be understood as comprising all volitional activities. These include volitions that lead to outward action or what we normally think of as the will. But they also include more internal processes, such as attention, *manasikāra* – literally, "making-in-the-mind." Thus we can understand *saṅkhāra* as referring to implicit and habitual processing routines that shape how we perceive and behave and that typically escape explicit, cognitive awareness.

Importantly, these habits of mind not only shape our inner and outer actions but are themselves formed through the repetition of certain kinds of inner and outer volitional activities. Thus, in addition to conditioning the other four aggregates, the *saṅkhāras* involve dynamic self-reference and self-conditioning: habits are formed and conditioned by habits (SN.III.87).[2] This conception parallels recent models of cognitive events as self-forming processes arising from non-linear interactions between components at neural and motor levels (Cosmelli et al. 2007). Complex (non-linear) dynamical systems have a feature known as sensitive dependence on initial conditions: a minute change in conditions at one point in time can greatly shift the trajectory of the system down the line. Similarly, the dynamic self-formation of the *saṅkhāras* allows for the possibility of radical transformation of one's personality traits. In the particular case of mindfulness meditation, the suggestion is that, by intentionally attending to present experience instead of dwelling in reactivity to the remembered past or the imagined future, we can radically transform the habits of attention that surface at moments of feeling threatened or tempted, and thereby transform the way we react outwardly to such situations.

Within this category of habits of mind, the role of attention is of particular interest for us here. In the *Mahāhatthipadopama Sutta* of the Majjhima Nikāya, for example, we find the following claim:

> If the internal eye-organ is intact, but an external form does not come into its range . . . If the internal eye-organ is intact, and an external form does come into its range, but there is not the bringing together born from that (*tajja samannāhāra*), there is not the appearance of a degree of consciousness born from that (*tajja viññāṇabhāga*). But when the internal eye-organ is intact, and an external form does come into its range, and there is the bringing together born from that, there is the appearance of a degree of consciousness born from that.
>
> (MN.I.190)

Despite other Pāli texts that omit the factor of "bringing together," *samannāhāra*, in the account of perceptual processes, this factor is clearly crucial in the above formulation: an external form coming into the range of an intact eye is said to result in a share or degree of consciousness only with the addition of this factor of bringing together. The traditional Pāli commentary glosses *samannāhāra* as here meaning *manasikāra* (attention).[3] As the above formulation suggests, *manasikāra* is understood in this theoretical framework as a universal kind of attention necessary for any moment of consciousness. It may therefore correspond in a rough way to the basic kind of alertness required for the basal, core-level consciousness that Parvizi and Damasio (2001) hypothesize to be dependent on subcortical structures such as the thalamus and brainstem, and which occurs independently of the direction of this consciousness to particular objects through selective attention.

This core level of consciousness, which we discuss briefly below, stands in contrast to the more cognitive functions that allow one to identify, recall, and report what one experiences. These cognitive processes are the function of the third aggregate, *saññā*. In the *Khajjaniya Sutta* (SN.III.87), *saññā* is defined as cognizing (*sañjānāti*) that there is blue, that there is red, yellow, or white. The term *saññā* is often glossed as "perception," but this interpretation is inadequate. As the Pāli scholar Peter Harvey explains, *saññā*

> is only one part of the perceptual process and . . . one can have a *saññā* of a mental object but cannot, in English, be said to "perceive" such an object . . . the word "*saññā*" and its verbal form "*sañ-jānāti*" clearly refer to some kind of knowledge or knowing which is done in an associative, connective, linking (*sa-*) way.
>
> (Harvey 1995, 141)

The Pāli texts contain some intriguing statements that suggest *saññā* may be akin to what the philosopher Ned Block (2007, 2008) calls "cognitive access," defined as the ability to recall, report, and deliberate on a perceptual event. The *Nibbedhika Sutta* (AN. III.413), for instance, defines *saññā* as that which results in spoken communication (*vohāra*): "As one identifies (*sañjānāti*) it, so one says 'I saw thus.' "

Saññā is differentiated in the Buddhist model of the mind from *viññāṇa*, the fifth aggregate, often glossed as "consciousness." It is tempting to relate this notion to what Block calls "phenomenal consciousness" (Block 2007, 2008). Whereas phenomenal consciousness consists in "what it is like" for a subject to have or to undergo an experience, cognitive access consists in having the content of an experience enter working memory so that one can identify and report on this content. Given this distinction, *viññāṇa*, defined as a moment of visual, auditory, tactile, olfactory, gustatory, or mental awareness, would be analogous to phenomenal consciousness, whereas *saññā*, defined as a recognitional ability, would be analogous to cognitive access.

Yet this tentative analogy between Pāli Buddhist and cognitive science conceptions of consciousness needs refinement. Block conceives of phenomenal consciousness as a state of experiencing in a rich and vivid way certain objects or properties – for instance, a state of seeing red. Without such a notion of phenomenally conscious states as essentially including modality-specific content, it would make little sense to suggest, as Block does, that visual phenomenal consciousness might be realized by certain patterns of recurrent neural activity in visual areas of the brain (Block 2005). In contrast, Parvizi and Damasio (2001) suggest that there is a basic, core level of consciousness, dependent on the thalamus and brainstem, that occurs independently of selective attentional processes in higher cortical areas. This core or ground-floor level of consciousness depends on a basic kind of alerting function distinct from the higher-level mechanisms of selective attention that come into play in determining what one is conscious of. On this view, the fact *that* there is a phenomenal feel – the fact that there is something it is like for a subject – depends on the basic alerting function. In contrast, the content of phenomenal consciousness – *what* it is like for a subject – depends also on how this consciousness is directed to particular objects and properties through selective attention. Put another way, the particular contents of phenomenal consciousness can be seen as modifications or modulations of a basal level of awareness dependent on the alerting function (see also Searle 2000). We suggested above that the Pāli Buddhist concept of *manasikāra* may be analogous to this alerting function, rather than to selective attention. Correspondingly, *viññāṇa* may be best understood from this cognitive science perspective as analogous to a basal level of awareness common to all phenomenally conscious states.

We need to be cautious, however, in drawing any of the foregoing parallels between the third and fifth aggregates and cognitive science conceptions of cognitive access and consciousness. Currently there is no consensus in cognitive science about whether phenomenal consciousness and cognitive access are two different phenomena, or whether phenomenal consciousness depends constitutively on cognitive access.[4] On the one hand, it seems odd to say that you can have a conscious experience that you do not know you are having. And if knowing that you are having a certain experience, such as a visual experience of the color red or a tactile experience of hardness, requires the cognitive functions of identifying the object or properties being experienced, then it seems problematic to postulate a type of experience that occurs independent of cognitive access. Furthermore, given that the principal scientific criterion for the presence of consciousness is behavioral report, and behavioral report requires cognitive access, how could such a subjective experience ever be investigated?

On the other hand, it seems unsatisfactory to assume, in advance of the evidence, that having a conscious experience consists wholly in various cognitive operations, such as identifying its content or identifying oneself as having experienced that content. Proponents of drawing a distinction between phenomenal consciousness and cognitive access need only posit that some instances of phenomenal consciousness happen not to be cognitively accessed; they need not posit that there are subjective experiences that the subject cannot access or know about. Indeed, one function of phenomenal consciousness may be to make its content accessible for encoding in working memory, for the purposes of identification, recall, deliberation, and report (Prinz 2005, 2011; see also Block 2011, 567). Certain experiences may be too fleeting and rapid to stabilize in working memory, as various kinds of evidence have sometimes been taken to suggest (see Block 2011; Kouider et al. 2010). Nevertheless, such experiences may not be inaccessible in principle; for instance, it may be possible to gain greater cognitive access to them through the kind of mental training central to mindfulness meditation.

We believe this last point indicates a major shortcoming in the current cognitive science discussions. These discussions have proceeded without significant consideration being given to the possibility that specific forms of mental training might be able to produce new data about attention and consciousness. Mental training and its relevance for understanding consciousness are areas where Buddhist theory and meditation practice have much to contribute, as we discuss in the next section.

Varieties of Attention Training

Many Buddhist traditions distinguish between meditation practices aimed primarily at concentrating the mind and meditation practices aimed primarily at developing wisdom. In a Buddhist context, concentration practices range from cultivating states such as lovingkindness or, literally, friendliness (*mettā*) to practices aimed simply at cultivating a settled and unified state of mind (*samādhi*) through concentration on a meditative object, such as the sensations of the breath or a visualized image of a colored disk or a light. In these forms of meditation, practitioners counteract mind-wandering by repeatedly bringing the mind back to the subject of meditation.

Concentration practices may have important contributions to make to our understanding of the processes responsible for stabilizing particular contents in consciousness. We can use studies of the perceptual phenomenon known as binocular rivalry to illustrate this point.

In normal vision, the brain receives visual images from each eye that present slightly differing views on the same scene. In the experimental paradigm known as binocular rivalry, however, each eye is presented with a different image at the same time. For example, one eye may receive the image of a house while the other eye receives the image of a face. Subjects generally report seeing one image at a time but also that their perception switches unpredictably between the two images. Thus, although the stimulus remains constant, visual consciousness changes as the two stimuli compete for perceptual dominance. On the one hand, the visual image that is not consciously seen provokes significant neural responses selective to its particular features. For example, the image of a fearful face has been found to activate the amygdala, an area of the brain associated with perceiving emotionally salient stimuli (Williams et al. 2004). On the other hand, voluntary shifts in attention have been shown to affect which image becomes consciously seen (Ooi and He 1999). For this reason, binocular rivalry paradigms have provided an important source of evidence for debates over consciousness and its relation to attention.

In an intriguing study of meditation and binocular rivalry, Olivia Carter and her colleagues found that long-term Tibetan Buddhist practitioners of concentration meditation were able to change the perceptual switching rate when they viewed the images while practicing this type of meditation (with eyes open focused on the display as the meditative object) (Carter et al. 2005). A large number of the practitioners reported that the amount of time one image remained perceptually dominant increased considerably while practicing concentration meditation as well as immediately after meditation. Three individuals reported that the image remained completely stable, with no switching, for an entire 5-minute period of concentration meditation. In some cases, one of the two images was completely dominant; in other cases, the non-dominant image remained faintly or partially visible behind the dominant one, so that the conscious perception was of two superimposed images. As Carter and her colleagues observe, "These results contrast sharply with the reported observations of over 1000 meditation-naïve individuals tested previously" (ibid., 412). Thus, it may be that meditative training of voluntary attention enables long-term practitioners of concentration meditation to stabilize consciousness of one or the other image, or even to maintain conscious awareness of the non-dominant image, in a way that normal subjects are unable to do. If so, investigations of brain activity in meditators with expertise in concentration meditation may help shed light on the processes that make particular contents phenomenally conscious.

The use of various methods of attention training for developing altered states of consciousness through strong concentration was widespread at the time of the Buddha. Buddhist texts relate how, before his enlightenment, the Buddha studied techniques for concentrating the mind under teachers such as Ālāra Kālāma and Uddaka Rāmaputta (MN.I.237–51). Yet these early Buddhist texts also emphasize that the method of mind training that the Buddha went on to discover for himself was novel, with results that differ importantly from those that were being taught by his contemporaries. In a modern context, we can take this claim to be an empirical one, subject to experimental test, and hence one that may be best approached through a cross-cultural cognitive science based on both Buddhist and cognitive scientific models of attention and consciousness.

In addition to what cognitive scientists describe as the endogenous orienting network, which voluntarily allocates selective attention to a chosen object (Corbetta and Shulman 2002), concentration or "focused attention" styles of meditation involve a "monitoring" function necessary to detect when attention has wandered away from the chosen object (Lutz et al. 2008). Lutz and colleagues distinguish such "focused attention" practices from "open monitoring" practices, which may involve focused attention training at early stages of practice but use the development of the monitoring skill to be able eventually to drop any intentional selection or deselection within the field of present experience. Instead, meditators aim to remain attentive to whatever arises in moment-to-moment experience, without becoming lost in mind-wandering. Open monitoring styles of meditation include certain Tibetan Buddhist and Chan/Zen practices, as well as Theravāda mindfulness practices.

Theravāda mindfulness meditation, or, more literally, the establishment of *sati* (*sati-upaṭṭhāna*), involves returning the mind again and again to present-moment experience (for a discussion of this term, see Anālayo 2004, 29–30; Bodhi 2011). This practice thus includes an element of concentration, though different teachers emphasize the concentrative aspect to differing degrees. In other concentrative practices, one might return the attention again and again to a particular feeling of friendliness, or a particular mental image of color or light, thereby cultivating the continuity and stability of a particular object in the mind. In contrast, Theravāda mindfulness practice aims to develop a settled type of attention on objects that are constantly changing. Present experiences of heat or cool in the body, of anger or of joy, of concentration or of distractedness, constantly arise and pass away again. Theravāda Buddhist teachings claim that experiencing for oneself in this direct and lucid way the impermanent and unstable nature of all aspects of experience brings about a profound change in how one relates to oneself and others (e.g., Mahasi Sayadaw 1994).

In our discussion of the five aggregates model above, we made a distinction between the particular sensory and mental contents of phenomenal consciousness and a basal level of consciousness dependent on an alerting function. Theravāda mindfulness meditation may hold particular promise for investigating this basal level of consciousness because this type of meditation is said to enhance the clear awareness of whatever arises but without using focused attentional selection. One way such enhanced phenomenal consciousness may be achieved is by a reduction in elaborative cognitive processes – the proliferation of evaluative thoughts about moment-to-moment stimuli – combined with increased alertness. Recent experimental studies of Theravāda mindfulness meditation are consistent with this idea.

Consider first a study of the effects of Theravāda mindfulness meditation on the so-called attentional blink. In this experimental paradigm, subjects have to identify two visual targets presented within 200 to 500 milliseconds of each other in a rapid sequence of other distracting visual stimuli. Subjects often notice the first target but fail to notice the second one, as if their attention had blinked. The standard explanation is that detecting the first target uses up the available attentional resources, so the second target is missed and not reported. A recent study showed that the ability to detect the second target was greatly improved after a three-month intensive Theravāda mindfulness meditation retreat, and that this improvement correlated with EEG measures showing more efficient neural responses to the first target (Slagter et al. 2007). Importantly, the participants were instructed not to meditate during the task, so the improved performance indicates that mindfulness meditation has lasting effects on attention outside of the context of meditation practice. The authors of this study suggest that mindfulness meditation may lead to less elaborative cognitive processing of the first visual target – less "mental stickiness" to it – and that this reduction facilitates the ability to identify and report the second rapidly occurring target.

The idea that enhanced phenomenal consciousness is linked to a reduction in elaborative cognitive processing as a result of mindfulness practice is also supported by recent work on mind-wandering and its association with the brain's so-called default mode network. The default mode network comprises a set of brain regions active in the resting state but whose activity decreases during externally directed and attention-demanding perceptual tasks (Buckner et al. 2008); these regions have also been shown to be active during mind-wandering (Mason et al. 2007; Christoff et al. 2009), including mind-wandering during focused attention meditation conditions (Hasenkamp et al. 2012). Mindfulness meditation practice is associated with decreases in default mode network activation (Brewer et al. 2011; Berkovich-Ohana et al. 2012) and, importantly, with corresponding increased activation in visceral and somatic areas associated with interception (Farb et al. 2007, 2010).

According to traditional descriptions, mindfulness becomes effortless at advanced stages of practice. As the Burmese meditation master Mahasi Sayadaw (1994) puts it, "in the act of noticing, effort is no longer required to keep formations before the mind or to understand them." We noted above that, in the Pāli Buddhist framework, a basic and universal kind of attention, *manasikāra*, is held to be necessary for consciousness. The scholar-practitioner Anālayo suggests that *sati* "can be understood as a further development and temporal extension of this type of attention [*manasikāra*], thereby adding clarity and depth to the usually too short fraction of time occupied by bare attention in the perceptual process" (Anālayo 2004, 59). Whereas the focusing of attention in concentration practices involves activation of voluntary orienting networks, mindfulness practice may consist in enhancing the processes involved in sustaining alert consciousness more generally. If this were the case, then we should expect that long-term trait increases in one's consciousness of subtle stimuli (as opposed to transitory state increases) would be evident even in resting states.

Conclusion

To study the effects of therapeutic interventions on the brain and the rest of the body, scientists need to employ conceptual constructs of the phenomenon under investigation that guide where and how they look. Thus, in studying the health benefits and psycho-physiological processes underlying mindfulness meditation, scientists have had to ask what precisely mindfulness is (Davidson 2010). Yet attempts in the scientific literature to define mindfulness have often proceeded in almost total independence from theoretical formulations of mindfulness practice contained in Buddhist textual traditions. Fortunately, a new conversation between Buddhist textual scholars and cognitive scientists about the construct of mindfulness is gaining momentum (see the collection of articles in the June 2011 issue of *Contemporary Buddhism*).

Our goal in this chapter has been to provide some useful tools for this new conversation. In particular, building bridges between the five aggregates model and contemporary cognitive science can offer a way to understand more precisely the roles of attention, consciousness, and memory in Theravāda mindfulness meditation. Like other concentration practices, many forms of mindfulness meditation begin by employing working memory in directing selective attention – for instance, to the sensations of breathing. As we suggested above, however, the reduction of elaborative cognitive processing in mindfulness meditation may play a central role in advanced mindfulness practice, in particular by allowing for an increase in phenomenal consciousness of current stimuli. This mental transformation in turn has implications for what psychologists call "episodic memory" (the memory of particular experienced events), because increased phenomenal consciousness can facilitate accurate identification of what is experienced, as well as later recall and report. Drawing on the relation between the concepts of *manasikāra* and *sati* in the Pāli Nikāyas, we have further speculated that mindfulness meditation may function by enhancing the alerting function crucial for phenomenal consciousness.

As we noted at the outset of this chapter, however, these texts allow multiple interpretations, and the conception of *manasikāra* that we employ may not line up neatly with traditional interpretations in the Theravāda Buddhist commentaries. We suggest that the proposed relation between *manasikāra* and *sati* be treated as a testable hypothesis. Whatever value our model may have lies in its ability to suggest fruitful directions for future work in the cross-cultural cognitive science of consciousness.

We conceive of the discussion that we have undertaken here as one tentative step in a larger project of developing a cross-cultural cognitive science of Buddhist therapeutic interventions. One way to build on our discussion would be to develop a cognitive science perspective on the Buddhist claim that mindfulness counteracts not knowing, by increasing awareness of presently arising stimuli, and also counteracts knowing wrongly, by attenuating emotional distortions of attention, perception, and memory. Having taken that step from cognitive to emotional functions, a further project would be to examine critically, in the light of empirical work on attention, emotion, and moral psychology, the central Buddhist claim that certain emotional motivations are unskillful (*akusala*) and to be abandoned (*pahātabbaṃ*); that other qualities are skillful (*kusala*) and to be cultivated (*bhavitabbaṃ*); and that we can discern the difference for ourselves.

Notes

1 The term *satipaṭṭhāna* has commonly been rendered as a (plural) noun, the (four) "foundations of mindfulness." But the primary sense of the term is verbal and refers to the active practice of establishing mindfulness, as noted recently by prominent translators such as Bhikkhu Bodhi (2011, 25) and Thanissaro Bhikkhu (2011). For a critique of the more standard gloss of *satipaṭṭhāna* as "foundations of mindfulness" and the commentarial derivation of the term from *paṭṭhāna* on which this gloss is based, see Anālayo (2004, 29–30).

2 SN.III.87, "*saṅkhāre saṅkhārattāya saṅkhatam abhisaṅkharonti.*"

3 MN-a.II.229 (commentary to MN.I.190). In support of this interpretation, Harvey (1995, 129–30) notes that these terms are used as synonyms in the *suttas*, as at MN.I.445.

4 For a sampling of the debate, see Block (2005, 2011); Cohen and Dennett (2011); Kouider et al. (2010); and Lamme (2003).

References

Anālayo (2004). *Satipaṭṭhāna: The Direct Path to Realization.* Cambridge: Windhorse.

Berkovich-Ohana, Aviva, Glicksohn, Joseph, and Goldstein, Abraham (2012). Mindfulness-Induced Changes in Gamma Band Activity – Implications for the Default Mode Network, Self-Reference and Attention. In *Clinical Neurophysiology* 123, 700–10. doi: 10.1016/j.clinph.2011.07.048.

Block, N. (2005). Two Neural Correlates of Consciousness. In *Trends in Cognitive Sciences* 9(2), 46–52. doi: 10.1016/j.tics.2004.12.006.

Block, N. (2007). Consciousness, Accessibility, and the Mesh between Psychology and Neuroscience. In *Behavioral and Brain Sciences* 30, 481–548. doi: 10.1017/S0140525X07002786.

Block, N. (2008). Consciousness and Cognitive Access. In *Proceedings of the Aristotelian Society* 108(3), 289–317. doi: 10.1111/j.1467-9264.2008.00247.x.

Block, N. (2011). Perceptual Consciousness Overflows Cognitive Access. In *Trends in Cognitive Sciences* 15, 567–75. doi: 10.1016/j.tics.2011.11.001.

Bodhi, Bhikkhu (2011). What Does Mindfulness Really Mean? A Canonical Perspective. In *Contemporary Buddhism* 12(1), 19–39. doi: 10.1080/14639947.2011.564813.

Brewer, Judson A., Worhunsky, Patrick D., Gray, Jeremy R., Tang, Yi-Yuan, Weber, Jochen, and Kober, Hedy (2011). Meditation Experience is Associated with Differences in Default Mode Network Activity and Connectivity. In *Proceedings of the National Academy of Sciences* 108, 20254–9. doi: 10.1073/pnas.1112029108.

Buckner, Randy L., Andrews-Hanna, Jessica R., and Schacter, Daniel L. (2008). The Brain's Default Network. In *Annals of the New York Academy of Sciences* 1124(1), 1–38. doi: 10.1196/annals.1440.011.

Carter, O. L., Presti, D. E., Callistemon, C., Ungerer, Y., Liu, G. B., and Pettigrew, J. D. (2005). Meditation Alters Perceptual Rivalry in Tibetan Buddhist Monks. In *Current Biology* 15, R412–R413.

Christoff, K., Gordon, A. M., Smallwood, J., Smith, R., and Schooler, J. W. (2009). Experience Sampling During fMRI Reveals Default Network and Executive System Contributions to Mind Wandering. In *Proceedings of the National Academy of Sciences* 106, 8719.

Cohen, Michael A., and Dennett, Daniel C. (2011). Consciousness Cannot Be Separated from Function. In *Trends in Cognitive Sciences* 15, 358–64. doi: 10.1016/j.tics.2011.06.008.

Colombetti, G. (2005). Appraising Valence. In *Journal of Consciousness Studies* 12(8–10), 103–26.

Corbetta, M., and Shulman, G. L. (2002). Control of Goal-Directed and Stimulus-Driven Attention in the Brain. In *Nature Reviews Neuroscience* 3, 201–15.

Cosmelli, D., Lachaux, J. P., and Thompson, E. (2007). Neurodynamical Approaches to Consciousness. In *The Cambridge Handbook of Consciousness*. Cambridge: Cambridge University Press.

Damasio, A. R. (2000). *The Feeling of What Happens: Body and Emotion in the Making of Consciousness*. London: Heinemann.

Davidson, R. J. (2010). Empirical Explorations of Mindfulness: Conceptual and Methodological Conundrums. In *Emotion* 10(1), 8–11.

Dreyfus, Georges (2011). Is Mindfulness Present-Centred and Non-Judgmental? A Discussion of the Cognitive Dimensions of Mindfulness. In *Contemporary Buddhism* 12(1), 41–54. doi: 10.1080/14639947.2011.564815.

Farb, N. A. S., Anderson, A. K., Mayberg, H., Bean, J., McKeon, D., and Segal, Z. V. (2010). Minding One's Emotions: Mindfulness Training Alters the Neural Expression of Sadness. *Emotion* 10(1), 25–33.

Farb, N. A. S., Segal, Z. V., Mayberg, H., Bean, J., McKeon, D., Fatima, Z., and Anderson, A. K. (2007). Attending to the Present: Mindfulness Meditation Reveals Distinct Neural Modes of Self-Reference. In *Social Cognitive and Affective Neuroscience* 2, 313.

Gethin, Rupert (2011). On Some Definitions of Mindfulness. In *Contemporary Buddhism* 12(1), 263–79. doi: 10.1080/14639947.2011.564843.

Hamilton, Sue (2000). *Early Buddhism: A New Approach: The I of the Beholder. Richmond*, Surrey: Curzon Press.

Harvey, Peter (1995). *The Selfless Mind: Personality, Consciousness and Nirvana in Early Buddhism*. London: Routledge.

Hasenkamp, Wendy, Wilson-Mendenhall, Christine D., Duncan, Erica, and Barsalou, Lawrence W. (2012). Mind Wandering and Attention during Focused Meditation: A Fine-Grained Temporal Analysis of Fluctuating Cognitive States. In *NeuroImage* 59, 750–60. doi: 10.1016/j.neuroimage.2011.07.008.

James, William (1884). What Is an Emotion? In *Mind* 9, 188–205.

Kabat-Zinn, Jon (2004). *Wherever You Go, There You Are*. New York: Hyperion.

Kouider, Sid, Gardelle, Vincent de, Sackur, Jérôme, and Dupoux, Emmanuel (2010). How Rich Is Consciousness? The Partial Awareness Hypothesis. In *Trends in Cognitive Sciences* 14, 301–7. doi: 10.1016/j.tics.2010.04.006.

Lamme, Victor A. F. (2003). Why Visual Attention and Awareness Are Different. In *Trends in Cognitive Sciences* 7(1), 12–18. doi: 10.1016/S1364-6613(02)00013-X.

LeDoux, J. E. (2000). Emotion Circuits in the Brain. In *Annual Review of Neuroscience* 23, 155–84.

Loewenstein, G., and Lerner, J. S. (2003). The Role of Affect in Decision Making. In *Handbook of Affective* Sciences. Ed. R. J. Davidson, K. R. Scherer, and H. H. Goldsmith. Oxford: Oxford University Press.

Lutz, Antoine, Dunne, John D., and Davidson, Richard J. (2007). Meditation and the Neuroscience of Consciousness. In *The Cambridge Handbook of Consciousness.* Ed. P. D Zelazo, Morris Moscovitch, and Evan Thompson. Cambridge: Cambridge University Press.

Lutz, Antoine, Slagter, Heleen A., Dunne, John D., and Davidson, Richard J. (2008). Attention Regulation and Monitoring in Meditation. In *Trends in Cognitive Sciences* 12, 163–9. doi: 10.1016/j.tics.2008.01.005.

Mahasi Sayadaw (1994). The Progress of Insight: (Visuddhiñana-katha). Trans. Nyanaponika Thera. At www.accesstoinsight.org/lib/authors/mahasi/progress.html#ch6.11.

Mason, M. F., Norton, M. I., Van Horn, J. D., Wegner, D. M., Grafton, S. T., and Macrae, C. N. (2007). Wandering Minds: The Default Network and Stimulus-Independent Thought. In *Science* 315, 393–5. doi: 10.1126/science.1131295.

Ooi, T. L., and He, Z. J. (1999). Binocular Rivalry and Visual Awareness: The Role of Attention. In *Perception* 28, 551–74.

Parvizi, J., and Damasio, A. (2001). Consciousness and the Brainstem. In *Cognition* 79, 135–60.

Prinz, Jesse J. (2004). *Gut Reactions: A Perceptual Theory of Emotion.* New York: Oxford University Press.

Prinz, Jesse J. (2005). A Neurofunctional Theory of Consciousness. In *Cognition and the Brain: The Philosophy and Neuroscience Movement.* Cambridge: Cambridge University Press, 381–96.

Prinz, Jesse J. (2011). Is Attention Necessary and Sufficient for Consciousness? In *Attention: Philosophical and Psychological Essays.* Oxford: Oxford University Press, 174.

Searle, John R. (2000). Consciousness. In *Annual Review of Neuroscience* 23, 557–78. doi: 10.1146/annurev.neuro.23.1.557.

Slagter, Heleen A, Lutz, Antoine, Greischar, Lawrence L., Francis, Andrew D., Nieuwenhuis, Sander, Davis, James M., and Davidson, Richard J. (2007). Mental Training Affects Distribution of Limited Brain Resources. In *PLOS Biology* 5(6), e138. doi: 10.1371/journal.pbio.0050138.

Thanissaro Bhikkhu (2011). Translator's introduction to Maha-satipatthana Sutta: The Great Frames of Reference. *Access to Insight.* Retrieved December 16, 2011, from http://www.accesstoinsight.org/tipitaka/dn/dn.22.0.than.html

Thompson, E. (2007). *Mind in Life: Biology, Phenomenology, and the Sciences of Mind.* Cambridge, MA: Belknap Press.

Varela, F. J., Thompson, E., and Rosch, E. (1991). *The Embodied Mind: Cognitive Science and Human Experience*. Cambridge, MA: MIT Press.

Williams, Mark A., Morris, Adam P., McGlone, Francis, Abbott, David F., and Mattingley, Jason B. (2004). Amygdala Responses to Fearful and Happy Facial Expressions under Conditions of Binocular Suppression. In *Journal of Neuroscience* 24, 2898–904. doi: 10.1523/JNEUROSCI.4977-03.2004.

Part V

Contemporary Issues and Applications

39

Buddhism and Environmental Ethics

SIMON P. JAMES

Ecological Holism

Like Buddhism, environmental ethics encompasses a wide variety of approaches, positions, and traditions. The seminal works of the field – most of which, not incidentally, were written by North Americans, Scandinavians, and Australians – often gave the impression that environmental ethics is primarily about our moral relations with the wilder parts of the biosphere – the lofty crags and dark forests so beloved by John Muir, rather than the softer, intensively managed landscapes of Belgium, say, or China's Northeast Plain. In recent years, however, an increasing number of environmental ethicists have turned their attention to those parts of the world which, although not wholly artifactual, have been deliberately and substantially shaped by human actions – "human" or "cultural" environments such as hedgerows, heaths, fields, and gardens (see, e.g., Arntzen and Brady 2008). Some, indeed, have urged that environmental ethicists should extend their sphere of concern to incorporate our moral relations with built environments (see, e.g., Fox 2006).

From its earliest days, moreover, environmental ethics has been closely associated with ecology. This is not to say that all environmental ethicists have endorsed the philosophical presuppositions of ecology – many have not. Nor is it to say that many environmental ethicists have engaged with cutting-edge developments of the sort that appear in journals such as *Oecologia* and *Ecological Monographs* – few have. But a number of them have been inspired by what they take to be the fundamental discovery of ecology: that all things in the biosphere – from humans to plants to soil – are intimately interconnected. "From the point of view of mature ecological science," writes one environmental ethicist, "the biological reality seems to be . . . more fluid and integrally patterned and less substantive and discrete than it had been previously represented." Organisms, for instance, must be conceived as "knots in the web of life, or temporary formations or perturbations in complex flow patterns" (Callicott 2010 [1986], 404–5).

A Companion to Buddhist Philosophy, First Edition. Edited by Steven M. Emmanuel.

To be sure, much more would need to be said to explain the meaning of such claims; however, the basic picture is clear: the physical world is not a collection of discrete objects, but a dynamic web of intimately interconnected elements.

In certain respects, this "ecological" conception of the world chimes with the worldview of early Buddhism. First, that worldview is, in one sense of the term, *naturalistic*. In many philosophical and religious traditions, human beings are thought to be essentially non-natural beings, imbued with supernatural souls. In early Buddhism, by contrast, all things, bar *nibbāna* (Skt *nirvāṇa*), are regarded as natural, in that all sentient beings – even the gods or *devas* – are thought to be bound up in *saṃsāra*, a single cycle of birth, death, and rebirth (see Holder 2007, 118, n.13; Harvey 2000, 152). Second, the worldview of early Buddhism is *holistic*. According to the central teachings of "non-self" (P. *anattā*) and "conditioned arising" (P. *paṭicca-samuppāda*), any phenomenal thing – understanding the term "thing" broadly – is thought to be what it is not on account of its possessing some intrinsic nature or "self," but because of the coincidence of certain conditions. Hence Buddhist thinkers maintain that any phenomenal thing, be it a hydrangea, hornbill, or human being, must be conceived holistically – that is, in terms of its relations to its manifold conditions. All such things are said to be "empty" of intrinsic nature (P. *sabhāva*; Skt *svabhāva*). Third, the early Buddhist worldview is *dynamic*, in that all phenomenal things are held to be impermanent (P. *anicca*). For the Buddha, as for Heraclitus, flux rather than stasis is the rule.

In the light of such observations, it might be tempting to conclude that Buddhist thinkers anticipated the most recent findings of ecological science (see Callicott 2008). And one might be tempted to draw the further conclusion that Buddhist philosophy qualifies as environmentally friendly precisely because it recognizes the ethical insight, founded on the empirical findings of ecology, that we human beings ought to care for nature because we are fundamentally part of it. Yet all this is much too fast. It is true that Buddhist ontologies – not just the ones indicated by early teachings of conditioned arising and non-self but also later ones such as the Madhyamaka account of emptiness (Skt *śūnyatā*) – are in certain respects holistic. Yet holistic ontologies are not all alike, and it is a further question whether any Buddhist "holisms" are equivalent to those envisaged by modern ecologists and their admirers in academic departments of philosophy or religion. In fact, there are several important differences between Buddhist and ecological varieties of holism. Most notably, Buddhist naturalism is not materialist, and in this respect it differs from many of the accounts of naturalism currently popular among philosophers and philosophically inclined scientists (see Holder 2007, 117–18). Moreover, when Mādhyamikas proclaim the emptiness of all things, they are not promoting anything like the picture of reality one might associate with ecological science. Whatever Nāgārjuna was up to (and determining that is beyond the scope of this essay), he certainly was not espousing the view that the world is a collection of physical objects bound together by causal connections.

So there are reasons to doubt the claim that the Buddhist teachings of non-self, conditioned arising, and emptiness amount to anything like an ecological view of nature. What is more, even if the Buddhist worldview *did* resemble that of modern ecological science, and even if, moreover, the Buddhist teachings *did* suggest that humans were in some sense "one" with the rest of nature, these points would not suffice to prove that Buddhism is environmentally friendly. For one can endorse an ecological view of nature – one can even insist on the unity or "oneness" of humans and nature – and yet at the same time consistently regard nature as being devoid of value. One could fully appreciate the intimate ecological connections between all things in nature, humans included, and yet not care at all about habitat depletion, over-hunting and global climate change (see, further, Cooper and James 2005, 108–13).

Nature and its Value

We have seen that Buddhism is, in one sense of the term, naturalistic. However, references to nature and what is natural can be interpreted in several different ways. In environmental ethics, for its part, nature is often contrasted with the human or human-made world rather than with the supernatural. What can Buddhist philosophy tell us about nature in this sense, the world of fur, feathers, scales, leaves, roots, and soil?

In his influential paper "The Early Buddhist Tradition and Ecological Ethics," Lambert Schmithausen argues that, while modern-day environmental thinkers tend to accord value to nature (in this second sense), early Buddhists did not. For early Buddhism, he maintains, nature, like the rest of the conditioned realm, was marked by "suffering, decay, death and impermanence" (Schmithausen 1997, 11). Thus, he writes:

> the ultimate analysis and evaluation of existence in early Buddhism does not motivate *efforts* for *preserving* nature, not to mention restoring it, nor efforts for transforming or *subjugating* it by means of technology. It only motivates the wish and effort to *liberate* oneself (*vimutti*) from *all* constituents of both personal existence and the world . . .
>
> (Ibid.)

Schmithausen (ibid., 28) admits that a few early Buddhist texts, notably some verses of the *Theragāthā*, portray nature as beautiful – although here, it may be added, natural things are regarded with a cool and detached eye and not with Wordsworthian or Muir-like passion (see Harris 2000, 127). What is more, he concedes the presence of a "hermit strand" in early Buddhism, a tendency to regard wild places as conducive to the meditative practices that enable awakening. Yet even here, he contends, nature is valued not as an end in itself, but merely because it can afford the meditator a welcome respite from the hubbub of social life (Schmithausen 1997, 26). Schmithausen's overall verdict remains unchanged: while, for modern environmental thinkers, nature is brimfull of value, for early Buddhism, and thus for those modern traditions which regard early Buddhism as the definitive statement of the Dhamma, it is for the most part a realm of impermanence and dis-ease from which the wise individual will seek to escape (a judgment echoed in Harris 2000, 122).

Not everyone has been convinced by this assessment. John Holder, for one, argues that Schmithausen has offered "an unwarrantedly pessimistic interpretation of the early texts" which obscures the fact that the early Buddhist path "is a way of living in this (natural) world . . . not an escape from it" (Holder 2007, 121, 122–3). Yet although Holder's arguments are strong and his conclusions well taken, it is nonetheless clear that early Buddhist conceptions of nature, while perhaps not as bleak as Schmithausen maintained, were still more downbeat than those that would emerge in later traditions of Buddhism, and in particular those that were to develop in East Asia (Eckel 1997, 339). In China, Korea, and Japan, nature and natural things often came to be accorded a spiritual meaning and value that would have been quite out of place in many Indian traditions of Buddhism. This is particularly apparent in East Asian art. It is evident, for example, in East Asian traditions of poetry – from the verses attributed to the T'ang dynasty Buddhist recluse Han Shan (said to have been scrawled onto cliffs and trees) to the highly stylized but nonetheless nature-focused *haiku* of figures such as Bashō (1644–1694) and Kikaku (1661–1707). The connections between Buddhist spirituality and the appreciation of nature are evident, too, in the ink and wash paintings of artists such as Sesshū (Japan, 1420–1506) and Bada Shanren (China, 1626–1705) as well as in Chinese and Japanese gardening, from the mossy paths and burbling streams of the *tsukiyama* kind of garden to the raked sand and bare rocks which epitomize the *kare-sansui* style.

The reasons for this shift towards the appreciation of nature are many and various. The key Mahāyāna teaching that *nirvāṇa* is not different from *saṃsāra* must have played its part, for instance. But one important factor must surely be the influence of certain indigenous and more "this-worldly" East Asian religious and philosophical traditions. The most important of these was Daoism. When Buddhism began to establish itself in the East, Chinese philosophers came to interpret its central teachings in Daoist and Neo-Daoist terms. The teaching of emptiness, for instance, was interpreted – rightly or wrongly, as the case may be – in terms of the Neo-Daoist concept of *wu* or non-being, a term often used to denote the nature of the mysterious *Dao* which was thought to run through and give rise to all things. Similarly, the ineffability of the seed of buddhahood, the buddha-nature, was compared with accounts of the ineffability of the *Dao*. In the wake of such interpretations, new, more world-directed forms of Buddhism began to take shape. The idea began to form that the fundamental truths of Buddhism could be found in the world, rather than in its transcendence.

This affirmation of nature and natural things was expressed most vividly in a transformed conception of Buddhist soteriology. Indian Mahāyānists had declared theirs the Great Vehicle, since it proclaimed that all sentient beings were destined for the greatest awakening – namely, the realization of buddhahood. Yet, as William LaFleur has shown, what in India had been vaunted as a welcome *expansion* of the vehicle was regarded in China as an unwarranted *restriction*. For why, the Chinese asked, should we deny the promise of buddhahood to plants and other apparently non-sentient beings? (LaFleur 1973, 95) Indeed, Chinese Buddhists such as Chan-jan (711–782) maintained that the Great Vehicle should be expanded to include not just grass and trees but even soil (see James 2004, 65).

Such ideas proved popular in Japan, where they resonated with indigenous Shintō notions that natural beings such as mountains and trees were inhabited by divine spirits (*kami*). From Japan's medieval period onwards, they would evolve into the teaching that all entities, not just human beings but also animals and plants, are inherently enlightened. In this manner, the Great Vehicle grew and grew, a tendency which reached its translogical conclusion in the claim of the Zen master Dōgen that all beings, not just sentient ones, do not *have* the buddha-nature, but *are* buddha-nature (see, further, James 2004, 22, 65–6).

Explaining the meaning of these claims is beyond the scope of this chapter (for a good introduction, see Parkes 1997). For present purposes, it will suffice to note one upshot of the transformed conception of the Great Vehicle: that non-human beings occasionally came to be portrayed as being spiritually superior to humans. Whereas human beings had to work at becoming enlightened, trees and other non-human beings were thought to be "in full possession of what man only still partially possesses" (LaFleur 2001, 112). Hence it came to be thought that the aspiring practitioner should look to, and try to emulate, natural things – the strength and dignity of pine trees, for instance, or the spontaneity of a clover's production of pollen (see James 2004, 67–8).

The ethical significance of these developments is, however, unclear. They certainly do not justify D. T. Suzuki's questionable claim that, in "the Orient," nature has never been conceived "in the form of an opposing power," but rather as a "constant friend and companion, who is to be absolutely trusted" (quoted in Harris 2000, 130). Nor do Buddhist conceptions of nature's spiritual significance entail that all individual beings, from deer to acorns to clods of soil, are legitimate objects of direct moral concern. In no Buddhist traditions has the first precept (non-violence or *ahiṃsā*) been thought to apply to our relations with rocks and clods of soil. Be that as it may, in many East Asian traditions of Buddhism, nature was regarded as valuable – it was thought to have value as a source of spiritual lessons. Is this enough to prove that East Asian Buddhism is inherently "green"? Many would contend that it is not, for to see nature as a spiritual resource is – they would add – nonetheless to see it as a resource and thus to have adopted an anthropocentric theory of value which is at odds with properly "green" or "environmental" concern.

This conclusion invites at least two responses. First, it must be acknowledged that, even if some Buddhist traditions portray non-sentient nature as a spiritual resource, individual sentient beings, whether human or non-human, are always regarded as objects of direct moral concern. A comparison with Kant's moral philosophy may prove helpful here. Unlike Descartes and Spinoza, Kant held that there are moral reasons to treat non-human animals well. Yet he added that any moral duties we have to non-human animals are in fact indirect duties to human beings. So the reason we should not harm a particular animal is not because doing so would wrong the creature. We should not harm it because doing so will incline us to mistreat our fellow human beings (see, further, O'Neill et al. 2008, 94–6). For Buddhist ethics, by contrast, animals are objects of both indirect and direct moral concern. By the lights of Buddhist ethics, one should not beat one's horse, not just because doing so will tend to make it harder to ride, nor simply because it will tend to warp one's own character, but also – and especially – because it will be bad for the horse (of which more presently).

Second, even if the Buddhist account of the value of non-sentient nature is in some sense anthropocentric, it is a further question whether the relevant sort of human-centeredness must disqualify it from serving as part of an adequate environmental ethic. For it could be argued that, in trying to justify moral concern for nature, what matters is not exactly whether nature is or is not thought to have value because, and to the extent that, it serves human interests, but what the interests in question are. If they reflect greed and narrow-mindedness, then the anthropocentrism in question might legitimately be regarded as pernicious. But if they testify to a broader and richer family of human hopes and aspirations – the aspiration to realize awakening, perhaps

– then it is less clear that the relevant sort of anthropocentrism should be a cause for concern. After all, there would seem to be a world of moral difference between valuing nature as a source of short-term profit and valuing it as a source of spiritual lessons.

Environmental Virtue

One way to consider the relations between Buddhist philosophy and environmental ethics is to ask what value Buddhist philosophical traditions have attributed to – or, for theorists of a realist inclination, discovered in – nature. But that is not the only way to proceed.

So let us begin anew, not by considering what Buddhist thinkers have had to say about nature and its value, but with the question of what they have said about the living of a good life. The Buddha's general conclusion is, of course, well known. To live an awakened or "nirvanic" life, one needs neither great wealth nor privileged birth. One needs to develop oneself. Like Aristotle or the Stoics, the Buddha maintains that living a good life is in large part a matter of becoming a certain sort of person, one who is compassionate, wise, generous, mindful, and so forth.

These observations have led some writers to conclude that Buddhist ethics is basically virtue ethical in form, in that it takes judgments of character to be primary, and eudaimonistic, in that it takes the virtues to be character traits a person needs if she is to live a genuinely fulfilling life. If these claims are correct and Buddhist ethics is basically virtue ethical in form, an interesting possibility presents itself: that, in assessing the environmental implications of Buddhist ethics, one should begin by considering not what sort of value Buddhist philosophers have attributed to nature, but what they have had to say about the virtues an awakened life is thought to exemplify. The possibility presents itself that a Buddhist virtue ethic could be – or could at least provide the basis for – what is sometimes referred to as an "environmental virtue ethic."

At first glance, this might seem an unpromising suggestion. It might appear that, while the notion of a Buddhist virtue ethic is dubious, that of a Buddhist *environmental* virtue ethic is doubly so – "nonsense on stilts," to adapt Jeremy Bentham. First, it might seem that a focus on improving one's character and leading a good life is at odds with the Buddhist teaching of non-self. If all things are void of self, how can a virtuous individual aim to improve her*self*? Doesn't self-improvement presuppose the existence of an abiding self to be improved? Second, talk of character and the good life might seem disturbingly human-centered or anthropocentric. To speak of character is, after all, to refer to the character of *human* beings; to speak of the good life is to speak of how we *humans* ought to live. Yet if we are looking for an environmental ethic, then surely we should be thinking not of what is good for us humans, but what is good for nature, for the *non*-human world?

But these objections presuppose a mistaken conception of the relation between virtue ethics and moral motivation. To say that Buddhism takes the form of a eudaimonist virtue ethic is to say that according to Buddhism the virtues tend to benefit the possessor. But it is not to say that the virtuous person will be *motivated* by a desire to secure some benefit for herself. For example, it might be good for a person to be compassionate, since thinking, feeling, and acting in an appropriately compassionate way when circumstances demand is part of what it means to lead a good life. Yet that does not mean that the compassionate person is motivated by a desire to lead a good life. The benefit comes as an unsought for by-product; the truly compassionate person simply sees suffering to be alleviated.

There is, moreover, no anthropocentrism here. Compassion is considered an integral part of the good life, as Buddhists envision it; and it is true that, so far as we know, all Buddhists are human. But this is not to say that the compassionate person will be motivated by a desire to alleviate the suffering of humans *rather than* non-humans. She will simply see suffering to be alleviated, and the question of whether it is the suffering of a dog or a monkey or a human being will, all things being equal, be of no account.

Talk of compassion for animals might seem to smack of sentimentality. It might seem that, in considering the rights and wrongs of our treatment of animals, one ought to base one's judgments on good hard facts and eschew spurious appeals to the heart. But it would be a mistake to dismiss Buddhist appeals to compassion on these grounds. For one thing, in Buddhist traditions compassion is thought to have a cognitive component: as stressed in the Mahāyāna, true compassion, the *mahā-karuṇā* of the bodhisattva, is internally related to *mahā-prajñā*, insight into the emptiness of all things. For another, in Buddhist contexts, concern for others is always conditioned by another virtue, equanimity. Thus compassion is supposed to extend to all animals – not just charismatic megafauna such as tigers, pandas, and whales, but also creatures that scamper, scuttle, or slither (Harvey 2000, 170). Thus Gary Snyder imagines a "depth ecology" which would "go to the dark side of nature – the ball of crunched bones in the scat, the feathers in the snow, the tales of insatiable appetite . . . the nocturnal, anaerobic, cannibalistic, microscopic, digestive [and] fermentative" (Snyder 2000, 136–7). From the standpoint of Buddhist ethics, all these beings, no matter how repellent or insignificant they might seem, live lives afflicted by *duḥkha*, and so all of them are legitimate objects of compassion.

Since it can be exhibited in one's dealings with the natural world, compassion qualifies as a Buddhist *environmental* virtue (as cruelty and callousness count as Buddhist environmental vices). Other such virtues could be *mettā* (Skt *maitrī*), the settled disposition to wish sentient beings happiness, and *muditā*, the tendency to take pleasure in their happiness. Another might be the mindfulness (P. *sati*; Skt *smṛti*) that the good person is supposed to exercise not just in her relations with her fellow humans, but in her dealings with her fellow non-humans, and indeed in her relations with the environment as a whole. The mindful person, in this sense, takes care to switch off electric lights when they are not needed, to walk when she doesn't need to drive, to recycle when she can, and so forth. And in considering the implications of her actions she may have recourse to the principle of universal mutual causality, as developed in East Asian Buddhist traditions such as Hua-Yen and adapted more recently by thinkers such as Joanna Macy. "Even this small action," she might think, "is a crystallisation or a condensation of a vast network of conditions" (see, further, Cooper and James 2005, 114–17).

A virtue intimately related to mindfulness – and another candidate environmental virtue – is selflessness or humility: not the tendency to judge oneself to be either worse than or equal to others, but the trait exhibited by the person who has become released from the self-centeredness apparent, among other things, in the tendency to rank oneself relative to one's fellows. To be humble in this sense is to be freed from the inveterate tendency to regard the world through the distorting prism of self-interest: to use Iris Murdoch's apt expression, it is to have undergone the "unselfing" that enables one to see things clearly (Murdoch 1971, 82). But it is also to be released from the tendency to see all things in terms of human interests. As Malcolm David Eckel observes, to follow the Buddhist path is not just to "challenge the naïve patterns of self-centredness from which the fabric of ordinary life is woven" but also to cultivate "concern for a wider network of life" (Eckel 1997, 342). Condemnations of anthropocentric hubris are there in the canonical texts – in, for example, the Buddha's criticisms of the priests of his day who regarded cows primarily as sacrificial offerings. But they could also be brought to bear upon certain modern attitudes and practices. Most obviously, the general tendency to regard nature as nothing more than a stock of resources could be criticized on such grounds. But anthropocentric hubris might also be thought to be evident in the popular tendency to regard nature as a repository of "natural capital" or a provider of "ecosystem services." For while it is true that those who speak, write, and think in such terms often wish sincerely to protect nature, their rhetoric both reflects and fosters a hubris of the sort one might associate with those who brazenly proclaim that nature is valuable only when it can be converted into dollars and pounds.

The virtue ethical approach sketched above has several merits. In particular, it allows one to justify moral concern for nature without appealing to certain contentious philosophical claims. First, it does not require one to postulate that natural beings have moral rights. This counts as an advantage, since talk of rights is difficult (though perhaps not impossible) to square with the basic principles of Buddhist ethics and, in any case, arguably presupposes a context of law and convention within which beings can claim their rights – a presupposition which is difficult to uphold when the beings under consideration are not rational and autonomous (see, further, O'Neill et al. 2008, 36–9). Second, adopting a virtue ethical approach does not require one to claim that natural beings have value "in themselves," intrinsic value. Such claims are, to be sure, unproblematic if they are taken to indicate merely that certain parts of nature are valuable as ends and not simply as means. But if they are taken to suggest that the value in question is non-relational, then they are hard to justify. Many of the properties that are central to the evaluation of natural environments, such as rarity, species richness, and biodiversity, are relational (ibid., 118), and in any case appeals to non-relational properties of any sort are difficult to accommodate within Buddhist conceptual frameworks (in which relationality is, of course, the rule). References to intrinsic value are also contentious if they are taken to suggest that nature's value can be defined without reference to the presence of actual or potential valuers, not least because it is unclear how such strongly objective values could exert any sort of "pull" upon moral agents (ibid., 120). Third, a virtue ethical approach does not presuppose extravagant "deep ecological" claims to the effect that it is possible to identify with other beings and in this way realize one's true Self. Again, this is to its credit, since, as well as being open to a variety of metaphysical and ethical objections, such claims are difficult to reconcile with the key Buddhist teaching of non-self and hence difficult to accommodate within a recognizably Buddhist environmental ethic (James 2004, 76–82; cf. Henning 2002). By contrast, if the virtue ethical reading sketched above is correct, then it would be wrong nonchalantly to squash a beetle, not because the beetle has either moral rights or intrinsic value, and not because all things, beetle included, are ultimately parts of a single Self – it would be wrong to squash the beetle because doing so would evince a cluster of moral vices, including callousness and hubris. (For virtue ethical readings of Buddhist environmental ethics, see Sponberg 1997; James 2004; Cooper and James 2005; and Sahni 2008.)

The Scope of Moral Concern

Not all writers think that Buddhist ethics is best thought of as a virtue ethic. Some think it more closely resembles certain other moral theories, such as utilitarianism. Others have rejected the very notion of trying to interpret Buddhist ethics through the lenses provided by Western moral theories on the grounds that such transcultural comparisons can encourage misinterpretations. However, whether or not Buddhism is thought to provide an environmental *virtue* ethic, it is clear that Buddhist ethics sanctions direct moral concern for at least some parts of the more or less natural (as opposed to artifactual) world. It is clear that Buddhist ethics qualifies as an environmental ethic. It is a further question, however, whether its conclusions are in tune with what we nowadays think of as environmental views.

Consider Buddhist views on our moral relations with (non-human) animals. Animals are regarded as fellow travellers in *saṃsāra*, which is to say that it is possible for an animal to be reborn as a human and a human as an animal. In this sense, any particular animal could have been one's mother, father, brother, sister, son, or daughter, and *saṃsāra* really is like one big unhappy family. Furthermore, as noted above, animals are regarded as objects of direct moral concern. In this respect, the general conclusions of Buddhist ethics – if not the arguments used to support them – are in line with those of modern-day opponents of "speciesism" such as Tom Regan and Peter Singer. But this is not to say that talk of animal *rights* – which is favored by Regan, if not by Singer – can easily be accommodated within a Buddhist ethical framework. Nor is it to say that Buddhist thinkers have tended to hold animals in high regard. On the contrary, while some texts – notably the *Jātaka* tales – depict animals in a positive light, the overall impression, in early Buddhism at least, is much less favorable. Animals are frequently portrayed as leading lives ruled by vice and hence *duḥkha* ("constitutionally disposed to acts of violence and sexual misconduct," as Harris [2000, 121] puts it). Rebirth as an animal is, moreover, generally regarded as a bad thing, a punishment for past misdeeds (ibid.; cf. Schmithausen 1997, 29; see, further, Waldau 2002, Part III). Hence the legendary "pure lands" or heavens envisaged by the devotees of some Buddhist traditions are thought to be devoid of animals. Since these lands are *heavens*, none of their inhabitants has to suffer rebirth as a non-human animal (Harris 2000, 121–2).

Buddhist views on vegetarianism also diverge from those of modern pro-animal thinkers. Both Singer and Regan oppose meat-eating – Singer on the grounds that it causes a vast amount of unnecessary suffering, Regan because it involves regarding and treating conscious beings as mere means. By contrast, although many Mahāyāna

Buddhists are vegetarians, even Theravādin monks and nuns tend to eat meat (see, further, Harvey 2000, 157–65). Indeed, they are urged not to refuse meat that is freely given as alms, so long as they can be confident that the animal was not killed specifically to feed them. It would be wrong to refuse, since (as Harvey explains) doing so "would deprive the donor of the karmic fruitfulness engendered by giving alms-food" (ibid., 160).

In certain respects, then, Buddhist views of animals diverge from those of modern-day opponents of speciesism. And in other respects, too, Buddhist ethics seems at odds with modern green or environmentalist agendas. Take species. The conservation of endangered species of animal is one of the primary objectives of some of the most influential environmental organizations. But it is difficult to see why, on Buddhist principles, one should conserve certain individuals simply because the species of which they are members happens to be endangered. At first glance, it would seem that, for Buddhists, *duḥkha* is *duḥkha*, and whether it is experienced by a white rhino or a rat is of no moral consequence at all (cf. Schmithausen 1997, 20; Harvey 2000, 183–4). Moreover, it is hard to see why, on Buddhist principles, efforts should be made to conserve a species *per se*. There is a great deal of controversy about what a species is – in fact some thinkers maintain that the concept ought to be eliminated altogether; however, just about all commentators agree that, whatever they are, species are not sentient. Individual flesh and blood pandas can amble around forests in southern China and chew on bamboo shoots, and, *pace* Descartes and Malebranche, they are evidently sentient. However, the species *Ailuropoda melanoleuca* cannot wander around forests or chomp on bamboo. Neither can it experience anything. Talk of compassion for species would therefore seem to indicate a category error.

The question of our moral relations to species *per se* points to a more general issue. While Buddhist ethics is able to sanction direct moral concern for individual sentient beings, many modern environmental thinkers propose that we have direct moral duties to *non*-sentient nature. Such thinkers tend to adopt one of two strategies. The first is to argue that all individual living beings, sentient and non-sentient, are objects of direct moral concern. The second is to argue that direct moral concern can be extended not merely to individuals but also to collectives such as ecosystems (see, further, O'Neill et al. 2008, ch. 6). Yet neither the first ("biocentric") nor the second ("ecocentric") strategy can easily be justified on Buddhist principles. It is true that there was some debate about the sentience of plants in early Buddhism; even so, ancient doctrinal disputes aside, it is difficult to justify the claim that plants are sentient. While a sunflower might be said to have certain interests (in receiving sufficient water, nutrients, and sunlight, for instance), the interests in question are not consciously held. Likewise, a forest or an area of wetland is incapable of thinking or feeling anything. Hence it is difficult to see how such entities could be legitimate objects of compassion (cf. Schmithausen 1997, 20; on the sentience of plants, see the discussion of Schmithausen's findings in Harvey 2000, 175).

One must take care not to conclude too much from this, however. For instance, some writers have suggested that non-violence (*ahiṃsā*) should be interpreted not simply as a moral precept or rule, but as a moral virtue that can be exhibited in one's relations with both sentient and non-sentient beings (James 2004, 69–72; Cooper and James 2005, 101–3, 132–5). And this interpretation would seem to be supported by the fact that plants are afforded a certain degree of protection under the *Vinaya* code governing the conduct of monks and nuns (Cooper and James 2005, 134). Yet whether or not this interpretation of *ahiṃsā* is found to be compelling, it is clear that extending compassion to sentient beings requires a certain degree of moral concern for the non-sentient world. Consider the conservation of tigers, for example. As we saw, Buddhist ethics can furnish us with moral reasons to protect individual tigers. We should treat tigers in some ways and not others because, like us, tigers are sentient beings and therefore legitimate objects of other-regarding moral virtues such as compassion and *mettā*. Yet Buddhist thinkers would affirm that, like all "things," any individual tiger is void of intrinsic nature, and that, as such, it is what it is because of the coincidence of certain conditions. In order to preserve tigers, then, one needs to preserve the network of conditions that gives rise to and constitutes the creatures – not just so many pounds of flesh, bone, and fur, but vast stretches of forest, brush, and wetland (cf. Holder 2007, 125–6). For these reasons, the Buddhist ethicist will be disinclined, in practice, to make a sharp distinction between the sentient and non-sentient parts of the world; she will not wish to etch the moral circle too deeply. Recognizing the interdependence of all things, she will realize that such sharp lines cannot be drawn.

The Social and Political Dimensions of Environmental Issues

We have considered the broadly virtue ethical question of how one ought to live one's life, and we have seen that part of the Buddhist answer is that we ought to try, all things being equal, to alleviate suffering – not just our own suffering, nor simply that of our fellow humans, but the suffering of all sentient beings. And in certain respects this conclusion chimes with what is usually thought of as environmental concern. But of course much more would need to be said if one were to articulate and defend an adequate Buddhist-inspired environmental ethic. For one thing, something would need to be said about the social, economic, and political dimensions of environmental problems. What, for instance, might a Buddhist ethic be able to tell us about Aristotle's old concern, the ways in which different sorts of political order can foster or hinder the development of good character? What, moreover, could it tell us about consumerism and its environmental implications? What might it have to say about the popular tendency to conceive our relations with nature in quasi-economic terms – in terms of "natural capital," for example, and "ecosystem services"? And what could a Buddhist environmental ethic tell us about the social and political arrangements that distance us from the unwelcome consequences of our actions – the carefully concealed abattoirs, the waste sent overseas to be treated in poorer countries? With Zen teacher Philip Kapleau, one might ask what use there is in "a Buddhism that lectures individuals on their delusions, but has nothing to say about the deluding political and economic conditions that reinforce these" (Kapleau 2000, 244). The social, economic, and political dimensions of environmental issues have, it is true, received some attention in the literature on Buddhism (see, for instance, Ophuls 2000; Payne 2010). Yet on these topics, as on much else pertaining to Buddhist ethics and the environment, much work remains to be done.

References

Arntzen, S., and Brady, E. (eds) (2008). *Humans in the Land: The Ethics and Aesthetics of the Cultural Landscape*. Oslo: Oslo Academic Press.

Callicott, J. Baird (2008). The New New (Buddhist?) Ecology? In *Journal for the Study of Religion, Nature and Culture* 2, 166–82.

Callicott, J. Baird (2010 [1986]). The Metaphysical Implications of Ecology. In *Environmental Ethics: The Big Questions*. Ed. D. R. Keller. Oxford: Wiley-Blackwell, 400–8. Originally pubd in *Environmental Ethics* 8, 301–16.

Cooper, D. E., and James, S. P. (2005). *Buddhism, Virtue and Environment*. Aldershot: Ashgate.

Eckel, M. D. (1997). Is there a Buddhist Philosophy of Nature? In *Buddhism and Ecology: The Interconnection of Dharma and Deeds*. Ed. M. E. Tucker and D. R. Williams. Cambridge, MA: Harvard University Press, 327–49.

Fox, W. (2006). *A Theory of General Ethics: Human Relationships, Nature, and the Built Environment*. Cambridge, MA: MIT Press.

Harris, I. (2000). Buddhism and Ecology. In *Contemporary Buddhist Ethics*. Ed. D. Keown. Richmond, Surrey: Curzon Press, 113–36.

Harvey, P. (2000). *An Introduction to Buddhist Ethics*. Cambridge: Cambridge University Press.

Henning, D. H. (2002). *Buddhism and Deep Ecology*. Bloomington, IN: First Books.

Holder, J. (2007). A Suffering (But Not Irreparable) Nature: Environmental Ethics from the Perspective of Early Buddhism. In *Contemporary Buddhism* 8, 113–30.

James, S. P. (2004). *Zen Buddhism and Environmental Ethics*. Aldershot: Ashgate.

Kapleau, P. (2000). Responsibility and Social Action. In *Dharma Rain: Sources of Buddhist Environmentalism*. Ed. S. Kaza and K. Kraft. Boston: Shambhala.

LaFleur, W. (1973). Saigyō and the Buddhist Value of Nature. In *History of Religions* 13, 93–128. Repr. in *Nature in Asian Traditions of Thought*. Ed. J. Baird Callicott and Roger T. Ames. Albany: State University of New York Press, 2001, 183–209.

Murdoch, I. (1971). *The Sovereignty of Good*. London: Routledge & Kegan Paul.

O'Neill, J., Holland, A., and Light, A. (eds) (2008). *Environmental Values*. London: Routledge.

Ophuls, W. (2000). Notes for a Buddhist Politics. In *Dharma Rain: Sources of Buddhist Environmentalism*. Ed. S. Kaza and K. Kraft. Boston: Shambhala, 369–78.

Parkes, G. (1997). Voices of Mountains, Trees, and Rivers: Kūkai, Dōgen, and a Deeper Ecology. In *Buddhism and Ecology: The Interconnection of Dharma and Deeds*. Ed. M. E. Tucker and D. R. Williams. Cambridge, MA: Harvard University Press, 111–28.

Payne, R. K. (ed.) (2010). *How Much is Enough? Buddhism, Consumerism, and the Human Environment*. Somerville, MA: Wisdom.

Sahni, P. (2008). *Environmental Ethics in Buddhism: A Virtues Approach*. London: Routledge.

Schmithausen, L. (1997). The Early Buddhist Tradition and Ecological Ethics. *Journal of Buddhist Ethics* 4, 1–42. Repr. in *How Much is Enough? Buddhism, Consumerism, and the Human Environment*. Ed. R. K. Payne. Somerville, MA: Wisdom, 2010.

Snyder, G. (2000). Blue Mountains Constantly Walking. In *Dharma Rain: Sources of Buddhist Environmentalism*. Ed. S. Kaza and K. Kraft. Boston: Shambhala, 125–41.

Sponberg, A. (1997). Green Buddhism and the Hierarchy of Compassion. In *Buddhism and Ecology: The Interconnection of Dharma and Deeds*. Ed. M. E. Tucker and D. R. Williams. Cambridge, MA: Harvard University Press, 351–76.

Waldau, P. (2002). *The Specter of Speciesism: Buddhist and Christian Views of Animals*. New York: Oxford University Press.

40

Buddhism and Biomedical Issues

DAMIEN KEOWN

The first problem which presents itself when discussing biomedical issues from a Buddhist perspective is whether we can speak of a "Buddhist view." Because of its internal variety and the absence of any central authority, some scholars prefer to speak of "Buddhisms" (plural) as opposed to "Buddhism" in the singular, which seems to preclude statements of the kind "The Buddhist view on issue *x* is . . ." without considerable qualification. Despite the differences among schools, however, I believe we can speak of a "Buddhist view" at least as far as our present purposes are concerned. This is because there is a good deal of consistency among the major schools in the field of ethics, both in terms of the dominant patterns of reasoning employed and in the conclusions reached on specific issues. Indeed, there is some reason for regarding ethics (particularly monastic ethics) as a more cohesive force in Buddhism than doctrine. Paul Williams has suggested that "in spite of the considerable diversity in Buddhism there is a relative unity and stability in the moral code" (Williams 1989, 6). However, even if we can postulate a common moral core as suggested above, it does not mean it will be an easy matter to ascertain the Buddhist view on particular contemporary issues.

One factor hindering progress has been the reluctance of the Buddhist Sangha (monastic order) to involve itself publicly in scientific controversies. The traditional monastic education does not include science, and many monks are ignorant of medical advances and the issues they raise. They can be uncomfortable discussing such subjects both from a lack of knowledge and on account of the fact that certain medical matters, especially those involving sex and reproduction, are seen as inappropriate subjects of conversation for those who have renounced home and family life. In general monks are seen by the laity as being "above" such matters, and laymen (and particularly lay women) would find a conversation on topics such as contraception, assisted reproduction, or abortion to be awkward and inappropriate. Accordingly, Buddhist monks, who

A Companion to Buddhist Philosophy, First Edition. Edited by Steven M. Emmanuel.

are the traditional source of authority on Buddhist teachings for most lay Buddhists, have been largely silent on bioethics (a notable exception is the Thai monk the Venerable Mettanando, who is also an MD). The practice in Buddhist countries has been for such matters to be devolved to the secular medical authorities, and few questions are raised publicly about the morality of contemporary medical research and practice. This attitude is changing slowly as more Westerners join the Order as monks and nuns.

A further factor may be a cultural one – namely, that Buddhists do not perceive any threat or challenge to their traditional beliefs from scientific discoveries in the way this was experienced by Christians. Indeed, it was primarily the response of Christian thinkers to new medical technologies in the 1960s that gave rise to the field of bioethics. Many Buddhists, by contrast, feel that their religion – which is generally perceived as adopting a rational and empiricist outlook – is in harmony with modern science and so they have little to fear from it (Ratanakul 2001). Also, Buddhists in general seem more flexible and "situational" in their interpretation of moral norms and less confident that the "correct" choice can be derived in advance through the application of moral logic. As Jeff Wilson notes, "Many commentators explicitly frame Buddhism in terms of open-armed compassion rather than boundary-drawing dogma, and as driven by ritual and practice rather than doctrine or rule" (Wilson 2009, 188). Adopting this more contextual approach means that Buddhists are reluctant to press a moral analysis in order to derive universal principles in the systematic way this is done in the West. This makes it harder to find position papers or authoritative statements of opinion by ecclesiastical authorities.

The study of Buddhist bioethics has evolved only within the last decade and the academic literature is extremely limited.[1] The main forum for the discussion of bioethics in Asian countries is a secular one – namely, the Asian Bioethics Association (founded in 1995 as the East Asian Association of Bioethics), an organization that has done much to promote awareness of and debate around bioethical issues, including hosting panels on Buddhist bioethics at its annual conferences.[2] The 2005 adoption by UNESCO of the Universal Declaration on Bioethics and Human Rights has been an important catalyst in promoting interest and raising awareness about bioethics both in the region and globally, an initiative that received further impetus from the establishment of the UNESCO Bangkok Bioethics Roundtable in 2006.

Buddhism and Medicine

Although Buddhism has only a short history of involvement in bioethics, it has a much longer history of involvement in the practice of medicine. R. L. Soni has written: "It is indeed a matter of supreme interest that the noble profession of medicine and the corpus of thought known as Buddhism are both concerned in their own way in the alleviation, control and ultimately the removal of human sufferings" (Soni 1976, 137). In a similar vein, under its entry on "Buddhism," the *Dictionary of Medical Ethics* points out that "The principles governing Buddhism and the practice of medicine have much in common" (Duncan et al. 1981).

The Buddhist Sangha has a claim to be the world's oldest and most widespread continuous social institution. For over 2,000 years it has, among its other activities, maintained a close involvement with the treatment of the sick. Several centuries before Christ, Buddhist monks were developing treatments for many kinds of medical conditions, and, it seems, Buddhism can claim much of the credit for the development of traditional Indian medicine known as *Āyurveda* (Zysk 1991, 4).[3] According to Zysk, the early Buddhist monasteries of India were the places where the most significant developments in Indian medicine took place (ibid., 6). The first beneficiaries of Buddhist medical expertise were therefore monks themselves. The Buddha pointed out that, since monks had severed all other social ties, it was incumbent on them to care for one another:

> You, O monks, have neither a father nor a mother who could nurse you. If, O monks, you do not nurse one another, who, then, will nurse you? Whoever, O monks, would nurse me, he should nurse the sick.[4]

Given the close connection between medicine and monasticism, it will come as no surprise to find that the Buddhist attitude to the treatment and care of patients is deeply influenced by its religious beliefs. What is to be done and not to be done by the physician will be determined by the same moral principles that determine what is to be done and not to be done by a monk, since the physician is a monk first and a physician second. Thus, as we might expect, medical ethics in Buddhism involves essentially the application of the wider principles of religious ethics to problems in a more specialized field.

The First Noble Truth

If we seek a doctrinal basis for the link between medical practice and Buddhist doctrine we will find it in the Four Noble Truths. It is under the First Noble Truth that the Buddha sets out the basic problem faced by mankind. The First Noble Truth points out that all forms of embodied existence are unsatisfactory by virtue of the physical and mental suffering which is inherent in them. It states: "Birth is suffering, sickness is suffering, old age is suffering, death is suffering; pain, grief, sorrow, despair and lamentation are suffering." The four physical aspects of suffering mentioned – namely, birth, sickness, old age, and death – may involve physical pain to a greater or lesser degree. The word translated as "suffering" (*duḥkha*) includes physical pain but denotes more broadly the profound unsatisfactoriness of the very mode of being within which birth and death occur. Against the background of the doctrines of karma and rebirth and the long cycle of lifetimes which, according to Buddhism, all experience, no one can expect that their lives will remain free of pain and disease. Whatever advances are made by medical science, it is unlikely that there will be a cure for every complaint. No one is immune from illness, and even the Buddha received medical treatment during his lifetime. In the final analysis it is unlikely that medical science will ever conquer sickness or death, though it may succeed in extending the average lifespan far beyond its present limits. The *psychological* problems mentioned under the First Noble Truth ("grief, sorrow, lamentation and despair") are perhaps even more intractable, and conditions involving anxiety and depression can be more debilitating and difficult to treat than physical infirmities. The point need not be labored, and the extensive catalogue of human mental and physical afflictions is well known to physicians and laymen alike.

Non-Self

The Truth of Suffering concludes with the cryptic statement "the five factors of individuality are suffering." This is a reference to a teaching expounded by the Buddha in his second sermon (Vin.I.13), which analyzes human nature into five factors (*skandhas*) – namely, the physical body (*rūpa*), sensations and feelings (*vedanā*), cognitions (*saṃjñā*), character traits and dispositions (*saṃskāra*), and consciousness or sentiency (*vijñāna*). There is no need to discuss the five factors individually, since the important point for us here is not so much what the list includes as what it does not. Specifically, the doctrine makes no mention of a soul or Self, understood as an eternal and immutable spiritual essence. By adopting this position the Buddha set himself apart from the orthodox Indian tradition as well as from other religions which teach that each person possesses an eternal soul (*ātman*). The Buddha's approach was practical and empirical, akin more to psychology than to theology. He explained human nature as constituted by the five factors much in the way that an automobile is constituted by its wheels, transmission, engine, steering, and chassis. Unlike science, of course, he believed that a person's moral identity – what we might call the individual's "spiritual DNA" – survives death and is reborn. This "person in process" view of the individual has important implications for the Buddhist perspective on bioethical issues, as will be seen below. A recent article by Michael Brannigan (Brannigan 2010) explores the influence of the non-self doctrine on North American bioethics.

Virtues

Two important Buddhist virtues that come to the fore particularly in Mahāyāna Buddhism are wisdom (*prajñā*) and compassion (*karuṇā*). Wisdom embraces the secular arts and sciences as well as religious teachings, and Buddhism has no objection to scientific research and investigation aimed at enhancing human well-being. The Dalai Lama is a frequent participant in scientific discussions and has expressed the view that, if science shows Buddhist beliefs to be wrong, those beliefs would have to be changed. Compassion (*karuṇā*) is a virtue which is of importance in all schools of Buddhism but which is particularly emphasized by the Mahāyāna, which sees selfless identification with the suffering of others as a defining quality of the bodhisattva or saint. In early Buddhism, *karuṇā* figures as the second of the four *Brahmavihāras* or "Divine Abidings." These states of mind, cultivated especially through the practice of meditation, are lovingkindness (*maitrī*), compassion (*karuṇā*), sympathetic joy (*muditā*), and equanimity (*upekṣā*).

A corollary of this compassionate identification with living things is the attitude of respect for life encapsulated in the term *ahiṃsā*, meaning "non-harming" or "non-injury." The imperative to respect life is enshrined in the first of the Five Precepts, and *ahiṃsā* plays a fundamental role in Buddhist bioethics. This belief in the "sanctity of life"[5] should be understood not as a commitment to "vitalism" (the belief that life must be preserved at all costs) but as the notion that intentional killing always represents a failure to respect the inalienable dignity of living creatures. In the context of bioethics, "life" means human life, but some, particularly Far-Eastern, schools of Buddhism come close to adopting a Schweitzerian "reverence for life" position in terms of which plants, micro-organisms, and even natural phenomena are given moral status. Indo-Tibetan schools, on the other hand, tend to see the relationship between plant, animal and human life as hierarchical rather than equalitarian. Human life occupies a place at the top of the hierarchy and is regarded as the most auspicious of all rebirths.

The conduct of monks, including medical practice, is regulated by a monastic code made up of some 250 rules. The rules emphasize non-harming, truthfulness, non self-aggrandizement, respect, modesty, and decorum, and although these virtues are intended for those in monastic orders they may also be thought appropriate to the members of any professional body, among them scientists, physicians, and nurses. Other important Buddhist virtues that should inform the practice of any profession in addition to those already mentioned are generosity (with one's time and resources), sobriety, and self-restraint. One classical formulation of important virtues includes generosity (*dāna*), kindly speech (*priya-vākya*), helpful action (*tatthārthacaryā*), and impartiality (*samānārthatā*) (Harvey 2000, 110). Informed by these virtues, the medical or other professional should act at all times in a manner consistent with his or her conscience. Another quality of great importance in one's personal and professional life is heedfulness (*appamāda*). This is described as the basis of all the virtues and is said to be composed of energy (*viriya*) and mindfulness (*sati*). Mindfulness is alert presence of mind that enables one to be both focused on the action in hand and aware of one's inner mental states, including intentions and motives. Buddhism recommends the practice of meditation as a means of cultivating all the above qualities.

The "Four Principles"

An obvious theoretical starting point for an inquiry into biomedical issues in Buddhism is to ask if the popular "Four Principles" approach (Beauchamp and Childress 1989) can be applied successfully to Buddhist bioethics. This very influential methodology prioritizes the four principles of benevolence, non-maleficence, autonomy, and justice in the resolution of moral dilemmas in health care. These principles are thought to be universal and to reflect moral convictions shared by people around the world. Robert E. Florida (1994) has discussed the merits of the "Four Principles" with specific reference to Buddhism and concludes that Buddhist bioethics is strongly compatible with two of these principles – namely, non-maleficence and beneficence – since these map directly onto the established Buddhist virtues of non-injury (*ahiṃsā*) and compassion (*karuṇā*). He is more circumspect about the role of the other two, since autonomy and justice are rarely mentioned in Buddhist teachings and it is difficult to think of translations for these terms in Buddhist languages. The Buddhist doctrine of non-self, furthermore, seems to undermine the notion of autonomous agency, and the important doctrine of dependent origination (*pratītya-samutpāda*) depicts not a world of autonomous individuals but one consisting of an interrelated and interdependent social network. In Asian societies, moreover, the requirements of justice are typically expressed in the form of duties rather than rights. While some accommodation between Western and Eastern concepts may be possible in these two areas, the fit is awkward at first sight.

The "Four Principles" approach, therefore, can be only partially successful in the context of Buddhism. This approach also has its own internal theoretical problems, not the least being how to prioritize and resolve conflicts between the four principles in any given situation.[6]

Other Theoretical Approaches

To gain further analytical traction, scholars have sought parallels with Western models beyond the "Four Principles" approach. The three most influential theories of ethics in the West have been deontology, utilitarianism, and virtue ethics. My own view is that Buddhist ethics bears a greater resemblance to virtue ethics than to any other Western theory, but not all scholars would agree with this identification. Some commentators have noted that the Buddhist belief in karma, according to which moral deeds always entail good and bad future consequences, gives Buddhism a utilitarian flavor and have drawn parallels between Buddhism and one or other of the variants of utilitarianism (Goodman 2009). The Mahāyāna doctrine of Skillful Means, which allows bodhisattvas considerable moral leeway, also has a utilitarian aspect, since it seems to prioritize successful outcomes over respect for the precepts.

We could add that Buddhism also possesses features associated with deontological ethics, such as the emphasis placed on the Five Precepts as moral rules that should never be infringed. The "no harm" principle (*ahiṃsā*) in Buddhism appears to be a near absolute constraint on action. Evidence of this kind suggests there is room for a deontological construction of Buddhist ethics, perhaps drawing on Kant's notion of the "categorical imperative" to explain absolutist features of the kind mentioned (Olson 1993). Finally, some scholars favour a "no theory" view of Buddhist ethics, in terms of which none of the available Western candidates adequately does justice to the complexity of the subject matter and characterize Buddhist ethics as a form of "ethical particularism," in terms of which moral judgments are made by drawing on different elements of Buddhist teachings as the situation requires (Hallisey 1996).

Transcultural Ethics

Before making comparisons of any kind we should pause to reflect on the methodological problems which such comparisons raise. It may be that the assumptions and presuppositions of Western thought are not compatible with those of Buddhism, and an insufficiently sensitive or nuanced comparison may simply force Buddhism into a Procrustean bed. However, while as yet there is no agreed methodology for undertaking a comparative study,[7] there seem to be sufficient common denominators between Buddhist and Western thought to begin an intercultural dialogue on medical ethics. The ethics of medicine provides an important bridgehead, since disease is a cultural universal (Deepadung 1992, 197). As Pellegrino puts it:

> As the biosphere expands to embrace the whole globe, every nation has a stake in every other nation's health. For these reasons, the practical and conceptual questions of transcul-

tural biomedical ethics are more sharply defined than in some other domains of knowledge.

(Pellegrino et al. 1992, 14)

Those, like Tom Beauchamp, who believe in a transcultural "common morality" speak of the "raw data for moral thinking" (Beauchamp 2001, 612) shared by people all over the world, which manifests itself in moral imperatives of the kind found in religious precepts everywhere, such as the Buddhist Five Precepts. Supporters of the "common morality" thesis, such as Veatch, believe "there are common 'pre-theoretical' insights – moral laws, rules, feelings, intuitions or perceptions of maxims – that are shared by peoples throughout the world" (Veatch 2004, 38). Such an understanding, indeed, is what grounds the "Four Principles" method, as mentioned above. There is not space here to discuss these unresolved theoretical questions further, and we turn now to a consideration of substantive biomedical issues.

Abortion

It may be thought that Buddhism is not well equipped to contribute to one specific area of bioethics – namely, reproductive medicine. William LaFleur has drawn attention to the lack of interest shown by early Buddhism in fecundity and reproduction. He points out that its early literature has no place for the water-based myths of origin so common in other religions, and that it associates water with purity rather than fertility. If anything, it was fire rather than water which became the emblem of early Buddhism. LaFleur comments: "Fire sermons, a distaste for myths about fecund waters, a dissociation of *right* religion from anything having to do with sexuality and reproductivity – these were all constitutive of the Buddhism that is often thought to have been *original* or, at least, constitutive of the early stage" (LaFleur 1992, 19). Another factor is that most Buddhist monks are celibate and, as noted above, will lack personal experience of the problems which arise in connection with reproduction and family life.

With respect to the Buddhist perspective on abortion, a number of preliminary questions present themselves. For example, is Buddhism "pro-life" or "pro-choice," and how do Buddhist ethical teachings such as *ahiṃsā* affect its approach to this issue? The Buddhist belief in rebirth clearly introduces a new dimension to the abortion debate. For one thing, it puts the question "When does life begin?" – a key question in the context of abortion – in an entirely new light. For Buddhism, life is a continuum with no discernible starting point, and birth and death are like a revolving door through which an individual passes again and again.

Early Buddhists shared the beliefs of the ancient Indian medical tradition regarding the human reproductive process, which taught that conception took place at the time of intercourse. By comparison with ancient Western notions, these ideas were quite advanced for the time and are more in line with the contemporary epigenetic model of fetal development. Interpreting the traditional teachings in the light of modern scientific discoveries such as ovulation, the most common view among Buddhists today, particularly those from traditional countries, is that fertilization is the point at which individual human life commences. As a consequence, abortion is widely seen as contrary to the first precept.

In the contemporary debate around abortion and the moral status of the fetus, much of the philosophical discussion of abortion in the West has focused on the criteria of moral personhood and the point at which a fetus acquires the capacities which entitle it to moral respect. Some philosophers argue that what we value about human beings is not life *per se* in the biological sense but rather the various faculties and powers which human beings possess, such as reason, self-consciousness, autonomy, the capacity to form relationships, and similar abilities. When these faculties are present, they say, we can speak of a moral "person," and when they are absent there is only biological life. As an example of this approach, feminist writers such as Mary Anne Warren have identified five features central to personhood – consciousness, reasoning, self-motivated activity, the capacity to communicate, and self-awareness. Warren claims that a fetus is no more conscious or rational than a fish, and that accordingly abortion is not immoral (Warren 1973). A recent Buddhist feminist perspective on abortion has been provided by Gross (2010).

A Buddhist pro-choice argument paralleling that based on the concept of personhood could be mounted by reference to the doctrine of the five aggregates (Skt *skandhas*; P. *khandhas*). As noted above, these are the five factors that constitute the individual human being. If it could be shown, for instance, that these five endowments were acquired gradually rather than all at once, it might be possible to argue that the life of an early fetus, which possessed fewer of the five, was less valuable than that of a more mature one, which possessed them all. This argument faces the problem that, according to the early commentarial tradition,[8] all five *skandhas* are present from the moment of rebirth (in other words, from conception). The doctrine of rebirth, moreover, sees the new conceptus not just as a "potential person" evolving for the first time from nothing but as a continuing entity bearing the complete karmic encoding of a recently deceased individual. If we rewind the karmic tape a short way, perhaps just a few hours to the point where death occurred in the previous life, we would typically find an adult man or woman fulfilling all the requirements of "personhood." According to traditional Buddhist teachings, what we have before us at conception is the same individual, only now at an immature state of physical development. Given the continuity of the human subject through thousands of lifetimes, it seems arbitrary to apply labels such as "actual" or "potential" to any given stage and to claim that the individual repeatedly gains and then loses the moral protection of the first precept.

Abortion in Buddhist Countries

In terms of contemporary practice, there is considerable variety across the Buddhist world and a fair amount of "emotional dissonance," whereby individuals experience themselves as pulled in contradictory directions. The early scriptural view that abortion is a breach of the first precept is generally followed in South Asian countries despite the evidence that large numbers of "back-street" abortions are carried out. In North Asian countries where Buddhism is practiced, such as Japan and South Korea, abortion occurs on a large scale.

What many see as a constructive contribution to the dilemma posed by abortion has been evolved in recent decades by Japanese Buddhists in the form of the *mizuko kuyō* memorial service for miscarried or aborted fetuses. The ritual became popular in the 1960s and 1970s in Japan and has since also spread to America.[9] Some of the larger Japanese sects oppose the ritual, regarding it as based on dubious theology, but Japanese Buddhist organizations have neither campaigned to change the law on abortion nor sought to influence the practice of the medical profession. Japan has not seen the kinds of attacks on abortion clinics and their personnel which have taken place in the USA. This approach is in line with the non-judgmental stance which Buddhism traditionally adopts on moral issues. It recognizes that the pressures and complexities of daily life can cloud the judgment and lead people to make wrong choices. The appropriate response in these cases, however, is thought to be compassion and understanding rather than vociferous condemnation.

Death and Dying

Turning from the beginning to the end of life, Buddhism teaches that the dying person's state of mind can influence the circumstances of rebirth in the next life. Accordingly, it sees it as desirable to approach death in a clear and mindful state rather than in a drugged or comatose condition. Nonetheless, there is no objection in principle to administering narcotics as part of a program of pain control. Where patients are in great pain it may be necessary to administer drugs and other medication, although recognizing that the quantities involved may shorten the patient's life. The doctor's aim here, however, in contrast to euthanasia, is to kill the pain, not the patient, and death is neither intended nor chosen as either a means or an end. In contrast to euthanasia, the physician wills the enhancement of life through the elimination of pain, while accepting that his efforts may hasten the advent of death. The Buddha forbade monks to take their own lives or to play a direct or indirect part in assisting or inciting others to commit suicide (see Keown 1996, 1998). Such acts were declared to be wrong even when motivated by compassion, in the light of which it seems that suicide, euthanasia, and physician-assisted suicide are contrary to canonical teachings.

In terminal care, and in cases where a permanent vegetative state (PVS) has been diagnosed, there is no need to go to extreme lengths to provide treatment where there is little or no prospect of recovery. Patients in the PVS condition cannot be regarded as dead (for reasons discussed below), and Buddhist principles appear to require that such patients should continue to receive at least basic care, including nutrition and hydration.[10] However, there would be no requirement to treat subsequent complications – for example, pneumonia or other infections – by administering antibiotics. While it might be foreseen that an untreated infection would lead to the patient's death, it would also be recognized that any course of treatment that is contemplated must be assessed against the background of the prognosis for overall recovery. Rather than embarking on a series of piecemeal treatments, none of which would produce a net improvement in the patient's overall condition, it would often be appropriate to reach the conclusion that the patient was beyond medical help and allow events to take their course. In such cases it is justifiable to refuse or withdraw treatment that is either futile or too burdensome in the light of the overall prognosis for recovery.

Brain Death and Organ Donation

In Asian countries outside of Japan there has been little public discussion of the ethics of organ transplantation or the definition of death from a Buddhist perspective.[11] Medical practice in Asian countries where Buddhism has a significant following tends to be determined more by conventions imported alongside the practice of Western medicine. In Japan, where there has been considerable opposition to organ transplantation despite recent (2009) legislation recognizing the concept of brain death, public disquiet seems based on indigenous beliefs and values which are not specifically Buddhist in nature.[12]

As far as I am aware, there are no formal declarations or official statements by professional associations representing Buddhist medical practitioners on these issues. The only published Buddhist medical opinion I have been able to locate is by the physician-monk Mettanando (1991), who believes Buddhism would accept a definition of death based on the loss of the functions of the brain stem. Although I once shared this view (Keown 2001 [1995]), my current understanding of the Buddhist position anticipates reservations concerning the concept of brain death and the current medical practice of cadaver organ transplantation, whether based on brain death or donation after cardiac death (DCD). This is not because Buddhism is opposed to organ donation *per se*, but because its traditional teachings on death and dying conflict with the Western protocols used to determine death prior to the harvesting of organs.

Early canonical sources make reference to three criteria that distinguish a living body from a dead one. The three are vitality (*āyu*), heat (*usmā*), and consciousness (*viññāṇa*) (SN.III.143). There is not space here to provide an exegesis of these terms, but suffice it to say, based on these criteria, the only practical method for determining death recognized by the ancient authorities is the loss of heat in the body. I suggest that this restrictive and conservative approach has much to do with Buddhist meditational practice and the knowledge that individuals could enter trance-like states resembling death and remain there for some considerable length of time without respiration or heartbeat. Early canonical sources speak of a state known as "the cessation of perception and feeling" (*saññāvedayitanirodha*) in which all of the normal physiological processes subside and the subject exists in a state of suspended animation. The Buddha himself entered such a state close to the time of his death, and his followers were perplexed as to whether or not he had actually passed away (DN.II.156). The phenomenon of the state of cessation – a state in which the subject is alive but where the body generates no vital signs – presents obstacles to any methodology which claims it can define the moment of death with precision. Buddhist sources, accordingly, are extremely hesitant as to when death can be declared, and in some traditions, such as Tibetan Buddhism, it is customary to wait for a period of three days before disposal of the body to be sure that death has taken place.

Buddhist psychology, furthermore, holds that the animating consciousness (*viññāṇa*) of an individual suffuses the entire body and is not located in any single organ. The

Buddhist concept of death, accordingly, would be the loss of integrated organic functioning rather than the absence of function in any one bodily component. For this reason Buddhists would likely be suspicious of any concept of death, or test for death, which placed undue weight on the failure of a single bodily organ such as the heart or brain. Further concerns alleging an underlying lack of scientific rigor surrounding these concepts have been pointed out by critics (Potts et al. 2000). For example, the criterion of brain death as enshrined in the US Uniform Definition of Death Act holds that death can be equated with "irreversible cessation of all functions of the entire brain," but, as critics point out, total cessation of brain function is rare in transplant candidates and residual vital signs continue to be registered. Brain-dead bodies undergo respiration at the cellular level, assimilate nutrients, fight infections, maintain body temperature, heal wounds, exhibit cardiovascular and hormonal stress responses, and can even gestate a fetus. While some experts dismiss these functions as residual biological activities, they seem sufficient at least to exclude *moral* certainty in declaring that brain-dead bodies are corpses. Second, the loss of function in an organ is not the same as the destruction of that organ: function can come and go in the way that a computer can be turned on and off while remaining fully serviceable: the fact that function is not presently observed does not mean that it cannot return. A third difficulty is that the requirement for irreversibility is problematic, since irreversibility is a prognosis, not a demonstrable medical fact (many conditions once deemed "irreversible" are today easily curable). Fourth, and finally, the tests for brain death are incapable by themselves of confirming the condition for which they are testing without the prior exclusion of a range of other possible causes of coma, such as barbiturate poisoning or hypothermia.

Similar objections can be made about the practice of DCD. The temporary loss of heartbeat during the short time this is monitored (typically from 2 to 5 minutes) does not mean that the heart will not restart, and, although heart transplantation is uncommon in these cases, the reuse of the very organ employed to determine the death of the donor seems to undermine the concept of death on which DCD is based. From a Buddhist perspective, both brain death and DCD place too much emphasis on a single bodily organ. Vital though these organs are, it seems to be going too far to equate the life of a human being with either one of them. In fact for one period of our lives – namely, during the early stages of fetal development – we exist without a brain or heart: an early embryo lacks both these organs but is undeniably alive. This suggests that a more holistic concept of death is required. So what tests for death would Buddhism accept? A robust set of tests would seem to be one that referenced the cardiovascular, respiratory, and nervous systems. The breakdown of these three major bodily systems would confirm the irreversible loss of structural integrity that the Buddhist concept of death requires. The delay in obtaining such confirmation would, however, rule out the practice of cadaver organ transplantation as it is performed today.[13]

Cloning

The birth of Dolly the sheep caused a furor when it was announced to the world on 24 February 1997. Dolly was the first mammalian clone, and her genetic proximity to the human species gave cause for deep reflection and concern as the implications for human beings were assessed. Dolly has since been followed by mice, goats, pigs, cats, and horses, and it seems only a matter of time until the technique is perfected for use on human beings. However, cloning is not a simple technique, and the successful birth of Dolly was preceded by 276 failed attempts. Human cloning may prove to be even more difficult, and the world has not awoken to another shock announcement quite as soon as some expected.

The type of cloning that produced Dolly is known as "reproductive cloning." An alternative type of procedure is known as "therapeutic cloning." Here the aim is not to produce a living copy of an individual, but to carry out experimentation on early embryos as part of a program of scientific research. The broad aim of this research is to understand better the process of genetic development in order to prevent abnormalities and to develop treatments using gene therapy to alleviate chronic hereditary diseases such as Huntington's disease and cystic fibrosis. Treatments of this kind, which are known as somatic therapies, work by targeting and repairing genetically abnormal cells – for example, by introducing missing genes.

In the furor that followed the birth of Dolly, cloning met with widespread condemnation by churchmen and politicians from across the globe. In this general wave of disapproval, religious opposition was led by the theistic traditions – notably, Christianity, Judaism, and Islam. These religions teach that life is a gift from God, and for them the creation of life in the laboratory seems to usurp the divine authority of the creator. Reproductive cloning is also in conflict with the biblical model of sexual generation. Cloning respects none of these religious precedents and, in the eyes of many believers, threatens to undermine divinely sanctioned norms governing family and social life.

Many of these theological objections disappear when cloning is viewed from a Buddhist perspective. Since Buddhism does not believe in a supreme being, there is no divine creator who might be offended by human attempts to duplicate his work. Nor does Buddhism believe in a personal soul or teach that human beings are made in God's image. Its view of creation and cosmology is very different from that of the Bible and does not seem to carry with it any normative principles or obligations relating to reproduction. There is no theological reason, then, why cloning could not be seen as just another way of creating life, neither intrinsically better nor worse than any other. One member of a research team, Professor Yong Moon from Korea's Seoul National University, was quoted in news reports as saying "Cloning is a different way of thinking about the recycling of life – it's a Buddhist way of thinking."[14]

The objection that cloning involves "playing God" in the literal sense (by creating life) goes hand in hand with a similar objection to playing God in a metaphorical sense. Such objections depict the creator of the clone as having godlike powers over the creature to which he has given life, to the extent of controlling virtually every aspect of its development. The parallel with the story of Frankenstein has been drawn by several commentators who see cloning as based on a "producer–product" type of relationship, rather than as one of respect for the equal dignity of human beings. Supporters of cloning regard such concerns as overstated and point out that clones have been with us throughout history in the form of identical twins. Some of the more horrific scenarios which have been expressed about cloning may accordingly be overstated. Even if this is the case, however, the advent of cloning is likely to influence traditional views of human nature and human dignity in complex ways. The benefits of cloning identified so far fall into two main groups: as an aid to current in-vitro fertilization techniques and in its use for genetic selection or eugenics purposes. The numbers who would benefit from the first are very small, and history has shown the potentially grave consequences of the latter.

Stem Cell Research

Many researchers believe that human stem cells have an important role to play in the development of genetic therapies. Stem cells have the ability to divide for indefinite periods in culture and to give rise to other more specialized cells. Because of the power they have to grow into any kind of somatic cell – such as a brain cell, a liver cell, a heart or blood cell – they are described as "pluripotent." This means they function a bit like the joker in a pack of playing cards, which can take on any value as the context requires. The use of embryonic stem cells raises moral problems of the kind discussed in connection with abortion, and it has not so far produced the breakthroughs many expected. Recent experiments have shown that adult stem cells can be reprogramed and induced to become pluripotent (hence they are termed "induced pluripotent stem cells," or IPSC, and more funding is now being directed towards this alternative technique of IPSC. In 2010, the world's best-funded institute for stem cell research, the California Institute for Regenerative Medicine, received $230 million for 14 research grants, only one of which involved embryonic stem cells. The use of adult cells or induced pluripotent stem cells removes one of the major ethical objections to stem cell research, and in this case science itself may have found a solution to the moral dilemma it created.

Brain Science: Psychology and Neuroscience

Since its origins, Buddhism has had a particular interest in the analysis and classification of mental phenomena and in the generation of altered states of consciousness through meditational practice. These interests coincide with those of Western psychologists and neuroscientists eager to understand the mechanisms in the brain responsible for the generation of cognitive and emotional experience. The Dalai Lama has been an enthusiastic proponent and participant in discussions and research projects designed to study the neurophysiology associated with meditative experience and to discover new therapeutic avenues for psychology. The dialogue between neuroscientists, psychologists, and Buddhist practitioners of meditation is now well established and has been comprehensively reviewed by Lutz, Dunne, and Davidson (2007).

Interest in meditation on the part of Western scientists began in the 1950s, and three decades later the Mind and Life Institute was set up with the participation of the late neuroscientist Francisco Varela. In 2003 the institute co-sponsored a conference with the McGovern Institute for Brain Research at MIT called "Investigating the Mind." Here, neuroscientists and Buddhist scholars spent two days with the Dalai Lama discussing attention, mental imagery, and the emotions. Some Buddhist neuroscientists such as James Austin, author of *Zen and the Brain* (1999), and the Buddhist scholar and former monk B. Alan Wallace, president of the Santa Barbara Institute for the Interdisciplinary Study of Consciousness, have been pioneers in this rapidly emerging field. Another well-known participant as both subject and collaborator is Matthieu Ricard, a former molecular biologist at the Pasteur Institute in Paris who was later ordained as a Tibetan Buddhist monk. Meditators who have been trained to observe their minds make excellent research subjects, since they are able to recall with greater clarity the mental phenomena they experience, making it easier to correlate these experiences with the measurements recorded by scientists during brain scans. The data obtained in this way can be useful in developing programs to teach attention skills and the control of emotions. The positive mental states cultivated in meditation, such as lovingkindness, compassion, sympathetic joy, and equanimity (the four *Brahmavihāras*), can be used to train the brain to shift gear and leave behind negative states like anger, fear, and depression. Richard Davidson and his colleagues at the University of Wisconsin, Madison, have demonstrated a high correlation between activity in the left versus the right frontal areas of the brain and positive emotional states generated in meditation. Based on these findings, psychologists have developed programs for Westerners to help promote emotional health and mental well-being, and a number of self-help books (e.g., Hanson 2009) claim to show how readers can change their lives by changing their brains using the ancient Buddhist teachings now validated by science.

But what if these effects could be duplicated by pharmacological means – for instance, simply by taking a "happy pill"? The discipline of neuroethics emerged in the last decade as a subfield of bioethics in order to address questions of this kind. The use of "mind enhancing" drugs common in earlier decades, notably in the 1960s, and as described in the book *Zig Zag Zen* (Badiner 2002), provided a gateway into Buddhist practice for many Westerners. It is well known that many college students in America today use prescription drugs such as Ritalin and Adderall to enhance their performance in examinations, and, in a commentary in *Nature* in 2008 written in conjunction with several other prominent bioethicists and neuroscientists, the journal's editor, Philip Campbell, wrote: "Safe and effective cognitive enhancers will benefit both the individual and society." He apparently regards their use as similar to traditional educational methods in improving intellectual performance and takes the view that such techniques are "morally equivalent to other, more familiar, enhancements" (Campbell 2008). Writing from a Buddhist perspective, the philosopher Andrew Fenton has expressed the view that, if a consequence of the development or use of pharmaceutical enhancements is further insight into our self-nature or the reduction or alleviation of suffering, then Buddhist traditions – and particularly Mahāyāna traditions which accept the use of "skillful means" – should support their use (Fenton 2009).

Buddhism is by no means hostile to either human enhancement or scientific progress, and indeed its entire rationale as a religion could be summed up as the fulfillment of human potential. However, it sees this as a long-term project which will not be advanced by short-term solutions. Although psychotropic drugs had been employed for religious purposes in India since ancient times and the use of marijuana by holy men was – and remains – widespread, the Buddha did not have recourse to any such substances to achieve his goal, and their use has never been countenanced by the Sangha. The Buddhist view has always been that the clarity of mind and intellectual lucidity needed to attain nirvana is best achieved through natural methods, and the primary technique relied on is meditation. While some schools of Buddhism believe there are shorter and longer paths to nirvana, there are none that teach that a drug-induced short-cut exists. Instead, Buddhism has developed its own toolkit for human enhancement and has always taught that progress must be cumulative, as opposed to sporadic, and situated in the context of a structured path to fulfillment. By contrast with traditional practice, when using pharmaceutical-based solutions the subject is a passive recipient of treatment as opposed to an active agent who engages in disciplined self-directed activity. Because of the effort and commitment they require, the traditional forms of practice have the power to transform the personality, in contrast to the administering of medication, where something is simply "done" to the actor as passive subject. While brief enhancement or palliation of symptoms may not be harmful in the short term, it can lead to dependency and undermine the achievement of a more permanent solution. Buddhist psychology detects a cyclic pattern in such conditions and observes that, unless the causal sequence is reset, the effects will recur indefinitely. What is needed is insight into the underlying causes through deep reflection and analysis of the kind facilitated by meditative practice.

Conclusion

Caution must be exercised when drawing conclusions about Buddhist perspectives on bioethics, as there is a risk of inadvertently superimposing Western categories on the discussion. The doctrine of karma and the belief in rebirth make Buddhism distinctive from an ethical perspective, and it is also renowned for its emphasis on benevolence and compassion and a scrupulous respect for living beings. As Buddhism continues to spread in the West there is an urgent need for dialogue with Western bioethicists in order to develop a framework in terms of which Buddhist responses to bioethical issues can be articulated with greater clarity and precision.

Notes

1 For a bibliographical survey, see Hughes and Keown (1995). Publications subsequent to the compilation of this bibliography include Harvey (2000); Keown (1999, 2000).
2 For a sample of current topics of interest, see the UNESCO publication *Asia Pacific Perspectives on Medical Ethics* (available online at www.eubios.info/APPME.pdf; accessed 20 October 2010).
3 Mitra (1985, 21) points out that the Pāli canon does not contain the word "*Āyurveda*," though it makes reference to all of its traditional branches of treatment.
4 Trans. Zysk (1991, 41), slightly amended.
5 For a brief statement of the Buddhist position, see Ratanakul (1985, 289f.).
6 For a more general critique of this methodology, see Schone-Seifert (2010).
7 A good introduction to the issues in transcultural medical ethics can be found in Pelligreno et al. (1992). For more recent reflections, see Coward and Ratanakul (1999), and for methodological questions see the essays in Rehmann-Sutter et al. (2005). A thorough discussion of the possibility of universal medical ethics is available in Engelhardt (2006).

8 See, for example, *Vinaya-Aṭṭhakathā*, II, 437f.
9 The appropriation of the ritual by Westerners was the subject of a recent book by Jeff Wilson (2009) entitled *Mourning the Unborn Dead: A Buddhist Ritual comes to America*. In it, Wilson writes: "All of the priests consulted for this book stated clearly that abortion is against fundamental Buddhist principles. However, many were more equivocal about its legal status. The majority felt that abortion is wrong morally but is a matter for the woman to decide for herself" (pp. 46f.).
10 Mettanando (1991); Keown (2001 [1995], 158–68).
11 For a fuller Buddhist critique of brain death, see Keown (2010).
12 For a discussion of the contrast between Japanese and North American attitudes to organ transplants, see Lock (2001).
13 It appears that Buddhism is not the only religion to have doubts about current practice in this respect, and after eight years of debate the United Kingdom's chief rabbi, Jonathan Sacks, issued an edict that carrying donor cards is unacceptable and that the UK organ donor system based on the criterion of brain stem death is incompatible with Jewish law (Wise 2011). Islamic scholars have expressed similar doubts about the concept of brain death (Bedir and Aksoy 2011).
14 Comments made at the conference of the American Association for the Advancement of Science, Seattle, 2004.

References

Badiner, A. H. (ed.) (2002). *Zig Zag Zen: Buddhism on Psychedelics*. San Francisco: Chronicle Books.

Beauchamp, T. L. (2001). Internal and External Standards for Medical Morality. In *Journal of Medicine and Philosophy* 26, 601–19.

Beauchamp, T. L. and Childress, J. F. (1989). *Principles of Biomedical Ethics*. New York: Oxford University Press.

Bedir, A., and Aksoy, S. (2011). Brain Death Revisited: It Is Not 'Complete Death', According to Islamic Sources. In *Journal of Medical Ethics*, 37, 290–4.

Brannigan, M. C. (2010). What Can Buddhist Non-Self Contribute to North American Bioethics? In *American Buddhism as a Way of Life*. Ed. G. Storhoff and J. Whalen-Bridge. New York: State University of New York Press, 69–82.

Campbell, P. (2008). Beyond Therapy. *Nature*, December 10.

Coward, H., and P. Ratanakul (1999). *A Cross-Cultural Dialogue on Health Care Ethics*. Waterloo, Ontario: Wilfrid Laurier University Press.

Deepadung, A. (1992). The Interaction between Thai Traditional and Western Medicine in Thailand. In *Transcultural Dimensions in Medical Ethics*. Ed. E. Pellegrino, P. Mazzarella, and P. Corsi. Frederick, MD: University Publishing Group, 197–212.

Duncan, A. S., Dunstan, G. R., and Welbourn, R. B. (1981). *Dictionary of Medical Ethics*. London: Darton, Longman & Todd.

Engelhardt, H. T. (2006). *Global Bioethics: The Collapse of Consensus*. Salem, MA: M&M Scrivener Press.

Fenton, A. (2009). Buddhism and Neuroethics: The Ethics of Pharmaceutical Cognitive Enhancement. In *Developing World Bioethics* 9(2), 47–56.

Florida, R. E. (1994). Buddhism and the Four Principles. In *Principles of Health Care Ethics*. Ed. R. Gillon and A. Lloyd. Chichester: John Wiley & Sons, 105–16.

Goodman, C. (2009). *Consequences of Compassion: An Interpretation and Defense of Buddhist Ethics*. New York: Oxford University Press.

Gross, R. M. (2010). A Contemporary North American Discussion of Abortion. In *American Buddhism as a Way of Life*. Ed. G. Storhoff and J. Whalen-Bridge. New York: State University of New York Press, 83–100.

Hallisey, C. (1996). Ethical Particularism in Theravada Buddhism. In *Journal of Buddhist Ethics* 3, 32–43.

Hanson, R. (2009). *Buddha's Brain: The Practical Neuroscience of Happiness, Love & Wisdom*. Oakland, CA: New Harbinger.

Harvey, P. (2000). *An Introduction to Buddhist Ethics: Foundations, Values and Issues*. Cambridge: Cambridge University Press.

Hughes, J. J., and Keown, D. (1995). Buddhism and Medical Ethics: A Bibliographic Introduction. In *Journal of Buddhist Ethics* 2, 105–24.

Keown, D. (1996). Buddhism and Suicide: The Case of Channa. In *Journal of Buddhist Ethics* 3, 8–31.

Keown, D. (1998). Suicide, Assisted Suicide and Euthanasia: A Buddhist Perspective. In *Journal of Law and Religion* 12, 385–405.

Keown, D. (1999). *Buddhism and Abortion*. London: Macmillan; Honolulu: University of Hawai'i Press.

Keown, D. (ed.) (2000). *Contemporary Buddhist Ethics*. Richmond, Surrey: Curzon Press.

Keown, D. (2001 [1995]). *Buddhism & Bioethics*. London: Palgrave.

Keown, D. (2010). Buddhism, Brain Death and Organ Transplantation. In *Journal of Buddhist Ethics* 17, 1–36.

LaFleur, W. A. (1992). *Liquid Life: Abortion and Buddhism in Japan*. Princeton, NJ: Princeton University Press.

Lock, M. (2001). *Twice Dead: Organ Transplants and the Reinvention of Death*. Berkeley: University of California Press.

Lutz, A., Dunne, J. D., and Davidson, R. J. (2007). Meditation and the Neuroscience of Consciousness. In *The Cambridge Handbook of Consciousness*. Cambridge: Cambridge University Press, 499–544.

Mettanando, B. (1991). Buddhist Ethics in the Practice of Medicine. In *Buddhist Ethics and Modern Society: An International Symposium*. Ed. C. Wei-hsun Fu and S. A. Wawrytko. New York: Greenwood Press, 195–213.

Mitra, J. (1985). *A Critical Appraisal of Ayurvedic Materials in Buddhist Literature (with special reference to Tripitaka)*. Varanasi: Jyotirlok Prakashan.

Olson, P. (1993). *The Discipline of Freedom: A Kantian View of the Role of Moral Precepts in Zen Practice*. Albany: State University of New York Press.

Pellegrino, E., Mazzarella, P., and Corsi, P. (1992). *Transcultural Dimensions in Medical Ethics*. Frederick, MD: University Publishing Group.

Potts, M., Byrne, P. A., and Nilges, R. G. (2000). *Beyond Brain Death: The Case against Brain Based Criteria for Human Death*. Dordrecht and Boston: Kluwer Academic.

Ratanakul, P. (1985). The Buddhist Concept of Life, Suffering and Death and their Meaning for Health Policy. In *Health Policy, Ethics and Human Values*. Ed. Z. Bankowski and J. H. Bryant. Geneva: CIOMS, 286–95.

Ratanakul, P. (2001). Buddhism – an Ally of Science? In *When Worlds Converge: Science and Religion in the Third Millennium*. Ed. C. N. Matthews, M. E. Tucker, and P. Hefner. Peru, IL: Open Court, 338–42.

Rehmann-Sutter, C., Düwell, M., and Mieth, D. (2005). *Bioethics in Cultural Contexts: Reflections on Methods and Finitude*. Dordrecht: Springer.

Schöne-Seifert, B. (2010). Danger and Merits of Principlism: Meta-Theoretical Reflections on the Beauchamp/Childress-Approach to Biomedical Ethics. In *Bioethics in Cultural Contexts:*

Reflections on Methods and Finitude. Ed. C. Rehmann-Sutter, M. Düwell, and D. Mieth. Dordrecht: Springer.

Soni, R. L. (1976). Buddhism in Relation to the Profession of Medicine. In *Religion and Medicine, 3*. Ed. D. W. Millard. London: SCM Press, 135–51.

Veatch, Robert (2004). Common Morality and Human Finitude. In *Weltanschauliche Offenheit in der Bioethik*. Ed. E. Baumann, P. Schröder et al. Berlin: Duncker & Humblot, 37–50.

Warren, M. A. (1973). On the Moral and Legal Status of Abortion. *The Monist* 57(1), 43–61.

Williams, P. (1989). *Mahayana Buddhism: The Doctrinal Foundations*. London: Routledge.

Wilson, J. (2009). *Mourning the Unborn Dead: A Buddhist Ritual Comes to America*. New York: Oxford University Press.

Wise, J. (2011). Chief Rabbi rules against donor cards and organ donation after brain stem death. In *British Medical Journal* 342, d275.

Zysk, K. G. (1991). *Asceticism and Healing in Ancient India: Medicine in the Buddhist Monastery*. Oxford: Oxford University Press.

41

War and Peace in Buddhist Philosophy

SALLIE B. KING

Textual Passages and Major Issues

Despite the fact that Buddhist countries have always had armies and always fought wars, the popular perception of Buddhists and non-Buddhists alike is that Buddhism as a religion and an ethical system is inherently opposed to violence. The reason for this lies primarily in the ethical teachings and values of the historical Buddha and early Buddhism, together with the bodhisattva ethic of the Mahāyāna.[1]

Theravāda

1 The first of the Buddhist lay precepts, the foundation of Theravāda Buddhist morality, is: "I undertake the precept to abstain from the taking of life" (Saddhatissa 1987, 73), which indicates that it is morally wrong to take life *at all*. Thus it is unlike the First Commandment of the Bible, which prohibits murder but not necessarily the taking of life in war. The Buddhist precept is clear that one should abstain from taking life under any and all circumstances.

2 One of the reasons why one is told that one should not take life in Buddhism is that to do so plants a negative karmic seed. That seed, once planted, causes the person who planted it to experience a painful karmic consequence later in this life or in a subsequent life. Therefore, for one's *own* sake, one should not kill. To kill another is to harm oneself as well as the one killed. Karma and its consequences are a major theme in Buddhism, as shown in these representative quotations from the *Dhammapada* (Carter and Palihawadana 1987, 9, 14):

A Companion to Buddhist Philosophy, First Edition. Edited by Steven M. Emmanuel.

What a foe may do to a foe,
or a hater to a hater –
Far worse than that
The mind ill held may do to him. (Verse 42)

The childish one thinks it is like honey
While the bad [he has done] is not yet matured.
But when the bad [he has done] is matured,
Then the childish one comes by suffering. (Verse 69)

3 Buddhist practice, if one engages in it seriously and over time, is intended to function to make one less and less capable of intentionally causing harm to any sentient being (any being capable of experiencing suffering), much less killing a human being. That is, Buddhist practice purposely cultivates feelings of universal benevolence, shared joy with others, feelings of closeness or kinship with others, and compassion – i.e., the heart that cannot bear to see others suffer. Moreover, it also is intended steadily to build one's self-control and to weaken feelings of fear, anger, enmity, and separation or alienation. Thus, in theory, the more serious one is about Buddhism and its practice, the less capable one should become of participating in war.

4 Monks are required by the Vinaya to keep their distance from the military. They may neither stay with the military nor watch an army fighting. Active soldiers may not ordain as monks.

5 The Right Livelihood component of the Eightfold Path does not directly discuss soldiering. To be a soldier is not on the list of occupations specified as falling outside the norms of Right Livelihood. However, to manufacture weapons (such as those used by soldiers) is specifically named as an occupation to be avoided by Buddhists. The Buddha does directly state in the *Saṃyutta Nikāya* that a soldier fighting with the intention of killing others who is himself killed in the course of battle will be born in the "Battle-Slain Hell." The text reads:

> When . . . a mercenary is one who strives and exerts himself in battle, his mind is already low, depraved, misdirected by the thought: "Let these beings be slain, slaughtered, annihilated, destroyed, or exterminated." If others then slay him and finish him off while he is striving and exerting himself in battle, then with the breakup of the body, after death, he is reborn in the "Battle-Slain Hell."
>
> (Bodhi 2000, 1335)

That is to say, the soldier who dies in battle is in a depraved state of intention-to-kill; that intention earns the negative karma that causes him to be born in this hell. In sum, individuals clearly are enjoined by the Buddha to avoid violence in their own personal behavior, on the battlefield or off.

6 Turning to the Buddha's social teachings, we find more guidance on this issue. The *Dhammapada* teaches that not only is killing morally wrong and harmful to oneself, it is also inefficacious. In the long run, it does not work. The text famously states:

Not by enmity are enmities quelled,
Whatever the occasion here.
By the absence of enmity are they quelled.
This is an ancient truth. (Verse 5)

(Carter and Palihawadana 1987, 3)

Due to the law of karma, violence produces further violence. Violent acts sow karmic seeds that bear fruit in retaliatory violence from the one who suffered the original blow. One may win today, only to suffer the revenge of the defeated later. There is no final victory in the use of arms, but only in laying them down. This passage, like all the passages cited on individual behavior, expresses a negative view towards violence, in this case using a pragmatic argument.

7 Very different is a passage from the *Cakkavatti Sīhanāda Sutta* of the *Dīgha Nikāya*, in which the Buddha gives the following advice to an aspiring *cakkavatti*:

> Yourself depending on the Dhamma, honouring it, revering it, cherishing it, doing homage to it and venerating it, having the Dhamma as your badge and banner, acknowledging the Dhamma as your master, you should establish guard, ward and protection according to Dhamma for your own household, your troops, your nobles and vassals, for Brahmins and householders, town and country folk, ascetics and Brahmins, for beasts and birds.
>
> (Walsh 1995 [1987], 396–7)

Thus is justified the existence of a military force for the purpose of protection. It is noteworthy that this is to be done "according to Dhamma," which apparently means in this context that the military should operate in some sense within the bounds of Buddhist morality (though the specifics of those limits are not given). Clearly, the phrasing here implies that it is a duty of the king to protect those humans and animals in his domain. The Buddha seems simply to assume that the king will have such an army and that what he wants to tell the king is that the army should be used only for defensive purposes and "according to Dhamma."

Mahāyāna

1 The mainstream of Mahāyāna values strongly emphasizes universal compassion – i.e., caring equally about the suffering of all sentient beings, with no distinction or favoritism, and making this caring one's greatest concern. Indeed, the doctrine of the bodhisattva may develop universal compassion to its logical extreme. A representative text from Śāntideva reads:

> At first one should meditate intently on the equality of oneself and others as follows: "All equally experience suffering and happiness. I should look after them as I do myself." . . . I should dispel the suffering of others because it is suffering like my own suffering. I should help others too because of their nature as beings, which is like my own being. . . . Without exception, no sufferings belong to anyone. They must be warded off simply because they are suffering. Why is any limitation put on this?
>
> (Śāntideva 1996, 96–7)

Particularly noteworthy here is the articulation of a universalistic ethic: the bodhisattva sees that objectively there are no grounds whatsoever for favoring one person over another. This is by far the dominant view in Mahāyāna texts.

2 On the other hand, the Mahāyāna has a small number of texts that open up the possible use of violence. The *Upāya-kauśalya Sūtra* tells the story of a bodhisattva (Śākyamuni Buddha in a past life) who is the captain of a boat. His name is "Great Compassionate." This bodhisattva learns that there is a bandit on board who is planning to murder the 500 merchants on the boat, all of whom are advanced bodhisattvas, in order to steal from them. The captain considers what he should do and ultimately decides that he should kill the bandit before the latter has a chance to kill the 500 merchant bodhisattvas. His decision is based upon his reasoning that, if the bandit kills the 500 merchant bodhisattvas, he (the bandit) will earn himself terrible negative karma from which he will suffer greatly in the future. Thus it is out of compassion for the bandit that the captain kills him. The text goes on to raise the question of whether this bodhisattva, in killing the bandit, earned himself negative karma. It answers in the negative: the bodhisattva actually curtailed his time in samsara by 100,000 eons with this act of skill in means and great compassion (Tatz 1994, 73–4). This teaching is the origin of the idea of "compassionate killing" in the Mahāyāna. Quite similar stories are told in a few other Mahāyāna texts, including the *Yogācārabhūmi* and *Bodhisattvabhūmi*.

Buddhist Violence and Warfare

When discussing war and peace in a Buddhist context, it is particularly important to distinguish Buddhist philosophy on the subject from the practice of Buddhists in historical and present fact. This is because Buddhist philosophy on the subject, especially in the teachings of the Buddha and the mainstream Mahāyāna teachings, so heavily emphasizes non-violence, while Buddhists themselves have frequently participated in violence and warfare. As Schmithausen puts it, there is here a remarkable "compartmentalization of values" (Schmithausen 1999, 53). Herein lies another set of philosophical questions: When Buddhists engage in violence, do they try to justify themselves in Buddhist terms? If so, how do they go about it?

Aśoka

When the question of Buddhism and war is raised, Buddhists frequently cite the example of the great King Aśoka (c. 270–232 BCE). Before his conversion to Buddhism, Aśoka was by no means averse to the use of war as a tool of statecraft. According to his thirteenth Rock Edict, in the eighth year of his reign, Aśoka conquered the neighboring country of Kalinga. Looking back, he was moved to profound remorse over the extensive carnage and grief he had caused. This remorse caused him to embrace Buddhism, to give up war, and progressively to move away from violence altogether, giving up hunting and promoting vegetarianism.

Aśoka is taken as the paradigmatic example of a king who embodies the moral principles of Buddhism – indeed, as the historical example most closely approaching the *cakkavatti* ideal, the ideal Buddhist monarch who rules by Dhamma, by Buddhist principles. It is important to note, however, that, in his rock edict, Aśoka makes it clear that his firm intention to avoid taking life has a limit. He publicly announces to the "[peoples in the remote sections of the conquered territory] . . . that he exercises the power to punish, despite his repentance, in order to induce them to desist from their crimes and escape execution" (Nikam and McKeon 1978, 28–9). In other words, he tells them that he will not passively tolerate violent deeds on their part but will retaliate with force to ensure the peace of the empire.

Buddhism and State Violence

Buddhist countries have always had armies and Buddhists have in large numbers always served in those armies and killed other human beings. It has, moreover, been common, often normative, in Buddhist countries for the state and institutional Buddhism to have a mutually supportive relationship, with the Sangha giving its blessings to the ruler and state, and the ruler supporting the Sangha and its properties. This has put Buddhism in the position of implicitly supporting the potential and actual violence of the state. Such a system was formalized in Thailand, for example, early in the twentieth century, when the motto of the state became: "Nation, Religion, King," with "Religion" referring to Buddhism, and the three together representing the three foundations of Thai society. At times national rhetoric blurs the line between religion and state and allows both state and religious actors to speak of the defense of the state and the Dhamma as a single thing, as occurred in Sri Lanka in the twentieth and early twenty-first centuries.

It is noteworthy that Buddhist soldiers, rulers, and others who have killed often do something afterwards to make merit, such as making a substantial offering to a pagoda or temple or subscribing to a major building project (Schmithausen 1999, 53). Such donors hope that the merit resulting from their gifts will compensate for the negative karma they earned by killing. This widespread practice betrays an awareness that acts of violence, including acts of military violence, however necessary or unavoidable one may have found them, are nonetheless incompatible with Buddhist ethical precepts. In other words, the "compartmentalization" of values mentioned above is sufficiently shaky that it may require supplementation, especially after egregious violations of the norm of non-violence. Though it may frequently be violated, a norm is still a norm.

Theravāda Efforts to Justify Participation in State Violence

As we have seen, the Buddha's teaching clearly indicates that killing another human being will earn the killer significant negative karma. This would seem to preclude a Buddhist justification for going to war or killing for other reasons of statecraft. Nonetheless, such killing frequently occurs. Two examples of Theravāda attempts to address the karma problem directly as part of an effort to justify war are instructive. These two cases are similar, as Peter Harvey notes (Harvey 2000, 261). First, in Sri Lanka, the chronicle *Mahāvaṃsa* tells the story of the Sinhalese Buddhist King Duṭṭhagāmaṇi in his war against the Hindu Tamil King Elara. When the war was over, King Duṭṭhagāmaṇi was greatly distressed over the large number of deaths for which he was responsible. (Thus far, the King's situation is like Aśoka's; however, the story now moves dramatically in the opposite direction.) The *Mahāvaṃsa* claims that *arhats*, enlightened Buddhist monks, told the king not to be concerned:

> That deed presents no obstacle on your path to heaven. You caused the death of just one and a half people, O king. One had taken the refuges . . . , the other the Five Precepts as well. The rest were wicked men of wrong view who died like (or: as considered as) beasts. You will in many ways illuminate the Buddha's teaching, so stop worrying.
>
> (Cited ibid., 256)

That is, the king is counseled that the non-Buddhist dead were not human beings but mere beasts, so he need not worry about any negative karmic consequences from killing human beings other than the "one and a half" Buddhists who died. It is further suggested that, since one consequence of the war is that Buddhism will be strengthened, this will create positive karmic fruit that will cancel out the negative karma resulting from the "one and a half" deaths. These claims can in no way be linked to anything the Buddha taught; indeed, they are directly contradicted by the teachings of the Buddha. The Buddha in no way differentiates between Buddhists and non-Buddhists when it comes to the wrongness of doing harm. The first precept, urging us not to take life, is clearly universal in scope (and includes animals). In addition, the Buddha does not say that positive karmic fruit can wipe out negative karmic fruit; both must be lived out.[2]

The second case is more modern, but takes the same approach. A Thai Buddhist monk named Kittivuḍḍho stated in 1976 that "killing Communists is not demeritorious":

> such killing is not the killing of persons (*khon*). Because whoever destroys the nation, religion and the monarchy is not a complete person, but mara (evil). Our intention must not be to kill people but to kill the Devil. It is the duty of all Thai.
>
> (Cited in Harvey 2000, 260)

The author here assumes that "nation, religion and the monarchy" are a tri-partite single entity of great value and urges Thais to be ready to kill to protect it. Kittivuḍḍho went on, like the *Mahāvaṃsa*, to claim that "the merit accrued from protecting the nation, the religion and the monarchy was greater than the demerit from taking the life of a communist" (Swearer 1981, 57). The Kittivuḍḍho and *Mahāvaṃsa* statements thus both justify killing with two devices: (1) the humanity of the enemy is negated; (2) the claim is made that the good produced outweighs the evil.

These statements have had quite different fates in the Buddhist world. Kittivuḍḍho's statements caused an uproar in Thailand, where the Sangha and the public recognized how incompatible they were with the Buddha's teaching. The Supreme Patriarch of Thai Buddhism denounced Kittivuḍḍho's statements and there were attempts to have him disciplined, though these came to naught (Harvey 2000, 261). In Sri Lanka, on the other hand, the *Mahāvaṃsa* is an ancient text, and people have grown up regarding it as authoritative. In recent decades, the right wing of Sinhalese Buddhism drew upon the *Mahāvaṃsa* to create a kind of just war theory in which ethnic group (Sinhalese), religion (Buddhism), and state (Sri Lanka) were melded into a single entity which was justified in aggressively defending itself against Sri Lankan Tamils (see Bartholomeusz

2002). This stance was opposed by progressive Sri Lankan Buddhists such as the Sarvodaya Shramadana.

Throughout the Theravāda Buddhist world, karmic consequences remain a barrier, probably the major barrier, to Buddhist efforts to justify war. As Demieville claimed, and subsequent researchers have confirmed, the main justification used by Theravāda Buddhist soldiers for killing in war is to defend the country and/or Buddhism (the two are often conflated in Buddhist majority countries) (Jerryson and Juergensmeyer 2010, 38). Recent evidence indicates that, when Theravāda Buddhists participate in war, their concerns do not focus on the morality of their possible involvement in killing *per se*, but on the karmic consequences for themselves of killing. Contemporary Theravāda soldiers, and some monks, argue that a soldier who kills will not earn negative karma from that act because his intention (*cetanā*) is not anger, hatred, or even the desire to kill *per se*, but the desire to protect the country and/or Buddhism. Other soldiers and monks are unconvinced by this argument and strongly believe that any act of killing will earn negative karma, regardless of motivation. Many soldiers remain highly concerned about the karmic consequences for themselves of killing in the line of duty (ibid., 164–5, 189).

China in the Sino-Japanese War

In the twentieth century, as China faced the prospect of an imminent invasion by Japan, a tide of fear swept the country that the Chinese would become slaves to the Japanese, a fear that brought in its wake a surge of nationalism and sentiment that such a fate must by all means be averted.[3] The Buddhist monkhood participated in this surge of nationalistic sentiment and desire to defend the country from devastation and slavery and passionately debated what their role should be. Some argued that they should engage in the traditional prayers and ceremonies to defend the nation. That option seemed rather feeble to many in the face of Japanese military might. Others argued that they should take up arms alongside the laity. This option troubled even many of those who were considering it, as it seemed to be a direct violation of their precepts to avoid killing and observe non-violence. Moreover, they felt keenly that their training as monks made them personally ill-prepared to engage in battle. Many felt torn between two imperatives: the imperative of their Buddhist practice, which they felt required them to maintain the precept against killing and non-violence at a level higher than that required of the laity; and the imperative to rise to the demands of the hour and defend the nation.

These issues were debated by the younger monks in the journals of the time. In the end, justification for participation in the war effort was composed of the following elements: (1) Buddhists are not only to avoid evil but also to do good – that is, passivity should be avoided; (2) compassion required the monks to help save the lives of the people; (3) the monks should repay their debt to the people and nation who give them the requisites that sustain them as monks; (4) the Mahāyāna principle of "compassionate killing" permitted "killing one with compassion in order to save many"; and (5) to abstain from participation in the war effort was a Hīnayāna-like attitude of preferring self-benefit over other-benefit (Yu 2005, 44–64). Thus, participation in the war effort was felt to be a form of self-sacrifice; not only did one risk one's life, one also jeopardized one's status as a monk by potentially violating one's precepts in case one did kill another.

After considerable intra-monastic debate, the Venerable Taixu, who was the leading voice at that time calling for many reforms in monastic Chinese Buddhism, articulated a compromise according to which monks and nuns would participate in the war effort but would not be required to engage in killing. This seemed to represent the consensus of the majority of at least the younger monastics, the older religious tending to be more conservative and wishing to maintain the traditional prohibition on participation in the military. Some monks fled or committed suicide rather than undergo military training and violate their precepts. However, the Sangha as a whole (monks and nuns) accepted military training and went on to make substantial contributions in the areas of propaganda (promoting nationalistic and patriotic sentiments in their sermons and public speeches and urging the laity to participate actively in resisting the Japanese invasion); campaigning for donations for the military; and forming Buddhist rescue squads, providing relief and medical assistance on the battlefield. Thus, while the Sangha did participate in the war effort (itself a violation of precepts), only a small minority took up arms and engaged in killing.

In his study of the Chinese monks' deliberations over participation in the Sino-Japanese War, the scholar Xue Yu offers important criticisms of their use of the idea of "compassionate killing" (Yu 2005, 201–3). First, he notes, "the overwhelming majority of Buddhist texts categorically advocate the supreme importance of non-killing, while only a very few texts endorse compassionate killing." The monks, he writes, are guilty of selectively quoting a very few passages over and over again, while by-passing the non-killing imperative that most texts stress. Second, the monks ignore the fact that even those few texts that endorse "compassionate killing" state that only a highly advanced bodhisattva with perfect wisdom and compassion is able to kill "compassionately" – i.e., with no hatred or thought of "enemy"; ordinary monks on a battlefield filled with carnage would hardly be in this condition. Third, Yu argues that "war can no longer be called war and an enemy cannot be regarded as the enemy if people are compassionate to each other. In fact, there will [be] no war and no one will have an enemy if everyone acts like a bodhisattva." In short, he is arguing that the notion of "compassionate killing" cannot apply to warfare – that is, the universal compassion of the bodhisattva and war are mutually incompatible.

Warrior Monks

It was common in East Asian Buddhist countries for warrior monks, quasi-monks, or outright mercenaries to be engaged to defend the monasteries. In China, in ages of widespread banditry, monasteries situated in remote locations no doubt felt they had no other choice if they were to survive. Certain Chinese and Korean monks and monasteries became famous for developing martial arts. Korean warrior monks fought repeatedly and in large numbers in defense of the country when called upon.

Japan's warrior monks (*sōhei*) were born out of a necessity to defend monasteries from bandits, but in that country's feudalistic era the monasteries themselves took on feudalistic qualities, notably attitudes of feudalistic loyalty. The armies of warrior monks soon began threatening secular authorities who did not extend desired appointment and other favors towards their monasteries and attacking each other in a direct struggle for pre-eminence among the sects. Bushido (the "Way of the Samurai"), a synthetic ethos built of feudalistic neo-Confucian, samurai, and Zen Buddhist values and principles, developed among the samurai class. It admonished the samurai to work selflessly and tirelessly, sacrificing their own interest for that of the feudal lord, to enter battle and fight fearlessly and honorably, and to be prepared to die at any moment on behalf of the feudal lord. Zen contributions included the principles of selflessness, fearlessness, and No Mind (here adapted to mean that one should enter battle without strategy and fight by means of pure valor alone). The feudalistic neo-Confucian element dedicated all this to the service of one's feudal lord.

In addition, the Zen sect was close to the samurai warrior class. Some Zen masters instructed the samurai in swordsmanship. In a letter to a master swordsman, the Zen master Takuan Sōhō Zenji wrote the following advice:

> Set your mind free as you would set the cat free; then your mind will work freely, unfixed, wherever it may go. Apply this to the mastery of swordsmanship: Do not let your mind stop, trying to figure out how to strike; forget how; strike without fixing your mind on the opponent. The man who opposes you is empty, and you yourself are empty; regard your striking hands and the sword as empty, yet do not be seized by [the concept of] emptiness. . . . The same can be said of dancing. Merely hold your fan and take steps. . . .
>
> Do not forget, day or night, your grave obligations [to your lord, Shōgun Iemitsu]; think only of how you can repay these obligations and fulfill your duty of loyalty.
>
> (deBary 1969, 377)

Here we see the Zen understanding of No Mind applied to swordsmanship. The swordsman is advised to strike spontaneously, without thought, intention, or strategy of any kind. From a moral point of view, it is stunning that the same advice is given a few lines later with respect to dancing, as if striking another with a sword and dancing were the same kind of action. It is clear that Takuan's concern is not with the morality of killing or with moral issues at all but solely with mental discipline. Takuan goes on to speak of the swordsman and his opponent as empty, seeming to understand by this that they are unreal or dreamlike and therefore one need not worry about harming this illusory other. This is an incorrect and nihilistic interpretation of emptiness. As Mahāyāna doctrine emphasizes and Vajrayāna ritual expresses again and again, wisdom (realizing the truth of emptiness) and universal compassion are two sides of a single coin. As early Buddhism taught, there is no self, but suffering is real. As the Mahāyāna taught, there are no sentient beings, but the bodhisattva nonetheless vows to save them all. In fact, Takuan's ethics are not Buddhist ethics. We see in the last lines quoted that he urges a neo-Confucian ethics of particularist loyalty and duty upon his correspondent.

Traditionally, few raised questions from a Buddhist point of view about the morality of the ethos that made Buddhism into the handmaiden of warfare. The contemporary American Zen master Robert Aitken voiced his objections when he wrote:

> The Devil quotes scripture, and *Māra*, the incarnation of ignorance, can quote the *Abhidharma*. The fallacy of the Way of the Samurai is similar to the fallacy of the Code of the Crusader. Both distort what should be a universal view into an argument for partisan warfare. . . . The [bodhisattva] vow of Takuan Zenji to save all beings did not encompass the one he called the enemy.
>
> (Aitken 1984, 5–6)

That is, the ethic of the bodhisattva is a universal ethic of compassion for all sentient beings without distinction. Bushido replaces this universalistic ethic with Confucian particularism: greater concern and dedication are due those with whom one has an important relationship. It is only a short step by way of samurai values to reach enmity towards the enemies of those with whom one has an important relationship.

Japanese Buddhism in World War II

In 1997, Brian Daizen A. Victoria powerfully raised questions about the morality of Japanese Buddhist behavior during World War II with his book *Zen at War*. He demonstrated that Japanese Buddhist leaders were involved in expansionist imperialism and militarism, apparently not only in order to survive in a wartime Japan where dissent was not permitted, but with conviction and real enthusiasm. He analyzed their rhetoric, showing an ideology that had much in common with Bushido. Here again was "Buddhist" language stripped of its universalism, steeped instead in particularism, though the selflessness and self-sacrifice, fearlessness, and No Mind valor which was expected during World War II was in the service of the Japanese emperor rather than of the feudal lord, and the ethical values were Shinto as well as Confucian, but scarcely Buddhist, though Buddhist language was used. An example of this rhetoric can be seen in the following passage written by the longtime Zen student Lieutenant Colonel Sugimoto Gorō:

> Zen Master Dōgen said, "To study the Buddha Dharma is to study the self. To study the self is to forget the self." To forget the self means to discard both body and mind. . . . This is the unity of the sovereign and his subjects, the origin of faith in the emperor.
>
> (Victoria 1997, 120)

Here we see that Zen Buddhist practice is held to remove the elements of "self" that separate the Japanese subject from the emperor, unifying the two. Whereas Dōgen's passage goes on to say that the result of forgetting the self is to "have the objective world prevail in you" – i.e., to be in a non-dualistic state of unity with the whole world – here one is in a state of unity only with the emperor. The result of such unity with the emperor can be seen in the words of the Zen master Harada Daiun Sōgaku: "[If ordered to] march: tramp, tramp, or shoot: bang, bang. This is the manifestation of the highest Wisdom [of Enlightenment]" (ibid., 137). Here the unity of subject and sovereign – or his extension, the soldier's commanding officer – is such that the commander's will automatically becomes the soldier's will; the soldier manifests his Zen state of "No Mind" by unhesitatingly – certainly without moral scruples – obeying his commander's orders.

Victoria's book demonstrated the twisting and manipulation of Zen philosophical language to serve a purpose incompatible with Buddhist ethics. Victoria judged Zen wartime language and behavior as "thoroughly and completely morally bankrupt" (Victoria 2003, 144); however, its perpetrators perceived themselves as being eminently moral. The morality in terms of which they were moral, though, was Shinto-Confucian morality, not Buddhist. This is an important example of the "over tolerance" characteristic of Buddhism in many times and places that allowed Buddhism to synthesize with other views, here Confucianism and Shinto – views which a more analytic approach might have regarded as ethically incompatible with Buddhism. Victoria's book delivered a shock to many Buddhists in Japan and the West; it has prompted some serious self-examination and a few apologies from Japanese Zen leaders and institutions in a process that is still ongoing.

Buddhist Self-Immolation

In Vietnam during the years of the American war, there were individual monks who left the Sangha to fight on one side or the other. However, by far the greater part of the Sangha declared itself in support of a non-violent stance that was nonetheless committed to trying to protect the people from suffering. Yet among those who were most profoundly committed to non-violence were some who committed self-immolation, burning themselves to death as an act of self-sacrifice which they hoped would hasten the war's end.

Buddhist self-immolation has never been understood as suicide. A suicide is committed out of grief, anger, or despair; a self-immolation is done out of love and compassion. In the Vietnamese war context, it was recognized as the act of a bodhisattva who was prepared to sacrifice his or her life out of compassion for the suffering of others. It was felt to be the most powerful action that could be taken by a person who was, on principle, committed not to harm another. The Vietnamese interpreted self-immolation as an act that might communicate very powerfully to one who was intent on perpetrating the war: "this is what war is; this is the consequence of your actions." It was hoped that this might touch such a person so deeply that she or he would be unable to continue prosecuting the war. Thus the self-immolators would not fire a shot or drop a bomb, but they would, with their burning bodies, attempt an action just as powerful, or perhaps more powerful, in bringing the war to an end, thereby saving untold numbers of lives on all sides.

The rationale for Vietnamese self-immolation drew upon two major threads, one historical and the other ideological. Historically, self-immolation (offering part or all of one's body) was introduced in a mythical context in the *Lotus Sūtra* but put into actual practice in China and, to a lesser extent, in Vietnam, both as an offering to the Buddha and as an act of protest when the Dharma was under attack (see Jan 1964–5). Such acts were rare and highly esteemed. Ideologically, the self-immolators drew upon Mahāyāna texts such as the *Upāya-kauśalya Sūtra*, which justified a bodhisattva's killing out of compassion in order to save many lives. In that text, the bodhisattva kills another, while the Vietnamese self-immolators killed themselves, but the latter well understood and accepted that all killing, whether of another or oneself, is equally prohibited by the first precept. The rationale that the Vietnamese self-immolators gave to justify their action was the same as the rationale in the *sūtra* – namely, the utilitarian argument that, when motivated by compassion, one may kill a person in order to prevent far more extensive killings. At the same time, the *sūtra* implicitly recognizes the morally and karmically troubling element in the act of "compassionate killing" by raising the question of whether there will be karmic retribution for the act. Thus, the bodhisattva in the *sūtra* says that he is willing to accept karmic retribution in the future for his act of killing – a retribution that must be acknowledged, at least in passing, inasmuch as one is violating the precept. Similarly, shortly before she immolated herself, a young

Vietnamese woman, Nhat Chi Mai, discussed with a close friend and fellow activist the possibility that she might fast to death. Her friend, shocked, tried to dissuade her, asking her who would care for her aged mother. The young woman replied, "I know that I would commit the sin of impiety towards my mother by killing myself, but if my death could help shorten the war and save lives, I would be willing to pay for the sin of impiety in another life" (King 1999, 289). As in the *sūtra*, it is part of the altruistic motivation that one will be ready to accept the negative karmic retribution that will follow from one's act.

Among Mahāyāna and Vajrayāna Buddhists, properly motivated and properly carried out self-immolation is widely admired, even revered. This kind of response was possible in Vietnam during the war years because the act was established in historical precedent and culturally understood.

In recent years, Tibetan monks, ex-monks, and nuns have begun to use self-immolation as an important act of protest against the Chinese occupation of Tibet. The Dalai Lama attempts to discourage these acts, emphasizing that every life is precious. A scholarly lama stresses that such acts should be undertaken only by the most advanced bodhisattvas, with nothing but pure love and compassion in their hearts, and that the teaching of "compassionate killing" is an advanced teaching that is not for the public (King 1999, 293). The Tibetan population responds to the self-immolations with sorrow and reverence.

Among Theravāda Buddhists there are more mixed feelings regarding the practice of self-immolation. Some simply consider it wrong, inasmuch as it violates the first precept. Some consider it wrong for Theravādans, but acceptable for Mahāyānists, with their principles of skillful means and bodhisattvic self-sacrifice. This seems to express an understanding of morality as faithfulness to the precepts of one's sect. One prominent Theravāda monk, upon being asked if the self-immolations were morally good, responded: "Yes. The self-immolations were *dāna-pāramitā* [the perfection of giving]; the greatest gift is to give a life" (King, 1999 292–3). In this way, he translated the Mahāyāna bodhisattva ethic into the language of giving, a moral virtue more familiar in the Theravāda context.

Buddhist Ideals and Buddhist Realities, I: Buddhist Non-Violence and Peacemaking

Since the 1960s, Buddhists have made major contributions to the world in the areas of peacemaking and non-violent political engagement. The most significant efforts have been the non-violent "Struggle Movement," also known as the "Third Way," during the war in Vietnam; the Tibetan Liberation Movement; the struggle to bring about non-violent regime change in Burma/Myanmar, including the monk-led Saffron Revolution as well as the lay leadership of Aung San Suu Kyi; and the effort by A. T. Ariyaratne and the Sarvodaya Shramadana to bring the civil war in Sri Lanka to a peaceful end. All four of these efforts were born of the necessity of responding to military and political situations of a devastating magnitude of violence. All four maintain(ed) strict standards of principled non-violence.

These four movements are all a part of the larger movement of engaged Buddhism, also known as socially engaged Buddhism. It is characteristic of that movement that it attempts to put the ideals of Buddhism into practice in the realm of active engagement with social and political issues. Thus, while above we have seen Buddhists in various ways compromising Buddhist ideals in the interest of perceived needs of self-defense or statecraft, the engaged Buddhist movement is an effort to take Buddhist ideals seriously and not compromise them while engaged with some often highly difficult and dangerous real-world struggles, including struggles for self-defense.

Non-Adversariality

There are fundamentally two traditional Buddhist ideals upon which all of these engaged Buddhists have based their non-violent movements: the ideal of *mettā-karuṇā* (lovingkindness and compassion) and the ideal of non-violence. The key factor in making these struggles what they are is that these two ideals are both interpreted and applied in the manner taught by the Buddha: as applying to all sentient beings (in these cases, especially all humans) equally and without distinction. When lovingkindness or compassion and non-violence are applied universally and without distinction, the result is a stance of non-enmity or non-adversariality, even in the midst of a life-and-death struggle. Moreover, even in the midst of a life-and-death struggle, the goal of these struggles has been envisioned not as victory for one's own side, but as a state of reconciliation, a win–win situation in which the well-being of both sides is enhanced.

The Vietnamese Buddhists were the first to articulate the non-adversarial stance to the global community, with Thich Nhat Hanh being one of the most eloquent spokespersons advocating this approach. In the midst of the war, Nhat Hanh wrote a poem that became the lyrics of a song widely sung throughout South Vietnam as part of the anti-war "Third Way" movement. It declares, in part,

Our enemy has the name of hatred
Our enemy has the name of inhumanity
Our enemy has the name of anger
Our enemy has the name of ideology . . .
Our enemy is not man.
If we kill man, with whom shall we live?

(Forest 1978, 12)

The "Third Way" movement that this song celebrates was a movement that declared itself to be neither on the side of the North and the communists (the first "way") nor on the side of the South and the anti-communists (the second "way"), but on the side of life (the third "way"). Even when members of their movement were killed, they maintained their ideals and declared that they would not hate those who had killed their comrades.

Both the Dalai Lama and the movement associated with him also embody the stance of non-enmity in their struggle with the Chinese. As in the Vietnamese and Burmese cases, the foundation of this stance is compassion applied equally to all. One learned lama close to the Dalai Lama put it this way:

> The main thing is to have compassion for mistakes made from an egocentric viewpoint, from ignorance. Sometimes you have a wrong view that fills you with hatred and you do something out of hatred that earns you negative karma. That must be subject to our compassion, our love. The Chinese are now earning terrible karma for what they are doing to us. We must feel compassion for *all* who are suffering, on both sides. We don't look at the Chinese as evil, but try to find a peaceful solution and make them happy and peaceful.[4]

Non-adversariality also infuses the Burmese movement. Aung San Suu Kyi tells the story of one of her colleagues being interrogated by the fearsome military intelligence:

> When Uncle U Kyi Maung was under detention, one of the Military Intelligence officers interrogating him asked, "Why did you decide to become a member of the Natonal League for Democracy?" And he answered, "For your sake." That's what our struggle is about: everybody's everyday lives, including those of the MI.
>
> (Aung San Suu Kyi 1997, 121)

Being Peace

A second contribution of the engaged Buddhists to the art of non-violent peacemaking came from Thich Nhat Hanh with his signature idea of "being peace," an idea that has been greatly influential in both Buddhist and non-Buddhist thinking about non-violence.[5] Thich Nhat Hanh reported being dismayed when he visited the United States during the Vietnam War years and observed the American anti-war movement and its angry, adversarial approach to trying to end American military involvement in Vietnam. He felt that such an approach could not possibly bring peace but would only open a new front in the war, between the pro-war and anti-war groups. He insisted that, in order to make peace, peacemakers must "be peace" – that is, they must have inner peace and calm and they must approach those with whom they struggle with a friendly, non-adversarial demeanor. In other words, for Thich Nhat Hanh, the end is already implicitly present in the means used to reach that end; thus, one can bring about peace only in a peaceful way. Here, Thich Nhat Hahn draws upon one of Buddhism's traditional strengths – the focus on developing inner peace – and applies it directly to the effort to make peace in the world. He furthermore encourages some traditional Buddhist practices – notably the practice of mindfulness – as tools for cultivating such inner peace, even in the midst of life-and-death situations.

The Four Noble Truths

A. T. Ariyaratne and the Sarvodaya Shramadana movement of Sri Lanka engaged in an extensive effort to bring that country's bloody civil war to an end, utilizing perhaps the most characteristic Buddhist analysis possible. The Sarvodayans had for decades used the Four Noble Truths as a template for analysis that guided their efforts to bring Sri Lanka out of deep poverty. On the basis of that experience, Ariyaratne and the Sarvodayans went on to apply the same method to guide their efforts to try to end the civil war in Sri Lanka by non-violent means. The analysis worked in the following way. The First Noble Truth states the problem one is trying to eliminate – classically, *dukkha*. In the context of Sri Lanka's civil war, when they asked themselves what problem they were trying to eliminate, the answer was violence. The Second Noble Truth, which states the cause of the problem (classically, craving), here disclosed that the cause of the war was poverty and ethnic hatred. The Third Noble Truth, which expresses the hoped-for goal (classically, nirvana), here envisioned a state of peace, "a sustainable, spiritually balanced island that works for all." Finally, the Fourth Noble Truth, the means to achieve the goal (classically, the Eightfold Path) here was identified as a substantial group of Sarvodaya development and peacemaking programs targeting poverty and ethnic hatred. Sarvodaya's understanding of how the Sri Lankan war could be ended is classical Buddhist cause and effect thinking: remove the fuel and the fire goes out; remove the causes of war and the war will end.

It must be acknowledged that these Buddhist non-violent movements have not yet seen a success. However, the Tibetan and Burmese struggles are, at the time of writing, ongoing.

Buddhist Ideals and Buddhist Realities, II: Investigating the Potential for a Buddhist Just War Theory

Tessa Bartholomeusz (2002) raised the possibility of a Buddhist just war theory with her study of Sri Lankan Buddhist rhetoric supporting the Buddhist war against the Tamil separatists in that country. While she made a good case that Sri Lankan Buddhists were using a *de facto* just war theory, the Sri Lankan case depends heavily upon use of the *Mahāvaṃsa*, a text that is authoritative only in Sri Lanka. In probing the potential for compatibility between Buddhist ideals and Buddhist realities, an interesting test case to consider is whether it might be possible to compose a Buddhist just war theory elsewhere in the Theravāda Buddhist world. This requires an effort to find some flexibility in Buddhist principles on the basis of which one could morally justify the defensive warfare that, in practice, most Buddhists want.

A central Buddhist tenet seems to make a serious Buddhist just war theory impossible: karma. Especially in the Theravāda context it remains clear that to kill a person violates the first precept and earns the one who kills significant bad karma. Thus, if one kills, one is harming oneself. If one takes the basic principles of Buddhism seriously, this is a very difficult problem for any serious effort to create a just war theory.

Three principles may be considered for their potential to reconcile Buddhist philosophical non-violence with Buddhist actual engagement in violence – i.e., Buddhist ideals and Buddhist realities. These three principles are the Two Wheels of Dhamma – intention and degree.

The Two Wheels of Dhamma

The popular idea of the Two Wheels of Dhamma holds that the Dhamma manifests itself in two realms: the *lokiya* (mundane or worldly) and the *lokuttara* (trans-mundane or religious) realms. Does this idea permit Buddhist ideals and realities to reconcile, perhaps allowing a lower ethical standard, or more flexibility, in the *lokiya* realm?

The Two Wheels of Dhamma concept does not in fact mandate two different standards for the mundane and trans-mundane realms, but rather looks to the very same Dhamma being *applied* in the two realms. The duty of a Buddhist king (and presumably other Buddhist rulers) is to actualize the Dhamma, to make it present in the world. Buddhism hopes for a *dhammarāja*, the righteous ruler who rules the *lokiya* realm according to Dhamma. Thus the intent of the two wheels doctrine is not to compromise the Dhamma, but to bring the world *up to* the standard of the Dhamma. It does not reconcile Buddhist ideals and Buddhist realities.

This is demonstrated in the ideal of the *cakkavatti* (wheel-turning) king. The *cakkavatti* is a version of the *dhammarāja*; he is the Buddhist ideal king who rules the *lokiya* realm by Dhamma, and he does have an army. The *Cakkavatti Sīhanāda Sutta* portrays the army of the *cakkavatti* entering a neighboring country, yet that army *does not kill* anyone. Neighboring rulers welcome the *cakkavatti* and willingly submit to his rule as soon as he enters their countries as a result of the power of the Dhamma which he manifests. Thus, Buddhist scriptural ideals recognize an ideal king, but he is portrayed in terms so mythological, so *lokuttara* in nature, that he gives no real guidance for the *lokiya* realm. The *cakkavatti* ideal does not address the question of how far the world *can* be brought up to the standard of Dhamma. It gives no guidance on the question of defensive violence.

Volition

Volition (*cetanā*), or the intention behind an action, plays an important role in Buddhist ethics in partially determining the karmic nature of the deed committed under the influence of that volition. In the *Aṅguttara Nikāya* the Buddha says, "It is mental volition, O monks, that I call karma. Having willed, one acts through body, speech or mind!" (Saddhatissa 1987, 20). The intention behind the act can never be ignored in considering the karmic nature of the act.

As we have seen, engaged Buddhists attempt to put the ideals of Buddhism into real-world practice. Theirs is a genuine Two Wheels of Dhamma attempt to bring *lokiya* worldly action up to the standard of the Dhamma. engaged Buddhist Aung San Suu Kyi's thoughts on defensive violence are thus instructive. Despite the fact that she is the leader of a non-violent movement, Aung San Suu Kyi by no means sees herself disbanding the army if she were ever to come to power. She speaks for many, probably most, Buddhists in defending the existence of an army:

> As I see it, the main responsibility of the army is to protect and defend the people. If we lived in a world where it was not necessary to defend ourselves, there would be no need for armies. But I do not envisage that in the near future the world would be such that we can afford to be without protection. I would like to think of the army as a force of protection rather than a force of destruction.
>
> And there's always the question of *cetena* [*cetanā*; right intention]. The *cetena* of the army should be right. I once had a talk with an army officer who was full of hatred for the Communists whom he had fought. And I said, "I find this very disturbing that you fought them out of a sense of hatred. I would like to think that you were fighting motivated by a love

> for the people you were defending rather than out of hate for those whom you were attacking." That's what I mean by *cetena*.
>
> (Aung San Suu Kyi 1997, 21–2)

We have seen above other Theravādans attempting to defend killing in war by arguing that a soldier's intention is to defend, not to kill. Aung San Suu Kyi clearly shares that view and justifies the existence of an army on that ground.

Certainly a soldier's act of killing in defense of his countrymen is karmically very different from an act such as murdering one's spouse's lover in a jealous rage – precisely because of the difference in the mental states behind the acts. Nonetheless, the Buddha has said that the soldier's act of killing can never be totally free of hatred and delusion; the implication is that it would be impossible intentionally to kill without such mental elements. We have seen that the tradition regards killing as always wrong and always earning some negative karmic fruit. Thus, recognition of the role played by intention in Buddhist ethics helps, but does not fully resolve, the Buddhist's dilemma. A Buddhist could express limited moral approval of the intention to defend, while having to continue to disapprove of the act of killing.

Moreover, Buddhism endeavors to transform people in such a way that they become more and more incapable of committing acts of violence. This is the point at which the contradiction between Buddhist ideals and realities is direct. Who will join the army – the segment of society that is least developed (from a Buddhist point of view), those who are willing and able to kill? This is not the kind of army that Aung San Suu Kyi envisages, as she shows in this exchange with her interviewer:

> ALAN CLEMENTS: Assuming democracy is achieved, what will happen to SLORC's [the Burmese military government's] army, of course with the generals removed?
>
> AUNG SAN SUU KYI: It will be a better and more honourable army and one that will be loved by the people. That is what you want an army to be.
>
> (Aung San Suu Kyi 1997, 41)

An honorable army that will be loved by the people probably will not be made up of the least developed elements in society.

Degree

Another attempt at resolving the dilemma is to consider degrees of violence. Thich Nhat Hanh writes:

> Depending on our state of being, our response to things will be more or less nonviolent. Even if we take pride in being vegetarian, for example, we have to acknowledge that the water in which we boil our vegetables contains many tiny microorganisms. We cannot be completely nonviolent, but by being vegetarian, we are going in the direction of nonviolence. If we want to head north, we can use the North Star to guide us, but it is impossible to arrive at the North Star. Our effort is only to proceed in that direction.

> Anyone can practice some nonviolence, even army generals. They may, for example, conduct their operations in ways that avoid killing innocent people. To help soldiers move in the nonviolent direction, we have to be in touch with them. If we divide reality into two camps – the violent and the nonviolent – and stand in one camp while attacking the other, the world will never have peace.
>
> (Thich Nhat Hanh 1993, 16–17)

Building upon Gandhi's observation that it is impossible to be entirely non-violent, Thich Nhat Hanh argues that all of us commit acts of violence; the difference is a matter of degree. It is not helpful for some to imagine themselves perfectly non-violent and from this position to criticize others. What is useful and pertinent, he argues, is for each of us to move as far as we are capable, from our various individual starting places, in the direction of the unattainable ideal of perfect non-violence.

Thich Nhat Hanh's comment gives Buddhism a way to express moral approval of a general who avoids killing non-combatants. This moral approval must remain limited, however, inasmuch as that general could always move further towards the ideal of non-violence.

In the end, the Buddhist tradition offers no clear answer to the question of self-defensive violence. Probably combining the intention to defend, rather than destroy, with actions that seek always to minimize violence is the best one can do in adjusting Theravāda Buddhism to the perennial Buddhist desire to act violently, when necessary, in self-defense. Recognizing intention and degree allows Buddhists to express limited moral approval of minimal defensive acts of violence. One wonders whether this is what the Buddha had in mind in his advice to the *cakkavatti* to have an army for the purpose of protection, acting "according to Dhamma."

Conclusion

Though Buddhism developed a robust personal ethic, it may well be accused of never having developed a systematic and comprehensive social ethic. Buddhist personal ethics do not translate directly or realistically into a fully functional social ethic. People want and expect their governments to defend them. Historically, Buddhist majority countries drew upon non-Buddhist philosophies to fashion their governmental institutions and functions. Buddhism's major contribution, the paradigmatic example of King Aśoka, is philosophically unhelpful. It is quite obvious that offensive warfare is unjustifiable from a Buddhist perspective. The real question before the Buddhist world is whether, to what extent, and how a Buddhist can justify engaging in self-defensive warfare.

The advent of engaged Buddhism places the dilemma of Buddhist violence in a new context. Insofar as it does not compromise the non-violent and non-particularist ideals of Buddhism, engaged Buddhism is an ongoing experiment in reconciling Buddhism's ideals with the reality of Buddhist behavior, in translating Buddhist personal ethics into a social ethic, and in determining how far Buddhist non-violence can be taken on the societal level.

Notes

1 Parts of the present chapter were previously published by the present author as "Buddhism and War," in *Socially Engaged Spirituality: Essays in Honor of Sulak Sivaraksa on His 70th Birthday*. Ed. David W. Chappell. Bangkok: Sathirakoses-Nagapradipa Foundation, 2003, 356–70. These passages are used with permission of the publisher.

2 See AN.V.292. Bhikkhu Bodhi (trans.), *The Numerical Discourses of the Buddha: A Translation of the Aṅguttara Nikāya* (Boston: Wisdom, 2012), p. 1535.

3 This account of Buddhist monastic participation in war is summarized from Yu (2005).

4 Geshe Sopa, in an interview with the author, May 2–4, 2000, Jerusalem. From notes taken by the author and reviewed by Geshe Sopa.

5 See Thich Nhat Hanh (1987) and the *film Peace Is Every Step*, by Gaetano Kazuo Maida.

References

Aitken, Robert (1984). *The Mind of Clover: Essays in Zen Buddhist Ethics*. San Francisco: North Point Press.

Aung San Suu Kyi (1997). *The Voice of Hope: Conversations with Alan Clements*. London and New York: Penguin.

Bartholomeusz, Tessa (2002). *In Defense of Dharma: Just-War Ideology in Buddhist Sri Lanka*. New York: Routledge.

Bodhi, Bhikkhu (trans.) (2000). *The Connected Discourses of the Buddha: A New Translation of the Saṃyutta Nikāya*. Boston: Wisdom.

Carter, John Ross, and Palihawadana, Mahinda (1987). *The Dhammapada*. Oxford and New York: Oxford University Press.

deBary, Theodore (ed.) (1969). *The Buddhist Tradition in India, China and Japan*. New York: Modern Library.

Forest, James H. (1978).*The Unified Buddhist Church of Vietnam: Fifteen Years for Reconciliation*. Hof van Stony, Netherlands: International Fellowship of Reconciliation.

Harvey, Peter (2000). *An Introduction to Buddhist Ethics*. Cambridge and New York: Cambridge University Press.

Jan Yun-hua (1964–5). Buddhist Self-Immolation in Medieval China. In *History of Religions* 4, 243–68.

Jerryson, Michael K., and Mark Juergensmeyer, (eds) (2010). *Buddhist Warfare*. Oxford and New York: Oxford University Press.

King, Sallie B. (1999). They Who Burn Themselves for Peace: Buddhist Self-Immolation. In *Socially Engaged Buddhism for the New Millennium: Essays in Honor of The Ven. Phra Dhammapitaka (Bhikkhu P. A. Payutto) On his 60th Birthday Anniversary*. Ed. Sulak Sivaraksa et al. Bangkok: Sathirakoses-Nagapradipa Foundation, 283–96.

Nikam, N. A., and McKeon, R. (1978). *The Edicts of Asoka*. Chicago and London: University of Chicago Press.

Saddhatissa, Hammalawa (1987). *Buddhist Ethics: The Path to Nirvana*. London: Wisdom.

Śāntideva. *The Bodhicaryāvatāra*. Trans. Kate Crosby and Andrew Skilton. Oxford and New York: Oxford University Press.

Schmithausen, Lambert (1999). Aspects of the Buddhist Attitude towards War. In *Violence, Non-Violence and the Rationalization of Violence in South Asian Cultural History*. Ed. Jan E. M. Houben and Karel R. Van Kooij. Leiden: Brill, 45–67.

Swearer, Donald K. (1981). *Buddhism and Society in Southeast Asia*. Chambersburg, PA: Anima Books.

Tatz, Mark (1994). *The Skill in Means (Upāyakauśalya) Sūtra*. Delhi: Motilal Banarsidass.

Thich Nhat Hanh (1987). *Being Peace*. Berkeley, CA: Parallax Press.

Thich Nhat Hanh (1993). *For a Future to be Possible: Commentaries on the Five Wonderful Precepts*. Berkeley, CA: Parallax Press.

Victoria, Brian Daizen (1997). *Zen at War*. New York and Tokyo: Weatherhill.

Victoria, Brian Daizen (2003). *Zen War Stories*. New York: Routledge.

Walsh, Maurice (trans.) (1995 [1987]). *The Long Discourses of the Buddha: A Translation of the Dīgha Nikāya*. Boston: Wisdom.

Yu, Xue (2005). *Buddhism, War and Nationalism: Chinese Monks in the Struggle against Japanese Aggressions, 1931–1945*. New York: Routledge.

42

Buddhist Perspectives on Human Rights

KARMA LEKSHE TSOMO

Buddhists generally have invested little time or effort in developing political or moral philosophy, as Damien Keown and other philosophers have pointed out (Keown 1998, 16). Yet, an assessment of Buddhist ethical theory through a Western lens can run the risk of overlooking or dismissing some of the more pertinent aspects of the Buddhist traditions. Although the latter do not speak with one voice, for hundreds of years they all have directed their attention towards liberation from suffering, which is also the presumed goal of human rights theories. Each tradition defines the pursuit of liberation as mental cultivation, learning and teaching the path to liberation, generating lovingkindness (*maitrī*) and compassion (*karuṇā*) towards all living beings, and social welfare activities on an immediate, practical level. Early Buddhist political ideals focused on the qualities of the good king as an archetype of enlightened leadership, rather than providing a framework for governance. At the time of the Buddha, there were no historical circumstances as widespread and horrible as those of the twentieth century that have served as a catalyst for the creation of human rights theory. Instead, followers of the Buddha were encouraged to behave according to the Noble Eightfold Path, the five precepts, the ten virtuous actions, and other moral guidelines for moral behavior that naturally lead to happiness, well-being, and ultimately liberation. In following these guidelines, Buddhists act as autonomous individuals who are also interconnected with countless other individuals whose happiness and well-being are equally important.

Today, many Buddhists express a deep concern for the welfare of all living beings, but few have recognized the importance of addressing the structural causes of suffering on a social or political level. Buddhists might argue that, in societies that are concerned primarily about the evolutionary process of spiritual liberation, there will naturally be fewer injustices and less need for social justice efforts because it is understood that, no

A Companion to Buddhist Philosophy, First Edition. Edited by Steven M. Emmanuel.

matter how many reforms are made, inequalities will naturally arise in human societies on account of mental afflictions (*kleśa*) such as greed, hatred, and ignorance. Working to eliminate these root causes of suffering is generally regarded as more beneficial than trying to redress social, political, racial, and economic injustices piecemeal, since the mental afflictions are the true structural causes of social inequities. It has been assumed that charitable activities bring temporary benefits but will not ultimately solve the world's problems, whereas human beings working to eliminate their mental afflictions will address these problems on a systemic level, resulting in social transformation and the benefit of all living beings. Perhaps as a consequence of having neglected political concerns, over the past 60 years human rights violations have occurred on a massive scale in many traditionally Buddhist lands: Burma, Buryatia, Cambodia, China, Kalmykia, Laos, Mongolia, Tibet, Vietnam, as well as elsewhere. Because millions of Buddhists have been the victims of egregious human rights violations, they have an enormous stake in forging a human rights theory that is at once universal, compatible with their worldview, and practical enough to protect their interests.

There is no precise definition of human rights in the Buddhist lexicon and no concept that can be mapped without problem in any of the Buddhist canonical languages. No matter how we parse the word "rights," it remains a foreign concept when translated into Buddhist languages. This does not mean that Buddhists do not support human rights; in fact, His Holiness the Fourteenth Dalai Lama and others have been strong supporters of human rights. Nor does it mean that the Buddhist lexicon lacks concepts that approximate and can be used to explain the notion. In fact, a Buddhist perspective may help to clarify what exactly is intended by the term "human rights."

Legalistic interpretations of human rights are commonplace, but this approach does not fit comfortably with Buddhist ways of thinking about and responding to moral dilemmas. Instead, the ethical ideals that served as a standard for good rulers can serve as a basis for human rights amid new pluralistic social and political realities. As Stephen McCarthy points out, the rule of the mythical *cakravartin* (wheel-turning monarch) took the form of a social contract founded on Dharma principles (McCarthy 2004, 69). These ideal monarchs (all male) acquired their status on the basis of merit in past lives and ruled benevolently according to the ten duties of Buddhist kingship, thus ensuring justice, happiness, and prosperity for all.[1] Similar to the *cakravartin* ideal, righteous kings (*dharmarāja*) were expected to rule according to ten moral precepts, the four laws of kings, and other codes of conduct that provided for and protected the well-being of the people (ibid., 71). The Burmese democracy advocate Aung San Suu Kyi refers to the ten duties of kings in defining a human rights doctrine for Burma that integrates Buddhist values in governance – what she calls a "spiritual revolution" – to ensure justice and compliance with human rights standards (ibid., 73).

Buddhists may hesitate to calculate human rights in terms of rights and duties, but these must be included in the conversation on human rights. Human rights is the language of contemporary global society, spoken in the most elevated international gatherings; it both serves an important function in human communications and is analogous to what the Dalai Lama has called a "universal sense of responsibility" (Dalai Lama 1998 [1993], xvii–xxi).

Establishing a Philosophical Framework

According to Buddhist teachings on dependent co-arising, all composite phenomena are interrelated, arising and perishing as a result of causes and conditions. Among myriad interdependently arising phenomena, sentient beings are especially valued. The goal of the Buddhist path is awakening, and only beings with consciousness and awareness have the potential to purify their consciousness and awaken to the true nature of things. All sentient beings, including animals, gods, hungry ghosts, and hell beings, possess this unique capability. All sentient beings also have the capacity to feel and to experience suffering; therefore, a basic Buddhist principle is to avoid harm to any sentient being.

Among sentient beings, it is especially human beings that are capable of progressing towards awakening. Because of their intelligence, their powers of reasoning, and their ability to act upon that reasoning, human beings, it is believed, have a special potential to evolve and ultimately to achieve the highest goal of awakening. The lifetime of a human being, with senses intact, who is born in an era when a buddha has taught, and when the teachings are still extant, understood, and practiced, is referred to as a "precious human rebirth." The most precious thing about such a rebirth is that human beings have the ability to purify their minds of mental afflictions and the intelligence to make good decisions about their actions (*karma*), to avoid unwholesome actions, to engage in wholesome actions, and to work for the welfare of others.

The Buddha claimed that nothing is so precious to any living being as its life and that no being wishes to experience harm or suffering. In accordance with the principle of *ahiṃsā* (non-harm), Buddhists believe that no living being should be harmed or transgressed, much less killed, especially those with a precious human rebirth. To do so not only causes suffering to sentient beings but also creates the causes of future suffering for oneself, since actions have consequences, either in this life or the next. The reasoning here is that the consequences of unwholesome actions rebound on oneself, in accordance with the Buddhist understanding of the law of cause and effect. Engaging in unwholesome actions not only causes suffering to others but also results in unpleasant experiences for the agent of the actions, including the possibility of intense suffering, and delays one's own awakening and liberation. The reverse is also true; it is beneficial to engage in wholesome actions, since they result in pleasant experiences, including personal well-being, and hasten one's own awakening. The logical conclusion is to refrain from harming any living being and instead to treat all living beings with lovingkindness and compassion. A moral framework of kindness and compassion in no way contradicts either the teachings of the major world religions or human rights theory; on the contrary, it supports them.

The ideals of any specific worldview provide a lens for understanding the system's values. For Buddhists, realized beings – *arhats*, bodhisattvas, or buddhas – pledge not to harm living beings, but instead to treat beings as if they were their own precious children. The universality of this concern may seem to be a distant goal for ordinary, deluded beings, but it provides insight into what Buddhists consider noble, worthy conduct and provides a model for everyday behavior. The idea is to generate universal concern for all sentient beings, desiring their happiness and never their harm. This ideal of universal responsibility for all sentient beings is an apt corollary of the notion of human rights. The fact that all sentient beings are equally liable to suffering, just like oneself, gives rise to thoughts of compassion, though this certainly requires practice. Compassion for all sentient beings and the law of *karma* (cause and effect) provide a sound foundation for developing a Buddhist theory of human rights.

Keown defines a right as "a benefit which confers upon its holder either a claim or a liberty" (Keown et al. 1998, 19), and he draws on early Buddhist descriptions of reciprocal duties between husband and wife, in texts such as the *Sigalovada Sutta*, as a source of human rights (ibid., 21). Apart from the exclusive nature of this heterosexist configuration, from a feminist perspective, the use of these reciprocal duties as a prototype is problematic because of the unequal duties expected of husbands and wives.[2] These reciprocal responsibilities were defined within a specific society that no longer exists and need to be reconsidered within a contemporary context. When we begin to formulate rules, laws, dues, and obligations within any specific cultural context, we open a can of worms. In the current, continually evolving multicultural community, it is imperative to arrive at some agreement of good will on a global level to prevent slaughter, torture, oppression, and other violations of decent human behavior.

A Buddhist perspective on human rights is integrally related to the concept of human responsibility and the recognition of human suffering. The concept of human responsibility is grounded in the law of *karma* (actions and their consequences), according to which individuals are responsible for their own actions of body, speech, and mind and also experience the consequences. The workings of cause and effect are very complicated, given that human beings create myriad actions every day and their actions are interrelated, but the principle is the basis of Buddhist moral theory and a guideline for everyday actions, even when the results of specific actions cannot be predicted. The point is to reduce and eventually to eliminate suffering for oneself and others, and therefore, pre-emptively, to refrain from actions that cause suffering. The salient point is intention, since the consequences of actions (*karma*) depend largely on the intention that motivates the action; if an action is accidental, the karmic consequences are minimal.[3] When individuals act together, the consequences for the individuals involved depend on the intentions of each. A Buddhist concept of human rights thus rests on the responsibility each individual has to create actions that are conducive to the well-being of all.

In a response to Keown, Craig K. Ihara raises two important issues with a thought experiment involving a male lead who is accused of a human rights violation for failing to catch the prima ballerina during a performance (see Ihara 1998, 43–4). As absurd as the accusation may sound, the example raises several important issues. From a Buddhist point of view, the most salient issue in this case is not whether or not the lead dancer's failure can be assigned the designation of "human rights violation," but whether or not he intended to drop the prima ballerina. If he did, and if he intended to cause her injury, his action could be considered morally culpable and would have unpleasant consequences, in accordance with the law of *karma*.

The history of the modern concept of human rights is indisputably rooted in Western intellectual history. It can also be argued that, whereas the concept of human rights may be liberating to colonized peoples, it may also be used to further the interests of Western powers.[4] However, the claim that the modern concept of human rights is illegitimate and is not applicable to non-Western societies because it is a Western construct is flawed. Good ideas have been borrowed back and forth since the dawn of human society, and human rights theory is a valid attempt to ensure its continuity. At the same time, a legitimate claim can be made for culturally specific concepts of human rights in order to respect and accommodate the cultural histories and worldviews of Buddhists, Hindus, Muslims, Daoists, indigenous peoples, and other non-Europeans. In our pluralistic global society, we have no option but to develop multiple, multicultural interpretations of human rights that are compatible with the principles already enshrined in the United Nations Declaration of Human Rights (UNDHR). Without these principles, in an interdependent world, weaker sectors of society are vulnerable to abuses, not only in international trade, but at all levels of global interaction. This allows the privileged to close their eyes to the abuses of multinational corporations, sex trafficking, child labor, and environmental degradation, often with the complicity of governments and the obscenely wealthy. For Buddhists, to ignore these concerns is a tragedy that contravenes the noble intention to do no harm, not just to individuals, but on a global scale.

It is legitimate to claim that the Buddhists already had their own culturally constructed concept of human rights in the fifth century BCE. If indeed the modern concept of human rights "elevates the individual human person and his [*sic*] freedom and happiness to the goal and end of all human association," as Eugene Kamenka (1978) contends (quoted in Junger 1998, 53), then the goals of Buddhism and human rights are identical. For Buddhists, the mental consciousness of each human being is individuated, not communal, and the immediate goal of the individual human person is to achieve freedom and happiness. This goal is not only compatible with modern human rights theory but it also expands to all of humanity. When Buddhists talk about achieving the welfare of oneself *and* others, or achieving perfect awakening in order to liberate all sentient beings from suffering, they expand the goal beyond their own individual freedom and happiness to include the freedom and happiness of all individual human persons.

Critics may counter that multiple disparate worldviews will result in multiple potentially conflicting theories of human rights, and that a pluralistic concept of human rights leaves us with nothing universally applicable and nothing enforceable. It is certainly true that enforcement is a critical and controversial issue in any human rights doctrine, especially when human rights violations are used as a pretext for empire. But diverse perspectives on human rights are not necessarily counterproductive, and may even be fruitful as long as all parties can agree on the basics: the right to be free of hunger, thirst, torture, rape, detention without due cause or due process, and so on. No human being wishes to be deprived of health, education, freedom of expression, freedom of assembly, and the other provisions of the United Nations Charter on Human Rights of 1945. Since human rights are already enshrined in the UNDHR, the task is simply to demonstrate that Buddhism has such a theory or a viable basis for such a theory.

Peter D. Junger's critique of the UNDHR as being "a peculiar mix of vagueness and specificity" (Junger 1998, 59) is well taken. What does "the right to security in the event of unemployment, sickness, disability, widowhood, old age, or other lack of livelihood in circumstances beyond his [*sic*] control" (ibid., 60–1) mean, especially to the unemployed, sick, disabled, widowed, aged, and destitute? But his suggestion that the rights specified in the UNDHR are incoherent and deny the truth of suffering does not follow. On the contrary, the document seems to support the First Noble Truth by pointing out the *dukkha* (suffering, unsatisfactoriness) entailed in these conditions. The aspiration to liberate beings from suffering is not an example of clinging to rights but a realistic recognition of the causes of human suffering. So, although the rights set forth in the UNDHR are idealistic and impractical, the obligation to protect the interests of human beings in danger of rape and slaughter remains. "Respect" is a vague, contested notion, but, in a nuclear world of pre-emptive militancy, a responsibility to preserve the human community from annihilation is something that most thinking human beings can support. The Dalai Lama goes so far as to claim that "Universal responsibility is the key to human survival (Dalai Lama 1998 [1993], xx).

The Limits of "Human" and "Rights"

The Parliament of the World's Religions held in 1993 resulted in the promulgation of a *Declaration towards a Global Ethic*, which expresses the necessity of "human rights, freedom, justice, peace, and the preservation of the Earth" and "the obligation to respect human dignity, human rights, and fundamental values" (Küng and Kuschel 1993, 18, 30). These are values to which almost all Buddhists would ascribe. "By a global ethic," it says, "we do not mean a global ideology or a single unified religion beyond all existing religions, and certainly not the domination of one religion over all others" (ibid., 21). With this statement, too, Buddhists would have little argument. But when it states: "By a global ethic we mean a fundamental consensus on binding values, irrevocable standards, and personal attitudes," we encounter what may be a serious problem. If by "irrevocable standards" the declaration refers to the killing of innocent human beings, most thinking people would probably agree. But the proposal that all human beings can reach consensus on "binding values" and "personal attitudes" does not seem likely. To find a globally recognized set of ethical standards, as daunting as that may appear, is a reasonable goal, however, and avoids some of the problems intrinsic in the term "rights."

One problem with the word "rights" is that it appears to assume an origin. From where do rights arise or descend? The notion of "God-given" rights may make sense in a context that assumes a creator or a bestower of boons. It falls flat in a system that assumes no beginning and no source of creation. Among Buddhists it is assumed that phenomena arise and perish momentarily and continually without the need of a prime mover. The notion of "inherent dignity" is similarly problematic, since Buddhists admit of nothing inherent. However, these concepts have parallels in Buddhist thinking. In place of creation and divine arbitration, Buddhists substitute the efficacy of cause and effect, with enlightenment replacing heaven teleologically. In place of "inherent human dignity," they substitute the concept of the precious human rebirth with its potential for awakening, later known as buddha-nature. Hence, although not "God-given" or "inherent," the potential for human fulfillment is equally recognized.

Another problem arises with the use of the word "sacred." In his excellent study *The Idea of Human Rights: Four Inquiries*, Michael J. Perry begins by asking whether the idea of human rights is "ineliminably religious." He claims, in agreement with R. H. Tawney, that "the conviction that every human being is sacred is inescapably religious" and that no secular version of this conviction is intelligible (Perry 1998, 11). Perry contends that only the religious perspective on the sacredness of human beings makes sense, and that a secular perspective on human rights makes no sense. He further claims that human rights doctrine is "a point of convergence among people from different religious traditions," based on a common "ecumenical" ground. As it happens, the matter is not so easily resolved, since this supposed ecumenical ground is not as solid as it may appear. All religions do not rest on similar assumptions, nor do they speak with one voice. Setting aside the many debates about what religion is and whether Buddhism, Daoism, and Confucianism rightly deserve to be categorized as such,[5] each undoubtedly has religious elements and each usually has a chapter in world religions books. Unfortunately for felicitous agreements, each of these ancient traditions also has its own view of reality, a worldview that is quite distinct from the Abrahamic faith traditions that have underwritten many discussions of human rights thus far. One quite glaring distinction is their lack of agreement about a concept that resembles "the sacred" and possibly even the adjective "sacred." If human rights are contingent on the notion that human beings are sacred, the enterprise of finding common ground for the concept of human rights falters. If a convincing argument can be made for a theory of human rights that does not hinge on the notion that human beings are sacred, a more universal argument for human rights can be made – one that will be acceptable to secularists as well as to religionists.

Defining the word "sacred" is tricky. For pantheists, the matter is simple: all that exists, whether animate or inanimate, is imbued with the divine and therefore sacred by nature. For monotheists, while the matter may seem relatively simple – all of creation is sacred because it is created by God – it is not, since human beings are accorded priority (even dominion) over other forms of life. Be that as it may, at least human beings are regarded as sacred, imbued with dignity and a right to inviolability. In the absence of a creator God, it is difficult to make a case for a notion of "the sacred" in Buddhism. While the blessing of babies, prayer beads, the consecration of images, and "sacred sites" are common in popular Buddhist practice in diverse contexts, it is impossible to find any theoretical basis for a concept of "the sacred" or "sacredness" in the absence of a creator god or supreme being to imbue his or her creation with such a quality or essence. If "the sacred" cannot exist apart from the notion of a supreme being, even if the notion of "the sacred" were sufficient and necessary to justify a theory of human rights, it is not a plausible foundation for a Buddhist theory of human rights. From a non-theistic Buddhist perspective, a secular concept of human rights makes perfect sense, because of human suffering. Just as each of us suffers subjectively, so do others also suffer; just as each of us wishes to be free of suffering, so do others. An awareness of this very basic reality of life should naturally give rise to compassion and respect for human dignity.

If the concept of the sacred or sacredness is absent in the Buddhist context, can we establish an equivalent concept? I propose that we begin with the notion of sentience, because it characterizes all beings as having the capacity to suffer. Because the Buddha warned against causing sentient beings harm, we could then undertake defining which harms are untenable. In classical Buddhist thought, sentient beings are not only capable of feeling and suffering, they also have the capacity to awaken from ignorance and free themselves from suffering. The capacity to feel – to feel heat, cold, joy, suffering, contentment, frustration, tranquility, anger, boredom, and the gamut of sensations and emotions – is not something that is endowed by a creator, but is simply a component or constituent quality of sentient life. To what extent other animals and other sentient beings feel these sensations and emotions is open to question, but human beings are aware of their capacity to feel and respond to sensations and emotions. Moreover, human beings have the special capacity to reflect on their sensations and emotions and are able to regulate their responses to stimuli. From a Buddhist perspective, this capacity sets human beings apart from other animals and other sentient beings. The capacity to make intelligent judgments enables human beings consciously to avoid destructive actions and to engage in beneficial actions in ways that are superior to most other forms of life. This capacity for intelligent judgment gives human beings special responsibilities and opportunities that are not feasible for other living beings.

A discussion of human rights naturally raises questions about the rights of non-human animals, but such a discussion is circumscribed by definition. From a Buddhist perspective, it could be argued that, until all human beings agree to extend the benefits of dignity and rights to all sentient beings – for example, by becoming vegetarians – human rights are compromised, in that speciesism limits human compassion by circumscribing the scope of its concern. This discussion is beyond the purview of this chapter, but it is a question that can and must be considered by Buddhists who are concerned with the welfare of all sentient beings. Here we begin by limiting our discussion to human rights, since it is necessary to start somewhere, and hope that the arguments can be extended, by analogy, in good time.

A Philosophical Qualm

In the Buddhist worldview, all compounded phenomena are characterized by *dukkha* (suffering, unsatisfactoriness), *anitya* (impermanence), and *anātman* (the absence of an independent self or soul). One might argue that the Buddhist deconstructionist concept of persons is a shaky foundation for deontology in general and human rights in particular. Some argue that Buddhism has no ethics, much less grounds for a theory of human rights, because the non-self (*anātman*) theory leaves no one to be wronged and no one to commit a transgression. Indeed, a nihilistic misinterpretation of the concept of *anātman* would have serious ethical implications and make any concept of human rights or human dignity untenable and incomprehensible. The idea that persons lack any permanent essence does not mean that they do not exist at all or that their actions have no consequences. Nāgārjuna's explanation of the two truths – conventional truth and ultimate truth – is helpful here. Phenomena exist on a conventional or relative level, but not ultimately – that is, although phenomena appear to exist concretely, substantially, or truly, in fact no inherent or enduring, independently existent essence can be found. Ideas such as compassion and universal responsibility are not undermined by the idea of non-self (*anātman*), because the self that is being refuted here is not the conventionally existent, living, breathing person but the idea of a self or soul that exists apart from its constituent parts (the body, feelings, consciousness, and so on). The Buddhist concept of persons as constituted of aggregates without independent existence does not undermine moral agency, since interdependent persons are responsible for their actions. The conventional-level understanding of the self is perfectly serviceable as a ground for human rights, since it is the conventional self that feels pain, suffers oppression, bleeds, and dies.

The Buddhist concept of non-self does challenge the notion of moral absolutes, however, since persons are contingent, interdependent, and dependent upon causes and conditions. Instead, Buddhist moral reasoning takes into account the complex circumstances in which decision-making occurs. Buddhist ethics is not simply situational, since it rests on well-defined moral guidelines such as non-harm, but it is flexible in response to social custom, human difference, and other unique conditions. Despite human diversity and the complexity of ethical decision-making, many people have not had a hand in crafting documents such as the UNDHR. In the task of gaining traction for human rights, it is necessary to listen to these voices, for the people whose voices are muted are the very people whose human rights are most frequently violated.

The Sum of Compassion and Reason

The concept of human rights as a normative moral principle is both meaningful and necessary. It is transcultural, in that certain principles such as kindness and compassion transcend cultural boundaries, and it is also culturally specific, in that it is applicable and actionable in multiple cultural settings. Formulating actionable policies that are both coherent and enforceable is a matter for another day, but the framework within which a Buddhist concept of human rights can be formulated is clear. Recognizing the vulnerability of beings to suffering and the potential of all beings for liberation from suffering should spur Buddhist nations and societies to address human needs and aspirations through formal political policy and action. The Buddhist moral framework of compassion and lovingkindness for all beings is rational, but not simply rational, since developing compassion requires sufficient empathy to recognize and experience the sufferings of others as being similar to one's own. Perhaps the quest to find an equivalent to human rights in Buddhism will have the unintended advantage of furthering the quest to construct a Buddhist social ethics analogous to other systems of social ethics.

In formulating a viable social ethics and speaking as advocates of human rights, Buddhists have one serious problem, however. If human rights translate to universal responsibility, Buddhists need to address the issue of gender discrimination within their own ranks. Human rights cannot be applied selectively – only to human beings of a particular color, gender, or ethnicity – but must apply universally. To argue for human rights for men but not for women, for whites but not for blacks, or only for members of one's own ethnic group is inadequate and renders one's advocacy of human rights hypocritical. Silence on the issue of women's rights constitutes an inexcusable lacuna.

The Convention on the Elimination of All Forms of Discrimination against Women, which was adopted by the United Nations General Assembly in 1979 and went into effect in 1981, argues for equal rights for women and men and the protection of these rights by law.[6] The convention does not specifically mention religious rights, but Article 2 of the UNDHR states: "Everyone is entitled to all the rights and freedoms set forth in this Declaration, without distinction of any kind, such as race, colour, sex, language, religion, political or other opinion, national or social origin, property, birth or other status." Article 18 further states: "Everyone has the right to freedom of thought, conscience and religion; this right includes freedom to change his religion or belief, and freedom, either alone or in community with others and in public or private, to manifest his religion or belief in teaching, practice, worship and observance." To my mind, it is a natural corollary of human rights to eliminate practices that subordinate women, including the practice of denying women the right to manifest their religious beliefs. Denying women equal access and opportunities institutionalizes their inferiority in society and hence supports everything from inferior education for girls to sex trafficking.

If human rights are guiding moral principles, then it is incumbent on religious organizations to allow and support women to achieve equal moral and religious authority, and hence to fulfill their human potential. Unfortunately, some religious traditions have reserved the right to discriminate against women on the basis of their gender, refusing to ordain them and blocking them from positions of authority. Even now, Buddhist women are barred from full ordination in Tibetan and Theravāda Buddhist societies. Religious and government institutions that ignore the negative effects of denying religious rights to women are complicit in maintaining institutionalized forms of gender injustice, in violation of women's human rights. For example, Lucinda Joy Peach (1999, 2001, 2005) and Chatsumarn Kabilsingh (now Bhikkhuni Dhammananda) (1991) present cogent evidence that links sex trafficking and the flourishing sex trade in Thailand to women's lack of religious rights and opportunities for full ordination.

Ironically, in an era when women's rights to participate freely in all sectors are widely recognized and celebrated, male religious leaders in some Buddhist traditions are overseeing the last bastion of gender discrimination. By clinging to an outdated worldview that maintains preconceived notions of women as inferior, they are blatantly out of step with the times, at the cost of their own credibility and the credibility of Buddhist insights on moral psychology. Gender discrimination in Buddhist societies is especially glaring, since it contradicts the tradition's own message of equality. It also conflicts with Buddhist scriptures, where the Buddha is on record as affirming women's equal potential for awakening and personally instituting full ordination for women. Buddhists are faced with the paradox that, although monks are theoretically the exemplars of moral purity, many are simultaneously morally deficient, in that they routinely deny religious rights to women. Monks who deny religious rights to women are not only guilty of transgressing internationally recognized standards of human rights, they are also transgressing the very moral values that they are charged to protect, such as compassion and lovingkindness.

Women are not the only ones in Buddhist societies whose human rights are not being protected. Millions live with poverty, illiteracy, inadequate health care, and political oppression. Yet, as for corporations, for some Buddhist traditions human rights seems to be off the table, even though religion is frequently supported by political institutions that perpetuate human rights violations (see, e.g., Philp 2009). To me, this raises the issue of "passive *karma*," or the *karma* of doing nothing. The theory of *karma* is central to Buddhist ethics and concepts of human rights. If *karma* is action, what are the consequences of inaction in a situation that urgently needs to be addressed?[7] If one were to stand by and watch children drown without moving a muscle to save them, most would deem such an action culpable or unethical. Extending this logic, to stand by and do nothing while millions suffer is similarly culpable or unethical. It seems that this logic would extend even further in a tradition premised on the values of lovingkindness and compassion and the vow to liberate all sentient beings from suffering and to effect their enlightenment. If this is the case, a Buddhist theory of human rights would involve not only thoughtful discussions but also an action plan to bring equal opportunities to women, children, and all miserable and marginalized beings.

Notes

1 The ten duties of a righteous ruler (*dasa rāja dharma*) are generosity (*dāna*), ethics (*sīla*), self-sacrifice (*pariccāga/parithyaga*), integrity (*ājjava/irju*), gentleness (*maddava/murdu*), self-discipline (*tapa/thapasa*), non-enmity (*akkodha/akrodaya*), non-harm (*avihiṃsā/ahiṃsā*), patience (*khanti/kṣānti*), and non-opposition (to the popular will) (*avirodha/avirodita*).

2 In the *Sigālaka Sutta*, the duties prescribed for a husband towards his wife are honoring her, not disparaging her, not being unfaithful to her, giving authority to her, and giving her adornments. The duties prescribed for a wife towards her husband are properly organizing her work, being kind to servants, not being unfaithful, protecting provisions, and being skillful and diligent in her work. Only the duty of faithfulness pertains to both. See Walshe (1995, 467).

3 In his lectures, U. S. N. Goenka, an Indian Burmese lay teacher of *vipassana* ("insight") meditation, points out the stark difference between the karmic consequences of the actions of two people with very different motivations: a doctor who unintentionally kills a patient during surgery and a thief who deliberately kills a convenience store clerk during a robbery.

4 For example, see Bricmont (2006). For a nuanced study of human rights and British colonialism, see Ibhawoh (2007).

5 If, as Perry contends, religion is necessarily connected with the idea of Ultimate Reality "in a profoundly intimate way," then Buddhism certainly does not qualify as a religion, since it eschews such a concept. The closest runner would be the concept of emptiness (*sunyata*), which is itself empty and thus ultimately not Ultimate at all.

6 While some countries have qualified their support with certain declarations and reservations, the United States is the only developed country that has not yet ratified the convention.

7 The morality of inaction has been raised by Kolnai (2005).

References

Bricmont, Jean (2006). *Humanitarian Imperialism: Using Human Rights to Sell War*. New York: Monthly Review Press.

Dalai Lama (1998 [1993]). Human Rights and Universal Responsibility, Statement to the Non-Governmental Organizations' United Nations World Conference on Human Rights, June 15, 1993. Vienna, Austria. In *Buddhism and Human Rights*. Ed. Damien Keown, Charles S. Prebish, and Wayne R. Husted. Richmond, Surrey: Curzon Press.

Ibhawoh, Bonny (2007). *Imperialism and Human Rights: Colonial Discourses of Rights and Liberties in African History*. Albany: State University of New York Press.

Ihara, Craig K. (1998). Why There are No Rights in Buddhism: A Reply to Damien Keown. In *Buddhism and Human Rights*. Ed. Damien Keown, Charles S. Prebish, and Wayne R. Husted. Richmond, Surrey: Curzon Press, 43–52.

Junger, Peter (1998). Why the Buddha Has No Rights. In *Buddhism and Human Rights*. Ed. Damien Keown, Charles S. Prebish, and Wayne R. Husted. Richmond, Surrey: Curzon Press, 53–96.

Kabilsingh, Chatsumarn (1991). *Thai Women in Buddhism*. Berkeley, CA: Parallax Press.

Kamenka, Eugene (1978). The Anatomy of an Idea. In *Human Rights*. Ed. E. Kamenka and Alice Ehr-Soon Tay. New York: St. Martin's Press, 1–12.

Keown, Damien (1998). Are There Human Rights in Buddhism? In *Buddhism and Human Rights*. Ed. Damien Keown, Charles S. Prebish, and Wayne R. Husted. Richmond, Surrey: Curzon Press.

Keown, Damien, Prebish, Charles S., and Husted, Wayne R. (eds) (1998). *Buddhism and Human Rights*. Richmond, Surrey: Curzon Press.

Kolnai, Aurél (2005). Actions and Inactions. In *Exploring the World of Human Practice: Readings in and about the Philosophy of Aurél Kolnai*. Ed. Zoltan Balazs and Francis Dunlop. Budapest: Central European University Press.

Küng, Hans, and Kuschel, Karl-Josef (eds) (1993). *A Global Ethic: The Declaration of the Parliament of the World's Religions*. London: SCM Press.

McCarthy, Stephen (2004). The Buddhist Political Rhetoric of Aung San Suu Kyi. In *Contemporary Buddhism* 5(2), 67–81.

Peach, Lucinda Joy (1999). Buddhism and Human Rights in the Thai Sex Trade. In *Religious Fundamentalisms and the Human Rights of Women*. Ed. Courtney W. Howland. New York: St. Martin's Press.

Peach, Lucinda Joy (2001). Are Women Human? The Promise and Perils of "Women's Rights as Human Rights." In *Negotiating Culture and Human Rights*. Ed. Lynda S. Bell, Andrew J. Nathan, and Ilan Peleg. New York: Columbia University Press.

Peach, Lucinda Joy (2005). Women's Rights as Human Rights. In *Universal Human Rights: Moral Order in a Divided World*. Ed. David A. Reidy, Mortimer N. S. Sellers, and Kenneth Henley. New York: Rowman & Littlefield.

Perry, Michael J. (1998). *The Idea of Human Rights: Four Inquiries*. New York: Oxford University Press.

Philp, Janette (2009). The Political Appropriation of Burma's Cultural Heritage and its Implication for Human Rights. In *Cultural Diversity, Heritage, and Human Rights: Intersections in Theory and Practice*. Ed. Michele Langfield, William Logan, and Máiréad Nic Craith. New York: Routledge.

Walshe, Maurice (1995). *The Long Discourses of the Buddha: A Translation of the Digha Nikaya*. Boston: Wisdom.

43

Buddhist Perspectives on Gender Issues

RITA M. GROSS

Gender studies in religion is a relatively recent development. Before the current feminist movement, religious studies, like most other disciplines, paid little attention to gender because the only human beings studied seriously were men. Beginning in the late 1960s, fueled in large part by innovative work being undertaken by female graduate students and younger scholars, people finally began to wonder what the other half of humanity – the women – did and thought. A large body of literature has now emerged which makes our information somewhat more balanced. Because we already had a great deal of information about what men have done and thought, much of the new research on religion and gender deals primarily with women.

By and large, sustained discussion of Buddhism and gender did not begin until the 1980s. Since then, four areas have emerged as especially important foci for discussions of Buddhism and gender. First is simply gathering the information about women and gender – given that most Buddhists, especially Western Buddhists, were quite unaware of how male-dominated Buddhism has traditionally been. Second, especially for Asian Buddhists, deep concern about the status of nuns and the need to restore full ordination for them in some parts of the Buddhist world has taken center stage. Third, especially for Western Buddhists, who are usually converts to Buddhism and are generally lay practitioners, a whole gamut of questions about how to live as Buddhists in a non-Buddhist culture became dominant. Finally, Buddhists, especially in the West, have taken up the issue of why there have been so few women teachers and leaders throughout Buddhist history and have begun to change that situation dramatically.

Gathering the Information

Superficially, it seems that Buddhism should not have a gender problem. There is no deity, and therefore no male deity, short-circuiting an issue that has been very difficult

---

A Companion to Buddhist Philosophy, First Edition. Edited by Steven M. Emmanuel.

for feminists in Western religions. Its teachings on human nature and its path and goal would seem to apply equally to all human beings. Indeed, Buddhist teachers are fond of saying, when asked about gender, that enlightened mind is beyond gender. This slogan, however, hides a multitude of problems centered in Buddhism's institutional male dominance, not the least of which is that the enlightened mind beyond gender was usually thought to reside in a male body. Though teachers have claimed that an enlightened mind has no gender, many traditional Buddhists believe it is unfortunate to be reborn as a woman, but that women who behave properly will be rewarded with a male body in their next rebirth. For example, when I gave a very early talk on Buddhism and feminism in 1980 at a conference in Hawai'i on Buddhist–Christian dialogue, the Japanese Buddhist male delegates told my Western (male) friends, who then told me, that they were having a very difficult time understanding how there could be anything for feminists to take issue with in Buddhism. "We can understand why Christian women have problems," they said. "After all, God is male and all the priests are men. But we Buddhists solved those problems long ago. Deserving women are reborn as men!" An enlightened mind is more likely to wind up in a male body because that mind receives a multitude of perks regarding access to Buddhist education and practice that are not usually accorded to minds located in female bodies.

In gathering the information about Buddhism and gender, the first and most important task was the consciousness-raising involved in proving that there are indeed gender issues in Buddhism. At first, Western Buddhists, who saw relative equality in their fledgling communities, refused to believe that traditional Buddhisms had been incredibly male-dominated for over two millennia. This truth undermined their starry-eyed enthusiasm for their new religion. Some Asian Buddhists thought that they should try to keep the information about Buddhism's male dominance hidden from wider view, while others, both women and men, accepted it as the norm. The few pioneers who fearlessly saw and named these gender disparities initially faced a good deal of hostility from other Buddhists.

In the 1980s and early 1990s, several important books laid the foundations for a widespread and detailed exploration of gender issues in Buddhism. The first of these was Diana Y. Paul's book (1979) about images of women in Indian Buddhist literature, the first book about women and Buddhism in over 30 years. In 1988, Sandy Boucher released the first edition of her account of contemporary American Buddhist women and their contributions to changing Buddhist attitudes and practices surrounding gender (see Boucher 1993). My *Buddhism after Patriarchy: A Feminist History, Analysis, and Reconstruction of Buddhism* (1993) was the first somewhat comprehensive book on Buddhism and gender, dealing with history and contemporary issues in both Asian and Western Buddhisms and making many suggestions for how a post-patriarchal Buddhism might look.

These books have been followed and supplemented by a veritable deluge of research about women in all aspects of Buddhism – all Buddhist denominations and cultures and all the issues facing Buddhist women, from monasticism to motherhood. These books, and many articles as well, not only delineate Buddhism's traditional male dominance and remedies for that problem, they also explore the many ways in which women have coped with their situations and the many outstanding Buddhist women throughout history who had been largely forgotten. Thus, there is no longer any excuse for any teacher or practitioner to be ignorant or negligent about the issues surrounding Buddhism and gender.

In addition to these publications, a series of conferences organized by Sakyadhita International has provided a gathering place for Buddhists interested in gender issues. Beginning with a meeting in Bodhgaya, India, in 1987, these biennial conferences have been held somewhere in Asia for most of the intervening period. Both lay and monastic practitioners, both Asians and Westerners, both men and women, attend these well-organized conferences, which are usually followed by an informative tour of local Buddhist places of interest. Many of them have also resulted in publications, usually edited by Karma Lekshe Tsomo, the founder of Sakyadhita and one of its major leaders. Immense amounts of information about Buddhism and gender have been gathered at these meetings, which often give Asian and younger scholars a supportive environment in which to present their research results.

The Nuns' Sangha: Past and Present

For many contemporary Buddhists, the status of nuns, and especially the need for their full ordination to be restored or initiated in several forms of Buddhism, is of great concern and interest. In some Asian contexts, this is the dominant question regarding Buddhism and gender. While Western Buddhists, by and large, are not monastics, many Westerners are also well informed on this issue and support various movements to improve the status of nuns worldwide.

Understanding this issue requires some historical framing. One of the better known passages in the early scriptures narrates that the Buddha's foster-mother and aunt, Prajapati, petitioned the Buddha to allow women to take monastic vows and practice that lifestyle. The Buddha refused three times and was finally persuaded only when his attendant Ananda argued that, because women could be enlightened, they should be allowed to follow the lifestyle that had been so helpful to men in pursuing that goal. The Buddha relented, but also imposed eight so-called "heavy rules" (the literal translation of *gurudharma*) on the nuns that would subordinate them completely to monks. He also added that his Dharma would now last only 500 years, rather than the 1,000 years it would have lasted had women not been allowed to "go forth from home to homelessness" (the traditional phrase used to describe becoming a monk or a nun). In current debates about reviving the nuns' order, some argue that it is not important to do so because the Buddha himself did not really want women to be able to become nuns. However, much current scholarship suggests that this particular passage was a later interpolation into the texts. One of the arguments in favor of this interpretation is that there is a great deal of internal contradiction in early scriptures between this passage and frequent statements by the Buddha indicating that he regarded the fourfold Sangha (monks, nuns, laywomen, laymen) as normative. In addition, the impressive accomplishments of the early nuns, recorded in the *Therigatha* (Rhys-Davids and Norman 1989) and other texts, would be difficult to explain if the Buddha had been so hostile to them.

Today three different sets of monastic rules are followed in different Buddhist communities. In two of these, the ordination of nuns had died out. East Asian Buddhists have always maintained the full ordination of nuns, but the practice died out in Theravāda Buddhism about 1,500 years after the Buddha's death. Until recently, the only quasi-monastic option for women was to live as a monastic without ordination, whether novice or final ordination, a position that has much lower status and receives far less economic support than is given to ordained monastics. It is unclear whether full nuns' ordination was ever practiced in Tibetan Vajrayāna Buddhism, but now only the novice ordination is available. Novice nuns shave their heads and wear maroon robes, so they look like monastics, a situation quite different from the one in Theravāda Buddhist countries, where even wearing monastic colors could be dangerous for a woman seeking to live as a nun. However, until recently, standards for economic support and education for nuns was extremely low. Many of them had to support themselves by undertaking childcare or manual labor, leaving little time for study and practice – the main point of becoming a nun in the first place.

As part of the worldwide women's movement of the late twentieth century, both men and women in all forms of Buddhism became concerned about the status and well-being of nuns. East Asian Buddhists did not have to struggle to reinstate full ordination for nuns, but they did need to revive their institutions in order to improve the latter's economic position and educational opportunities. This effort has been very successful in Korea, Taiwan, Vietnam, and other places where East Asian monasticism is dominant. Becoming a nun and receiving a good education, as well as economic support and some independence, is an attractive alternative for many women to a male-dominated marriage. Because women do not have as many opportunities as men in the prosperous secular economies of East Asia, today there are many more nuns than monks in these countries. But pious and successful laypeople still want to "earn merit" by donating to monastics, and East Asian nuns are reaping the benefits of their generosity. Their educational and meditation centers are prospering. Women receive good training and become confident spokespersons and teachers for their traditions. Much of their well-being and success is due to the fact that they become fully ordained rather than second-class monastics, as is the case when full ordination is lacking. Comparing the confidence and well-being of East Asian nuns to that of both Tibetan and Theravāda "nuns" is one of the strongest arguments for restoring full ordination in both of those communities.

The situation for Theravāda Buddhist nuns differs somewhat from country to country. In Sri Lanka, which had a long history of nuns before their order died out, ordination has been successfully reintroduced. The first ordination in almost 1,000 years took place in 1998, and since then small numbers of women have become nuns. Though they continue to face some opposition from male monastics and the hierarchy of monastic leaders, they are fully accepted by other monastics and many lay people. The situation is much more difficult in South-East Asian Buddhist countries, most of which did not receive nuns' ordination lineages when Buddhism came to their countries, and particularly difficult in Thailand, where it is illegal for monks to assist in ordination ceremonies for nuns and where monastic opposition to initiating a nuns' Sangha is very strong. Nevertheless, some women, led by the Venerable Dhammananda (formerly Chatsumarn Kabilsingh), have managed to receive full ordination, and every year a few more women are ordained and live as Buddhist nuns wearing monastic colors. Meanwhile, large numbers of women continue to wear the white robes of the non-ordained *maechi*, living a quasi-monastic life without ordination.

In Tibetan Vajrayāna Buddhism, novice nuns wear robes in monastic colors, and recently their situation regarding education and support has improved dramatically. Nevertheless there are many fewer nuns than monks and very few highly respected female teachers. As in Theravāda Buddhism, there has been a well-organized, respectful, but vocal movement, often led by Western convert nuns who have received full ordination in an East Asian lineage, to institute full ordination for nuns in Tibetan Buddhism. The Dalai Lama himself is greatly in favor of the movement and has stated so publicly (Mohr and Tsedroen 2010). He says that he is sure the Buddha would be in favor of it, but that he cannot make it happen by himself, against the opposition of some of his senior advisors and leaders. The issue has been under study now for decades, always with the promise that a solution will soon be found – though it never appears. Despite universal high regard for the Dalai Lama, many have become frustrated with his reticence on this issue.

Those who oppose reinstating or initiating the nuns' Sangha usually cite concern over purity of the ordination lineages as the reason for their opposition. Because ordination rules state that nuns should be ordained by a dual Sangha of both monks and nuns, and there are currently no fully ordained Theravāda or Tibetan nuns, East Asian Buddhists would have to be involved initially to restart the ordinations. Either Theravāda and Tibetan women could receive ordination from East Asians and then serve as the required quorum of nuns in Theravāda or Tibetan ordination ceremonies, or East Asian nuns could initially serve as the nuns' quorum. However, many object to these possible procedures, saying they have doubts about the purity of East Asian ordination lineages, an argument that is particularly problematic in Theravāda contexts. Historical records indicate that East Asian nuns' ordination lineages stem from a group of Sri Lankan nuns who went to China specifically to serve as a quorum to establish those lineages. The situation is equally problematic for Tibet. Some scholarship indicates that the men's ordination lineages at one time had been so stressed that even a quorum of Tibetan monks was no longer available, but that it was filled by relying on several Chinese monks ordained in a different lineage to make up the requisite number of monks for ordinations to begin again.

Others, both women and men, object because they claim that full ordination is not necessary for women's practice and spiritual attainments to flourish – an argument that could have merit, were it not for the fact that most laypeople are far more willing to give economic support to fully ordained monastics. Still others claim that they have more freedom as non-monastic renunciants than they would have if they were ordained. They can handle money more easily, which helps them minister among ordinary people and do charity work. It also means that they are not subject to the eight "heavy rules" and thus have more freedom to run their own institutions. Still others claim that the movement for women's full ordination is an offshoot of feminism, and they do not want to be identified with that movement in any way. Many who have long been acculturated to accept male dominance as the norm simply cannot bring themselves to defy or contradict the male monastics who are their teachers and with whom they have had long associations.

Living as a Lay Buddhist, Especially in the Western World

At the present time, Western Buddhists are not following the usual Asian paradigm of interdependence and division of labor between monastics and laypeople, with monastics doing most of the "spiritual" work and laypeople earning merit for a better future by supporting monastics economically and also receiving religious teachings from them. For Buddhism to be so heavily dependent on lay practitioners is an experiment never before tried in the Buddhist world, except perhaps for aspects of more recent Japanese Buddhist history. It remains to be seen how well the experiment will turn out or whether, as Buddhism becomes better established in the West, more people will take up monastic life. Currently, most Western Buddhists are not very enthusiastic about monasticism for themselves, though they generally respect Asian monastics. Given that economic support is difficult to come by in the West, it is probably a fortunate coincidence that so few people currently wish to live as monastics.

Beginning in the early 1970s, many young, well-educated Westerners began to convert to Buddhism and to pursue their new religion with great enthusiasm. They joined a much older, much more numerous, and much better established, but much less innovative, group of ethnic Asian Buddhists who had been in the West, in some cases for generations. Especially in terms of engagement with gender issues, this group of recent converts faced many questions that, for two reasons, were quite new for Buddhist practitioners. First, they were trying to combine serious Buddhist practice, which is quite time-consuming, with the demands of lay life, especially the need to have a job or a career and the expectation or desire to form families and reproduce, which are also time-consuming. Either of these alone can easily be a full-time pursuit. Second, these Buddhists came of age during and were influenced by the feminist movement, even though many of them tried to deny that feminism was relevant to them or their lives. Nevertheless, many patterns of domestic work and childcare common to both Asian cultures and pre-feminist Western lifestyles were called into question. For example, the young women practiced and studied side by side with their boyfriends – something that was not the norm in Asian cultures. The way in which these young women took it for granted that they should also study and practice had a deep impact on Western Buddhism years later.

In trying to negotiate their lifestyle as lay Buddhists who were also serious practitioners, the new Buddhists felt they had little guidance and often complained vociferously about this perceived lack. Classic Buddhist texts were written mainly for monastic audiences and consequently did not deal with issues of fair distribution of domestic labor and childcare or how to combine Buddhist practice with the demands of livelihood. Probably Asian lay Buddhists had received advice from their teachers about how to deal with their domestic lives, but this material was not part of textual tradition and so was not available to Western students. Many Asian teachers were not sure how to work with their Western students concerning such questions, particularly because the gender roles with which they were familiar were so different and so much more traditional. These Asian teachers did not want to discourage the students who were flocking to their meditation programs, and, to their great credit, they usually dealt with female and male students in a fairly even-handed manner. But that did not mean that they could help their students figure out how to combine livelihood, family life, and Buddhist practice.

The first lesson the new Buddhists had to absorb was that it is impossible to do everything one might want to do within one short lifetime, because they simply did not have enough time or energy. While most Westerners rejected the radical Indian Buddhist solution of renouncing career and family completely, they swiftly learned that it is probably not possible to have a large family, to pursue a successful, high-powered career, and to become enlightened all in one lifetime. Some choices would have to be made. Serious Buddhist practice does entail cutting back somewhere else, at least from the usual expectations many Westerners have for themselves. Whether or not one becomes a monastic, renunciation is important in Buddhism. In fact, renunciation is sometimes said to be "the foot of meditation" – meaning that it is the basis for any progress on the Buddhist path.

I always tell my new meditation students that, if they become serious about their Buddhist practice, there will be consequences in other areas of their lives. One will probably need to limit the size of one's family if one has a family at all. If a person discovers Buddhist practice after having established a marriage and family, it often causes some stress to the relationship from a partner who is not sympathetic to requests for time and money to attend retreats and other Buddhist programs. Livelihood presents real problems because pursuing the Buddhist path costs money. Westerners often complain that Dharma should be "free," as they think it is in Asia. What they forget is that the lay Buddhist population there has been trained for generations to donate generously to religious institutions in order to improve their own karmic balance sheet in hopes of better future rebirths. Meditation centers cannot offer programs for "free." In the absence of donors who will give money in exchange for more merit and better karma, such things as electricity bills have to be paid by those who receive the teachings – meditators and practitioners themselves. As it is, Buddhist teachers usually are paid very little for their work. Nevertheless, most centers do have a policy of never turning people away for lack of funds and asking that everyone contribute what they can. So, despite the temptation to put career on the back burner to have more time for practice, one must have some livelihood to support one's Dharma activities. But a high-powered position demanding all of one's time and energy is not going to work either. Negotiating all these limitations can be very demanding. Such difficulties apply equally to women and to men in a situation in which the two-income family has become the norm and in which many women are self-supporting, if not the sole support for their children as well. Single people with children are in an especially difficult position.

Most of the new adherents were childless when they became involved in Buddhism, but many did have children eventually. Children brought another set of issues for which most Western Buddhists felt they did not have good precedents or advice. The basic issue is that silent, sitting meditation is not a very child-friendly activity. Silence and motionlessness are not usual for children. Perhaps babies can sleep through a meditation session, but very quickly that becomes impossible. In a situation of traditional gender roles, the solution would have been obvious and easy: women would have dropped out of active participation in meditation centers and taken care of children while men continued their training. But, despite their wary attitudes towards feminism, this group of practitioners was not about to opt for that solution. Instead, they asked for teachings on parenting as a dimension of Buddhist practice, and they requested childcare at meditation centers and during meditation programs.

Though results were somewhat slow in coming regarding both concerns, now children's programs and activities are commonplace, both in urban meditation centers, which usually hold shorter weekly activities, and at rural residential centers, which typically hold longer programs. Such activities also helped solve another problem: how to raise Buddhist children in a non-Buddhist culture. In majority Buddhist cultures in Asia, such problems are non-existent. Regular holiday celebrations held at local Buddhist centers are attended by whole families. In those situations, children imbibe Buddhism in much the same way that Christian children absorb Christianity in Western cultures. Granted, majority religions, which can easily gain adherents by default, often have followers who are uninformed and lukewarm. But Western Buddhist parents had few ideas about how to present their highly adult religion to children, never having been Buddhist children themselves and never having had any experience with Buddhist children. While solving their own problems – being able to continue their training by having children's activities during adult programs – they also began to solve the difficult problem of raising Buddhist children in a non-Buddhist culture. Now a generation of Buddhist children, sometimes colloquially called "dharma brats," has grown up. Many of them continue to identify as Buddhists, even though Western Buddhism is still growing mainly through conversion.

Theoretical writings on how to regard domestic work and childcare as part of one's ongoing meditation have been slower in coming, though recently a book on parenthood as a spiritual path has finally appeared (Miller 2006). However, intuitively, many lay Buddhists have always felt that work so important to keeping the world going cannot be off the radar as Buddhist practice. What many people have not noticed is that, while there is in Buddhism a traditional division of labor between monastics and householders, it actually requires a great deal of domestic labor, identical with that done by householders, to maintain a monastery or nunnery. Large amounts of food must be prepared and all the buildings must be cleaned and maintained. In addition, monastics in some forms of Buddhism are famous for their skill in gardening and grow much of their own food. Mindful weeding is definitely part of Buddhist practice in such contexts. Many monasteries also function as orphanages, and young monks and nuns are common. While very young children are not found in such contexts, nevertheless, many children must be educated and cared for. If such work is part of spiritual practice when done in a monastery, why not when it is done in a domestic household? The only difference would involve not the location in which it takes place but the extent to which every activity is done with a meditative mind. Thus, a householder who is well trained in meditation could use housework and childcare as meditative practices.

Actually Western Buddhists could be well prepared to make the transition into using ordinary domestic work as a meditation practice because they have been trained at meditation centers to do so. A great deal of domestic work is also required for a residential meditation retreat to happen, and this labor is not hired out but done by participants in the retreat. Thus, "rota" is part of every meditation program, and meditation students are frequently told that doing their rota is as much part of their meditation training as is sitting on their cushions. If this insight becomes part of mainstream Buddhist wisdom, Western lay practitioners will have made a significant contribution to the ongoing development of Buddhist thought.

Finally, for non-celibate practitioners, some guidelines regarding sexual ethics must be part of an evolving Western Buddhism. During the 1970s and 1980s, a good bit of sexual license prevailed, including multiple sexual scandals concerning teachers having affairs with their students. Though such incidents continue to occur, most meditation centers have initiated formal guidelines regarding them, and teachers usually suffer severe penalties for infractions. Most teachers no longer permit sexual indiscretions on the part of their students, especially when they are in residence at a meditation center. In a departure from public Asian pronouncements, most Western Buddhist centers are also welcoming to openly gay, lesbian, or transgender people. Most teachers emphasize faithfulness and integrity in relationships much more than conventional heterosexual pairing.

The Acid Test: Fostering Women Teachers

In non-theistic Buddhism, teachers and the Sangha itself perform the functions usually filled by deities in theistic religions. Sangha provides companionship on the path and feedback about one's behavior and demeanor. It is no accident that, in non-theistic Buddhism, the Sangha is the third Refuge. The other two Refuges are the Buddha and the Dharma (the teachings of the Buddha). Because the Buddha is no longer available to teach the Dharma and to guide the Sangha, therefore, Buddhist teachers must perform those absolutely vital tasks. Without teachers, who must be properly trained and authorized, Buddhism could not endure. There is no role more important, central, and vital in Buddhism than that of the teacher. While Vajrayāna Buddhism is famous for its emphasis on the *guru*/teacher, this generalization holds for all forms of Buddhism.

But throughout Buddhist history the vast majority of teachers have been men. This was also the case when Western students first began to practice Buddhism. Without exception, their Asian teachers were men, despite the fact that their students were women and men in equal numbers. Because teachers must be highly developed spiritually, if not enlightened, this lack of female teachers played into traditional Buddhism's overall views regarding women – that the best option for a woman was to be reborn as a man.

For many Western women, their main hesitation regarding Buddhism was this lack of female teachers. It made no sense at all. If enlightened mind is genderless, as all the teachers claimed, why does it so consistently reside in male bodies? The only feasible answer is that Buddhist institutions have failed women, and failed them seriously, by not providing them with the thorough training required to become a teacher. To counter that objection, we were often told that many Asian women were, in fact, highly accomplished; they simply did not function in public as teachers, leaving that role to the men. But that made no sense either. Why would highly accomplished practitioners, who surely would teach if they were men, not be teaching in their female bodies? Given that many Western women felt keenly that they lacked relevant role models – *women* role models – this attempt to explain why there were so few women teachers seemed extremely hollow and unconvincing. In fact, it seemed that there was a vicious circle concerning the lack of female teachers and the explanations given for it. Many stories circulated colloquially about qualified, competent women and girls being denied training simply because they were female. Why were they denied this training despite their competence? Simply because, as women, they would not be teaching anyway, so they did not need the training!

Women who were not convinced or deterred by any of these answers responded with two tactics. The first could be seen as part of the "information gathering" required to rethink gender issues in Buddhism. As feminist scholarship regarding other religions had proved, there could well be hidden resources – highly accomplished women teachers about whom records simply had not been kept or whose records were hidden in largely androcentric lineage records. Already in the mid-1980s, Buddhist women who longed for female role models successfully began to unearth long-buried stories of accomplished women (Allione 1984). Since that time, much research has been done in all forms of Buddhism with impressive results.

Though the importance of women teachers as role models for female students has been emphasized greatly, other dimensions of this issue may be more important. Female role models are important, not only for women but also for men, especially in a culture in which men are accustomed to being in charge and to having most of the authority and prestige. Men need to learn how to relate to a woman as *guru*, as spiritual master and director. Such training would go far to undercut the easy assumptions of men that they are more competent than women, that they simply deserve power and prestige automatically. However, there is an even more important reason why women need to become authorized teachers and to be recognized as such. Enlightened mind is beyond gender, but unenlightened men and women are not. The more sex-segregated a culture is, the more the cultures of women and men will be somewhat different, with stereotypical women's and men's ways of being. In such a situation, men have little access to women's wisdom. Only women can teach this to men and to the culture at large, as well as to other women. If we do not have women teaching publicly, this women's wisdom may well be lost, or at least be inaccessible to anyone except women of that specific culture.

Women who were not satisfied with the conventional answers to their questions about why there were so few women teachers also responded in another way. We insisted on being trained ourselves, in not dropping out of the meditation center's activities to take care of domestic work and childcare while the men continued their training. That is why it is so important that, early in the history of Western Buddhism, young women assumed that the teachings were meant for them, too, and trained alongside their male friends. Later on, when they already had some facility with Dharma, at the stage of their lives when their foremothers would have dropped out of formal training in order to take care of everyone else, these women insisted instead that men do their fair share of domestic work and childcare, and that meditation centers also provide programs for children. Given that these women were usually contributing to the economic support of their domestic units, such expectations of men and Dharma centers were completely reasonable.

By and large, women were aided by sympathetic and supportive male teachers, both Asian and Western. These men may not have always understood the frustrations and sadness their female students experienced about Buddhism's record of male dominance and lack of support for female accomplishment, and they may not always even have had a good understanding of how to work with female students who had been beaten down by millennia of male dominance. But at least they did not discourage female students from having high aspirations or withhold training from them, and they did authorize them to teach when the women's understanding warranted such trust. In some cases, they very skillfully threw our frustration and feelings of being cheated back at us. Very early in my practice path, I asked a teacher why there were so few women teachers – always my most serious misgiving about Buddhism. He was rather taken aback, but he responded, "Because you haven't become one yet!" That was a good answer. Unfortunately, he also went on to claim that his wife was a good teacher (though her status was nowhere nearly as high as his) and that someone needed to take care of the children – thus betraying his own limitations in understanding the problem. In another case in which a woman expressed misgivings because there were so few female role models, the teacher shot back, "That's history! Now it's up to you." These kinds of challenges were very helpful in the long run.

What has happened now that Buddhism has been seriously practiced in the West for more than 40 years? In all forms of Buddhism, large numbers of women have now been authorized to teach, so many that about half the teaching at most Dharma centers is done by women. Some women, such as Pema Chodron, have become immensely popular and well known – one could say as well known as very popular male teachers. This is an immense change in only a short period and something unprecedented in Buddhist history. At the same time, there is still a downside. Much of the introductory and intermediate teaching is done by women, while men still dominate the top ranks of popular, highly visible teachers, despite the popularity of a few female teachers. In this sense, Buddhism mirrors many other enterprises, in which, despite all their training and accomplishments, most women seem to hit a glass ceiling at a certain point. This seems to be even more the case for Asian women. Especially in the world of Tibetan Buddhism, the international teaching circuit has become a major source of teachings and revenue for the monasteries-in-exile in India. But only one woman participates prominently in this international circuit.

Is the glass half empty or half full? It would not be wise to become complacent at this point in time, but it also would be unwise not to recognize how much has been accomplished in passing the acid test for whether or not Buddhism is solving its gender issues – the presence or absence of female teachers teaching both women and men publicly. What will happen in the next 40 years?

References

Allione, Tsultrim (1984). *Women of Wisdom.* London: Routledge & Kegan Paul.

Boucher, Sandy (1993). *Turning the Wheel: American Women Creating the New Buddhism.* Rev. and expanded edn. Boston: Beacon Press.

Gross, Rita M. (1993). *Buddhism after Patriarchy: A Feminist History, Analysis, and Reconstruction of Buddhism.* Albany: State University of New York Press.

Miller, Karen Maezen (2006). *Momma Zen: Walking the Crooked Path of Motherhood*. Boston: Shambhala.

Mohr, Thea, and Tsedroen, Jampa (2010). *Dignity and Discipline: Reviving Full Ordination for Buddhist Nuns*. Boston: Wisdom.

Paul, Diana Y. (1979). *Women in Buddhism: Images of the Feminine in Mahayana Tradition*. Berkeley, CA: Asian Humanities Press.

Rhys-Davids, C. A. F., and Norman, K. R. (1989). *Poems of the Early Buddhist Nuns (Therigatha)*. Oxford: Pali Text Society.

44

Diversity Matters

Buddhist Reflections on the Meaning of Difference

PETER D. HERSHOCK

The need to recognize and respect differences – especially differences in terms of gender, ethnicity, religion, culture, political persuasion, cognitive style, and core values – is now widely accepted as crucial for realizing productive relations both within and among societies. Although concerns about the divisive potential of differences and appeals for greater unity remain powerful, these are now being actively counterbalanced. "Diversity" is no longer something to be noted in passing. It is something to be celebrated as a positive signifier of the rejection of social, political, and cultural exclusion – a goal worthy of being affirmed and actively pursued in our schools, businesses, political alliances, and cultural aspirations.

This positive engagement with difference is historically recent, however, and often lacking in the kind and depth of critical acuity needed to pass from positively acknowledging differences to productively appreciating them. It is only over the last 30 or 40 years – perhaps reflecting growing respect for ecological understanding – that "diversity" has come to be broadly regarded not only as denoting a factual condition that has intrinsic value but also as a core contemporary value that merits significant social and political attention. Yet, for many, it remains unclear why greater "diversity" is a good thing if it amounts to nothing more than a numerical increase along some category or other. As the idiom goes, more is not always better.

Indeed, some have come to see growing attention to differences of identity and cultural values as detracting from critical engagement with the structural issues of class and race differences that previously had been central to the pursuit of social justice. With this in mind, social theorists such as Nancy Fraser (2002) have argued explicitly against any decoupling of the cultural politics of difference from the social politics of equality, rightly rejecting any either/or choice between *recognition* and *redistribution*. Differences in "who we are" and "where we stand" in the local, national, regional, and global geographies of power, wealth, and opportunity – themselves highly differentiated and uneven – are not unrelated. In short, the conceptual link between affirming

A Companion to Buddhist Philosophy, First Edition. Edited by Steven M. Emmanuel.

diversity and pursuing both greater justice and human-with-planetary flourishing remains tenuous and contested.

This is not unusual. New concepts are often coined in familiar terms and are only gradually freed from the constraints of customary usages. In the case of adopting "diversity" to designate a core contemporary value, this is doubly so. While we are now comfortable using the word "values" to direct attention to qualitative resolutions of what is personally, socially, politically, and culturally *worthwhile* – a metaphorical extension of the economic conception of "value" as a purely quantitative measure of *worth* – its first usage in this fashion can be dated to an anthropology paper published in 1918.[1] Here, as in other such cases of linguistic and conceptual rehabilitation, the familiar term "value" served as a basis for cantilevering discourse out from the known (exchange relations) into the unknown (the factors orienting the appreciative dynamics of cognition and conduct) – an exploratory and typically gradual process. As it happens, we are still very much in the beginning stages of moving from a purely quantitative understanding of diversity to understanding it qualitatively as a distinctive and central twenty-first-century value.

In what follows, I want to make use of Buddhist resources to contribute to this process. More specifically, I want to employ Buddhist conceptions of karma and nonduality to generate movement oblique to the ontologically freighted opposition of sameness and difference – opening a "middle way" beyond the contrariety of modern valorizations of global unification and postmodern valorizations of free variation. In doing so, my aim is both conceptual clarification and critical integration. If modern and postmodern valorizations of autonomy have been crucial to empowering distinctive responses to social, economic, political, and cultural coercion, a non-dualistic conception of diversity has potential for strengthening and more equitably orienting the interdependence of these spheres – a value for relational transformation from the personal sphere to the environmental.

The Contemporary Aporia of Difference: Historical Contexts

As noted by John Rawls in his seminal book *A Theory of Justice* (1971), plurality has from the outset been a key feature of modern societies. The historical reality – neatly and ironically epitomized by Rawls's method of retreating behind a "veil of ignorance" to make justice-promoting decisions – has, however, been one of treating differences among the members of modern polities as contingent matters of fact to be dissolved in pursuit of universal ideals. In the American context, this broadly assimilationist understanding of difference is epitomized by the Latin phrase emblazoned on every American coin and bill: *e pluribus unum*, or "oneness out of many." As might well be expected in the context of self-conscious efforts to craft geographically bounded and ethnically varied nation-states, modern engagements with difference have focused predominantly on the functional subordination of difference to sameness.

This homogenizing dimension of modernization has been associated most visibly with the impacts of nationalization, industrialization, and globalization, all of which have served as powerful forces for structural integration and values convergence from at least the mid-nineteenth century. By the 1960s, however, at the height of Cold War competition between opposing development ideologies, growing skepticism emerged about the viability and fairness of globally implementing any universalist vision of human flourishing – whether capitalist or communist. In addition to explicitly political movements for civil rights and massing commitments to gender and racial equality, there developed an increasingly articulated range of postmodern challenges to all master narratives and to the social, cultural, and cognitive violence implied by their subordination of real differences to foundational ideals of inherent sameness.

Yet, by the late 1980s and the end of the Cold War, it became clear that, while identity politics and postmodern discourses were important counters to the "flattening" effects of industrialization and globalization, these were not the only – and perhaps not the most critically relevant – effects of these processes. Alongside their homogenizing impacts, there has been a proliferation of challenges to top-down articulations of the nation-state; the emergence of globally divisive terrorist movements and competing fundamentalisms; an ever intensifying, market-driven proliferation of consumption and lifestyle options; the linked production of ever expanding market delivered goods and services and ever more finely differentiated populations in need of them; the displacement of organically sustained natal communities by fully elective communities-on-demand; and the social subordination of relationally focused commitment to individually and independently exercised choice. In sum, as ubiquitous as the homogenizing/integrating effects of industrial modernization and globalization have been, these processes have also been inseparable from a historically unprecedented *multiplication* and *magnification* of *differences*, both among and within societies.

At a material level, these trends towards differentiation have manifested most strikingly as increasingly uneven geographies of development. In sharp contrast with modern ideals of increasing universality and equality, global realities are now characterized by dramatically expanding inequalities of wealth, income, and resource use. In 1820, the wealth and income gap between the richest 20 percent of countries in the world and the poorest 20 percent stood at a ratio of 3 to 1. By 1913, according to the United Nations Development Programme's 1999 *Human Development Report*, that ratio had increased to 11 to 1; in 1950 it was 35 to 1; in 1973, 44 to 1; and in 1998, 86 to 1. Today, that ratio is estimated at 126 to 1, with the top 1 percent of the world's households now owning 40 percent of global wealth and the top 5 percent holding 75 percent. The bottom 50 percent of the world's people – some 3.5 billion men, women, and children – own less than 1 percent of global wealth (Davies et al. 2008).

While personal, corporate, and national greed may be factors in this stunning transfer of wealth and income from the global majority to an increasingly thin minority, greed is not all that is at work. Over the course of especially the past four decades, a profound structural transformation has been occurring in association with the emergence of truly complex systems of global economic, social, political, and cultural interdependence. For present purposes, let me mention just two aspects of this transformation: the advent of *global networks* and *reflexive modernization*.

As a result of advances in communications and computing, the organizational dynamics of power have shifted from the global predominance of relatively centralized military-industrial complexes towards what Manuel Castells (1996, 1997, 1998) has termed global informational capitalism, or the network society. Among the crucial features of networks is that their growth is a non-linear function of both negative (i.e., stabilizing) feedback and positive feedback that accelerates interactions and amplifies differentiation. This suggests that network-facilitated global informational capitalism will accelerate flows of goods, services, and people in ways that unpredictably intensify and amplify both integration and fragmentation – a characteristic brought home very dramatically by the 2008 global financial meltdown and subsequent recession.

This systemic pairing of vitality and volatility is central to what Ulrich Beck, Anthony Giddens, and Scott Lash (Beck et al. 1994; Beck, 1992; 1999) have referred to as *reflexive modernization* or *world risk society*: the emergence of conditions in which continued industrial/economic growth entails the production of unpredictable threats, risks, and hazards in the face of which responsible decisions nevertheless must be made. That is, beyond certain thresholds of scale, scope, and complexity, it is no longer possible either to externalize the environmental, social, economic, and cultural costs of sustained growth or to inhibit their percolation into virtually every aspect of life. The result is an amplification of the tensions between freedom and control that have characterized modernity from its earliest European iterations (Wagner, 1994) – an expansion of "emancipatory" (often market-mediated) freedoms of choice, accompanied by an intensification of "disciplinary" compulsions to choose under conditions of continuously heightening ambiguity, uncertainty, and risk.

As would be expected with the rise of global networks and reflexive modernization, the trajectory of contemporary globalization has involved both intensifying interdependence and the accelerating multiplication/magnification of differences: a progressive differentiation of globalization "winners" and "losers" as a function not of the failures of our modern techno-economic systems, but rather of their successes. That is, the kinds of instability and inequality that are now being experienced are results not of primarily external factors but rather of recursively amplifying internal ones.

This invites recognition that we are not just in an era of change, but are changing from an era characterized by *problem solution* to one characterized by *predicament resolution*. Problems mark the advent of conditions in which existing practices and techniques fail to bring about aims and interests that we fully intend to continue pursuing. Solutions are innovative responses to such conditions that enable existing values and interests to be successfully promoted. Predicaments occur when conditions force recognition of conflicts among our own values, aims, and interests. Unlike problems, predicaments cannot be solved; they can only be resolved, where resolution implies both clarity (about how the circumstances of experienced conflict have arisen) and commitment (to a reconfiguration of our aims and priorities). Predicament resolution, in other words, entails improvising new constellations of values and intentions – a redefinition of both the means-to and meanings-of success. Global climate change, for example, is not a problem. We know precisely what is needed to rein in the climate impacts of human activity and have the technical ability to act on that understanding. Climate change is a predicament that can be sustainably addressed only by reconciling historically grounded conflicts among globally prevailing economic, social, political, cultural, and environmental interests and values.

Stated otherwise, ours is an era in which we are both individually and collectively experiencing a shift from the predominance of the *technical* to that of the *ethical*.

The predicaments being generated by the complex "difference engines" of industrial modernization and globalization are forcing shared confrontation with a deepening aporia, an impasse or paradox. On the one hand, in keeping with the still emerging dynamics of the politics of identity, we now need to recognize and respect differences more fully, enabling differences to matter more, not less, than before. On the other hand, we also need to engage in increasingly robust and globally coherent collective action, incorporating differences within shared and deepening commitments.

This aporia is a defining condition of what we might call climax modernity – our global arrival at a historical juncture beyond which further modernization will result in ever more strikingly ironic consequences. It is not an aporia that is readily addressed on the basis of the spectrum of currently prevailing ethical biases. At one end are ethical stances expressing commitment to some version of modern universalism and its root assumption that everyone is essentially "just like me." At the other end are stances expressing commitment to the inversion of modern values and to endorsing some version of postmodern particularism rooted in assertions that "no one is ultimately just like me." The former run the considerable and well-recognized risks of justifying ethnocentric coercion and cosmopolitan conformity; the latter run no less considerable and apparent risks of justifying increasingly divisive tribalisms that render substantially shared commitments unintelligible. Ironically, then, in spite of their profound polarization regarding the critical scopes of equality and autonomy, modern universalism and postmodern particularism have in common a strategic bias towards disarming difference, in effect rendering it critically impotent. What is needed, instead, is deepening clarity about effectively committing to working out from within our differences, establishing shared movement "oblique" to the opposition of sameness and difference.

Restoring the Excluded Middle: Moving Oblique to the Opposition of Sameness and Difference

To date, many good intentions notwithstanding, global inequalities have continued to grow, and little critical headway has been made in determining the point at which expanding inequality constitutes deepening inequity. I would submit that this failure is, at least to some extent, a function of the ontological bias towards individual existents that is part of the conceptual toolkits through which the contrary conditions of modernity and postmodernity have been constructed and practically adumbrated. Addressing the contemporary aporia of difference requires critical engagement with the qualitative dynamics of interdependence itself, rather than with the impacts of global integration and fragmentation on various kinds and scales of individuals – whether persons, communities, corporations, or nation-states. Under present conditions, continued allegiance to taking the individual to be ethically, economically, socially, and politically foundational is like insisting on the necessity and merits of eating soup with a fork. We are in need of critical resources developed on the basis of affirming the ontological primacy of relationality as such.

Buddhism's 2,500-year history of practicing how most keenly and fruitfully to become aware of the interdependence or ultimately relational nature of all things provides considerable warrant for turning to Buddhist traditions in search of such critical resources. Further warrant is, I think, offered by the fact that Buddhist practice has not aimed at generating or validating a "god's eye" view of the dynamics of interdependence – a presumptively "objective" pursuit – but has instead been conceived and undertaken as a process of embodied engagement in authoring our own liberation from trouble and suffering. In this sense, Buddhism is less like science (an ostensibly neutral pursuit of knowledge) than it is like technology (the purposeful application of knowledge for practical problem-solving). But the analogy goes only so far. Buddhist practice involves the recursive and predicament-resolving transformation of both self and circumstance.

As recounted at various places in the canonical literature of early Buddhism, the Buddha's pivotal insight on the eve of his awakening was that all things arise interdependently. That is, he realized that there are no independently existing things or beings, no foundational entities or elements, and no first causes. Strongly interpreted, relationality is "ontologically" more basic than things related. Interdependence is not an external, contingent relation; it is an internal or constitutive one. Crucially, this means that the advent of trouble and suffering cannot be attributed to the operation of chance, fate, or the linearly imposed whims of other beings – whether animal, human, or divine. Trouble and suffering are functions or expressions of errant patterns of interdependence, and liberation from them is ultimately a matter of reconfiguring and reorienting relational dynamics.

In the teaching encounters recounted in the early Buddhist canon, the Buddha advises those who would bring about such a relational transformation to begin by seeing ignorance (*avijjā*), habit formations (*saṅkhāra*), and craving forms of desire (*taṇhā*) as root conditions for the arising and persistence of trouble and suffering. That is, he advises the adoption of a critical stance with respect to thinking, acting, and feeling as interlinked fields of progressive training. More generally, however – and for present purposes, more importantly – he also recommends seeing the experience of trouble and suffering as a function of karma.[2]

"Karma" is now widely used to mean something like "what goes around, comes around" – a euphemism that translates roughly into "everyone ultimately gets what they deserve." But this usage, with its implication of a linear pattern of morally inflected payback, has little to do with the Buddhist conception of karma. Rather than detailing a system of just deserts – a conception of karma with roots in the Vedic tradition – the Buddhist teaching of karma was developed as a central element in the practice of liberation from trouble and suffering. Indeed, much to the dismay of interlocutors subscribing to Vedic conceptions of the cosmos, when the Buddha was asked on what basis it was possible to lead the noble life of awakening (*bodhi*), he responded that it was precisely karma that made liberation possible (*Lonaphala Sutta*, AN.III.99).

According to the Buddhist teaching of karma, if we pay close and sustained enough attention to the dynamic complexion of our lives, we will discern a meticulous consonance obtaining between the patterns of our own values–intentions–actions and the patterns of outcome and opportunity we experience. This means that experienced realities always imply some degree of responsibility. Ethical disengagement is not an option. But it also means nothing is absolutely destined or fated to be, and that we have no warrant for claiming any situation in which we find ourselves to be intractable. It is always possible to change our values, intentions, and actions, revising the meaning of interdependence to realize and sustain liberating relational dynamics.

One of the practical implications of the teaching of karma is that the path of realizing untroubled and untroubling patterns of interdependence necessarily entails both a critique of self and a critique of culture. While attending to and carefully reconfiguring the complexion of our values, intentions, and actions is perhaps of paramount importance, the fact is that many of our most deeply held values have historically framed, familial, cultural, social, economic, and political origins. Our lives as persons-in-community are profoundly shaped by values embedded within social, economic, political, cultural, and technological institutions, in the structures of intentionality that they embody and facilitate, and in the patterns of practice that they encourage and regulate. As a process of dissolving troubling karma, Buddhist practice has always and necessarily been socially engaged.

The traditional approach to dissolving troubling karma and realizing a liberating redirection of the dynamics of interdependence is through the integrated cultivation of wisdom (*paññā*), attentive mastery (*samādhi*), and moral clarity (*śīla*). Especially in Mahāyāna contexts, in which the bodhisattva ideal supplants that of *arahant*, this is understood in explicitly relational terms as the progressive embodiment of appreciative and contributory virtuosity – the realization of improvisational genius aimed at fostering the situational emergence of liberating commitments and conduct. But, in both cases, the mark of high quality engagement in the path of Buddhist practice is not essentially private. Asked how one could tell if a practitioner was faring well on the path, the Buddha responded that his or her situation would be thoroughly suffused with the four relational headings of compassion, lovingkindness, equanimity, and joy in the good fortune of others – a publicly manifest transformation of relational dynamics.

It is thus important to stress the situated nature of embarking upon and navigating the Buddhist path of liberation from trouble and suffering. Dissolving the conditions that bring about errant or troubled/troubling patterns of interdependence can be successfully and sustainably undertaken only on the basis of things as they have come to be (*yathābhūtam*) and not simply as they are at present. Not only do histories make a difference, there can be no one-size-fits-all solutions or universal blueprints. The origins of the Middle Way are not in some timeless space of absolutes, but rather here in our midst, and coursing on the Way is not a matter of escaping from circumstances, but rather of working out from within them in new and liberating directions.[3]

Difference and Sameness Revisited: Getting Beyond Opposition

The synoptic view of contemporary global dynamics sketched out earlier suggests that increasing differentiation is a crucial part of how things "have come to be" under conditions of climax modernity – politically, economically, socially, culturally, and technologically. Seen from a certain angle, this differentiation is in apparent accord with such core modern values as autonomy, sovereignty, choice, and control. The shift from the predominance of natal communities and socio-culturally ascribed identities to increasingly elective communities and individually subscribed patterns of identification is part of a vast expansion of options, not only in order to lead lives worth living but also to determine what kind of life is worthwhile. At the same time, however, there is overwhelming evidence that the differentiation processes being driven by contemporary patterns of modernization, industrialization, and globalization are *not* aligned with creating more equitable distributions of either the benefits or the costs of continued growth. On the contrary, they are resulting in ever more dramatically uneven geographies of opportunity, liability, wealth, and power.

Because of the causal complexity of the systems of interdependence that characterize contemporary realities, it is tempting to regard the synergy among economic growth, expanding freedoms of choice, hazard proliferation, increased volatility, and rising inequality as an unavoidable matter of either historical accident or developmental necessity. According to such a view, this synergy and the trouble and suffering it is causing for an ever larger global majority are ultimately no one's responsibility. The Buddhist teaching of karma instructs us to consider otherwise. In considerable agreement with some of the more insightful critics of modernization, industrialization, and globalization (Beck et al. 1994; Harvey 1996, 2006), a karmic perspective on this troubling synergy is that it is a function not of the failures of modernization, industrialization, and globalization but rather of their successes – evidence of profound conflicts within and among globally dominant patterns of values–intentions–actions.

Earlier, we framed this conflict in terms of an aporetic tension between the needs to recognize and respect differences and to subsume differences within robustly shared commitments of the kind and depth required for local-to-global scaled predicaments. But, from a karmic perspective, this specific combination of needs itself reflects a values tension between independence and autonomy, on one hand, and commonality and cooperation, on the other; between postmodern, market valorizations of free variation and modern, democratic valorizations of progressive unification; and between locating ethical consciousness in awareness of being different (as in Levinas) or in awareness of being essentially the same (as in Kant).

Put in these elemental conceptual terms, it could be said that the interlinked processes of modernization, industrialization, and globalization are forcing confrontation with the limits of dualism as a framework for critical engagement and of conceiving equity in terms of equality of opportunity. Ironically, while a key technological bias of the late twentieth and early twenty-first centuries has been towards increasing digitalization (a mapping of the world through the primal contrast of 1s and 0s in *de facto* celebration of the logic of the excluded middle), the experiential trajectory of this bias has been in the direction of intensifying imperatives practically and appreciatively to bridge difference and sameness – a bridge without which failures to resolve the predicaments being generated by continued growth will only increase the scale and scope of trouble and suffering being caused thereby, further eroding our prospects for global developmental justice.

Buddhism on Emptiness and the Non-Duality of Sameness and Difference

One of the seminal contributions of the Mahāyāna Buddhist traditions that were in full flower by the second century CE was to see interdependence (*pratītya-samutpāda*) as implying emptiness (*śūnyatā*) or the absence of essential natures or fixed identities. As understood, for example, by the great Mahāyāna thinker Nāgārjuna, seeing this was to see that there are ultimately no grounds for any opposition or dualism, including the opposition of samsara and nirvana. In the words of the *Heart Sutra* – still chanted daily in Mahāyāna temples around the world – "form is nothing other than emptiness" and "emptiness is nothing other than form."

This affirmation of non-duality comes to full fruition, perhaps, in the Chinese Huayan tradition and the work of the monk Fazang (643–712). Building on the four-fold meditation of Dushun (557–640) on the *dharmadhātu* or realm of truth/ultimate reality as *shi* or experiential matters (事法界, *shi fajie*), as *li* or informing patterns/principles (理法界, *li fajie*), as the mutual non-obstruction of *li* and *shi* (理事無礙法界, *li-shi wuai fajie*), and as the mutual non-obstruction of *shi* and *shi* (事事無礙法界, *shi-shi wuai fajie*), Fazang argued that, if mutual causality is inseparable from emptiness, then there is no interdependence without interpenetration. This implies that – in contrast to "vertical" non-dualisms affirming the identity of the divine and the mundane or "horizontal" non-dualisms affirming a monistic metaphysics (both of which had been formulated in non-Buddhist India) – Buddhist non-duality consists in an ecological matrix of all things that is not grounded in some common essence or substance, but rather emerges through the *shared functioning* of each thing or being as a distinctive *cause of the totality* of the real.

To facilitate understanding the non-duality of all things, in the final section of his "Huayan Essay on the Five Teachings" (*Huayan wujiao zhang*, T.45, no. 1866), Fazang makes metaphorical use of a traditional, timber-framed building. Such a building comprises a number of poles that rest on stone foundation blocks and are linked together into a stable unit by bracketed tiers of beams and rafters which are jointed to a central ridge beam. Atop this array of major timbers is a latticework of purlins onto which are layered clay roofing tiles, the immense weight of which compresses and stabilizes the entire construction. For Fazang, the complex relationship among the components in such a wood-framed building is analogous to that which obtains among all things. Insofar as the removal of rafters would cause the entire building to collapse, the rafters can be said to be the cause of the totality of the building. At the same time, it is only when bracketed into the beams that band together the building's poles that an individual timber becomes a rafter. Prior to that, it is simply a length of planed and shaped wood. The same relationship of mutual causation of part and whole obtains, of course, with respect to the beams, the purlins, the roofing tiles, and so on. More generally stated, each particular in the world (*shi*) consists at once in causing and being caused by the totality and, ultimately, *is* precisely what it contributes functionally to the patterning articulation (*li*) of that totality.

From the Huayan Buddhist perspective, all things are the same, precisely insofar as they differ meaningfully from one another. Or, stated otherwise, each thing ultimately *is* what it *means* for all others. Realizing the non-duality of all things is not an erasure of differences, a final collapse of all distinctions into an all-frozen sameness; it is a restoration of the logically excluded middle between "sameness" and "difference" – the irreducibly dynamic totality of mutual contribution. In this sense, to make use of a conceptual contrast framed by Jean-Luc Nancy (2000), the *dharmadhātu* is not something we have in *common* (a foundational essence); it is something in which we each have a distinct and indispensible contributory *share*.

Fazang's stress on the contributory potential of difference resonates powerfully with the bodhisattva ideal of Mahāyāna soteriology – the ideal of beings who demonstrate unlimited clarity about and commitment to realizing liberating relational dynamics. To realize the non-duality of all things is to realize that whether we live in samsara (relationships fraught with trouble and suffering) or nirvana (liberating patterns of relationality) is a function of precisely how we *differ-from* and *differ-for* one another. Liberation is not dissolution into an eternal space of the same. It is a process of continually discerning how best to differ-for others through concrete acts of sharing that demonstrate both appreciative and contributory virtuosity.

From Difference to Diversity: Qualitatively Transforming Differentiation Processes

According to Buddhist non-dualism, difference is not the conceptually vacuous opposite of sameness. On the contrary, difference is always dynamic and qualitatively differentiated. As a bridge to contemporary issues associated with the multiplication and magnification of differences, and in particular to considering how the matrix of differentiations generated by modern industrialization and globalization might be more equitably structured, let me introduce a heuristic contrast between *variety* and *diversity*.

Variety is a *quantitative* index of factual multiplicity. It entails nothing more than things being-different from one another – a function of simply or complicatedly structured *coexistence*. As a process, variation is passive or neutral with respect to relational quality or direction and implies only increasing, numeric plurality.

Diversity is a *qualitative* index of mutual contribution to sustainably shared welfare. It marks the emergence of complex and coordination-enriching *interdependence*. As a process, diversification implies a recursively structured process of becoming-different, changing in ways that are situationally significant and meaning-generating. That is, diversification involves opening new modalities of interaction.

Whereas variety can be seen at a glance, diversity is a relational achievement that becomes evident (if at all) only over time. Variety can be forcibly realized; diversity emerges only when conditions are conducive to a shift from merely *differing-from* one another to significantly *differing-for* one another – the activation of difference as the basis of mutual contribution.

This contrast can be illustrated by the kinds of difference that obtain among the various species in a zoo and in a naturally occurring ecosystem. A well-funded and properly designed zoo will enable a wide range of complex organisms to live in secure coexistence, maintained by steady infusions of externally originated expertise, construction materials, energy, food, medicines, and so on. An ecosystem consists in the emergence of a complex and resource-maximizing pattern of interdependencies among a similarly wide range of complex organisms and their naturally occurring environments. Unlike zoos, ecosystems are self-sustaining, self-organizing, and creatively adaptive systems in which species differentiation contributes recursively to enhancing the vitality of the total system's constitutive dynamics. Zoos are exhibitions of species variety; ecosystems are expressions of species diversity.

Appealing to a contrast between zoos and ecosystems is useful in illustrating the conceptual distinction between variety and diversity. But biodiversity is a particular and relatively limited iteration of diversification processes and should not be understood as either foundational or exemplary. Ecological relations are but one expression of diversity. The emergence of fully reflexive cultures, for example, has vastly expanded the domains within which mutual contribution is possible – entirely new domains of qualitatively transformative systems of differentiation. Moreover, technological advances, particularly in transportation and communication, have made integrative dynamics possible at historically unprecedented scales, vastly increasing potentials for diversity.

It is nevertheless useful to note that biodiversity is greatest not in the geographical center of a given ecosystem, but rather in the *ecotone* or zone of interfusion between/among ecosystems. Stated more generally, both needs and potentials for diversity tend to be greatest where autopoetic, complex systems of interdependence converge. Granted that the behavior and structural organization of complex systems are an expression of adaptively sustained values (Lemke, 2000), this means that potentials for diversity will tend to be greatest in spaces of *uncommon interests* and heightened likelihoods of predicament-rich encounter. Thus, it is not surprising that the great trade nexuses – such as the pre-modern cities of Chang'an and Baghdad at the eastern and western ends of the famed "silk roads," or London and New York at the eastern and western horizons of Atlantic trade – have also been spaces of great cultural vitality and diversity.

Of course, just as predicaments are not always resolved, potentials for diversity are not always fully realized. Indeed, the widening gaps of wealth, income, resource use, opportunity, and risk are arguably a telling index of the extent to which existing regimes of modernization, industrialization, and globalization bias differentiation processes towards variety. From this point of view, the aporetic experience of historically unprecedented needs both to recognize and respect differences and to subsume our differences within robustly and ever more globally shared commitments is *not* anomalous – a critically irrelevant fluctuation in the field of contemporary global dynamics. It is proof of abiding (and perhaps deepening) needs and potentials for reorienting the karma of global interdependence in the ways needed to reconcile growth with equity.

Equity and Diversity: Going Beyond Equality of Opportunity

It is now customary to define equity in terms of individual equality of opportunity – a conception of equity that is rooted in modern convictions that all human beings have the same universal nature. On this basis, all individuals are understood as endowed at birth with a common set of rights or entitlements, including equal rights to pursue lives worth living. Thus defined, equity is at the conceptual crux of a powerful set of values that have incited and informed much of the emancipatory dynamics of modernity. Yet, conceptually grounding equity in our essential sameness is at considerable odds with the dynamics of a world systemically disposed towards the multiplication and magnification of differences, leading to a kind of agnosticism about whether the differentiation processes needed to sustain economic growth are inflected towards greater variety or diversity. In effect, such a conception runs the risk of directing our attention to generic, absolute gains in terms of access and life options while at the same time contributing to expanding and deepening distinctively experienced forms of relational degradation.

We are in need of a conception of equity in which difference is not ignored but, rather, taken into productive, critical account. The rudiments of such a conception of equity can be traced back at least to Aristotle in Western traditions of thought. While Aristotle was convinced of the overarching merits of the universal application of laws binding all within society, he was also aware of the fact that there are times when the universal application of law will result in injustice. Rights of appeal to considerations of equity were needed, in other words, to ensure that real and important differences among those living under the law were given the kind of consideration needed for applications of the law to result in truly fair judgments.

This identification of equity with critically informed considerations of difference and the limits of universality persisted in the European and American contexts through the early modern era, but were gradually (and for reasons beyond the scope of our current discussion) superseded by a more explicitly political conception of equity in terms of rights of participation. The modern identification of equity with equality of opportunity reflects the growing dominance of what Stephen Toulmin (1990) has termed the "hidden agenda of modernity" – a powerfully "cosmopolitan" agenda emerging in the context of virulent ethnic and religious conflicts and shaped by widespread convergence on a set of values including universality, equality, sovereignty, autonomy, precision, competition, choice, and control. Consonant with this cosmopolitan turn, the shift from seeking equity through explicit and particular considerations of difference to seeking it through generic guarantees of equal opportunity marks a turn from the *concrete* to the *abstract* – a turn that has proved conducive to a sublimation of fairness into justice.

Equality is never total. Claims of equality necessarily involve an editorial or abstracting process that excludes as irrelevant anything that would specify differences among the things being compared. Equality claims are, in other words, a function of selective ignorance. We can be equal as citizens or as human beings, but not as unique persons with distinct heritages, talents, and aspirations. Equality is not a natural fact but, rather, a construct, a fiction. It is without question a very powerful fiction. And it has proven effective, for example, in inspiring challenges to traditional gender constructions and conceptually grounding universal human rights regimes. Yet, the power of equality derives precisely from the constraints that the pursuit of equality places on scopes of consideration – constraints without which the pursuit of equality would be waylaid by the legions of insistent particularities that characterize the experienced realities of being human and what it is like to be a woman or a minority or disabled. Just as there are emotional registers that cannot be intimated in a major key, or through rhythm alone, as a distinctive value or modality of appreciation, there are things that equality (or any other value) simply cannot do.

To take a specific case, the valorization of equality has clearly played an important role in galvanizing commitment to universal literacy and legally guaranteed rights to education for all. But actually to achieve universal literacy, it is no less clearly necessary to address the cultural, social, economic, political, and historical factors that continue to limit the educational achievements of girls and women, even when they are legally guaranteed "equal" educational opportunities. Educational equity requires going well beyond assurances of non-exclusion. More generally, the fictional narrative of universal human equality has not proven to be effective in generating real-world responses to growing inequalities of wealth, income, resource use, opportunity, and risk, or to specifying conceptually the thresholds beyond which inequalities become inequitable.

There is, of course, room for debate about what constitutes poverty or an excessive burden of risk, and at what precise point these cannot be seen simply as facts but, rather, as evidence of structural arrangements that are systematically unfair. But when the world's 1,210 billionaires have combined holdings in excess of $4.5 trillion, or nearly 2.4 percent of total global wealth (Kroll and Dolan 2011), even as one in every five people on the planet lives on less than $1 per day (calculated according to purchasing power parity) in conditions so degraded and degrading that the World Bank deems these 1.4 billion people not to have even the hope of a dignified life, I would argue that we are well beyond any reasonable debate about whether global realities are fairly structured. Conceptually delinking equity and equality is crucial to developing practically effective clarity-about and shared commitments-to addressing the effects of such predicaments as global hunger, poverty, and climate change.

Working out from the Buddhist concepts of karma and non-duality, this can be seen as a two-part process: (1) a move from taking equity to be a generically obtainable, factual state of affairs to seeing it as a distinctive value operative (or not) in concretely experienced relational dynamics; and (2) a move from seeing equity as the achievement of a common ground for individually attaining lives worth living to seeing it as a function of the degree to which the totality of local, national, regional, and global relational dynamics are oriented towards enhanced mutual contribution and more inclusively and intensely shared flourishing.

With these moves, inequity ceases to be a conceptually vacuous *absence* and comes to be understood as a measure of the degree to which differentiation means (results in) the instantiation or further proliferation of degraded and/or degrading relational patterns. In this sense, inequity consists in the *presence* of situational conditions conducive to experienced asymmetries of control and contribution – progressively compromised relational strengths and depleted resources for relating freely and for shared predicament resolution. In contrast, equity will be enhanced when and where further differentiation means (results in) the instantiation or further adumbration of an ennobling relational pattern – the situational heightening of strengths/capacities for relating freely and for significant mutual contribution. That is, equity consists in the presence of viable approaches to acting resolutely in one's own self-interest in ways that are also deemed valuable by others. Equity in this sense is *not* a correlate of achieved sameness but, rather, an ongoing, values-driven reconfiguration of relational dynamics to conserve maximally and appreciate differences of the sort needed for mutual contribution and shared flourishing. In short, there ultimately can be no equity without diversity.

The now dominant conception of equity suggests that achieving equity is a finite game – an endeavor that is undertaken in order to balance individual/collective powers, where power is understood as a capacity for determining situational outcomes. In this sense, equity is an end result, a target to be reached. Realizing relational equity can only be undertaken as an infinite game of enhancing interactive strengths, where strength is understood as a capacity for relating freely in such a way that the "game" remains interesting (and increasingly so) for all involved.[4] Relational equity is not a destination, it is a direction – a process of orienting differentiation as needed for it to serve as a generative nexus of creative and coordinative strength, shifting emphasis from whether or how much we *differ-from* one another to how best we might *differ-for* one another.

Equity as an Ethos of Virtuosity

A relational approach to conceiving equity along these lines begs the question of how to know whether our attempts to differ-for one another will not – perhaps ironically – result in greater inequity, trouble, and suffering. In idiomatic English, how do we ensure that we do not "pave a road to hell" with our own very good intentions? In the early Buddhist tradition, the rudiments of a response to the question are offered in the Buddha's response to a question about the origins of conflict and the means to cease producing the conditions through which conflict arises. In the *Sakkapañha Sutta* (DN.21) the Buddha locates the ultimate origins of conflict in *papañca*, or the obsessive, mental proliferation of relational blockages. To dissolve our propensities for *papañca* and realize conditions free from propensities for conflict, he enjoins paying close attention to the relationally manifest outcomes of our values–intentions–actions – outcomes that may be physical, emotional, cognitive, social, economic, or political. Whenever these outcomes are *akusala*, we should withdraw commitment to the values–intentions–actions implicated in their occurrence. At the same time, we should deepen commitment to those values–intentions–actions that result in *kusala* eventualities.

Now, although the Pali term *kusala* is often translated as "wholesome" or "skilled," and *akusala* as "unwholesome" or "unskilled," they do not in fact form a dichotomous pair of opposites. The term *kusala* functions as a superlative and connotes the active realization of exemplary conduct and relational dynamics. That is, the *kusala/akusala* contrast cannot be accurately mapped onto the contrast of what is either wholesome or unwholesome or what is either good or bad. Whatever can be located within an existing set of established standards – all that is good, good enough, and bad – is *akusala*. Realizing *kusala* eventualities entails realizing a superlative arc of change, moving beyond "good and evil" in the direction of the manifestly virtuosic.

In music – especially music that is improvised – virtuosity is not something that one has, a particular trait or possession; it is present only as something demonstrated. Although practice is certainly needed to reach the point of demonstrating virtuosity, it is less a function of the (necessarily finite) time a musician spends in practice as it is his or her quality of engagement and creative openness – his or her capacities for at once unpredictably abandoning and musically exceeding the known. Virtuosity is, in other words, a demonstration not of musical power but rather of musical strength. Musical virtuosity is not a moment of finality, the achievement of musical closure; it is the occasion of a surprising opening of musical space. Publicly demonstrated, it is the occasion of spontaneous applause, serving as a catalytic force for the shared eruption of bodily, emotional, and cognitive appreciation – a sense of having experienced something of inordinate value and hence of being extraordinarily valuably situated.

As values, relational equity and diversity are distinctive modalities of realizing virtuosic interdependence. In much the same way that realizing Buddhist non-dualism dissolves the opposition of samsara and nirvana and opens prospects for bodhisattva action beyond the strictures of likes and dislikes, valuing relational equity and diversity dissolves the opposition of self and other, opening prospects for realizing virtuosic relational dynamics both within and across scales from the personal to the environmental.

A Practical Coda

This is a quite sweeping claim, and it is natural to wonder whether it is not just a philosophically clad pipe dream, both insubstantial and impossible to instantiate. After all, as an emergent relational quality, diversity (and hence equity) cannot be imposed at will. And since it is also part of the conceptions of diversity and equity offered here that working towards their practical articulation cannot be undertaken singly, we would seem to be faced with a "catch 22." Getting sufficient numbers of people to share in the pursuit of greater equity and diversity with the depths of coordination needed to address a global predicament such as climate change would seem to require already having achieved personal and structural appreciation of precisely these values.

But this "catch 22" – like the logical error of asking which comes first, the chicken or the egg – is itself an artifact of failing to recognize the interdependence of all things and remaining wedded to a linear understanding of causality. In Buddhist contexts, the specters of this dilemma of needing the results of a process in order to start that very process most commonly appear in relation to doubts about the efficacy of practice – doubts, ultimately, about the connection between practice and enlightenment. The assumption on which such doubts are constructed is, of course, that practice is a means to the end of enlightenment. And, given our human ignorance and conditioning by karma created over countless lifetimes, it is natural to wonder how it could ever be possible to close the gap between means and end. How do we even know what constitutes effective practice if we do not already know what enlightenment is, which clearly we do not?

The Buddhist response, perhaps most succinctly and unequivocally stated, is in Huineng's Chan Buddhist declaration that "it is precisely Buddhist practice that is Buddha." Buddhist practice is not, in other words, a means to the end of realizing Buddhist enlightenment; it is the demonstration of enlightenment. This is not to deny, of course, that there is a difference between the practice of a novice and a master – that difference is, indeed, what enables the master to mentor the novice and for the novice to inspire the teaching of the master. Rather, the point is that practicing/demonstrating enlightenment is an irreducibly recursive process that does not allow us to talk about either a neatly delineated beginning or a distant and yet-to-be achieved end. Hence the iconic formula in Chan Buddhism that the *bodhimaṇḍala* – the place of enlightenment – is not somewhere else to which we must journey; it is here and now, wherever we happen to be walking, standing, sitting, or reclining. Or, stated in the terms of our present discussion: the recursively evolving path to more equitable and diversity-rich global interdependence is always and everywhere accessible.

Still, just as it is natural and valid for novices to ask how they can deepen their Buddhist practice, it is natural and valid to ask how to accelerate the recursive process of structurally amplifying the valorization of diversity and relational equity. As an example of how this question might be answered, let me offer a suggestion relevant to realizing less dualistically framed electoral and policy-making processes. Elections and policy development already play central roles in shaping the dynamics of the public sphere and will inevitably be major factors in framing and implementing locally, nationally, regionally, and globally integrated responses to the kinds and depths of predicament that seem likely to characterize the realities of the twenty-first century.

There is now a growing body of work (Page 2007) that indicates that cognitively diverse working groups outperform non-diverse groups of experts in situations where predicament-resolving improvisation rather than problem-solving innovation is required. There is also a growing body of work (see, for example, Gutmann and Thompson 1996) that mounts powerful arguments on behalf of deliberative democracy as a means to offset some of the recognized liabilities of electorally focused representative democracy. In such procedural democracies, major frameworks for policy decisions are commonly forwarded in the form of specific bills, which elected representatives either accept or reject. In multi-party democratic systems, individual citizens exercise similarly dualistic options in voting for one candidate (and implicitly against all others). This essentially dualistic system of yes/no voting is deeply flawed and dramatically constrains the potential for realizing diversity-enriching forms of government of the sort needed to enact and sustain freely deliberative predicament resolution.

An alternative consonant with Buddhist non-dualism and suited to generating responses to issues that cannot be addressed in solely technical terms is to replace for/against voting systems with systems that allow for the expression of weighted evaluations. One model for doing so is that of majority judgment, developed by Balinski and Laraki (2011). This approach allows voters – whether individual citizens, members of committees, or elected officials – to grade candidates or policies as excellent, very good, good, acceptable, poor; to reject these candidates or policies; or to voice the position of having no opinion at all in the vote. Importantly, such a system is mathematically immune to the Condorcet and Arrow paradox, as well as to strategic manipulation, offering a "social decision function" that allows even very large populations to share in the process of evaluating and not merely approving/disapproving candidates (whether persons or policies).

Although such a voting system cannot be expected to deliver diversity dividends like those that might be achieved in small working groups, it would institutionalize public practices of considering and expressing convictions about the meaning of excellence rather than delivering crude statements of like and dislike. The evolution of such a system would arguably involve the movement away from an "all or nothing" mentality and efforts to refine the evaluative sensitivities of the voting public. In the long run, especially if applied within governments in voting on specific bills, it would tend to depoliticize decision-making by providing an alternative to voting that shows whether one is "for or against" a given party.

It is not likely that such a system would, by itself, initiate substantial public movement in the direction of both conscientiously refraining from conduct leading to *akusala* eventualities and vigorously engaging in practices conducive to eventualities that are *kusala*, or to shifting from dualistic to non-dualistic engagements with sameness and difference – particularly with respect to important life values. Yet the overall likelihood of such movement would greatly increase if, for example, a change in voting mechanisms were paralleled by complementary changes in other domains. Here, I might mention the possibility of orienting education away from the globally dominant, curricular model that is organized around separate "bodies of knowledge" towards approaches suited to the emergence of new "ecologies of knowledge" and to fostering the kinds of capabilities and commitments needed to recognize and critically engage complex and predicament-rich systems of interdependence.

These are, of course, simply suggestions made from one particular perspective on the ways in which the contemporary dynamics of global interdependence are both magnifying and multiplying differences among and within our societies, forcing confrontation with our *uncommon* assumptions about how best to address the predicaments arising with our pursuits of enriching lives for all. Buddhist thought and practice suggest that these very differences, if acknowledged and skillfully appreciated, also afford potent opportunities for realizing globally shared resolve on the most just and fair means-to and meanings-of human-with-planetary flourishing. The task of how we best shift from merely differing-from one another (variety) to differing-for one another in the ways needed for the emergence of ever greater scales and scopes of diversity is, fortunately, one to which each and every one of us can distinctively contribute.

Notes

1 The first systematic exposition of values in the contemporary sense implying both social origins and psychological attitudes was originally published just after World War I as a methodological aside in a work on Polish peasants by Thomas and Znaniecki (1958 [1918–20]).

2 An extensive discussion of my own thinking about karma can be found in Hershock (2008).

3 The social engagement required by Buddhist practice should not be construed, however, as necessarily or primarily oppositional in nature. Instead, in keeping with the way the Buddhist monastic community aspired neither to independence from the rest of society nor to the universal imposition of its own organizational structures, but rather to realizing an arc of mutually beneficial interdependence between the Sangha and the rest of society, the critique of culture entailed by Buddhist practice is best understood as a countercultural one – a critique conducted from within.

4 My use of finite and infinite games in relation to strength and power is derived from Carse (1987).

References

Balinski, Michel, and Laraki, Rida (2011). *Majority Judgment: Measuring, Ranking, and Electing.* Boston: MIT Press.

Beck, Ulrich (1992). *Risk Society: Towards a New Modernity*. London: Sage.

Beck, Ulrich (1999). *World Risk Society*. Cambridge: Polity.

Beck, Ulrich, Giddens, Anthony, and Lash, Scott (1994). *Reflexive Modernization: Politics, Tradition and Aesthetics in the Modern Social Order*. Stanford, CA: Stanford University Press.

Carse, James P. (1987). *Finite and Infinite Games: A Vision of Life as Play and Possibility*. New York: Balantine Books.

Castells, Manuel (1996). *The Information Age: Economy, Society and Culture, Vol. 1: The Rise of the Network Society*. Oxford, and Cambridge, MA: Blackwell.

Castells, Manuel (1997). *The Information Age: Economy, Society and Culture, Vol. 2: The Power of Identity*. Oxford, and Cambridge, MA: Blackwell.

Castells, Manuel (1998). *The Information Age: Economy, Society and Culture, Vol. 3: End of Millennium*. Oxford, and Cambridge, MA: Blackwell.

Davies, James B., Sandström, Susanna, Shorrocks, Anthony, and Wolff, Edward N. (2008). *World Distribution of Household Wealth*. Discussion Paper 2008/3. Helsinki: UNU-WIDER.

Fraser, Nancy (2002). Recognition without Ethics. In *Recognition and Difference: Politics, Identity, Multiculture*. Ed. Scott Lash and Mike Featherstone. Thousand Oaks, CA: Sage.

Gutmann, Amy, and Thompson, Dennis (1996). *Democracy and Disagreement*. Cambridge, MA: Belknap Press of Harvard University Press.

Harvey, David (1996). *Justice, Nature and the Geography of Difference*. Oxford: Blackwell.

Harvey, David (2006). *Spaces of Global Capitalism: Towards a Theory of Uneven Geographical Development*. London: Verso.

Hershock, Peter D. (2008). Valuing Karma: A Critical Concept for Orienting Interdependence toward Personal and Public Good. In *Revisioning Karma – the eBook*. Ed. Charles Prebish, Damien Keown, and Dale S. Wright. JBE Online Books.

Kroll, Luisa, and Dolan, Kerry A. (2011). World's Billionaires 2011: A Record Year in Numbers, Money and Impact. *Forbes.Com*, March 9. At www.forbes.com/2011/03/08/world-billionaires-2011-intro.html.

Lemke, Jay (2000). Material Sign Processes and Ecosocial Organization. In *Downward Causation: Self Organization in Biology, Psychology and Society*. Ed. P. B. Andersen, C. Emmeche and N. O. Finnemann-Nielsen. Aarhus: Aarhus University Press.

Nancy, Jean-Luc (2000). *Being Singular Plural*. Trans. Robert D. Richardson and Anne E. O'Byrne. Stanford, CA: Stanford University Press.

Page, Scott (2007). *The Difference: How the Power of Diversity Creates Better Groups, Firms, Schools and Societies*. Princeton, NJ: Princeton University Press.

Rawls, John (1971). *A Theory of Justice*. Cambridge, MA: Harvard University Press.

Thomas, William I., and Znaniecki, Florian (1958 [1918–20]). *The Polish Peasant in Europe and America*, Vols 1–2. New York: Dover.

Toulmin, Stephen (1990). *Cosmopolis: The Hidden Agenda of Modernity*. Chicago: University of Chicago Press.

Wagner, Peter (1994). *A Sociology of Modernity, Liberty and Discipline*. London: Routledge.

Further Reading

Bareau, André (1955). *Les Sectes bouddhique du Petit Véhicule*. Paris: École française d'Extrême-Orient. *The Buddhist Schools of the Small Vehicle*. Trans. S. Boin-Webb, ed. A. Skilton. Honolulu: University of Hawai'i Press.

Brassard, Francis (2000). *The Concept of Bodhicitta in Śāntideva's "Bodhicaryāvatāra"*. Albany: State University of New York Press.

Broughton, Jeffrey Lyle (2009). *Zongmi on Chan*. New York: Columbia University Press.

Chakrabarti, Kisor Kumar (1999). *Classical Indian Philosophy of Mind: The Nyāya Dualist Tradition*. Albany: State University of New York Press.

Chappell, David (ed.) (1983). *T'ien-t'ai Buddhism: An Outline of the Fourfold Teachings*. Tokyo: Daiichi Shobō.

Clayton, Barbra (2006). *Moral Theory in Śāntideva's Śikṣāssamuccaya: Cultivating the Fruits of Virtue*. New York: Routledge.

Cleary, Thomas F. (1995). *Entry into the Inconceivable: An Introduction to Hua-Yen Buddhism*. Honolulu: University of Hawai'i Press.

Cone, Margaret (2001). *A Dictionary of Pāli, Parts 1, 2*. Oxford: Pali Text Society.

Cook, Francis H. (1989). *Sounds of Valley Streams: Enlightenment in Dōgen's Zen*. Albany: State University of New York Press.

De Jong, J. W. (1977). *Nāgārjuna's Mūlamadhyamakakārikā Prajñā Nāma*. Rev. Christian Lindtner, 2004. Chennai: Adyar Library.

Eckel, Malcolm D. (2008). *Bhāviveka and His Buddhist Opponents*. Cambridge, MA: Harvard University Press.

Faure, Bernard (2009). *Unmasking Buddhism*. Oxford: Wiley-Blackwell.

Ganeri, Jonardon (2007). *The Concealed Art of the Soul: Theories of Self and Practices of Truth in Indian Ethics and Epistemology*. Oxford: Clarendon Press.

Gimello, Robert M., and Gregory, Peter (eds) (1983). *Studies in Ch'an and Hua-Yen*. Honolulu: University of Hawai'i Press.

Gregory, Peter N. (1995). *Inquiry into the Origin of Humanity: An Annotated Translation of Tsung-Mi's Yuan Jen Lun with a Modern Commentary*. Honolulu: University of Hawai'i Press.

A Companion to Buddhist Philosophy, First Edition. Edited by Steven M. Emmanuel.

Gregory, Peter N. (2002). *Tsung-Mi and the Sinification of Buddhism*. Honolulu: University of Hawai'i Press.

Heine, Steven (1994). *Dōgen and the Kōan Tradition: A Tale of Two Shōbōgenzō Texts*. Albany: State University of New York Press.

Hoffman, F. J. (1987). *Rationality and Mind in Early Buddhism*. Delhi: Motilal Banarsidass.

Jayatilleke, K. N. (1963). *Early Buddhist Theory of Knowledge*. London: George Allen & Unwin.

Johansson, R. E. A. (1969). *The Psychology of Nirvana*. London: George Allen & Unwin.

Johansson, R. E. A. (1979). *The Dynamic Psychology of Early Buddhism*. Oxford: Curzon Press.

Kalupahana, D. J. (1992). *A History of Buddhist Philosophy: Continuities and Discontinuities*. Honolulu: University of Hawai'i Press.

Karma Phuntsho (2005). *Mipham's Dialectics and the Debates on Emptiness*. London: Routledge.

Keown, Damien (2003). *Dictionary of Buddhism*. Oxford: Oxford University Press.

King, Winston L. (2001 [1964]). *In the Hope of Nirvana: The Ethics of Theravada Buddhism*. Seattle: Pariyatti Press.

Kraft, Kenneth (ed.) (1992). *Inner Peace, World Peace: Essays on Buddhism and Nonviolence*. Albany: State University of New York Press.

LaFleur, W. R. (1988). *Buddhism: A Cultural Perspective*. Englewood Cliffs, NJ: Prentice-Hall.

Lang, K. (2003). *Four Illusions: Candrakīrti's Advice to Travelers on the Bodhisattva Path*. New York: Oxford University Press.

Loizzo, J. (2007). *Nāgārjuna's Reason Sixty (Yuktiṣaṣṭikā) with Candrakīrti's Reason Sixty Commentary*. New York: American Institute of Buddhist Studies at Columbia University.

Lopez, D. (ed.) (1988). *Buddhist Hermeneutics*. Honolulu: University of Hawai'i Press.

Matilal, Bimal K. (1971). *Epistemology, Logic, and Grammar in Indian Philosophical Analysis*. The Hague: Mouton.

Ñāṇananda, Bhikkhu (1986). *Concept and Reality in Early Buddhist Thought*. Kandy, Sri Lanka: Buddhist Publication Society.

Odin, Steven (1995). *Process Metaphysics and Hua-Yen Buddhism: A Critical Study of Cumulative Penetration vs. Interpenetration*. Albany: State University of New York Press.

Pettit, John (1999). *Mipham's Beacon of Certainty: Illuminating the View of Dzogchen, the Great Perfection*. Boston: Wisdom.

Ruegg, D. Seyfort (2002). *Studies in Indian and Tibetan Madhyamaka Thought, Part II: Two Prolegomena to Madhyamaka Philosophy*. Vienna: Arbeitskreis für Tibetische und Buddhistische Studien.

Saratchandra, E. R. (1958). *Buddhist Psychology of Perception*. Colombo, Sri Lanka: Associated Newspapers of Ceylon.

Siderits, Mark, Thompson, Evan, and Zahavi, Dan (2011). *Self, No Self? Perspectives from Analytical, Phenomenological, and Indian Traditions*. Oxford: Oxford University Press.

Sparham, Gareth (2005). *Tantric Ethics*. Boston: Wisdom.

Sprung, M. (1979). *Lucid Exposition of the Middle Way: The Essential Chapters from the Prasannapadā of Candrakīrti*. Boulder, CO: Prajñā Press.

Tillemans, T. (1990). *Materials for the Study of Āryadeva, Dharmapāla and Candrakīrti*. 2 vols. Vienna: Arbeitskreis für Tibetische und Buddhistische Studien.

Tola, Ferdando, and Dragonetti, Carmen (1995). *Nāgārjuna's Refutation of Logic*. Delhi: Matilal Banarsidass.

Tsomo, Karma Lekshe (ed.) (2000). *Innovative Buddhist Women: Swimming Against the Stream*. Richmond, Surrey: Curzon Press.

Vaidya, P. L. (ed.) (1961). *Samādhirajasūtra*. Darbangha: Mithila Institute of Post Graduate Studies and Research in Sanskrit Learning.

van der Kuijp, Leonard W. J. (1983). *Contributions to the Development of Tibetan Buddhist Epistemology from the Eleventh to the Thirteenth Century*. Wiesbaden: Franz Steiner.

Walser, Joseph (2005). *Nāgārjuna in Context: Mahāyāna Buddhism and Early Indian Culture*. New York: Columbia University Press.

Wright, Dale S. (2009). *The Six Perfections: Buddhism and the Cultivation of Character*. New York: Oxford University Press.

Yotsuya, K. (1999). *The Critique of Svatantra Reasoning by Candrakīrti and Tsongkha-pa: A Study of Philosophical Proof According to Two Prāsaṅgika Madhyamaka Traditions of India and Tibet*. Stuttgart: Franz Steiner.

Index

Abbot's Quarter 351–4
Abe, Masao 195
abhidhamma-pitaka 2, 74, 75
Abhidhamma 8
  causation 244
  in China 112–13, 115
  commentaries on 80–3
  creative mental activity 384
  focus and canon of 78–80
  Hinayana schools 193–4
  interpreting reality 117
  Kathavatthu 78
  language and reality 469
  literature 367–8
  meaning of 377
  metaphysics of 130–4
  as a method 387
  on *nirvana* and *samsara* 334–55
  open and dynamic nature 388–9
  partite things 216
  path shown by *arahats* 462
  philosophical school of 129
  relational reality 218–19
  taxonomies of existence/experience 246
  Two Truths theory 256
Abhidhammatthasangaha (Anuruddha) 81–2
Abhidhammavatara/Introduction to the Abhidhamma (Buddhadatta) 82
Abhidharmakosa (Vasubandhu) 398–9, 422
Abhinavagupta 106
abortion 619–21
absorption *(jhananga)* 390
accumulation, path of 96
act *(kriya)* 279
action
  disposition to 232
  good and bad 435–6
  worldly activity 334–5
    see also karma/kamma
action-rebirth *(karma-samsara)* 525
  engaged Buddhism 530–1
Adhimutta 41
Advaita Vedanta 106, 153, 586
Advice for Travelers on the Bodhisattva Path (Candrakirti) 442
aesthetics, Zen 124
afterlife 396
Agganna Sutta 497
aggregates *see* five aggregates
ahisma *see* non-harm
Aiken, Robert 639–40
akrodha 466
Aksapada
  "Aphorisms on Logic"/*Nyaya-sutra* 311
Alara Kalama 565, 592
alcohol 446
Alexander the Great 500, 543
Alice in Wonderland (Carroll) 357

A Companion to Buddhist Philosophy, First Edition. Edited by Steven M. Emmanuel.

altruism
compassion and 467–8
Mahayana tradition 86–7
Ambattha Sutta 498
Ambedkar, B. R.
The Buddha and His Dhamma 524–5, 530
engaged Buddhism 526, 527, 530–1
Ames, William 337
Amitabha Sutra/Smaller Sutra of Immeasurable Life 122
Amitayurdhyana Sutra/Meditation Sutra 122
Amoghavajra 120
Amstutz, Galen 486, 488
Analayo 593–4
Ananda 461–2, 500
character of 457
life of 452
anatta/anatman *see* non-self
Anatta-lakkhana Sutta 34, 35–6
anger
absence of/*akrodha* 466
bodhisattvas and 402–3
Anguttara Nikaya 74
pain 31
wheel of state 499
anicca/anitya *see* impermanence
annihilationism 64
Anuruddha
on Buddha's nirvana 335
commentaries/little finger manuals 81–2
Apadana 463
"Aphorisms on Logic" *see Nyaya-sutra* (Gautama/Aksapada)
appearance
emptiness and 100
sutras compared to tantra 105
apprehension, non- 297
arahats/arahants (awakened disciples)
Buddha's companions 452, 455–7
categories of 454–5
collecting teachings 1–2
compassion and 512–13
contrasted with bodhisattvas 442–3
culmination of noble states 40
ethical training 439–40
experience of *nirvana* 43
female 457–8
five path system 96–7
free of distress 42–3
individual stories of 455–62
language of teaching 366–74
Mahayana penultimate goal 87
nature of in Theravada Abhidhamma 78
silent buddhas/*paccekabuddha* 454–5
state of Noble Ones 28–9
teaching with narrative 462–3
Aristotle 121, 431, 432
language and reason 307, 308
on law 498
moral philosophy 433
Nichomachean Ethics 478–9
realism 214
syllogisms 309–10
universal laws and injustice 686
virtue ethics 477, 478–81, 487
ariya-sacca *see* Four Noble Truths; truth
Ariyaratna, A. T. 527, 642
ariyasangha 453
armaments 532
artha 373
Arthasastra (Kautalya) 492–3
Arthavadins 165
Arya-Sura
Compendium of the Perfections 442
Aryadeva 89
Candrakirti's commentary on 331
Catuhsataka 347
comments on Nagarjuna 91
Four Hundred Verses 442
One Hundred Verses Treatise 114
referencing worldly things 332–3
self and nirvana 339
Aryan outlook 14–15, 18–19
Aryavimuktsena 95
Asanga 89, 90, 95, 112
Bodhisattva Stage 442
principles of reason 245–6
Yogacara school 93–4
asceticism
Indian views 14
Jainism 23
Yasodhara denounces 460
Asian Bioethics Association 614
Asoka, King
character of 496
model of political Buddhism 536
Pillar Edict 493
political paradigm of 542–5
punishment 547
sponsors doctrine debates 274

Asoka, King (*cont'd*)
violence and warfare of 634–5
a wheel-turning monarch 502
Asvaghosa
Awakening of Faith in the Mahayana 119
Atisa (Dipamkarasrijnana)
pramana as a waste of time 281–2
attachment *(upadana)*
calm and insight 62
cause of *dukkha* 39
compassion and 466–7
conditional co-arising 57–8
to emptiness 204–6
as a fetter 569–70
letting go of *dukkha* 32
to opinions 57–8
Pure Land giving in to fate 122
Sanlun classification of 115
sensory experience of the world 231
Atthakavagga (Section of Eights) 77
Atthasalini/The Expositor (Buddhaghosa) 81
Aung San Suu Kyi 527, 642, 644
army for self-defense 646–7
human rights 652
Austin, J. L. 245
How to Do Things with Words 369
Austin, James
Zen and the Brain 626
Avalokitesvara 507
Avatamsaka Sutra 518
avijja *see* ignorance, spiritual
awakened disciples *see arahats*
awakening
Buddha's quest for 26, 567–8
Chan/Zen understanding 123–4
to emptiness 190
engaged Buddhism 529
four stages towards 28, 118
innate 296–7
metaphors of light for 250
non-action 203
Tiantai reading of *Lotus Sutra* 265
ultimate truth 262
Awakening of Faith in the Mahayana (Asvaghosa) 119, 121
Dasheng Qixin Lun translated by Paramartha 187–9
Huayan tradition and 186–9
meditation 199
Suchness 207
awareness *(cittavithi)*
Buddhaghosa's commentary on 81

Badiner, A. H.
Zig Zag Zen 626
Baizhang 350
monastic rules 353
paradoxes 360
Zen monastic code 352
Balinski, Michel 690
Bangladesh 71
Bankei, Yotaku 202
Barthes, Roland 359
Bartholomeusz, Tessa 645
Beauchamp, Tom 619
Beck, Ulrich 678
becoming or being *(bhava)* 48
conditioned co-arising 59–60
"Becoming the Buddha in this Body" 120
Bendall, Cecil
A Compendium of Buddhist Doctrine (with Rouse) 442
Bentham, Jeremy 481
Berkeley, George 155–6, 214
Berling, Judith 360
"Between the Horns of Idealism and Realism" (Priest) **214–21**
Bhartrhari
language and empiricism 246
theory of *sabdabrahma* 279
Vakyapadiya 309
Bhavanakrama 296
bhavanga 385 *see* continuum
Bhaviveka 89–90, 94, 114, 317
comments on Buddhapalita 92
sense and sense data 397
syllogisms and inferences 342–4
Bielefeldt, C. 371
Bimbisara, King of Magadha 493
biomedical issues
abortion 619–21
brain death and organ donation 622–3
Buddhist virtues and 616–17
cloning 623–5
death and dying 621–2
diversity of thought 613–14
Four Principles approach 617–18
medical practice 614–15

psychology and neuroscience 625–7
sangha medical practice 614–15
stem cell research 625
transcultural ethics 618–19
birth *(jati)*
conditioned co-arising 60
Biyan lu
"Mazu's Four Affirmations and Hundred Negations" 361–2
bla 576
bliss
awareness of 169
gnosis 169–70
im/perishable 172–3
Block, Ned 589
The Blue Cliff Record/Biyan lu/Hekiganroku (Xuedou) 200, 201, 351
Blumenthal, James
"Indian Mahayana Buddhism" **86–97**
Bodhi, Bhikkhu 7, 82, 527, 561, 563, 632
on feeling 235
grasping at rules 58
Bodhicaryavatara (Santideva) 176, 271, 402–3, 470
bodhicitta 86–7, 120, 173
Mahayana telos 480
Bodhidharma 112
attributed Zen motto 351
introduces Chan/Zen 123
bodhisattvas
any skilful means 446–7
Chinese differences 114
compassion 471, 482–3
contrasted with *arahats* 442–3
as cosmic beings 443–4
emperors of Tibet 504–6
ethical qualities of 281–2
five paths system 96
kings and 502–3
The Lotus Sutra 513
Lotus Sutra truth parable 260–2
Mahayana tradition and 86–7, 442
precepts 484
Santideva's manual for 402–3
self-immolation 641–2
study of logic 275
teaching ideal of 430
virtual acts 486–7
Yasodhara as partner 460
Bodhisattvayogaracatuhsatakatika (Candrakirti) 346–7
bodily existence *(rupa)*
arahat's pain 40–1
birth, aging and death 40
development in womb 54
energy of 576
five aggregates 232, 419
formless beings 175–6
not "owned" 38
particular individuals and 6
physical change and 6–7
process pluralism 63
scientific framework for 587
tantra 100
Book of Changes 357–8
The Book of Equanimity 205
"The Book of Gradual Sayings/*Anguttara Nikaya*" 492
"The Book of Long Sayings/*Digha Nikaya*" 492
"The Book of the Fours" 496
Bötrül 103
Boucher, Sandy 664
Brahmadatta, King 497
Brahmajalasutta
mind-body dualism 396
Brahmanas
satya 27–8
scriptural interpretation 22
self and non-Self 35
Brahmanism
the All 231
ariya/noble 28–9
Buddha reconstructs 237
"The Discourse on Threefold Knowledge" 226–7
Indian social hierarchy 493–4
knowledge and 223
self/*atman* 425, 426
study of logic 273–4
view of self/*atman* 419–21
women and 494
"The Brahmins of Sala" 434
Brannigan, Michael 616
Buddha (Siddhattha Gotama)
Ambedkar questions 530
anti-dogmatism 227
arahat companions 458
armed bodyguard 472

Buddha (Siddhattha Gotama) (*cont'd*)
awakening of 5, 182
on compassion 466
cultural context of 15–16
on death 39, 229
on difficulty of conditioned co-arising 46–7
"Discourse on Threefold Knowledge" 226–7
"Discourse to Prince Abhaya" 228
"Discourse to the Kalamas" 225–6
"Discourse to Vacchagotta on Fire" 228–9
ethical themes in original teachings 434–41
faeces of 78–9
Four Noble Truths 437–40
goal of teaching 257
as Greatly Compassionate ship captain 473
on his awakening 567–8
identification with in present 100–1
immanent presence 104
intellectual biography 13–14
intention and karma 383
as Knower of Worlds 392
knowledge for liberation 224–5
leaves no texts 5–6, 13
life of 429–30
on meditation 378
metaphysical questions 228–30
nature of in Theravada Abhidhamma 78
origins of Buddhism 1–2
own *nirvana* 334
parable of the burning house 87–8
physical pain of 41–2
progressive leader 494
reluctant to accept nuns 665
silence of 370
split in followers after death of 72
step-by-step discourse 27
taught to mother 80
teaches only two things 230
therapeutic role of emptiness 336
thought upon awakening 118
trusting 400
unanswered questions 77, 350
unorthodox view 24
Yasodhara as partner 460

Buddha Amitabha/Amitayus 122
The Buddha and His Dhamma (Ambedkar) 524–5, 530
buddha-nature *(tathagata-garbha)* 513
bliss and gnosis 171–6
emptiness without defilements 156–8
Kalacakra tantric tradition 164–5
making manifest 295–6
no-mind 202
Sanlun 116
Zhenyan tradition 120–1
Buddha Vairocana 118, 119
Buddhabhadra 112
Buddhadasa, Bhikkhu
quenching *dukkha* 526
Buddhadatta 82
Buddhaghosa
Abhidhamma commentaries 80–1, 377–8, 387
arahat ethical training 439
cetasikas and *citta* 384–5
classification of phenomena 377–8
false sense of self 389
on feeling and craving 65
meditating on mental experience 378–9
nama-rupa 391–2
The Path of Purification 434
on sensory contact 379, 382
buddhahood
Candrakirti's *Madhyamakavatara* 331
language on path to 331–2
The Lotus Sutra 513
Madhyamakavatara on 340
silent buddhas/*paccekabuddha* 454–5
skillful means and 372
universal 518
universality of *The Lotus Sutra* 515–16
Buddhapalita 89
Candrakirti defends 331
comments on Nagarjuna 91–2
prasanga arguments 343
Prasangika school 114
Buddhism after Patriarchy: A Feminist History, Analysis, and Reconstruction of Buddhism (Gross) 664
"Buddhism and Biomedical Issues" (Keown) **613–27**
"Buddhism and Environmental Ethics" (James) **601–11**

Buddhism, engaged 532–4
Ambedkar on 524–5, 530–1
compassion and universality 539–40
core concepts of 525–7
The Five Precepts 531–2
scope of 527–8
"Buddhism in Khotan"/*Li yul lung bstan pa* 504
"Buddhist Ethics and Western Moral Philosophy" (Edelglass) **476–88**
Buddhist Global Relief 527
Buddhist Logic (Stcherbatsky) 272
"Buddhist Meditation: Theory and Practice" (Goodman) **555–71**
Buddhist Peace Fellowship 527
"Buddhist Perspectives on Gender Issues" (Gross) **663–73**
"Buddhist Perspectives on Human Rights" (Tsomo) **651–61**
Buddhist philosophy
commentaries on Abhidhamma 80–3
comparisons with Hobbes 538
contemporary scholarship 3
context of realism *versus* idealism 214–17
four Indian intellectual streams of 129–30
inconsistency of 526
letting go rather than aversion 57
as living tradition 6
as *nastika*/deniers 22
origins of 1–2
path and attainments of 78
as religion 657
spread to China and Tibet 2
therapeutic purpose of 161–2
view of reality 6
"Buddhist Philosophy of Logic" (Tanaka) **320–7**
Burma (Myanmar)
commentaries/little finger manuals 81–2
democracy movement 652
liberation movement 527, 645
meditation on mental experience 378
Theravada school 71
Burton, David
"Emptiness in Mahayana Buddhism" **151–62**
Byrom, Thomas 571
Cage, John
Silence: Lectures and Writings 357–8
cakkavatti *see under* kings and statecraft
Cakkavatti Sihanada Sutta 494, 495, 498, 646
on warfare 633
calm *(samatha)*
conditioned co-arising 61
development of 41
see also jhana/dhyana
Calming and Contemplation in the Five Teachings of Huayan (Dushun) 182
Cambodia
liberation movement 527
Theravada school 71–2
Campbell, Philip 626
Candrakirti 91
Advice for Travelers on the Bodhisattva Path 442
Bodhisattvayogaracatuhsatakatika 346–7
comments on Buddhapalita 92
contradictory language about emptiness 336–9
doctrine of two truths 332–4
emptiness of emptiness 206
four positions *(catuskoti)* 340–2
influence on Atisa 281
Introduction of Madhyamaka 271
life and works 331
Madhyamakavatara 176, 331, 340
Madhyamakavatarabhasya 346–7
on nirvana 339–40
praises compassion 471
Prasangika-Madhyamaka 99–100
Prasannapada 346
seeing *versus* "seeing as" 247
sense and sense data 397
syllogistic inferences of Bhaviveka 343–4
teaching emptiness 335–6
two aspects of reality 220
valid means of cognition 344–6
on worldly activity 334–5
"Candrakirti on the Limits of Language and Logic" (Lang) **331–47**
Carroll, Lewis 357
Carter, Olivia 591

Carvaka school 14
heterodox views 22
materialist views of 23–4
caste system
Ambedkar and Dalits 530
Dalit Buddhists 524–5
hierarchy of 493–4
Indian views 14
Castells, Manuel 677
Catuhsataka (Aryadeva)
Candrakirti's commentary on 347
catuskoti 340–2
causality
Abhidharma non-/existence 133
act and result 279
Buddhist empiricism 243–4
causal efficacy *(karyakaranayukti)* 245–6
causal generation *(tadutpatti)* 253
conditioning the mind 155
dependent co-origination 526
Huayan two theories of 118–19
interdependent 181
logic and 315
Madhyamaka concepts of 135, 137–8
between mental and physical events 397
mental-only reality 140, 141–2
not moral 396
see also conditional co-arising
Cavell, Stanley
Cities of Words 366
The Central Conception of Buddhism and the Meaning of the word "Dharma" (Stcherbatsky) 526
The Central Philosophy of Buddhism (Murti) 525
Cessation and Contemplation in the Five Teachings of Huayan/Huayan wujiao zhiguan 181
cessationism *(ucchedavada)* 396
cetana *see* intention
Chaba
cognitive criterion 413
correspondence criterion 414–15
disjunctivism 410–11
sense-datum theory 409
Chaba Chokyi Senge 405
phenomenal objects and perception 406–7
Chan Buddhism *see* Zen/Chan/Seon Buddhism
Chan-jan 604
chance 279
Chang, Garma 183
emptiness 204, 205–6
chants
"Praise to Amitabha Buddha" 122
see also mantras
Chanyuan chingquei/Zen'en shingi 353
"Character, Disposition and the Qualities of the *Arahats* as a Means of Communicating Buddhist Philosophy in the *Suttas*" (Shaw) **452–63**
Chatsumarn Kabilsingh *see* Dhammananda, Venerable Chatsumarn
Chengguan 118
commentary on *Meditative Approaches* 184–5
China
arrival and establishment of Buddhism 110–12
Buddhism spreads to 2
Confucian tradition 110
eccentric oral teachings 349
expressions on nature 604
Five Mountain monastic system 354
oldest versions of *Lotus Sutra* 513
P'an-Chiao system 88
Sino-Japanese war 637–8
Theravada school in Yunnan 71
traditions and founders 112
Chinese Buddhist Association 527
Chinese language
Pali canon and 2
Chisholm, Roderick 276–7
Chodron, Pema 673
Chögyal Namkhai Norbu Rinpoche 573
Chos-rgyal 'Phags-pa 506
Chronicle of Buddhas/Buddhavamsa 455
Chrysippus 433
Chuan faboa ji/Den hoboki 350
Chulalongkorn, King 545
Ciji Gongdehui 527
Cities of Words (Cavell) 366
citta *see* mind
Citta (disciple) 453, 461
cittamatra *see* mental-only reality
Cittamatra school *see* Yogacara school
clarity 104

Cleary, Thomas 181–2, 566
cloning 623–5
co-dependent arising *see* conditioned co-arising
cognition *(pramana)* 21
  affective modes of experience 234–5
  Candrakirti on valid means of 344–5
  and consciousness 385–6
  deconstructive analysis 246–8
  false 415–16
  Faxiang's four elements 113
  five aggregates and *samjna* 419
  inference and 322–3
  Kadam school 406
  non-conceptual 407
  phenomenal character of 406–7
  pragmatic reasoning and 252–3
  six criteria of 412–13
  Tibet 99
  types of episodes 412
"Cognition, Phenomenal Character, and Intentionality in Tibetan Buddhism" (Stoltz) **405–16**
coherence
  coherentism 243
  Three Truths theory 266
Collected Writings on Sources of Knowledge/ Pramanasamuccaya (Dignaga) 400
Collection on Higher Knowlege/ Abhidharmasamuccaya II 245
Collection on the Sources of Knowledge (Dignaga) 251
Collins, Steven 3, 454
communications technology 677–8
"Comparative Reflections on Buddhist Political Thought" (Cummiskey) **536–49**
compassion *(karuna)* 439
  benefitting self and others 467–8
  biomedical issues 616, 618
  bodhisattvas 513
  Buddha on 400, 466
  as Buddha's motive 278
  consequentialism and 483
  Dalai Lama 544–55
  engaged Buddhism 531, 532–4, 539
  for environment 606–7
  "great" 467
  linguistic deconstruction 469
  Mahayana tradition 86–7
  in modern culture 681
  peacemaking 643–4
  Shambhalan political model 536
  Tiantai *tathata* 116–17
  Vajrayana 106
  violence and 472–4
  virtue ethics 479
  warfare and 633–4, 637
"Compassion and the Ethics of Violence" (Jenkins) **466–74**
A Compendium of Buddhist Doctrine (Bendall and Rouse) 442
Compendium of the Perfections (Arya-Sura) 442
"Compendium on Epistemic Cognition"/ *Pramanasamuccaya* (Dignaga) 312
concepts
  correspondence criterion 416–17
  as mental phenomena 406, 407
  as phenomena 406, 407
Concepts of Deity (Owen) 105–6
Le Concile de Lhasa (Demiéville) 290, 292–3
conditioned co-arising *(pratityasamutpada)* 37, 91, 181
  12 links/*nidanas* 50–60
  calm 61–2
  concept of 5
  fathoming 61
  feelings causing suffering 234–5
  Four Noble Truths and 46–7
  Four True Realities 49–50
  general nature of 66–7
  khandhas and 50
  Mahayana school and 67
  meaning and nature of 48–9
  the Middle Way 62–5
  principle of conditionality 47–8
  relationships of condition for arising 65–6
  sensory input 379
  similes in the *suttas* 65–6
  spiritual practice 49–50
  temporal links over lives 60–1
  Theravada doctrine 76
"The Conditioned Co-arising of Mental and Bodily Processes" (Harvey) **46–67**
Confucianism 110, 514
  Chan Buddhism and 124
  neo- 351
  as religion 657

consciousness *(vinnana/vijnana)* 77
attention 585, 589
cetasikas and *citta* 385
changing and variable nature 385
conditioned co-arising 47, 52–4
development of body 54–5
eight types of mind 143
five aggregates 232, 419, 589
five Mahayana paths 96
foundational 143
four divisions of reality 384
nama bending and 391
particular individuals and 6
and physical processes 63
reflexive awareness 95
scientific framework for 589–90
of self 424–5
sensory modes of 233
"stream of" 233
support for 52
types of 94
unconscious no-mind 203
Vijnanavadins 169
Yogacara school 93
consequences
seeds and fruit 17–18
consequentialism 477, 478
Buddhist ethics as 481–3
constructing activities *(sankhara/samskara)* 33
accumulation and karma 384
cessation of 48
cosmology 392
the "I am conceit" 37
ontological constructivism 154
spiritual ignorance arising from 49
contact/impingment *(phassa)* 47, 77
continuity *(bhavanga)*
male/female 457
Convention on the Elimination of All forms of Discrimination against Woman 659–60
conversation, pure *(qingtan)*
development in China 110
correspondence
cognition criterion 413, 414–15
conceptual thought and 416–17
Coseru, Christian
"Reason and Experience in Buddhist Epistemology" **241–54**
cosmology
hierarchy 392–3
mind as microcosm of 390–1
in Theravada Abhidhamma 78
cosmopolitanism 686
craving and thirst *(tanha/trsna)*
for being 38
cause of suffering 37–8, 77
compassion and 466–7
conditioned co-arising 47–8, 55–7
grasping 57–8
for non-existence 38
rooted in delusion 38
Second Noble Truth 430, 438, 568
senses and 38, 231
spiritual ignorance 65
Theravada doctrine 77
volition and free will 427
Critical Buddhism 157
Culasaccaka Sutta 472
Cummiskey, David
"Comparative Reflections on Buddhist Political Thought" **536–49**
Cunningham, Alexander 455
cybernetics 152

Dadaism 356, 357
Dalai Lama 506–7, 539
afflictive emotions 538
Buddha of Compassion 545
encourages democracy 547
human rights and 652
non-adversarial peacemaking 643–4
science and 616, 625
support for nuns 667
types of transformation 540
universal responsibility 533
Damasio, Antonio 587, 589–90
Daoan 111
Daoism 514
appreciation of nature 604
Chinese blend with Buddhism 110
language 350
nothingness 195
as religion 657
darsanas
nine schools of thought 14–15, 19–20
the "orthodox" six 20–2
Dasabhumika Sutra 373, 471, 502

Dasyus
  pre-Vedic outlook 14, 15, 17–18
Davidson, Richard 626
Davis, Bret W.
  "Forms of Emptiness in Zen" **190–208**
Davis, Jake H.
  "From the Five Aggregates to Phenomenal Consciousness" (with Thompson) **585–95**
death
  biomedical issues 621–2
  Buddha's silence on 39
  existence of *Tathagata* 229
The Death of Ivan Illyich (Tolstoy) 569
defilements *(klesa)*
  buddha-nature and emptiness 156–8
  conceptuality 157
Delhi-Topra Pillar Edict 493
delusion *(moha)* 39, 395
Demiéville, Paul
  Le Concile de Lhasa 290, 292–3
democracy
  Buddhist 548
  difference/sameness non-duality 690–1
  the general will 546
  resistance to 545–6
Dengyo Daishi (Saicho) 514
deontology 477
dependence 245
dependent arising *see* co-dependent arising
dependent origination *(pratitya-samutpada)* 617
Derrida, Jacques 154
  ethics 484
  linguistic idealism 215
Descartes, René
  self and 420
  subject of mental states 425
desire *see* thirst and craving *(tanha/trsna)*
determinism
  Carvaka school 24
  self and free will 425–8
Devadatta 515–16
Devendrabuddhi 90, 94, 299
Dewey, Thomas 300
dGe-lugs-pa school 506
Dhamma-cakka-ppavatana Sutta
  Buddha's first sermon 26, 29
  five bundles of grasping-fuel 32–4
  on true reality 37, 39
dhamma/dharma
  Abhidharma real/unreal distinction 130–4
  Ambedkar questions 530
  Aryan views of 19
  cessation and *nirvana* 50
  compassion and 469
  definition of 193
  engaged Buddhism 528
  Faxiang tradition 112–13
  function of 77
  general nature of conditioned co-arising 66–7
  Indra's jeweled net 182–3
  kings and justice 497, 499–501
  The Lotus Sutra 517
  meaning of 26, 152
  non-Self 36
  realism and 216
  Setting in Motion of the Wheel 5
  in Theravada Abhidhamma 79
  Two Wheels of 645–6
Dhammanadna, Bhikkhuni (Chatsumarn Kabilsingh) 666
  sex trade and discrimination 660
Dhammapada stories
  arahats 455
  meditation as empty room 198
  on warfare 631–3
Dhammapala 80, 82
dhammaraja *see under* kings and statecraft
Dhammasangani (Buddhist Psychological Ethics) 74, 79
  56 mental factors 379
  Buddhaghosa's commentary on 81
  lists of mental factors 386
  other factors 388–9
Dhammayuttika Nikaya 75
Dharma Hall
  Zen literature 351–4
Dharma, One Vehicle of
  The Lotus Sutra 514
dharmadhatu
  dependent co-arising 119
  four stages towards awakening 118
  Huayan tradition 117–19
  Zhenyan tradition 120
dharmakaya
  Shingon tradition 120–1

Dharmakirti 90, 94, 242
epistemology of 95, 129, 297
"Gloss on the Means of Epistemic Cognition" 309
influence on Kamalasila 291
mental events 399–402
metaphysics of 144–9
pragmatic reasoning 253–4
Pramana-varttika 317, 320, 399
"Proof of the Criterion" 278
rejects realism 405
seeing *versus* "seeing as" 247
valid cognition 99
yogic perception 299, 300
Dharmapala 90, 112
Dharmaraksa 110, 112, 116
Dharmottara 299
dhatu *see* realm/context
Dhatukatha (Discourse on Elements) 74, 79
Buddhaghosa's commentary on 81
difference *see* diversity
digha-nikaya
mind-body 74, 396
Dignaga 90, 94, 112, 242
"Compendium on Epistemic Cognition" 312
criterion of reason 276
develops logic system 91
epistemological-logical school 129
Indian syllogisms 312–14
Kadam school disagrees with 411
language and reason 307
metaphysics of 144–9
moral philosophy 431
personal experience 399
Pramanasamuccaya 320, 400
rejects realism 405
seeing *versus* "seeing as" 247
triple inferential mark 251–2
valid cognition 345
Dionysius Thrax 308
discernment, three degrees of 280–1
The Discipline of Freedom (Olson) 484–5
discourse
liberating *(paramartha satya)* 180
"Discourse at Kitagiri" 566–7
"Discourse of the Honeyball" 232–3, 234
"Discourse on Fear and Dread" 567
"Discourse on Mindfulness of Breathing" 558
"Discourse on Mindfulness of the Body" 563–4, 566
"Discourse on Right View" 237
"Discourse on the All" 231
"Discourse on the Simile of the Snake" 562
"Discourse on Threefold Knowledge" 226–7
"Discourse to Prince Abhaya" 228
"Discourse to Subha" 567
"Discourse to the Kalamas" 225–6
"Discourse to Vacchagotta on Fire" 228–9
"Discourse to Vacchagotta on the Threefold Knowledge" 237
disjunctivism
illusion and 410–11
Kadam school 408, 410–11
distress 387
diversity
democracy and 690–1
differing-for and differing-from 684–5, 688
ecosystems 685
emptiness of identity 682–4
equity and 686–8, 696–9
historical perspective 676–9
modern sameness/difference 679–82
variety and 684
see also gender; women
"Diversity Matters: Buddhist Reflections on the Meaning of Difference" (Hershock) **675–91**
Dogen
admires Rujing 353
"Empty Space" 198
illusory conceptions 359
seated meditation 200–1
Shobogenzo 353
temples 354
use of speech 208
Dolce, Linda 518
Dölpopa 102
Dongshan Shouchu 351, 356, 359
Dosho 112, 114
doubt
Buddhas endorsement of 243
teaching emptiness 335–6
dravyasat *see under* existence: primary
dreams of sex 175
Dreyfus, George 481

"The Drum Wheel of Reason"/*Hetu-cakra-damaru* (Dignaga) 312
dualities 201–2
  arguing about *nirvana* 339
  equity and diversity 688–9
  illusion of 202
  non-conceptual meditation and 301
  see also mind-body dualism
Duckworth, Douglas
  "Tibetan Mahayana and Vajrayana" **99–106**
dukkha *see* suffering
"*Dukkha,* Non-Self, and the Teaching on the Four 'Noble Truths'" (Harvey) **26–44**
Dumoulin, Heinrich 351
Dunhuang school 291
Durgatiparisodhana Tantra 503
Dus-gsum mKhyen-pa 506
Dushun 112, 181
  Calming and Contemplation 182
Dutthagamani, King 473
Dylan, Bob 358

East Asia
  nuns in 666
  Yogacara school 89, 90
  see also individual countries
"East Asian Buddhism" (Green) **110–24**
Eckel, Malcolm David 608
Edelglass, William
  "Buddhist Ethics and Western Moral Philosophy" **476–88**
"Effacement" 434
efficiency 277
"Eight Chapters"/*Astadhyayi* (Panini) 308, 315
Eight Thousand-Lined Perfection of Wisdom Sutra 165
Eight Thousand-Lined Perfection of Wisdom Sutra (Sariputra) 170–2
Eightfold Path 430
  conditioned co-arising 50
  elements of 40
  ethics and 440–1
  good mental factors 387
  karma as a law of nature 526
  Mahayana bodhisattvas 446–7
  moral philosophy 433
  Six Perfections and 444
  warfare 632
elements
  dhatus in Theravada doctrine 76
  five 121
  Kalacakratantra interpretation 172
  mind-body relationship 63
  physical *dharmas* 130
  rupa 392
  in Theravada Abhidhamma 79
Eliot, T. S.
  The Waste Land 357
Empedocles 121
empiricism
  supersensory powers and 237
emptiness (*sunnata/sunyata*) 271
  of all phenomena 164
  attachment to 205–6
  beyond Madhyamaka reality 136
  buddha-nature 156–8
  Candrakirti on 335–6
  Chinese translation 111
  compassion and 469–70
  criticism of Zen teaching 195
  dhamma/dharma 89
  dharmadhatu 117, 184–6
  ecological holism and 602
  the empty form 167–8
  emptying of 204–6
  formlessness of reality 194–8
  freedom of 204
  gnosis 167–70
  independent inference 92
  inexpressible 103
  is *nirvana* 340
  lack of own-being 192–4
  language of 336–9
  like noumena and phenomena 484–5
  like space 167
  The Lotus Sutra 513
  Madhyamaka school 90–1, 152–4
  Mahayana bodhisattvas 442
  meanings of 151–2
  misunderstanding 258
  non-dual subject and object of gnosis 165–6
  not nihilism 335
  of objects 199
  as "openness" 194
  origin of phenomena from 175

emptiness *(sunnata/sunyata)* *(cont'd)*
other-emptiness 102, 103
path of preparation 96
of sameness/difference duality 682–4
Sanlun buddha-nature 116
self-emptiness 102–3
six forms of 191–2
sixteen kinds of 166
subject-object duality 154–6
teaching 335–6
as therapeutic 161–2, 336
Three Truths theory 266–7
transcendence 104
translation of *sunyata* 196–7
unity with appearance 100
wisdom of gnosis 167–76
without views 158–61
of words 206–8
Yogacara school 92–3, 93, 155–6
"Emptiness in Mahayana Buddhism" (Burton) **151–62**
energy/activity 20
"The Enlightened Sovereign: Buddhism and Kingship in India and Tibet" (Halkias) **491–507**
enlightenment
arahats 463
practicing 689–90
without theology or metaphysics 539
see also awakening; Eightfold Path; *nirvana/nibbana*
Enni Ben'en 354
environmental ethics
climate change 678
holistic Buddhist teachings 602–3
intrinsic value 608
moral relations 601, 609–11
reconciling with non-self 606–9
social and political issues 611
value of nature 603–6
Epicureanism 161, 432, 433, 498
epistemology
affective and cognitive experience 234–5
the All of sensory experience 230–2
anti-reflexivity principle 249
Buddha's teaching on 223–5, 224–5
Buddhist context of 8, 241–3
Buddhist logic in 321–4
Dharmakirti and 276–9
disjunctivism and illusions 410–11
experience as natural process 232–3
experience *versus* reasoning 251–3
four intellectual Indian streams 129
four positions 340–2
human limitations 228–30
idealism 161
inference 324–6
Kadam school 405–6
Kamalasila's degrees of discernment 280–1
knowledge and liberation 235–9
knowledge of mind from meditation 567
modes of knowing 248
non-Buddhist philosophy 283
non-conceptual knowledge 157–8
personal verification of knowledge 225–8
phenomenal disjunctivism 408
principles without support 250–1
refuting self-establishment thesis 248–9
rejecting views on reality 159–61
rise of Buddhist scholarship in 273–6
role of inference in 321
Santaraksita's 26 topics 279–80
seeing *versus* "seeing as" 246–50
spiritual value of 273, 281–4
theory of exclusion 149
value of meditative states 297–8
yogic perception 291
see also logic
equality
diversity and equity 686–8
equity as relational 687–8
injustices in universalities 686
esoteric teachings
mikkyo 120
essentialism 102
The Essentials of Buddhist Philosophy (Takakusu) 526
eternalism 64
"Ethical Thought in Indian Buddhism" (Gowans) **429–49**
ethics *see* moral action *(sila)* and ethics
ethnicity and race 675
eudaimonia 478–80
Europe
Theravada school 72
evidence
cognition criterion 413
exclusion, theory of *(apoha)* 148–9, 315–17

existence
  Abhidharma real/unreal distinction 130–4
  conceptual *(prajnaptisat)* 152
  conditioned co-arising as middle way 62–3
  emptiness of all things 152
  everything as phenomena 237
  extra-mental 144–5
  gnosis of wisdom 168–70
  intrinsic *(svabhava)* 152
  language and 342–3
  Madhyamaka *svabhava* 134–9
  of non-existence 170
  of *pramanas* 344–5
  primary *(dravyasat)* 152
  true emptiness of 103
experience
  affective modes and cognition 234–5
  Buddha's grounding in 224–5
  Buddhist notion of 241, 242
  construction world from senses 234
  doctrine of five aggregates 386
  mental factors 390
  as natural process 232–3
  realization of evidence 246
  versus reasoning 251–3
  in Theravada Abhidhamma 78
extrasensory perception 279

Fagushan 527
fangzhang/hojo 354
fatalism 24
Faure, Bernard 360
Faxiang *(Hosso/Beopsang)* tradition 112–14
Fazang/Fa-tsang 119, 186
  commentary on *Awakening of Faith* 187
  emptiness of identity 683
  golden lion analogy 195–6
feelings *(vedana)*
  afflictive 538, 541
  aspects of suffering 40
  conditioned co-arising 47, 55–7
  consciousness 382
  five aggregates 33, 232, 419
  Four Divine Abidings 566
  giving rise to suffering 234–5
  good, bad and neutral 380–1
  impermanence of 31
  particular individuals and 6
  scientific framework for 587–8
  Theravada doctrine 77
Ferrer, Jorge
  Participatory Turn 575
fishing net (Indra's) metaphor 118
five aggregates *(khandhas/skandhas)* 421–2
  abortion and 620
  Buddha's concept of person 232–3
  bundles of grasping-fuel 33
  causal and conditioning factors 244
  concept of "person" 332
  conditioned co-arising 50
  doctrine of 386
  dukkha 32–4
  dynamic person 573
  empty of intrinsic nature 339
  end of 43
  essentials for moral character 447
  human rights and 659
  Kalacakratantra interpretation 172
  meditation and 593
  model of mind 585, 587–91
  non-self theory 419, 421
  not abstraction 462
  the particular individual and 6
  person like a fist 181
  positive overturn 101
  sanna/perception 33
  Sariputta and 455
  suffering and 40
  Theravada doctrine 76–7, 79
  types of emptiness and 166
  Vasubandhu on non-self 422–4
  vedana/feeling 33
  the will 425
  see also body; consciousness; feelings; perceptions; person; volitions
five paths 96–7
five precepts
  engaged Buddhism questions 531–2
Florida, Robert E. 617
Flower Garland Sutra/Avatamsaka 87, 120, 181
  Huayan tradition 117–18
Fodor, Jerry 246–7
Foguangshan 527
form
  empty 168
  like Kantian noumena 485

"Forms of Emptiness in Zen" (Davis) **190–208**
Forster, E. M. 463
Foucault, Michel 215
Foulk, Griffith 352
Foundations of Mindfulness Sutra 576–7, 578
Four Divine Abidings 566
Four Divine Abidings/*Brahmaviharas* 616
Four Hundred Verses (Aryadeva) 442
Four Noble Truths *(arya-satyani)*
  Buddha's teaching 26–7, 29, 437–40, 476
  conditioned co-arising 46–7, 49–50
  Dharmakirti's epistemology 278
  engaged Buddhism questions 529, 530
  knowledge from meditation 568
  Madhyamaka *svabhava* 135
  meaning of *ariya-sacca* 27–9
  moral philosophy 430, 432
  role of inference 321
  spiritual ignorance 51
Fox, Alan
  "The Huayan Metaphysics of Totality" **180–9**
Franco, Eli 344
Frankfurt, Harry 426–8
Fraser, Nancy 675
Frauwallner, Erich 311
free will, non-self theory and 425–8
freedom, emptiness and 204
"From the Five Aggregates to Phenomenal Consciousness" (Davis and Thompson) **585–95**
Fruits of the Homeless Life/Samannaphala Sutta 274
Fundamental Verses on the Middle Way (Nagarjuna) 114

Gadamer, Hans-Georg 187
Gandavyuha Sutra 181–2
Gandhi, Mohandas K. (Mahatma)
  degree of violence 648
  satyagraha 28
Ganeri, Jonardon 245
Garfield, Jay 338, 347
The Gateless Barrier 201, 208
Gathering of the Quiddities/Tattvasamgraha (Santaraksita) 279, 280–1
Gautama *see* Gotama, Siddhattha (the Buddha)
Gavampati 457
gay, lesbian and transgender people 670
Geluk/Svatantrika school 100, 102–3, 114
  differences with Prasangika 342
  Prasangika-Madhyamaka 105
  yogic meditation 291
Gelukpa order 281
gender issues
  equality and equity 686–7
  little doctrinal problem 663–4
  recent development and awareness 663–5
    see also women
generosity *(dana)*
  one of Six Perfections 443, 444
  virtue ethics 479
Gethin, Rupert 4, 388–9, 390–1
Giddens, Anthony 678
Gillon, Brendan S.
  "Language and Logic in Indian Buddhist Thought" **307–318**
globalization, development of 677–9
"Gloss on the Means of Epistemic Cognition"/*Pramana-varttika* (Dharmakirti) 309
gnosis
  the apprehended mind 167
  emptiness and 165–6
  five aspects of 166
  self-aware 172–4
  supreme 165
  of wisdom 167–76
God/supreme being
  bestowing "sacred" "rights" 656–8
  cloning and 624
  creation 279
  Dharmakirti's epistemology 278
  Hegel on 104
  negative theology 205
  pantheism 105–6
  Yogic metaphysics 21
Gombrich, Richard 227
  on accepting the texts 4–5
  fire imagery 32
  What the Buddha Thought 525–6
Gómez, Luis O. 3

good *(kusala)*
Buddhaghosa defines 379
human nature 119
Goodman, Charles 486–7
"Buddhist Meditation: Theory and Practice" **555–71**
consequentialism 482–3
Gosala 24
gotra theory 113
Gowans, Christopher W.
"Ethical Thought in Indian Buddhism" **429–49**
Philosophy of the Buddha 4
grasping *see* attachment *(upadana)*
Great Calming and Contemplating (Zhiyi) 115
Great Perfection school 101
innate enlightenment 296
no-thinking meditation and 295
Great Vehicle *see* Mahayana Buddhism
"Greater Discourse on Questions and Answers" 235
greed 538
Green, Ronald S.
"East Asian Buddhism" **110–24**
Gross, Rita M.
Buddhism after Patriarchy 664
"Buddhist Perspectives on Gender Issues" **663–73**
ground *(hetu)* 311–12
grub rje, mKhas 176
Gu-shri Khan 506
Guanyin, bodhisattva 515
Guhyasamajatantra 173
A Guide to the Bodhisattva's Way of Life (Santideva) 87
Gunaratana, Bhante Henepola 558
gunas
three qualities of reality 20–1
Gyonen 122

Hadot, Pierre 273
Hakeda, Yoshito S. 196
Hakuin, Ekaku
Praise of Zazen 190
use of *koans* 201–2
Halkias, Georgios T.
"The Enlightened Sovereign" **491–507**
Hallisey, Charles 485
hallucinations
disjunctivism 408
intentionalist theory 410
as phenomenal objects 406–7
Hamilton, Sue
on concept of self 462
on constructing world 234
personal destiny and philosophy 16
Han Shan 604
Harris, I. 609
Harvey, Peter 487, 589
"The Conditioned Co-arising of Mental and Bodily Processes" **46–67**
"*Dukkha*, Non-Self, and the Teaching on the Four 'Noble Truths'" **26–44**
free flowing mind 202
hatred
cause of *dukkha* 39
self-destructive 538
Haughton, Hugh 357
Hayes, Richard P. 313
"Philosophy of Mind in Buddhism" **395–404**
Heart Sutra 190, 193
emptiness even of Buddhist doctrine 207
Thich Nhat Hanh's commentary 194
Hegel, Georg W. F.
idealism 214
on the infinite 106
Lectures on the Philosophy of Religion 104
Heim, Maria
"Mind in Theravada Buddhism" **377–93**
Heine, Steven
"On the Value of Speaking and Not Speaking" **349–62**
hell realms 399
hermeneutics
Vasubandhu's *Commentary* 275
Hershock, Peter D.
"Diversity Matters: Buddhist Reflections on the Meaning of Difference" **675–91**
virtuosity 16
Heshang
deadly debate in Tibet 290
making Buddha-nature manifest 295–6
Samyé debate 291–4
hetu 387

hetuvidya *see* logic
Hinayana Buddhism (Lesser Vehicle) 441
- *The Lotus Sutra* 513
- Solitary Realizers and Hearers 87–8, 193–4

Hisamatsu Shin'ichi
- "Oriental Nothingness" 194–5

Hobbes, Thomas
- Buddhist political critique of 536
- concept of nature 542
- individualism 540–1
- *Leviathan* 537–8

Holder, John J. 603
- "A Survey of Early Buddhist Epistemology" **223–39**

Homer 491
Honda Nissho 519
Honen 122–3
Hong Kong Buddhist Association 527
Hongzhou school 350
Hori, Victor Sogen 208, 356
How to Do Things with Words (Austin) 369
Howard, Angela Falco 499
Howe, Elias 141–2
Hua-Yen 607
Hua Yen Sutra 189
Huangbo 350, 352, 360
Huayan Jing 181, 182, 183, 186
Huayan/Kegon/Hwaeom school 112, 117–19
- awakening and cultivation 188–9
- conditioned co-arising 67
- metaphysics of 180–8
- non-duality of difference/sameness 683
- Zen/Chan and 180, 194

"The Huayan Metaphysics of Totality" (Fox) **180–9**
Huayan Sutra
- *dharmadhatu* 184

Huiguo 120
Huike/Eka 123, 208, 358–9
Huineng
- on Buddhist practice 689
- meditation and liberation 199
- mind-only 200
- non-abiding mind 204
- things arising in mind 202

Huiwen 112
human rights
- bestowed "sacred" "rights" 656–8
- compassion and reason 659–61
- concept of 652
- non-self and 658–9
- philosophic framework for 653–6
- universality 686

Hume, David
- Buddhist political critique of 536–7
- on self 6–7, 420, 425
- use of justice 541, 548

humility *(nirmana)*
- virtue ethics 479

Hurvitz, Leon 371

The Idea of Human Rights (Perry) 657
idealism 161
- Buddhist context of 217–18
- compassion and 469
- Madhyamaka school 218–19
- two aspects of reality 220
- Western philosophy and 214–15
- Yogacara differences from 155–6

identity *(tadatmya)*
- Dharmakirti's notion of 253

ignorance, spiritual *(avijja/avidya)*
- condition for craving 65
- conditioned co-arising 47, 51
- constructing activities 52
- different views on 91
- Mahayana tradition 86
- perception of duality from 94
- self-destructive 538
- Theravada doctrine 77

Ihara, Craig K. 654
Ikeda Daisaku 521
Ikkyu, Sojun 197
illusion
- aspects of reality 220
- disjunctivism 410–11
- as phenomenal objects 406–7

immanence
- tantra 104

impermanence *(anitya/anicca)*
- Buddhaghosa's commentaries on 81
- Buddha's death and 41
- concept of 5
- *dukkha* and non-self 34–7
- inversion of perceptions 38

Mahayana tradition 89
meditation on 165
non-self 462
suffering and 40
impingement *see* contact/impingement
India and Indian thought
context of Gotama's life 15–16
nine classic schools 14–15
philosophy or religion? 15
post-Alexander Indo-Greeks 500
small monarchies 493–4
Theravada school 71
view of reality 14–15
view of the world 20
"Indian Mahayana Buddhism" (Blumenthal) **86–97**
individualism 540–1
the general will and 546
Western philosophy 537
see self
Indra's Net 118, 182, 194
inference *(anumana)* 279, 320
Candrakirti accepts as valid 344–5
learning from others 317–18
as logic 324–6
from others 321
role in epistemology 321, 323–4
theory of 147–8
triple conditions of 324–6
infinite
pantheism and 106
Inoue Nissho 520
intention *(cetana)*
intentional objects 415
intentionalist theory of perception 409–10
Kantian ethics 484–5
and karma 383–4
mental formations and 398–9
right 440
Theravada view of mind 382–3
violence and 472–3
International Network of Engaged Buddhists (INEB) 527
intoxicants
modern problems worse than 532
Introduction to Enlightened Conduct (Santideva) *see Bodhicaryavatara*
"Introduction to Logic"/*Nyaya-mukha* (Dignaga) 312
Introduction to the Madhyamaka (Candrakirti) 271

Jainism 14
heterodox views 22, 23
logic of "may be" 279
self and the life principle 35
James, Simon P.
"Buddhism and Environmental Ethics" **601–11**
James, William 300, 587
Japan
abortion issue 620–1
expressions about nature 604
Huayan/Kegon tradition 117
The Lotus Sutra 514
Nichiren and *Lotus Sutra* 516–19
Nichirenism 519–21
Sino-Japanese war 637–8
True Pure Land/Jodo Shinshu 121
World War II 640–1
jara-marana *see also:* bodily existence; death
Jataka and *avadana* literature
arahats 454–5
on Khema 458–9
kingship 492, 497
role of narrative 463
on Uppalavanna 459
violence and Buddha 472
on Yasodhara 460–1
jati *see* birth
Jayatilleke, K. N. 243
Jenkins, Stephen
"Compassion and the Ethics of Violence" **466–74**
jhanas/dhyanas 564–5
Buddha's insights from 27
Jigme Lingpa
Wisdom Chats 573
Jigme Sangye Wangchuk 504
Jingde chuandeng/Keitoku dentoroku 351
Jinpa, Geshe Thupten 579
Jizang 112, 114, 115
Jnanasrimitra 317
Jogye Order 124
Johnson, Mark 100
Jonang school 101–3
tantra 105
joy *(somanassa)* 387
Junger, Peter D. 656–7

justice
  Buddhist theory of 541–2

Kabat-Zinn, Jon 556, 586
Kadam school
  correspondence and perception 414–5
  development of 405–6
  disjunctivism 408
Kaginushi Ryokei 205
Kalacakra tantric tradition 101
  achieving buddhahood 164–5
  interpretation of emptiness 172–3
Kalama Sutra 243
Kalupahana, David 231
Kamalasila 90, 95
  Bhavanakrama III on Heshang 292, 293–5
  deadly Samyé debate 290–5
  degrees of discernment 280–1
  non-conceptual meditation 301
  Salistambasutratika 370
  "Stages of Meditation" 95–6, 291
  theory of exclusion 317
  thick description of buddha-nature 297–8
  yogic perception 299, 300
Kamenka, Eugene 655
Kant, Immanuel
  categorical imperative 618
  deontology 477
  idealism 214
  moral duty to non-humans 605
  morality and intention 484–5
Kapleau, Philip 611
Kapstein, Matthew T.
  " 'Spiritual Exercise' and Buddhist Epistemologists in India and Tibet" **270–84**
karma/kamma
  Aryan view of 19
  becoming and being 59
  Buddha's own teachings 434–7
  constructing activities 52
  Dasyu view of 17–18
  denial of 395
  diversity and 676
  engaged Buddhism 530–1
  forward-looking 437
  guiding present actions 122
  human rights and 654, 660–1
  intention and 383–4
  as a law of nature 18, 526
  as a material force 396
  modern society and culture 681
  moral conduct and 430, 435–7
  no-mind and non-action 203–4
  relation to sensory experience 156
  seeds in consciousness 143
  taking life 631
  ten realms 116
  Theravada Abhidhamma 78
  transferring merit 444
  Vaibhasika school 398–9
  violence and intention 472–3
  volition and 646
  without thinking 293
    see also rebirth
Karma Pak-shi 506
Karnakagomin 317
karuna *see* compassion
Kassapa (Mahakassapa) 82, 452–3, 457
Kasulis, Thomas 203
Kasyapamatanga 110
Kasyapaparivarta 336
Kathavatthu (Points of Controversy) 74, 77–8
  Buddhaghosa's commentary on 81
Katsura, Shoryu 252, 342
Kautalya
  Arthasastra 492–3
Kawamura, Kodo 359
Keer, Dhananjay 524, 533–4
kenology *see* emptiness
Keown, Damien 487, 651
  "Buddhism and Biomedical Issues" **613–27**
  human rights 654
  The Nature of Buddhist Ethics 478, 479–81
Ketsumeidan (Blood Pledge Corps) 520
Khajjaniya Sutta 589
khandha/skandha *see* five aggregates
Khandhaka 74
Khema 82, 453, 458–9
Khotan 504
Khri gTsug-lde-brtsan (Ral-pa-can) 505
Khri Srong-lde-btsan 505
King, Sallie B.
  "War and Peace in Buddhist Philosophy" **631–48**

kings and leadership
buddhahood of kings 502–3
early Buddhist views of 491–3
elected king/Mahasammata 497–8
Greek political philosophy 498
incarnation succession of Tibet 506–7
Jataka literature 497
The Lotus Sutra 514–15, 517–19
monastic communities and 492–3
qualities of kings 496
righteous king/*dhammaraja* 498
Sangha check on king 549
socially progressive Buddhism 493–7
spread of Buddhism and 502–3
Tibetan bodhisattva-emperors 504–6
warfare 634–41
wheel-turning king/*cakkavatti* 498–501, 502, 503–4, 646, 652
Klein, Anne Carolyn
"Seeing Mind, Being Body" **572–82**
klesa *see* defilements
knowledge 236, 237
Atisa's scepticism 281
human limitations 228–30
measure of 271
from meditation 567–71
non-conceptual 157–8
pragmatic context 253–4
role in path to liberation 235–9
from senses 574–5
threefold 226–7
transcendent *versus* perceptions 236
triple conditions of inference 324–5
see also epistemology
koans 201–2, 208
meaning of non-sense 354, 359–60
as monastic narrative 360–2
transcendence of words and 349, 350
Koestler, Arthur
The Lotus and the Robot 355
Koller, J. M. 21
Kondanna 452, 457
Korea
Huayan/Hwaeom tradition 117
Jogye order 124
nuns 666
koro 142
Kublai Khan 506
Kuiji 112, 113–14
Kukai
"Becoming the Buddha in this Body" 120
Kumarajiva 111, 112, 114, 116
Kumarila Bhatta 317
kusala/akusala 688
Kutadanta Sutta 494

LaFleur, William 518, 604, 619
Lakoff, George 100
Lam rim chen mo (Tsong kha pa) 291
Lamotte, Étienne 5
Lang, Karen C.
"Candrakirti on the Limits of Language and Logic" **331–47**
language
analysis of compassion 469
construction of the world 215
empiricism and 246
emptiness of words 206–8
emptiness paradoxes 336–9
human reasoning and 307–9
metaphoric 333–4
name-and-form *(nama-rupa)* 53–4
non-conceptual knowledge 158
path to buddhahood 331–2
radical irreverence 350–1
Sanskrit to Chinese 111
of "self" 37
silence and 358–9
skillful means for teaching 8, 366–74
techniques of Zen discourse 356
transforms consciousness 120
word and meaning 279
and Zen silence 249–51
"Language and Logic in Indian Buddhist Thought" (Gillon) **307–318**
Language and Phrases of the Lotus Sutra (Zhiyi) 115
Lankavatara Sutra/Entrance to Lanka Sutra 89, 123, 199, 502
Lanxi temples 354
Laos
Theravada school 71–2
Laozi 350
Laraki, Rida 690
The Large Sutra on Perfect Wisdom 442
Larger Emptiness Sutra 198
Lash, Scott 678

Laumakis, Stephen J.
  "The Philosophical Context of Gotama's Thought" **13–24**
law
  enforcement 547–8
  necessity of 538
Laws of Manu/Manusmrti 492–3
learning, path of no more 96
Lectures on the Philosophy of Religion (Hegel) 104
Leibniz, Gottfried Wilhelm 218
Leviathan (Hobbes) 537–8
Levinas, Emmanuel 484
Levine, Michael
  Pantheism 106
Lewis, Stephen J. 486, 488
lHa Lama Ye-shes-'od 506
lHa-lde 506
Lhasa, Council of *see* Samyé debate
liberation *(moksa)*
  cessation of all 447
  Indian outlook 14
  knowledge central to 223–4
  Mahayana path system 95–6
  supreme value of 280
lightness 388
Lingpa, Jigme 580–1
Linji 196, 350
literature
  nature and poetry 604
  Zen 352–4
living beings
  Mahayana compassion for 86–7
Locke, John 214
logic
  Bhaviveka's syllogistic inferences 342–4
  Buddhist context of 271–3, 320
  developments by Dignaga 91
  Dignaga's theory of exclusion 315–17
  double negation 309
  four intellectual streams 129
  four positions/*catuskoti* 340–2
  Indian syllogisms 310–14
  linguistic approach 309
  ontic approach 309
  place in Buddhist philosophy 8
  questioning universals 314–18
  significance in epistemology 321–4
  thesis/ground/corroboration 311–12
  universals 315–17
  use of inference 324–6
  validity of syllogisms 322–3
  Western forms of argument 322
  wheel of grounds 313
Lokayata school 278
Long chen pa 101, 301, 581
"Longer Discourse on Mindfulness" 586
The Lotus and the Robot (Koestler) 355
The Lotus Sutra/Saddharma Pundarika 87–8, 116, 503
  commentaries and interpretation 513–14
  influence of 512
  models of truth 259, 260–2
  modern interpretations 519–21
  Nichiren school 516–19
  origins of 512–13
  radicalism of left and right 521–2
  skillful means and 518–19
  Tiantai reading of 265
  universal buddhahood 515–16, 518
  Vietnamese self-immolation 641
loving kindness *(metta-bhavana)* 559–61
  biomedicine and 616
  in modern culture 681
  peacemaking 643–4
Low, Albert 198

McCagney, Nancy 194, 196–7
McCarthy, Steven 652
MacDonald, Anne 344–6
McLeod, Kenneth 561, 578
McRae, John 360
Macy, Joanna 607
Madhyamaka (Middle Way) Buddhism 62, 88, 89, 90–2
  commentaries on emptiness 91–2
  concept of emptiness 152–4
  conceptual reification 484
  conditioned co-arising as 62–5
  constructivism 154–5
  deconstructing compassion 469
  ecological holism 602
  ethics 484
  the fourth true reality and 40
  Geluk tradition 102
  hierarchy of tantra 103–5
  inference arguments 342–4
  interest in good lives 270–1
  Kalacakra tradition 164

moral practice over justification 448
Nagarjuna 193
Nyingma tradition 102
overcoming ignorance 91
philosophical school of 129
realism *versus* idealism 218–19
Santaraksita blends with Yogacara 95
Tiantai tradition 117
variations and interpretations 101–4
against views of reality 158–61
see also Candrakirti; Nagarjuna; Sanlun tradition
Madhyamakavatara (Candrakirti) 176, 346–7
existence of *svabhava* 337
towards buddhahood 340
two truths doctrine 332–4
Maha Ghosananda, Samdech Preah 527
Maha-nidana Sutta
craving and grasping 58
my "Self" and feeling 57
name-and-form 53–4
Mahabheriharaka-parivarta-sutra 503
Mahahatthipadopama Sutta 456, 588
Mahakasyapa 351
mahamudra 165
Mahamudra school
no-thinking meditation and 295
Mahaparinibbana Sutta 500
Mahavairocana 121
Mahavedallasutta 366
Mahavihara school
history of 72–3
Pali texts 73
Sri Lanka 75
Mahavihara Temple, Anuradhapura 72
Mahayana Awakening of Faith Treatise/Dasheng Qixin Lun 181, 187
Mahayana Buddhism
altruism and compassion 86–7
compassion 471
conditioned co-arising 67
diversity of schools 88
emptiness of fixed identities 682–3
ethics 429
Four Noble Truths 27
idealism and 217
importance of *Lotus Sutra* 512–13
influence in Zen 192
Kamalasila on 293–4
kings and 502–4
in modern global society 681
moral philosophy 433
natural world 604–5
non-abiding *nirvana* 44
the One Vehicle 525
origins of 441–2
path system 95–7
Santaraksita's thinking 95
Six Perfections and 443–6, 446
skillful means towards enlightenment 446–7
sky/space emptiness 196–7
study of logic 274
teaching and practices of 2
therapeutic purpose of 161–2
transformation in meditation 569
value of liberation 280
Mahayanasutralankara (Asanga/Maitreya) 371–2
Maitreya 165, 504
The Ornament of Clear Realization 95–6
Majig Lapdron 577
Majjhima Nikaya 74, 235, 588
mental factors 382
Makiguchi Tsunesaburo 521
Malaysia 71
mandalas (visual symbols) 503
the six elements 121
Zhenyan tradition 119–21
manifestation 413
Manjusri 516
Manjusrimulakalpa 502
mantras
system of 164
Zhenyan tradition 119–21
Manu 492–3
Laws of 494
Marx, Karl 214
material world
Buddhaghosa's commentary on 81
consumerism 677
consumption 547
fourfold division of reality 378
male/female 457
material beings 23
matter/*prakriti* as mode of reality 20
and mind 391–3
nature of 78
rupa/material form of person 33

materialism
  Carvaka school 22
  Santaraksita and 279
  self and 425
matika 79
Matrceta 368–9
Maturana, Humberto 154
may be *(syadvada)* 279
Mazu 350
  mind is Buddha 200
meaning of life
  Aryan accounts of 19–20
meditation 9
  abandoning the fetters 569–70
  advanced 391
  analytical 291
  the *arahats* and 453
  attention training 585, 588, 591–4
  bhavanamayi 271
  boredom 563–4
  breaking dualities 201–2
  breathing mindfulness 556–8
  calm/*samatha* 459
  in China 110
  continuity thesis 298
  deadly Samyé debate 290–5
  development of calm 41
  on *dharmadhatu* 184–5
  disidentification 561–3
  dynamic body 572–3
  dynamics of 576–83
  Eightfold Path 430
  epistemological value of 297–8
  fixed 291
  the four *jhanas* 564–5
  Four Noble Truths and 568
  importance in Buddhism 555
  independence thesis 298, 299–300
  Kalacakra tantric tradition 165
  Kamalsila sees stupefaction in 294–5
  like water 199
  on loving kindness 559–61
  meditative contemplation 479
  on mental experience 378
  mindfulness of body 563–4
  no-thought/mind 292–5
  non-conceptual 301
  non-duality of *samadhi* 202
  one of Six Perfections 443, 445
  part of Three Forms of Training 555–6
  path of 96
  pragmatism 300
  psychology and 626
  samatha 456
  scientific investigation 591–4
  seated 200–1
  serenity and/or insight 441
  sitting/*zazen* 124, 485
  Six Perfections 430
  as source of knowledge 567–71
  on space 167
  states of *samadhi* 198–9
  as therapy 300
  in Theravada Abhidhamma 78
  threefold truth 117
  Tibetan teachings 2
  use of *koans* 201–2, 208
  walking 558–9
  women 671
  Yoga 21
  yogic perception 291
  Zen/Chan 123, 198–202
Meditative Approaches to the Huayan Dharmadhatu 181, 184–5
Menander *see* Milinda
Mencius 119
mental concentration *(samadhi)* 224, 236
  Eightfold Path 440
  Four Noble Truths 476
  non-duality of 202
  states of 198–9
mental factors *(cetasika)*
  factors of absorption/*jhananga* 386–7
  four divisions of reality 378, 384
  good, bad and neutral 379, 380–1, 386–9
  lists of 379, 380–1
  meditation on 378
mental formations *(samskara/sankhara)* 33
  dreams and hallucinations 399
  factors of experience 234
  five aggregates 419
  influence on unawakened experience 390
  intentions 398–9
  Theravada doctrine 77
  world denial 106
mental-only reality *see* mind-only reality

mental states
teaching emptiness 335–6
un-/wholesome 243–4
see also mind *(citta)*
Mercier, Cardinal 271, 276–7, 278
Merleau-Ponty, Maurice 100
meta-ethics *see under* moral conduct *(sila)* and ethics
"Metaphysical Issues in Indian Buddhist Thought" (Westerhoff) **129–49**
metaphysics
atheistic naturalism 21
Buddha's lack of interest in 234
Dignaga and Dharmakirti schools 144–9
four intellectual streams 129–30
of Huayan Buddhism 180–8
Madhyamaka 134–9
unanswered questions 228–30
Yogacara 139–44
method *(nyaya)* 241, 294
abhidhamma 377
Abhidhamma as 387
Pali tradition 377
metta-citta
compassion and 467
Metta Sutta 468
Mettanando, Bhikkhu 614, 623
Middle Length Discourses 434
mikkyo 120
Milinda (Menander), King 421–2
conversion of 500–1
Milindapanha 421–2, 473
Mill, John Stuart 477
Mimamsa school 14
inference arguments 343
"orthodox" *darsanas* 20, 21–2
scriptural interpretation 21–2
mind *(citta)*
apprehending/apprehended 167
calm and 62
causally conditioned 155
creates all things 194
defiled 143
Faxiang tradition 112
five aggregates model 585, 587–91
four divisions of reality 378, 384
impurities *(cittamala)* 169
is Buddha 200
learning from meditation 567
and matter 391–3
as microcosm of cosmos 390–1
no-mind 191, 202–4, 292–5
One Mind 187–8
of others 245
Pali tradition 377–8
physical events and causality 397
purity of mind 51
self and non-Self 35–6
varied Buddhist positions on 403–4
wuxin (no-mind) 115
Yogacara school 93, 143
see also awareness; consciousness; mental factors; mind-only reality
Mind and Life Institute 625
mind-body relationship 395
Dharmakirti 400–2
processes of 63–4
"Mind in Theravada Buddhism" (Heim) **377–93**
mind-only reality *(cittamatra)* 395
causality 140, 141–2
control of perceptions 140–1, 142–3
great mirror wisdom 199–200
interpersonal regularity 140, 142
spatio-temporal regularity 139–40, 141
tantra 103
mindfulness *(sati/smrti)* 52, 479, 586
breathing and meditation 556–8
increasing perception 570
for non-humans 607
Mindfulness-Based Stress Reduction programs 556, 586
Mipam 102
Mishima, Yukio
The Temple of the Golden Pavilion 355–6
misunderstanding *(avidya)*
cause of suffering 395
mKhas pa'i dga ston 296
Moggaliputta Tissa
"Points of Controversy"/*Katha-vatthu* 310
Moggallana (Mahamoggallana) 452, 455, 456–7
Mohanty, J. N. 21
moksa
ritual practice 21
Moksakaragupta
theory of exclusion 317

monastic community *(sangha)*
Abbot's Quarter 353
appeal of non-monasticism 540
Asokan model 536
Baizhang rules 353
balancing political power 548
biomedical issues 613–14, 614–15, 617
Dharma Halls 353
ethical conduct 485
five precepts 479
history of Theravada school 72–3
narration of *koans* 360–2
nikaya 72–3
political relations 492–3, 501, 506, 539, 544
representing Buddha 352
rules of 541
status of nuns 665–7
warrior monks 638–40
see also monks and nuns
monism
mind-only 395
monks and nuns
abandoning ignorance 237
Theravada school 71
moral conduct *(sila)* and ethics 224
aggregates essential to 447
antithetical approach 448
arahat training 439
Aristotle's virtue theory 487
Aryan view of 19
Buddha teachings 334
Buddha's original teachings 434–41
compassion 470
consequentialism 481–3
Eightfold Path 430, 440–1
escaping suffering 7
eudaimonia 478–80
five precepts 479
Four Noble Truths 437–40, 476
human nature 119
Indian outlook 14, 447–9
Mahayana Buddhism 430–1, 442–7
meta-ethics 477–8
in modern culture 681
moral philosophy in Indian Buddhism 431–4
natural patterns and 17–18
not systematized by Buddhists 476–7
one of Six Perfections 443
reconstructive approach 448
Shambalanan political model 539
six ethical stances of *Samannaphalasutta* 396–7
themes of 429–31
three Cardinal Virtues 480
Three Forms of Training 555
utilitarianism 481–2
virtue ethics 477, 478–81
Western – Buddhist dialogue 485–8
see also biomedical issues; environmental ethics
Mu 201–2, 349, 350
mudras (hand gestures)
the six elements 121
Zhenyan tradition 119–21
mula 387
Mulamadhyamakakarika/The Fundamental Verses of the Middle Way (Nagarjuna) 90–1
Murdoch, Iris 608
Murti, T. V. R.
The Central Philosophy of Buddhism 526
mystics, silence and 350

Naganuma Myoko 521
Nagarjuna 89–92, 165, 191, 192
absence of identities 683
all ceases in liberation 447
on bodhisattvas 442
Candrakirti's commentaries on 331, 332, 346–7
causality 397
challenges rationality 245
emptiness 602
emptiness of emptiness 206
four positions/*catuskoti* 341, 342
The Fundamental Verses of the Middle Way 90
grasping emptiness wrongly 258
influence on Atisa 281
on kings 503
Madhyamaka school 193
moral philosophy 431
Mulamadhyamakakarika 90, 397
negative statements 342
philosophy of mind as distraction 403
Precious Garland 442, 579

refuting self-establishment thesis 248–50
Sanlun treatises 114, 115
Santaraksita and 279
self and nirvana 339
Stanzas on the Middle Way 247
suchness 207
two truths 658
Two Truths theory 257, 259–62
Vigrahavyavartani 344
Nagasena 421–2
and Milinda 500
Naiyayika school
existence of *pramanas* 344–5
logic 317
logic and 314
nama-rupa 391–2 *see* name-and-form
Namacaradipaka/"Illuminating the Action of the Mind" (Saddhamma-jotipala) 82
Namarupapariccheda/"The Determination of the Mental and Physical Aggregates" (Anuruddha) 82
Namarupasamasa/The Summary of Mind and Matter (Khema) 82
name-and-form *(nama-rupa)* 53–4
language and 53–4
the sentient body 54–5
Nanamoli, Bhikkhu 7, 561, 563
Nance, Richard F.
"The Voice of Another" **366–74**
Nancy, Jean-Luc 683
Naropa
Sekoddesatika 165
nationalism 546–7
naturalism, atheistic 21
nature
absence of intrinsic nature 297
constructed/*parikalpitasvabhava* 89, 93
dependent/*paratantrasvabhava* 89, 93, 143
dualist modes of 20
Hobbes on 537–8, 542
imagined 143
intrinsic 339
non-natures *(asvabhava)* 93
perfected/*parinispannasvabhava* 89, 93, 143
Samkhya doctrine 279
three types of 143–4
Treatise on Three Natures 217
see also reality
The Nature of Buddhist Ethics (Keown) 478, 479–81
Navayana (New Vehicle) Buddhism *see* Buddhism, socially engaged
negation
negation of 205
true existence 103
two kinds of 148–9
neo-Buddhism *see* Buddhism, socially engaged
Nepal, Theravada school in 71
Net of Indra 182
Newton, Isaac 218
Ngag-dbang blo-bzang rgya-mtsho 507
Ngog Loden Sherab 405, 411
Nhat Chi Mai 642
Nhat Hanh *see* Thich Nhat Hanh
Nibbedhika Sutta 589
Nichio 518–19
Nichiren school
lay movement 521
The Lotus Sutra 514, 515
modern Nichirenism 519–21
socio-political attitudes 515–19
Nichomachean Ethics (Aristotle) 478–9
nidanas
conditioned co-arising 47, 50–60
nihilism
compared to emptiness 335
counteracting 347
Madhyamaka tradition 101–2
negativity of emptiness 206
not real/non-existent 132
Nikayas *see sutta-pitaka*
Nipponzan Myohoji 527
nirodha
conditioned co-arising 48
nirvana/nibbana
as alternative to birth 60
Buddha's primary teaching 230
cessation of suffering 7
classic views of 20
conditioned co-arising 49–50
determinism 24
disengaging with the world 334–5
as emptiness 340
four divisions of reality 378, 384
goal achieved by knowledge 224

nirvana/nibbana (*cont'd*)
highest value of 280
immersion of two minds 167
like *eudaimonia* 479
Madhyamaka's potency 164–5
Mahayana tradition 86
meaning of 39
non-abiding 44
non-Self 35, 36
not obtained by seekers 339
Pure Land tradition 121–2
pursuit of 512–13
recognition of "true names" 529
role of knowledge 235–9
signless state 43
soteriological value of emptiness 339–40
Third Noble Truth 430, 438–9
in this world 339
unconditioned *dharma* 197
virtue ethics and 480
Nirvana Sutra 116
Nishida, Kitaro 197–8, 203
Nishitani, Keiji 197, 206
Niwano Nikkyo 521
nominalism
Dignaga and Dharmakirti 144–5, 147
non-being *(wu)* 604
non-dualism
emptiness of fixed identities 683
non-harm *(ahisma)* 466
biomedical ethics 616, 618
violence and compassion 472–3
non-self *(anatman)* 89, 190, 279
Abhidharma existence 132
arahat's freedom 40–1
biomedical issues and 616
Buddha's goal of teaching 258
concept of 5, 215
dukkha and impermanence 34–7
free will and 425–8
"how" rather than "who" 50
human rights and 658–9
King Milinda 421–2
meaning of 36
not abstract 462–3
not "no self" 36
outline of theory 419–21
pudgala and 422–4
soteriology and 7
Theravada doctrine 76, 78
"The Non-Self Theory and Problems in Philosophy of Mind" (Tuske) **419–28**
novelty
cognition criterion 413
Nyala Padma Dudul 579
Nyanaponika
on *dhammas* 378
mental factors 385, 386, 390
perception of objects 382
Nyaya school 14, 273, 332
"orthodox" *darsanas* 20, 22–3
theism of 278
Nyaya-sutra/"Aphorisms on Logic" (Gautama/Aksapada) 311
Nyingma school 102–3
tantra 105

obscurations *(niravaranata)*
emptiness and 166
Oetke, Claus 313
on *Milindapanha* 422
on non-self theory 419–21
Ogawa Takashi 361–2
Olson, Philip
The Discipline of Freedom 484–5
On Sentences and Words/Vakyapadiya (Bhartrhari) 309
"On the Value of Speaking and Not Speaking" (Heine) **349–62**
One Hundred Verses Treatise (Aryadeva) 114, 115
ontology
Abhidhamma 388–9
Buddha doesn't explore 7
compassion and emptiness 469–70
Dasyu view of purpose 17
Jain pluralism 23
Madhyamaka 104, 152–3
nihilism 132, 154
paradoxes of 338
Zen non-being and emptiness 191–2
see also existence
oral and vernacular tradition
reliability of 3
Owen, H. P.
Concepts of Deity 105–6
on the infinite 106

paccekabuddha *see under arahats*
pacifism
  Western ideas of Buddhism 472
Padma Kathang 505
Padmasambhava 505
pain *see* suffering *(dukkha)*
Pali texts and language
  Buddhaghosa's writing on 80
  canonical and para-canonical literature 74–5
  centrality of knowledge 223–4
  five aggregates 585
  four *jhanas* 564
  lack of capitals 37
  Pali Text Society 75, 79
  Six Perfections 443
  Three Baskets/*Tipitaka*/*Tripitaka* 429
    see also under "Discourse" titles; texts, canonical; Theravada school
P'an-Chiao system 88
Pancappakarana/Exposition of the Five Books (Buddhaghosa) 81
Panini
  "Eight Chapters"/*Astadhyayi* 308, 315
pantheism
  Vajrayana as 105–6
Pantheism: A Non-Theistic Concept of Deity (Levine) 106
"Parable of the Arrow" 229–30
"Parable of the Raft" 256, 257
Parakramabahu I
  reforms under 72
Paramartha 119, 187
Paramarthasamudgata 93
Paramatthavinicchaya/"The Discrimination of Ultimate Meaning" (Anuruddha) 82
Parivara 74
Park, Jin 484
Parliament of the World's Religions
  Declaration towards a Global Ethic 656
Participatory Turn (Ferrer) 575
particular *(visesa)* 279
Parvizi, J. 589–90
Path of Purification *see Visuddhimagga*
paticca-samuppada *see* conditioned co-arising
patience *(ksanti)* 479
  one of Six Perfections 443, 445
Patrul Rinpoche
  Words of my Perfect Teacher 577
Patthana (Conditional Relations) 74, 79, 80
  Buddhaghosa's commentary on 81
Paul, Diana Y. 664
peacemaking
  being peace 644
  Four Noble Truths 644–5
  liberation movements 642–3
  non-adversariality 643–4
    see also warfare and violence
Peach, Lucinda Joy 660
Pellegrino, E. 618–19
perception *(pratyaksa or sanna)* 279
  acquiring knowledge from 243
  direct of the yogin 298–9
  disjunctive theory of 406
  duality from ignorance 94
  factor in consciousness 382
  five aggregates 33, 589
  intentionalist theory of 409–10
  Kadam realism 416
  learning about the world 317–18
  mental control of 140–1, 142
  modes of consciousness 232–3
  particular individuals and 6
  phenomenal objects 406
  sense-datum theory of 409
  six supersensory powers 236–7
  source of knowledge 321
  temporal aspect 385
  theory of exclusion 148–9
  of ultimate 345–6
  as valid means of cognition 345–6
  yogic 299
perfection *(paramita)* 479
  Perfection of Wisdom Sutras 2
  Six Perfections 430–1
  system of *(paramita-naya)* 164
The Perfection of Wisdom in Eight Thousand Lines 442
The Perfection of Wisdom Sutras/ Prajnaparamita Sutras 2, 87, 89, 93, 116, 167, 190–1, 193, 196, 429, 441, 442
  compassion 469
  the Tathagata 171, 172

perpetual wandering *(samsara)* 435
compassion and 467, 471
entrapment in 175, 260, 383, 387
habitual propensities 169, 174
hierarchy of the cosmos 390
karma and 531
liberation from 14, 96, 293, 369
like an unhappy family 609
and *nirvana* 117, 262, 334–5, 339
nirvana and 683
world of 89
see also rebirth
Perry, Michael J.
The Idea of Human Rights 657
personal responsibility 396
persons
Buddha's analysis of 232–3
continuity and identity 233
philosophical debates about 215–16
see also five aggregates
pessimism 31
pesticides 532
phassa see contact/impingement
phenomena *(dharmadhatu)* 185
cessation of 48–9
character of cognition 406–7
classification of 377
concept and real object 412
concepts 406, 407
dependently arisen 237
disjunctivism 408
emptiness of 171
fourfold division of reality 378
hallucinations/illusion 406
noumena and 485
origin from emptiness 175
real particulars 406, 407
Yogacara school 94
Zen emptiness 196–7
"The Philosophical Context of Gotama's Thought" (Laumakis) **13–24**
philosophy
bridges between Buddhists and West 8–9
therapeutic purpose of 161–2
philosophy, Western
ethical dialogue with Buddhism 485–8
human rights 654–5
living well as goal of 270
meta-ethics 477
morality and ethics 431–2, 433
One Truth position 256
"Philosophy of Mind in Buddhism" (Hayes) **395–404**
Philosophy of the Buddha (Gowans) 4
physicalism 396
Pindapataparisuddhi Sutta 455
Platform Sutra 360
The Platform Sutra of the Sixth Patriarch 200
Plato
Meno 250
political thought 494
Protagoras 498
The Republic 501, 518
"Please Call Me by My True Names" (Thich Nhat Hanh) 528–9
Plutarch 501
"Points of Controversy"/*Katha-vatthu* 244–5, 310
"Political Interpretations of the *Lotus Sutra*" (Shields) **512–22**
politics
Asokan model 536, 542–3, 549
democracy 545–6
the general will 546–7
Shambhalan model 536, 539–42, 548, 549
see also Buddhism, engaged; kings and statecraft
poverty and wealth
inequalities 677
power
other-power *(tariki)* 122
self-power *(jiriki)* 122
Powers, John 545
"Practical Applications of the *Perfection of Wisdom Sutra* and Madhyamaka in the Kalacakra Tantric Tradition" (Wallace) **164–76**
pragmatism 347
meditation and 300
reasoning 252–4
truth 256
Praise of Zazen (Hakuin) 190
Prajapati 665
Prajnakaragupta
interprets Dharmakirti 278–9
Prajnakaramati
sentient beings and compassion 471

Prajnaparamita Sutra *see The Perfection of Wisdom Sutras*
prajnaptisat *see under* existence: conceptual
Pramana-varttika (Dharmakirti) 317, 320, 400
Pramanasamuccaya/"Compendium on Epistemic Cognition" (Dignaga) 320
pramanavada *see* epistemology
Pramanaviniscaya (Dharmakirti) 320
Prasangika-Madhyamaka school 105, 114, 176
  differences with Svatantrika 342
  roots in Tibet 99
  Tsongkhapa's interpretation 102
Prasannapada (Candrakirti) 346
Prasenajit, King of Kosala 493
pratijna *see* thesis
pratityasamutpada *see* conditioned co-arising
"Precepts of Debate" (Vasubandhu) 311
Precious Garland (Nagarjuna) 442, 579
preparation, path of 96
Priest, Graham
  accepting true contradictions 338
  "Between the Horns of Idealism and Realism" **214–21**
Principles of Commentary/Vyakhyayukti (Vasubandhu) 275
Prinz, Jesse 587
The Profound Meaning of the Lotus Sutra (Zhiyi) 115, 117
pudgala *see* five aggregates; self
Pudgalavadins 165
Puggalapannatti (A Designation of Human Types) 74, 79
  Buddhaghosa's commentary on 81
Pundarika
  bliss and buddhahood 172–5
  commentary on *Kalacakratantra* 165
  on formless beings 175–6
  unthinking gnosis 171–2
  Vimalaprabha 172
Pure Land Buddhism 527
Pure Land *(Jingtuzong/Jodo/Jeongtojong)* school 112, 121–3
Pyrrhonian Skepticism 432
Pythagoreans 121

Quakers 532
quality *(guna)* 279
quantum mechanics
  Huayan *dharmadhatu* 185
Queen, Christopher S.
  "Socially Engaged Buddhism" **524–34**
The Questions of King Milinda 434
questions, unanswered 244
  Zen and 350

race and ethnicity
  human rights and 659
Rahula 453, 459
Rahula, Walpola
  What the Buddha Taught 4
Randle, Herbert Niel 311
Raparupavibhaga/The Classification of Forms and Formless Things (Buddhadatta) 82
rationality *see* reason
Ratnakarasanti 95
Rawls, John 537, 542
  A Theory of Justice 676
realism
  Buddhist context of 215–16
  Madhyamaka school 218–19
  rejection of direct 405
  relational reality 218–19
  scientific 155
  Vaisesika pluralism 22
  Western philosophy and 214–15
reality
  Abhidharma 130–4, 388–9
  the "All" 231
  appearance of mental propensities 166
  Brahman error 237
  buddha-nature as Absolute 157
  central Buddhist view of 6
  common-sense position 145
  constructivism 154
  dualist modes of 20
  emptiness and 219–21
  eternity and infinity 228–9
  general nature of conditioned co-arising 66–7
  Indian view of (Dasyus) 14–15
  interdependent causality 181
  language and 469
  mind-only/*cittamatra* 139–44, 161
  of momentary perceptions 144–5
  non-duality of two 167
  the oneness of the universe 121
  patterns of nature 17–18

reality (*cont'd*)
pre-Vedic 16–18
principle of natural reasoning 246
rejecting any views concerning 158–61
second True Reality 37–9
Tiantai interpretation 117
transcendent *versus* perceived 170, 237
ultimate 345–6
universals as fiction 144–5
universals in logic 315–17
water, fire and air 20
world denial 106
Yogacara three aspects 155–6
see also dhammas/dharmas
reason
examination/ground *(yukti)* 241, 245, 246
versus experience 251–3
five perspectives of 308–9
human rights and 659–61
internal, objective and immediate criteria 276–8
language and 307–9
logical inquiry *(tarka)* 241
Nagarjuna's challenge 245
natural 246
Nyaya school 22
pragmatic 252–4
reasoned reflection *(cintamayi)* 271
"Reason and Experience in Buddhist Epistemology" (Coseru) **241–54**
rebirth *(samsara)*
arahat's state 40–1
Aryan view of 19
Buddha's own teachings 434–7
craving for annihilation 38
Dasyu view of 17
Dharmakirti on 278
engaged Buddhism 531
eternalism or annihilationism 64
femininity/masculinity 457
gender value 664
holism of cycle 602
Indian views of reality 14
Jainism 23
pessimistic view of life 30–1
as purifying 653
without material form 63–4
see also karma/kamma
Reeves, Gene 518
Regan, Tom 609–10
Reiyukai Kyodan 520
relativism
Madhyamaka reality 136
religion
Buddhism as 657
Indian thought and 15, 16
self-validation 279
Repetti, R. 426, 427, 428
The Republic (Plato) 501
reverence *(adara)*
virtue ethics 479
Rewata Dhamma 82
Ricard, Matthieu 626
Rinzai school 353
dualities 201–2
koans 201
Rissho Gokokudo (Righteous National Defense Temple) 520
Rissho Koseikai 520, 521, 527
rites and rituals
grasping at 58
Mimamsa school 21–2
Rorty, Richard 300
Rouse, W. H. D.
A Compendium of Buddhist Doctrine (with Bendall) 442
Rousseau, Jean-Jacques
Buddhist political critique of 536, 537
the general will 546–7, 549
Rujing 353
"Rules of Debate"/*Vada-vidhi* (Vasubandhu) 311
Rumi 582
rupa *see* material world

Sa-skya school 506
Saccasankhepa/"Brief Account of the Truths" (Dhammapala) 82
Saddhamma-jotipala 82
Saddhatissa 631
Sadhuputra
Sekoddesa-tippani 167–8
Saffron Revolution 642
Saicho (Dengyo Daishi) 514
Saivism 106
Sakkapanha Sutta 688
Sakya
yogic meditation 291

Sakyabuddhi 90, 94
Sakyadhita International 527, 665
Sakyamuni 351, 492, 518, 565
buddhahood of 502
iconography of 501
intellectual streams of thought 129
life and work of 493
on previous life 500
teachings as a raft 207
Salistambasutratika (Kamalasila) 370
Salistambha Sutra 280
Salzberg, Sharon 539
samadhi *see* mental concentration
Samadhiraja Sutra
Candrakirti on nirvana 339
metaphoric language 333–4
Samannaphalasutta
six ethical stances 396–7
Samdhinirmocana Sutra/*The Sutra Unraveling the Thought* 89
Samkhya school 14
five elements 121
metaphysics of 21
"orthodox" *darsanas* 20–1
Sammaditthi Sutta 456
Sammohavinodani/Dispeller of Delusion (Buddhaghosa) 81
samsara *see* perpetual wandering
Samyé monastery 505
debate 290–5
Samyutta Nikaya /Connected Discourses of the Buddha 58, 74
metaphoric language 333–4
Sangiti Sutta 456
Sangpu Monastery 405
sankhara/*samskara* *see* constructing activities; mental formations; mental volitions
Sanlun/Sanron/Samnon school 112, 114–15
sanna *see* perception
Sanskrit language
lack of capitals 37
Mahavihara tradition and 73
Pali canon and 2
translation into Chinese 111
Santaraksita 90, 94
Gathering of the Quiddities/*Tattvasamgraha* 279
influence in Tibet 99
Tattvasamgraha 424
theory of exclusion 317
Yogacara-Madhyamaka 95
Santideva
benefitting self and others 468
Bodhicaryavatara 87, 176, 271, 402–3, 470, 581
on compassion 471
controlling mind 484
pain of self and others 448
positive aspect of suffering 483
on Six Perfections 445
universal compassion 633–4
Sariputta 518
on Buddha's death 41
character of 455–6
on conditioned co-arising 46–7
on feelings 31
importance of 455
Khema and 458
life of 452
truth parable 260
Sarvastivada school 193
conditioned co-arising 60
Sarvodaya Shramadana 527, 642, 644–5
satya
doctrine of 216, 219–21
meaning of 27–8
Satyadvayavatarasutra
ultimate and conventional truth 339
Satyakaparivarta Sutra 473
Sautrantika school 88, 139
extra-mental existence 144–5
perceptions 146–7
tantra 103
Sayadaw, Mahasi 593
Schmithausen, Lambert 603–4
science
Dalai Lama and 616, 625
theoretical frameworks 585–7
see also biomedical issues
Searle, John 154
Seeds of Peace: A Buddhist Vision for Renewing Society (Sivaraksa) 532
"Seeing Mind, Being Body" (Klein) **572–82**
seeing, path of 96
Sekoddesa-tippani 167–8, 169

self *(atman)* 237
  agency and 424–5
  arahants and 442–3
  Aryan view of 19
  awareness in meditation 169
  Brahman 22, 419, 420
  Chan/Zen 123
  dukkha 38–9
  false sense of 389
  as a fetter 569–70
  five aggregates 6, 32–4
  grasping at 57–8
  Hume on 6–7
  I-consciousness 424–5
  liberation of 34–5
  metaphorical language and 333, 334
  nature of 279
  power of 122
  "spirit self" 21
  Western "ownership" theory 420
  see also name-and-form; non-self
self-awareness
  critiques of Kalacakra tradition 176
self-cherishing 466
self-love
  Hobbes on 537–8
semantics
  non-dualistic interpretation 135–6
Seno'o Giro 520–1
senses
  awareness of sense data 397–8
  bases in Theravada Abhidhamma 79
  conditional co-arising 55
  consciousness of 143
  constructing world from 234
  dharmadhatus 183–4
  extrasensory 279
  Kalacakratantra interpretation 172
  knowledge from 574–5
  mental factors 379, 382
  rejection of "All" 230–2
  Santaraksita and 279
  seeing *versus* "seeing as" 246–7
  self-aware gnosis and 172–4
  sense-datum theory 409
  sense fields *(ayatanas)* 47, 55, 76
  six sense fields *(salayatana)* 77
  ultimate 377
  see also feeling; perception
Seon *see* Zen/Chan/Seon Buddhism
Setting in Motion of the Wheel Dhamma 5
sex
  bestiality 173
  in dreams 141–2, 175
  at meditation centers 671
  modern problems worse than 532
  non-human *arahants* 79
  renunciation of sensual 440
  sex trade and women 660
  as skillful means 446
  on spiritual path 460
  yoga 172–5
Shambhalan kingdom 548
  model of political Buddhism 536
  political model 539–42
Shandao 122
Sharf, Robert 340
Shaw, Sarah
  "Character, Disposition, and the Qualities of the *Arahats*" **452–63**
Shenxiu
  The Platform Sutra of the Sixth Patriarch 200
Shibayama, Zenkei
  on speech 208
Shields, James Mark
  "Political Interpretations of the *Lotus Sutra*" **512–22**
Shin school
  moral teachings 488
Shingon school *see* Zhenyan/Shingon tradition
Shinran 123
Shinto school 604
Shobogenzo (Dogen) 353
"The Shorter Discourse on the Lion's Roar" 237
"The Shorter Exposition of Action" 434
Shotoku Taishi 514
Siderits, Mark 315, 338–9
Siksananda 119
Silabhadra 112
silence
  Zen and 358–9
Silence: Lectures and Writings (Cage) 357–8
sin, Buddhist view of 51
Singapore, Theravada school in 71
Singer, Peter 609–10

Sivaraksa, Sulak 540
engaged Buddhism 525
Seeds of Peace 532
Six Perfections *(Paramitas)*
ethical teachings 443–6
Mahayana morality 442
moral philosophy 433
"The Six-phased Yoga of the *Abbreviated Wheel of Time Tantra*" (Vajrapani) 167
skandhas *see* five aggregates
skepticism/doubt *(vicikiccha)* 161
as a fetter 569–70
Madhyamaka 160
Pyrrhonian 160
see also doubt
skillful means *(upaya)* 180, 195
arhat speech for teaching 370–3
biomedicine and 618
The Lotus Sutra 513, 515, 518–19
Mahayana tradition 87–8, 446
Two Truths model 262–3
virtuous acts 483
Skilling, Peter 83
Skilton, Andrew
"Theravada" **71–83**
sleep
wind of *prana* 175
Smaller Emptiness Sutra 198
Smith, A. D. 411
Snyder, Gary 607
Soames, Scott 270, 271
social justice 532–4
compassion and 467
difference 675–6
progressive Buddhism 494–7
see also Buddhism, socially engaged
social norms, Aryan view of 19
socialism, Seno'o Nichirenism and 520–1
"Socially Engaged Buddhism" (Queen) **524–34**
softness 388
Soka Gakkai 520, 521, 527
solipsism 156
Soni, R. L. 614
soteriology
concept of non-self 7
Four Noble Truths 430
Madhyamaka potency 164
Mahayana tradition 86, 95–7
non-Self 36
problem of suffering 5
value of emptiness 339–40
Soto school 353
soul, identity with body 229
South-East Asia
Theravada school 71–2
space and time
emptiness like space 167
mental-only reality 139–40, 141
reality of objects 146
sky/space emptiness 196–7
Spinoza, Baruch
blessedness 106
pantheistic ontology 104
spirit *(purusa)*
mode of reality 20, 21
spiritual beings 23
"'Spiritual Exercise' and Buddhist Epistemologists in India and Tibet" (Kapstein) **270–84**
spiritual practice
conditioned co-arising 49–50
see also meditation
Sri Lanka
just war 645
Mahavihara Temple, Anuradhapura 72
Mahavihara tradition 75
nuns 666
Theravada school 71
Yasodhara as folk heroine 461
Srimala, Queen 503
Srimaladevi Simhanada-sutra 503
Srong-brtsan-sgam-po, King 504
"Stages of Meditation" (Kamalasila) 291
Stanzas on the Middle Way/ Mulamadhyamakakarika (Nagarjuna) 247
statecraft *see* kings and leadership; politics
Stcherbatsky, Theodore 278, 284
Buddhist Logic 272
The Central Conception of Buddhism 526
Stengs, Irene 545
Sthavira community 72–3
Sthiramati 90
Stoicism 161, 273, 432
common ground with Buddhism 484
craving and 433

Stoltz, Jonathan
"*Cognition, Phenomenal Character,* and Intentionality in Tibetan Buddhism" **405–16**
Stone, Jacqueline 517
Strawson, P. F.
on self 420, 421
Struggle Movement/Third Way 642
Subhakarasimha
Zhenyan tradition 120
Subhuti 165, 167
subjectivity
being aware 104
Madhyamaka tantra 104
substance *(dravya)*
six categories of 279
suchness
inexpressibility of 207
"The Sudden Awakening to the Originally Real" 291–2
Suddenists 296
suffering *(dukkha)*
all of nature 607, 609
arising from feelings 234–5
Buddha's primary teaching 230
causes of 7, 56–7, 395, 651–2
central to canonical texts 5
cessation of 7, 40–4
Chinese worldview and 111
common-sense view of reality and 146–7
conditioned co-arising 49, 64
conventional versu ultimate real 132
engaged Buddhism 525
First Noble Truth 430, 437–8
five aggregates 32–4
Four Noble Truths 29, 476
human rights and 654–7
institutional causes of 492–3
meaning of 26, 29–31, 43–4
medicine and 615
meditating upon 568
metaphysics of 181
nirvana and 43
non-self 462
past, present and future 367
positive aspects of 483
pragmatic approach to ending 256–7
quenching 526
of self and others 448
sensory input 55
social engaged view of 526, 528–31
supersensory understanding 237
threefold practice 7
see also Four Noble Truths
suicide, craving for 38
Sukhavativyuha Sutra/Larger Sutra of Immeasurable Life 122
Suksamran, Somboon 542
sunyata *see* emptiness
superimpositions
cognition criterion 413
supersensory powers 236–7
Surangama Sutra 195
The Surta Unraveling the Thought 93
"A Survey of Early Buddhist Epistemology" (Holder) **223–39**
Sutra of Cosmology/Shih chi ching 499
Sutra of Golden Light 503
Sutra of the Humane Kings/Renwang jing 503
sutta-pitaka (Pali Nikayas) 4
Sutta-vibhanga 74
suttas/sutras
on being 59–60
Buddha-nature 101
Buddhaghosa 389
concept of self 36
critical understanding of 275
illusory appearance 105
language of teaching 370
Mahayana teaching 88–9
narratives of paths 463
not moral philosophy 442
Pure Land tradition 122
roots of *dukkha* 56
similies for *nidanas* 65–6
sutta-pitaka discourses 73–5
Zen defiling 350
Suzuki, D. T. 605
no-mind as unconscious 203
svabhava
existence of 337
intrinsic nature of *dharmas* 130, 132
Madhyamaka existence 134–9
see also under existence: intrinsic
svalaksana
dharma characteristics 130
Svatantrika *see* Geluk/Svatantrika school
Swearer, Donald 525

Taiwanese nuns 666
Takakusu, Junjiro
The Essentials of Buddhist Philosophy 526
Takuan Soho Zenji 639
tama (inertia/dullness) 20
Tanaka Chigaku 519–20
Restoration of Our Sect/*Shumon no ishin* 520
Tanaka, Koji
"Buddhist Philosophy of Logic" **320–7**
tanha see craving and thirst
Tanluan 112, 122
tantras
associations with term 120
Buddha-nature 101
clarity 104
divine appearances 105
Madhyamaka hierarchy of 103–5
physical being 100
practice in Tibet 99
self-awareness and 169
Tantric Buddhism (Vajrayana) 2
Tathagatagarbha tradition
Guhyasamajatantra 173
meditation 199
Perfection of Wisdom Sutra 171, 172
tathata (thatness) 116–17, 217
Chan/Zen 123
power to cleanse 119
Tattvasamgraha (Santaraksita) 424
Tawney, R. H. 657
Taylor, Mark 356
The Temple of the Golden Pavilion (Mishima) 355–6
Tendai school 517
texts
abandoning dualistic thinking 301
abhidhamma 377
abhidhamma-pitaka 74
anguttara-nikaya 74
authority of 279
Buddha and 1–2
commentaries on 80–3
Dhatukatha 74, 79
digha-nikaya 74
Kathavatthu 74, 79
Khandhaka 74
khuddaka-nikaya 74
language of teaching 370–74
letting go of 5–6
majjhima-nikaya 74
moral philosophy 442
Pali 2, 73–6, 74
Parivara 74
Patthana 74, 79, 80
Puggalapannatti 74, 79
reliability of 3
samyutta-nikaya 74
scriptural interpretation 21–2
sources of 1–3
Sutta-vibhanga 74
Tipitaka 2
Vibhanga 74, 79
Yamaka 74, 79
see also suttas/sutras; individual titles
Thailand
monarchy of 545
Sarvastivada school 75
Theravada school 71
A Theory of Justice (Rawls) 676
Theragatha 603
"Theravada" (Skilton) **71–83**
Theravada Buddhism
arahat's experience of *nirvana* 43, 44
Asokan paradigm 542–5
becoming and being 59–60
Dhammasangani 57
doctrine 76–7
"doctrine of the Elders" 72
ethics 485
Four Noble Truths and 27
grasping 57, 58
history and context 71–3
mindfulness meditation 592, 593, 594
moral philosophy 433
"new" 83
nirvana like *eudaimonia* 479
non-returners 63–4
nuns 666, 667
Pali texts 2, 3, 73–6
Sivaraksa questions 532
Stream-Winners 569, 578
structure and focus of Abhidhamma 77–80
warfare and violence 473, 631–3, 635–7, 648
Therigatha 665
thesis *(pratijna)*
see also logic

Thich Nhat Hanh 193
commentary on *Heart Sutra* 194
degree of violence 647–8
emptiness of water 198
engaged Buddhism 525, 526, 527
non-adversarial peacemaking 643, 644
"Please Call Me by My True Names" 528–9
social transformation 539, 540
Thich Quang Duc 533
things, thingness of 65
thirst and craving *see* craving and thirst
Thompson, Evan
"From the Five Aggregates to Phenomenal Consciousness" (with Davis) **585–95**
thought
consciousness of 143
Huayan four patterns of 118
"Three Baskets"/*Sutta Pitaka*
ethical themes 434
"Three Baskets"/*Tipitaka*/*Tripitaka* 429
three natures *(svabhavas)*
rejection of 90
Yogacara school 93–4
"The Three Truths in Tiantai Buddhism" (Ziporyn) **256–69**
three truths model 117, 256
understanding conventional truth 263–4
threefold knowledge 226–7, 236, 237
Tiansheng guangdeng lu/*Tensho dentoroku* 351, 358
Tiantai (Tendai/Cheontae) school 112, 115–17, 193
conventional truth as obstructing 262
The Lotus Sutra 513, 514
Three Truths model 256, 262–9
Tibet
Bodhisattva-Emperors 504–6
Buddhism spreads to 2
deadly Samyé debate 290
incarnation succession 506–7
Madhyamaka school 89, 90–2
nuns 666–7
realist view of perception 405
resistance to democratic rule 545
scholastic traditions 272
study of *pramana* 282
tantra traditions 99
teachings and practices of 2
Wheel of Life 61
see also Kadam school
Tibetan Liberation Movement 642, 645
"Tibetan Mahayana and Vajrayana" (Duckworth) **99–106**
Tillemans, Tom J. F.
"Yogic Perception, Meditation, and Enlightenment" **290–301**
time
Santaraksita and 279
Tissa
abhidhamma text 78
"To Potaliya" 434
Tolstoy, Leo
The Death of Ivan Illyich 569
Toulmin, Stephen 686
training, threefold *(tisikkha)* 224, 555
tranquility *(ataraxia)* 382, 387–8
like Greek *eudaimonia* 432–3
suspending judgment 160
Treatise on Consciousness-Only 113
Treatise on the Prajnaparamita Sutra 116
Treatise on Three Natures/*Trisvabhavanirdesa* (Vasubandhu) 217
"Treatise on Truth"/*Rú shí lù* (Vasubandhu) 311
Trungpa, Chogyam 539
truth *(satya)*
Aristotelian syllogisms 309–10
ariya-sacca 27–9
Candrakirti's two truths doctrine 332–4
concealing 403
conventional 89, 153, 258–62, 263–4, 332–3, 339
direct perception 346
doctrine of two *satyas* 216, 219–21
emptiness 102
four positions/*catuskoti* 340–2
highest goal 403
human use of language 307–8
Madhyamaka traditions 103
modifier theory of 216
moral claims 396
multiple forms of validity 256–8
One Truth position 256
rejecting views on 159–61
of religious teaching 225–7
Santaraksita's thoughts on 95

semantic non-dualist interpretation 135–6
skillful means *(upaya)* 180
three truths model 117, 263–9
two truths theory 256, 257, 259–62
ultimate 89, 153, 259–62, 339, 471, 658
Yogacara 143–4
Tsomo, Karma Lekshe 665
"Buddhist Perspectives on Human Rights" **651–61**
Tsongkhapa 176, 295, 506
commentary 92
Geluk tradition 102
Lam rim chen mo 291
philosophical Vajrayana 100
"Proof of *Pramana*" 281, 282–4
Tuske, Joerg
"The Non-Self Theory and Problems in Philosophy of Mind" **419–28**
Twelve Gate Treatise (Nagarjuna) 114, 115
Two Truths doctrine 332–4

Uddyotakara 317
UNESCO
Bangkok Bioethics Roundtable 614
Universal Declaration on Bioethics and Human Rights 614
uniqueness
cognition criterion 413
United Nations Declaration of Human Rights 655–6
United Nations Development Programme
1999 *Human Development Report* 677
universality
engaged Buddhism 539
global vision of values 676–9
injustice from 686
The Lotus Sutra 514, 515–16
Shambhalan model 540
Upanishads
absolute being *versus* emptiness 204
the All 231
being and self 27
Chandogya Upanishad 54
five elements 121
knowledge for liberation 223
meaning of life 19
monism 23
name and form 54
self and non-Self 35
transcendent knowledge 236
upaya *see* skillful means
Upaya-kausalya Sutra 371, 372, 634
Buddha's past life 473
Uppalavanna 453, 458
character of 459
utilitarianism 481–2, 618

vacaspatimisra 291
Vaibhasika school 88
karma and intentions 398
overcoming ignorance 91
primary and conceptual existence 152
Vairocana Buddha 120
Vaisesika school 14
categories of substance 279
five elements 121
"orthodox" *darsanas* 20, 22–3
pluralist realism 22
theism of 278
Vajira
five aggregates 35
Vajrabodhi
Zhenyan tradition 120
Vajrapani
"The Six-phased Yoga" 167
Vajrayana school
guru/teacher 671
identification with the Buddha 100–1
kings and 502–4
nuns 666, 667
as pantheistic 105–6
philosophical 100–1
subjectivity 104
tantra 103–5
in Tibet 100
see Tantric Buddhism
Valleé Poussin, Louis de La 346
varna (color) 19
see also caste system
Vasubandhu 90, 95, 112, 141–2
Abhidharmakosam 398–9
meanings and phrases 367
moral philosophy 431
Principles of Commentary 275
rejects existence of self 422–4
"Rules of Debate"/*Vada-vidhi* 311
Tarka-sastra 311, 312

Vasubandhu (*cont'd*)
Thirty Verses on Consciousness-Only 113
Treatise on Three Natures 217
Yogacara school 93–4
Vatsiputriyas
self/*pudgala* 423
Veatch, Robert 619
vedana *see* feeling/sensation
Vedanta school 14
Vedas
orthodoxy of 20
veda as knowledge 223
Vedic outlook
Indian context 14–15
pre-Vedic 14, 15, 17–18
primordial Cosmic Man 279
Velez de Cea, Abraham 481
Vibhanga (The Book of Analysis) 74, 79, 81
Victoria, Brian Daizen A. 640
Vietnam
Buddhist self-immolation 641–2
nuns 666
Theravada school 71
Third Way movement 642, 643, 644
viewpoints
right and wrong 57–8
vigor *(virya)*
one of Six Perfections 443, 445
Vigrahavyavartani (Nagarjuna) 344
vihesa
meaning of 42
Vijnanavadins 165, 169
Vimalakirti Sutra 124, 208, 350, 353–4
Vimalaprabha (Pundarika) 172
Vimsika/Vimsatikakarika 399
Vinaya (monastic code)
collected after Buddha's death 1–2
vinnana *see* consciousness
violence *see* peacemaking; warfare and violence
virtues 19
Visakha 453
Visuddhimagga /Path of Purification 74, 391
commentary by Buddhaghosa 75, 80, 434
vitalism 616–17
"The Voice of Another: Speech, Responsiveness and Buddhist Philosophy" (Nance) **366–74**
volition *(cetana)* 588
consciousness 53
five aggregates 33
non-self and free will 425–8
particular individuals and 6
in Theravada Abhidhamma 78
in warfare 646–7
vyanjana 373

Wallace, B. Alan 626
Wallace, Vesna A.
"Practical Applications of the *Perfection of Wisdom Sutra*" **164–76**
Wang Xi
and the deadly debate 292
memoir of Samyé debate 290, 294
"War and Peace in Buddhist Philosophy" (King) **631–48**
warfare and violence
Buddhists engaging in 634–41
compassion and 472–4
degree 647–8
intention and 472–3
just war theory 645–8
Mahayana 633–4
self-immolation 641–2
Theravada and 631–3
Two Wheels of Dhamma 645–6
wrong views and 57–8
see also peacemaking
Warren, Mary Anne 620
The Waste Land (Eliot) 357
Watson, Burton 187
Watts, Alan 358
Westerhoff, Jan
"Metaphysical Issues in Indian Buddhist Thought" **129–49**
modes of knowing 248
What the Buddha Taught (Rahula) 4
What the Buddha Thought (Gombrich) 526
wheel of life 76
illustration of ten realms 116
Wheeler, J. R. 154
Wieger, Leon 355, 360
Williams, Paul 613
approaches to emptiness 199
willing *(ceteti)* 52
Wilson, Jeff 614

Winograd, Terry 154
wisdom *(panna/prajna)* 224
  achieving knowledge 236
  biomedicine 616
  bodhisattvas and 403
  Chinese developments 110
  Eightfold Path 430, 440
  of emptiness 170–6
  escaping suffering 7
  forms of 167
  Four Noble Truths 476
  immeasurable/*amitabha* 122
  from meditation 568–9
  mirror 200
  in modern culture 681
  Sanlun levels of 115
  the Six Perfections 430, 443, 445–6
  Three Forms of Training 555
  three grades of 271
  virtue ethics 479
women
  arahats 457
  in Buddhist doctrine 457
  as Buddhist teachers 671–3
  discrimination against 659–61
  engaged Buddhism 532
  lay Buddhists 668–71
  The Lotus Sutra 516
  progressive Buddhist views 494
  scholarship 672
  Theravada nuns 71
Woncheuk 114
Wonhyo 189
  bodhisattva precepts 484
workableness 388
world, eternity and infinity of 228–9
Wright, Dale 352
  Zen discourse 354–5
Wu, Empress 186
Wu, John 362
Wu Zetian, Empress 119
Wumen 200
  attachment to emptiness 205–6
  on speech and silence 207, 208
Wumenguan koans 358, 359
wuxin (no-mind) 115

Xuanzang 111, 112, 113–14, 186
Xue Yu 638
Xuedou
  The Blue Cliff Records 200

Yamada Koun 196
Yamaka ("The Pairs") 74, 79
  Buddhaghosa's commentary on 81
Yanagida, Seizan
  mirror mind 200
Yasodhara (Rahulamata)
  varied stories and importance of 459–62
Yasutani, Hakuun 198
Yeshé wang po 296
Yogacara school 88
  conditioned co-arising 67
  denies extra-mental existence 144–5
  East Asian strains 113
  emptiness of subject-object duality 154–6
  Fazang influenced by 186
  gotra theory 113
  idealism of 217–18, 219
  Indian schools of thought 14
  within Madhyamaka tradition 92–4
  meditation 21, 199
  metaphysics of 21, 139–44
  mind-only *(cittamatra)* 154–5, 161
  "orthodox" *darsanas* 20, 21
  philosophical school of 129
  "Proponents of False Representations" 94
  Santaraksita blends with Madhyamaka 95
  three aspects 155–6
  three natures 93
    see also Faxiang
"Yogic Perception, Meditation, and Enlightenment" (Tillemans) **290–301**
yogic practices
  deadly debate over 291–5
  Indian views 14
  perception of 299, 345–6
  six-phased meditation on space 167
  Tibetan teachings 2
  truth and 403
yogipratyaksa
  direct perception 298–9
Youth League for Revitalizing Buddhism 520

Yuanwu 200
yukti *see under* reason
Yuktisastika (Nagarjuna) 345

zazen (seated meditation) 124
Zen and the Brain (Austin) 626
Zen/Chan/Seon Buddhism 112, 123–4
  Abbot as Buddha's representative 352
  awakening to emptiness 190
  buddha-nature in environment 604
  compared to Huayan 180
  cultural practices 124
  Dharma Hall/Abbot's Quarter literature 351–4
  discourse sense and nonsense 354–60
  Heshang's debate 291–2
  influence on Western culture 356–7
  koan 351
  lack of own-being 192–4
  meaning of emptiness 196–8
  meditation 592
  meditative consciousness 198–202
  non-verbal sounds 349
  practicing enlightenment 689–90
  seated meditation 200–1
  silence and 358–9
  sitting meditation *(Zazen)* 485
  temples 354
  warrior monks 639–40
  Zongmi on awakening 187–9
Zen Peacemakers 527
Zhenyan/Shingon tradition 112, 119–21, 517
Zhiyi 193
  commentaries on *The Lotus Sutra* 513–14
  Lotus Sutra truth parable 260–2
  The Profound Meaning of the Lotus Sutra 117
  Tiantai doctrine 115–17
Zhuangzi 186–7
  forgetting ordinary thought 350
  looking for wordless man 359
  rigid boundaries of language 207
Zig Zag Zen (Badiner) 626
Ziporyn, Brook 197
  "The Three Truths in Tiantai Buddhism" **256–69**
Zongmi 187–8, 187–9